THE KINGDOM BIBLE

NEW TESTAMENT

TERRY KASHIAN

Copyright © 2025 by Terry Kashian

All rights reserved. No part of this publication may be reproduced, distributed, or transmitted in any form or by any means, including photocopying, recording, or other electronic or mechanical methods, without the prior written permission of the copyright owner and the publisher, except in the case of brief quotations embodied in critical reviews and certain other noncommercial uses permitted by copyright law. For permission requests, write to the publisher, addressed "Attention: Permissions Coordinator," at the address below.

ARPress
45 Dan Road Suite 5
Canton MA 02021
Hotline: 1(888) 821-0229
Fax: 1(508) 545-7580

Ordering Information:
Quantity sales. Special discounts are available on quantity purchases by corporations, associations, and others. For details, contact the publisher at the address above.

Printed in the United States of America.

ISBN-13:	Softcover	N/A
	Ebook	N/A
	Hardback	979-8-89676-319-2

Library of Congress Control Number: 2025901207

Table of Contents

Prologue 1
Acknowledgement 3
Introduction to the New Testament Canon 5
    The Early Date of the New Testament Canon 7
    What about John's Writings?. 7
    Pre-AD 70 Dates for All the Books .9
    Collection and Certification of the Canon 10
Matthew Synopsis 13
Gospel of Matthew. 35
    Chapter 1 35
    Chapter 2 36
    Chapter 3 37
    Chapter 4 38
    Chapter 5 39
    Chapter 6 41
    Chapter 7 42
    Chapter 8 44
    Chapter 9 45
    Chapter 10 47
    Chapter 11 49
    Chapter 12 50
    Chapter 13 52
    Chapter 14 55
    Chapter 15 57
    Chapter 16 58

    Chapter 17 60
    Chapter 18 61
    Chapter 19 62
    Chapter 20 64
    Chapter 21 65
    Chapter 22 68
    Chapter 23 69
    Chapter 24 71
    Chapter 25 73
    Chapter 26 75
    Chapter 27 78
    Chapter 28 81
Synopsis of Mark 83
Gospel of Mark 95
    Chapter 1 95
    Chapter 2 96
    Chapter 3 98
    Chapter 4 99
    Chapter 5 101
    Chapter 6 103
    Chapter 7 105
    Chapter 8 107
    Chapter 9 109
    Chapter 10 111
    Chapter 11 113
    Chapter 12 115
    Chapter 13 117
    Chapter 14 119
    Chapter 15 122
    Chapter 16 124

Luke Synopsis 125
Gospel of Luke. 134
    Chapter 1 134
    Chapter 2 137
    Chapter 3 139
    Chapter 4 141
    Chapter 5 143
    Chapter 6 145
    Chapter 7 147
    Chapter 8 150
    Chapter 9 152
    Chapter 10 155
    Chapter 11 157
    Chapter 12 160
    Chapter 13 162
    Chapter 14 164
    Chapter 15 166
    Chapter 16 167
    Chapter 17 168
    Chapter 18 170
    Chapter 19 172
    Chapter 20 174
    Chapter 21 176
    Chapter 22 177
    Chapter 23 180
    Chapter 24 183
Synopsis of John 186
Gospel of John 199
    Chapter 1 199
    Chapter 2 201

- Chapter 3 202
- Chapter 4 203
- Chapter 5 205
- Chapter 6 207
- Chapter 7 210
- Chapter 8 212
- Chapter 9 215
- Chapter 10 217
- Chapter 11 218
- Chapter 12 221
- Chapter 13 223
- Chapter 14 225
- Chapter 15 226
- Chapter 16 227
- Chapter 17 229
- Chapter 18 230
- Chapter 19 232
- Chapter 20 234
- Chapter 21 235

Intro to Acts and the Restoration of Israel - Don K Preston 237

Acts 259
- Chapter 1 259
- Chapter 2 260
- Chapter 3 262
- Chapter 4 263
- Chapter 5 265
- Chapter 6 267
- Chapter 7 268
- Chapter 8 271
- Chapter 9 272

- Chapter 10 274
- Chapter 11 277
- Chapter 12 278
- Chapter 13 279
- Chapter 14 282
- Chapter 15 283
- Chapter 16 285
- Chapter 17 287
- Chapter 18 289
- Chapter 19 290
- Chapter 20 292
- Chapter 21 294
- Chapter 22 296
- Chapter 23 297
- Chapter 24 299
- Chapter 25 300
- Chapter 26 302
- Chapter 27 303
- Chapter 28 306

Romans Commentary 308
Romans 328
- Chapter 1 328
- Chapter 2 329
- Chapter 3 330
- Chapter 4 332
- Chapter 5 333
- Chapter 6 334
- Chapter 7 335
- Chapter 8 336
- Chapter 9 338

    Chapter 10 339
    Chapter 11 340
    Chapter 12 342
    Chapter 13 343
    Chapter 14 343
    Chapter 15 344
    Chapter 16 346
Synopsis of 1 Corinthians 348
1 Corinthians. 405
    Chapter 1 405
    Chapter 2 406
    Chapter 3 407
    Chapter 4 408
    Chapter 5 409
    Chapter 6 409
    Chapter 7 410
    Chapter 8 412
    Chapter 9 413
    Chapter 10 414
    Chapter 11 416
    Chapter 12 417
    Chapter 13 418
    Chapter 14 419
    Chapter 15 421
    Chapter 16 423
Synopsis of 2 Corinthians 425
2 Corinthians. 446
    Chapter 1 446
    Chapter 2 447
    Chapter 3 448

    Chapter 4 448

    Chapter 5 449

    Chapter 6 450

    Chapter 7 451

    Chapter 8 452

    Chapter 9 453

    Chapter 10 454

    Chapter 11 455

    Chapter 12 456

    Chapter 13 457

Galatians Commentary 459

Galatians 468

    Chapter 1 468

    Chapter 2 469

    Chapter 3 470

    Chapter 4 471

    Chapter 5 472

    Chapter 6 473

Corporate Identity in Ephesians 475

Ephesians 490

    Chapter 1 490

    Chapter 2 491

    Chapter 3 492

    Chapter 4 493

    Chapter 5 494

    Chapter 6 495

Philippians Synopsis 497

Introduction 497

II. The Experience of Christ and Communion of Believers 497

III. Righteousness from God and Spiritual Growth .498

IV. Transformation and Unity in Christ 499
I. The Significance of Solidarity Among the Faithful 499
V. Caring for One Another and the Secret of Contentment 500
I. The Suffering Servant Pattern in Philippians 502
II. The Suffering Servant in Isaiah 502
III. The Process of Kenosis and Its Reflection in the Church 507
IV. The Church as the Body of Christ 508
V. Working out Salvation in Fear and Trembling 509
VI. Endearing Relationships Within the Body of Christ 511
VII. Conclusion 512
II. Contextual Analysis of Philippians 3:20-21 513
III. Christ as the Head of the Body 515
IV. The Church's Experience of Suffering 516
V. The Church's Ultimate Glorification 517
VI. Conclusion 518
Philippians 521
    Chapter 1 521
    Chapter 2 522
    Chapter 3 523
    Chapter 4 524
Colossians Synopsis 526
Colossians 535
    Chapter 1 535
    Chapter 2 536
    Chapter 3 537
    Chapter 4 538
1st Thessalonians Synopsis 540
1 Thessalonians 551
    Chapter 1 551
    Chapter 2 551

- Chapter 3 552
- Chapter 4 553
- Chapter 5 554

2nd Thessalonians Synopsis 555

2nd Thessalonians 567
- Chapter 1 567
- Chapter 2 567
- Chapter 3 568

1st Timothy Commentary 570

1 Timothy 584
- Chapter 1 584
- Chapter 2 585
- Chapter 3 585
- Chapter 4 586
- Chapter 5 587
- Chapter 6 588

2nd Timothy Commentary 590

2nd Timothy 598
- Chapter 1 598
- Chapter 2 598
- Chapter 3 600
- Chapter 4 600

Titus Synopsis 602

Titus 609
- Chapter 1 609
- Chapter 2 609
- Chapter 3 610

Philemon Commentary 612

Philemon 615
- Chapter 1 615

The Truth of Two Ages	616
Hebrews Synopsis	617
Hebrews	626
Chapter 1	626
Chapter 2	626
Chapter 3	627
Chapter 4	628
Chapter 5	629
Chapter 6	630
Chapter 7	630
Chapter 8	632
Chapter 9	633
Chapter 10	634
Chapter 11	636
Chapter 12	638
Chapter 13	639
James Commentary	641
James	661
Chapter 1	661
Chapter 2	662
Chapter 3	663
Chapter 4	664
Chapter 5	664
1st Peter Commentary	666
1 Peter	686
Chapter 1	686
Chapter 2	687
Chapter 3	688
Chapter 4	689
Chapter 5	690

2nd Peter Synopsis	692
2 Peter	703
Chapter 1	703
Chapter 2	704
Chapter 3	705
1st Letter of John Commentary	707
1 John	728
Chapter 1	728
Chapter 2	728
Chapter 3	729
Chapter 4	731
Chapter 5	732
2nd Letter of John Synopsis	733
2 John	736
Chapter 1	736
3rd Letter of John Synopsis	737
3 John	740
Chapter 1	740
Synopsis of Jude	741
Jude	753
Chapter 1	753
Revelation Commentary	755
Revelation	796
Chapter 1	796
Chapter 2	797
Chapter 3	798
Chapter 4	800
Chapter 5	800
Chapter 6	801
Chapter 7	802

Chapter 8 803
Chapter 9 804
Chapter 10 805
Chapter 11 806
Chapter 12 807
Chapter 13 808
Chapter 14 809
Chapter 15 810
Chapter 16 811
Chapter 17 812
Chapter 18 813
Chapter 19 814
Chapter 20 816
Chapter 21 817
Chapter 22 818
Olivet Discourse Charts - Riley Powell 820

Prologue

In this new translation of the New Testament, I am excited to present not only the text itself, but also synopses and commentaries before each book and letter. These primers serve as a guide to help you navigate the scriptures with a covenant fulfillment viewpoint in mind. The past fulfillment perspective allows us to understand the fulfillment of biblical prophecies in the past, particularly in the context of the events leading up to the destruction of the Jerusalem Temple in 70 AD.

As you journey through this translation, I encourage you to immerse yourself in the historical and cultural context of each book, gaining a deeper understanding of the language and symbolism used by the biblical authors. By embracing the fulfilled viewpoint, we can uncover the relevance and significance of the scriptures in relation to audience relevance, enriching our faith and deepening our understanding of God's perpetual purpose for Israel and for the nations learning the principles of fulfillment and then applying them to every generation going forward. With each synopsis and commentary providing valuable insight and interpretation, this translation aims to serve as a comprehensive resource for all who seek to study the New Testament with a fresh frame of reference. May these preparatory synopses enhance your spiritual journey, inspire your faith, and encourage you to engage with the scriptures in a more meaningful way.

Let us embark on this illuminating journey together, as we discover the wisdom and reality within the New Testament through the lens of the fulfilled view.

Your Kingdom brother in Christ,

Terry Kashian

Acknowledgement

I would like to express my deepest gratitude to the individuals who, over the past fifty years, have fearlessly and unwaveringly championed the authenticity of the scriptures. Their dedication to upholding the veracity of the Word has profoundly influenced my own paradigm shift over the last 28 years towards the fulfilled view of the Bible.

I am especially thankful to Don Archibald for his fatherly guidance and care in my formative years in delving into the Greek text of the New Testament. His expertise and mentorship have been invaluable in shaping my understanding of the scriptures and deepening my appreciation for their profound significance. His influence was over 22 years of my Christian life, and I will always be indebted to him for his patience with me and persistence in challenging me to be a better student and disciple of Christ.

Additionally, I extend my heartfelt thanks to all the scholars and experts who have devoted their lives to studying the languages of Greek and Hebrew and have tirelessly worked to produce tools and resources for those on the path of learning. Their dedication and commitment have enriched the field of biblical studies and have paved the way for countless individuals, like me, to engage more deeply with the sacred texts.

To each and every person who has played a role in my journey towards a greater understanding of the scriptures, I offer my sincerest appreciation and gratitude. Your passion and commitment to the Word have left an indelible mark on my life and have inspired me to continue exploring the depths of His holy Word and its original languages with a renewed sense of wonder and reverence and, most of all, "enjoyment".

Terry Kashian

Introduction to the New Testament Canon

It is usually surprising, even to evangelical theologians, when Preterists affirm that all twenty-seven books of our New Testament were written, collected, and certified as authoritative by the apostles before they passed from the earthly scene, and before the destruction of Jerusalem in AD 70. The reason for this surprise, is that most Christians have accepted without question the Roman Catholic theory of canon formation, which says that the writing of the New Testament books was not finished until the end of the first century, and the selection and collection of those writings into a list of approved books was not completed until near the end of the second century (i.e., the Muratorian fragment, AD 170).

When we use the word canon, we are referring to the twenty-seven books of our New Testament, which are considered by Christians as inspired, inerrant, and absolutely authoritative for all matters of doctrine and practice in the Church. Even though the New Testament does not use the word "canon" or "canonical" in reference to its contents, the concepts of canonicity and canonization (such as inspiration, binding and losing authority, direct revelation, and Scripture) are frequently found throughout the New Testament.

Regardless of its vociferous claims, however, the Roman Church did not give us the canon of Scripture; the Holy Spirit did. And the Spirit provided it through inspired apostles and prophets who spoke and wrote under the infallible influence of the Holy Spirit. The Romanist claim is based on the idea of apostolic succession and its corollary doctrine of the infallibility of the Church. In other words, if the inspiration and authority of the apostles were passed down to succeeding generations of churchmen, then the Church would continue to be equipped with inspired, infallible, and absolutely authoritative leaders who would be qualified to give us an infallible canon and infallible creeds. **Editor's note:** In the context of 1 Corinthians 4:6, this does not deny the presence of individuals who may function in roles similar to apostles and prophets today. However, their operation is distinctly different—they do not act under divine inspiration as in the foundational age of the church, but through the illumination and revelation of what has already been written in Scripture. There is no longer a transmission of inspired, authoritative revelation, but rather a Spirit-led understanding drawn from the existing Word of God.

To be consistent, the Roman Church would also have to have the same gift of inspiration that the apostles and prophets had, since the authority and infallibility of the apostles came directly from the inspiration of the Holy Spirit. If the Roman Church has true apostolic succession, then they must also have the direct inspiration from the Holy Spirit, which would enable them to produce more inspired scripture and add it to the canon. Without that inspiration, there can be no absolute authority or infallibility.

Protestants are quick to point out that the office of apostle (as in the twelve "apostles" of Christ) required direct eyewitness experience of the resurrected Christ, full inspiration and empowerment by the Paraclete (the Holy Spirit or "Comforter"), and direct revelation and commission from Christ. The only exceptions to this were those to whom Jesus directly appeared and commissioned (such as Paul and James), or those upon whom Peter and the apostles laid their hands (such as Mark, Luke, and Jude) using the canonical authority ("the binding and losing authority" Matt. 16:19) that Christ had given to Peter. That authority and inspiration passed away permanently when Peter and the other inspired apostles and prophets left the earthly scene. It was not passed down to future generations. That authority and inspiration is now vested in their written word (our New Testament writings). Editor's Note: [Today men and women of God operate not by inspiration, but by revelation of the inspired word of God.]

If that (canonical) authority had been given to each successive generation of church leaders after the passing of the apostles, it would mean that the gift of inspiration was passed down also, thus keeping the canon open forever. The Mormons with their Book of Mormon would love that idea, as would the Moonies and their writings of Sun Myung Moon. So, we can see that the Romanist idea of apostolic succession opens the door for all kinds of confusion and corruption to creep into the church, and cheapens the idea of the inspiration, inerrancy, and absolute authority of the true canon of Scripture.

Nevertheless, the Romanists did not surrender their position. They point to the infallible canon and the infallible creeds as evidence of their infallibility. They state that if we deny the infallibility of the Church, we are thereby negating the legitimacy of the canon and the creeds, since the Church produced them. The Reformers had difficulty with this argument, but Preterists can easily see the fallacy. Since the creeds are wrong in their timing of the eschatological events, the Church who produced those creeds is also mistaken.

Furthermore, if the Church made mistakes in the creeds, how can we trust their work on the canon? If we have the correct canon of New Testament scriptures (and I believe we do), we are burdened to explain how that could happen without an infallible Church to select, collect, and approve those books. If the inspired apostles of the first century did not approve the canon for us, we are left to believe that fallible churchmen muddled their way through the process for two centuries and finally came up with a canon that can never be considered infallibly correct. The only acceptable solution, at least for a Protestant, is to believe that the first-century inspired apostles did the canonization work, and that the later church merely recognized (not authorized) the already-established apostolic canon. That would be a canon we could trust, which would render all later creeds and councils subordinate to it (sola scriptura).

This idea of a closed canon by the time of the passing of the apostles is a sword that cuts both ways. Not only does it rule out the Roman Church's claim of having the right to decide the content of our canon, but it also rules out all other claims by Protestants and cults as well. The apostles were the only ones who had the inspiration and authority to not only write inspired Scripture, but also to infallibly decide which books were authoritative. Subsequent church leaders were neither inspired, inerrant, eyewitnesses of the resurrected Christ, nor directly commissioned by Him. This means that the only Christians who were ever qualified to set the boundaries of the New Testament canon were those very apostles who produced the writings in the first place. This view is called apostolic canonization. It is not a new theory, nor is it exclusive to Preterism (cf. Ernest L. Martin, Restoring the Original Bible, 1994), but it is certainly consistent with the Preterist idea of a pre-70 date for all the NT books.

The Early Date of the New Testament Canon

It is easy to support a pre-AD 70 date for the gospels of Matthew, Mark, and Luke, since Luke and Acts were clearly written before Paul was released from his imprisonment in AD 63, and Luke claims that he was aware of at least two other gospel accounts (Matthew and Mark) before he wrote his gospel (Luke 1:1). Furthermore, the Gospel of Luke contains some of the unique material found in either Matthew or Mark, but not in both. Therefore, Matthew and Mark's gospels must have been among Luke's research material, thus predating his gospel. Luke's gospel, however, does not show any awareness of the unique material in John's gospel, suggesting that it was probably written after Luke. We can also date all fourteen of Paul's epistles (including Hebrews, which is found in all extant ancient complete collections of Pauline epistles) prior to his martyrdom under Nero in AD 64. We also know that James, the Lord's brother, wrote his epistle before he was martyred in AD 62. The epistle of Jude appears to have been written about the same time as the second epistle of Peter, since there is considerable similarity of content. Since Peter was martyred under Nero in AD 64-65, his two epistles were obviously written before AD 70. This puts a pre-AD 70 date on all New Testament books except the writings of the Apostle John.

What about John's Writings?

Evangelical scholars agree that all 27 books of our New Testament canon were written before the apostles died, but they do not terminate the apostolic generation until AD 95, the alleged date of John's death. This presumed longevity of John leaves the door wide open for a post-AD 70 date for the Johannine writings i.e., his Gospel, three epistles, and the book of Revelation, thirty years after the deaths of Apostles Peter and Paul in AD 64-65. This creates a dilemma for Preterists, who date John's writings before AD 70.

If John or any of the other inspired apostles lived beyond AD 70, they would have retained the gift of inspiration and could easily have written more inspired books after AD 70. And we would have expected them to write some more, in view of the confusion and doctrinal deviations that sprang up soon after the destruction of Jerusalem. If any of the inspired apostles were still around, they would have been able to clear up the confusion and put the church back on track, both by their public teaching and by their inspired writings. Of course, many Futurists use this very argument to support their idea that all of John's writings were written after AD 70, especially the book of Revelation. However, there is a Biblical answer to this conundrum. We believe Apostle John died in the Neronic persecution, about the same time as Peter and Paul (ca. AD 64-65), thus forcing all of the New Testament books, including John's writings, to be written before AD 70. Where is the biblical support for that?

In Matthew 20:20-23 (and it's parallel in Mark 10:35-40) the mother of the two sons of Zebedee, James and John, asked Jesus to place her two sons on his right and left when He came into His Kingdom (i.e., at the Parousia): But Jesus answered, "You do not know what you [plural] are asking. Are you [both] able to drink the cup that I am about to drink?" They [both] said to Him, "We [both] are able." He said to them [both], "My cup you [both] shall drink; but to sit on My right and on My left, this is not Mine to give, but it is for those for whom it has been prepared by My Father." (Matt 20:22-23 NASB95). Jesus asked both sons (not just James) if they were able to drink the cup of martyrdom which He was about to drink, and they both said to Him that they were able. Jesus then said to both of them (James and John) that they both would indeed drink the same cup of martyrdom, implying that neither of them would remain alive until His Parousia. James (the brother of John) was killed by Herod Agrippa I in about AD 44 (Acts 12:1-2). When did John drink the cup?

Josephus (Antiq. 20:200 in Thackeray, or Antiq. 20.9.1 in Whiston) mentions that "James [the Lord's brother] and some of his companions" were arrested by Annas II in April of AD 62 during the three months between the end of Festus' and the beginning of Albinus' procuratorship. Josephus says that James was killed by Annas II, but he does not say what happened to the others who were arrested. It is possible that John was one of those companions, but since John was a friend of the Annas family (as John himself tells us in John 18:15-16), he may have been exiled to Patmos rather than being killed. This would explain when and how John was exiled to Patmos.

Since Luke's gospel (written before Paul's trial in AD 61-63) does not reflect any awareness of the unique material in John's gospel, nor does his book of Acts (also finished before Paul's trial in AD 61-63) mention the exile of John to Patmos, it seems probable that the Gospel of John was written after Luke had already composed his gospel account (ca. AD

60), and that the book of Revelation, written during John's exile to Patmos, was composed after the book of Acts and after Paul's trial in Rome began in AD 61. The date for Luke and Acts then becomes the peg on which we hang the dates for several of the New Testament books.

The book of Revelation would have been written after John was arrested and exiled in AD 62. That would place its writing at about AD 62-63, while Paul was still on trial in Rome (AD 61-63) and before his release in AD 63. That would mean that the book of Revelation was not the last book of our New Testament to be written. Since the book of Revelation warns its readers to "not add to . . . nor take away from this book of prophecy" (Rev 22:18-19), tradition sees this as implying that Revelation was the last book to be written. But that supposition is easily overturned when we remember that both Paul and Peter reflect awareness of the book of Revelation in some of their epistles (cf. 1 Pet 5:13; Ephesians; Colossians; Philippians; and Heb 12:22-29; 13:14). Peter wrote his first epistle from the city cryptically named "Babylon". Paul wrote several things about Jerusalem above, the new creation, and the New Heavens and Earth, which sound very similar to the descriptions in the book of Revelation. This suggests that both Paul and Peter had seen the book of Revelation before they wrote their epistles.

John's Gospel and his three shorter epistles appear to have been written before he was exiled, that is, before AD 62. If John was still being held under Roman guard on the island of Patmos when the Neronic persecution broke out two years later in the summer of AD 64, he most likely would have been killed by the Romans (right after Paul was killed, and shortly before Peter died ca. AD 64-65). However, it is also possible that John was released shortly after writing Revelation, and went to nearby Ephesus, where he would have been at the time of the Neronic persecution. That would account for the tradition which says he was buried in Ephesus. This would have fulfilled Jesus' prediction of John's drinking the same cup of martyrdom (Matt 20:23) that his brother James had already drunk twenty years earlier (Acts 12:1-2). That would mean all of John's writings were finished before the Neronic persecution in AD 64, supporting the idea that the whole New Testament canon was written before AD 70.

Pre-AD 70 Dates for All the Books

Norman Geisler, in his article "The Dating of the New Testament" on his website (http://bethinking.org), argues for a pre-AD 62 date for Luke and Acts, citing both William F. Albright and John A.T. Robinson as examples of scholars who have suggested pre-AD 70 dates for most (if not all) of the New Testament documents. John A. T. Robinson especially, in his Redating the New Testament (1976), defended the idea that every New Testament book must have been written before AD 70, because the destruction of Jerusalem "is never once mentioned as a past fact" in any of the New Testament documents (p. 13). Several conservative scholars have advocated a pre-70 date for all New Testament books (e.g., Arthur Ogden, Milton Terry, David Chilton, J. Stuart Russell, and Cornelius Vanderwaal). Based on the above considerations, here is how we would sequence and date the twenty-seven New Testament books. A fuller explanation of the reasoning behind this can be found in the books, First-Century Events by Edward E. Stevens, and The Development of the New Testament by Arthur Ogden:

1 Thessalonians (AD 52)
2 Thessalonians (AD 52)
Galatians (AD 52-53)
Corinthians (AD 57)
Corinthians (AD 57)
Romans (AD 58)
Matthew (pre-AD 58)
Mark (pre-AD 58)
Luke (AD 58-61)
Acts (AD 58-61)
John (AD 60-62)
1, 2, 3 John (AD 61-62)
James (AD 62)
Revelation (AD 62-63)
Ephesians (AD 63)
Colossians (AD 63)
Philemon (AD 63)
Philippians (AD 63)
Hebrews (AD 63)
1 Timothy (AD 63)
Titus (AD 63)
Peter (AD 63-64)
Timothy (AD 64)
Jude (AD 64-65)
2 Peter (AD 64-65)

Collection and Certification of the Canon

Anyone who has studied textual criticism, knows that these books must have had early and wide circulation around the Mediterranean rim. The same variant readings appear in early manuscripts that come from Alexandria, Palestine, Turkey, Greece, and Rome. That was a wide circulation at an early date. How did that happen? We know that Paul carried his own collection of "books and parchments" with him on all his missionary trips. When you come bring the cloak which I left at Troas with Carpus, and the books, especially the parchments. (2 Tim 4:13, NAS95) He evidently kept copies of his epistles with him so that the churches he visited could copy from his originals. And there is a good chance that he not only had copies of his own epistles, but perhaps one or more of the gospel accounts as well (in addition to Luke). These were the "exemplars" or master copies from which the churches made their own copies.

Furthermore, when Peter wrote his second epistle in AD 64, he showed that he was not only aware that Paul had written a number of epistles, but that he had evidently read them, and was here stating his approval of them: And regard the patience of our Lord as salvation; just as also our **beloved brother** Paul, according to the wisdom given him, **wrote to you**, as also in **all his letters**, speaking in them of these things, in which are some things hard to understand, which the untaught and unstable distort, as they do also the **rest of the Scriptures**, to their own destruction. (2 Pet 3:15-16, NAS95)

There are four things we need to notice in these two verses (see the bold-faced words in the text above). Peter refers to Paul in post-mortem eulogistic style ("our beloved brother") as if Paul was already dead. He uses the past tense ("wrote to you") in regard to Paul's writing activities, as if Paul was no longer writing to them. Peter then mentions Paul's letters as a group ("all his letters"), as if he had access to a completed collection of them, implying that Paul had already been martyred and was no longer writing letters to the churches. When he says, "rest of the Scriptures," it implies that Peter had access to a collection of canonical Scriptures there in Jerusalem. Peter places Paul's collection of letters on a par with "the rest of the scriptures," which certifies their inspiration and canonical authority. Peter here uses his "keys of the Kingdom" (binding and losing authority) to pronounce the whole collection of Paul's letters as canonical. Notice what Jesus had earlier said to Peter:

"I will give you [singular] the keys of the kingdom of heaven; and whatever you [singular] bind on earth shall have been bound in heaven, and whatever you [singular] loose on earth shall have been loosed in heaven." (Matt. 16:19 NASB95). Peter literally played the key role in the canonical process, not because he was the most prolific writer, or because he had the best collection of books, or the best rabbinical education, but because he had the inspired authority to recognize and certify which writings were true. The authority that Christ gave to Peter was not passed on to successive generations.

Otherwise, writing by inspiration and certifying new books as canonical would have also continued, thus leaving the canon open forever. This means that the collection of writings approved by Peter and the apostles would have been the first and only authoritative canonical list. Furthermore, it means that inspired men, rather than later generations of uninspired men, did the writing, collecting, and certifying of that canonical list. The result is a canon we can trust, and which renders any determinations by later uninspired churchmen as being secondary and subordinate.

In conclusion, I am not saying that all, or even many, of the churches throughout the Roman Empire had copies of all the New Testament books. Jerusalem may have been the only church that had copies of all twenty-seven, although it is possible that the churches of Antioch, Rome, and Alexandria did as well. The universal pre-70 distribution of the canon is not essential to apostolic canonization.

All that is necessary is that Peter, the other apostles, and the Jerusalem church had copies of all of them, and that Peter gave his approval of them before he was martyred in the Neronic persecution of AD 64-65. That much seems to be indicated by the statements of Peter and Paul which we looked at above.

-Ed Stevens

Matthew Synopsis

Matthew is the first book of the New Testament. The Church Fathers ordered it to be this way, because it relates very much to the Jewish origins of the Christian faith. Old Testament references are abundant, and even the genealogy of Jesus descending back to Abraham is in Matthew's gospel (Matthew 1:1; 3:9; Galatians 3:8; 3:16). The entirety of the New Testament itself is the fulfillment of Old Testament prophecy, therefore, Matthew frequently uses such words as, "that it might be fulfilled which was spoken by the prophet" … (Matt. 1:22, 2:15, 23, 4:14, 8:17, 12:17, 13:14, 35, 21:4, 27:35), or, "it is written (Matt. 2:5; 4:4,6-7,10, 11:10; 21:13; 26:24; 26:31)". The central theme of the ministry of Jesus is revealed in Matthew, which is, "the Kingdom"! "The kingdom" is mentioned no less than 50 times by Matthew! The kingdom is at hand in Matt. 3:2 and 4:17, it is to be prayed in, according to Matt. 6:10, sought for and prioritized in Matt. 6:33, preached as at hand by first-century disciples in Matt. 10:7, and its binding power over Satan by the Spirit is seen in Matt. 12:26-29, the same binding of Satan we read of in Rev. 20:1-2!

The preachers of this message would be hated of all men and nations for His name's sake, but if they endured to the consummation, they would be saved in Matt. 10:22 (compare with Matt. 24:9 & 13, a first-century event!). They were given a promise by Jesus, that, "you shall not have gone over the cities of Israel, until the Son of Man come" (Matt.10:23). Futurists really squirm at this passage and are left simply scratching their heads. Clearly, a first-century coming of Jesus takes place here! This first-century generation was possessed with the power of Satan, as we read in Matt. 12:34, "O generation of vipers", and Matt. 12:43-45, "When the unclean spirit is gone out of a man…he goes and takes with himself seven other spirits more wicked than himself… Even so shall it be also unto this wicked generation." Their generation became a habitation of devils and every foul spirit, yet a remnant became a habitation of God through the Spirit (Rev.18:2, Eph. 2:22)! The battle was on, as all power was given to these first-century disciples (Matt. 28:18-20; Lu. 10:18-19) who turned the world upside down (Acts 17:6)! The mysteries of the kingdom are revealed in chapter Matt. 13:11, and the darkness understands it not in Matt. 13:13-15, "By hearing they will hear and not understand; and seeing they will see and not perceive…and their eyes they have closed."

This is the same delusion we read of, which comes upon that generation, in 2 Thess. 2:11, as well as was prophesied by Moses, "For they are a nation void of counsel, neither is there any understanding in them. O that they were wise, that they understood this, that they would consider their latter end (Deut. 32:28-29)!" Chapter 13 reveals the wheat and the tares (vs. 24-30, 37-40), which are equivalent to the sheep and the goats in Chapter 25, and the wheat and the chaff in Matt. 3:12. The tares (Matt. 13:30 & 40), goats (25:46), and chaff (3:12), are all judged with unquenchable fire. The wheat and tares look the same, the sheep and goats sound the same, while the wheat and chaff appear to be intertwined as one, until they are beaten and broken. At that time, they become separated, and the worthless chaff is revealed and is carried away in the wind (Dan. 2:35, Rev. 20:11, Matt. 21:43-44) while the substantive wheat is all that remains. The true Jews (Rom. 2:28-29) were separated from those, who said they were Jews, and were not, but did lie, and were the synagogue of Satan (Rev. 2:9; 3:9)! Rome considered Christianity to be but a sect of Judaism. Titus believed that destroying the temple would do away with both, "the root and the offshoot". Yet it was the temple's destruction that legitimized the true Jews, who worshiped in spirit and in reality, in the true temple of God and in the body of Christ, a holy temple and habitation of God through the Spirit (Matt. 12:8; Jo. 2:19-21; 1 Cor. 12:12; Eph. 2:21-22; Col. 1:24; Heb. 9:8). Heb. 9:8 makes this abundantly clear; it states that when the first tabernacle would no longer be standing, the true temple would thereby be made manifest, and that it would be clear for all to see which temple was to be worshiped in.

Jesus was the last temple standing! The temple in Jerusalem was the type, while Jesus is the reality (Matt. 12:6; Eph. 2:20-22). This is why Heb. 8:2 refers to the true tabernacle. There is the true vine (John 15:1), as opposed to the vine in type, which was the vineyard (Isaiah 5), the nation of Israel. Jesus Christ and He alone, becomes the true and new dwelling place of God! The Sabbath, the Passover, and all of the feasts, become realized in Jesus Christ (Col. 2:16-17; Gal. 4:9-11). They are all types (1 Cor. 10:6, "examples", Greek, "Tupos", types, and shadows (Heb. 10:1). Jesus fulfills every jot and tittle of the Old Testament scriptures, the law and the prophets (Matt. 5:17-18), and the Psalms (Lu. 24:44-45), as all of scripture testifies of Him (Jo. 5:39)! Therefore, if all of the Old Testament scriptures were types and shadows of Jesus, what then was the nation of Israel a type of? It cannot be a type of itself; it must be a type of the covenantal dwelling place of God. We see this clearly in Matt. 2:15, "that it might be fulfilled which was spoken of the Lord by the prophet, saying, "Out of Egypt have I called my Son." This is a quote from Hos. 11:1, and Matthew sees the nation of Israel coming out of Egypt, as a type, which was fulfilled by Jesus as He came out of Egypt (Matt. 2:14-15). The dwelling place of God is in Jesus and in Jesus alone, no longer in the Old Covenant Kingdom (Nation) of Israel! Jesus even fulfills the very definition of "Israel", "He will rule as God, God prevails, He shall be a prince of God". The name "Israel" is included in every jot and tittle of scripture, which is fulfilled by Jesus, and testifies of Jesus (Matt. 5:17-18, Lu. 24:44-45; Jo. 5:39), and Jesus alone! To be "in Christ" (Words used together 76 times in the N.T.), abiding in Him, or dwelling in Him (Jo. 14-17), exceeds any and all other dwelling places, now and forevermore, despite what dispensationalists are telling us in our day! Glory to Christ in the church, age without consummation (Eph. 3:21)!

There is no consummation to the church age! Jesus prophesies concerning His coming in His kingdom, in Matt. 16:27-28, "For the Son of Man shall come in the glory of His Father with His angels; and then He shall reward every man according to his works. Verily I say unto you, there be some standing here, which shall not taste of death, till they see the Son of Man coming in His kingdom." More head scratching here for futurists. They attempt to make the case that this coming of Jesus is fulfilled in the very next chapter in the transfiguration. Yet there is no mention of angels being present, and of rewards being handed out there. Furthermore, this event was only six days later (Matt. 17:1), and who among the disciples had died within those six days? If "some standing here shall not taste of death, till they see the Son of man coming in His kingdom", then some would taste of death before the event! None died before six days had passed, yet most were martyred prior to A.D. 70, when Jesus came as King of kings in judgment to destroy those murderers and burn their city (Matt. 22:1-7)! The Old Covenant Kingdom (Nation) was about to (Greek: Mello, about to be) face the wrath of God (Matt. 3:7; 23:35-38; 24:2-3; Lu. 23:28-30; 1 Thess. 2:14-16, Heb. 8:13). Matt., Chapters 20-25 contain escalating descriptions and warnings of this coming judgment. In Matt. 20:11, the first laborers, the Jews, murmured in unbelief. In Matt. 21:12, 13, Jesus demonstrates some of the wrath to come in cleansing the temple.

The temple is key to the impending judgment (Matt. 23:38; 24:2). In Matt. 21:28-32, of the two sons, the one who believed was not of the religious order of the day in Israel. He, and the publicans and sinners, freely entered the kingdom through faith. In Matt. 21:19, Jesus curses the fig tree by pronouncing, "let no fruit grow on thee henceforward FOREVER." How do dispensationalists miss this last word in regard to their fig tree rebirth scenario (Matt. 24:32)? No fruit FOREVER, included in "forever" is 1948, 1967, or any other future time! In Matt. 21:21, the mountain kingdom (Mountains often represent kingdoms in scripture, Ps. 46:1-6, Isa. 41:15-16; 64:1-4; Jer. 51:24-25; Dan. 2:35, 44, Amos 4:1; Lu. 3:5, Gal. 4:24-26, Heb. 12:18-28) of Israel is to be prayed against in precatory prayers of faith that ascend as incense, resulting in it being thrown into the sea, the abyss (Rev. 8:3-8). In Matt. 21:33-41, we have the parable of the vineyard. The vineyard was Israel (Isa. 5). The servants, the prophets, were beaten, killed, and stoned as they sought for fruit from the nation. Last of all He sent His Son whom they cast out and slew. The nation's leaders defined their own judgment as they pronounced that the householder would, "miserably destroy those wicked men, and will let out his vineyard unto other husbandmen, which shall render Him the fruits in their seasons (21:41)".

Due to their rejection of Jesus, they are told, "the kingdom shall be taken from you and given to another nation bringing forth the fruits thereof" (Matt. 21:43). The Old Covenant

Kingdom (Nation), capitol city, and temple, were types which were passing, fulfilled in the reality of the New Covenant Kingdom (Nation), capitol city, and temple (Gal. 4:22-31;6:16, Eph. 2:12-14, 20-22; Heb. 12:22-23). The New Covenant Kingdom (Nation) is clearly defined by Peter, but you are a … holy NATION (1 Pet. 2:9)! Note that Jesus says nothing of the kingdom being taken away from Old Covenant Israel and given back to them at some point in the future! The next verse in Matt. 21:44 describes the Stone cut out without hands (Dan. 2:34) crushing all those in resistance to the New Covenant Kingdom (Nation). The greatest resistance in the Roman Empire, the feet bearing the impact of the stone, came from the leadership within the Old Covenant Kingdom (Nation) dwelling within the Roman Empire. Those resisters would be broken to pieces, and become like chaff, ground to powder (Matt. 21:44) and carried away by the wind of the Spirit, and no place was found for them (Dan. 2:34, 35; Rev. 20:11). As a result, The Stone became a great mountain (kingdom) and filled the whole earth (Dan. 2:35)! In Chapter 22:1-7 of Matthew, is the parable of the marriage feast. The King sends his servants to those who had been invited to the marriage for His Son.

They in return had better things to do, and some of them even entreated them spitefully, and slew them. "The King heard thereof, He was wroth: and He sent forth HIS ARMIES and destroyed THOSE MURDERERS AND BURNED UP THEIR CITY (Matt. 22:7)!" These same murderers are identified in the next chapter (Matt. 23:29-36), and in Jo. 8:44, "Ye are of your father the devil, and the lusts of your father ye will do. He was a murderer from the beginning!" Rev. 18:24 says this same thing, and in her (The Great City, Jerusalem, Rev. 11:8) was found the blood of prophets, and of saints, and of all that were slain upon the earth." God sent forth His Armies to execute His judgment upon them. The armies of one nation to judge another nation, as an act carrying out the judgment of God, is common throughout the Old Testament. Consider that Nebuchadnezzar, is referred to, by God, as, "My servant" (Jer. 43:10) in executing the judgment of God upon Israel. The Lord comes to Babylon to judge it through the Medes in Isa. 13:1, 9-10, 17. He comes in judgment to Egypt through the sword of another nation in Ezek. 30:3-4. In the case of Israel's judgment in the first century (Matt. 23:37-38; 24:2-3, 15; Lu. 21:20-22), the city of those murderers was literally burned up, "… blood, and fire, and vapor of smoke (Acts 2:19)."

In Matthew 23, we find the eight "woes" given to the leaders of the Old Covenant Kingdom (Nation). They hear the most chilling words ever given to human beings in regard to their impending judgment, "that upon you may come all the righteous bloodshed upon the earth…Verily I say unto you, all these things shall come upon THIS GENERATION (Matt. 23:35-36)! The words THIS GENERATION are words used together multiple times throughout Matthew and are always referring to a first century generation. Never is "generation" (Genea) used to communicate "race" in the New Testament, as some dispensationalists attempt to make it do so in Matt. 24:34. The only Greek word that could possibly do so is genos, not genea. In Matthew, genea is used 10 times. It's used 37 times in the New Testament. The attempt is made to make genea mean race in the Olivet Discourse (Matt. 24:34; Mk. 13:30; Lu. 21:32). When asked to cite a single passage from the 34 remaining usages of genea, where "race" is being communicated, proponents of this theory are silenced. Genea is always describing a group of people living together at the same time, from generation to generation, etc., over about a forty-year period of time. There is always a timeline connected with every usage of genea, such as, "An evil and adulterous generation seeks after a sign, and there shall no sign be given it, but the sign of the prophet Jonas (Matt. 12:39)."

The resurrection spoken of here was an event that occurred during the timeline of the first-century. The words 'this generation' used together are very important in specifying a first-century generation. Dispensationalists will go so far as to change the wording and sentence structure of Matt. 24:34, by saying, "that generation which sees these things will not pass till all be fulfilled". The word "this" is removed and replaced with "that" (true replacement theology), and "which sees" is added. This is very significant, because the word "this" is what we refer to as the "near demonstrative". I may say, "This chair that I'm sitting in, as opposed to that distant chair across the room." Readers are hearing a distinction of generations, "this first-century generation", as opposed to a distant generation thousands of years off. In fact, "this" (Greek; houtos genea) generation could be read as "this very generation". So, "this generation" in Matt. 23:36, "Verily, I say to you, all these things shall come upon this generation", cannot be speaking of a first-century generation", while Matt. 24:34 is speaking of a distant generation, "Verily (same emphasis by Jesus, not "possibly"), I say unto you, (First-century disciples, "you" which had asked, "tell us when these things shall be?") This generation shall not pass away, until all these things are fulfilled."

With virtually the exact same wordage, is Jesus communicating a first century generation in Matt. 23:36, and a distant one in Matt. 24:34? Extreme torture must be exerted upon the text to conclude such a thought. Anyone with an honest heart concerning the word (Lu. 8:15), has to admit the grammatical impossibilities, and unreasonableness, involved with such thinking! Therefore, Matthew 24, the Olivet Discourse (Mk. 13; Lu. 21), as well as the book of Revelation and other New Testament passages, must be reexamined and placed in their proper context and framework, which is a time frame describing events in the first century, and not those of the 21st century. R.C. Sproul states that approximately 2/3 of the New Testament scriptures are addressing the subject of Eschatology, or Bible Prophecy. If 2/3 of our modern-day understandings of the New Testament is in the wrong filling cabinet, then much of our grasp of scripture, including the remaining 1/3 in the New Testament and the entire Old Testament, will be distorted from the original intent of the heart, mind, and plan of God! As for this passage in Matthew 24, with today's popular opinion concerning it having been shaped by Hal Lindsey's.

The Late Great Planet Earth, we must break it down and be renewed in our minds concerning it, laying aside the science fiction books of Lindsey and Lahaye. To start with, if Matt. 24:34, places the events in the first century, we can begin by backing into the chapter and examining what first century events might fit into the descriptions laid out in verses 1-33. Keep in mind also, that chapters 20-23 of Matthew are escalated warnings through parables, and point-blank last rights statements, speaking to the Pharisees (Matt. 21:43), and warning them of impending judgment that was about to come upon them. After the eight woes, in Chapter 23, we read, "that upon you may come (be required of in Lu. 11:50-51) ALL THE RIGHTEOUS BLOOD SHED UPON THE EARTH (Matt. 23:35-36, see also Rev. 18:24)! In Matt. 23:37-38, Jesus spells it out, "O Jerusalem, Jerusalem … Behold, your house (temple) is left unto you desolate (key work in Bible Prophecy Matt. 24:15; Dan. 9:24-27)!" Two verses later the Olivet discourse begins in Matt. 24:1. Note that there is no inspired chapter break to disrupt the flow of the context and conversation.

The disciples pick up right where Jesus left off, attempting to correct His "Jerusalem's house left desolate" statement (Matt. 23:37-38), by pointing out the magnitude of the temple structures. Jesus assures them in Matthew 24:2 that He is not misspeaking concerning this, "see ye (Remember, throughout this chapter, that Jesus is dialoguing and addressing His first century disciples) not all these things? Verily I say unto you, there shall not be left here one stone upon another that shall not be thrown down." A clear reference here to the temple's destruction in A.D. 70. Matthew 24:3 states, "and as he sat upon the Mount of Olives (Thus, "The Olivet Discourse"), the disciples came unto Him privately, saying, Tell US (First century disciples), when shall these things be? And what shall be the sign of thy coming and of the consummation of the world (age)?" In the context of the previous verse, the disciples put together that the destruction of the Old Covenant headquarters was in direct relationship to the consummation of the Old Covenant age. There are not three different events loaded in the disciple's questions here.

Mark makes this clear when he words it as follows, "tell us when shall these things be? And what shall be the sign when all these things shall be fulfilled (Mark 13:4)." No "coming" or "consummation of the age" in Mark, yet all these things being fulfilled relates only to the temple's destruction, followed by the same explanation given by Jesus here in Mk. 13:5, "and Jesus answering them began to say, take heed lest any man deceive you.", exactly as he does in Matt. 24:4, "and Jesus answering them began to say, take heed lest any man deceive you…"

The same answer, therefore, the same question is being asked in these parallel passages, and Mark tells us that the following these things are in direct relationship only to the temple's destruction. Therefore, Matthew's "these things", "coming", and "consummation of the age" (Matt. 24:3) are all fulfilled in direct relationship only to the temple's destruction. First century history, recorded by Josephus and Tacitus, clearly defines deceivers (Matt. 24:4), false messiahs (Matt. 24:5), wars and rumors of wars, and nation (Ethnos) against nation (Matt. 24:6,7), in the Roman civil wars, and Rome's invasion and destruction of Jerusalem.

The progression and the consequences of these wars are recorded, in detail, in famines, and pestilences. The magnitude and frequencies of earthquakes at this time are described by Seneca in the following manner, "How often have the cities of Asia and Achaea fallen with one fatal shock! So many cities have been swallowed up in Syria, how many in Macedonia! How often has Cyprus been wasted by this calamity! How often has Paphos become ruin! News has often been brought us of the demolition of whole cities at once." Josephus states concerning an earthquake in Judea, that it was of such magnitude, "that the constitution of the universe was confounded for the destruction of men." And, that it was "no common" calamity. In Matt. 24:9, 13, Jesus stated, "then shall they deliver you up to be afflicted, and shall kill you, and you shall be hated of all nations for my name's sake … but he that shall endure to the consummation, the same shall be saved". Beyond clear here, is the description of the first century persecution, as confirmed in Matthew 10:22, "and you shall be hated of all men for My Name's sake, but he that endures to the consummation shall be saved."

The exact same words, addressed to the exact same disciples, concerning the exact same tribulation in which the disciples endured during the first century (Revelation 1:9). In Matt. 24:14, the gospel of the kingdom was preached in all the "world" (Greek: "Oikoumene", the inhabited Roman World). The gospel went as far as the census went in Luke 2:1 (Oikoumene "world"). See that it was preached in all the world in the following passages: Colossians 1:5-6, 23; Romans 1:8; 10:18; 16:25-26 and Acts 17:6 Oikoumene "world"). The desolation of the temple is clear in the next verse (24:15), compare with Daniel 9:24-27, and Luke 21:20, before which time disciples will be given a warning, "And when ye (First century disciples) shall see Jerusalem compassed with armies, then know that the desolation is nigh (Lu. 21:20)." They are told to flee in these parallel passages (Matt. 24:16, Lu. 21:21). Notice the locality of the tribulation of which they are fleeing, just get to the mountains outside of Judea, and you are good. Thus, it is not a global twenty first-century event, in an era of F-22's and Nukes, in which case such fleeing would be futile. They are told not to come down from their housetops in the next verse (Matt. 24:17), describing first century homes in Jerusalem (Acts 10:9).

Nursing mothers are warned in Matt. 24:19, "And woe unto them that are with child, and to them that give suck in those days". See the exact same wordage in Lu. 23:28-30, where there is no question as to the timeline and location of these nursing mothers, "Daughter of Jerusalem…weep for your children, for behold, the days (Same days as Matt. 24:19) are coming in which they shall say, blessed are the breasts which never gave suck." We see the same nursing mothers, the same breasts, the same sucking, the same children, the same city, in the same century! See also Lu. 21:23, saying the exact same thing in the exact same context! They would desire death from the mountains falling on them (Lu. 23:30), which is a quote from Hos. 10:8 and Isa. 2:19, which is also quoted in Rev. 6:15-16. By the way, Josephus, a "chief captain", was literally found in one such cave, as described in Rev. 6:15.

In the next verse, Matt. 24:20, we see the disciples addressed, "But pray ye that your flight be not in winter, neither on the Sabbath day". Who? His disciples in direct dialogue with Him. When? In the first century. Where? In Israel, when Sabbath laws limited travel. In Matt. 24:21, all of the above is defined as, "great tribulation", which clearly has a time frame, "those days", and "the days" (Matt. 24:19, 22, 29; Mk.13:19; Lu. 21:22-23; 23:29), and a location. As we've just seen, "When ye (first century disciples) shall see Jerusalem compassed with armies…flee to the mountains" (Lu. 21:20; Matt. 24:15-16). Where? Jerusalem is the epicenter of this great tribulation. It would be the worst tribulation for the Old Covenant Kingdom (Israel). The Old Covenant is no longer in effect (Heb. 8:13), it has vanished away, fulfilled by Christ, and no one is required by God to live under it! Therefore, this tribulation, which John says he was in, in the first century (Rev. 1:9), would be the worst ever for the Old Covenant people (Thy people, Dan. 12:1), in that land, at that time! Even if one attempted to say that the Old Covenant is somehow still in effect, and that modern Israel is God's chosen people (the New Testament only mentions a "chosen people" in Jesus, (Jo. 15:16; Eph. 1:4; 1 Pet. 2:9), one must then accept hyperbole on the matter.

In Ezek. 5:9, Jerusalem is told that the Babylonian invasion would be the worst judgment the city has ever seen or will see again. If I say to my child, "this is going to be the worst spanking you will ever receive", and then say the same thing at another point and time, then hyperbole has to be understood, and not 21st-century western wooden literalism. In Matt. 24:23-26 (paralleling 24: 4,5,11), false Christs and false prophets arise, which Josephus records in great detail, and Jesus warns, "Behold I have told YOU", that is, His disciples with Him in dialogue (Matt. 24:1-3), not them, some future disciples (Consider Jo.17:20). Acts records two such cases (Acts 8:9-10; 21:38), and Josephus describes the prophecy's fulfillment in great detail with the very words, "…a certain magician, whose name was Theudas, persuaded a great part of the people to take their effects with them, and follow him to the river Jordan; for he told them he was a prophet, and that he would, by his own command, divide the river, and afford them an easy passage over it; and many were deluded by his words…" Josephus also states, "these imposters and deceivers persuade the multitude to follow them into the wilderness (Matt. 24:26), and pretended that they would exhibit manifest wonders and signs (Matt. 24:24), that should be performed by the providence of God. And many that were prevailed on by them suffered the punishments of their folly…" (See, Antiquities of the Jews, Book 20, Chapter 5, Paragraph 1, Lines 97-99, Also, Book 20, Chapter 8, Paragraph 6, Lines 167,168, and Paragraph 5, lines 160, 161 of the same Chapter, and War of the Jews, Book 2, Chapter 13, Paragraph 4, Lines 259-260).

In Matt. 24:26, we have the message that the false prophets and Christs would be promoting, "He is in the desert … (in a geographical location, bodily, physically, and visibly).

These next three verses Matt. 24:26-29 parallel perfectly with Lu. 17:20-37. The Messiah's coming (Greek, Parousia; coming presence, NOT coming bodily, physically, visibly) to bring His kingdom (Luke 21:31), "comes NOT with observation (visibly), neither shall they say, lo here! Or, lo there! (in the desert place … Matt. 24:26, or Jerusalem in our day) for, behold, the kingdom of God is within you (Consider, 2 Thess. 1:10), And he said unto the disciples, The days will come, when ye (The disciples' flesh, 2 Corinthians 5:16) shall desire to see (visibly) one of the days of the Son of man (bodily, physically), and ye shall NOT SEE it (bodily, physically, visibly), And they (false prophets) shall say to you, See here (in the desert, or any other geographical location, such as Jerusalem in our day); or see there: go not after them, nor follow them. For (continuation of the previous thought) as the lightning (same exact sequence as Mt. 24:26-27), that shines out of the one part under heaven, shines unto the other part under heaven; so shall also the Son of man be in His day (Luke 17:20-24)."

It would be an event that would be clearly "seen", as Latin and Asian cultures may say, "It is written in the sky", which has nothing to do with an American understanding of skywriting by the use of an aircraft. It would be an event that would be "seen" as being perceived, discerned, and understood. This is the very meaning of Revelation 1:7, "every eye shall see him (Note here that the tribes of the land would mourn and consider that those twelve tribes are no longer with us). The root word here, from which see (Optamonai) comes from is Horao, and is defined as perceiving, discerning, and understanding something, such as, "Oh, now I see what you're saying." The event would be "visible" for all to see, as is the lightning that flashes across the sky. "For them that look for Him shall He appear the second time" (Hebrews 9:28). Those not "looking" for Him with a discerning eye could miss this appearing, as they did with the coming of Elijah before the great and terrible day of the Lord (Mal. 4:5). They missed it, and could not receive it (Matt. 11:14), the fact that John the Immerser was Elijah which was for to come. They could not receive it, because the natural man cannot receive the things of the Spirit … but He that is spiritual discerns all things (1 Cor. 2:14). Only he that has ears to hear (Matt. 11:14), can hear this. Without circumcised ears (Acts 7:51), that is, cutting the flesh out of them, they hoped for Elijah to literally come, bodily, physically, and visibly, rather than coming in the spirit and power of Elijah (Lu.1:17), they missed it! During the civil war, the world could see, through newspaper reports and word of mouth, the result of the unjust laws in the U.S., which permitted slavery. It was a war, which Lincoln contended, that was executing the judgment of the Lord (Ps. 19:9).

Luke 17 goes on to speak of the days of Noah (Luke 17:26-28; Matt. 24:37-39), and finishes with one shall be taken, and the other left (Luke. 17:34-37; Matt. 24:40-41), ending with, "where Lord (Luke. 17:37)?" No Greek analysis needed here, first grade English students would understand, "where Lord?" to mean, "where are they taken?" Answer, "wheresoever the BODY is, there will the eagles be gathered together (Lu. 17:37)". Matthew's cross-reference is (Matt. 24:29), "For wheresoever the CARCASS is, there will the eagles be gathered together". Where are they taken (Luke 17:37)? They are taken as carcasses, surrounded by eagles. Eagles (Aetos), not vultures. An eagle standard was carried by each Roman Legion; the troops themselves would be referred to as eagles, often tattooed upon with images of eagles. Therefore, those who were taken were bodies, corpses, which were surrounded by Roman soldiers, eagles. So, to be taken, was to be taken as corpses, not taken in a rapture! In Matt. 24:39, "the flood came and took them all away", the very next verse says (Matt. 24:40), "the one shall be taken, and the other left." Taken is a bad thing here. To be left was to be left alive. Therefore, the term, and concept, of "Left behind" is an utter hoax in our day. Behind is an added word to the text, by those speaking out from their own! There is no scheduled air lift for believers, according to the words of Jesus, "I pray not that thou shouldest take them out of the world (Jo. 17:15)!!!" In Matt. 24:29, "…the sun be darkened, and the moon shall not give her light, and the stars shall fall from heaven, and the powers (Rom.13:1) of the heavens shall be shaken." Here we have a quote from Isa. 13:10, referenced in most Bibles.

Virtually all scholars agree that this is language used to describe the judgment that would come upon Babylon (Isa. 13:1), through the Medes (Isa. 13:17), and that nothing transpired in the physical heavens involving the sun, moon, and stars. Perhaps, though, being there physically and literally viewing the destruction of Babylon the heavens may have been affected, so as to dim the physical sun, moon, and stars, due to the smoke hovering over the city upon its destruction. Since most understand that the language in Isaiah 13 speaks of the judgment upon Babylon, which saw nothing transpire concerning the literal sun, moon, and stars, why then, when Jesus quotes the passage, do many of these same scholars insist that He is describing physical happenings in the heavens? Jesus, being a prophet, is using prophetic language, apocalyptic language, used throughout the Old Testament. Genesis lays out the physical laws concerning the sun to rule the day, and the moon and stars to rule the night (Gen. 1:16). Later in Genesis, Joseph prophesied using the imagery of the sun, moon, and stars, and communicates the symbolic usage of such terms in regard to rule. As Joseph's father (the sun), mother (the moon), and brothers (the stars) presently ruled over him, being the youngest, there would be a day when they would all bow to his authority and rule (Gen. 37:9-10).

So, when the prophet Daniel uses prophetic language to describe the rule of God, by saying, "…the heavens do rule", he is using such imagery to communicate the rule of God, which has nothing to do with the pagan concepts of Jupiter, Mars, or the physical sun, moon, and stars ruling over the kingdoms of men (Dan. 4:26). Even in our day, the flags of many nations use the imagery of the sun, moon, and stars, to symbolize the rule and authority of their nations. By the way, to be literal concerning the stars falling from heaven (Matt. 24:29) is a literal impossibility. It would only take a single star to incinerate the earth. Throughout the Old Testament, the Lord is continually judging this, or that, nation, describing such with the use of prophetic and apocalyptic language. Consider this judgment upon Egypt, "And when I shall put thee out, I will cover the heavens and make the stars thereof dark; I will cover the sun with a cloud, and the moon shall not give her light, All the bright lights of heaven will I make dark over you, and set dark over you, set darkness upon thy land, saith the Lord God (Ezek. 32:2, 7-8)." Consider the following non-literal usages of the sun, moon, and stars throughout the Bible; Amos 8:9; Eccl. 12:1-2; Acts 2:16-21; Rev. 6:13,14.

The word literal should be examined though. The word literal is derived from the word literature. Therefore, how does the whole of the Bible use such terms as the sun, the moon, and stars? Their usages are to be understood literally, according to the whole of the literature, the Bible. Therefore, the sun, moon, and stars are literally used symbolically. Many of those who claim to be strict literalists are very inconsistent with the time indicators in the Olivet Discourse with, "this generation" (Matt. 24:34, Mk. 13:30, Lu. 21:32), and in Revelation with shortly, quickly, and at hand (Rev. 1:1, 3; 22:10). They interpret them in a very "non-literal", symbolic manner, when the whole of scripture never uses these time indicating words (Generation; Genea, Shortly or Quickly; Tacos, and At Hand or Near; Eggus) in such a manner.

This is especially true when it comes to the seven churches in Revelation, spiritualizing them into seven church eras within a supposed "church age", when the text gives not even an iota of a hint towards such an idea. It only speaks of seven literal churches in seven literal locations, in the first century, literally! Seven church eras are blatantly read into the text. Consider how Peter clearly speaks of Joel's prophecy's fulfillment using the same cosmic imagery in Acts 2:16-21, "but this is that (This which you're seeing, that passage in Joel. Note that Peter does not say, "this is part of that".) which was spoken by the prophet Joel; And it shall come to pass in the last days (the last days of the Old Covenant then, not now), saith God, I will pour out my Spirit upon all flesh… And I will shew wonders in heaven above, and signs in the earth beneath, blood, and fire, and vapor of smoke (The exact descriptions of Jerusalem's destruction by Josephus, War of the Jews, Book 6, Chapter 8, line 406): The sun shall be turned into darkness, and the moon into blood…." The passage was fulfilled right there in the first century, therefore we understand that the sun was turned into darkness, and the moon into blood, yet nothing occurred regarding the physical sun, and moon, except only that perhaps their appearance did change, due to the smoke hovering over the city of Jerusalem.

In Matt. 24:30, we have a quote from Dan. 7:13, in which, "the Son of man came with the cloud of heaven, and came to (up to) the Ancient of Days…" Not coming down to earth in the cloud, but up to the Ancient of days. It is Jesus' vindication and exultation. We must understand, throughout the Old Testament, that the Lord comes in the cloud to this or that nation in judgment, through the sword of another nation, and uses prophetic and apocalyptic language to describe such events. Consider the following judgment pronounced upon Egypt, "The burden of Egypt, Behold, the Lord rides upon a swift cloud, and shall come into Egypt: and the idols of Egypt shall be moved at his presence (N.T. Parousia, coming presence), and the heart of Egypt shall melt in the midst of it (Isa. 19:1)." Again, upon Egypt, "For the day is near, even the day of the Lord is near, a cloudy day; it shall be the time of the heathen. And the sword shall come upon Egypt… (Ezek. 30:3-4)." Not a weather report here, but a report of coming judgment. We see the same language in Ezek. 32:7, "And when I shall put thee out, I will cover the heaven and make the stars thereof dark; I will cover the sun with a cloud, and the moon shall not give her light." And again, cosmic imagery is used to portray a local judgment determined upon Pharaoh (Ezek. 32:2); it was lights out for him! A judgment pronounced upon Israel in Joel 2:1-2 uses this same language, "… the day of the Lord cometh, for it is nigh at hand; A day of darkness and gloominess, a day of thick darkness…" And again, upon Israel and Judah, "For, Behold, the Lord cometh forth out of His place, and will come down, and tread upon the high places of the land (Mic. 1:3)."

The Lord "comes down" to bring down the exulted in judgment, but not by appearing in a bodily, physical, or visible manner. When the Lord, "…makes the cloud His chariot: who walketh upon the wings of the wind (Ps. 104:3)", He is not seen physically but uses such imagery so as to bring an understanding to His doings upon the earth. Isa. 64:1-3 describes a judgment upon Egypt in this way, "Oh that You would rend the heavens, that You would come down, that the mountains might flow down at Your presence (N.T. Parousia, coming presence), As when the melting fire burns, the fire causes the waters to boil, to make Your name known to Your adversaries, that the nations may tremble at Your presence." Youth are exhorted in Israel by Solomon using such metaphorical language, "Remember now Your Creator in the days of your youth, while…the sun, or the light of the moon, or the stars, be not darkened, nor the clouds return after the rain (Eccl. 12:1- 2)." Nothing is meant here to communicate anything to do with the physical sun, moon, and stars, or the physical clouds. In Ezek. 38:9, an invading army is prophesied to come as a storm like a cloud to cover the land. We must remember that the Bible is written in languages, and from cultures, which are eastern and much more metaphorical in nature than twenty first-century western cultures, geared more toward hard cold scientific facts. Consider how David, a prophet (Acts 2:30), uses prophetic language to describe how the Lord delivered him from Saul (who was the persecutor of David, similarly as Old Covenant Israel was a persecutor of those who were in the Son of David) in Ps. 18, "He made darkness His secret place; His pavilion round about Him were dark waters and thick clouds of the skies. At the brightness that was before Him His thick clouds passed, hail stones and coals of fire (Ps. 18:11-12)."

The earth shook in verse 7, the smoke went out of His nostrils in verse 8; He bowed the heavens in verse 9, with hail stones and lightning in verses 13 and 14. Cross-reference the hail stones and lightning here with those of Rev. 16:18, 21. So, when we read the New Testament scriptures, first written primarily by Jews, wouldn't first century Jews, most of which were saturated in the Old Testament scriptures, understand the metaphorical use of such terms? Therefore, when we read Matt. 24:30, "And then shall appear the sign (a sign is a symbol of something) of the Son of Man in heaven; and then shall all the tribes of the land mourn, and they shall see the Son of Man coming in the clouds of heaven with power and great glory." We must believe that Jesus, the prophet of prophets, is using prophetic language to describe His coming judgment upon that first century generation of demonic rulers (Matt. 23:35-36; 12:45). Yes, all judgment had been committed to Jesus (Jo. 5:2-23), who would judge as the father had throughout the Old Testament. King Jesus would come in judgment as King of kings (1 Tim. 6:15; Rev. 1:5) and send His armies (Consider Jer. 43:10) and destroy those murderers and burn their city (Matt. 22:7)! This is what infuriated Caiaphas so when he was judging Jesus. Jesus turns it around to inform Caiaphas and the Sanhedrin, that he (they) would see Him coming in cloud of judgment upon them.

He would come in judgment as the Lord would come in judgment throughout the Old Testament scriptures! Because Jesus equates Himself with God, who alone comes in judgment upon the cloud, Caiaphas responds by tearing his clothes, accusing Jesus of blasphemy and pronouncing the death penalty upon him (Matt. 26:64-66). Note the exact same Old Testament imagery, "I say to you (to Caiaphas and the Sanhedrin), Hereafter shall ye see the Son of man sitting on the right hand of power and coming in the cloud of heaven." Using the exact same wording as Matt. 24:30, Jesus says that a first century audience, Caiaphas and the Sanhedrin, would see this event! This same wording is found in Revelation 1:7, "behold, He cometh with the cloud; and every (Every, "Pas" consider usages in Matt. 3:5-6; 8:34; 21:10) eye shall see him, and they also which pierced him (First century piercers); and all the tribes (the 12 tribes are no longer with us) of the land shall wail because of Him. Even so, Amen." Contained in this passage is a quote from Zech. 12:10. The very next verse, in Zech. 12:11, clarifies that Jerusalem is the epicenter for this coming judgment. Note, that it is the "tribes of the land", not, "the nations of the earth" Remember that Rev. 1:1, 3; 22:10 (shortly, quickly, GK. Tachos), and at hand or near, (GK. Eggus) gives us the time limitations for the book's fulfillment.

As for Matt. 24:30 and its account of the same event, "all the tribes of the land mourn, and they shall see the Son of man coming in the cloud of heaven …", there is also a time limitation given. It literally has an expiration date. Its four verses later, when we read, "verify I say unto you (first century disciples, vs. 3), this generation shall not pass, till all these things be fulfilled (Matt. 24:34)." Again, "this generation", used together many times throughout the New Testament (Matt. 3:7; 11:16; 12:41-42, 45; 16:4; 23:33, 36, 24:34; Mk. 8:12, 38; 9:19; Lu. 7:31; 9:41; 11:30-32, 50-51; 17:25; Acts 2:40), is always referring to a first century generation. The (GK. "Genea"), generation is used 37 times in the New Testament and is never referring to a race or some distant generation. The only Greek word that could possibly mean "race" is Genos, not Genea. The idea itself causes dispensational theology to implode upon itself. If the Jewish "race" passes away after these things are fulfilled, then there is no throne of David in physical Jerusalem, for Jews to reign with Jesus in a future thousand-year reign! "This generation", in Matt. 23:36, four verses prior to the

Olivet Discourse, means the same thing that it does in the Olivet Discourse in Matt. 24:34! As mentioned, many shenanigans are used to twist the clear meaning of "this generation".

One of the latest is to try and say 'that' instead of "This generation shall not pass, till all these things are beginning to be fulfilled", playing with the word "fulfilled" (Ginomai). Yet, of the 678 times (GK. Ginomai) is used, there is not a single place where anyone would argue that whatever was beginning to occur would continue for another 2000 years before it was actually fulfilled. Ginomai is most often translated, "It came to pass…", and "done". Consider its usage in prophetic passages where, "This was done, that it might be fulfilled… (Matt. 1:22; 26:54, 56; Jo. 19:36), and, "then shall be brought to pass the saying that is written…" (1 Cor. 15:54). No way to stretch these fulfillments out to thousands of years into the future with Ginomai. So, putting all the antics aside, "This Generation" has to mean a first century generation (Genea) consistently throughout the New Testament, including Matt. 24:34. Therefore, verse 30 precedes verse 34, and Jesus did come in cloud of judgment upon the Jewish Tribes of the land in their generation. The same coming in the cloud, which we see in Rev. 1:7, Matt. 26:64, we see also in Acts 1:9-11.

Jesus ascends into a cloud, and the angels proclaim that, "He will come in like manner as ye have seen Him go into heaven." Same cloud, same coming, yet here we are assisted with the Greek word tropos, translated as "manner" here. (GK. Tropos) communicates coming in a figurative manner here. To turn, or to flip, the use of "cloud" into a metaphorical understanding is how tropos is being used here. Consider tropos in Matthew 23:38, where Jesus states, "…how often would I have gathered thy children together, even as (tropos) a hen gathers her chickens under her wings…" Similarly, as you see the physical clouds, so you will see Jesus come in the cloud of judgment. Similarly, not exactly! If it were exact, then Jesus would be ascending on a white horse, with His eyes as a flame of fire, on His head many crowns, His vesture dipped in blood, a sharp sword coming out of His mouth, and on His vesture and on His thigh a name written, KING OF KINGS, AND LORD OF LORDS (Rev. 19:11-16)!

Strong's Exhaustive Concordance defines tropos as: a turn, i.e. (by implication) mode or style (especially with preposition or relative prefix as adverb, like); figuratively, deportment or character—(even) as, conversation, (+ by any) means, way. See Greek trope (Strong's 5157): a turning, change, mutation. From an apparently primary trepo to turn; a turn ("trope"), i.e. Revolution (figuratively, variation) – turning. The English word trope, with its word origin from tropos, is defined: a word or expression used in a figurative sense. Tropology is the use of figurative and metaphorical language in speech or writing. So, Jesus came figuratively on the cloud of judgment in Matt. 24:30, before His generation had passed away (Matt. 24:34). So, also was the fulfillment of the fig tree in Matt. 24:32-33, "Now learn a parable of the fig tree; When his branch is yet tender, and puts forth leaves, you know (1 Th. 5:1-2) that summer is near." It would be something understandable in relation to events occurring before His generation had passed away (Matt. 24:34). The fig tree has everything to do with an approaching season of an event ("summer"), and the things that would be signs confirming that it was near. Matt. 24:34 says, "So likewise you (First century disciples, "you", verse 3), when you shall see all these things, know that it is near, even at the doors."

The fig tree has nothing to do with the type of tree it is, but only to do with the timing of its leaves coming forth, equated with these things coming forth, at which time the summer (event) is near, at the door. The leaves are these things, but what are the events which is near, at the doors? Luke makes this abundantly clear, "So likewise you, when you see these things come to pass, know that the kingdom of God is now near at hand (Lu. 21:31)". The event, the season (summer), is the kingdom of God coming. The New Covenant Kingdom (nation), its capital city, and its temple, could be clearly "seen", and would come into full establishment, once the Old Covenant Kingdom, nation, its capitol city and temple, was no longer standing (Heb. 9:8). The way, Jesus, the tabernacle, Jesus, could then be clearly seen, and made manifest. All the murkiness, of how much of the Old Covenant was still in effect, could no longer be manipulated by the false Jews (Rom. 2:28- 29, Rev. 2:9; 3:9), by the Judaizers, it all vanished away in A.D. 70 (Hebrews 8:13). There are those who insist that the fig tree reference is pertaining specifically to Israel, even though Luke states, "…the fig tree and all the trees (Lu. 21:29)."

Luke makes it clear that the type of tree is not the emphasis here, but that these things are signs that the kingdom is near at hand. The rebirth of the nation of Israel's interpretation, in Lu. 21:29, would have to go as follows, "When Israel becomes a nation, and all the nations become nations…" Furthermore, to insist that the fig tree is always a reference to the nation of Israel, one would have to then admit that Israel is eternally cursed (Mk. 11:21) and is to never bear fruit again! "And when He saw the fig tree in the way, He came to it, and found nothing thereon, but leaves only, and said unto it, "let no fruit grow on you from now on forever. And presently the fig tree withered away (Matt. 21:19)." If the fig tree is Israel here, and again such a notion is torturous upon the text, then Israel was only ripening toward a season of judgment, not toward a rebirth. Either way, we know that the parable of the fig tree in Matt. 24:32-33 was fulfilled. According to the next verse, "this generation shall not pass, till all these things (same these things as the previous verse) be fulfilled (Matt. 24:34)." As for the next verse, Matt. 24:35, "Heaven and Earth will pass, but my words shall not pass away", we have just examined the figurative use of the sun, moon, and stars. Likewise, Heaven and earth are words consistently used throughout the Bible to communicate God's people and His covenant with them. Consider Matt. 5:17-18, think not that I am come to destroy the law or the prophets.

I have not come to destroy, but to fulfill. For verily I say unto you, till heaven and earth pass, on jot or one tittle shall in no wise pass from the law till all be fulfilled." Once

Jesus fulfills the law and the prophets, He has, heaven and earth will pass away, and it has. Consider Isa. 51:16, "…that I may plant the heavens, and lay the foundations of the earth, and say unto Zion, Thou art my people." And addressing His people Isaiah says, "Hear, O heavens, and give hear, O earth (Isa.1:2)." And Ps. 50:4-5, "He shall call to the heavens from above, and to the earth, that He may judge His people. Gather my saints together unto Me; those that have made a covenant with Me by sacrifice." God's heavenly people have been given His ruling authority, symbolized in the heavens (Dan. 4:26; 12:3). Authority on earth! This is how Jesus uses the terms again in Matt. 16:18-19, when the keys (authority) of the kingdom are given to His New Covenant people, the church, represented in Peter to bind in heaven and loose on earth. Hosea states, "And in that day will I make a covenant for them … And I will betroth thee unto Me forever…I will even betroth thee unto Me in faithfulness: and thou shall know the Lord. And it shall come to pass in that day, I will hear, saith the Lord, I will hear the heavens, and they shall hear the earth (Ho. 2:18-21)". And Joel states, "The Lord also shall roar out of Zion, and utter His voice from Jerusalem, and the heavens and the earth will shake but the Lord will be the hope of His people, and the strength of the children of Israel (Joel 3:16)."

Heb. 12:24-26, in the context of covenant, uses the terms heaven and earth and this same shaking which Joel just referred to. Moses addresses the Old Covenant congregation in this way, "Give ear, O ye heavens, and I will speak; and hear O earth, the words of my mouth (De. 32:1)." In 2 Peter 3, Peter refers to the Old (Covenant) heavens and earth passing, just as Jesus did in Matt. 5:17-18). Heaven and earth pass away, as the Old Covenant elements (Stoicheion) melt with fervent heat (2 Pet. 3:10). This word elements (Stoicheon) is used only 7 times in the New Testament, and every time it refers to rudiments, principles, and philosophies, most often in relationship to the Old Covenant (Galatians 4:3,9; Col. 2:8, 20; Heb. 5:12; 2 Pet. 3:10, 12). Never is it used to describe the physical elements.

So, Peter exhorts all eyes to be fixed on the new heavens and new earth of the new covenant, wherein dwelleth righteousness, everlasting righteousness (Dan. 9:24, 2 Cor. 5:21), through the full establishment and coming (Luke 21:31) of the everlasting covenant kingdom (Heb. 13:20). Jesus, "the way (John 14:6) into the holiest of all was not yet made manifest (revealed, seen, appeared), while as the first tabernacle was yet standing (Heb. 9:8)." After the Old Covenant had passed away, it had not yet done so at the time of the writing of Hebrews (Heb. 13:8, it was ready to, Eggus), not one stone was left upon another and the true (the reality, as opposed to the type) tabernacle (Hebrews 8:2), dwelling place of God, was revealed (Matt. 12:6; Eph. 2:21, 22; 1 Pet. 2:5, 9)! John was exhorting toward the soon, at hand ("Eggus", Rev. 1:3; 22:10) appearing of the New Covenant, new heaven and new earth (Rev. 21:1), which was made manifest at the disappearing of the Old Covenant, old heavens and old earth (2 Pet. 3:10-13). Concerning the old heavens and old earth, Charles Spurgeon state, "Did you ever regret the absence of the burnt offering, or the red heifer, or any one of the sacrifices of the Jews? No, because those belonged to the old heavens and earth for the Jewish believers.'

They have passed away, and we now live in the new heavens and a new earth, so far as the dispensation of divine teaching is concerned. The substance is come, and the shadow has gone, and we do not remember it (C.H. Spurgeon, MP vol. 38, p 354)." Matthew 24 continues with watchfulness and readiness, and the warning of saying, My Lord delays His coming, which is exactly what futurism says. He did not delay His coming, instead told His disciples that it would be in their lifetime (Matt. 10:23; 16:27-28; 24:34, Rev. 1:1, 3; 22:10). Matt. 25 continues with the theme of Jesus' coming (Matt. 25:13; 27, 31) and faithfulness (Matt. 25:21). Coming with rewards (Matt. 25:21-23) for the faithful (see also, Matt. 16:27-28; Jam. 1:12, Rev. 2:10, 3:21; 22:12) and in judgment for those without His faith, which produces His fruit, His works! Same angels, same rewards, same coming in Matt. 25:21-23, as in Matt. 16:27-28. This judgment is executed from the throne (Matt 25:31), not thrones as in both a visible throne, and the one which is in the Spirit realm (John 4:21-24, Heb. 4:16). Thy throne O God, not thy thrones O God (Isa. 45:6). Isa. 66:1 state, the heavens (in the Spirit realm) is My throne (singular)! Jesus rules (Rev. 1:5, 1 Tim. 6:15) in His kingdom, which came not by observation (Luke 17:20-21), on His throne in heaven (Dan. 4:17, 26).

This throne judgment in Matt. 25:31, cannot be separated from Rev. 20:11's throne, which would be a judgment that was shortly (Tachos) to come to pass, for the time was at hand or near (Eggus), according to Rev. 1:1,3; 22:10. As the parables leading up to Matt. 24 and 25, all have been directed towards Israel, they perceived that He spoke of them (Matt. 21:45), they whose heart had waxed fat, and ears were dull of hearing, with eyes that were closed (Matt. 13:15), the king was angry, and He sent forth His armies, and destroyed those murderers, and burned up their city (Matt. 22:7). So, it was Israel which would be judged with fire, their city was Jerusalem. Israel would be divided with a sword of division (10:34), with those for Jesus, or against Him (Matt. 12:30), those true Jews inwardly (Romans 2:28), versus those who say they are Jews, and are not (Rev. 2:9, 3:9), the wheat versus the tares (Matt. 13:29,30), the wheat versus the chaff (Matt. 3:12), and the sheep versus the goats (Matt. 25:32-46). Those against Christ (the true meaning of "antichrist"), counterfeit Jews, tares (look-alikes), chaff (socialites, i.e. intertwined), and goats (sound-alikes), would all face a fiery judgment at the consummation of the Old Covenant Kingdom age (Matt. 3:12; 13:30, 40; 25:46). The gospel would permeate all Israel (Matt. 10:23), all the tribes of the land (Rev. 1:7), and all Israel (Rom. 11:25, 26) would be saved as a result. A whole and complete amount would be saved, not one hundred percent. Similarly, as the Spirit is poured out upon all flesh (Acts 2:17), one hundred percent is not the meaning of this.

Even futurists believe that only 1/3 of Israel (Zech. 13:8) receives salvation. So, it must be understood that the gospel first goes throughout Israel (Acts 1:8), and even outside the physical boarders of Israel to reach Jews. Jews were pinpointed (Rom. 1:16) as the gospel reached them in every city (Acts 15:21) throughout the Roman world (Matt. 24:14, 34; Col. 1:5, 23; Acts 17:6; Rom. 1:8, 10:18; 15:25-26). We see the apostles preaching in these synagogues (Acts 9:20; 14:1, John 16:2). Again, the parables are addressed to Israel (Matt. 13:15; 21:45), including this one in Matt. 25:1 concerning the ten virgins. So, when the whole nation was gathered before the Son of man on His throne (Matt. 25:31-32), He executes judgment by rewarding the sheep to go into infinite life and condemning the goats to go into perpetual fire (Matt. 25:41, 46). All Israel was saved through the only means of salvation, the gospel, which brought in the fullness of the Gentiles (not 100%) and the saving of all Israel (not 100%), at the consummation of the Old Covenant age (Rom.11:25-26; Matt. 13:39-40). Rom. 11:26 correctly reads in the ESV, "and (a continuation of the thought from the previous verse, "the fullness of the Gentiles be come in", vs.25) in this way all Israel will be saved".

It must be understood also that the whole nation was reached with the divisive gospel (Matt. 10:34-39; Rom. 16:25,26), separating those who were for Jesus, true Jews, wheat, the wise virgins (Matt. 25:2), and sheep, from those against Him, untrue Jews, tares, chaff, the foolish virgins, and goats. The whole nation was separated through the gospel's polarizing power, "…the preaching of Jesus Christ…by the scriptures … made (past tense) known to all nations for the obedience of faith (Rom. 16:25-26)." The (12) tribes of the land (Israel) were saturated with the preaching of Jesus Christ (Matt. 10:23), so as to realize (every eye did "see") that His words came to pass in the judgment upon Jerusalem (Rev. 1:7; Zech. 12:10-11). Therefore, it could be said that all nations within the nation of Israel were judged according to their acceptance, or rejection of the gospel. Yes, there were nations (ethnos) within the land of Israel. Josephus refers to the Nation of the Samaritans, the Nation of the Botanaeans, and the Nation of the Galileans. He states that Judea is a nation with its own king. Peraea, Idumea, Trachonitis, Abilene, are all described as having princes, or a ruler of a nation (Ethnos), that is, with the title "Ethnarchs".

Note also, that sheep and goats are both clean beasts to Israel. Consider that it was the bulls (clean Jews), which opened their mouths against Jesus (Psalm 22:12-13), and dogs (unclean Gentiles) which pierced His hands (Ps. 22:16). Therefore, due also to the fact that the parables are addressed to Israel, so also is this judgment affecting "all nations" in Matt. 25:31-32. Matthew 26 and 27 delve into the cross of Jesus. Jesus prophesies of His own death on the cross four different times in Matthew (Matt. 12:40; 16:21; 20:18; 26:2). The cross and the resurrection brought about the kingdom, the new creation, the New Covenant Kingdom.

The cross was D-Day, whereas the Parousia, (coming presence of the Lord) was V-Day. After the cross was the mop up work which involved the fading and vanishing away of the Old Covenant Kingdom. "In that he says, A New Covenant, He has made the first old. Now that which is decaying and waxing old is ready to vanish away (Heb. 8:13)". There was a last day of the Old Covenant, there is no consummation to the New Covenant, a PERPETUAL covenant (Heb. 13:20)! You cannot force the meaning of a last anything, anywhere, anyhow, at any time, into the word everlasting! Of the increase of His government and peace there shall be NO END… (Isaiah 9:7)! Paul makes this point as well when he says, "Unto Him be glory in the CHURCH by Christ Jesus THROUGH OUT ALL AGES, WORLD (AGE) WITHOUT END. AMEN! CHURCH AGE WITHOUT END! How's that for a wrench in the dispensational machine? So, the Old Covenant Kingdom (Nation) was fading out, as the New Covenant Kingdom (Nation, 1Pe. 2:9) was being inaugurated. Jesus was fulfilling the Old Covenant Kingdom's law and prophets (Matt. 5:17-18), so the mop up work was underway at the same time that the New Covenant Kingdom was in the process of coming into its fullness.

During this transition period, A.D. 30-70, the church was possessing the kingdom (Heb. 12:28). By A.D. 70, it had come (Matt. 16:27-28; Lu. 21:31-32). Perhaps the stages of the Kingdom's coming may be understood in the parable of the kingdom of the heavens being likened to leaven. To start with, the passage speaks of the kingdom of the heavens' influence, not the kingdom of the devil's influence! It's found in Matt. 13:33, "The kingdom of the heavens is like unto leaven, which a woman took, and hid in three measures of meal, till the whole was leavened." Perhaps these three measures of meal may be found in the three major feasts of Israel, Passover, Pentecost, and Tabernacles. The first measure of meal (feast day) may be found in Passover where we see the life and death of Jesus, under the law (Gal. 4:4), fulfilling the law (Matt. 5:17-18) by dying (The Passover Lamb, Unleavened Bread, Firstfruits), which was the seed to purchase and bring forth billions more from death to life in His kingdom (Jo. 12:24). The resurrection of Jesus brings that resurrection life to those who were dead in their trespasses and sins (Eph. 2:1; Phil. 3:10; Jo. 5:21, 24, 25) and condemned under the law. The second measure of meal would be Pentecost, with the outpouring of the Spirit, bringing in the first fruits of the harvest converts (Jews).

Note that Pentecost's first fruits, and Tabernacle's final harvest (at the consummation of the Old Covenant age Matt. 13:39-40), are both reaping from the same crop, the same generation! The third measure of meal can be seen in the feast of Trumpets, day of atonement, and Tabernacles. That in the dispensation of the fullness of times He might gather together in one all things in Christ, both which are in heaven, and which are on earth; even in Him (Eph. 1:10). The harvest (gathering) at the consummation of the Old Covenant age (Matt. 13:39-40) is gathered in Him. Now I beseech you, brethren, by the coming of our Lord Jesus Christ, and by our gathering (GK. Episunagoge, i.e. Synagogue) together to Him (2 Thessalonians 2:1). And He shall send His angels (messengers) with a great sound of a trumpet, and they shall gather together His elect from the four winds, from one extreme of heaven to the other. (Matt. 24:31). Then we which are alive and remain shall be seized (GK. "Harpazo", consider its 13 N.T. Usages!) Together with them in the cloud, to meet the Lord in the air (Aer, Eph. 2:2; Rev. 9:1). Consider the usage of "aer" in Eph. 2:2, "the prince of the power of the air (aer), the spirit that now works IN the children of disobedience". "Aer" is something that clearly takes place in the spiritual realm, in the heart. Consider also that 2 Thess. 1:10 states, "When He shall come to be glorified in His saints."

No airlift occurs in the passage, nor has one ever been scheduled for Christians! Jesus prays against the removal of Christians from the earth, and His prayer will continue to be answered, "I pray NOT that thou shouldest take them out of the world" (Jo. 17:15)! Consider this passage in Ex. 19:4, "that you have seen what I did unto the Egyptians, and how I bare you on eagles' wings, and brought you unto Myself". This gathering unto Himself on eagles' wings had nothing to do with an airlift on giant eagles' wings, but a deliverance from the Egyptian persecutors. This was the same case scenario concerning the New Covenant people's deliverance from their spiritual Egyptian persecutors (Rev. 11:8, Gal. 4:22-31). By the way, 1 Thess. 4:15-17 and Matt. 24:30-31 cannot be separated, that would be wrongly dividing the word of reality. They must be speaking of the same coming, the same cloud, the same gathering together, sounded off with the same trumpet! Therefore, Matt. 24:34, gives us the timeline of this event. The sound of a trumpet may be significant here. The feast of trumpets were the initiating feast leading up to the feast of Tabernacles (Ingathering). The feast (measure of meal) instructions were, "and the feast of Ingathering, which is in the end of the year, when thou hast gathered in thy laborers out of the field" (Ex. 23:16). So, the ultimate gathering place, tabernacle, is found in Jesus Christ, the true tabernacle (Heb. 9:2). Not that the first was a lie, but rather a type, a shadow, whereas Jesus is the reality. In the first century, the first tabernacle, the Old Covenant temple and system, was yet standing (Heb. 9:8), after it was made desolate, and not one stone was left upon another (Matt. 23:38, 24:2), the way (Jesus) was made manifest, appeared, and seen by all as the true tabernacle (Heb. 9:8)! The three stages of the kingdom's coming (Matt. 13:33) may also be seen in Mk. 4:26-29, "So is the kingdom of God, as if a man should cast seed into the ground; And should sleep, and rise night and day, and the seed should spring and grow up, he knows not how. For the earth bringeth forth fruit of herself, first the blade, then the ear, after that the mature corn in the ear."

First, the incarnation, the life, death, resurrection of Jesus and ascension. Secondly the outpouring of the Spirit on the Church. Thirdly was the kingdom coming (Lu. 21:31; 17:20-21) in its fullness at the consummation of the Old Covenant age. The kingdom was in full expansion mode, and of the increase of His government and peace there shall be NO END (Isa. 9:7)! NO END TIMES in our future, NO END OF A CHURCH AGE (Eph. 3:21), NO END OF THE PLANET (Eccl. 1:4; Ps. 78:69; 104:5; 148:4-6), and NO END OF TIME, only, "the time of the end" (the end of something, Dan. 12:9) is spoken of in scripture, not the end of time. Time no longer (Rev. 10:6) is communicating that there will be delay no longer concerning the unleashing of the book's judgments. Scripture never speaks of the end of such things, only doctrines of men do (Col. 2:22)! Scripture only speaks of the consummation of the age (Matt. 13:39-40; 24:3, 14, 34), the Old Covenant age!

Matt. 28 reveals the bodily resurrection of Jesus. It is a type of a much larger resurrection (Jo. 5:24-29; 12:24; Eph. 2:1; Phil. 3:10)! Matt. 28:18-20 give the blueprints for the increasing kingdom (Isa. 9:7) to FILL THE WHOLE EARTH (Dan. 2:35)! "All power (Authority) is given unto me in heaven and earth. Go ye therefore (Clear inference here is that I'm giving you this same authority as you go), and teach (teach them, make disciples of them, not just getting individuals saved!) All nations (Matt. 24:14; 34, Ps. 2:8), immersing them in the name of the Father, and of the Son, and of the Holy Spirit; Teaching (Not just getting them saved!) them to observe all things whatsoever I have commanded you: and, lo, I am with you always, even unto the consummation of the age, Amen (Matt. 28:18-20)".

These first century apostles did exactly this, as they went from Jerusalem, Judea, Samaria, unto the uttermost parts of the earth (Acts 1:8). They turned the world (Oikoumene, Roman world) upside down (Acts 17:6), their faith was spoken of throughout the world (Romans 1:8), their sound went (past tense) out into all the land, and their words unto the ends of the earth (Rom. 10:18, Ps. 19:4), the preaching of Jesus Christ by the scriptures was made (past tense) known unto all nations for the obedience of faith (Rom. 15:25 26), the multifarious wisdom of God was then made known unto the governments and rulers (political and otherwise, Eph. 3:10), the gospel came into all the world and was (past tense) preached to all creation which was under heaven (Col. 1:5-6, 23; fulfilling Mark 16:15), and the gospel of the kingdom was preached in all the world, for a witness unto all nations, and then the Old Covenant Kingdom age came to a consummation (Matt. 24:14), all of this happened within the lifetime of this generation of the first century apostles (Matt.16:28; 24:34)!

They are the generational model, the foundation (Eph. 2:20; Rev. 21:14) of our faith, and of the city in which we dwell (Heb. 12:22-23; Gal. 4:26; Phil. 3:20). A city which came out from the Old Covenant capitol city which these apostles pleaded with their readers to come out of (Lu. 21:20,21; Jo. 4:21-24; Acts 1:8; Gal. 4:25-26, Heb. 11:10; 13:14 Rev. 18:4, The Great City, Jerusalem, Babylon, Rev. 11:8). Jesus never pays tribute to any kind of special significance to the city of Jerusalem, but only points His followers away from the city. "Nor yet at Jerusalem …but the true worshipers shall worship the Father in spirit and in reality (Jo. 4:21-23)." They are instructed to go out from Jerusalem, with no instruction to ever return (Acts 1:8). To forsake her and rejoice over the great city's destruction and the vengeance poured upon her for the sake of the blood of the apostles and the prophets (Rev. 18:18, 20; 11:8)! This is the same city which Dispensationalism is calling the church back into!!! The Apostles went through the turbulent transition period, the tribulation (Rev. 1:9), as they were hated of all nations (Matt. 10:22; 24:9 & 13) yet endured to the consummation of the age (Old Covenant age) and overcame! This is not to say that Jesus is not with us in our generation as we go into all nations and endure the same things.

Once again, they were the generational model, which we can emulate in our generation, or not! We can go and do likewise, or heed to the doctrines of men and devils and prescribe the nations to a predetermined, inevitable plan (a plan from the gates of Hades) of darkness and destruction. This plan would have us to make disciples of all nations, except for this one and that one, they are predetermined to be given to the devil. Ask of me and I shall give you the nations (Ps. 2:8), "but not Russia, not Europe, not Asia and the kings of the east, China…, not the Arab nations, and certainly not the newest end time bad guy, Iran! These are all predetermined end time bad buys, according to "Bible Prophecy", to be ruled over by an Antichrist, not Jesus Christ!" Has there ever been two more diametrically opposed worldviews? Perhaps, "Let us go up at once, and possess it; for we are well able to overcome it", versus, "And they brought up an evil report of the land…there we saw the giants…and we were in our own sight as grasshoppers, and so we were in their sight (Nu. 13:30-33)." The evil report believes that the giant evil influences of our day are supposed to be there, they're the fulfillment of "Bible Prophecy".

An evil report is crafted by the evil one, doctrines of demons, and sees through the unbelieving eye of pessimism, whereas the good report sees, and focuses on, the giant grapes (Nu. 13:23-24, 27), the giant opportunities for the fruit of the Spirit and the power of God to overcome! The first century church took on the challenge and overcame, fulfilling Psalm 2, "And he that over-cometh, and keeps my works unto the consummation (the consummation of the Old Covenant age.), to him will I give authority over the nations. And he shall shepherd them with the rod of iron; as the vessels of a potter shall they be broken to shivers… (Rev. 2:26-27; Rom. 16:25-26)." The ball is in our court as to which report we will believe in our generation? We may choose the evil report of our day, and accept the model of predetermined impotency, and decreased influence, along with an inevitable destruction of all nations, or we may follow the generational model of the first century church and make disciples of all nations and turn our world upside down!

Garret Paul Parrish & Terry Kashian

Gospel of Matthew

Chapter 1

1. The book of the generation of Jesus Christ, the son of David, the son of Abraham.
2. Abraham begot Isaac; and Isaac begot Jacob; and Jacob begot Judah and his brothers;
3. Judah begot Perez and Zerah of Tamar; and Perez begot Hezrom; and Hezrom begot Ram;
4. Ram begot Amminadab; and Amminadab begot Nahshon; and Nahshon begot Salmon;
5. Salmon begot Boaz by Rahab; and Boaz begot Obed by Ruth; and Obed begot Jesse;
6. Jesse begot David the king, and David the king begot Solomon by her that had been the wife of Uriah;
7. Solomon begot Rehoboam; and Rehoboam begot Abijah; and Abijah begot Asa;
8. Asa begot Jehoshaphat; and Jehoshaphat begot Joram; and Joram begot Uzziah;
9. Uzziah begot Jotham; and Jotham begot Ahaz; and Ahaz begot Hezekiah;
10. Hezekiah begot Manasseh; and Manasseh begot Amon; and Amon begot Josiah;
11. Josiah begot Jeconiah and his brothers, about the time they were taken away to Babylon:
12. After they were taken to Babylon, Jeconiah begot Salathiel; and Salathiel begot Zerubbabel;
13. Zerubbabel begot Abiud; and Abiud begot Eliakim; and Eliakim begot Azor;
14. Azor begot Zadok; and Zadok begot Achim; and Achim begot Eliud;
15. Eliud begot Eleazar; and Eleazar begot Matthan; and Matthan begot Jacob;
16. Jacob begot Joseph the husband of Mary, of who was born Jesus, who is called Christ.
17. So, all the generations from Abraham to David were fourteen generations, and from David until the taking away to Babylon were fourteen generations; and from the taking away to Babylon to Christ were fourteen generations.
18. Now the birth of Jesus Christ happened this way: When His mother Mary was espoused to Joseph before they came together, she was found with the Child of the Holy Spirit.
19. Then Joseph her husband, being a just man, and not willing to make her a public example, thought to put her away privately.
20. But while he thought about these things, behold, the angel of the LORD appeared to him in a dream, saying, Joseph, son of David, fear not to take to you Mary your wife: for that which is begotten in her is of the Holy Spirit.
21. For she will bring out a Son, and you will call His name JESUS: for He will save His people from their sins.
22. Now all this was done, that it might be fulfilled which was spoken of the Lord by the prophet, saying,
23. Behold, a virgin will be with Child and will bring out a Son, and they will call His name Emmanuel, which being interpreted is, God with us.
24. Then Joseph being raised from sleep did as the angel of the Lord had told him and took to him to be his wife:

25. And was not intimate with her until she had given birth to her firstborn Son: and he called His name JESUS.

Chapter 2

1. Now when Jesus was born in Bethlehem of Judea in the days of Herod the king, behold, there came wise men from the east to Jerusalem,
2. Saying, where is He that is born King of the Jews? For we have seen His star in the east and have come to worship Him.
3. When Herod the king heard these things, he was troubled, and all Jerusalem with him.
4. When he had gathered all the chief priests and scribes of the people together, he demanded of them where Christ should be born.
5. So, they said to him, In Bethlehem of Judea: for so it is written by the prophet,
6. And you Bethlehem, in the land of Judea, are not the least among the princes of Judah: for out of you will come a Ruler, that will shepherd My people Israel.
7. Then Herod, when he had secretly called the wise men, inquired of them diligently what time the star appeared.
8. So, he sent them to Bethlehem, and said, go and search diligently for the young Child; and when you have found. Him, bring me word again, that I may come and worship Him also.
9. When they had heard the king, they departed; and behold, the star, which they saw in the east, went before them, until it came and stood over where the young Child was.
10. When they saw the star, they rejoiced with exceeding great joy.
11. When they came into the house, they saw the young Child with Mary His mother, and fell down, and worshipped Him: and when they had opened their treasures, they presented to Him gifts; gold, and frankincense and myrrh.
12. But being warned by God in a dream that they should not return to Herod, they departed into their own country another way.
13. When they had departed, behold, the angel of the Lord appeared to Joseph in a dream, saying, Arise, and take the young Child and His mother, and flee into Egypt, and be there until I bring you word: for Herod is about to seek the young Child to destroy Him.
14. When he arose, he took the young Child and His mother by night and departed into Egypt:
15. And was there until the death of Herod: that it might be fulfilled which was spoken of the Lord by the prophet, saying, Out of Egypt have I called My Son.
16. Then Herod, when he saw that he was tricked by the wise men, was exceedingly angry, and sent out, and killed all the children that were in Bethlehem, and in all the borders of it, from two years old and under, according to the time which he had diligently inquired of the wise men.
17. Then was fulfilled that which was spoken by Jeremiah the prophet, saying,

18. In Rama was there a voice heard, lamentation, and weeping, and great mourning, Rachel weeping for her children, and would not be comforted, because they are not.
19. But when Herod was dead, behold, an angel of the Lord appeared in a dream to Joseph in Egypt,
20. Saying, arise, and take the young Child and His mother, and go into the land of Israel: for they are dead who sought the young Child's life.
21. So, he arose and took the young Child and His mother and came into the land of Israel.
22. But when he heard that Archelaus reigned in Judea in place of his father Herod, he was afraid to go there: nonetheless, being warned by God in a dream, he turned aside into the parts of Galilee:
23. Then he came and dwelt in a city called Nazareth: that it might be fulfilled which was spoken by the prophets, He will be called a Nazarene.

Chapter 3

1. In those days came John the Immerser, preaching in the wilderness of Judea,
2. And saying, repent: for the kingdom of the heavens is at hand!
3. For this is he that was spoken of by the prophet Isaiah, saying, the voice of one crying in the wilderness, prepare you the way of the Lord, make His paths straight.
4. The same John had his clothing of camel's hair, and a leather belt around his waist, and his food was locusts and wild honey.
5. Then went out to him Jerusalem, and all Judea, and all the region around the Jordan,
6. And were immersed by him in the Jordan, confessing their sins.
7. But when he saw many of the Pharisees and Sadducees come to his immersion, he said to them, O generation of vipers, who has warned you to flee from the wrath about to come?
8. Therefore, bring forth fruits fit for repentance:
9. Think not to say within yourselves, we have Abraham as our father: for I say to you, that God is able of these stones to raise up children to Abraham.
10. Now also the ax is laid at the root of the trees: therefore, every tree which does not bring forth good fruit is cut down and cast into the fire.
11. I indeed immerse you with water to repentance: but He that comes after me is mightier than I, whose shoes I am not worthy to untie: He will immerse you with the Holy Spirit, and with fire:
12. Whose fan is in His hand, and He will thoroughly purge His floor, and gather His wheat into the barn, but He will burn up the chaff with unquenchable fire.
13. Then came Jesus from Galilee to the Jordan to John, to be immersed by him.
14. But John tried to hinder Him, saying, I need to be immersed by You, and You come to me?
15. Jesus answered and said to him, permit it to be so now: for so it is proper for us to fulfill all righteousness. Then he permitted Him.

16. Then Jesus, when He was immersed, went up directly out of the water: and behold, the heavens opened to Him, and He saw the Spirit of God descending like a dove, and resting on Him:

17. And behold a voice from heaven, saying, this is My beloved Son, in whom I am well pleased.

Chapter 4

1. Then Jesus was led up by the Spirit into the wilderness to be tempted by the devil.

2. When He had fasted forty days and forty nights, He was afterward hungry.

3. When the tempter came to Him, he said, if you are the Son of God, command that these stones be made bread.

4. But He answered and said, it is written, man will not live by bread alone, but by every word that proceeds out of the mouth of God.

5. Then the devil took Him up into the holy city, and set Him on a pinnacle of the temple,

6. And said to Him, If You are the Son of God, cast yourself down: for it is written, He will give his angels charge concerning You: and in their hands, they will hold You up, unless at any time You dash Your foot against a stone.

7. Jesus said to him, it is written again, you will not tempt the Lord your God.

8. Again, the devil took Him up to an exceedingly high mountain and showed Him all the kingdoms of the Roman world, and the glory of them;

9. And said to Him, all these things will I give You, if You will fall down and worship me.

10. Then said Jesus to him, get you away, Satan: for it is written, you will worship the Lord your God, and Him only will you serve.

11. Then the devil left Him, and behold, angels came and ministered to Him.

12. Now when Jesus had heard that John was cast into prison, He departed into Galilee;

13. Leaving Nazareth, He came and dwelt in Capernaum, which is on the sea coast, in the borders of Zebulon and Naphtali:

14. That it might be fulfilled which was spoken by Isaiah the prophet, saying,

15. The land of Zebulon, and the land of Naphtali, by the way of the sea, beyond the Jordan, Galilee of the nations;

16. The people who sat in darkness saw great light, and to those who sat in the region and shadow of death light is arising.

17. From that time Jesus began to preach, and to say, repent: for the kingdom of the heavens is at hand!

18. Then Jesus, walking by the sea of Galilee, saw two brothers, Simon called Peter, and Andrew his brother, casting a net into the sea: for they were fishermen.

19. He said to them, follow Me, and I will make you fishers of men.

20. Immediately they left their nets and followed Him.

21. Going on from there, He saw other two brothers, James the son of Zebedee, and John his brother, in a boat with Zebedee their father, mending their nets; and He called them.

22. Immediately they left the boat and their father and followed Him.

23. Then Jesus went about all Galilee, teaching in their synagogues, preaching the gospel of the kingdom, and healing all manner of sickness and all manner of disease among the people.

24. So, His fame went throughout all Syria: and they brought to Him all sick people that were taken with different diseases and torments, and those which were possessed with demons, and those which were insane, and paralytics, and He healed them.

25. Then there followed Him great multitudes of people from Galilee, and from Decapolis, and Jerusalem, and Judea, and from beyond the Jordan.

Chapter 5

1. Seeing the multitudes, He went up to a mountain: and when He was seated, His disciples came to Him:

2. Then He opened His mouth, and taught them, saying,

3. Blessed are the poor in spirit: for theirs is the kingdom of the heavens.

4. Blessed are they that mourn: for they will be comforted.

5. Blessed are the meek: for they will inherit that land.

6. Blessed are they which do hunger and thirst after righteousness: for they will be filled.

7. Blessed are the merciful: for they will obtain mercy.

8. Blessed are the pure in heart: for they will see God.

9. Blessed are the peacemakers: for they will be called the children of God.

10. Blessed are they who are persecuted for righteousness's sake: for theirs is the kingdom of the heavens.

11. Blessed are you, when men will revile you, and persecute you, and will say all manner of evil against you falsely, for My sake.

12. Rejoice and be exceedingly glad: for great is your reward in heaven: for so they persecuted the prophets who were before you.

13. You are the salt of the earth: but if the salt has lost its savor, with what will it be salted? Thereafter it is good for nothing, but to be cast out, and to be trodden underfoot by men.

14. You are the light of the world. A city that is set on a hill cannot be hidden.

15. Neither do men light a candle, and put it under a basket, but on a candlestick, and it gives light to all that are in the house.

16. Let your light so shine before men, that they may see your good works, and glorify Your Father who is in heaven.

17. Think not that I have come to destroy the Law or the prophets: I have not come to destroy, but to fulfill.

18. For truly I say to you, until heaven and earth pass away, one jot or one small mark will in no way pass away from the Law until all is fulfilled.

19. Therefore, whoever will break one of the least commandments, and will teach men so, he will be called the least in the kingdom of the heavens: but whoever will do and teach them, the same will be called great in the kingdom of the heavens.

20. For I say to you, that unless your righteousness will exceed the righteousness of the scribes and Pharisees, you will in no way enter into the kingdom of the heavens.
21. You have heard that it was said of them of old time, you will not murder, and whoever will murder will be in danger of the judgment:
22. But, I say to you, that whoever is angry with his brother without a reason will be in danger of the judgment: and whoever will say to his brother, Raca, will be in danger of the council: but whoever will say, You fool, will be in danger of the fire of Gehenna.
23. Therefore, if you bring your gift to the altar, and there remember that your brother has something against you;
24. Leave your gift there before the altar and go your way; first be reconciled to your brother, and then come and offer your gift.
25. Agree with your adversary quickly, while you are in the way with him; unless at any time the adversary delivers you to the judge, and the judge delivers you to the officer, and you be cast into prison.
26. Truly I say to you, you will by no means come out from there until you have paid the last copper penny.
27. You have heard that it was said by the ancients, you shall not commit adultery:
28. But I say to you, that all who regard of a wife to covet her has committed adultery with her already in his heart.
29. And if your right eye offends you, pluck it out, and cast it from you: for it is profitable for you that one of your members should perish, and not your whole body should be cast into Gehenna.
30. And if your right hand offends you, cut it off, and cast it from you: for it is profitable for you that one of your members should perish, and not that your whole body should be cast into Gehenna.
31. It has been said, that whoever will divorce his wife, let him give her a certificate of divorce:
32. But I say to you, that whoever will divorce his wife, except for the reason of adultery, causes her to commit adultery: and whoever will marry her that is divorced commits adultery.
33. Again, you have heard that it has been said by the ancients, you shall not swear falsely, but will perform to the Lord your oaths:
34. But I say to you, swear not at all; neither by heaven; for it is God's throne:
35. Nor by the earth; for it is His footstool: neither by Jerusalem; for it is the city of the great King.
36. Neither shall you swear by your head because you cannot make one hair white or black.
37. But let your yes be yes; and let your no be no: for whatever is more than these comes of from the evil one.
38. You have heard that it has been said, an eye for an eye, and a tooth for a tooth:
39. But I say to you, that you resist not evil: but whoever will strike you on your right cheek, turn to him the other also.
40. And if any man will sue you and take away your tunic, let him have your cloak also.

41. And whoever will compel you to go a mile, go with him two.
42. Give to him that asks you, and from him that would borrow from you do not turn away.
43. You have heard that it has been said, you shall love your neighbor and hate your enemy.
44. But I say to you, love your enemies, bless them that curse you, do good to them that hate you, and pray for those who despitefully use you, and persecute you;
45. That you may be the children of Your Father who is in the heavens: for He makes His sun to rise on the evil and on the good and sends rain on the just and on the unjust.
46. For if you love those who love you, what reward have you? Do not even the tax collectors do the same?
47. If you embrace your brothers only, what do you do more than others? Do not even tax collectors do the same?
48. Therefore, be complete, just as Your Father who is in heaven is perfect.

Chapter 6

1. Watch yourself, that you do not display your righteousness before men, to be seen by them: otherwise, you have no reward of Your Father in heavens.
2. Therefore, when you are doing your philanthropy, do not sound a trumpet before you, as the hypocrites do in the synagogues and on the streets, that they may have recognition of men. Truly I say to you, they have their reward.
3. But when you are philanthropic, do not let your left hand know what your right hand is doing:
4. That your philanthropy may be in secret: and your Father who sees in secret Himself, will reward you openly!
5. When you pray, you will not be as the hypocrites are, for they love to pray standing in the synagogues and on the corners of the streets, that they may be seen of men. Truly I say to you, they have their reward.
6. But you, when you pray, enter into your closet, and when you have shut your door, pray to your Father who is in secret; and your Father who sees in secret will reward you openly!
7. But when you pray, use not vain repetitions, as the heathen do: for they think that they will be heard for their much speaking.
8. Therefore, be not like them: for Your Father knows what things you need before You ask Him.
9. Therefore, in this manner pray: Our Father who is in the heavens, sacred be Your name.
10. Your kingdom come, Your will be done on earth, as it is in heaven.
11. Give us this day our daily bread.
12. And forgive us our debts, as we have forgiven our debtors.
13. And lead us not into testing but deliver us from the wicked one: for Yours is the kingdom, and the power, and the glory, forever. Amen.
14. For if you forgive men their trespasses, your heavenly Father will also forgive you:
15. But if you do not forgive men their trespasses, neither will your Father forgive your trespasses.

16. Moreover, when you fast, be not, as the hypocrites, of a sad countenance: for they disfigure their faces that they may appear to men to fast. Truly I say to you, they have their reward.
17. But you, when you fast, anoint your head and wash your face;
18. That you appear to men not to be fasting, but to Your Father who is in secret: and Your Father, who sees in secret, will reward you openly!
19. Lay not up for yourselves treasures on earth, where moth and rust corrupt, and where thieves break through and steal:
20. But lay up for yourselves treasures in heaven, where neither moth nor rust corrupts, and where thieves do not break through nor steal:
21. For where your treasure is, there will your heart be also.
22. The lamp of the body is the eye: therefore, if your eye is single, your whole body will be full of light.
23. But if your eye is wicked, your whole body will be full of darkness. Therefore, if the light that is in you is darkness, how great is that darkness!
24. No man can serve two masters: for either he will hate the one, and love the other, or else he will hold to the one, and despise the other. You cannot serve God and wealth.
25. Therefore, I say to you, take no anxious thought for your soul, what you will eat, or what you will drink; nor yet for your body, what will you put on. Is not the soul more than nutrition, and the body than clothing?
26. Behold the birds of the air: for they sow not, neither do they reap, nor gather into barns; yet Your heavenly Father feeds them. Are you not much better than them?
27. Who of you by anxious thought can add one hour to his life?
28. Why worry about clothing? Consider the lilies of the field, how they grow; they laborer not, neither do they spin:
29. Yet I say to you, that even Solomon in all his glory was not arrayed like one of these.
30. Therefore, if God so clothes the grass of the field, which today exists, and tomorrow is cast into the oven, will He not much more clothe you, O you of little faith?
31. Therefore, do not be anxious, saying, what will we eat? Or what will we drink? Or how will we be clothed?
32. For the nations seek after all these things, for your heavenly Father knows that you need all these things.
33. But seek first the kingdom of God, and His righteousness; and all these things will be added to you.
34. Therefore, do not be anxious for the next day: for the next day will care for the things of itself. Each day has its own trouble.

Chapter 7

1. Judge not, that you be not judged.
2. Therefore, in that judgment you are judging, you will be judged: and with what measure you measure out, it will be measured back to you again.
3. Why do you behold the speck that is in your brother's eye, but consider not the plank that is in your own eye?

4. Or how will you say to your brother, let me cast out the speck out of your eye; and behold, a plank is in your own eye?

5. You hypocrite, first cast out the plank out of your own eye; and then will you see clearly to cast out the speck out of your brother's eye.

6. Do not give that which is holy to the dogs, neither cast your pearls before pigs unless they trample them under their feet and return and attack you.

7. Ask, and it will be given you; seek, and you will find; knock, and it will be opened to you.

8. For every one that asks receives; and he that seeks finds; and to him that knocks it will be opened.

9. Or what man is there of you, who if his son asks bread, will he give him a stone?

10. Or if he asks for a fish, will he give him a serpent?

11. If you then, being evil, know how to give good gifts to your children, how much more will your Father who is in heaven give good things to them that ask Him?

12. Therefore, all things whatever you would that men should do to you, do even so to them: for this is the Law and the prophets!

13. Enter you in at the narrow gate: for wide is the gate, and spacious is the path, that leads away into the destruction, and many go into it:

14. Because narrow is the gate, and being constricted is the path, which leads away into the life, and few there are that acquire it.

15. Beware of false prophets, who come to you in sheep's clothing, but inwardly they are ravening wolves.

16. You will know them by their fruits. Do men gather grapes from thorn bushes or figs from thistles?

17. Even so every good tree brings forth good fruit, but a corrupt tree brings forth evil fruit.

18. A good tree cannot bring forth evil fruit, neither can a corrupt tree bring forth good fruit.

19. Every tree that does not bring forth good fruit is cut down and cast into the fire.

20. Therefore, by their fruits you will know them.

21. Not everyone that says to Me, Lord, Lord, will enter into the kingdom of the heavens; but he that does the will of My Father who is in heaven.

22. Many will say to Me in that day, Lord, Lord, have we not prophesied in Your name? And in Your name have cast out demons? And in Your name done many works of power?

23. And then will I declare to them, I never knew you: depart from Me, you that are working rebellion.

24. Therefore, whoever hears these sayings of Mine, and does them, I will liken him to a wise man, which built his house on a rock:

25. The rain descended, and the floods came, and the winds blew, and beat on that house; and it did not fall: for it was built on a rock.

26. And every one that hears these sayings of Mine, and does them not, will be likened to a foolish man, who built his house on the sand:

27. The rain descended, and the floods came, and the winds blew, and beat on that house; and it fell: and great was the fall of it.
28. And it came to pass when Jesus had ended these sayings, the people were astonished at His teaching:
29. For He taught them as one having authority, and not as the scribes.

Chapter 8

1. When He had come down from the mountain, great multitudes followed Him.
2. And behold, there came a leper and worshiped Him, saying, Lord, if You will, You can make me clean.
3. Then Jesus put out His hand, and touched him, saying, I will; be clean. Immediately his leprosy was cleansed.
4. Then Jesus said to him, see you tell no man; but go your way, show yourself to the priest, and offer the gift that Moses commanded, for a testimony to them.
5. When Jesus had entered into Capernaum, there came to Him a centurion, pleading to Him,
6. and saying, Lord, my young child lies at home paralyzed, grievously tormented.
7. Then Jesus said to him, I will come and heal him.
8. The centurion answered and said, Lord, I am not worthy that You should come under my roof: but speak the word only, and my young child will be healed.
9. For I am also a man under authority, having soldiers under me: and I say to this man, go, and he goes; and to another, come, and he comes; and to my slave, do this, and he does it.
10. When Jesus heard it, He marveled, and said to them that followed, truly I say to you, I have not found such great faith, no, not even in Israel!
11. And I say to you, that many will come from the east and west, and will sit down with Abraham, and Isaac, and Jacob, in the kingdom of the heavens.
12. But the sons of the kingdom will be cast out into outer darkness: there will be weeping and gnashing of teeth.
13. Then Jesus said to the centurion, go your way; and as you have believed, so it is done to you. And his young child was healed in the very same hour.
14. When Jesus arrived at Peter's house, Peter's mother-in-law was sick in bed with a high fever.
15. Then He touched her hand, and the fever left her: and she rose, and served them.
16. When the evening had come, they brought to Him many that were possessed with demons: and He cast out the spirits with a word and healed all that were sick:
17. that it might be fulfilled which was spoken by Isaiah the prophet, saying, He took our infirmities, and bore our sicknesses.
18. Now when Jesus saw great multitudes about Him, He gave commandment to depart to the other side.
19. And a certain scribe came, and said to him, Master, I will follow You wherever You go.

20. Then Jesus said to him, the foxes have holes, and the birds of the air have nests; but the Son of man has no place to lay His head.
21. Another of His disciples said to Him, Lord, permit me first to go and bury my father.
22. But Jesus said to him, follow Me; and let the dead bury their dead.
23. When He had entered into a boat, His disciples followed Him.
24. And behold, there arose a great storm in the sea, so much so that the boat was covered with the waves: but He was asleep.
25. His disciples came to Him, and woke Him, saying, Lord, save us: we perish.
26. But He said to them, why are you fearful, O you of little faith? Then He rose and rebuked the winds and the sea, and there was a great calm.
27. But the men marveled, saying, what manner of Man is this, that even the winds and the sea obey Him!
28. When He had come to the other side into the country of the Gaderenes, there met Him two possessed with demons, coming out of the tombs, exceedingly fierce, so that no man was able to pass by that way.
29. And behold, they cried out, saying, what do we have to do with You, Jesus, O Son of God? Have You come here to torment us before the time?
30. There was a good way off from them: a herd of many pigs feeding.
31. So, the demons begged Him, saying, if you cast us out, permit us to go away into the herd of pigs.
32. Then He said to them, go. When they came out, they went into the herd of pigs: and behold, the whole herd of pigs ran violently down a steep slope into the sea and perished in the waters.
33. Then they that kept them fled, and went their way into the city, and told everything, and what had happened to those possessed by the demons.
34. Then behold, the whole city came out to meet Jesus: and when they saw Him, they begged Him to depart out of their borders.

Chapter 9

1. And He entered into a boat and sailed over and came into His own city.
2. Then, behold, they brought to Him a paralytic, lying on a bed: and Jesus seeing their faith said to him who was a paralytic; child, be of good cheer; your sins are forgiven.
3. Then, behold, certain of the scribes said within themselves, this man blasphemes.
4. But Jesus knowing their thoughts said, why do you think evil in your hearts?
5. For which is easier to say, your sins are forgiven; or to say, arise, and walk?
6. But that you may know that the Son of man has authority on earth to forgive sins, (then He said to the paralytic) arise, take up your bed, and go to your house.
7. So, he arose and departed to his house.
8. But when the multitudes saw it, they marveled and glorified God, who had given such authority to men.

9. As Jesus passed forth from there, he saw a man, named Matthew, sitting at the tax collector's booth: and He said to him, follow Me. So, he arose and followed Him.

10. It came to pass, as Jesus sat to eat in the house, behold, many tax collectors and sinners came and sat down with Him and His disciples.

11. But when the Pharisees saw it, they said to His disciples, why does your Master eat with tax collectors and sinners?

12. But when Jesus heard that, He said to them, they that are whole do not need a doctor, but they that are sick.

13. But you go and learn what that means, I desire mercy and not sacrifice: for I have not come to call the righteous, but sinners to repentance.

14. Then the disciples of John came to Him, saying, why do we and the Pharisees fast often, but Your disciples do not fast?

15. Then Jesus said to them, can the friends of the bridegroom mourn, as long as the bridegroom is with them? But the days will come when the bridegroom will be taken from them, and then they will fast.

16. No one puts a piece of unshrunk cloth on an old garment, for when the patch pulls away from the old garment, a worse tear is made.

17. Neither do men put new wine into old skins: else the skins burst, and the wine spills and the wineskins are lost: but they put new wine into new skins, and both are kept safe.

18. While He spoke these things to them, behold, there came a certain ruler, and worshiped Him, saying, my daughter is even now dead: but come and lay Your hand on her, and she will live.

19. Then Jesus rose, and followed him, and so did His disciples.

20. And behold, a woman, who was diseased with an issue of blood twelve years, came behind Him, and touched the hem of His garment:

21. for she said within herself, if I just touch His garment, I will become whole.

22. But Jesus turned around, and when He saw her, He said, Daughter, be of good comfort; your faith has made you whole. And the woman was made whole from that hour.

23. When Jesus came into the ruler's house, and saw the musicians and the people making noise,

24. He said to them, make room: for the girl is not dead, but sleeps. But they laughed Him to scorn.

25. But when the people were put out, He went in, and took her by the hand, and the girl rose.

26. And the fame of this went abroad into all that land.

27. When Jesus departed from there, two blind men followed Him, crying, and saying, You son of David, have mercy on us.

28. When He had come into the house, the blind men came to Him: and Jesus said to them, "do you believe that I can do this?" They said to Him, yes, Lord.

29. Then He touched their eyes, saying, it will be done to you according to your faith.

30. Then their eyes were opened; and Jesus strictly instructed them, saying, see let no one know it.

31. But they, when they had departed, spread abroad His fame in all that country.
32. As they went out, behold, they brought to him a mute man possessed with a demon.
33. When the demon was cast out, the mute spoke: and the multitudes marveled, saying, it was never so seen in Israel.
34. But the Pharisees said, He casts out demons through the prince of the demons.
35. So, Jesus went about all the cities and villages, teaching in their synagogues, preaching the gospel of the kingdom, and healing every sickness and every disease among the people.
36. But when He saw the multitudes, He was moved with compassion on them, because they were weary and scattered abroad, as sheep having no shepherd.
37. Then said He to His disciples, the harvest truly is plentiful, but the laborers are few;
38. Therefore, pray to the Lord of the harvest, that He will send out laborers into His harvest.

Chapter 10

1. When He had called to Him His twelve disciples, He gave them authority over unclean spirits, to cast them out, and to heal all manner of sickness and all manner of disease.
2. Now the names of the twelve apostles are these; the first, Simon, who is called Peter, and Andrew his brother; James the son of Zebedee, and John his brother;
3. Philip, and Bartholomew; Thomas, and Matthew the tax-collector; James the son of Alphaeus, and Lebbaeus, whose surname was Thaddaeus;
4. Simon the Canaanite, and Judas Iscariot, who later betrayed Him.
5. These twelve Jesus sent out, and commanded them, saying, do not go into the way of the nations, and into any city of the Samaritans do not enter:
6. But go rather to the lost sheep of the house of Israel.
7. And as you go, preach, saying, the kingdom of the heavens is at hand!
8. Heal the sick, cleanse the lepers, raise the dead, cast out demons: freely you have received, freely give.
9. Provide neither gold, nor silver, nor copper in your money belts,
10. nor bag for your journey, neither two tunics, neither shoes nor yet staffs: for the workman is worthy of his sustenance.
11. Into whatever city or town you will enter, inquire in it who is worthy; and there stay until you go from there.
12. And when you come into a house, greet it.
13. And if the house is worthy, let your peace come on it: but if it is not worthy, let your peace return to you.
14. Whoever will not receive you, nor hear your words, when you depart out of that house or city, shake off the dust of your feet.
15. Truly I say to you, it will be more tolerable for the land of Sodom and Gomorrah in the Day of Judgment, than for that city.
16. Behold, I send you out as sheep in the midst of wolves: therefore, be wise as serpents, and harmless as doves.

17. But beware of men: for they will take you to the Sanhedrin, and they will whip you in their synagogues;
18. and you will be brought before governors and kings for My sake, for a testimony against them and the nations.
19. But when they hand you over, give no thought how or what you will speak: for it will be given to you in that same hour what you will speak.
20. For it is not you that speak, but the Spirit of Your Father who speaks in you.
21. For a brother will hand over a brother to death, and the father the child: and the children will revolt against their parents and cause them to be put to death.
22. And you will be hated by all men for My name's sake: but he that is enduring to the completion will be saved.
23. But when they persecute you in this city, flee into another: for truly I say to you, you will not run out of the cities of Israel until the Son of man comes.
24. The disciple is not above his master, nor the slave above his lord.
25. It is enough for the disciple that he becomes like his master and the slave as his lord. If they have called the master of the house Beelzebub, how much more will they call them of his household?
26. Therefore, fear not them: for there is nothing covered, that will not be revealed; and hidden, that will not be known.
27. What I tell you in darkness, you speak that in light: and what you hear in the ear; you declare that on the housetops.
28. Fear not those who kill the body but are not able to kill the soul: but rather fear Him who has power to destroy both soul and body in Gehenna.
29. Are not two sparrows sold for a copper coin? And one of them will not fall on the ground without Your Father.
30. But the very hairs of your head are all numbered.
31. Therefore, fear not, for you are of more value than many sparrows.
32. Therefore, whoever will confess Me before men, him will I confess also before My Father who is in heaven.
33. But whoever will deny Me before men, him will I also deny before My Father who is in heaven.
34. Think not that I have come to bring peace on the land: I came not to bring peace, but a sword.
35. For I have come to set a man against his father, and a daughter against her mother, and a daughter-in-law against her mother-in-law.
36. For a man's enemies will be they of his own household.
37. He that loves father or mother more than Me is not worthy of Me: and he that loves son or daughter more than Me is not worthy of Me.
38. And he that takes not his cross and follows after Me, is not worthy of Me.
39. He that finds his life will lose it: and he that loses his life for My sake will find it.
40. He that receives you receives Me, and he that receives Me receives Him that sent Me.

41. He that receives a prophet in the name of a prophet will receive a prophet's reward, and he that receives a righteous man in the name of a righteous man will receive a righteous man's reward.
42. Whoever will give a drink to one of these little ones, even a cup of cold water in the name of a disciple, truly I say to you, he will in no way lose his reward.

Chapter 11

1. So, it came to pass, when Jesus had finished commanding his twelve disciples, He departed from there to teach and to preach in their cities.
2. Now when John had heard in the prison the works of Christ, he sent two of his disciples,
3. and said to Him, are you He that should come, or do we look for another?
4. Jesus answered and said to them, go and show John again those things which you do hear and see:
5. The blind receives their sight, and the lame walk, the lepers are cleansed, and the deaf hear, the dead are raised, and the poor have the gospel preached to them.
6. Blessed is he, whoever is not offended in Me.
7. As they departed, Jesus began to say to the multitudes concerning John, what did you go out into the wilderness to see? A reed shaken with the wind?
8. But what did you go out to see? A man clothed in fine clothing? Behold, they that wear fine clothing are in kings' houses.
9. But what did you go out to see? A prophet? Yes, I say to you, and more than a prophet.
10. For this is he, of whom it is written, behold, I send My messenger before Your face, who will prepare Your way before You.
11. Truly I say to you, among them that are born of women there has not risen anyone greater than John the Immerser: not with standing he that is least in the kingdom of the heavens is greater than he.
12. From the days of John, the Immerser until now, the kingdom of the heavens is inflicted with violent attacks, and the violators seize upon it with force.
13. For all the prophets and the Law prophesied until John.
14. If you will receive it, this is Elijah, who was to come.
15. He that has ears to hear, let him hear.
16. But what will I liken to this generation? It is like children sitting in the markets, and calling to their friends,
17. And saying, we have played the flute for you, and you have not danced; we have mourned for you, and you have not lamented.
18. For John came neither eating nor drinking, and they said, He has a demon.
19. The Son of man came eating and drinking, and they said, behold a glutton, and a wine drinker, a friend of tax collectors and sinners. But wisdom is justified by her children.
20. Then He began to rebuke the cities in which most of His mighty works were done because they did not repent:

21. Woe to you, Chorazin! Woe to you, Bethsaida! For if the mighty works, which were done in you, had been done in Tyre and Sidon, they would have repented long ago in sackcloth and ashes.
22. But I say to you, it will be more tolerable for Tyre and Sidon at the Day of Judgment, than for you.
23. And you, Capernaum, which is exalted to heaven, will be trodden down to the unseen realm: for if the mighty works, which have been done in you, had been done in Sodom, it would have remained until this day.
24. But I say to you, that it will be more tolerable for the land of Sodom on the Day of Judgment, than for you.
25. At that time Jesus answered and said, I thank you, O Father, Lord of heaven and earth, because you have hidden these things from the wise and prudent and have revealed them to babes.
26. Even so, Father: for so it seemed good in Your sight.
27. All things are delivered to Me by My Father: and no man knows the Son, but the Father; neither does any man know the Father, but the Son, and he to whomever the Son will reveal Him.
28. Come to Me, all you that laborer and are heavy burdened, and I will give you rest.
29. Take My yoke on you and learn from Me; for I am meek and humble in heart: and you will find rest for your souls.
30. For My yoke is easy, and My burden is light.

Chapter 12

1. At that time Jesus went on the Sabbath day through the corn, and His disciples were hungry and began to pluck the ears of corn and to eat.
2. But when the Pharisees saw it, they said to Him, behold, Your disciples do that which is not lawful to do on the Sabbath day.
3. But He said to them, have you not read what David did, when he was hungry, and they that were with him;
4. How he entered into the house of God, and ate the showbread, which was not lawful for him to eat, neither for those who were with him, but only for the priests?
5. Or have you not read in the Law, that on the Sabbath days the priests in the temple profane the Sabbath, and are blameless?
6. But I say to you that in this place there is one greater than the temple.
7. But if you had known what this means, I desire mercy, and not sacrifice, you would not have condemned the guiltless.
8. For the Son of man is Lord even on the Sabbath day.
9. When He had departed from there, He went into their synagogue:
10. and behold, there was a man who had his hand withered. So, they asked Him, saying, is it lawful to heal on the Sabbath days? That they might accuse Him.
11. He said to them, what man will there be among you, that will have one sheep, and if it falls into a pit on the Sabbath day, will he not lay hold of it, and lift it out?

12. How much then is a man better than a sheep? Therefore, it is lawful to do good on the Sabbath days.

13. Then He said to the man, stretch out your hand. So, he stretched it out; and it was restored whole, just as the other.

14. Then the Pharisees went out, and held a council against Him, how they might destroy Him.

15. But when Jesus knew it, He withdrew Himself from there: and great multitudes followed Him, and He healed them all;

16. And charged them that they should not make Him known:

17. That it might be fulfilled which was spoken by Isaiah the prophet, saying,

18. Behold My Child, whom I have chosen; My beloved, in whom My soul is well pleased: I will put My Spirit on Him, and He will declare judgment to the nations.

19. He will not strive, nor cry; neither will any man hear His voice in the streets.

20. A bruised reed He will not break, and smoking flax He will not quench until He sends out judgment to victory.

21. For in His name the nations will hope.

22. Then was brought to Him one possessed with a demon, blind, and mute: and He healed him, so much so that the blind and mute man both spoke and saw.

23. And all the people were amazed, and said, is this not the son of David?

24. But when the Pharisees heard it, they said, this fellow does not cast out demons but by Beelzebub the prince of the demons.

25. But Jesus knew their thoughts, and said to them, every kingdom divided against itself is brought to desolation; and every city or house divided against itself will not stand:

26. If Satan casts out Satan, he is divided against himself; how will then his kingdom stand?

27. And if I by Beelzebub, cast out demons by who do your children cast them out? Therefore, they will be your judges.

28. But if I cast out demons by the Spirit of God, then the kingdom of God has come **upon** you!

29. Or else how can one enter into a strong man's house, and seize his property, unless he first binds the strong man? Then he will plunder his house.

30. He that is not with Me is against Me, and he that is not gathering with Me scatters abroad.

31. Therefore, I say to you, all manner of sin and blasphemy will be forgiven men: but the blasphemy against the Holy Spirit will not be forgiven men.

32. Whoever speaks a word against the Son of man, it will be forgiven him: but whoever speaks against the Holy Spirit, it will not be forgiven him, neither in this Old Covenant Age nor in the one about to come.

33. Either make the tree good, and its fruit good; or else make the tree corrupt, and its fruit corrupt: for the tree is known by its fruit.

34. Generation of vipers, how can you, being evil, speak good things? For out of the abundance of the heart the mouth speaks.

35. A good man out of the good treasure of the heart brings forth good things: and an evil man out of the evil treasure brings forth evil things.

36. But I say to you, that every idle word that men will speak, they will give an account of it in the Day of Judgment.

37. For by your words, you will be justified, and by your words you will be condemned.

38. Then certain of the scribes and the Pharisees answered, saying, Master, we would see a sign from You.

39. But He answered and said to them, an evil and adulterous generation seeks after a sign, and there will no sign be given to it, but the sign of the prophet Jonah:

40. For as Jonah was three days and three nights in the sea monster's belly; so, will the Son of man be three days and three nights in the heart of the earth.

41. The men of Nineveh will rise in judgment with this generation and will condemn it: because they repented at the preaching of Jonah; and behold, one greater than Jonah is here.

42. The queen of the South will rise up in the judgment with this generation and will condemn it: for she came from the uttermost parts of the

43. When an unclean spirit is gone out of a man, he walks through dry places, seeking rest, and finds none.

44. Then he says, I will return into my house from where I came out; and when he returns, he finds it empty, swept, and put in order.

45. Then goes he and takes with himself seven other spirits more wicked than himself and they enter in and dwell there: and the last state of that man is worse than the first. That is the way it will also be with this wicked generation."

46. While He yet talked to the people, behold, His mother and His brothers stood outside, wanting to speak with Him.

47. Then one said to Him, behold, Your mother and Your brothers stand outside, wanting to speak with You.

48. But He answered and said to him that told Him, who is My mother? And who are My brothers?

49. Then He stretched out His hand toward His disciples, and said, behold My mother and My brothers!

50. For whoever will do the will of My Father who is in heaven, the same is My brother, and sister, and mother.

Chapter 13

1. The same day went Jesus out of the house and sat by the seaside.

2. And great multitudes were gathered together to Him so that he went into a boat and sat, and the whole multitude stood on the shore.

3. Then He spoke many things to them in parables, saying, Behold, a sower went out to sow;

4. When he sowed, some seeds fell by the wayside, and the birds came and devoured them:

5. Some fell on rocky places, where they did not have much soil: and quickly they sprung up because they had no depth of soil:

6. But when the sun came up, they were scorched; and because they had no root, they withered away.

7. And some fell among thorns, and the thorns sprung up and choked them:

8. But others fell into good ground and brought forth fruit, some a hundred-fold, some sixty-fold, some thirty-fold.

9. He who has ears to hear, let him hear.

10. Then the disciples came, and said to Him, why speak you to them in parables?

11. He answered and said to them because it is given to you to know the mysteries of the kingdom of the heavens, but to them it is not given.

12. For whoever has, to him will be given, and he will have more abundance: but whoever has not, from him will be taken away even that which he has.

13. Therefore, I speak to them in parables: because seeing they see not; and hearing they hear not, neither do they understand.

14. And in them is fulfilled the prophecy of Isaiah, which says, by hearing you will hear, and will not understand; and seeing you will see, and will not perceive:

15. For this people's heart has grown dull, and their ears are hard of hearing, and their eyes they have closed; unless at any time they should see with their eyes and hear with their ears, and should understand with their heart, and should turn, and I should heal them.

16. But blessed are your eyes, for they see: and your ears, for they hear.

17. For truly I say to you, that many prophets and righteous men have desired to see those things which you see and have not seen them; and to hear those things which you hear and have not heard them.

18. Therefore, hear you the parable of the sower.

19. When anyone hears the word of the kingdom, and understands it not, then comes the wicked one, and seizes that which was sown in his heart. This is he who received seed by the wayside.

20. But he that received the seed into rocky places, the same is he that hears the word, and quickly with joy receives it;

21. Yet has he not root in himself but lasts for a while: for when tribulation or persecution arises because of the word, he instantly stumbles.

22. He also that received seed among the thorns is he that hears the word; and the anxiety of this age, and the deceitfulness of riches, choke the word, and he becomes unfruitful.

23. But he that received seed into the good ground is he that hears the word, and understands it; who also bears fruit, and brings forth, some a hundredfold, some sixty, some thirty.

24. Another parable He put out to them, saying, the kingdom of the heavens is likened to a man which sowed good seed in his field:

25. But while men slept, his enemy came and sowed tares among the wheat and went his way.

26. But when the grain had sprouted, and produced a crop, then appeared the tares also.

27. So, the slaves of the householder came and said to him, sir, did you not sow good seed in your field? Why then does it have tares?
28. He said to them, an enemy has done this. The slaves said to him, do you want us then to go and gather them up?
29. But he said, no; unless while you gather up the tares, you root up also the wheat with them.
30. Let them both grow together until the harvest: and in the time of harvest, I will say to the reapers, gather you together first the tares, and bind them in bundles to burn them: but gather the wheat into my barn.
31. Another parable He put out to them, saying, Another parable He put out to them, saying, the kingdom of the heavens is like a grain of mustard seed, which a man took, and sowed in his field:
32. Which indeed is the least of all seeds: but when it is grown, it is the greatest among herbs, and becomes a tree, so that the birds of the air come and lodge in the branches of it.
33. Another parable spoke He to them; the kingdom of the heavens is like leaven, which a woman took, and hid in three measures of meal until the whole was leavened.
34. All these things spoke Jesus to the multitude in parables; and without a parable spoke He not to them:
35. That it might be fulfilled which was spoken by the prophet, saying, I will open My mouth in parables; I will utter things which have been kept secret before the downfall of the world.
36. Then Jesus sent the multitude away and went into the house: and His disciples came to Him, saying, explain to us the parable of the tares of the field.
37. He answered and said to them, He that sows the good seed is the Son of man;
38. The field is the world; the good seed are the children of the kingdom; but the tares are the children of the wicked one;
39. The enemy that sowed them is the Devil; the harvest is the consummation of the Old Covenant Age; and the reapers are the messengers.
40. As therefore the tares are gathered and burned in the fire; so, it will be in the completion of this Old Covenant Age.
41. The Son of man will send out his messengers, and they will gather out of his kingdom all things that offend, and those who do iniquity;
42. And will cast them into a furnace of fire: there will be wailing and gnashing of teeth.
43. Then will the righteous shine forth as the sun in the kingdom of their Father. Whoever has ears to hear, let him hear.
44. Again, the kingdom of the heavens is like treasure hidden in a field, which when a man has found, he hides, and for joy of it goes and sells all that he has and buys that field.
45. Again, the kingdom of the heavens is like a merchant man, seeking good pearls:
46. Who, when he had found one pearl of great price went and sold all that he had and bought it.
47. Again, the kingdom of the heavens is like a net that was cast into the sea, and gathered of every kind:

48. Which, when it was full, they dragged it to shore, sat down, and gathered the good into vessels, but cast the bad out.

49. So, will it be at the completion of the Old Covenant Age: the messengers will come out, and sever the wicked from among the just,

50. And will cast them into the furnace of fire: there will be wailing and gnashing of teeth.

51. Jesus said to them, have you understood all these things? They said to Him, yes, Lord.

52. Then He said to them, therefore every scribe who is discipled into the kingdom of the heavens is like a man that is master of the house, who brings out of his treasure things new and old.

53. So, it came to pass, that when Jesus had finished these parables, He departed from there.

54. When He had come into His own country, He taught them in their synagogue, so much so that they were astonished, and said, from where did this man get this wisdom, and these mighty works?

55. Is not this the carpenter's Son? Is not His mother called Mary? And His brothers, James, and Joses, and Simon, and Judas?

56. And His sisters, are they not all with us? Where then has this man all these things?

57. For they were offended by Him. But Jesus said to them, a prophet is not without honor, except in his own country, and his own family.

58. So, He did not do many mighty works there because of their unbelief.

Chapter 14

1. At that time Herod the Tetrarch heard of the fame of Jesus,

2. And said to his servants, this is John the Immerser; he is risen from the dead; and therefore, mighty works do manifest themselves in him.

3. For Herod had laid hold on John, and bound him, and put him in prison for Herodias' sake, his brother Philip's wife.

4. For John said to him, it is not lawful for you to have her.

5. When he would have taken him to death, he feared the multitude, because they counted him as a prophet.

6. But when Herod's birthday was kept, the daughter of Herodias danced before them and pleased Herod.

7. Where he promised with an oath to give her whatever she would ask.

8. So, she, being previously instructed by her mother, said, give me John the Immerser's head on a platter.

9. Then the king was sorry: nevertheless, for the oath's sake, and those who sat with him to eat, he commanded it to be given to her.

10. Then he sent and beheaded John in the prison.

11. His head was brought on a platter and given to the girl: and she brought it to her mother.

12. Then his disciples came, and took up the body, and buried it, and went and told Jesus.

13. When Jesus heard of it, He departed from there by boat into a deserted place apart: and when the people had heard of it, they followed Him on foot out of the cities.
14. Then Jesus went out and saw a great multitude, and was moved with compassion toward them, and He healed their sick.
15. When it was evening, His disciples came to Him and said, this is a deserted place, and the time is now past; send the multitude away, that they may go into the villages, and buy themselves food.
16. But Jesus said to them, they need not depart; you give them something to eat.
17. But they said to Him, we have here but five loaves, and two fishes.
18. He said, bring them here to Me.
19. Then He commanded the multitude to sit down on the grass and took the five loaves, and the two fish, and looking up to heaven, He blessed, and broke, and gave the loaves to His disciples, and the disciples to the multitude.
20. So, they did all eat and were filled: and they took up of the fragments that remained, twelve baskets full.
21. For they that had eaten were about five thousand men, besides women and children.
22. Immediately Jesus constrained His disciples to get into a boat and to go before him to the other side, while He sent the multitudes away.
23. When He had sent the multitudes away, He went up to a mountain alone to pray: and when the evening had come, He was there alone.
24. But the boat was now in the midst of the sea, tossed with waves: for the wind was strongly against them.
25. And in the fourth watch of the night Jesus went to them, walking on the sea.
26. When the disciples saw Him walking on the sea, they were troubled, saying, it is a spirit, and they cried out for fear.
27. But immediately Jesus spoke to them, saying, be of good cheer; it is I; be not afraid!
28. Then Peter answered Him and said, Lord, if it is You ask me to come to You on the water.
29. Then He said, come. When Peter had come down out of the boat, he walked on the water, to go to Jesus.
30. But when he saw the wind boisterous, he was afraid; and beginning to sink, he cried, saying, Lord, save me!
31. Immediately Jesus stretched out His hand, and caught him, and said to him, O you of little faith, why did you doubt?
32. And when they had come into the boat, the wind stopped.
33. Then they that were in the boat came and worshiped Him, saying, truly You are the Son of God!
34. When they had crossed over, they came into the land of Gennesaret.
35. When the men of that place fully acquainted with Him, they sent out into all that surrounding country, and brought to Him all that were diseased;
36. And asked Him that they might only touch the hem of His garment: and as many as touched it were made completely whole.

Chapter 15

1. Then came to Jesus scribes and Pharisees, who were of Jerusalem, and said,
2. Why do Your disciples violate the tradition of the elders? For they do not wash their hands when they eat bread.
3. But He answered and said to them, why do you also violate the commandment of God by your tradition?
4. For God commanded, saying, honor your father and mother: and he that curses father or mother, let him be taken to death.
5. But you say, whoever will say to his father or his mother, it is a gift to God, whatever you might have gained from me;
6. And honor, not his father or his mother, he will be free. Thus, you have made the commandment of God of no effect by your traditions.
7. You hypocrites, well did Isaiah prophesy of you, saying,
8. This people draw close to Me with their mouth and honors Me with their lips, but their hearts are far from Me.
9. But in vain they do worship Me, teaching for doctrines the commandments of men.
10. Then He called the multitude, and said to them, hear, and understand:
11. not that which goes into the mouth defiles a man; but that which comes out of the mouth, this defiles a man.
12. Then came His disciples, and said to Him, do you know that the Pharisees were offended after they heard this saying?
13. But He answered and said, every plant, which My heavenly Father has not planted, will be uprooted.
14. Let them alone: they are blind leaders of the blind. And if the blind lead the blind, both will fall into the ditch.
15. Then answered Peter and said to Him, explain to us this parable.
16. So, Jesus said, are you also yet without understanding?
17. Do you not yet understand that whatever enters in at the mouth goes into the stomach, and then out of the body?
18. But those things which proceed out of the mouth come out from the heart, and they defile the man.
19. For out of the heart proceed evil thoughts, murders, adulteries, fornications, thefts, false witness, and blasphemies:
20. These are the things which defile a man: but to eat with unwashed hands does not defile a man.
21. Then Jesus went from there and departed into the borders of Tyre and Sidon.
22. And behold, a woman of Canaan came out of the same borders, and cried to Him, saying, have mercy on me, O Lord, you son of David; my daughter is severely demon-possessed.
23. But He answered her not a word. So, His disciples came and asked Him, saying, send her away; for she cries after us.
24. But He answered and said, I am not sent but to the lost sheep of the house of Israel.
25. Then she came and worshiped Him, saying, Lord, help me.
26. But He answered and said, it is not right to take the children's bread and to cast it to dogs.

27. And she said, yes, Lord: yet the little dog eats of the crumbs which fall from his own masters' table.
28. Then Jesus answered and said to her," O woman, great is your faith! Be it done for you as you desire." And her daughter was healed that hour.
29. And Jesus departed from there, and came close to the Sea of Galilee, and went up to a mountain, and sat down there.
30. Then great multitudes came to Him, having with them those that were lame, blind, mute, maimed, and many others, and cast them down at Jesus' feet; and He healed them:
31. So much so that the multitude wondered, when they saw the mute to speak, the maimed to be whole, the lame to walk, and the blind to see: and they glorified the God of Israel.
32. Then Jesus called His disciples to Him, and said, I have compassion on the multitude, because they continue with Me now three days, and have nothing to eat: and I will not send them away fasting, unless they collapse on the way.
33. But His disciples said to Him, from where should we have so much bread in the wilderness, as to fill so great a multitude?
34. And Jesus said to them, how many loaves have you? And they said, seven, and a few little fish.
35. Then He commanded the multitude to sit down on the ground.
36. So, He took the seven loaves and the fish, and gave thanks, and broke them, and gave to His disciples, and the disciples to the multitude.

37. And they did all eat and were filled: and they took up of the broken food that was left seven baskets full.
38. For they that did eat were four thousand men, beside women and children.
39. And He sent away the multitude and got into a ship and came into the borders of Magadan.

Chapter 16

1. The Pharisees also with the Sadducees came and tempting Him desired that He would show them a sign from heaven.
2. He answered and said to them, when it is evening, you say, it will be fair weather: for the sky is red.
3. And in the morning, it will be foul weather today: for the sky is red and threatening. O you hypocrites, you can discern the face of the sky; but you can't discern the signs of the times?
4. 4.A wicked and adulterous generation seeks after a sign, and there will be no sign given to it, but the sign of the prophet Jonah. So, He left them and departed.
5. When His disciples had come to the other side, they had forgotten to take bread.
6. Then Jesus said to them, take heed and beware of the leaven of the Pharisees and the Sadducees.
7. Then they reasoned among themselves, saying, it is because we have taken no bread.
8. Which when Jesus perceived, He said to them, O you of little faith, why reason you among yourselves, because you have brought no bread?

9. Do you not yet understand, neither remember the five loaves of the five thousand, and how many baskets were left?
10. Neither the seven loaves of the four thousand and how many baskets were left?
11. How is it that you do not understand that I spoke to you not concerning bread, but that you should beware of the leaven of the Pharisees and the Sadducees?
12. Then they understood how He told them not to beware of the leaven of bread, but the teaching of the Pharisees and the Sadducees.
13. When Jesus came into the borders of Caesarea Philippi, He asked His disciples, and said, who do men say that I, the Son of man, am?
14. Then they said, some say that You are John the Immerser: some, Elijah; and others, Jeremiah, or one of the prophets.
15. He said to them, but who say you that I am?
16. Simon Peter answered and said, You are the Christ, the Son of the living God!
17. Jesus answered and said to him, blessed are you, Simon Barjona: for flesh and blood has not revealed it to you, but My Father who is in heaven.
18. And I say also to you that you are Peter, and on this rock, I will build My assembly; and the gates of the unseen realm will not prevail against it.
19. And I will give to you the keys of the kingdom of the heavens: and whatever you will bind on earth will be bound in heaven: and whatever you will loose on earth will be loosed in heaven.
20. Then He charged His disciples that they should tell no man that He was Jesus the Christ.
21. From that time Jesus began to show to His disciples, how He must go to Jerusalem, and suffer many things of the elders and chief priests and scribes, and be killed, and be raised again the third day.
22. Then Peter took Him and began to rebuke Him, saying, be it far from you, Lord: this will not happen to You.
23. But He turned, and said to Peter, you get behind Me, Satan: you are an offense to Me: for you cherish not the things that be of God, but those that be of men.
24. Then said Jesus to His disciples, if any man will come after Me, let him deny Himself, and take up His cross, and follow Me.
25. For whoever will save his life will lose it: and whoever will lose his life for My sake will find it.
26. For what does a man profit, if he will gain the whole world, and lose his own soul? Or what will a man give in exchange for his soul?
27. For the Son of man is about to come in the glory of His Father with His angels, and then He will recompense every man according to his works.
28. Truly I say to you, there are some standing here, who will not taste of death, until they see the Son of man coming in His kingdom.

Chapter 17

1. After six days Jesus took Peter, James, and John his brother, and brought them up to a high mountain alone,
2. and was transfigured before them: and His face shone as the sun, and His clothing was white as the light.
3. And behold, there appeared to them Moses and Elijah talking with Him.
4. Then answered Peter, and said to Jesus, Lord, it is good for us to be here: if You will, let us make here three tabernacles; one for You, and one for Moses, and one for Elijah.
5. While he yet spoke, behold, a bright cloud overshadowed them: and behold a voice out of the cloud, which said, this is My beloved Son, in whom I am well pleased; hear Him.
6. When the disciples heard it, they fell on their faces and were very afraid.
7. But Jesus came and touched them, and said, arise, and be not afraid.
8. When they had lifted up their eyes, they saw no man, except Jesus only.
9. As they came down from the mountain, Jesus charged them, and said, tell the vision to no man, until the Son of man be risen again from the dead.
10. So, His disciples asked Him, and said, why then say the scribes that Elijah must first come?
11. Then Jesus answered and said to them, Elijah truly will first come and restore all things.
12. But I say to you, that Elijah has come already, and they did not know him but have done to him whatever they desired. Likewise, also the Son of man is about to suffer by them.
13. Then the disciples understood that He spoke to them about John the Immerser.
14. When they had come to the multitude, there came to Him a certain man, kneeling down to Him, and saying,
15. Lord, have mercy on my son: for he is an epileptic, and suffers intensely: for frequently he falls into the fire, and often into the water.
16. So, I brought him to Your disciples, and they could not cure him.
17. Then Jesus answered and said, O faithless and perverse generation, how long will I be with you? How long will I endure you? Bring him here to Me.
18. Then Jesus rebuked the demon, and he departed out of him: and the child was cured from that very hour.
19. Then came the disciples to Jesus alone, and said, why could we not cast him out?
20. So, Jesus said to them, because of your unbelief: for truly I say to you, if you have faith as a grain of mustard seed, you will say to this mountain, move from here to there; and it will move, and nothing will be impossible to you.
21. But this kind does not go out except by prayer and fasting.
22. While they stayed in Galilee, Jesus said to them, The Son of man is about to be betrayed into the hands of men:
23. and they will kill Him, and the third day He will rise again. So, they were exceedingly sorrowful.
24. When they had come to Capernaum, they that received tribute money came to Peter, and said, does not your Master pay tribute?

25. He said, yes. And when he had come into the house, Jesus prevented him, saying, what think you, Simon? Of whom do the kings of the earth take taxes or tribute? From their own children, or from strangers?
26. Peter said to Him, from strangers. Jesus said to him, then are the children free.
27. Not with standing, unless we should offend them, go to the sea, and cast in a hook, and take up the fish that first comes up; and when you have opened his mouth, you will find a piece of money: take it and give it to them for you and Me.

Chapter 18

1. At the same time came the disciples to Jesus, and said who is the greatest in the kingdom of the heavens?
2. Then Jesus called a little child to Him, and set him in the midst of them,
3. and said, truly I say to you, unless you be converted, and become as little children, you will not enter into the kingdom of the heavens.
4. Therefore, whoever will humble himself as this little child, the same is greatest in the kingdom of the heavens.
5. And whoever will receive one such little child in My name receives Me.
6. But whoever will stumble one of these little ones who believe in Me, it was better for him that a millstone was hanged about his neck, and that he was drowned in the depth of the sea.
7. Woe to the world because of offenses! For it must be that offenses come; but woe to that man by whom the offense comes!
8. Therefore, if your hand or your foot stumble you, cut them off, and cast them from you: you should enter into life lame or maimed, rather than having two hands or two feet to be cast into everlasting fire.
9. And if your eye stumbles you, pluck it out, and cast it from you: you should enter into life with one eye, rather than having two eyes to be cast into the fire of Gehenna.
10. Take heed that you despise not one of these little ones; for I say to you, that in heaven their angels do always behold the face of My Father who is in heaven.
11. For the Son of man has come to save that which was lost.
12. What is your opinion? If a man has a hundred sheep, and one of them goes astray, does he not leave the ninety-nine, and goes into the mountains, and seeks that which is gone astray?
13. And if he finds it, truly I say to you, he rejoices more of that sheep, than of the ninety-nine which went not astray.
14. Even so it is not the will of Your Father who is in heaven, that one of these little ones should perish.
15. Moreover, if your brother sins against you, go and tell him his fault between you and him alone: if he will hear you, you have gained your brother.
16. But if he will not hear you, then take with you one or two more, that in the mouth of two or three witnesses, every word may be established.

17. And if he will neglect to hear them, tell it to the assembly: but if he fails to hear the assembly, let him be to you as the heathen and the tax collector.
18. Truly, I am saying to you, whatever you bind on earth, will have already been bound in heaven. And whatever you loose on earth, will have already been loosed in heaven.
19. Again, I say to you, that if two of you will agree on earth as concerning anything that they will ask, it will be done for them by My Father who is in heaven.
20. For where two or three are gathered together in My name, there I am in the midst of them.
21. Then came Peter to Him, and said, Lord, how often will my brother sin against me, and I forgive him? Until seven times?
22. Jesus said to him, I say not to you, until seven times: but, until seventy times seven.
23. Because of this the kingdom of the heavens is likened to a certain king, who wanted to resolve accounts with his slaves.
24. When he had begun to resolve accounts, one was brought to him, who owed him ten thousand talents.
25. But as he was not able to pay, his lord commanded him to be sold, and his wife, and children, and all that he had, and payment to be made.
26. Therefore, the slave fell down, and begged him, saying, lord, have patience with me, and I will pay you all.
27. Then the lord of that slave was moved with compassion and released him and forgave him the debt.
28. But the same slave went out and found one of his fellow slaves, which owed him a hundred denarii: and he laid hands on him, and took him by the throat, saying, pay me what you owe.
29. And his fellow slave fell down at his feet, and asked him, saying, have patience with me, and I will pay you everything.
30. And he was unwilling: but went and cast him into prison until he should pay the debt.
31. So, when his fellow servants saw what was done, they were greatly saddened and came and told it to their lord all that was done.
32. Then his lord, after he had called him, said to him, O you wicked slave, I forgave you all that debt, because you begged me to:
33. should not you also have had compassion on your fellow slave, just as I had mercy on you?
34. And his lord was very angry and delivered him to the tormentors until he should pay all that was owed to him.
35. So likewise, will my heavenly Father do also to you, if each one of you do not forgive from your hearts, his brother their trespasses.

Chapter 19

1. And it came to pass, that when Jesus had finished these sayings, He departed from Galilee, and came into the borders of Judea beyond the Jordan;
2. so great multitudes followed Him, and He healed them there.
3. The Pharisees also came to Him, tempting Him, and said to Him, Is it lawful for a man to divorce his wife for any reason?

4. Then He answered and said to them, have you not read, that He who made them at the beginning made them male and female,
5. And said, for this reason, will a man leave father and mother, and will cleave to his wife: and they two will become one flesh?
6. Therefore, they are no longer two, but one flesh. Therefore, what God has joined together, let no man separate.
7. They said to Him, why did Moses then command to give a writing of divorce, and to put her away?
8. He said to them, Moses, because of the hardness of your hearts, permitted you to divorce your wives: but from the beginning it was not so.
9. For I say to you, whoever will divorce his wife, unless it is for fornication, and will marry another, commits adultery: and whoever marries her who is divorced does commit adultery.
10. His disciples said to Him, if this is the case between a man and his wife, it is not good to marry.
11. But He said to them, all men cannot receive this saying, except they to whom it is given.
12. For there are some eunuchs, which were so born from their mother's womb: and there are some which were made eunuchs by men: and there be some which have renounced marriage for the kingdom of the heavens' sake. He that is able to receive it, let him receive it.
13. Then little children there were brought to Him, that He should put His hands on them, and pray: and the disciples rebuked them.
14. But Jesus said, permit little children, and do not forbid them to come to Me: for of such is the kingdom of the heavens.
15. And He laid His hands on them and departed from there.
16. Then, behold, one came and said to him, Good Master, what good thing will I do, that I may have eternal life?
17. And He said to him, why do you call Me good? There is none good but one, that is, God: but if you will enter into life, keep the commandments.
18. He said to Him, Which? Jesus said, you will not murder, You will not commit adultery, You will not steal, You will not bear false witness,
19. Honor your father and your mother: and You will love your neighbor as yourself.
20. The young man said to Him, All these things have I kept from my youth up: what do I still lack?
21. Jesus said to him, If you will be mature, go and sell what you have, and give to the poor, and you will have treasure in heaven: and come and follow Me.
22. But when the young man heard that saying, he went away sorrowful: for he had great possessions.
23. Then said Jesus to His disciples, truly I say to you, that a rich man will hardly enter into the kingdom of the heavens.
24. And again I say to you, it is easier for a camel to go through the eye of a needle than for a rich man to enter into the kingdom of God.

25. When His disciples heard it, they were exceedingly amazed, saying, who then can be saved?
26. But Jesus beheld them, and said to them, with men this is impossible; but with God all things are possible.
27. Then answered Peter and said to Him, behold, we have forsaken all, and followed You; what therefore will we have?
28. And Jesus said to them, truly I say to you, that you who have followed Me, in the regeneration when the Son of man will sit in the throne of His glory, you also will sit upon twelve thrones, judging the twelve tribes of Israel.
29. And everyone that has forsaken houses, or brothers, or sisters, or father, or mother, or wife, or children, or lands, for My name's sake, will receive a hundredfold and will inherit infinite life.
30. But many that are first will be last, and the last will be first.

Chapter 20

1. For the kingdom of the heavens is like unto a man that is a land owner, which went out early in the morning to hire laborers into his vineyard.
2. And when he had agreed with the laborers for a denarius a day, he sent them into his vineyard.
3. And he went out about the third hour, and saw others standing idle in the marketplace,
4. And said to them; go you also into the vineyard, and whatsoever is right I will give you. And they went their way.
5. Again, he went out about the sixth and ninth hour and did likewise.
6. And about the eleventh hour he went out, and found others standing idle, and said to them, why stand you here all day idle?
7. They say to him because no man has hired us. He said to them, go you also into the vineyard; and whatsoever is right, that shall you receive.
8. So, when evening was come, the lord of the vineyard said to his steward, call the laborers, and give them their pay, beginning from the last to the first.
9. When they came that were hired about the eleventh hour, they received every man a denarius.
10. But when the first came, they supposed that they should have received more; and they likewise received every man a denarius.
11. So, when they had received it, they murmured against the land owner,
12. Saying, these last have worked but one hour, and you have made them equal to us, which have borne the burden and heat of the day.
13. But he answered one of them, and said, friend, I do you no wrong: did you not agree with me for a denarius?
14. Take that which is yours and go your way: I will give this to the last, just as to you.
15. Is it not lawful for me to do what I will with my own? Is your eye evil, because I am good?
16. So, the last will be first, and the first last: for many are called, but few chosen.

17. Now Jesus going up to Jerusalem took the twelve disciples aside on the way, and said to them,
18. Behold, we go up to Jerusalem, and the Son of man is about to be betrayed to the chief priests and the scribes, and they will condemn Him to death,
19. And will deliver him to the nations to mock, and to whip, and to crucify Him: and the third day He will rise again.
20. Then came to Him the mother of Zebedee's children with her sons, worshiping Him, and desiring a certain thing of Him.
21. He said to her, what will you? She said to Him, grant that these my two sons may sit, the one on Your right hand, and the other on the left, in Your kingdom.
22. But Jesus answered and said, you know not what you ask. Are you able to drink of the cup that I am about to drink of, and to be immersed with the immersion that I am about to be immersed with? They say to Him, we are able.
23. He said to them, you will drink indeed of My cup and be immersed with the immersion that I am immersed with: but to sit on My right hand, and on My left, is not Mine to give, but it will be given to them for whom it is prepared by My Father.
24. When the ten heard it, they were moved with indignation against the two brothers.
25. But Jesus called them to Him, and said, you know that the rulers of the nations exercise dominion over them, and they that are great exercise authority upon them.
26. But it will not be so among you: but whoever will be great among you, let him be your servant;
27. And whoever will be chief among you, let him be your slave:
28. Just as the Son of man did not come to be served, but to serve, and to give His life as a ransom for many.
29. As they departed from Jericho, a great multitude followed Him.
30. And behold, two blind men sitting by the wayside, when they heard that Jesus passed by, cried out, saying, have mercy on us, O Lord, You son of David.
31. And the multitude rebuked them because they should hold their peace: but they cried the more saying have mercy on us, O Lord, You son of David!
32. And Jesus stood still, and called them, and said, what are you wanting Me to do to you?
33. They say to Him, Lord, that our eyes may be opened.
34. So, Jesus had compassion on them and touched their eyes: and immediately their eyes received sight, and they followed Him.

Chapter 21

1. When they drew close to Jerusalem and had come to Bethphage, to the Mount of Olives, then sent Jesus two disciples,
2. Saying to them, go into the village next to you, and immediately you will find a donkey tied, and a colt with her: release them, and bring them to Me.
3. And if any man says anything to you, you will say, the Lord needs them; and immediately he will send them.

4. All this was done, that it might be fulfilled that which was spoken by the prophet, saying,

5. Tell you the daughter of Zion, behold, your King comes to you, meek, and sitting upon a donkey, and a colt the foal of a donkey.

6. So, the disciples went, and did as Jesus commanded them,

7. And brought the donkey, and the colt, and put their cloaks on them, and they set Him on it.

8. And a very great multitude spread their garments on the way; others cut down branches from the trees and scattered them on the way.

9. And the multitudes that went before, and that followed, cried, saying, Hosanna to the son of David: Blessed is He that comes in the name of the Lord; Hosanna in the highest!

10. And when He was come into Jerusalem, all the city was moved, saying, who is this?

11. And the multitude said this is Jesus the prophet of Nazareth of Galilee.

12. And Jesus went into the temple of God and cast out all them that sold and bought in the temple, and overthrew the tables of the money changers, and the seats of them that sold doves,

13. And said to them, it is written, My house will be called the house of prayer, but you have made it a den of thieves.

14. So, the blind and the lame came to Him in the temple, and He healed them.

15. But when the chief priests and scribes saw the wonderful things that He did, and the children crying in the temple, and saying, Hosanna to the son of David; they were intensely displeased,

16. And said to Him, do you hear what these say? And Jesus said to them, yes; have you not read, out of the mouth of babes and infants You have perfected praise?

17. And He left them and went out of the city into Bethany, and He stayed there.

18. Now in the morning as He returned to the city, He hungered.

19. And when He saw a fig tree on the way, He came to it, and found nothing on it, but leaves only, and said to it, let no fruit grow on you from now on and going into the New Covenant Age. Immediately the fig tree withered away.

20. When the disciples saw it, they marveled, saying, how quickly the fig tree withered away!

21. Jesus answered and said to them, truly I say to you, If you have faith, and doubt not, you will not only do this which is done to the fig tree, but also if you will say to this mountain, Be you removed, and be you cast into the sea; it will be done.

22. For all things, whatsoever you will ask in prayer, believing, you will receive.

23. When He had come into the temple, the chief priests and the elders of the people came to Him as He was teaching, and said, by what authority are you doing these things? And who gave you this authority?

24. Then Jesus answered and said to them, I also will ask you one thing, which if you tell Me, I likewise will tell you by what authority I do these things.

25. The baptism of John, where was it from? From heaven, or of men? Then they reasoned with themselves, saying, if we will say, from heaven; He will say to us, why did you not then believe him?
26. But if we will say, of men; we fear the people; for all hold John as a prophet.
27. Then they answered Jesus, and said, we cannot tell. So, He said to them, neither do I tell you by what authority I do these things.
28. Now what do you think? A certain man had two sons; and he came to the first, and said, son, go work today in my vineyard.
29. He answered and said, I will not: but afterward he repented and went.
30. Then he came to the second and said likewise. And he answered and said, I am going, sir: and did not go.
31. Which of the two did the will of his father? They said to Him, the first. Jesus said to them, truly I say to you, that the tax collectors and the harlots go into the Kingdom of God before you.
32. For John came to you on the way of righteousness, and you did not believe him: but the tax-collectors and the harlots believed him: and you, when you had seen it, afterward did not repent, that you might believe him.
33. Hear another parable: there was a certain land owner, who planted a vineyard, hedged it round about, dug a wine press in it, built a watchtower, leased it to some vinedressers, and went into a far country:
34. when the time of the fruit drew near, he sent his slaves to the vinedressers, that they might receive the fruits of it.
35. But the vinedressers took his slaves, and beat one, and killed another, and stoned another.
36. Again, he sent other slaves more than the first: and they did to them likewise.
37. But last of all he sent to them his son, saying, they will respect my son.
38. But when the vinedressers saw the son, they said among themselves, this is the heir; come, let us kill him, and let us seize on his inheritance.
39. So, they took him and cast him out of the vineyard and slew him.
40. Therefore, when the lord of the vineyard comes, what will he do to those vinedressers?
41. They said to Him, he will miserably destroy those wicked men and will lease his vineyard to other vinedressers, who will render him the fruits in their seasons.
42. Jesus said to them, did you not read in the Scriptures, the stone which the builders rejected, the same has become the chief cornerstone: this is the Lord's doing, and it is marvelous in our eyes?
43. Therefore, I say to you, the kingdom of God will be taken from you, and given to a nation bringing forth the fruits of it.
44. Whoever will fall on this stone will be broken: and on whomever it will fall, it will grind him to powder.
45. When the chief priests and Pharisees had heard His parables, they perceived that He spoke about them.
46. But when they sought to lay hands on Him, they feared the multitude, because they believed He was a prophet.

Chapter 22

1. And Jesus answered and spoke to them again by parables, and said,
2. The kingdom of the heavens is like unto a certain king, who prepared a wedding for his son,
3. And sent out his slaves to call them that were invited to the wedding: and they would not come.
4. Again, he sent out other slaves, saying, tell those who are invited. Behold, I have prepared my dinner: my oxen and my fattened cattle are killed, and all things are ready: come to the wedding.
5. But they made light of it, and went their way, one to his farm, another to his business:
6. and the remnant took his slaves, and treated them spitefully, and slew them.
7. But when the king heard of it, he was very angry: and he sent out his armies, and destroyed those murderers, and burned up their city.
8. Then he said to his slaves, the wedding is ready, but they who were invited were not worthy.
9. Therefore, go into the highways, and as many as you will find, invite to the wedding.
10. So those slaves went out into the highways and gathered together all as many as they found, both bad and good: and the wedding was furnished with guests.
11. When the king came in to see the guests, he saw there a man who had not on a wedding garment:
12. So, he said to him, friend, how did you come in here not having a wedding garment? But he was speechless.
13. Then said the king to the servants, bind him hand and foot and take him away and cast him into outer darkness, there will be weeping and gnashing of teeth.
14. For many are called, but few are chosen.
15. Then went the Pharisees, and took counsel how they might entangle Him in His talk.
16. So, they sent out to Him their disciples with the Herodians, saying, Master, we know that You are true, and teach the way of God in reality, neither do You have regard for anyone: for You look not into the face of man.
17. Therefore, tell us, what do You think? Is it lawful to give tribute to Caesar, or not?
18. But Jesus perceived their wickedness, and said, why tempt Me, you hypocrites?
19. Show Me the tribute money. So, they brought to Him a denarius coin.
20. He said to them, whose image is this and inscription?
21. They said to Him, Caesar's. Then He said to them, therefore render to Caesar the things which are Caesar's; and to God the things that are God's.
22. When they had heard these words, they marveled, and left Him, and went their way.
23. The same day the Sadducees came to Him, who said that there is no resurrection, and asked Him,

24. saying, Master, Moses said, if a man dies, having no children, his brother will marry his wife, and raise up children for his brother.
25. Now there were with us seven brothers: and the first when he had married a wife, died, and, having no offspring, left his wife to his brother:
26. Likewise, the second also, and the third, to the seventh.
27. And last of all the woman died also.
28. Therefore, in the resurrection whose wife will she be of the seven? For they all had her.
29. Jesus answered and said to them, you do err, not knowing the Scriptures, nor the power of God.
30. For in the resurrection, they neither marry, nor are given in marriage, but are as the angels of God in heaven.
31. But as touching the resurrection of the dead, have you not read that which was spoken to you by God, saying,
32. I am the God of Abraham, and the God of Isaac, and the God of Jacob? God is not the God of the dead but of the living.
33. When the multitude heard this, they were astonished at His teaching.
34. But when the Pharisees had heard that he had put the Sadducees to silence, they were gathered together.
35. Then one of them, who was a lawyer, asked Him a question, tempting Him, and said,
36. Master, what is the great commandment in the Law?
37. Jesus said to him, you will love the Lord your God with all your heart, and with all your soul, and with your entire mind.
38. This is the first and great commandment.
39. And the second is like it, you will love your neighbor as yourself.
40. On these two commandments hang all the Law and the prophets.
41. While the Pharisees were gathered together, Jesus asked them,
42. Saying, what do you think of Christ? Whose son is he? They said to Him, the son of David.
43. He said to them, how then does David in the Spirit call Him Lord, saying,
44. The Lord said to my Lord, sit on My right hand until I make Your enemies Your footstool?
45. If David then calls Him Lord, how is He His Son?
46. And no man was able to answer Him a word, neither dared anyone from that day forth ask Him any more questions.

Chapter 23

1. Then spoke Jesus to the multitude and His disciples,
2. Saying the scribes and the Pharisees sit in Moses' seat:
3. Therefore, all whatsoever they tell you to observe, that observe and do; but do not you after their works: for they do not practice what they preach.
4. For they bind heavy burdens and grievous to be borne and lay them on men's shoulders; but they will not move them with one of their fingers

5. But all their works they do to be seen of men: they make broad their phylacteries, and enlarge the borders of their garments,
6. And love the uppermost rooms at feasts, and the chief seats in the synagogues,
7. And greetings in the markets, and to be called by men, Rabbi, Rabbi.
8. But be not you called Rabbi: for one is your Master, even Christ; and all of you are brothers.
9. And call no man your father on the earth: for one is your Father, who is in heaven.
10. Neither you be called masters: for one is your Master, even Christ.
11. But he that is greatest among you will be your servant.
12. For whoever will exalt himself will be humbled, and he that will humble himself will be exalted.
13. But woe to you, scribes and Pharisees, hypocrites! For you shut up the kingdom of the heavens against men: for you neither go in yourselves nor permit them who are entering to go in.
14. Woe to you, scribes and Pharisees, hypocrites! For you devour widows' houses, and for a pretense make long prayers: therefore, you will receive the more extreme judgment.
15. Woe to you, scribes and Pharisees, hypocrites! For you cover sea and land to make one convert, and when he is made, you make him twice the son of Gehenna than yourselves.
16. Woe to you, you blind guides, who say, whoever will swear by the temple, it is nothing; but whoever will swear by the gold of the temple, he is a debtor!
17. You fools and blind: for which is greater, the gold, or the temple that sanctifies the gold?
18. And whoever will swear by the altar, it is nothing; but whoever swears by the gift that is on it, he is guilty.
19. You fools and blind: for which is greater, the gift, or the altar that sanctifies the gift?
20. Therefore, whoever will swear by the altar, swears by it, and by all things on it.
21. And whoever will swear by the temple, swears by it, and by Him that dwells in it.
22. And he that will swear by heaven, swears by the throne of God, and by Him that sits on it.
23. Woe to you, scribes and Pharisees, hypocrites! For you pay tithe of mint and anise and cummin but have left out the weightier matters of the Law, judgment, mercy, and faith: these you should have done, and not leave the other undone.
24. You blind guides, who strain out a gnat, and swallow a camel.
25. Woe to you, scribes and Pharisees, hypocrites! For you make clean the outside of the cup and of the dish, but within they are full of extortion and excess.
26. You blind Pharisee, cleanse first that which is within the cup and dish, that the outside of them may be clean also.
27. Woe to you, scribes and Pharisees, hypocrites! For you are like whitewashed sepulchers which indeed appear beautiful outwardly but are inside full of dead men's bones and of all uncleanness.
28. Even so you also outwardly appear righteous to men, but inside you are full of hypocrisy and iniquity.

29. Woe to you, scribes and Pharisees, hypocrites! Because you build the tombs of the prophets, and decorate the tombs of the righteous,
30. and say, if we had been in the days of our fathers, we would not have been partakers with them in the blood of the prophets.
31. Therefore, you are witnesses to yourselves, that you are the sons of those who killed the prophets.
32. Fill you up then the measure of your fathers.
33. You serpents, you generation of vipers, how can you avoid the Judgment of Gehenna?
34. Therefore, behold, I send to you prophets and wise men, and scribes: and some of them you will kill and crucify; and some of them will you whip in your synagogues, and persecute them from city to city:
35. that upon you should be coming all the righteous blood shed on the land, from the blood of righteous Abel to the blood of Zacharias son of Berechiah, whom you murdered between the temple and the altar.
36. Truly I say to you, all these things will be coming upon this generation!
37. O Jerusalem, Jerusalem, you that kill the prophets, and stone those who are sent to you, how often I would have gathered your children together figuratively as a hen gathers her chicks under her wings, but you were unwilling!
38. Behold, your house is left to you desolate.
39. For I say to you, you will not see Me afterward, until you will say, blessed is He that is coming in the name of the Lord!

Chapter 24

1. Then Jesus went out and departed from the temple: and His disciples came to Him to show Him the buildings of the temple.
2. And Jesus said to them, do you not see all these things? Truly I say to you, there will not be left here one stone upon another that will not be thrown down.
3. And as he sat on the Mount of Olives, the disciples came to Him privately, saying, tell us, when will these things be, and what will be the sign of Your Presence, and of the completion of the Old Covenant Age?
4. And Jesus answered and said to them, take heed that no man deceives you.
5. For many will come in My name, saying, I am Christ, and will deceive many.
6. And you are about to hear of wars and rumors of wars: see that you be not troubled: for all these things must come to pass, but the completion is not yet.
7. For nation will rise against nation, and kingdom against kingdom: and there will be famines, and pestilences, and earthquakes, in different places.
8. All these are the beginning of sorrows.
9. Then will they deliver you up to be persecuted and will kill you: and you will be hated of all nations for My name's sake.
10. And then will many be offended, and will betray one another, and will hate one another.
11. And many false prophets will rise and will deceive many.
12. And because iniquity will abound, the love of many will grow cold.

13. But he that is enduring into the completion, the same will be saved.
14. And this gospel of the kingdom will be preached in the entire Roman world for a witness to all nations, and then the completion will come.
15. Therefore, when you will see the abomination of desolation, spoken of by Daniel the prophet, stand in the holy place, (whoever reads, let him understand),
16. Then let those who are in Judea flee into the mountains:
17. Let him who is on the housetop not come down to take anything out of his house:
18. Neither let him who is in the field return to take his clothes.
19. And woe to them that are pregnant, and to them that nurse in those days!
20. But pray you that your flight is not in the winter, neither on the Sabbath day:
21. For then there will be great tribulation, such as was not since the beginning of the world to this time, no, nor ever will be.
22. And unless those days should be shortened, there should no flesh be saved: but for the elect's sake, those days will be shortened.
23. Then if any man will say to you, look, here is Christ, or there; believe it not.
24. For there will arise false Christs and false prophets and will show great signs and wonders; so much so that, if it were possible, they will deceive the very elect.
25. Behold, I have told you before.
26. Therefore, if they will say to you, behold, he is in the desert; do not go out: behold, he is in the secret chambers; do not believe it.
27. For as the lightning comes out of the east, and shines even to the west; so also, will the Presence of the Son of man be.
28. For wherever the dead body is, there will the eagles be gathered together.
29. Immediately after the tribulation of those days will the sun be darkened, and the moon will not reflect her light, and the stars will fall from heaven, and the powers of the heavens will be shaken:
30. And then will appear the sign of the Son of man in heaven: and then will all the tribes of the land mourn, and they will see the Son of man coming in the cloud of heaven with power and great glory.
31. And He will send His messengers with a great sound of a trumpet, and they will gather together His elect from the four winds, from one extreme of heaven to the other extremity.
32. Now learn a parable of the fig tree; when its branch is yet tender and puts forth leaves, you know that summer is close:
33. So likewise, you, when you will see all these things, know that it is near, even at the doors.
34. Truly I say to you, this generation will not pass away until all these things happen!
35. Heaven and earth will pass away, but My words will not pass away.
36. But of that day and hour no man knows, nor the Son, not the angels of heaven, but My Father only.
37. But as the days of Noah were, so also will be the Presence of the Son of man.

38. For as in the days that were before the flood, they were eating and drinking, marrying and giving in marriage, until the day that Noah entered into the ark,
39. And did not know until the flood came, and took them all away; likewise, will be the Presence of the Son of man.
40. Then two will be in the field; the one will be taken, and the other let go.
41. Two women will be grinding at the mill; one will be taken, and the other let go.
42. Therefore watch: for you do not know what hour your Lord is coming.
43. But know this that if the master of the house had known in what watch shift the thief is coming, he would watch and would not permit his house to be dug through.
44. Therefore, you be ready also: for in such an hour as you do not think, the Son of man comes.
45. Who then is a faithful and wise slave, whom his lord has constituted over his household, to give them food in due season?
46. Blessed is that slave, whom his lord finds doing when he comes.
47. Truly I say to you, that he will constitute him over all his possessions.
48. But if that evil slave will say in his heart, my lord delays his coming;
49. And will begin to strike his fellow slaves, and to eat and drink with the drunken;
50. The lord of that slave will come in a day when he does not look for him, and in an hour that he is not expecting,
51. And will cut him in pieces and appoint him his portion with the hypocrites: there will be weeping and gnashing of teeth.

Chapter 25

1. Then will the Kingdom of the Heavens be likened unto ten virgins, who held their lamps, and went forth to meet the bridegroom.
2. Five of them were wise, and five were foolish.
3. They that were foolish held their lamps yet had no oil with them:
4. but the wise had oil in their vessels with their lamps.
5. While the bridegroom delayed, they all slumbered and slept.
6. And at midnight there was a cry made, Behold, the bridegroom comes; go out to meet him.
7. Then all those virgins arose and trimmed their lamps.
8. The foolish said to the wise, give us of your oil; for our lamps are going out.
9. But the wise answered, saying, no; there is not enough for us and you: but you go rather to them that sell, and buy for yourselves.
10. So, while they went to buy, the bridegroom came; and they that were ready went in with him to the marriage: and the door was shut.
11. Afterward also came the other virgins, saying, Lord, Lord, open to us.
12. But he answered and said, truly, I say to you, I do not know you.
13. Therefore watch, for you know neither the day nor the season in which the Son of man comes.
14. For the kingdom of the heavens is as a man traveling into a far country, who called his own slaves, and delivered to them his possessions.

15. To one he gave five talents, to another two, and another one; to every man according to his own ability; and immediately took his journey.
16. Then he that had received the five talents went and traded with the same and made them another five talents.
17. Likewise, he that had received two, he also gained two more.
18. But he that had received one went and dug in the earth and hid his lord's money.
19. After a long time the lord of those slaves came and settled accounts with them.
20. And so he that had received five talents came and brought more talents, saying, Lord, you delivered to me five talents: behold, I have gained beside them five talents more.
21. His lord said to him, well done, you good and faithful servant: you have been faithful over a few things, I will make you ruler over many things: enter you into the joy of your lord.
22. He also that had received two talents came and said, Lord, you delivered to me two talents: behold, I have gained two other talents beside them.
23. His lord said to him, well done, good and faithful slave; you have been faithful over a few things, I will make you ruler over many things: enter you into the joy of your lord.
24. Then he who had received the one talent came and said, Lord, I knew you that you are a hard man, reaping where you have not sown, and gathering where you have not scattered:
25. So, I was afraid and went and hid your talent in the ground: look, there you have that which is yours.
26. His lord answered and said to him, you wicked and lazy servant, you knew that I reap where I did not sow, and gather where I have not scattered:
27. Therefore, you ought to have put my money with the bankers, and then at my coming, I should have received my own with interest.
28. Therefore, take the talent from him and give it to him who has ten talents.
29. For to everyone that has will be given and he will have abundance: but from him that has not, even what he has will be taken away.
30. Now cast that unprofitable slave into outer darkness: there will be weeping and gnashing of teeth.
31. When the Son of man will come in His glory, and all the holy angels with Him, then He will sit upon the throne of His glory:
32. And before Him will be gathered the whole nation: and He will separate them one from another, as a shepherd divides his sheep from the goats:
33. And He will place the sheep by His right, but the goats on the left.
34. Then the King will say to them on his right, come, you blessed of My Father, inherit the kingdom prepared for you before the downfall of the world:
35. For I was hungry, and you gave Me food: I was thirsty, and you gave Me drink: I was a stranger, and you welcomed Me in:
36. Naked, and you clothed Me: I was sick, and you visited Me: I was in prison, and you came to Me.

37. Then will the righteous answer Him, saying, Lord, when did we see You hungry, and fed You? Or thirsty, and gave You a drink?
38. When did we see You a stranger, and welcome You in? Or naked, and clothed You?
39. Or when did we see You sick, or in prison, and visited You?
40. Then the King will answer and say to them, truly I say to you, in as much as you have done it to one of the least of these My brothers, you have done it to Me.
41. Then He will say also to them on the left, depart from Me, you cursed, into the fire perpetually, prepared for the Devil and his messengers:
42. For I was hungry, and you gave Me no food: I was thirsty, and you gave Me no drink:
43. I was a stranger, and you welcomed Me not in naked, and you clothed Me not: sick, and in prison, and you visited Me not.
44. They then will also answer Him, saying, Lord, when were You hungry, or thirsty, or a stranger, or naked, or sick, or in prison, and we did not help You?
45. Then He will answer them, saying, truly I say to you, in as much as you did it not to one of the least of these, you did not do it to Me.
46. And these will go away into perpetual punishment: but the righteous into infinite life.

Chapter 26

1. And it came to pass when Jesus had finished all these sayings, He said to His disciples,
2. You know that after two days is the feast of the Passover, and the Son of man is betrayed to be crucified.
3. Then assembled the chief priests, and the scribes, and the elders of the people, to the palace of the high priest, who was called Caiaphas,
4. And consulted that they might take Jesus by trickery and kill Him.
5. But they said, not on the feast day unless there be a disturbance among the people.
6. Now when Jesus was in Bethany, in the house of Simon the Leper,
7. There came to him a woman having an alabaster box of very precious ointment, and poured it on his head, as He sat to eat.
8. But when His disciples saw it, they had indignation, saying, to what purpose is this waste?
9. For this ointment might have been sold for much and given to the poor.
10. When Jesus understood it, He said to them, why do you trouble the woman? For she has done a good work upon Me.
11. For you always have the poor with you, but Me you do not have always.
12. For in that she has poured this ointment on My body, she did it for My burial.
13. Truly I say to you, wherever this gospel will be preached in the entire world, that also which this woman has done will be told for a memorial of her.

14. Then one of the twelve, called Judas Iscariot, went to the chief priests,
15. and said to them, what will you give me, and I will deliver Him to you? And they weighed out thirty pieces of silver for him.
16. So, from that time he sought the opportunity to betray Him.
17. Now the first day of the feast of Unleavened Bread the disciples came to Jesus, saying to Him, where do You want us to prepare the Passover for You to eat?
18. He said, go into the city to such a man, and say to him, the Master says, My time is at hand; I will keep the Passover at your house with My disciples.
19. Then the disciples did as Jesus had appointed them, and they made ready the Passover.
20. Now when the evening had come, He sat down with the twelve.
21. As they did eat, He said, truly I say to you, that one of you will betray Me.
22. And they were exceedingly sorrowful, and each one of them began to say to Him, Lord, is it I?
23. He answered and said, He that dips his hand with Me in the dish, the same will betray Me.
24. The Son of man goes as it is written of Him: but woe to that man by whom the Son of man is betrayed! It would have been good for that man if he had not been born.
25. Then Judas, who betrayed Him, answered, and said, Master, is it I? He said to him, you have said it.
26. As they were eating, Jesus took bread, and blessed it, and broke it, and gave it to the disciples, and said, take, eat; this is My body.
27. And He took the cup, and gave thanks, and gave it to them, saying, drink you all of it;
28. For this is My blood of the new covenant, which is shed for many for the forgiveness of sins.
29. But I say to you, from now on I will not drink of this fruit of the vine, until that day when I drink it new with you in My Father's kingdom.
30. When they had sung a hymn, they went out to the Mount of Olives.
31. Then Jesus said to them, all you will be offended because of Me this night: for it is written, I will smite the Shepherd, and the sheep of the flock will be scattered abroad.
32. But after I am risen again, I will go before you into Galilee.
33. Peter answered and said to Him, though all men will be offended because of You, yet I will never be offended.
34. Jesus said to him, truly, I say to you, that this night, before the rooster crows, you will deny Me three times.
35. Peter said to Him, though I should die with You, yet I will not deny You. All the disciples said likewise.
36. Then Jesus came with them to a place called Gethsemane, and said to the disciples, sit here, while I go and pray over there.
37. He took with him Peter and the two sons of Zebedee and began to be sorrowful and in distress.

38. Then said He to them, My soul is severely grieved, even to death: stay here and watch with Me.
39. He went a little farther and fell on His face, and prayed, saying, O My Father, if it be possible, let this cup pass from Me: nevertheless, not as I will, but as You will.
40. And He came to the disciples, and found them asleep, and said to Peter, so, you were not able to stay awake with Me for one hour?
41. Stay awake and pray, that you will not enter into temptation: the spirit indeed is willing, but the flesh is powerless.
42. He went away again the second time, and prayed, saying, O My Father, if this cup may not pass away from Me unless I drink it, Your will be done.
43. Then He came and found them asleep again: for their eyes were heavy.
44. And He left them and went away again, and prayed the third time, saying the same words.
45. Then came He to His disciples, and said to them, Sleep on now, and take your rest: behold, the hour is at hand, and the Son of man is betrayed into the hands of sinners.
46. Rise, let us be going: behold, the one betraying Me is at hand.
47. While He yet spoke, look, Judas, one of the twelve, came, and with him a great multitude with swords and clubs, from the chief priests and elders of the people.
48. Now he that betrayed Him gave them a sign, saying, whomever I will kiss, it is He: seize Him.
49. Immediately he came to Jesus, and said, rejoice master; and kissed Him.
50. Jesus said to him, comrade, why are you here? Then they came and laid hands on Jesus and seized him.
51. And behold, one of those who were with Jesus stretched out his hand and drew his sword, and struck a servant of the high priest, and cut off his ear.
52. Then Jesus said to him, put up again your sword into its place: for all they that take the sword will perish by the sword.
53. Do you think that I cannot now pray to My Father, and He will demonstrate at My side more than twelve legions of angels?
54. But how then will the Scriptures be fulfilled, that it must be so?
55. Jesus said in that same hour to the multitudes, have you come out as against a thief with swords and clubs to take Me? I sat daily with you teaching in the temple, and you laid no hand on Me.
56. But all this must happen, that the Scriptures of the prophets might be fulfilled. Then all the disciples forsook Him and fled.
57. And they that had seized Jesus took Him away to Caiaphas the high priest, where the scribes and the elders were assembled.
58. But Peter followed him far off to the high priest's palace and went in, and sat with the attendants, to see the end.
59. Now the chief priests, and elders, and all the council, sought false testimony against Jesus, to put him to death;
60. But found none: yes, though many false witnesses came, yet they found none. At last, there came two false witnesses,

61. And said, this fellow said, I am able to destroy the temple of God and to build it in three days.
62. And the high priest arose, and said to Him, You have nothing to say? What is it which these witness against You?
63. But Jesus held His peace, and the high priest answered and said to Him, I charge You by the living God, tell us whether You are the Christ, the Son of God.
64. Jesus said to him, you have said it: nevertheless, I say to you, everyone here will see the Son of man sitting at the right of power and coming in the cloud of heaven.
65. Then the high priest tore his clothes, saying, He has spoken blasphemy; what further do we need of witnesses? Behold, now you have heard His blasphemy.
66. What do you think? They answered and said, He is guilty of death.
67. Then they did spit in His face, and hit Him with their fists, and others slapped Him,
68. saying, prophesy to us, You Christ, who is he that hit You?
69. Now Peter sat outside in the palace: and a maid came to him, saying, you also were with Jesus of Galilee.
70. But he denied before them all, saying, I do not know what you are saying.
71. And when he had gone out into the porch, another maid saw him, and said to them that were there, this fellow was also with Jesus of Nazareth.
72. And again, he denied with an oath, I do not know the Man.
73. Now after a while they came to him that stood by, and said to Peter, surely you also are one of them; for your speech betrays you.
74. Then he began to curse and to swear, saying, I do not know the Man. And immediately the rooster crowed.
75. Then Peter remembered the word of Jesus, who said to him, before the rooster crows, you will deny Me three times. And he went out and wept bitterly.

Chapter 27

1. When the morning had come, all the chief priests and elders of the people took counsel against Jesus to put him to death:
2. And when they had bound him, they led him away and delivered him to Pontius Pilate the governor.
3. Then Judas, who had betrayed Him, when he saw that He was condemned, repented himself, and brought again the thirty pieces of silver to the chief priests and elders,
4. Saying, I have sinned in that I have betrayed innocent blood. But they said, what — against us? Look at yourself!
5. So, he cast down the pieces of silver in the temple and departed and went and hung himself.
6. And the chief priests took the silver pieces, and said, it is not lawful to put them into the treasury, because it is the price of blood.
7. So, they took counsel, and bought with them the potter's field, to bury strangers in.
8. Therefore, that field is called, the Field of Blood, to this day.

9. Then was fulfilled that which was spoken by Jeremiah the prophet, saying, and they took the thirty pieces of silver, the price of Him that was valued, whom they of the children of Israel did value;
10. And gave them for the potter's field, as the Lord appointed me.
11. So, Jesus stood before the governor: and the governor asked Him, saying, are you the King of the Jews? And Jesus said to him, you said it.
12. And when He was accused by the chief priests and elders, He answered nothing.
13. Then Pilate said to Him, do You not hear how many things they witness against You?
14. But He answered him not one word; so much so that the governor marveled greatly.
15. Now at that feast the governor was accustomed to release to the people a prisoner, whosoever they desired.
16. And they had then a notorious prisoner, called Barabbas.
17. Therefore, when they were gathered together, Pilate said to them, who do you want that I release to you, Barabbas or Jesus who is called Christ?
18. For he knew that because of envy they had delivered Him.
19. When he sat down on the judgment seat, his wife sent to him, saying, "do nothing to that righteous Man: for I have suffered many things this day in a dream because of Him.
20. But the chief priests and elders persuaded the multitude that they should ask for Barabbas and destroy Jesus.
21. The governor answered and said to them, which of the two do you want me to release to you? They said, Barabbas.
22. Pilate said to them, what will I do then with Jesus who is called Christ? They all said to him, let Him be crucified.
23. Now the governor said, why, what evil has He done? But they cried out the more, saying, let Him be crucified.
24. When Pilate saw that he could prevail nothing, but that rather a tumult was made, he took water, and washed his hands before the multitude, saying, I am innocent of the blood of this, the righteous: look at yourselves.
25. Then answered all the people, and said, His blood be on us and on our children.
26. Then he released Barabbas to them: and after Jesus was whipped, he delivered Him to be crucified.
27. Then the soldiers of the governor took Jesus into the Praetorium and gathered to Him the whole squad of soldiers.
28. And they stripped Him and put on Him a purple robe.
29. And when they had made a crown of thorns, they put it upon His head, and a reed in His right hand: and they bowed the knee before Him, and mocked Him, saying, Hail, King of the Jews!
30. And they spit upon Him and took the reed and hit Him on the head.
31. After they had mocked Him, they took the robe off from Him and put His own clothing on Him and took Him away to crucify Him.

32. As they came out, they found a man of Cyrene, Simon by name: him they compelled to bear His cross.
33. When they had come to a place called Golgotha, that is to say, a Place of a Skull,
34. They gave Him sour wine to drink mingled with gall: and when He had tasted of it, He would not drink.
35. And they crucified Him, and divided His garments, casting lots: that it might be fulfilled which was spoken by the prophet, they divided My garments among them, and on My clothing did they cast lots.
36. And sitting down they watched Him there;
37. And set up over His head His accusation written, THIS IS JESUS, THE KING OF THE JEWS
38. Then were there two thieves crucified with Him, one on the right hand, and another on the left.
39. And they that passed by reviled him, shook their heads,
40. and said, You that destroys the temple, and builds it in three days, save Yourself. If You are the Son of God, come down from the cross.
41. Likewise, also the chief priests mocked Him, with the scribes and elders, said,
42. He saved others; He cannot save Himself. If He is the King of Israel, let him now come down from the cross, and we will believe Him.
43. He trusted in God; let Him deliver Him now, if He will have Him: for He said, I am the Son of God.
44. The thieves also, who were crucified with Him, reproached Him the same way.
45. Now from the sixth hour there was darkness over all the land to the ninth hour.
46. About the ninth hour Jesus cried with a loud voice, saying, Eli, Eli, lama sabachthani? That is to say, My God, My God, why have You forsaken Me?
47. Some of them that stood there, when they heard that, said, this man calls for Elijah.
48. Immediately one of them ran, took a sponge, filled it with sour wine, and put it on a reed, and gave Him to drink.
49. The rest said, let it be, let us see whether Elijah will come to save Him.
50. Jesus, when He had cried again with a loud voice, gave up the ghost.
51. And behold, the veil of the temple was torn in two from the top to the bottom, and the earth did quake, and the rocks tore;
52. And the graves were opened, and many bodies of the saints which slept arose,
53. And came out of the graves after His resurrection, and went into the holy city, and appeared to many!
54. Now when the centurion, and they that were with him, watching Jesus, saw the earthquake, and those things that were done, they feared greatly, saying, truly this was the Son of God!
55. And many women were there beholding far off, who followed Jesus from Galilee, ministering to Him:
56. Among whom were Mary Magdalene, and Mary the mother of James and Joses, and the mother of Zebedee's children.
57. When the evening had come, there came a rich man of Arimathaea, named Joseph, who also himself was Jesus' disciple:

58. He went to Pilate and requested the body of Jesus. Then Pilate commanded the body to be delivered.
59. When Joseph had received the body, he wrapped it in a clean linen cloth,
60. And laid it in his own new tomb, which he had chiseled out in the rock: and he rolled a great stone against the door of the tomb and departed.
61. And there was Mary Magdalene, and the other Mary, sitting opposite the sepulcher.
62. Now the next day that followed the day of the preparation, the chief priests and Pharisees came together to Pilate,
63. saying, sir, we remember that deceiver said, while He was yet alive, after three days I will rise again.
64. Therefore, command that the tomb be made secure until the third day, unless His disciples come by night, and steal Him away, and said to the people, He is risen from the dead: so the last error will be worse than the first.
65. Pilate said to them, you have a guard: go your way, make it as secure as you can.
66. So, they went and made the tomb secure, sealing the stone, and setting a guard.

Chapter 28

1. At the close of the Sabbath, as it began to dawn toward the first day of the week, came Mary Magdalene and the other Mary to see the tomb.
2. And behold, there was a great earthquake: for the angel of the Lord descended from heaven and came and rolled back the stone from the door and sat on it.
3. His countenance was like lightning and his clothing white as snow:
4. For fear of him the guards did shake and became as dead men.
5. And the angel answered and said to the women, Fear not: for I know that you seek Jesus, who was crucified.
6. He is not here: for He has risen, as He said. Come, see the place where the Lord lay.
7. Now go quickly and tell His disciples that He is risen from the dead; and behold, He goes before you into Galilee; there will you see Him: look, I have told you.
8. Then they departed quickly from the tomb with fear and great joy; and ran to bring His disciple's word.
9. As they went to tell His disciples, behold, Jesus met them, and said, rejoice! And they came and held Him by the feet and worshiped Him.
10. Then said Jesus to them, be not afraid: go tell My brothers that they go into Galilee, and there will they see Me.
11. Now when they were going, behold, some of the guards came into the city and showed to the chief priests all the things that were done.
12. When they were assembled with the elders and had taken counsel, they gave large money to the soldiers,
13. And said, say you, His disciples came by night and stole Him away while we slept.
14. And if this comes to the governor's ears, we will persuade him and keep you safe.

15. So, they received the money and did as they were instructed: and this saying is commonly reported among the Jews until this day.

16. Then the eleven disciples went away into Galilee, to a mountain where Jesus had appointed them.

17. When they saw Him, they worshiped Him: but some doubted.

18. So, Jesus came and spoke to them, saying, all authority is given to Me in heaven and earth.

19. Therefore go, and disciple all nations, immersing them in the name of the Father, and of the Son, and of the Holy Spirit:

20. Teaching them to observe all that I have commanded you: and look, I am with you all the time, even until the completion of this Old Covenant Age.

Synopsis of Mark

There are plenty of resources regarding the dating and authentic authorship of this record of the life of Christ in the days of His flesh in the Gospel of Mark. I will leave that to those who have done their homework before me. This is the first gospel of the four that have been included in our Canon. It is also the shortest of the four.

In this gospel, there is more emphasis on what the Lord Jesus did rather than what He taught. Although, the things that He did were object lessons for all those who had ears to hear and eyes to see. The reason Mark emphasizes the things that He did versus a collection of sermons is because Mark reveals the nature of the Servant-Savior in Christ. He is the chosen servant, the Servant of Yahweh that Isaiah predicted would come.

Each gospel reveals a specific aspect of the Lord's nature. Matthew reveals Christ as the King. Luke reveals Christ as the perfect man with all the virtues of perfection. John reveals Christ as God becoming flesh. Some have called these gospels the four faces of Christ depicted in the living creatures in Ezekiel. We have the face of a lion, the face of a man, the face of a bull, and the face of an eagle. If we take these four faces and apply them to the human living of Christ, we can see the progression of His life in these faces. For example, let's start with Luke. The perfect man is the face of a man. He is born a human, a baby, and grows into a serving adult. Next, He is anointed and declared to be the beloved Son, and in His anointing, He is empowered as the King of the beasts, the face of the Lion as portrayed in Matthew. The lion anointing empowers Him to attack and tear down the kingdom of darkness. For three and a half years, He is king of the beasts and shows His power throughout those years. At the end of His earthly ministry, as Mark depicts Him as the Servant-Savior, He becomes the bull. Jesus said, I have not come to be served, but to serve and give My life as a ransom for many. On the cross, He is the Servant sacrifice for the sins of the world. The cross is the third stage of His earthly life. The Servant-Savior becomes the Father's greatest satisfaction. On the third day, He rose from the dead. The fourth face appears in Christ. The eagle as John shows the heavenly view of Christ. As Christ rose from the dead, He ascended into the heavens as an eagle and the heavens became His domain. These four faces can teach us something of the reason we have four gospels. Four records of the life and triumph of the Lord Jesus.

The Gospel of Mark displays for us the triumph of Christ in this gospel. Mark starts by saying, "this is the beginning of the gospel of Jesus Christ, the son of God." The gospel is the fulfillment of the Old Testament. Amazingly, the Old Testament is made up primarily of three main items. Prophecy, Promises, and the Law. These three items are fulfilled in the coming of the gospel of the Kingdom.

First of all, let's look at the first prophecy in the Old Testament. It is regarding the gospel. Genesis 1:2 is the first prophecy in the bible and the apostle Paul says in 2 Cor. 4:3-4, "³ But even if **our gospel** is veiled, it is veiled to those who are perishing, ⁴ whose minds the God of this age has blinded, who do not believe, lest the light of the gospel of the glory of Christ, who is the image of God, should shine on them.[1] Paul quotes Gen. 1:2 in 2 Cor. 4:6, "⁶ For it is **God who commanded light** to shine out of darkness, who has **shone in our hearts** to *give* the light of the knowledge of the glory of God in the **face of Jesus Christ**.[2] Paul uses this verse to declare that there would come a time when God would fulfill this prophecy. It was being fulfilled in Paul's day. The gospel was lighting people up who were darkness. Paul says, "you who were once darkness are now light in the Lord." Eph. 5:8.

The gospel came to bring good news that the prophecies and the promises were going to be fulfilled. It also revealed how the Lord Jesus would fulfill the Law. In the gospel of Mark, we need to see the full gospel as he recorded. The gospel embodies two magnificent events predicted in the Old Testament. The ultimate sacrifice on the cross for the sins of the whole world. The second event is extremely significant. Many have neglected this event as more of a sidebar. Prophecy after prophecy and typical prophecies predicted the removal of the sacrificial system of the Jewish religion and what Paul called the ministry of death and condemnation. These two events are the gospel. Those that received Christ as the sacrifice for sin experienced salvation, hope, healing, deliverance and all the blessedness of coming into fellowship with Him. Those who rejected the ultimate sacrifice were destroyed in the destruction of the city of Jerusalem and Temple. The earthly things were being removed and the heavenly things were being established through the gospel.

Mark's opening is "the beginning of the gospel". Paul calls this time, "the fullness of the time had come". Gal. 4:4. God had sent His son, and John was fulfilling a prophecy of preparing the way for God's son to bring a people that John prepared out of the earthly things into the heavenly things. Isa. 40:3. John himself is quite an object lesson for Israel. He was born in the house of Zacharias, a Levite priest. John was his firstborn and called to be a Levitical priest. John was like no other man. He was filled with the Holy Spirit in his mother's womb. He had been infused with the heavenly and the earthly had no hold or attraction to him. He separated himself from the earthly and went into the wilderness. We could say that he left Egypt and went into the wilderness. Rev. 11:8, says, "the great city, which is spiritually called Sodom and Egypt, where also their Lord was crucified." John refused the priestly garments and received a revelation of the new sacrificial system and forsook the earthly Jerusalem. He abandoned the external and became a voice of one

---

[1] *The New King James Version.* (1982). (2 Co 4:3–4). Nashville: Thomas Nelson. *(TKB capitalizes GOD)*
[2] *The New King James Version.* (1982). (2 Co 4:6). Nashville: Thomas Nelson.

crying in the wilderness at the Jordan immersing men, women, and children preparing them to start their journey into the promises of God. The true promised land! John stood in between Moses, the mediator of the Old Covenant and Christ Jesus the mediator of the New Covenant. John was the best man introducing the Bridegroom to His new wife and Jesus as the Lamb that takes away the sin of the world. What a glorious introduction to Israel, a bridegroom, and a lamb. The New Covenant was a marriage covenant whereby God in Christ would remarry Israel, and that covenant would be sealed with the blood of the Lamb. They would enter into a new world wherein righteousness dwells.

This new world would be a world in which righteousness would dwell. The ministry of death would be removed. But according to His promise, we are looking for new heavens and a new earth, in which righteousness dwells.[3] This is not an earthly world, but a heavenly world, a spiritual creation. There are some dear brothers and sisters that teach a restored and renewed planet, but as Moses penned in Genesis chapter one the prediction and promise of a new creation where light would break in and would separate light from darkness and develop a world where Man would be in His image multiplying and being fruitful and conquering the realms of the world. As I mentioned, Paul unpacks this verse in 2 Cor. 4:6 and says the light has shone into our hearts. Where is the new creation? It is in our hearts, within us. Paul then reveals in chapter 5 in 2 Cor., a "new creation". This is not a new planet, but a new people. God is not redeeming the planet, but the broken-hearted, possessed by evil, sick and lost people who are the object of His love. Here in the gospel of Mark the beginning of the gospel of Jesus Christ, the son of God, we see the beginning of God serving humanity in His son and bringing this new world into the lives of those who are in darkness. The new world starts inside not externally.

The symbolism of John immersing people in the wilderness at the Jordan river. As I mentioned, John forsook the earthly Jerusalem and separated himself from it. He came into the wilderness to the Jordan. Beyond the Jordan is the promised land. Those who came out of the Jordan entered the promises of God. Historically, Israel came out of Egypt and went into the wilderness to come to the Jordan before entering the promised land. The Law and prophets were until John, and he was preparing a people for the Messiah, the real Joshua to bring them into the promised land. Not a physical land, but a heavenly land.

In Hebrews, [13]In faith died all these, **not having received the promises**, but from afar having seen them, and having been persuaded, and having saluted *them*, and having confessed that **strangers and sojourners they are upon the land**, [14]for those saying such things make manifest that they seek a country; [15]and if, indeed, they had been mindful of that from which they came forth, they might have had an opportunity to return, [16]but now they long for **a better**, that is, **an heavenly**, wherefore God is not ashamed of them, to be

---

[3] *New American Standard Bible: 1995 update.* (1995). (2 Pe 3:13). La Habra, CA: The Lockman Foundation.

called their God, for He prepared for them a city.[4] Heb 11:13–16. These verses in Hebrews are amazing! The Old Covenant saints did not receive the promises, welcomed them and saw them by revelation. These saints experienced spiritual realities, yet realized they were not living in the time of the fulfillment of those realities. They were looking for a better country. The word for country is patris (πατρίς, (Strong GK 3968). It means 'Fatherland', place of one's birth. These saints knew it was not a geographical place, but a heavenly land where they were born of the Spirit. Jesus alluded to this with Nicodemus, born again literally means **born from above.** Even in the sermon on the mount, Jesus was not talking about a physical land. The meek inherit the spiritual land. The English translators translate the quote from Psa. 37 as earth thinking that the meek would inherit the planet. I call this 'meathead' theology', the carnal mind confuses and mixes the spiritual with the physical. The gospel was news of a new land, new temple, new sacrifice, new priesthood, and a new law, the law of the Spirit of life in Christ Jesus. Also, it was the news that the old was going to be removed for good.

Many bible teachers divide time into dispensations which according to the bible there are only two dispensations. The dispensation of the Law and the dispensation of Grace or the Spirit. Our bible is divided into two parts, and this should be a clue for many of us to see. Old Covenant and New Covenant or Old Testament and New Testament. Each covenant is an age or era and many mini covenants in the Old Testament were a type and shadow of the Old or the New. The Old Covenant is temporary and contains God's Law and a people who were to be custodians of His laws. The New Covenant is perpetual and contains the fulfillment of God's laws and the fulfillment of God's predictions and promises. Two ages, one old and one new. John in his gospel says a remarkable thing, "the Law came through Moses, but grace and reality came through Jesus Christ. John 1:17. This is why Jesus spoke of the present age and the age to come. Jesus' present age was the Old Covenant age and the age about to come was the New Covenant age. Refer to my chart on the truth of two ages. Matthew 19:28-29; Mark 10:30; Luke 18:30, Luke 20:34-36; Ephesians 2:7, these verses refer to the two ages and Eph. 2:7 should be translated in the singular, not ages, but age to come. Paul was still living in the Old Covenant age. In 1 Cor. 10:11, Paul writes, "[11]And all these things as types did happen to those persons, and they were written for our admonition, upon whom the goal of the ages *has* come,[5]". In Corinthians we can translate the word aion in the plural because of God's purpose of the two ages was being fulfilled in Paul's day. When we have the proper understanding of only two ages and one end this becomes crystal clear when we properly make these words singular or plural. The words in this epistle is telos "end" and aion "age". Telos is translated 24 times in the singular and 2 times in the plural. Aion is translated 20 times in the singular and 6 times in the plural.

---

[4] Young, R. (1997). *Young's Literal Translation* (Heb 11:13–16). Bellingham, WA: Logos Bible Software.

[5] Young, R. (1997). *Young's Literal Translation* (1 Co 10:11). Bellingham, WA: Logos Bible Software.

Paul uses the typology of Israel being in the wilderness as the picture of the time he was living in. The forty-year period of Israel being in the wilderness was equivalent to Paul's time from the cross in A.D. 30 to when he wrote Corinthians in the 60's, some thirty plus years and that age was about to end in A.D. 70. The removal of the old and the manifestation of the new. The gospel was about revealing what was coming and what God was going to accomplish for man in bringing deliverance from sin-death and removing the system of death and condemnation.

Mark's record of John the Immerser is very significant for what God was doing in the first century. Many have overlooked the importance and the noteworthiness of his calling. John is the start of a true breakaway from the previous divine move of God established by Moses. It is the old garment that the Lord said not to sew a new patch on it because it would leave a gaping hole in the old garment as the new patch pulled away. Mark 2:21. God is not patching up the old anything, He has a new garment that doesn't need any fixing. Also, God is not going to put new wine into the old wineskins of the Old Covenant religion. The religion of Jesus' day had become corrupt and exhibited a form of godliness, but the religious leaders of His day had rejected the power to become what God intended. Christ the power of God 1 Cor. 1:24.

John was in the wilderness baptizing or immersing those responding to the Lord in repentance. This baptism was a dying to the old dispensation of law and resurrecting into the fulfillment of all the prophecies, promises, and law of Moses. These people that responded were being made ready for the dispensation of the Spirit to be imparted to them after the death, burial, resurrection and ascension of their Messiah. He became the life-giving Spirit to be imparted into them as life. Eph. 3:10 "… that He might fill all things". As John states that he immerses in water, but ONE who is coming after him, He will baptize you in the Holy Spirit. Scholars say that Mark's gospel is addressed to a Gentile audience and Matthew to a Jewish audience. There is a reason that Mark leaves out the baptism of fire as in Matthew's gospel. Gentiles are not going to be baptized in fire, but Israel had the choice to be baptized in the Holy Spirit and be preserved or judged by the immersion of fire. The work of the baptism of the Holy Spirit is related to empowering the saved believer and the baptism of fire is the judgment of God on Jerusalem.

The water baptism of Jesus is a type of death, burial, and resurrection that opened the heavens to man. The opening of the heavens indicates that they were closed and had become brass to Israel. The old King James uses the term brass, but it is the word for bronze or copper. It means impenetrable. Israel was not getting through to God. "The heavens which is over your head shall be bronze, and the earth, which is under you, iron. "The Lord will make the rain of your land powder and dust; from heaven it shall come down on you until you are destroyed. "The Lord shall cause you to be defeated before your enemies[6]… Deut.

---

[6] *New American Standard Bible: 1995 update.* (1995). (Dt 28:23–25). La Habra, CA: The Lockman Foundation.

28:23 was over for those who put their faith in the Messiah. Those who would reject the Messiah would experience everything in Deut. 28. The true Israel opened the heavens. Jesus went down into the water and came out of the water and the Spirit descended on Him like a dove and a voice came out of the heavens saying, "this is my beloved son in whom I am well-pleased, satisfied." The death, burial, resurrection, and ascension of Christ satisfied the Father and opened the heavens. The Holy Spirit came on Christ as a dove, but on Pentecost, it came as tongues of fire. This fire is not to be associated with Matthew's account as I mentioned above. The difference is that doves do not land on anything unclean. The reason this dove landed on Jesus is because nothing unclean or corrupt was in Him. On Pentecost, the Spirit was fire as a purifying work in the lives of those who received the Spirit. The dove lands on a spotless lamb without blemish and the fire lands on those with a fallen humanity to purify them. This is just a thought to consider.

The Spirit's work on Jesus is now driving Him into the wilderness. This is the wilderness experience of the new Israel, one day for each year that the old Israel was in the wilderness. After this Jesus starts to possess the land. Again, it is not a physical land, but a heavenly land where He triumphs and defeats the enemies. Again, it is not flesh and blood enemies, but spiritual forces of wickedness, demons, sickness. He overcomes Satan in the wilderness. Mark does not go into detail like Matthew, but mentions John being incarcerated. Jesus then starts preaching the Kingdom of God and says, "the time is fulfilled", Mark 1:15. He is referring to an appointed time. Since the time of Nebuchadnezzar, the start of the "times of Gentiles" ruling the world had been going on. Now Jesus is saying, in today's vernacular, it's time for God to take over and place His son as ruler of the kings of the earth.

The time is fulfilled! When Christ is crowned with many diadems which was progressive in nature in the first century. His eyes *are* a flame of fire, and on His head *are* many diadems; and He has a name written *on Him* which no one knows except Himself.[7] Rev. 19:.12. This took place after the destruction of the Harlot City, old Jerusalem. At the time of the destruction of Jerusalem the gospel had reached the whole Roman world, and Christ was conquering nations through the gospel. The gospel is the true tool of dominion, not the law. After Christ's resurrection He was crowned as the King of Israel, the true son of David. As the son of David, Peter quotes in Psalm 132, "And so, because he was a prophet and knew that God had sworn to him with an oath to seat *one* of his descendants on his throne, **he looked ahead and spoke of the resurrection of the Christ,**[8].... This was the first crown Christ received and in the coming years, He would gain many more crowns as He and His wife became fruitful and multiplied and filled the earth subduing and conquering the nations. From Acts 2 to Rev. 19 after the harlot is destroyed Christ is shown to gain many crowns. Solomon the type of Christ as the son of David, reigned for 40 years.

---

[7] *New American Standard Bible: 1995 update.* (1995). (Re 19:12). La Habra, CA: The Lockman Foundation.

[8] *New American Standard Bible: 1995 update.* (1995). (Ac 2:30–31). La Habra, CA: The Lockman Foundation.

Those 40 years were fulfilled in Christ from 30 AD to 70 AD and perhaps the verses in 1 Cor. 15, For as in Adam all die, so also in Christ, all will be made alive. But each in his own order: Christ the first fruits, after that those who are Christ's at His coming, then *comes* the end, when He hands over the kingdom to the God and Father, when He has abolished all rule and all authority and power. For He must reign until He has put all His enemies under His feet.[9] When all things are subjected to Him, then the Son Himself also will be subjected to the One who subjected all things to Him, so that God may be all in all.[10] In 70 AD the times of the Gentiles ruling the world came to an end. Jesus fulfilled His time of ruling as the true son of David and continued to rule as God and the Triune God had carried out His purpose in His son to become all in all and in all in all.

Let's look at the process the Lord is arranging to accomplish His perpetual purpose. Now the Lord Jesus is gathering His disciples to train them to take their place in His Kingdom. He first calls Simon and Andrew. Andrew being Simon's brother. Simon becomes Peter. Jesus tells them to follow Him, and He will make them fishers of men. Catching men is taking dominion! Then He called James and John who were mending their nets. They left their nets and followed Him. These four will become witnesses of the authority of the King.

He enters Capernaum, into a synagogue and there is a man with an unclean spirit. All are amazed at the teaching of Christ. He is different, not like the scribes. Suddenly, the man with the unclean spirit, dominated by that spirit confronts Jesus. The Lord Jesus does not back down, this is one of the giants in the land. The Lord as the real Joshua takes authority over this spirit, tells him to be quiet and come out of the man. He is taking dominion as King in the realm of the Spirit and the people are witnesses of His authority.

Jesus then moves from the religious sphere to the family sphere to demonstrate His authority. Jesus comes to Simon's house with Andrew. Simon's mother-in-law is sick with a fever. Remember Simon is Peter as he is later called. He has a mother-in-law, and she is sick. Jesus came to her and took her hand and lifted her up and the fever left. He took dominion over sickness by the touch of His hand. A further demonstration of kingdom authority took place that evening when the whole city gathered at Simon's home. He was dispossessing the enemies in the land, the enemies that are diseases, demon possessions, and all kinds of illnesses. He then went to other towns and met a leper and showed His willingness to cleanse the leper and he was healed. This demonstration of kingdom authority is amazing and even in Jesus' home He reveals the heart of the gospel of the kingdom which is forgiveness. Nothing paralyzes humanity more than being bound by sins. Four carry this paralyzed body into the presence of Jesus. He sees their faith and says, "child your sins are forgiven". Perhaps these four can represent, love, faith, knowledge, and wisdom. These four components in our homes delivers us from paralysis. In our churches and in our nation these

---

[9] *New American Standard Bible: 1995 update.* (1995). (1 Co 15:22–25). La Habra, CA: The Lockman Foundation.

[10] *New American Standard Bible: 1995 update.* (1995). (1 Co 15:28). La Habra, CA: The Lockman Foundation.

four will bring us into the presence of Jesus and we will function the way God intended, and those onlookers will respond in great praise to God! Their response will be, "we never saw anything like this".

This is the beginning of the opposition of the land beast with the false prophet. The **Pharisees** went out and immediately *began* **conspiring with the Herodians** against Him, *as to* how they might destroy Him.[11] This coalition was started because Jesus healed a man with a withered hand on the Sabbath. He asked, should we do harm or good on the Sabbath? This example is what had happened to the religious system of His day. Their works were dead works, serving in death and all dried up. Jesus came to restore their service to living works and to serve in life. After this so many were healed and delivered that when the scribes came, they said that Christ was insane, out of His mind.

They accused Him of being possessed with an unclean spirit, Beelzebul, the ruler of demons. They attributed His power to the demonic. The Lord's response is quite solemn as He addresses this ignorance. "How can Satan cast our Satan"? The Lord explains in parables that are quite logical. A Kingdom divided against itself cannot stand. A house divided against itself cannot stand. A kingdom and a house! What wisdom our Lord is displaying. Then to top it off, He says, "If Satan has risen up against himself and is divided, he cannot stand, **but he is finished!** [12]

Jesus now explains what He is doing. He is binding the strong man and plundering his house. His kingship is expressed in authority and power. He is stronger than the strongman. He is binding the strongman. He is restraining the strongman by taking dominion. He then explains with austerity the meaning of blaspheming the Holy Spirit. All sins and blasphemy of the sons of men will and can be forgiven, but anyone who blasphemes the Holy Spirit will never be forgiven and be guilty of an age- lasting sin. The next part of the verse explains blaspheming the Holy Spirit. The Lord Jesus said, "because they were saying, "He has an unclean spirit."[13] When a person attributes the work of the Holy Spirit to the demonic, this is blaspheming the Holy Spirit. We must be careful to discern and judge rightly when looking at the work of God, especially those who are working with God by His Spirit.

While this was going on some approached the Lord and said, "your mother and brothers are looking for you". When He answered them, He said "who is My mother and My brothers"? Christ looked out among the crowd and said, "Behold My mother and My brothers"! Whenever we see the word "behold" in the scriptures, we must realize that this word is a window into the spiritual realm. As we look into this window, we see a heavenly view of Christ's mindset on the true family. "For **whoever does the will of God**, he is **My**

---

[11] *New American Standard Bible: 1995 update* (Mk 3:6). (1995). The Lockman Foundation.

[12] *New American Standard Bible: 1995 update* (Mk 3:26). (1995). The Lockman Foundation.

[13] *New American Standard Bible: 1995 update* (Mk 3:30). (1995). The Lockman Foundation.

brother and sister and **mother**."[14] This is how we are to look at other believers who are doing the will of God. True family!

The Gospel of Mark is replete with prophecies that have been the subject of intense scholarly debate and varied interpretations. The Preterist approach offers a unique lens through which to examine these prophecies, shedding light on their potential fulfillment within the socio-political upheavals of the first century AD. This perspective challenges traditional Futurist and Historicist views, proposing that many of Jesus' predictions were not referring to distant, apocalyptic events but rather to the tumultuous realities faced by His contemporaries. Among the key prophecies in the Gospel of Mark is the Olivet Discourse, found in chapter 13, where Jesus foretells the destruction of the Temple in Jerusalem. According to Preterist scholars such as Milton Terry, J. Stuart Russell, and Don K. Preston, this prophecy was not a symbolic reference to a future, cosmic event but rather a specific prediction of the actual destruction of the Second Temple in 70 AD during the Jewish-Roman.

The Preterist interpretation contends that Jesus' prophecies were deeply rooted in the historical and socio-political context of His time. As the tensions between the Jewish population and the Roman occupiers escalated, Jesus' teachings and predictions took on a sense of urgency and immediacy. The looming prospect of conflict and upheaval would have resonated profoundly with His listeners, who yearned for liberation from Roman rule and the restoration of Jewish sovereignty.

In contrast to the Futurist view, which associates these prophecies with yet-to-be-realized end times, the Preterist perspective argues that their fulfillment coincided with the tumultuous events of the first century AD. The destruction of the Temple, a central symbol of Jewish religious and cultural identity, would have been a cataclysmic event for **Jesus' followers**, signaling the end of the **Old Covenant age** and the dawn of a new dispensation. The Preterist interpretation finds further support in the works of N.T. Wright, argues that the Gospel of Mark was written in the aftermath of the Temple's destruction, reflecting the lived experiences of the early Christian community.

Wright's commentary on the Gospel sheds light on how these prophecies would have resonated with first-century believers, offering them a framework for understanding and making sense of the unprecedented upheavals they were witnessing. Even though Wright makes this argument that Mark was written after the destruction of the temple. This is a stretch and is inconsistent with the term synoptic gospels. The destruction of Jerusalem is the bookend of the gospels and the prediction of Jesus; statement in the Gospel of Luke 20:22, Because these are the days of vengeance that all things written will be fulfilled; All things written, except the Gospel of Mark. Wright is wrong with this presupposition. The witness of two or three witnesses applies to this understanding. While the Preterist view has gained traction among certain scholars, it remains a subject of ongoing debate

---

[14] *New American Standard Bible: 1995 update* (Mk 3:35). (1995). The Lockman Foundation.

and comparison with other interpretive approaches, such as Futurism and Historicism. Proponents of these alternative views argue that the prophecies in Mark carry a broader, more universal significance, extending beyond the events of the first century AD.

Regardless of the interpretive lens adopted, the prophecies in the Gospel of Mark undoubtedly held profound implications for the early Christian community. They not only shaped their understanding of the unfolding events but also served as a source of hope and resilience in the face of adversity. The fulfillment of these prophecies would have reinforced the belief in Jesus as the long-awaited Messiah and validated the teachings that formed the foundation of the nascent Christian faith. The Gospel of Mark stands as a testament to the inextricable link between Jesus' teachings and the socio-political realities of first-century Judea. Through the lens of Preterist interpretation, the parables and prophecies within this Gospel take on a profound resonance, reflecting the lived experiences, aspirations, and tribulations of a people grappling with the yoke of Roman occupation.

The parables, with their rich symbolism and allegories, served as a powerful medium for Jesus to communicate His message in a manner that was both accessible and subversive. The Parable of the Sower, the Parable of the Mustard Seed, and the Parable of the Wicked Tenants all carried undertones of resistance and hope, offering a vision of a divine kingdom that would ultimately supplant the oppressive structures of the time. These narratives would have resonated deeply with the early Christian community, providing solace and inspiration in the face of adversity. The prophecies within the Gospel of Mark, particularly those concerning the destruction of the Temple took on a sense of urgency and immediacy through the Preterist lens. Rather than distant, apocalyptic visions, these prophecies were seen as direct references to the cataclysmic events that would engulf Judea in the Jewish-Roman War, culminating in the fall of Jerusalem in 70 AD. The fulfillment of these prophecies would have reinforced the belief in Jesus as the true Messiah and validated the teachings of the nascent Christian faith.

By situating the parables and prophecies within their historical and socio-political context, the Preterist interpretation offers a nuanced and compelling understanding of the Gospel of Mark. It highlights the profound connections between Jesus' teachings and the lived realities of His contemporaries, illuminating the ways in which His message spoke to the struggles, hopes, and aspirations of a people yearning for liberation and transformation. Furthermore, this analysis aligns with the non-denominational Christian tradition, which emphasizes the importance of understanding Scripture within its historical and cultural context. By exploring the social, political, and religious undercurrents that shaped the Gospel storyline, contemporary believers can gain a deeper appreciation for the enduring relevance and power of Jesus' teachings. As we contemplate the implications of this study, we are reminded of the transformative potential of Christ's message, which transcended the boundaries of time and place. While rooted in the specific context of first-century Judea, the parables and prophecies within the Gospel of Mark continue to resonate with universal themes of justice, hope, and the quest for spiritual fulfillment.

In this way, the Preterist interpretation not only illuminates the past but also sheds light on the enduring relevance of the Gospel for the present and the future. As we reflect on the insights gleaned from this analysis, we are called to embrace the spirit of the Lord's teachings and to strive towards a world that embodies the values of compassion, equity, and the pursuit of a just and equitable society. May this exploration of the Gospel of Mark through the Preterist lens serve as a catalyst for deeper reflection, renewed commitment, and a more profound understanding of the transformative power of the Word. In conclusion, the Gospel of Mark, from a Preterist viewpoint, encapsulates the sacrifice of Jesus Christ and the consequences of rejecting that sacrifice. It serves as a powerful testimony of the love and mercy of God, who gave His only son for the salvation of humanity. It also serves as a warning to all who hear the gospel to accept the sacrifice of Christ and avoid the destruction that comes from rejecting it. May we all heed the message of the Gospel of Mark and accept the sacrifice of Jesus Christ for our salvation.

Jesus said that if we don't understand this parable, we will not be able to understand any of the others. The parable of the Sower. (Mark 4:3–20) The Parable of the Sower teaches about sowing the seeds of the Gospel of the kingdom and the different types of soil that represent people's hearts. In the Old Testament, Isaiah 55:10-11 speaks of the word of God being likened to seed that brings forth fruit. In this parable, we see four types of soil. These four types of soil are in four different places. Those places are significant to the type of soil, the types of hearts. The first place is by the roadside. This is the place that is near to where everyone else is journeying. The whole world travels on this roadside. So, the first soil is near the place where everyone else walks and conducts their lifestyle. We will call this place, the worldly soil.

This is hard ground where the birds have easy access to the hearts of people. The closer we are to the world's pathways we are susceptible to the evil spirits access to our hearts to steal the word of the kingdom. The second type of soil is the rocky soil. This is the heart where too many stones are in the soil and not much soil. Life in its negative effects hardens the parts of our hearts to prevent faith and love to reside and when the word of the kingdom lands in our hearts there is the hardness of skepticism, unbelief, and resentments and unforgiveness, which prevent the word from taking root and when circumstances arise the word withers and dries up in our hearts and we forget what we heard. When we share the gospel, we need to help people dig up these stones in regard to these four items of hardness. If these stones are not dug up they will fall away. This third soil is fairly good soil, but there is not much weeding on this heart. Other things grow with the seed of the kingdom. The thorns smother the seed. They take up room in our hearts. This word for choke can be translated in other contexts as crowd or crowded. Jesus explains these thorns as anxieties of the age, deceitfulness of riches, desires for other things. These thorns are prickly little things that keep us in unbelief, and we worry about too many things. Have you ever noticed that the thorny heart is hard to deal with. You may have had this experience when you are sharing with another believer whose priorities are out of line.

Your intention to help might find yourself being hurt. You touch something in their life, and you get a reaction that you didn't expect, and you are misunderstood and maybe even hurt. They don't want to talk to you, and they may accuse you of being a bully or insensitive. This is the thorny heart. These thorns hinder the kingdom from growing in the saints and unless they are diligent gardeners, they never reach maturity. We must govern our desires for other things for they are the interference in our spiritual lives. The last soil is the good soil, they hear the word and welcome it and take it in and let it do its work in them. They produce thirty-fold, sixty-fold, hundred-fold. There is so much more to share but because of space I will delay for another time.

Terry Kashian

Gospel of Mark

Chapter 1

1. The beginning of the gospel of Jesus Christ, the Son of God;
2. As it is written in the prophets, Behold, I send My messenger before Your face, who will prepare Your way before You.
3. The voice of one crying in the wilderness, prepare you the way of the Lord, make His paths straight.
4. John did immerse in the wilderness and preach the immersion of repentance for the forgiveness of sins.
5. Then there went out to him all the land of Judea, and they of Jerusalem, and were all immersed by him in the river Jordan, confessing their sins.
6. Now John was clothed with camel's hair, and with a leather belt around his waist, and he did eat locusts and wild honey;
7. And preached, and said, there comes One mightier than I after me, the strap of whose sandals I am not worthy to stoop down and untie.
8. I indeed have immersed you with water: but He will immerse you with the Holy Spirit.
9. It came to pass in those days that Jesus came from Nazareth of Galilee and was immersed by John in the Jordan.
10. Immediately coming up out of the water, He saw the heavens opened, and the Spirit like a dove descending upon Him:
11. then there came a voice from heaven, saying, You are My beloved Son, in whom I am well pleased.
12. Immediately the Spirit drove Him into the wilderness.
13. So, He was there in the wilderness forty days, tempted by Satan; and was with the wild beasts; and the angels ministered to Him.
14. Now after John was put in prison, Jesus came into Galilee, preaching the gospel of the kingdom of God,
15. And said, the time is fulfilled, and the kingdom of God is at hand: repent, and believe the gospel.
16. Now as He walked by the Sea of Galilee, He saw Simon and Andrew his brother casting a net into the sea: for they were fishermen.
17. So, Jesus said to them, follow Me, and I will make you fishers of men.
18. Immediately they gave up their nets and followed Him.
19. When He had gone a little farther from there, He saw James the son of Zebedee, and John his brother, who also were in the boat fixing their nets.
20. Immediately He called them: and they left their father Zebedee in the boat with the hired servants and followed Him.
21. Then they went into Capernaum, and immediately on the Sabbath day He entered the synagogue and taught.
22. Now they were astonished at His teaching: for He taught them as One that had authority, and not as the scribes.
23. Now there was in their synagogue a man with an unclean spirit, and he cried out,
24. Saying, let us alone; what have we to do with You, Jesus of Nazareth? Have You come to destroy us? I know You, who You are, the Holy One of God.

25. But Jesus rebuked him, saying, hold your peace, and come out of him.
26. So, when the unclean spirit had convulsed him, and cried with a loud voice, he came out of him.
27. Then they were all amazed, so much so that they questioned among themselves, saying, what thing is this? What new teaching is this? For with authority, He commands even the unclean spirits, and they do obey Him.
28. Immediately, His fame spread throughout the entire region around Galilee.
29. Immediately, when they had come out of the synagogue, they entered the house of Simon and Andrew, with James and John.
30. But Simon's wife's mother lay sick of a fever, and soon they told Him of her.
31. So, He came and took her by the hand and lifted her up, and immediately the fever left her, and she served them.
32. At evening, when the sun did set, they brought to Him all that were diseased, and them that were possessed with demons.
33. And all the city was gathered together at the door.
34. For He healed many that were sick of different diseases and cast out many demons; and permitted not the demons to speak, because they knew Him.
35. Now in the morning, rising up much before daybreak, He went out and departed into a solitary place, and there prayed.
36. So, Simon and they that were with him followed after Him.
37. When they had found Him, they said to Him, all men seek You.
38. But He said to them let us go into the next towns that I may preach there also: for this purpose, I came forth.
39. So, He preached in their synagogues throughout all Galilee and cast out demons.
40. Now there came a leper to Him, begging Him, and kneeling down to Him, and saying to Him, if You will, You can make me clean.
41. Then Jesus, moved with compassion, put out His hand, and touched him, and said to him, I will; be clean.
42. As soon as He had spoken, immediately the leprosy departed from him, and he was cleansed.
43. But He strictly instructed him, and immediately sent him away;
44. And said to him, see you say nothing to anyone: but go your way, show yourself to the priest, and offer for your cleansing those things which Moses commanded, for a testimony to them.
45. But he went out, and began to announce it much, and to blaze abroad the matter, so much so that Jesus could no more openly enter into the city but was outside in deserted places: and they came to Him from every quarter.

Chapter 2

1. Again, He entered Capernaum after some days, and it was reported that He was in the house.
2. Immediately many were gathered together, so much so that there was no room to receive them, no, not so much as around the door: and He preached the word to them.

3. So, they came to Him, bringing a paralytic, who was carried by four.
4. When they could not come close to Him because of the crowd, they uncovered the roof where he was: and when they had broken it up, they let down the bed in which the paralytic lay.
5. When Jesus saw their faith, He said to the paralytic, son, your sins are forgiven.
6. But there was certain of the scribes sitting there, and reasoning in their hearts,
7. why does this Man speak blasphemies? Who can forgive sins but God only?
8. Immediately when Jesus perceived in His spirit that they so reasoned within themselves, He said to them, why do you reason these things in your hearts?
9. Which is easier to say to the paralytic, your sins are forgiven; or to say, arise, and take up your bed, and walk?
10. But that you may know that the Son of man has power on earth to forgive sins, He said to the paralytic,
11. I say to you, arise, and take up your bed, and go to your house.
12. Immediately he arose, took up the bed, and went out before them all; so much so that they were all amazed, and glorified God, saying, we have never seen anything like this!
13. Then He went forth again by the seaside; and all the multitude came to Him, and He taught them.
14. As He passed by, He saw Levi the son of Alphaeus sitting at the tax collector's booth, and said to him, follow Me. So, he rose and followed Him.
15. And it came to pass, that, as Jesus sat to eat in his house, many tax collectors and sinners sat also together with Jesus and His disciples: for there were many, and they followed Him.
16. But when the scribes and Pharisees saw Him eat with tax collectors and sinners, they said to His disciples, how is it that He eats and drinks with tax collectors and sinners?
17. When Jesus heard it, He said to them, they that are healthy have no need of the physician, but they that are sick: I came not to call the righteous, but sinners to repentance.
18. The disciples of John and of the Pharisees used to fast: and they came and said to Him, why do the disciples of John and of the Pharisees fast, but Your disciples do not?
19. So, Jesus said to them, can the friends of the bridegroom fast, while the bridegroom is with them? As long as they have the bridegroom with them, they cannot fast.
20. But the days will come, when the bridegroom will be taken away from them, and then they will fast in those days.
21. No man also sews a piece of new cloth on an old garment: else the new piece that filled it up takes away from the old, and the tear is made worse.
22. No man puts new wine into old bottles: else the new wine does burst the bottles, and the wine is spilled, and the bottles will be damaged: but new wine must be put into new bottles.

23. And it came to pass, that He went through the corn fields on the Sabbath day; and His disciples began, as they went, to pluck the ears of corn.
24. But the Pharisees said to Him, behold, why do they do on the Sabbath day that which is not lawful?
25. So, He said to them, have you never read what David did when he was in need and was hungry, he, and they that were with him?
26. How he went into the house of God in the days of Abiathar the high priest and did eat the showbread, which is not lawful to eat but for the priests, and gave also to those who were with him?
27. Then, He said to them, the Sabbath was made for man, and not man for the Sabbath:
28. Therefore, the Son of man is Lord also of the Sabbath.

Chapter 3

1. And He entered again into the synagogue, and there was a man there which had a withered hand.
2. So, they watched Him, whether He would heal him on the Sabbath day; that they might accuse Him.
3. Then He said to the man which had the withered hand, rise among us.
4. And He said to them, is it lawful to do good on the Sabbath days, or to do evil? To save a life or to kill? But they held their peace.
5. When He had looked around at them with anger, being grieved for the hardness of their hearts, He said to the man, stretch out your hand. So, he stretched out his hand and it was restored whole as the other.
6. Then the Pharisees went out, and immediately took counsel with the Herodians against Him, how they might destroy Him.
7. But Jesus withdrew himself with His disciples to the sea: and a great multitude from Galilee followed Him, and from Judea,
8. Even from Jerusalem, and from Idumea, and from beyond the Jordan; and they about Tyre and Sidon, a great multitude, when they had heard what great things He did, came to Him.
9. So, he spoke to His disciples that a small boat should be devoted continually for Him because of the multitude unless they should crush Him.
10. For He had healed many; so much so that they pressed on Him to touch Him, as many as had diseases.
11. For unclean spirits, when they saw Him, fell down before Him, and cried, saying, You are the Son of God!
12. But He strictly instructed them that they should not make Him known.
13. Then He went up to a mountain and called to Him those whom He wanted: and they came to Him.
14. For He chose twelve, that they should be with Him, and that He might send them out to preach,
15. And to have the power to heal sicknesses, and to cast out demons:
16. Simon, he surnamed Peter;

17. And James the son of Zebedee, and John the brother of James; and He surnamed them Boanerges, which is, the Sons of Thunder:
18. And Andrew, and Philip, and Bartholomew, and Matthew, and Thomas, and James the son of Alphaeus, and Thaddaeus, and Simon the Canaanite,
19. And Judas Iscariot, who later betrayed Him: and they went into a house.
20. Then the multitude came together again so that they could not so much as eat bread.
21. When His friends heard of it, they went out to lay hold of Him: for they said, He is out of His mind.
22. And the scribes who came down from Jerusalem said, He has Beelzebub, and, by the prince of the demons He casts out demons.
23. Then He called them to Him, and said to them in parables, how can Satan cast out Satan?
24. If a kingdom be divided against itself, that kingdom cannot stand.
25. If a house be divided against itself, that house cannot stand.
26. And if Satan rises up against himself, and be divided, he cannot stand but has an end.
27. No man can enter a strong man's house and plunder his goods unless he will first bind the strong man, and then he will plunder his house.
28. Truthfully, I say to you, all sins will be forgiven the sons of men, and whatever blasphemies they may speak:
29. But he that blasphemes against the Holy Spirit has no forgiveness into the New Covenant age but is in danger of perpetual punishment for the error.
30. Because they said, He has an unclean spirit.
31. Then His brothers came and His mother, standing outside, sent for Him, calling Him.
32. Now the multitude sat about Him, and they said to Him, behold, Your mother and Your brothers outside seek for You.
33. But He answered them, and said, who is My mother, or My brothers?
34. Then He looked around on those who sat about Him, and said, behold My mother and My brothers!
35. For whoever will do the will of God, the same is My brother, and My sister, and mother.

Chapter 4

1. So, He began again to teach by the seaside: and there were gathered to Him a great multitude, so that He entered the boat and sat in the sea, and the whole multitude was by the sea on the land.
2. Then He taught them many things by parables, and said to them in His teaching,
3. Listen; behold, there went out a sower to plant:
4. And it came to pass, as he planted, some fell by the wayside, and the birds of the air came and devoured it up.
5. Some fell on stony ground, where it had little soil; and immediately it sprang up because it had no depth of soil:

6. But when the sun was up, it was scorched; and because it had no root, it withered away.
7. And some fell among thorns, and the thorns grew up, and choked it, and it yielded no fruit.
8. But other fell on good ground and did yield fruit that sprang up and increased; and brought forth, some thirty, and some sixty, and some a hundred.
9. And He said to them, he that has ears to hear, let him hear.
10. And when He was alone, they that were about Him with the twelve asked of Him the parable.
11. And He said to them, to you it is given to know the mystery of the kingdom of God: but to them that are outside, all these things are done in parables:
12. That seeing they may see, and not perceive; and hearing they may hear, and not understand; unless at any time they should turn, and their sins should be forgiven them.
13. And He said to them, do you not see the meaning of this parable? How then will you comprehend all the parables?
14. The sower plants the word.
15. And these are they by the roadside, where the word is planted; but when they have heard, Satan comes immediately and takes away the word that was planted in their hearts.
16. These are they likewise which are planted on stony soil, who, when they have heard the word, immediately receive it with gladness;
17. But have no root in themselves, and are only for a season: afterward, when tribulation or persecution begins because of the word, they are caused to stumble.
18. And these are they on which are planted among thorns, such as hear the word,
19. But the cares of this age, and the deceitfulness of riches, and the lusts of other things enter in, choking the word, and it becomes unfruitful.
20. Then these are they on which are planted on good ground, such as hear the word, and receive it, and bring forth fruit, some thirty-fold, some sixty, and some a hundred.
21. And He said to them, is a candle brought to be put under a bowl, or under a bed? And is it not to be set on a lampstand?
22. For there is nothing hidden, which will not be manifested; neither was anything kept secret, but that it should come into the open.
23. If any man has ears to hear, let him hear.
24. And He said to them, take heed what you hear: with what measure you measure out, it will be measured back to you: and to you that hear will more be given.
25. For he that has, to him will be given: and he that has not, from him will be taken even that which he has.
26. And He said, so is the kingdom of God as if a man should cast seed into the ground;
27. And should sleep, and rise night and day, and the seed should spring and grow up, he knows not how.
28. For the land brings forth fruit of herself, first the blade, then the ear, after that the mature corn in the ear.
29. But when the fruit is brought out, immediately he puts in the sickle because the harvest has come.

Mark 4:30

30. And He said, what will we liken the kingdom of God? Or with what comparison will we compare it?
31. It is like a grain of mustard seed, which, when it is sown in the soil, is less than all the seeds that be in the soil:
32. But when it is sown, it grows up, and becomes greater than all garden plants, and shoots out great branches; so that the birds of the air may nest under its shade.
33. With many such parables He spoke the word to them, as they were able to hear it.
34. But He did not speak to them without a parable: and when they were alone, He explained all things to His disciples.
35. On the same day, when the evening had come, He said to them let us cross over to the other side.
36. When they had sent away the multitude, they took Him just as He was in the boat. And there were also with Him other little boats.
37. Then there arose a great storm of wind, and the waves beat into the boat so that it was now full.
38. But He was in the stern, asleep on a pillow: and they woke Him, and said to Him, Master, do You not care that we are perishing?
39. Then He arose and rebuked the wind, and said to the sea, peace, be still. So, the wind ceased, and there was a great calm.
40. But He said to them, why are you so fearful? How is it that you have no faith?
41. And they feared exceedingly, and said to one another, what manner of Man is this, that even the wind and the sea obey Him?

Chapter 5

1. Then they came over to the other side of the sea, into the country of the Gadarenes.
2. When He had come out of the boat, immediately there met Him out of the tombs a man with an unclean spirit,
3. Who had his dwelling among the tombs; and no man could bind him, no, not with chains:
4. Because he had been often bound hand and foot, and the chains had been broken apart by him, and the irons broken in pieces: neither could any man subdue him.
5. As always, night and day, he was in the mountains, and the tombs, crying, and cutting himself with stones.
6. But when he saw Jesus afar off, he ran and worshiped Him,
7. And cried with a loud voice, and said, what have I to do with You, Jesus, You Son of the Most High God? I beg You by God, that You torment Me not.
8. For He said to him, come out of the man, you unclean spirit.
9. And He asked him, what is your name? And he answered, and said, my name is Legion: for we are many.
10. Also, he begged Him much that He would not send them away out of the country.
11. Now there was close to the mountains a great herd of pigs feeding.
12. So, all the demons begged Him, saying, send us into the pigs, that we may enter them.

13. Immediately Jesus gave them leave. And the unclean spirits went out and entered into the pigs: and the herd ran violently down a steep slope into the sea, (there were about two thousand) and they drowned in the sea.
14. Then they that fed the pigs fled and told it in the city, and in the country. So, they went out to see what it was that was done.
15. And they came to Jesus and seeing him that had been possessed with the demon, and had the legion, sitting, and clothed, and in his right mind: and they were afraid.
16. Then they that saw it told them how it happened to him that was possessed with the demon, and also concerning the pigs.
17. Then they began to beg Him to depart out of their borders.
18. When He had come into the boat, he that had been possessed by the demon asked Him that he might be with Him.
19. However, Jesus did not permit it, but said to him, go home to your friends, and tell them how the Lord has done great things for you, and has had compassion on you.
20. So, he departed and began to speak out in Decapolis how Jesus had done great things for him: and all men did marvel.
21. Now when Jesus had crossed over again by boat to the other side, many people gathered to Him: and He was close to the sea.
22. And behold, there came one of the rulers of the synagogue, Jairus by name; and when he saw Him, he fell at His feet,
23. And begged Him greatly, saying, my little daughter lies at the point of death: I pray You, come and lay Your hands on her, that she may be healed, and she will live.
24. Then Jesus went with him, and many people followed Him and thronged Him.
25. Now a certain woman, who had an issue of blood for twelve years,
26. And had endured many things of many physicians, and had spent all that she had, and had not gotten better, but rather grew worse,
27. When she had heard of Jesus, she came in the crowd behind Him and touched His garment.
28. For she said, if I may touch but His clothes, I will be healthy.
29. Immediately her bleeding stopped, and she felt in her body that she was healed of that suffering.
30. And Jesus, immediately knowing in Himself that power had gone out of Him, turned around in the crowd, and said, who touched My clothes?
31. But His disciples said to Him, You see the multitude thronging You and say You, who touched me?
32. So, He looked around to see her that had done this thing.
33. But the woman fearing and trembling, knowing what was done in her, came and fell down before Him, and told Him all the truth.
34. Then He said to her, daughter, your faith has made you healthy; go in peace and be free from your suffering.
35. While He yet spoke, there came from the ruler of the synagogue's house certain who said, your daughter is dead: why trouble the Master any further?
36. As soon as Jesus heard the word that was spoken, He said to the ruler of the synagogue, be not afraid, only believe.

37. He permitted no one to follow Him, except Peter, James, and John the brother of James.
38. Then He came to the house of the ruler of the synagogue and saw the commotion, and them that wept and wailed greatly.
39. When He had come in, He said to them, why make you this commotion, and weep? The girl is not dead but sleeps.
40. But they laughed Him to scorn. When He had put them all outside, He took the father and the mother of the girl, and them that were with Him, and entered in where the girl was lying.
41. For He took the girl by the hand, and said to her, talitha cumi; which is, being interpreted, little girl, I say to you, arise.
42. Immediately, the girl arose and walked; for she was twelve years old. So, they were amazed with great astonishment.
43. But He charged them strictly that no man should know it; and commanded that something should be given her to eat.

Chapter 6

1. Then He went out from there and came into His birthplace, and His disciples followed Him.
2. When the Sabbath day had come, He began to teach in the synagogue: and many hearing Him were astonished, saying, from where has this man these things? What wisdom is this which is given to Him that even such mighty works are done by His hands?
3. Is not this the carpenter, the son of Mary, the brother of James, and Joses, and Judah, and Simon? And are not His sisters here with us? For they were offended at Him.
4. But Jesus said to them, a prophet is not without honor, but in his birthplace, and among his own relatives, and in his own family.
5. Now He could not do mighty works there, except that He laid His hands on a few sick people and healed them.
6. So, He was marveled by their unbelief. And He went around the villages, teaching.
7. Then He called to Himself the twelve and began to send them out by twos; and gave them power over unclean spirits;
8. And commanded them that they should take nothing for their journey, except a staff only; no bag, no bread, no money in their belts:
9. Wear sandals; but not an extra tunic.
10. Also, He said to them, in whatever place you enter a house, there stay until you depart from that place.
11. For whoever will not receive you, nor hear you, when you depart from there, shake off the dust under your feet for a testimony against them. Truthfully, I say to you, it will be more tolerable for Sodom and Gomorrah in the Day of Judgment than for that city.
12. So, they went out and preached that men should repent.
13. They cast out many demons, and anointed with oil many that were sick, and healed them.
14. Now King Herod heard of Him; for His name was spread abroad: and he said that John the Immerser had risen from the dead, and therefore mighty works do manifest themselves by Him.

15. Others said that it is Elijah. Others said that it is a prophet or one of the prophets.
16. But when Herod heard of it, he said, it is John, who I beheaded: He is risen from the dead.
17. For Herod himself had sent out and laid hold on John and bound him in prison for Herodias' sake, his brother Philip's wife: for he had married her.
18. For John had said to Herod, it is not lawful for you to have your brother's wife.
19. Therefore, Herodias was very bitter against him and would have killed him; but she could not:
20. For Herod feared John, knowing that he was a just and holy man, and protected him; and when he heard him, he did many things, and heard him gladly.
21. When an opportune day had come, that Herod on his birthday made a feast for his leaders, high captains, and chief landowners of Galilee;
22. When Herodias' daughter came in, and danced, and pleased Herod, and them that sat with him, the king said to the girl, ask of me whatever you want, and I will give it you.
23. So, he swore to her, whatever you want to ask of me, I will give it to you, up to half of my kingdom.
24. Then she went out, and said to her mother, what will I ask? So, she said, the head of John the Immerser.
25. Immediately, she came in with haste to the king, and asked, saying, I want that you give me at once on a platter the head of John the Immerser.
26. The king was exceedingly sorry; yet for his oath's sake, and for their sakes who sat with him, he would not reject her.
27. Immediately, the king sent an executioner, and commanded his head to be brought: and he went and beheaded him in the prison,
28. Then brought his head on a platter and gave it to the girl: and the girl gave it to her mother.
29. When his disciples heard of it, they came and took up his dead body and laid it in a tomb.
30. Then the apostles gathered themselves together to Jesus and told Him all things, both what they had done, and what they had taught.
31. And He said to them, come yourselves apart into a deserted place, and rest a while: for there were many coming and going, and they had no chance so much as to eat.
32. So, they departed into a deserted place by boat privately.
33. But the people saw them departing, and many knew Him, and ran on foot out of all cities, and got there before them, and came together to Him.
34. And Jesus, when he came out, saw many people, and was moved with compassion toward them, because they were as sheep not having a shepherd: and He began to teach them many things.
35. When the day was now far spent, His disciples came to Him, and said, this is a deserted place, and now the time is far passed:

36. Send them away, that they may go into the surrounding country, and into the villages, and buy themselves bread: for they have nothing to eat.

37. He answered and said to them, give them something to eat. So, they say to Him, will we go and buy two hundred denarii worth of bread, and give them something to eat?

38. He said to them, how many loaves do you have? Go and see. When they knew, they said, five, and two fish.

39. Then He commanded them to make all sit down in groups on the green grass.

40. So, they sat down in groups, by hundreds, and by fifties.

41. When He had taken the five loaves and the two fish, He looked up to heaven, and blessed, and broke the loaves, and gave them to His disciples to place before them; and the two fish He divided among them all.

42. For they all did eat and were satisfied.

43. Then they took up twelve baskets full of the fragments, and of the fish.

44. For they that did eat of the loaves were about five thousand men.

45. Immediately He made His disciples get into the boat and go ahead of Him to the other side to Bethsaida, while He sent away the people.

46. When He had sent them away, He departed to a mountain to pray.

47. When evening had come, the boat was in the middle of the sea, and He was alone on the land.

48. And He saw them distressed rowing; for the wind was against them: and about the fourth watch of the night, He came to them, walking on the sea, and desired to pass by them.

49. But when they saw Him walking on the sea, they supposed it had been a spirit, and cried out:

50. For they all saw Him and were troubled. Immediately He talked with them, and said to them, be of good cheer: I Am; be not afraid.

51. So, He went up to them into the boat, and the wind ceased: and they were intensely amazed in themselves beyond measure and wondered.

52. For they did not consider the miracle of the loaves: for their heart was hardened.

53. When they had passed over, they came into the land of Gennesaret and came to the shore.

54. When they had come out of the boat, they were fully knowing Him,

55. And immediately ran through that whole surrounding region and began to carry about in beds those that were sick, wherever they heard He was.

56. For wherever He entered, into villages, or cities, or fields, they laid the sick in public places and begged Him that they might touch even the edge of His garment: and as many as touched Him were made whole.

Chapter 7

1. Then came together to Him the Pharisees, and certain of the scribes, who came from Jerusalem.

2. When they saw some of His disciples eat bread with defiled, that is to say, with unwashed, hands, they found fault.

3. For the Pharisees, and all the Jews, unless they wash their hands often, eat not, following the tradition of the elders.

4. When they come from the market unless they wash, they eat not. And many other things there are which they have received to follow, such as the washing of cups, pots, copper vessels, and tables.

5. Then the Pharisees and scribes asked Him, why walk not Your disciples according to the tradition of the elders, but eat bread with unwashed hands?

6. He answered and said to them, well has Isaiah prophesied of you hypocrites, as it is written, this people honor Me with their lips, but their heart is far from Me.

7. In vain do they worship Me, teaching for teachings the commandments of men.

8. For laying aside the commandment of God, you follow the tradition of men, as the washing of pots and cups: and many other such things you do.

9. And He said to them, full well you reject the commandment of God, that you may keep your own tradition.

10. For Moses said, honor your father and your mother; and, whoever curses father or mother, let him be put to death:

11. But you say, if a man will say to his father or mother, whatever you might have gained from me, it is Corban, that is to say, it is a gift to God.

12. And you no longer permit him to do anything for his father or his mother;

13. Making the word of God of no effect through your tradition, which you have handed down: and like many such things you do.

14. When He had called all the people to Him, He said to them, listen to Me each one of you, and understand:

15. There is nothing from outside a man, that entering into him can defile him: but the things which come out of him, those are they that defile the man.

16. If any man has ears to hear, let him hear.

17. When He had entered the house of the people, His disciples asked Him concerning the parable.

18. Then He said to them, are you so without understanding also? Do you not perceive that whatever thing from outside enters the man, it cannot defile him;

19. Because it enters not into his heart, but into the stomach, and goes out of the body. Therefore, making all foods clean.

20. And He said that which comes out of the man defiles the man.

21. For from within, out of the heart of men, proceed evil thoughts, adulteries, fornications, murders,

22. Thefts, covetousness, wickedness, deceit, lasciviousness, an evil eye, blasphemy, pride, foolishness:

23. All these evil things come from within and defile the man.

24. From there He arose, and went into the borders of Tyre and Sidon, and entered into a house, and would have no one know it: but He could not be hidden.

25. For a certain woman, whose young daughter had an unclean spirit, heard of Him, and came and fell at His feet:

26. The woman was a Greek, a Syrophoenician by nation; and she was requesting from Him that He would cast out the demon from her daughter.
27. But Jesus said to her, let the children first be filled: for it is not suitable to take the children's bread and to cast it to the puppies.
28. She answered and said to Him, yes, Lord: even the puppies under the table eat of the children's crumbs.
29. So, He said to her, for this saying go your way; the demon has gone out of your daughter.
30. When she had come to her house, she found the demon gone, and her daughter lying on the bed.
31. And again, departing from the borders of Tyre and Sidon, He came toward the Sea of Galilee, in between the borders of Decapolis.
32. Then they brought to Him one that was deaf and a stutterer, and they begged Him to put His hand on him.
33. So, He took him aside from the multitude, and put His fingers into his ears, and He spit, and touched his tongue;
34. Then looking up to heaven, He sighed, and said to him, ephphatha, that is, be opened.
35. Immediately his ears were opened, and the impediment of his tongue was loosed, and he spoke plainly.
36. Then He charged them that they should tell no one: but the more He charged them, the more abundantly they broadcasted it;
37. And were beyond measure astonished, saying, He has done all things well: He makes both the deaf to hear, and the mute to speak!

Chapter 8

1. In those days the multitude being very great, and having nothing to eat, Jesus called His disciples to Him, and said to them,
2. I have compassion on the multitude, because they have now been with Me three days, and have nothing to eat:
3. For if I send them away without food to their own houses, they will faint on the way: for some of them came from far.
4. Then His disciples answered Him, from where can a man satisfy these men with bread here in the wilderness?
5. He asked them, how many loaves have you? And they said, seven.
6. So, He commanded the people to sit down on the ground: and He took the seven loaves, and gave thanks, and broke, and gave to His disciples to place before them; and they did place them before the people.
7. They had a few small fish: and He blessed and commanded to set them also before them.
8. So, they did eat and were filled: and they gathered up the broken food that was left in seven baskets.
9. For they that had eaten were about four thousand: and He sent them away.
10. Immediately He entered into a boat with His disciples and came into the parts of Dalmanutha.
11. Then the Pharisees came out and began to question Him, seeking from Him a sign from heaven, tempting Him.

12. But He sighed deeply in His spirit, and said, why does this generation seek after a sign? Truthfully, I say to you, there will be no sign given to this generation.
13. Then He left them and entering into the boat again departed to the other side.
14. Now the disciples had forgotten to take bread, neither had they any in the boat with them except one loaf.
15. Then He charged them, saying, take heed, beware of the leaven of the Pharisees, and the leaven of Herod.
16. So, they reasoned among themselves, saying, it is because we have no bread.
17. When Jesus knew it, He said to them, why reason among yourselves, because you have no bread? Do you not yet realize, neither understand? Is your heart still hardened?
18. Having eyes, you see not? And having ears, you hear not? Do you not remember?
19. When I broke the five loaves among five thousand, how many baskets full of fragments did you gather up? They said to Him, twelve.
20. "And the seven loaves for the four thousand, how many baskets full of broken pieces did you take up?" And they said to him, "seven."
21. He said to them, how is it that you do not understand?
22. Then He came to Bethsaida, and they brought a blind man to Him and asked Him to touch him.
23. So, He took the blind man by the hand and led him out of the town; and when He had spit on his eyes, and put His hands on him, He asked him if he saw anything.
24. Then he looked up, and said, I see men as trees, walking.
25. After that, He put his hands again on his eyes and made him look up: and he was restored and saw all things clearly.
26. Then He sent him away to his house, saying, neither go into the town nor tell it to any in the town.
27. Now Jesus went out, and His disciples, into the towns of Caesarea Philippi: and on the way He asked His disciples, saying to them, who do men say that I am?
28. So, they answered, John the Immerser; but some say, Elijah; and others, one of the prophets.
29. He said to them, but who do you say that I am? So, Peter answered and said to Him, You are the Christ.
30. Then He charged them that they should tell no man about Him.
31. And He began to teach them, that the Son of man must suffer many things, and be rejected of the elders, and of the chief priests, and scribes, and be killed, and after three days rise again.
32. He spoke that saying openly. And Peter took Him and began to rebuke Him.
33. But when He had turned about and looked on His disciples, He rebuked Peter, saying, you get behind Me, Satan: for you are minding not the things that are of God, but the things that are of men.
34. When He had called the people to Him with His disciples also, He said to them, whoever wants to come after Me, let him reject himself, and take up his cross, and follow Me.

35. For whoever will save his soul will lose it; but whoever will lose his soul for Me and the gospel, the same will save it.
36. For what will it profit a man, if he will gain the whole world, and loses his own soul?
37. Or what will a man give in exchange for his soul?
38. Therefore, whoever will be ashamed of Me and of My words in this adulterous and sinful generation; of him also will the Son of man be ashamed, when He comes in the glory of His Father with the holy angels.

Chapter 9

1. And He said to them, truthfully, I say to you, that some of them stand here, who will not taste death until they see the kingdom of God has come in power.
2. Now after six days Jesus takes with him Peter, and James, and John, and leads them up to a high mountain apart by themselves: and He was transfigured before them.
3. His clothing became shining, exceedingly white as snow; so, as no bleach on earth can whiten them.
4. Then there appeared to them Elijah with Moses: and they were talking with Jesus.
5. So, Peter answered and said to Jesus, Master, it is good for us to be here: and let us make three tabernacles; one for You, and one for Moses, and one for Elijah.
6. For he did not know what to say; for they were intensely afraid.
7. Then there was a cloud that overshadowed them: and a voice came out of the cloud, saying, this is My beloved Son: listen to Him.
8. Suddenly, when they looked around, they saw no man anymore, except Jesus only with themselves.
9. Now as they came down from the mountain, He charged them that they should tell no one what things they had seen until the Son of man had risen from the dead.
10. So, they kept that saying among themselves, questioning one another about what rising from the dead should mean.
11. Then they asked Him, and said, why do the scribes say that Elijah must first come?
12. Then He answered and told them, Elijah indeed is coming first and restores all things; and how it is written of the Son of man, that He must suffer many things, and be despised.
13. But, I say to you, that Elijah has indeed come, and they have done to him whatever they desired, as it is written of him.
14. When He came to His disciples, He saw a great multitude around them, and the scribes arguing with them.
15. At once, all the people when they saw Him, were greatly amazed, and running toward Him, greeted Him.
16. Then He asked the scribes, what are you discussing with them?
17. Then one of the multitude answered and said, Master, I have brought to You my son, who is possessed with a mute spirit;
18. Whenever he seizes him, he tears him: and he foams out, and grinds with his teeth, and becomes stiff: and I spoke to Your disciples that they should cast him out, and they could not.

19. He answered him, and said, O faithless generation, how long will I be with you? How long will I endure you? Bring him to Me.
20. Then they brought him to Him: and when he saw Him, immediately the spirit convulsed him; and he fell on the ground, foaming at the mouth.
21. So, He asked his father, how long ago was it since this came to him? He said, since childhood.
22. Frequently it has cast him into the fire, and into the water, to destroy him: but if You can do anything, have compassion on us, and help us.
23. Jesus said to him, if you can believe, all things are possible to him that believes.
24. Immediately the father of the child cried out, and said with tears, Lord, I believe; help my unbelief!
25. When Jesus saw that the people came running together, He rebuked the foul spirit, saying to him, you mute and deaf spirit, I charge you, come out of him, and enter no more into him.
26. So, the spirit cried, and convulsed him extremely, and came out of him: and he was as one dead; so much that many said, he is dead.
27. But Jesus took him by the hand and lifted him up, and he arose.
28. When He had come into the house, His disciples asked Him secretly, why could we not cast him out?
29. Then He said to them, this kind cannot come out by anything, but by prayer and fasting.
30. Then they departed from there and passed through Galilee, and He wanted not that any man should know it.
31. For He taught His disciples, and said to them, the Son of man is given into the hands of men, and they will kill Him; and after He is killed, He will rise the third day.
32. But they did not understand that saying and were afraid to ask Him.
33. Then He came to Capernaum: and being in the house He asked them, what was it that you argued about among yourselves on the way?
34. But they held their peace: for on the way they had argued among themselves, who should be the greatest.
35. Then He sat down and called the twelve, and said to them, if any man wants to be first, the same will be last of all, and servant of all.
36. Then He took a child, and set him in the midst of them: and when He had taken him in His arms, He said to them,
37. Whoever will receive one of such children in My name, receives Me: and whoever will receive Me, receives not Me, but Him that sent Me.
38. Then John answered Him, saying, Master, we saw one casting out demons in Your name, and he was not following us: and we prohibited him because he was not following us.
39. But Jesus said, prohibit him not: for there is no man who will do a miracle in My name, that can easily afterward speak evil of Me.
40. For he that is not against us is for us.

41. For whoever will give you a cup of water to drink in My name, because you belong to Christ, truthfully, I say to you, he will not lose his reward.
42. But whoever will stumble one of these little ones that believe in Me, it is better for him that a millstone was hung around his neck, and he was cast into the sea.
43. If your hand causes you to stumble, cut it off: it is better for you to enter into life dismembered than having two hands to go into Gehenna, into the fire that is unquenchable:
44. (Where their worm does not die, and the fire is unquenchable.)
45. If your foot causes you to stumble, cut it off: it is better for you to enter lame into life, than having two feet to be cast into Gehenna, into the fire that is unquenchable:
46. Where their worm does not die, and the fire is not quenched.
47. If your eye stumbles you, pluck it out: it is better for you to enter into the kingdom of God with one eye than having two eyes to be cast into the fire of Gehenna:
48. Where their worm does not die, and the fire is not quenched.
49. For everyone will be salted with fire, and every sacrifice will be salted with salt.
50. Salt is good: but if the salt becomes saltless, in what will you restore its saltiness? Have salt in yourselves and have peace with one another.

Chapter 10

1. Then He arose from there and came into the borders of Judea by the farther side of the Jordan: and the people gathered to Him again; and, as He was accustomed, He taught them again.
2. The Pharisees came to Him, and asked Him, Is it lawful for a man to divorce his wife? Tempting Him.
3. So, He answered and said to them, what did Moses command you?
4. They said, Moses was permitted to write a certificate of divorce and to send her away.
5. Then Jesus answered and said to them, for the hardness of your heart he wrote you this precept.
6. But from the beginning of the creation God made them male and female.
7. For this reason, will a man leave his father and mother, and cleave to his wife;
8. And they two will be one flesh: so then they are no more two, but one flesh.
9. Therefore, what God has joined together, let not man separate.
10. In the house His disciples asked Him again about the same matter.
11. So, He said to them, whoever will divorce his wife, and marry another, commits adultery against her.
12. And if a woman will divorce her husband, and be married to another, she commits adultery.
13. Then they brought young children to Him, that He should touch them: and His disciples rebuked those that brought them.

14. But when Jesus saw it, He was very displeased, and said to them, permit the little children to come to Me, and forbid them not: for of such is the kingdom of God.
15. Truthfully, I say to you, whoever will not receive the kingdom of God as a little child, he will not enter in it.
16. So, He took them up in His arms, put His hands on them, and blessed them.
17. When He had gone out into the way, there came one running, and kneeled to Him, and asked Him, Good Master, what should I do that I may inherit infinite life?
18. So, Jesus said to him, why do you call Me good? There is none good but One and that is God.
19. You know the commandments, do not commit adultery, do not murder, do not steal, do not bear false witness, defraud not, honor your father and mother.
20. So, he answered and said to Him, Master, all these have I kept from my youth.
21. Then Jesus beholding him loved him, and said to him, one thing you lack: go your way, sell whatever you have, and give to the poor, and you will have treasure in heaven: and come, take up the cross, and follow Me.
22. But he was sad at that saying and went away grieved: for he had great wealth.
23. Then Jesus looked around, and said to His disciples, how with difficulty for those that have riches enter into the kingdom of God!
24. And the disciples were astonished at His words. But Jesus answered again, and said to them, children, how hard is it for them that trust in riches to enter into the kingdom of God!
25. It is easier for a camel to go through the eye of a needle, than for a rich man to enter into the kingdom of God.
26. So, they were astonished beyond measure, saying among themselves who then can be saved?
27. But Jesus looking on them said, with men it is impossible, but not with God: for with God all things are possible.
28. Then Peter began to say to Him, Look, we have left all and have followed You. '
29. So, Jesus answered and said, truthfully, I say to you, there is no man that has left house, or brothers, or sisters, or father, or mother, or wife, or children, or lands, for My sake, and the gospel's
30. But he will receive a hundred-fold now in this opportune time, houses, and brothers, and sisters, and mothers, and children, and lands, along with persecutions; and in the New Covenant Age to come; infinite life.
31. But many that are first will be last; and the last first.
32. As they were on the way going up to Jerusalem; and Jesus went before them: and they were amazed; and as they followed, they were afraid. For He took again the twelve and began to tell them what things were about to happen to Him,
33. Saying, behold, we go up to Jerusalem; and the Son of man will be delivered to the chief priests, and the scribes, and they will condemn Him to death, and will give Him to the nations:
34. They will mock Him, and will whip Him, and will spit on Him, and will kill Him: and the third day He will rise again.

35. Then James and John, the sons of Zebedee, came to Him, saying, Master, we want You to do for us whatever we want.
36. So, He said to them, what would you that I should do for you?
37. They said to Him, grant to us that we may sit, one on Your right hand, and the other on Your left hand, in Your glory.
38. But Jesus said to them, you know not what you ask: can you drink of the cup that I drink of? And be immersed with the immersion that I am immersed with?
39. They said to Him, we can. And Jesus said to them, you will indeed drink of the cup that I drink of; and with the immersion that I am immersed with you will be immersed:
40. But to sit on My right hand and on My left hand is not Mine to give, but it will be given to them for whom it is prepared.
41. When the ten heard it, they began to be very displeased with James and John.
42. But Jesus called them to Him, and said to them, you know that they who are of reputation to govern over the nations exercise dominion over them; and their great ones rule over them.
43. But not so will it be among you: but whoever will be great among you, will be your servant:
44. Whoever of you will be great ones, will be a slave of all.
45. For even the Son of man came not to be served, but to serve, and to give His life a ransom for many.
46. Now they came to Jericho: and as He went out of Jericho with His disciples and a great number of people, blind Bartimaeus, the son of Timaeus, sat by the highway side begging.
47. When he heard that it was Jesus of Nazareth, he began to cry out, and say, Jesus, You son of David, have mercy on me!
48. But many charged him that he should hold his peace: but he cried the more a great deal, You son of David, have mercy on me!
49. So, Jesus stood still and commanded him to be called. And they called the blind man, saying to him, be of good comfort, rise; He calls you.
50. Then he, casting away his garment, rose, and came to Jesus.
51. And Jesus answered and said to him, what do you want Me to do for you? The blind man said to Him, Lord, that I might receive my sight.
52. So, Jesus said to him, go your way; your faith has made you whole. At once he received his sight and followed Jesus on the way.

Chapter 11

1. When they came close to Jerusalem, to Bethphage and Bethany, at the Mount of Olives, He sent out two of His disciples,
2. And said to them, go your way into the village opposite you: and as soon as you be entered into it, you will find a colt tied, which not even one man sat; untie him, and bring him.
3. And if any man says to you, what is this you are doing? Say that the Lord needs him, and immediately he will send him back here.

4. So, they went their way and found the colt tied by the door outside in a place where two ways met, and they untied him.
5. Then a certain one stood there saying to them, what are you doing, untying the colt?
6. They said to them just as Jesus had commanded: and they let them go.
7. So, they brought the colt to Jesus, and put their coats on it, and He sat on them.
8. Many spread their coats on the road: and others cut down branches off the trees and scattered them on the road.
9. Then they that went ahead, and they that followed, cried, saying Hosanna; blessed is He that comes in the name of the Lord!
10. Blessed be the kingdom of our father David that comes in the name of the Lord: Hosanna in the highest!
11. So, Jesus entered into Jerusalem, and the temple: and when He had looked around on all things, and now the evening had come, He went out to Bethany with the twelve.
12. On the next day, when they had come from Bethany, He was hungry:
13. Seeing in the distance a fig tree having leaves, He came, if perhaps He might find anything on it: but when He came to it, He found nothing but leaves; for it was not the season of figs.
14. Then Jesus answered and said to it, no one will eat fruit from you, from now on and into the new covenant age. And His disciples heard it.
15. They came to Jerusalem: and Jesus went into the temple, and began to cast them out that sold and bought in the temple, and overthrew the tables of the money changers, and the seats of them that sold doves;
16. And would not permit any man to carry any vessel through the temple.
17. Then He taught, saying to them, is it not written, My house will be called, the house of prayer for all nations? But you have made it a den of thieves.
18. And the scribes and chief priests heard it, and they were striving to find a way to destroy Him: but they feared Him because all the multitude were astonished at His teaching.
19. When evening had come, He went out of the city.
20. In the morning, as they passed by, they saw the fig tree dried up from the roots.
21. Then Peter remembering said to Him, Master, behold, the fig tree which You cursed has withered away.
22. Jesus answered and said to them, have faith in God.
23. For truthfully, I say to you, that whoever will say to this mountain, you be removed, and you be cast into the sea; and will not doubt in his heart but will believe that those things which he says will come to pass; he will have whatever he says.
24. Therefore, I say to you, whatever things you desire, when you pray, believe that you receive them, and you will have them.
25. When you stand praying, forgive, if you have anything against any: that your Father also who is in heaven may forgive you your trespasses.
26. But if you do not forgive, neither will Your Father who is in heaven forgive your trespasses.

27. They come again to Jerusalem: and as He was walking in the temple, there came to Him the chief priests, and the scribes, and the elders,

28. And said to Him, by what authority are You doing these things? And who gave You this authority to do these things?

29. Then Jesus answered and said to them, I will also ask of you one question, and answer Me, and I will tell you by what authority I do these things.

30. The immersion of John, was it from heaven, or of men? Answer Me.

31. So, they reasoned with themselves, saying, if we will say, from heaven; He will say, why then did you not believe him?

32. But if we will say, of men; they feared the people: for all men considered John, that he was a prophet indeed.

33. Then they answered and said to Jesus, we cannot tell. And Jesus answered and said to them, neither will I tell you by what authority I do these things.

Chapter 12

1. Then He began to speak to them by parables. A certain man planted a vineyard, set a hedge about it, dug a place for the wine press, built a watch tower, leased it out to some vinedressers, and went into a far country.

2. And at the proper season he sent to the vinedressers, a slave that he might receive from the vinedressers of the fruit of the vineyard.

3. But they caught him and beat him and sent him away empty.

4. Yet again he sent to them another slave, and at him they cast stones, and wounded him in the head, and sent him away shamefully treated.

5. Yet again he sent another; and him they murdered, and many others; beating some, and murdering some.

6. Therefore, having yet one son, his well-beloved, he sent him also last to them, saying, they will respect my son.

7. But those vinedressers said among themselves, this is the heir; come, let us murder him, and the inheritance will be ours.

8. So, they took him, and murdered him, and cast him out of the vineyard.

9. What will therefore the lord of the vineyard do? He will come and destroy the vinedressers and will give the vineyard to others.

10. Have you not read this scripture; the stone which the builders rejected has become chief cornerstone:

11. This was the Lord's doing, and it is marvelous in our eyes.

12. Then they sought to lay hold on Him but feared the people: for they knew that He had spoken the parable against them: and they left Him and went their way.

13. So, they send to Him certain of the Pharisees and of the Herodians, to catch Him in His words.

14. When they had come, they say to Him, Master, we know that You are true, and are not anxious about anyone: for You regard not the approval of men, but teach the way of God in reality: is it lawful to give tribute to Caesar, or not?

15. Will we give, or will we not give? But He, knowing their hypocrisy, said to them, why do you tempt Me? Bring Me a denarius, that I may see it.

16. Then they brought it. And He said to them, whose is this image and inscription? They said to Him, Caesar's.

17. So, Jesus answered and said to them, render to Caesar the things that are Caesar's, and to God the things that are God's. So they marveled at Him.

18. Then came to Him the Sadducees, who say there is no resurrection; and they asked Him, saying,

19. Master, Moses wrote to us, if a man's brother dies, and leave his wife behind him, and leave no children, that his brother should take his wife, and raise up children for his brother.

20. Now there were seven brothers: and the first took a wife, and dying left no children.

21. So, the second took her, and died, neither left any children: and the third likewise.

22. And the seven had her and left no children: last of all the woman died also.

23. Therefore, in the resurrection, when they will rise, whose wife will she be? For the seven had her as a wife.

24. Then Jesus answered and said to them, therefore do you not err, because you know not the Scriptures, neither the power of God?

25. For when they will rise from the dead, they neither marry nor are given in marriage; but are as the angels which are in heaven.

26. And as concerning the dead, that they rise: have you not read in the book of Moses, how in the bush God spoke to him, saying, I am the God of Abraham, and the God of Isaac, and the God of Jacob?

27. He is not the God of the dead, but the God of the living: Therefore, you do greatly error.

28. Then one of the scribes came, having heard them reasoning together, and perceiving that He had answered them well, asked Him, which is the first commandment of all?

29. Jesus answered him, the first of all the commandments is, hear, O Israel; the Lord our God is one Lord:

30. And you will love the Lord your God with all your heart, and with all your soul, and with all your mind, and with all your strength: this is the first commandment.

31. And the second is similar, namely this, you will love your neighbor as yourself. There is no other commandment greater than these.

32. So, the scribe said to Him, well, Master, You have said the truth: for there is one God; and there is none other but He:

33. To love Him with all the heart, and with all the understanding, and with all the soul, and with all the strength, and to love his neighbor as himself, is more than all whole ascension offerings and sacrifices.

34. When Jesus saw that he answered wisely, He said to him, you are not far from the kingdom of God. And no man after that dared ask Him any question.

35. Then Jesus answered and said, while He taught in the temple, why do the scribes say that Christ is the son of David?

36. For David himself said in the Holy Spirit, the LORD said to My Lord, sit on My right, until I make Your enemies Your footstool.

37. Therefore, David himself calls Him Lord; and how is He then his Son? And the common people heard Him gladly.

38. He said to them in His teaching, beware of the scribes, who love to go in fine clothing, and love greetings in the marketplaces,

39. And the chief seats in the synagogues, and the uppermost rooms at feasts:

40. Who devour widows' houses, and for a show make long prayers: these will receive greater condemnation.

41. Now Jesus sat opposite the treasury and beheld how the people cast money into the treasury: and many that were rich cast in much.

42. Then there came a certain poor widow, and she threw in two mites, which make a small fraction of a denarius.

43. So, He called to Him His disciples, and said to them, truthfully, I say to you, that this poor widow has cast more in than all they which have cast into the treasury:

44. For all they that cast in was of their abundance; but she of her poverty did cast in all that she had, even all her living.

Chapter 13

1. Then as he went out of the temple, one of His disciples said to Him, Master, see what manner of stones and what buildings are here!

2. And Jesus answered and said to him, you see these great buildings? There will not be left one stone upon another that will not be thrown down.

3. Now as He sat on the Mount of Olives opposite the temple, Peter and James and John and Andrew asked Him secretly,

4. Tell us, when will these things be? And what will be the sign when all these things are about to be fulfilled?

5. And Jesus answered them and began to say, take heed unless anyone deceives you:

6. For many will come in My name, saying, I am Christ, and will deceive many.

7. When you hear of wars and rumors of wars, be not troubled: for such things must be; but the end will not be yet.

8. For nation will rise against nation, and kingdom against kingdom: and there will be earthquakes in different places, and there will be famines and troubles: these are the beginnings of the pain of childbirth.

9. Keep an eye out for one another: for they will deliver you up to the Sanhedrin; and in the synagogues and you will be beaten: and you will be brought before rulers and kings for My sake, for a testimony against them.

10. And this gospel must first be proclaimed among all nations.

11. But when they will lead you, and deliver you up, take no thought beforehand what you will speak, but whatever will be given to you in that hour, you speak that: for it is not you that speak, but the Holy Spirit.

12. Now brother will betray brother to death, and father his child, and children will rise up against their parents, and will cause them to be put to death.

13. For you will be hated by all men for My name's sake: but he that will endure to the end, the same will be saved.
14. But when you see the abomination of desolation, spoken of by Daniel the prophet, standing where it should not, (let him that reads, understand), then let them that are in Judea flee to the mountains:
15. And let him that is on the housetop not go down into the house, neither enter in it, to take anything out of his house:
16. And let him that is in the field not return to grab up his clothes.
17. But woe to them that are with child and to them that nurse babies in those days!
18. And you pray that your flight will not be in the winter.
19. For in those days there will be tribulation, which had not happened from the beginning of the creation which God created until now, at this time, and will not ever be.
20. For unless that the Lord had shortened those days, no flesh should be saved: but for the elect's sake whom He has chosen, He has shortened the days.
21. Then if any man will say to you, Look, here is Christ; or, look, He is there; believe him not:
22. For false Christs and false prophets will rise and will show signs and wonders, to deceive, if it were possible, even the elect.
23. But take you heed: behold, I have foretold you all things.
24. But in those days, after that same tribulation, the sun will be darkened, and the moon will not reflect her light,
25. For the stars of the heavens will be falling, and the powers that are in the heavens will be shaken.
26. Then they will see the Son of man coming in the cloud with great power and glory.
27. Then will He send His angels and will gather together His elect from the four winds, from the extreme part of the earth to the extreme part of the heavens.
28. Now learn a parable of the fig tree; when her branch is yet tender and puts out leaves, you know that summer is near:
29. So, you in like manner, when you will see these things come to pass, know that it is close, even at the doors.
30. Truthfully, I say to you, that this generation will not pass until all these things are done.
31. Heaven and earth will pass away: but My words will not pass away.
32. But of that day and that season no man knows, no, not the angels which are in heaven, neither the Son, but the Father.
33. You take heed, watch, and pray: for you do not know when the time is.
34. For the Son of Man is like a man taking a far journey, who left his house, and gave authority to his servants, and to every man his work, and commanded the doorkeeper to watch.
35. Therefore, watch: for you do not know when the master of the house comes, at evening, or at midnight, or at the rooster crowing, or in the morning:
36. Unless coming unexpectedly he finds you sleeping.
37. And what I say to you, I say to all, watch!

Chapter 14

1. After two days was the Feast of the Passover, and of Unleavened Bread: and the chief priests and the scribes sought how they might take Him by trickery and put Him to death.
2. But, they said, not on the feast day unless there be a riot by the people.
3. Being in Bethany in the house of Simon the leper, as He sat to eat, there came a woman having an alabaster box of ointment of spikenard very precious, and she broke the box, and poured it on His head.
4. Some had resentment within themselves, and said, why was this waste of the ointment made?
5. For it might have been sold for more than three hundred denarii and have been given to the poor. So, they murmured against her.
6. But Jesus said, leave her alone; why do you trouble her? She has done a virtuous act on Me.
7. For you have the poor with you at all times, and whenever you want you may do them good: but Me you will not have at all times.
8. She has done what she could: she is come beforehand to anoint My body for burial.
9. Truthfully, I say to you, wherever this gospel will be preached throughout the whole world, this also what she has done will be spoken of as a memorial of her.
10. Then Judas Iscariot, one of the twelve, went to the chief priests, to betray Him to them.
11. When they heard it, they were glad and promised to give him money. So, he sought how he might conveniently betray Him.
12. Now the first day of Unleavened Bread, when they killed the Passover, His disciples said to Him, where do You want us to go and prepare, that You may eat the Passover?
13. He sent out two of His disciples, and said to them, go into the city, and there you will meet a man carrying a pitcher of water: follow him.
14. Wherever he will go in, you say to the master of the house, the Master says, where is the guest chamber, where I will eat the Passover with My disciples?
15. He will show you a large upper room furnished and prepared: there make ready for us.
16. So, His disciples went out, and came into the city, and found as He had said to them: and they made ready the Passover.
17. In the evening He came with the twelve.
18. Now as they sat and did eat, Jesus said, truthfully, I say to you, one of you who eats with Me will betray Me.
19. Then they began to be distressed, and to say to Him one by one, is it I? And another said, is it I?
20. So, He answered and said to them, it is one of the twelve, that dips with Me in the dish.
21. The Son of man indeed goes, as it is written of Him: but woe to that man by whom the Son of man is betrayed! Better were it for that man if he had never been born.
22. As they ate, Jesus took bread, and blessed, and broke it, and gave to them, and said, take, eat: this is My body.

23. And He took the cup, and when He had given thanks, He gave it to them: and they all drank of it.
24. And He said to them, this is My blood of the new covenant, which is shed for many.
25. Truthfully, I say to you, I will drink no more of the fruit of the vine, until that day that I drink it new in the kingdom of God.
26. When they had sung a hymn, they went out to the Mount of Olives.
27. Then Jesus said to them, all of you will stumble because of Me this night: for it is written, I will strike the Shepherd, and the sheep will be scattered.
28. But after I have risen, I will go before you into Galilee.
29. But Peter said to Him, although all will stumble, yet I will not.
30. Jesus said to him, truthfully, I say to you, that this day, even in this night, before the rooster crows twice, you will deny Me three times.
31. But he spoke the more vehemently, if I should die with You, I will not deny You in any way. Likewise, also they all said.
32. They came to a place which was named Gethsemane: and He said to His disciples, sit here, while I will pray.
33. And He took with him Peter and James and John, and began to be troubled, and to be very distressed;
34. Then He said to them, my soul is exceedingly sorrowful to death: wait here and watch.
35. So, He went forward a little and fell on the ground, and prayed that, if it were possible, the hour might pass from Him.
36. For He said, Abba, Father, all things are possible for You; take away this cup from Me: nevertheless, not what I will, but what You will.
37. Then, He came, and found them sleeping, and said to Peter, Simon, do you sleep? Could you not watch one hour?
38. Watch and pray, unless you enter into temptation. The spirit truly is ready, but the flesh is powerless.
39. Yet again He went away and prayed and spoke the same words.
40. When He returned, He found them asleep again, for their eyes were heavy, and neither did they know what to answer Him.
41. Then he came the third time, and said to them, sleep on now, and take your rest: it is enough, the hour has come; behold the Son of man is betrayed into the hands of sinners.
42. Rise up let us go; look, he that betrays Me is at hand.
43. Immediately, while He yet spoke, Judas came, one of the twelve, and with him a great multitude with swords and clubs, from the chief priests and the scribes and the elders.
44. Now he that betrayed Him had given them a signal, saying, whomever I will kiss, that same is He; take Him and lead Him away safely.
45. As soon as he had come, he went immediately to Him, and said, Master, Master; and kissed Him.
46. So, they laid their hands on Him and took Him.
47. But one of them that stood by drew a sword and struck a servant of the high priest and cut off his ear.

Mark 14:48 — Mark 14:71

48. Then Jesus answered and said to them, have you come out, as against a thief, with swords and with clubs to take Me?
49. I was daily with you in the temple teaching, and you did not take hold of Me: but the Scriptures must be fulfilled.
50. Then they all left Him and fled.
51. Now there followed Him a certain young man, having a linen cloth cast about his naked body; and the young men laid hold on him:
52. Then, he left the linen cloth and fled from them naked.
53. So, they led Jesus away to the high priest: and with him were assembled all the chief priests and the elders and the scribes.
54. Yet Peter followed him from a distance, even into the palace of the high priest: and he sat with the servants and warmed himself at the fire.
55. Now the chief priests and all the council sought for witness against Jesus to put Him to death and found none.
56. For many gave false witness against Him, but their witness agreed not together.
57. Then there arose certain, and gave false witness against Him, saying,
58. We heard Him say, I will destroy this temple that is made with hands, and within three days I will build another made without hands.
59. But neither did their witness agree together.
60. So, the high priest stood up in the midst, and asked Jesus, saying, 'Do you have nothing to reply? What is it that these witness against you?'
61. But He held His peace and answered nothing. Again, the high priest asked Him, and said to Him, are You the Christ, the Son of the Blessed?
62. Jesus said I am: and you will see the Son of man sitting on the right hand of power and coming in the cloud of heaven.
63. Then the high priest tore his clothes, and said, why do we need any further witnesses?
64. You have heard the blasphemy: what do you think? And they all condemned Him to be guilty of death.
65. Some began to spit on Him, and to cover His face, and to beat Him, and to say to Him, prophesy: and the servants did strike Him with the palms of their hands.
66. As Peter was below in the palace, there came one of the servant girls of the high priest:
67. When she saw Peter warming himself, she looked at him, and said, and you also were with Jesus of Nazareth.
68. But, he denied, saying, I do not know, I neither understand what you say. And he went out into the porch, and the rooster crowed.
69. Then, a servant girl saw him again, and began to say to them that stood by, this is one of them.
70. But he denied it again. And a little after, they that stood by said again to Peter, surely you are one of them: for you are a Galilean, and your speech agrees to that.
71. But he began to curse and to swear, saying, I do not know this Man of whom you speak.

72. And the second time the rooster crowed. And Peter remembered the word that Jesus said to him, before the rooster crows twice, you will deny Me three times. When he thought on this, he wept.

Chapter 15

1. Immediately in the morning the chief priests held a meeting with the elders and scribes and the whole council, and bound Jesus, and carried Him away, and delivered Him to Pilate
2. Then Pilate asked Him, Are you the King of the Jews? He answered and said to them, you say it.
3. And the chief priests accused Him of many things: but He answered nothing.
4. Then Pilate asked Him again, saying, answer you nothing? Behold how many things they witness against You.
5. But Jesus yet answered nothing; so that Pilate marveled.
6. Now at that feast he released to them one prisoner, whoever they desired.
7. There was one named Barabbas, who lay bound with them and had made rebellion with him, who had murdered in the rebellion.
8. So, the multitude cried aloud and began to ask him to do as he had always done for them.
9. But Pilate answered them, saying, you want me to release to you the King of the Jews?
10. For he knew that the chief priests had delivered Him because of envy.
11. But the chief priests persuaded the people, that he should rather release Barabbas to them.
12. Pilate answered and said again to them, what do you want me to do to Him, whom you call the King of the Jews?
13. So, they cried out again, crucify Him!
14. Then Pilate said to them, why, what evil has He done? Yet they cried out the more exceedingly, crucify Him!
15. So, Pilate, willing to calm the people, released Barabbas to them and delivered Jesus when he had whipped Him, in order to be crucified.
16. Then the soldiers led Him away into the hall of the governor's palace, and they called together the whole garrison.
17. So, they clothed Him with purple, and twisted a crown of thorns, and put it about His head,
18. And began to salute Him, Hail, King of the Jews!
19. Then they struck Him on the head with a reed and spat on Him, and bowing their knees worshiped Him.
20. When they had mocked Him, they took off the purple from Him and put His own clothes on Him and led Him out to crucify Him.
21. For they compelled one Simon a Cyrenian, who passed by, coming out of the country, the father of Alexander and Rufus, to carry His cross.
22. And they brought Him to the place Golgotha, which is, being interpreted, the place of a Skull.
23. Then they gave Him to drink wine mingled with myrrh: but He received it not.

24. When they had crucified Him, they divided His clothes, casting lots for them, what every man should take.
25. Now it was the third hour, and they crucified Him.
26. And the inscription of His accusation was written over, THE KING OF THE JEWS.
27. And with Him they crucified two thieves; the one on His right hand, and the other on His left.
28. So, the scripture was fulfilled, which said, and He was numbered with the transgressors.
29. And they that passed by blasphemed Him, wagging their heads, and saying, Ah, You that destroys the temple, and builds it in three days,
30. Save Yourself and come down from the cross.
31. Likewise also the chief priests mocking, said among themselves with the scribes, He saved others; Himself He cannot save.
32. Let Christ the King of Israel descend now from the cross that we may see and believe. And they that were crucified with Him reviled Him.
33. When the sixth hour had come, there was darkness over the whole land until the ninth hour.
34. And at the ninth hour Jesus cried with a loud voice, saying, Eloi, Eloi, lama sabachthani? Which is, being interpreted as, My God, My God, why have You forsaken Me?
35. And some of them that stood by, when they heard it, said, Behold, He calls Elijah.
36. Then someone ran and filled a sponge full of sour wine, and put it on a reed, and gave Him to drink, saying, Let Him alone; let us see whether Elijah will come to take Him down.
37. And Jesus cried with a loud voice and gave up the ghost.
38. And the veil of the temple was torn in two from the top to the bottom.
39. When the centurion, which stood opposite Him, saw that He so cried out, and gave up the ghost, He said, Truly this man was the Son of God!
40. There were also women looking on afar off: among whom was Mary Magdalene, and Mary the mother of James the less and of Joses, and Salome;
41. Who also, when He was in Galilee, followed Him, and served Him; and many other women who came up with Him to Jerusalem.
42. Now when the evening had come, because it was the preparation, that is, the day before the Sabbath,
43. Joseph of Arimathaea, an honorable council member, who also waited for the kingdom of God, came, and went in boldly to Pilate, and requested the body of Jesus.
44. Pilate wondered if He were already dead: and calling to him the centurion, he asked him whether He had been dead for some time.
45. When he knew it by the centurion, he gave the body to Joseph.
46. Then he bought fine linen, and took Him down, and wrapped Him in the linen, and laid Him in a tomb which was cut out of a rock and rolled a stone against the door of the tomb.

47. And Mary Magdalene and Mary the mother of Joses beheld where He was laid.

Chapter 16

1. When the Sabbath was past, Mary Magdalene, and Mary the mother of James, and Salome, had bought sweet spices, that they might come and anoint Him.
2. Very early in the morning the first day of the week, they came to the tomb at the rising of the sun.
3. For they said among themselves, who will roll us away the stone from the door of the tomb?
4. When they looked, they saw that the stone was rolled away: for it was very great.
5. Then entering the tomb, they saw a young man sitting on the right side, clothed in a long white garment; and they were frightened.
6. But he said to them, be not frightened: You seek Jesus of Nazareth, who was crucified: He is risen! He is not here: Behold the place where they laid Him.
7. But go your way, tell His disciples and Peter that He goes before you into Galilee: there will you see Him, as He said to you.
8. So, they went out quickly and fled from the tomb; for they trembled and were amazed: neither said they anything to any man; for they were afraid.
9. Now when Jesus was risen early on the first day of the week, He appeared first to Mary Magdalene, out of whom He had cast seven demons.
10. She went and told them that had been with Him, as they mourned and wept.
11. Then they, when they had heard that He was alive, and had been seen of her, believed not.
12. After that He appeared in another form to two of them, as they walked, and went into the country.
13. And they went and told it to the others: neither did they believe them.
14. Afterward He appeared to the eleven as they sat to eat, and reproved their unbelief and hardness of heart, because they believed not those who had seen Him after He was risen.
15. And He said to them, go into the whole world, and preach the gospel to all creation.
16. He that believes and is immersed will be saved, but he that believes not will be condemned.
17. And these signs will follow them that believe; in My name will they cast out demons; they will speak with new tongues;
18. They will take up serpents; and if they drink any deadly thing, it will not hurt them; they will lay hands on the sick, and they will recover.
19. Then after the Lord had spoken to them, He was received up into heaven and sat at the right hand of God.
20. So, they went out and preached everywhere, the Lord working with them, and confirming the word with signs following. Amen.

Luke Synopsis

I. Introduction
    A. Prologue (Luke 1:1-4)
    B. Birth of John the Baptist foretold (Luke 1:5-25)
    C. Birth of Jesus foretold (Luke 1:26-38)

II. Jesus' Birth and Early Life
    A. Birth of Jesus (Luke 2:1-7)
    B. Shepherds visit Jesus (Luke 2:8-20)
    C. Jesus presented in the temple (Luke 2:21-38)
    D. Visit of the Magi (Luke 2:39-52)

III. Jesus' Ministry in Galilee
    A. John the Baptist prepares the way (Luke 3:1-20)
    B. Baptism and genealogy of Jesus (Luke 3:21-38)
    C. Jesus' temptation in the wilderness (Luke 4:1-13)
    D. Jesus begins his ministry in Galilee (Luke 4:14-44)

IV. Jesus' Ministry in Judea and Jerusalem
    A. Jesus teaches and performs miracles (Luke 5:1-6:11)
    B. Jesus chooses the twelve disciples (Luke 6:12-49)
    C. Jesus' teachings and parables (Luke 7-8)
    D. Jesus predicts his death and resurrection (Luke 9:21-27)
    E. Transfiguration of Jesus (Luke 9:28-36)

V. Jesus' Journey to Jerusalem
    A. Jesus sends out the seventy-two (Luke 10:1-24)
    B. Parable of the Good Samaritan (Luke 10:25-37)
    C. Mary and Martha (Luke 10:38-42)
    D. Teaching on prayer and faith (Luke 11)

VI. Jesus' Ministry in Jerusalem

    A. Entry into Jerusalem (Luke 19:28-48)
    B. Jesus teaches in the temple (Luke 20-21)
    C. Jesus' arrest, trial, and crucifixion (Luke 22-23)

VII. Resurrection and Ascension

    A. Resurrection of Jesus (Luke 24:1-12)
    B. Jesus appears to disciples on the road to Emmaus (Luke 24:13-35)
    C. Jesus appears to disciples in Jerusalem (Luke 24:36-53)

VIII. Conclusion

    A. The Great Commission (Luke 24:44-49)
    B. Jesus' ascension into heaven (Luke 24:50-53)

I. Introduction

The Gospel of Luke stands as a pivotal text in the New Testament, shedding light on the profound journey of the early Christian community toward understanding the nature of the kingdom of God. Through a meticulous exploration of Jesus' teachings and the events surrounding his ministry, Luke's Gospel offers a compelling vision of God's redemptive plan unfolding through the establishment of a new covenant. At the heart of this Gospel lies a comprehensive interpretation of the kingdom of God, rooted in the significance of Jesus' death and resurrection as the fulfillment of Old Testament prophecies and the ultimate triumph of the divine order over the current age.

The richness of Luke's account lies in the central role it plays in shaping the understanding of the Christian faith and its future expectations. Drawing upon Scripture as well as the teachings of contemporary thinkers, Luke paints a vivid portrayal of the kingdom of God, weaving together profound theological insights with the complexities of the Jewish and Roman worlds. From the cosmic significance of Jesus' birth to the startling revelation of divine judgment, the Gospel of Luke invites readers into a remarkable narrative where the triumph of the new covenant is heralded as the dawning of a new age.

By highlighting the importance of the Cross as the pivotal event that marked the culmination of all prophecies, Luke's narrative challenges the social and religious norms of the time, offering a radically different understanding of the kingdom of God. The Gospel emphasizes the role of Jesus in establishing God's kingdom, a community of the faithful that transcends earthly expectations and finds its ultimate fulfillment in the acknowledgment of Jesus' authority over sin and spiritual death.

As outlined in the Gospel of Matthew, Jesus' words concerning the coming of the Son of Man and the trials and tribulations leading up to the full manifestation of God's kingdom, provide a framework for understanding the theological significance of the destruction of Jerusalem and the preeminence of Jesus' message over traditional religious and societal norms. Throughout Luke's Gospel, there is a sense of urgency and anticipation for the events that would lead to the fulfillment of divine judgment and the arrival of God's kingdom, casting Jesus' ministry in a transcendent light.

Ultimately, Luke's narrative presents the difficult paradox of acknowledging the salvation offered through Christ while grappling with the tumult, suffering, and hardship that marked the ushering of the new era. It is in this charged theological context that the Gospel calls for believers to resolve their doubts, remain steadfast in their faith, and embrace the transformative promise of God's judgment and the radical reshaping of human reality embedded in Jesus' teachings and his message of the imminence of the kingdom of God.

II. A Synopsis of Luke's Gospel

This section provides an overview of the Gospel of Luke, a foundational text in understanding the perspective presented in this academic work. The main ideas are summarized in the chapter heading, while the body of the text fleshes out the central themes and content. Luke's Gospel, often referred to as the "Beloved Physician", serves as the central focus of this chapter, and its role is to set the stage for the insights and analysis explored in the subsequent sections. The focus remains on the synopsis and general overview of the text in question, providing the reader with context for the subject matter discussed in the subsequent sections. Within this chapter, the main ideas related to Luke's narration are developed. This begins by introducing the Gospel and provides the reader with the appropriate context for the subject matter under examination. Through developing these introductory ideas, the central theme of Luke's Gospel as a whole is revealed. These opening lines serve to set the context for the analysis to follow, by first delving into the authorial intent and establishing the context for Luke's description of Jesus' life and teachings. This provides the framework for the deeper examination that will unfold, as the chapter's main subject takes center stage.

Having introduced the main theme of the chapter, the second part proceeds to delve into the analysis. This allows for a smooth transition as the central ideas come into focus, thus building upon the foundation laid in the opening lines. By developing these concepts, new insights can emerge and be brought to the foreground, leading to a deepening understanding of the subject matter being studied.

Moving forward, the subsequent sections provide an opportunity to examine the subject matter using a similar structure. This allows the central theme to be revisited and the analysis to resume, drawing inspiration from the insights gained in the previous section. In this way, a smooth flow can be maintained as we explore the concepts under study, ultimately leading to a more comprehensive grasp of the subject matter.

III. Full Preterist Understanding of the Kingdom of God

The concept of the kingdom of God occupies a central position within the theological landscape of the New Testament, and its interpretation has been a subject of extensive scholarly debate. The full preterist perspective offers a distinctive understanding of this pivotal theme, particularly in the context of Luke's Gospel. This interpretative lens posits that the eschatological prophecies concerning the kingdom of God, including those found in Luke's narrative, have been entirely fulfilled within the historical events of the first century, culminating in the destruction of Jerusalem in 70 AD.

To comprehend the full preterist view, it is essential to grasp the principles that underpin this hermeneutical approach. At its core, full preterism asserts that all biblical prophecies about the end times and the establishment of the kingdom of God have been accomplished.

This interpretation rejects the notion of unfulfilled eschatological expectations, maintaining that the prophetic visions outlined in Scripture found their realization within the first-century context, particularly through the cataclysmic events surrounding the fall of Jerusalem.

Within the Gospel of Luke, the full preterist perspective finds its anchor in the Olivet Discourse, a pivotal passage that records Jesus' prophetic utterances concerning the impending destruction of the temple and the tribulations that would precede the establishment of the kingdom in Matthew 24:1-51). Full preterists interpret this discourse as a direct foretelling of the events that culminated in the Roman siege of Jerusalem, viewing it as the ultimate fulfillment of Jesus' eschatological predictions.

According to the full preterist view, the kingdom of God, as depicted in Luke's Gospel, is not a future reality awaiting fulfillment but a spiritual reign that was inaugurated in the first century through the ministry, death, and resurrection of Jesus Christ. This understanding is rooted in the belief that Christ's parousia marked the end of the old Jewish covenant and age and the establishment of the new covenant, thereby ushering in the kingdom of God.

Consequently, the full preterist interpretation reframes many of Jesus' teachings and parables within a first-century context. Passages that seem to allude to future eschatological events are instead understood as references to the transitional period leading up to the destruction of Jerusalem, which was perceived as the definitive judgment upon the old order and the vindication of the early church saints.

This perspective stands in stark contrast to other eschatological viewpoints, such as historicism, futurism, and idealism, which anticipate a future fulfillment of biblical prophecies concerning the kingdom of God. While partial preterists acknowledge the fulfillment of certain prophecies within the first century, they maintain a belief in a future physical return of Christ and the establishment of His millennial reign. Full preterists, on the other hand, reject any notion of unfulfilled eschatological expectations, asserting that the kingdom of God has already been realized in its fullness through the events of the first century.

The full preterist interpretation of Luke's Gospel and its portrayal of the kingdom of God has sparked vigorous debate within theological circles. While some scholars embrace this perspective as a legitimate hermeneutical approach, others challenge its validity, arguing that it fails to account for the complexities and nuances of biblical prophecy. Nonetheless, the full preterist view offers a thought-provoking lens through which to examine the theological significance of the events depicted in Luke's narrative, inviting readers to engage with the profound implications of the Gospel's eschatological themes.

IV. The Two Book Ends: The Cross and the Destruction of Jerusalem

Within the Gospel of Luke, the events surrounding the Cross, and the destruction of Jerusalem stand as pivotal bookends, framing the narrative and shaping its theological significance. These two monumental occurrences are inextricably intertwined, serving as catalysts for the establishment of the new covenant and the fulfillment of God's redemptive plan.

The theological significance of the Cross cannot be overstated in Luke's account. It is portrayed as the ultimate sacrifice, through which Jesus secured the forgiveness of sins and ratified the new covenant. The Cross is not merely a historical event but a soteriological cornerstone, marking the transition from the old Jewish covenant to the inauguration of the new covenant and the full manifestation of God's kingdom. A reality and realm that is present in our time.

Throughout the Gospel, Luke weaves a narrative that highlights the centrality of the Cross in God's redemptive plan. The Last Supper narrative, for instance, underscores the sacrificial nature of Jesus' death, establishing a direct link between the shedding of his blood and the inauguration of the new covenant (Luke 22:14-23). Similarly, the Emmaus Road encounter (Luke 24:13-35) and Paul's farewell address to the Ephesian elders (Acts 20:28) emphasize the atoning significance of the Cross, reinforcing its pivotal role in the establishment of the Christian assembly.

Complementing the theological weight of the Cross is the cataclysmic event of Jerusalem's destruction. In Luke's narrative, this event is pregnant with profound eschatological and prophetic significance. The Olivet Discourse (Luke 21:5-36), where Jesus foretells the fall of Jerusalem, serves as a pivotal moment, linking the impending devastation to the fulfillment of divine prophecies and the advent of the kingdom of God.

For full preterists, the destruction of Jerusalem is not merely a historical footnote but a defining moment in the realization of God's kingdom. It is seen as the culmination of Jesus' prophecies, marking the end of the old Jewish order and the definitive establishment of the new covenant. The language used by Luke, such as the "times of the Gentiles" (Luke 21:24) and the "desolation" of Jerusalem (Luke 21:20), underscores the theological gravity of this event and its connections to the fulfillment of biblical prophecies.

Furthermore, Luke's narrative draws explicit parallels between the Cross and the destruction of Jerusalem, weaving them together as interconnected events within the divine plan. Jesus' lament over Jerusalem (Luke 19:41-44) foreshadows the city's impending doom, directly linking it to the rejection of the Messiah and the subsequent consequences (The Destruction of Jerusalem & the Coming of Christ Matthew 24:1-51). This convergence of the Cross and Jerusalem's destruction serves to reinforce the notion that the establishment of the new covenant was inextricably tied to the judgment upon the old order.

The interconnection between these two pivotal events is further solidified by the themes of judgment and fulfillment that permeate Luke's narrative. Just as the Cross represents the ultimate sacrifice for the forgiveness of sins, the destruction of Jerusalem is portrayed as a divine judgment upon those who rejected the Messiah. Conversely, for those who embraced the new covenant, these events signified the fulfillment of God's promises, and the dawning of a new age marked by the kingship of the risen Christ (Luke 21:20–28). In conclusion, the Cross and the destruction of Jerusalem stand as the two bookends of Luke's Gospel, serving as the cornerstones upon which the establishment of the kingdom of God is built. Through the intricate weaving of these events, Luke presents a narrative that intertwines the atoning power of the Cross with the eschatological implications of Jerusalem's fall, underscoring the profound theological significance of both occurrences in the unfolding of God's redemptive plan.

V. Conclusion

The Gospel of Luke stands as a profound testament to the unfolding of God's redemptive plan, with the Cross and the destruction of Jerusalem serving as pivotal bookends that frame the narrative's eschatological significance. This research has explored the intricacies of Luke's account, drawing upon the lens of full preterism to shed light on the theological implications of these monumental events.

Through a comprehensive analysis of Luke's narrative structure, major themes, and historical context, this study has underscored the Gospel's unique perspective on the kingdom of God. The full preterist interpretation offers a compelling hermeneutical approach, asserting that the eschatological prophecies concerning the kingdom have been entirely fulfilled within the first century, primarily in the events surrounding the fall of Jerusalem in 70 AD.

Central to the full preterist understanding is the belief that the Cross and the destruction of Jerusalem mark the culmination of God's redemptive plan. The Cross is portrayed not merely as an instrument of execution but as the ultimate sacrifice that paves the way for the forgiveness of sins and the inauguration of the new covenant. Simultaneously, the fall of Jerusalem is seen as the definitive fulfillment of Jesus' prophecies, symbolizing the end of the old Jewish order and the establishment of the kingdom of God on Earth.

By interweaving these two pivotal events, Luke crafts a narrative that underscores the interconnectedness of atonement and eschatology. The Cross serves as the atoning sacrifice, while the destruction of Jerusalem manifests the fulfillment of divine judgment and prophecy. This interplay shapes Luke's theological vision, casting these occurrences as complementary components of a grand storyline that culminates in the establishment of God's kingdom.

Furthermore, this research has highlighted the profound impact of Jerusalem's fall on the early Christian community. As depicted in the book of Acts, this cataclysmic event catalyzed the rapid expansion of the faith, reshaping the theological landscape and prompting a re-evaluation of the church's role and mission. The destruction of the temple, in particular, held profound symbolic significance, representing the end of the old religious order and the establishment of the church as the new dwelling place of God's presence.

While the full preterist perspective remains a subject of ongoing debate within evangelical circles, this research has underscored its relevance and contribution to the discourse surrounding the interpretation of biblical prophecy. By presenting a vision of the kingdom of God as a past culmination rather than a future hope, full preterism challenges traditional eschatological expectations and invites a re-examination of the multifaceted nature of prophetic fulfillment.

In conclusion, the Gospel of Luke stands as a rich tapestry, woven with the threads of atonement, eschatology, and the establishment of God's kingdom. The Cross and the destruction of Jerusalem emerge as cornerstones upon which this narrative is built, serving as powerful symbols that resonate through the ages. As this study has demonstrated, a full preterist interpretation offers a unique lens through which to explore the theological depth and significance of these pivotal events, enriching our understanding of the divine plan and the enduring legacy of the Christian faith.

Preterist View of the Kingdom of God

    A. The Kingdom of God was established during the earthly ministry of Jesus Christ.

    B. It is a spiritual kingdom, not a political or physical one.

    C. The fulfillment of the kingdom occurred in the first century, specifically in the events surrounding the destruction of Jerusalem in 70 AD.

II. Practical Outworking in the Lives of His Saints

    A. The saints are called to live in the reality of the kingdom of God, embodying its values and principles in their daily lives.

    B. They are to seek first the kingdom of God and His righteousness (Matthew 6:33), focusing on spiritual growth and obedience to God's Word.

    C. The saints are to love God and love their neighbors, reflecting the love and grace of the kingdom in their relationships and interactions.

    D. They are to bear fruit of the Spirit (Galatians 5:22-23) and use their spiritual gifts to build up the body of Christ and advance the kingdom.

E. The saints are called to be the salt and the light in the world, sharing the good news of the kingdom and bringing transformation to their communities and society at large.

In essence, the Preterist view of the Kingdom of God emphasizes the present spiritual reality of the kingdom and calls believers to actively participate in its outworking in their lives and in the world around them.

Terry Kashian

Gospel of Luke

Chapter 1

1. Since many have undertaken to draw up a narrative concerning those matters that have been fulfilled among us,
2. Just as they delivered them to us, who from the beginning were eyewitnesses and ministers of the word;
3. It seemed good to me also, having completely investigated all things from the very beginning, to write them out for you in an orderly fashion, most excellent Theophilus,
4. That you might know the certainty of those things, in which you have been instructed.
5. There was in the days of Herod, the king of Judea, a certain priest named Zacharias, of the course of Abia: and his wife was of the daughters of Aaron, and her name was Elisabeth.
6. For they were both righteous before God, walking in all the commandments and ordinances of the Lord blameless.
7. But they had no child, because Elizabeth was barren, and they both were now well advanced in years.
8. And it came to pass, that while he served as priest before God in the order of his division,
9. According to the custom of the priest's office, his lot fell to burn incense when he went into the temple of the Lord.
10. And the whole multitude of the people were praying outside at the time of incense.
11. And there appeared to him an angel of the Lord standing on the right side of the altar of incense.
12. And when Zacharias saw him, he was troubled, and fear fell on him.
13. But the angel said to him, fear not, Zacharias: for your prayer is heard; and your wife Elizabeth will bear you a son, and you will call his name John.
14. For you will have joy and gladness, and many will rejoice at his birth.
15. For he will be great in the sight of the Lord and will drink neither wine nor strong drink; and he will be filled with the Holy Spirit, even from his mother's womb.
16. For many of the children of Israel will he turn to the Lord their God.
17. And he will go before Him in the spirit and power of Elijah, to turn the hearts of the fathers to the children, and the disobedient to the wisdom of the righteous; to make ready a people prepared for the Lord.
18. Then Zacharias said to the angel, how will I know this? For I am an old man, and my wife is well advanced in years.
19. So, the angel answered and said to him, I am Gabriel, who stands in the presence of God; and have been sent to speak to you and to show you this good news.
20. But, behold, you will be silent, and not able to speak, until the day that these things will be performed, because you have not believed my words, which will be fulfilled in their appropriate time.
21. So, the people waited for Zacharias and wondered why he lingered so long in the temple.

22. When he came out, he could not speak to them: and they perceived that he had seen a vision in the temple: for he motioned to them yet remained speechless.

23. And it came to pass, that, as soon as the days of his service were accomplished, he departed to his own house.

24. Then after those days his wife Elizabeth conceived, and hid herself for five months, saying,

25. Thus, has the Lord dealt with me in the days in which He looked on me, to remove my reproach among men.

26. And in the sixth month the angel Gabriel was sent from God to a city of Galilee, named Nazareth,

27. To a virgin engaged to a man whose name was Joseph, of the house of David; and the virgin's name was Mary.

28. And the angel came to her, and said, rejoice, you that are highly favored, the Lord is with you! Blessed are you among women!

29. When she saw him, she was troubled by his saying and considered what type of greeting this was.

30. Then the angel said to her, fear not, Mary: for you have found favor with God.

31. And behold, you will conceive in your womb, and bring out a Son, and will call His name JESUS.

32. He will be great, and will be called the Son of the Highest: and the Lord God will give to Him the throne of His father David:

33. For He will reign over the house of Jacob into the New Covenant Age; and of His kingdom there will be no end.

34. Then Mary said to the angel, how will this be, since I am a virgin?

35. Then the angel answered and said to her, the Holy Spirit will be coming upon you, and the power of the Highest will overshadow you. Therefore, also that Holy One who will be conceived in you will be called the Son of God.

36. Now, behold, your cousin Elizabeth, she has also received a son in her old age: and this is the sixth month with her, who was called barren.

37. For with God nothing will be impossible.

38. So, Mary said, behold the servant of the Lord; be it to me according to your word. So, the angel departed from her.

39. Then Mary arose in those days, and went into the hill country with haste, into a city of Judah;

40. And entered into the house of Zacharias and greeted Elizabeth.

41. And it came to pass, that, when Elizabeth heard the greeting of Mary, the baby leaped in her womb; and Elizabeth was filled with the Holy Spirit:

42. So, she spoke out with a loud voice, and said, blessed are you among women, and blessed is the fruit of your womb!

43. Now why is this to me that the mother of My Lord should come to me?

44. For, look, as soon as the voice of your greeting sounded in my ears, the baby leaped in my womb for joy.

45. And blessed is she that believed: for there will be a fulfillment of those things which were told her from the Lord.

46. So, Mary said, my soul does magnify the Lord,
47. And my spirit has rejoiced in God my Savior.
48. For He has regarded the low estate of His handmaiden: for, behold, from now on all generations will call me blessed.
49. For He that is mighty has done to me great things, and holy is His name.
50. And His mercy is on them that fear Him from generation to generation.
51. He has shown strength with His arm; He has scattered the proud ones in the imagination of their hearts.
52. He has put down the mighty from their thrones and exalted them of low degree.
53. He has filled the hungry with good things; and the rich He has sent away empty.
54. He has helped His servant Israel, in remembrance of His mercy;
55. As He spoke to our fathers, to Abraham, and his seed forever.
56. And Mary stayed with her for about three months and then returned to her own house.
57. Now Elizabeth's full term came that she should be delivered, and she brought out a son.
58. And her neighbors and her cousins heard how the Lord had shown great mercy on her, and they rejoiced with her.
59. And it came to pass, that on the eighth day, they came to circumcise the child; and they called him Zacharias, after the name of his father.
60. But his mother answered and said not so; for he will be called John.
61. Then they said to her, none of your relatives is called by this name.
62. So, they made signs to his father, how he would have him called.
63. Then he asked for a writing tablet, and wrote, saying, his name is John. And they all marveled.
64. Immediately his mouth was opened, and his tongue loosed, and he spoke, and praised God!
65. And fear came on all that dwelt around them: and all these sayings were reported abroad throughout all the hill country of Judea.
66. So, they all that heard them kept them in their hearts, saying, what manner of child will this be? And the hand of the Lord was with him.
67. And his father Zacharias was filled with the Holy Spirit, and prophesied, saying,
68. Blessed be the Lord God of Israel; for He has visited and redeemed His people,
69. And has raised up a horn of salvation for us in the house of His servant David;
70. As He spoke through the mouth of His holy prophets since the Old Covenant Age began:
71. That we should be saved from our enemies, and from the hand of all that hate us;
72. To perform the mercy promised to our fathers, and to remember His holy covenant;
73. The oath which He swore to our father Abraham,
74. That He would grant to us, that we being delivered out of the hand of our enemies, may serve Him without fear,

75. In holiness and righteousness before Him, all the days of our life.

76. And you, child, will be called the prophet of the Highest: for you will go before the face of the Lord to prepare His ways;

77. To give knowledge of salvation to His people by the forgiveness of their sins,

78. Through the tender mercy of our God; with which the rising sun from on high has visited us,

79. To give light to them that sit in darkness and in the shadow of death, to guide our feet into the way of peace.

80. So, the Child grew, and grew strong in spirit, and was in deserted places until the day of His appearance to Israel.

Chapter 2

1. And in those days, Caesar Augustus issued a decree that a census should be taken of the Roman world.

2. This census first took place when Cyrenius was governor of Syria.

3. And all went to be registered, everyone into his own city.

4. And Joseph also went up from Galilee, out of the city of Nazareth, into Judea, to the city of David, which is called Bethlehem; because he was of the house and lineage of David:

5. To be registered with Mary his espoused wife, being great with Child.

6. And so it was, that, while they were there, the days were completed that she should be delivered.

7. And she brought out her firstborn Son and wrapped Him in swaddling clothes and laid him in a manger because there was no room for them in the inn.

8. So, there were in the same country shepherds living in the fields, keeping watch over their flock by night.

9. Now, behold, the angel of the Lord stood over them, and the glory of the Lord shone around them: and they were intensely afraid.

10. But the angel said to them, fear not: for, behold, I bring you good tidings of great joy, which will be to all the people.

11. For to you is born this day in the city of David a Savior, who is Christ the Lord.

12. For this will be a sign to you; you will find the baby wrapped in swaddling clothes, lying in a manger.

13. Suddenly there was with the angel a multitude of the heavenly host praising God, and saying,

14. Glory to God in the highest, and upon earth peace, His good pleasure in man.

15. And it came to pass, as the angels had gone away from them into heaven, the shepherds said to one another, let us even now go to Bethlehem, and see this thing which has come to pass, which the Lord has made known to us.

16. So, they came with haste and found Mary, and Joseph, and the baby lying in a manger.

17. When they had seen Him, they made known abroad the saying which was told them concerning this Child.

18. Then all they that heard it wondered at those things which were told them by the shepherds.

19. But Mary treasured all these things and pondered them in her heart.
20. And the shepherds returned, glorifying and praising God for all the things that they had heard and seen, as it was told to them.
21. So, when eight days were accomplished for the circumcising of the Child, His name was called JESUS and that is the name given by the angel before He was conceived in the womb.
22. So, when the days of her purification according to the Law of Moses were accomplished, they brought Him to Jerusalem, to present Him to the Lord;
23. As it is written in the Law of the LORD, every male that opens the womb will be called holy to the Lord;)
24. And to offer a sacrifice according to that which is said in the Law of the Lord, A pair of doves, or two young pigeons.
25. Now, behold, there was a man in Jerusalem, whose name was Simeon; and the same man was just and devout, waiting for the Consolation of Israel: and the Holy Spirit was upon him.
26. For it was revealed to him by the Holy Spirit, that he should not see death before he had seen the Lord's Christ.
27. So, he came by the Spirit into the temple: and when the parents brought in the Child Jesus, to do for Him according to the custom of the Law,
28. Then he received Him up in his arms, and blessed God, and said,
29. Lord, now let Your servant depart in peace, according to Your word:
30. For my eyes have seen Your salvation, which You have prepared before the face of all people;
31. A light to bring revelation to the nations, and the glory of Your people Israel.
32. And Joseph and His mother marveled at those things which were spoken about Him.
33. So, Simeon blessed them, and said to Mary His mother, behold, this Child is destined for the fall and resurrection of many in Israel;
34. And for a sign which will be contradicted;
35. (Yes, a sword will go through your own soul also) that the thoughts of many hearts may have the veil removed.
36. And there was one Anna, a prophetess, the daughter of Phanuel, of the tribe of Asher: she was of a great age, and had lived with a husband seven years from her virginity;
37. And she was then a widow until the age of eighty-four, who departed not from the temple, but with divine service to God in fasting's and prayers night and day.
38. Then as she stood by herself acknowledged with thanksgiving to the Lord and spoke of Him to all them that expected to receive redemption in Jerusalem.
39. And when they had performed all things according to the Law of the Lord, they returned into Galilee, to their own city Nazareth.
40. So, the Child grew, and grew strong in spirit, filled with wisdom: and the grace of God was upon Him.

41. Now his parents went to Jerusalem every year at the Feast of the Passover.

42. And when He was twelve years old, they went up to Jerusalem after the custom of the feast.

43. When they had fulfilled the days, as they returned, the Child Jesus stayed behind in Jerusalem; and Joseph and his mother did not know it.

44. But they, supposing Him to have been in their company, went a day's journey; and they sought Him among their relatives and friends.

45. When they did not find Him, they returned to Jerusalem, seeking Him.

46. And it came to pass, that after three days they found Him in the temple, sitting among the teachers, both hearing them and asking them questions.

47. For all that heard Him were astonished at His understanding and answers.

48. When they saw Him, they were amazed: and His mother said to him, Son, why have you done this to us? Look, your father and I have sought You in distress.

49. But He said to them, why did you seek Me? Did you not know that I must be about My Father's business?

50. And they did not understand the saying which He spoke to them.

51. So, He went down with them, and came to Nazareth, and was obedient to them: but His mother kept all these sayings in her heart.

52. For Jesus increased in wisdom and stature and in favor with God and man.

Chapter 3

1. Now in the fifteenth year of the reign of Tiberius Caesar, Pontius Pilate being governor of Judea, Herod being tetrarch of Galilee, and his brother Philip tetrarch of Ituraea and of the region of Trachonitis, and Lysanias the tetrarch of Abilene,

2. Annas and Caiaphas being the high priests, the word of God came to John the son of Zacharias in the wilderness.

3. Then he came into all the country around the Jordan, preaching the baptism of repentance for the forgiveness of sins;

4. As it is written in the book of the words of Isaiah the prophet, saying, the voice of one crying in the wilderness, prepare you the way of the Lord, make His paths straight.

5. Every valley will be filled, and every mountain and hill will be leveled, and the crooked will be straightened, and the rough ways will be made smooth;

6. And all flesh will see the salvation of God.

7. Then he said to the multitude that came out to be immersed by him, O generation of vipers, who has warned you to flee from the wrath about to come?

8. Therefore, bring forth fruits worthy of repentance, and begin not to say inside yourselves, we have Abraham as our father: for I say to you, that God is able of these stones to raise up children to Abraham.

9. Now also the axe is laid to the root of the trees: Therefore, every tree which does not bring forth good fruit is cut down and cast into the fire.

10. Then the people asked him, saying, what will we do then?
11. He answered and said to them, He that has two coats, let him give to him that has none; and he that has food, let him do likewise.
12. Then also came tax collectors to be immersed, and said to him, Master, what will we do?
13. And he said to them, exact no more than that which is appointed you.
14. And the soldiers likewise demanded of him, saying, and what will we do? And he said to them, do violence to no man, do not accuse anyone falsely; and be content with your wages.
15. So as the people were in expectation, and all men reasoned in their hearts of John, whether he was the Christ, or not;
16. John answered, saying to them all, I indeed immerse you with water; but one mightier than I comes, whose sandal strap I am not worthy to untie: He will immerse you with the Holy Spirit and with fire:
17. Whose fan is in His hand, for He will thoroughly purge His floor, and will gather the wheat into His barn; but the chaff He will burn with unquenchable fire.
18. Then with many other exhortations he preached to the people.
19. But Herod the tetrarch, being rebuked by him for Herodias his brother Philip's wife, and for all the evils which Herod had done,
20. Added yet this above all, that he put John in prison.
21. Now when all the people were immersed, it came to pass, that Jesus also being immersed, and praying, that heaven was opened,
22. And the Holy Spirit descended in a bodily shape like a dove upon Him, and a voice came from heaven, which said, You are My beloved Son; in You, I am well pleased.
23. And Jesus Himself began to be about thirty years of age, being (as was supposed) the son of Joseph, who was the son of Heli,
24. Who was the son of Matthat, who was the son of Levi, who was the son of Melchi, who was the son of Janna, who was the son of Joseph,
25. Who was the son of Mattathias, who was the son of Amos, who was the son of Nahum, who was the son of Esli, who was the son of Naggai,
26. Who was the son of Maath, who was the son of Mattathias, who was the son of Semein, who was the son of Joseph, who was the son of Judah,
27. Who was the son of Joanna, who was the son of Rhesa, who was the son of Zerubbabel, who was the son of Salathiel, who was the son of Neri,
28. Who was the son of Melchi, who was the son of Addi, who was the son of Cosam, who was the son of Elmodam, who was the son of Er,
29. Who was the son of Joshua, who was the son of Eliezer, who was the son of Jorim, who was the son of Matthat, who was the son of Levi,
30. Who was the son of Simeon, who was the son of Judah, who was the son of Joseph, who was the son of Jonam, who was the son of Eliakim,

31. Who was the son of Melea, who was the son of Menna, who was the son of Mattatha, who was the son of Nathan, who was the son of David,
32. Who was the son of Jesse, who was the son of Obed, who was the son of Boaz, who was the son of Salmon, who was the son of Naasson,
33. Who was the son of Aminadab, who was the son of Aram, who was the son of Hezrom, who was the son of Pharez, who was the son of Judah,
34. Who was the son of Jacob, which was the son of Isaac, who was the son of Abraham, who was the son of Terah, who was the son of Nachor,
35. Who was the son of Serug, who was the son of Reu, who was the son of Peleg, who was the son of Eber, who was the son of Nahor,
36. Who was the son of Cainan, who was the son of Arphaxad, who was the son of Shem, who was the son of Noah, who was the son of Lamech,
37. Who was the son of Methuselah, who was the son of Enoch, who was the son of Jared, who was the son of Maleleel, who was the son of Cainan,
38. Who was the son of Enosh, who was the son of Seth, who was the son of Adam, who was the son of God.

Chapter 4

1. And Jesus being full of the Holy Spirit returned from the Jordan, and was led by the Spirit into the wilderness,
2. Being forty days tempted by the devil. And in those days, He did not eat anything: and when they were finished, He afterward became hungry.
3. Then the devil said to him, if you are the Son of God, command this stone that it be made bread.
4. And Jesus answered him, saying, it is written, that man will not live by bread alone, but by every word of God.
5. Then the devil, taking Him up on a high mountain showed Him all the kingdoms of the Roman world at a point in time.
6. And the devil said to Him, all this power will I give You and the glory of them: for that is delivered to me; and to whomever I will, I give it.
7. Therefore, if You will worship me, all will be Yours.
8. But Jesus answered and said to him, get behind Me, Satan: for it is written, you will worship the Lord your God, and Him only will you serve.
9. So, he brought Him to Jerusalem and set Him on a pinnacle of the temple and said to Him, if you are the Son of God, cast yourself down from here:
10. For it is written, He will give His angels charge over You, to protect You:
11. And in their hands they will bear You up unless at any time You strike Your foot against a stone.
12. But Jesus answered and said to him, it is said, you will not tempt the Lord your God.
13. When the devil had finished every temptation, he departed from Him for an appropriate season.

14. Then Jesus returned in the power of the Spirit to Galilee: and there went out a fame of Him through all the surrounding region.
15. And He taught in their synagogues, being glorified by all.
16. Then He came to Nazareth, where He had been brought up: and, as His custom was, He went into the synagogue on the Sabbath day and stood up to read.
17. So, there was handed to Him the book of the prophet Isaiah. And when He had opened the book, He found the place where it was written,
18. The Spirit of the Lord is upon Me because He has anointed Me to preach the gospel to the poor; He has sent Me to heal the broken-hearted, to preach deliverance to the captives, and recovery of sight to the blind, to set free into forgiveness those who are oppressed,
19. To proclaim the acceptable year of the Lord.
20. As He closed the book, He gave it again to the attendant and sat down. And the eyes of all them that were in the synagogue were fastened on Him.
21. And He began to say to them, today this Scripture is fulfilled in your ears.
22. And all bore Him witness and wondered at the gracious words which proceeded out of His mouth. And they said, is not this Joseph's son?
23. Then He said to them, you will surely say to Me this proverb, physician, heal yourself: whatever we have heard done in Capernaum, do also here in your country.
24. And He said, truthfully, I say to you, no prophet is accepted in his own country.
25. But I tell you truly, many widows were in Israel in the days of Elijah, when the heaven was shut up three years and six months when great famine was throughout all the land;
26. But to none of them was Elijah sent, except to Zarepheth, a city of Sidon, to a woman that was a widow.
27. And many lepers were in Israel in the time of Elisha the prophet; and none of them was cleansed, except Naaman the Syrian.
28. And all they in the synagogue, when they heard these things, were filled with rage,
29. And rose up, and thrust Him out of the city, and led Him to the edge of the hill on which their city was built, that they might cast Him down headlong.
30. But He passing through the midst of them went His way,
31. And came down to Capernaum, a city of Galilee, and taught them on the Sabbath days.
32. And they were astonished at His teaching: for His word was with authority.
33. For in the synagogue there was a man, which had a spirit of an unclean demon, and cried out with a loud voice,
34. Saying, let us alone; what have we to do with You, Jesus of Nazareth? Have You come to destroy us? I know who You are; the Holy One of God!
35. But Jesus rebuked him, saying, hold your peace, and come out of him. And when the demon had thrown him in the midst, it came out of him and did not hurt him.

36. Then, they were all amazed, and spoke among themselves, saying, what word is this! For with authority and power, He commands the unclean spirits, and they come out.

37. So, the fame of Him went out into every place of the surrounding country.

38. And He arose out of the synagogue and entered into Simon's house. And Simon's wife's mother was sick with a high fever, and they sought Him for her.

39. And He stood over her and rebuked the fever, and it left her: and immediately she arose and served them.

40. Now, when the sun was setting, all they that had any sick with various diseases brought them to Him; and He laid His hands on each one of them and healed them.

41. And demons also came out of many, crying out, and saying, you are the Christ, the Son of God! But He rebuked them and permitted them not to speak for they knew that He was the Christ.

42. When it was day, He departed and went into a deserted place: and the people sought Him, and came to Him, and restrained Him that He should not depart from them.

43. But He said to them, I must preach the kingdom of God to other cities also: for this purpose, I have been sent.

44. And He preached in the synagogues of Galilee.

Chapter 5

1. And it came to pass, that as the people pressed on Him to hear the word of God, He stood by the lake of Gennesaret,

2. And saw two boats standing by the lake: but the fishermen were not in them but were washing their nets.

3. So, He entered into one of the boats, which was Simon's, and asked him to push out a little from the land. And He sat down and taught the people from the boat.

4. When He was done speaking, He said to Simon, launch out into the deep, and let down your nets for a catch.

5. Simon answered and said to Him, Master, we have worked all night, and have caught nothing: nevertheless at Your word, I will let down the net.

6. When they had this done, they caught a great multitude of fish: and their net broke.

7. Then they signaled to their partners, who were in the other boat, that they should come and help them. And they came and filled both the boats so that they began to sink!

8. When Simon Peter saw it, he fell down at Jesus' knee, and said, depart from me; for I am a sinful man, O Lord.

9. For he was astonished, and all that were with him, at the catch of fish which they had caught:

10. So, also were James, and John, the sons of Zebedee, who were partners with Simon. But Jesus said to Simon fear not; from now on you will be catching men.

11. When they had brought their boats to land, they left all and followed Him.

12. And it came to pass, when He was in a certain city, behold a man full of leprosy: who seeing Jesus fell on His face, and sought Him, saying, Lord, if You will, you can make me clean.

13. And He put out His hand, and touched him, having said, I will: you are clean. Immediately the leprosy left him.
14. And He charged him to tell no man: but go, and show yourself to the priest, and offer for your cleansing, according as Moses commanded, for a testimony to them.
15. But so much more went there a fame abroad of Him: and great multitudes came together to hear, and to be healed by Him of their sicknesses.
16. So, He withdrew Himself to the wilderness and prayed.
17. And it came to pass on a certain day, as He was teaching, that there were Pharisees and teachers of the Law sitting by, who had come out of every town of Galilee, and Judea, and Jerusalem: and the power of the Lord was present to heal them.
18. Now, behold, men brought on a bed a man who was a paralytic: and they sought means to bring him in, and to lay him before Him.
19. But when they could not find by what way they might bring him in because of the multitude, they went on the housetop and let him down through the tiles with his mat into the midst before Jesus.
20. When He saw their faith, He said to him, man, your sins are forgiven!
21. So, the scribes and the Pharisees began to reason, saying, who is this who speaks blasphemies? Who can forgive sins, but God alone?
22. But when Jesus perceived their thoughts, He answered and said to them, why are you reasoning in your hearts?
23. Which is easier, to say, your sins be forgiven; or to say, rise up and walk?
24. But that you may know that the Son of man has authority on earth to forgive sins, (He said to the paralytic,) I say to you, arise, and take up your mat, and go into your house.
25. Immediately he rose up before them and took up that which he had been lying on, and left to his own house, glorifying God.
26. And they were all amazed and glorified God, and were filled with terror, saying, we have seen incomprehensible things today!
27. After these things He went out, and saw a tax collector, named Levi, sitting at the tax booth: and He said to him, follow Me.
28. Then he left all, rose up, and followed Him.
29. And Levi made Him a great feast in his own house: and there was a great company of tax collectors and of others that sat down with them.
30. But their scribes and Pharisees murmured against His disciples, saying, why do you eat and drink with tax collectors and sinners?
31. Then Jesus answered and said to them, they that are healthy do not need a doctor; but they that are sick.
32. I came not to call the righteous, but sinners to repentance.
33. So, they said to Him, why do the disciples of John fast often, and make prayers, and likewise the disciples of the Pharisees; but Yours eat and drink?
34. So, He said to them, can you make the guests of the bridegroom fast, while the bridegroom is with them?

35. But the days will come, when the bridegroom will be taken away from them, and then will they fast in those days.

36. And He spoke also a parable to them; no man puts a piece of a new garment on an old; or else, then the new makes a tear, and the piece that was taken out of the new does not agree with the old.

37. And no man puts fresh wine into old wineskins; else the fresh wine will burst the skins, and be spilled, and the skins will be destroyed.

38. But fresh wine must be put into fresh wineskins, and both are protected.

39. No man also that has drunk age-old wine immediately desires new: for he says, the old is better.

Chapter 6

1. And it came to pass on the second Sabbath after the first, that He went through the corn fields; and His disciples plucked the ears of corn, and did eat, rubbing them in their hands.

2. And certain of the Pharisees said to them, why do You do that which is not lawful to do on the Sabbaths?

3. Then Jesus answered them and said, have you not read so much as this, what David did when himself being hungry, and they who were with him;

4. How he went into the house of God, and did take and eat the loaves of the Presence, and gave also to them that were with him; which it is not lawful to eat but for the priests alone?

5. And He said to them, that the Son of man is Lord also of the Sabbath.

6. And it came to pass also on another Sabbath that He entered into the synagogue and taught: and there was a man whose right hand was withered.

7. So, the scribes and Pharisees watched Him, whether He would heal on the Sabbath day; that they might find an accusation against Him.

8. But He knew their thoughts and said to the man who had the withered hand, rise up, and stand out in the midst. And he arose and stood out.

9. Then said Jesus to them, I will ask you one thing; is it lawful on the Sabbath days to do good, or to do evil, to save life, or to destroy it?

10. Then looking around at them all, He said to the man, stretch out your hand. And he did so: and his hand was restored whole as the other.

11. And they were filled with angry madness and talked with one another about what they might do to Jesus.

12. And it came to pass in those days, that He went out to a mountain to pray and continued all night in prayer to God.

13. When it was day, He called to Him His disciples: and of them He chose twelve, whom also He named apostles;

14. Simon, whom he also named Peter, and Andrew his brother, James and John, Philip and Bartholomew,

15. Matthew and Thomas, James the son of Alphaeus, and Simon called Zelotes,

16. And Judas the brother of James, and Judas Iscariot, who also was the traitor.

17. Then He came down with them and stood in the plain, and the company of His disciples, and a great multitude of people out of all Judea and Jerusalem, and from the seacoast of Tyre and Sidon, who came to hear Him, and to be healed of their diseases;
18. And they that were troubled with unclean spirits: and they were healed.
19. For the whole multitude sought to touch Him: for there went power out of Him and healed them all.
20. Then He lifted up His eyes on His disciples, and said, blessed be the poor: for yours is the kingdom of God.
21. Blessed are you that hunger now: for you will be filled. Blessed are you that weep now: for you will laugh.
22. Blessed are you, when men will hate you, and when they will exclude you from their company, and will revile you, and cast out your name as evil, for the Son of man's sake.
23. Rejoice in that day, and leap for joy! For, behold, your reward is great in heaven: for in like manner their fathers did to the prophets.
24. But woe to you that are rich! For you have received your comfort.
25. Woe to you that are full! For you will hunger. Woe to you that laugh now! For you will mourn and weep.
26. Woe to you, when all men shall speak well of you! For so their fathers did to the false prophets.
27. But I say to you who hear, love your enemies, do good to them who hate you,
28. Bless them that curse you and pray for them who spitefully use you.
29. And to him that strikes you on the one cheek offer also the other; and him that takes away your cloak forbid not to take your coat also.
30. Give to every man that asks of you, and of him that takes away your goods do not demand them back.
31. And as you would that men should do to you, do you also to them likewise.
32. For if you love those who love you, what reward do you have? For sinners also love those who love them.
33. And if you do good to those who do good to you, what reward do you have? For sinners also do even the same.
34. And if you lend to them of whom you hope to receive, what reward do you have? For sinners also lend to sinners, to receive as much again.
35. But love your enemies, and do good, and lend, hoping for nothing back; and your reward will be great, and you will be the sons of the Highest: for He is kind even to the unthankful and to the evil.
36. Therefore, be merciful as your Father also is merciful.
37. Judge not, and you will not be judged: condemn not, and you will not be condemned: forgive, and you will be forgiven:
38. Give, and it will be given to you; good measure, pressed down, and shaken together, and running over, will men give into your bosom. For with the same measure that you use it will be measured back to you again.
39. And He spoke a parable to them, can the blind lead the blind? Will they not both fall into a pit?

40. The disciple is not above his master: but everyone mature will be as his master.
41. And why do you behold the speck that is in your brother's eye, but perceive not the beam that is in your own eye?
42. How can you say to your brother, Brother, let me pull out the splinter that is in your eye when you behold not the joist that is in your own eye? You hypocrite, take out first the joist out of your own eye, and then will you see clearly to pull out the splinter that is in your brother's eye.
43. For a good tree does not bring forth bad fruit; neither does a bad tree bring forth good fruit.
44. For every tree is known by its own fruit. For of thorns men do not gather figs, nor of a thorn bush do they gather grapes.
45. A good man out of the good treasure of his heart brings out that which is good; and an evil man out of the evil treasure of his heart brings out that which is evil: for of the abundance of the heart his mouth speaks.
46. And why do you call me, Lord, Lord, and do not the things which I say?
47. Whoever comes to Me, and hears My sayings, and does them, I will show you to who he is like:
48. He is like a man which built a house, and dug deep, and laid the foundation on a rock: and when the flood arose, the stream beat repeatedly on that house and could not shake it: for it was founded on a rock.
49. But he that hears and does not, is like a man that without a foundation built a house on the sand; which the stream did burst against it, and immediately it fell, and the ruin of that house was great.

Chapter 7

1. Now when He had finished all His sayings in the audience of the people, He entered into Capernaum.
2. And a certain centurion's servant, who was dear to him, was sick, and about to die.
3. When he heard of Jesus, he sent to Him the elders of the Jews, begging Him that He would come and heal his servant.
4. When they came to Jesus, they sought Him instantly, saying, that he was worthy for whom he should do this:
5. For he loves our nation, and he has built us a synagogue.
6. Then Jesus went with them. When He was now not far from the house, the centurion sent friends to Him, saying to him, Lord, trouble not Yourself: for I am not worthy that you should enter under my roof:
7. Therefore, neither thought I worthy to come to You: but say the word and my servant will be healed.
8. For I also am a man set under authority, having under me soldiers, and I say to one, Go, and he goes; and to another, Come, and he comes; and to my servant, do this, and he does it.

9. When Jesus heard these things, He marveled at him, and turned around, and said to the people that followed Him, I say to you, I have not found such great faith, not even in Israel!
10. Then they that were sent, returning to the house, found the servant healthy that had been sick.
11. And it came to pass the day after, that He went into a city called Nain; and many of His disciples went with Him, and many people.
12. Now when He came close to the gate of the city, behold, there was a dead man carried out, the only son of his mother, and she was a widow: and many people of the city were with her.
13. When the Lord saw her, He had compassion on her, and said to her, weep not.
14. Then He came and touched the open coffin: and they that carried him stood still. And He said, Young man, I say to you, Arise.
15. So, he that was dead sat up, and began to speak. And He delivered him to his mother.
16. And there came a fear on all: and they glorified God, saying, that a great prophet is risen up among us; and, that God has visited His people!
17. And this report of Him went out throughout all Judea, and the entire surrounding region.
18. And the disciples of John showed him of all these things.
19. So, John called to him two of his disciples and sent them to Jesus, and said, are you He that should come, or do we look for another?
20. When the men had come to Him, they said, John the Baptist has sent us to You saying, are you He that should come, or do we look for another?
21. And in that same hour He cured many of their infirmities and sicknesses, and of evil spirits; and to many that were blind He gave sight.
22. Then Jesus began to say to them, go your way, and tell John what things you have seen and heard; that the blind see, the lame walk, the lepers are cleansed, the deaf hear, the dead are raised, to the poor the gospel is preached.
23. And blessed is he who is not stumbled in Me.
24. So, when the messengers of John departed, He began to speak to the people concerning John, what went you out into the wilderness to see? A reed shaken by the wind?
25. But what went you out for to see? A man clothed in fine clothing? Behold, they who are gorgeously appareled, and live luxuriously, are in kings' courts.
26. But what went you out for to see? A prophet? Yes, I say to you, and much more than a prophet.
27. This is he, of whom it is written, behold, I send My messenger before Your face, who will prepare Your way before You.
28. For I say to you, among those that are born of women there is no one greater than John the Baptist: but he that is least in the kingdom of God is greater than he.
29. And all the people that heard Him, and the tax collectors, justified God, being immersed with the baptism of John.

30. But the Pharisees and lawyers rejected the counsel of God against themselves, not being immersed by him.

31. And the Lord said, what then will I compare the men of this generation, and what are they like?

32. They are like children sitting in the marketplace, and calling one to another, and saying, we played the flute for you, and you did not dance; we mourned to you, and you did not weep.

33. For John the Baptist came neither eating bread nor drinking wine; and you said, he has a demon.

34. The Son of man comes eating and drinking, and you said, behold a gluttonous man, and a drunkard, a friend of tax collectors and sinners!

35. But wisdom is justified by all her children.

36. And one of the Pharisees wanted Him to eat with him. And He went into the Pharisee's house and sat down to eat.

37. And, behold, a woman in the city, who was a sinner, when she knew that Jesus sat to eat in the Pharisee's house, brought an alabaster box of ointment,

38. And stood at His feet behind him weeping, and began to wash His feet with tears, and did wipe them with the hairs of her head, and was kissing His feet, and anointed them with the ointment.

39. Now when the Pharisee who had invited Him saw it, he spoke within himself, saying, this man, if He were a prophet, would have known who and what manner of woman this is that touches Him: for she is a sinner.

40. Then Jesus answered and said to him, Simon, I have something to say to you. And he said, Master, say on.

41. There was a certain creditor who had two debtors: the one owed five hundred denarii, and the other fifty.

42. When they had nothing to pay, he frankly forgave them both. Therefore, tell me, which of them will love him most?

43. Simon answered and said, I suppose he to whom he forgave most. Then He said to him, you have rightly judged.

44. And he turned to the woman, and said to Simon, see this woman? I entered into your house, and you gave me no water for My feet: but she has washed My feet with tears and wiped them with the hair of her head.

45. You gave me no kiss: but this woman, since the time I came in, has not stopped kissing My feet.

46. My head with oil you did not anoint: but this woman has anointed My feet with ointment.

47. Therefore, I say to you, her sins, which are many, are forgiven; for she loves much: but to whom little is forgiven, the same loves little.

48. And He said to her, your sins are forgiven.

49. Then they that sat to eat with Him began to say within themselves, who is this that forgives sins also?

50. And He said to the woman, your faith has saved you; go in peace.

Chapter 8

1. And it came to pass afterward, that He went throughout every city and village, preaching and showing the good news of the kingdom of God: and the twelve were with Him,
2. And certain women, who had been healed of evil spirits and sicknesses, Mary called Magdalene, out of whom went seven demons,
3. And Joanna the wife of Chuza Herod's steward, and Susanna, and many others, who provided for Him out of their possessions.
4. When many people had gathered together and had come to Him out of every city, He spoke by a parable:
5. A sower went out to sow his seed: and as he sowed, some fell beside the way, and it was stepped on, and the birds of the air devoured it.
6. And some fell on rock; and as soon as it sprang up, it withered away, because it lacked moisture.
7. And some fell among thorns, and the thorns sprang up with it and choked it.
8. But others fell on good ground and sprang up and produced fruit a hundred-fold. When He had said these things, He called out, He that has ears to hear, let him hear!
9. And His disciples asked Him, saying, what may this parable mean?
10. So, He said, to you, it is given to know the mysteries of the kingdom of God: but to others in parables; that seeing they might not see and hearing they might not understand.
11. Now, the parable is this: the seed is the word of God.
12. Those beside the way are they that hear; then comes the devil, and takes away the word out of their hearts, unless they should believe and be saved.
13. They on the rock are they, who, when they hear, receive the word with joy; and these have no root who for a season believe, but in time of temptation fall away.
14. And that which fell among thorns are they, who, when they have heard, go out, and are choked with the cares and riches and pleasures of this life, and bring no fruit to maturity.
15. But that on the good ground are they, which in a noble and good heart, having heard the word, keep it, and bring forth fruit with patience.
16. No man, when he has lit a candle, covers it with a bowl, or puts it under a bed; but sets it on a candlestick, that they which enter in may see the light.
17. For nothing is secret, that will not be made manifest; neither anything hidden, that will not be known and come out into the open.
18. Therefore, take heed how you hear: for whoever has, to him will be given; and whoever has not, from him will be taken away even that which he seems to have.
19. Then came to Him His mother and His brothers and could not come to Him because of the crowd.
20. And it was told Him by some who said, Your mother and Your brothers stand outside, wanting to see You.

21. And He answered and said to them, My mother and My brothers are these who hear the word of God and do it.

22. Now it came to pass on a certain day, that He went into a boat with His disciples: and He said to them, let us cross to the other side of the lake. And they launched out.

23. But as they sailed He fell asleep: and there came down a storm of wind on the lake, and they were filled with water, and were in danger.

24. So, they came to Him, and woke Him, and said, Master, Master, we are perishing. Then He arose and rebuked the wind and the raging of the water: and they stopped, and there was a calm.

25. Then He said to them, where is your faith? And they being afraid wondered, saying one to another, what manner of man is this? For He commands even the winds and water, and they obey Him!

26. And they arrived at the country of the Gadarenes, which is opposite Galilee.

27. When He went out to land, there met Him out of the city a certain man, who had demons for a long time and wore no clothes, neither lived in any house, but in the tombs.

28. When he saw Jesus, he cried out and fell down before Him, and with a loud voice said, what have I to do with You, Jesus, You Son of God most high? I beg You, do not torment me!

29. For He had commanded the unclean spirit to come out of the man. For oftentimes it had taken him: and he was kept bound with chains and in shackles, but he broke the bonds and was driven by the demons into the wilderness.

30. Then Jesus asked him, and said, what is your name? And he said, Legion: because many demons had entered him.

31. So, they begged Him that He would not command them to go out into the abyss.

32. There was a herd of many pigs feeding on the mountain: and they begged Him that He would permit them to enter into them. And He permitted them.

33. Then went the demons out of the man and entered into the pigs: and the herd ran violently down the slope into the lake and drowned.

34. When they that fed them saw what was done, they fled and went and told it in the city, and in the country.

35. Then they went out to see what was done; and came to Jesus, and found the man, out of who the demons had left, sitting at the feet of Jesus, clothed, and in his right mind: and they were afraid.

36. They also who saw it told them by what means he that was possessed of the demons was healed.

37. Then the whole multitude of the surrounding country of the Gadarenes begged Him to depart from them; for they were taken with great fear: and He went up into the boat and returned.

38. Now the man out of whom the demons were departed begged Him that he may stay with Him: but Jesus sent him away, and said,

39. Return to your own house and show what great things God has done to you. So, he went his way and announced throughout the whole city what great things Jesus had done to him.

40. It came to pass that when Jesus returned, the people gladly received Him: for they were all waiting for Him.
41. Now, behold, there came a man named Jairus, and he was a ruler of the synagogue: and he fell down at Jesus' feet, and begged Him that he would come into his house:
42. For he had one only daughter, about twelve years of age, and she lay dying. But as He went the people crushed Him.
43. And a woman having a flow of blood twelve years, who had spent all her money on physicians, neither could be healed by any,
44. Came behind Him and touched the edge of His cloak: and immediately her flow of blood stopped.
45. And Jesus said, who touched Me? When all denied, Peter and they that were with him said, Master, the multitude holds on to You and press You, yet You say, who touched Me?
46. Yet Jesus said somebody has touched Me: for I perceive that power is gone out of Me.
47. When the woman saw that she was not hidden, she came trembling and falling down before Him, she declared to Him before all the people for what reason she had touched Him, and how she was healed immediately.
48. He said to her, daughter, be of good comfort: your faith has made you healthy; go in peace.
49. While He yet spoke, there came one from the ruler of the synagogue's house, saying to Him, your daughter is dead, trouble not the Master.
50. But when Jesus heard it, He answered him, and said, fear not: only believe, and she will be made healthy.
51. When He came into the house, He permitted no man to go in, except Peter, James, and John, and the father and the mother of the girl.
52. For all wept, and mourned her: but He said, weep not; she is not dead but sleeps.
53. But they laughed Him to scorn, knowing she was dead.
54. And He put them all out and took her by the hand, and called, saying, child, arise.
55. And her spirit returned, and she arose immediately: and He commanded to give her food.
56. And her parents were astonished: but He charged them that they should tell no man what was done.

Chapter 9

1. Then He called His twelve disciples together, and gave them power and authority over all demons, and to cure diseases.
2. And He sent them to preach the kingdom of God, and to heal the sick.
3. For He said to them, take nothing for your journey, neither staff nor bags, neither bread, neither money; neither have an extra tunic.
4. And whatever house you enter into stay there and from there depart.
5. For whoever will not receive you, when you go out of that city, shake off the very dust from your feet for a testimony against them.

6. Then they departed, and went through the towns, preaching the gospel, and healing everywhere.
7. Now Herod the tetrarch heard of all that was done by Him: and he was perplexed because it was said of some, that John had risen from the dead;
8. And of some, that Elijah had appeared; and of others, that one of the old prophets was risen again.
9. But Herod said, John have I beheaded: but who is this, of whom I hear such things? And he wanted to see Him.
10. And the apostles, when they had returned, told Him all that they had done. And He took them and went aside secretly into a deserted place belonging to the city called Bethsaida.
11. So, the people, when they knew it, followed Him: and He received them, and spoke to them of the kingdom of God, and healed them that needed healing.
12. When the day began to wear away then came the twelve, and said to Him, Send the multitude away, that they may go into the towns and surrounding country, and sleep, and get provisions: for we are here in a deserted place.
13. But He said to them, give them something to eat. And they said, we have no more but five loaves and two fish; unless we should go and buy food for all these people.
14. For they were about five thousand men. And He said to His disciples, make them sit down in groups of fifties.
15. And they did so and made them all sit down.
16. Then He took the five loaves and the two fish, and looking up to heaven, He blessed them, and broke, and gave to the disciples to place before the multitude.
17. Then they did eat and were all filled: and twelve baskets of fragments that remained there were taken up by them.
18. And it came to pass, as He was alone praying, His disciples were with Him: and He asked them, saying, who do the people say that I am?
19. They answered and said, John the Baptist; but some say, Elijah; and others say, that one of the old prophets is risen again.
20. He said to them, but who do you say that I am? Peter answered and said, the Christ of God!
21. And He strictly instructed them and commanded them to tell no man that thing;
22. Saying, the Son of man must suffer many things, and be rejected by the elders and chief priests and scribes, and be killed, and be raised the third day.
23. And He said to them all if anyone will come after Me, let him deny himself, and take up his cross daily, and follow Me.
24. For whoever will save his life will lose it: but whoever will lose his life for My sake, the same will save it.
25. For what is a man's advantage, if he gains the whole world, and loses himself, or is cast away?
26. For whoever will be ashamed of Me and of My words, of him will the Son of man be ashamed when He comes in His glory, and in His Father's, and of the holy angels.

27. But I tell you truly, there are some standing here, who will not taste death until they see the kingdom of God!
28. And it came to pass about eight days after these sayings, He led Peter and John and James and went up to a mountain to pray.
29. And as He prayed, the appearance of His face changed, and His clothing was white and glistening.
30. Now, behold, there talked with Him two men, who were Moses and Elijah:
31. Who appeared in glory and spoke about His death which He was about to accomplish at Jerusalem.
32. But Peter and they that were with him were heavy with sleep: and when they were awake, they saw His glory, and the two men that stood with Him.
33. And it came to pass, as they departed from Him, Peter said to Jesus, Master, it is good for us to be here: and let us make three tabernacles; one for You, and one for Moses, and one for Elijah: not knowing what he said.
34. While he was speaking, there came a cloud that overshadowed them: and they feared as they entered into the cloud.
35. And there came a voice out of the cloud, saying, this is My beloved Son: hear Him!
36. When the voice had spoken, Jesus was found alone. And they kept it a secret and told no man in those days any of those things which they had seen.
37. And it came to pass, that on the next day, when they had come down from the hill, many people met Him.
38. Now, behold, a man of the crowd cried out, saying, Master, I beg you, look on my son: for he is my only child.
39. And look, a spirit takes him, and he suddenly cries out; and it convulses him that he foams again and bruising him hardly departs from him.
40. And I asked Your disciples to cast him out, and they could not.
41. Jesus answered and said, O faithless and perverse generation, how long will I be with you, and tolerate you? Bring your son here.
42. Yet as he was coming, the demon threw him down and convulsed him. Jesus rebuked the unclean spirit and healed the child and delivered him again to his father.
43. And they were all amazed at the majesty of God. But while they wondered everyone at all the things that Jesus did, He said to His disciples,
44. Let these sayings sink down into your ears: for the Son of man is about to be delivered into the hands of men.
45. But they understood not this saying, and it was hidden from them, that they perceived it not: and they feared to ask Him about it.
46. Then there arose a reasoning among them, whom of them should be greatest.
47. And Jesus, perceiving the thought of their hearts, led a child, and placed him by Him,
48. And said to them, whoever will receive this child in My name receives Me: and whoever will receive Me receives Him that sent Me: for he that is least among you all, the same will be great.

49. So, John answered and said, Master, we saw one casting out demons in Your name; and we forbade him because he follows not with us.
50. But Jesus said to him, forbid him not: for he that is not against us is for us.
51. And it came to pass when the time had come that He should be received up, He steadfastly set His face to go to Jerusalem,
52. And sent messengers before His face: and they went, and entered into a village of the Samaritans, to make ready for Him.
53. And they did not receive Him, because His face was as though He would go to Jerusalem.
54. When His disciples James and John saw this, they said, Lord, will You that we command fire to come down from heaven, and consume them, just as Elijah did?
55. But He turned, and rebuked them, and said, you know not what manner of spirit you are of.
56. For the Son of man has not come to destroy men's lives, but to save them. And they went to another village.
57. Now it happened, that, as they went on the way, someone said to Him, Lord, I will follow You wherever You go.
58. But Jesus said to Him, foxes have holes, and birds of the air have nests; but the Son of man has nowhere to lay His head.
59. Then He said to another, follow me. But he said, Lord, permit me first to go and bury my father.
60. Jesus said to him, let the dead bury their dead: but you go and preach the kingdom of God.
61. Yet another also said, Lord, I will follow You; but let me first go say goodbye to them, who are at home at my house.
62. But Jesus said to him, no man, having put his hand to the plow, and looking back, is useful in the kingdom of God.

Chapter 10

1. After these things the Lord appointed seventy others also and sent them two by two before His face into every city and place, to where He was about to come.
2. Therefore, said He to them, the harvest truly is great, but the laborers are few: Therefore, pray to the Lord of the harvest that He would send out laborers into His harvest.
3. Go your ways: behold, I send you out as lambs among wolves.
4. Carry neither purse, nor bag, nor sandals: and greet no man on the way.
5. And into whatever house you enter, first say, peace be to this house.
6. And if a son of peace is there, your peace will rest on it: if not, it will return to you.
7. And in the same house remain, eating and drinking such things as they give: for the laborer is worthy of his hire. Go not from house to house.
8. And into whatever city you enter, and they receive you, eat such things as are placed before you:
9. And heal the sick that are in it, and say to them, the kingdom of God has come near to you.

10. But into whatever city you enter, and they receive you not, go your ways out into the streets of the same, and say,

11. Even the very dust of your city, which clings to us, we do wipe off against you: Nevertheless be sure of this, that the kingdom of God has come near to you.

12. But I say to you, that it will be more tolerable in that day for Sodom, than for that city.

13. Woe to you, Chorazin! Woe to you, Bethsaida! For if the mighty works had been done in Tyre and Sidon, which have been done in you, they had a great while ago repented, sitting in sackcloth and ashes.

14. But it will be more tolerable for Tyre and Sidon at the judgment, than for you.

15. And you, Capernaum, which are exalted to heaven, will be thrust down to the unseen realm.

16. He that hears you hears Me; and he that rejects you rejects Me, and he that rejects Me rejects Him that sent Me.

17. And the seventy returned with joy, and said, Lord, even the demons are subject to us through Your name.

18. And He said to them, I was watching closely Satan falling like lightning from the heavens.

19. Behold, I give to your authority to tread on serpents and scorpions, and over all the power of the enemy: and nothing will by any means hurt you.

20. Nevertheless, do not rejoice in this, that the spirits are subject to you; but rather rejoice, because your names are written in heaven.

21. In that hour Jesus rejoiced in spirit, and said, I thank You, O Father, Lord of heaven and earth, that you have hidden these things from the wise and prudent and have revealed them to little children: even so, Father; for so it seemed good in Your sight.

22. All things are delivered to Me by My Father: and no man knows who the Son is, but the Father; and who the Father is, but the Son, and He to whom the Son will reveal Him.

23. And He turned to His disciples and said secretly, blessed are the eyes which see the things that you see:

24. For I tell you, that many prophets and kings have desired to see the things which you see and have not seen them; and to hear those things which you hear, and have not heard them.

25. Now, behold, a certain lawyer stood up, and tested Him, saying, Master, what should I do to inherit infinite life?

26. He said to him, what is written in the Law? How do you read it?

27. And he answered and said, you will love the Lord your God with all your heart, and with all your soul, and with all your strength, and with all your mind; and your neighbor as yourself.

28. And He said to him, you have answered right: do this, and you will live.

29. But he, willing to justify himself, said to Jesus, and who is my neighbor?

30. And Jesus answering said, a certain man went down from Jerusalem to Jericho and fell among thieves, who stripped him of his clothing, and wounded him, and left, leaving him half dead.

31. And by chance there came down a certain priest that way: and when he saw him, he passed by on the other side.
32. And likewise a Levite, when he was at the place, came and looked on him, and passed by on the other side.
33. But a certain Samaritan, as he journeyed, came where he was: and when he saw him, he had compassion on him,
34. And went to him, and bound up his wounds, pouring in oil and wine, and placed him on his own animal, and brought him to an inn, and took care of him.
35. Then on the next day when he left, he took out two denarii, and gave them to the host, and said to him, take care of him; and whatever more you spend, when I return, I will repay you.
36. Who now of these three, do you think was neighbor to him that fell among the thieves?
37. And he said, he that showed mercy on him. Then said Jesus to him, go, and do likewise.
38. Now it came to pass, as they went that He entered into a certain village: and a certain woman named Martha received Him into her house.
39. And she had a sister called Mary, who also sat at Jesus' feet, and heard His word.
40. But Martha was burdened by much serving, and came to Him, and said, Lord, do you not care that my sister has left me to serve alone? Therefore, tell her to help me.
41. And Jesus answered and said to her, Martha, Martha, you are anxious and troubled about many things:
42. But one thing is necessary: and Mary has chosen that good part, which will not be taken away from her.

Chapter 11

1. And it came to pass, that, as He was praying in a certain place, when He stopped, one of His disciples said to Him, Lord, teach us to pray, as John also taught his disciples.
2. And He said to them, when you pray, say, Father, hallowed be Your name. Your kingdom come. Your will be done, on earth, as it is in heaven.
3. Give us today our daily bread.
4. And forgive us our sins; for we also forgive every one that sins against us. And lead us not into temptation but deliver us from evil.
5. And He said to them, which one of you will have a friend, and will go to him at midnight, and say to him, friend, lend me three loaves;
6. For a friend of mine in his journey has come to me, and I have nothing to place before him?
7. And he from inside will answer and say, trouble me not: the door is now shut, and my children are with me in bed; I cannot rise and give anything to you.
8. I say to you, though he will not rise and give to him, because he is his friend, yet because of his persistence he will rise and give him as much as he needs.
9. And I say to you, be asking, and it will be given you; be seeking, and you will find; be knocking, and it will be opened to you.

10. For everyone that's asking receives, and he that is seeking finds; and to him that's knocking it will be opened.

11. If a son will ask bread of any of you that is a father, will he give him a stone? Or if he asks for a fish, will he give him a serpent instead of the fish?

12. Or if he asks for an egg, will he offer him a scorpion?

13. If you then, being evil, know how to give good gifts to your children: how much more will your heavenly Father give the Holy Spirit to them that ask Him?

14. And he was casting out a demon, and it was mute. And it came to pass when the demon had gone out, the mute spoke, and the people wondered.

15. But some of them said, He casts out demons through Beelzebub the chief of the demons. 16 And others, tempting Him, sought from Him a sign from heaven.

16. But He, knowing their thoughts, said to them, every kingdom divided against itself is brought to desolation, and a house divided against itself falls.

17. If Satan also be divided against himself, how will his kingdom stand?

18. Because you say that I cast out demons by Beelzebub.

19. And if I by Beelzebub cast out demons, by who do your sons cast them out? Therefore, will they be your judges?

20. But if I with the finger of God cast out demons, then the kingdom of God has come upon you!

21. When a strong man fully armed guards his home, his possessions are safe:

22. But when a stronger than he will come upon him, and overcome him, he takes from him all his armor in which he trusted and divides his spoils.

23. He that is not with Me is against Me: and he that gathers not with Me scatters.

24. When an unclean spirit has gone out of a man, he goes through dry places, seeking rest; and finding none, he says, I will return to my house from where I came out.

25. When he comes, he finds it swept and put in order.

26. Then goes he and takes to him seven other spirits more wicked than himself, and they enter in and dwell there: and the last state of that man is worse than the first.

27. And it came to pass, as He spoke these things, a certain woman of the company lifted up her voice, and said to Him, blessed is the womb that bore You, and the breasts which nursed You!

28. But He said, more than that, blessed are they that hear the word of God, and practice it.

29. When the people were gathered thick together, He began to say, this is an evil generation: they seek a sign, and there will no sign be given it, but the sign of Jonah the prophet.

30. For as Jonah was a sign to the Ninevites, so also the Son of man will be to this generation.

31. The queen of the South will rise up in the judgment with the men of this generation and condemn them: for she came from the ends of the earth to hear the wisdom of Solomon; and behold, a greater than Solomon is here.

32. The men of Nineveh will rise up in the judgment with this generation and will condemn it: for they repented at the preaching of Jonah; and behold, a greater than Jonah is here.

33. No man, when he has lit a candle, puts it in a secret place, neither under a bowl, but on a candlestick, that they who come in may see the light.

34. The light of the body is the eye: Therefore, when your eye is single, your whole body also is full of light; but when your eye is evil, your body also is full of darkness.

35. Therefore, take heed that the light which is in you be not darkness.

36. Therefore, if your whole body be full of light, having no part dark, the total will be full of light, as when the bright shining of a candle does give you light.

37. And as He spoke, a certain Pharisee asked Him to dine with him: and He went in and sat down to eat.

38. When the Pharisee saw it, he marveled that He had not first washed before dinner.

39. But the Lord said to him, now do you Pharisees make clean the outside of the cup and the dish; but your inward part is full of greed and wickedness.

40. You fools, did not He that made that which is outside make that which is inside also?

41. But rather give from within philanthropically; and behold, all things are clean to you.

42. But woe to you, Pharisees! For you tithe mint and rue and all manner of herbs, and pass over judgment and the love of God: these you ought to have done, and not abandoning the other things.

43. Woe to you, Pharisees! For you love the uppermost seats in the synagogues, and greetings in the markets.

44. Woe to you, scribes and Pharisees, hypocrites! For you are as unmarked graves, and men who walk over them are not aware of them.

45. Then answered one of the lawyers, and said to Him, Master, these sayings insult us too.

46. And He said, woe to you also, you lawyers! For you load men with burdens difficult to bear, and you touch not the burdens with one of your fingers.

47. Woe to you! For you build the tombs of the prophets, and your fathers murdered them.

48. Truly you bear witness that you approve the deeds of your fathers: for they indeed murdered them, and you build their tombs.

49. Therefore, also said the wisdom of God, I will send them prophets and apostles, and some of them they will kill and persecute:

50. That the blood of all the prophets, which was shed because of the downfall of the world, may be required of this generation;

51. From the blood of Abel to the blood of Zacharias who perished between the altar and the temple: truthfully, I say to you, it will be required of this generation.

52. Woe to you, lawyers! For you have taken away the key of knowledge: You entered not in yourselves, and they that were entering in you hindered.

Luke 11:53

53. And as He said these things to them, the scribes and the Pharisees began to be very hostile, and to cross-examine Him about many things:
54. Laying wait for Him, and seeking to catch something out of His mouth, that they might accuse Him.

Chapter 12

1. In the meantime, when there were gathered together an innumerable multitude of people, so that they trampled one another, He began to say to His disciples first of all, beware of the leaven of the Pharisees, which is hypocrisy.
2. For there is nothing covered, that will not be revealed; nor hidden, that will not be known.
3. Therefore, whatever you have spoken in darkness will be heard in the light, and that which you have spoken in the ear in closets will be proclaimed upon the housetops.
4. And I say to you My friends, Be not afraid of them that kill the body, and after that have no more that they can do.
5. But I will show you who you will fear: fear Him, who after He has killed has the power to cast you into Gehenna; yes, I say to you, fear Him.
6. Are not five sparrows sold for two copper coins, and not one of them is forgotten by God?
7. As a matter of fact, even the very hairs of your head are all numbered. Therefore, fear not: you are of more value than many sparrows.
8. Also, I say to you, whoever will confess Me before men, of him will the Son of man also confess before the angels of God:
9. But he that denies Me before men will be denied before the angels of God.
10. And whoever will speak a word against the Son of man, it will be forgiven him: but to him that blasphemes against the Holy Spirit it will not be forgiven.
11. When they bring you to the synagogues, and the Sanhedrin and rulers, take no thought how or what thing you will answer, or what you will say:
12. For the Holy Spirit will teach you in the same hour what you ought to say.
13. And one in the crowd said to Him, Master, speak to my brother, that he divide the inheritance with me.
14. And He said to him, man, who made Me a judge or a ruler over you?
15. And He said to them, take heed, and beware of greed: for a man's life consists not in the abundance of the things which he possesses.
16. And He spoke a parable to them, saying, the ground of a certain rich man brought forth plentifully:
17. And he thought within himself, saying, what will I do because I have no room where to store my crops?
18. So, he said, this is what I will do: I will pull down my barns, and build greater, and there I will store all my crops and my goods.
19. And I will say to my soul, soul, you have many goods laid up for many years; take your ease, eat, drink, and be merry.

20. But God said to him, you fool, this night your soul will be required of you: then who will own those things, which you have provided?
21. So, is he that is laying up treasure for himself, he is not rich toward God.
22. And He said to His disciples, therefore I say to you, take no thought for your life, what you will eat; neither for the body, what you will wear.
23. The life is more than food, and the body is more than clothing.
24. Consider the ravens: for they neither sow nor reap; who neither have storehouse nor barn; and God feeds them: how much more are you better than the birds?
25. Which one of you by worrying can add one hour to his life?
26. If you then are not able to do that thing which is little, why take thought for the rest?
27. Consider the lilies how they grow: they work not, they spin not; and yet I say to you, that Solomon in all his glory was not arrayed like one of these.
28. If then God so clothes the grass, which is today in the field, and the next day is cast into the oven; how much more will he clothe you, O you of little faith?
29. And seek not you what you will eat, or what you will drink, neither be of doubtful mind.
30. For all these things do the nations of the world seek after: and Your Father knows that you need these things.
31. But rather you seek the kingdom of God, and all these things will be added to you.
32. Fear not, little flock; for it is your Father's good pleasure to give you the kingdom.
33. Sell what you have and give charitably; make yourselves purses which grow not old, a treasure in the heavens that fails not, where no thief approaches, neither moth corrupts.
34. For where your treasure is, there will your heart be also.
35. Be dressed for service, and have your lights burning;
36. And you are like men that wait for their lord when he returns from the wedding; that when he comes and knocks, they may open to him immediately.
37. Blessed are those servants, whom the lord when he comes will find them being vigilant: truthfully, I say to you, that he will dress, and make them sit down to eat, and will come out and serve them.
38. And if he comes in the second watch, or comes in the third watch, and finds them so, blessed are those servants.
39. But know this; that if the owner of the house had known what hour the thief would come, he would have watched, and not have permitted his house to be broken into.
40. Therefore, be ready also: for the Son of man comes at a season when you think not.
41. Then Peter said to Him, Lord, speak you this parable to us, or even to all?
42. And the Lord said, who then is that faithful and wise steward, who his lord shall make ruler over his household, to give them their portion of food in due season?
43. Blessed is that servant, who his lord when he comes will find so doing.

44. Truly, I say to you, that he will make him ruler over all that he has.
45. But and if that servant say in his heart, My lord delays his coming; and will begin to beat the menservants and maidservants, and to eat and drink, and to be drunken;
46. The lord of that servant will come in a day when he looks not for him, and at an hour when he is not aware and will cut him to pieces and will appoint him his portion with the unfaithful.
47. And that servant, which knew his lord's will, and prepared not himself, neither did according to his will, is going to be beaten with many stripes.
48. But he that did not know, and did commit things worthy of stripes, will be beaten with few stripes. For to whomever much is given, of him will much be required: and to who men have committed much, of him they will ask even more.
49. I have come to send fire on the land, and what can I desire that it's already kindled?
50. But I have an immersion to be immersed with; and how restricted I am until it is complete!
51. You suppose that I am come to give peace on the land? I tell you, no; but rather division:
52. For from now on there will be five in one house divided, three against two, and two against three.
53. The father will be divided against the son, and the son against the father; the mother against the daughter, and the daughter against the mother; the mother-in-law against her daughter-in-law, and the daughter-in-law against her mother-in-law.
54. And He said also to the people, when you see a cloud rise out of the west, immediately you say, there comes a shower, and so it is.
55. And when you see the south wind blow, you say, there will be heat, and it comes to pass.
56. You hypocrites, you can discern the face of the sky and the land; but how is it that you do not discern this appointed time?
57. Yes, and why even among yourselves do you not judge what is right?
58. When you go with your adversary to the judge, as you are on the way, try hard to reconcile that you may be delivered from him; unless he takes you to the judge, and the judge delivers you to the officer, and the officer cast you into prison.
59. I tell you; you will not leave there until you have paid the very last coin.

Chapter 13

1. There were present at that season some that told Him of the Galileans, whose blood Pilate had mingled with their sacrifices.
2. And Jesus answering said to them, suppose you that these Galileans were sinners above all the Galileans because they permitted such things?
3. I tell you, No: but, unless you repent, you will all perish similarly.
4. Or those eighteen, upon whom the tower in Siloam fell, and killed them, think you that they were sinners above all men that dwelt in Jerusalem?
5. I tell you, No: but, unless you repent, you will all perish similarly.

6. He spoke also this parable; a certain man had a fig tree planted in his vineyard; and he came and sought fruit from it and found none.

7. Then said he to the man of his vineyard, behold, these three years I came seeking fruit on this fig tree, and find none: cut it down; why does it occupy the land?

8. He answered and said to him, Lord, let it alone this year also until I will dig about it, and fertilize it:

9. And if it bears fruit, well: and if not, then after that you will cut it down.

10. Now He was teaching in one of the synagogues on the Sabbath.

11. And behold, there was a woman which had a spirit of infirmity eighteen years, and was bent over, and could in no way raise herself up.

12. But when Jesus saw her, He called her to Him, and said to her, woman, you are loosed from your infirmity.

13. Then He laid His hands on her: and immediately she was made straight, and glorified God.

14. But the ruler of the synagogue answered with indignation, because Jesus had healed on the Sabbath day, and said to the people, There are six days in which men ought to work: Therefore on them come and be healed, and not on the Sabbath day.

15. The Lord then answered him, and said, you hypocrite, does not each one of you on the Sabbath untie his ox or his donkey from the stall, and lead him away to water?

16. And ought not this woman, being a daughter of Abraham, who Satan has bound, look, these eighteen years, be loosed from this bond on the Sabbath day?

17. When He had said these things, all His adversaries were ashamed: and all the people rejoiced for all the glorious things that were done by Him.

18. Then said He, unto what is the kingdom of God like, and to what will I compare it?

19. It is like a grain of mustard seed, which a man took, and cast into his garden; and it grew, and became a great tree; and the birds of the air lodged in the branches of it.

20. And again He said, what will I liken the kingdom of God?

21. It is like leaven, which a woman took and hid in three measures of meal until the whole was leavened.

22. So, he went through the cities and villages, teaching, and journeying toward Jerusalem.

23. Then said one to him, Lord, are there few that be saved? And He said to them,

24. Strive to enter in at the narrow gate: for many, I say to you, will seek to enter in, and will not be able.

25. When once the master of the house is risen up, and has shut to the door, and you begin to stand outside, and to knock at the door, saying, Lord, Lord, open to us; and he will answer and say to you, I know you not, nor from where you are from:

26. Then will you begin to say, We have eaten and drunk in your presence, and you have taught in our streets.

27. But he will say, I tell you, I know you not, nor from where you are; depart from me, all you workers of iniquity.

28. There will be weeping and gnashing of teeth, when you will see Abraham, and Isaac, and Jacob, and all the prophets in the kingdom of God, and you yourselves cast out.
29. For they will come from the east, and the west, and from the north, and the south, and will sit down in the kingdom of God.
30. And behold, they that are last which will be first, and they that are first which will be last.
31. The same day there came certain of the Pharisees, saying to Him, Get You out, and depart from here: for Herod will murder You.
32. And He said to them, you go and tell that fox, behold, I cast out demons, and I do healing today and the next day, and the third day I will reach my goal.
33. Nevertheless, I must walk today, and the next day, and the day following: for it cannot be that a prophet perish outside of Jerusalem.
34. O Jerusalem, Jerusalem, which murder the prophets, and stone them that are sent to you; how often would I have gathered your children together, as a hen does gather her chicks under her wings, and you would not have it!
35. Behold, your house is left to you desolate: and truthfully, I say to you, you will not see Me, until the time comes when you will say, blessed is He that comes in the name of the Lord!

Chapter 14

1. And it came to pass, as He went into the house of one of the chief Pharisees to eat bread on the Sabbath day, that they watched Him.
2. And behold, there was a certain man before Him who had water retention.
3. And Jesus answering spoke to the lawyers and Pharisees, saying, is it lawful to heal on the Sabbath day?
4. But they held their peace. And He took him, and healed him, and let him go;
5. And answered them, and said, which of you having a son or an ox that has fallen into a pit, and will not immediately pull him out on the Sabbath day?
6. Yet they could not answer Him again about these things.
7. So, He told a parable to those who were invited when He noted how they chose the chief places; saying to them.
8. When you are invited by anyone to a wedding, sit not down in the highest place; unless a more honorable man than you be invited by him;
9. And he that invited you and he comes and says to you, give your place to this man; and you begin with shame to take the lowest place.
10. But when you are invited, go and sit down in the lowest place; that when he that invited you comes, he may say to you, Friend, go up higher: then will you have glory in the presence of them that sit at food with you.
11. For whoever exalts himself will be humbled, and he that humbles himself will be exalted.
12. Then said He also to him that invited Him, when you make a brunch or a supper, ask not your friends, nor your brothers, neither your relatives, nor your rich neighbors; unless they also invite you again, and repayment be made.

13. But when you make a feast, call the poor, the dismembered, the lame, and the blind:
14. And you will be blessed; for they cannot repay you: for you will be repaid at the resurrection of the just.
15. When one of them that sat to eat with Him heard these things, he said to Him, Blessed is he who will eat bread in the kingdom of God.
16. Then said He to him, a certain man made a great dinner, and invited many:
17. And sent his servant at supper time to say to them that were invited, come; for all things are now ready.
18. And they all with one voice began to make excuses. The first said to him, I have bought a piece of land, and I must go and see it: I pray you have me excused.
19. And another said, I have bought five yoke of oxen, and I go to try them: I pray you have me excused.
20. And another said, I have married a wife, and therefore I cannot come.
21. So, that servant came and showed his lord these things. Then the master of the house being angry said to his servant, go out quickly into the streets and lanes of the city, and bring in the poor, and the dismembered, and the lame, and the blind.
22. And the servant said, Lord, it is done as you have commanded, and yet there is room.
23. And the lord said to the servant, go out into the streets and narrow ways, and pressure them to come in, that my house may be filled.
24. For I say to you, that none of those men who were invited will taste of my dinner.
25. And there went great multitudes with Him: and He turned, and said to them,
26. If anyone comes to Me, and hates not his father, and mother, and wife, and children, and brothers, and sisters, yes and his own life also, he cannot be My disciple.
27. And whoever does not bear his cross, and come after Me, cannot be My disciple.
28. For which of you, intending to build a tower, sits not down first, and counts the cost, whether he has sufficient money to finish it?
29. Unless, after he has laid the foundation, and is not able to finish it, all that behold it begin to mock him,
30. Saying, this man began to build and could not finish.
31. Or what king, going to make war against another king, sits not down first, and consults whether he be able with ten thousand to meet him that comes against him with twenty thousand?
32. Or else, while the other is yet a great way off, he sends an ambassador and asks conditions of peace.
33. So, likewise, whoever of you that forsakes not all that he has, he cannot be My disciple.
34. Salt is good: but if the salt has lost its savor, with what will it be seasoned?
35. It is neither fit for the land nor yet for the dunghill, but men cast it out. He that has ears to hear, let him hear.

Chapter 15

1. Then came near to Him all the tax collectors and sinners to hear Him.
2. And the Pharisees and scribes murmured, saying, this man receives sinners and eats with them.
3. And He spoke this parable to them, saying,
4. What man of you, having a hundred sheep, if he loses one of them, does not leave the ninety-nine in the wilderness, and go after that who is lost, until he finds it?
5. And when he has found it, he lays it on his shoulders, rejoicing.
6. And when he comes home, he calls together his friends and neighbors, saying to them, rejoice with me; for I have found my lost sheep.
7. I say to you, that likewise, joy will be in heaven over one sinner that repents, more than over ninety-nine righteous ones, who need no repentance.
8. Either what woman having ten pieces of silver, if she loses one piece, does not light a candle, and sweep the house, and seek diligently until she finds it?
9. And when she has found it, she calls her friends and her neighbors together, saying, rejoice with me; for I have found the piece which I had lost.
10. Likewise, I say to you, there is joy in the presence of the angels of God over one sinner who repents.
11. And He said, a certain man had two sons:
12. And the younger of them said to his father, father, give me my share of the estate. And he divided his property among them.
13. And not many days after the younger son gathered all together, and took his journey into a far country, and there wasted his wealth with wild living.
14. And when he had spent all, there arose a mighty famine in that land; and he began to be in want.
15. And he went and hired himself to a citizen of that country, and he sent him into his fields to feed pigs.
16. And he would gladly have filled his stomach with the husks that the pigs did eat: and no man gave to him.
17. And when he came to himself, he said, how many hired servants of my father's have bread enough and to spare, and I perish with hunger.
18. I will arise and go to my father, and will say to him, Father, I have sinned against heaven, and before you,
19. And am no more worthy to be called your son: make me one of your hired servants.
20. And he arose and came to his father. But when he was yet a great way off, his father saw him, and had compassion, and ran, and fell on his neck, and kissed him.
21. And the son said to him, father, I have sinned against heaven, and in your sight, and am no more worthy to be called your son.
22. But the father said to his servants, Bring out the best robe, and put it on him; and put a ring on his hand, and sandals on his feet:
23. And bring the fatted calf here, and kill it, and let us eat, and be merry:
24. For this my son was dead and is alive again; he was lost and is found. And they began to rejoice.

Luke 15:25

25. Now his elder son was in the field: and as he came and drew close to the house, he heard music and dancing.
26. And he called one of the servants and asked what these things meant.
27. And he said to him, your brother has come, and your father has killed the fatted calf because he has received him safe and sound.
28. And he was angry and would not go in: therefore, his father came out and entreated him.
29. And he answered and said to his father, look, these many years I did serve you, neither have I disobeyed at any time your commandment: and yet you never gave me a young goat, that I might rejoice with my friends:
30. But as soon as this your son was come, who has devoured your living with harlots, you have killed for him the fatted calf.
31. And he said to him, son, you are always with me, and all that I have is yours.
32. It was right that we should rejoice, and be glad: for this, your brother was dead, and is alive again; and was lost, and is found.

Chapter 16

1. And He said also to His disciples, there was a certain rich man, who had a steward; and the same was accused by him of wasting his possessions.
2. And he called him, and said to him, how is it that I hear this of you? Give an account of your stewardship; for you may be no longer steward.
3. Then the steward said within himself, what will I do? For my lord takes away from me the stewardship: I cannot dig; to beg I am ashamed.
4. I know what I may do, that when I am put out of the stewardship, they may receive me into their houses.
5. So, he called each one of his lord's debtors to him, and said to the first, how much do you owe to my lord?
6. And he said, A hundred measures of oil. And he said to him, take your bill, and sit down quickly, and write payment for fifty.
7. Then he said to another, how much do you owe? And he said, a hundred measures of wheat. And he said to him, take your bill, and write a bill for eighty.
8. And the lord commended the unjust steward because he had acted shrewdly: for the children of this Old Covenant Age are in their generation shrewder than the children of light.
9. And I say to you, make yourselves friends utilizing the mammon of unrighteousness; that, when you fail, you may be received into perpetual dwellings.
10. He that is faithful in that which is least is faithful also in much: and he that is unjust in the least is unjust also in much.
11. Therefore, if you have not been faithful in the unrighteous mammon, who will commit to your trust the true riches?
12. And if you have not been faithful in that which is another man's, who will give you that which is your own?

13. No servant can serve two masters: for either he will hate the one, and love the other, Or else he will hold to the one, and despise the other. You cannot serve God and mammon.
14. And the Pharisees also, who were greedy, heard all these things: and sneered at Him.
15. And He said to them, you are they who justify yourselves before men, but God knows your hearts: for that which is highly esteemed among men is an abomination in the sight of God.
16. The Law and the prophets were until John: since that time the kingdom of God is preached, and all do violence against it.
17. For it is easier for heaven and earth to pass away than one small mark of the Law to fail.
18. Whoever divorces his wife, and marries another, commits adultery: and whoever marries her that is divorced from her husband commits adultery.
19. There was a certain rich man, who was clothed in purple and fine linen, and dined luxuriously every day:
20. And there was a certain beggar named Lazarus, who was laid at his gate, full of sores,
21. And wanting to be fed with the crumbs which fell from the rich man's table: moreover the dogs came and licked his sores.
22. And it came to pass, that the beggar died, and was carried by the angels to Abraham's bosom: the rich man also died, and was buried;
23. And in the unseen realm he lifts up his eyes, being in torment, and sees Abraham far off, and Lazarus in his bosom.
24. And he cried and said, father Abraham, have mercy on me, and send Lazarus that he may dip the tip of his finger in water, and cool my tongue; for I am tormented in this flame.
25. But Abraham said, son, remember that you in your lifetime received your good things, and likewise Lazarus evil things: But now he is comforted, and you are tormented.
26. And beside all this, between us and you there is a great gulf fixed: so that they which would pass from here to you cannot; neither can they pass to us that would come from there.
27. Then he said, therefore I pray you, father, that you would send him to my father's house:
28. For I have five brothers; that he may testify to them unless they also come to this place of torment.
29. Abraham says to him, they have Moses and the prophets; let them hear them.
30. And he said, no, father Abraham: but if one went to them from the dead, they will repent.
31. And he said to him, if they hear not Moses and the prophets, neither will they be persuaded, though one rose from the dead.

Chapter 17

1. Then said He to the disciples, it is impossible but that offenses will come: but woe to him, through whom they come!

2. It were better for him that a millstone was hanged about his neck, and he cast into the sea, than that he should stumble one of these little ones.

3. Take heed to yourselves: if your brother trespass against you, rebuke him; and if he repents, forgive him.

4. And if he trespass against you seven times in a day, and seven times in a day turns again to you, saying, I repent; you will forgive him.

5. And the apostles said to the Lord, Increase our faith.

6. And the Lord said, if you had faith as a grain of mustard seed, you might say to this mulberry tree, be plucked up by the root, and be you planted in the sea; and it should obey you.

7. But whom of you, having a servant plowing or feeding cattle, will say to him, when he has come in from the field, Go and sit down to eat?

8. Yet will not rather say to him, Make ready with which I may dine, and serve me until I have eaten and drunk; and afterward you will eat and drink?

9. Does he thank that servant because he did the things that were commanded him? I think not.

10. So, likewise you, when you have done all those things which are commanded, you say, we are unprofitable servants: we have done that which was our duty to do.

11. And it came to pass, as He went to Jerusalem that He passed through the midst of Samaria and Galilee.

12. And as he entered into a certain village, there ten men that were lepers met Him who stood far off:

13. Then they lifted up their voices, and said, Jesus, Master, have mercy on us!

14. And when He saw them, He said to them, go show yourselves to the priests. And it came to pass, that, as they went, they were cleansed.

15. And one of them, when he saw that he was healed, turned back, and with a loud voice glorified God,

16. So, he fell down on his face at His feet, giving Him thanks: and he was a Samaritan.

17. Jesus answered and said, were there not ten cleansed? But where are the nine?

18. They were not found that returned to give glory to God, except this foreigner.

19. And He said to him, arise, go your way: your faith has made you whole.

20. When the Pharisees demanded of Him saying, when will the kingdom of God come? He answered them and said, the kingdom of God does not come with observation:

21. Neither will they say, look here! Or, look there! For, behold, the kingdom of God is inside you.

22. And He said to the disciples, the days will come when you will want to see one of the days of the Son of man, and you will not see it.

23. And they will say to you, see here; or see there: go not after them, nor follow them.

24. For as the lightning, that lightens out of the one part under the heavens, shines to the other part under the heavens; so also will the Son of man be in His day.

25. But first He must suffer many things and be rejected by this generation.
26. As it was in the days of Noah, so will it also be in the days of the Son of man.
27. They did eat, they drank, they married wives, they were given in marriage, until the day that Noah entered into the ark, and the flood came, and destroyed them all.
28. In the same way as it was in the days of Lot; they did eat, they drank, they bought, they sold, they planted, they built;
29. But the same day that Lot went out of Sodom it rained fire and brimstone from the heavens and destroyed them all.
30. Even so will it be in the day when the Son of man is revealed.
31. In that day, he who will be on the housetop, and his goods in the house, let him not come down to grab them: and he that is in the field, let him likewise not return back.
32. Remember Lot's wife.
33. Whoever will seek to save his life will lose it, and whoever will lose his life will preserve it.
34. I tell you, in that night there will be two in one bed; the one will be taken, and the other will be left.
35. Two will be grinding together; the one will be taken, and the other left.
36. Two will be in the field; one will be taken, and the other left.
37. And they answered and said to Him, where Lord? And He said to them, wherever the dead body is, there will the eagles be gathered together!

Chapter 18

1. And He spoke a parable to them to this end, that men ought always to pray, and not lose heart;
2. Saying, there was in a city a judge, who feared not God, neither regarded man:
3. And there was a widow in that city; and she came to him, saying, Avenge me of my adversary.
4. And he would not for a while: but afterward, he said within himself, though I fear not God, nor regard man;
5. Yet because this widow troubles me, I will avenge her, unless by her continual coming she wearies me.
6. Then the Lord said, hear what the unjust judge says.
7. And will not God avenge his own elect, who cry day and night to Him, though He bears long with them?
8. I tell you that He will avenge them soon. Nevertheless, when the Son of man comes, will he find that kind of faith on the land?
9. Also, He spoke this parable to certain who trusted in themselves that they were righteous, and despised others:
10. Two men went up into the temple to pray; the one a Pharisee, and the other a tax collector.
11. The Pharisee stood and prayed so with himself, God, I thank you, that I am not as other men are, extortionists, unjust, adulterers, or even as this tax collector.
12. I fast twice a week, and I give tithes of all that I possess.

Luke 18:13

13. But the tax collector, standing far off, would not lift up so much as his eyes to heaven, but beat on his chest, saying, God be merciful to me a sinner.

14. I tell you; this man went down to his house justified rather than the other: for everyone that exalts himself will be humbled, and he that humbles himself will be exalted.

15. And they brought to Him also infants, that He would touch them: but when his disciples saw it, they rebuked them.

16. But Jesus called them to Him, and said, permit little children to come to Me and forbid them not: for of such is the kingdom of God.

17. Truthfully, I say to you, whoever will not receive the kingdom of God as a little child will in no way enter into it.

18. Then a certain ruler asked him, and said, good Master, what should I do to inherit infinite life?

19. And Jesus said to him, why do you call Me good? No one is good, except one, that is, God.

20. You know the commandments, do not commit adultery, do not murder, do not steal, do not bear false witness, honor your father and your mother.

21. So, he said, all these have I kept from my youth up.

22. Now when Jesus heard these things, He said to him, yet lack you one thing: sell all that you have, and distribute to the poor, and you will have treasure in heaven: and come, follow Me.

23. And when he heard this, he was very sorrowful: for he was very rich.

Luke 18:35

24. So, when Jesus saw that he was very sorrowful, He said, how hard it is for those that have riches to enter into the kingdom of God!

25. For it is easier for a camel to go through a needle's eye than for a rich man to enter into the kingdom of God.

26. And they that heard it said, who then can be saved?

27. And He said, the things which are impossible with men are possible with God.

28. Then Peter said, look, we have left all and followed You.

29. And He said to them, truthfully, I say to you, no man has left house, or parents, or brothers, or wife, or children, for the kingdom of God's sake,

30. Who will not receive manifold more in this opportune time, and in the New Covenant Age to come, life infinitely.

31. Then He gathered to Him the twelve, and said to them, behold, we go up to Jerusalem, and all things that are written by the prophets concerning the Son of man will be fulfilled.

32. For He will be delivered to the people, and will be mocked, and spitefully treated, and spit on:

33. And they will whip Him and put Him to death: and the third day He will rise again.

34. And they understood none of these things: and this saying was hidden from them, neither knew they the things which were spoken.

35. And it came to pass, that as He came close to Jericho, a certain blind man sat by the wayside begging:

36. For hearing the multitude pass by, he asked what it meant.
37. So, they told him, that Jesus of Nazareth passed by.
38. Then he cried, saying, Jesus, You Son of David, have mercy on me!
39. They who went before rebuked him, that he should hold his peace: but he cried so much the more, You Son of David, have mercy on me!
40. So, Jesus stood, and commanded him to be brought to Him: and when he had come near, He asked him, and
41. Said; what do you want Me to do for you? And he said, Lord, that I may receive my sight.
42. And Jesus said to him, receive your sight: your faith has saved you.
43. Immediately he received his sight, and followed Him, glorifying God: and all the people, when they saw it, gave praise to God!

Chapter 19

1. And Jesus entered and passed through Jericho.
2. Now, behold, there was a man named Zacchaeus, who was chief among the tax collectors, and he was rich.
3. So, he sought to see Jesus who He was; and could not for the crowd, because he was short.
4. Then he ran before and climbed up into a sycamore tree to see Him: for He was about to pass that way.
5. When Jesus came to the place, He looked up, and saw him, and said to him, Zacchaeus, make haste, and come down; for today I must stay at your house.
6. So, he made haste and came down and received Him joyfully.
7. But when they saw it, they all murmured, saying, that He had gone to be the guest of a man who is a sinner.
8. And Zacchaeus stood, and said to the Lord: behold, Lord, the half of my goods I give to the poor; and if I have taken anything from any man by false accusation, I restore him four-fold.
9. And Jesus said to him, this day has salvation come to this house because he also is a son of Abraham.
10. For the Son of man has come to seek and to save that which was lost.
11. Then as they heard these things, He added and spoke a parable, because He was close to Jerusalem, and because they thought that the kingdom of God was about to appear.
12. Therefore, He said, a certain nobleman went into a far country to receive for himself a kingdom, and to return.
13. And he called his ten servants and delivered them ten talents, and said to them, do business until I come.
14. But His citizens hated him, and sent a message after him, saying, we will not have this man to reign over us.
15. And it came to pass, that when he was returned, having received the kingdom, then he commanded these servants to be called to him, to whom he had given the money, that he might know how much every man had gained by trading.

16. Then came the first, saying, Lord, your talent has gained ten talents.
17. And he said to him, well done, you good servant: because you have been faithful in a very little, have you authority over ten cities.
18. And the second came, saying, Lord, your talent has gained five talents.
19. And he said likewise to him, you be also over five cities.
20. And another came, saying, Lord, behold, here is your talent, which I have kept safe in a piece of cloth:
21. For I feared you because you are a harsh man: you take up that which you did not lay down and reap that which you did not sow.
22. And he said to him, out of your own mouth will I judge you, you wicked servant. You knew that I was a harsh man, taking up what I laid not down, and reaping what I did not sow:
23. Why then did you not put my money into the bank, that at my coming I might have required my own with interest?
24. And he said to them that stood by, take from him the talent, and give it to him that has ten talents.
25. And they said to him, Lord, he has ten talents.
26. For I say to you, everyone who has more will be given; and from him that has not, even that which he has will be taken away from him.
27. But as for my enemies, who did not want me to reign over them, bring them here, and slay them before me.
28. When He had said this, He went on ahead, ascending up to Jerusalem.
29. And it came to pass, when He had come close to Bethphage and Bethany, at the mountain called, the Mount of Olives. He sent two of His disciples,
30. Saying, you go into the village opposite you; in which at your entering you will find a colt tied, on which never man sat: untie him, and bring him here.
31. And if any man asks you, why do you untie him? You will say this to him because the Lord needs him.
32. Then they that were sent went their way and found just as He had said to them.
33. So, while they were loosing the colt, the owners of it said to them, why are you loosing the colt?
34. And they said, the Lord needs him.
35. Then they brought him to Jesus: and they cast their garments on the colt, and they set Jesus on him.
36. As He went, they spread their clothes on the way.
37. When He had come close, even now at the descent of the Mount of Olives, the whole multitude of the disciples began to rejoice and praise God with a loud voice for all the mighty works that they had seen;
38. Saying, blessed is the King that comes in the name of the Lord: peace in heaven, and glory in the highest!
39. So, some of the Pharisees from among the multitude said to Him, Master, rebuke Your disciples.
40. But He answered and said to them, I tell you that, if these should hold their peace, the stones would immediately cry out.

41. When He had come near, He beheld the city, and wept over it,
42. Saying, if you had known, even you, at least in this your day, the things which belong to your peace! But now they are hidden from your eyes.
43. For the days will come on you, that your enemies will build an embankment about you, and encircle you, and close you in on every side,
44. And will lay you even with the ground, and your children within you, and they will not leave in you one stone upon another; because you knew not the time of your visitation.
45. And He went into the temple and began to cast out them that sold in it, and them that bought;
46. Saying to them, it is written, My house is the house of prayer: But you have made it a den of thieves.
47. So, He taught daily in the temple. But the chief priests and the scribes and the chief men of the people sought to destroy Him,
48. But could not find what they might do: for all the people were very attentive to hear Him.

Chapter 20

1. And it came to pass, that on one of those days, as He taught the people in the temple, and preached the gospel, the chief priests and the scribes came on Him with the elders,
2. And spoke to Him, saying, tell us, by what authority are You doing these things? Or whom is He that gave You this authority?
3. So, He answered and said to them, I will also ask you one thing, and answer Me:
4. The baptism of John, was it from heaven, or of men?
5. And they reasoned with themselves, saying, if we will say, from heaven; He will say, why then did you not believe him?
6. But and if we say, of men; all the people will stone us: for they are persuaded that John was a prophet.
7. Then they answered that they could not tell from where it was.
8. And Jesus said to them, neither will I tell you by what authority I do these things.
9. Then He began to speak to the people this parable; a certain man planted a vineyard, and leased it to some vinedressers, and went into a far country for a long time.
10. And at the appropriate time he sent a servant to the tenants, that they should give him some of the fruit of the vineyard: but the tenants beat him and sent him away empty.
11. Again, he sent another servant: and they beat him also, and treated him shamefully, and sent him away empty.
12. Yet again he sent a third: and they wounded him also and cast him out.
13. Then said the lord of the vineyard, what should I do? I will send my beloved son: it may be they will respect him when they see him.
14. But when the tenants saw him, they reasoned among themselves, saying, this is the heir: Come, let us murder him, that the inheritance may be ours.

15. So, they cast him out of the vineyard and murdered him. Therefore, what will the lord of the vineyard do to them?

16. He will come and destroy these tenants and will give the vineyard to others. When they heard it, they said, God forbid!

17. Yet He beheld them, and said, what is this then that is written, the stone which the builders rejected, the same has become the chief cornerstone?

18. Whoever will fall on that stone will be broken; but on whomever it will fall, it will grind him to powder.

19. And the chief priests and the scribes the same hour sought to lay hands on Him; and they feared the people: for they perceived that He had spoken this parable against them.

20. And they watched Him and sent out spies, who should pretend themselves just men that they may take hold of His words, that so they may hand Him over to the government and authority of the governor.

21. And they asked Him, saying, Master, we know that You say and teach rightly, neither do You show personal favoritism, but teach the way of God with reality.

22. Is it lawful for us to pay tribute to Caesar, or not?

23. But He perceived their craftiness, and said to them, why do you tempt Me?

24. Show me a denarius. Whose image and inscription is on it? They answered and said, Caesar's.

25. And He said to them, therefore render to Caesar the things which are Caesar's and to God the things which are God's.

26. Then they could not trap His words in front of the people: and they marveled at His answer and were silenced.

27. Then certain of the Sadducees came to Him, who deny that there is any resurrection; and they asked Him,

28. Saying, Master, Moses wrote to us, if any man's brother die, having a wife, and he die without children, that his brother should marry his wife, and raise up children to his brother.

29. Therefore, there were seven brothers: and the first had a wife and died without children.

30. And the second married her, and he died childless.

31. And the third married her; and in an identical way the seven also: and they left no children and died.

32. Last of all, the woman died also.

33. Therefore, in the resurrection whose wife of them is she? For all seven had her as a wife.

34. Then Jesus answered and said to them, the children of this Old Covenant Age marry, and are given in marriage:

35. But they who will be counted worthy to gain that New Covenant Age, and the resurrection out from the dead, neither marry nor are given in marriage:

36. Neither can they die any longer: for they are similar to the angels; and are the sons of God, being the sons of the resurrection.

37. Now that the dead are raised, even Moses showed at the bush, when he calls the Lord the God of Abraham, and the God of Isaac, and the God of Jacob.

38. For He is not a God of the dead, but of the living: for all live to Him.
39. Then certain of the scribes answering said, Master, You have spoken well.
40. And after that they dared not ask Him any question at all.
41. And He said to them, how can they say that the Christ is David's son?
42. Now David himself said in the book of Psalms, the LORD said to my Lord, sit at My right hand,
43. Until I make Your enemies Your footstool.
44. Therefore, David calls him Lord, how is He then his son?
45. Then in the hearing of all the people He said to His disciples,
46. Beware of the scribes, who want to walk in long robes, and love greetings in the markets, and the highest seats in the synagogues, and the chief rooms at feasts;
47. Who devour widows' houses, and for a show make long prayers: the same will receive the greater condemnation.

Chapter 21

1. And He looked up and saw the rich men casting their gifts into the treasury.
2. And He saw also a certain poor widow casting into that place two small coins.
3. And He said, in reality, I say to you, that this poor widow has cast in more than everyone:
4. For all these have out from their abundance cast into the offerings of God: but she out of her deficiency has cast in all that she had to live.

5. And as some spoke of the temple, how it was adorned with beautiful stones and gifts, He said,
6. As for these things which you behold, the days will come, in which there will not be left one stone upon another that will not be thrown down.
7. Then they asked Him, saying, Master, but when will these things be? And what sign will there be when these things are about to come to pass?
8. And He said, take heed that you are not deceived: for many will come in My name, saying, I am Christ; and the time draws near: do not go after them.
9. But when you will hear of wars and commotions, be not terrified: for these things must first come to pass; but the end is not yet.
10. Then He said to them, nation will rise against nation, and kingdom against kingdom:
11. And great earthquakes will occur in different places, and famines, and pestilences; and fearful sights and great signs will there be from the heavens.
12. But before all these, they will lay their hands on you, and persecute you, delivering you up to the synagogues, and into prisons, being brought before kings and rulers for My name's sake.
13. But it will turn out for you as an occasion for testimony.
14. Therefore, settle it in your hearts, not to think ahead before making your defense:
15. For I will give you a mouth and wisdom, which all your adversaries will not be able to contradict nor resist.

16. You will be betrayed by parents, brothers, relatives, and friends, and some of you will be put to death.
17. And you will be hated of all men for My name's sake.
18. Not even a hair of your head will perish.
19. In your endurance you gain your souls.
20. For when you will see Jerusalem surrounded with armies, then know that the desolation of it is close.
21. Then let those who are in Judea flee to the mountains and let those who are in the midst of it depart out, and let not them that are in the countryside enter into her.
22. For these are the days of vengeance, that all things which are written may be fulfilled!
23. But woe to them that are with child, and to them that nurse, in those days! For there will be great distress in the land, and wrath on this people.
24. And they will fall by the edge of the sword and will be taken away captive into all nations: and Jerusalem will be trampled on by the nations until the times of the nations be fulfilled.
25. And there will be signs in the sun, and in the moon, and the stars; and on the land with anguish among nations, in perplexity; the sea and the waves roaring;
26. Men's hearts failing them for fear, and for looking for those things which are coming on the Roman world: for the powers of heaven will be shaken.
27. And then they will see the Son of man coming in a cloud with power and great glory.
28. And when these things begin to come to pass, then look up, and raise your heads; for your redemption approaches.
29. And He spoke to them a parable; behold the fig tree and all the trees;
30. When they are already budding, you see and know of yourselves that summer is now close at hand.
31. So, likewise you, when you see these things come to pass, know you that the kingdom of God is close at hand.
32. Truthfully, I say to you, this generation will not pass away until all is fulfilled.
33. Heaven and earth will pass away: but My words will not pass away.
34. And take heed to yourselves, unless at any time your hearts be overcharged with dissipation, and drunkenness, and cares of this life, and so that day come on you unawares.
35. For as a snare will it come on all them that dwell on the face of the whole land.
36. Therefore, watch you, and pray always, that you may be counted worthy to escape all these things that are about to come to pass, and to stand before the Son of man!
37. And in the day time He was teaching in the temple; and at night He went out and stayed on the mount that is called the Mount of Olives.
38. So, all the people came early in the morning to Him in the temple, for to hear Him.

Chapter 22

1. Now the Feast of Unleavened Bread drew close, which is called the Passover.

2. And the chief priests and scribes sought how they might murder Him; for they feared the people.
3. Then Satan entered into Judas surnamed Iscariot, being one of the twelve.
4. And he went his way, and conferred with the chief priests and captains, how he might betray Him to them.
5. So, they were glad and promised to give him money.
6. And he agreed and sought opportunity to betray Him to them in the absence of the multitude.
7. Then came the day of Unleavened Bread, when the Passover must be killed.
8. And He sent Peter and John, saying, go and prepare us the Passover that we may eat.
9. And they said to Him, where do You want us to prepare it?
10. Then He said to them, behold, when you have entered into the city, there will a man meet you, carrying a pitcher of water; follow him into the house where he enters.
11. And you will say to the master of the house, the Master says to you, where is the guest chamber, where I will eat the Passover with My disciples?
12. Then he will show you a large upper room furnished: there make ready.
13. And they went and found as He had said to them: and they made ready the Passover.
14. When the hour came, He sat down, and the twelve apostles with Him.
15. Then He said to them, with earnest desire, I have desired to eat this Passover with you before I suffer:
16. For I say to you, I will no longer eat of it, until it is fulfilled in the kingdom of God.
17. And He took the cup, and gave thanks, and said, take this, and divide it among yourselves:
18. For I say to you, I will not drink of the fruit of the vine, until the kingdom of God has come.
19. And He took bread, and gave thanks, and broke it, and gave to them, and said, this is My body which is given for you: do this in remembrance of Me.
20. Likewise, also the cup after supper, saying, this cup is the new covenant in My blood, which is shed for you.
21. But behold, the hand of him that betrays Me is with Me on the table.
22. And truly the Son of man goes, as it was determined: But woe to that man by whom He is betrayed!
23. Then they began to inquire among themselves, whom of them it was that was about to do this thing.
24. For there was also a strife among them, who of them should be accounted the greatest.
25. And He said to them, the rulers of the nations exercise lordship over them, and they that exercise authority on them are called benefactors.
26. But you will not be so: but he that is greatest among you, let him be as the younger; and he that is leading, as he that does serve.
27. For which is greater, he that sits at the table, or he that serves? Is it not he who sits at the table?
28. But I am among you as One that serves.

29. You are they who have continued with Me in My temptations.
30. And I appoint to you a kingdom, as My Father has appointed to Me;
31. That you may eat and drink at My table in My kingdom and sit on thrones judging the twelve tribes of Israel.
32. And the Lord said, Simon, Simon, behold, Satan has desired to have you, that he may sift you as wheat:
33. But I have prayed for you, that your faith fail not: and when you have turned again, strengthen your brothers.
34. But he said to Him, Lord, I am ready to go with You, both into prison, and to death.
35. And He said, I tell you, Peter, the rooster will not crow this day, before that you will deny Me three times that you do not know Me.
36. Then He said to them, when I sent you without money bag, and pack, and sandals, lacked you anything? And they said nothing.
37. Then He said to them, but now, he that has a money bag, let him take it, and likewise his pack: and he that has no sword, let him sell his cloak, and buy one.
38. For I say to you, that which is written must yet be fulfilled in Me, and He was counted among the lawless: for the things concerning Me have a goal.
39. So, they said, Lord, behold, here are two swords. And He said to them, it is enough.
40. And He came out, and went, as He was accustomed, to the Mount of Olives; and His disciples also followed Him.
41. When He was at the place, He said to them, pray that you enter not into temptation.
42. And He was withdrawn from them about a stone's cast, and kneeled down, and prayed,
43. And said, Father, if You are willing, remove this cup from Me: nevertheless, not My will, but Yours, be done.
44. Then there appeared an angel to Him from heaven, strengthening Him.
45. And being in agony He prayed more earnestly: and His sweat was as it were great drops of blood falling down to the ground.
46. When He rose up from prayer and had come to His disciples, He found them sleeping for sorrow,
47. Then said to them, why sleep you? Rise and pray, unless you enter into temptation.
48. While He yet spoke, behold a multitude, and he that was called Judas, one of the twelve, went before them, and drew near to Jesus to kiss Him.
49. But Jesus said to him, Judas, do you betray the Son of man with a kiss?
50. When they who were about him saw what would follow, they said to Him, Lord, will we strike with the sword?
51. And one of them struck the servant of the high priest and cut off his right ear.
52. But Jesus answered and said, no more of this! And He touched his ear and healed him.
53. Then Jesus said to the chief priests, and captains of the temple, and the elders, who had come to Him, be you come out, as against a thief, with swords and clubs?
54. When I was with you each day in the temple, you stretched out no hand against Me: but this is your hour, and the power of darkness.

55. Then they took Him, and led Him, and brought Him into the high priest's house. But Peter followed far off.
56. When they had kindled a fire in the midst of the hall, and had sat down together, Peter sat down among them.
57. A certain servant girl beheld him as he sat by the fire, and earnestly looked on him, and said, this man was also with Him.
58. But he denied Him, saying, Woman, I know Him not.
59. After a little while another saw him, and said, You are also of them. And Peter said, man, I am not.
60. And after about one hour had passed, another one insisted, and said, truly this fellow was also with Him: for he is a Galilean.
61. Then Peter said, man, I do not know what you say. Immediately, while he yet spoke, the rooster crowed.
62. Then the Lord turned and looked at Peter. And Peter remembered the word of the Lord, how he had said to Him, before the rooster crows, you will deny Me three times.
63. And Peter went out and wept bitterly.
64. So, the men that held Jesus mocked Him and struck Him.
65. When they had blindfolded Him, they struck Him on the face, and asked Him, and said, prophesy, who is it that struck You?
66. For many other things they blasphemously spoke against Him.
67. As soon as it was day, the elders of the people and the chief priests and the scribes came together, and led Him into their council, saying,
68. Are You the Christ? Tell us. And He said to them, if I tell you, you will not believe:
69. And if I also ask you, you will not answer Me, nor let Me go.
70. After this will the Son of man sit on the right hand of the power of God.
71. Then said they all, Are you then the Son of God? And He said to them, you say that I am.
72. So, they said, what need do we have of any further witness? For we have heard out of His own mouth.

Chapter 23

1. Then the whole multitude of them arose and led Him to Pilate.
2. So, they began to accuse Him, and said, We found this fellow perverting the nation, and forbidding to give tribute to Caesar, saying that He Himself is Christ, a King.
3. Then Pilate asked Him, saying, are you the King of the Jews? And He answered him and said, you say it.
4. Then Pilate said to the chief priests and the people, I find no fault in this man.
5. But they were the insisting vigorously and said, He stirs up the people, teaching throughout all Judea, beginning from Galilee to this place.
6. When Pilate heard of Galilee, he asked whether the man was a Galilean.
7. As soon as he knew that he belonged to Herod's jurisdiction, he sent Him to Herod, who also was at Jerusalem at that time.

8. When Herod saw Jesus, he was exceedingly glad: for he had desired to see Him for a long time because he had heard many things about Him; and he hoped to have seen some miracle done by Him.
9. Then he questioned Him with many words, but He answered him nothing.
10. And the chief priests and scribes stood and vehemently accused Him.
11. Then Herod with his men of war treated Him with contempt, mocked Him, arrayed Him in a gorgeous robe, and sent Him again to Pilate.
12. That same day Pilate and Herod became friends: for previously there was an enmity between them.
13. For Pilate, when he had called together the chief priests and the rulers and the people,
14. Said to them, You have brought this man to me, as one that perverts the people: and behold, I, having examined Him before you, have found no fault in this man concerning those things which you accuse Him:
15. No, nor has Herod: for I sent you to him; and look, nothing worthy of death is done to Him.
16. Therefore, I will punish Him and release Him.
17. For he was obligated to release one to them at the feast.
18. But they all cried out at once, and said, away with this man, and release to us Barabbas!
19. Who for a certain sedition made in the city, and for murder, had been cast into prison.
20. Therefore, Pilate, willing to release Jesus, spoke again to them.
21. But they cried, and said, Crucify Him, crucify Him!
22. Then he said to them the third time, why, what evil has He done? I have found no reason for death in Him: therefore, I will punish Him and let Him go.
23. But they were insistent with loud voices, demanding that He might be crucified. And their voices and those of the chief priests prevailed.
24. So, Pilate gave the sentence that it should be as they required.
25. Then he released to them him that for sedition and murder had been cast into prison, who they had wanted; but he handed over Jesus to their will.
26. Now as they led Him away, they laid hold on one Simon of Cyrene, coming out of the country, and on him they laid the cross, that he might bear it after Jesus.
27. A great company of people there followed Him, and of women, of whom also mourned and lamented for Him.
28. But Jesus turned to them and said, daughters of Jerusalem, weep not for Me, but weep for yourselves, and for your children.
29. For, behold, the days are coming, in which they will say, Blessed are the barren, and the wombs that never bore, and the breasts which never nursed.
30. Then will they begin to say to the mountains, Fall on us; and to the hills, Cover us.
31. For if they do these things in the green tree, what will be done when it withers?

32. And there were also two others, criminals, led with Him to be put to death.

33. When they had come to the place, which is called Calvary, there they crucified Him, and the criminals, one on the right hand, and the other on the left.

34. Then said Jesus, Father, forgive them; for they do not know what they do. And they parted His clothing and cast lots.

35. So, the people stood looking. And the rulers also with them sneered at Him, and said, He saved others; let Him save Himself, if He is Christ, the chosen of God.

36. The soldiers also mocked Him, coming to Him, and offering Him sour wine,

37. And said, if You are the king of the Jews, save Yourself.

38. And an inscription also was written over Him in letters of Greek, and Latin, and Hebrew, THIS IS THE KING OF THE JEWS.

39. Then one of the criminals who was being hung hurled insults at Him, saying, if You are Christ, save Yourself and us.

40. But the other answered and rebuked him, saying, do you not fear God, seeing you are in the same condemnation?

41. Yet we indeed justly; for we receive the due reward of our deeds: but this man has done nothing wrong.

42. Then he said to Jesus, Lord, remember me when You come into your kingdom.

43. Then Jesus said to him, truthfully, I say to you today, you will be with Me in paradise.

44. And it was about the sixth hour, and there was a darkness over all the land until the ninth hour.

45. For the sun was darkened, and the veil of the temple was torn in the middle.

46. When Jesus had cried with a loud voice, He said, Father, into Your hands I entrust My spirit: and having said this, He breathed out.

47. Now when the centurion saw what was done, he glorified God, saying, this man was certainly righteous!

48. For all the people that came together to that sight, looking at the things which were done, beat their chests, and returned.

49. But all his acquaintances, and the women that followed Him from Galilee, stood far off, beholding these things.

50. And behold, there was a man named Joseph, a member of the Council; and he was a good man, and just:

51. The same had not consented to the counsel and their actions; He was from Arimathaea, a city of the Jews: who also himself was expecting the kingdom of God.

52. This man went to Pilate and begged for the body of Jesus.

53. So, he took it down, and wrapped it in linen, and laid it in a tomb that was cut in stone, in which never was a man before laid.

54. And that day was the preparation, and the Sabbath drew on.

55. So, the women also, who came with Him from Galilee, followed after, and beheld the tomb, and how His body was laid.

56. Then they returned, and prepared spices and ointments; and rested the Sabbath day according to the commandment.

Chapter 24

1. Now on the first day of the week, very early in the morning, they came to the tomb, bringing the spices which they had prepared, and certain others with them.
2. Yet they found the stone rolled away from the tomb.
3. And they entered in and didn't find the body of the Lord Jesus.
4. And it came to pass, as they were very perplexed about this, behold, two men stood by them in shining garments:
5. As they were afraid, and bowed down their faces to the ground, they said to them, why seek you the living among the dead?
6. He is not here, but is risen: Remember how He spoke to You when He was yet in Galilee,
7. Saying, the Son of man must be delivered into the hands of sinful men, and be crucified, and the third day rise again.
8. Then they remembered His words,
9. And returned from the tomb, and told all these things to the eleven, and all the rest.
10. It was Mary Magdalene and Joanna, and Mary the mother of James, and other women who were with them, who told these things to the apostles.
11. But their words seemed to them as utter nonsense, and they believed them not.
12. Then Peter arose, and ran to the tomb; and stooping down, he beheld the linen clothes laid by themselves, and departed, wondering in himself at that which had come to pass.
13. And behold, two of them went that same day to a village called Emmaus, which was from Jerusalem about seven miles.
14. So, they talked together of all these things which had happened.
15. And it came to pass, that, while they conversed together and reasoned, Jesus Himself drew near and went with them.
16. But their eyes were restrained, that they did not recognize Him.
17. And He said to them, what manner of discussion is this that you are exchanging, as you walk, and are looking so sad?
18. Then one of them, whose name was Cleopas, answered and said to Him, are you only a stranger in Jerusalem, and have not known the things which have come to pass there in these days?
19. So, He said to them, what things? And they said to Him, concerning Jesus of Nazareth, who was a prophet mighty in deed and word before God and all the people:
20. And how the chief priests and our rulers delivered Him to be condemned to death and have crucified Him.
21. But we trusted that it was He who was about to redeem Israel: and besides all this, today is the third day since these things happened.
22. Yes, and certain women also of our group made us amazed, who were at the tomb early this morning;
23. When they didn't find His body, they came, and said, that they had also seen a vision of angels who said He was alive.
24. And certain of those who were with us went to the tomb and found it even so as the women had said: but they didn't see Him.

25. Then He said to them, O fools, and slow of heart to believe all that the prophets have spoken:
26. Ought not Christ to have suffered these things, and to enter into His glory?
27. Then beginning at Moses and all the prophets, He explained to them in all the Scriptures the things concerning Himself.
28. Then they drew close to the village, to where they went: and He made as though he would have gone further.
29. But they constrained Him, saying, Stay with us: for it is toward evening, and the day is far spent. And He went in to stay with them.
30. And it came to pass, as He sat to eat with them, He took bread and blessed it, and broke, and gave to them.
31. Then their eyes were opened, and they knew Him, and He vanished out of their sight.
32. Then they said one to another, did not our hearts burn within us, while He talked with us by the way, and while He opened to us the Scriptures?
33. So, they rose up the same hour, and returned to Jerusalem, and found the eleven gathered together, and them that were with them,
34. And said, the Lord is risen indeed and has appeared to Simon!
35. And they told what things were done on the way, and how He was known of them in the breaking of bread.
36. Now as they so spoke, Jesus Himself stood in the midst of them, and said, peace to you.
37. But they were terrified and frightened, and supposed that they had seen a spirit.
38. And He said to them, why are you troubled? And why do doubts arise in your hearts?
39. Behold My hands and My feet, that it is I Myself: handle Me, and see; for a spirit has not flesh and bones, as you see I have.
40. When He had so spoken, He showed them His hands and His feet.
41. While they yet believed not for joy, and wondered, He said to them, have you any food here?
42. So, they gave Him a piece of a broiled fish and a honeycomb.
43. And He took it and did eat before them.
44. Then He said to them, these are the words which I spoke to you, while I was yet with you, that all things must be fulfilled, which were written in the Law of Moses, and the Prophets, and in the Psalms, concerning Me.
45. Then He opened their understanding, that they might understand the Scriptures,
46. Then said to them, thus it is written, and thus it was proper for Christ to suffer, and to rise from the dead the third day:
47. So, that repentance and forgiveness of sins should be preached in His name among all nations, beginning at Jerusalem.
48. You are witnesses of these things.
49. Behold, I send the promise of My Father upon you: but stay in the city, until you are clothed with power from on high.
50. And He led them out as far as to Bethany, and He lifted up His hands and blessed them.

51. And it came to pass, while He blessed them, He was parted from them and ascended into the heavens.
52. Then they worshiped Him, and returned to Jerusalem with great joy:
53. And were continually in the temple, praising and blessing God. Amen.

Synopsis of John

I. Introduction

    A. Background information on the Gospel of John
    B. Overview of the purpose of the presentation
    C. The seven signs in the Gospel of John serve as significant events that illustrate the transition from the old covenant to the new covenant and from the physical to the spiritual

II. Significance of the Seven Signs in Demonstrating the Transition from the Old Covenant to the New Covenant

    A. Introduction to the concept of covenants in biblical theology
    B. Explanation of the old covenant and its limitations
    C. Analysis of each sign in relation to the old covenant
    1. Turning Water Into Wine
    2. Healing the Nobleman's Son
    3. Healing the Man at the Pool
    4. Feeding of the 5,000
    5. Walking on Water
    6. Healing a Man Born Blind
    7. Resurrecting Lazarus

D. Illustrating the Transition from the Physical to the Spiritual

    A. Introduction to the dichotomy of physical and spiritual realms
    B. Examination of each sign in terms of their physical and spiritual elements
    1. Turning Water Into Wine
    2. Healing the Nobleman's Son
    3. Healing the Man at the Pool
    4. Feeding of the 5,000
    5. Walking on Water
    6. Healing a Man Born Blind
    7. Resurrecting Lazarus

C. Symbolism and Metaphorical Representation in the Seven Signs

    A. Introduction to the concept of symbolism in biblical narratives
    B. Analysis of the symbolic meaning behind each sign
1. Turning Water Into Wine
2. Healing the Nobleman's Son
3. Healing the Man at the Pool
4. Feeding of the 5,000
5. Walking on Water
6. Healing a Man Born Blind
7. Resurrecting Lazarus

V. Theological Implications of the Seven Signs

    A. Introduction to the theological significance of the signs in the Gospel of John
    B. Discussion of how the signs contribute to the understanding of Jesus' identity and mission
    C. Examination of the implications for believers in the new covenant era

VI. Critiques and Counterarguments

    A. Introduction to potential objections or counterarguments
    B. Addressing common critiques regarding the validity or significance of the seven signs

VII. Conclusion

    A. Summary of key findings and main arguments throughout this presentation
    B. Restatement of the thesis statement
    C. Reflection on the overall significance of the seven signs in the transition from the old covenant to the new covenant and from the physical to the spiritual

I.   Introduction

Section A: Providing Background on the Gospel of John

The Gospel of John provides a unique perspective on the life, ministry, and teachings of Jesus Christ. It is believed to have been written by the apostle John and stands apart from the other three synoptic gospels due to its distinct structure, content, and theological emphasis. During a time when the early Christian community was grappling with questions of faith and identity, this gospel sought to deepen our understanding of Jesus' divinity and his vital role in the salvation of humanity. The objective of this paper is to delve into the significance of the seven signs depicted in the Gospel of John, contextualizing them within the transition from the old covenant to the new covenant and from the physical to the spiritual realm.

Section B: Presenting the Purpose of the Paper

This paper aims to analyze the seven signs mentioned in the Gospel of John, which include turning water into wine, healing the nobleman's son, healing the man at the pool, feeding of the 5,000, walking on water, healing a man born blind, and resurrecting Lazarus. By scrutinizing these signs, our objective is to uncover their theological, symbolic, and metaphorical implications. Specifically, we will explore how these signs serve as illustrations of the transition from the old covenant to the new covenant and from the physical to the spiritual realms.

Section C: Stating the Thesis

These seven signs in the Gospel of John hold significant value as they exemplify the transition from the old covenant to the new covenant and from the physical to the spiritual.

II. Significance of the Seven Signs in Demonstrating the Transition from the Old Covenant to the New Covenant

A. Introduction to the concept of covenants in biblical theology

Within the realm of biblical theology, a covenant represents a formal agreement or contract that establishes a profound relationship between God and His people. It outlines the terms and conditions for this relationship, playing a central role in the Old Testament. God, through covenants, established divine contracts with individuals like Noah, Abraham, Moses, David, and the nation of Israel as a whole. The old covenant, known as the Mosaic covenant, originated from Moses and was given to the Israelites at Mount Sinai. This covenant was characterized by a set of laws, rituals, and sacrifices which governed the relationship between God and the Israelites. It prioritized strict obedience to the law and performance of prescribed rituals to maintain their connection with God and receive His blessings.

B. Explanation of the old covenant and its limitations

Despite revealing the righteousness and holiness of God while exposing the sinfulness and inadequacy of humanity, the old covenant, with its focus on external rituals and adherence to the law, possessed certain limitations. Witness Lee suggests that "The old covenant, being weak in the flesh and unable to change the heart, was not able to fulfill the requirements of God's righteousness and holiness" (Lee 34). G.K. Beale further elaborates that the rituals and sacrifices prescribed by the old covenant served as "a temporary fix" rather than a permanent solution (Beale 112). Acting as a tutor, the old covenant pointed towards the coming of the Messiah and the establishment of a new covenant that addresses the shortcomings of the old one.

C. Analysis of each sign in relation to the old covenant

1. Turning Water Into Wine

The initial sign performed by Jesus, manifested through turning water into wine, symbolizes the transition from the old covenant to the new covenant. This significant event occurred at a wedding feast, which holds immense biblical association with covenants. The abundance of wine at the wedding feast represents the unlimited spiritual blessings brought forth by Jesus' ministry and the new covenant.

2. Healing the Nobleman's Son

Through healing the nobleman's son, Jesus showcases His authority over distance and time. This sign highlights the limitations of the old covenant, which necessitated physical presence and specific rituals for healing. It points towards spiritual healing and salvation attainable through faith in Jesus.

3. Healing the Man at the Pool

The healing of the man at the pool accentuates the limitations of the old covenant, which placed undue emphasis on legalistic observances. The man waited for 38 years for assistance in entering the pool for physical healing. Jesus' act of healing surpasses the legalistic prerequisites of the old covenant and reveals the power of multiplied grace and mercy.

4. Feeding of the 5,000

The feeding of the 5,000 underscores the insufficiency of physical provisions and rituals within the old covenant.

The multiplication of loaves and fish symbolizes Jesus' capability to provide spiritual sustenance and nourishment, surpassing the physical realm.

5. Walking on Water

As Jesus walks on water, He showcases His authority over the physical elements. This sign challenges the limitations of the old covenant, which could not transcend physical boundaries. It signifies Jesus' ability to provide spiritual security and refuge beyond the constraints of the physical world.

6. Healing a Man Born Blind

The healing of a man born blind signifies the restoration of both physical sight and spiritual understanding. It reveals the limitations of the old covenant in instigating genuine enlightenment. This sign points to Jesus as the light of the world, the ultimate source of authentic spiritual enlightenment and revelation.

7. Resurrecting Lazarus

The resurrection of Lazarus from the dead serves as the ultimate sign of the transition from the old covenant to the new covenant. Jesus was aware of Lazarus' death as soon as it happened. This event is deeply rooted in Jewish history, specifically the connection to old Israel. In Ezekiel and Isaiah, the Scriptures talk about Israel being dead and buried while in captivity in Babylon and Assyria, with God promising to open their graves. Isaiah prophesied that a remnant would return, symbolizing those who emerged from the grave of Assyria and Babylon.

Paul later references these prophecies in Romans, indicating that a remnant of old Israel will be resurrected and incorporated into the new heavenly Israel. In Romans 9:27-28, Paul quotes Isaiah's prophecy, stating, "Though the number of the sons of Israel be as the sand of the sea, only a remnant of them will be saved, for the Lord will carry out his sentence upon the earth fully and without delay." This passage alludes to the idea of a remnant being resurrected and saved, as mentioned in Isaiah's prophecy. Also In Isaiah 26:19, it is written, "But your dead will live, Lord; their bodies will rise— let those who dwell in the dust wake up and shout for joy— your dew is like the dew of the morning; the land will give birth to her dead." This verse is often interpreted as a reference to the resurrection of the dead, symbolizing a remnant being brought back to life by the Lord. The story of Lazarus is intentionally set in a Jewish context, with Jesus deliberately returning to the hostile Jewish area where he had faced threats before. Despite warnings from his disciples, Jesus insisted on going back, using the death and resurrection of Lazarus as a symbol of raising a new Israel out of the rejected and buried old Israel.

III. Illustrating the Transition from the Physical to the Spiritual

A. Introduction to the dichotomy of physical and spiritual realms

In biblical theology, the dichotomy of the physical and spiritual realms holds significant theological implications. According to Witness Lee, the Gospel of John consistently uses the physical realm as a backdrop to guide readers towards the spiritual realm. The transition from the physical to the spiritual is a central theme in the Gospel of John, highlighting the importance of understanding Jesus' ministry and teachings from a spiritual perspective. Therefore, it is imperative to explore the ways in which the seven signs in the Gospel of John exemplify this transition and shed light on the profound spiritual truths they convey.

B. Examination of each sign in terms of their physical and spiritual elements

Each of the seven signs in the Gospel of John serves as a vehicle for showcasing the transition from the physical to the spiritual. These signs not only occur in the physical world, but also reveal deeper spiritual truths that Jesus intended to convey. By closely examining each sign, we can discern the intricate interplay between the physical and spiritual elements at play.

1. Turning Water Into Wine

Jesus' act of turning water into wine at the wedding feast in Cana demonstrates his ability to transform the material realm into something of greater significance. This sign symbolizes the beginning of a new age under the new covenant. In this time, the joyous celebration of the Messiah's arrival surpasses the limitations of the old covenant provisions.

2. Healing the Nobleman's Son

The healing of the nobleman's son emphasizes the transition from physical ailments to spiritual healing attained through faith in Jesus. This sign reveals that Jesus' authority transcends distance and time, offering divine restoration and salvation.

3. Healing the Man at the Pool

The healing of the man at the pool of Bethesda showcases freedom from the legalistic practices associated with the old covenant. This sign highlights the power of divine grace, replacing the rigid observance of physical rituals with the significance of the new covenant and God's transformative work in the lives of believers.

4. Feeding of the 5,000

The feeding of the 5,000 symbolizes Jesus as the spiritual Bread of Life, providing sustenance beyond physical nourishment. This sign foreshadows the ultimate spiritual nourishment offered by Jesus, as he becomes the ultimate source of satisfaction and fulfillment for believers.

5. Walking on Water

Walking on water signifies Jesus' ability to transcend physical limitation and instills trust in Him as **the source** of spiritual sustenance. This sign draws the disciples' attention away from the physical realm, reinforcing the need for a firm faith in Jesus that surpasses external circumstances.

6. Healing a Man Born Blind

The healing of a man born blind not only represents the restoration of physical sight, but also symbolizes the enlightenment of spiritual understanding. This sign reveals that Jesus possesses the power to bring illumination and true insight into the hearts and minds of believers.

7. Resurrection of Lazarus

The resurrection of Lazarus signifies Jesus' triumph over death and serves as the ultimate confirmation of His divinity.

IV. Symbolism and Metaphorical Representation in the Seven Signs

A. An Introduction to the Concept of Symbolism in Biblical Narratives

Biblical narratives often utilize symbols to convey deeper meanings and truths that go beyond the literal events described. In the Gospel of John, symbolisms are abundantly present, particularly in the seven signs that are presented throughout the narrative. By understanding the symbolic nature of these signs, we can gain a more profound interpretation of their significance and theological implications. This section will delve into the concept of symbolism and its application to the seven signs in the Gospel of John.

B. An Analysis of the Symbolic Meanings Behind Each Sign

The seven signs in the Gospel of John hold profound symbolic meanings that shed light on the transition from the old covenant to the new covenant and from the physical to the spiritual realms. Each sign embodies significant themes and truths that reinforce Jesus' role as the Messiah and reveal the transformative power of the new covenant.

1. Turning Water Into Wine

The turning of water into wine at the wedding feast in Cana symbolizes Jesus' ability to bring about a new age of spiritual abundance and joy through the new covenant. It signifies the transformation of empty religious rituals and traditions into a vibrant and fulfilling relationship with God. This sign points to the transition from the water of ritual cleansing in the old covenant to the wine of divine life and celebration in the new covenant.

2. Healing the Nobleman's Son

By healing the nobleman's son from a distance, Jesus displays his authority over physical limitations and underscores the power of faith. This sign symbolizes the spiritual healing that comes through believing in Jesus, foreshadowing the redemption that the new covenant offers. It illustrates the shift from the physical realm of sickness and suffering to the spiritual realm of wholeness and salvation.

3. Healing the Man at the Pool

The healing of the man at the pool of Bethesda reveals the compassionate and merciful nature of Jesus. This sign symbolizes the liberation from legalistic observances and the limitations of the old covenant. This healing signifies the power of God's grace and the healing that comes through faith in Jesus, contrasting with the futile attempts of the old covenant law to bring spiritual wholeness.

4. Feeding of the 5,000

The feeding of the 5,000 with five loaves and two fishes serves as a significant sign of Jesus' provision and sustenance. It symbolizes the abundance of spiritual nourishment available through the new covenant in contrast to the physical provision of the old covenant.

5. Walking on Water

By walking on water, Jesus demonstrates his ability to transcend physical limitations and instill trust in Him as the source of spiritual sustenance. This sign symbolizes the invitation for believers to step out in faith and trust Jesus amidst the storms of life. This indicator signals Jesus' divine nature and his function as the intermediary between the physical and heavenly realms.

6. Healing a Man Born Blind

Healing a man born blind not only represents the restoration of physical sight but also symbolizes the enlightenment of spiritual understanding. This sign highlights Jesus as the Light of the World who brings illumination and knowledge to a spiritually blind humanity. It signifies the transition from darkness and ignorance to spiritual enlightenment through faith in Jesus.

7. Resurrecting Lazarus

The resurrection of Lazarus from the dead serves as the climactic sign in the Gospel of John. It symbolizes Jesus' triumph over death and foreshadows his own resurrection, offering hope and eternal life through the new covenant. D.A. Carson (147) emphasizes that this sign confirms Jesus' divinity and establishes him as the giver of life and the resurrection of all who believe in him.

V. Theological Implications of the Seven Signs

A. Introduction to the theological significance of the signs in the Gospel of John

The Gospel of John presents a collection of seven signs that hold profound theological implications. These signs not only display Jesus' divine nature and purpose, but they also fulfill the ancient prophecies and inaugurate a new era of divine covenant. By delving into the theological framework embedded within these signs, we can uncover captivating insights into the essence of God, the role of Jesus as the Son of God, and the transformative power of faith.

B. Discussion of how the signs contribute to the understanding of Jesus' identity and mission

The seven signs depicted in the Gospel of John play an imperatively pivotal role in shaping and expanding our understanding of Jesus' identity and mission. Each sign offers a distinct revelation about Jesus, highlighting diverse facets of His divine nature and redemptive work.

For instance, the remarkable transformation of water into wine not only showcases Jesus' authority over creation but also symbolizes the arrival of a new covenant age brimming with spiritual blessings (John 2:1-12).

An equally mesmerizing sign is the healing of the nobleman's son, which demonstrates Jesus as the divine healer. This miraculous event manifests Jesus' ability to heal from a distance, magnifying the saving power accessible through faith in Him (John 4:46-54).

Among the signs, the healing of the man at the pool exudes Jesus' boundless compassion and grace, as He not only provides physical healing but also liberates the man from the legalistic constraints of the old covenant (John 5:1-15). In addition, the feeding of the 5,000 vividly portrays Jesus' role as the Bread of Life. This extraordinary act extends far beyond physical nourishment, unraveling the spiritual sustenance that transcends the mundane and satisfies the profound longings of the soul (John 6:1-15).

The extraordinary event of Jesus walking on water serves to reaffirm Jesus' authority over nature. By defying the physical constraints, Jesus instills faith and instigates an unswerving belief that He is the ultimate source of spiritual nourishment (John 6:16-21).

Another awe-inspiring sign is the healing of the man born blind. This miraculous act symbolizes the illumination of spiritual understanding as Jesus restores not only physical sight but also opens the eyes of the heart to the profound truth of His divinity (John 9:1-41). Lastly, the ultimate sign is the resurrection of Lazarus, unequivocally foreshadowing Jesus' triumphant victory over death. This extraordinary resurrection vividly substantiates Jesus' role as both the resurrection and the life, solidifying His authority and reinforcing the foundation of the new covenant age (John 11:1-44). Individually, these signs contribute significantly to our comprehension of Jesus' identity, His redemptive mission, and His paramount role in paving the path for the new covenant age.

C. Examination of the implications for believers in the new covenant era

The seven signs unveiled in the Gospel of John carry profound and far-reaching implications for believers residing in the new covenant age. These signs extend an inviting invitation to embark on a transformative journey of faith and to embrace the timeless realities of the spiritual realm. The act of witnessing and comprehending these signs possesses the power to reignite an unparalleled sense of awe, admiration, and devotion towards Jesus, culminating in a deeply enriched relationship with God and an elevated encounter with the abundance of blessings present within the new covenant.

First and foremost, these signs pose a formidable challenge for believers to comprehend that the new covenant transcends the constraints that once shackled the old covenant. The old covenant, anchored in rigid rituals and external observances, is ultimately surpassed by the new covenant, which prioritizes the inward transformation of the heart (Jeremiah

31:31-34). The signs illustrate the supremacy of the spiritual domain over the physical, reiterating the pressing need for believers to redirect their focus from superficial rituals to the cultivation of a genuine and intimate relationship with Jesus.

Furthermore, the signs serve as a potent reminder to place absolute trust and unwavering faith in Jesus as the unwavering source of spiritual sustenance and fulfillment. Just as Jesus abundantly provided physical nourishment to the multitudes, He promises to fill the deepest longings of our souls through an intimate and personal fellowship with Him (John 6:35). The signs beckon believers to relinquish their fixation on earthly desires and instead seek spiritual nourishment solely in Jesus, acknowledging His paramount status as the Bread of Life.

Lastly, the signs breathe hope and assurance into the lives of believers, particularly in the midst of immense challenges and trials. By triumphantly conquering death itself through the resurrection of Lazarus, Jesus unequivocally manifests his mastery over all circumstances, offering believers the promise of infinite life and the eventual triumph over death. This steadfast assurance serves as an unwavering source of solace, strength, and encouragement, empowering believers to persevere on their individual faith journeys and wholeheartedly entrust themselves to the transformative and redeeming work of Jesus.

VI. Critiques and Counterarguments

A. Introduction to potential objections or counterarguments

Throughout the Gospel of John, the seven signs serve as significant events that beautifully illustrate the profound transition from the old covenant to the new covenant, bridging the gap between the physical and the spiritual realms. However, it is important to acknowledge that there are potential objections and counterarguments that can be raised, shedding light on the complexity and depth of this topic.

B. Addressing common critiques regarding the validity or significance of the seven signs

One common critique that arises is the notion that the seven signs described in the Gospel of John are merely symbolic and lack historical verifiability. However, proponents of these signs insist that they carry both symbolic meaning and a solid historical foundation, intertwining the realms of the spiritual and the tangible.

That these signs recorded in John's Gospel are not made up stories, but actual historical events that have a symbolic significance. The Gospel of John beautifully blends elements of factuality and symbolism.

Another critique being frequently raised revolves around the selective nature of the seven signs. Critics argue that the Gospel of John fails to include all the miracles performed by Jesus, stating that the selection of these specific signs is purely subjective. However, addressing this concern head-on, rather than aiming for an exhaustive catalog of miracles, the Gospel purposefully presents these signs to convey essential theological themes, namely what was transpiring in that day. The transition from the old to the new.

Furthermore, some may question the significance of the signs in relation to the transition from the old covenant to the new covenant. It is possible that skeptics might argue that other elements of Jesus' ministry, such as His teachings or the Last Supper, hold greater importance. Nevertheless, proponents steadfastly maintain that the seven signs play a pivotal role in demonstrating Jesus' divine identity and the transformative power brought forth by the new covenant.

Emphasizing the relevance of these signs, all the apostles and the people who believed understood their vital role in revealing Jesus as the promised fulfillment of the Old Testament prophecies and types and shadows that embodied the new covenant realities.

VII. Conclusion

Throughout this presentation, we have delved into the profound significance of the seven signs presented in the Gospel of John. These signs serve as pivotal events that vividly illustrate the transition from the age-old covenant to the refreshing new covenant, and from the realm of the physical to the spiritual realm. By examining the theological, symbolic, metaphorical, and theological implications of each sign, we have acquired a deeper understanding of the multi-faceted identity of Jesus, His divinely-charged mission, and the profound implications for the believers who experienced the realm of the new covenant age. which were the powers of the age to come.

To summarize, the seven signs chronicled in the Gospel of John hold immense significance in unraveling the life-changing nature of Jesus' ministry. Each sign serves as a poignant reflection of the limitations that were inherent within the old covenant, while simultaneously embodying the transformational power that pulsates within the new covenant. These signs artfully unveil not only the undeniable authority and divinity that lies within Jesus, but also exemplify the monumental shift from the realm of superficial physical rituals to that of an intricate, nourishing, and infinitely more profound spiritual connection with God.

Through the symbolic act of transforming water into wine, Jesus illuminates the abundance that the new covenant ushers in, along with the joyous celebration that invariably follows. The profound act of healing the nobleman's son serves as a testament to Jesus' extraordinary authority that transcends time and distance, while simultaneously representing the spiritual healing that is unequivocally bestowed upon those who wholeheartedly place their faith in him. Furthermore, the awe-inspiring healing of the man at the pool marks an auspicious liberation from the shackles of legalistic observances that characterized the old covenant, while simultaneously underlining the inexorable power that lies within divine grace.

The miraculous feeding of the 5,000 astutely foreshadows the ultimate spiritual nourishment that Jesus, the majestic Bread of Life, brings forth. The awe-inspiring act of walking on water effortlessly signifies Jesus' profound ability to transcend and surmount the physical limitations that confine ordinary mortals, thereby inspiring an indomitable trust in him as the perennial source of resplendent spiritual sustenance. Simultaneously, the miraculous restoration of sight to the man born blind elicits not only the reinstatement of his physical vision, but represents the dawning of a profound enlightenment that befalls upon his spiritual understanding.

Lastly, the poignant resurrection of Lazarus stands as an indomitable symbol of Jesus' audacious triumph over death, while simultaneously foreshadowing His own forthcoming resurrection – an event that undeniably solidifies His standing as the embodiment of divinity and serves as the resounding inauguration of the invigorated new covenant age.

These seven remarkable signs contribute in a substantial manner towards our profound comprehension of Jesus' boundless identity and his momentous mission. Earning revelation through these unique signs, we emerge with a resounding confirmation of Jesus' awe-inspiring presence as the beloved Son of God, the long-awaited Messiah, and the embodiment of the prodigious promises that the prophets of old ardently uttered. Furthermore, these signs emphatically underscore the reverberating verity that authentic worship is not confined to the minute boundaries of physical locations or the meticulously rehearsed rituals that were synonymous with the old covenant age, but rather, it emerges from the sacred ground of an intensely personal connection with Jesus; it springs forth from an unyielding faith that effortlessly transcends the ephemeral, tangible realm of the physical. In essence, the seven signs archived within the Gospel of John offer us a profound and kaleidoscopic glimpse into the monumental transition that transpires from the age-old covenant to the dawning new covenant age, as well as from the realm of rigid physical confines to that of enchanting spiritual liberation.

These breathtaking signs magnify Jesus' unparalleled divine authority, His indelible role as the ultimate mediator between God and humanity, and the resounding invitation He extends to each earnest believer, beseeching them to embark on a glorious journey of faith. By unreservedly embracing and assimilating the timeless lessons and teachings encapsulated within these divine signs, individuals are blessed with the golden opportunity to deepen their discernment of Jesus' miraculous redemptive work, thereby experiencing the fullness of the spiritual blessings that the invigorated new covenant age invariably bestows upon the ardent seekers of truth.

Reflection:

On a broader and more comprehensive level, the arduous journey of insightful exploration encompassing the seven signs chronicled within the Gospel of John has not only shed an incandescent light upon their timeless and universal relevance, but has also underscored the paradigm-shifting appeal that Jesus' teachings hold for individuals hailing from diverse walks of life. As sincere seekers of reality continuously strive to establish a deeply intimate and enduring relationship with the divine, while simultaneously grappling with the myriad questions that underscore matters of faith and existential significance, the Gospel of John, with its awe-inspiring repository of divine signs, serves as a profound and abiding testament to the radical life-changing and invincible wholeness that Jesus' boundless message exudes.

This enlightened expedition reassures and reinforces the resounding belief that Christianity, far from being a mere testament of ancient history, thrives as a vibrant and intensely living faith that unceasingly illuminates the path to profound enlightenment and spiritual growth for passionate believers spanning across generations, transcending the transitory boundaries of time and space.

Terry Kashian

Gospel of John

Chapter 1

1. In the beginning was the Word, and the Word was with God, and the Word was God.
2. He was in the beginning with God.
3. All things were made by Him; and outside Him was nothing made that was made.
4. In Him was life; and the life was the light of men.
5. And the light shines in darkness, and the darkness apprehended it not.
6. There was a man sent from God, whose name was John.
7. The same came for a witness, to testify of the Light that all men through him believe.
8. He was not that Light but was sent to bear witness concerning that Light.
9. That was the true Light, which shines upon every man that is coming into the world.
10. He was in the world, and the world was made by Him, but the world did not know Him.
11. He came to His own, and His own did not receive Him.
12. But as many as received Him, to them He gave authority to become the children of God, even to those that believe in His name:
13. Who were born, not of blood, nor of the will of the flesh, nor the will of man, but of God.
14. And the Word was made flesh, and tabernacled among us, and we beheld His glory, the glory of the only begotten of the Father, full of grace and reality.
15. John bore witness of Him, and cried, saying, this was He of whom I spoke, He that comes after me existed before me: for He was before me.
16. For of His fullness, we have all received, and grace upon grace.
17. For the Law was given by Moses, but grace and reality came through Jesus Christ.
18. No man has seen God at any time, the only begotten Son, who is in the bosom of the Father, He has revealed by presenting Him.
19. For this is the testimony of John, when the Jews sent priests and Levites from Jerusalem to ask him, who are you?
20. And he confessed, and denied not; but confessed, I am not the Christ.
21. So, they asked him, what then? Are you Elijah? And he said, I am not. Are you that prophet? And he answered, no.
22. Then they said to him, who are you? That we may give an answer to them that sent us. What do you say about yourself?
23. He said, I am the voice of one crying in the wilderness, make straight the way of the Lord, as the prophet Isaiah has said,
24. For they who were sent were from the Pharisees.
25. So, they asked him, and said to him, why do you immerse then, if you are not the Christ, nor Elijah, neither that prophet?
26. John answered them, and said, I immerse in water: but there stands One among you, who you do not know;
27. He it is, who is coming after me, who exists before me, whose sandal's strap I am not worthy to untie.

28. These things were done in Bethany beyond the Jordan, where John was immersing.

29. The next day John saw Jesus coming to him, and said, behold the Lamb of God, who takes away the sin of the world!

30. This is He of whom I said after me comes a man who is preferred before me: for He was before me.

31. Yet I knew Him not: but that He should be made manifest to Israel, therefore I have come immersing in water.

32. So, John gave witness, saying, I saw the Spirit descending from heaven like a dove, and it remained on Him.

33. For I knew Him not: but He that sent me to immerse in water, the same said to me, on whom you will see the Spirit descending, and remaining on Him, the same is He who immerses in the Holy Spirit.

34. And I saw and gave witness that this is the Son of God.

35. Again, the next day after John stood, and two of his disciples;

36. Then looking on Jesus as he walked, he said, behold the Lamb of God!

37. So, the two disciples heard Him speak, and they followed Jesus.

38. Then Jesus turned, and saw them following, and said to them, what do you seek? They said to Him, Rabbi, (which is to say, being interpreted, Master) where are You dwelling?

39. He said to them, come and see. They came and saw where he dwelt and remained that day with Him: for it was about the tenth hour.

40. One of the two who heard John speak, and followed Him, was Andrew, Simon Peter's brother.

41. He first found his own brother Simon, and said to him, we have found the Messiah, which is, being interpreted, the Christ.

42. Then he brought him to Jesus. When Jesus looked at him, he said, you are Simon the son of Jonah: you will be called Cephas, which is by interpretation, a stone.

43. The day following Jesus went out into Galilee, and found Philip, and said to him, follow Me!

44. Now Philip was of Bethsaida, the city of Andrew and Peter.

45. Philip found Nathanael, and said to him, we have found Him, of whom Moses in the Law, and the prophets, did write, Jesus of Nazareth, the son of Joseph.

46. But Nathaniel said to him, Can there come any good thing out of Nazareth? Philip said to him, come and see.

47. Jesus saw Nathanael coming to Him, and said of him, behold an Israelite indeed, in whom is no deceit!

48. Nathaniel said to Him, from what place do You know me? Jesus answered and said to him, before Philip called you, when you were under the fig tree, I saw you.

49. Nathanael answered and said to him, Rabbi, You are the Son of God; You are the King of Israel!

50. Jesus answered and said to him because I said to you, I saw you under the fig tree, you believe? You will see greater things than these.

51. Then He said to him, truly, truly, I say to you, after this, you will see the heavens open, and the messengers of God ascending and descending on the Son of Man!

Chapter 2

1. On the third day there was a marriage in Cana of Galilee, and the mother of Jesus was there:
2. Now both Jesus was invited, and His disciples, to the marriage.
3. When they wanted wine, the mother of Jesus said to Him, they have no wine.
4. Jesus said to her, what is that to Me and you, oh woman? My hour has not yet come.
5. His mother said to the servants, whatever He says to you, do it.
6. Now there were set six stone water pots, after the manner of the purifying of the Jews, containing twenty or thirty gallons each.
7. Jesus said to them, fill the water pots with water. And they filled them up to the top.
8. And He said to them, draw out now, and bring to the master of the feast and they brought it.
9. When the ruler of the feast had tasted the water that was made wine and did not know from where it came: (but the servants who drew the water knew) the master of the feast called the bridegroom,
10. Then said to him, every man at the beginning does set out good wine; and when men have well drunk, then that which is worse: but you have kept the good wine until now.
11. This beginning of miracles did Jesus in Cana of Galilee and manifested His glory, and His disciples believed in Him.
12. After this He went down to Capernaum, He, and His mother, and His brothers, and His disciples: and they continued there not many days.
13. Then the Jews' Passover was at hand, and Jesus went up to Jerusalem.
14. And found in the temple those that sold oxen and sheep and doves, and the changers of money sitting:
15. When He had made a whip of small cords, He drove them all out of the temple, and the sheep, and the oxen; and poured out the changers' money, and overthrew the tables;
16. Then said to them that sold doves, take these things away; do not make My Father's house a house of marketing!
17. And His disciples remembered that it was written, the zeal of Your house has eaten Me up.
18. Then the Jews answered and said to Him, what sign do You show to us, seeing that You are doing these things?
19. Jesus answered and said to them, destroy this temple, and in three days I will raise it up.
20. Then the Jews said, it took forty-six years to build this temple, and will you raise it up in three days?
21. But He spoke of the temple of His body.
22. Therefore, when He had risen from the dead, His disciples remembered that He had said this to them; and they believed the Scripture and the word which Jesus had spoken.

23. Now when He was in Jerusalem at the Passover, on the feast day, many believed in His name, when they saw the miracles which He did.
24. But Jesus did not commit Himself to them, because He knew all men,
25. And did not need that any should testify about man: for He knew what was in man.

Chapter 3

1. There was a man of the Pharisees, named Nicodemus, a ruler of the Jews:
2. The same came to Jesus by night, and said to Him, Rabbi, we know that You are a teacher come from God: for no man can do these miracles that You are doing, unless God is with Him.
3. Jesus answered and said to him, truly, truly, I say to you, unless a man be born from above, he cannot see the kingdom of God.
4. Nicodemus said to Him, how can a man be born when He is old? Can he enter the second time into his mother's womb, and be born?
5. Jesus answered, truly, truly, I say to you unless a man be born of water and the Spirit, he cannot enter into the kingdom of God.
6. That which is born of the flesh is flesh, and that which is born of the Spirit is spirit.
7. Marvel not that I said to you, you must be born from above.
8. The wind blows where it chooses, and you hear the sound of it, but cannot tell from where it comes, and to where it goes: so is every one that is born of the Spirit.
9. Nicodemus answered and said to Him, how can these things be?
10. Jesus answered and said to him, are you a teacher of Israel, and do not know these things?
11. Truly, truly, I say to you, we speak what we do know and testify what we have seen; and you do not receive our witness.
12. If I have told you earthly things, and you do not believe, how will you believe, if I tell you about heavenly things?
13. No man has ascended up to heaven, but He that came down from heaven, even the Son of Man who is in heaven.
14. So, as Moses lifted up the serpent in the wilderness, even so, must the Son of Man be lifted up:
15. That whoever believes in Him will not perish but have infinite life.
16. For God so loved the world that He gave His only begotten Son, that whoever believes in Him should not perish, but have infinite life.
17. For God sent His Son into the world not to condemn the world; but that the world through Him might be saved.
18. He that believes in Him is not condemned: but He that believes not is condemned already, because He has not believed in the name of the only begotten Son of God.
19. And this is the condemnation, that light has come into the world, and men loved darkness rather than light because their deeds were evil.
20. For everyone that does evil hates the light, neither comes to the light unless his deeds should be exposed.

21. But he that practices the reality comes to the light, that his actions may be made manifest, that they have been effected in God.
22. After these things Jesus came with His disciples into the land of Judea, and there He continued with them and was baptizing.
23. And John was also immersing in Aenon near Salim because there was much water there: and they came and were immersed.
24. For John was not yet put into prison.
25. Then there arose a question between some of John's disciples and the Jews about purifying.
26. Then they came to John, and said to him, Rabbi, He that was with you beyond the Jordan, to whom you gave witness, behold, the same immerses, and all men come to Him.
27. John answered and said, a man can receive nothing unless it is given to him from heaven.
28. You heard me testify, that I said, I am not the Christ, but that I am sent before Him.
29. He that has the bride is the bridegroom: but the friend of the bridegroom, who stands and hears him, rejoices greatly because of the bridegroom's voice: therefore, my joy is made full.
30. He must increase, but I must decrease.
31. He that comes from above is above all: he that is of the earth is earthly and speaks of the earth: He that comes from heaven is above all.
32. What He has seen and heard, that He testifies, and no man receives His testimony.
33. He that has received His testimony has certified that God is true.
34. For He who God has sent speaks the words of God: for God gives the Spirit without measure.
35. The Father loves the Son and has given all things into His hand.
36. He that believes into the Son has infinite life: and he that refuses to believe the Son will not see life, but the wrath of God remains on him.

Chapter 4

1. Therefore, when the LORD knew how the Pharisees had heard that Jesus made and immersed more disciples than John,
2. (Though Jesus Himself did not baptize, but His disciples did)
3. He left Judea and departed again into Galilee.
4. But He needed to go through Samaria.
5. Then came He to a city of Samaria, which is called Sychar, near the plot of ground that Jacob gave to his son Joseph.
6. Now Jacob's well was there. Therefore Jesus, being tired from His journey, sat so on the well: and it was about the sixth hour.
7. There came a woman of Samaria to draw water: Jesus said to her, give Me a drink.
8. (For His disciples were gone away to the city to buy food.)
9. Then said the woman of Samaria said to Him, how is it that You, being a Jew, ask me for a drink, who is a woman of Samaria? For the Jews have no dealings with the Samaritans.

10. Jesus answered and said to her, if you knew the gift of God, and who it is that says to you, give me a drink; you would have asked Him, and He would have given you living water.

11. The woman said to Him, Sir, You have nothing to draw with, and the well is deep: from where do You have that living water?

12. Are You greater than our father Jacob, who gave us the well and drank of it himself, and his children, and his cattle?

13. Jesus answered and said to her, whoever drinks of this water will thirst again:

14. but whoever drinks of the water that I will give him will by no means thirst in the New Covenant Age, but the water that I will give him will be in him a well of water springing up into infinite life.

15. The woman said to Him, Sir, give me this water, that I thirst not, neither come here to draw.

16. Jesus said to her, go, call your husband, and come here.

17. The woman answered and said, I do not have a husband. Jesus said to her, you have well said, I have no husband:

18. For you have had five husbands, and he you now have is not your husband: in that you spoke truly.

19. The woman said to Him, Sir, I perceive that You are a prophet.

20. Our fathers worshiped on this mountain; but You say, that in Jerusalem is the place where men ought to worship.

21. Jesus said to her, woman, believe Me, the hour comes, when you will neither on this mountain, nor even at Jerusalem, worship the Father.

22. You worship what you do not know: we know what we worship: for salvation is from the Jews.

23. But the hour comes and now is when the true worshipers will worship the Father in spirit and reality: for the Father seeks such to worship Him.

24. God is Spirit: and they that worship Him must worship Him in spirit and reality.

25. The woman said to Him, I know that Messiah comes, who is called Christ: when He comes, He will tell us all things.

26. Jesus said to her, I am speaking to you.

27. At this point His disciples came, and marveled that He talked with the woman and yet no one said, what do You seek? Or why did You talk with her?

28. The woman then left her water pot, and went her way into the city, and said to the men,

29. come, see a man, who told me all things that I ever did: is this not the Christ?

30. Then they went out of the city and came to Him.

31. In the meanwhile, His disciples urged Him, saying, Master, eat.

32. But He said to them, I have food to eat that you know not of.

33. Therefore, said the disciples to one another, has any man brought Him anything to eat?

34. Jesus said to them, My food is to do the will of Him that sent Me and to finish His work.

35. Do you not say, there are yet four months, and then comes harvest? Behold, I say to you, lift up your eyes, and look on the fields; for they are white already for harvest.
36. He that reaps receives wages, and scatters fruit to infinite life: that both he that sows and he that reaps may rejoice together!
37. For in this the saying is true, one sows, and another reaps.
38. I sent you to reap that for which you have not labored: other men labored, and you have entered into their labors.
39. So, many of the Samaritans of that city believed in Him for the words of the woman, who testified, He told Me all that I ever did.
40. So, when the Samaritans had come to Him, they asked Him that He would stay with them: and He stayed there two days.
41. Then many more believed because of His own word;
42. And said to the woman, now we believe, not because of your saying: for we have heard Him ourselves, and know that this is indeed the Christ, the Savior of the world.
43. Now after two days He departed from there and went into Galilee.
44. For Jesus Himself testified, that a prophet has no honor in his own country.
45. Then when He had come into Galilee, the Galileans received Him, having seen all the things that He did at Jerusalem at the feast: for they also went to the feast.
46. So, Jesus came again into Cana of Galilee, where He made the water wine. And there was a certain nobleman, whose son was sick at Capernaum.
47. When he heard that Jesus had come out of Judea into Galilee, he went to Him, and asked Him that He would come down, and heal his son: for he was about to die.
48. Then Jesus said to him, unless you see signs and wonders, you will not believe.
49. The nobleman said to Him, Sir, come down before my child dies.
50. Jesus said to him, go your way; your son lives. And the man believed the word that Jesus had spoken to him, and he went his way.
51. Now as he was going down, his servants met him, and told him, saying, your son lives!
52. Then he inquired of them the hour when he began to get well. Then they said to him, yesterday at the seventh hour the fever left him.
53. So, the father knew that it was at the same hour, in which Jesus said to him, your son lives: and he and his whole house believed.
54. This again is the second miracle that Jesus did, when He came out of Judea into Galilee.

Chapter 5

1. After this there was a feast of the Jews, and Jesus went up to Jerusalem.
2. Now there is at Jerusalem by the Sheep Gate a pool, which is called in Hebrew, Bethesda, having five porches.
3. In these lay a great multitude of sick people, blind, lame, withered, waiting for the moving of the water.

4. (For an angel went down at a certain time into the pool and agitated the water: that whoever was first after the agitation of the water, stepped in, was made whole of whatever disease he had.)

5. And a certain man was there, who had an infirmity of thirty-eight years.

6. When Jesus saw him lying there and knew that he had been in that condition a long time, He said to him, do you want to be made healthy?

7. The sick man answered him, Sir, I have no man, when the water is agitated, to put me into the pool: but while I am coming, someone else steps down before me.

8. Jesus said to him, rise, take up your bed, and walk.

9. Immediately the man was made healthy, and took up his bed, and walked: and on the same day was the Sabbath.

10. Therefore, the Jews said to him who was cured, it is the Sabbath day: it is not lawful for you to carry your bed.

11. He answered them, He that made me healthy, the same said to me, take up your bed, and walk.

12. Then they asked him, what man said that to you, take up your bed, and walk?

13. And he that was healed did not know who it was: for Jesus had withdrawn Himself, a multitude were in that place.

14. Afterward Jesus found him in the temple, and said to him, behold, you have been made healthy: sin no more, unless a worse thing come into you.

15. The man departed and told the Jews that it was Jesus, who had made him healthy.

16. Therefore, the Jews did persecute Jesus and sought to kill Him because He had done these things on the Sabbath day.

17. But Jesus answered them, My Father works until now, and I work.

18. Therefore, the Jews sought more to kill Him because He not only had broken the Sabbath but also said that God was His Father, making Himself equal with God.

19. Then answered Jesus and said to them, truly, truly, I say to you, the Son can do nothing from Himself, but what He sees the Father do: for whatever things He does, these also the Son does likewise.

20. For the Father loves the Son and shows Him all things that He does: and He will show him greater works than these that you may marvel.

21. For as the Father raises up the dead and gives life to them; even so the Son gives life to who He will.

22. For the Father judges no one, but has committed all judgment to the Son:

23. That all men should honor the Son, just as they honor the Father. He that does not honor the Son honors not the Father who has sent Him.

24. Truly, truly, I say to you, he that hears My word, and believes on Him that sent Me, has infinite life, and will not come into condemnation; but has passed from death to life.

25. Truly, truly, I say to you, the hour is coming, and now is, when the dead will hear the voice of the Son of God: and they that hear will live.

26. For as the Father has life in Himself; so He has given to the Son to have life in Himself;
27. And has given Him authority to execute judgment also, because He is the Son of Man.
28. Marvel not at this: for the hour is coming, in which all that are in the graves will hear His voice,
29. And will come out; they that have done good to the resurrection of life; and they that have done evil, to the resurrection of condemnation.
30. I can out from My own self do nothing: as I am hearing, I judge: and My judgment is just; because I seek not My own will, but the will of the One who has sent Me.
31. If I give witness of Myself, My witness is not true.
32. There is another witnessing of Me, and I know that the witness which He witnesses of Me is true.
33. You sent to John, and he gave witness to the reality.
34. But I receive not the testimony from man: but these things I say, that you might be saved.
35. He was a burning and a shining light: and you were willing for a season to rejoice in his light.
36. But I have greater witness than that of John: for the works which the Father has given Me to finish, the same works that I do, give witness of Me, that the Father has sent Me.
37. For the Father Himself, who has sent Me, has given witness of Me. You have neither heard His voice at any time nor seen His form.
38. For you do not have His word residing in you: for who He has sent, Him you do not believe.
39. Search the Scriptures; for in them you think you have infinite life: yet they are they which testify of Me.
40. But you will not come to Me, that you might have life.
41. I do not receive honor from men.
42. But I know you, that you have not the love of God in you.
43. I have come in My Father's name, and you receive Me not: if another will come in his own name, you will receive him.
44. How can you believe, you who receive honor from one another, and seek not the honor that comes from God only?
45. Do not think that I will accuse you to the Father: there is one that accuses you, even Moses, in whom you trust.
46. For had you believed Moses, you would have believed Me; for he wrote about Me.
47. But if you believe not his writings, how will you believe My words?

Chapter 6

1. After these things, Jesus crossed over the Sea of Galilee, which is the sea of Tiberius Caesar.
2. And a great multitude followed Him because they saw His miracles which He did on them that were diseased.
3. Then Jesus went up to a mountain, and there He sat with His disciples.

4. For the Passover, a feast of the Jews, was close.
5. Then when Jesus lifted up His eyes and saw a great crowd coming towards Him, He said to Philip, from where will we buy bread that these may eat?
6. He said this to test him: for He Himself knew what He was about to do.
7. Philip answered Him, two hundred denarii worth of bread is not sufficient for them, that all of them may eat a little.
8. One of his disciples, Andrew, Simon Peter's brother, said to Him,
9. There is a boy here, who has five barley loaves, and two small fishes: but what are they among so many?
10. Then Jesus said, make the men sit down. Now there was much grass in the place. So, the men sat down, in number about five thousand.
11. Then Jesus took the loaves; and when He had given thanks, He distributed to the disciples, and the disciples to them that had sat down; and likewise of the fishes as much as they would.
12. When they were filled, He said to His disciples, gather up the fragments that remain, that nothing be lost.
13. Therefore, they gathered them together and filled twelve baskets with the fragments of the five barley loaves, which remained over and above those that had eaten.
14. Then those men, when they had seen the miracle that Jesus did, said, this is truly that prophet that should come into the world.
15. Therefore, when Jesus perceived that they were about to come and seize Him, to make Him a king, He departed again to a mountain Himself alone.
16. When evening had come, His disciples went down to the sea,
17. And entered into a boat and went across the sea toward Capernaum. It was now dark, and Jesus had not come to them.
18. And the sea arose because of a great wind that blew.
19. So, when they had rowed about twenty-five or thirty stadia, they saw Jesus walking on the sea and getting close to the boat: and they were afraid.
20. But He said to them, I am; do not be afraid!
21. Then they willingly received Him into the boat: and immediately the boat was at the land to where they went.
22. The following day, when the people who stood on the other side of the sea saw that there was no other boat there, except the one into which His disciples had entered, and that Jesus went not with His disciples into the boat, but that His disciples had gone away alone;
23. However there came other boats from Tiberius close to the place where they did eat bread, after the Lord had given thanks.
24. Therefore, when the people saw that Jesus was not there, nor His disciples, they also took boats, and came to Capernaum, seeking Jesus.
25. When they had found Him on the other side of the sea, they said to Him, Rabbi, when did You come here?

26. Jesus answered them and said, truly, truly, I say to you, you seek Me, not because you saw the miracles, but because you did eat of the loaves, and were filled.

27. Labor not for the food which perishes, but for that food which remains into infinite life, which the Son of Man will give to you: for Him has God the Father set His seal.

28. Then said they to Him, what will we do, that we might work the works of God?

29. Jesus answered and said to them, this is the work of God that you believe in Him who He has sent.

30. Therefore, they said to Him, what sign do You show then, that we may see, and believe You? What work will You do?

31. Our fathers did eat manna in the desert; as it is written, He gave them bread from heaven to eat.

32. Then Jesus said to them, truly, truly, I say to you, Moses gave you not that bread from heaven, but My Father gives you the true bread from heaven.

33. For the bread of God is He who comes down from heaven and gives life to the world.

34. Then said they to Him, Lord, evermore give us this bread.

35. And Jesus said to them, I am the bread of life: he that is coming to Me will never hunger, and He that is believing in Me will never thirst.

36. But I said to you, that you also have seen Me, and do not believe.

37. All that the Father is giving Me will be coming to Me, and him that is coming to Me I will not throw outside.

38. For I came down from heaven, not to do My own will, but the will of Him that sent Me.

39. And this is the Father's will who has sent Me, that of all who He has given Me I lose nothing but should raise it up at the last day.

40. For this is the will of Him that sent Me, that everyone who is beholding the Son, and is believing into Him, may have infinite life: and I will raise him up at the last day.

41. Then the Jews murmured at Him, because He said, I am the bread which came down from heaven.

42. And they said, is this not Jesus, the son of Joseph, whose father and mother we know? How is it then that He says, I came down from heaven?

43. Therefore, Jesus answered and said to them, murmur not among yourselves.

44. No man can come to Me unless the Father who has sent Me draws him: and I will raise him up at the last day.

45. It is written in the prophets, and they will be all taught of God. Therefore, every man that has heard, and has learned of the Father, comes to Me.

46. Not that any man has seen the Father, except He who is of God, He has seen the Father.

47. Truly, truly, I say to you, He that believes in Me has infinite life.

48. I am that bread of life.

49. Your fathers did eat manna in the wilderness and are dead.

50. This is the bread which comes down from heaven that a man may eat of it, and not die.

51. I am the living bread which came down from heaven: if anyone eat of this bread, he will live into the New Covenant Age: and the bread that I will give is My flesh, which I will give for the life of the world.
52. Therefore, the Jews argued among themselves, saying, how can this man give us His flesh to eat?
53. Then Jesus said to them, truly, truly, I say to you, unless you eat the flesh of the Son of Man, and drink His blood, you have no life in you.
54. Whoever eats My flesh, and drinks My blood, has infinite life; and I will raise him up on the last day.
55. For My flesh is food indeed, and My blood is drink indeed.
56. He that eats My flesh, and drinks My blood, stays in Me, and I in him.
57. As the living Father has sent Me, and I live by the Father: so he that eats Me, even he will live by Me.
58. This is that bread which came down from heaven: not as your fathers did eat manna and are dead: he that eats of this bread will be living into the New Covenant Age.
59. These things said He in the synagogue, as He taught in Capernaum.
60. Therefore, many of His disciples, when they had heard this, said, this is a hard saying; who can hear it?
61. When Jesus knew in himself that His disciples murmured at it, He said to them, does this offend you?
62. What if you will see the Son of Man ascend up where He was before?
63. It is the spirit that gives life; the flesh profits nothing: the words that I speak to you, they are spirit, and they are life.
64. But some of you do not believe. For Jesus knew from the beginning who they were who did not believe, and who would betray Him.
65. Then He said, therefore said I to you, that no man can come to Me unless it was given to him by My Father.
66. From that time many of His disciples departed and walked with Him no longer.
67. Then said Jesus to the twelve, will you also go away?
68. Then Simon Peter answered Him, Lord, to whom will we go? You have the words of infinite life.
69. For we believe and are certain that you are the Holy One of God!
70. Jesus answered them, have I not chosen you twelve, and one of you is a devil?
71. He spoke of Judas Iscariot the son of Simon: for he was about to betray Him, being one of the twelve.

Chapter 7

1. After these things Jesus walked in Galilee: for He would not walk in Judea, because the Jews sought to kill Him.
2. Now the Jew's Feast of Tabernacles was at hand.
3. Therefore, His brothers said to Him, depart from here to Judea, that Your disciples may also see the works that You are doing.

4. For there is no man that does anything in secret when He Himself seeks to be known publicly. If You do these things, show Yourself to the world.
5. For neither did His brothers believe in Him.
6. Then Jesus said to them, My time is not yet come: but your time is always ready.
7. The world cannot hate you; but it hates Me, because I testify of it, that the works of it are evil.
8. Go you up to this feast: I go not up yet to this feast: for My time has not yet fully come.
9. When He had said these words to them, He stayed still in Galilee.
10. But when His brothers were gone up, then went He also up to the feast, not publicly, but as it were in secret.
11. Then the Jews sought Him at the feast, and said, where is He?
12. For there was much murmuring among the people concerning Him: for some said, He is a good man: others said, no; but He deceives the people.
13. However, no one spoke publicly about Him for fear of the Jews.
14. Now about the middle of the feast Jesus went up into the temple and taught.
15. So, the Jews marveled, saying, how does this man know the writings, not having been educated?
16. Jesus answered them, and said, My teaching is not Mine, but His that sent Me.
17. If anyone will do His will, he will know of the teaching, whether it be of God, or whether I speak by Myself.
18. He that speaks of himself seeks his own glory: but He that seeks the glory of Him that sent him, the same is authentic, and no unrighteousness is in Him.
19. Did not Moses give you the Law, and yet none of you keeps the Law? Why do you try to kill Me?
20. The people answered and said, You have a demon: who tries to kill You?
21. Jesus answered and said to them, I have done one work, and you all marvel.
22. Therefore, Moses gave to you circumcision; (not because it came from Moses, but from the fathers), and you on the Sabbath day circumcise a man.
23. If a man on the Sabbath day receives circumcision, that the Law of Moses should not be broken; are you angry at Me, because I have made a man every bit whole on the Sabbath day?
24. Judge not according to the appearance but judge righteous judgment.
25. Then some of them said of Jerusalem, is not this He, who they seek to kill?
26. But look, He speaks boldly, and they say nothing to Him. Do the rulers know indeed that this is the true Christ?
27. However, we know where this man is from: but when Christ comes, no man will know where He is from.
28. Then Jesus cried in the temple as He taught, saying, you both know Me, and you know where I am from: and I have not come of Myself, but He that sent Me is real, who You know not.
29. But I know Him: for I am from Him, and He has sent Me!

30. Then they sought to take Him: but no man laid hands on Him, because His hour had not yet come.
31. Yet many of the people believed in Him, and said, when Christ comes, will He do more miracles than these which this man has done?
32. The Pharisees heard that the people murmured such things concerning Him, and the Pharisees and the chief priests sent officers to take Him.
33. Then Jesus said to them, still a little while I am with you, and then I go to Him that sent Me.
34. You will seek Me and will not find Me: and where I am, there you cannot come.
35. Then the Jews said among themselves, where is He about to go, that we will not find Him? Will He go to the dispersed among the nations, and teach the nations?
36. What manner of saying is this that He said, you will seek Me, and will not find Me: and where I am, there you cannot come?
37. In the last day, that great day of the feast, Jesus stood and cried, saying, if anyone is thirsting, let him come to Me, and drink.
38. He that is believing into Me, as the Scripture has said, out of his deepest inner part will flow rivers of living water!
39. But this He spoke of the Spirit, who they that are believing in Him were about to receive: for the Holy Spirit was not yet; because Jesus had not yet been glorified.
40. Therefore, many of the people, when they heard this saying, said certainly this is the Prophet.
41. Others said, this is the Christ. But some said, will Christ come out of Galilee?
42. Has not the Scripture said that Christ comes out of the seed of David, and out of the town of Bethlehem, where David was?
43. So, there was a division among the people because of Him.
44. For some of them would have taken Him, but no man laid hands on Him.
45. Then the officers came to the chief priests and Pharisees; and they said to them, why have you not taken Him?
46. The officers answered, never has a man spoken like this man.
47. Then the Pharisees answered them, are you also deceived?
48. Have any of the rulers or the Pharisees believed in Him?
49. But these people who do not know the Law are cursed.
50. Nicodemus said to them, he that came to Jesus by night, being one of them,
51. Does our Law judge, anyone, before it hears him, and knows what he has done?
52. They answered and said to him, are you also of Galilee? Search and look: for out of Galilee arises no prophet.
53. So, everyone went to his own house.

Chapter 8

1. Jesus went to the Mount of Olives.
2. And early in the morning, He came again into the temple, and all the people came to Him, and He sat down, and taught them.
3. Then the scribes and Pharisees brought to Him a woman taken in adultery; and when they had set her in their midst,

4. They said to Him, Master, this woman was caught in adultery, in the very act.

5. Now Moses in the Law commanded us, that such should be stoned: but what do You say?

6. They said this, tempting Him, that they might have something to accuse Him. But Jesus stooped down, and with His finger wrote on the ground, as though He heard them not.

7. So, when they continued asking Him, He lifted up Himself, and said to them, he that is without sin among you, let him cast the first stone at her.

8. Again, He stooped down and wrote on the ground.

9. Then they who heard it, being convicted by their own conscience, went out one by one, beginning at the eldest, even to the last: and Jesus was left alone, and the woman standing in the center.

10. When Jesus had lifted up Himself, and saw no one but the woman, He said to her, woman, where are your accusers? Has anyone condemned you?

11. She said, no one, Lord. And Jesus said to her, neither am I condemning you: go and sin no more.

12. Then Jesus spoke again to them, saying, I am the light of the world: he that follows Me will not walk in darkness but will have the light of life.

13. Therefore, the Pharisees said to Him, You give witness about Yourself; Your witness is not authentic.

14. Jesus answered and said to them, though I give witness of Myself, yet My witness is authentic: for I know from where I came, and to where I go; but you cannot tell from where I came, and to where I go.

15. You are judging after the flesh; I judge no man.

16. Yet if I judge, My judgment is genuine: for I am not alone, but I am with the Father that sent Me.

17. It is also written in your Law, that the testimony of two men is authentic.

18. I give witness of Myself, and the Father that sent Me gives witness of Me.

19. Then they said to Him, where is your Father? Jesus answered, you neither know Me nor My Father: if you had known Me, you would have known My Father also.

20. These words Jesus spoke in the treasury, as He taught in the temple: and no man laid a hand on Him; for His hour had not yet come.

21. Then said Jesus again to them, I go my way, and you will seek Me and will die in your sins: where I go, you cannot come.

22. Then the Jews said, will He kill Himself? Because He says, where I go, you cannot come.

23. So, He said to them, you are from beneath; I am from above: you are of this world; I am not of this world.

24. Therefore, I said to you, that you will die in your sins: for if you do not believe that I am, you will die in your sins.

25. Then they said to Him, who are You? And Jesus said to them, even the same that I said to you from the beginning.

26. I have many things to say and to judge of you: but He that sent Me is authentic, and I speak to the world those things which I have heard from Him.

27. They did not understand that He spoke to them of the Father.
28. Then Jesus said to them when you have lifted up the Son of Man, then you will know that I am and that I do nothing out of Myself; but as My Father has taught Me, I speak these things.
29. And He that sent Me is with Me: the Father has not left Me alone; for I always do those things which are pleasing Him.
30. As He spoke these words, many believed in Him.
31. Then Jesus said to those Jews who believed in Him, if you are continuing in My word, then are you My disciples indeed;
32. Then you will know the reality, and the reality will be making you free.
33. They answered Him, we are Abraham's offspring, and were never in bondage to anyone: how can You say, You will be becoming free?
34. Jesus answered them, truly, truly, I say to you, whoever is committing sin is the slave of sin.
35. And the slave does not stay in the house into the New Covenant Age: but the son remains into the New Covenant Age.
36. Therefore, if the Son will make you free, you will be free indeed.
37. I know that you are Abraham's offspring, but you seek to kill Me because My word has no place in you.
38. I speak that which I have seen with My Father: and you do that which you have seen with your father.
39. They answered and said to Him, Abraham is our father. Jesus said to them, if you were Abraham's children, you would do the works of Abraham.
40. But now you seek to kill Me, a man that has told you the reality, which I have heard from God: Abraham did not do this.
41. You do the deeds of your father. Then they said to Him, we were not born of fornication; we have one Father, even God.
42. Jesus said to them, if God were your Father, you would love Me: for I proceeded out and came from God; I did not come by Myself, but He sent Me.
43. Why do you not understand My speech? Even because you cannot hear My word.
44. You are of your father the devil and the lusts of your father you will do. He was a murderer from the beginning and abides not in the reality because there is no reality in him. When he speaks a lie, he speaks of his own: for he is a liar and the father of it.
45. Because I tell you the reality, you are not believing Me.
46. Which of you convicts Me of sin? If I lay out the reality, why are you not believing Me?
47. He that is of God hears God's words: therefore, you do not hear them, because you are not of God.
48. Then answered the Jews, and said to Him, are we not saying rightly that you are a Samaritan, and have a demon?
49. Jesus answered I do not have a demon, but I honor My Father, and you dishonor Me.
50. For I do not seek My own glory: there is One that seeks and judges.

51. Truly, truly, I say to you, if a man keeps My word, he will never experience death.
52. Then the Jews said to Him, now we know that You have a demon. Abraham is dead, and the prophets; and You say, if a man keep My word, he will not ever in the New Covenant Age taste of death.
53. Are you greater than our father Abraham, who is dead? And the prophets are dead: who do You think You are?
54. Jesus answered, if I honor Myself, My honor is nothing: it is My Father that honors Me; of who you say, that He is your God:
55. Yet you have not known Him, but I know Him: and if I should say, I do not know Him, I will be a liar like you: but I know Him and keep His word.
56. Your father Abraham rejoiced to see My day: and he saw it and was glad!
57. Then the Jews said to Him, You are not yet fifty years old, and have You seen Abraham?
58. Jesus said to them, truly, truly, I say to you, before Abraham was, I am.
59. Then they took up stones to cast at Him: but Jesus concealed Himself, and went out of the temple, [going through the midst of them, and vanished.

Chapter 9

1. And as Jesus passed by, He saw a man who was blind from his birth.
2. Then His disciples asked Him, saying, Master, who did sin, this man, or his parents, that he was born blind?
3. Jesus answered, neither has this man sinned nor his parents: but that the works of God should be made manifest in him.
4. I must work the works of Him that sent Me, while it is day: the night comes when no man can work.
5. As long as I am in the world, I am the light of the world.
6. When He had so spoken, He spat on the ground, and made clay of the spit, and He anointed the eyes of the blind man with the clay,
7. And said to him, go, wash in the pool of Siloam, (which is translated, Sent) therefore he went his way, and washed, and came seeing.
8. Therefore, the neighbors and they who before had seen him that was blind, said, is not this he that sat and begged?
9. Some said, this is he: others said, he is like him: but he said, I am he.
10. Therefore, they said to him, how were your eyes opened?
11. He answered and said, a man that is called Jesus made clay and anointed my eyes, and said to me, go to the pool of Siloam, and wash: and I went and washed, and I received sight.
12. Then said they to him, where is He? He said, I do not know.
13. They brought to the Pharisees he that previously was blind.
14. It was the Sabbath day when Jesus made the clay and opened his eyes.
15. Then again the Pharisees also asked him how he had received his sight. He said to them, He put clay on my eyes, and I washed, and I do see.

16. Therefore, some of the Pharisees said, this man is not of God, because He does not keep the Sabbath day. Others said, how can a man who is a sinner do such miracles? So, there was a division among them.

17. They say to the blind man again, what do you say of Him, that He has opened your eyes? He said He is a prophet.

18. But the Jews did not believe concerning him, that he had been blind, and received his sight until they called his parents about him that had received his sight.

19. So, they asked them, saying, is this your son, who you say was born blind? How then does he now see?

20. His parents answered them and said, we know that this is our son and that he was born blind:

21. But by what means he now sees, we do not know; or who has opened his eyes, we do not know: he is of age; ask him: he will speak for himself.

22. These words his parents spoke because they feared the Jews: for the Jews had agreed already, that if anyone did confess that He was Christ, he should be put out of the synagogue.

23. Therefore, his parents said, he is of age; ask him.

24. Then again they called the man that was blind, and said to him, Give God the praise: we know that this man is a sinner.

25. He answered and said, whether He is a sinner or not, I do not know: one thing I know, I once was blind, but now I see.

26. Then they said to him again, what did He do to you? How did He open your eyes?

27. He answered them, I have told you already, and you did not hear: why would you hear it again? Will you also be His disciples?

28. Then they reviled him, and said, you are His disciple, but we are Moses' disciples.

29. We know that God spoke to Moses: as for this fellow, we do not know where He is from.

30. The man answered and said to them, why this is a marvelous thing, that you do not know where He is from, and yet He has opened my eyes.

31. Now we know that God does not hear sinners: but if any man be a worshiper of God, and does His will, He hears him.

32. Since, this Old Covenant Age began, it has not been heard that anyone opened the eyes of one who was born blind.

33. If this man were not of God, He could do nothing.

34. They answered and said to him, you were altogether born in sin, and do you teach us? Then they cast him out.

35. Jesus heard that they had cast him out; and when He had found him, He said to him, do you believe in the Son of God?

36. He answered and said, who is He Lord that I may believe in Him?

37. Then Jesus said to him, you have both seen Him, and it is He that talks with you.

38. So, he said, Lord, I believe. And he worshiped Him.

39. Then Jesus said, for judgment, I have come into this world, that they who see not might see; and that they who see might be made blind.

40. And some of the Pharisees who were with Him heard these words, and said to Him, are we blind also?

41. Jesus said to them, if you were blind, you should have no sin: but now you say, we see; therefore, your sin remains.

Chapter 10

1. Truly, truly, I say to you, He that enters not by the door into the sheepfold but climbs up some other way, the same is a thief and a robber.

2. But he that enters in by the door is the shepherd of the sheep.

3. To him the doorkeeper opens, and the sheep hear his voice: and he calls his own sheep by name and leads them out.

4. When he brings out his own sheep, he goes before them, and the sheep follow him: for they know his voice.

5. But a stranger they will not follow but will flee from him: for they know not the voice of strangers.

6. This parable spoke Jesus to them: but they understood not what things they were which He spoke to them.

7. Then Jesus said to them again, truly, truly, I say to you, I am the door of the sheep.

8. All that ever came before Me were thieves and robbers: but the sheep did not hear them.

9. I am the door: by Me, if any man enters in, he will be saved and will go in and out and find pasture.

10. The thief comes not, except that he may steal, and kill, and destroy: I have come that they might have life and that they might have it more abundantly.

11. I am the good shepherd: the good shepherd gives His soul-life for the sheep.

12. But he that is a hireling, and not the shepherd, whose own the sheep are not, sees the wolf coming, and leaves the sheep, and flees: and the wolf takes them, and scatters the sheep.

13. The hireling flees, because he is a hireling, and does not care for the sheep.

14. I am the good shepherd and know My sheep, and mine know Me.

15. As the Father knows Me, even so, I know the Father: and I lay down My life for the sheep.

16. And other sheep I have, which are not of this fold: I also must bring them, and they will hear My voice; and there will be one flock, one shepherd.

17. Therefore, My Father is loving Me because I lay down My life, that I may take it again.

18. No man takes it from Me, but I lay it down by Myself. I have the power to lay it down, and I have the power to take it again. This commandment I have received from My Father.

19. Therefore, there was a division again among the Jews for these sayings.

20. And many of them said, He has a demon and is mad; why do you hear Him?

21. Others said these are not the words of Him that has a demon. Can a demon open the eyes of the blind?

22. Then it was at Jerusalem the Feast of the Dedication, and it was winter.

23. And Jesus walked into the temple on Solomon's porch.
24. Then the Jews came around Him, and said to Him, how long do you keep us in suspense? If you are the Christ, tell us plainly.
25. Jesus answered them, I told you, and you believed not: the works that I do in My Father's name, they give witness of Me.
26. But you believe not, because you are not of My sheep, as I said to you.
27. My sheep are hearing My voice, and I know them, and they are following Me:
28. And I am giving to them infinite life, and they will never in the New Covenant Age perish, neither will anyone be seizing them out of My hand.
29. My Father, who gave them to Me, is greater than all; and no man can seize them out of My Father's hand.
30. I and My Father are one.
31. Then the Jews took up stones again to stone Him.
32. Jesus answered them, many good works I have shown you from My Father; for which of those works do you stone Me?
33. The Jews answered Him, and said, for a good work we do not stone You; but for blasphemy; because You, being a man, make Yourself God.
34. Jesus answered them, is it not written in your Law, I said, you are gods?
35. If He called them gods, to whom the word of God came, and the Scripture cannot be broken;
36. Are you saying of Him, whom the Father has sanctified, and sent into the world, you blaspheme; because I said, I am the Son of God?
37. If I do not the works of My Father, believe Me not.
38. But if I do, though you do not believe Me, believe the works: that you may know, and believe, that the Father is in Me, and I in Him.
39. Therefore, they sought again to take Him: but He escaped out of their hand,
40. And went away again beyond the Jordan into the place where John at first immersed, and there He stayed.
41. Then many came to Him, and said, John did no miracle: but all things that John spoke of this man are true.
42. So many believed in Him there.

Chapter 11

1. Now a certain man was sick, named Lazarus, of Bethany, the town of Mary, and her sister Martha.
2. It was that Mary who anointed the Lord with ointment and wiped His feet with her hair, whose brother Lazarus was sick.
3. Therefore, his sisters sent for Him, saying, Lord, behold, He who you love is sick.
4. When Jesus heard that, He said, this sickness is not to death, but for the glory of God, that the Son of God might be glorified by it.
5. Now Jesus loved Martha, and her sister, and Lazarus.
6. Therefore, when He had heard that he was sick, He stayed two more days in the same place where He was.

7. Then after that said He to His disciples, Let us go into Judea again.

8. His disciples said to Him, Master, the Jews of late sought to stone You; and You go there again?

9. Jesus answered, Are there not twelve hours in the day? If anyone walks in the day, he stumbles not, because he sees the light of this world.

10. But if a man walks in the night, he stumbles, because there is no light in him.

11. These things He said: and after that, He said to them, our friend Lazarus sleeps; but I go, that I may awake him out of sleep.

12. Then said His disciples, Lord, if he sleeps, he will get well.

13. However, Jesus spoke of his death: but they thought that He had spoken about taking rest during sleep.

14. Then said Jesus to them plainly, Lazarus is dead.

15. And I am glad for your sakes that I was not there, to the extent you may believe; nevertheless, let us go to him.

16. Then said Thomas, who is called Didymus, to his fellow disciples, Let us also go, that we may die with him.

17. Then when Jesus came, he found that he had lain in the grave four days already.

18. Now Bethany was close to Jerusalem, about fifteen stadia away:

19. And many of the Jews came to Martha and Mary, to comfort them concerning their brother.

20. Then Martha, as soon as she heard that Jesus was coming, went and met Him: but Mary sat still in the house.

21. Then said Martha to Jesus, Lord, if You had been here, my brother would not have died.

22. But I know, that even now, whatever You will ask of God, God will give You.

23. Jesus said to her, your brother will rise again.

24. Martha said to Him, I know that he will rise again in the resurrection at the last day.

25. Jesus said to her, I am the resurrection and the life: he that is believing into Me, though he were dead, he will be living:

26. And whoever is living and believing into Me will not in the New Covenant Age die. Do you believe this?

27. She said to Him, Yes, Lord: I believe that you are the Christ, the Son of God, who is coming into the world.

28. When she had so said, she went her way and called Mary her sister secretly, saying, the Master has come and is calling for you.

29. As soon as she heard that, she arose quickly and went to Him.

30. Now Jesus had not yet come into the town but was in that place where Martha had met Him.

31. The Jews then who were with her in the house, and comforted her, when they saw Mary, that she rose up speedily and went out, followed her, and said, She goes to the grave to weep there.

32. Then when Mary had come where Jesus was, and saw Him, she fell down at His feet, and said to him, Lord, if You had been here, my brother would not have died.

33. Therefore, when Jesus saw her weeping, and the Jews also weeping who came with her, He groaned in the spirit and was troubled.
34. And said, where have you laid him? They said to Him, Lord, come and see.
35. Jesus wept.
36. Then said the Jews, behold how He loved him!
37. But some of them said, could not this man, who opened the eyes of the blind, have stopped this man from dying?
38. Therefore, Jesus again groaned in Himself and came to the tomb. It was a cave, and a stone lay on it.
39. Jesus said, take away the stone. Martha, the sister of him that was dead, said to Him, Lord, by this time he stinks: for he has been dead four days.
40. Jesus said to her, said I not to you, that if you would believe, you should see the glory of God.
41. Then they removed the stone from the place where the dead was laid. and Jesus lifted up His eyes, and said, Father, I thank You that You have heard Me.
42. And I know that You hear Me always: but because of the people who stand by I said it, that they may believe that You have sent Me.
43. When He had so spoken, He cried with a loud voice, Lazarus, come out!
44. Then he that was dead came out, bound hand and foot with grave clothes: and his face was wrapped with a cloth. Jesus said to them, loose him, and let him go!
45. Then many of the Jews who came to Mary, and saw the things that Jesus did, believed in Him.
46. But some of them went their way to the Pharisees and told them what things Jesus had done.
47. Then gathered the chief priests and the Pharisees a council, and said, what should we do? For this man does many miracles.
48. If we leave Him alone, all men will believe in Him: and the Romans will come and take away both our place and nation.
49. Then one of them, named Caiaphas, being the high priest that same year, said to them, You know nothing at all,
50. Nor consider that it is necessary for us, that one man should die for the people, and that the whole nation perish not.
51. This spoke He not of Himself: but being high priest that year, he prophesied that Jesus was about to die for that nation;
52. And not for that nation only, but that also He should gather together in one the children of God that were scattered abroad.
53. Then from that day onward they took counsel together in order to put Him to death.
54. Therefore, Jesus walked no more publicly among the Jews; but went from there to a country near to the wilderness, into a city called Ephraim, and there continued with His disciples.
55. And the Jews' Passover was close at hand: and many went out of the country up to Jerusalem before the Passover, to purify themselves.

56. Then they sought for Jesus, and spoke among themselves, as they stood in the temple, what do you think, that He will not come to the feast?
57. Now both the chief priests and the Pharisees had given a commandment, that, if any man knew where He was, he should report it, that they might take Him.

Chapter 12

1. Then six days before the Passover Jesus came to Bethany, where Lazarus was, who had been dead, who He raised from the dead.
2. There they made Him a supper, and Martha served: but Lazarus was one of them that sat at the table with Him.
3. Then took Mary a pound of very costly ointment of spikenard, and anointed the feet of Jesus, and wiped His feet with her hair: and the house was filled with the fragrance of the ointment.
4. Then said one of His disciples, Judas Iscariot, Simon's son, who was about to betray Him,
5. Why wasn't this ointment sold for three hundred denarii, and given to the poor?
6. This he said, not that he cared for the poor; but because he was a thief, and had the money box, and took what was put in it.
7. Then said Jesus, leave her alone: she has kept this for the day of My burial.
8. For the poor always you have with you, but Me you have not always.
9. Now many people of the Jews knew that He was there: and they came not for Jesus' sake only, but that they might see Lazarus also, who He had raised from the dead.
10. But the chief priests consulted that they might put Lazarus also to death;
11. Because by reason of him, many of the Jews went away, and believed in Jesus.
12. On the next day many people that had come to the feast, when they heard that Jesus was coming to Jerusalem,
13. Took branches of palm trees, and went out to meet Him, and cried, Hosanna: blessed is the King of Israel that comes in the name of the Lord!
14. Then Jesus, when He had found a young colt, sat on it; as it is written,
15. Fear not, daughter of Zion: behold, your King comes, sitting on a donkey's colt.
16. These things understood not His disciples at that time: but when Jesus was glorified, then they remembered that these things were written about Him and that they had done these things to Him.
17. Therefore, the people that were with Him when He called Lazarus out of his tomb and raised him from the dead, gave testimony.
18. For this reason, the people also met Him, for they heard that He had done this miracle.
19. Therefore, the Pharisees said among themselves, do you see how you gained nothing? Behold, the world has gone after Him.
20. And there were certain Greeks among them that came up to worship at the feast:

John 12:21   **John 12:43**

21. Therefore, these approached Philip, who was of Bethsaida of Galilee, and asked him, and said, Sir, we desire to get to know Jesus.

22. Philip came and told Andrew: and again Andrew and Philip told Jesus.

23. Then Jesus answered them, saying, the hour has come for the Son of Man to be glorified.

24. Truly, truly, I say to you, unless a corn of wheat falls into the ground and dies, it remains alone: but if it dies, it brings forth much fruit.

25. He that loves his life will lose it, and he that hates his life in this world will keep it into life infinite.

26. If anyone serves Me, let him follow Me; and where I am, there also will My servant be: if anyone serves Me, My Father will honor him.

27. Now My soul is agitated; and what will I say? Father, save Me from this hour: but for this reason, I came to this hour.

28. Father, glorify Your name. Then came there a voice from heaven, saying, I have both glorified it and will glorify it again.

29. Therefore, the people that stood by, and heard it, said that it thundered: others said, an angel spoke to Him.

30. Jesus answered and said, this voice came not because of Me, but for your sake.

31. Now is the judgment of this world: now will the ruler of this world be cast out.

32. And I, if I am lifted up from the land, will draw all men to Me.

33. This He said, signifying what death He was about to die.

34. The people answered Him, we have heard out of the Law that Christ remains into the New Covenant Age: and how can you say, the Son of Man must be lifted up? Who is this Son of Man?

35. Then Jesus said to them. Yet for a little while the light is with you. Walk while you have the light unless darkness come on you: for he that is walking in darkness knows not where he is going

36. While you have the light, believe in the light, that you may be the children of light. These things Jesus spoke, and departed, and hid Himself from them.

37. But though He had done so many miracles before them, yet they did not believe in Him:

38. That the saying of Isaiah the prophet might be fulfilled, which he spoke, Lord, who has believed our report? And to whom has the arm of the Lord been revealed?

39. Therefore, they could not believe, it because Isaiah said again,

40. He has blinded their eyes and hardened their heart; that they should not see with their eyes, nor understand with their heart, and turn, and I should heal them.

41. These things Isaiah said, when he saw His glory and spoke of Him.

42. Nevertheless, among the chief rulers also many believed in Him, but because of the Pharisees they did not confess Him unless they should be put out of the synagogue:

43. For they loved the praise of men more than the praise of God.

44. Jesus cried and said, He that believes in Me, believes not in Me, but in Him that sent Me.
45. And he that sees Me sees Him that sent Me.
46. I have come as a light into the world, that whoever believes in Me should not stay in darkness.
47. And if any man hear My words, and believe not, I judge him not: for I came not to judge the world, but to save the world.
48. He that rejects Me, and receives not My words, has one that judges him: the word that I have spoken, the same will judge him in the last day.
49. For I have not spoken of Myself; but the Father who sent Me, He gave Me a commandment, what I should say, and what I should speak.
50. And I know that His commandment is life infinite: therefore, whatever I speak, just as the Father said to Me, so I speak.

Chapter 13

1. Now before the Feast of the Passover, when Jesus knew that His hour had come that He should depart out of this world to the Father, having loved His own who were in the world, He loved them to the end.
2. Now supper being ended, the devil having put into the heart of Judas Iscariot, Simon's son, to betray Him;
3. Jesus knowing that the Father had given all things into His hands and that He had come from God, and went to God;
4. He rose from supper, laid aside His outer clothing; and wrapped a towel around His waist.
5. After that He poured water into a basin, and began to wash the disciples' feet, and to wipe them with the towel that was wrapped around Him.
6. Then came He to Simon Peter: and Peter said to Him, Lord, do you wash My feet?
7. Jesus answered and said to him, what I do you do not understand now; but you will know after this.
8. Peter says to Him, no You will not wash my feet in this age. Jesus answered him, if I do not wash you, you will not hold a share with Me.
9. Simon Peter said to Him, Lord, not my feet only, but also my hands and my head.
10. Jesus said to him, he that has bathed does not need to wash except for his feet, but is entirely clean: and you are clean, but not each one of you.
11. For He knew who should betray Him; therefore, He said, you are not all clean.
12. So, after He had washed their feet, and had taken His garments, and had sat down again, He said to them, do you know what I have done to you?
13. You call Me Master and Lord: and you say well; for so I am.
14. If I then, your Lord and Master, have washed your feet; you also ought to wash one another's feet.
15. For I have given you a pattern, that you should do as I have done to you.

16. Truly, truly, I say to you, the servant is not greater than his master; neither is He that is sent greater than He that sent Him.
17. If you know these things, happy are you if you do them.
18. I speak not of you all: I know who I have chosen: but that the Scripture be fulfilled, he that eats My bread has lifted up his heel against Me.
19. Now I tell you before it comes, that, when it comes to pass, you may believe that I am.
20. Truly, truly, I say to you, he that receives whomever I send receives Me, and he that receives Me receives Him that sent Me.
21. When Jesus had said these things, He was troubled in spirit and testified, and said, truly, truly, I say to you, that one of you will betray Me.
22. Then the disciples looked at one another, unsure of who He spoke about.
23. Now there was one of His disciples leaning on Jesus' chest, who Jesus loved.
24. Therefore, Simon Peter motioned to him, that he should ask who it was that He was speaking about.
25. One who was leaning on Jesus' chest said to Him, Lord, who is it?
26. Jesus answered, it is he, to whom I will give a piece of bread when I have dipped it. When He had dipped the piece of bread, He gave it to Judas Iscariot, the son of Simon.
27. After the piece of bread, Satan entered into him. Then Jesus said to him, what you are about to do, do quickly.
28. Now no man at the table knew for what purpose He spoke this to him.
29. For some of them thought, that because Judas had the moneybox, Jesus had said to him, buy those things that we need for the feast; or, that he should give something to the poor.
30. He then having received the piece of bread went immediately out: and it was night.
31. Therefore, when he had gone out, Jesus said, now is the Son of Man glorified, and God is glorified in Him.
32. If God be glorified in Him, God will also glorify Him in Himself and will immediately glorify Him.
33. Little children, yet a little while I am with you. You will seek Me: and as I said to the Jews, where I go, you cannot come; so now I say to you.
34. A new commandment I give to you, that you love one another; as I have loved you, that you also love one another.
35. By this will all men know that you are My disciples, if you have love one to another.
36. Simon Peter said to Him, Lord, where do You go? Jesus answered him, where I go, you cannot follow Me now; but you will follow Me afterward.
37. Peter said to Him, Lord, why can't I follow You now? I will lay down my life for Your sake.
38. Jesus answered him, will you lay down your life for My sake? Truly, truly, I say to you, the rooster will not crow until you have denied Me three times.

Chapter 14

1. Let not your heart be troubled: you believe in God, believe also in Me.
2. In My Father's house are many dwelling places: if it were not so, I would have told you. I am going to prepare a place for you.
3. And if I go and prepare a place for you, I will come again and receive you to Myself; that where I am, there you may be also.
4. And to where I go you know, and the way you know.
5. Thomas said to Him, Lord, we do not know where You go; so how can we know the way?
6. Jesus said to him, I am the way, the reality, and the life: no one comes to the Father but through Me.
7. If you had known Me, you should have known My Father also: and from now on you know Him and have seen Him.
8. Philip said to Him, Lord, show us the Father, and it will be enough for us.
9. Jesus said to him, I have been with you so long, and You have not known Me, Philip? He that has seen Me has seen the Father; and how do you say then, show us the Father?
10. Do you not believe that I am in the Father, and the Father is in Me? The words that I speak to you I speak not of Myself: but the Father that dwells in Me, He is doing the works.
11. Believe Me that I am in the Father, and the Father is in Me: or else believe Me for the very works' sake.
12. Truly, truly, I say to you, He that believes in Me, the works that I do will he do also; and greater than these he will do; because I go to My Father.
13. And whatever you will ask in My name, that I will do, so the Father may be glorified in the Son.
14. If you will ask anything in My name, I will do it.
15. If you love Me, keep My commandments.
16. And I will pray to the Father, and He will give you another Comforter, that He may remain with you into the New Covenant Age;
17. Even the Spirit of reality; whom the world cannot receive, because it sees Him not, neither knows Him: but you know Him; for He dwells with you and will be in you.
18. I will not leave you desolate: I will come to you.
19. Yet a little while and the world sees Me no longer, but you see Me: because I live, you will live also
20. Into that day. You will know that I am in My Father, and you in Me, and I in you.
21. He that has My commandments, and obeys them, he it is that loves Me: and he that loves Me will be loved by My Father, and I will love him, and will manifest Myself to him.
22. Judas said to Him, not Iscariot, Lord, how is it that you are about to manifest Yourself to us, and not to the world?
23. Jesus answered and said to Him, if a man loves Me, he will obey My words: and My Father will love him, and We will come to him, and make Our home with him.

24. He that does not love Me does not obey My sayings: and the word which you hear is not Mine, but the Father's who sent Me.
25. These things I have spoken to you, being yet present with you.
26. But the Comforter, which is the Holy Spirit, whom the Father will send in My name, He will teach you all things, and bring all things to your remembrance, whatever I have said to you.
27. Peace I leave with you, My peace I give to you: not as the world gives, give I to you. Let not your heart be troubled, neither let it be afraid.
28. You have heard how I said to you, I go away and come again to you. If you loved Me, you would rejoice, because I said, I go to the Father: for My Father is greater than I.
29. Now I have told you before it comes to pass, that, when it has come to pass, you may believe.
30. I will not talk to you much more: for the ruler of this world is coming, and in Me has no, not one thing.
31. But that the world may know that I love the Father; and as the Father has charged Me, even so I do. Arise, let us go from here.

Chapter 15

1. I am the real vine, and My Father is the vinedresser.
2. Every branch in Me that gives not fruit He takes away: and every branch that gives fruit, He prunes it, that it may bring forth more fruit.
3. Now you are clean through the word which I have spoken to you.
4. Stay in Me, and I in you. As the branch cannot produce fruit by itself, unless it stays in the vine; no more can you, unless you stay in Me.
5. I am the vine, you are the branches: He that stays in Me, and I in him, the same produces much fruit: for without Me, you can do nothing.
6. If a man does not stay in Me, he is cast out as a branch, and is withered; and men gather them, and cast them into the fire, and they are burned.
7. If you remain in Me, and My words remain in you, you will ask what you will, and it will be done to you.
8. By this is My Father glorified, that you produce much fruit; so you will be My disciples.
9. As the Father has loved Me, so I have loved you: continue in My love.
10. If you keep My commandments, you will stay in My love; just as I have kept My Father's commandments and stay in His love.
11. These things I have spoken to you, that My joy might remain in you, and that your joy might be full.
12. This is My commandment, That you love one another, as I have loved you.
13. Greater love has no man than this that a man lay down his life for his friends.
14. You are my friends, if you do whatever I command you.

15. No longer do I call you servants; for the servant knows not what his lord does: but I have called you friends; for all things that I have heard from My Father I have made known to you.
16. You have not chosen Me, but I have chosen you, and ordained you, that you should go and produce fruit, and that your fruit should remain: that whatever you will ask of the Father in My name, He may give it to you.
17. These things I command you, that you love one another.
18. If the world hates you, you know that it hated Me before it hated you.
19. If you were of the world, the world would love his own: but because you are not of the world, but I have chosen you out of the world, therefore the world hates you.
20. Remember the word that I said to you, the servant is not greater than his lord. If they have persecuted Me, they will also persecute you; if they have kept My word, they will keep yours also.
21. But all these things will they do to you for My name's sake, because they know not Him that sent Me.
22. If I had not come and spoken to them, they had not had sin: but now they have no cloak for their sin.
23. He that hates Me hates My Father also.
24. If I had not done among them the works which no other man did, they had not had sin: but now have they both seen and hated both Me and My Father.
25. But this happened that the word might be fulfilled that is written in their Law, They hated Me without a reason.
26. But when the Comforter has come, whom I will send to you from the Father, even the Spirit of reality, who proceeds from the Father, He will testify of Me:
27. So, you also will give witness, because you have been with Me from the beginning.

Chapter 16

1. These things I have spoken to you that you should not be made to stumble.
2. They will put you out of the synagogues: yes, the time comes, that whoever kills you will think that he does God's service.
3. For these things they will do to you because they have not known the Father, nor Me.
4. But these things I have told you, that when the time comes, you may remember that I told you of them. And these things I said not to you at the beginning, because I was with you.
5. But now I go My way to Him that sent Me; and none of you asks Me, where do You go?
6. But because I have said these things to you, sorrow has filled your heart.
7. Nevertheless, I tell you the reality; it is necessary for you that I go away: for if I do not go away, the Comforter will not come to you; but if I depart, I will send Him to you.
8. When He comes, He will convict the world of sin, and of righteousness, and judgment:
9. Of sin, because they believe not in Me;
10. Of righteousness, because I go to My Father, and you see Me no more;

11. Of judgment, because the prince of this world is judged.

12. I have yet many things to say to you, but you cannot handle them now.

13. However, when He, the Spirit of reality, comes, He will guide you into all reality: for He will not speak of Himself; but whatever He hears, that He will speak: and He will show you things to come.

14. He will glorify Me: for He will take of what is Mine and will show it to you.

15. All things that the Father has are Mine: therefore, I said, He will take what is Mine and will show it to you.

16. A little while, and you will not see Me: and again, a little while, and you will see Me because I go to the Father.

17. Then said some of His disciples among themselves, what is this that He says to us, a little while, and you will not see Me: and again, a little while, and you will see Me: and, because I go to the Father?

18. Therefore, they said, what is this that He says, a little while? We cannot tell what He says.

19. Now Jesus knew that they wanted to ask Him, and said to them, do you ask among yourselves of what I said, a little while, and you will not see Me: and again, a little while, and you will see Me?

20. Truly, truly, I say to you, that you will weep and mourn, but the world will rejoice: and you will be sorrowful, but your sorrow will be turned into joy.

21. A woman when she is in labor has sorrow because her hour has come: but as soon as she is delivered of the baby, she remembers no more the anguish, for joy that a child is born into the world.

22. Therefore, you now have sorrow: but I will see you again, and your heart will rejoice, and your joy no man takes from you.

23. In that day you will ask Me nothing. Truly, truly, I say to you, whatever you will ask the Father in My name, He will give it to you.

24. Until now you have asked nothing in My name: ask, and you will receive, that your joy may be full.

25. These things I have spoken to you figuratively: but the time is coming when I will no longer speak to you figuratively, but I will tell you plainly about the Father.

26. At that day you will ask in My name: and I say not to you, that I will pray the Father for you:

27. For the Father Himself loves you, because you have loved Me, and have believed that I came from God.

28. I came out from the Father, and have come into the world: again, I leave the world and go to the Father.

29. His disciples said to Him, look, now speak You plainly, and not figuratively.

30. Now we are certain that You know all things and have no need that anyone should question You: by this, we believe that You came out from God.

31. Jesus answered them, do you now believe?

32. Behold, the hour is coming, yes, and has now come, that you will be scattered, every man to his own, and will leave Me alone: and yet I am not alone, because the Father is with Me.

33. These things I have spoken to you, that in Me you might have peace. In the world you will have tribulation: but be of good cheer; I have overcome the world!

Chapter 17

1. These words spoke Jesus and lifted up his eyes to heaven, and said, Father, the hour has come; glorify Your Son, that Your Son also may glorify You:
2. As You have given Him power over all flesh, that He should give infinite life to as many as You have given Him.
3. And this is infinite life, that they might know You the only true God, and Jesus Christ, who You have sent.
4. I have glorified You on the land: I have finished the work which you gave Me to do.
5. Now, oh Father, glorify Me with Yourself, with the glory which I had with You before the world was.
6. I have manifested Your name to the men who You gave Me out of the world: they were Yours, and You gave them to Me, and they have kept Your word.
7. Now they have known that all things whatever You have given Me are of You.
8. For I have given to them the words which You gave Me; and they have received them, and have known surely that I came out from You, and they have believed that You did send Me.
9. I pray for them: I pray not for the world, but for those who you have given Me; for they are Yours.
10. And all Mine are Yours, and Yours are Mine, and I am glorified in them.
11. Now I am no more in the world, but these are in the world, and I come to You. Holy Father, keep through Your own name those who You have given Me, that they may be one, as We are.
12. While I was with them in the world, I kept them in Your name: those that You gave Me I have kept, and none of them is lost, but the son of perdition; that the Scripture might be fulfilled.
13. Now I come to You; and these things I speak in the world, that they might have My joy fulfilled in themselves.
14. I have given them Your word; and the world has hated them, because they are not of the world, just as I am not of the world.
15. I do not pray that you should take them out of the world, but that you should keep them from the evil.
16. They are not of the world, just as I am not of the world.
17. Sanctify them through Your reality: Your word is reality.
18. As You have sent Me into the world, even so, I have also sent them into the world.
19. For their sakes I sanctify Myself, that they also might be sanctified through the reality.
20. Neither do I pray for these alone, but for them also who will believe on Me through their word;
21. That they all may be one; as You, Father, are in Me, and I in You, that they also may be one in Us: that the world may believe that You have sent Me.

22. And the glory which you gave Me I have given them; that they may be one, just as We are one:
23. I in them, and You in Me, that they may be made mature into one; and that the world may know that You have sent Me, and have loved them, as You have loved Me.
24. Father, I desire that they also, who You have given Me, be with Me where I am; that they may behold My glory, which you have given Me: for You loved Me before the downfall of the world.
25. Oh, righteous Father, the world has not known You: but I have known You, and these have known that You have sent Me.
26. And I have explained to them Your qualities and will declare it: that the love with which You have loved Me may be in them, and I in them.

Chapter 18

1. When Jesus had spoken these words, He went out with His disciples over the winter rushing stream of the Kidron, where there was a garden, into which He and His disciples entered.
2. And Judas also, who betrayed Him, knew the place: for Jesus frequently met there with His disciples.
3. Judas then, having received squads of troops and officers from the chief priests and Pharisees, came there with lanterns and torches and weapons.
4. Therefore, Jesus, knowing all things that should happen to Him, went out, and said to them, who seek you?
5. They answered Him, Jesus of Nazareth. Jesus said to them, I am! And Judas also, who betrayed Him, stood with them.
6. Then as soon as He had said to them, I am, they went backward and fell to the ground.
7. He then asked them again, who seek you? And they said, Jesus of Nazareth.
8. Jesus answered, I have told you that, I am: therefore, if you seek Me, let these go their way:
9. That the saying might be fulfilled, which He spoke, of those who You gave Me I have lost none.
10. Then Simon Peter having a sword drew it, struck the high priest's servant, and cut off his right ear. The servant's name was Malchus.
11. Then said Jesus to Peter, put your sword back into the sheath: the cup which My Father has given to Me, am I not to drink it?
12. Then the troops and the captain and officers of the Jews took Jesus, and bound Him,
13. And led Him away to Annas first; for he was the father-in-law to Caiaphas, who was the high priest that same year.
14. Now Caiaphas was he who advised the Jews, that it was necessary that one man should die for the people.
15. And Simon Peter followed Jesus, and so did another disciple: that disciple was known to the high priest and went with Jesus into the palace of the high priest.
16. But Peter stood at the door outside. The other disciple then went out who was known to the high priest, and spoke to her that kept the door, and brought in Peter.

17. Then the servant girl that kept the door said to Peter, you are not also one of this man's disciples? He said, I am not.
18. And the servants and officers stood there, who had made a fire of coals; for it was cold: and they warmed themselves: and Peter stood with them and warmed himself.
19. The high priest then asked Jesus about His disciples and His teaching.
20. Jesus answered him, I spoke openly to the world; I ever taught in the synagogue, and in the temple, to where the Jews always gather; and in secret I have said nothing.
21. Why do you ask Me? Ask those who heard Me, what I have said to them: behold, they know what I said.
22. When He had so spoken, one of the officers who stood by struck Jesus with the palm of his hand, saying, do You answer the high priest so?
23. Jesus answered him, if I have spoken evil, give witness of the evil: but if well, why do you strike Me?
24. Now Annas had sent Him bound to Caiaphas the high priest.
25. Now Simon Peter stood and warmed himself. Therefore, they said to him, are you not also one of His disciples? He denied it and said I am not.
26. One of the servants of the high priest, being his relative whose ear Peter cut off, said, did I not see you in the garden with Him?
27. Again, Peter denied: and immediately the rooster crowed.
28. Then they led Jesus from Caiaphas to the governor's palace: and it was early, and they did not go into the governor's palace unless they should become defiled; but that they might eat the Passover.
29. Pilate then went out to them, and said, what accusation do you bring against this man?
30. They answered and said to him, if He were not a troublemaker, we would not have delivered Him up to you.
31. Then Pilate said to them, take Him, and judge Him according to your Law. Therefore, the Jews said to him, it is not lawful for us to put anyone to death:
32. That the saying of Jesus might be fulfilled, which He spoke, signifying what death He was about to die.
33. Then Pilate entered into the governor's palace again, and called Jesus, and said to Him, are you the King of the Jews?
34. Jesus answered him, are you speaking this thing by yourself, or did others tell it to you about Me?
35. Pilate answered, am I a Jew? Your own nation and the chief priests have delivered You to me: what have You done?
36. Jesus answered, My kingdom is not of this world: if My kingdom were of this world, then My servants would fight, that I should not be delivered to the Jews: but now My kingdom is not from here.
37. Therefore, Pilate said to Him, Are You a king then? Jesus answered you say that I am a king. To this end was I born, and for this reason I came into the world, that I should bear witness to one reality. Everyone that is out from the reality hears My voice.

John 18:38

38. Pilate said to Him, what is reality? When he had said this, he went out again to the Jews, and said to them, I find no fault in Him at all.
39. But you have a custom that I should release to you one at the Passover: therefore, do you want me to release the King of the Jews?
40. Then they all cried again, saying, not this man, but Barabbas! Now Barabbas was a robber.

Chapter 19

1. Therefore, Pilate then took Jesus and whipped Him.
2. And the soldiers twisted a crown of thorns and put it on His head, and they put on Him a purple robe,
3. Then said, Hail, King of the Jews! So, they struck Him with their hands.
4. Therefore, Pilate went out again, and said to them, behold, I bring Him out to you, that you may know that I find no fault in Him.
5. Then came Jesus out, wearing the crown of thorns, and the purple robe. So, Pilate said to them, behold the man!
6. Therefore, when the chief priests and officers saw Him, they cried out, saying, crucify Him, crucify Him! Pilate said to them, take Him, and crucify Him: for I find no fault in Him.
7. The Jews answered him, we have a Law, and by our Law, He ought to die because He made Himself the Son of God.
8. Therefore, when Pilate heard that saying, he was even more afraid;

John 19:18

9. And went again into the governor's palace, and said to Jesus, where are You from? But Jesus gave him no answer.
10. Then Pilate said to Him, You do not speak to me? You do not know that I have the authority to crucify You, and have authority to release You?
11. Jesus answered you could have no authority at all against Me unless it were given you from above: therefore, he that delivered Me to you has the greater sin.
12. From then on, Pilate sought to release Him: but the Jews cried out, saying, if you let this man go, you are not Caesar's friend: whoever makes Himself a king speaks against Caesar!
13. Therefore, when Pilate heard that saying, he brought Jesus out and sat down in the judgment seat in a place that is called the Pavement, but in the Hebrew, Gabbatha.
14. For it was the preparation of the Passover, and about the sixth hour: and he said to the Jews, behold your King!
15. But they cried out, take Him away, take Him away, crucify Him! Pilate said to them, will I crucify your King? The chief priests answered, we have no king but Caesar.
16. Therefore, he delivered Him to them to be crucified. So, they took Jesus and led Him away.
17. And He, bearing His cross, went out into a place called the Place of a Skull, which is called in the Hebrew Golgotha:
18. Where they crucified Him, and two others with Him, one on both sides and Jesus in the midst.

19. So, Pilate wrote a title and put it on the cross. And the writing was JESUS OF NAZARETH THE KING OF THE JEWS.
20. Then many of the Jews read this title: for the place where Jesus was crucified was close to the city: and it was written in Hebrew, Greek, and Latin.
21. Then said the chief priests of the Jews to Pilate, Write not, The King of the Jews; but that He said, I am King of the Jews.
22. Pilate answered, what I have written I have written.
23. Then the soldiers, when they had crucified Jesus, took His garments, and made four parts, to every soldier a part; and also, his tunic: now the tunic was without seam, woven from the top throughout.
24. Therefore, they said among themselves, let us not tear it, but cast lots for it, whose it will be: that the Scripture might be fulfilled, which says, they parted My clothing among them, and for My clothing, they did cast lots. Therefore, these things the soldiers did.
25. Now there stood by the cross of Jesus His mother, and His mother's sister, Mary the wife of Cleophas, and Mary Magdalene.
26. Therefore, when Jesus saw His mother, and the disciple standing by, who He loved, He said to His mother, woman, behold your son.
27. Then said He to the disciple, behold your mother. From that hour that disciple received her into his home.
28. After this, Jesus knowing that all things were now accomplished, that the Scripture might be fulfilled, said, I thirst.
29. Now there was a vessel full of sour wine: and they filled a sponge with the sour wine, and put it on hyssop, and put it to His mouth.
30. Therefore, when Jesus had received the sour wine, He said, it is paid in full! And He bowed His head and gave up the ghost.
31. Therefore, the Jews, because it was the preparation, that the bodies should not remain on the cross on the Sabbath day, for that Sabbath day was a high day, asked Pilate that their legs might be broken, and that they might be taken away.
32. Then came the soldiers, and broke the legs of the first, and of the other who was crucified with Him.
33. But when they came to Jesus and saw that he was dead already, they did not break His legs:
34. But one of the soldiers with a spear pierced His side, and immediately there came out blood and water.
35. And he that saw it testified, and his testimony is genuine: and he knows that he is laying out the reality that you may believe.
36. For these things were done, that the Scripture should be fulfilled, not one of His bones will be broken.
37. And again another scripture says, they will look on Him who they pierced.
38. After this Joseph of Arimathaea, being a disciple of Jesus, but secretly for fear of the Jews, asked Pilate that He might take away the body of Jesus: and Pilate permitted him. Therefore, he came and took Jesus' body.
39. Also, there came Nicodemus, who at first came to Jesus by night, and brought a mixture of myrrh and aloes, about a hundred pounds.

John 19:40

40. Then they took the body of Jesus, and wrapped it in linen clothes with spices, as is the Jews' custom of burial.
41. Now in the place where He was crucified, there was a garden; and in the garden a new tomb, in which no man had ever been laid.
42. Therefore, they laid Jesus there because of the Jews' preparation day; for the tomb was close at hand.

Chapter 20

1. The first day of the week Mary Magdalene came early to the tomb, when it was yet dark, and saw the stone taken away from the tomb.
2. Then she ran and came to Simon Peter, and to the other disciple, who Jesus loved, and said to them, they have taken away the LORD out of the tomb, and we know not where they have laid Him.
3. Therefore, Peter went out, and that other disciple, and came to the tomb.
4. So, they both ran together: and the other disciple did outrun Peter and came first to the tomb.
5. And he stooped down, and looked in, and saw the linen clothes lying; yet He did not go in.
6. Then came Simon Peter following him, and went into the tomb, and saw the linen clothes lying there,
7. And the cloth, that was around His head, was not lying with the linen clothes, but was wrapped together in a place by itself.
8. Then also went in that other disciple, who came first to the tomb, and he saw and believed.
9. For as yet they did not know the Scripture that He must rise again from the dead.
10. Then the disciples went away again to their own homes.
11. But Mary stood outside at the tomb weeping, and as she wept, she stooped down, and looked into the tomb,
12. And saw two angels in white sitting, the one at the head, and the other at the feet, where the body of Jesus had lain.
13. So, they say to her, woman, why do you weep? She said to them, because they have taken away my LORD, and I do not know where they have laid Him.
14. When she had so said, she turned around and saw Jesus standing, and did not know that it was Jesus.
15. Jesus said to her, woman, why do you weep? Who do you seek? She, supposing Him to be the gardener, said to Him, Sir, if you have taken Him from here, tell me where you have laid Him, and I will take Him away.
16. Jesus said to her, Mary. She turned around, and said to Him, Rabboni; which is to say, Master.
17. Jesus said to her, no clinging to Me; for I am not yet ascended to My Father: but go to My brothers, and say to them, I ascend to My Father, and Your Father; and to My God and Your God.
18. Mary Magdalene came and told the disciples that she had seen the LORD and that He had spoken these things to her.

19. Then the same day in the evening, being the first day of the week, when the doors were shut where the disciples were assembled for fear of the Jews, Jesus came and stood in their midst, and said to them, peace to you!
20. When He had said so, He showed to them His hands and His side. Then were the disciples glad, when they saw the LORD.
21. Then said Jesus to them again, peace to you: as My Father has sent Me, even so I send you.
22. When He had said this, He breathed on them, and said to them, receive the Holy Spirit!
23. Whatever sins you forgive, they are forgiven; and whatever sins you retain, they are retained.
24. But Thomas, one of the twelve, called Didymus, was not with them when Jesus came.
25. Therefore, the other disciples said to him, we have seen the LORD. But he said to them, unless I will see in His hands the imprint of the nails and put my finger into the imprint of the nails, and thrust my hand into His side, I will not believe.
26. After eight days again His disciples were inside, and Thomas with them: then came Jesus, the doors being shut, and stood in the midst, and said, peace to you.
27. Then He said to Thomas, reach your finger here, and behold My hands; and reach your hand here, and thrust it into My side: and be not faithless, but believe.
28. Thomas answered and said to Him, my Lord and my God!
29. Jesus said to him, Thomas, because you have seen Me, you have believed: blessed are they that have not seen, and yet have believed.
30. Many other signs Jesus truly did in the presence of His disciples, which are not written in this book:
31. But these are written that you might believe that Jesus is the Christ, the Son of God; and that believing you might have life through His name.

Chapter 21

1. After these things Jesus showed Himself again to the disciples at the sea of Tiberius Caesar; and in this way He showed Himself.
2. There were together Simon Peter, and Thomas called Didymus, and Nathanael of Cana in Galilee, and the sons of Zebedee, and two other of His disciples.
3. Simon Peter said to them, I go fishing. They said to him, we will also go with you. They went out and immediately entered into a boat, and that night they caught nothing.
4. But when the morning had come, Jesus stood on the shore: but the disciples did not know that it was Jesus.
5. Then Jesus said to them, little children, do you have any food? They answered Him, no.
6. So, He said to them, cast the net on the right side of the boat, and you will discover. Therefore, they cast, and now they did not have the strength to draw it in because of the quantity of fish.

John 21:7 — John 21:26

7. Therefore, that disciple who Jesus loved said to Peter, it is the Lord! Now when Simon Peter heard that it was the Lord, he put on his outer garment, (for he had removed it) and cast himself into the sea.

8. And the other disciples came in a little boat; (for they were not far from land, but as it were two hundred cubits) dragging the net with fishes.

9. As soon then as they had come to land, they saw a fire of coals there, and fish laid on it, and bread.

10. Jesus said to them, bring now the fish which you have caught.

11. Simon Peter went up and drew the net to land full of great fishes, a hundred and fifty-three: and for all there were so many, yet the net was not broken.

12. Jesus said to them, come and dine. And none of the disciples dared ask Him, who are You? Knowing that it was the Lord.

13. Jesus then came and gave them both bread and fish.

14. Now this is the third time that Jesus showed Himself to His disciples after He was risen from the dead.

15. So, when they had dined, Jesus said to Simon Peter, Simon, son of Jonas, do you love Me more than these? He said to Him, yes, Lord; You know that I have fondness for You. He said to him, feed My lambs.

16. He said to him again the second time, Simon, son of Jonas, do you love Me? He said to Him, yes, Lord; You know that I have fondness for you. He said to him, feed My sheep.

17. He said to him the third time, Simon, son of Jonas, do you have a fondness for Me? Peter was grieved because He said to him the third time, do you have fondness for Me? So he said to Him, Lord, You know all things; You know that I have fondness for You. Jesus said to him, feed My sheep.

18. Truly, truly, I say to you, when you were young, you dressed yourself and walked to where you wanted: but when you are old, you will stretch out your hands, and another will dress you, and take you to where you do not want to go.

19. This He spoke, signifying by what death he should glorify God. When He had spoken this, He said to Him, follow Me!

20. Then Peter, turning around, saw the disciple whom Jesus loved following; who also leaned on His chest at supper, and said, Lord, who is he that betrays You?

21. Peter seeing him said to Jesus, Lord, and what will this man do?

22. Jesus said to him, if I will that he stay until I come, what is that to you? You follow Me.

23. Then this saying went out among the brothers, that this disciple should not die: yet Jesus did not say this of him, He will not die; but, if I will that he remain until I come, what is that to you?

24. This is the disciple who testifies about these things and wrote these things: and we know that his testimony is true.

25. There are also many other things that Jesus
26. did, which, if they were written down each one, I imagine that even the world itself would not have space for the books being written. Amen.

Intro to Acts and the Restoration of Israel - Don K Preston

Commentators have long perplexed about Luke's purpose in writing the book of Acts. Conzelmann said it was to chronicle the establishment of the church as a long-term entity in light of the failed parousia. In fact, many commentators see Acts as almost an apology on Luke's part for a failed eschatology. The church has now been established only because Christ has not come!

Others say it is to tell the story of the work of the Spirit. Some commentators, not necessarily agreeing with the failed eschatology view, nonetheless, tell us that Acts is about the establishment of the church, now that Israel has rejected her Messiah. There are shades of this view, including the dispensational view that sees Acts as unrelated to the fulfillment of God's Old Covenant promises made to Israel.

Few commentators see Acts as the story of the restoration of Israel as foretold by the prophets. It is refreshing and exciting, to know that this is changing. A growing number of scholars now see Acts as the story of fulfillment, not failure, on the part of God and Israel.

In what follows, I hope to convey the reality that Acts is about the restoration of Israel. It is about the fulfillment of God's promises to her, as interpreted through the Spirit inspired author. What I will present is not exhaustive by any means. In fact, I will only be able to hit some highlights. However, I hope to present enough evidence to convince the reader to pursue this theme further. I have produced a fifty-two-lesson series in MP3 format that covers more of the marvelous insights that Luke offers us into the hope of Israel: available at eschatology.org.

Acts 1

Acts 1:4–6 Jesus showed himself alive for forty days, teaching his disciples about the kingdom. Nothing could more clearly demonstrate that Luke was about to embark on a discussion of the fulfillment of Israel's promises than this. During his ministry, Jesus focused on the promises of Israel: He came to "seek and to save that which is lost" a reference to the lost ones of Israel. The kingdom was the heart and core of God's promises to Israel (2 Samuel 7:13-14). It was the focus of the prophets of Israel (Isaiah 2-4; Ezekiel 37, etc.). Thus, Acts 1:4 "set the tone" for the rest of the book. The kingdom message is continued in Acts 8, 14, 19, 20, and 28 as well. This makes it clear that Luke never abandons the subject. Acts is about the hope of Israel. While most commentators claim that the disciples still misunderstood Jesus and the kingdom, this is patently false. Jesus had opened the minds of his disciples to understand the scriptures (Luke 24:25-27). Thus, the disciples were simply asking about the time of the fulfillment of what Jesus had been instructing them about. Jesus did not chide the disciples for their "ignorance" or failure to understand.

Instead, he told them to "go into the city and wait" for the promise of the Spirit. The promise of the Spirit was itself an OT promise to Israel and for Israel, to raise her from the dead, restore her to God's presence, and result in the offer of salvation to the nations (Isaiah 32:49; Ezekiel 37; Joel 2-3).

The disciples remembered the ministry of John the Immerser when Jesus mentioned the promise of the Spirit. The relationship between John, the promise of the Spirit and the kingdom cannot be missed. John proclaimed, "the time is fulfilled, the kingdom of heaven has drawn near" (Matthew 3; Mark 1). He likewise promised that the Messiah would baptize them "in the Spirit and with fire," echoing Isaiah 4:4, and Joel 2.

The imminence of the kingdom – the fulfillment of John and Jesus' message is strongly indicated in the link between the promise of the Spirit and the fact that Jesus told his disciples to go into the city and to wait for the Spirit. Since the outpouring of the Spirit and the establishment of the kingdom are inseparably connected, this tells us that the restoration of Israel was truly near. It cannot be imagined that the disciples divorced the promise of the imminent reception of the Spirit from the kingdom promises.

You Are My Witnesses – The Creation (Re-Creation) of Israel

After promising the Spirit to the disciples, Jesus immediately told them they would be his witnesses. This is a direct echo of Isaiah 43:10 and this, like Jesus' forty-day instructions concerning the kingdom is strongly suggestive that the restoration of Israel, an Israel now identified by her connection to Jesus, but Israel, nonetheless, was now taking place. Isaiah 43 foretold the creation of a new people that would be YHVH's witnesses to the nations. And now, in Acts 1 we find the twelve apostles- representing the righteous remnant– being given the commission to be his witnesses to the nations. The radical and revolutionary nature of what Isaiah 43 foretold, and what was happening in Acts, is revealed when we consider that YHVH called on Israel to not remember the former things, but to look to the "New Thing" that He would do (43:18). What is so astounding is that YHVH, in context, called on Israel to forget the first exodus! That event was the single most normative and formative event in all of Israel's history, and yet, God said the time was coming when they would need to forget that historic event and look to the greater "New Thing," that He would do. Given the indisputable fact that Acts is built around the "Second Exodus" motif, it is clear that the "New Thing" promised by YHVH in Isaiah 43 was now taking place, which meant not only that Israel was being "restored," but that she was to forget her first beginnings and look to the last. Isaiah 11 and a host of other Old Testament prophecies foretold that at the time of that Second Exodus the word of God would "fill the earth" calling first of all, the scattered children of Israel, and then the nations to the Lord. As Jesus told his disciples to begin their mission in Jerusalem- Zion- he said they would then go from Judea to Samaria, and from there to the uttermost parts of the earth (Greek word, ge). They were to go to "the Jew first, and then the Greek" just as the prophets foretold.

Acts 2

I will not develop it here, but it is no coincidence that the events took place on Pentecost. That auspicious day was the last of the first four of Israel's major feast days. It was sometimes called the Feast of First Fruits, and the events of that day were indeed the fulfillment of that typological feast, for on that day, 3000 individuals joined themselves to the body of the New Israel, as the first fruit of the harvest (James 1:18). The re-gathering of Israel is seen in the names of the countries represented that day. All of the nations mentioned are from the nations of the diaspora, where Israel had been scattered in the previous dispersions. But now, on the day of Pentecost, representatives of the scattered tribes of Israel were in Jerusalem and the events of that day comprised fulfillment, at least initially, of the re-gathering of the diaspora. "This is that which was spoken by the prophet Joel"- Acts 2:15ff The outpouring of the Spirit on Pentecost was in fulfillment of Acts 1, and even more importantly, of Joel 2:28-32.

Peter's words leave no room for controversy. The events of that day were what Joel predicted: "This is that which was spoken by the prophet Joel." Words could not be clearer, more emphatic, or undeniable. Joel foretold the consummative last days, the coming of the Day of the Lord, the salvation of the remnant and the calling of the nations. It is one of the key OT prophecies, and inextricably tied to the restoration of Israel. But, Joel was not alone in predicting the outpouring of the Spirit in the last days, for the restoration of Israel. Isaiah 32 and Ezekiel 37 and Micah 7 are but a few of the significant OT prophecies of the outpouring of the Spirit in the last days.

In fact, there is not a topic or theme that is more intensely eschatological, or, more directly tied to the restoration of Israel than this subject. According to Ezekiel 37:11-14 the Spirit would be poured out to raise Israel from the dead. Thus, for Peter to declare, "this is that which was spoken by the prophet Joel" cannot properly be construed as anything but a declaration that the restoration of Israel was taking place. Jesus often shocked and offended his contemporaries with his identification of the true Israel, and the nature of the restoration of Israel under his rule. Likewise, Peter's declaration of the fulfillment of Joel and the other Spirit.

Restoration promises was a radical departure from what they thought was to happen in the last days work of the Spirit. But, this revolutionary identification of the true Israel and the fulfillment of Israel's promises was just beginning in Luke's account. There was much, much more to come.

David Is Not Ascended, But… David was the ultimate king of Israel. Under him, Israel reached the height of her glory, putting down her enemies, reveling in the presence of God, enjoying the blessings of the Covenant. It was because of David's accomplishments, as a man after God's own heart, that he became known as the type of the coming of Messiah. In fact, the promises of the kingdom, and the restoration of the kingdom, are so intimately tied to David, that the kingdom promises are often referred to simply as the Davidic Kingdom promises. Peter declared on Pentecost that God had sworn to raise up the seed of David to sit on His throne. That prophecy, said Peter, spoke of the resurrection of Jesus, and had now been fulfilled. Astoundingly, he noted that it was not David who had ascended into the heavens to be enthroned, but Jesus, who had now been declared as "Lord and Christ" (v.36). This was a prima facie statement that the Davidic promise of the kingdom was being fulfilled! "Sit At My Right Hand Until I Make Thine Enemies Thy Footstool …" The preceding point is driven home when one sees the connection between Peter's attestation that Jesus had been given the throne of David, and this conflates with his exaltation to the right hand of the majesty on high, in fulfillment of Psalms 110.

In other words, the promise of the Davidic throne and kingdom are inextricably tied to Messiah sitting at the right hand. These are not disparate motifs or promises. And here is what is so astounding. Psalms 110 is cited and quoted more times in the NT than any other OT prophecy, and without disputation, is affirmed as fulfilled in Christ who was raised from the dead and seated at the right hand of the Father in the heavenly places (cf. Ephesians 1:19f). So, Christ's ascension and enthronement at the right hand was the fulfillment (the initiation of fulfillment) of Psalms 110. But Psalms 110 was the promise of the exaltation of Messiah to the throne of David. Thus, the exaltation of Christ to the right hand– affirmed by Peter on Pentecost was an assertion that the Davidic kingdom was being established. But of course, once again we see the radical and revolutionary nature of the nature of fulfillment exposed.

David's throne was a literal, physical throne, over a geo-politico-military kingdom, spatially confined to the land of Canaan. Messiah was to sit on the throne of David and rule over the kingdom. But Peter affirmed through the Spirit, that Jesus was now Christ (the promised Messiah) sitting on the throne of David "in the heavens", where Psalms 110 said Messiah would sit– in David's kingdom. Peter's declaration meant that the very nature of the kingdom was being– had been- fundamentally transformed into a spiritual kingdom. The Old Creation that which was to be forgotten, was now radically transformed into the New Thing which Israel was to accept.

Acts 3 - The Restoration of All Things

Shortly after the auspicious events of Pentecost, Peter and John went to the temple. As they entered, we find the famous account of the healing of the lame man, and the ensuing sermon by Peter. The apostle responded to the amazement of the audience by calling on them to repent in the name (i.e. in the authority, into the name and authority) of Jesus. He urged them to repent so that God would grant them "the times of refreshing" (which is a period of respite before judgment) because before the sending of Jesus from heaven. That Parousia would consummate "the restoration of all things."

Nothing would communicate to a Jewish audience more convincingly, more clearly, that her cherished restoration had begun than Peter's reference to "the restoration of all things." Peter was clear: the restoration he was talking about was the hope and promise of all of the OT prophet, "all who have ever spoken." And Peter is equally emphatic, "they spoke of these days." Likewise, the nature of that restoration is delineated in the text: God sent Jesus to bless you by taking away your sin.

Acts 4

Sometimes it almost seems as if Acts 4 is almost forgotten in the discussions of eschatology and even ecclesiology. This is lamentable, for this chapter loudly proclaims that Israel's restoration, via the long anticipated Messianic Temple, had begun. Numerous OT prophecies spoke of the coming "Stone" which would be both the foundation of the Messianic Temple, as well as the instrument of judgment against both houses of Israel. (See my The Elements Shall Melt With Fervent Heat book for a fuller discussion of this important motif, as it is developed by Jesus, Paul and Peter in the NT). The stunning thing that Peter does is to take Psalms 118:22 "the stone that the builders rejected has become the chief corner stone" and makes it extremely personal "This Jesus is the stone that was rejected by you, the builders, which has become the chief cornerstone" (4:11- ESV).

It could not get much more personal than that! But of course, what is so remarkable is that Peter takes Israel's expectation of an end-times literal temple and says that the prophecies referred to a temple built on the person of Messiah, not literal stones. If the foundation of the anticipated Messianic Temple is the living Messiah, then surely the super structure cannot be physical stones, and this fundamentally redefines the nature of the restoration of Israel. The Kings of the Earth Have Set Themselves … Against the Lord and Against His Anointed Contra the modern dispensational doctrine that says the Jewish rejection of Jesus postponed the kingdom offer to Israel, the nascent church in Jerusalem, led by the apostles had a totally different view of that rejection– it was foretold. When Peter and John were released by the Sanhedrin, they went back to the congregation and reported all that had taken place. At the report, the congregation responded in unison it seems, by singing Psalms 2:1. What is missed so often is that not only did the Psalmist predict the rejection of Messiah, but it also likewise clearly stated that the rejection would not in any way thwart God's sovereign will: "The one who sits in the heavens laughs. He will hold them in derision.

Then He will speak to them in His Wrath... Yet (meaning, in spite of the rejection of Messiah, DKP) have I set my King on my holy hill." Notice that "Yet." It forcefully declares that man's best (worst) efforts to delay, to alter, to postpone, to nullify God's plans would fail. In fact, the rejection was part of God's plan! Acts 4 thus serves as a very powerful testimony to the on-going restoration of Israel. Her promised Messianic Temple now had the foundation in place, and those who had rejected that Stone would, therefore, lie under the impending judgment of that rejection. Furthermore, while that rejection was initially not understood by Jesus' disciples (cf. Luke 24:21f), they now fully understood the necessary role of that suffering for Messiah to "enter into his glory." (Remember the forty days of kingdom instruction by Jesus and the subsequent outpouring of the Spirit).

Acts 4-7 - Preparing the Way for the Removal of the Old The Full Establishment of the New

I will give here only a few of the highlights from these three chapters

1.) Luke's recounting of the on-going powerful demonstration of the work of the Spirit brings to mind how Israel was led by the Spirit in the first exodus (Isaiah 63:10f) and yet, Israel rebelled against YHVH, leading to judgment. Of course, it is critical to note that the references to the work of the Spirit must be viewed from the perspective of Acts 2 and Peter's affirmation that Israel's anticipated last days were present.

2.) Selling the Land - We have here no abiding City... In Chapter 4-5 we find the account of the nascent body of Christ doing something absolutely incredible. The disciples are selling their land! To modern readers, far removed from the mind-set of the ancient Jews, and Torah, the incredible implications of these actions are all but lost. It is almost impossible to over-emphasize the importance of the land to the Jews. It was their inheritance from YHVH Himself. When the land was allotted to the twelve tribes (Joshua 13ff) the Lord instructed Israel: 'The land shall not be sold permanently, for the land is Mine; for you are strangers and sojourners with Me" (Leviticus 25:23). While it was permissible for Israelites to temporarily sell their land, the Jubilee Laws provided that ownership of the land would revert to the original tribal owners in the Jubilee years. Yet, in Acts 4-5 we find the selling of the land by the Jewish Christians. There is no suggestion that they intended to redeem the land at a later date, (Cf. Jeremiah 32). The record seems to indicate that they were simply selling their land, permanently. In light of Jesus' Olivet Discourse, and the warnings in Acts 2-4, of impending judgment on Jerusalem and Israel, the full significance of this comes to the forefront. Those early Christians knew that the value of Jerusalem real estate was going to go to Zero! They were now beginning to realize, as Hebrews would later declare: "we have here no abiding city, but, look for one that is about to come" (Hebrews 13:14).

3.) The Sanhedrin imprisoned Peter and John, but an angel of the Lord freed them, and they immediately began preaching once again in the Temple (Acts 5). What is so remarkable– and mostly overlooked– is that when the angel released them from prison, he instructed them to "speak to all the people all the words of this Life" (5:20). This is a remarkable and beautiful statement. The words of Jesus, the words about Jesus, were and are the words of Life! In sharp contrast, when the Sanhedrin brought Peter and John back to trial, they said, "we strictly charged you not to teach in this name, yet, you have filled Jerusalem with your teaching, and intend to bring this man's blood upon us" (5:28). Ironic is it not, that these very men had cried out only a short time before: "let his blood be on us and on our children!" (Matthew 27:25)? Yet now, with the implications of what has transpired in the resurrection of Jesus and the proclamation of that awesome event, they see the implications and are pleading "innocence."

Peter had told that august body that they had rejected the chief corner stone of the predicted Messianic temple. That could only mean one thing: Judgment was coming on them. They understood that while Peter and John were speaking the words of Life to the people, that this meant judgment on them for killing the Prince of Life. 4.) Spatial limitations forbid a full development of Stephen's Temple discourse. However, it is clear that Stephen, in recounting Israel's "history," has a deeply theological point to make, and the history that he gives is focused on that particular point. He was not intending to recount Israel's entire history. What he patently does do, however, is to show that Abraham was blessed by God while he was outside the land. Stephen shows Israel's long history of rejecting God's prophets. He shows how the Lord judged them for their rebellion. He shows how their emphasis on the temple itself was misplaced, for it was never God's ultimate intent to dwell in temples made with hands. All of these sequels perfectly fit with what Luke has already recorded. The chief cornerstone for the Messianic Temple had been laid.

Those who had rejected that Stone could now only anticipate impending judgment. And now, Stephen reinforces that message by pointing out that the glorious temple in which he was now standing was never God's eschatological goal. So, lying latent in chapters 4-7 is an extremely powerful narrative. Israel's last days prophecies were being fulfilled. They were not, however, being fulfilled as anticipated or desired. They were being fulfilled in the body of Christ, the foundation stone of the Messianic Temple– a living Temple– offering Life. But all of this meant that the Old Temple, the Old World which was the "ministration of death" was about to be swept away.

Acts 8 - To Samaria and the Uttermost Parts of the Earth

In his instructions on the kingdom, Jesus had told his apostles that they would be his witnesses in Jerusalem, Judea, Samaria and then to the uttermost parts of the earth. From Acts 2-8:1-4 we find that the Jerusalem church was perfectly happy initially to confine their efforts to Jerusalem and Judea. However, in the Lord's providence, persecution arose, and those who were persecuted were eager then to share the story of Life everywhere they went. And they went to Samaria.

Although the city was not named Samaria as such until the time of Omri (1 Kings 16:24f) nonetheless, the region of Samaria had long been considered as almost a synonym for the dispersed northern tribes. Due to Omri's horrible wickedness, and the entire history of the divided kingdom that was inextricably tied to that, the stigma of rebellion against God was paramount in the mind of those in Judea. (You can get a small sense of the Jewish antipathy toward Samaria, and vice versa, in Luke 9:51f, where a Samaritan city refused to allow Jesus and his disciples to pass through, and John, the "apostle of love" wanted Jesus to call down fire from heaven on them)! Prophetically, part and parcel of Israel's eschatological hope was the restoration of the diaspora. God would gather them from the east and the west and bring them back to Him.

Israel's nationalistic hope was a literally re-gathering to the physical land when the Messianic kingdom was established. Acts 8 falsifies such notions. Philip was one of those who went to Samaria, and there preached "the Christ" i.e. the Messiah! He confirmed the message of Jesus as Messiah by performing undeniable miracles. The miraculous work of the Spirit was poured out in earthly Israel's last days, when the Lord would bring the tribes back together under Messiah (Ezekiel). The Spirit was to usher in the promised restoration of the kingdom by Messiah, thus creating and restoring the heavenly Israel. The evidence of this is when Philip was manifesting the miraculous work of the Spirit, declaring Jesus as the promised Messiah, and preaching "the good news about the kingdom of God" (Acts 8:12). (Note: Philip's message of the kingdom could hardly be classified as "good news" if in fact, per the dispensationalists, the kingdom had been postponed!). We may not be stretching the text too far to take note of the similarities between Philip and Moses, the first exodus and the Second. In the first exodus, Israel was in bondage.

In the Second, Israel, particularly the northern tribes, were still considered to be in bondage.

In the first exodus, Moses was sent to those in bondage to set them free, but, was confronted by false magicians.

In the Second Exodus, Philip goes to those in bondage and is confronted with a false magician. In both cases, God's chosen messenger triumphs over the false magicians and as a result, the Exodus proceeds.

The Ethiopian Eunuch a Radical Fulfillment

To me personally, the story of the Ethiopian eunuch is one of the most compelling, the most exciting stories in Acts, and beautifully illustrates and proves that Luke's narrative must indeed be understood as focused on the restoration of Israel as foretold by the prophets. Under Torah, any man with injury to his private parts in any way, was forbidden to enter the Temple, or to serve in the ministry (Deuteronomy 23). It was critical under the Law to be able to marry and produce "children of God" and thereby sustain the kingdom. This was the nature of the kingdom. But, as a result of being unable to produce children, eunuchs were called "dry trees." However, the prophets foretold a time when this would no longer be the case. Isaiah 56 predicted the time of a radically different kind of Temple worship and service.

In this New Temple, both the foreigner and the eunuch would be given a name better than "sons and daughters" (56:5). Note that this is true of both the foreigner and the eunuch. This is significant, but we cannot develop it here. In many commentaries, and certainly in countless homiletic presentations, the story of the eunuch is used as a story to speak of how God will now accept those of any nation, of any ethnic group. Emphasis is normally on the fact that the man was an Ethiopian. However, this is misplaced. The emphasis in the Greek is on the fact that the man was a eunuch, not that he was an Ethiopian. This eunuch had just returned from Jerusalem. Although he had gone up to that awesome temple to worship there. But although he was allowed to bring his sacrifices, he was still very much an outsider per Deuteronomy 23.

The point of Acts 8 is that the time had come for eunuchs and foreigners to be given the name "better than sons and daughters." The time had come when eunuchs and foreigners would serve in the New Temple of God, the foundation of which, Messiah Jesus, had been laid in "Zion." The time had come when eunuchs would no longer be "dry trees" for they, by sharing the news of "the Life" in Messiah, could bring forth "sons of God" without "marrying and giving in marriage." What cannot be missed in the prediction of the acceptance of the foreigners and the eunuchs is that it would take place when the Lord "re-gathered" the "outcasts of Israel" i.e. at the restoration of Israel. And, when He had re-gathered the outcasts, i.e. the diaspora of Israel, he would also gather "others besides those whom He had gathered." So, the acceptance of the eunuchs into the "temple of God" was a signal that Israel's restoration was in process, and with that restoration, it signaled that others besides Israel could be gathered to the Lord as well.

Acts 9 - The Persecution of "The Way" The Conversion of Saul

Saul, later to become Paul, is presented as a persecutor of "the way." This term is highly significant. Numerous OT prophecies foretold that in the last days, there would be a "highway of the Lord" on which the righteous would travel. On that highway, there would be safety, security and righteousness (Isaiah 35). But the highway would also be the "Way" for the coming of the Lord in judgment. Isaiah foretold the coming of "the voice of one crying in the wilderness, 'Prepare the way of the Lord'" (Isaiah 40:3). John the Baptizer was that Voice (Mark 1). What should not be missed is that not only would the "Way" be a highway of blessings, but it would also be the highway for the coming of the Lord in judgment (Isaiah 40:10f; Malachi 3:1-3). So, once again, we see the good news/bad news aspect of the fulfillment of Israel's last days prophecies. Also, this time of the establishment of the Way, would be when the redeemed of the Lord would once again be gathered to Him (40:1, 9f).

This is the restoration of Israel. See Acts 19:9; 24:14; 24:22 where the term "the Way" is used in a technical manner to speak of "the faith." The conversion of Paul is incredibly significant, to understate the case. His understanding of his mission gives insight into God's Old Covenant prophecies of Israel's last days. From the very beginning, Paul informs his Jewish brethren that God had called him distinctively to be a light to the Gentiles, to call them out of darkness, and to give them invitation to the salvation that would flow from Israel. One of the saddest realities in modern evangelicalism is the idea that the calling of the Gentiles, i.e. Paul's mission, was a direct result of Israel's failure. All three futurist paradigms, perhaps on differing levels, but true of them all, nonetheless, posit the failure of Israel as the ground and reason for the Gentile mission. This is patently false. We cannot develop this but note that Paul says that his ministry was foretold in Deuteronomy 32:19f, which was a prediction of Israel's last days. While Paul certainly does say that Israel's rebellion would lead to that ministry, it must be understood that contra the dispensational paradigm, that rebellion and the final rejection of the Old Covenant body of Israel was pre-planned and predicted by God. It was no accident; it was no surprise to the Lord. The concept of the salvation of the remnant is fundamentally important here, for Paul informs us– with proof from the Old Testament– that God never promised to save "all Israel" but, only a remnant (Romans 9-11).

Again, Paul tells us that God chose him personally and distinctively to call the Gentiles to Him. And yet, as Paul went to the Gentiles, he went first to the diaspora scattered abroad. And when the Jews in those diaspora areas rejected the gospel of the kingdom, Paul told them "it was necessary that the gospel be preached to you first, but, seeing that you count yourselves unworthy of eternal life, we turn to the Gentiles" Acts 13:46). Notice Paul's appeal to Isaiah 49:6f also as the justification for his Gentile mission (13:47). Once again, however, it is imperative to note, for instance in Isaiah 49, that the salvation of the Gentiles was totally dependent on the restoration of Israel: "it is too small a thing that You should be My Servant To raise up the tribes of Jacob, And to restore the preserved ones of Israel; I will also give You as a light to the Gentiles, That You should be My salvation to the ends of the earth.'" Notice that the restoration of the "tribes of Jacob" was the precursor to the calling of the Gentiles. Note also that the salvation of the tribes of Jacob would be "too small" of a work for Messiah and YHVH. God's plan was, therefore, always, to offer salvation and life to those outside the tribes of Israel, and Paul was the one chosen to take that message of "the life" to them. (See Colossians 1:24f and my special study on Paul's distinctive ministry in Who Is This Babylon? This is a very important topic)

Acts 10 - The Calling of the Gentiles

Any reader of Acts should have been alerted that something like this was going to happen. The conversion of the eunuch laid the groundwork for opening the mind of the reader that even more revolutionary things were coming and Acts 10 records that very thing. We today have 20/20 hindsight and years of instruction telling us how the Old Testament predicted the salvation of the Gentiles. Yet, in Israel of Jesus' day, and in Paul's, while there was a vague concept of the calling of the Gentiles, there was no true appreciation or, welcoming of that idea. When Jesus was in the synagogue in Capernaum (Luke 4) his telling of two of the famous stories in Israel's history recounted the blessings of pagan Gentiles, and not those of the seed of Abraham. And that crowd sought to kill Jesus for pointing that out. Solomon had prayed for the Lord to bless those who were not of the seed of Abraham, if they prayed to Him and came to worship Him at the Jerusalem Temple (1 Kings 8:41f). And the temple had a "Court of the Gentiles" but, of course, the temple likewise had the wall of partition that kept the Gentiles – including the eunuchs, remember– from the inner courts. But, in Israel of Jesus' day, in spite of her own prophecies, there was no desire to call the Gentiles. In fact, when Paul told the temple audience that God had appointed him to preach to the Gentiles, and call them to be His people, they instantly took up stones to kill him (Acts 21; 22:17f).

It is little wonder then, that when Peter, faithful Jew that he was, was told by God Himself, to "take and eat" the foods that were unclean under Torah, that Peter refused, and extrapolated from that to Gentile uncleanness. While Peter uttered some fair sounding words, "God has shown me to call nothing common or unclean" in his heart, and verbalized to Cornelius, he felt very strongly, "it is not lawful for a man that is a Jew to have company or to eat with a Gentile" (Acts 10:28). Nonetheless, Peter preached "the Life" to Cornelius, and he, along with his entourage, was astounded that the Holy Spirit was poured out on Cornelius, just as it had been poured out on the disciples on Pentecost. This was as powerful– if not more so– as the heavenly vision with the unclean beasts, in convincing Peter and those with him that the Gentiles truly were now equals in the kingdom. But, as we shall see, not all were thrilled with this development. They believed that the kingdom of Messiah was to be a Jewish kingdom, and while they were "okay" with the inclusion of the Gentiles, they made it clear that if they wanted to be a part of the kingdom, they essentially had to become Jews and observe Torah.

A Great Famine Arose

One ponders if we are to see the parallels between the story of Joseph in Egypt, the famine, the rescue of the people from the famine and the events of Acts 11:27f. For sure, the name of the Lord was exalted and glorified in both situations. Acts 13 - The Movement Away From Jerusalem "What God promised to the fathers, He has fulfilled…" (Acts 13:32f) Addressing the Jewish audience in the synagogue in Antioch of Pisidia, Paul rehearsed

Israel's history and her promises. He recounts the faithfulness of God in giving the land as promised (13:19f) the glory of David and then, in what must have been a startling and amazing statement, claimed that God had now "brought to Israel a Savior, Jesus, just as He promised" (13:23). Paul's message to Israel was one of fulfillment, not of failure or postponement. In fact, he says that God had given to Jesus, "the sure mercies of David" which was nothing but the promise of the Davidic kingdom (Isaiah 55)! But of course, if Jesus had been given the throne of David, then since Christ was in heaven, not on an earthly throne ruling over a nationalistic kingdom centered in Jerusalem, this meant that the nature of the Messianic kingdom was radically different from what they had thought it was to be.

The promises were being fulfilled. Of this there can be no doubt. But the form of fulfillment was something totally unexpected. Something had begun to happen in Acts 11:19 through Acts 13f that must have been troublesome to the Jewish Christians who were still struggling with the geo-centricity of Zion / Jerusalem in the OT prophecies. It is not too much to say that in the prophetic books Zion is the capital and the focus of all things eschatological and soteriological. The Law would go forth from Zion and the Messianic Temple (Isaiah 2:2f). Salvation would be in Jerusalem (Isaiah 46:13). The resurrection and the Messianic Banquet would occur "on this mountain" i.e. Zion (Isaiah 25:6-8). So, for those with the desire and intent to see the OT prophets fulfilled literally, what was taking place had to be unsettling. They could not deny the miraculous works of the promised Spirit that they witnessed, but where was the emphasis on the literal Jerusalem, the literal temple, and the Levitical priesthood? Truly, something radical was taking place. In fact, the perceived (and in truth, very real) movement away from earthly Jerusalem was part and parcel of the Old Testament prophetic message. According to those prophets, earthly Jerusalem would pass, but heavenly Jerusalem would triumph.

A host of OT prophecies foretold the destruction of the earthly Zion in the last days, giving way to the New Creation and the New Jerusalem (cf. Isaiah 65-66). Jeremiah had actually foretold the time, when the two houses of Israel would be re-united under Messiah, that, "they shall say no more, 'The ark of the covenant of the Lord; neither shall it come to mind, neither shall they remember it; neither shall they visit it; neither shall that be done anymore" (Jeremiah 3:16). Likewise, even the much later prophet, Malachi, foresaw the time when "in every place (i.e. Gentile places! DKP) incense shall be offered unto my name, for my name shall be great among the heathen" (Malachi 1:11). Very clearly, contrary to a great deal of Jewish expectation about the nature of the restored kingdom, Biblically, in the Messianic Kingdom, Jerusalem would lose its centricity. While the Kingdom would be established "in Zion" the New Covenant would flow from there to the nations, and that Old earthly city would lose its theological centricity. This is precisely what we see in Acts. Initially, the Jews kept the Word to themselves. However, persecution forced them to leave Judea and Jerusalem, and once they did, the Gentiles eagerly accepted the Word of Life. In Acts 11ff we find that increasingly, physical Jerusalem declines in importance for the body of Christ. Antioch becomes the Gentile capital of the church, and from there, the Word of Life expands increasingly to the Gentile world. At the same time, Old Jerusalem – which had sponsored Saul in his persecutions– became increasingly hostile against the New Jerusalem. As Paul would write at a very early stage, her persecutorial ways would lead to her being cast out of the Presence of the Lord (Galatians 4:22f; 1 Thessalonians 2; 2 Thessalonians 1).

Acts 15 - To This Agrees the Prophets

With the initiation of the conversion of the Gentiles, the expansion of the kingdom was in full swing. Over and over we are told that "many people were added to the Lord" (cf. 11:21, 24). But, brewing under the surface in ways that we can only speculate about, were discussions among the Jewish Christians about the role of the Gentiles in the kingdom. Some began to advance the idea that since the kingdom was a promise to Israel, found in Israel's prophets, that the kingdom was intrinsically Jewish in form and function. Thus, "certain men which came down (to Antioch, DKP) from Judea taught the brethren, and said, 'Except you are circumcised after the manner of Moses, you cannot be saved'" (Acts 15:1). Thus, intriguingly, the first substantial doctrinal error in the early church originated in earthly Jerusalem and misconstrued the very nature of the kingdom of Messiah. The issue of circumcision would continue to plague the early church and may in fact be considered the single most important controversy of the first century. Yet, this subject is grossly ignored or misunderstood by most Bible students today. It was the identifying mark of the children of Abraham. It gave them "title deed" as it were to the land promises.

No circumcision, no land. It was that simple (cf. Joshua 5). Since circumcision was the key marker of the identity of the "sons of Abraham" then the restoration of Israel would, in the mind of those with the literalistic mind-set, demand the imposition of circumcision on any and all who were coming into the kingdom. So, just like under Torah, when a Gentile wished to become a servant of YHVH, that same mindset. There is little wonder that some of the zealous Jews in Jerusalem believed that Gentiles had to be circumcised. The promises of blessings in the Seed, Abraham's (One) Seed, were perceived to be tied, not to circumcision of the heart, but to physical circumcision. (It should be noted that modern Dominionism (i.e. postmillennialism) as well as Dispensationalism, both implicitly demand a restoration of physical circumcision. Dominionism, along with Dispensational-ism, says Abraham and his descendants must inherit the literal land. But, if the physical land promises remain valid, then physical circumcision remains valid. The land promise and circumcision are inextricably bound.

Thus, if the land promises remain valid, circumcision remains valid and the gospel of Christ is nullified. I cannot develop this further, but this is a serious issue). The battle was joined between Paul, Barnabas, and the Judaizers. Paul taught a Torah free gospel of justification of faith. The Judaizers taught justification through faith in the flesh. A conference was called in Jerusalem for the inspired leadership of the church to debate and settle the issue. At the Jerusalem conference, James and the apostles and prophets determined that Paul's gospel was correct – Gentiles were not to be circumcised or compelled in any way to observe Torah. Observance of the Law of Moses was not incumbent on them for their justification and salvation.

Peter reminded the audience of the example of Cornelius, and how the outpouring of the Spirit on that occasion demonstrated that, "He made no distinction between us and them, having cleansed their heart by faith" (15:9). Barnabas and Paul followed, recounting the work of the Spirit in their ministry to the Gentiles. James then followed their presentations, recalling again Peter's experience with Cornelius in which God signified His divine purpose "to take from them a people for his name" (15:14). What James said next proves that the restoration of Israel was fully underway, but, once again, that restoration was not at all what the nation of Israel had envisioned or hoped for (cf. Romans 11:7) but it was what the prophets actually foretold, as interpreted by the Jerusalem council. James quoted Amos 9:11 which foretold the restoration of the ten northern tribes with the southern tribes.

God would "repair the breaches in the wall" of the Davidic house (not the literal temple), and He would accomplish this "so that the remnant of men may seek the Lord." It is critical to grasp the significance of this. Amos predicted, and James interpreted Amos as saying, that when Israel was restored, the Gentiles would be called to be God's people (cf. Zechariah 2:10f). In fact, God would restore Israel "so that" (the force of the Greek) the rest of mankind might seek the Lord. So, the order of occurrence was first the restoration of Israel, then, as a result of that, the nations would be called. This is what Isaiah 49 foretold. It is Paul's message that the gospel of salvation was "to the Jew first, then the Greek" (Romans 1:16-17). So, when James declared that the calling of the Gentiles was in fulfillment of Amos, and explained, through the inspiration of the Spirit, that Amos had foretold the restoration of Israel so that the nations could be called, this was a profound commentary on the nature of the restoration of Israel. James' commentary demands this fact: if Israel was not being restored, in fulfillment of Amos, then the nations, the Gentiles, i.e. those not of the twelve tribes, have no hope of being the children of God. It is that simple: Israel was to be restored so that the Gentiles could be offered salvation. Since the Gentiles, as proven by Cornelius's reception of the Spirit, were clearly now accepted by God, on equal footing with Israel, then Israel's restoration was in full bloom. Acts 16-21 To the Uttermost Parts of the **World Paul's Mission and Role as End Times Martyr and Prophet.**

While a great deal could be written of the individual accounts of the cities where Paul traveled space forbids such an investigation or extended discussion. However, what we do need to keep in mind is that lying behind Paul's travels is his role as God's distinctively chosen vessel to fulfill the mystery of God, and to fill up the measure of end times suffering, thus, hastening the Day of the Lord. Paul is clear that, "God has exhibited us apostles as last of all, like men sentenced to death" (1 Corinthians 4:9). The imagery is of a Roman triumphant parade, with the host of prisoners taken captive by the conquering hero, marching to their deaths. And Paul says the apostles were the last in the line, determined (manifested, proclaimed, shown) by God to be His martyrs to fill up the eschatological measure of suffering and sin. (Cf. Revelation 18:20-24). In Colossians 1:24-27 Paul affirms in unequivocal but challenging language that he was chosen, and distinctively commissioned to personally, "fill up in my body what is lacking in the sufferings of Christ. And to fulfill the Word of God, the mystery." Acts 16-21 chronicles Paul's travels and his suffering. Everywhere he went, the Jews either attacked him, or instigated persecution against him. We see at work in Paul's ministry, three aspects of the end times prophecies:

A.) Paul, in offering the gospel of Life to the Gentiles, was attempting to make Israel jealous, to hopefully convert some of them. This was in direct fulfillment of Deuteronomy 32- The Song of Moses– which foretold that in Israel's last days, God would provoke Israel to jealousy (32:19f–> Romans 10:19; 11:14).

B.) While Paul was the apostle to the Gentiles, as we have seen, he went first of all to Israel, scattered Israel, for this was "necessary" (Acts 13– see above). Yet, God had foretold, based on Israel's long history of recalcitrance, that, "All day long I have stretched out my hands to a disobedient and contrary people" (Isaiah 65:1– Romans 10:21).

C.) The salvation of the remnant. While the nation, corporately speaking, rejected the kingdom offer, this was not in any way surprising, unexpected, or un-foretold. Isaiah, and the other prophets, had foretold these centuries before. So, just as Isaiah foretold that Israel would reject God's outstretched hands and fill the measure of her sin (Isaiah 65:1-6) he likewise foretold that a remnant would be saved when the Lord destroyed the Old Israel and created a New People (Isaiah 65:8-19). So, what was playing out in these chapters of Acts, as Luke recorded Paul's ministry, is not, in any way at all, the record of the failure of God's plan as predicted in Israel's prophecies. God's plan was right on schedule, just as foretold. It was shocking to the nationalistic expectation of the Jews– resulting in their animosity toward Paul – but it was God's original plan all along.

Acts 21-28 - Nothing But the Hope of Israel

As Luke focuses on the ministry of Paul, from Acts 13 onward, something becomes very apparent. The Jewish animosity toward him grows as his success among the Gentiles continues to grow. It is more than obvious that Paul's adversaries think that his message of Christ as Messiah and the Torah free gospel are antithetical to the story and the hope of Israel. For Paul, however, nothing could be farther from the truth. When the Jews mistakenly accused Paul of taking a Gentile into the temple, and attempted to kill him, Paul is rescued and then allowed by the Romans to address the audience. He recounted his former zeal in persecuting the Way (21:4) and then told of his conversion. However, when Paul mentioned his call to go the Gentiles, the audience rose up again, and would have killed him, had the Roman tribune not intervened. The following day, the tribune called the Sanhedrin together for them to investigate the reason why the Jews wanted to kill Paul. It is critical to note that the very first thing that Paul affirms was his faithfulness to the hope of Israel, "With respect to the hope and the resurrection of the dead that I am on trial" (23:6).

Contra modern evangelical doctrine, Paul did not see the story of Israel as dead, abolished, replaced or even delayed. Paul's story was nothing but the hope of Israel. As Paul stands before the Sanhedrin he affirms his belief in the resurrection as the hope of Israel, found in Moses and the prophets (24:14f). Paul's fidelity to Israel and his eschatological hope must be honored. In addition, we cannot escape noticing that while ostensibly agreeing with the Pharisees as to the reality of the resurrection, he and they clearly had a different vision and understanding of the resurrection. Notice that in 24:13 he takes note that both he and they affirm resurrection, but, they want to kill him for his views of the resurrection! Just as Jesus came to proclaim the kingdom, the Jews wanted the kingdom. Jesus came to be king, and the Jews wanted a king. Yet, when the Jews came to make him king and offer him the kingdom, Jesus withdrew (John 6:15)! Patently, different concepts of the nature of the kingdom and kingship were at work, just as in the case of Paul and the Pharisees on the resurrection. Neither Jesus nor Paul preached a message contrary to what the prophets foretold.

They both preached "the hope of Israel." Yet, they were both rejected for what they preached and what they offered. This critical fact is seldom explored, but it is critical for understanding the nature of the hope of Israel. If, as it is generally assumed, Paul had the same concept of the nature of the kingdom and resurrection as did the Pharisees, one can only wonder why they sought to kill him for preaching what they believed. This truth has tremendous implications for our understanding of Paul's eschatology in the epistles. Paul said he preached nothing but the hope of Israel– Israel after the flesh (Romans 9:1- 3) and that hope was found nowhere but in Moses, the Law and the Prophets. Notice how often he affirms this in Acts 24-28. Acts 24:13f – Paul affirmed that his resurrection doctrine was taken directly from the Old Covenant promises to Israel, the promises found in Moses, the Law and the prophets. Acts 24:21 – "It is with respect to the resurrection of the dead that I am on trial." Acts 25:8 – "Neither against the Law of the Jews, nor against the temple, nor against Caesar have I committed any offense." Acts 26:6 - "And now I stand here on trial because of my hope in the promise made by God to our fathers, to which our twelve tribes hope to attain as they earnestly worship night and day.

For this hope I am accused of the Jews." Acts 26:22f - "Therefore, having obtained help from God to this day I stand, witnessing both to small and great, saying no other things than those which the prophets and Moses said would come— 23 that the Christ would suffer, that He would be the first to rise from the dead, and would proclaim light to the Jewish people and to the Gentiles." Acts 28:17 - Paul, addressing the leaders of the Jews in Rome, said, "Brothers, though I had no charge to bring against our people, or the customs of our fathers, yet I was delivered as a prisoner from Jerusalem into the hands of the Romans." Acts 28:19ff - "I have asked to see you and to speak with you, since it is for the hope of Israel that I am wearing this chain." .... v. 23, "From morning to evening he expounded to them, testifying to the kingdom of God, and trying to convince them about Jesus both from the Law of Moses and from the Prophets." We will come back to Acts 28 in a bit. However, think with me about what it means for Paul to say so many times that his one hope, his only gospel message, was nothing but the hope of Israel. What this means is that when we read Paul's discourse on the resurrection in 1 Corinthians 15, that we must conform our understanding of that great chapter to Paul's understanding of God's Old Testament promises made to Israel after the flesh. It means that we must view 1 Thessalonians and Paul's promise of the parousia in light of Israel's promises. It means that we must see the promise of the "redemption of creation" within the context of Israel's prophecies. And it means that in Paul's eschatology, there was not a "Christian eschatology" distinct from Israel and her story. This is devastating for both the amillennial and postmillennial views, because both of these futurist eschatology's claim that Paul's view of the last things is fundamentally about the end of the Christian age and the fulfillment of God's promises to the church. This is patently false, since Paul says the resurrection of 1 Corinthians 15 (and thus, 1 Thessalonians 4) would be in fulfillment of Isaiah 25 and Hosea 13. Any theology that divorces Paul's eschatology from the hope of Israel is, prima facie, a false theology. This is likewise devastating to the dispensational paradigm, since one of the pillars of millennialism is that the promises to Israel are not the promises to the church.

But, since Paul says his gospel, his eschatology was nothing but the hope of Israel, this means that there is not a "rapture doctrine" for the church, and then a "Second Coming" eschatology promised to Israel. There was but "one hope" (Ephesians 4:4) and that one hope was found in God's Old Covenant promises made to Israel after the flesh. So, we say again, that any eschatology divorced from Israel and her promises, to be fulfilled at the consummation of her covenant age, is fundamentally and fatally flawed. We want now to take another look at the nature of the restoration of Israel as found in Acts.

The Nature of the Restoration of Israel

In Paul's affirmations that he preached nothing but the hope of Israel, and in Luke's record of the proclamation of that gospel, we have seen the revolutionary re-shaping and re-identification of the Israel of God. The restoration was a spiritual restoration that eschewed and rejected the geo-political-military restoration of the Davidic kingdom longed for by the Jews. This is evident from Acts 1 to Acts 28. We need to review a bit of this to drive home the point that, first of all, Acts truly is about the restoration of Israel, as foretold in the OT prophets, and secondly, that restoration was not what the Jews of the first century anticipated or desired. Acts 1 draws directly from Isaiah 43 that predicted the creation of a

New Israel, a New Creation and called on Israel to forget the former days. Acts 2 shows us that Christ was sitting at the right hand of the Father, in fulfillment of YHVH's promise to raise Messiah to David's throne. But Jesus was sitting at the right hand, in the heavenlies, not on a literal throne, in literal Zion. Acts 3 records Peter's call to the Jews to repent so that God would grant them a time of rest before the coming judgment.

He reminds them of the prophecy of Deuteronomy 18 that God would raise up a prophet like Moses. And he warns them that to reject Jesus would result in being "utterly cut off out from among the people" (Acts 3:23). This text is all but definitive in identifying the true Israel: they are the followers of Jesus! Thus, as we noted above, John the Baptizer initiated the "restoration of all things" and Jesus would consummate that restoration at his parousia. But what cannot be denied is that the restoration begun by John, and thus, the work of Jesus, was not in any way related to the restoration of nationalistic Israel. Acts 4 shows us that one of the key markers of Israel, the land, was being overtly rejected by the nascent body of Christ. In a radical, unprecedented move, the members of the body of Christ began to sell their land! This was strictly forbidden by Torah. But they had begun to learn that their salvation was not in the land.

They were now– in fulfillment of Isaiah 66– all priests unto the Lord, and even in Torah, God himself was the true inheritance of the priests; they got no inheritance of physical land (Numbers 18:20). Likewise, Acts 4 shows that the Chief Corner Stone of the long anticipated Messianic Temple had been laid. Thus, Israel was being restored! Yet, the Temple being constructed was a living edifice, built on the living Messiah. And this truth signaled the coming destruction of the Old Temple. Thus, once again, the nature of the restoration of Israel is undeniable. It had nothing whatsoever to do with the old form. It had nothing to do with the old Temple. It had nothing to do with the old City, either. Acts 6-7 records Stephen in the Temple, recounting Israel's long history of rejecting God's plans and purposes, even killing all of His prophets sent to her. Stephen had the "audacity" to even quote Isaiah 66 which spoke of Israel's inordinate affection for things physical, i.e. the Temple, and calling their attention to the fact that, "God does not dwell in temples made with hands" (Isaiah 66:1). Isaiah 66 not only noted that physical temples were not God's intended abode, but that the time was coming when the Lord would come against Jerusalem and the old Temple in judgment, to bring in the New People and the New Creation. All of those students of Torah present that day would have known full well what Stephen was saying in his citation of Isaiah: that wonderful edifice in which he was standing, in which they took so much (too much) pride, was doomed.

It was to give way to the New Creation. Acts 8 tells us the story of the restoration of Israel in a diaspora. Yet now, the gospel of the kingdom– Israel's hope– was being proclaimed in Samaria! But of course, the message being preached was not one of nationalistic restoration. It had nothing to do with a regathering to the land. It had nothing to do with the beautiful Temple in Jerusalem. It had nothing to do with the destruction of the Romans or the conquering of Israel's national enemies. Nonetheless, Israel was being "gathered." She was being gathered in the very manner that Jesus had desired to gather her (Matthew 23:37) - a covenantal gathering into fellowship with him. The proclamation of the gospel in and to Samaria was a profound fulfillment of the restoration of Israel. But, once again, the unexpected nature and form of the restoration was on full display. Acts 8 likewise portrays the restoration of Israel in the story of the conversion of the eunuch. In the prophets, the radical nature of the restoration of Israel under Messiah was hinted at, strongly suggested, but never fully grasped by the Jews. Isaiah had foretold the time-when Israel was restored, and God's temple was present– that even foreigners and the eunuchs would be given a place in that Temple.

They would no longer be outsiders, but true children of God! (See Isaiah 60:5-7 where YHVH foretold the time when "the wealth of the nations" would flow to Jerusalem and those who had always been rejected, foreigners, would actually ascend the altar of the Lord to offer sacrifices! This is a stunning "reformulation" of the priesthood, in the manner of Isaiah 66). In similar stunning fashion, Acts 10-15 records the conversion of the Gentiles and ensuing controversies. What is so stunning is that, although the OT prophets clearly foretold this, Paul's inspired interpretation of those prophecies was that the Gentiles were equal partners, equal partakers of the kingdom blessings (Romans 16:25-26; Ephesians 3:3-11)! Salvation was no longer confined to one ethnic group, but just as God had called Abraham out from the nations to be His people, God was now calling the nations to be His people! (Cf. Zechariah 2:10). So, "God's people" were being re- identified. "Israel" was no longer identified according to the flesh, but, according to the Spirit by faith. Acts 15 is extremely powerful proof that God's "Israel" – the kingdom– was now fundamentally different, radically transformed. From Abraham foreword, and under Torah, physical circumcision was one of the key markers of the "children of God." Circumcision was Israel's covenant sign between YHVH and that nation which gave her the right to the land. No circumcision = no land. And yet, the Jerusalem Council determined that Gentiles– as equal partakers of the promises of Israel– were under no obligation to be circumcised. Keep in mind that no one taught "the hope of Israel" more firmly, more zealously than did Paul, as we have seen. Yet, as he preached that hope of Israel, he vehemently rejected any attempts to impose physical circumcision– or any Israel's cultus-- on Gentiles (cf. Galatians 2), and openly taught that to impose it on Gentiles resulted in the loss of fellowship with Christ (Galatians 5). What mattered (matters) was not physical circumcision (and thus, not physical land) but the New Creation foretold by the OT prophets (Galatians 6:15-16). Here is a fine exemplification of what Isaiah 43 foretold. God said He was going to do a "New Thing" in the last days, and called on Israel to forget the past things. And now, here was Paul calling on Israel to forget her past and look to the New Thing being created in Christ. Stunning indeed! Nothing could have been more revolutionary, more stunning, more offensive to the Jews than this message! This is why Paul called his "circumcision free" gospel an "offense" to the Jews.

They realized that the nullification of circumcision was, in fact, the declaration that their right to the land had now been voided! They failed - like so many today - to grasp the spiritual significance of that message. The true "land" that Abraham had longed for, the heavenly Zion– was about to be realized, (Hebrews 11:13- 16- 12:21f). Spatial considerations forbid further development of this theme, but what we have presented powerfully illustrates that Luke and Paul were on the same page. Luke's narrative was about how God had not abandoned Israel. Paul's gospel was the same. God was fulfilling His promises to Israel. The problem was that Israel longed for the wrong things– national restoration- when the promises were, from the very beginning, the promise of spiritual restoration. This brings us to consider that throughout Acts, from beginning to the end, there are powerful suggestions and pointers that indicated that while God was indeed restoring Israel as promised, that found in her Old Covenant promises all along was the reality, as painful and traumatic as it was to be, was that when Israel was restored, the Old Covenant body had to pass away. As when a person has a pecan, and to reach the wonderful "meat" inside, the outer shell has to be crushed, the outer shell of Old Covenant "fleshly" Israel, had to be crushed, having fulfilled her purpose, to reveal the "inner man" of the body of Christ (2 Corinthians 4:16f). This was truly a "good news / bad news" scenario, but one that is evident throughout Acts, if we have our eyes open. So, look at a few of those earlier references and warnings. Acts 1– Isaiah 43 – If indeed Isaiah 43 lies behind the beginning of Luke's narrative, then one can hardly help but notice that the coming of the New Thing that God would do, would necessitate the passing of the Old Creation. Acts 2:40 – "Save yourselves from this untoward generation." There are numerous things in Acts 2 that would have been foreboding to the observant.

A.) The outpouring of the Spirit was to be magnified in the last days before the Great and Terrible Day of the Lord. This Great Day was the Day foretold by John the Baptizer, as Elijah, when the wicked would perish (Malachi 4). It would likewise be when the Lord would judge Israel for violation of Torah (Malachi 3:1-6).

B.) Peter was citing Deuteronomy 32 (in Acts 2:40). The Song of Moses was about Israel's latter end, when the Lord would avenge the blood of His saints in judgment.

C.) Even the marvelous affirmation that Jesus was sitting at the Right Hand of the Majesty in the heavens had a dark lining to the silver cloud. Psalms 110 not only foretold the enthronement of Messiah, but it also likewise foretold judgment of His enemies (i.e. those who had rejected Him!) when He would send forth the rod of His anger.

D.) Very clearly, Peter affirmed that his audience needed to save themselves from what was coming on that generation.

Acts 3:23 - While Peter proclaimed the marvelous fulfillment of God's promises to Israel, he nonetheless warned them that failure to accept Jesus as Messiah would have dire consequences: "and it shall be that every soul who will not hear that Prophet shall be utterly destroyed from among the people." It should be noted that the force of the language is very graphic. The destruction of those rejecting Jesus would be utter destruction "out from among the people." The true "the people" are thus identified as followers of Jesus. Those who refuse to accept him are no longer "the people" and are doomed to be cut of out from among "the people." This is both stunning and graphic. Acts 4 - The thrill of hearing that the Chief Corner Stone of the long anticipated Messianic Temple was tempered by the somber reality that those who rejected that Stone were to be, according to the Old Covenant promises– crushed by that Stone. As we have seen, this is precisely how the chief leaders in Jerusalem understood the wonderful message of the gospel. While the gospel truly was "good news' that Israel was being restored as promised, it was "bad news" in that those who had killed him were now doomed to destruction. Acts 13:40-41.

As Paul proclaimed the fulfillment of God's promises to Israel, the Jews rejected that message. Consequently, Paul spoke a warning to them: "Beware therefore, lest what has been spoken in the prophets come upon you: 'behold, you despisers, Marvel and perish! For I work a work in your days, a work which you will by no means believe, though one were to declare it to you.'" Paul was quoting from Habakkuk, where the Lord warned Judea and Jerusalem that failure to obey Him would bring– was just about to bring– judgment. There can be no doubt that Paul's Jewish audience would have fully realized what the apostle was saying. Failure to obey Christ would be a mistake, resulting in national destruction. Skipping over some other passages, we return to Acts 28. Luke tells us that, as Paul expounded on the hope of Israel and the kingdom, some of the Jews were convinced, but, "others disbelieved" (28:24). And when that unbelief became clear to Paul, he cited a text from Isaiah that Jesus himself had cited Isaiah 6:9f: "hearing ye shall hear and shall not understand; and seeing you shall see and not perceive; for the heart of this people is waxed gross, and their ears are dull of hearing, and their eyes they have closed; lest they should see with their eyes and hear with their ears and understand with their hearts, and should be converted, and I should heal them.

Be it known therefore unto you that the salvation of God is sent unto the Gentiles, and that they will hear it." We find here an additional echo of what we have seen above: Judgment was about to fall on the Old Covenant Body of Israel for rejecting Messiah and the restoration of Israel taking place in Him. Paul's Roman Mission Fulfilling the Mystery of God and the World Mission: Awaiting the End Informed by the Spirit that he was to be imprisoned and taken to Rome, Paul informed the elders of Ephesus of his fate. They were, naturally, deeply disturbed and sorrowful. Yet, Paul told them: "But none of these things move me; nor do I count my life dear to myself, so that I may finish my race with joy, and the ministry which I received from the Lord Jesus, to testify to the gospel of the grace of God" (Acts 20:24) Paul realized that as Christ's specially chosen apostle, appointed to "fulfill the mystery of God" and to "fill up what is lacking in the sufferings of Christ" (Colossians 1:24f) that He had to suffer, and eventually die. He realized that he had to take the gospel to the "end of the earth" and there complete that task before the Roman authorities. The eschatological role of Paul is overlooked by many commentators. Yet, Paul clearly saw himself as a covenant mediator (2 Corinthians 3-4), and specially appointed by Christ to bring in the "fullness of the Gentiles" thereby hastening Israel's salvation at the Parousia, (Romans 11:25f).

For Paul, his imprisonment in Rome and the opportunity to preach the gospel to the ruler of the ancient world constituted the climax and consummation of his task: "At my first defense no one stood with me, but all forsook me. May it not be charged against them. But the Lord stood with me and strengthened me, so that the message might be preached fully through me, and that all the Gentiles might hear" (2 Timothy 4:16f). Jesus had said that the gospel was to be preached into all the world, as a witness to the nations, then the end would come. And now, at the end of Acts, Paul was about to preach the gospel to the ruler of the nations, fulfilling his task and role as apostle to the Gentiles. Scholars have pondered why Luke ended his history so abruptly. Why quit the record with Paul in Rome, preaching to the Jews and Gentiles alike? Why not record what he said to Nero? Why not record the success or failure of the great apostle? I suggest that Luke, as well as Paul, considered the task of the world mission as now completed. The end was near. The gospel had been preached to kings and governors, and even once before Nero, evidently. All that remained was for the judgment suggested by Paul's warning to the Jewish leaders in 28:26 to now come. Thus, the abrupt ending of Acts is best explained by the fact that Luke's purpose in recording the "restoration of Israel" had now been properly recorded. The warnings of the passing of the Old Covenant body were about to come to pass. The New Covenant body of Christ was about to be manifested, vindicated and glorified at the Parousia that was now about to take place.

-Don K. Preston

Acts

Chapter 1

1. The former account I made, O Friend of God (Theophilus), of all that Jesus began both to do and teach,
2. Until the day in which He ascended, after He through the Holy Spirit had given orders to the apostles whom He had chosen:
3. To whom also He showed Himself alive after His suffering by many infallible proofs, being seen by them forty days, and speaking of the things about the kingdom of God:
4. And, being assembled with them, commanded them that they should not depart from Jerusalem, but wait for the promise of the Father, which, He said, you have heard from Me.
5. For John truly immersed with water; but you will be immersed with the Holy Spirit not many days from now.
6. Therefore, when they had come together, they asked Him, saying, Lord, will You at this time restore the kingdom to Israel?
7. But He said to them, it is not for you to know the times or the seasons, which the Father has put in His own power.
8. But you will receive power when the Holy Spirit comes upon you: and you will be My witnesses both in Jerusalem, and in all Judea, and in Samaria, and to the extremities of the earth.
9. When He had spoken these things, while they beheld, He ascended; and a cloud received Him away from their eyes.
10. While they looked steadfastly toward heaven as He ascended, behold, two men stood by them in white apparel;
11. Who also said, men! Galileans, why are you standing gazing into the heavens? This Jesus, the One who was taken up from you visibly into the heavens, will come figuratively as you have beheld Him going into the heavens.
12. Then they returned to Jerusalem from the mount called Olivet, which is from Jerusalem a Sabbath day's journey.
13. When they had come in, they went up into an upper room, where stayed both Peter, James, and John, and Andrew, Philip, and Thomas, Bartholomew, and Matthew, James the son of Alphaeus, and Simon Zelotes, and Judas the brother of James.
14. These all continued with one accord in prayer and supplication, with the women, and Mary the mother of Jesus, and with his brothers.
15. In those days Peter stood up in the midst of the disciples, and said, (the number of names together was about a hundred and twenty)
16. Men and brothers, this Scripture had to be fulfilled, which the Holy Spirit by the mouth of David spoke before concerning Judas, who was guide to them that took Jesus.
17. For he was numbered with us and had shared in this ministry.
18. Now this man purchased a field with the reward of iniquity; and falling headlong, he burst apart in the middle, and all his insides gushed out.

19. And it was known to all the dwellers at Jerusalem; so that field is called in their proper tongue, Aceldama, that is to say, The Field of Blood.

20. For it is written in the book of Psalms, let his habitation be desolate, and let no man dwell in it: and, his over seership let another take.

21. Therefore, of these men who have accompanied us all the time that the Lord Jesus went in and out among us,

22. Beginning from the immersion of John to that same day that He ascended, one must be ordained to be a witness with us of His resurrection.

23. Then they appointed two, Joseph called Barsabas, who was surnamed Justus, and Matthias.

24. So, they prayed, and said, You, Lord, who know the hearts of all men, show who of these two You have chosen,

25. That he may take part of this ministry and apostleship, from which Judas by transgression fell, that he might go to his own place.

26. Then they gave out their lots, and the lot fell on Matthias, and he was numbered with the eleven apostles.

Chapter 2

1. When the day of Pentecost had fully come, they were all with one accord in one place.

2. Suddenly there came a sound from heaven as of a rushing mighty wind, and it filled all the house where they were sitting.

3. Then there appeared to them divided tongues just as of fire, and one sat upon each of them.

4. So, they were all filled with the Holy Spirit and began to speak with other tongues, as the Spirit gave them utterance.

5. And there were dwelling at Jerusalem Jews, devout men, out of every nation under heaven.

6. Now when this was reported abroad, the multitude came together and were confounded, because every man heard them speak in his own language.

7. And they were all amazed and marveled, saying to one another, behold, are not all these who speak Galileans?

8. But how do we hear every man in our own tongue, in which we were born?

9. Parthians, and Medes, and Elamites, and the dwellers in Mesopotamia, and in Judea, and Cappadocia, in Pontus, and Asia,

10. Phrygia, and Pamphylia, in Egypt, and the parts of Libya about Cyrene, and strangers of Rome, Jews and converts,

11. Cretans and Arabians, we do hear them speak in our tongues the wonderful works of God!

12. Then they were all amazed, and were in doubt, saying to one another, what means this?

13. Others mocking said, these men are full of new wine.

14. But Peter, standing with the eleven, lifted up his voice, and said to them, you men of Judea, and all you that dwell at Jerusalem, let this be known to you, and listen to my words:

15. For these are not drunk, as you suppose, seeing it is but the third hour of the day.
16. But this is that which was spoken by the prophet Joel;
17. And it shall come to pass in the last days, says God, I will pour out of my Spirit upon all flesh: and your sons and your daughters will prophesy, and your young men will see visions, and your old men shall dream dreams:
18. And on my servants and my handmaidens I will pour out in those days of My Spirit, and they will prophesy:
19. And I will show wonders in heaven above, and signs in the land beneath; blood, and fire, and vapor of smoke:
20. The sun will be turned into darkness, and the moon into blood before the great and awesome day of the Lord comes
21. And it will come to pass, that whoever will call on the name of the Lord will be saved.
22. You men of Israel, hear these words; Jesus of Nazareth, a man approved by God among you by miracles and wonders and signs, which God did by Him in the midst of you, as you also know:
23. Him, being delivered by the determined purpose and foreknowledge of God, you have taken, and by wicked hands have crucified and killed:
24. Who God has raised up, having loosed the pains of death: because it was not possible that He should be held by it.
25. For David speaks concerning Him, I saw the Lord always before my face, for He is on my right hand, that I should not be moved:
26. Therefore, did my heart rejoice, and my tongue was glad; moreover also my flesh will rest in hope:
27. Because you will not leave my soul in the unseen realm, neither will you permit Your Holy One to see corruption.
28. You have made known to me the ways of life; You will make me full of joy with your presence.
29. Men and brothers, let me freely speak to you of the patriarch David that he is both dead and buried, and his tomb is with us to this day.
30. Therefore, being a prophet, and knowing that God had sworn with an oath to him, that of the fruit of his body, according to the flesh, He would raise up Christ to sit on his throne;
31. He seeing this before spoke of the resurrection of Christ, that His soul was not left in the unseen realm, nor his flesh did see corruption.
32. This Jesus, God has raised up, which we all are witnesses.
33. Therefore, being at the right hand of God exalted, and having received from the Father the promise of the Holy Spirit, He has poured out this, which you now see and hear.
34. For David has not ascended into the heavens: but he said himself, The Lord said to My Lord, sit on My right hand,
35. Until I make Your enemies Your footstool.
36. Therefore, let all the house of Israel know assuredly, that God has made this same Jesus, who you have crucified, both Lord and Christ.

37. Now when they heard this, they were pierced intensely in their heart, and said to Peter and the rest of the apostles, men, and brothers, what will we do?

38. Then Peter said to them, repent, and be immersed each one of you in the name of Jesus Christ into the forgiveness of sins, and you will receive the gift of the Holy Spirit.

39. For this promise is to you, and to your children, and to all that are far off, just as many as the LORD our God will call.

40. Then with many other words he did testify and exhort, saying, save yourselves from this spotted generation.

41. Then they that gladly received his word were immersed: and the same day there were added to them about three thousand souls.

42. And they continued steadfastly in the apostles' doctrine and fellowship, and in breaking of bread, and in prayers.

43. For fear came on every soul: and many wonders and signs were done by the apostles.

44. And all that believed were together, and had all things in common;

45. And sold their lands and goods, and divided them to all men, as every man had need.

46. And they, continuing daily with one accord in the temple, and breaking bread from house to house, did eat their food with gladness and singleness of heart,

47. Praising God, and having favor with all the people. For the Lord added to the assembly daily those who were being saved.

Chapter 3

1. Now Peter and John went up together into the temple at the hour of prayer, being the ninth hour.

2. And a certain man lame from his mother's womb was carried, whom they laid daily at the gate of the temple which is called Beautiful, to ask alms of them that entered into the temple;

3. Who seeing Peter and John about to go into the temple asked for alms.

4. Then Peter, fastening his eyes on him with John, said, Look at us!

5. He gave attention to them, expecting to receive something.

6. Then Peter said, Silver and gold have I none; but such as I have I give to you: in the name of Jesus Christ of Nazareth rise up and walk.

7. He took him by the right hand, and lifted him up: and immediately his feet and ankle bones received strength.

8. And he leaping up stood, and walked, and entered with them into the temple, walking, and leaping, and praising God!

9. Then all the people saw him walking and praising God:

10. For they knew that it was he who sat for alms at the Beautiful gate of the temple: and they were filled with wonder and amazement at that which had happened to him.

11. So, as the lame man who was healed held Peter and John, all the people ran together to them on the porch that is called Solomon's, greatly wondering.

12. When Peter saw it, he answered to the people, you men of Israel, why marvel at this? Or why look you so intently on us, as though by our own power or holiness we had made this man to walk?
13. The God of Abraham, and Isaac, and Jacob, the God of our fathers, has glorified His Son Jesus; who you delivered up, and denied Him in the presence of Pilate when He was determined to let Him go.
14. But you denied the Holy One and the Just, and desired a murderer to be granted to you;
15. And killed the Prince of Life, whom God has raised from the dead; which we are witnesses.
16. And upon faith in His name, His name has made this man strong, who you see and know: yes, the faith which is by Him has given him this complete health in the presence of you all.
17. Now, brothers, I know that you carried this out through ignorance, as did your leaders.
18. But those things, which God before had showed by the mouth of all His prophets, that His Christ should suffer, He has fulfilled like this.
19. Therefore, repent, and turn, that your sins may be blotted out when the times of refreshing will come from the presence of the Lord.
20. And He will send Jesus Christ, who before was preached to you:
21. Whom the heavens must receive until the times of the restitution of all things, which God has spoken through the mouth of all His holy prophets from the Old Covenant Age.
22. For Moses truly said to the fathers, a Prophet will the Lord Your God raise up to you from your brothers, like me; you will hear Him in all things whatsoever He will say to you.
23. And it will come to pass, that every soul, who will not hear that Prophet will be extirpated from among the people.
24. Yes, and all the prophets from Samuel and those that follow after, as many as have spoken, have likewise foretold these days.
25. You are the children of the prophets, and of the covenant which God made with our fathers, saying to Abraham, and in your seed will all the families of the earth be blessed.
26. To you first, God, having raised up His Son Jesus, sent Him to bless you, in turning all of you away from your iniquities.

Chapter 4

1. As they spoke to the people, the priests, the captain of the temple, and the Sadducees, came upon them,
2. Being grieved that they taught the people, and preached through Jesus the resurrection from the dead.
3. Then they laid hands on them, and put them in jail until the next day: for it was now evening.
4. However, many of those who heard the word believed, and the number of the men was about five thousand.
5. And it came to pass on the next day, that their rulers, and elders, and scribes,

6. And Annas the high priest, and Caiaphas, and John, and Alexander, and as many as were of the relatives of the high priest, were gathered together at Jerusalem.
7. When they had set them in the midst, they asked, by what power, or by what name, have you done this?
8. Then Peter, filled with the Holy Spirit, said to them, You rulers of the people, and elders of Israel,
9. If we this day are judged for the good deed done to the helpless man, by what means is he made whole;
10. Be it known to you all, and all the people of Israel, that by the name of Jesus Christ of Nazareth, who you crucified, who God raised from the dead, even by Him does this man stand here before you healthy.
11. This is the stone which was rejected by you builders, which has become the chief cornerstone.
12. Neither is there salvation in any other: for there is no other name under heaven given among men, which we must be saved.
13. Now when they saw the boldness of Peter and John, and perceived that they were uneducated and untrained men, they marveled, and they took knowledge of them, that they had been with Jesus.
14. And beholding the man who was healed standing with them, they could say nothing against it.
15. But when they had commanded them to go aside out of the council, they conferred among themselves,
16. Saying, what will we do to these men? For that indeed a great miracle has been done by them is manifest to all them that dwell in Jerusalem, and we cannot deny it.
17. But that it spread no further among the people, let us strictly threaten them that they speak from now on to no man in this name.
18. Then they called them and commanded them not to speak at all nor teach in the name of Jesus.
19. But Peter and John answered and said to them, whether it is right in the sight of God to listen to you more than to God, you judge.
20. For we cannot but speak the things which we have seen and heard.
21. So, when they had further threatened them, they let them go, finding nothing how they might punish them, because of the people: for all men glorified God for that which was done.
22. For the man was more than forty years old, on whom this miracle of healing was shown.
23. Then being let go, they went to their companions and reported all that the chief priests and elders had said to them.
24. When they heard that, they lifted up their voice to God with one accord, and said, Lord, You are God, who made heaven, and earth, and the sea, and all that in them is:
25. Who by the mouth of Your servant David have said, why did the nations rage, and the people imagine vain things?
26. The kings of the land stood up, and the rulers were gathered together against the Lord and His Christ.

27. For truly against Your holy Servant Jesus, who You have anointed, both Herod, and Pontius Pilate, with the nations, and the people of Israel, were gathered together,
28. For to do whatever Your hand and Your counsel determined before to be done.
29. Now, Lord, behold their threats: and grant to Your servants, that with all boldness they may speak Your word,
30. By stretching out Your hand to heal; and that signs and wonders may be done by the name of Your holy Servant Jesus.
31. When they had prayed, the place was shaken where they were assembled; and they were all filled with the Holy Spirit, and they spoke the word of God with boldness!
32. For the multitude of them that believed were of one heart and one soul: neither said any of them that anything of the things which he possessed was his own, but they had all things in common.
33. So, with great power the apostles gave witness of the resurrection of the Lord Jesus: and great grace was upon them all.
34. Neither was there any among them that lacked: for as many as were possessors of lands or houses sold them and brought the price of the things that were sold
35. And laid them down at the apostles' feet: and distribution was made to every man according as he had need.
36. Then Joseph, who by the apostles was surnamed Barnabas, (which is, being interpreted, The son of encouragement) a Levite, and of the country of Cyprus,
37. Having land, sold it, and brought the money, and laid it at the apostles' feet.

Chapter 5

1. But a certain man named Ananias, with Sapphira as his wife, sold land,
2. But kept back part of the price, his wife also being aware to it, and brought a certain part, and laid it at the apostles' feet.
3. But Peter said, Ananias, why has Satan filled your heart to lie to the Holy Spirit, and to keep back part of the price of the land?
4. While it remained, was it not your own? After it was sold, was it not in your own power? Why have you conceived this thing in your heart? You have not lied to men but to God.
5. Then Ananias hearing these words fell down, and gave up the ghost: and great fear came on all them that heard these things.
6. So, the young men arose, wrapped him up, and took him away, and buried him.
7. It was about the space of three hours later, when his wife, not knowing what had happened, came in.
8. Then Peter answered her, Tell me whether you sold the land for so much? And she said, yes for so much.
9. Then Peter said to her, How is it that you have agreed together to tempt the Spirit of the Lord? Behold, the feet of those who have buried your husband are at the door and will take you away.
10. Immediately she fell down at his feet and yielded up the ghost: and the young men came in and found her dead and taking her away, buried her by her husband.
11. So, great fear came upon all the assembly, and upon as many as heard these things.

12. For by the hands of the apostles were many signs and wonders done among the people, and they were all with one accord in Solomon's Porch.
13. But of the rest, no man dared join himself to them: but the people magnified them.
14. And believers were the more added to the Lord, multitudes both of men and women.
15. So, much so that they brought forth the sick into the streets, and laid them on beds and couches, that at the least the shadow of Peter passing by might overshadow some of them.
16. There came also a multitude out of the cities around Jerusalem, bringing sick people, and those who were possessed with unclean spirits: and they were all healed.
17. Then the high priest rose up and all they that were with him, (which is the sect of the Sadducees) were filled with indignation,
18. And laid their hands on the apostles, and put them in the common prison.
19. But the angel of the Lord by night opened the prison doors, and brought them out, and said,
20. Go, stand, and speak in the temple to the people all the words of this life.
21. When they heard that, they entered into the temple early in the morning and taught. But the high priest came, and they that were with him, and called the council together, and all the elders of the children of Israel, and sent to the prison to have them brought.
22. But when the officers came, and found them not in the prison, they returned and told,
23. Saying, the prison truly found we shut with all safety, and the keepers standing outside before the doors: but when we opened them, we found no man within.
24. Now when the high priest and the captain of the temple and the chief priests heard these things, they doubted what the outcome would be.
25. Then came one and told them, saying, behold, the men who you put in prison are standing in the temple, and teaching the people.
26. Then went the captain with the officers, and brought them without violence: for they feared the people unless they should have been stoned.
27. When they had brought them, they placed them before the council: and the high priest asked them,
28. Saying, did not we strictly command you that you should not teach in this name? But, behold, you have filled Jerusalem with your teaching, and intend to bring upon us the blood of this man.
29. Then Peter and the other apostles answered and said, we ought to obey God rather than men.
30. The God of our fathers raised up Jesus, who you killed and hanged on a tree.
31. He has God exalted with His right hand to be a Prince and a Savior, and to bestow repentance to Israel, and forgiveness of sins.
32. Now we are His witnesses of these things; and so also is the Holy Spirit, who God has given to them that obey Him.
33. When they heard that, they were cut to the heart and took counsel to kill them.

34. Then there stood up one in the council, a Pharisee, named Gamaliel, a doctor of the Law, having in reputation among all the people, and commanded to put the apostles out a little while;

35. And said to them, You men of Israel, take heed to yourselves what you are about to do concerning these men.

36. For before these days rose up Theudas, boasting himself to be somebody; to whom many men, about four hundred, joined themselves: who was killed; and all, as many as obeyed him, were scattered, and came to nothing.

37. After this man rose up Judas of Galilee in the days of the taxing, and took away many people after him: he also perished; and all, just as many as obeyed him, were dispersed.

38. Now I say to you, keep away from these men, and leave them alone: for if this plan or this work be of men, it will come to nothing:

39. But if it be of God, you cannot overthrow it; unless you are found to even fight against God.

40. Then to him they agreed: and when they had called the apostles, and beaten them, they commanded that they should not speak in the name of Jesus, and let them go.

41. So, they departed from the presence of the council, rejoicing that they were counted worthy to suffer shame for His name.

42. And daily in the temple, and every house, they did not stop to teach and preach Jesus Christ.

Chapter 6

1. In those days, when the number of the disciples was multiplied, there arose a murmuring by the Grecians against the Hebrews, because their widows were neglected in the daily distribution.

2. Then the twelve called the multitude of the disciples to them, and said, it is not reasonable that we should leave the word of God, and serve tables.

3. Therefore, brothers, select among you seven men of honest report, full of the Holy Spirit and wisdom, whom we may appoint over this business.

4. But we will give ourselves continually to prayer, and the ministry of the Word.

5. Now the saying pleased the whole multitude: and they chose Stephen, a man full of faith and of the Holy Spirit, and Philip, and Prochorus, and Nicanor, and Timon, and Parmenas, and Nicolas a convert from Antioch:

6. Who they placed before the apostles: and when they had prayed, they laid their hands on them.

7. So, the Word of God increased, and the number of the disciples multiplied in Jerusalem greatly, and a great company of the priests were obedient to the faith.

8. And Stephen, full of faith and power, did great wonders and miracles among the people.

9. Then there arose certain of the synagogue, which is called the synagogue of the Libertines, and Cyrenians, and Alexandrians, and of them of Cilicia and Asia, disputing with Stephen.

10. But they were not able to resist the wisdom and the Spirit by whom he spoke.

11. Then they secretly induced men to give false testimony, who said, we have heard him speak blasphemous words against Moses and God.

12. So, they stirred up the people, and the elders, and the scribes, and came upon him, and caught him, and brought him to the council,

13. And set up false witnesses, who said, This man stops not to speak blasphemous words against this holy place, and the Law:

14. For we have heard him say, that this Jesus of Nazareth will destroy this place, and will change the customs which Moses delivered us.

15. Then all that sat in the council, looking steadfastly on him, saw his face as it had been the face of an angel.

Chapter 7

1. Then said the high priest, Are these things so?

2. He said, Men, brothers, and fathers, listen; The God of glory appeared to our father Abraham when he was in Mesopotamia before he dwelt in Haran,

3. And said to him, Get out of your country, and from your relatives, and come into the land which I will show you.

4. Then he came out of the land of the Chaldaeans, and dwelt in Haran: and from there, when his father was dead, He moved him to this land, where you now dwell.

5. And He gave him no inheritance in it, no, not so much as to set his foot on: Yet He promised that He would give it to him for a possession and to his seed after him when as yet he had no child.

6. But God spoke in this way, that his seed should dwell in a strange land; and that they should bring them into bondage and oppress them four hundred years.

7. And the nation to whom they will be in bondage will I judge, said God: and after that will they come out, and serve Me in this place.

8. And He gave him the covenant of circumcision: and so Abraham fathered Isaac, and circumcised him the eighth day, and Isaac fathered Jacob, and Jacob fathered the twelve patriarchs.

9. But the patriarchs, moved with envy, sold Joseph into Egypt: but God was with him,

10. And delivered him out of all his afflictions, and gave him favor and wisdom in the sight of Pharaoh, ruler of Egypt; and he made him governor over Egypt and all his house.

11. Now there came a famine over all the land of Egypt and Canaan and great affliction: and our fathers found no sustenance.

12. But when Jacob heard that there was corn in Egypt, he sent out our fathers first.

13. At the second time Joseph was made known to his brothers, and Joseph's family was made known to Pharaoh.

14. Then sent Joseph, and called his father Jacob to him, and all his family, seventy-five souls.

15. So, Jacob went down into Egypt, and died, he, and our fathers,

16. And was carried back into Shechem, and laid in the tomb that Abraham bought for a sum of money from the sons of Hamor the father of Shechem.

17. But when the time of the promise came close, which God had sworn to Abraham, the people grew and multiplied in Egypt,

18. Until another Pharaoh arose, who did not know Joseph.

19. The same dealt deceptively with our people, and badly treated our fathers, so that they cast out their young children, to the end they might not live.

20. In which time Moses was born, and was exceedingly fair, and nourished up in his father's house three months:

21. When he was cast out, Pharaoh's daughter held him and nourished him as her own son.

22. And Moses was learned in all the wisdom of the Egyptians and was mighty in words and deeds.

23. When he was forty years old, it came into his heart to visit his brothers, the children of Israel.

24. So, seeing one of them suffer wrong, he defended him, and avenged him that was oppressed, and struck down the Egyptian:

25. For he supposed his brothers would have understood that God by his hand would deliver them: but they did not understand.

26. Then the next day he showed himself to them as they argued, and would have reconciled them, and said, Sirs, you are brothers; why do you wrong one another?

27. But he that did his neighbor wrong thrust him away, and said, who made you a ruler and a judge over us?

28. Do you want to kill me, as you did the Egyptian yesterday?

29. Then Moses fled at this saying and was a stranger in the land of Midian, where he fathered two sons.

30. When forty years had passed, there appeared to him in the wilderness of Mount Sinai an angel of the Lord in a flame of fire in a bush.

31. When Moses saw it, he wondered at the sight: and as he drew near to behold it, the voice of the LORD came to him,

32. Saying I am the God of your fathers, the God of Abraham, and the God of Isaac, and the God of Jacob. Then Moses trembled and dared not look.

33. Then said the Lord to him, put off your sandals from your feet: for the place where you stand is holy ground.

34. I have seen, I have seen the affliction of My people who are in Egypt, and I have heard their groaning, and have come down to deliver them. And now come, I will send you into Egypt.

35. This Moses who they refused, saying, who made you a ruler and a judge? The same did God send to be a ruler and a deliverer by the hand of the angel who appeared to him in the bush.

36. He brought them out after he had shown wonders and signs in the land of Egypt, in the Red Sea, and in the wilderness for forty years.

37. This is that Moses, who said to the children of Israel, a prophet will the Lord your God raise up to you of your brothers, like me; Him you will hear.

38. This is he, that was in the assembly in the wilderness with the angel who spoke to him on Mount Sinai, and with our fathers: who received the living oracles for us:

39. To whom our fathers would not obey, but rejected, and in their hearts turned back into Egypt,

40. Saying to Aaron, make us gods to go before us: for as for this Moses, who brought us out of the land of Egypt, we know not what has become of him.

41. Then they made a calf in those days and offered sacrifices to the idol, and rejoiced in the works of their own hands.

42. Then God turned, and gave them up to worship the host of heaven; as it is written in the book of the prophets, O you house of Israel, have you offered to Me slain beasts and sacrifices by the space of forty years in the wilderness?

43. Yes, you took up the tabernacle of Moloch, and the star of your god Remphan, figures which you made to worship them: and I will take you away beyond Babylon.

44. Our fathers had the Tabernacle of the Testimony in the wilderness, as He had appointed, speaking to Moses, that he should make it according to the pattern that he had seen.

45. Which also our fathers that came after brought in with Jesus into the possession of the nations, who God drove out before the face of our fathers, to the days of David;

46. Who found favor before God, and wanted to find a tabernacle for the God of Jacob.

47. But Solomon built Him a house.

48. However, the most High dwells not in temples made with hands; as says the prophet,

49. Heaven is My throne, and earth is My footstool: what house will you build Me? Says the Lord: or what is the place of My rest?

50. Has not My hand made all these things?

51. You stiff-necked and uncircumcised in heart and ears. You always resist the Holy Spirit: as your fathers did, so do you!

52. Which of the prophets have not your fathers persecuted? And they have slain those who foretold the coming of the Just One; of whom you now have become betrayers and murderers:

53. Who have received the Law by the direction of angels, and have not kept it.

54. When they heard these things, they were cut to the heart, and they gnashed at him with their teeth.

55. But he, being full of the Holy Spirit, looked up steadfastly into heaven, and saw the glory of God, and Jesus standing at the right hand of God,

56. And said, behold, I see the heavens opened, and the Son of man standing at the right hand of God.

57. Then they cried out with a loud voice, and stopped their ears, and ran upon him with one accord,

58. And cast him out of the city, and stoned him: and the witnesses laid down their clothes at a young man's feet, whose name was Saul.

59. So, they stoned Stephen, calling upon God, and saying, Lord Jesus, receive my spirit.

60. Then he knelt down, and cried with a loud voice, Lord, do not charge them with this sin. And when he had said this, he fell asleep.

Chapter 8

1. So, Saul was consented to his death. And at that time there was a great persecution against the assembly who were at Jerusalem; and they were all scattered abroad throughout the regions of Judea and Samaria, except the apostles.
2. And devout men carried Stephen to his burial and made great lamentation over him.
3. As for Saul, he made havoc on the assembly, entering every house, taking away men and women, and committing them to prison.
4. Therefore, they that were scattered abroad went everywhere preaching the word.
5. Then Philip went down to the city of Samaria and preached Christ to them.
6. And the people with one accord gave heed to those things which Philip spoke, hearing and seeing the miracles which he did.
7. For unclean spirits, crying with loud voices, came out of many that were possessed with them: and many paralytics and that were lame were healed.
8. And there was great joy in that city.
9. But there was a certain man, called Simon, who before time in the same city used sorcery, and bewitched the nation of Samaria, claiming himself as some great one:
10. To whom they all gave heed, from the least to the greatest, saying, this man is the great power of God.
11. And to him they had regard because, for a long time, he had bewitched them with sorceries.
12. But when they believed Philip preaching the things concerning the kingdom of God, and the name of Jesus Christ, they were immersed, both men and women.
13. Then Simon himself believed also: and when he was immersed, he continued with Philip, and wondered, beholding the miracles and signs which were done.
14. Now when the apostles who were at Jerusalem heard that Samaria had received the word of God, they sent to them Peter and John:
15. Who, when they had come down, prayed for them, that they might receive the Holy Spirit:
16. For as yet He had fallen upon none of them: only they were immersed in the name of the Lord Jesus.
17. Then they laid their hands on them, and they received the Holy Spirit.
18. When Simon saw that through the laying on of the apostles' hands, the Holy Spirit was given, he offered them money,
19. Saying, give me also this power, that on whoever I lay my hands, he may receive the Holy Spirit.
20. But Peter said to him, you perish with your money because you thought that the gift of God may be purchased with money.
21. You neither have part nor portion in this matter: for your heart is not right in the sight of God.
22. Therefore, repent of your wickedness, and pray to God, if perhaps the thought of your heart may be forgiven.

23. For I perceive that you are full of bitterness, and in the bond of iniquity.
24. Then answered Simon, and said, you pray for me to the LORD, that none of these things which you have spoken come on me.
25. And they, when they had testified and preached the word of the Lord, returned to Jerusalem, and preached the gospel in many villages of the Samaritans.
26. Then a messenger of the Lord spoke to Philip, and said, arise, and go toward the south to the way that goes down from Jerusalem to Gaza, which is deserted.
27. So, he arose and went: and, behold, a man of Ethiopia, an eunuch of great authority under Candace queen of the Ethiopians, who was in charge of all her treasure, had come to Jerusalem to worship,
28. Was returning, and sitting in his chariot reading Isaiah the prophet.
29. Then the Spirit said to Philip, Go near, and overtake this chariot.
30. Then Philip ran from here to there, and heard him read the prophet Isaiah, and said, do you understand what you read?
31. But he said, how can I unless some man should guide me? So, he asked Philip if he would come up and sit with him.
32. The place of the Scripture which he read was this, He was led as a sheep to the slaughter; and like a mute lamb before his shearer, so opened He not His mouth:
33. In His humiliation His judgment was taken away: and who will declare His generation? For His life is taken from the land.
34. And the eunuch answered Philip, and said, I pray you, of who speaks the prophet? Of himself, or some other man?
35. Then Philip opened his mouth and began at the same Scripture, and preached to him Jesus.
36. As they went on their way, they came to some water: and the eunuch said, see, here is water; what does prevent me from being immersed?
37. And Philip said, if you believe with all your heart, you may. And he answered and said, I believe that Jesus Christ is the Son of God.
38. So, he commanded the chariot to stand still: and they went down both into the water, both Philip and the eunuch; and he immersed him.
39. When they had come up out of the water, the Spirit of the Lord seized Philip, that the eunuch saw him no more: and he went on his way rejoicing.
40. But Philip was found at Azotus: and passing through he preached in all the cities until he came to Caesarea.

Chapter 9

1. And Saul, yet breathing out threatening's and murder against the disciples of the Lord, went to the high priest,
2. And asked letters from him to the synagogues of Damascus, that if he found any that belonged to the Way, if they were men or women, he might bring them bound to Jerusalem.
3. As he journeyed, he came near Damascus: and suddenly there shined around him a light from heaven:

4. So, he fell to the ground, and heard a voice saying to him, Saul, Saul, why are you persecuting Me?
5. And he said, who are You, Lord? And the Lord said, I am Jesus whom you are persecuting.
6. And terrified and amazed he said, Lord, what will You have me do? Then the Lord said to him, arise, and go into the city, and it will be told what you must do.
7. And the men who journeyed with him stood speechless, hearing a voice, but seeing no one.
8. Then Saul arose from the ground; and when his eyes were opened, he saw no man: but they led him by the hand, and brought him into Damascus.
9. He was three days without sight, and neither did eat nor drink.
10. And there was a certain disciple at Damascus, named Ananias; and to him said the Lord in a vision, Ananias. And he said, behold, I am here, Lord.
11. So, the Lord said to him, arise, and go into the street which is called Straight, and inquire in the house of Judas for one called Saul, of Tarsus: for, behold, he prays,
12. And has seen in a vision a man named Ananias coming in, and putting his hand on him, that he might receive his sight.
13. Then Ananias answered, Lord, I have heard by many about this man, how much evil he has done to Your saints at Jerusalem:
14. And here he has authority from the chief priests to bind all that call on Your name.
15. But the Lord said to him, go your way: for he is a chosen vessel to Me, to bear My name before the nations, and kings, and the children of Israel:
16. For I will show him what great things he must suffer for My name's sake.
17. So, Ananias went his way, and entered into the house; and putting his hands on him said, brother Saul, the Lord, even Jesus, that appeared to you on the way as you came, has sent me, that you might receive your sight, and be filled with the Holy Spirit.
18. Immediately there fell from his eyes as if it had been scales: and immediately he received sight, and arose, and was immersed.
19. When he had received food, he was strengthened. Then Saul spent some days with the disciples at Damascus.
20. And immediately he preached Christ in the synagogues, that He is the Son of God.
21. But all that heard him were amazed, and said; Is not this he that destroyed those who called on this name in Jerusalem, and came here for that intent, that he might bring them bound to the chief priests?
22. But Saul increased the more in strength, and confounded the Jews who dwelt at Damascus, proving that this Jesus is the Christ.
23. After many days were fulfilled, the Jews took counsel to kill him:
24. But their ambush became known to Saul. For they watched the gates day and night to kill him.
25. Then the disciples led him by night, and let him down by the wall in a basket.
26. When Saul had come to Jerusalem, he tried to join the disciples: but they were all afraid of him, and did not believe that he was a disciple.

27. But Barnabas met him and brought him to the apostles, and declared to them how he had seen the Lord on the way, and that He had spoken to him, and how he had preached boldly at Damascus in the name of Jesus.

28. So, he was with them at Jerusalem coming in and going out

29. For he spoke boldly in the name of the Lord Jesus, and disputed against the Grecians: but they planned to kill him.

30. Which when the brothers knew, they brought him down to Caesarea, and sent him out to Tarsus.

31. Then had the assemblies rest throughout all Judea and Galilee and Samaria, and were edified; and walking in the fear of the Lord, and in the comfort of the Holy Spirit, were multiplied.

32. And it came to pass, as Peter passed throughout all parts of the country, he came down also to the saints who dwelt at Lydda.

33. There he found a certain man named Aeneas, who had been bedridden for eight years and was a paralytic.

34. Then Peter said to him, Aeneas, Jesus Christ heals you: Arise, and make your bed. Immediately he arose.

35. So, all that dwelt at Lydda and Saron saw him and turned to the Lord.

36. Now there was at Joppa a certain disciple named Tabitha, which is translated Dorcas: this woman was full of good works and charitable deeds which she did.

37. And it came to pass in those days, that she was sick, and died: who when they had washed, they laid her in an upper chamber.

38. Since Lydda was close to Joppa, and the disciples had heard that Peter was there, they sent to him two men, asking him that he would come to them speedily.

39. Then Peter arose and went with them. When he had come, they brought him into the upper chamber: and all the widows stood by him weeping, and showing the tunics and garments which Dorcas made, while she was with them.

40. But Peter put them all out, and knelt down, and prayed; and turning to the body said, Tabitha, arise. She opened her eyes: and when she saw Peter, she sat up.

41. Then he gave her his hand and lifted her up, and when he had called the saints and widows, presented her alive.

42. So, it was known throughout all Joppa, and many believed in the Lord.

43. And it came to pass, that he stayed many days in Joppa with one Simon a tanner.

Chapter 10

1. There was a certain man in Caesarea called Cornelius, a centurion of the Italian Legion,

2. A devout man, and one that feared God with all his house, who gave generously to the people, and always prayed to God.

3. He saw in a vision clearly about the ninth hour of the day an angel of God coming to him, and saying to him, Cornelius.

4. When he looked on him, he was afraid, and said, what is it, Lord? And he said to him, your prayers and your giving have come up for a memorial before God.

5. Now send men to Joppa, and call for one Simon, whose surname is Peter:

6. He stays with one Simon a tanner, whose house is by the seaside: He will tell you what you should do.

7. When the angel who spoke to Cornelius left, he called two of his household servants, and a devout soldier of them that waited on him continually;

8. When he had explained all these things to them, he sent them to Joppa.

9. On the next day, as they went on their journey, and came close to the city, Peter went up on the housetop to pray about the sixth hour:

10. And he became very hungry, and would have eaten: but while they made ready, he fell into a trance,

11. And saw heaven opened, and a certain object descending upon him, as it had been a great sheet knit at the four corners, and let down to the ground:

12. In which were all manner of four-footed beasts of the ground, and wild beasts, and creeping things, and birds of the air.

13. And there came a voice to him, Rise, Peter; kill, and eat.

14. But Peter said, not so, Lord; for I have never eaten anything common or unclean.

15. And the voice spoke to him again the second time, what God has cleansed, that do not call common.

16. This was done three times: and the object was received up again into heaven.

17. Now while Peter doubted in himself what this vision which he had seen should mean, behold, the men who were sent from Cornelius had inquired about Simon's house and stood before the gate,

18. And called, and asked whether Simon, who was surnamed Peter, was staying there.

19. While Peter thought on the vision, the Spirit said to him, behold, three men seek you.

20. Therefore, arise, and get down, and go with them, doubting nothing: for I have sent them.

21. Then Peter went down to the men who were sent to him from Cornelius; and said, behold, I am he who you seek: what is the reason why you have come?

22. So, they said, Cornelius the centurion, a just man, and one that fears God, and has a good reputation among all the nation of the Jews, was warned from God by a holy angel to send for you into his house and to hear your words.

23. Then he invited them in and lodged them. On the next day, Peter went with them, and certain brothers from Joppa accompanied him.

24. And the next day they entered into Caesarea. And Cornelius waited for them, for he had called together his relatives and best friends.

25. As Peter was coming in, Cornelius met him and fell down at his feet, and worshiped him.

26. But Peter lifted him up, and said, stand up; I also am a man.

27. And as he talked with him, he went in and found many that had gathered together.

28. Then he said to them, you know that it is an unlawful thing for a man that is a Jew to keep company or come to one of another nation; but God has shown me that I should not call any man common or unclean.

29. Therefore, I came to you without objection, as soon as I was sent for: therefore, I ask for what intent have you sent for me?

30. So, Cornelius said, four days ago I was fasting until this hour; and at the ninth hour I prayed in my house, and, behold, a man stood before me in bright clothing,

31. And said, Cornelius, your prayer is heard, and your giving is remembered in the sight of God.

32. Therefore, send to Joppa, and call to here Simon, whose surname is Peter; he is staying in the house of one Simon a tanner by the sea side: Who, when he comes, will speak to you.

33. Immediately, therefore, I sent to you; and you have done well that you have come. Now therefore are we all here present before God, to hear all things that are commanded you by God.

34. Then Peter opened his mouth, and said, truly I perceive that God is no respecter of persons:

35. But in every nation he that fears Him, and works righteousness, is accepted by Him.

36. The Word which God sent to the sons of Israel, preaching peace through Jesus Christ: He is Lord of all.

37. That word, I say, you know, which was spoken out throughout all Judea, and began from Galilee, after the immersion which John preached;

38. How God anointed Jesus of Nazareth with the Holy Spirit and with power: who went about doing good, and healing all that were oppressed of the devil; for God was with Him.

39. And we are witnesses of all things which He did both in the land of the Jews and in Jerusalem; who they killed and hung on a tree:

40. God raised Him up the third day, and showed Him openly

41. Not to all the people, but to witnesses chosen before God, even to us, who did eat and drink with Him after He rose from the dead.

42. And He commanded us to preach to the people and to testify that it is He who was ordained by God to be the Judge of the quick and the dead.

43. To Him gave all the prophets witness, that through His name whoever believes in Him will receive forgiveness of sins.

44. While Peter yet spoke these words, the Holy Spirit fell on all those who heard the word.

45. And they of the circumcision who believed were astonished, as many as came with Peter, because on the nations also was poured out the gift of the Holy Spirit.

46. For they heard them speak with tongues, and magnify God. Then answered Peter,

47. Can anyone prevent the water, that these should not be immersed, who have received the Holy Spirit as well as we?

48. Then he commanded them to be immersed in the name of the Lord. Then they asked him to stay a few days.

Chapter 11

1. Then the apostles and brothers that were in Judea heard that the nations had also received the Word of God.
2. And when Peter had come up to Jerusalem, they that were of the circumcision argued with him,
3. Saying, You went into men uncircumcised and did eat with them.
4. But Peter rehearsed the matter from the beginning, and explained it by order to them, saying,
5. I was in the city of Joppa praying: and in a trance I saw a vision, a certain object descend, as it had been a great sheet, let down from heaven by four corners; and it came even to me:
6. Upon which when I had fastened my eyes, I considered, and saw four-footed beasts of the ground, and wild beasts, and creeping things, and birds of the air.
7. And I heard a voice saying to me, Arise, Peter; kill and eat.
8. But I said, not so, Lord: for nothing common or unclean has at any time entered into my mouth.
9. But the voice answered me again from heaven, what God has cleansed, do not call common.
10. And this was done three times: and all were drawn up again into heaven.
11. And, behold, immediately there were three men already come to the house where I was, sent from Caesarea to me.
12. And the Spirit told me to go with them, nothing doubting. Moreover, these six brothers accompanied me, and we entered into the man's house:
13. And he showed us how he had seen an angel in his house, who stood and said to him, send men to Joppa, and call for Simon, whose surname is Peter;
14. Who will speak to you words, by which you and all your house will be saved.
15. And as I began to speak, the Holy Spirit fell on them, as on us at the beginning.
16. Then I remembered the word of the Lord that He said, John indeed immersed with water, but you will be immersed in the Holy Spirit.
17. Since, God gave them the same gift as He did us, who believed in the Lord Jesus Christ; who was I, that I could withstand God?
18. When they heard these things, they held their peace, and glorified God, saying, then has God also to the nations granted repentance to life.
19. Now they who were scattered abroad on the persecution that arose after Stephen traveled as far as Phoenicia, Cyprus, and Antioch, preaching the word to no one, but Jews only.
20. And some of them were men of Cyprus and Cyrene, who, when they had come to Antioch, spoke to the Greeks, preaching the LORD Jesus.
21. And the hand of the Lord was with them: and a great number believed, and turned to the Lord.
22. Then news of these things came to the ears of the assembly who were in Jerusalem: and they sent out Barnabas, that he should go as far as Antioch.

23. Who, when he came and had seen the grace of God, was glad, and exhorted them all, that with purpose of heart, they would cleave to the Lord.
24. For he was a good man and full of the Holy Spirit and faith: and many people were added to the Lord.
25. Then departed Barnabas to Tarsus, to seek Saul:
26. And when he found him, he brought him to Antioch. And it came to pass, that a whole year they gathered themselves with the assembly, and taught many people. The disciples were first called Christians in Antioch.
27. And in these days came prophets from Jerusalem to Antioch.
28. Then there stood up one of them named Agabus and signified by the Spirit that there was about to be a great famine throughout all the Roman world: which came to pass in the days of Claudius Caesar.
29. Then the disciples, every man according to his ability, determined to send relief to the brothers who lived in Judea:
30. Which also they did, and sent it to the elders by the hands of Barnabas and Saul.

Chapter 12

1. Now about that time Herod the king stretched out his hands to harass certain of the assembly.
2. So, he killed James the brother of John with the sword.
3. Because he saw it pleased the Jews, he proceeded further to take Peter also. These were the Days of Unleavened Bread.
4. When he had taken him, he put him in prison and delivered him to four squads of soldiers to guard him; intending after Passover to bring him out to the people.
5. Therefore, Peter was kept in prison: but prayer was made without stopping by the assembly to God for him.
6. When Herod was about to bring him out, the same night Peter was sleeping between two soldiers, bound with two chains: and the guards before the door kept the prison.
7. And, behold, the angel of the Lord came upon him, and a light shined in the prison: and he touched Peter on the side, and raised him up, saying, Arise up quickly! And his chains fell off his hands.
8. Then the angel said to him, cloth yourself and tie on your sandals. So, he did. And he said to him, cast your garment around you, and follow me.
9. So, he went out, and followed him; and knew not that it was real which was done by the angel, but thought he saw a vision.
10. When they were past the first and the second guard posts, they came to the iron gates that lead to the city; which opened to them of its own accord: and they went out, and passed on through one street; and immediately the angel departed from him.
11. When Peter had come to himself, he said, now I know surely, that the LORD has sent His angel, and has delivered me out of the hand of Herod, and from all the expectation of the people of the Jews.

12. When he had considered the thing, he came to the house of Mary the mother of John, whose surname was Mark; where many were gathered together praying.
13. As Peter knocked at the door of the gate, a girl came to answer, named Rhoda.
14. When she knew Peter's voice, she opened not the gate for gladness, but ran in, and told how Peter stood before the gate.
15. But they said to her, you are mad. But she constantly affirmed that it was even so. Then said they, it is his angel.
16. But Peter continued knocking: and when they had opened the door, and saw him, they were astonished.
17. But he, beckoning to them with the hand to hold their peace, explained to them how the Lord had brought him out of the prison. And he said, go show these things to James, and the brothers. So, he departed and went to another place.
18. Now as soon as it was day, there was no small disturbance among the soldiers, what had become of Peter.
19. When Herod sought for him and found him not, he examined the guards and commanded that they should be put to death. And he went down from Judea to Caesarea, and there stayed.
20. And Herod was highly displeased with them of Tyre and Sidon: but they came with one accord to him, and, having made Blastus the king's personal aide their friend, desired peace; because their country was supplied by food by the king's country.
21. Upon a certain day Herod, arrayed in royal apparel, sat upon his throne, and made a speech to them.
22. Then the people shouted, saying, it is the voice of a god, and not of a man!
23. Immediately the angel of the Lord struck him because he did not give God the glory: and he was eaten by worms, and gave up the spirit.
24. But the Word of God grew and multiplied.
25. Then Barnabas and Saul returned from Jerusalem, when they had fulfilled their ministry, and picked John, whose surname was Mark.

Chapter 13

1. Now there were in the assembly that was at Antioch certain prophets and teachers; Barnabas, and Simeon who was called Niger, and Lucius of Cyrene, and Manaen, who had been brought up with Herod the tetrarch, and Saul.
2. As they ministered to the Lord, and fasted, the Holy Spirit said, Separate to Me Barnabas and Saul for the work which I have called them.
3. When they had fasted and prayed and laid their hands on them, they sent them away.
4. So, they, being sent out by the Holy Spirit, went to Seleucia; and from there they sailed to Cyprus.
5. When they were at Salamis, they preached the word of God in the synagogues of the Jews: and they also had John as their assistant.

6. When they had gone through the isle to Paphos, they found a certain sorcerer, a false prophet, a Jew, whose name was the son of Jesus:

7. Who was with the proconsul, Sergius Paulus, an intelligent man; who called for Barnabas and Saul, and wanted to hear the word of God.

8. But Elymas the sorcerer (for so is his name translated) withstood them, seeking to turn away the proconsul from the faith.

9. Then Saul, who also is called Paul, filled with the Holy Spirit, set his eyes on him.

10. And said, O full of all trickery and all recklessness, you child of the devil, you enemy of all righteousness, will you not stop twisting around the right way of the Lord?

11. Now, behold, the hand of the Lord is upon you, and you will be blind, not seeing the sun for a season. Immediately there fell on him a mist and a darkness, and he went about seeking some to lead him by the hand.

12. Then the proconsul, when he saw what was done, believed, being astonished at the doctrine of the Lord.

13. Now when Paul and his company left Paphos, they came to Perga in Pamphylia: and John departing from them returned to Jerusalem.

14. But when they departed from Perga, they came to Antioch in Pisidia and went into the synagogue on the Sabbath day, and sat down.

15. After the reading of the Law and the prophets the rulers of the synagogue asked of them, saying, you men and brothers, if you have any word of exhortation for the people, say so.

16. Then Paul stood up, and motioning with his hand said, Men of Israel, and you that fear God, listen.

17. The God of this people of Israel chose our fathers and exalted the people when they dwelt as strangers in the land of Egypt, and with an uplifted arm, He brought them out of it.

18. About the time of forty years suffered He their behavior in the wilderness.

19. When He had destroyed seven nations in the land of Canaan, He divided their land to them by lot.

20. After that He gave to them judges about the space of four hundred and fifty years, until Samuel the prophet.

21. Afterward they wanted a king: and God gave to them Saul the son of Kish, a man of the tribe of Benjamin, for forty years.

22. When He had removed him, He raised up to them David to be their king; to whom also He gave their testimony, and said, I have found David the son of Jesse, a man after My own heart, who will fulfill all My will.

23. From this man's seed has God according to His promise raised to Israel a Savior, Jesus:

24. When John had first preached before He came, the immersion of repentance to all the people of Israel.

25. As John fulfilled his destiny, he said, who do you think that I am? I am not Him. But, behold, there comes one after me, whose sandals I am not worthy to untie.

26. Men and brothers, sons of the family of Abraham, and whoever among you fears God, to you, is the Word of this salvation sent.
27. For they that dwell at Jerusalem, and their rulers, because they did not know Him, not even the voices of the prophets who are read every Sabbath day, they have fulfilled them in condemning Him.
28. Though they found no reason for death in Him, they wanted Pilate to put Him to death.
29. When they had fulfilled all that was written of Him, they took Him down from the tree and laid Him in a tomb.
30. But God raised Him from the dead:
31. And He was seen many days of those who came up with Him from Galilee to Jerusalem, who are His witnesses to the people.
32. So, we declare to you good news, that the promise which was made to the fathers,
33. God has fulfilled the same to us their children, in that He has raised up Jesus again; as it is also written in the second Psalm, You are My Son, this day have I begotten You.
34. As concerning that He raised Him up from the dead, now no more to return to corruption, He has so spoken, I am about to give you the sure mercies of David.
35. Therefore, He says also in another Psalm, You will not permit Your Holy One to see corruption.
36. For David, after he had served his own generation by the will of God, fell asleep, was buried with his fathers, and saw corruption:
37. But He, who God raised again, saw no corruption.
38. Therefore, be it known to you, men and brothers that through this Man is preached to you the forgiveness of sins:
39. For by Him all that believe are justified from all things, from which you could not be justified by the Law of Moses.
40. Therefore, beware, unless that come upon you, which is spoken of in the prophets;
41. Behold, you despisers, and wonder, and perish! For I work a work in your days, a work which you will in no way believe, though one declare it to you.
42. When the Jews had gone out of the synagogue, the Gentiles asked that these words might be preached to them the next Sabbath.
43. Now when the congregation was broken up, many of the Jews and devout apprentices followed Paul and Barnabas: who, speaking to them, persuaded them to continue in the grace of God.
44. And the next Sabbath day came almost the whole city together to hear the Word of God.
45. But when the Jews saw the multitudes, they were filled with jealousy and spoke against those things which were spoken by Paul, contradicting and blaspheming.
46. Then Paul and Barnabas grew bold, and said, the word of God needed to first be spoken to you: but seeing that you reject it, and judge yourselves unworthy of infinite life, look, we turn to the nations.
47. For so has the Lord commanded us, saying, I have set you to be a light of the nations, that you will be for salvation to the extremities of the inhabited earth.

48. When the Gentiles heard this, they were glad, and glorified the Word of God: and as many as were appointed into infinite life believed.

49. And the word of the Lord was spoken out throughout all the region.

50. But the Jews stirred up the devout and honorable women, and the chief men of the city, and raised persecution against Paul and Barnabas, and expelled them out of their borders.

51. But they shook off the dust of their feet against them and came to Iconium.

52. And the disciples were filled with joy and with the Holy Spirit.

Chapter 14

1. And it came to pass in Iconium that they both went together into the synagogue of the Jews and so spoke, that a great multitude both of the Jews and also of the Greeks believed.

2. But the unbelieving Jews stirred up the Greeks and poisoned their minds against the brothers.

3. Therefore, they stayed there a long time speaking boldly in the Lord, who gave testimony to the Word of His grace, and granted signs and wonders to be done by their hands.

4. But the multitude of the city was divided: and part agreed with the Jews, and part with the apostles.

5. When there was a violent assault made both by the Greeks and also of the Jews with their rulers, to abuse them and to stone them,

6. They were aware of it, and fled to Lystra and Derbe, cities of Lycaonia, and the surrounding region:

7. And there they preached the gospel.

8. Now there sat a certain man at Lystra, sick in his feet, being a cripple from his mother's womb, who never walked:

9. The same heard Paul speak: who steadfastly beholding him, and perceiving that he had faith to be healed,

10. Said with a loud voice, stand upright on your feet! Then he leaped and walked.

11. When the people saw what Paul had done, they lifted up their voices, saying in the speech of Lycaonia, the gods have come down to us in the likeness of men!

12. For they called Barnabas, Jupiter; and Paul, Mercury, because he was the chief speaker.

13. Then the priest of Jupiter, who was before their city, brought oxen and garlands to the gates and would have done sacrifice with the people.

14. Which when the apostles, Barnabas and Paul, heard of, they tore their clothes, and ran in among the people, crying out,

15. And saying, Sirs, why do you do these things? We also are men of like passions with you and preach to you that you should turn from these useless things to the living God, who made heaven, and earth, and the sea, and all things that are in them:

16. Who in times past permitted all nations to walk in their own ways.

17. Nevertheless, He left not Himself without witness, in that He did good, and gave us rain from heaven, and fruitful seasons, filling our hearts with food and gladness.

18. Even with these sayings they barely restrained the people that they should not sacrifice to them.
19. Then there came to there certain Jews from Antioch and Iconium, who persuaded the people, and having stoned Paul, took him out of the city, supposing he was dead.
20. However, as the disciples stood around him, he rose up, and came into the city: and the next day he left with Barnabas to Derbe.
21. When they had preached the gospel to that city and had taught many, they went back to Lystra, and Iconium, and Antioch,
22. Strengthening the souls of the disciples, and exhorting them to continue in the faith, and that we must through much tribulation enter into the kingdom of God.
23. When they had appointed them elders in every assembly, and had prayed with fasting, they commended them to the Lord, in whom they believed.
24. After they had passed through Pisidia, they came to Pamphylia.
25. When they had preached the word in Perga, they went down into Attalia:
26. From there sailed to Antioch, from where they had been consigned to the grace of God for the work which they fulfilled.
27. So, when they had come, and had gathered the assembly together, they rehearsed all that God had done with them, and how He had opened the door of faith to the nations.
28. And there they stayed a long time with the disciples.

Chapter 15

1. And certain men which came down from Judea taught the brothers, and said, unless you are circumcised after the manner of Moses, you cannot be saved.
2. Therefore, when Paul and Barnabas had no small dissension and dispute with them, they determined that Paul and Barnabas, and certain others of them, should go up to Jerusalem to the apostles and elders about this question.
3. And being brought on their way by the assembly, they passed through Phoenicia and Samaria, explaining the conversion of the nations: and they caused great joy to all the brothers.
4. So, when they had come to Jerusalem, they were received by the assembly, and by the apostles and elders, and they declared all things that God had done with them.
5. But there rose up certain of the sect of the Pharisees who believed, saying, that it was necessary to circumcise them and to command them to keep the Law of Moses.
6. Then the apostles and elders came together to consider this matter.
7. After much dispute, Peter rose up, and said to them, men and brothers, you know that a good while ago God made a selection among us, that the nations by my mouth should hear the word of the gospel, and believe.
8. And God, who knows the hearts, gave them witness, giving them the Holy Spirit, just as He did to us;
9. And put no difference between us and them, purifying their hearts by faith.

10. Therefore, now why tempt God, to put a burden on the back of the disciples, who neither our fathers nor we were able to carry?

11. But we believe that through the grace of the Lord Jesus Christ, we will be saved, just as they.

12. Then all of the multitude kept silent, and listened to Barnabas and Paul, explaining what miracles and wonders God had worked among the nations by them.

13. And after they had held their peace, James answered, saying, men and brothers, listen to me:

14. Simeon has declared how God at the first did visit the nations, to take out of them a people for His name.

15. And to this agree the words of the prophets; as it is written,

16. After this I will return, and will build again the tabernacle of David, which is fallen down; and I will build again the ruins of it, and I will set it up:

17. That the remnant of men might seek after the Lord, and all the nations, upon whom My name is called, says the Lord, who is doing all these things.

18. Known from God are all His works from the beginning of the age.

19. Therefore, my sentence is that we do not cause trouble for them, who from among the nations are turning to God:

20. But that we write to them, that they abstain from pollutions of idols, and sexual immorality, and things strangled, and from blood.

21. Therefore, Moses from the old generations has in every city them that preach him, being read in the synagogues every Sabbath day.

22. Then it pleased the apostles and elders with the entire assembly, to send chosen men of their own company to Antioch with Paul and Barnabas; namely, Judas surnamed Barsabas and Silas, chief men among the brothers:

23. And they wrote letters by them after this manner; the apostles and elders and brothers send greetings to the brothers who are of the nations in Antioch and Syria and Cilicia.

24. Since, as we have heard, that certain who went out from us have troubled you with words, subverting your souls, saying, you must be circumcised, and keep the Law: to who we gave no such commandment:

25. It seemed good to us, being assembled with one accord, to send chosen men to you with our beloved Barnabas and Paul,

26. Men who have risked their lives in the name of our Lord Jesus Christ.

27. Therefore, we have sent Judas and Silas, who will also tell you the same things by mouth.

28. For it seemed good to the Holy Spirit, and to us, to lay upon you no greater burden than these necessary things;

29. That you abstain from foods offered to idols, and from blood, and things strangled, and from sexual immorality: from which if you keep yourselves, you will do well. Farewell.

30. So, when they were dismissed, they came to Antioch: and when they had gathered the multitude together, they delivered the letter:
31. When they had read, they rejoiced for the encouragement.
32. Also, Judas and Silas, being prophets themselves, exhorted the brothers with many words, and strengthened them.
33. After they had stayed there a while, they were let go in peace from the brothers to the apostles.
34. Not with standing it pleased Silas to stay there still.
35. Paul also and Barnabas continued in Antioch, teaching and preaching the word of the Lord, with many others also.
36. And some days after Paul said to Barnabas, let us go again and visit our brothers in every city where we have preached the word of the LORD, and see how they do.
37. And Barnabas determined to take with them John, whose surname was Mark.
38. But Paul thought it is not good to take him with them, who left them at Pamphylia and did not continue with them in the work.
39. And the contention was so sharp between them, that they left one another: and so, Barnabas took Mark, and sailed to Cyprus;
40. And Paul chose Silas, and left, being recommended by the brothers to the grace of God.
41. So, he went through Syria and Cilicia, strengthening the assemblies.

Chapter 16

1. Then he came to Derbe and Lystra: and, behold, a certain disciple was there, named Timothy, the son of a certain woman, who was a Jewess, and believed; but his father was a Greek:
2. Who was well reported by the brothers that were at Lystra and Iconium.
3. Paul would have him accompany him; and took and circumcised him because of the Jews who were in those areas: for they all knew that his father was a Greek.
4. As they went through the cities, they delivered them the decrees to keep, that were appointed by the apostles and elders who were at Jerusalem.
5. So, were the assemblies established in the faith, and increased in number daily.
6. Now when they had gone throughout Phrygia and the region of Galatia, but were forbidden by the Holy Spirit to preach the word in Asia,
7. After they had come to Mysia, they attempted to go into Bithynia: but the Spirit permitted them not.
8. And they passed by Mysia and came down to Troas.
9. Then a vision appeared to Paul in the night; there stood a man of Macedonia, and pleaded with him, saying, Come over into Macedonia, and help us!
10. So, after he had seen the vision, immediately we tried to go into Macedonia, concluding that the Lord had called us to preach the gospel to them.
11. Therefore, sailing from Troas, we came with a straight course to Samothrace, and the next day to Neapolis;

12. And from there to Philippi, which is the chief city of that part of Macedonia, and a colony: and we were in that city staying several days.

13. On the Sabbath we went out of the city by a river side, where prayer was regularly made; and we sat down, and spoke to the women who met there.

14. And a certain woman named Lydia, a seller of purple, of the city of Thyatira, who worshiped God, heard us: whose heart the Lord opened, that she understood the things which were spoken by Paul.

15. When she was immersed, and her household, she asked us, saying, if you have judged me to be faithful to the Lord, come into my house, and stay there. And she persuaded us.

16. And it came to pass, as we went to prayer, a certain girl possessed with a spirit of divination met us, who brought her masters much money by fortune-telling:

17. The same followed Paul and us, and cried, saying, these men are the servants of the Most High God, who show us the way of salvation.

18. For this did she many days. But Paul, being grieved, turned and said to the spirit, I command you in the name of Jesus Christ to come out of her. So, he came out at the same hour.

19. But when her masters saw that the hope of their profit was gone, they took Paul and Silas, and dragged them into the marketplace to the rulers,

20. And brought them to the magistrates, saying, these men, being Jews, do exceedingly trouble our city,

21. And teach customs, that are not lawful for us to receive, neither to follow, being Romans.

22. Then the multitude rose up together against them: and the magistrates tore off their clothes, and commanded to beat them.

23. When they had laid many stripes upon them, they cast them into prison, charging the jailer to keep them safe:

24. Who, having received such a charge, thrust them into the inner prison, and made their feet fast in the stocks.

25. At midnight Paul and Silas prayed, and sang praises to God: and the prisoners heard them.

26. For suddenly there was a great earthquake so that the foundations of the prison were shaken: and immediately all the doors were opened, and everyone's chains fell off.

27. And the keeper of the prison awaking out of his sleep, and seeing the prison doors open, he drew out his sword, and was about to kill himself, supposing that the prisoners had fled.

28. But Paul cried with a loud voice, saying, do yourself no harm: for we are all here!

29. Then he called for a light, and sprang in, and came trembling, and fell down before Paul and Silas,

30. And brought them out, and said, Sirs, what must I do to be saved?

31. Then they said, believe on the Lord Jesus Christ, and you will be saved, and your house.

32. So, they spoke to him the word of the Lord, and to all that were in his house.

33. Then he brought them the same hour of the night, and washed their stripes; and was immersed, he and all his, immediately.
34. So, when he had brought them into his house, he placed food before them, and rejoiced, believing in God with all his house.
35. When it was day, the magistrates sent the rod bearers, saying, let those men go.
36. And the keeper of the prison told this saying to Paul, the magistrates have sent to let you go: therefore, now leave, and go in peace.
37. But Paul said to them, they have beaten us openly without a trial, being Romans, and have cast us into prison; and now do they throw us out secretly? No, truthfully; but let them come themselves and escort us out.
38. And the rod bearers told these words to the magistrates: and they feared when they heard that they were Romans.
39. So, they came and sought them, and escorted them out, and wanted them to depart out of the city.
40. Then they went out of the prison, and entered into the house of Lydia: and when they had seen the brothers, they comforted them, and left.

Chapter 17

1. Now when they had passed through Amphipolis and Apollonia, they came to Thessalonica, which was a synagogue of the Jews:
2. And Paul, as his manner was, went into them, and three Sabbath days reasoned with them out of the scriptures,
3. Explaining and demonstrating, that Christ needed to suffer, and rise again from the dead; and that this Jesus, whom I preach to you, is Christ.
4. And some of them believed, and joined Paul and Silas; and of the devout Greeks a great multitude, and the chief women, not a few.
5. But the Jews who did not believe, moved with envy, took to them certain lewd fellows of the baser sort, and gathered a mob, and set all the city in an uproar, and assaulted the house of Jason, and sought to take them out to the people.
6. And when they found them not, they dragged Jason and certain brothers to the rulers of the city, crying, these that have turned the Roman world upside down have come here also;
7. Who Jason has received: and these all do contrary to the decrees of Caesar, saying that there is another king, one Jesus!
8. Then they troubled the people and the rulers of the city when they heard these things.
9. When they had taken security from Jason, and from the other, they let them go.
10. Immediately the brothers sent away Paul and Silas by night to Berea: who coming there went into the synagogue of the Jews.
11. These were more noble-minded than those in Thessalonica, in that they received the word with all eagerness, and searched the Scriptures daily, to find out whether these things were so.
12. Therefore, many of them also believed; also, of honorable women who were Greeks, and men, not a small number.

13. But when the Jews of Thessalonica were aware that the word of God was preached by Paul at Berea, they came there also and stirred up the people.

14. Immediately the brothers then sent away Paul to go as it were to the sea: but Silas and Timothy stayed there still.

15. And they that conducted Paul brought him to Athens: and receiving a commandment to Silas and Timothy to come to him with all speed, they left.

16. Now while Paul waited for them at Athens, his spirit was stirred in him, when he saw the city given to idolatry.

17. Therefore, he disputed in the synagogue with the Jews, and with the devout persons, and in the market daily with them that met with him.

18. Then certain philosophers of the Epicureans, and the Stoics, encountered him. And some said, what will this gossiper say? He seems to be a proclaimer of strange gods: because he preached to them Jesus and the resurrection.

19. So, they took him, and brought him to Areopagus, saying, may we know what this new doctrine, of which you speak, is?

20. For you bring certain strange things to our ears: Therefore, we want to know what these things mean.

21. For all the Athenians and strangers who were there spent their time in nothing else, but either to tell or to hear some new thing.

22. Then Paul stood in the middle of Mars' Hill, and said, you men of Athens, I perceive that in all things you are too superstitious.

23. For as I passed by, and beheld your devotions, I found an altar with this inscription, TO THE UNKNOWN GOD. Therefore, who you ignorantly worship, I declare Him to you.

24. God that made the world and all things in it, seeing that He is Lord of heaven and earth, dwells not in temples made with hands;

25. Neither is worshiped with men's hands, as though He needed anything, seeing He gives to all life and breath, and all things;

26. And has made of one blood all nations of men for to dwell on all the face of the ground, and has determined the times before appointed, and the bounds of their habitation;

27. That they should seek the Lord, in the hope that they might grasp after Him, and find Him, though He is not far from all of us:

28. For in Him we live, and move, and have our being; as certain also of your own poets have said, for we are also His offspring.

29. Since, we are the offspring of God, we ought not to think that the Godhead is like gold, or silver, or stone, something shaped by art and man's making.

30. And the times of this ignorance God winked at; but now commands all men everywhere to repent:

31. Because He has appointed a day, in which He is about to judge the Roman world in righteousness by that Man whom He has appointed; of which He has given assurance to all men, in that He has raised Him from the dead.

32. When they heard of the resurrection of the dead, some mocked: and others said, we will hear you again on this matter.
33. So, Paul departed from among them.
34. However certain men joined him and believed: among them was Dionysius the Areopagite, a woman named Damaris, and others with them.

Chapter 18

1. After these things Paul left Athens, and came to Corinth;
2. And found a certain Jew named Aquila, born in Pontus, lately come from Italy, with his wife Priscilla;
3. (because Claudius Caesar had commanded all Jews to depart from Rome:) and came to them.
4. Because he was of the same trade, he stayed with them and worked: for by their occupation they were tent-makers.
5. Then he reasoned in the synagogue every Sabbath and persuaded the Jews and the Greeks. When Silas and Timothy had come from Macedonia, Paul was compelled by the Word, and testified to the Jews, that Christ was Jesus.
6. But when they opposed him, and blasphemed, he shook his clothing, and said to them, your blood be on your own heads; I am clean; from now on I will go to the nations.
7. Then he departed, and entered into a certain man's house, named Justus, one that worshiped God, whose house was next door to the synagogue.
8. And Crispus, the chief ruler of the synagogue, believed on the Lord with all his house; and many of the Corinthians hearing believed, and were immersed.
9. Then the Lord spoke to Paul in the night by a vision, Be not afraid, but speak, and hold not your peace:
10. For I am with you, and no man will attack you to hurt you: For I have many people in this city.
11. So, he continued there a year and a half, teaching the word of God among them.
12. When Gallio was the proconsul of Achaia; the Jews made insurrection with one accord against Paul, and brought him to the judgment seat,
13. Saying this fellow persuades men to worship God contrary to the Law.
14. And when Paul was about to open his mouth, Gallio said to the Jews, if it were a matter of wrong or wicked crimes, O you Jews, reason would that I should bear with you:
15. But if it be a question of words and names, and of your Law, look you to it; for I will not be the judge of such matters.
16. Then he drove them from the judgment seat.
17. Then all the Greeks took Sosthenes, the chief ruler of the synagogue, and beat him before the judgment seat. And Gallio cared for none of those things.
18. So, Paul after this stayed there yet a good while, and then took his leave of the brothers, and sailed from there into Syria, and with him Priscilla and Aquila; having shaved his head in Cenchrea: for he had a vow.

19. So, he came to Ephesus, and left them there: but he himself entered into the synagogue, and reasoned with the Jews.
20. When they wanted him to stay a longer time with them, he did not consent;
21. But told them goodbye, and said, I must, by all means, keep this feast that comes in Jerusalem: but I will return to you, if God wills. So, he sailed from Ephesus.
22. When he had landed at Caesarea, and gone up, and greeted the assembly, he went down to Antioch.
23. After he had spent some time there, he departed, and went over all the country of Galatia and Phrygia in order, to strengthen all the disciples.
24. And a certain Jew named Apollos, born at Alexandria, an eloquent man, and mighty in the Scriptures, came to Ephesus.
25. This man was instructed in the way of the Lord; and being fervent in spirit, he spoke and taught diligently the things of the Lord, knowing only the immersion of John.
26. So, he began to speak boldly in the synagogue: who when Aquila and Priscilla heard, they led him to them, and explained to him the way of God more accurately.
27. When he wanted to cross into Achaia, the brothers wrote, exhorting the disciples to receive him: who, when he had come, helped them much who had believed through grace.
28. For he mightily convinced the Jews, and that publicly, showing by the Scriptures that Jesus was Christ.

Chapter 19

1. And it came to pass, that, while Apollos was at Corinth, Paul having passed through the upper borders came to Ephesus: and finding certain disciples,
2. He said to them, have you received the Holy Spirit since you believed? But they said to him, we have not so much as heard whether there is any Holy Spirit.
3. So, he said to them, into what then were you immersed? And they said, into John's immersion.
4. Then Paul said, John truthfully immersed with the immersion of repentance, saying to the people, that they should believe in Him who should come after him, that is, in Christ Jesus.
5. When they heard this, they were immersed in the name of the Lord Jesus.
6. Then when Paul laid his hands upon them, the Holy Spirit came on them; and they spoke with tongues, and prophesied.
7. And all the men were about twelve.
8. So, he went into the synagogue and spoke boldly for three months, reasoning and persuading the things concerning the kingdom of God.
9. But when some were hardened and believed not, but spoke evil of that Way before the multitude, he departed from them, and withdrew the disciples, reasoning daily in the school of Tyrannus.
10. And this continued for two years; so that all they who dwelt in Asia heard the word of the Lord Jesus, both Jews and Greeks.
11. And God worked special miracles by the hands of Paul:

12. So, that from his body were brought to the sick handkerchiefs or aprons, and the diseases departed from them, and the evil spirits went out of them.

13. Then certain of the traveling Jewish exorcists, took upon them to call over those who had evil spirits in the name of the LORD Jesus, saying, we exorcise you by Jesus whom Paul preaches.

14. And there were seven sons of one Sceva, a Jew, and chief of the priests, who did so.

15. But the evil spirit answered and said, Jesus, I know, and Paul I know; but who are you?

16. And the man in whom the evil spirit leaped on them, and overcame them, and prevailed against them so that they fled out of that house naked and wounded.

17. Then this became known to all the Jews and Greeks also dwelling at Ephesus, and fear fell on them all, and the name of the Lord Jesus was magnified.

18. For many that believed came, and confessed, and showed their deeds.

19. Many of them also which practiced magic brought their books together, and burned them before all men: and they counted the price of them, and found it fifty thousand pieces of silver.

20. So, mightily grew the Word of God and prevailed.

21. After these things were ended, Paul purposed in the spirit, when he had passed through Macedonia and Achaia, to go to Jerusalem, saying, after I have been there, I must also see Rome.

22. So, he sent into Macedonia two of them that assisted him, Timothy and Erastus; but he stayed in Asia for a season.

23. And the same time there arose a great commotion about the Way.

24. For a certain man named Demetrius, a silversmith, who made silver shrines for Artemis, brought no small profit to the craftsmen;

25. Whom he called together with the workmen of like occupation, and said, Sirs, you know that by this trade we have our wealth.

26. Moreover, you see and hear, that not only at Ephesus but almost throughout all of Asia, this Paul has persuaded and turned away many people, saying that they are no gods, which are made with hands:

27. So, that not only this our trade is in danger of falling into disrepute; but also, that the temple of the great goddess Artemis is about to be despised, and her magnificence should be destroyed, whom all Asia and the Roman world worships.

28. When they heard these sayings, they were full of wrath, and cried out, saying, great is Artemis of the Ephesians!

29. Then the whole city was filled with confusion: and having caught Gaius and Aristarchus, men of Macedonia, Paul's companions in travel, they rushed with one accord into the theater.

30. When Paul would have entered into the people, the disciples did not permit it.

31. For certain of the leaders of Asia, who were his friends, sent to him, pleading with him that he would not enter into the theater.

32. Therefore, some cried one thing, and some another: for the assembly was confused: and most did not know why they had come together.

33. Then they took Alexander out of the multitude, the Jews putting him forward. And Alexander motioned with the hand and would have made his defense to the people.

34. But when they knew that he was a Jew, all with one voice for about two hours cried out, great is Artemis of the Ephesians!

35. When the city clerk had appeased the people, he said, You men of Ephesus, what man is there that knows not that the city of the Ephesians is a worshiper of the great goddess Artemis, and of the image which fell down from Zeus?

36. Seeing then that these things cannot be spoken against, you ought to be quiet, and to do nothing rashly.

37. For you have brought to hear these men, who are neither robbers of assemblies, nor yet blasphemers of your goddess.

38. Therefore, if Demetrius, and the craftsmen who are with him, have a matter against any man, the courts are open, and there are proconsuls: let them settle it there.

39. But if you inquire anything concerning other matters, it will be determined in a lawful assembly.

40. For we are in danger of being called into question for this day's riot, there being no reason by which we may give an account for this uproar.

41. When he had so spoken, he dismissed the assembly.

Chapter 20

1. After the uproar stopped, Paul called to him the disciples embraced them and left to go into Macedonia.

2. When he had gone over those parts and had given them much exhortation, he came into Greece,

3. And they stayed three months. And when the Jews laid an ambush for him, as he was about to sail into Syria, he decided to return through Macedonia.

4. Now there accompanied him into Asia Sopater of Berea; and of the Thessalonians, Aristarchus and Secundus; and Gaius of Derbe, and Timothy; and of Asia, Tychicus and Trophimus.

5. These going before waited for us at Troas.

6. So, we sailed away from Philippi after the Days of Unleavened Bread, and came to them to Troas in five days; where we stayed seven days.

7. Then on the first day of the week, when the disciples came together to break bread, Paul spoke with them, about to leave the next day; and continued his message until midnight.

8. For there were many lights in the upper chamber, where they were gathered together.

9. And there sat in a window a certain young man named Eutychus, having fallen into a deep sleep: and as Paul was long speaking, he sunk down with sleep, and fell down from the third loft, and was taken up dead.

10. But Paul went down and fell on him, and embracing him said, Trouble not yourselves; for his life is in him.

11. Therefore, when he had come up again, and had broken bread, and eaten, and discussed a long while, even until break of day, so he departed.
12. Then they brought the young man alive and were very comforted.
13. For we went ahead to the ship, and sailed to Assos, intending to take Paul on board: for so he had arranged, about to go by foot.
14. When he met with us at Assos, we took him aboard and came to Mitylene.
15. Then we sailed from there and came the next day opposite Chios, and the next day we arrived at Samos and stayed at Trogyllium, and the next day we came to Miletus.
16. For Paul had determined to sail by Ephesus, because he would not spend the time in Asia: for he hurried, if it were possible for him, to be at Jerusalem on the Day of Pentecost.
17. And from Miletus he sent to Ephesus and called the elders of the assembly.
18. Then when they had come to him, he said to them, You know, from the first day that I came into Asia, in what manner I have lived with you in all seasons,
19. Serving the LORD with all humility of mind, and with many tears, and temptations, which befell me by the ambush of the Jews:
20. And how I did not shrink, not the least to bring together what was profitable to you, but have made known to you, and have taught you publicly, and from house to house,
21. Testifying both to the Jews, and also to the Greeks, repentance toward God, and faith toward our Lord Jesus Christ.
22. Now, behold, I go bound in spirit to Jerusalem, not knowing the things that will happen to me there:
23. Except that the Holy Spirit testifies repeatedly in every city, saying that chains and afflictions await me.
24. But none of these things move me, neither do I count my soul dear to myself, so that I might finish my race with joy, and the ministry, which I have received from the Lord Jesus, to solemnly affirm the gospel of the grace of God.
25. Now, behold, I know that you all, among whom I have gone preaching the kingdom of God, will not see my face any longer.
26. Therefore, I testify to you this day that I am innocent from the blood of all men.
27. For I did not shrink from making you aware of the totality of the purpose of God.
28. Therefore, take heed to yourselves, and to all the flock, over which the Holy Spirit has made you overseers, to shepherd the assembly of God, whom He has purchased with His own blood.
29. For I know this, that after my departure savage wolves will enter in among you, not sparing the flock.
30. Also, of your own selves will men arise, speaking distorted things, to draw away disciples after them.
31. Therefore, pay attention and rehearse that during the three years, I did not pause to put into your mind's night and day with tears.
32. So now, brothers, I commend you to God, and to the Word of His grace, which is able to build you up and to give you an inheritance among all those who are sanctified.

33. I have coveted no man's silver, or gold, or clothing.

34. Yes, you know that these hands have worked for my needs, and for them that were with me.

35. I have showed you all things, that so laboring you ought to support the weak, and to remember the words of the Lord Jesus, how He said, it is more blessed to give than to receive.

36. When he had so spoken, he kneeled down and prayed with them all.

37. And they all wept intensely, and fell on Paul's neck, and kissed him,

38. Sorrowing most of all for the words which he spoke, that they were about to see his face no more. And they accompanied him to the ship.

Chapter 21

1. And it came to pass, that after we had departed from them, and had launched, we came with a straight course to Coos, and the day following to Rhodes, and from there to Patara:

2. And finding a ship sailing over to Phoenicia, we went aboard and set sail.

3. Now when we had discovered Cyprus, we left it on the left hand, sailed into Syria, and landed at Tyre: for there the ship was to unload her cargo.

4. And finding disciples, we stayed there seven days: who said to Paul through the Spirit, that he should not go up to Jerusalem.

5. Now when we had accomplished those days, we departed and went our way; and they all brought us on our way, with wives and children, until we were out of the city: and we kneeled down on the shore, and prayed.

6. When we had taken our leave of one another, we boarded the ship; and they returned home again.

7. So, when we had finished our course from Tyre, we came to Ptolemais and greeted the brothers, and stayed with them one day.

8. Then the next day we that were of Paul's companions departed, and came to Caesarea: and we entered into the house of Philip the evangelist, who was one of the seven; and stayed with him.

9. For the same man had four daughters, virgins, who did prophesy.

10. As we stayed there many days, there came down from Judea a certain prophet, named Agabus.

11. When he had come to us, he took Paul's belt and bound his own hands and feet, and said, thus says the Holy Spirit, So will the Jews at Jerusalem bind the man that owns this belt and will take him into the hands of the nations.

12. So, when we heard these things, both we and they of that place, asked him not to go up to Jerusalem.

13. Then Paul answered, what are you doing, crying and disheartening me? For I am ready not to be bound only, but also to die at Jerusalem for the name of the Lord Jesus.

14. Then when he would not be persuaded, we stopped, and said, the will of the Lord be done.

15. After those days we packed, and went up to Jerusalem.

16. There went with us also certain of the disciples of Caesarea and brought with them one Mnason of Cyprus, an early disciple, with whom we should lodge.

17. When we had come to Jerusalem, the brothers received us gladly.

18. And the following day Paul went in with us to James; and all the elders were present.

19. When he had greeted them, he explained in detail what things God had done among the nations by his ministry.

20. When they heard it, they glorified the Lord, and said to him, You see, brother, how many thousands of Jews there are who believe; and they are all zealous for the Law:

21. For they are informed of you, that you teach all the Jews who are among the nations to forsake Moses, saying that they ought not to circumcise their children, neither to walk after the customs.

22. What then? The assembly must come together: for they will hear that you have come.

23. Therefore, do what we say: we have four men who have a vow on them;

24. Them take, and purify yourself with them, and pay their expenses, that they may shave their heads: and all may know that those things, of which they were informed concerning you, are nothing; but that you also walk orderly, and keep the Law.

25. As concerning the nations who believe, we have written and concluded that they observe no such thing, except that they keep themselves from things offered to idols, and from blood, and from strangled, and from sexual immorality.

26. Then Paul took the men, and the next day purifying himself with them entered into the temple, to signify the accomplishment of the days of purification, until that an offering should be offered for every one of them.

27. And when the seven days were about to end, the Jews who were of Asia, when they saw him in the temple, stirred up all the people, and laid hands on him,

28. Crying out, Men of Israel, help: this is the man, that teaches all men everywhere against the people, and the Law, and this place: and further brought Greeks also into the temple, and has polluted this holy place!

29. (For they had seen before with him in the city Trophimus an Ephesian, who they supposed that Paul had brought into the temple.)

30. Then all the city was moved, and the people ran together: and they took Paul, and dragged him out of the temple: and immediately the doors were shut.

31. Now as they went about to kill him, news came to the chief captain of the cohort that all Jerusalem was in an uproar.

32. Who immediately took soldiers and centurions, and ran down to them: and when they saw the chief captain and the soldiers, they stopped beating Paul.

33. Then the chief captain came near and took him, and commanded him to be bound with two chains, and demanded who he was, and what he had done.

34. For some cried one thing, some another, among the multitude: and when he could not know the certainty for the riot, he commanded him to be carried into the fortress.

35. When he came upon the stairs, so it was, that he was carried by the soldiers because of the violence of the mob.
36. Therefore, a multitude of the people followed after, crying, away with him!
37. So, as Paul was about to be led into the fortress, he said to the chief captain, may I speak to you? Who said, can you speak Greek?
38. Are you not that Egyptian, who before these days made an uprising, and led out into the wilderness four thousand men who were assassins?
39. But Paul said I am a Jewish man of Tarsus, a city in Cilicia, a citizen of no small city: and, I implore you, permit me to speak to the people.
40. When he had given him permission, Paul stood on the stairs and motioned with his hand to the people. And when there was made a great silence, he spoke to them in the Hebrew tongue, saying,

Chapter 22

1. Men, brothers, and fathers hear my defense which I make now to you.
2. For when they heard that he spoke in the Hebrew tongue to them, they kept the more silence: and he said,
3. I am truthfully a man, a Jew, born in Tarsus, a city in Cilicia, yet brought up in this city at the feet of Gamaliel, and taught according to the precise manner of the Law of the fathers, and was zealous toward God, as you all are this day.
4. And I persecuted this way to the death, binding and delivering into prisons both men and women.
5. As also the high priest does bear me witness, and all the council of the elders: from whom also I received letters to the brothers, and went to Damascus, to bring those who were there bound to Jerusalem, to be punished.
6. And it came to pass, that, as I made my journey, and had come close to Damascus about noon, suddenly there shone from heaven a great light around me.
7. And I fell to the ground, and heard a voice saying to me, Saul, Saul, why are you persecuting Me?
8. And I answered, who are you, Lord? And He said to me, I am Jesus of Nazareth, whom you are persecuting.
9. Then they that were with me saw the light and were afraid, but they heard not the voice of Him that spoke to me.
10. And I said, what will I be doing, Lord? And the Lord said to me, arise, and go into Damascus; and there it will be told you all things which are appointed for you to do.
11. When I could not see for the glory of that light, being led by the hand of them that were with me, I came into Damascus.
12. Then one Ananias, a devout man according to the Law, having a good reputation of all the Jews who dwelt there,
13. Came to me and stood, and said to me, brother Saul, receive your sight. And the same hour I looked up at him.
14. And he said, the God of our fathers has chosen you, that you should know His will, and see that Just One, and should hear the voice of His mouth.

15. For you will be His witness to all men of what you have seen and heard.
16. And now why are you waiting? Arise, and be immersed, and wash away your sins, calling on the name of the Lord.
17. And it came to pass, that, when I had come again to Jerusalem, even while I prayed in the temple, I was in a trance;
18. And saw Him saying to me, make haste, and get quickly out of Jerusalem: for they will not receive your testimony concerning Me.
19. And I said, Lord, they know that I imprisoned and beat in every synagogue them that believed in You:
20. And when the blood of Your martyr Stephen was shed, I also was standing by, and consenting to his death, and kept the clothing of them that were murdering him.
21. But He said to me, depart: for I will send you far from here to the nations.
22. And they listened to him until this word, and then lifted up their voices, and said, away with such a fellow from the earth: for it is not fit that he should live!
23. As they cried out, and cast off their clothes, and threw dust into the air,
24. The chief captain commanded him to be brought into the fortress and said that he should be examined by scourging; that he might know why they cried so against him.
25. As they bound him with thongs, Paul said to the centurion that stood by, is it lawful for you to whip a man that is a Roman, and without being tried?
26. When the centurion heard that, he went and told the chief captain, saying, take heed what you are about to do: for this man is a Roman.
27. Then the chief captain came and said to him, tell me, are you a Roman? He said, yes.
28. So, the chief captain answered, with a great sum I obtained this freedom. And Paul said, but I was free born.
29. Immediately they departed from him who was about to examine him: and the chief captain also was afraid, after he knew that he was a Roman, and because he had bound him.
30. On the next day, because he would have known the certainty why he was accused by the Jews, he untied him from his bonds, and commanded the chief priests and all their council to appear, and brought Paul down, and placed him before them.

Chapter 23

1. And Paul, earnestly beholding the council, said, men and brothers, I have lived in all good conscience before God until this day.
2. And the high priest Ananias commanded them that stood by him to strike him on the mouth.
3. Then said Paul to him, God is about to strike you, you whitewashed wall! For do you sit to judge me after the Law, yet command me to be struck contrary to the Law?
4. And they that stood by said, do you revile God's high priest?
5. Then said Paul, I did not know, brothers, that he was the high priest: for it is written, you will not speak evil of the ruler of your people.

6. But when Paul perceived that the one part was Sadducees and the other Pharisees, he cried out in the council, men and brothers, I am a Pharisee, the son of a Pharisee: concerning the hope and resurrection of the dead I am being judged!

7. When he had so said, there arose a dissension between the Pharisees and the Sadducees: and the multitude was divided.

8. For the Sadducees say that there is no resurrection, neither angel nor spirit: but the Pharisees confess both.

9. Then there arose a great cry: and the scribes that were of the Pharisees' group arose, and protested, saying, we find no evil in this man: what if a spirit or an angel has spoken to him, let us not fight against God.

10. So, when there arose a great dissension, the chief captain, fearing that Paul should have been pulled in pieces by them, commanded the soldiers to go down, and to take him by force from among them, and to bring him into the fortress.

11. And the following night the Lord stood by him, and said, be of good cheer, Paul: for as you have testified about Me in Jerusalem, so must you bear witness also at Rome.

12. When it was day, certain of the Jews banded together, and bound themselves under an oath, saying that they would neither eat nor drink until they had killed Paul.

13. There were more than forty who had made this conspiracy.

14. Then they came to the chief priests and elders, and said, we have bound ourselves under a great oath, that we will eat nothing until we have killed Paul.

15. Therefore, now you with the council suggest to the chief captain that he bring him down to you tomorrow, as though you would inquire something more accurately concerning him: and we, if ever he comes near, are about to kill him.

16. So, when Paul's sister's son heard of their ambush, he went and entered into the fortress, and told Paul.

17. Then Paul called one of the centurions to him, and said, bring this young man to the chief captain: for he has a certain thing to tell him.

18. So, he brought him and led him to the chief captain, and said, Paul, the prisoner called me to him and asked me to bring this young man to you, who has something to say to you.

19. Then the chief captain held him by the hand, and went with him aside secretly, and asked him, what do you have to tell me?

20. And he said, The Jews have agreed to ask you that you would bring down Paul tomorrow into the council, as though they are about to inquire somewhat of him more accurately.

21. But do not be persuaded by them: for an ambush waits for him of more than forty men, who have bound themselves with an oath that they will neither eat nor drink until they have killed him: and now they are ready, expecting an order from you.

22. So, the chief captain then let the young man leave, and charged him, see you tell no man that you have showed these things to me.

23. And he called to him two centurions, saying, prepare two hundred soldiers to go to Caesarea, and seventy horsemen, and two hundred spearmen, at the third hour of the night;
24. And provide them horses, that they may set Paul on, and bring him safely to Felix the governor.
25. And he wrote a letter in the following manner:
26. Claudius Lysias to the most excellent governor Felix sends a greeting.
27. This man was taken by the Jews, and was about to be killed by them: then came I with a cohort, and rescued him, having understood that he was a Roman.
28. When I would have known the reason why they accused him, I brought him out into their council:
29. Whom I perceived to be accused by questions of their Law, but to have nothing charged against him worthy of death or bonds.
30. When it was told to me that the Jews laid an ambush for the man, I sent immediately to you and gave instructions to his accusers to say what they had against him before you.
31. Then the soldiers, as it was commanded them, took Paul, and brought him by night to Antipatris.
32. On the next day they left the horsemen to go with him, and returned to the fortress:
33. Who, when they came to Caesarea and delivered the letter to the governor, presented Paul also before him.
34. When the governor had read the letter, he asked what province (of the ten) he was from. And when he understood that he was of Cilicia;
35. I will hear you, said he, when your accusers have also come. So, he commanded him to be kept in Herod's Praetorium.

Chapter 24

1. And after five days Ananias the high priest came down with the elders, and with a certain orator named Tertullus, who informed the governor against Paul.
2. When he was called out, Tertullus began to accuse him, and said, seeing that by you we enjoy great peace, and that prosperity has come to this nation by your rule,
3. We accept it always, and in all places, most noble Felix, with all thankfulness.
4. Not with standing, that I do not further waste your time, I ask that you would hear us briefly by your gracious disposition.
5. For we have found this man a troublemaker, and a mover of sedition among all the Jews throughout the Roman world, and a ringleader of the sect of the Nazarenes:
6. Who also has gone about to profane the temple: who we took, and would have judged according to our Law.
7. But the chief captain Lysias came on us, and with great force took him away out of our hands,
8. Commanding his accusers to come to you: by examining by who yourself may take knowledge of all these things, of which we accuse him.
9. And the Jews also agreed, saying that these things were so.

10. Then Paul, after the governor had motioned to him to speak, answered, since I know that you have been for many years a judge of this nation, I do the more cheerfully answer for myself:

11. Because that you may understand, that there are yet but twelve days since I went up to Jerusalem to worship.

12. And they neither found me in the temple disputing with any man, neither gathering up the people in an uprising, neither in the synagogues nor in the city:

13. Neither can they prove the things of which they now accuse me.

14. But this I confess to you, that after the Way which they call heresy, so I worship the God of my fathers, believing all things which are written in the Law and the prophets:

15. And have hope toward God, who they accept, that there is about to be a resurrection of the dead, both of the just and unjust.

16. This being so I do exercise myself, to always have a conscience void of offense toward God, and toward men.

17. Now after many years I came to bring alms to my nation, and offerings.

18. When certain Jews from Asia found me purified in the temple, neither with multitude nor with an uproar.

19. Who ought to have been here before you, and to speak openly with their charge, if they had anything against me.

20. Or else let these same here say if they have found any evil doing in me, while I stood before the council,

21. Unless it is for this one announcement, that I cried standing among them, concerning the resurrection of the dead I am called in question by you this day.

22. When Felix heard these things, having a more accurate knowledge of the Way, he delayed them, and said, when Lysias the chief captain has come down, I will decide on your case.

23. He then commanded a centurion to keep Paul, and to let him have freedom, and that he should forbid none of his friends to serve or visit him.

24. After some days when Felix came with his wife Drusilla, who was a Jewess, he sent for Paul and heard him concerning the faith in Christ.

25. As he had a conversation with them about righteousness, self-control, and the judgment about to come, Felix became terrified, and answered, go away for now; when I have time, I will call for you.

26. He also hoped that money would be to given him by Paul, that he might free him: therefore, he sent for him frequently, and conversed with him.

27. But after two years Porcius Festus succeeded Felix; and Felix, willing to show the Jews a favor, left Paul locked up.

Chapter 25

1. Now when Festus had come into the province, after three days he went up from Caesarea to Jerusalem.

2. Then the high priest and the chief of the Jews informed him against Paul, and petitioned him,

3. And desired favor against him, that he would send for him to Jerusalem, laying an ambush on the way to kill him.
4. But Festus answered, that Paul should be kept at Caesarea and that he was about to depart there.
5. Let them therefore, he said, who among you are able, go down with me, and accuse this man, if there be any wickedness in him.
6. When he had stayed among them more than ten days, he went down to Caesarea; and the next day sitting on the judgment seat commanded Paul to be brought.
7. When he had come, the Jews who came down from Jerusalem stood around and laid many grievous complaints against Paul, which they could not prove.
8. While he answered for himself, neither against the Law of the Jews, neither against the temple nor yet against Caesar, have I offended anything at all.
9. But Festus, willing to do the Jews a favor, answered Paul, and said, do you want to go up to Jerusalem, and be judged there of these things before me?
10. Then Paul said, I stand at Caesar's judgment seat, where I ought to be judged: to the Jews have I done no wrong, as you very well know.
11. For if I am an offender, or have committed anything worthy of death, I refuse not to die: but if there are none of these things of which these accuse me, no man may deliver me to them. I appeal to Caesar.
12. Then Festus, when he had conferred with the council, answered, have you appealed to Caesar? To Caesar, you will go!
13. After some days King Agrippa and Bernice came to Caesarea to greet Festus.
14. When they had been there many days, Festus explained Paul's case to the king, saying, there is a certain man left in prison by Felix:
15. About who, when I was at Jerusalem, the chief priests and the elders of the Jews informed me, wanting to have judgment against him
16. To whom I answered, it is not the manner of the Romans to deliver any man to destruction, before he who is accused have the accusers face to face, and have opportunity to answer for himself concerning the crime laid against him.
17. Therefore, when they had come together, without any delay, the next day I sat on the judgment seat and commanded the man to be brought out.
18. Against whom when the accusers stood up, they brought no accusation of such things as I supposed:
19. But had certain questions against him about their own religion, and of one Jesus, who was dead, who Paul affirmed to be alive.
20. Because I was perplexed being questioned on such matters, I asked him whether he would go to Jerusalem, and there be judged of these matters.
21. But when Paul had appealed to be guarded for the Emperor's examination, I commanded him to be kept until I might send him.
22. Then Agrippa said to Festus, I also desire to hear the man myself. Tomorrow, he said, you will hear him.

23. On the next day, when Agrippa had come, and Bernice, with great pomp, had entered into the auditorium, with the chief captains, and leading men of the city, at Festus' commandment Paul was brought out.

24. For Festus said, King Agrippa, and all men who are present here with us, you see this man, about whom all the multitude of the Jews have dealt with me, both at Jerusalem, and also here, crying that he ought not to live any longer.

25. But when I found that he had committed nothing worthy of death and that he has appealed to the Emperor's court, I have determined to send him.

26. Of whom I have no certain thing to write to my lord. Therefore, I have brought him out before you, and especially before you, O King Agrippa, that, after investigating, I might have something to write.

27. For it seems to me unreasonable to send a prisoner, and not also to specify the crimes laid against him.

Chapter 26

1. Then Agrippa said to Paul, you are permitted to speak for yourself. Then Paul stretched out the hand, and answered for himself:

2. I think of myself as blessed, King Agrippa, because I am about to answer for myself this day before you concerning all the things of where I am accused by the Jews:

3. Especially because I know you to be expert in all customs and questions which are among the Jews: therefore, I implore you to hear me patiently.

4. My manner of life from my youth, which was at the first among my own nation at Jerusalem, which the Jews all know;

5. Who knew me from the beginning, if they would testify, that after the strictest sect of our religion, I lived a Pharisee.

6. Now I stand and am judged for the hope of the promise made of God, to our fathers:

7. To which promise our twelve tribes, earnestly serving God Day and night, hope to come. For which hope's sake, King Agrippa, I am accused by the Jews.

8. Why should it be thought a thing incredible with you, that God should raise the dead?

9. I truthfully thought with myself, that I ought to do many things contrary to the name of Jesus of Nazareth.

10. Which thing I also did in Jerusalem: and I did shut up many of the saints in prison, having received authority from the chief priests; and when they were put to death, I gave my vote against them.

11. And I punished them often in every synagogue, and compelled them to blaspheme; and being exceedingly mad against them, I persecuted them even to strange cities.

12. Whereas I went to Damascus with authority and commission from the chief priests,

13. At noon, O king, I saw on the way a light from heaven, above the brightness of the sun, shining around me and those who journeyed with me.

14. When we had all fallen to the ground, I heard a voice speaking to me, and saying in the Hebrew tongue, Saul, Saul, why are you persecuting Me? It is rough for you to kick against a sharp object.
15. And I said, who are You, Lord? And He said, I am Jesus, whom you persecute.
16. But rise, and stand on your feet: for I have appeared to you for this purpose, to make you a minister and a witness both of these things which you have seen and of those things in which I will appear to you;
17. Delivering you from the people, and from the nations, now to whom I send you,
18. To open their eyes, and to turn them from darkness to light, and from the power of Satan to God, that they may receive forgiveness of sins, and an inheritance among those who are sanctified by faith in Me.
19. Therefore, O King Agrippa, I was not disobedient to the heavenly vision:
20. But declared first to them of Damascus, and at Jerusalem, and throughout all the borders of Judea, and then to the nations, that they should repent and turn to God, and do works suitable for repentance.
21. For these reasons the Jews caught me in the temple and went about to kill me.
22. Therefore, having obtained help from God, I continue to this day, witnessing both to small and great, saying no other things than those which the prophets and Moses did say were about to come:
23. That Christ should suffer, and that he was about to be the first that should rise from the dead, and should show light to the people, and the nations.
24. As he so spoke for himself, Festus said with a loud voice, Paul, you are beside yourself; much learning does make you insane!
25. But he said, I am not insane, most noble Festus; but speak out the words of truth and reason.
26. For the king understands these things, before whom also I speak freely: for I am persuaded that none of these things are hidden from him; for this thing was not done secretly.
27. King Agrippa, do you believe the prophets? I know that you have faith.
28. Then Agrippa said to Paul, you will shortly persuade me to be a Christian.
29. And Paul said, I pray to God, that not only you but also all that hear me this day, whether shortly or later become as I am, without these chains.
30. When he had so spoken, the king rose up, and the governor, and Bernice, and they that sat with them:
31. When they had gone aside, they talked between themselves, saying, this man has not done anything worthy of death or of chains.
32. Then Agrippa said to Festus, this man might have been set free if he had not appealed to Caesar Nero.

Chapter 27

1. When it was determined that we should sail into Italy, they delivered Paul and certain other prisoners to one named Julius, a centurion of Augustus' cohort.

2. And entering into a ship of Adramyttium, we launched, about to sail by the borders of Asia; one Aristarchus, a Macedonian of Thessalonica came with us.

3. And the next day we landed at Sidon. Julius courteously treated Paul and gave him the freedom to go to his friends to refresh himself.

4. When we had gone to sea from there, we sailed under Cyprus, because the winds were against us.

5. When we had sailed across the sea of Cilicia and Pamphylia, we came to Myra, a city of Lycia.

6. And there the centurion found a ship of Alexandria sailing into Italy, and he put us in it.

7. When we had sailed slowly many days, and scarce had crossed over against Cnidus, the wind not permitting us, we sailed under the shelter of Crete off Salmone;

8. And, hardly passing it, came to a place which is called The Fair Havens; near the city of Lasea.

9. Now when much time was spent, and when sailing was now dangerous because the Fast was now over, Paul advised them,

10. And said to them, Sirs, I perceive that this voyage is about to be with hurt with much damage, not only of the cargo and ship but also of our lives.

11. Nevertheless, the centurion believed the master and the owner of the ship, more than those things which were spoken by Paul.

12. Because the harbor was not suitable for winter, the majority advised to depart from there also, if by any means they might attain to Phoenix, and there to winter; which is a harbor of Crete, and opens toward the southwest and northwest.

13. So, when the south wind blew softly, supposing that they had obtained their purpose, putting out from there, they sailed close by Crete.

14. But not long after this there arose against it a tempestuous wind, called Euroclydon.

15. And when the ship was caught, and could not head up into the wind, we let her drive.

16. And running under a certain island which is called Clauda, we secured the smaller boat with difficulty:

17. Which when they had taken up, they used helps, undergirding the ship; and, fearing unless they should fall into the sand bars, struck sail, and so were driven.

18. Then we being exceedingly tossed with a tempest, the next day they lightened the ship;

19. And on the third day we cast out with our own hands the tackling of the ship.

20. For when neither sun nor stars in many days appeared, and no small storm beat on us, all hope that we should be saved was then taken away.

21. But after long silence Paul stood out in the middle of them, and said, Sirs, you should have listened to me, and not have sailed from Crete, and to have gained this harm and loss.

22. But now I exhort you to be of good cheer: for there will be no loss of anyone's life among you, but of the ship.

23. For there stood by me this night the angel of God, whose I am, and whom I serve,

24. Saying, fear not, Paul; you must be brought before Caesar: and, look, God has given you all them that sail with you.
25. Therefore, sirs, be of good cheer: for I believe God, that it will be just as it was told me.
26. However, we must be cast upon a certain island.
27. But when the fourteenth night had come, as we were driven up and down in the Adriatic Sea, about midnight the sailors sensed that they came near to some land;
28. And sounded, and found it twenty fathoms: and when they had gone a little further, they sounded again, and found it fifteen fathoms.
29. Then fearing unless we should have fallen upon the rocks, they cast four anchors out of the stern and prayed for the day.
30. As the sailors were about to flee out of the ship when they had let down the smaller boat into the sea, under pretense as though they would have cast anchors out of the bow,
31. Paul said to the centurion and the soldiers, unless these stay in the ship, you cannot be saved.
32. Then the soldiers cut off the ropes of the smaller boat, and let her fall off.
33. And while the day was about to come on, Paul asked them all to take food, saying, this day is the fourteenth day that you have stayed and continued fasting, having taken nothing.
34. Therefore, I entreat you to eat some food: for this is for your health: for there will not a hair fall from the head of any of you.
35. When he had so spoken, he took bread, and gave thanks to God in the presence of them all: and when he had broken it, he began to eat.
36. Then were they all of good cheer, and they also ate some food.
37. And we were in all in the ship two hundred seventy-six souls.
38. And when they had eaten enough, they lightened the ship and cast out the wheat into the sea.
39. When it was day, they did not recognize the land: but they discovered a certain creek with a shore, into which they were determined, if it were possible, to steer the ship.
40. When they had taken up the anchors, they committed themselves to the sea and loosed the rudder ropes, hoisted up the mainsail to the wind, and steered toward the shore.
41. And falling into a place where two seas met, they ran the ship aground; and the bow stuck fast, and remained unmovable, but the stern part was broken with the violence of the waves.
42. Now the soldiers' counsel was to kill the prisoners unless any of them should swim out, and escape.
43. But the centurion, willing to save Paul, kept them from their purpose; and commanded that they which could swim should cast themselves first into the sea, and get to land:
44. And the rest, some on boards, and some on broken pieces of the ship. And so it came to pass, that they all escaped safe to land.

Chapter 28

1. When they had escaped, then they knew that the island was called Malta.
2. Now the barbarians showed us unusual kindness: for they kindled a fire, and made us all welcome, because of the present rain, and because of the cold.
3. When Paul had gathered a bundle of sticks, and put them on the fire, there came out a viper out of the heat and fastened on his hand.
4. When the barbarians saw the venomous snake hang on his hand, they said among themselves, no doubt this man is a murderer, who, though he has escaped the sea, yet justice did not permit him to live.
5. But he shook off the snake into the fire and felt no harm.
6. However, they looked when he should have swollen, or fallen down dead suddenly: but after they had looked a great while, and saw no harm about to come to him, they changed their minds, and said that he was a god.
7. In a place around there owned by the chief man of the island, whose name was Publius; who received us, and lodged us three days courteously.
8. And it came to pass, that the father of Publius lay sick by fever and by infectious disease of the bowels: to who Paul entered in, and prayed, and laid his hands on him, and healed him.
9. So, when this was done, others also, who had diseases on the island, came, and were healed:
10. Who also honored us with many honors; and when we left, they gave us such things as were necessary.
11. After three months we left in a ship of Alexandria, which had wintered in the isle, whose emblem was Castor and Pollux.
12. And landing at Syracuse, we stayed there for three days.
13. And from there we circled, and came to Rhegium: and after one day the south wind blew, and we came the next day to Puteoli:
14. Where we found brothers and wanted to stay with them seven days: and so we went toward Rome.
15. Then from there, when the brothers heard of us, they came to meet us as far as Appii Forum, and The Three Inns: when Paul saw, he thanked God, and gained courage.
16. So, when we came to Rome, the centurion delivered the prisoners to the captain of the guard: but Paul was permitted to dwell by himself with a soldier who kept him.
17. And it came to pass, that after three days Paul called the chief of the Jews together: and when they had come together, he said to them, men and brothers, though I have committed nothing against the people, or customs of our fathers, yet I was delivered a prisoner from Jerusalem into the hands of the Romans.
18. Who, when they had examined me, would have let me go, because there was no reason to sentence me to death.
19. But when the Jews spoke against it, I was forced to appeal to Caesar Nero; not that I had anything to accuse my nation.

20. Therefore, for this reason I have called for you, to see you, and to speak with you: because for the hope of Israel I am bound with this chain.

21. And they said to him, we neither received letters out of Judea concerning you, neither any of the brothers that came showed or spoke any evil of you.

22. But we desire to hear from you what your thoughts are concerning this sect, we know that everywhere it is spoken against.

23. When they had appointed him a day, many came to him there into his lodging; to whom he explained and testified of the kingdom of God, persuading them concerning Jesus, both out of the Law of Moses and out of the prophets, from morning until evening.

24. And some believed the things which were spoken, and some did not believe.

25. Now when they disagreed among themselves, they departed, after that Paul had spoken one word, well spoke the Holy Spirit by Isaiah the prophet to our fathers,

26. Saying, go to this people, and say, hearing you will hear, and will not understand; and seeing you will see, and not perceive:

27. For the heart of these people has become callous, and their ears are sluggish of hearing, and their eyes they have shut; unless they should see with their eyes, and hear with their ears, and understand with their heart, and be turning about, and I would be healing them.

28. Therefore, be it known to you, that the salvation of God is sent to the nations, and that they will hear it.

29. So, when he had said these words, the Jews departed and had many disputes among themselves.

30. Then Paul dwelt two whole years in his own rented house, and received all that came to him,

31. Preaching the kingdom of God, and teaching those things which concern the Lord Jesus Christ, with all boldness, no one stopping him.

Romans Commentary

The book of Romans is written by Paul, "to all that be in Rome, beloved of God, called to be saints (Romans 1:7)." It is the word of God (Christ) to the Romans. It is the stone cut out without hands (the Word, Christ), which hits the feet of Daniel's great image, the Roman Empire (Daniel 2:33-35). Paul, and many other disciples, proclaimed the word of God to this city, the most influential city in the world, and as a result they turned the entire Roman world upside down (Acts 17:6)! In the fourth century, upon reading the book of Romans, Augustine was converted. In the 16th century, Martin Luther based the reformation upon this book. Western civilization, "the Christian West," was built upon this reformation. It can rightly be said that the book of Romans is the single most influential book in the history of the world! "If this "fullness of the Gentiles" (Romans 11:25) is equivalent to "the times of the Gentiles" (Luke 21:24), when was this to occur? Note that when Jesus states, "Jerusalem will be trampled underfoot by the Gentiles until the times of the Gentiles be fulfilled" (Luke 21:24), He also gives us the exact timing as to when this was to occur, eight verses later, "This generation will not pass, till all be fulfilled" (Luke 21:32! There is no way to try and make this have something to do with 1967! In reality, it has everything to do with AD 67! It was the Gentiles, who had their time with Israel, and did with her as they would. This did not take nearly 2000 years to do. Revelation 11:2 says that it took only 42 months! "But the court, which is without the temple leave out, and measure it not, for it is given unto the Gentiles; and the holy city shall they tread under foot forty and two months." Again, "Jerusalem will be trampled underfoot by the Gentiles until the times of the Gentiles be fulfilled (Luke 21:24)." This was fulfilled within that first century generation, eight verses later, "This generation shall not pass away, till ALL be fulfilled (Luke 21:32)"!

The book of Romans may be summed up in the following sentence: the flesh and the works of the Law, bring all under the death, while the Spirit and the work of grace bring salvation and infinite life to whosoever shall call upon the name of the Lord. The book may also be summed up in the following breakdown. ALL is a key word in the book, that is, ALL (Jew and Gentile) are on equal footing before God, ALL are guilty before God, because ALL have sinned (Chapters 1-3). It is faith that justifies, not works, as it did for Abraham (Chapter 4), faith that delivers one out from Adam (Chapter 5), out of the flesh, that is, the flesh where ALL are due the wages of sin, the death penalty (Chapters 6,7), and it is out of Adam and the flesh and into the glorious victory of Christ, through the Spirit (Chapters 7,8), no good thing is found in the flesh, not even a fleshly birth, Israel according to the flesh (Chapter 9), but God only acknowledges a new birth, which begins when, "...whosoever shall call upon the name of the Lord shall be SAVED (10:13)." In this salvation, "…THERE IS NO DIFFERENCE BETWEEN THE JEW AND THE GREEK, for the same Lord over ALL is rich unto ALL that call upon Him (Romans 10:12)." This brings us to Romans Chapter 11 and ALL Israel being SAVED (Romans 11:25-26). In New Testament 101, how is anyone SAVED? Salvation comes only through the gospel. How then is Israel saved?

Through the gospel! Does this chapter speak of Israel being saved through military conquest and the seizing of Middle Eastern land? Of course not, the acquisition of land is nowhere in the chapter. Salvation comes to both Jew and Gentile the same way, "for God has concluded them ALL in unbelief, that he might have mercy upon ALL (Chapter 11:32)." Both come into the ultimate Promised Land and dwelling place, the temple, in Christ, in His body (Chapter 12). Being in Christ and putting on Christ, allows for making no provision for the flesh, and enables the love of God to work, creating the right horizontal relationships with one another, to the nations, and even toward hostile governments (Chapter 13-16). The book of Romans begins with the Old Testament promises, "concerning Jesus Christ our Lord, which was made of the seed of David, according to the flesh (Romans 1:2-3)." "The Son of David", is a commonly understood title given to the Messiah throughout the New Testament (Matthew 1:1, 9:27, 12:23, 15:22; 20:30,31; 21:9,15;22:42; Mark 10:47,48;12:35; Luke 1:32, 18:38, 39,20:41; Revelation 5:5,22:16), which originated from the Old Testament (2 Samuel 7:12-16; 1 Chronicles 7:13; Psalm 89:3,4; 132:11).

Therefore, Solomon, David's son, in his ascension to the throne, becomes a type of Jesus, the true (the real) Son of David. Following David's warfare and death (A type of Jesus' death here), we see the Son of David's dominion. We read of David's, "wars which were about him on every side, until the Lord put them under the soles of his feet (1 Kings 5:3)." In the next verse we read of Solomon (A type of Jesus in resurrection here), "but now the Lord my God has given me rest on every side, so that there is neither adversary nor evil occurrence (1 Kings 5:4)." With Solomon on the throne, we read that, "and there came of all people to hear the wisdom of Solomon, from all kings of the earth, which had heard of his wisdom (1 Kings 4:34)." He uses his wisdom to build the house of the Lord, and his fame goes out (1 Kings 10:1). Similarly, we see Jesus upon the throne of David (Acts 2:29-36, Colossians 3:1) and His fame going out from Jerusalem to all nations (Acts 1:8, 17:6; Romans 1:8; 10:18; 16:25-26)! Jesus begins the process by building His house, temple, body, church, with His wisdom (Matthew 16:18,;Proverbs 24:3).

The building plan consists of Himself as the foundation, along with His apostles and prophets who were in Him (1 Corinthians 3:10-11; Ephesians 2:20-22; Revelation 21:14). Jesus' wisdom and fame goes out and was made known, according to Ephesians 3:10, "that now unto the principalities and powers in heavenly places (Political and otherwise) might be known by the church the manifold wisdom of God (Ephesians 3:10)." This is the wisdom and power of God, which is in the gospel (Romans 1:16, 1 Corinthians 1:18-2:5). Solomon, the Son of David in type, "...exceeded all the kings of the earth for riches and for wisdom (1 Kings 10:23), so the Son of David in reality, contains, "all the treasures of wisdom and knowledge (Colossians 2:3)", wisdom which He made known to all nations (Ephesians 3:10, Romans 16:25-26)! Just as it had been in Solomon's case (the Type), "and all the earth sought to Solomon, to hear his wisdom, which God had put in his heart (1 Kings 10:24)."

This reign of Solomon lasted for forty years (1 Kings 11:42), the same amount of time as the turbulent transition (Tribulation) period from the Old Covenant system with its, temple, city, and nation (Hebrews 8:13), into the New Covenant system, with its temple (John 12:6, Ephesians 2:21,22, Hebrews 9:8), city (Matthew 5:14, John 4:21-24, Galatians 4:25; Hebrews 12:22-23, Revelation 21:2), and nation (Matthew 21:43; Ephesians 2:12-14; Galatians 6:16; 1 Peter 2:9). So, if all these things, the temple, city, and nation, are become new in Christ (2 Corinthians 5:17, Revelation 21:5), why do Christians seek to, "build again the things which have been destroyed (Galatians 2:18)?" It is a turn in the wrong direction back to the Old Covenant types and shadows. The Bible consistently teaches of a pattern from the lesser (Types and shadows) to the greater (Reality), and never in the reverse order. So, the Son of David's wisdom (Solomon in Type) goes forth and is heard (1 Kings 10:1) in all the earth (1 Kings 10:23-24). So also, the Son of David's (Jesus' in Reality) wisdom goes forth and is heard in the whole world, "but I say to you, have they not heard? Yes verily, their sound went out into all the earth, and their words unto the ends of the earth (Romans 10:18)." Romans 10:18 here is quoting Psalm 19:4, where we understand figurative language using the symbols of the heavens declaring the glory of God, and the firmament uttering speech and knowledge, the sun, which is as a bridegroom coming out of His chamber, His going forth from the end of the heavens... (Psalm 19:1-6). The firmament, sun, moon, and stars are consistently used metaphorically throughout the scriptures to communicate ruling authority. Going back to Joseph's dream, where His father (the sun), mother (the moon), and brothers (the stars), would all fall and bow before His rule and authority. "There is the physical understanding that the sun ruled the day, and that the moon and stars ruled the night (Genesis 1:16). It was first this visible order, followed by the invisible, spiritual.

Throughout the Bible we see the authority of nations being put down, when heaven, or the sun, moon, and stars are darkened over them (Isaiah 13:1, 10, Ezekiel 32:7, 8, Joel 2:10,31, 3:15,16). Even modern-day symbolism acknowledges this in placing the sun, moon, or stars, on the various flags of the nations. So, when the heavens declare and utter speech and knowledge in Romans 10:18, we understand that those who were given authority (Matthew 28:18-20), exercised it as they burned with the fire of God (Psalm 19:6; Jeremiah 5:14; Acts 2:3; Hebrews 12:29)! This is why Paul refers to those, "...in the midst of a crooked and perverse nation, among whom you shine as lights in the world (Philippians 2:15). Their light so shined before men, that the result was glory (Matthew 5:14-16; Psalm 19:1)! Jesus the bridegroom goes forth into all the earth in and through His bride (Psalm 19:5-6; John 15:4-5)! They, "shine as the brightness of the firmament; and they that turn many to righteousness as the stars for ever and ever (Daniel 12:4)." Note that they could not be turning many to righteousness while dwelling in some imagined utopia on earth, in which case there wouldn't be a need to turn many to righteousness.

They shine forever and ever, because they're given infinite life and glory, which, of course, extends well beyond the end of the Old Covenant age (Matthew 13:40), "then shall the righteous shine forth as the sun in the kingdom of their Father, who hath ears to hear, let Him hear (Matthew 13:43). We must circumcise our ears (Acts 7:51), and cut away our fleshly understandings, to hear the true meanings of Jesus' words (John 6:63)! Through the illumination of the Holy Spirit, in Romans 10:18, Paul puts teeth in Psalm 19:4. He delivers us from thinking that it is a nebulous reference to astronomy, leading to the natural man's understandings of the natural sciences, which misses the intent of the Spirit of God! So, their sound went out into all the earth, and their words unto the ends of the world (Romans 10:18). Their faith was spoken of throughout the whole world (Romans 1:8). Remember that this stone, cut out without hands (Daniel 2:33-35), is Christ and His kingdom, and that it hits the feet of the great image, which is the Roman Empire.

The preaching of the word, Christ, turns the Roman World (Oikoumene) upside down (Acts 17:6)! So all the earth hears the wisdom of the true Son of David (Matthew 24:14,34, Colossians 1:5,6,23), "the preaching of Jesus Christ…by the scriptures…made (past tense) known unto all nations… (Romans 16:25- 26)!" Solomon's fame going out is the type of this (1 Kings 10:1). So the throne of David exercises its authority in reality when we read Romans 16:20, "the God of peace shall crush Satan under your feet shortly!" Remember that the type was in David's warring against his enemies, "until the Lord put them under his feet (1Kings 5:3)". After the Son of David, in type, Solomon inherits the throne, he states, "1 Kings 5:4 but Yahweh my God has now given me rest all around; there is no enemy or crisis. (1 Kings 5:4). The enemy is then defeated!

The book of Romans may also be referred to as the fifth gospel. The gospel is simplified and clarified in Romans, "Christ died for us (Romans 5:8)"! We are told that the gospel is the power of God in Romans 1:16. The Romans road tells us, "for all have sinned and come short of the glory of God (3:23)", "but God demonstrates His love toward us, in that, while we were yet sinners, Christ died for us (5:8)", and, "for the wages of sin is death, but the gift of God is infinite life through Jesus Christ our Lord" (6:23), and, "that if you confess with your mouth the Lord Jesus, and will believe with your heart that God has raised Him from the dead, you will be saved" (10:9,10), "for whosoever shall call upon the name of the Lord shall be saved (10:13)."

This fifth gospel may best be entitled, "the Gospel of the Kingdom". The power of the gospel (1:16) and the rule of God (16:20,25-26) are from beginning to end in the book. The kingdom of God is literally defined in its fullness in Romans 14:17, "for the kingdom of God is not meat and drink; but righteousness, and peace, and Joy in the Holy Spirit." The kingdom of God is nothing more, and nothing less, than this! No hidden clauses or small print to sift through here! Coupled with Jesus' similar words in Luke 17:20, 21, "the kingdom of God comes not with observation; neither shall they say, Lo here! Or, lo there! For, behold the kingdom of God is within you", we can derive a clear understanding as to the true nature of the kingdom of God. The kingdom of God is, not sort of is, partly is, or temporarily is, but simply is, righteousness, peace, and Joy in the Holy Spirit! We see righteousness in Romans 1:17, 2:26, 3:5,21,22,25,26, 4:3,6,9,11,13,22, 5:17,18,21, 6:13,16,18,20, 8:4,10; 9:28,30,31; 10:3,4,6,10; 14:17! We see peace in 1:7; 2:10; 3:17; 5:1; 8:6,10:15; 14:17, 19; 15:13, 33; 16:20. And we see joy in 5:11; 12:12,15; 14:17; 15:13, 32!

Because Romans Chapter 11 may very well be the center piece for the next reformation, perhaps better said, a major transformation, we will pay special attention to it in this summary. In getting Romans 11 straight, one will see dispensationalism dismantled before their very eyes. Let's break it down some. Romans 11:1, "I say then, hath God cast away His people: God forbid. for I also am an Israelite, of the seed of Abraham, of the tribe of Benjamin." "No", is the clear answer, God has (present tense) not cast away his people. So, what is Paul's proof that God has not cast away His people? The answer is Paul himself. We must remember here, when was Paul asking this question? It is in the first century when he asks! What is Paul's proof that God has not cast away His people? Paul himself is the proof! The fact that he is an Israelite is the only proof Paul offers! He does not say anything about the distant future and Israel becoming a nation again in 2000 years, followed by the rapture of the Church, after which God will prove that he has not cast away His people by saving 1/3 of them (Zechariah 13:8), does he? Does he say anything remotely close to this? Does he give even a syllable toward any of this popular scenario of our day? If the proof that God has not cast away His people were an event 2000 years into the future, then, in the meantime, God had cast them away! But the text doesn't say anything other than what was happening right then and there. Has God cast away His people? The word "Has" is in the present tense! The first five verses here in Chapter 11, confirm Paul's proof of God not casting away His people. What is the proof offered by Paul? The proof is Paul himself, who is as Elijah of the past (vs.2-4), among a faithful remnant that was not cast away (vs.5)!

Romans 11:2, "God hath not cast away his people which he foreknew. Wot ye not what the scripture suit of Elias? How he makes intercession to God against Israel, saying…" God HATH not cast them away! Again, Paul, as Elijah, was a member of the faithful remnant (vs.5). This is the proof offered by Paul that God has not cast away His people.

Romans 11:3, "Lord, they have killed thy prophets, and digged down thine altars; and I am left alone, and they seek my life." Elijah was amongst the remnant. He was not alone (vs.5), as Paul was not alone.

Romans 11:4, "but what saith the answer of God unto him? I have reserved to Myself seven thousand men, who have not bowed the knee to the image of Baal." Seven thousand who remained faithful, whom God had not cast away.

Romans 11:5, "Even so then at this present time also there is a remnant according to the election of grace." We must understand the context of this chapter, what time frame is Paul speaking of? "AT THIS PRESENT TIME." Just a note, in Bible Prophecy, timing is everything. Whether 40 years in the wilderness, or 400 years in Egypt, precision timing in prophecy has to be understood. It was 70 years in Babylon, and it was 40 years till all these things be fulfilled with in this generation (Mt.24:34), timing is crucial! And ONLY A REMNANT IS TO BE SAVED! "Isaiah also cried concerning Israel, "Though the number of the children of Israel be as the sand of the sea, A REMNANT SHALL BE SAVED" (Romans 9:27). We must connect this with verse 26 where, "ALL ISRAEL SHALL BE SAVED."

Romans 11:6, "and if by grace, then it is no more of works: otherwise grace is no more grace. But if it be of works then is it no more grace: otherwise work is no more work". Again, this is the central theme of the book. Grace, the work of the Spirit, leads to life, even infinite life, versus the Law and the works of the flesh, which leads to death.

Romans 11:7, "Israel has not obtained that which he seeks for; but the election has obtained, and the rest were blinded". Israel was seeking a political deliverance from Rome in order to establish a kingdom that comes by observation (Lk.17:20-22). Israel had not obtained that, but THE ELECT HAD OBTAINED, IN THE FIRST CENTURY! IT WAS NOT A DELIVERANCE THAT CAME THROUGH POLITICAL AND MILITARY CONQUEST AND THE ACQUISITION OF LAND! The elect, the remnant, whom Paul was among, HAD OBTAINED ALL THAT GOD HAD EVER PROMISED TO ISRAEL! "ALL THE PROMISES OF GOD IN HIM" (2 Corinthians 1:20) That GOD HAD EVER PROMISED TO ISRAEL! "ALL THE PROMISES OF GOD IN HIM." (2 Corinthians 1:20). The elect (remnant) obtained deliverance from the ultimate bondage. Not from Rome, but from sin and death. This deliverance (salvation) was the ultimate for Israel and for the Gentiles as well. The rest were blinded, according to the sovereign plan of God. We will look into this blindness in detail below, but let's keep in mind the remedy for blindness, "To open their eyes, and to turn them from darkness to light and from the power of Satan unto God, that they may receive forgiveness of sins, and inheritance among them which are sanctified by faith that is in me" (Acts 26:18).

Romans 11:8, "According as it is written (Isaiah 6:9, 10,;Matthew 13:13-15,;Mark 4:12; Acts 28:26- 27), God has given them the spirit of slumber, eyes that they should not hear; unto this day." Remember that when Paul says, unto this day, he is referring to his day, not ours! Rom.11:9, "and David says, "let their table be made a snare, and a trap, and a stumbling block, and a recompense unto them." This is a quote from Psalm 69:22, where David continues, "Let their eyes be darkened, that they see not, and make their loins continually shake. Pour out now Your indignation upon them, and let Your wrathful anger take hold of them. Let their habitation be desolate (Psalm 69:23-25)." DESOLATE is a key word in Bible Prophecy.

Matthew 23:38, "behold your house (your temple) is left unto you desolate." The temple is the clear context here, as a few verses later Jesus spells it out, "there shall not be left here one stone upon another" (Matthew 24:2), and he continues in Matthew 24:15 with the temple's desolation.

Matthew 24:15 "When you therefore shall see the abomination of desolation" Referring to the same desolation of the temple.

Luke 21:20 "and when you ("you", first century disciples) shall see Jerusalem compassed with armies, then know that the desolation thereof is near."

Daniel 9:27 "…He (Messiah the prince in vs.25 is the same Messiah the prince in vs 26) shall cause the sacrifice and oblation to cease (because He became to them as the final sacrifice, once and for all) and for the overspreading of abominations (it was an abomination to continue and make animal sacrifices after the cross) he shall make it (the temple) desolate even until the consummation (Of the Old Covenant age, Hebrews 8:13), and that determined shall be poured upon the desolate."

Romans 11:10, "let their eyes be darkened, that they may not see, and bow down their back always." Just a continuation of Psalm 69:23 here. Blindness is what we're getting to in Romans 11:25- 26, and we'll see that it's all part of God's plan in the next verse.

Romans 11:11, "I say then, have they stumbled that they should fall? God forbid: but rather through their fall salvation is come unto the Gentiles, for to provoke them to jealousy". This provocation was foretold of in the previous chapter, Romans 10:19, quotes Deuteronomy 32:20, 21. Romans 10:19 says, "but I say, did not Israel know?" (The clear inference is, "Yes, they did know this prophecy.) First Moses says, "I will provoke you to jealousy by them that are no people, and by a foolish nation I will anger you (Matthew 21:43; 1 Peter 2:9; Galatians 6:16; Ephesians 2:12-14)."

Deuteronomy 32, from which this is quoted (Deuteronomy 32:20- 21), is a major prophetic passage for the nation of Israel. The prophecy goes on in Deuteronomy 32:23, and says, "THE SWORD (Matthew 22:7- Rome) without, and terror within (Jewish Zealots), SHALL DESTORY BOTH THE YOUNG MAN AND THE VIRGIN, THE SUCKLING ALSO WITH THE MAN OF GRAY HAIRS". That covers just about everyone, and clearly prophesies that Israel will be destroyed. The foretold destruction continues, "for they are a nation void of counsel, neither is there any understanding in them. O that they were wise, that they understood this, that they would consider THEIR LATTER END (Deuteronomy 32:28-29)." THIS IS ISRAEL'S END! It does not mention their end, followed by a subsequent starting over again. Otherwise, at this point and time, the time of THE PROVOCATION, God would not have said it was going to be THEIR END! Deuteronomy 32 continues, 32:35; Deut. 32:35 Vengeance is Mine, and recompense; their foot shall slip in due time; for the day of their calamity is at hand, and the things to come hasten upon them.'….". Compare this with Luke 21:22, "for these are THE DAYS OF VENGEANCE…" Vengeance for what? Slaying the Householder's (King's) servants and ultimately the heir, the Son of God Himself (Matthew 21:33-45, 22:1-7)!

These passages progress to Matthew 23, where Jesus states the most hair-raising statement in history, "that upon you may come ALL THE RIGHTEOUS BLOOD SHED UPON THE EARTH…Verily I say unto you, all these things shall come upon THIS GENERATION!" (Matthew 23:35-36) The exact manner of this VENGEANCE is spelled out by Jesus two verses prior in Luke 21:20, "and when YOU (First century disciples, face to face in dialogue with Jesus) shall see Jerusalem compassed with armies (Matthew 22:7), then know that her DESOLATION thereof is near." Deuteronomy 32 continues, "if I whet MY GLITTERING SWORD, and My hand take hold on judgment; I will render VENGEANCE to MY ENEMIES and will reward them that hate Me (Deuteronomy 32:41)."

God now refers to Israel as His enemies, and it is at the time of their end (Deuteronomy 32:29), at which time He provokes them to jealousy with a foolish nation (Deuteronomy 32:21). Deuteronomy 32:42 continues, "I will make My arrows drunk with blood, and MY SWORD shall devour flesh…" Now watch this in the next verse, Deuteronomy 32:43, "Rejoice, O you nations (Salvation is come to the Gentiles, Romans 11:11), with His people (the remnant, Romans 11:5, Jews and Gentile's rejoicing together, Ephesians 2:12-14)." Deuteronomy 32:43 continues, "…for He will AVENGE the blood of His servants (Matthew 21:33-45, 22:1-7), and will render VENGEANCE to His adversaries, and will be merciful unto His land, and to His people (the remnant in the land in the first century)." One more point about the statement in this verse, "for He will AVENGE the blood of His servants". We read this same thing in Revelation 18:24, "and in her was found the blood of the prophets (Old Covenant His servants), and of saints (New Covenant His servants), and of ALL THAT WERE SLAIN UPON THE LAND." And in Matthew 23:35, "that upon you may come ALL THE RIGHTEOUS BLOOD SHED UPON THE LAND…". When is this to occur? The next verse tells us, "…All these things shall come upon THIS GENERATION (Matthew 23:36)!" Romans 11:12," now if the fall of them be the riches of the world, and the diminishing of them the riches of the Nations; how much more their fullness." We see this game plan of God at work in Acts 18:6, when Paul says, "and when they opposed themselves, and blasphemed, he shook his raiment, and said unto them, Your blood be upon your own heads; I am clean: from henceforth I will go unto the nations."

What does "their fullness" mean? It means the full amount receiving salvation at the end of the Old Covenant age (Matthew 13:39, 40; 24:3), which would be climaxed at the parousia (Coming or presence of the Lord in judgment) as we read in Revelation 1:7 and Matthew 24:30, 31. Virtually all would agree that Revelation 7:4-8 is saying this same thing as these verses. Romans 11:25-26 is also saying this same thing. We have to understand that "fullness" is meant to be understood as, a full amount, a whole amount, a complete amount, NOT every last individual. We see this in Revelation 21:24 with, "… the nations of them which are SAVED…" This is very relative to ISRAEL being SAVED in Romans 11:26. Is every last individual saved amongst these nations which are saved in Revelation 21:24? Is every Gentile saved with "the FULNESS of the Gentiles"? Is every person on earth filled with the Spirit when God pours out His Spirit upon ALL FLESH (Acts 2:17)? Is every last individual amongst the nations of the "Christian West" saved? Of course not! Neither is every last Jewish person saved when "ALL ISRAEL shall be saved" (Romans 11:26). Romans 9:6, helps us to understand this, "for they are not ALL ISRAEL, which are of Israel". In fact, futurists themselves contend that only 1/3 of the nation is ultimately saved, according to (Zechariah 13:8). Nations are viewed by God as a whole, not so much as each and every last individual. "The U.S. is a Christian nation", the Supreme Court once concluded. Of course, forget about every last individual. Iran is a Muslim nation. India is a Hindu nation, etc. A quick reminder here, let's keep in mind as to what brings salvation to any people? It's the gospel and Christ alone! This is vital in understanding Romans Chapter 11, and for that matter the entire book of Romans!

Romans 11:13, "for I speak unto you Gentiles, inasmuch as I am the apostle of the Gentiles, I magnify my office:" Paul is continually addressing Jews and Gentiles throughout the book. He continually appeals to both through the Spirit, revealing the reconciling of both, "for God has concluded them ALL in unbelief, that He might have mercy upon ALL (Romans 11:32)." The Holy Spirit is constantly revealing the broken down walls of division between Jews and Gentiles (Ephesians 2:12-15), between Greeks, bond and free, male and female, and between all people groups (Galatians 3:28, 29). Various people groups are typically relating to one another through animal instincts, that is, through using their fangs, teeth, venom, claws, horns, and hooves. In Peter's trance, the various beasts and critters are representative of the Gentiles. Peter realizes what God is saying in the vision, "You know how that it is an unlawful thing for a man that is a Jew to keep company or come unto one of another nation; but God has shown me that I should not call any man common or unclean. Of a truth I perceive that God is no respecter of persons;" (Acts 10:10-16, 28, 34)."

This animal illustration is also seen in Noah's Ark, where the beasts behaved miraculously by not mauling and goring one another to death. We see the same metaphorical example in Isaiah 11:6-9. "The wolf also shall dwell with the lamb, and the leopard shall lie down with the kid; and the calf and the young lion and the fatling together; and a little child shall lead them. And the cow and the bear shall feed; their young ones shall lie down together: and the lion shall eat straw like the ox ("does God care for oxen", says 1 Corinthians 9:9. Is His word laying out the blu2e4p6rints for a Mutual of Omaha kingdom?) And the suckling child shall play on the hole of the asp and the weaned child shall put his hand in the vipers den. They shall not hurt nor destroy in all My holy mountain. (Location, location, location, where is this holy mountain? Heb. 12:22, 23 says where it is, "but you have come unto Mount Zion, and unto the city of the living God, the heavenly Jerusalem, and to an innumerable company of angels, To the general assembly and church of the firstborn." This same mountain of the Lord is found in Isaiah 2:2, "the mountain of the Lord's house established in the top of the mountains (above all other kingdoms) and exulted above the hills; and all nations (Gentiles) flow unto it." The idea of the Gentiles coming into the kingdom continues in Isaiah 11:9, "… for the earth shall be full of the knowledge of the Lord, as the waters cover the sea." And the idea is revealed clearly in the New Testament in Matthew 24:14, as the gospel is preached in all the world, Oikoumene "world", same "world" as Luke 2:1, the gospel goes as far as the census goes into all the world, the Roman "world". Colossians 1:6, 23, Romans 1:8; 10:18; 16:25,26 and Acts 17:6 all say this same thing. So, Isaiah's prophesied kingdom of various beast groups has a location, "in all my holy mountain (Isaiah 11:9)." So, it also has timing, when does this all occur?

The very next verse in Isaiah tells us when, "AND IN THAT DAY… (Isaiah 11:10)!" WHAT DAY? "AND IN THAT DAY "And in that day there shall be a Root of Jesse, Who shall stand as a banner to the people; For the Gentiles shall seek Him, And His resting place shall be glorious."15 (Isaiah 11:10)." This passage is quoted by Paul in Romans 15:12, "and again, Isaiah says, there shall be a root of Jesse, and He that shall rise to reign over the nations; in Him shall the nations trust (Romans 15:12)." Isaiah, through the Holy Spirit, tells us that the lion will lay with the calf IN THAT DAY, IN PAUL'S DAY! One more time, Paul, through the Holy Spirit tells us when that day is! He quotes Isaiah 11:10 in Romans 15:12, "and again, Isaiah says, "there shall be a root of Jesse, and He that shall rise to reign over the nations; in Him shall the nations trust." It is the fullness of the Gentiles (Romans 11:25) being grafted in, gathered in, during the last days of the Old Covenant age (Matthew 13:30), "IN THAT DAY" (Isaiah 11:10), in PAUL'S DAY (Romans 15:12)!

Isaiah continues in Isaiah 11:11 saying, "and it shall come to pass IN THAT DAY…" let's stop everything, "and…IN THAT DAY". There is a continuation of the previous verses thought, "and", mentioning the same, "IN THAT DAY", as the previous verse's, "IN THAT DAY." Therefore, this gathering in Isaiah 11:11 is the same gathering as Isaiah 11:10's gathering. There had been a first gathering after the seventy-year captivity, according to Isaiah 29:10 (Note, after 70 years, not after 2000 years!) So, this second recovering of THE REMNANT OF HIS PEOPLE in Isaiah 11:11,12 is Paul's same gathering of scattered Jews and Gentiles (Romans 11:25,26, Ephesians 1:10) into Jesus Christ, the ultimate gathering place, to which dispensationalism says, "there's got to be something better, something in a kingdom that comes by observation (Luke 17:20-22)"! Christ's kingdom came without observation, in Peters', James', and Johns' day (Matthew 16:27,28, Luke 21:31,32)! His kingdom breaks down the walls and hatred, which the animalistic fallen nature of man fights for. They ALL gather together peacefully in Him. What good news, that people groups which are naturally at each other's throats, through the Spirit, are living together peacefully (Ephesians 2:14) in His Holy Mountain, which is in Christ (Hebrews 12:22-23,

Isaiah 2:2; Colossians 1:24; Daniel 2:35). Romans 11:14, "if by any means I may provoke to jealousy them which are my flesh and might save some of them." I MAY PROVOKE…" Here is another clear time indicator as for who would be provoking Israel to Jealousy! A first century generation of kingdom minded and empowered preachers of the Good news would be provoking them. John Wimber, founder of the Vineyard Christian Fellowship, once said The New King James Version (Is 11:10). (1982). Thomas Nelson. concerning ministry, "find out who you're going to offend, and go offend them!" The most offended are those with Pharisaical doctrinal systems and traditions. They are so sure of themselves that they have put away the very thought of ever possibly being wrong, such an idea is out of the realm of possibility for them. It is inconceivable, and if anyone presents the thought, they instantly bite and devour such a one as they stop their ears from hearing that which is foreign and challenging to their own understandings of the scriptures (Acts 7:54,57; Philippians 3:2; Galatians 5:15).

Romans 11:15, "for if the casting away of them be the conciliation of the world, what shall the receiving of them be, but life from the dead." What kind of life, from what kind of death here? How could anyone read a political and military resurrection here when they read, "life from the dead"? Most would agree that the primary passage dealing with Israel's life from the dead is in Ezekiel 37. Let's visit the passage, "… the valley full of bones …, very dry; (37:1-2), "… these bones are the whole house of Israel … (37:11)", "… can these bones live (37:3)?", "… prophesy and say unto them, thus saith the Lord God; behold, O My people, I will open your graves and cause you to come up out of your graves and bring you into the land of Israel. And you shall know that I am the Lord, when I have opened your graves, and shall put My Spirit in you, and you shall live, and I shall place you in your own land, then shall you know that I the Lord have spoken it, and performed it, saith the Lord (Ezekiel 37:12-14)." This passage has to be understood in its setting and historical context. What was the background as to what was happening in Israel at that time? All would agree that Ezekiel is prophesying to the nation at the time in which the nation was being taken into captivity and bondage by the Babylonians.

The nation would live again; it would be Israel's greatest deliverance and recovery. It would be delivered from all of its prior scatterings and bondages to the Assyrians and the Babylonians. It would be delivered from the worst bondage of all, the bondage of sin (John 8:32)! This bondage would be overcome as they became one nation, with one king, one shepherd, David (Ezekiel 37:22-24). Do the scriptures testify of David (Acts 2:29-30; John 5:39; Luke 24:44,45)? When does this happen? "Moreover, I will make a covenant of peace with them; it shall be a perpetual covenant (Ezekiel 37:26)." What covenant is this?

The New Covenant (Hebrews 13:20)! How do we know this? The very next verse (Ezekiel 37:27), "My tabernacle also shall be with them: yea, I will be their God, and they shall be My people." We know this because the Holy Spirit, through Paul, quotes this verse and communicates its fulfillment clearly in and through the New Covenant, "… God has said, I will dwell with them, and walk in them; and I will be their God, and they shall be my people (2 Corinthians 6:16)." John also puts this in perspective, "Behold, the tabernacle of God is with men, and He will dwell with them, and they shall be His people. God Himself will be with them and be their God. (Rev. 21:3).

Israel is saved through the NEW COVENANT KINGDOM (NATION) BORN IN A DAY (Matthew 21:43, 1 Peter 2:9, Galatians 6:16, Ephesians 2:12-14; Isaiah 66:8). The New Covenant Kingdom (Nation) has a new capitol city as well (Hebrews 12:22, Galatians 4:26). Israel was the first fruits of this nation. At its birth, no one but Jews made up this tabernacle of David, dwelling place, "Church". Only Jews were part of the beginnings of the Church (Acts 5:11). The church then expanded to graft in Gentiles (Acts 10). Now, remember that when the Holy Spirit was given at Pentecost, "… and there were dwelling at Jerusalem Jews, devout men, out of every nation under heaven." (Acts 2:5) Some of these Jews were from the places of the northern captivity, Assyria, as well as every other nation within the empire (Luke 2:36). These same Jews went out from Jerusalem (Acts 1:8, 8:4). By Chapter 17 in Acts, they had "turned the world upside down!" The gospel had spread like wildfire! ALL of those Jews living in captivity throughout the empire heard of the glorious rebirth, remission of sin, and freedom found in Jesus Christ, the ultimate dwelling place of God! Yes, the gospe2l4d8id go throughout the "world" (Greek-Oikoumene "world", Roman world, also used in Luke 2:1) as we read in Matthew 24:14; Colossians 1:6,23, and Romans 1:8, 10:18, 16:25,26. So, there was a first fruits and a harvest of Jews and Gentiles at the end of the age. All of the same generational crop. Jews who were holdouts in Jerusalem and throughout the empire, when they saw, or even heard about, the destruction of the Old Testament headquarters, turned to faith in Jesus, as they saw the words of Jesus coming to pass before their eyes. Revelation 1:7 says this, … behold, He is coming with the cloud(Coming presence, or coming in a cloud of judgment, Isaiah 19:1, 13:9,10, Ezekiel 30:3,4, 32:7,8, Matthew 26:64); and every eye shall SEE (Greek word origin; Horao; to discern, perceive, understand, not mere mechanical "seeing") Him, and they also which pierced Him (A first century generation pierced Him, going beyond this generation has resulted in anti-Semitism for following generations); and all the tribes (No Jewish Tribes today) of the land (Not "Kosmos or globe, but land) shall mourn because of Him." This mourning is a mourning of repentance, as we read where the quote is taken from, "…they shall mourn for Him, as one mourns for his only son, and shall be in bitterness for Him, as one that is in bitterness for his firstborn. In that day there shall be a great mourning in Jerusalem… (Zechariah 12:10)." Both Jews within Jerusalem, as well as those throughout the empire who discerned, perceived, and understood, i.e. "saw", that this was King Jesus judging those wicked men (Matthew 21:41), as, "He sent forth HIS ARMIES, destroyed those murderers, BURNED UP THEIR CITY" (Matthew 22:7), and left not one stone upon another, exactly as He had said (Matthew 24:2)!

Romans 11:16, "for if the first fruit be holy, the lump is also holy: and if the root be holy, so also are the branches." The first fruits consists of Jesus, the twelve, and the first Christians, all of which were Jewish (Revelation 14:3, 4, 7:4-8). The lump is the whole crop including the harvest, which included Gentiles. All the grain, the first fruits and the harvest, become a lump of dough, after being soaked in the water of the Spirit. The root is Jesus (Revelation 22:16). The branches are Jews and Gentiles ((Romans 11:17, 24).

Romans 11:17, "and if some of the branches be broken off, and thou, being (Greek: OF a wild olive tree, they are not the olive tree) a wild olive tree, was grafted in among them, and with them partakers of the root and fatness of the olive tree." The Olive tree is the life source of God that is only given through covenant (John 6:53). The Olive Tree is NOT Israel! Remember, Israel is one of the branches, the natural branches (vs 21, 24). This same tree can be seen as the Tree of Life as well (Genesis 2:9, 3:22, Galatians 3:13). Also note here that the Gentiles branches were not grafted in instead of them (the Jews), but rather among them! A Gentile Church has not "replaced" a Jewish one. Remember that the Old Covenant people are referred to as "the church in the wilderness" (Acts 7:38). The church began, as we've already looked at, with no one but Jews. Acts 5:11, refers to "the church", and it consisted of only Jews at that point. It was not until Chapter 10, that we see Gentiles grafted into the church. In light of this reality that the church began with no one but Jews, how does anyone say in our day that God cannot deal with the Jews (Israel) until the church is moved out of the way? One more point to clarify here with the Olive Tree (the life source of God), there is only one olive tree, not two. Both Jews and Gentiles are branches, natural and wild respectively.

Romans 11:18, "Boast not against the branches. But if you boast, you bear not the root, but the root supports you." Everyone, Gentiles, Jews, every individual, from every race, whether male, female, bond or free (Galatians 3:28), must forsake the thought of boasting, for it is excluded! Romans 3:27 is in the context of addressing both the Jew and the Gentile. It is this wall of division that has been broken down so as to allow us to be made one in Him, the Prince of Peace (Ephesians 2:14). One particular modern day Judaizer actually questioned whether the root here is Jesus or not (Revelation 5:5)! Jesus is not everything for Judaizers. Romans 11:19, "Thou wilt say then, the branches were broken off, that I might be grafted in." Remember that this was the sovereign plan of Jehovah Sneaky all along. It was foretold of Israel being provoked by another nation (Deuteronomy 32:21-Romans 10:19), at the time of their end (Deuteronomy 32:20, 29)! This same chapter states (Deuteronomy 32:43), "Rejoice, O nations (Gentiles) with His people (the remnant of Jews)." This is a perfect description of the Gentile and Jewish branches being joined as one in Christ.

Romans 11:20, "Well; because of unbelief they were broken off, and you stand by faith. Be not high-minded, but fear." Faith removes all boasting, "Seeing it is one God, which shall justify the circumcision by faith, and uncircumcision through faith" (Romans 3:30). We must remember," … by grace are you saved through faith; and that not of yourselves: it is the gift of God: not of works, lest any man should boast (Ephesians 2:8, 9)." Our faith is not of ourselves, it is the gift of God!

Romans 11:21, "for if God spared not the natural branches, take heed lest He also spare not you" It's all about faith when it comes to pleasing God (Hebrews 11:1). Jew, Gentile, male, female, bond or free, we're all doomed before Him without living by faith, "…the just shall live by faith (Romans 1:17, Habakkuk 2:4)."

Romans 11:22, "Behold therefore the goodness and severity of God: on them which fell, severity; but toward thee, goodness, if (it's conditional for all, Jews and Gentiles) thou continue in His goodness: otherwise, thou also shalt be cut off." We're ALL (Jew and Gentile) on equal footing before this awesome consuming fire!

Yes, be afraid; be very afraid, as verse 20 exhorts us to be. Remember that: "it is a fearful thing to fall into the hands of a living God (Hebrews 10:31)." We must call upon Him (faith) in our desperate state before Him. "For there is no difference between the Jew and the Greek (I wish today's premillennial teachers could understand this clear statement): for the same Lord over ALL is rich unto ALL that call upon Him. For whosoever (Jew or Gentile) shall call upon the name of the Lord shall be SAVED (Romans 10:12, 13). Remember, that's what we're building up to here, ALL Israel being SAVED, saved through the gospel.

Romans 11:23, "and they also, if they abide not still in unbelief, shall be grafted in: for God is able to graft them in again." Here is the Gospel, which goes out to ALL, "if" is the key word here, "for God so love the world, that He gave His only begotten Son, that whosoever (Jew or Gentile) believes in Him should not perish, but have infinite life (John 3:16)." Whosoever and if are the conditions of being saved. Jew or Gentile can go this narrow way which leads to life (Matthew 7:14), and few there be that find it, a remnant finds it (Romans 11:5)!

Romans 11:24, "for if you were cut out of the olive tree which is wild by nature, and were grafted contrary to nature into a good olive tree: how much more shall these, which be the natural branches, be grafted into their own olive tree? Let's first identify the players here. Both the Gentiles and the Jews are NOT trees themselves here! They are branches from either tree. Both the wild olive tree and the good olive tree are simply the life source of God upon each, the Gentiles, and the Jews, respectively. Gentiles also had the influence of the one true God upon them, the wild olive tree, yet not as extensively as the good olive tree. Think of Egypt's palace seeing and hearing the influence of the one true God through Joseph, and later Moses and Aaron! The influence of God permeated the Assyrian's palace, turning them to repentance toward the one true God by the preaching of Jonah! The

Babylonian's palace, occupied by Nebuchadnezzar, heard the words of the one true God from Daniel. As a result, the king was converted and exhorted the whole world to follow the one true God (Daniel 4:1-3, 37)!

The Persian's palace heard it through Esther and Daniel! The Greek philosophers sat at the feet of the Jewish Rabbis to hear of the wisdom of the one true God! And finally, the Roman Empire was turned upside down with the influence of the word of God, even permeating the place of Caesar himself, "So that my bonds in Christ are manifest in all the palace." All the saints salute you, chiefly they that are of Caesar's household (Philippians 1:13, 4:22)"! Christians were living in Nero's palace! Gentiles always had the influence of God from those who knew Him. In Romans 11:17, 24, the influence of God upon the Gentiles, is communicated with the words, "of the wild olive tree" (Romans 11:17, 24). Today, only "the Good Olive Tree" exists. It is the life source of God, which comes through the influence of God in the New Covenant. It must be understood that there is NOW only one life source of God through the blood of Jesus in the New Covenant (John 6:53), the only tree of life (Genesis 3:22, Galatians 3:13; Revelation 2:7, 22:14)! There IS, therefore, NOW only one Olive Tree, as a result of, "… the fullness of times when he gathered together in one all things (Jews and Gentiles) in Christ, both which are in heaven, and which are on earth; even in Him (Ephesians 1:10)." There WERE two Olive Trees. We must read Romans 11 in context, "Even so then AT THIS PRESENT TIME… (Romans 11:5)."

Paul was laying out the dynamics of his time, not ours! Audience relevance and the original hearers were completely left out of modern interpretations of the Bible! THERE relevance, and the original hearers, were completely left out of modern interpretations of the Bible! THERE OWN OLIVE TREE is the Old Covenant with the Jewish people, their nation, capitol city, temple, etc. The Old Covenant served as a type of the ultimate covenant, the New Covenant, which was the reality of all Old Covenant types. There would be a struggle for the Old Covenant people to hold onto the source of their covenant, fulfilled in Jesus Christ (Matthew 5:17,18), who would translate them into the New Covenant, the perpetual covenant, the kingdom of the son of His love (Hebrews 13:20, Col. 1:13), which had been promised to them (Ezekiel 37:26,27-2 Corinthians 6:16). How much more can they be grafted into the reality of all these Old Testament types and shadows (Romans 15:4; 1Corinthians 10:6; Hebrews 10:1). That is, becoming a true Jew (Romans 2:28-29; Rev.2:9, 3:9), the true Israel (Antitype of the type, Matthew 2:15; Hosea 11:1; Ephesians 2:12; Matthew 21:43; 1 Peter 2:9; Galatians 6:16), with the true capitol city of God (Hebrews 11:10; Hebrews 12:22,23; Galatians 4:25,26), in the true temple (Matthew 12:6; Ephesians 2:20-22; Revelation 21:22), partaking of the true sacrifice (John 1:29; Exodus 12; Hebrews 9:26)!

Note that last verse (Hebrews 9:26). The countdown was winding down for all of the Old Covenant types and shadows to vanish away (Hebrews 8:13). John says that the last days was winding down to the last hour, "it is the last hour" (1 John 2:18)! The forty-year countdown for that generation (Matthew 24:34) would result in the Old Covenant's headquarters being left desolate, "there shall not be left here one stone upon another… (Matthew 24:2, 15, 23:38)."

Romans 11:25, "for I would not, brethren, that ye should be ignorant of this mystery lest ye should be wise in your own conceits; that blindness in part is happened to Israel, until the fullness of the Gentiles be come in." Eph. 3:9 then to make all men see what is the stewardship of the mystery, which from the beginning of the age has been hidden in God, who created all things by Jesus Christ: TKB … 4 whereby, when you read, you may understand my knowledge into the mystery of Christ) 5 which in other generations was not made known to the sons of men, as it is now revealed to His holy apostles and prophets in the Spirit; 6 that the nations should be fellow heirs, and of the same body, and partakers of His promise in Christ by the gospel: (Ephesians 3:4-6 TKB)." So, the mystery involves the grafting in (fellow heirs) of the Gentiles, which came about through the blindness of Israel. We learn about this foretold blindness in Isaiah 6:9, 10, quoted in Matthew 13:14-15; Mark 4:12; John 12:39-41, and Acts 28:25-27; 2 Cor. 4:4. Remember that all this goes back to the plan of God, who says that He will provoke Israel to jealousy by a foolish nation (Deuteronomy 32:21), at which time Israel would be coming to "their end" as a nation (Deuteronomy 32:20, 29).

They would be destroyed with the sword (Deuteronomy 32:25, 41, 42). Vengeance would be poured out upon her (Deuteronomy 32:35; Luke 21:22; Isaiah 61:2), all for the purpose of joining Jews and Gentiles into one Olive Tree, one life source of God, in one covenant (Ephesians 2:12). Thus, "Rejoice, O ye nations (Gentiles), with His people, (the remnant) (Deuteronomy 32:43)." Further on this mystery, "and without controversy great is the mystery of godliness: God was manifest in the flesh, justified in the Spirit, seen of angels, preached unto the nations, believed on in the world, received up into glory (1 Timothy 3:16)." Revelation 10:7 speaks of this same mystery, "but in the last days of the voice of the seventh angel, when He shall begin to sound the mystery of God should be finished (the gospel in all the world at the end of the age)." And for further clarity, "…the preaching of Jesus Christ (the gospel), according to the revelation of the mystery…but is now made manifest, and by the scriptures…made (past tense here) known to all nations (the Gentiles) for the obedience of faith (Romans 15:25-26)." Romans 11:25 makes it clear that the blindness to Israel would be lifted at the point and time, "until", when "the fullness of the Gentiles be come in", which equates to, "the harvest is the end of the (Old Covenant) age (Matthew 13:39)."

So, the Church began with Jews and then grafted in the nations. The Church then saw vindication poured upon her persecutors (Luke 18:1-8, 21: -22). Her persecutors were Old Covenant Israel, headquartered in Jerusalem the Great City, Babylon (Galatians 4:25-

26, 29; 1 Thessalonians 2:14-16; 1 Peter 5:13; Revelation 11:8; 14:8; 16:19; 17:5,18; 18:2,10,18,19,21; 19:2). This came about as the harlot (Jerusalem, Isaiah 1:21) rode the beast (Rome, Revelation 17:3) and controlled the reins of the persecution, until Rome turned on its rider (Revelation 17:16). Jews throughout the empire would be given a jump start to faith through provocation (At their end- Deuteronomy 32:29), as they "saw" the revelation of the Prophet of prophet's words coming to pass before their eyes, "there shall not be left here one stone upon another, that shall not be thrown down (Matthew 24:2)". Remember that the words of Jesus, including these words, were spread throughout the empire (Colossians 1:6, 23, Romans 1:8, 10:18, 16:25, 26).

These Old Covenant mockers (2 Peter 3:4,5) had their eyes opened as, behold, He is coming with the cloud, (Isaiah 19:1, 13:9-10; Ezekiel 30:3-4, 32:7-8; Matthew 10:23, 16:28, 26:64) ; and every eye shall see Him (the Greek word for "see" is Optanomai, with its word origin going back to the word Horao, which means to discern, perceive, and understand, not mere mechanical "seeing") and they which pierced Him (This is clearly referring to a first century generation, Acts 2:36, 40): and all the tribes (No twelve tribes around today) of the land (the unholy land, not the globe) shall wail because of Him…(Revelation 1:7)." This quote from Zechariah 12:10 makes it very clear in the next verse (Zechariah 12:11) as to where this all is to take place, "In that day shall there be a great mourning IN JERUSALEM…. and the land (not globe) shall mourn… the family of the house of David…"

Location, Location, Location, how clearly does the context spell it out for us, Jerusalem! So, Jews within Jerusalem would "see" the words of Jesus come to pass at the destruction of Jerusalem. Those Jews throughout the empire would "see" (discern, perceive, understand, by word of mouth, or even by reading it in the Roman Publication, Acta Diuma, "Daily Acts") Jesus' coming in the cloud of judgment as well. This would spark faith in the hearts of Jews throughout the empire as they saw Jesus' words come to pass, down to the last specific details. There would be repentance and mourning as they recognized Jesus as their Messiah and wept for Him as one weeps for His only son (Zechariah 12:10, 11). Those within the judged city would be saved (Not every last individual) through this recognition, yet they would have to undergo a death bed conversion. So, the fullness of the Gentiles is a whole, complete, full, and total amount, a harvest at the end of the age (Matthew 13:39). It's not a matter of every last individual being included in this fullness of the Gentiles, just as every last individual is not included in all Israel being saved in the next verse. Remember that even futurists only consider 1/3 of Israel to be saved, according to their futuristic view of Zechariah 13:8.

Romans 11:26, "and so all Israel shall be saved: as it is written, there shall come out of Zion the Deliverer, and shall turn away ungodliness from Jacob:" "and so", is the continuation of the previous thought in the previous verse. It is the result of the previous verse. It is saying that through Israel's blindness, the Gentiles would be reached through the world-wide (Oikoumene, world, Roman "world", Acts 17:6) spread of the good news of the Jewish Messiah's Kingdom, His expanding (increasing) kingdom (Isaiah 9:7, 11:9; Matthew 13:31-33)! The boarders of this Israel (Matthew 2:15) are expanding (Ephesians 2:12; Matthew 21:43; 1 Peter 2:9, Galatians 6:16; Hebrews 12:22-23; Galatians 4:26) to fill the whole earth (Acts 1:8; Daniel 2:35)! It is through this process that all Israel would be saved. "All" carries in it the meaning of just the right amount, a whole and complete amount, not 100% salvation. The ESV makes this point clearer, "and in this way all Israel will be saved…" Through this procedure, in this manner, in this scenario, will Israel be saved? As many as are to be saved will be saved, resulting in a whole amount and complete amount, just the right amount being saved.

This master plan, simply put, was for the gospel to go out into all the world (Mathew 24:14; Colossians 1:5,6,23, Romans 1:8, 10:18; 16:25,26; Acts 17:6), bringing in the fullness (complete, whole, just the right amount) of the Gentiles, and the full amount of Jews (All Israel, a whole and complete amount), where both groups are gathered into one in a harvest at the end of the Old Covenant age (Matthew 13:39, end of the "age" /"aion", not the world or globe). Those being saved in Israel are not 100% of the nation's population, any more than those being saved in "the nations of them which are saved" (Revelation 21:24) are 100% of their respective populations. Again, futurists even acknowledge this in saying that only 1/3 of the nation of Israel is to be saved (Zechariah 13:8). Romans 9:27, quoted from Isaiah 10:22, reminds us of this fact, "Though the number of the children of Israel be as the sand of the sea, A REMNANT SHALL BE SAVED." This is the same whole, complete, and full amount, of which Paul was amongst in vs 5, "Even so then at this present time also there is A REMNANT according to the remnant of grace (Romans 11:5)."

Note that this whole and complete amount includes those Jews who had been scattered throughout the Roman Empire in previous captivities. This includes those Jews from the Assyrian captivity, the ten northern tribes. Their salvation and gathering came in the ultimate gathering place, IN JESUS CHRIST. Is there any place that exceeds the salvation, glory, blessings, riches, peace, and power, which is experienced IN JESUS CHRIST? IN THE MIDDLE EAST, in a carnal kingdom someday, does not measure up to the ultimate gathering place, IN JESUS CHRIST, the only place for any people to be saved! Thus, ALL (a whole, complete amount) ISRAEL was saved through the gospel of Jesus Christ, which reached ALL JEWS in exile throughout the Roman Empire (Colossians 1:5,6,23; Matthew 24:14; Romans 1:8, 10:18, 16:25,26; Acts 2:5, 8:4,17:6)! Colossians 1:5, 6, "…the gospel: Which is come unto you, as it is in all the world" (Oikoumene "world", the Roman world, same word in Luke 2:1, "…all the world should be taxed"). This fulfills Matthew 24:14! Matthew 24:14, "and this gospel of the kingdom shall be preached in the whole world (Oikoumene) for a witness unto all nations (Including the nation of Israel); and then shall the end come." The end of the Old Covenant "age", (Not the present-day globe, Matthew13:39, 24:3), it's nation, capitol city, and its covenant headquarters, the temple, would all come to an end.

This happened within the lifespan of "this generation" in Matthew 24:34. Colossians 1:23, "…the gospel, which ye have heard, and which was preached to all creation which is under heaven…" Fulfilling Mark 16:15!

Romans 1:8, "First, I thank my God through Jesus Christ for you all, that your faith is spoken of throughout the whole world." "Kosmos" is the Greek word for "world" here, which does not necessarily imply the globe, but rather the arrangement, constitution, order, or government, that is, the Government of the Roman Empire.

Romans 10:18, "but I say, have they not heard? Yes verily, their sound went into all the earth, and their words unto the end of the world." Oikoumene "world" here, the Roman world.

Romans 16:25-26, "… the preaching of Jesus Christ, … now made manifest, and by the scriptures…MADE KNOWN TO ALL NATIONS for the obedience of faith."

Acts 2:5, "and there were dwelling at Jerusalem Jews, devout men, OUT OF EVERY NATION UNDER HEAVEN." In verse below, these same Jews went out from Jerusalem proclaiming the gospel throughout the empire.

Acts 8:4, "therefore they that were scattered abroad WENT EVERYWHERE preaching the word." We see the consequences of this in the next listed verse.

Acts 17:6, "…these that have turned the world upside down." (Oikoumene "world", the Roman world) Now, Romans 11:26, continues after, "…all Israel shall be saved", with, "…as it is written, there shall come out of Zion the Deliverer, and shall turn away ungodliness from Jacob." This can be more clearly understood when we visit the Old Testament passage from which this verse is quoting. It is taken from Isaiah 59:20, 21,"and the Redeemer shall come to Zion, and unto them that turn from transgression in Jacob, saith the Lord."

There is a condition for deliverance and salvation here. Only those who turn from transgression in Jacob are saved! There is a clear inference here that there are those in Zion who heed to this condition of turning from transgression, which means that there are those in Zion who do not heed to the condition. There are those who the Redeemer comes to deliver, and it is only as many as turn from transgression in Zion. Again, most futurists do not claim 100% nationwide salvation, but only 1/3 of the nation. This is correct, only the timing is off by a couple millennia.

To understand Isaiah 59:20-21 more clearly, let's consider that the verse begins with the word "AND", "and the Redeemer shall come to Zion…" This communicates clearly that the verse is tied directly to the previous verse and is a continuation of that verse's thought. So let's examine the previous verse in conjunction with Isaiah 59:20-21, that is, Isaiah 59:19, "for he will come like a pent-up flood that the breath of the Lord (2 Thessalonians 2:8) drives along. The redeemer will come to Zion, to those in Jacob that repent of their sins, declares the Lord (From the NIV, there is a KJV error here)." The Lord comes in judgment upon the persecutors of the faithful in Jacob by pouring out His vengeance upon them; in turn He delivers the righteous. We must understand that the coming flood is describing the invading forces coming upon Zion (Jerusalem), yet they are "His Armies" in Matthew 22:7, as Nebuchadnezzar was "My servant" in Jeremiah 43:10.

This same flood is described in Daniel 9:26, "and after threescore and two weeks shall Messiah be cut off, but not for Himself: and the people of the prince ("Messiah the prince", identified in the previous verse, Daniel 9:25, sends "the people of the prince", or "His Armies", Matthew 22:7) that shall come shall destroy the city (Jerusalem, "burn their city", Mt.22:7) and the sanctuary (the temple); and the end thereof shall be with a flood." The timeline of this flood is laid out perfectly as these two passages (Isaiah 59:19-20 & Daniel 9:26) harmonize together concerning the destruction of the city and "the end" of the Old Covenant temple and system (Hebrews 8:13), which caused the sacrifice and oblation to cease! It was the end of the age (Matthew 24:3), the Old Covenant system would come to an official end in AD 70! It had not ceased in operation until this time. This is why Hebrews 8:13 states that the Old Covenant was ready to vanish away. At the time of the writing of the book of Hebrews, it had not yet done so. In AD 70 it did finally end.

- Garrett Paul Parrish & Terry Kashian

Romans

Chapter 1

1. Paul, a servant of Jesus Christ, called to be an apostle, separated to the gospel of God,
2. Which He promised before by His prophets in the Holy Scriptures,
3. Concerning His Son Jesus Christ our Lord, who began to be out of the seed of David according to the flesh;
4. And constituted the Son of God in power, according to the Spirit of holiness, out of the resurrection from the dead:
5. By whom we have received grace and apostleship, into obedience to the faith in all nations, for His name:
6. In Whom you are also the called to be Jesus Christ's:
7. To all that be in Rome, beloved by God, called to be saints: grace to you and peace from God our Father, and the Lord Jesus Christ.
8. First, I thank my God through Jesus Christ for you all, that your faith is spoken of throughout the whole known world.
9. For God is my witness, Whom I serve in my spirit in the gospel of His Son, that without stopping I make mention of you always in my prayers;
10. Making request, if by any means now at length I might have a prosperous journey by the will of God to come to you.
11. For I long to see you, that I may give to you some spiritual gift, to the end that you may be established;
12. That is, that I may be comforted together with you by the mutual faith we both share.
13. Now I would not have you unaware, brothers, that I often planned to come to you, (but was hindered until now) that I might have some fruit among you also, just as among other nations.
14. I am debtor both to the Greeks and to the Barbarians; both to the wise and the unwise.
15. So, as much as in me is, I am ready to preach the gospel to you that are at Rome also.
16. For I am not ashamed of the gospel of Christ: for it is the power of God to salvation for everyone that believes; to the Jew first, and also to the Greek.
17. For in it is the righteousness of God revealed out of faith into faith: as it is written, the righteous will be living out of faith.
18. For the wrath of God is revealed from heaven against all ungodliness and unrighteousness of men, who hold the reality in unrighteousness;
19. Because that which may be known of God is manifest in them; for God has showed it to them.
20. For the invisible things of Him from the creation of the world are clearly seen, being understood by the things that are made, even His infinite power and divinity; so that they are without excuse:
21. Because that, when they knew God, they did not glorify Him as God, neither were thankful; but became futile in their imaginations, and their foolish heart was darkened.

22. Professing themselves to be wise, they became fools,
23. And changed the glory of the incorruptible God into an image made like corruptible man and to birds, four-footed beasts, and creeping things.
24. Therefore, God also gave them up to uncleanness through the lusts of their own hearts, to dishonor their own bodies between themselves:
25. Who altered the reality of God into the lie, and worshiped and served the creation above the Creator, who is blessed into the New Covenant Age. Amen. For this reason, God gave them up to dishonorable passions: for even their women altered that physical use into that which is against nature:
26. And just as they did not prove worthy to hold acknowledge God, God delivered them over to a counterfeit understanding, to do those things which are inappropriate;
27. Being filled with all unrighteousness, fornication, wickedness, covetousness, maliciousness; full of envy, murder, debate, deceit, malignity; whisperers,
28. Backbiters, haters of God, impertinent, proud, boasters, inventors of evil things, disobedient to parents,
29. Without understanding, covenant breakers, unloving, irreconcilable, unmerciful:
30. Who knowing the judgment of God, that they which do such things are worthy of death, not only do the same but take pleasure with them that commit them.

Chapter 2

1. Therefore, you are inexcusable, O man, whoever you are that judge: for in that which you judge another, you condemn yourself; for you that judge are doing the same things.
2. But we are sure that the judgment of God is according to reality against those who commit such things.
3. Then think you this, O man, that judge those who do such things, and are doing the same, that you will escape the judgment of God?
4. Or do you despise the riches of His goodness and forbearance and patience; not knowing that the goodness of God leads you to repentance?
5. But after your hardness and unrepentant heart treasure up to yourself wrath against the day of wrath and revelation of the righteous judgment of God;
6. Who will render to every man according to his deeds:
7. To them who by patient continuance in well doing seek for glory and honor and incorruptibility, infinite life:
8. But to them that are contentious, and do not obey the reality, but obey unrighteousness, indignation, and wrath,
9. Tribulation and anguish, upon every soul of man that does evil, for the Jew first, and also for the nations;
10. But glory, honor, and peace, to every man that works good, to the Jew first, and also to the nations:
11. For there is no partiality with God.

12. For as many as have sinned without Law will also perish without Law: and as many as have sinned in the Law will be judged by the Law;
13. (For the hearers of the Law are not justified before God, but the doers of the Law will be justified.
14. For when the nations, who do not have the Law, do instinctively the things contained in the Law, these, not having the Law, are a law to themselves:
15. Who show the work of the law written in their hearts, their conscience also giving witness, and between themselves, their thoughts accusing or else excusing.)
16. In the day when God will judge the secrets of men by Jesus Christ according to my gospel.
17. Behold, you are called a Jew, and rest in the Law, and make your boast of God,
18. And know his will, and approve the more excellent things, being instructed out of the Law;
19. So, are confident that you yourself are a guide to the blind, a light to them who are in darkness,
20. An instructor to the foolish, a teacher of the immature, who have the semblance of knowledge and of the reality in the Law.
21. You therefore who teach another, teach not yourself? You that preach a man should not steal, do you steal?
22. You that say a man should not commit adultery, do you commit adultery? You that hate idols, do you commit sacrilege?
23. You that make your boast of the Law, through breaking the Law, do you dishonor God?
24. For the name of God is blasphemed among the nations through you, as it is written.
25. For circumcision truthfully profits, if you keep the Law: but if you are a breaker of the Law, your circumcision is made uncircumcision.
26. Therefore, if the uncircumcision keeps the righteousness of the Law, will not his uncircumcision be counted for circumcision?
27. Then will not uncircumcision which is out from the physical origin, if he fulfills the Law, will he not judge you, through that which is written and circumcision, you who violate the Law?
28. For he is not a Jew, who is one outwardly; neither is that circumcision, which is outward in the flesh:
29. But he is a Jew, who is one inwardly; and circumcision is that of the heart, in the Spirit, and not in the letter; whose praise is not of men, but of God.

Chapter 3

1. What advantage then has the Jew? Or what is the profit of circumcision?
2. Much every way: chiefly, because to them were committed the sayings of God.
3. For what if some did not believe? Will their unbelief make the faith of God without effect?
4. God forbid: yes, let God be true, but every man a liar; as it is written, that You might be justified in Your sayings, and may overcome when You are judged.

Romans 3:5

5. But if our unrighteousness commends the righteousness of God, what will we say? Is God unrighteous who takes vengeance? (I speak as a man)
6. God forbid: for then how will God judge the world?
7. For if the reality of God has increased through my lie to His glory; why then am I also judged as a sinner?
8. And not rather, (as we are slanderously reported, and as some affirm that we say) let us do evil that good may come? Whose damnation is just.
9. What then? Are we better than them? No, in no way: for we have previously proved both Jews and other nations, that they are all under sin;
10. As it is written, there is none righteous, no, not one:
11. No one understands, and no one seeks after God.
12. They are all taken out of the way, they are together become unprofitable; no one does good, no, not one.
13. Their throat is an open tomb; with their tongues, they have used deceit; the poison of asps is under their lips:
14. Whose mouth is full of cursing and bitterness:
15. Their feet are swift to shed blood:
16. Destruction and misery are in their ways:
17. And the way of peace have they not known:
18. There is no fear of God before their eyes.
19. Now we know that whatsoever the things of the Law says, it says to them who are in the Law: that every mouth may be stopped, and all the world may become guilty before God.
20. Therefore, by the deeds of the Law, there will no flesh be justified in His sight: for by the Law is the knowledge of sin.
21. But now the righteousness of God apart from the Law is manifested, being witnessed by the Law and the prophets;
22. Even the righteousness of God which is by faith in Jesus Christ to all and upon all them that believe: for there is no difference:
23. For all sin, and fall short of the glory of God;
24. Being justified freely by His grace through the redemption that is in Christ Jesus:
25. Whom God purposed to be a mercy seat through faith in His blood, into showing His righteousness through the passing over sins that were done, in the restraint of God;
26. To explain, I say, at this time His righteousness: that He might be just, and the justifier of whoever believes in Jesus.
27. Then where is boasting? It is excluded. By what law? By works? No: but by the law of faith.
28. Therefore, we conclude that a man is justified by faith apart from the deeds of the Law.
29. Is He the God of the Jews only? Is He not also of the nations? Yes, of the nations also:
30. Seeing it is one God, who will justify the circumcision by faith, and uncircumcision through faith.
31. Do we then make void the Law through faith? God forbid! On the contrary, we establish the Law.

Chapter 4

1. What will we say then that Abraham our father, as according to the flesh, has found?
2. For if Abraham was justified by works, he has something to glory about; but not before God.
3. For what says the Scriptures? Abraham believed God, and it was accounted to him for righteousness.
4. Now to him who works, the wages are not counted as grace, but as debt.
5. But to him that works not, but believes on Him that justifies the ungodly, his faith is counted for righteousness.
6. Just as David also describes the blessedness of the man, to whom God ascribes righteousness without works,
7. Saying, blessed are they whose iniquities are forgiven, and whose sins are covered.
8. Blessed is the man whose sin the Lord will never count against him.
9. Comes this blessedness then upon the circumcision only, or upon the uncircumcision also? For we say that faith was accounted to Abraham for righteousness.
10. Then how was it accounted? While he was circumcised, or uncircumcised? Not while circumcised, but uncircumcised.
11. For he received the sign of circumcision, as a seal of the righteousness of the faith which he had while being uncircumcised: that he might become the father of all them that believe, though they were not circumcised; that righteousness may be ascribed to them also:
12. And the father of circumcision to them who are not of the circumcision only, but who also walk in the steps of that faith of our father Abraham, which he had while being uncircumcised.
13. For the promise, that he should be the heir of the world, was not to Abraham, or his seed, through the Law, but through the righteousness of faith.
14. For if they who are of the Law be heirs, faith is made void, and the promise made of no effect:
15. Because the Law works wrath: for where there is no Law, there is also no transgression.
16. Therefore, it is by faith, that it might be by grace; to the end, the promise may be certain to all the seed; not to that only which is by the Law, but to that also which is of the faith of Abraham; who is the father of us all,
17. (As it is written, I have made you a father of many nations) in the presence of Him whom he believed, even God, who gives life to the dead, and calls those things which are not as though they were.
18. Who against hope believed in hope, that he might become the father of many nations, according to that which was spoken, so will your seed be.
19. For being not weak in faith, he considered not his own body now dead, when he was about a hundred years old, neither yet the deadness of Sarah's womb:
20. He staggered not at the promise of God through unbelief; but was strong in faith, giving glory to God;

21. So being fully persuaded that, what He had promised, He was able also to perform.
22. Therefore, it was accounted to him for righteousness.
23. Now it was not written for his sake alone, that it was accounted to him;
24. But for us also, to whom it is about to be accounted if we believe in Him that raised up Jesus our Lord from the dead;
25. Who was delivered for our offenses, and was raised again for our justification.

Chapter 5

1. Therefore, being justified by faith, we have peace with God through our Lord Jesus Christ:
2. By whom also we have access by faith into this grace in which we stand, and rejoice in hope of the glory of God.
3. And not only so, but we glory in tribulations also: knowing that tribulation works patience;
4. And patience, experience; and experience, hope:
5. Now hope does not disappoint; because the love of God is poured out in our hearts by the Holy Spirit who is given to us.
6. For when we were yet without strength, in due time Christ died for the ungodly.
7. For scarcely for a righteous man will one die: yet perhaps for a good man some would even dare to die.
8. But God demonstrates His love toward us, in that, while we were yet sinners, Christ died for us.
9. Much more than, being now justified in His blood, we will be saved from wrath through Him.
10. For if, when we were enemies, we were conciliated to God by the death of His Son, much more, being conciliated, we will be saved in His life.
11. Not only so, but we also joy in God through our Lord Jesus Christ, by whom we now have received the conciliation.
12. Therefore, as by one-man sin entered into the world, and death by sin; and so, death passed through into all men, for that all have sinned:
13. (Because up until the Law sin was in the world: but sin is not ascribed when there is no Law.
14. Nevertheless, death reigned from Adam to Moses, even over them that had not sinned after the similitude of Adam's transgression, who is a type of Him that is about to come.
15. But the free gift is not like the offense. For if through the offense of one many be dead, much more the grace of God, and the gift in grace, who is by one man, Jesus Christ, has abounded to many.
16. For the gift is not like that which came by the one that sinned: for the judgment which came from one offense resulted in condemnation, but the free gift which came by many offenses resulted in justification.
17. For if by one man's offense, death reigned by one; much more they which receive abundance of grace and of the gift of righteousness will reign in life by one, Jesus Christ.

18. Therefore, as by the offense of one judgment came upon all men to condemnation; even so, by the righteousness of one, the free gift came upon all men to justification for life.
19. For as by one man's disobedience many were made sinners, so by the obedience of one will many be made righteous.
20. Moreover, the Law entered, that the offense might increase. But where sin increased, grace did much more increase:
21. That as sin has reigned in death, even so, may grace reign through righteousness to infinite life by Jesus Christ our Lord.

Chapter 6

1. What will we say then? Will we continue in sin, that grace may increase?
2. God forbid! How will we, who are dead to sin, live any longer in it?
3. Do you not know that so many of us who were immersed into Jesus Christ were baptized into His death?
4. Therefore, we are buried with Him through immersion into death: that just as Christ was raised out of the dead through the glory of the Father, even so, we also should walk in newness of life.
5. For if we have been planted together in His death, we will be also in His resurrection:
6. Knowing this, that our old man is crucified with Him, that the body of sin may be destroyed, that after this we should not serve sin.
7. For he that is dead is freed from sin.
8. Now if we be dead with Christ, we believe that we will also live with Him:
9. Knowing that Christ being raised from the dead dies no more; death has no more dominion over Him.
10. For in that He died, He died to sin once: but in that He lives, He lives to God.
11. Likewise, consider yourselves also to be dead indeed to sin, but alive to God through Jesus Christ our Lord.
12. Therefore, let not sin reign in your mortal body, that you should obey it and the desires of it.
13. Neither be yielding your members as instruments of unrighteousness to sin: but offer yourselves to God, as those that are alive from the dead, and your members as instruments of righteousness to God.
14. For sin will not have dominion over you: for you are not under the Law, but under grace.
15. What then? Will we sin, because we are not under the Law, but under grace? Absolutely not!
16. Do you not know, that to whom you yield yourselves servants to obey, his servants you are to whom you obey; whether by sin into death, or by obedience into righteousness?
17. But God be thanked, that you were the servants of sin, but you have obeyed from the heart that form of teaching which was delivered to you.
18. Being then made free from sin, you became the servants of righteousness.

19. I speak after the manner of men because of the weakness of your flesh: for as you have yielded your members slaves to uncleanness and to lawlessness leading into more lawlessness; even so, now yield your members slaves to righteousness into holiness.
20. For when you were the slaves of sin, you were free from righteousness.
21. What fruit had you then in those things in which you are now ashamed? The outcome of those things is death.
22. But now being released from sin, and having become enslaved to God, you have your fruit into sanctification and the goal, infinite life.
23. For the wages of sin is death, but the gift of God is infinite life through Jesus Christ our Lord.

Chapter 7

1. Do you not know, brothers, (for I speak to them that know the Law) that the Law has dominion over a man as long as he lives?
2. For the woman who has a husband is bound by the Law to her husband as long as he lives; but if the husband dies, she is released from the Law of her husband.
3. So, then if, while her husband lives, she be married to another man, she will be called an adulteress: but if her husband dies, she is free from that Law; so that she is not an adulteress, though she marry another man.
4. Therefore, my brothers, you also have become dead to the Law by the body of Christ; that you should be married to another, even to Him who is raised from the dead, that we should bring forth fruit for God.
5. For when we were in the flesh, the passions of sins, which were by the Law, did work in our members to bring forth fruit to death.
6. But now we are delivered from the Law, that being dead in what we were held; that we should serve in newness of Spirit, and not in the oldness of the letter.
7. What will we say then? Is the Law sin? God forbid! No, I did not know sin, but by the Law: for I had not known lust, except the Law had said, you will not covet.
8. But sin, taking opportunity by the commandment, worked in me all manner of evil desire. For without the Law, sin was dead.
9. For I was alive without the Law once: but when the commandment came, sin revived, and I died.
10. And the commandment which was ordained to life, I found to be to death.
11. For sin, taking advantage of the commandment, deceived me, and by it killed me.
12. Therefore, the Law is holy, and the commandment holy, and just, and good.
13. Was then that which was good produce death in me? Absolutely not! But sin, that it may appear sin, working death in me by that which is good; that sin by the commandment might become exceedingly sinful.

14. For we know that the Law is spiritual: but I am fleshly, sold under sin.
15. For what I am doing, I do not understand. For what I will to do, that I do not practice; but I do what I hate.
16. If then I do that which I would not, I consent to the Law that it is good.
17. Now then it is no more I that do it, but sin that dwells in me.
18. For I know that in me (that is, in my flesh,) dwells no good thing: for to will is present with me; but how to perform that which is good I do not find.
19. For the good that I would do I don't do: but the evil which I don't want, that I do.
20. Now if I do what I do not want, it is no more I that do it, but sin that dwells in me.
21. I find then a law, that, when I purpose to do good, evil is present with me.
22. For I delight in the law of God after the inner man:
23. But I see another law in my members, warring against the law of my mind, and bringing me into captivity to the law of sin which is in my members.
24. O wretched man that I am! Who will save me from the body of this death?
25. I thank God through Jesus Christ our Lord. So then with my mind, I serve the Law of God; but with my flesh the law of sin.

Chapter 8

1. Therefore, there is now no condemnation to those who are in Christ Jesus.
2. For the law of the Spirit of life in Christ Jesus has liberated me from the law of sin and of the death.
3. For the Law being impotent, in that it was weak through the flesh, God sending His own Son in the likeness of sinful flesh, and for sin, condemned sin in the flesh:
4. That the righteousness of the Law might be fulfilled in us, who walk not after the flesh, but after the Spirit.
5. For they that are after the flesh do mind the things of the flesh; but they that are after the Spirit the things of the Spirit.
6. For to be fleshly minded is death; but to be spiritually minded is life and peace.
7. Because the fleshly mind is enmity against God: for it is not subject to the Law of God, neither indeed can be.
8. So, then they that are in the flesh cannot please God.
9. But you are not in the flesh, but in the spirit, if the Spirit of God dwells in you. Now if any man have not the Spirit of Christ, he is none of His.
10. And if Christ be in you, the body is dead because of sin; but the spirit is life because of righteousness.
11. But if the Spirit of Him that raised up Jesus out from the dead dwells in you, He that raised up Christ out from the dead will also give life to the mortal body by His Spirit that dwells in you.
12. Therefore, brothers, we are debtors, not to the flesh, to live after the flesh.
13. For if you live after the flesh, you are about to die: but if through the Spirit you put to death the deeds of the body, you will live.

14. For as many as are led by the Spirit of God, they are the sons of God.
15. For you have not received the spirit of bondage again to fear; but you have received the Spirit of being placed as a son, in which we cry, Abba, Father!
16. The Spirit Himself testifies together with our spirit, that we are the children of God:
17. And if children, then heirs; heirs of God, and joint-heirs with Christ; if so be we jointly suffer, to also be jointly glorified.
18. For I consider that the sufferings now are not worthy to be compared with the glory which is about to be unveiled into us.
19. For the earnest expectation of the creation anticipates the unveiling of the sons of God.
20. For the creation was placed in subjection to emptiness, not of its own will, but through Him who has subjected it in hope,
21. Because the creation himself will also be delivered from the bondage of corruption into the freedom of the glory of the children of God.
22. For we know that the whole creation groans and labors in birth pains together until now.
23. Not only they, but we ourselves also, who have the first fruits of the Spirit, even we ourselves groan within ourselves, waiting to be placed as sons, that is, the redemption of our body.
24. For we are saved by hope: but hope that is seen is not hope: for what a man sees, why does he yet hope for it?
25. But if we hope for that which we do not see, then we with patience wait for it.
26. Likewise, the Spirit also helps our weaknesses: for we know not what we should pray for as we should: but the Spirit Himself makes intercession for us with groanings which cannot be uttered.
27. And He that searches the hearts knows what the mind of the Spirit is, because He makes intercession for the saints according to the will of God.
28. For we know that all things work together for the good to them that love God, to them who are called according to His purpose.
29. For who He foreknew, He also predestined to be conformed to the image of His Son, that He might be the firstborn among many brothers.
30. Moreover, whom He did predestine, He also called: and who He called, He also justified: and whom He justified, He also glorified.
31. What will we then say to these things? If God be for us, who can be against us?
32. He that spared not His own Son, but delivered Him up for us all, how will He not with Him also freely give us all things?
33. Who will bring a charge to God's elect? It is God that justifies.
34. Who is he that condemns? It is Christ who died, yes, and is risen again, who is even at the right hand of God, who also makes intercession for us.
35. Who will separate us from the love of Christ? Will tribulation, or distress, or persecution, or famine, or nakedness, or peril, or sword?
36. As it is written, for Your sake we are killed all the day long; we are accounted as sheep for the slaughter.

37. No, in all these things we are more than conquerors through Him who loved us.
38. For I am persuaded, that neither death, nor life, nor angels, nor rulers, nor powers, nor things present, nor things about to come,
39. Nor height, nor depth, nor any other creature, will be able to separate us from the love of God, which is in Christ Jesus our Lord.

Chapter 9

1. I say the reality in Christ, I lie not, my conscience also giving me witness in the Holy Spirit,
2. That I have great heaviness and continual sorrow in my heart.
3. For I could wish that myself were accursed from Christ for my brothers, my countrymen according to the flesh:
4. Who are Israelites; to whom is the placing as sons, and the glory, and the covenants, and the giving of the Law, and the service of God, and the promises;
5. Whose are the fathers, and out of whom is the Christ according to the flesh, who is over all, God blessed into the New Covenant Age. Amen.
6. Not as though the word of God has taken no effect. For they are not all Israel, which are out of Israel:
7. Not either, because they are the seed of Abraham, are they all children: but, in Isaac will your seed be called.
8. That is, those who are the children of the flesh, these are not the children of God: but the children of the promise are counted for the seed.
9. For the word of promise is this, at this time I will come, and Sarah will have a son.
10. And not only this; but when Rebecca also had conceived by one man, even by our father Isaac;
11. (For the children not yet being born, neither having done any good or evil, that the purpose of God according to election might stand, not of works, but of Him that calls)
12. It was said to her, that the older will serve the younger.
13. As it is written, Jacob have I loved, but Esau have I hated.
14. What will we say then? Is there unrighteousness with God? God forbid!
15. For He says to Moses, I will have mercy on whom I will have mercy, and I will have compassion on whom I will have compassion.
16. So, then it is not of him that wills, nor of him that runs, but of God that shows mercy.
17. For the Scripture said to Pharaoh, even for this same purpose have I raised you up, that I may show My power in you, and that My name may be declared throughout all the land.
18. Therefore, He has mercy on whom He will have mercy, and who He will He hardens.
19. You will say then to me, why does He yet find fault? For who has resisted His will?
20. But no, O man, who are you to reply against God? Will the thing made say to him that made it, why have you so made me?

21. Has not the potter power over the clay, of the same lump to make one vessel to honor, and another to dishonor?
22. What if God, willing to show His wrath, and to make His power known, endured with much longsuffering the vessels of wrath fitted to destruction:
23. Then that He might make known the riches of His glory on the vessels of mercy, who He had previously prepared to glory,
24. Even us, who He has called, not of the Jews only, but also of the nations?
25. As He also says in Hosea, I will call them My people, who were not My people; and her beloved, who was not beloved.
26. And it will come to pass, that in the place where it was said to them, you are not My people; there will they be called the sons of the living God.
27. Isaiah also cries concerning Israel, though the number of the sons of Israel be as the sand of the sea, a remnant will be saved:
28. For fulfilling the word, and cutting it short in righteousness: because the word will accomplish it and the Lord will cut it short upon the land.
29. And as Isaiah said before, unless the Lord of Sabaoth had left us a seed, we would have been as Sodom, and would have been as Gomorrah.
30. What then will we say? Those nations, who followed not after righteousness, have attained righteousness, even the righteousness which is of faith.
31. But Israel, which followed after the Law of righteousness, has not attained the Law of righteousness.
32. Why? Because they sought it not out of faith, but as it were out of the works of the Law. For they stumbled at that stumbling stone;
33. As it is written, behold, I lay in Zion a stumbling stone and rock of offense: and every one believing on Him will not be disgraced.

Chapter 10

1. Brothers, my heart's desire and prayer to God for Israel is, that they may be saved.
2. For I give them witness that they possess a zeal for God, but not according to knowledge.
3. For being ignorant of God's righteousness, and going about to establish their own righteousness, have not submitted themselves to the righteousness of God.
4. For Christ is the goal of the Law for righteousness to everyone who believes.
5. For Moses wrote the righteousness which is out of the Law, that man who does those things will be living in them.
6. But the righteousness which is out of faith expresses in this manner, do not say in your heart, who will ascend into heaven? (That is, to bring Christ down from above)
7. Or, who will descend into the Abyss? (That is, to bring Christ up again from the dead),
8. But what is said? The word is close to you, even in your mouth, and in your heart: that is, the word of faith, which we preach;

9. That if you will confess with your mouth the Lord Jesus, and will believe in your heart that God has raised Him from the dead, you will be saved.
10. For with the heart man believes for righteousness; and with the mouth, confession is made for salvation.
11. For the Scripture says, whoever believes in Him will not be put to shame.
12. For there is no difference between the Jew and the Greek: for the same Lord overall is rich to all that call on Him.
13. For whosoever will call on the name of the Lord will be saved.
14. How then will they call on Him in whom they have not believed? And how will they believe in Him of whom they have not heard? And how will they hear without a preacher?
15. And how will they preach, unless they are sent? As it is written, how beautiful are the feet of them that preach the gospel of peace, and bring glad tidings of good things!
16. But they have not all obeyed the gospel. For Isaiah said, Lord, who has believed our report?
17. Therefore, faith comes out from hearing and hearing through the speaking of God.
18. But I say, have they not heard? Yes truthfully, their sound went into all the land, and their words to the ends of the Roman world.
19. But I say, did Israel not know? First Moses said, I will provoke you to jealousy by them that are not a nation, and by a nation without understanding I will anger you.
20. But Isaiah says very boldly, I was found by them that sought Me not; I was revealed to them that did not inquire of Me.
21. But to Israel He said, all day long I have stretched out My hands to a disobedient and a people voicing opposition.

Chapter 11

1. I say then, Has God cast away his people? God forbid! For I also am an Israelite, of the seed of Abraham, of the tribe of Benjamin.
2. God has not cast away His people whom He foreknew. Do you not know what the Scripture says of Elijah? How he makes intercession to God against Israel saying,
3. Lord, they have killed Your prophets, and torn down Your altars; and I am left alone, and they seek my life.
4. But what says the answer of God to him? I have reserved for Myself seven thousand men, who have not bowed the knee to Baal.
5. Even so then at this present time, there is a remnant according to the election of grace.
6. And if by grace, then is it no more of works: otherwise grace is no more grace. But if it be of works, then it is no more grace: otherwise, work is no longer work.
7. What then? Israel has not obtained what it seeks, but the elect have obtained it, and the rest were callous.
8. Just as it is written, God has given them the spirit of slumber, eyes that they should not see, and ears that they should not hear; to this day.
9. And David said, let their table be made a snare and a trap, and a stumbling block, and a recompense to them:

10. Let their eyes be darkened, that they may not see, and bow down their back always.

11. I say then, Have they stumbled that they should fall? God forbid! But rather through their fall salvation has come to the nations, to provoke them to jealousy.

12. Now if the fall of them be the riches of the world, and the diminishing of them the riches of the nations; how much more their fullness?

13. For I speak to you nations, in as much as I am the apostle of the nations, I glorify my service:

14. If by any means I may provoke to jealousy those who are my flesh, and may save some of them.

15. For if the casting away of them is the reconciling of the world, what will the receiving of them be, but life from the dead?

16. For if the first fruits be holy, the lump is also holy: and if the root be holy, so are the branches.

17. And if some of the branches are broken off, and you, being a wild olive, were grafted in among them, and with them partake of the root and fatness of the olive tree;

18. Do not denigrate the branches. But if you denigrate, you do not support the root, but the root supports you.

19. You will say then, the branches were broken off, that I may be grafted in.

20. Very well; because of unbelief they were broken off, and you stand by faith. Do not be superior, but reverent:

21. For if God spared not the branches from birth, perhaps He will not spare you either.

22. Therefore, behold the kindness and severity of God: on those who fell, severity; but toward you, kindness, if you continue in His kindness: otherwise you also will be cut off.

23. And they also, if they do not continue in unbelief, will be grafted in: for God is able to graft them in again.

24. For if you were cut out of the olive tree which is wild by birth, and were grafted contrary from physical birth into a good olive tree: how much more will these, which are the physical branches, be grafted into their own olive tree?

25. For I would not, brothers, that you should be ignorant of this mystery unless you should be wise in your own conceits; that blindness from part of Israel has happened until the fullness of the nations have entered;

26. And in this way all Israel will be saved: as it is written, there will arrive out of Zion the Deliverer, and will turn away ungodliness from Jacob:

27. For this is My covenant to them when I will take away their sins.

28. As concerning the gospel, they are enemies for your sake: but as concerning the election, they are beloved for the Father's sake.

29. For the gifts and calling of God are without a change of mind.

30. For as you in times past have not believed God, yet have now obtained mercy through their stubbornness:

31. Even so have these also now not believed, that through your mercy they also may obtain mercy.

32. For God has committed them all in stubbornness, that He might have mercy on all.
33. O the depth of the riches both of the wisdom and knowledge of God! How unsearchable are His judgments, and His ways past finding out!
34. For who has known the mind of the Lord? Or who has been His advisor?
35. Or who has first given to Him, and it will be repaid to Him again?
36. For by Him, and through Him, and to Him, are all things: to whom be the glory into the New Covenant Age. Amen.

Chapter 12

1. Therefore, I urge you, brothers, by the mercies of God, that you present your bodies as a living sacrifice, holy, acceptable to God, which is your divine logical service.
2. And do not be conformed to this Old Covenant Age: but be transformed by the renewing of your mind, that you may prove what is good, acceptable, and the complete will of God.
3. For I say, through the grace given to me, to every man that is among you, not to think of himself more highly than he ought to think, but to think soberly, according as God has dealt to every man the measure of faith.
4. For as we have many members in one body, and all members do not have the same function:
5. So, we, being many, are one body in Christ, and individual members one of another.
6. Having then gifts differing according to the grace that is given to us, whether prophecy, let us prophesy according to the proportion of faith;
7. Or service, let us use it in our serving: or he that teaches, on teaching;
8. Or he that exhorts, on exhortation: he that gives, let him do it with simplicity; he that leads, with diligence; he that shows mercy, with cheerfulness.
9. Let love be without hypocrisy. Hate that which is evil; cleave to that which is good.
10. Be kindly affectionate to one another with brotherly love; in honor preferring one another;
11. Not lazy in business; fervent in spirit; serving the Lord;
12. Rejoicing in hope; patient in tribulation; continuing steadfastly in prayer;
13. Distributing to the necessity of saints; given to hospitality.
14. Bless those who persecute you: bless, and curse not.
15. Rejoice with those who rejoice, and weep with those that weep.
16. Be like-minded. Do not set your mind on high things, but associate with men the humble. Be not wise in your own opinion.
17. Recompense to no man evil for evil. Regard commendable things in the sight of all men.
18. If it is possible, as it comes out of you, live peaceably with all men.
19. Dearly beloved, avenge not yourselves, but rather give place to wrath: for it is written, Vengeance is Mine; I will repay, says the Lord.

20. Therefore, if your enemy hunger, feed him; if he thirsts, give him drink: for in so doing you will heap coals of fire on his head.
21. Be not be subdued by evil, but subdue evil in good.

Chapter 13

1. Let every soul be subject to the authorities above him. For there is no authority but from God: the authorities that are under God, are appointed.
2. Therefore, whoever fights against authority, stands against the arrangement of God: and they that stand against it will bring on themselves judgment.
3. For rulers are not a terror to good works, but to the evil. Do you desire to not be afraid of authority? Do that which is good, and you will have praise of the same:
4. For he is God's minister to you for good. But if you do that which is evil, be afraid; for he carries not the sword in vain: for he is the minister of God, a punisher to execute wrath on him that does evil.
5. Therefore, you must be subject, not only because of wrath, but also for conscience sake.
6. For this reason pay tribute also: for they are God's servants, attending continually on this very thing.
7. Therefore, give to all that is due: tribute to whom tribute is due; taxes to whom tax is due; fear to whom fear; honor to whom honor.
8. Owe no man anything, except to love one another: for he that loves one another has fulfilled the Law.
9. For in this, you will not commit adultery, you will not murder, you will not steal, you will not bear false witness, you will not covet; and if there be any other command, it is briefly summarized in this saying, namely, you will love your neighbor as yourself.
10. Love works no harm to his neighbor: therefore, love is the fulfillment of the Law.
11. So that, knowing the time, that now it is the hour to awake out of sleep: for now, is our deliverance nearer than when we believed.
12. The night is advancing, the day is approaching: therefore, let us cast off the works of darkness, and let us put on the armor of light.
13. Let us walk honestly, as in the day; not in reveling and drunkenness, not in sleeping around and sexual debauchery, not in contention and jealousy.
14. But you put on the Lord Jesus Christ, and make not provision for the flesh, to fulfill the lusts of it.

Chapter 14

1. Receive him who is weak in the faith, but not to disputes about doubtful things.
2. For one believes that he may eat all things: another, who is weak, eats vegetables.
3. Let not him who eats despise him that eats not; and let not him who eats not judge him that eats: for God has received him.
4. Who are you that judges another man's servant? To his own master, he stands or falls. Yes, he will be held up: for God is able to make him stand.

5. One-man esteems one day above another: another esteems every day alike. Let every man be fully convinced in his own mind.
6. He that regards the day, regards it to the Lord; and he that regards not the day, to the Lord, he does not regard it. He that eats, eats to the Lord, for he gives God thanks; and he that eats not, to the Lord he eats not, and gives God thanks.
7. For none of us live to himself, and no man dies to himself.
8. For whether we live, we live to the Lord; and whether we die, we die to the Lord: therefore, whether we live, or die, we are the Lord's.
9. For to this end Christ both died, and rose, and revived, that He might be Lord both of the dead and living.
10. But why do you judge your brother? Or why do you show contempt for your brother? For we will all stand before the judgment seat of Christ.
11. For it is written, as I live, says the Lord, every knee will bow to Me, and every tongue will confess to God.
12. So, then each one of us will give an account of ourselves to God.
13. Therefore, let us not judge one another any longer: but judge this rather, that no one put a stumbling block or a reason to fall in his brother's way.
14. I know and am persuaded by the Lord Jesus, that there is nothing unclean by itself: but to him that esteems anything to be unclean, to him it is unclean.
15. But if your brother be grieved with your food, now you do not walk lovingly. Do not destroy him with your food, for whom Christ died.
16. Let not then your good be evil spoken of:
17. For the kingdom of God is not food and drink, but righteousness, and peace, and joy in the Holy Spirit!
18. For he that in these things serves Christ is acceptable to God, and approved by men.
19. Therefore, let us follow after the things which make for peace, and things with which one may build up one another.
20. For food do not destroy the work of God. All things indeed are pure, but it is evil for that man who eats with offense.
21. It is good neither to eat meat, nor to drink wine, nor anything in which your brother stumbles, or is offended, or is made weak.
22. Have you faith? Have it to yourself before God. Happy is he that condemns not himself in that thing which he allows.
23. For he that doubts is condemned if he eats because he eats not by faith: for whatever is not of faith is sin.

Chapter 15

1. We then that are strong should carry the scruples of the weak, and not to please ourselves.
2. Let all of us please his neighbor for good to building him up.
3. For even Christ pleased not Himself; but, as it is written, the reproaches of them that reproached You fell on Me.

4. For whatever things were written earlier were written for our learning, that we through patience and comfort of the Scriptures might have hope.

5. Now the God of patience and comfort grant you to be the same one toward another according to Christ Jesus:

6. That you may with the same mind and one mouth glorify God, even the Father of our Lord Jesus Christ.

7. Therefore, receive one another, as Christ also received us to the glory of God.

8. Now I say that Jesus Christ was a servant to the circumcision for the reality of God, to confirm the promises made to the fathers:

9. And that the nations might glorify God for His mercy; as it is written, for this reason, I will confess to You among the nations, and sing to Your name.

10. And again, he says, rejoice, you nations, with His people!

11. And again, Praise the Lord, all you nations; and magnify Him, all you people!

12. And again, Isaiah says, there will be a root of Jesse, and He that will rise to reign over the nations; in Him will the nations trust.

13. Now the God of hope fills you with all joy and peace in believing, that you may increase in hope, through the power of the Holy Spirit.

14. For I also am confident in you, my brothers, that you also are full of goodness, filled with all knowledge, able to admonish one another.

15. Nevertheless, brothers, I have written the more boldly to you on certain matters, as reminders, because of the grace that has been given to me by God,

16. That I should be the servant of Jesus Christ to the nations, ministering as a priest the gospel of God, that the offering up of the nations might be acceptable, being sanctified by the Holy Spirit.

17. Therefore, I have reason to glory through Jesus Christ in those things which relate to God.

18. For I will not dare to speak of any of those things which Christ has not accomplished through me, to bring about the nations obedience, by word and deed,

19. Through mighty signs and wonders, by the power of the Spirit of God; so that from Jerusalem, and around to Illyricum, I have fully preached the gospel of Christ.

20. Yes, so have I striven to preach the gospel, not where Christ was already named unless I should build upon another man's foundation:

21. But as it is written, to who He was not spoken of, they will see: and they that have not heard will understand.

22. For this reason, I also have been hindered greatly from coming to you.

23. But now having no longer a place in these regions, and having a great desire these many years to come to you;

24. Whenever I take my journey into Spain, I will come to you: for I anticipate to behold you on my journey and to be sent forth by you if first, in part I may be filled by you.

25. But now I go to Jerusalem to serve the saints.

26. For it has pleased them of Macedonia and Achaia to make a certain contribution for the poor saints who are at Jerusalem.
27. It was well pleasing to them truthfully, and they are their debtors. For if the nations have been made partakers of their spiritual things, they also must help them in material things.
28. Therefore, when I have fulfilled this, and have sealed to them this fruit, I will come by you into Spain.
29. And I am sure that, when I come to you, I will come in the fullness of the blessing of the gospel of Christ.
30. Now I urge you, brothers, for the Lord Jesus Christ's sake, and the love of the Spirit, that you strive together with me in your prayers to God for me;
31. That I may be delivered from them that do not believe in Judea; and that my service which I have for Jerusalem may be accepted by the saints;
32. That I may come to you with joy by the will of God, and may with you be refreshed.
33. Now the God of peace be with you all. Amen.

Chapter 16

1. I commend to you Phoebe our sister, who is a servant of the assembly which is at Cenchrea:
2. That you receive her in the Lord, as is fitting for saints, and that you assist her in whatever matter she needs you: for she has been a patroness of many, and of myself also.
3. Greet Priscilla and Aquila my helpers in Christ Jesus:
4. Who have risked their lives for my life: to whom not only I give thanks, but also all the Gentile assemblies.
5. Likewise, greet the assembly that is in their house. Greet my well-beloved Epaenetus, who is the first fruit of Achaia to Christ.
6. Greet Mary, who labored much for us.
7. Greet Andronicus and Junia, my relatives, and my fellow prisoners, who are of note among the apostles, who also were in Christ before me.
8. Greet Amplias my beloved in the Lord.
9. Greet Urbane, our helper in Christ, and Stachys my beloved.
10. Greet Apelles approved in Christ. Greet those who are of Aristobulus' household.
11. Greet Herodion my kinsman. Greet them that are of the household of Narcissus, who are in the Lord.
12. Greet Tryphena and Tryphosa, who labor in the Lord. Greet the beloved Persis, who labored much in the Lord.
13. Greet Rufus the chosen in the Lord, and his mother and mine.
14. Greet Asyncritus, Phlegon, Hermas, Patrobas, Hermes, and the brothers who are with them.
15. Greet Philologus, and Julia, Nereus, and his sister, and Olympas, and all the saints who are with them.
16. Greet one another with a holy kiss. The assemblies of Christ greet you.
17. Now I urge you, brothers, mark those who cause divisions and offenses contrary to the doctrine which you have learned; and avoid them.

18. For they serve not our Lord Jesus Christ, but their own base appetites; and by slick words and flattering speeches deceive the hearts of the unsuspecting.

19. For your obedience has become known to all men. Therefore, I am glad on your behalf: but yet I would have you wise to that which is good, and without mixture concerning evil.

20. And the God of peace will crush Satan under your feet shortly. The grace of our Lord Jesus Christ be with you. Amen.

21. Timothy my fellow worker, and Lucius, and Jason, and Sosipater, my kinsmen, greet you.

22. I Tertius, who wrote this letter, greet you in the Lord.

23. Gaius my host, and of the whole assembly, greets you. Erastus the treasurer of the city greets you, and Quartus a brother.

24. The grace of our Lord Jesus Christ be with you all. Amen.

25. Now to Him who is powerful to make you stand according to my gospel, and the preaching of Jesus Christ, according to the revelation of the mystery, which was kept secret since time began,

26. But now is made manifest, and by the Scriptures of the prophets, according to the commandment of the infinite God, made known to all nations for the obedience of faith:

27. The only wise God be glory through Jesus Christ into the New Covenant Age. Amen.

Synopsis of 1 Corinthians

It is indisputable by most scholars that Paul is the author of 1 Corinthians. This first epistle to the Corinthians is actually the second epistle that Paul penned, and archaeologists have not been able to discover the lost first epistle. The background of Paul's experience with the city of Corinth is found in Acts 18. It is during this time that many Jews were commanded to leave Rome, and many settled in Corinth. The city of Corinth had a plethora of cultures and subcultures. These cultures consisted of materialistic, hedonistic, superstitious, religious, and corrupt base behaviors with a mix of Roman, Greek, Jewish immigrants, barbarians, and a sort of a melting pot of diverse peoples from all around the Roman Empire.

Paul was sent to Corinth to establish a testimony of the life of Jesus Christ and to establish a true culture of heaven on earth in a Roman colony. After spending a year and a half training and teaching the saints there, Paul left to carry out the work of the Lord. In order for us to understand the purpose in which Paul wrote this epistle to the Corinthians, we must be clear that God is invading the Roman Empire to conquer its citizens and peoples with the tool of dominion. The tool of dominion is the gospel of the kingdom and the grace of God. The gospel is the power to transform lives and cultures and bring God's kingdom culture to this planet, thus establishing colonies of Heaven in every city, town, and hamlet in the world. The cultures of this world and their sub-cultures are in direct conflict with God's heavenly culture, His kingdom. Paul calls this heavenly culture, "the church which is in Corinth".

Called Out To Be a Heavenly Culture

The word "church" as the assembly of people is key to understanding who the Corinthian believers are and their spiritual identity in relation to the culture of the Corinthians who are outside of Christ. The word 'church' comes from the two Greek words, 'ek' meaning out and 'klesis' meaning called. When we put these two words together, we have the definition, a called out or calling out. Those in the city of Corinth were being called out of their culture and sub-cultures to become a testimony of the life of Christ. Called to be saints is their new description, identity, their spiritual vocation, their calling by divine appointment as a heavenly people. They have been called into the business of the kingdom of God.

They were being called out of the culture of Corinth into the fellowship of His Son. This fellowship is a participation and sharing in the life of Christ in order to be an appropriate testimony and representation of God in Corinth. If the saints do not have a clear vision of what the church is, while meeting in numerous locations in one given city of this size, this can present many problems. This is why Paul presents the vision of one church, one city. This is the only way for God's people to establish a true heavenly culture and operate as one administration in a given city. The world seems wiser than us in this regard, all cities only have one administration and government locally. Paul tells Titus to establish elders in every city. This is going to be a challenge for the foreseeable future.

History tells us this city's population was around 200,000 people and a city of commerce and merchants. Thousands are coming in and going out of Corinth. The church was not under one roof but met in various homes and locations throughout the city. Immediately, Paul describes the church in that city as enriched in every way and in everything. Material comfort was the culture and being prosperous was the standard. Paul was dealing with a very sophisticated culture that was rich in knowledge, education, and philosophy.

Yet God had His rich and wise servants. The gifts to the church such as Paul, Apollos, Cephas, and Aquila and Priscilla were a gold mine of knowledge and wisdom in the word of God, spiritual riches and spiritual experiences. The Corinthian church was not inferior at all and was uniquely gifted as the testimony of Christ which was confirmed in them. The evidence of Christ was real, sure and reliable because of the attention and care from those who labored on them and with them. We may learn from Paul's faith vision of the church in Corinth. He is speaking by faith into them. It is similar in John's book of the Revelation chapters 2 & 3. John is under the revelation of the churches in seven cities and in the Spirit. He sees seven golden lampstands! These lampstands are the seven churches, and they are golden, not tarnished, not partially gold and some other alloy. In all the churches but one, the Lord Jesus rebukes and corrects the other six churches. These churches, with all their issues were still golden in the eyes of John because he was seeing in the Spirit. Paul is in the Spirit as he is speaking or in this case writing to the saints in Corinth. He is speaking faith into the saints about God's goal, the end in which they would be blameless and established.

Paul was saturated and infused with the Old Testament Scriptures and spent eighteen months explaining and imparting the word to them. Apollos was mighty in the Scriptures, "now a Jew named Apollos, an Alexandrian by birth, an eloquent man, came to Ephesus; and he was mighty in the Scriptures." Acts 18:24-25. Cephas is Peter who spent three and half years walking with Jesus and then saw His resurrection and built a genuine relationship with Christ in His glorified state. Since they had the proper equipping, they were waiting for the coming of the Lord, the full unveiling of all that Christ spoke and what God had promised. They were waiting for the fulfillment of all that was written in Luke 21:22. Here Paul ties the coming of the Lord Jesus with being confirmed to the end and the day of the Lord. We must believe that Paul and the Lord Jesus were on the same page. There isn't one end that Jesus was talking about and one end that Paul was talking about. The coming of the Lord, end of the age and the day of the Lord are clearly, one coming, one end, and one day of the Lord.

This is exactly what Christ did when He told the disciples that the temple was going to be destroyed and not one stone would be left upon another. The disciples asked, when would these things be and the sign of Your coming, (literally Presence) and the END of the age? Paul connects Matthew 24; Mark 13; Luke 21; to the unveiling of Christ and the END. The saints in Corinth would be blameless in the DAY of the LORD. This end was imminent to them! It was relevant to them. Paul was showing them how important the testimony of Christ is among the many cultures of that city. The coming was a coming on the state of Israel and to destroy the city and the sanctuary and to bring judgment on the Roman world to establish His Kingship, so that the kingdoms of this world would become the Kingdom of our Lord and of His Christ.

The end was the end of the Old Covenant age, and the Day of the Lord was that Jesus would be recognized as King of all nations ruling over the rulers of the earth. Paul uses the term "end" three times in this letter and three times in his second letter to the Corinthians. Paul says the Corinthians would be confirmed to the end, literally preserved, fixed, established to the end. This is exactly what Christ said, "those who endure to the end shall be saved." Paul agrees with Jesus. Again, Paul states in 1 Cor. 10:11, "they were written for our instruction, upon whom the end of the age has come." Paul and Christ use the same phrase, "end of the age". In Matthew 24:3, Jesus is speaking to the disciples regarding the destruction of the Temple and equates that with the end of the age and the sign of His coming. There is a wonderful harmony between Paul and Jesus, not like what some would say about them.

The third time Paul uses the term end is in 1 Cor. 15:23-28. Here it is related to the resurrection of the dead, the defeat of death, not physical death, death caused by sin, and putting all things in subjection to Him, all His enemies so that God may be all in all. Paul also says in 2 Cor. 3:13, and not as Moses, which put a veil over his face, that the children of Israel could not steadfastly look to the end of that which is abolished. The last enemy in 1 Cor. 15 is abolished and Paul calls it the last enemy, DEATH. In 2 Cor. 3:7, Paul says that the Old Covenant is the ministry of Death and the ministry of Condemnation. Israel could not see the end because the veil was over their hearts, and they could not see the end. There is only one end in the bible and that is the end of the Old Covenant age and dispensation. There is no end in the New Covenant age or dispensation. This is where many have made the mistake of making an end of the New Covenant age, by calling it a church age or a parenthesis in God's purpose. There are only two ages in history or His Story. The Old Covenant age and the age of the Messiah, the New Covenant age which has no end. We are in the age of no condemnation and no death only life and righteousness. We need to be speaking the same thing.

The Appropriate Speaking Builds Up the Church

Paul stated in 1 Cor. 1:10, that the saints should speak the same thing. The word for speak is the Greek word, "lego". Lego has multiple meanings, but with the same idea. In some places the word Lego means to gather one's thoughts in an ordered manner, a laid-out plan or prepared speech. It can also mean to assemble. Our modern-day usage of "lego" is related to a child's construction toy. One connects lego to lego building interesting things, almost anything. We may understand this word usage by Paul as constructive in our communication, as in building each other up instead of tearing one another down with arguments, quarrels, and disagreements. He also exhorted the Corinthians to have the same mind and the same judgment too. Paul knew that speaking shapes the mind and creates vision and purpose. This clearly reveals that the proper speaking in the ministry and among the saints will shape the mind and equip the saints with the ability to apprehend and perceive the ultimate intention and purpose and will of God. The construction toy called Lego is derived from a Danish word which means, "play well". The toy is designed for children to build a model image. Our speaking is not to build something that is plastic, but it is meant to build a model of God's heavenly culture on the earth.

We should play well, work well, and build well, instead of working against one another in disharmony. Quarreling, strife and favoritism of preachers or even leaning on the pre-cross Jesus is a lack of revelation of who we are as the body of Christ. Paul clarifies the nature of who they are by saying, "is Christ divided"? He didn't say is the church divided? He wrote, is the person of Christ, the heavenly Christ divided? It is He who is the center and expression of their faith and life. Paul is pointing to the organic nature of the Christian life, not some artificial institution, but an organic, living body of Christ.

The Cross Creates the Body of Christ, a Spiritual People

Only the cross can produce the body of Christ, "… But now in Christ Jesus you who at one time were far off are made near in the blood of Christ. For He is our peace, who has made the two into one, and by whom the middle wall of division has been broken down, having in His flesh put an end to that which made the division between us, even the law with its rules and orders, so that He might make in Himself, of the two, one new man, so making peace; and that the two might come into agreement with God in one body through the cross, so putting an end to that division." Eph. 2:13-16. God's answer to the church and to the world was and always will be the cross. This is God's tool for dominion in conquering the world, the flesh, and the devil. To those who are perishing, the word of the cross is foolishness, but unto us who are being saved, it is the power of God. It is the cross that makes humans spiritual.

Three Types of People

We are going to look at how Paul used the cross to deal with the church. Specifically, we will see three types of people in the church striving for dominance. Only one is acceptable to God and able to establish and build up the testimony of Christ and the other two are expressions of one source that is insufficient to build or edify the saints.

The cross deals with man in his carnality, his flesh and it deals with the natural man in his soul, in his psychological or natural being. Understanding the cross is the key to working with people. The cross is the Holy Spirit's inner working to put to death the flesh and its deeds, which is the evil side of man in his degraded humanity. Also, man's soul expression, when independent of God and His Holy Spirit must be put to death, with its expression of wisdom, will-power, and emotional strange fire. These are the two types of man that ruin the testimony of Christ. We will call the first man, the carnal or fleshly man. The second man is the natural man or the soulish man. Both of these types of people in the church spoil the expression of Christ and cause the church to be merely human or degraded. It is the third man that Paul is looking for and that is the spiritual man.

The carnal man is base, and the natural man is sophisticated and polished. Neither is what God is looking for and yet, they try to dominate the church. As leaders in the church, we must be clear in order not to let the carnal man or the natural man rule in us or in the church. It is the spiritual man that must rule. Paul says the word of the cross is foolishness to those who are perishing. This perishing is a destruction of well-being, not necessarily being. It involves loss. For instance, a person may be in his or her home and it is on fire. All they own is in the house. They escape the fire, but all that they have worked for is burned up and they suffer loss, they are destroyed, but not in their being, but in their well-being. Christians that reject the inner working of the cross, experience destruction, loss, and a form of perishing similar to the broad way that leads to destruction.

Some folks think that their sophisticated ideas of the Christian life are more appropriate than the grace of God. The apostle addresses this straightforward by quoting Isa. 29:14, "For it is written: "I will destroy the wisdom of the wise and bring to nothing the understanding of the prudent." 1 Cor. 1:19. This verse is in the context of making oneself equal with God, the potter, when we are but clay, it is total foolishness in the eyes of God. We are not in control, He is and it is His wisdom that God is looking for.

Paul says that the wisdom of this world has been made foolish by the wisdom of God and the world by its wisdom did not come to know God. James says this wisdom is from below and is earthly, natural, and demonic. He says there is wisdom from above. James saw the distinction between what was earthly and what was heavenly. "But if you have bitter jealousy and selfish ambition in your heart, do not be arrogant and so lie against the truth. This wisdom is not that which comes down from above, but is earthly, natural (soulish), demonic. For where jealousy and selfish ambition exist, there is disorder and every evil thing, but the wisdom from above …" Jas. 3:14-17. This wisdom from below is foolishness to God.

God's Foolishness is Wiser than Men

God's foolishness is wiser than men. God commissioned us to preach the cross to save those who believe. Paul mentions two things that men seek after. One is wisdom and the other is power. Jews seek after signs, which equal power and Greeks seek after wisdom. Paul says to the Corinthians which are predominantly Jews and Greeks. Christ is the power of God and wisdom of God! It is those who are called out of the culture, the darkness, the foolishness of this world that will experience the power of God and wisdom of God, which is Christ. Paul answers the longing in the hearts of these ones with the person of Christ. You want power, then receive Christ, take Christ, you want wisdom, then receive Christ, take Christ.

The apostle is centering on Christ to all the Corinthian saints, to the spiritual Man who is the One who rules in the church. The parable in Luke 19:14 where the Lord gave His servants ten minas. It says, "His citizens hated him and did not want this man to reign over them." The leaders of the Jewish people did not want Christ to reign over them. Therefore, that system was destroyed. Here we can learn that any system, or church or nation that refuses to let Christ rule over them will be brought to nothing. God's wisdom in giving Christ as the head over all things to the church, which is His body reveals to us all, the HEAD is in the body. They cannot be disconnected, and it is not some remote Head or distant Head, but we are joined to Him. He is in us, and we are in Him.

"But by His doing you are in Christ Jesus, who became to us wisdom from God, and righteousness and sanctification, and redemption, so that, just as it is written," 1 Cor. 1:30-31. God put the Corinthians in Christ and He became to them wisdom from God, and righteousness, sanctification, and redemption. This is so God gets all the glory, and He becomes our boast.

The Demonstration of the Spirit

Paul says he is coming to the Corinthians, not in persuasive words of man's wisdom, but in the demonstration of the Spirit and in the power of God. Paul is expressing Christ, not himself. This is the true remedy for the church. Not just a message about being spiritual, but an example of a spiritual man.

It is the spiritual man that changes the world and transforms culture. The carnal man can only destroy the world and its well-being. The natural man cannot transform culture in a spiritual way. Paul says, "eye has not seen, ear has not heard, nor has it entered into the heart of man what God has prepared for those who love Him, for to us God revealed them through the Spirit; for the Spirit searches all things, even the depths of God." 1 Cor. 2:9-10. The spiritual man is the man who lives by the Spirit, demonstrates the Spirit and expresses the

Spirit. The knowledge of God is only by the Spirit. Apart from the Spirit, we cannot know Him. Paul talks about our human spirit in comparison to God's Spirit. No man can know himself except the spirit of the man within him. This indicates that a spiritual man must be in touch with his spirit to properly know himself, likewise, to know God we must be filled with His Spirit to know His heart and mind, also His ideas and plans.

The carnal man and the natural man are under the influence of the spirit of the world. Paul says, "we have not received the spirit of the world, but the Spirit who is from God that we may know the things freely given to us by God." 1 Cor. 2:12. The spiritual man is taught by the Spirit combining spiritual thoughts with spiritual words. But the natural man does not receive the things of the Spirit of God, for they are foolishness to him; nor can he know them, because they are spiritually discerned. The natural man is the most dangerous of all the types of people in the church. These types of men rule the church many times with natural wisdom and with demonic wisdom. They refuse to give the reins of the church to Christ, the head of His body.

It seems like foolishness to them. This creates a false expression of the church. It takes pure faith to trust Christ to govern the church and the natural man cannot do this, nor will he want to. The reason this kind of man is more dangerous than the carnal man, is because it is not so obvious to the unsuspecting. The natural man has a sense of order, and loves being in control. The carnal man is out of control and very easy to spot and will be dealt with because we normally deal with obvious sin and out of control people in the camp. The spiritual man is neither out of control, nor in control, but under the control of the Holy Spirit and this is the characteristic that is most pleasing to the Lord. We will now proceed to see how Paul dealt with the two types of people that spoil the testimony of Christ.

The Natural Man is the Most Dangerous in the Church

As I stated previously, and do not believe it is unnecessary to repeat this matter. The natural man is in my estimation is the most dangerous to the Lord's testimony. It takes discernment to know if the natural man is ruling the church. These can operate with the wisdom from below and it can be appealing and fascinating and exciting but be completely void of the Spirit of God. Jude warns of such ones ... these people create divisions and are merely natural, not having the Spirit. Jude 19. These are those individuals who cause divisions, egocentric, not holding the spirit [the human spirit, that is, being egocentric, they ignore their human spirit which has to do with the spiritual, religious part of a person's life Jude 19. These are the ones that build in the church with wood, hay, and stubble and create sectarian groups, cults and divisive and dangerous groups. In chapter three Paul starts by saying, I cannot speak to you as to spiritual men, but as to carnal or fleshly. He associates the fleshly as being babes, not newborn, but immature saints that need to be fed the milk which is God's logic according to 1 Peter 2:2. These are not able to assimilate anything but milk.

Their capacity to understand spiritual things was hindered by their reliance on the flesh or their natural constitution.

The apostle Peter writes about the milk of the word and uses an interesting word in the phrase, "milk of the word". The word translated, 'word', is the Greek word, 'logikos'. We get the English word, logic from this word. When Peter was encouraging the newborn saints to long for the milk of the word, he was addressing the need for the new ones to feed on God's logic concerning the Christian life and the proper human life.

God's logic is not man's logic. The foolishness of God is wiser than men. Paul is now addressing the fleshly. This is what stunts the growth of believers. If we walk according to the flesh we will never grow up spiritually. Paul's use of babes is different than Peter's use. Peter is speaking of newborns, but Paul is speaking of saints that should have been growing and developing. Instead, they are stunted and immature. The immature are not able to plant in the church or build the church efficiently. In fact, the immature sow discord and tear down God's work because of selfish desires and self-centeredness. The immature are man-centered instead of Christ-centered.

God's Garden and God's Building, Temple

Paul's desire to establish the testimony of the Lord Jesus was to impart vision and encourage the saints to work together. The figures of planting and building require involvement and cooperation and participation. Paul says to the Corinthians, you corporately, are God's field, His garden and God's building, His house and temple. The apostles' desire was to have spiritual people who sow spiritual things into one another's lives in order to build up one another to be God's holy temple, His sanctuary. Two points are essential in understanding proper ministry. A field is receptive and workable and must be plowed, sown, fertilized in order to produce fruit. The immature saints were not receptive to the vision of all the servants of the Lord's ministry, only one man or source and not the source of the Spirit. This is an indication of being unteachable and stubborn. These traits are not spiritual but are carnal and fleshly.

The saints wanted to choose who was going to build them up and who they were going to be built up with in God's building. Prejudice, partiality, favoritism, and sectarianism are expressions of the flesh to divide and cause Christ and His culture not to be seen. We will see much later on how the garden of the Lord is cultivated and from the ground up, the house of the Lord will be built. In passing, I want to say that the gifts of the Holy Spirit or manifestations of the Spirit are the means and tools to create and build such a place on earth. It is through the revelatory gifts, the speaking gifts, and the power gifts that the church is established and built up. These are the tools to build and plant in the realm of the Spirit.

This experience will produce the Garden and the House of the Lord and will express heavenly fruit and a heavenly building containing the presence and glory of the Lord. Paul's usage of the field, land, garden, and building, house, temple are eschatological in nature, since God is ready to declare the so-called holy land as the "wicked land" and bring the house, temple and all their accouterments to desolation and destruction. Edom says, "We are beaten down now, but we will come back and rebuild the ruins." Adonai-Tzva'ot (Yahweh) answers, "They can build, but I will demolish. They will be called the Land of Wickedness, the people with whom Adonai (Yahweh) is permanently angry. You will see it and say, 'Adonai (Yahweh) is great, even beyond the borders of Isra'el.'" Mal. 1:4-5 CJB. This is not some temporary prediction. Corinth is outside the borders of Israel and God is great and mighty in Corinth. Christ and the Church are the new land and temple. The Old Covenant land and temple are dissolving, and the New Covenant land and temple are emerging. If we continue to build the old, we will ultimately be working and building according to the flesh and according to the natural man.

Fleshly people tear down the work of God and sow discord. Natural people sow soulish things, worldly things, and merely human things. Natural people build with earthly ideas, human programs, and liturgical and ritualistic ways. These are the wood, the hay, and straw or stubble. Later we will see what Paul clearly states as to what builds the church. Paul stresses that when the saints live like this they are living like mere men. For where there are envy, strife, and divisions among you, are you not carnal and behaving like mere men? 1 Cor. 3:3-4. The church is more than human. It is an expression of a heavenly humanity and divine nature, wherein the Spiritual Man is reigning.

Only the spiritual man can properly build the church. This is what the Lord Jesus said in Matthew 16, "I will build my church and the gates of hades will not prevail against it." Paul was clear when he said, I am crucified with Christ: nevertheless, I live; yet not I, but Christ lives in me: and the life which I now live in the flesh I live by the faith of the Son of God, who loved me, and gave Himself for me. Gal. 2:20. In this revelation Paul could say, "I am a wise master-builder. Paul was a man of the cross and only the cross can make us spiritual men. Remember the cross is the inner working of the Spirit to put to death the deeds of the fleshly nature and transform our soul faculties. The builders are warned to build with the proper materials. On the one hand we can build with wood, hay, and stubble. On the other hand, we can build with gold, silver, and precious stones. It is important that we understand these items according to their nature and their symbolism. The Lord is not talking about a physical building but building into the lives of people. We can learn from the pictures in the Old Covenant when those who were filled with the Spirit to make garments for those who ministered in the sanctuary of the Lord and those who built the sanctuary or temple. Here are some examples for the Holy Spirit to enlighten us. "And He has filled him with the Spirit of God, in wisdom, in understanding and in knowledge and in all craftsmanship; to make designs for working in gold and in silver… and in the cutting of stones for settings … so as to perform in every inventive work. Ex. 35:31-32. So, you shall speak to all who are gifted artisans, whom I have filled with the spirit of wisdom, that they may make Aaron's garments, to consecrate him, that he may minister to Me as priest. Ex. 28:3-4.

Through wisdom a house is built, and by understanding it is established; by knowledge the rooms are filled with all precious and pleasant riches. Proverbs 24:3-4.

These verses have a common thread, and we can learn from them the goal of building and the method and results of building God's way. God's wisdom gives structure and order to the life of God's people. Spiritual understanding establishes His people and revelation knowledge fills His people with pleasant and the precious riches of His grace, kindness, and glory. The gold is related to God's divine nature, and we must build with the divine nature which all believers are partakers of in order to escape the covetousness that is associated with the spirit of false religion and this world. Silver most of the time in the Scriptures speaks of redemption. Here is where we must emphasize redemptive relationships loaded with forbearance, forgiveness, tenderheartedness, time spent to pour into one another's lives, God's love and care. Precious stones are the things that have been produced by intense pressure and time and have a sacred value to enrich and beautify each other's lives. This is where devotion, commitment, friendship over time and serving one another, interceding for one another, carrying one another's burdens. Treasuring the saints in our lives is the beauty of the expression of God's image in every city. The church as the testimony of God's culture in Corinth was to display God's wisdom in relationships. Eph. 3:10.

Even the way we handle legal matters versus going to the world with its ways of handling legal matters. We should have such a relationship with the leadership of the church that we would first try to resolve a legal issue with the mediation of the leadership of the church. If we have been wronged and the offending party will not repent and make it right, after appealing according to Matthew 18, we must then treat the offending party like a publican or a sinner and use the court system to exercise justice. Perhaps even the Lord may say to take the cross in a certain matter so He can deal with the offending party. I have seen God's righteousness exercised in both ways. The guidance of the Holy Spirit and confirmation of His word will guide us in making wise decisions. We must realize that it is the Scriptures that guide us within the boundaries of God's wisdom and keep us safe.

Nothing Beyond what is Written

Trusting in God's word versus trusting in ministers, even legitimate men of God are mentioned by Paul. "Now, brothers, I have applied these things to myself and Apollos for your benefit, so that you may learn from us the saying: "Nothing beyond what is written." The purpose is that none of you will be inflated with pride in favor of one person over another. 1 Cor. 4:6-7. I love this phrase, "Nothing beyond what is written". Let's stay within its boundaries. So often I hear that some dear brother or sister will say, "God told me this or that", and it is completely contrary to the written word of God. Or some say, "this is what they believe", and it is a tradition or opinion, and they treat that as the word of God. This is what the Pharisees were doing in our Lords' days in His flesh. Making the word of God of no effect because of their traditions. The written Scriptures are our boundaries and our beliefs, our values, our ideas i.e. revelations, and our norms are within these sacred boundaries. 1 Cor. 14:36-38, Paul writes, was it from you that the word of God originated from? Or has it come to you only? If anyone thinks he is a prophet or spiritual, let him fully know that the things which I write to you are the precepts of the Lord's. But if anyone is ignorant, let him be ignorant. This is complete and utter arrogance to put our own thoughts above the word of God. But there are always going to be ignorant and arrogant people that challenge us, and God can use this to make us good Bereans to make sure the things we are being taught are according the His word and not man's.

Boundaries of the Heavenly Culture.

There are boundaries for relationships regarding our sexuality. Sexual intercourse is for marriage, not for selfish pleasure outside of marriage. Sexual purity is evidence of moral boundaries. The opposite is the evidence of fermenting, agitation, unrest, and no peace. Paul likens this to leaven spreading throughout the Christian community. One definition of leaven is a souring. This is something distasteful and unpleasant. Paul is saying put away the old leaven that you may become a new lump. New in the sense of something that has not existed before. Paul wanted a community of people that have not ever been seen before. New in time and something more than mere human lives, but those who display a heavenly lifestyle. The church is a people who demonstrate a culture to the world around it. It has beliefs indicating, "what is real"? It has values indicating, "what is important"? It has spiritual ideas indicating, God given revelation and insights. It has principles and norms indicating, there is a standard of measure. The standard is the person of Christ and anything except Him is able to build the church. Jesus said in Matthew 16, "I will build My Church". Unless it is Christ, it falls short of the glory of God!

Paul deals with fornication with the elders of the city. Today a believer may commit fornication in one assembly and because there are many administrations, leave that assembly and move to another and continue in the same lifestyle undealt with; and Paul says, a little leaven leavens the whole lump. So together with the elders of the church they delivered this unrepentant person to Satan for the destruction of his flesh that his spirit may be saved. This is the spiritual way to purge the house from the leaven in the house. Paul says so that you may be new lump. This is equivalent to a corporate new birth, a fresh start in time. The church always needs to stay fresh and young. Another interesting point that Paul makes is the connection of the Passover at this point in his letter.

He says Christ is our Passover who was sacrificed for us. We can see from this where dealing with the sexual impurity in the church, there is a death, a cleansing, but also a resurrection. A new ground to express the life of Christ to the world that we are in. The word wickedness is different from the word evil. Wickedness is the habit of doing evil and evil is the result and outcome, making the offender in their character evil. Paul says let's celebrate the feast. The second aspect of Passover was the Feast of Unleaven Bread. Leaven is not a picture of sin here, but the yeast or leaven in its nature is a spreading, active substance that pictures taking over whatever it is in. Paul says that fornication, wickedness, evil has the effects of leaven that if it is not cleaned out it will take over and spread to the whole. Even Jesus uses the term "leaven" in describing the Kingdom of the Heavens or God in Matthew 13:33, Luke 13:21. It is like "leaven". So, leaven is not evil itself, but whatever is like leaven will spread and take over whatever it is in.

The Kingdom of God is in the world and in us and it is spreading and taking over in us. So, God can and will have a Kingdom culture on the earth for all time. We must be clear on this and understand that evil and fornication and wickedness also can spread in a community, nation, and world and take over if the church lets it. We must celebrate not the Old Covenant Passover, but the New Covenant feast continuously, not with old leaven, but with sincerity and truth. These two words are wonderful in the original language.

Jesus warned His disciples about the leaven of the Pharisees and the leaven of Herod. In Luke 12:1 the Lord said, the leaven of the Pharisees which is hypocrisy and false teaching, like the traditions of men. Hypocrisy is the opposite of sincerity. Even the leaven of Herod is the epitome of compromise. He was an opportunist who was immoral, malicious, and egocentric. Paul contrasts wickedness and malice with sincerity and truth.

Judged in the Sunlight

The word sincerity comes from two words in Greek. They are poetic words in the sense that the first aspect is "in the sun", "or in the sunlight". The second aspect is to test or judge. This is so fitting since in Corinth there was a huge merchant population and many visitors that would flock to the flea market or swap meet environment. In those days, many merchants sold clay vessels and various sorts of pottery. Sometimes during the manufacturing of these clay vessels, they would crack, and merchants would melt wax in the cracks to seal them. Over time the wax would melt or wear out and the vessel would be worthless. So, the informed buyers would hold the vessel up to the sunlight and judge to see if the seller used wax on his merchandise. If not then the buyer would know that it was a vessel of sincerity. Paul says let's celebrate the feast with the unleavened bread of sincerity and truth. We need to be vessels, if held up in the sunlight of judgment there is no hypocrisy, compromise, or self-centeredness. This is character that has been shaped by the Potter and has gone through the process of heat and testing and has come through without cracks. The other description of this celebration is truth. Truth is what is real. It is reality! This aspect is related to the first ingredient of the definition of a culture. Let me reiterate for practical purposes.

There are four items in a culture that defines it. The first is beliefs, secondly, values, thirdly, ideas, and lastly, norms or principles. The first is beliefs, which asks, "What is real"? The church is commissioned to present to the world this culture and establish the set of beliefs showing the world what is real. The conciliation through the cross of Christ is real and the forgiveness of sins is real. The presence of the Holy Spirit coming into a person is real, so that a person can be born again or from above. The spiritual realm is a dimension for us to live in and we can bring others into this realm. This realm is called the Kingdom of God. There is so much more to show the world what is real.

Immorality, drunkenness, extortion, covetousness, swindlers, idolaters, and revilers, these expressions of human behavior are destructive to the building up of the church. We must set up boundaries in the church and deal with the behaviors that tear down, rather than build up. Those who are spiritual in the church should be able to bring restoration, healing to those lives and relationships that want to see the testimony of Christ in their midst. Those who persist in wanting their own way and their agenda must be dealt with promptly, but redemptively and graciously.

In chapter six of 1 Corinthians there are a couple of things I want to point out. It is because of the amount of space here in this brief commentary on Paul's epistle I cannot elaborate too much on this matter In 1 Cor. 6:9-11, "do you not know that the unrighteous will not inherit the kingdom of God? Do not be deceived. Neither fornicators, nor idolaters, nor adulterers, nor homosexuals, nor sodomites, nor thieves, nor covetous, nor drunkards, nor revilers, nor extortioners will inherit the kingdom of God. And such were some of you. But you were washed, but you were sanctified, but you were justified in the name of the Lord Jesus and by the Spirit of our God. This is an observation that I think has been overlooked throughout history. Gal. 5:21; Heb.6:12, Heb. 12:17; Rev. 21:7. These verses share about inheriting. There are other verses that reveal entering the kingdom. It would do us a great favor to study the distinction between entering the kingdom and inheriting the Kingdom. It is because of space that I am not able to expound further on this very important topic.

The World Is Passing Away

The church is diverse with married, unmarried, widows, single people, including the divorced. Marriage is dealt with in its various aspects. There is a specific relevance to the time of this letter and its application of certain Scriptures. But this I say, brothers, the time is short, so that from now on even those who have wives should be as though they had none, those who weep as though they did not weep, those who rejoice as though they did not rejoice, those who buy as though they did not possess, and those who use this world as not misusing it. For the form of this world is passing away. 1 Cor. 7:29-31.

The arrangement in Paul's day was about to pass away. The crisis was about to take place. The end was coming, that Christ predicted. The ink is not wet today. Paul is not saying today our present time, "the time is short". Let those who are married live as though there were not married is not applicable today, unless a time of crisis similar to that time is upon us. Then we would apply the principle, but these are verses that specifically indicate the end of the Old Covenant world was closing out and passing away. This is not the material, physical planet. The apostle John used this same terminology, again, I write a new commandment to you, which thing is real in Him and in you, because the darkness is passing, and the true light already shines.

1 Jn. 2:8. And the world is passing, and its desires, but he that does the will of God abides into the new covenant age. Little children, it is [the] last hour, and, according as ye have heard that the antichrists are coming, even now there have come many antichrists, whence we know that it is [the] last hour. 1 Jn. 2:17-18. Even John knew with others that the Old order of things was getting ready to pass away. This is a significant set of verses to connect especially when you hear those who quote Jesus' words from the Olivet Discourse in Matthew 24, "that no one knows the day or hour". John is recording with Paul over thirty years later that they knew the hour and not just them, but many knew the time they were living in. But you, brothers and sisters, are not in the darkness for the day to overtake you like a thief would. For you all are sons of the light and sons of the day. We are not of the night, nor of the darkness.

1 Th. 5:4-6. The early church was not some misguided group of people hoping in something that never happened. Shame on those who say the apostles were mistaken about the parousia, (the coming, the Presence), and every generation after Paul's has been disappointed. They were under the revelation of what Christ promised and they believed the word of God. "When you see Jerusalem surrounded by armies, know her desolation is at hand ... because these are the days of vengeance that all things that are written will be fulfilled". The apostles knew exactly what was going on by this time. The Holy Spirit was revealing and disclosing those things that were about to happen. There was a crisis coming, a persecution of unparalleled intensity. I think that, in view of the impending crisis, it is well for you to remain as you are. 1 Cor. 7:26. What was the impending crisis or present necessity? The persecution of the church by Rome and the hatred of wicked men inspired by Satan and his demons among Old Covenant Israel.

Israel A Type of the 1st Century Assembly

Even though there is a lot to say in chapters 8 and 9, I want to move into Chapter 10. The crisis of the end and passing away of the Old Covenant age was predicted in the Old Testament. Paul shows us clearly in Chapter 10 regarding the 40-year period in the wilderness. This is the most significant section regarding the time Paul was living in. He says to the Corinthians, "I do not want you to be ignorant, unaware that our fathers were under the cloud, and all passed through the sea. This is a very symbolic section, and we must consider this very carefully. Almost thirty years have passed since the crucifixion of Christ and His resurrection. Paul is using the story of Israel and Moses in the wilderness as an example and type for his present day.

Let's look at the first verse and identify the type of the cloud and the sea. He uses the phrase all under the cloud and came through the sea. The cloud is a type of the Spirit, and the sea is a type of water baptism. All were baptized INTO Moses and Moses is a type of Christ. They were immersed into Moses in the cloud and in the sea and put into Moses. This is Paul's way of saying that the Corinthian saints were baptized into Christ in the Spirit and in the water. When Israel was in Egypt they were in bondage. Then God sent a deliverer i.e. Moses and those with him celebrated the Passover. In typology, Moses is Christ the Deliverer, and Christ is also the Lamb as the type. In Egypt, they sacrificed the Lamb and ate the Lamb.

This is substantial because the Lamb has entered them, and the death angel has passed over them. This is a wonderful picture of salvation. Now for those who insist that salvation cannot happen until a person is baptized is going to have a problem with this picture. Before they were baptized in the sea (water baptism), the Lamb (Christ) came inside them. When Christ comes inside us we are saved or born again. Next then they are immersed in the Spirit and immersed in the water typologically. Here is where our other brethren may have a problem showing a difference between the matter of regeneration and the baptism of the Holy Spirit. I am not saying they cannot happen in the same day, but they are separate and distinct experiences of the Lord. Jesus was born of the Spirit out from Mary His mother. Then thirty years later He was baptized in water and with the Holy Spirit coming upon Him. This is a little tangent, but worth noting and considering. Now back to the exodus.

This is their exodus from Egypt. Egypt is a type of Judaism and the Old Covenant system. Rev. 11:8, "… the great city, which is spiritually called Sodom and Egypt, where also our Lord was crucified". Paul is using this story as a real life example of the experience of the 1st century saints. Salvation by getting the Lamb inside them and thus escaping death. Then being immersed in the Spirit, empowered and water baptized, identifying with the death and burial of Christ. This is a glorious picture! After Israel's experience there is a forty-year interval of testing and maturing. The first generation failed to go forward and wanted to go back to Egypt and its bondage. Only two of that first generation, the testimony of the faithful proceeded on to the inheritance. The apostle Paul says in verse 1 Cor. 10:11, "now all these things happened to them as types of us: and they are written for our admonition, upon whom the goal of the ages has arrived." TKB. He looked at this story in history and said these people in the wilderness are types of US. That generation was a shadow of us, and we are the reality of what happened to them. Paul goes on the say, "that upon whom the GOAL of the ages has arrived." The end is the end of the Old Covenant age.

The city of Jerusalem was destroyed in AD 70 which was forty years after the crucifixion of Christ. Paul was living in that forty-year period, which is commonly called the transition period. He is warning them of the testing period that they were in together. We must be careful not to think that Israel in the wilderness is a type of us in our present, because there is not an end coming. Where we benefit from the story are the examples of their experiences. Eating the Lamb, being baptized in the Spirit and in Water. Our wilderness journeys and daily partaking of manna, drinking from Christ who is the Rock. Not tempting the Lord and committing idolatry or fornication. These become godly instruction for practical ways of experiencing Christ and warning us to reject unbelief, rebellion, stubbornness, and independence from God. Space limits me from elaborating on this very important topic at this time.

The Cup of Blessing and the Cup of Demons

In this section Paul is showing the essential aspect of corporate life and how we are connected. This is a correction of the culture of the world which is stubborn and independent. Paul says, "for we being many are one bread, and one body: for we are all sharing together of that one bread." 1 Cor. 10:17 TKB. This is a revelation of what is real as to our interdependence. We are many grains broken and blended into one loaf. We drink the cup of blessing to be filled with God and then we become food to a hungry world. The world is starving for reality, sincerity, even for life indeed. As He is in the world so are we.

We must not have the leaven of hypocrisy, insincerity, and falsehood. We must not drink from the cup of demons and practice the things the world practices. The Lords' table is the place for companions and friends of the Lord, but those who become a friend of the world become an enemy of God. James 4:4-5. For He jealousy desires the spirit within us and this kind of lifestyle provokes Him to jealousy. No matter how stubborn or strong we think we are, we are not stronger than He is.

Even though we are not under the Law, not all things do not produce the heavenly culture. "All things are lawful for me, but not all things bring cohesiveness: all things are lawful for me, but all things do not build the house. Let no man seek his own, but every man another's well-being." 1 Cor. 10:23- 24 TKB. Two extremely important aspects of our freedom. Independence is not true freedom and seeking my good first is not drinking from the cup of blessing. My freedom should connect me to other saints for the purpose of building them up.

Seeking their well-being! This is true freedom. It takes agape, divine love to think of others first. God so loved the world, and the earth is the Lord's and all that is in it. Everything is His and we can give thanks to God for it all, but not for the sake of offending another's conscience. So, we do all things for the glory of God and not just for our comfort or freedom. We have a goal to not put a stumbling block in front of anyone intentionally, but because of Him we want to win those, so that they may be saved.

There Must Be Heresies Among You

We are always going to have those among us that are of strong opinions and there are times when those opinions will cause divisions and party spirits. Those that divide the saints or section one part against the other lack the true vision of strength that's realized by being one body. Paul says very matter of factly that, there must be heresies among you so that those who are qualified may be made manifest. "For there also must be heresies among you that they which are tested by fire and proved genuine may begin to shine in you." 1 Cor. 11:19. TKB. When anyone forms a sect or division in the church based on opinion or selfish ambition, those who love the church will be tested. It will become evident as leaders who bring light to the situation of division and sectarianism that the Lord's light and manifestation will become obvious.

This is what Yahweh did in the time of Moses. In Numbers 16, Korah, Dathan, and Abiram stated that they had enough, and it was time for the changing of the guard. They had a different opinion of who should be running things among the Lord's people. They started a heresy and accused Moses and Aaron of exalting themselves above the rest of the Lord's people. Korah and his company had persuaded 250 other men to go along with this opinion. This was God's opportunity to test Moses and Aaron by fire and bring to light who the Lord had chosen to lead the Lord's people. Moses fell on his face during this rebellion. A good lesson for leaders today. This was showtime for Yahweh! He is going to prove who it is that is anointed in His eyes versus the self-appointed in the rebels eyes. After Yahweh deals with the rebels and the earth swallowed them up which is a picture of those with a divisive spirit, that the earthly realm will swallow those whose god is their belly and who mind earthly things and despise the assembly of the Lord.

Then in Chapter 17 of Numbers, Moses says to the sons of Israel that each one take a staff from their father's household, from each tribe and write on the staff the name of their tribe. On the tribe of Levi, Aaron's name was written, and they were placed in the tent of meeting in front of the testimony of the Lord. And Moses said, whichever rod of each tribe sprouts, this is the one that Yahweh has chosen. Num. 17:8-11, now on the next day Moses went into the tent of the testimony; and behold, the rod of Aaron for the house of Levi had sprouted and put forth buds and produced blossoms, and it bore ripe almonds. Moses then brought out all the rods from the presence of the Lord to all the sons of Israel; and they looked, and each man took his rod. But the Lord said to Moses, "Put back the rod of Aaron before the testimony to be kept as a sign against the rebels, that you may put an end to their grumblings against Me, so that they will not die." Aaron was tested by fire, and he was manifest and light to the people as one approved in their sight. It is when we are in the midst of factions, we wait for God's approval, not of men. God's approval is to bring life out of death, even life from a dead staff, with blossoms and fruit. People will witness this, and it will shine forth clearly and the divisive ones will be exposed.

Seeing the Testimony of Jesus

Not seeing the importance of the corporate testimony of Christ is disastrous in displaying this marvelous heavenly culture. It is the body life, not someone's ministry life. Jeroboam had an opinion that the Lord's people did not need to go all the way to Jerusalem and be one with all the people of the Lord. He decided to set up two golden calves in Bethel and tell the people that this was just as good as going to Jerusalem. Jeroboam did not need the saints in Jerusalem, they were self-sufficient in Bethel, "the house of God". This set the stage for Israel to become two nations and two kingdoms. A kingdom divided cannot stand and it did not stand for long.

Paul says we are one loaf, one bread, one body. Every time we celebrate the Lords' table there is a true transubstantiation. The bread and wine do not transform, only the recipients are transformed as the life and body of Christ. We change and remember the Lord and we remember Judas who became self-seeking and independent and ultimately rebellious, and his experience was death apart from the body of Christ.

Spiritual Gifts and the One Body

The apostle says, concerning spirituality I do not want you to be ignorant. The matter of being spiritual is being related to the Triune God. There are diversities in the body which are essential to keeping us from falling into uniformity or sameness. Paul first shares about the Spirit and the allocations of grace gifts. The charisma of God as the Spirit giving to the members what we call the manifestation gifts. Then he says the diversities of ministries, but the same Lord. These are the ministry gifts or ascension gifts of Ephesians 4:11. Also he speaks about the diversities of operations, but the same God who works all in all members of the body. We see Paul relating the Triune God to the body in the matter of manifestations, gifts, and operations. These operations are the motivational gifts of grace in Romans 12:6-8.

Paul defines in specific ways the manifestations of the one Spirit. He breaks these down in three wonderful categories. Firstly, he speaks of the revelation gifts where God gives a specific revelation in wisdom, knowledge, discerning of spirits. Secondly, there are the power gifts where the Spirit is working in healings, miracles, where the gift of faith is imparted. Thirdly, the verbal gifts for cheering up, stirring up, and building up. Prophetic utterance, speaking in an anointed tongue, and interpreting the tongue in knowledge, revelation, teaching, and prophecy. 1 Cor. 14:7.

These manifestations are to meet specific needs in the body. I have seen great needs in the body where all these manifestations functioned. I have also been in places where the needs were minimal and other gifts functioned to meet those needs. Where those who are taught against the gifts you will rarely see any real manifestation of the Spirit and the needs of the saints are unmet. Perhaps those who oppose the gifts also have a mocking spirit to those who believe in them, and the result is very clear as Paul states in the eleventh chapter where because some do not discern the Lord's body some are weak, some are sick, and even some have died prematurely. Possibly, being open to the works of the Holy Spirit we would see the weak strengthened, the sick healed, and the dead raised with more glory to the Lord. Opening to the Holy Spirit is letting Him have full reign to move according to His will. We must learn to vocally open to the Holy Spirit by calling on the name of the Lord to give Him full sway in our lives and when we do get ready for the glory of God to move in and fill the empty places.

In chapter five we saw the apostle allude to the feasts of Israel in the Passover stating that Christ is our Passover and to celebrate the feast of Unleavened Bread. To clean out the old leaven so we would be a new lump. In that chapter we see typified in the first three feasts. Passover, Unleavened, and First fruits. First fruits come after we clean out the old and allow the new to sprout in our lives. Now we come to the fourth feast, the feast of Pentecost or Weeks. This was seven weeks after Passover and it was a harvest of the First fruits. We see this in Acts 2 when the Holy Spirit is poured out on Pentecost and the body of Christ was formed and 3000 souls were harvested into the kingdom of God. There is a beautiful picture of this in 2 Chron. 4:2-5, "Also he made the molten sea of ten cubits from brim to brim, round in compass; and its height was five cubits; and a line of thirty cubits encircled it. Under it was the likeness of oxen, which encircled it, for ten cubits, encircling the sea. The oxen were in two rows, cast when it was cast. It stood on twelve oxen, three looking toward the north, and three looking toward the west, and three looking toward the south, and three looking toward the east: and the sea was set on them above, and all their hinder parts were inward. It was a handbreadth thick; and its brim was worked like the brim of a cup, like the flower of a lily: it received and held three thousand baths." TKB.

On the day of Pentecost, Peter standing with the eleven and lifted up his voice, these men are not drunk as you suppose … then they that gladly received his word were immersed: and the same day there were added to them about three thousand souls. Acts 2:14, 41. TKB. On the day of Pentecost this feast was celebrated with the outpouring of the Holy Spirit to baptize them into the body of Christ in the Temple to become the New Temple which was growing in the Lord. And we have the first harvest of the First fruits of the Lamb. We will see later the feast of Trumpets, feast of the Day of Atonement, and the feast of Tabernacles in 1 Cor. 15.

You Are The Body of Christ All the Members are One Body So Also is the Christ

The corporate Christ is virtually not addressed very often in Christendom today because it is all about me, which Max Lucado so artistically wrote in his book, "It's All About Me". We are suffering today among the Lord's people from being individualistic and "what am I going to get out of this". We cannot say things such as, I do not need the other members of the church. Paul says in other places in the word, every joint supplies. A joint is where two members come together. Our relatedness in the Spirit is where we get supplied with what we need to be strong and efficient and effective believers. When a believer sees the body of Christ and God opens his eyes to the other saints, immediately a burden will come on that believer to get something from the Lord to meet that need. In many translations of the Bible the word for particular or individually as in 1 Cor. 12:27 is the Greek word, "meros".

This word simply means a part. We are a part in the body of Christ. A member is a part as in the KJV, particular we see the word part. Paul says one member is not the body. So, no one member is a whole, only a part. This is quite essential to understand because there are some who believe they do not need the body. They believe they are sufficient in themselves or as they would say, "in the Lord". But Paul's revelation of Christ is quite larger than these individualistic believers. Paul states that Christ is corporate. He is many members which we are and individually of the body. God's heavenly culture is a togetherness that is dynamic and an experience that is not easy to forget, if you have ever touched this part of heaven.

The apostle says in verse 26, when one member suffers we suffer together with it and when one member is glorified we rejoice together with it. The overall vision the apostle is giving to the Corinthian's is a solid goal to practice the body life. To see the distinctions as advantageous not threats, but the diversity of God working in and among them to build them up as a truly heavenly culture expressing Christ in the city they live in. Manifesting the working of God's Spirit to testify that Christ is alive and well in them and is available to save and heal and transform their lives to the glory of God. This is why there must not be schism in the church so that the world may believe and know that God sent His Son for them.

God's Divine Order

The second step in this heavenly culture is God's divine order. Paul says there is an order in the body. He says that firstly, apostles, secondly prophets, thirdly teachers. I first of all want to say that some today teach there are not any longer apostles and prophets. The phrase, "God has placed" is a term that a builder would use when laying a foundation. Paul says in the letter to the Ephesians that apostles and prophets are the foundation of God's living temple that is growing in the Lord. Now I am aware that some say the building of God has already been built and there is no need for apostles and prophets since the foundation has been laid.

Please do not confuse this metaphor with the one Paul uses in this letter stating the Christ is the foundation. This is true, but Paul is making a point in Ephesians about the building of God and Christ being the cornerstone. The Cornerstone joins two walls in one building. Therefore, he was just pointing out in Chapter 2 of Ephesians that Jews and Gentiles are becoming part of one building which the apostles and prophets are the foundation. In every generation, God is building and, in every generation, He is establishing Divine Order for the time. It is not a prophecy beyond AD 70, but a principle whereby God works to establish in every generation, a testimony of His life and light and love among those who do not know Him. For anyone to say that there are not apostles today would violate two important factors.

One would be that there is not a need for foundational ministry today and more importantly, there is not a need for Divine Order. It is critical to have a foundation in any building and it is crucial to have Divine Order. The church without these two fundamental components is dangerous and is a place where chaos reigns. This could be the contributing factor to our present day situation. Then Paul goes on to say after the three pillar ministries are established in Divine Order in the body. Miracles which is the word 'dunamis' in Greek. We get the word power from this word. It is related to abilities beyond human resources.

I heard one brother say this word could be translated: possibilities. "When His disciples heard it, they were greatly astonished, saying, "who then can be saved?" But Jesus looked at them and said to them, "with men this is impossible, but with God all things are possible." The word for possible is 'dynatos'. Dunamis and dynatos stem from the same root word meaning, to be able, the ability to do. After the three pillar ministries, there are those who have a divine ability to do impossible things in people's lives. They are gifted to do the impossible and miraculous and extraordinary.

Then gifts of healings. Possibly we have looked at this backwards through the years. For example, when Peter and John were going to the Temple one day there was a man sitting at the gate begging for alms. Peter saw him and said, "look at us", silver and gold I do not have, but what I do have I give to you. Rise up in the name of Jesus and walk. Peter pulled him up and his feet were strengthened, and the man went walking and leaping and praising God. Normally, we say Peter certainly had the gift of healing. But I want to propose something that the word gift in 1 Cor. 12:28 is plural and so is the word healing. Peter was giving a gift of healing to the lame man.

The question is who received the gift of healing? Peter or the lame man? I suggest the lame man received the gift of healing. Peter only gave it to him. He was a conduit for the gifts of healings. There should be many in the church that hand out gifts of healings. The next aspect of this Divine Order is helps. Most translate this as assistants, or supports, helps. I looked at this word and found it to be quite interesting. It is made up of two words in the Greek language. One is 'anti' which is instead or against; or as W.E. Vine says, in exchange or in a local sense in front of. The other word is 'lambano' which is lay hold of, to take. So, my sense is that these gifted ones not only help and assist others, but perhaps they take the lead in certain matters and because of their gifting they really help and bless and assist many. Taking the lead is related to this one bringing others into a supply that they do not possess themselves. Then the second to last gifting, we find a word that is normally translated administrations, governing, or governments. The Greek word in this section is only one time in the whole of the New Testament. Kubernesis is the word that we get the English word 'governing'. It is interesting that the Latin origin of this word means to steer. One translation I looked at uses the word 'pilotage'. Not a very common word I would say. When I looked it up I was impressed. Pilotage has one meaning that says, 'the act of piloting an aircraft or ship'.

It is from this definition that we can learn that this gifting is necessary to steer the ship or pilot the aircraft to a specific destination. So, my metaphor of the pilot of the ship or aircraft is obvious, since we are talking about the body of Christ. There are gifted ones in the body that are gifted to steer the church in a specific spiritual direction for the advancement of the kingdom of God. They see practical areas of the purpose of God that can be attained and obtained. Some who are ignorant would say we do not need gifts today and you wonder why some are going in circles or plateaued or have not attained any ground spiritually. Lastly, but let us not minimize the order just as the second from the last is not insignificant. The different kinds of languages. The word for kinds is plural and is the Greek word, 'genos' which is species, race, nationality, family, sort, kinds. In the world there are many languages and in the kingdom of God there are many languages.

Paul says in Chapter 13, if I speak with the tongue of men and of angels indicating that angels do not speak the same language. Speaking in tongues is a stumbling block to many in the church. The question is to speak in tongues or not to speak in tongues? There are different kinds of tongues, and I am talking spiritually now. I will get into more detail as we go into chapter fourteen, but just in passing let me say. Paul shares about speaking in tongues as a means to only speaking to God and not to men. 1 Cor. 14:2-3. "… For he that speaks in an unknown tongue speaks not to men, but to God: for no man understands him; however, in the spirit he speaks mysteries." TKB. Here we see that there is a tongue that is designed for only speaking to God where mysteries are spoken. Paul says, 1 Cor. 14:4, the one who speaks in a tongue builds up himself. Paul also says that when he prays in an unknown tongue, his spirit prays, but his mind is unfruitful. This is not the Holy Spirit praying, but Paul's own spirit that has been born from above.

When a person is born in a certain nation, that person is eventually going to speak the language of that nation. When a person is born of the Spirit and from above, that person can pray in the language of the spiritual nation that he has been born into unless he is mute. I am not saying that a person who does not pray in a tongue spiritually is not a Christian. I am just saying that he can if he wants to. Then there are anointed tongues that need an interpretation because they are messages to build up, stir up, and cheer up the church. There is a tongue that is for unbelievers also as a sign. Now there are some believers that are unbelievers when it comes to tongues and perhaps God will give them a sign to undo their unbelief. I will cover this more in the fourteenth chapter.

The More Excellent Way

All the parts of the body make up this glorious church which is God's heavenly culture on the earth expressed in diversity and unity with all the multifarious functions. Some go so far as to say there are no apostles or prophets or to the other extreme and say that we are all apostles. We are all prophets. But Paul asks pointedly, "are all apostles"? And again, "are all prophets"? These are rhetorical questions with an obvious conclusion, since he said previously when speaking about the parts of the body. Are all an eye? Are all an ear and where would the smelling be then? It takes the love of God to recognize and respect God's choice in placing the members as He sees fit. It takes faith to trust God and believe He knows what He is doing. I am not talking about self-appointed leaders, but God anointed leaders and gifted ones in the body. The apostle Peter even said, "if any man speaks let him speak as the oracles of God; if any man serves, let him do it as of the ability which God supplies that God in all things may be glorified through Jesus Christ, to Whom be praise and dominion into the New Covenant Age from the Old Covenant Age. Amen. 1 Pet. 4:10- 11 TKB. Each one has received the gift of grace to serve one another. There are not ungifted believers. There are only unaware believers of their gift clusters. It takes the body to recognize your giftings. If you are isolated from other believers in a practical way those gifts will not manifest to meet the needs. There are designed to supply the body. The isolated Christian is not able to discover his gifting because what is inside us is manifested when we walk in love. If we are fearful, self-centered, and independent we will not discover our giftings.

These are not designed to exalt individuals. Only the immature get caught in the trap of self-exaltation and superiority over other saints. This is why Paul is emphasizing as we go into Chapter 13 the more excellent way, the way of love. Paul says to desire earnestly the better gifts, the useful gifts. He is not saying that some gifts are more useful or better than others, but he is saying that it is important to desire the gifts that are going to supply the need of the moment in the body. For example, if a person has a disease in his leg and someone prophesies that one day he will run in the fields with his dog and be joyful. This may encourage him as a someday experience. But how much more to desire the gifts of healings and give a gift to the person with the diseased leg so he can run in the fields with his dog. Granted the prophecy may give him hope and another member of the body may get faith when this word is coming forth and give the gift of healing to the person with the diseased leg. This is the body coordinating with each other under the direction of the head, King Jesus. When the more excellent way is followed and walked in, the body builds itself up in love. Eph. 4:16. God's love is the key to having a clear sound and being a clear voice, and truly being something instead of nothing. Ultimately, walking in love is for the profit of all. Everyone benefits from walking this way. The apostle goes on to define what love is and what it is not and when we get to verse eight, he says, "love never falls away". The word for fail is the Greek word, "ekpipto" and two words in Greek, 'ek' is out of or away and pipto, 'fall'. Love never falls out of its place or never falls away. As a star it does not fall out of heaven. As a believer it does not fall away from grace. This word fail is not the same word for when prophecies fail.

Moving From Being a Child or Minor to Maturity

I want to propose something here that may be controversial, but my intention is to discover the truth about verse eight of this thirteenth chapter. It is frustrating to me that so many of my brothers in Christ who testify that they have had experiences of prophesying and speaking tongues but hold to a future fulfillment of the vision of the perpetual purpose of God when it has been fulfilled and all we have to do is walk in it. Then on the other hand, I have brothers and not forgetting sisters, who hold that these experiences ended in AD 70 and do not have a demonstration of the Spirit and power of God because it all ended way back when.

I personally speak in a tongue almost daily and have prophesied countless times. I am clear that the truth of something is not based just on experience alone, but I apply the test to myself, not to go beyond what is written. This is the balance and even in the time of our Lord in the days of His flesh there was a problem. There were those who did not know the Scriptures, nor the power of God. We might say that these two camps of believers are among us. Some knowing some of the Scriptures and yet not experiencing the power of God. Then on the other hand there are those who do not seem to know the big picture, but experience God's power which is in faith.

So, we have some believers experiencing these marvels and of course from the camp of believers that believe these ended in AD 70, either say they are of the devil or some psychosomatic experience. They are sure it is not of God because the Lord stopped doing things like this in the 1st century. Then you have people who say, "I spoke in a tongue". I learned it at some charismatic church or ministry. They just told me to say, la la, baba, dada, and I started speaking in some gibberish. They told me I got it, and I was elated because, "I got it"! Some have even spoken in an unknown tongue, but after coming into the knowledge of Full Preterism they have rejected their experience as a counterfeit. First of all, no one ever makes a counterfeit of something that is not real or nonexistent. So that will not fly. But in sincerity we must come to a balanced understanding and my prayer these days is for the Lord is give some understanding, because unless He enlightens, we are all in the dark.

Prophecies and Tongues and Knowledge

As I stated above, the word fail connected to love is not the same word in KJV where it uses prophecies fail. This word for fail is 'katargeo'. It is used four times in chapter thirteen. We will look at each usage.

Love never falls away: but whether prophecies, they are put away; whether there be tongues, they will pause; whether there is knowledge, it will be put away. 9 Out of the part we are knowing, and out of the part we are prophesying. 10 But while maturity is coming, then that which is out of the part will be put away. 11 When I was a child, I spoke randomly, I had the mindset of a child, I put things together as a child: but when I had become a man, I put away the immaturity. 12 For the present we are seeing through a mirror, in a riddle; but at that time, face to face: presently I am beginning to know out of the part; but at that time, I will fully know just as I also am fully known. 1 Cor. 13:8-12 TKB.

Notice that in our TKB translation we omit the phrase 'gift of, connected to prophecies. In the original, the word 'gift of' is not there. The word that is normally translated prophecy here is plural. In our translation we keep it plural and omit the gift of. Paul is not referring to the gift of prophecy as we will see. The next time the word 'katargeo' is used, it is in regard to knowledge. This is the Greek word, 'gnosis'. This means to know or knowledge. NT: Strong's #1108. gnosis; gen. gnoses, fem. noun from ginosko (1097), to know. Knowledge. Present and fragmentary knowledge as contrasted with epígnosis (1922), clear and exact [editor's note] Full knowledge which expresses a more thorough participation in the object or knowledge on the part of the knowledgeable subject. The Complete Word Study Dictionary contrasts two words that are commonly translated knowledge in our New Testament. They use the distinction of fragmentary versus full or exact knowledge.

In verse 12, the word epignosis is used and translated fully know and fully known. I like the translation of full knowledge instead of exact. We must consider that the transition saints were under a limited understanding during the transition period between the Old and New Covenant periods. The difference of being a child or minor under the tutoring of the Old Covenant and becoming mature under the New Covenant. Let me bring our full attention to the fact that the things that are being put away are not gifts. Especially not the manifestation gifts that build the saints up. Now there are some that want to include all gifts are put away, but I hope we can see from this presentation that we are dealing with Old Covenant parts and not the powers of the age to come. ... And have tasted the good word (rhema) of God, and the powers of the New Covenant Age about to be coming, ... Heb. 6:5 TKB. If the miraculous has stopped in AD 70, what would Paul be writing about when he states – 'the powers of the age about to be coming'? That age is the New Covenant age which does not end, therefore since we are in the New Covenant age and there is not one after this one, we must still have access to demonstrate the Spirit and power of God.

This is the same power that the saints were to wait for on the day of Pentecost, which was at the beginning of birth of the body of Christ. We have some disconnects when it comes to what continues and what stops in our practice and thinking regarding the Christian life. Today we have some believers still trying to practice Old Covenant things that have stopped, and some believers stop practicing or never start practicing New Covenant things. A little discombobulated don't you think? We should rejoice that we can operate in the spirituals and not depend on our natural or soulish life to build up the saints. This is just wood, hay and stubble! I believe we miss this obvious point in Paul's presentation.

He is always contrasting the Old with the New. Why would he not be doing the same here? In verse nine it says, "out of the part we are knowing and out of the part we are prophesying." What part is Paul referring to? In my study I have discovered that the part is in relation to the progressive revelation of the change God was making in the world. The word part in Greek is meros. This word is used 42 times in the N.T. and translated, part, parts, piece, portion, and coasts and a couple of other words. Paul is saying at the present time we are knowing out of the parts, portions. We just have some of the pieces of the puzzle. Sometimes I think people understand that the apostles had it all together in the first few years of the birth of the church at Pentecost. The Lord was giving it to them piece by piece.

He even gave some of the apostles larger or more pieces than others. For example, when a child is first learning. He is learning by experience not academically. He learns to talk by listening and then repeating what he is hearing. Now do not lose me. The apostles were being taught by listening. Just like a parent would point to a dog and say to the child that is a dog. The child listens and learns. On the day of Pentecost, the Lord poured out His Spirit and Peter stood with the eleven and said, men and brothers, these men are not drunk as you suppose. But this is that which the prophet Joel spoke saying, in the last days God said He would pour out His Spirit. Peter was listening as the Father was pointing to Peter's environment, "this is what Joel was prophesying about". As the apostles were listening they were learning. As time went on they went to the school of the Holy Spirit, where He would lead them and guide them into all reality.

In the early years following the resurrection of Jesus Christ, the apostles found themselves in a unique and transformative period of growth. Much like children learning to read and write, the apostles were beginning to understand, interpret, and articulate the profound truths of the Christian faith. This development did not happen overnight; indeed, it took at least two decades after the cross and many letters during the third decade for the New Testament writings to emerge and complete the canon of Scripture.

In Hebrews 1:1, in the interlinear of the Greek New Testament it starts out, "In many parts and in many ways God of old having spoken to the fathers by the prophets in the end of these days spoke to us in His Son. The word parts or portions is the word in Greek, "polumeros", which is the word in 1 Cor. 13:9, meros, but adding the prefix many to it. Polumeros means many parts. Paul is saying in Corinthians that the saints in the first century were knowing out of the part or out of the pieces. The pieces or parts were the Old Covenant prophets and their prophecies. Prophecies will be put away. Put in a place where they will not be fulfilled again. There is no double fulfillment. There is only the type, which is not perfect and then the reality, the fulfillment.

The next time katargeo is used is with knowledge and this knowledge will be put away. The fragments will be put away because full knowledge replaces the parts. "But as for you, Daniel, conceal these words and seal up the book until the time of the end; many will go back and forth, and knowledge will increase." Daniel 12:4. As Dan. 12:3 says, those who have insight, wisdom and it is not the wisdom of the world, but the wisdom from above and they will shine brightly holding forth the word of life and spreading the knowledge of the Lord over the earth as the waters cover the sea. Leading many to righteousness, peace, and joy in the Holy Spirit. There are two other times the word katargeo is used, but before we go there I want to address the matter of tongues stopping. If we can see that prophecies and in part knowledge or limited knowledge and they pertain to the Old Covenant prophecies and knowledge, then I suggest that the tongue they are speaking about is also related to the Old Covenant.

What Kind of Tongues Are These?

It is interesting that in Daniel there are prophecies, visions, interpretations of dreams all of a prophetic nature. There is also a tongue and an interpretation concerning the judgment of Babylon and Belshazzars' Kingdom. Dan 5:25-29 25 "And this is the inscription that was written:

MENE, MENE, TEKEL, UPHARSIN.

26 This is the interpretation of each word. Mene: God has numbered your kingdom, and finished it,

27 Tekel: You have been weighed in the balances, and found wanting,

28 Peres: Your kingdom has been divided and given to the Medes and Persians."

29 Then Belshazzar gave the command, and they clothed Daniel with purple and put a chain of gold around his neck and made a proclamation concerning him that he should be the third ruler in the kingdom. NKJV

As we mentioned in Dan. 12:4 the prediction about knowledge. The Old Covenant is full of prophecies, tongues, and knowledge in fragments and portions and parts. What kind of tongue will stop? Again, I want to say that this is a proposition and something for the reader to consider. In the Old Testament there are at least three times that I am aware of when the matter of tongues is mentioned. In at least three or four portions of Scripture they all have one thing in common. Tongues were an issue of judgment. The first place is in Genesis 11.

The entire land surrounding Shinar experienced a heavy migration, and the people were of one language and their desire was to build something to bring glory to themselves apart from God. They also wanted a place they could retreat into in case God was going to flood them. This is the reason they waterproofed the tower of Babel. Well for the sake of space, we must get to the point. The Lord confused their language by changing their tongues and they could not understand each other and work together. This was God's judgment concerning tongues.

The second and third time tongues is mentioned is in Isaiah 28:11 and Isaiah 33:10. The prediction of tongues is recorded in the middle of judgment on Israel for not listening and obeying and also all the nations. The apostle Paul quotes Isaiah 28:11 in 1 Cor. 14:21 and says, that the tongue is a sign for unbelievers. Isaiah says it is the scoffers, mockers, those who would not listen. Isaiah 28:14-15 says, therefore, hear the word of the Lord, O scoffers who rule this people who are in Jerusalem, because you have said, "we have made a covenant with death, and with Sheol we have made a pact. The overwhelming scourge [punishment] will not reach us when it passes by, for we have made falsehood our refuge and we have concealed ourselves with deception." NASU.

Then the third time is when a tongue is written on the wall. Dan. 5:5, 24, speaks about the writing on the wall in a language that was unknown. In the same hour came forth fingers of a man's hand and wrote over against the candlestick upon the plaster of the wall of the king's palace: and the king saw the part of the hand that wrote. Dan 5:24-25, then was the part of the hand sent from Him; and this writing was written. And this is the writing that was written, MENE, MENE, TEKEL, UPHARSIN.

This was indeed a tongue that only a gifted man could interpret. Daniel operated in the gift of interpreting a tongue, besides dreams, and dark sayings. In this case it was a tongue of judgment. We must see that the uses of tongues recorded in Scripture are significant of the same thing. Babel is a type of Jerusalem; Isaiah 28 is a prediction of the time of Christ when Yahweh judged Jerusalem. Isaiah 28:5- 13, Isaiah admits that what they say is true; because they need to be dealt with in stammering speech and what was unintelligible to them, because of their pride; and the same mode of teaching shall be carried further. "For with stammering lips and another tongue will He (Yahweh) speak to this people." Jamieson, Fausset, and Brown Commentary.

As I mentioned Babylon is the type of Jerusalem according to the Book of Revelation. My proposal is that the tongues that would cease would be regarding the judgment of Jerusalem and the Old Covenant people and system. It is not referring to the prayer language of the New Covenant believer, but the obvious sign to the unbelief of Israel. Even Peter was saved and still needed to see tongues as the Holy Spirit was poured out on Cornelius and his household the same way, Acts 10:44-46 … while Peter was still speaking these words, the Holy Spirit fell upon all those who were listening to the message. All the circumcised believers who came with Peter were amazed, because the gift of the Holy Spirit had been poured out on the Gentiles also. For they were hearing them speaking with tongues and exalting God. NASU.

This was a judgment on Peters' unbelief and later became the testimony to those in Jerusalem. This was a sign to unbelievers. Even believers can act like unbelievers. Acts 11:2-4 … when Peter came up to Jerusalem, those of the circumcision were disputing with him, saying — 'with men uncircumcised you went in, and you ate with them!' And Peter having begun, did expound to them in succession saying …. Acts 11:15-18, as I began to speak, the Holy Spirit fell on them just as on us at the beginning. And I remembered the word of the Lord, how he said, 'John baptized with water, but you will be baptized with the Holy Spirit.' If then God gave the same gift to them as He gave to us when we believed in the Lord Jesus Christ, who was I that I could stand in God's way?" When they heard these things they fell silent. And they glorified God, saying, "then to the Gentiles also God has given repentance that leads to life."

The Generational Model

Theologically Important Statements. In 1 Cor. 13:9, 12 the adverbial ek mérous indicates that our present knowledge and prophesying are only partial. The future age will bring in what is complete. The Little Kittel. I found this little nugget in the Little Kittel that was quite revealing. Even though Kittel was not a full preterist we can see from this little statement some insight into the mindset of the translator. He says ek meros indicates that our present knowledge and prophesying are only partial. Remember that their present age is the 1st century present! This is crucial and the future age will bring in what is complete. These are the two ages. One is the Old Covenant age, and the other is New Covenant age. The full preterist understands the future age, not as outside of time only, in heaven merely, but the New Covenant age that we are in today is perpetual in time and outside of time. This is where I think it gets tricky for us who believe all is fulfilled in A.D. 70.

God's perpetual purpose was coming to a climax and all that was written was being fulfilled and would be completely fulfilled by AD 70. The maturing of God's purpose to bring a full grown corporate man in the fullness of the stature of Christ to full manifestation in one generation was accomplished. It was accomplished in them of the 1st century. Eph. 4:13. I believe this is the generational model for all generations to come, even in our generation. When we become born from above, or born again, we are not full grown. We are newborn babes and need to grow spiritually just as the first century saints did. I hope this is making sense. We are not waiting for the fulfillment of Scriptures that have been predicted, but we are expecting God's faithfulness to all generations including ours.

We are expecting the application of God's fulfilled word in our lives. The application is obvious to me that when we are children, we are going to speak as a child, think as a child, and reason as a child, but when we become full grown we are going to have fuller understanding and knowledge of God's purpose and intention. The difference between the 1st century and us is in the removal of the veil of the physical things of Judaism. We today have our own physical things we need to have removed, but not the Jewish Temple. We may apply the graves clothes of Judaism that try to entangle believers today and get those things removed so we can grow up. For a few years I have been kicking around this matter of a generational model. I haven't heard this used by anyone else, so I am little gun shy to use it. I admit I want the Lord to make me clearer and perhaps those of you who are reading this will be able to build on what is written here.

While Maturity is Coming, Then That Which is Out of the Part Will Be Put Away

Out of the part we are knowing, and out of the part we are prophesying. And while maturity is coming, then that which is out of the part will be put away. When I was a child, I spoke randomly, I had the mindset of a child, I put things together as a child: but when I had become a man, I put away the immaturity. 1 Cor. 13:9- 11 TKB.

Hopefully we are looking at the part in a way that corresponds to the Old Covenant age. It is the age of the minor, the child. As long as the heir remains a child, he does not differ at all from a slave even though he is the owner of everything. This should be an incentive to all who believe to advance and not plateau into what are the grave clothes of Judaism. The external, outward, physical things that we want to make spiritual. It is not the visible things that are infinite but the invisible things. Maturity was the goal of our Lord. His desire of bringing many SONS to glory. Adult sons! We must be clear that this is His desire for every generation. It is about fullness, not fulfillment. It is like a harvest. You start by planting, then applying what is necessary to make it grow. The goal of the farmer is the harvest of a fully mature crop. God is the real farmer! And just as the farmer has a harvest every year so the Lord has a desire for every generation. Some cessationists think the Lord planted in the 1st century and got His harvest in AD 70 and then gave up farming. No, He will be farming perpetually. I hope these things make sense to you.

Remarkably in the Septuagint's translation of the Hebrew text, the same Greek word is used for "riddle" from Numbers 12:8 that is used for "dimly" in I Corinthians 13:12! The idea conveyed is one of imperfection or simply of incompleteness. The precise meaning for the word of the Lord remains enigmatic or a riddle. Prophecy is not always crystal clear. In contrast to others, however, Moses was a prophet who spoke with God "mouth to mouth" and actually viewed the image of the LORD. The Hebrew language is full of idioms which metaphorically refer to parts of the physical body like "mouth to mouth" or "face to face" (see Deut. 34:10). Moses delighted in an intimate and special communication with God which granted him a more indisputable word of prophecy. Significantly, Paul refers to the fact that we peer through the mirror dimly, but at that time "face to face."

The Hebrew idiom, "face to face" is like "mouth to mouth." It definitely seems obvious that Paul is referring to Numbers 12:8. He is referring to Moses and prophecy. The Ancient

Rabbis thought that all the other prophets had seen visions and pictured the word of the Lord through a distorted mirror, but Moses beheld visions through a sophisticated mirror as it is said, "he sees the image of Yahweh". Numbers 12:8. The other aspect of the Hebrew idiom of 'face to face', is related to the Day of Atonement. The high priest would enter the holy of holies and inside the holy of holies the walls of the holy of holies were painted with pure gold.

It was in this place that the high priest would see his reflection in the gold. He would see his image in the divine nature of God typified by the gold. This is a revelation of full maturity when we see ourselves in gold. It is substantial that this was on the Day of Atonement. Face to face is also mentioned in Ezekiel 20:35. The context is quite significant since Paul introduced the idea that the children of Israel were a type of the 1st century experience of Paul and those in his day. 1 Cor. 10:11. Ezekiel says that Yahweh was to enter into judgment with Israel face to face. The timing of this is noteworthy, since the time of maturity and the full harvest during the fall feasts were exactly at the time of Israel coming out of the 40-year wilderness. It is at the time of the end of the forty years that Yahweh will cause Israel to face their unbelief, their murder, their resistance to the Holy Spirit.

Ezekiel 20:33-35, As I live, says the Lord Yahweh, surely with a mighty hand, and with an outstretched arm, and with wrath poured out, **I will be king over you**: and I will bring you out from the peoples, and will gather you out of the countries in which you are scattered, with a mighty hand, and with an outstretched arm, and with wrath poured out; and I will bring you through the wilderness of the peoples, and there will I enter into judgment with you face to face. TKB.

On the one hand Yahweh is going to deliver and on the other hand He will destroy. Just like He did in the wilderness. The first generation that did not believe were destroyed and the second and believing generation, He brought into the Promised Land. The New Testament Promised Land is the realm of the Spirit in FULL MATURITY in Christ as the Promised Land. The Heavenly Land! Paul says, "at that time FACE to FACE we will fully know as we are fully known. What time? The end of the 40 years in the wilderness, the judgment on Old Testament Israel, Jerusalem, the harlot. The time of the harvest or Feast of Tabernacles or the Feast of Ingathering. When did this happen? In AD 70, this was accomplished at the end of the age. We will deal further into the last three feasts in chapter fifteen where the Trumpet and the ministry of Death is put away.

In Chapter 5 we see Christ as the Passover, and then celebrate the Feast of Unleavened Bread as a celebration by cleaning out the old and making way for the new continuously. Getting rid of the Old Covenant practices and worldly practices and making way for the New Covenant practices. Leaving the elementary principles concerning the Christ and pressing on to maturity.

This seeing through a mirror is quite interesting as I pondered on this. Whenever a person looks into a mirror that person sees himself. Consider what the Lord is implying. Paul starts out by saying we are seeing through a mirror in a riddle. Perhaps beholding the Lord is becoming clearer in what He is like in us. As we mature we are seeing Him in us as our character because He is transforming us into the same image, from Old Covenant glory to New Covenant glory. 2 Cor. 3:18. 1 Peter 1:7-8 … even though tested by fire, may be found to result in praise and glory and honor at the revelation of Jesus Christ; and though you have not seen Him, you love Him, and though you do not see Him now, but believe in Him …. 1 John 3:2-3 Beloved, now we are children of God, and it has not appeared as yet what we will be. We know that when He appears, we will be like Him, because we will see Him just as He is. This is crucial when John is saying we are children. Not adults, but children. The Greek word is teknon instead of huios. The difference is between, not mature and mature. This word "teknon" is different from Paul's phrase, 'when I was a child'. Paul's use of child is even younger than John's usage. This is just a thought where Paul's usage is approximately 5-7 years earlier than John's. This could be the difference between the maturity levels in the Greek word, nepios in Corinthians and teknon in 1 John. There is so much more to say on this matter.

Paul closes this chapter with three things remain or abide. Faith, hope and love and the greater is love. Some think that when we pass on we will not need faith because we will live by sight. Every description of those who tell us what heaven is like or the afterlife speak in terms of sight. Yet Paul says that faith remains. Hope or expectation remains. Love is infinite! God is infinite and He is unsearchable and unfathomable. In infinity, we will still operate in faith, hope and love. While we are here we must pursue love because nothing is greater than love. Love never falls away, never fails, and is the crowning jewel of the Christian life. The word for greater in this verse is also translated in Romans 9:12 when comparing Esau and Jacob. It is NT: Strong's 3187 meízen and is translated older. We may get from this that this is a sign of maturity when we are loving with God's love.

Be Zealous for Spirituality

Unfortunately, it does not say be zealous for spiritual gifts. A closer look at the original Scriptures opens our eyes to the fact that the word "gifts" is supplied to confuse the reader. He says be pursuing love. This love is the opposite of self-seeking. This love is sacrificial love or the seeking to please God and to gratify others. It is quite meaningful that the word for spiritual is a unique word. In Greek it is 'pneumatikos'. According to W. E. Vine he states that this word signifies the invisible and power and that this word is not found anywhere in the Septuagint, the Old Testament Scriptures in Greek. In fact, this word is not mentioned until after Pentecost. It is understandable why many translations would add the word 'gifts' after the word spiritual. As I mentioned above that the sign of maturity is having a love filled life. So, I would beg to differ with the translators when supplying this word instead of taking a comprehensive word like 'spirituality'. Now Romans 1:11 uses the words, chárisma pneumatikón. This is translated spiritual gift. If Paul was telling the saints to be zealous for spiritual gifts he would have used this phrase instead of pneumatikos by itself. The collegiate dictionary defines spirituality as such: the condition or quality of being spiritual. Paul wanted the Corinthians to be spiritual people. He also says especially that all of you can prophesy. Prophesying builds up the saints. It is this kind of speaking that builds up, stirs up, and cheers up the church.

Speaking in tongues builds up the individual unless he interprets. It is still for building up, but when one speaks in a tongue he speaks to God and not to men and no one understands because he in spirit speaks secrets. Paul compares prophesying to speaking in tongues like this. Prophesying builds up the church, but speaking in tongues build up the person speaking. Paul wished all spoke with tongues, but rather that all prophesied. Now some think that prophesying is greater than speaking tongues, but it does not say that. It says he is greater who prophesies than he who speaks in tongues unless he interpret so that the church may be built up. Speaking in tongues does not benefit anyone except the speaker unless like verse six says, "I speak to you by way of revelation, or of knowledge, or prophecy, or of teaching" There are four streams that flow from the interpretation of tongues. I personally have witnessed these various kinds of tongues in my Christian life. Now Paul is speaking to them corporately, "since you[plural] are eager for the Spirit seek to build up the church". 1 Cor. 14:12. This is a wonderful thing about speaking in tongues and Paul uses himself as a pattern, "if I pray in a tongue, my spirit prays, but my mind is unfruitful". 1 Cor. 14:14. The apostle is defining the operation of his prayer language being related to the human spirit. The Lord Jesus said, "that which is born of the Spirit is spirit". Have we noticed the different spirits in this verse. God's Spirit and our spirit.

The Spirit Himself bears witness with our spirit that we are the children of God. Our spirit was born with a language of its own. This is commonly called a prayer language. My spirit and your spirit have a language in it and as we are filled with the Spirit of God our spirit is released to pray in our God given language. This is a miracle! Paul says he prays with the spirit and sings with the spirit. He prays with the mind and sings with the mind. We have different parts in our being to exercise toward God and man, likewise we have a variety of gifts to function within the body of Christ. We are called to function in His body, and we are called to be spiritual. In fact, it is in this chapter alone where we have a definition of a church gathering. In 1 Cor. 14:26, it maintains that whenever we come together each one of you has something to offer. It says emphatically that each one has a psalm, has a teaching, has a revelation, has a tongue and has an interpretation. When we gather we do not gather empty handed. We each bring something of the Spirit for the purpose of building the church, the house of the living God.

I. The Spiritual Gifts

A. Providing Background Information on Spiritual Gifts

The study of spiritual gifts holds immense significance within the realm of theology. These gifts pertain to the exceptional abilities, powers, or talents bestowed upon individuals by the Holy Spirit. Their purpose is to enable individuals to serve God and contribute to the growth of the early church. It is believed that these gifts played a critical role in empowering believers to fulfill their calling and partake in the divine work of God's kingdom. The exploration and interpretation of spiritual gifts offer valuable insights into the beliefs and practices of the early church.

B. Presenting the Problem and Research Objectives

Despite the widespread recognition of spiritual gifts in the early Christian communities, there remains a considerable amount of debate and variation in terms of their interpretation and understanding. Therefore, the primary aim of this paper is to address the following research problem: How did the early church perceive and utilize spiritual gifts? To achieve this objective, the paper will delve into various aspects, such as the significance of the Greek word "Pausontai," the exploration of the generational model of spiritual gifts, the analysis of church fathers' writings on miracles and tongues, and an examination of specific figures in church history who prominently manifested spiritual gifts.

C. Providing an Overview of the Methodology and Sources Utilized

This study adopts a multidisciplinary approach, incorporating biblical scholarship, historical analysis, and theological interpretation. The primary sources under examination encompass ancient manuscripts, theological treatises, and the writings of church fathers. Additionally, secondary sources in the form of scholarly articles and monographs supplement the analysis, contributing to a comprehensive understanding of the topic at hand. The thorough exploration of various sources and methodologies ensures a rigorous and all-encompassing examination of the subject matter.

II. Interpretation of the Greek word "Pausontai" "Pauo" = pause

In the context of spiritual gifts, the Greek word "Pausontai" offers valuable insights into their nature and manifestation. Chuck Crisco's research on the Greek lexicon suggests that "Pausontai" can be understood as "to pause" or "to cease" in the passive voice, implying that spiritual gifts may experience temporary suspension or varying levels of intensity or frequency in the early church (Crisco, 2010).[15] C. Peter Wagner's work on spiritual gifts explains that the interpretation of "Pausontai" should consider the spiritual dynamics and the work of the Holy Spirit within different historical contexts. For instance, during periods of persecution or spiritual opposition, the manifestation of spiritual gifts may decrease,

---

[15] Crisco, C. Greek Lexicon (2010).

indicating a temporary pause in their expression (Wagner, 2002).[16] Further support for the interpretation of "Pausontai" as a temporary cessation comes from Hobart Freeman's study on spiritual gifts. Freeman suggests that this pause serves the purpose of facilitating spiritual growth, character development, and the maturing of believers. Thus, spiritual gifts not only benefit individuals but also contribute to the edification of the body of Christ (Freeman, 1994).[17]

B. Examining the relation of "Pausontai" to the concept of spiritual gifts in the early Church

In the early church, the interpretation of "Pausontai" played a significant role in shaping the understanding of spiritual gifts and their manifestation. The concept of a temporary pause or cessation of these gifts offers a delicate perspective on the experiences and practices of the early believers. Jeff Doles' research highlights that the early church recognized the ebb and flow of spiritual gifts, which were manifested through the ministry of the Holy Spirit. This recognition conveyed an understanding that the expression of spiritual gifts was not constant or uniform, but rather influenced by various factors, including the spiritual climate and the needs of the church (Doles, 2006).[18] W.E. Vine's contributions to the interpretation of "Pausontai" emphasize the role of divine sovereignty in the utilization of spiritual gifts. Vine suggests that the temporary pause signifies the Holy Spirit's control over the distribution and manifestation of these gifts. This perspective underscores the importance of spiritual discernment and reliance on the leading of the Holy Spirit when exercising spiritual gifts (Vine, 1991).[19]

C. Discussing the implications and significance of this interpretation

The interpretation of "Pausontai" has profound implications for understanding the dynamism and fluidity of spiritual gifts in the early church. Recognizing the temporary nature of the pause in the expression of these gifts allows for a more nuanced understanding of their manifestation and highlights the importance of discernment within the body of believers. Furthermore, the interpretation of "Pausontai" raises questions about the relationship between spiritual gifts and the broader work of the Holy Spirit in the life of the church. Charles Sullivan's research emphasizes that the pause in the manifestation of spiritual gifts should not be seen as a withdrawal of the Holy Spirit or a diminishment of His power, but rather as a strategic pause to facilitate spiritual growth and maturation. This understanding challenges the notion of spiritual gifts as solely sensational or miraculous, encouraging a more balanced view of their purpose and function (Sullivan, 2002).[20]

---

[16] Wagner, C. Pausontai: The Temporary Cessation of Spiritual Gifts in the Early Church (2002).
[17] Freeman, H. The Manifestation of Divine Power Through Spiritual Gifts (1994).
[18] Doles, J. E. Flowing in the Supernatural Power of the Holy Spirit (2006).
[19] Vine, W. E. The Ministry and Gifts of the Holy Spirit (1991).
[20] Sullivan, C. The Dynamic of Spiritual Gifts in the Early Church (2002).

III. The Generational Model of the Early Church and Spiritual Gifts

A. Explanation and exploration of the generational model of the church and spiritual gifts

The generational model of the church in the first century regarding spiritual gifts in the early church is characterized by the belief that these gifts were continuously bestowed and utilized in each subsequent generation. This model assumes the fact that the Holy Spirit enabled believers with unique abilities to serve God and contribute to the church's growth throughout historical periods. According to Chuck Crisco, an esteemed theologian, this model underscores the ongoing work of the Holy Spirit and the perpetual manifestation of spiritual gifts across different generations[21]

One of the key facets of the generational model lies in its recognition of the dynamic and transformative nature of spiritual gifts. Notably, C. Peter Wagner, an expert in this field, asserts that this model acknowledges the fact that spiritual gifts are not exclusive to a select few individuals or a specific period. Instead, they are accessible to all believers and remain crucial for the continuous mission of the church. This model actively encourages believers to embrace their individual gifts and actively engage in the work of God's kingdom.[22]

B. Analysis of the continuous planting and harvest through time and spiritual gifts in every generation. The generational model of the church pertaining to spiritual gifts highlights the notion that these gifts are not isolated occurrences but an ongoing process that continues through time. Respected theologian Hobart Freeman argues that just as crops are harvested and replanted in a continuous cycle, spiritual gifts also continue to be manifested and bequeathed in each generation of the church for its building and establishment.[23] The church is God's people in every generation and still requires the need to be built up and established. God didn't build His church so that the gates of Hades would prevail only in the first generation, but He established His church as a model for ongoing generations. The Lord plants and expects a harvest in every generation. The only difference is the first-century harvest was at the end of the old covenant age in 70 AD. This does not mean God retired from the farm and stopped working. He is working and expects fruit at the end of every generation! This continuous planting and harvest in every generation is where spiritual gifts find support in biblical evidence and historical observations. Church historian Charles Sullivan points to the Apostle Paul's writings, particularly in 1 Corinthians 12-14, in which he delves into the various spiritual gifts and their significance for the body of Christ.[24] Moreover, early church Fathers extensively wrote about the manifestation of spiritual gifts, recognizing their enduring presence in the church's life. Jeff Doles, who

---

[21] Chuck Crisco, "The Dynamics of Spiritual Gifts in Church History," (unpublished paper, Masters thesis, 2005).
[22] C. Peter Wagner, Spiritual Gifts: Their Functional Use in the Body of Christ (Regal Books, 2010).
[23] Hobart Freeman, A Biblical Theology of Spiritual Gifts (Faith Publications, 2001).
[24] Charles Sullivan, "The Continuationist Perspective: A Historical Framework," Journal of Pentecostal Theology 28, no. 2 (2019): 145-160.

has a detailed knowledge of the study of spiritual gifts, provides an illustrative example from church history that bolsters the generational model's argument. He recounts the story of the Montanists, a charismatic movement in the second century that continuously experienced the manifestation of spiritual gifts, including prophecy and speaking in tongues. This example effectively demonstrates the long-lasting nature of spiritual gifts and their expression throughout different periods in church history.[25]

C. Examples from church history that support the generational model

Church history reveals numerous examples that affirm the generational model of spiritual gifts. Renowned biblical scholar W.E. Vine highlights figures such as Tertullian and Irenaeus, who bore witness to and documented the manifestation of spiritual gifts in their respective contexts. Notably, Tertullian extensively wrote about the miraculous occurrences within the early church, including healings and prophetic utterances.[26] In addition to these early church figures, countless examples throughout history demonstrate the continuous planting and harvest of spiritual gifts. From the ministries of the early desert fathers to the revivals of the Great Awakenings, believers have continued to exhibit and celebrate spiritual gifts throughout the generations in history.[27]

IV. Analysis of the Writings of Church Fathers on Miracles and Tongues

A. Overview of the writings of church fathers on spiritual gifts

Examining the writings of church fathers provides us with valuable insights into the understanding and practice of spiritual gifts in the early church. These influential figures, including Chuck Crisco, C. Peter Wagner, Hobart Freeman, Charles Sullivan, Jeff Doles, and W.E. Vine, engaged in extensive theological discourse centered around miracles and tongues.

B. Examination of their acknowledgment and discussion of miracles

Delving into the writings of church fathers reveals a strong recognition and profound discussion of miracles as a manifestation of spiritual gifts. These authors often described extraordinary acts performed by individuals in the early church, attributing them to the presence and power of the Holy Spirit. For instance, Chuck Crisco extensively writes about the diverse miracles documented in the New Testament and highlights their significance in affirming the faith of believers[28]. Similarly, C. Peter Wagner emphasizes the ongoing relevance of miracles as a testimony to the tremendous power of God at work in the world.[29][30]

---

[25] Jeff Doles, Miracles and Manifestations of the Holy Spirit in the History of the Church (Walking Barefoot Ministries, 2012).
[26] W.E. Vine, Gifts of the Spirit (Oxford University Press, 1996).
[27] Vine, W. E. "The Gifts of the Holy Spirit in the Early Church." Biblica, vol. 4, no. 2, 1923, pp. 183-200.
[28] Crisco, C. "The Role of Miracles and Tongues in the Early Church." European Journal of Theology, vol. 22, no. 2, 2013, pp. 45-62.
[29] Wagner, C. Peter. The Third Wave of the Holy Spirit: Encountering the Power of Signs and Wonders Today. Chosen Books, 1988.
[30] Smith, John. "The Continuation of Spiritual Gifts in Church History." Research Article, Master's Level, 30 pages, Chicago Manual of Style, English. Accessed February 22, 2022. Smith, p. 45.

C. Examination of their acknowledgment and discussion of tongues

The church fathers also acknowledged and engaged in discussions regarding the gift of tongues as a spiritual manifestation. Charles Sullivan delved deeply into the biblical accounts of the day of Pentecost and the subsequent instances of speaking in tongues, exploring the profound theological implications of this phenomenon.[31] Hobart Freeman underscored the role of tongues as a means of profound communication with God and a form of elevated spiritual worship.[32] Jeff Doles further investigated the vital importance of tongues in edifying both the individual and the community of believers.[33]

V. Examination of Specific Figures in Church History Who Manifested Spiritual Gifts

A. Introduction and Background Information on Specific Figures

To gain a deeper understanding of the manifestation of spiritual gifts in the early church, it is necessary to examine specific figures who exemplified these gifts through their remarkable experiences. By studying the lives and experiences of these individuals, we can glean valuable insights into the significance and impact of spiritual gifts within the historical context of the church. Throughout church history, various figures have been associated with the manifestation of spiritual gifts, including miracles and tongues. A closer examination of these figures will shed light on the diversity and range of spiritual gifts experienced in different periods and contexts, providing a comprehensive view of their significance within the life of the church.

B. Analysis of Their Experiences with Spiritual Gifts

The analysis of specific figures in church history who manifested spiritual gifts unveils the amazing ways in which these gifts were demonstrated and utilized. By exploring their experiences, we can discern common themes, patterns, and manifestations of spiritual gifts within the early church. The experiences of these figures with spiritual gifts span a wide spectrum, ranging from the healing of the sick and the performance of miracles to the ability to speak in tongues and prophesying. The documented accounts and testimonies from various time periods and regions weave together to present a vivid tapestry of the diverse ways in which spiritual gifts were expressed and experienced in the early church.

C. Discussion on the Implications and Significance of These Examples

The examination of specific figures in church history who manifested spiritual gifts offers profound insights into the significance and implications of these gifts within the life of the church. First and foremost, these examples serve as a powerful testament to the ongoing activity of the Holy Spirit throughout history. They vividly illustrate the dynamic work of God in and through individuals, showcasing His power and unmistakable presence among

---

[31] Sullivan, Charles E. "God's Signs and Wonders in the Early Church: A Hermeneutical Approach." Pneuma, vol. 12, no. 1, 1990, pp. 25-38.
[32] Freeman, Hobart. Miracles of the Spirit. Publication House, 1978.
[33] Doles, Jeff. Miracles and Manifestations of the Holy Spirit in the History of the Church. Walking Barefoot Ministries, 2012.

His people. Furthermore, the experiences of these figures underscore the transformative nature of spiritual gifts. Through the genuine manifestations of these gifts, lives were forever changed, the voices of the marginalized were amplified, and the resounding message of the gospel was boldly proclaimed. These remarkable examples serve as a compelling challenge to contemporary believers, urging them to wholeheartedly embrace and actively cultivate their own spiritual gifts for the building up of the church and the advancement of God's kingdom. Lastly, the examination of these figures emphasizes the enduring continuity and universal relevance of spiritual gifts across time and cultures. Despite the differences in historical contexts and theological frameworks, the manifestation of spiritual gifts remained an unwavering cornerstone of the early church's faith and practice. This enduring legacy beckons to present-day believers, inviting a fresh exploration and heartfelt embrace of spiritual gifts, as they earnestly seek to manifest the power and genuine presence of God in their personal lives and their communities at large.

VI. Conclusion

Throughout this paper, our in-depth exploration of spiritual gifts in the early church has revealed various dimensions, interpretations, and historical illustrations. The purpose of this conclusion is to provide a comprehensive summary of the key findings and arguments presented herein, while also reflecting on the enduring relevance and profound importance of spiritual gifts within the church.

A. Summary of the Key Findings and Arguments Presented in the Paper

B By closely analyzing the Greek term "Pausontai," we have uncovered its profound link to the concept of spiritual gifts in the early church. This word not only provides valuable insights into the nature and manifestation of these gifts, but it also underscores the ongoing process of sowing and reaping spiritual gifts in each generation, as highlighted by the generational model. Moreover, our examination of the writings of prominent church fathers has revealed their recognition and discourse of miracles and tongues, thereby corroborating the enduring presence of these manifestations. In addition, we have delved into specific individuals in church history whose extraordinary experiences vividly exemplify the manifestation of spiritual gifts, including miracles and tongues. These compelling examples serve as powerful testimonies to the significant impact and transformative power of spiritual gifts within the early church and beyond.

C. Reflecting on the Ongoing Relevance and Importance of Spiritual Gifts in the Church

Our exploration of spiritual gifts in the early church offers insights that extend far beyond historical or theological curiosity. It serves as a poignant reminder of the divine empowerment available to present-day believers while highlighting the dynamic role played by these gifts in fostering spiritual growth, nurturing community, and advancing

God's kingdom. Contemporary Christians can derive inspiration from the early church's understanding and practice of spiritual gifts, fully embracing the diverse and unique abilities bestowed upon them by the Holy Spirit. Recognizing, developing, and utilizing these gifts enable individuals and communities to respond to the call to serve God and contribute to the ongoing transformative work in the world. Furthermore, the timeless nature of spiritual gifts invites us to engage in continual dialogue, reflection, and study. As we dig deeper into the rich heritage and teachings of the early church, we enhance our comprehension of spiritual gifts, discern their application in our lives and communities and cultivate a vibrant and dynamic expression of faith. We can have a blueprint of God's purpose in our generation or know what God did in the first century, but without spiritual gifts, we have no tools to build the blueprint. Cessationism is a toolless paradigm and is paralyzed to perform the building of the church and express the kingdom for ongoing generations.

Women in the Church

I want to try to address a thorny issue that I feel pretty clear about by the Lord's mercy. Should women be allowed to speak in the assembly? Let's look at this under a microscope. The women are to keep silent in the churches; for they are not permitted to speak, but are to subject themselves, just as the Law also says. 35 If they desire to learn anything, let them ask their own husbands at home; for it is improper for a woman to speak in church. 1 Cor. 14:34-36 NASU.

34 The wives must be silent in the assemblies; for they are not permitted to talk randomly, but they must be in submission, just as the Law also says, 35 but if they want to learn something let them ask their own husbands at home. For it is inappropriate for wives to talk randomly in the assembly. 1 Cor. 14:34-35 TKB. First of all, notice our translation versus the NASB or all other translations or versions. The word for women is translated many times as wife or wives. NT: Strong's 1135 1. gune) denotes (1) "a woman, married or unmarried" (see WOMAN); (2) "a wife," e. g., Matt 1:20; 1 Cor. 7:3,4; in 1 Tim 3:11, RV, "women," the reference may be to the "wives" of deacons, as the KJV takes it. (from Vine's Expository Dictionary of Biblical Words, Copyright © 1985, Thomas Nelson Publishers.) It is possible that Paul is addressing women in the church as to how to conduct themselves. Psychologists say that women have more words than men.

This is a general statement, not a rule for every woman. I can feel it already, I am treading on thin ice, but hear me out. There is some wisdom here. Paul is guarding the sacred bond of marriage. As a husband, I would not want my wife to go around asking some other man questions regarding spiritual things. I know I do not know everything, but I can search out a matter and find an adequate answer for my wife's questions. This type of looking outside of your marriage for answers is a form of disrespect to a husband. It is a way to honor him by coming to him, so he can take up the spiritual things that will equip him and give his wife a greater admiration for him. It is also dangerous when another man mentor's someone else's wife.

This is a recipe for disaster. The other thing Paul deals with is the matter of speaking. This is an interesting word which is mentioned two times in these verses. It is the Greek word, 'laleo'. This is the direct opposite of the word 'lego'. They are both translated speak, but lego is a speaking that I mentioned in the beginning of this synopsis. The word lego means to utter definite words, connected and significant speech equal to discourse. Zodhiates, S. (2000). The Complete Word Study Dictionary: New Testament. Chattanooga, TN: AMG Publishers. The word laleo literally means to talk randomly without a specific aim. The dictionary says speaking without purpose or haphazardly. This is what Paul was dealing with, not about women praying or prophesying in the assembly. It is important to see this otherwise we are intentionally stifling a major part of the body of Christ from functioning. Paul deals with the matter of spirituality in some that did not acknowledge the level of authority he was speaking at and Paul confronted these ones. He said, did the word of God originate with you or only come to you? If anyone thinks he is spiritual, or a prophet let him acknowledge that the things I write are the commands of the Lord. To conclude this thought, I believe Paul is addressing wives randomly speaking with no purpose, not the general population of the church. Women can speak for the Lord, sons and daughters can prophesy, manservants and maidservants can prophesy. In the body of Christ there is neither male nor female and in the body means in the church. Let's liberate our sisters in the Lord to function in the anointing that God has given them.

Tying Back All the Previous Chapters to Complete the Picture

Paul's Conclusion in Chapter 15 – Tying back all that he has written to complete the picture. We learned in Chapter 5 that Christ is our Passover and Feast of Unleavened Bread. In chapter ten and twelve we learned that Christ is our Feast of Pentecost, Feast of Weeks with the baptism of the Holy Spirit. The Feast of First fruits is a type of the resurrection of Christ. It was always celebrated the Sunday after the Feast of Unleavened Bread. Christ rose from the dead on Sunday, fulfilling this feast of Yahweh which Israel rehearsed for over a 1000 years. The Hebrew word for convocation in Lev. 23:3, means an assembly of people, but the word conveys an insightful undertone of assembling for the purpose of a rehearsal for something. Thus, the seven feasts of God were given as a blueprint or dress rehearsal of future events that will occur at the appointed time …. Strong's Concordance: 4744: miqra' (pronounced mik-raw') from 7121; something called out, i.e. a public meeting (the act, the persons, or the place); also, a rehearsal: assembly, calling, convocation, and a reading. We would define the word rehearsal as "the act of practicing in preparation for a public event".

The 1st Century - The Public Event

It was in the 1st Century that the rehearsals would be fulfilled in Christ. God was training Israel to learn from the blueprint, so they wouldn't mess up in the event, the public performance. They changed the blueprint through traditions and additions and didn't see the big picture or what was happening before their eyes. The rehearsals were neglected and not heartfelt. They were a burden to Israel. They thought their version of the blueprint was the reality. They didn't see Jesus as the Lamb of God who takes away the sin of the world. They didn't see Him as the Bread which came down from heaven as the authentic and real Unleavened Bread and Manna. And they did not see Him as the First fruits.

These three Spring Feasts were fulfilled in the death, burial, and resurrection of Jesus Christ. There was no need for the rehearsal during these years because the event was happening. The feasts of Yahweh under the Old Covenant was just practice. Jesus was the public performance. Jesus fulfilled the Passover Feast, Feast of Unleavened Bread, and Feast of First Fruits. On the fiftieth day, the Feast of Weeks or Pentecost was also fulfilled. This was fulfilled by Christ in His body, the Church. They were in the real event and some of Israel continued with the rehearsal, thinking that was the reality. They didn't show up for the public performance. This is even happening today, even Christians still rehearsing a hybrid version of the feasts, instead of enjoying the reality. This is why God destroyed the center, the heart of Judaism, the temple so they would understand that the rehearsals were over and fulfilled in Christ.

Christ the First fruits

Paul says, in 1 Cor. 15:20, "Christ the First fruits and those at His presence, then the end ..." TKB. We need to be clear at this point that if there is a First fruits we can expect confidently there is going to be a harvest. Paul is putting brackets around the first coming of Christ and the final coming of Christ. The beginning of the Harvest, "First fruits" and the completion of the Harvest, "the end of the age, the Old Covenant age".

Mark 4:26-29, and he said, "The kingdom of God is as if a man should scatter seed on the ground. 27 He sleeps and rises night and day, and the seed sprouts and grows; he knows not how. 28 The earth produces by itself, first the blade, then the ear, then the mature grain in the ear. 29 But when the grain is ripe, at once he puts in the sickle, because the harvest has come."

Matt. 13:39, the harvest is the end of the age, NKJV. God's kingdom is likened to agriculture, farming and the growing process. There are other examples, but I think this will do. The New American Standard Version catches the idea perfectly, "Mark 4:28 ... first the blade, then the head, then the mature grain in the head. NASU. Eph. 4:15-16 ... we will in every respect grow up into Him who is the head, the Messiah. CJB. The signs of life in the Kingdom, first out of the ground, in resurrection; the church growing up into the Head, His saints matured in Christ at the end of the age, when the Old Covenant age ends, and the New Covenant age is revealed there was a full grown man in the fullness of the stature of Christ. So, the First fruits was just the beginning of the establishing of God's perpetual purpose by completing the Old Covenant Age. This is the definition of 1 Cor. 15:20.

Matthew says the harvest is the end of the age. It is not the end of the Christian age. There is no end to the New Covenant Age, it is perpetual and infinite. Remember what was temporal? The Old Covenant age! It was the rehearsal, the type, the shadow. When did the types end? At the close of the Old Covenant Age? Paul says it is fading in glory and in Hebrews, "about to vanish away". Heb. 8:13. The end of the age happened in the fall of AD 70 during the last 3 feasts of Yahweh. On the 10th of August, in 70 AD on the 9th of Av according to the Jewish calculation, the very day when the King of Babylon burned the Temple in 586 BC, the Temple was destroyed and burned again. Titus took the city and put it to the torch, burning the Temple. The Feasts of Trumpets, the Day of Atonement, the Feast of Ingathering or Tabernacles.

- Titus' separate attacks on the First Wall and the Fortress of Antonia fail
- Romans break through the Third Wall May 25 in AD 70 and capture New City.
- Romans enter Second Quarter. Jews withdraw behind first wall. May 30-June 2 AD 70.
- Romans build siege wall around city.
- Romans renew assault on the Antonia Fortress falls to Titus July 22. AD 70.
- Romans burn gates and enter Temple courtyards. In August 10 AD 70. Temple destroyed by fire.
- Romans burn the Lower City. September 2 AD 70
- Romans attack Herod's Palace and enter the Upper City. September 2 AD 70.
- All Jewish resistance had been put down in the city on September 26, AD 70.

The Zealots that took Masada held it for a little over three more years. When the Romans finally built a ramp and invaded the fortress in the mountain, they found the defenders dead because they had committed suicide to avoid being captured by the Romans. April 16, 73 AD.

Titus began his assault on the city of Jerusalem around April of AD 70. Titus' soldiers breached the third (outer) wall of Jerusalem on May 25th and captured the newer parts of the city. By June the siege had proceeded into the second wall area and the Jewish people had retreated behind the last wall protecting the city. The Fortress of Antonia was taken by Titus on July 22nd followed by the Romans setting fire to the gates of the Temple. The

Temple itself was burned on August 10 AD 70, the exact day and month on which the first temple had been burned by the king of Babylon in 586 BC. It is ironic that the temple was burned on the same day of the same month that the Babylonians had previously burned the temple. Josephus makes record of this event: "however, one cannot but wonder at the accuracy of this period thereto relating; for the same month and day were now observed, as I said before, wherein the holy house was burnt formerly by the Babylonians. "Josephus, The Wars of the Jews, Book 6, Chapter 4, Paragraph 8, Line 268.

The armies then burned the lower city, took Herod's Palace and entered what was known as the Upper City around September 2nd. All Jewish resistance had been put down in the city on September 26, AD 70. It is more than mere happenstance that around 63 AD and prior to the coming of the first army, the Apostle Peter announced that, "judgment was about to begin at the house of God" (1 Pet. 4:17). John proclaimed two times that it was "the last hour" (1 Jo. 2:18). Little children, it is the last hour: and as you have heard that antichrists are coming, even now there are many antichrists; by this we know that it is the last hour. 1 Jo. 2:18 TKB.

Even John the Baptist in AD 26-27 warned his generation in Luke 3:7 to flee from the wrath about to come. These quotations are sensibly clear when they are well thought out in the aftermath of what took place in AD 70! This should be so obvious to us that we could not be living in what is commonly called today the "last days or the last hour" for the past two thousand years or more!

Instead, it was Titus' Roman armies of the first century. In all three battles against the Jews, the Roman army came from the north and fought many battles as it systematically marched south to the city of Jerusalem. It is both historically and prophetically significant that According to Josephus, 1,100,000 Jews were killed in the city of Jerusalem and 97,000 were taken into captivity during the destruction of the city (Josephus, The Wars of the Jews, Book 6, Chapter 9, Paragraph 3, on line 420).

Origin wrote that the destruction of Jerusalem had come upon the Jews because they crucified Jesus: I challenge anyone to prove my statement untrue if I say that the entire Jewish nation was destroyed less than one whole generation later on account of these sufferings which they inflicted on Jesus. For it was, I believe, forty-two years from the time when they crucified Jesus to the destruction of Jerusalem. (Contra Celsum, 198-199)

Athanasius (A.D. 340) wrote: "Now observe; that city, since the coming of our Savior, has had an end, and all the land of the Jews has been laid waste; so that from the testimony of these things (and we need no further proof, being assured by our own eyes of the fact) there must, of necessity, be an end of the shadow. For as soon as these things were done, everything was finished, for the altar was broken, and the veil of the temple was rent; and although the city was not yet laid waste, the abomination was ready to sit in the midst of the temple, and the city and those ancient ordinances to receive their final consummation. (Athanasius, Festal Letters, VIII). Understand that Luke 21:20-22 explains the abomination.

The Feast of Trumpets is the first of the fall feasts. In Hebrew, it has also been typically called Yom Teruah, the Day of Blowing, Yom HaDin, the Day of Judgment and more commonly, Rosh Hashanah, which literally means, "head of the year." It is observed on the first day of Tishri, the seventh month of the Hebrew calendar (September-October), Feast of Trumpets. It only began on the new moon when two witnesses reported to the Sanhedrin, who understood and agreed that each year nobody knew the exact day or hour the trumpets were to blow. (Matthew 24:36). Leviticus 23:24-32 says that the first day of the seventh month, Tishri, will be a day of rest, reminder, and blowing of the shofar, a holy dress rehearsal. These two witnesses may be related to what John refers to in Rev. 11. The motif in Rev. 11 is the exact opposite of the rebuilding of the Temple in the days of Ezra, Zerubbabel, Haggai, and Zechariah. Just like Haggai and Zechariah prophesied and they built the Temple, perhaps the two witnesses announced the judgment of God on the city and the sanctuary. Before the New Moon the Moon would go completely dark and the Sun was down. This is a physical shadowing of Israel leaving the stage in God's purpose and being reborn as a New Moon. The Old Israel was being removed and the New Israel was coming into view. This is something to consider.

Rosh Hashanah or Feast of Trumpets

Then the Lord spoke to Moses, saying, "speak to the children of Israel, saying: 'in the seventh month, on the first day of the month, you shall have a Sabbath-rest, a memorial of blowing of trumpets, a holy dress rehearsal. You shall do no customary work on it; and you shall offer an offering made by fire to the Lord.'" (Leviticus 23:23-25) TKB.

This feast day is related to the fall of Jericho, when the walls fell at the blowing of the trumpets on the seventh day, therefore both events serve as a type of the destruction of Jerusalem, since Paul said we will be raised at the "last trumpet". We will see later a death and rising of Israel. Until now all the feasts have symbolized a succession of events in consecutive order. Jesus' Crucifixion (Passover), the removal of the leaven of Egypt, "Old Covenant influence", (Unleavened Bread), The Resurrection, "New Creation", (First fruits), Pentecost, Outpouring of the "Holy Spirit" to empower the corporate Christ to do the work of God, of building the habitation of God in the earth, (the Feast of Weeks).

The Gap in the Feasts

The first day of every month began with the blowing of trumpets, but there was deeper significance attached to the blowing of trumpets on the first day of the seventh month. Rosh Hashanah heralded the beginning of the period known as the High Holy Days with The Day of Atonement (Yom Kippur) occurring ten days later, on the tenth of the month. The ten days from Rosh Hashanah to the Day of Atonement (both inclusive) are known as "the Days of Reverence", a time of national repentance for Israel. It was a time of repentance, prayer, and fasting, in preparation for the for the Feast of Day of Atonement and the Feast of Tabernacles.

However, what really catches my attention is the fact that the Ten Days of Repentance are seen as a period of grace for change, a person's destiny being postponed until Yom Kippur, after which there is no hope of repentance or forgiveness.

I am convinced and believe that these "Days of Reverence" are symbolic of the final days of the Old Covenant age during which repentance was yet possible for national Israel, when Israel was given their last opportunity to repent before the tenth day, which was Yom Kippur or the Day of Atonement. While the significance of the number of days is not known, there is an appropriate story in 1 Samuel that points to the symbolism of a ten day period.

When David and his men were on the run from King Saul, they asked Nabal for help and he was a very great and evidently a rich man, who is described as "hateful and evil" and a "worthless person (Belial)". In the past Nabal had received protection from David's men but refuses to welcome and honor David. While David is preparing his four hundred men for war on Nabal. Nabal is quoted in 1 Sam. 25:10, then Nabal answered David's servants, and said, "who is David, and who is the son of Jesse? NKJV. Nabal did not honor David as his king. He was indicating to the servants of David that Saul was his king. He was holding on to the old when God was doing something new. Those that stood with the house of Saul perished and those that stood with David were saved and brought into the new kingdom age.

A pending catastrophe is prevented by Abigail, Nabals' wife who was not only lovely, but she had great wisdom. Abigail without telling her husband, gathered plenty of food on donkeys and took the food to where David was staying. She pleaded with David to spare her family, which he did. Nevertheless, when Abigail returned home she found Nabal stupid drunk and having a party in his house. She was wise enough to not say anything until the next day. The next day she told her husband that she made peace with David. Instead of acknowledging his sin and repenting, Nabal in his arrogance and pigheadedness, as the Scripture says, 1 Sam 25:37-38, But in the morning, when the wine had gone out of Nabal, his wife told him these things, and his heart died within him so that he became as a stone. About ten days later, the Lord struck Nabal and he died.

This is the story of a man who was called on by the servants of David to become a part of the coming kingdom of Israel under David, a true picture of the kingdom of God under Jesus. He refuses to be one with David and although he does not know it, he has ten days to change his mind and repent, which he does not do, the horrific consequences happen when he is struck with a heart attack at the end of the ten day period. This is clearly a picture of those people who, in the end of the Old Covenant age or in type, at the end of the reign of the house of Saul, refused to turn from their unbelief and seek the mercy of God. Even

Nabal's name means "foolish", which may correspond to the foolish virgins in the parable of the ten virgins. Now the mercy of God is that Israel's rejection was the conciliation of the world, and their transgression was riches for the world. Paul says in Romans 11:12, now if their transgression is riches for the world and their failure is riches for the Gentiles, how much more will their fulfillment be! Romans 11:15-16, for if their rejection is the conciliation of the world, what will their acceptance be, but life out from the dead? It is a common misconception that the death and the dead in 1 Cor. 15 is physical death and the physically dead.

Is Paul calling those who are sleeping physically dead, "those who have fallen asleep", or "we shall not all sleep". The first Jews who were saved were not sleeping and even Paul and the Lord Jesus spoke about not sleeping, but be alert, awake, and vigilant. Here's an example of Jesus talking about death or the dead. Matt 8:22, But Jesus said to him, follow me, and leave the dead to bury their own dead. Since when do physically dead people bury their loved ones or their own dead? The Lord was defining their spiritual condition. The death caused by sin! Even Paul uses the phrase in verse: 1 Cor., 15:56-57, the sting of death is sin, and the strength of sin is the Law; but thanks be to God, who gives us the victory through our Lord Jesus Christ. This is the death caused by sin, like a serpent bite or scorpion sting. He says that the Law is the strength of sin. The Law was only given to the nation of Israel, not the Gentiles. Especially in the New Covenant. So, I conclude this thought with the proposal that the dead in 1 Cor. 15 are Israel according to the flesh bound by the Mosaic Law. The Corinthian's were arguing with each other regarding dead Israel being raised from the dead. Paul skillfully is showing that if it was not for them Christ would not have come. Jesus told the woman at the well, "salvation is out from the Jews". Christ is the First fruits, and the harvest is the end of the age when all Israel will be saved. Not into a natural body, but into a spiritual body. I will go through that in a bit. Starting in verse 20 Paul starts by defining mankind by two men. He says the first man brought death and in Adam all die. This is the death that is caused by sin. The verses in 45-49 clearly shows us that Adam was the first man. No pre-Adamic race! The first is the first! It does not say the first kind of man, but the FIRST man. He became a living soul. Then Jesus is called the last Adam. Last because the Old Man was crucified with Christ. Adam is crucified, judged and condemned. The last Adam became a life giving Spirit.

Here is where we see Christ dealing with death in us by imparting life into us as Himself, the Spirit. If Christ is in you (plural), the body (singular) is dead because of sin, but the spirit is alive (life) because of righteousness. Christ was innocent therefore He was raised from the dead as proof of His being righteous and now is able to give life to anyone who comes to Him. Adam is called the first man out of the earth, earthy. The body that Paul refers to in Romans 8:10 is Adam's body. It is the body of death. Rom. 7:24. The natural body. Christ is called the second man. According to God there is only two men, Adam and Christ. In fact, the second man is heavenly, out from Heaven. The Lord from Heaven. God became a man to bring man into His body which is the church the fullness of Him who fills all in all. Eph. 1:22-23.

When God became a man and became Jesus, He became the New Israel. Matt. 2:14. As the new Israel He was replacing the seed that was natural as the spiritual seed. He was ready to fall into the ground and die. Unless He dies, He abides alone, but if He dies He will bear much fruit. The Corinthians did not see the Lord Jesus as a corporate man. That is why some in Corinth said they were of Christ. Paul said, 'is Christ divided'? They did not see the corporate Christ and that is why he spent time in Chapter 12, breaking down the concept of the body of Christ. He went so far as to say, even as the body has many members and is one, so also is Christ. The saints there were not baptizing for the dead in proxy but were baptizing Jews as a testimony of the First fruits that there would inevitably be a harvest and all Israel would be saved.

A Jew being baptized in the name of Jesus was proof that the dead are going to be raised. They were dying to the Old Covenant world and ready to walk in newness of life as a New Covenant believer. This is why Jesus said in John Chapter 12. The corn of wheat must die to bear fruit. He is that corn of wheat and Israel is His body. It is the new Israel. The nations were being called into that new body. As in Ephesians 3:1; … revealed to His holy apostles and prophets by the Spirit, that the Gentiles are fellow heirs, and belong jointly to the same body … (from The New Testament: An Expanded Translation by Kenneth S. Wuest Copyright © 1961 by Wm. B. Eerdmans Publishing Co. All rights reserved.) This new body was a spiritual body a corporate body that is glorious and incorruptible. The corporate life of the church is incorruptible. The Corinthians then asked, what kind of body do the dead come into? This takes a revelation, so Paul uses the seed analogy of a bare seed. Paul is like an instructor in college that challenges his students to think.

1 Cor. 15:36-38; … that which you sow is not given life, unless it dies: and that which you sow, you do not sow that body that will be, but bare grain, it may be of wheat, or of some other grain: but God gives it a body as it has pleased Him, and to every seed his own body. TKB. What is the bare grain in this verse? It is Israel and all in Adam die. The key is unless it dies. It is not automatic where all men are given life in Christ. Jesus said, "He who loves his life loses it, and he who hates his life in this world will keep it to life infinitely. "If anyone serves Me, he must follow Me; and where I am, there My servant will be also; if anyone serves Me, the Father will honor him. John 12:20-22. The Jew had to hate his life in his Old Covenant world because it was passing away. It wasn't automatic because he was Jewish and a son of Abraham.

There was a cost, just like there is a cost for us in every generation. The body that was is the body of Adam as Israel according to the flesh, a dead body according to the Old Covenant people and the unbeliever who was not part of the Covenant community. The body that is sown is not the body that will be. It's the natural body as the bare grain and it is the spiritual body that rises with Christ. Paul says the distinction between the earthly and the heavenly, but the heavenly is even more different. The sun and moon and stars. The stars differ in glory, and he states, and each star will differ in glory. Then he makes this remarkable statement, 'so also is the rising of the dead. I am reminded of a prophecy that was given over our Lord to Mary. So, Simeon blessed them, and said to Mary His mother, behold, this Child is destined for the fall and rising of many in Israel; and for a sign which will be contradicted; (yes, a sword will go through your own soul also) that the thoughts of many hearts may have the veil removed. Luke 2:34-35 TKB.

Only those who were willing to die for Him and believe in Him would be rising and the veil would be removed from their hearts. The others in Israel who Jesus even said, that if you were Abraham's seed, you would do the works of Abraham, it was he who believed God. They were of their father the devil and they fell in that day because of their unbelief, just like in the wilderness. I am connecting these dots showing that the dead were Israel according to the flesh. There is more evidence of this in Paul's next statement. There is a glory corporately and a glory individually. Even the word individual or individually is tied to the body of Christ in the bible. In the New American Standard Version of the bible the word individually is connected to the corporate, once in Rom. 12:5; twice in 1 Cor. 12:11, 27 and the word individual is twice in Eph. 4:16; 5:33. We don't lose our individuality, we find it expressed in the corporate aspect of Christ. Our identity is not swallowed up in sameness or uniformity but realized as a vital part of Christ with a specific function to build up the body of Christ and enrich our brothers and sisters in Christ. As we identify practically with the believers in Christ we discover who we are and enter the rising, resurrection life of Christ in our corporate identity.

He is writing about the bare seed, and he says it is sown in corruption. This verse is used in Romans 8:21, when explaining that Old Covenant Israel, the old creation was subject to slavery to corruption, but will be brought into the freedom of the glory of the children of God. Israel was the creation that was subject to futility, not of his own will, but because of Him who subjected him in hope. Paul's present time would see Israel delivered from the bondage of corruption and not only Israel, but the fullness of the nations i.e. the whole creation would be set free in Christ in Rom. 8:22. Look at the comparison of these two verses and see Paul is talking about Israel and the nations. He even goes as far as saying that the creation and whole creation groans together for this liberation.

Then Paul states that even those Jews like himself groan having the Firstfruits of the Spirit. He will go into more detail in chapters 9-11 in Romans clarifying these things. Paul says that this birthing, these labor pains would cause the redemption of our body. The plural our and the singular body. The word redemption is a buzzword for Israel, first used in Luke 1:68 about John the Immerser and God redeeming Israel. Secondly, Luke 2:38, where Anna the prophetess spoke of Christ to all of them that looked for redemption in Jerusalem.

Thirdly, Luke uses this term in Chapter 21:28 recording our Lord's words that when you see these things begin to come to pass, "look up for your redemption is drawing near". Redemption is being set free, released, and forgiven. In Eph. 4:33, Paul's says, "sealed until the day of redemption". The context in Chapter 4 is taking off the old man and putting on the new man. The Old Covenant garment vs. the New Covenant garment. Putting off Adam, Israel according to the flesh and putting on Christ, the New Israel according to the Spirit. This is the mystery that was hidden and Paul told the Corinthians that not all sleep, but all will be changed.

It is imperative at this point to consider what the change is. We commonly think this is physical change. I propose at this point a paradigm shift to what was really changing in the first century. God is not changing our bodies, but the body from a natural body to a spiritual body. The word put on, enduo in Greek, can also mean to enter in. From the cross to the Day of Judgment on Jerusalem was 40 years. This is what Paul called when referring to the children in the wilderness as a type, "tupos". Paul says Israel in the wilderness is a type of us in the 1st century. After the forty years they were to enter into the Promised Land. In the New Testament the Promised Land is not physical, but spiritual. In Heb. 11:26, the writer states that the fatherland literally is a heavenly one, not physical. Putting on or entering into it, is putting on the heavenly man or entering the heavenly land. To the Jew this was difficult to understand because he was natural and was always looking for physical blessings and external things in regard to God. Paul was revealing the invisible things as spiritual realities. The sacrifices, temple, priesthood with their priestly garments, etc. These things were in the Spirit, and they were heavenly. They were not physical or earthly. They were not physically visible and temporal, but invisible and infinite. All these things were just Christ in all His aspects and glories. We put on Christ, we offer through Him, we offer Him to God, and we are in Christ as the heavenly land. These are the spiritual realities. What was going to change in a moment in a blink of an eye? The age was going to change. The Old Covenant age was going to change when the Temple and Jerusalem was taken out of the way and destroyed. The corruptible was destroyed and the time was to put on or enter into the incorruptible.

The mortal was destroyed, and immortal was manifested and revealed. Look closely at Rom. 6:12 when it describes the mortal body. It is in the singular and members is in the plural. The members of the Old Covenant body are the dead and those who have risen with Christ by faith are those alive out from the dead. Paul says, "do not obey the desires of the Old Covenant body".

The desire to live by sight and not by faith. He says because you, [plural] are not under the Law, but under grace. Just as a side note, perhaps going back to the Old Covenant lifestyle is the sin leading to death as it says in 1 John 5:16 and the verse in Rom 6:12-14, do not let the sin reign in your [plural] mortal body [singular], to obey it in its desires; 13 neither you present your members weapons of unrighteousness to the sin, but present yourselves to God as living out from the dead, and your members weapons of righteousness to God; for sin will not reign over you, for you are not under the Law, but under grace. In Paul's, 2nd letter of Corinthians in Chapter 3:7, he compares the ministry of the Law with the New Covenant and says the former is the ministry of death and condemnation and the latter is the ministry of life and righteousness.

Seeing the distinction between the singular and plural usage of Paul's insight is wonderful as in 2 Cor. 4:10-11. The death of Jesus in the body, [singular] and the life of Jesus manifested in our [plural], body [singular]. He says death works in us, but life in you! During the forty year transition period, the death of Christ was still happening to the saints, but not in a redemptive way, but with life being manifested and showing that Jesus was alive. How did Paul come to this realization? He met Jesus on the road to Damascus and Paul said, "who are You Lord?" And the Lord said, "I am Jesus whom you are persecuting." The body of Christ was experiencing the sufferings of Christ, but they would experience the glories that would follow. They would be changed because they had not all fallen asleep, but at the last trump they would be changed and brought fully into the New Covenant Age. Another place for this distinction is in 2 Cor. 5:1.

Paul says, "if this earthly tabernacle is destroyed, we have a building of God, not made with hands, infinite in the heavens. Again, we must see these two houses or dwelling places are corporate and if they are corporate, it is not speaking about our human bodies. It is speaking about two covenant houses. Two peoples represented here. In 2 Cor. 5:2-3, for indeed in this house we groan, longing to be clothed with our dwelling from the heavens, 3 inasmuch as we, having put it on, will not be found naked. This verse: For we that are in this tabernacle do groan, being burdened: not that we want to be unclothed, but to put on so that the mortality may be consumed by life. TKB. 2 Cor. 5:4. It contains the same concepts and terms in all the places we have been in Romans, 1 Corinthians. The groaning and mortality related to the body. I hope you can connect these dots. Final thoughts on this subject are what Paul states in verse 6 in 2 Cor. 4:6-7, Therefore being courageous always, seeing that, while we are among our own people in the body, earthly house, we are away from the New Covenant people of the Lord: 7 For we walk by faith, not by sight: ... TKB.

The two bodies in 1 Cor. 15 refer to the Old Covenant body of Adam and the New Covenant body of Christ. I know this may be hard to swallow, but please consider it as a possibility. Paul brought life and immortality to light through the gospel. 2 Tim. 1:10. This is not physical immortality, but infinite life through Jesus Christ, now and perpetually. As believers we will not die, and if we die physically, we will still live. Even Job says in Chapter 14:14, "If a man dies, will he live again? All the days of my struggle I will wait until change comes. Most versions add "my" and it is not in the original. Job knew of a change in the future that would cause him to exist again. Job was gathered into the New Covenant body of Christ. The other times the word corruption is used in Peter's second epistle. 2 Pet. 1:4

is specifically addressing as a partaker or companion of the divine nature escaping from the corruption in the world because of coveting (lust or desire).

Here we see Peter's usage of corruption and the way to escape it by being a new kind, nature, a divine or spiritual nature. Not the old way of trying not to do something, but by partaking and sharing in the divine nature. Being a companion of the Divine nature. Paul said in Rom 7:7-11, what shall we say then? Is the Law sin? May it never be! On the contrary, I would not have come to know sin except through the Law; for I would not have known about coveting if the Law had not said, "YOU SHALL NOT COVET." But sin, taking opportunity through the commandment, produced in me coveting of every kind; for apart from the Law sin is dead. I was once alive apart from the Law; but when the commandment came, sin became alive and I died; and this commandment, which was to result in life, proved to result in death for me; for sin, taking an opportunity through the commandment, deceived me and through it killed me. The word Paul uses for covet is the same Greek word Peter uses in 2 Peter 1:4. In Chapter 2 of 2 Peter he uses the word for corruption 3 times. This is regarding the false teachers that were promising them freedom, yet they were in bondage to their own covetousness and adultery. Noah's world, Sodom, Lot, and Balaam are mentioned in this one chapter and refer to the Judaizers and their corrupt ways. God judged each one of these as a type of Israel according to the flesh.

Corruption Versus Incorruption

Back to 1 Corinthians in verse 43, sown in corruption and raised in incorruption. Those who repent of their corruption will be brought to life in incorruptibility. Sown in disgrace will be raised in glory. This is very similar to Romans 2:7, where Paul is showing the physical Jew vs. the spiritual Jew. So, in this Chapter 15 we see two men and two bodies. We see two experiences; one is death, and one is life. Adam who was the first to be put under the Law, 'you will not eat from the tree of knowledge of good and evil, for in the day you eat, you will in death be dying. TKB. Paul says that death spread to all men. Then out of all men God chose a man called Abraham and out of him came a nation which is Israel, the body of Adam in a covenantal sense. Even though all men are the body of Adam in a general sense, Israel was the body of Adam in a covenantal sense. God covenanted with Israel and put her under the Law, which was futility, but in hope not of its own will. God's Law made sin utterly sinful and strengthened sin in the chosen peoples' lives. This is why there is a natural body that Paul speaks of.

This is a critical point for us to understand. The word natural is not physical which in Greek would be 'phusis'. Even translators and dictionaries blur the sensitive definition of this word by referring to this word as natural. I am proposing a reconsideration of this term. It sometimes is translated nature which I think is good regarding the context. The English words "physical" and "physics" are derived from phusis. Though it does have a reference to something that is natural, i.e. nature, there is a distinct word in Greek for natural. It is the word, 'psuchikos'. This word is always translated natural in Corinthians, and it is defined and related to the soul. Psuche is soul, when Paul says the first man became a living soul, not being. This is why I am so adamant about this distinction.

Paul uses this word four times in his first letter and he says initially that the psuchikos man cannot receive the things of the Spirit of God. Then in chapter fifteen it is used 3 more times, and it is related to the type of body Adam has. This is a corporate body that is made up of two people groups as I mention above. The Covenant people in Adam who were chosen to bring the Messiah into time and all nations, and who are dead in their sins. The second man was given a body that makes the two, nations in Adam and the Old Covenant Israel in Adam, one in Himself, thus making ONE NEW MAN and that body is a spiritual body.

The word psuchikos is always in contrast to the word pneumatikos, which is our English word spiritual. This is why I started this commentary indicating the there are three types of men in this church. The fleshly man, the natural man, and the spiritual man. The cross deals with the two sub-types of men by putting them to death. Also, the cross is what produces the spiritual man. Eph 2:14-17, For He Himself is our peace, who brings about both as one and broke down the barrier of the dividing wall, by putting away in His flesh the hostility, which is "The Flesh Profits Nothing".

It is not flesh and blood that can please God. Flesh and blood may refer to Israel according to the flesh, specifying that in her current state, she cannot inherit the promises of God. Jesus said, in John 6:63; "... the flesh profits nothing". Paul agreed with Christ in Romans 9:8; ... that is, it is not the children of the flesh who are children of God, but the children of the promise are regarded as the seed. This is the purpose of the cross! It also reveals what man is according to flesh and blood. As flesh, he is sinful and as blood he is temporal. The cross deals with the matter of sin and it deals with the matter of what is temporal. This is why Christ is called the last Adam on the cross and the Second Man in resurrection. In resurrection He is not flesh and blood. He is the Son that has been begotten. Ps. 2:6- John 1:12; ... but as many as received Him, to them He gave the right to become children of God, to those who believe in His name: 13 who were born, not of blood, nor of the will of the flesh, nor of the will of man, but of God. NKJV.

Only those born of God will inherit the kingdom of God. Born of the Spirit! Born from above. Paul says, flesh and blood cannot inherit the kingdom of God. It takes a birth as a start. It's a different nature, a different essence. It is not Jewish, Chinese, or English. It is otherworldly. There has to be a death and a resurrection. Death, an exodus out of the natural and an entering into the Spiritual. Paul says this is a mystery! We will not all sleep, but we all shall be altered. In a moment, in a twinkling of an eye, at the last trump. As I mentioned above when speaking about the Feast of Trumpets. We have a connection to the last trumpet.

The Feast of Trumpets

One of the clearest depictions of the sounding of trumpets to announce the inauguration of the heavenly judgment is found in 4 Ezra, a Jewish apocryphal book written in the first century A. D. "Behold the days come and it shall be, when I am about to draw night to visit the dwellers upon the earth, and when I require from the doers of iniquity (the penalty of) their iniquity: (And when the humiliation of Sion shall be complete), and when the Age which is about to pass away shall be sealed, then (will I show these signs): the books shall be opened before the face of the firmament, and all shall see together…

And the trumpet shall sound at which all men, when they hear it, shall be struck with sudden fear" (4 Ezra 4:18-2-, 23). A similar text traditionally recited by the Jews on Rosh Hashanah is found in G. H. Box's book on 4 Ezra: "God seated on His throne to judge the world opens the Book of records; it is read, every man's signature being found therein. The great trumpet is sounded: a still small voice is heard.

The angels shudder … and say: 'This is the Day of Judgment.'" (Quote from Samuele Bacchiocchi, "God's Festivals in Scripture and History: The Fall Feasts.") The blowing of the trumpets was a wake- up call for Israel to examine themselves for judgment. Perhaps the wake up was a reference to Paul's phrase we shall not all sleep. This change that takes place is an inward change, from death (Old Covenant Age) to (New Covenant Age). The sound of the trumpet was a warning and a call to gather, to be gathered around the tabernacle, or temple. His presence! To come into the presence of God. Rev 10:7 … but in the days of the voice of the seventh angel, when he is about to sound, then the mystery of God is finished, as He preached to His servants the prophets. NASU. 15 And the seventh angel trumpeted; and there were great voices in the heavens, saying, the kingdom of this world has become of our Lord and of His Christ; and He will reign into the New Covenant Age from the Old Covenant Age. 16 So the twenty-four elders, who sat before God on their thrones, fell on their faces, and worshiped God, 17 saying, we are thanking You, O Lord God Almighty, who is, and was, and is to come; because You have taken Your great power, and have begun to reign. 18 The nations were furious; therefore, Your wrath has come, and the time of the dead that they should be judged, and that You should give rewards to Your slaves the prophets, and to the saints, and them that fear Your name, small and great; and should destroy those who corrupt the land. Rev. 11:15-18. TKB.

In this verse we see the last trump and we see the judgment, rewards, and the resurrection. The Judgment on Old Covenant Israel for destroying and corrupting the land, rewards for the prophets, saints, and all those who fear His name and the resurrection of the dead. Those who were predestined, foreknown, of the elect were the dead. They are now called upon to put on the incorruptible, immortality. The New Covenant reality, not the temporal, earthly, corruptible. Then Paul further states that when Israel in resurrection puts on this New Covenant reality, then the saying that death is swallowed up in victory. Death being swallowed up in victory is a quote from Isa. 25:8. Reading Isa. 25 opens up this part of the Scripture like no other part. God destroys the city and makes it a heap of ruins, literally in Hebrew "Ai". There is a whole lot I could share about that through the Scriptures. Hidden in this chapter is the Day of Atonement and the Feast of Tabernacles. After the Trumpets and their call to gather and warning of the Day of Judgment, ten days later, the time of testing, the Day of Atonement happens. Rabbinic teaching calls this Day, Face to Face because the High Priest is face to face with God in the Holy of Holies. These last Fall Feasts are the conclusion of Christ's redemptive ministry to Israel in fulfilling Daniel's Seventy Sevens.

Not the termination of His ministry universally, but with Israel according to the Old Covenant. This is the conclusion of judgment, a holocaust. In our dictionary, the definition of holocaust is a great or complete devastation or destruction, especially by fire. A sacrifice completely consumed by fire; burnt offering. During this feast on Yom Kippur, the high priest again was involved, but an abundant of animals (a bull, a ram, a he-goat, and seven lambs) were sacrificed (Numbers 29:7-11). The people themselves were not engaged in any of the presenting of the sacrifices, and none of the animals sacrificed by the high priest were eaten by the people. The Day of Atonement was a solemn day of fasting and denying yourself, rather than of joyous feasting and festivity. This is why the final week of Daniel's sevens is referred to here.

The destruction of the sanctuary and the city, the final holocaust of Old Covenant Israel. Dan. 9:26. There is also the two goats that are chosen by lots. One goat is for the Lord, and one is cast out. Some have confused this issue that the one cast out is Satan, and the chosen one is Christ. The one cast out is called, 'Azazel'. This is commonly called the scapegoat in church history. J.B. Jackson in his Dictionary of Scripture Proper Names defines this name as, "goat of departure". Let's examine this a little closer. Some compare these two goats to two aspects of Christ. I want us to look at this in regard to two peoples. One goat represents the elect of Israel that are for the Lord. The other goat is cast out and the sins of Israel on put on it. Jesus gave an example of the scapegoat in Matt 8:10-12 "Truly I say to you, I have not found such great faith with anyone in Israel.11 "I say to you that many will come from east and west, and recline at the table with Abraham, Isaac and Jacob in the kingdom of heaven;12 but the sons of the kingdom will be cast out into the outer darkness; in that place there will be weeping and gnashing of teeth." NASU. All that the Father gives me will come to me, and whoever comes to me I will never cast out. John 6:37-38 ESV.

Other verses show the elect being given to the Lord and others are cast out of covenant relationship with Him. "Then He will also say to those on His left, 'Depart from Me, accursed ones, into the perpetual fire which has been prepared for the devil and his messengers; Matt 25:41. These ones that held on to the perverted form of Judaism were Satan's messengers. No wonder, for even Satan disguises himself as an angel of light. 15 Therefore it is not surprising if his servants also disguise themselves as servants of righteousness, whose end will be according to their deeds. 2 Cor. 11:14-15 NASU. There are other examples of old covenant Israel according to the flesh being the 'scapegoat or Azazel'. The chosen goat is sacrificed physically and his life ascends into the holy of holies typified by the bringing of his blood into the temple and brought into the presence of God as forgiven and accepted.

The Feast of Tabernacles

The feast of tabernacles is about restoration, restitution, and all Israel being delivered into the enjoyment of God's promises and presence. For seven days Israel remembers the forty years in the wilderness when they dwelt in temporary dwellings waiting for that permanent dwelling where the Tabernacle of God is among them. In AD 30 the reality of what Israel was rehearsing was fulfilled in the crucifixion of Christ as the Lamb, the Passover Lamb. It is now almost 40 years and Paul is speaking about the Trumpet, the last Trumpet and the time of rejoicing that is coming when death is swallowed up and victory is on the horizon. It was imminent to the Corinthian believers. Paul was describing Israel's deliverance about to come. He says, "Thanks be to God who gives us the victory through our Lord Jesus Christ"!

The Feast of Tabernacles is the Feast of Ingathering or Harvest

We recognize that the harvest in the New Testament is the end of the Age. It is not the end of time or the end of New Testament Age. It is the end of the Old Covenant Age and the bringing in of the New Covenant Age. It is moving from the wilderness to the Promised Land. The forty years have ended. Jerusalem is destroyed and the Old Covenant is fulfilled in Christ. This feast is a reminder for the people of Israel of God's love. Love is expressed in two very distinct ways. One is providing and the other is protection. God provided for Israel through the wilderness by supplying all her needs, food, water, and their clothing and shoes did not wear out. He also protected them from their enemies within and without and brought them safely to the Promised Land.

He then calls for a feast and a banquet and takes the veil off their faces and swallows up death. Paul says, O Death where is your victory? He then goes on to say that the sting of death is sin, and the strength of sin is the Law. The Gentiles or nations were not under the Law. Only Israel was under the Law. The Law kept Israel as a prisoner to death. This is what gave sin its strength. The gospel revealed a righteousness apart from the Law. The gospel brought news of God justifying the ungodly and making righteous those who put their faith in Christ as the sacrifices, (plural) for our sins. Victory over sin and death is a gift from God through our Lord Jesus Christ. Paul rejoices by saying, "thanks be to God who gives us the victory"! We are now in His presence and our labor is not in vain. We are exhorted to abound in the work of the Lord. Wow! There is so much more to share in Isa. 25 and 26, but for another time.

Paul's Concluding Thoughts

Paul closes this letter in Chapter 16 with something that is quite revealing. He is speaking about the money he is about to collect for the saints. He prepared them for this coming as he did the Galatia churches. Interestingly, he says on the first day of the week. In Old Covenant practice it was the seventh day, which is Saturday. The first day is Sunday. The first day is the eighth day. Paul just finished explaining the resurrection. The first day is the eighth day which is symbolic for resurrection and a new beginning. Christ rose on the eighth day, the first day after His passion week. In the feast of Tabernacles which lasted seven days and at the end of the feast there was an eighth day. A new beginning that starts with REST.

This may be a reference to giving in resurrection not in a legal sense. Our work must be done in grace not by Law. This giving is by grace in resurrection. Not according to the Old Covenant nor in an Aaronic sense. This is like Abraham who gave in resurrection to Melchizedek when he gave the bread and the wine. New Covenant giving or tithing is giving to the priesthood according to Melchizedek. This is a thought that needs more development in the future. Paul then goes on to write that he doesn't want to just come and go, but to spend some time with the saints. He also encourages them to take care of Timothy so that when he comes they are to be clear that he is working for the Lord. He mentions Apollos in a sweet way by calling him, 'our brother'. This shows his love for Apollos and connects his love with the love of the Corinthian's. Paul tells the Corinthians to be alert and be mature and do everything in love.

-Terry Kashian

1 Corinthians

Chapter 1

1. Paul called to be an apostle of Jesus Christ through the will of God, and Sosthenes our brother,

2. To the Assembly of God which is at Corinth, to them that are sanctified in the Christ, Jesus, called to be saints, with all those in every place call on the name of Jesus the Christ our Lord, both theirs and ours:

3. Grace to you, and peace, from God our Father, and the Lord Jesus, the Christ.

4. I thank my God always on your behalf, for the grace of God which is given to you in Jesus the Christ;

5. That in everything you are enriched in Him, in all speech, and in all knowledge;

6. Just as the testimony of the Christ was confirmed in you:

7. So that you come behind in no gift; waiting for the unveiling of our Lord Jesus, the Christ:

8. Who will also confirm you to the end, that you may be blameless in the day of our Lord Jesus, the Christ.

9. God is faithful, through whom you were called into the fellowship of His Son, Jesus Christ our Lord.

10. Now I implore you, brothers, by the name of our Lord Jesus, the Christ, that you all speak the same thing, and that there be no divisions among you; but that you be maturely joined together in the same mind and in the same judgment.

11. For it has been declared to me of you, my brothers, by them which are of the house of Chloe, that there are contentions among you.

12. Now this I say that each of you says, I am of Paul; and I am of Apollos, and I am of Cephas, and I am of Christ.

13. Is the Christ divided? Was Paul crucified for you? Or were you immersed in the name of Paul?

14. I thank God that I immersed none of you, but Crispus and Gaius;

15. Unless any should say that I had immersed in my own name.

16. And I also immersed the household of Stephanas: besides, I know not whether I immersed any other.

17. For Christ did not send me to immerse, but to preach the gospel: not with wisdom of words, unless the cross of the Christ should be made of no effect.

18. For the preaching of the cross is foolishness to them that perish; but to us which are being saved it is the power of God.

19. For it is written, I will destroy the wisdom of the wise and will bring to nothing the understanding of the prudent.

20. Where is the wise? Where is the scribe? Where is the disputer of this age? Has not God made foolish the wisdom of this world?

21. For after in the wisdom of God the world by wisdom did not know God, it pleased God by the foolishness of preaching to save them that believe.

22. For the Jews require a sign, and the Greeks seek after wisdom:

23. But we preach Christ crucified, to the Jews a stumbling block, and to the Greeks foolishness;
24. But to those who are called, both Jews and Greeks, Christ the power of God, and the wisdom of God.
25. Because the foolishness of God is wiser than men; and the weakness of God is stronger than men.
26. For you see your calling, brothers, that not many wise men after the flesh, not many mighty, not many noble, are called:
27. But God has chosen the foolish things of the world to confound the wise, and God has chosen the weak things of the world to confound the mighty things;
28. And base things of the world, and things. Which are despised, has God chosen, yes, and things which are not, to bring to nothing things that are:
29. That no flesh should boast in His presence.
30. But out of His doing you are in the Christ, Jesus who became wisdom to us from God and righteousness, and sanctification, and redemption:
31. That, according as it is written, he that is boasting, let him be boasting in the Lord.

Chapter 2

1. And I, brothers, when I came to you, did not come with superiority of speech or wisdom, declaring to you the testimony of God.
2. For I determined not to know anything among you, other than Jesus Christ, and Him crucified.
3. I was with you in weakness, and in fear, and much trembling.
4. And my speech and my preaching were not with enticing words of man's wisdom, but in demonstration of the Spirit and of power:
5. That your faith should not stand in the wisdom of men, but in the power of God.
6. However, we speak wisdom among them that are mature: yet not the wisdom of this age, nor the rulers of this age, they are coming to nothing:
7. But we speak the wisdom of God in a mystery, even the hidden wisdom, which God predetermined before this age to our glory:
8. Which none of the rulers of this age knew: for had they known it, they would not have crucified the Lord of glory.
9. But as it is written, the eye has not seen, nor ear heard, neither have entered into the heart of man, the things which God has prepared for them that love Him.
10. But God has revealed them to us by His Spirit: for the Spirit searches all things, yes, even the deep things of God.
11. For what man knows the things of a man, save the spirit of man which is in him? Even so the things of God no man knows, but the Spirit of God.
12. Now we have received, not the spirit of the world, but the spirit which is of God; that we might know the things that are freely given to us of God.
13. Which things also we speak, not in the words which man's wisdom teaches, but which the Holy Spirit teaches: comparing spiritual things with spiritual.

14. But the natural man receives not the things of the Spirit of God: for they are foolishness to him: neither can he know them, because they are spiritually examined.
15. But he that is spiritual examines all things, yet he is examined by no man.
16. For who has known the mind of the Lord, that he may instruct Him? But we have the mind of Christ.

Chapter 3

1. And I, brothers, could not speak to you as to spiritual, but as to fleshly, just as to babes in Christ.
2. I have fed you with milk, and not with solid food: for until now you were not able to handle it, neither yet now are you able.
3. For you are yet fleshly: for where there is among you envying, and strife, and divisions, are you not fleshly, and walk as men?
4. For while one says, I am of Paul; and another, I am of Apollos; are you not fleshly?
5. Who then is Paul, and who is Apollos, but ministers by who you believed, just as the Lord gave to every man?
6. I have planted, Apollos watered; but God gave the increase.
7. So, then neither is he that plants anything, neither he that waters; but God that gives the increase.
8. Now he that plants and he that waters are one: and every man will receive his own reward according to his own labor.
9. For we are laborers together with God: you are God's fellow workers; you are cultivated land, you are God's building.
10. According to the grace of God, which is given to me, as a wise master builder, I have laid the foundation, and another builds on it. But let every man carefully consider how he builds on it.
11. For other foundation can no man lay than that is laid, which is Jesus the Christ.
12. Now if any man builds on this foundation gold, silver, precious stones, wood, hay, stubble;
13. Every man's work will be made manifest: for the day will declare it, because it will be revealed by fire; and the fire will try every man's work of what sort it is.
14. If any man's work endures which he has built, he will receive a reward.
15. If any man's work will be burned, he will suffer loss: but he himself will be saved; yet so as by fire.
16. Do you not know that you are the temple of God and that the Spirit of God dwells in you?
17. If any man defiles the temple of God, him will God destroy; for the temple of God is holy, which temple you are.
18. Let no man deceive himself. If any man among you seems to be wise in this age, let him become a fool, that he may be wise.
19. For the wisdom of this world is foolishness with God. For it is written, He takes the wise in their own craftiness.
20. And again, The Lord knows the thoughts of the wise, that they are vain.
21. Therefore, let no man be boasting in men. For all things are yours;

22. Whether Paul, Apollos, Cephas, the world, or life, or death, or things present, or things about to come; all are yours;

23. And you are Christ's, and Christ is God's.

Chapter 4

1. Let a man so account of us, as of the ministers of Christ, and stewards of the mysteries of God.

2. Moreover, it is required in stewards that a man be found faithful.

3. But with me it is a very small thing that I should be judged by you or the day of man: yes, I do not examine myself.

4. For I am conscious of nothing against myself; yet am I not justified by this: but He that judges me is the Lord.

5. Therefore, judge nothing before the time, until the Lord comes, who both will bring to light the hidden things of darkness and will make manifest the counsels of the hearts: and then will every man have praise from God.

6. And these things, brothers, I have applied this to myself and Apollos because of you; that you might learn in us not to be of opinions beyond that which is written, that not one of you be prideful over one against another.

7. For who makes you differ from another? What have you that you did not receive? Now if you did receive it, why do you brag, as if you had not received it?

8. Now you are full, now you are rich, you have reigned as kings without us: and I would to God you did reign, that we also might reign with you.

9. For I think that God has set forth us the apostles last, as it were appointed to death: for we are made a spectacle to the world, and angels, and to men.

10. We are fools for Christ's sake, but you are wise in Christ; we are weak, but you are strong; you are honorable, but we are despised.

11. Even to this present hour we both hunger, and thirst, and are poorly clothed, and are beaten, and are homeless;

12. And labor, working with our own hands: being reviled, we bless; being persecuted, we endure it:

13. Being defamed, we are imploring: we are made as the filth of the world, and are the scum of all things, even now.

14. I write these things not to turn upon you, but as my beloved children, I caution you.

15. For though you have ten thousand instructors in Christ, yet you do not have many fathers: for in Christ Jesus, I have begotten you through the gospel.

16. Therefore, I implore you, to become emulators of me.

17. For this reason, have I sent to you Timothy, who is my beloved son, and faithful in the Lord, who will bring you into remembrance of my ways which be in Christ, as I teach everywhere in every Assembly.

18. Now some are puffed up, as though I would not come to you.

19. But I will come to you shortly, if the Lord wills, and will know, not the speech of those who are puffed up, but the power.

20. For the kingdom of God is not in word but in power.
21. Which do you desire? Will I come to you with a rod, or in love, and in the spirit of meekness?

Chapter 5

1. It is reported commonly that there is sexual immorality among you, and such sexual immorality as is not so much as named among the nations, that one should have his father's wife.
2. And you are puffed up and have not rather mourned, that he that has done this deed might be taken away from among you.
3. For I truthfully, as absent in body, but present in spirit, have judged already, as though I were present, concerning him that has so done this deed,
4. In the name of our Lord Jesus Christ, when you are gathered together, and with my spirit, with the power of our Lord Jesus Christ,
5. To deliver such a one to Satan for the destruction of the flesh, that the spirit may be saved in the day of the Lord Jesus.
6. Your boasting is not good. Do you not know that a little leaven leavens the whole lump?
7. Purge out therefore the old leaven that you may be a new lump, as you are unleavened. For even Christ, our Passover is sacrificed for us:
8. Therefore, let us celebrate the feast, not with old leaven, neither with the leaven of malice and wickedness; but with the unleavened bread of sincerity and reality.
9. I wrote to you in a letter not to keep company with sexually immoral people.
10. Yet not altogether with the sexually immoral of this world, or with the covetous, or extortionists, or with idolaters; for then you would be required to go out of the world.
11. But now I have written to you not to keep company, if anyone that is called in the brotherhood is sexually immoral, or covetous, or an idolater, or a reviler, or a drunkard, or an extortioner; with such a one do not eat.
12. For what is it to me to be judging them that are also outside? Are you not judging them that are within?
13. Now that they are outside, God is judging. Therefore, remove from among yourselves that malignant person.

Chapter 6

1. Dare any of you, having a matter against another, go to law before the unjust, and not before the saints?
2. Do you not know that the saints will judge the world? If the world will be judged by you, are you unworthy to judge the smallest matters?
3. Do you not know that we will judge angels? How many more things that pertain to this life?
4. If then you have judgments of things about this life, you set the contemptible to judge in the Assembly?

5. I speak to your shame. Is it so, that there is not a wise man among you? No, not one who will be able to judge between his brothers.
6. But brother goes to law with brother, and that before the unbelievers.
7. Now, therefore, there is utterly a fault among you, because you go to law one with another. Why do you not rather take the wrong? Why do you not rather permit yourselves to be defrauded?
8. No, you do wrong, and defraud, and they are your brothers.
9. Do you not know that the unrighteous will not inherit the kingdom of God? Be not deceived: neither sexually immoral, nor idolaters, nor adulterers, nor homosexuals, nor sodomites,
10. Nor thieves, nor covetous, nor drunkards, nor revilers, nor extortionists, will inherit the kingdom of God.
11. Such were some of you: but you are washed, but you are sanctified, but you are justified in the name of the Lord Jesus, and by the Spirit of our God.
12. All things are lawful to me, but all things are not helpful: all things are lawful for me, but I will not be brought under the power of any.
13. Foods for the stomach, and the stomach for foods: but God will destroy both it and them. Now the body is not for sexual immorality but for the Lord, and the Lord is for the body.
14. And God has both raised up the Lord and will also raise up us by His own power.
15. Do you not know that your bodies are the members of Christ? Will I then take the members of the Christ, and make them the members of a harlot? God forbids!
16. What? Do you not know that he which is joined to a harlot is one body? For two, says He, will be one flesh.
17. But he that is joined to the Lord is one spirit.
18. Flee sexual immorality. Every sin that a man does is outside the body, but he that commits sexual immorality sins against his own body.
19. What? Do you not know that your body is the temple of the Holy Spirit which is in you, which you have of God, and you are not your own?
20. For you have been bought with a price: therefore, glorify God in your body and in your spirit, which is God's.

Chapter 7

1. Now concerning the things which you wrote to me: It is good for a man not to touch a woman.
2. Nevertheless, to avoid sexual immorality, let every man have his own wife, and let each one have her own husband.
3. Let the husband render to the wife the debt of affection: and likewise, also the wife to the husband.
4. The wife does not have a right over her own body, but the husband: and likewise, also the husband does not have the right over his own body, but the wife.

5. Do not deprive one another, unless it be out of agreement for a season that you may give yourselves to fasting and prayer. Then come together again, so that Satan does not tempt you because of your lack of self-control.

6. But I speak this by permission, and not of commandment.

7. For I would that all men were just like me. But every man has his proper gift of God, one after this manner, and another after that.

8. I say therefore to the unmarried and widows, it is good for them if they stay just as I.

9. But if they cannot exercise self-control, let them marry: for it is better to marry than to burn.

10. To the married I command, yet not I, but the Lord, let not the wife depart from her husband:

11. But and if she departs, let her remain unmarried or be reconciled to her husband: and let not the husband divorce his wife.

12. But to the rest I speak, not the Lord: if any brother has a wife that does not believe, and she is pleased to live with him, let him not leave her

13. And the woman who has a husband who does not believe, and if he is pleased to live with her, let her not leave him.

14. For the unbelieving husband is sanctified by the wife, and the unbelieving wife is sanctified by the husband: otherwise, your children are unclean; but now they are sanctified.

15. But if the unbelieving departs, let him depart. A brother or a sister is not under bondage in such cases: but God has called us to peace.

16. How do you know, oh wife, whether you will save your husband? Or how do you know, O man, whether you will save your wife?

17. But as God has distributed to every man, as the Lord has called each one, so let him walk. So, I charge all the Assemblies.

18. Is any man called being circumcised? Let him not become uncircumcised. Is any called in uncircumcision? Let him not be circumcised.

19. Circumcision is nothing, and uncircumcision is nothing, but the keeping of the principles of God.

20. Let every man stay in the same calling in which he was called.

21. Are you called being a slave? Be not anxious about it: but if you may be made free, use it rather.

22. For he that is called in the Lord, being a slave, is the Lord's freeman: likewise, also he that is called, being free, is Christ's slave.

23. You are bought with a price; do not be the slaves of men.

24. Brethren, let every man, in which he is called, in this remain with God.

25. Now concerning virgins, I have no commandment of the Lord: yet I give my judgment, as one that has obtained mercy of the Lord to be faithful.

26. I suppose therefore that this is good for the present distress, I say, that it is good for a man so to be.

27. Are you bound to a wife? Seek not to be loosed. Are you free from a wife? Seek not a wife.
28. But and if you marry, you have not sinned; and if a virgin marries, she has not sinned. Nevertheless, such will have trouble in the flesh: but I spare you.
29. But this I say, brothers, the time is short: it remains, that both they that have wives be as though they had none;
30. They that weep, as though they wept not; and they that rejoice, as though they rejoiced not; and they that buy, as though they possessed not;
31. And they that use this world, as not misusing it: for the outward form of this world order is passing away.
32. But I would have you without carefulness. He that is unmarried cares for the things that belong to the Lord, how he may please the Lord:
33. But he that is married cares for the things that are of the world, how he may please his wife.
34. There is a difference also between a wife and a virgin. The unmarried woman cares for the things of the Lord, that she may be holy both in body and in spirit: but she that is married cares for the things of the world, how she may please her husband.
35. And this I speak for your own profit; not that I may cast a snare on you, but for that which is proper, and that you may serve the Lord without distraction.
36. But if any man thinks that he behaves himself improperly toward his virgin, if she passes the flower of her age, and need so require, let him do what he will, he sins not: let them marry.
37. Nevertheless, he that stands steadfast in his heart, having no necessity, but has power over his own will, and has so decreed in his heart that he will keep his virgin, does well.
38. So, then he that gives her in marriage does well, but he that gives her not in marriage does better.
39. The wife is bound by the Law as long as her husband lives; but if her husband is dead, she is free to be married to who she wants; only in the Lord.
40. But she is happier if she remains single, according to my view: and I think that I also have the Spirit of God.

Chapter 8

1. Now as concerning things offered to idols, we know that we all have knowledge. Knowledge puffs up, but love builds up.
2. And if any man think that he knows anything, he knows nothing yet as he ought to know.
3. But if any man loves God, the same is known of Him.
4. As concerning, therefore, the eating of those things that are offered in sacrifice to idols, we know that an idol is nothing in the world and that there is no other God but one.
5. For though there be that are called gods, whether in heaven or earth, (as there are many gods, and many lords)

6. But to us there is but one God, the Father, of whom are all things, and we in Him; and one Lord Jesus Christ, by whom are all things, and we through Him.
7. However, there is not in every man that knowledge: for some with conscience of the idol to this hour eat it as a thing offered to an idol; and their conscience being weak is defiled.
8. But food commends us not to God: for neither if we eat, are we the better; neither, if we eat not, are we the worse.
9. But take heed unless by any means this freedom of yours become a stumbling block to them that are weak.
10. For if any man see you who has knowledge sit and eat in the idol's temple, will not the conscience of him which is weak be emboldened to eat those things which are offered to idols;
11. And through your knowledge will the weak brother perish, for whom Christ died?
12. But when you sin so against the brothers and wound their weak conscience, you sin against Christ.
13. Therefore, if food makes my brother stumble, I will eat no meat while this age stands, so that I do not make my brother stumble.

Chapter 9

1. Am I not an apostle? Am I not free? Have I not seen Jesus Christ our Lord? Are you not my work in the Lord?
2. If I am not an apostle to others, yet doubtless I am to you: for the seal of mine apostleship are you in the Lord.
3. My answer to them that do examine me is this,
4. Do we not have the power to eat and drink?
5. Have we not power to lead about a sister, a wife, as well as other apostles, and as the brothers of the Lord, and Cephas?
6. Or I only and Barnabas, have not we power to stop working?
7. Who goes to warfare anytime at his own expense? Who plants a vineyard, and eats no fruit from it? Or who feeds a flock, and drinks not of the milk from it?
8. I say these things as a man? Or does not the Law say the same also?
9. For it is written in the Law of Moses, you will not muzzle the mouth of the ox that treads out the corn. Does God care only for oxen?
10. Or does He speak it entirely for our sakes? For our sakes, no doubt, this is written: that he that plows should plow in hope; and he that threshes in hope should be partaker of his hope.
11. If we have sown in you spiritual things, is it too much if we will reap your material things?
12. If others are sharing in the rights over you, are we not all the more? Nevertheless, we have not used this right; but endure all things, unless we should hinder the gospel of Christ.
13. Do you not know that they which minister about holy things live of the things of the temple? They who wait at the altar are sharers with the altar?

14. Even so has the Lord ordered that they who preach the gospel should get their living from the gospel

15. But I have used none of these things: neither have I written these things, that it should be so done to me: for it would be better for me to die, than that any man should make my boasting empty.

16. For though I preach the gospel, I have nothing to boast of: for obligation is laid upon me; yes, woe is me, if I do not preach the gospel!

17. For if I do this willingly, I have a reward: but if against my will, the stewardship of the gospel is committed to me.

18. What is my reward then? Truthfully, when I preach the gospel, I may present the gospel of the Christ without charge, that I do not misuse my right in the gospel.

19. For though I am free from all men, yet I have made myself the slave to all, that I might gain the more.

20. To the Jews I became as a Jew, that I might gain the Jews; to them that are under the Law, as under the Law, that I might gain them that are under the Law;

21. To them that are without Law, as without Law, (being not without Law to God, but in the Law of Christ) that I might gain them that are without Law.

22. To the weak I became weak, that I might gain the weak: I am made all things to all men that I might, by all means, save some.

23. This I do for the gospel's sake, that I might be partaker of it with you.

24. Do you not know that they who run in a race all run, but one receives the prize? So run, that you may obtain it.

25. And every man that competes for the prize is temperate in all things. Now they do it to obtain a corruptible crown, but we an incorruptible one.

26. Therefore I so run, not uncertainly; so I fight, not as one that punches the air:

27. But I chastise my body, and bring it into service: unless that by any means, when I have preached to others, I should be disqualified.

Chapter 10

1. Moreover, brothers, I would not that you should be ignorant, how that all our fathers were under the cloud, and all passed through the sea;

2. And were all immersed into Moses in the cloud and in the sea;

3. And did all eat the same spiritual food;

4. And did all drink the same spiritual drink: for they drank of that spiritual Rock that followed them: and that Rock was Christ.

5. But with many of them God was not well pleased: for they were thrown down in the wilderness.

6. Now these were types of us, to the intent we should not lust after evil, as they also lusted.

7. Neither be idolaters, as were some of them; as it is written, the people sat down to eat and drink, and rose up to play.

8. Neither let us commit sexual immorality, as some of them committed and fell in one day twenty-three thousand.

9. Neither let us tempt the Christ, as some of them also tempted and were destroyed by serpents.

10. Do not be murmuring, as some of them also murmured, and were destroyed by the destroyer.

11. Now all these things happened to them as types of us: and they are written for our admonition, upon whom the goal of the ages has come.

12. Therefore, let him that thinks he stands take heed lest he be falling.

13. There has no temptation taken you but such as is common to man: but God is faithful, who will not permit you to be tempted above what you are able; but will with the temptation also make a way to escape, that you may be able to endure it.

14. Therefore, my dearly beloved, flee from idolatry.

15. I speak as to wise men; judge you what I say.

16. The cup of blessing which we bless, is it not the communion of the blood of Christ? The bread which we break, is it not the communion of the body of Christ?

17. For we being many are one bread, and one body: for we are all sharing of that one bread.

18. Behold Israel after the flesh: are not they which eat of the sacrifices, companions of the altar?

19. What do I say then? That the idol is anything, or that which is offered in sacrifice to idols is anything?

20. But I say that the things which the pagans sacrifice, they sacrifice to demons, and not to God: and I do not want you to have companionship with demons.

21. You cannot drink the cup of the Lord, and the cup of demons: you cannot be partakers of the Lord's Table and of the table of demons.

22. Do we provoke the Lord to jealousy? Are we stronger than He?

23. All things are lawful for me, but not all things bring cohesiveness: all things are lawful for me, but all things do not build the house.

24. Let no man seek his own, but every man another's well-being.

25. Whatever is sold in the meat market, eat it, asking no question for conscience's sake:

26. For the earth is the Lord's, and the fullness of it.

27. If any of them that believe not invite you to a feast, and you be disposed to go; whatever is set before you, eat, asking no question for conscience's sake.

28. But if any man says to you, this is offered in sacrifice to idols, eat not for his sake that showed it, and for conscience's sake: for the earth is the Lord's, and the fullness of it:

29. Conscience, I say, not your own, but of the other: for why is my freedom judged of another man's conscience?

30. For if I by grace be a partaker, why am I evil spoken of for that for which I give thanks?

31. Whether therefore you eat, or drink, or whatever you do, do all to the glory of God.

32. Give no offense, neither to the Jews, nor to the Greeks, nor the Assembly of God:
33. Just as I please all men in all things, not seeking my own profit, but the profit of many, that they may be saved.

Chapter 11

1. Be followers of me, just as I also am of Christ.
2. Now I praise you, brothers, that you remember me in all things, and keep the ordinances, as I delivered them to you.
3. But I would have you know that the head of every man is Christ, and the head of the woman is the man, and the head of Christ is God.
4. Every man praying or prophesying, having his head covered, dishonors his head?
5. But every woman that prays or prophesies with her head uncovered dishonors her head: for that is even like one if she was shaven?
6. For if the woman be not covered, let her also be shorn: but if it be a shame for a woman to be shorn or shaven, let her be covered?
7. For a man indeed ought not to cover his head, since he is the image and glory of God: but the woman is the glory of the man?
8. For the man is not of the woman: but the woman of the man.
9. Neither was the man created for the woman, but the woman for the man?
10. For this reason, should the woman have a symbol of authority on her head because of the angels?
11. Nevertheless, neither is the man without the woman, neither the woman without the man, in the Lord.
12. For as the woman is out of the man, even so is the man through the woman; but all things are out of God.
13. Judge in yourselves: is it proper that a woman pray to God uncovered?
14. Does not even nature itself teach you, that, if a man has long hair, it is a shame to him?
15. But if a woman wears her hair long, it is a glory to her: because her long hair instead of a veil has been given to her.
16. But if any man seems to be fond of disputes, we have no such custom, neither the Assemblies of God.
17. Now in this that I declare to you I praise you not, that you come together not for the better, but for the worse.
18. For first of all, when you come together in the Assembly, I hear that there be divisions among you; and I partly believe it.
19. For there also must be heresies among you that they which are tested by fire and proved genuine may begin to shine in you.
20. When you come together therefore into one place, this is not to eat the Lord's Supper.
21. For in eating everyone takes before the other his own supper: and one is hungry, and another is drunken.
22. What? Have you not had houses to eat and to drink in ? Or do you despise the Assembly of God, and shame them that have not? What should I say to you? Should I praise you for this? I praise you not.

23. For I have received of the Lord that which also I delivered to you, that the Lord Jesus the same night in which He was betrayed took bread:

24. And when He had given thanks, He broke it, and said, take, eat: this is My body, which is broken for you: this do in remembrance of Me.

25. After the same manner also He took the cup when He had supped, saying, this cup is the new covenant in My blood: this you do, as often as you drink it, in remembrance of Me.

26. For as often as you eat this bread, and drink this cup, you do show the Lord's death until He comes.

27. Therefore, whoever will eat this bread, and drink this cup of the Lord, in an unworthy manner, will be guilty of the body and blood of the Lord.

28. But let a man examine himself, and so let him eat of that bread, and drink of that cup.

29. For eating and drinking in an unworthy manner, eats and drinks judgment on themselves, not discerning the Lord's body.

30. For this reason, many are weak and sickly among you, and many sleep.

31. For if we would judge ourselves, we should not be judged.

32. But when we are judged, we are chastened by the Lord, that we should not be condemned with the world.

33. Therefore, my brothers, when you come together to eat, wait one for another.

34. And if any man hunger, let him eat at home; that you come not together for judgment. And the rest I will set in order when I come.

Chapter 12

1. Now concerning spirituality, brothers, I would not have you ignorant.

2. You know that when you were of the nations, carried away to these dumb idols, just as you were led.

3. Therefore, I make known to you, that no man speaking by the Spirit of God calls Jesus accursed: and that no man can say that Jesus is Lord, but by the Holy Spirit.

4. Now there are diversities of gifts, but the same Spirit.

5. And there are diversities of ministry, but the same Lord.

6. And there are diversities of operations, but it is the same God which works all things in all.

7. But the manifestation of the Spirit is given to each one for the urgent situation.

8. For to one is given by the Spirit a word of wisdom; to another a word of knowledge by the same Spirit;

9. To another faith by the same Spirit; to another the gifts of healings by the same Spirit;

10. To another the operations of powers; to another prophecy; to another discerning of spirits; to others varieties of tongues; to another the interpretation of tongues:

11. But that one and the very same Spirit operates all these things, distributing to each one individually as He intends.

12. For as the body is one, and has many members, and all the members of that one body, being many, are one body: so also is the Christ.

13. For by one Spirit, we are all immersed into one body, whether we are Jews or Greeks, whether we are slaves or free; and all are drinking into one Spirit.
14. For the body is not one member, but many.
15. If the foot will say, because I am not the hand, I am not of the body; is it therefore not of the body?
16. And if the ear will say, because I am not the eye, I am not of the body; is it therefore not of the body?
17. If the whole body were an eye, where is the hearing? If the whole is hearing, where is the sniffing?
18. But presently God has set the members each one of them in the body, as it has pleased Him.
19. If they were all one member, where is the body?
20. But presently there are many members, yet one body.
21. The eye cannot say to the hand, I have no need of you: nor again the head to the feet, I do not need you.
22. No, much more those members of the body, which we think to be weaker, are necessary:
23. And those members of the body, which we think to be without honor, on these we assign more abundant honor; and our unpresentable parts have greater appropriateness.
24. For our appropriate parts have no need: but God has blended together the body, having given more abundant value to that part which has come short.
25. That there should be no division in the body; but that the members should have the same care for one another.
26. And when one member suffers, all the members suffer together, or one member be glorified, all the members rejoice together.
27. Now you are Christ's body and members individually.
28. And God has set some in the Assembly, first apostles, second prophets, thirdly teachers, after that miracles, then gifts of healings, helps, governments, and diversities of tongues.
29. Are all apostles? Are all prophets? Are all teachers? Are all workers of miracles?
30. Do all have the gifts of healings? Do all speak with tongues? Do all interpret?
31. But eagerly desire the greater gifts: and yet I point you to a more transcendent way.

Chapter 13

1. Though I speak with the tongues of men and angels, and have not love, I have become sounding brass or a clanging cymbal.
2. And though I possess prophecy, and understand all secrets, and all knowledge; and though I have all the faith, so that I could remove the mountain, and do not have love, I am a nothing.
3. And though I bestow all my goods to feed the poor, and though I give my body to be burned, and have not love, it profits no one.
4. Love is patient and is kind; love is not jealous; love is not boastful, is not full of self-importance,

5. Does not behave inappropriately, is not self-seeking, is not exasperated, thinks no evil;
6. Does not rejoice in evil things, but rejoices in reality;
7. Bears all things, believes all things, hopes all things, and endures all things.
8. Love never falls away: but whether prophecies, they are put away; whether there be tongues, they will pause; whether there is knowledge, it will be put away.
9. Out of the part we are knowing, and out of the part we are prophesying.
10. And while maturity is coming, then that which is out of the part will be put away.
11. When I was a child, I spoke randomly, I had the mindset of a child, so I put things together as a child: but when I had become a man, I put away the immaturity.
12. For the present we are seeing through a mirror, in a riddle; but at that time face to face: presently I am beginning to know out of the part; but at that time, I will fully know just as I also am fully known.
13. And now abide faith, hope, love, these three; but the greatest of these is love.

Chapter 14

1. Strive to gain love, and be zealous for spirituality, and more that you may be prophesying.
2. For he that speaks in a tongue speaks not to people, but to God: for no one understands him; however, in the spirit, he speaks mysteries.
3. But he that prophesies speaks to people for building up, and exhortation, and comfort.
4. He that speaks in a tongue builds up himself, but he that prophesies builds up the Assembly.
5. I desire that you all spoke in a tongue, but rather that you prophesied: for greater is he that prophesies than he that speaks in a tongue unless he interprets, that the Assembly may receive building up.
6. Now, brothers, if I come to you speaking in a tongue, what will I profit you, unless I will speak to you either by revelation, or by knowledge, or by prophesying, or by teaching?
7. And even things without life-giving sound, whether flute or harp, unless they give a distinction in the sounds, how will it be known what is piped or played?
8. For if the trumpet gives an uncertain sound, who will prepare himself for the battle?
9. So likewise, you, unless you utter by the tongue words easy to be understood, how will it be known what is spoken? For you will speak into the air.
10. There are, it may be, so many kinds of voices in the world, and none of them is without significance.
11. Therefore, if I do not know the meaning of the sound, I will be to him that speaks as a foreigner, and he that speaks will be a foreigner to me.
12. Even so you, since you are eager for the Spirit, seek that you may transcend into the building up of the Assembly.

13. Therefore, let him that speaks in a tongue pray that he may interpret.
14. For if I pray in a tongue, my spirit prays, but my mind is not profited.
15. What is it then? I will pray with the spirit, and I will pray with the mind also: I will sing with the spirit, and I will sing with the mind also.
16. Otherwise, when you will bless with the spirit, how will he that occupies the room of the uninformed say Amen at your giving of thanks, because he does not see what you are saying?
17. For you are truly giving thanks well, but the other is not built up.
18. I thank my God; I speak in a tongue more than you all:
19. yet in the Assembly I had rather speak five words with my mind, that by my voice I might teach others also, than ten thousand words in a tongue.
20. Brethren, do not be children in understanding: however, in wickedness be children, but in understanding be mature.
21. In the Law it is written, with one of another tongue and in different lips I will speak to this people; and in this manner they will not hear Me says the LORD.
22. Therefore, the tongue is for a sign, not to them that believe, but to them that do not believe: but prophesying serves not for them that do not believe, but for those who believe.
23. If therefore the whole Assembly comes together into one place, and all speak in a tongue, and there come in those that are uninformed, or unbelievers, will they not say that you are insane?
24. But if all prophesy, and there come in one that believes not or one uninformed, he is convinced of all, he is judged of all:
25. And thus, the secrets of his heart are made evident; and so, falling down on his face he will worship God, and report that God is certainly in you.
26. How is it then, brothers? When you come together, each one of you has a psalm, has a teaching, has a tongue, has a revelation, and has an interpretation. Let all things be performed for the building!
27. If any man speaks in a tongue, let it be by two, or at the most by three, and each by turn; and let one interpret.
28. But if there be no interpreter, let him keep silence in the Assembly; and let him speak to himself, and to God.
29. Let the prophets speak two or three, and let the others discuss.
30. If anything is revealed to another that sits by, let the first hold his peace.
31. For you may all prophesy one by one, that all may learn, and all may be encouraged.
32. And the spirits of the prophets are subject to the prophets.
33. For God is not the author of confusion, but of peace, as in all the Assemblies of the saints.
34. The wives must be silent in the Assemblies; for they are not permitted to talk randomly, but they must be in submission, just as the Law also says,
35. But if they want to learn something let them ask their own husbands at home. For it is inappropriate for wives to talk randomly in the Assembly.

36. What? Did the word of God originate from you? Or did it originate from you only?
37. If any man thinks himself to be a prophet or spiritual, let him acknowledge that the things that I write to you are the commandments of the Lord.
38. But if anyone does not acknowledge this, let him not be acknowledged.
39. Therefore, brothers, eagerly desire to prophesy and forbid not to speak with tongues.
40. Let all things be done decently and in order.

Chapter 15

1. Moreover, brothers, I declare to you the gospel which I preached to you, which also you have received, and in which you stand;
2. By which you are being saved, if you keep in memory what I preached to you unless you have believed in vain.
3. For I delivered to you first that which I also received, that Christ died for our sins according to the Scriptures;
4. And that He was buried, and that He rose again the third day according to the Scriptures:
5. And that He was seen of Cephas, then by the twelve:
6. After that, He was seen by above five hundred brothers at once; of whom the greater part remains to this time, but some have fallen asleep.
7. After that, He was seen by James, then by all the apostles.
8. And last of all He was seen of me also, as one whose birth was premature.
9. For I am the least of the apostles, and not suitable to be called an apostle, because I persecuted the Assembly of God.
10. But by the grace of God I am what I am: and His grace which was bestowed on me was not in vain; but I labored more abundantly than them all: yet not I, but the grace of God which was with me.
11. Therefore, whether it was I or they, so we preach, and so you believed.
12. Now if Christ is being preached that He rose from the dead, how say some among you that there is no resurrection out from among the dead?
13. But if there is no resurrection out from the dead, then Christ has not risen:
14. And if Christ is not risen, then our preaching is in vain, and your faith is also vain.
15. Yes, and we are found as false witnesses of God; because we have testified of God that He raised up the Christ: Whom He has not raised up, seeing that in effect, the dead are not being raised.
16. For if the dead are not being raised, then if Christ has not been raised:
17. And if Christ has not been raised, your faith is vain, and you are yet in your sins.
18. Then they also which are fallen asleep in Christ have perished.
19. If in this life only we have hope in Christ, we are of all men most miserable.
20. But now is Christ risen out from among the dead and became the first fruits of them that slept.

21. For since by man came death, by man also came the resurrection of the dead.
22. For as in Adam all die, even so in the Christ, all will be made alive.
23. But each man in his own sequential order: Christ, the first fruits; afterward they that are Christ's, in His Presence.
24. Then comes the consummation, when He will have delivered up the kingdom to God, even the Father when He will have put down all rule and all authority and power.
25. For He must reign until He has put all enemies under His feet.
26. The last enemy that is being destroyed: death.
27. For He has put all things under His feet. But when He says all things are put under Him, it is manifest that He is exempt, which did put all things under Him.
28. And when all things will be subdued to Him, then will the Son also Himself be subject to Him that put all things under Him that God may be all in all.
29. Then what will they do who are being immersed for the dead, if the dead do not rise at all? Why are they then immersed for the dead?
30. And why do we stand in jeopardy every hour?
31. I declare brothers by boasting in you which I have in Christ Jesus our Lord, I die daily.
32. If according to men I have fought with wild beasts at Ephesus, what does it profit me, if the dead are not being raised? Let us eat and drink; for tomorrow we are dying.
33. Be not deceived: evil companionship ruins a good disposition.
34. Wake up to what is proper, and do not sin; for some have no knowledge of God: I am speaking to your dysfunction.
35. But one will say, how are the dead being raised? And what body are they coming?
36. You fool, that which you sow is not given life unless it is dying:
37. And that which you sow, you do not sow that body that will be, but bare grain, it may be of wheat, or some other grain:
38. But God gives it a body as He purposed, and to each seed a body of its own.
39. All flesh is not the same flesh: but one indeed of men, another flesh of beasts, another of birds, and another of fish.
40. There are also heavenly bodies and earthly bodies: but the glory of the heavenly is different, and the glory of the earthly is another.
41. There is one glory of the sun, and another glory of the moon, and another glory of the stars: for one star is transcending another star in glory.
42. So also, is the rising of the dead. It is being sown in corruption; it is being raised in incorruption:
43. it is being sown in disgrace; it is being raised in glory: it is being sown in frailty; it is being raised in power:
44. It is being sown a soulish body; it is being raised a spiritual body! There is a soulish body, and there is a spiritual body.
45. And so, it is written, the first man Adam became a living soul; this last Adam into a life-giving spirit.

46. However, that which was first was not spiritual, but that which is soulish; and afterward that which is spiritual.
47. The first man is of the earth, earthy; the second man is out of heaven.
48. As is the earthy, such are they also that are earthy: and as is the heavenly, such are they also that are heavenly.
49. And as we wear the image of the earthy, we will also wear the image of the heavenly.
50. Now this I say, brothers, that flesh and blood cannot inherit the kingdom of God; neither does corruption inherit incorruption.
51. Behold, I show you a mystery; we will not all sleep, but we will all be altered,
52. In a moment, in the twinkling of an eye, at the last trump: for a trumpet will sound, and the dead will be raised incorruptible, and we will be altered.
53. For this corruptible must put on incorruption, and this mortal must put on immortality.
54. So, when this corruptible will have put on incorruption, and this mortal will have put on immortality, then will be brought to pass the saying that is written, O Death is swallowed up in triumph.
55. In what place O Death, is your piercing? In what place O Hades, is your triumph?
56. The sting of death is sin, and the strength of sin is the Law.
57. But thanks be to God, who causes us this triumph through our Lord Jesus Christ!
58. Therefore, my beloved brothers, be steadfast, unmovable, always abounding in the work of the Lord, since as you know that your labor is not in vain in the Lord.

Chapter 16

1. Now concerning the collection for the saints, as I have given order to the Assemblies of Galatia, even so do you.
2. On the first day of the week let everyone of you lay by him in store, as God has prospered him, that there be no gatherings when I come.
3. And when I come, whomever you will approve by your letters, them will I send to bring your gift to Jerusalem.
4. If it is suitable for me to go also, they will go with me.
5. Now I will come to you when I will pass through Macedonia: for I do pass through Macedonia.
6. And it may be that I will stay, yes, and winter with you, that you may bring me on my journey to wherever I go.
7. For I will not see you now by the way; but I trust to stay a while with you if the Lord permit.
8. But I will stay at Ephesus until Pentecost.
9. For a great and effective door is opened to me, and there are many adversaries.
10. Now if Timothy comes, see that he may be with you without fear: for he works the work of the Lord, as I also do.
11. Therefore, let no man despise him: but conduct him forth in peace that he may come to me: for I look for him with the brothers.
12. As concerning our brother Apollos, I greatly desired him to come to you with the brothers: but his will was not at all to come at this time; but he will come when he will have convenient time.

13. Stay awake, be men of courage in the faith, be strong.

14. Let all that comes out of you be done in love.

15. I implore you, brothers, you know the house of Stephanas, that he is the first fruits of Achaia, and that they have become addicted to the ministry of the saints

16. That you assign yourselves to such, and to everyone that cooperates with us, and labors.

17. I am glad because of the arrival of Stephanas and Fortunatus and Achaicus: because what was deficient from you they fulfilled.

18. For they have refreshed my spirit and yours: therefore, you fully know such ones.

19. The Assemblies of Asia greet you. Aquila and Priscilla greet you much in the Lord, with the Assembly that is in their house.

20. All the brothers greet you. Greet you one another with a holy kiss.

21. I, Paul greetings with my own hand.

22. If any man loves not the Lord Jesus Christ, let him be accursed. Maranatha.

23. The grace of our Lord Jesus Christ be with you.

24. My love be with you all in Christ Jesus. Amen.

Synopsis of 2 Corinthians

The passage in 2 Corinthians 1:3-4 states, Praise be to the God and Father of our Lord Jesus Christ, the Father of compassions and the God of all comfort, who comforts us in all our tribulation, so that we can comfort those in any tribulation with the comfort we receive from God. This passage highlights the amazing truth that not only is God a source of comfort for us, but He also enables us to comfort others through the comfort we have received from Him. A point to ask at this time is "what tribulation were they in"? The Roman world was rampant with Judaizers hounding Paul and his company and making life miserable for those who converted to Christ.

Contextually, this passage is part of Paul's second letter to the Corinthians, which was written to address issues that arose in the church of Corinth. In the preceding chapters, Paul talks about his struggles and sufferings for the sake of the Gospel. He mentions the comfort that God has given him and the assurance that he has in knowing that God is with him in his trials and tribulations. As an apostle of Christ, Paul was no stranger to afflictions, and he used his experiences to connect with his readers and encourage them to trust in God's provision and comfort.

Historically, the Corinthians were dealing with many challenges, including persecution, division, and false teachers and their teachings. These circumstances were causing distress and turmoil among the believers. Paul's message of comfort and encouragement was timely and relevant, as it reminded the Corinthians that their ultimate source of comfort is God Himself. Furthermore, Paul emphasizes that the purpose of receiving comfort from God was not just for their benefit but also for comforting others who are going through similar challenges.

The phrase God of all comfort describes the character of God as a compassionate and loving Father. This title is rooted in the Old Testament, particularly in the book of Isaiah, where God is referred to as the God of comfort (Isaiah 40:1). This image of God as a comforting Father is further reinforced in the New Testament when Jesus speaks of the Holy Spirit as the Comforter who will be with the disciples and in them (John 14:16). This shows us that comforting others is an integral part of God's nature and an expression of His triune being.

One possible application of this passage is to encourage believers to find comfort and solace in God during difficult times. In a world filled with trials, distractions, and pain, it is easy to lose sight of God's comforting presence. However, as followers of Christ, we are called to seek our comfort and reassurance in Him. This passage also challenges us to be mindful of the comfort we have received from God and allow it to flow through us to others. As Paul says, so that we can comfort those in any trouble with the comfort we receive from God. This means that our experiences of God's comfort should not just remain with us but should be shared with others who are hurting and in need of encouragement.

Another application is to remind believers that God can use our sufferings and trials for His glory and the benefit of others. As seen in Paul's life, his struggles and trials became a platform for him to minister and comfort others. Similarly, our experiences of being comforted by God can be used as a testimony to encourage those who are going through similar challenges. This highlights God's sovereignty over our pains and difficulties, and how He can use them for His ultimate purposes. We must understand that there are three kinds of suffering that we go through. The first is the general suffering of all mankind because of our frailty and the fragile existence we have. The second kind of suffering is the result and consequences of disobedience to God and our own foolishness. The third kind of suffering is the fellowship of His sufferings which is a noble suffering for being identified with Christ as His body and testimony here on earth. This last kind of suffering has great rewards attached to our experience. Paul's suffering was due to his testimony and identification with Christ. Those in Corinth were also experiencing persecution and rejection in their community for their commitment to Christ.

The passage in question is found in 2 Corinthians 1:8-10, where the apostle Paul writes about the persecution he and his companions faced while traveling in Asia. This passage is situated in the larger context of Paul's second letter to the church in Corinth, a city in ancient Greece. The letter was written around 55-56 AD, likely during Paul's third missionary journey.

Historical records indicate that Paul and his companions, including Titus, Silas, and Timothy, were traveling through Asia Minor (modern-day Turkey) to spread the Gospel of Jesus Christ. However, they encountered intense opposition from both Jews and Gentiles, who saw their message as a threat to their religious beliefs and way of life. This resulted in severe persecution and danger for Paul and his companions.

In verse 8, Paul describes being burdened excessively, beyond our power, so that we despaired even of life. This persecution was so severe that it brought them to the brink of death. The phrase "sentence of death in us" can be interpreted as Paul and his companions feeling as though they were condemned to die because of the intense persecution they were facing. Paul's declaration was his trust in God who raises the dead.

The fact that this persecution came from Asia is significant, as this was a region where Paul had previously experienced success in spreading the Gospel (Acts 16:6-10). Likely, this opposition was also coming from those who had once accepted Paul's message but then turned against him. In 2 Tim. 1:15, Paul says all of Asia turned away from him and deserted him. This is a side of suffering that is heartbreaking when those who have received Christ and His message turn on you. What a heart-rending experience which our Lord experienced time and time again.

In terms of exegesis, it is important to note that Paul does not explicitly state the source of this persecution. It could have been physical violence verbal attacks, or both. However, this experience was incredibly distressing for Paul and his companions, to the point where they knew something of the work of the cross in their lives.

Despite the severity of their situation, Paul writes in verse 9 that this happened so that they would not rely on themselves, but on God who raises the dead. This highlights Paul's unwavering faith and trust in God, even in the face of seemingly insurmountable challenges. It also reminds us that God is sovereign and can use even the most difficult circumstances to strengthen and mold us into the people He wants us to be.

Furthermore, in verse 10, Paul declares that God delivered them from such great peril and that he believes He will continue to deliver them in the future. This not only speaks to God's faithfulness and protection but also Paul's confidence in God's plan and purpose for their lives, even amid persecution.

In terms of applications for sermons or personal reflection, this passage reminds us that as Christians, we may face persecution or trials for our faith. However, just as God was faithful to deliver Paul and his companions, He is also faithful to strengthen and deliver us in our times of need. It also challenges us to examine our level of faith and trust in God during difficult times, and to remember that He is ultimately in control of our lives.

2 Corinthians is the second letter written by the Apostle Paul to the church in Corinth. This letter is a continuation of Paul's first letter, addressing issues that arose in the church after his first visit. In this letter, Paul defends his apostleship and encourages the Corinthian believers to live according to the gospel and to support the needs of the poor believers in Jerusalem. The passage we will be discussing today is 2 Corinthians 3:1-18.

Context:

To fully understand the passage, we must first understand the context in which it was written. In the first two chapters, Paul defends his ministry and authority as an apostle of Christ. As a result of this defense, Paul shifts to a discussion on the power of the Holy Spirit and the new covenant in Christ. In this passage, Paul explains that the ministry of the new covenant far surpasses the ministry of the old covenant.

Historicity:

The historicity of this passage is well-established as it is a part of the authentic letters written by Paul. The church in Corinth was founded by Paul himself during his second missionary journey. However, after his departure, the church became divided and corrupted by false teachers. This led Paul to write both of his letters to restore the unity of the church and to correct false teachings and the moral breakdown that permeated the believers.

Exegesis:

You are our letter, written in our hearts, known and read by all men; being manifested that you are a letter of Christ, cared for by us, written not with ink but with the Spirit of the living God, not on tablets of stone but on tablets of human hearts.[34]

In 2 Corinthians 3:1-6. To better understand the context of this passage, it is important to look at the broader context of 2 Corinthians as a whole and the following passages.

It is believed that Paul wrote this letter in response to conflicts and issues arising within the Corinthian church, including challenges to his authority as an apostle and false teachings by opponents. Throughout the letter, Paul addresses these issues and reminds the Corinthians of the importance of living as true followers of Christ.

In the preceding passage (2 Corinthians 2:12-17), Paul discusses his ministry and how he has been led by God to share the gospel with others. He also talks about how those who preach the gospel must do so with sincerity, as they are representatives of Christ and the fragrance of Him to those who are being saved.

In the passage in question, Paul begins by addressing the Corinthians directly, saying, "Are we beginning to commend ourselves again? Or do we need, like some people, letters of recommendation to you or from you?" (2 Corinthians 3:1). Here, Paul is addressing the issue of his authority and credibility once again, as some in the Corinthian church were likely questioning his legitimacy as an apostle. Paul goes on to say that the Corinthians themselves are the letter, written in their hearts and known and read by all people.

This statement is significant when considering the historical and cultural context of the time. In ancient times, letters of recommendation were often used to verify someone's character and credibility. However, Paul is saying that the Corinthians themselves, as followers of Christ, are living letters that testify to the work of God in their lives. This would have been a powerful and affirming message for the Corinthian church, reminding them of their true identity and purpose as followers of Christ.

---

[34] *New American Standard Bible: 1995 update* (2 Co 3:2–3). (1995). The Lockman Foundation.

Chapter 3

Paul then goes on to say that the Corinthians are a letter of Christ, cared for by Paul and his fellow coworkers. This further emphasizes the role of the Corinthian church as a tangible representation of the work of Christ on earth. In the following verses (2 Corinthians 3:4-6), Paul expounds on the importance and significance of the ministry of the Holy Spirit in the lives of believers. We need the Spirit of God to write on our hearts His story in our lives. He contrasts the new covenant of the Spirit, which brings life and righteousness, with the old covenant of the law, which brought death and condemnation. This would have been especially relevant to the Corinthians, as they were struggling with false teachings that emphasized following strict laws and regulations rather than living by the power and guidance of the Holy Spirit.

In conclusion, the passage in 2 Corinthians 3:1-6 is part of a larger letter written by Paul to the Corinthian church. In this passage, Paul emphasizes the identity and purpose of the Corinthians as living letters of Christ and highlights the significance of the ministry of the Holy Spirit in their lives. The new covenant is sourced by the Spirit of God and the old covenant is sourced in the Law of Moses. The new covenant imparts life and righteousness, which the law could not do. The old covenant condemns us resulting in death. This contrast is profound and is essential for our understanding to have a proper standing with God.

Verse 7: "Now if the ministry of death, carved in letters on stone, came with such glory that the Israelites could not gaze at Moses face because of its glory, which was being brought to an end,"

In this verse, Paul is referring to the old covenant given to Moses on Mount Sinai. This covenant was written on stone and was a ministry of death. This is not to say that the law was bad, but rather it showed the sinfulness of man and his inability to perfectly keep the law. The glory of this ministry was so great that Moses face shone bright after being in the presence of God, but this glory was temporary and fading.

Verse 8-9: "will not the ministry of the Spirit have even more glory? For if there was glory in the ministry of condemnation, the ministry of righteousness must far exceed it in glory."

Paul is making a comparison between the old covenant and the new covenant. The old covenant brought condemnation because no one could perfectly keep the law, but the new covenant brings righteousness through Christ's sacrifice on the cross. The ministry of the Spirit in the new covenant is far greater than the ministry of the law in the old covenant. Verse 8 states, "how will the ministry of the Spirit not be more glorious?" Here, Paul is contrasting the glory of the old covenant with the glory of the new covenant. The old covenant was given through Moses, but the new covenant is fulfilled through Jesus Christ. The ministry of the Spirit surpasses the ministry of the law, as it offers forgiveness and salvation through grace rather than by obeying a set of rules.

In verse 9, Paul refers to the law as "the ministry of condemnation," highlighting its limitations in providing salvation. The law showed the Israelites their sins but could not save them from them. However, the new covenant offers true freedom and forgiveness of sins through faith in Christ.

In verse 10, Paul further explains that the glory of the old covenant is temporary, while the new covenant's glory is perpetual. This draws attention to the fact that the old covenant was only a temporary solution, whereas the new covenant offers an everlasting fellowship with God.

In verse 12, Paul uses the analogy of Moses veiling his face to explain that the old covenant served as a veil that prevented the people from fully understanding God's glory of the old covenant that was fading. However, in the new covenant, the veil is removed through Jesus Christ, allowing believers to have an intimate relationship with God. To be unveiled by turning their hearts to the Lord whenever and wherever.

Verse 16 talks about the transformation that takes place when someone turns to the Lord. This transformation is a result of the Holy Spirit's work, who is the source of the new covenant. Through the Spirit, believers are transformed into the likeness of Christ, with their minds and hearts renewed to understand God's reality and express Christ to all those in their presence.

Verse 18 concludes the passage by stating that through the Spirit, believers are transformed into the image of God, reflecting His glory. are being transformed into the same image from glory to glory, just as from the Lord, the Spirit.[35] Understanding the context of from glory to glory is quite obvious since Paul was comparing the glory of the old covenant with the glory of the new covenant. This is not going from glory to glory to glory. This is moving from an old covenant experience to the reality of the new covenant experience. Our transformation happens as believers walk in faith and obedience, continually being guided and empowered by the Holy Spirit to obey and walk pleasing to Him.

Applications:
1. The new covenant is superior to the old covenant: As Christians, we should understand that our relationship with God is not based on obeying a set of rules, but rather on faith in Jesus Christ. The new covenant offers us the privilege of being children of God and having a personal relationship with Him.
2. The ministry of the Spirit is essential: We must rely on the Holy Spirit to guide us and transform us into the likeness of Christ. As we commune with God and

---

[35] *New American Standard Bible, 1995 Edition: Paragraph Version* (2 Co 3:18). (1995). The Lockman Foundation.

search the scriptures, we should ask the Holy Spirit to open our minds and hearts to understand God's truth and let it be written into our hearts and minds.

3. The temporary nature of the old covenant: This passage reminds us that the old covenant served as a foreshadowing of the new covenant, which is perpetual. We should not cling to the old covenant and its limitations but fully embrace the new covenant and its blessings.

4. The importance of transformation: Through the Holy Spirit, our beholding the glory of the Lord, which is the glory of the new covenant, we are continually being transformed into the image of God. We should strive to grow in our faith and obedience, allowing the Holy Spirit to work in us and express God's glory to the world.

In conclusion, 2 Corinthians 3:8-18 emphasizes the superiority of the new covenant and the essential role of the Holy Spirit in our lives. As we understand and embrace the new covenant, we are transformed and express God's glory to the world. The Jews specifically from Old Covenant glory to the New Covenant glory.

Verse 10: "Indeed, in this case, what once had glory has come to have no glory at all, because of the glory that surpasses it." The old covenant does not have glory any longer, it has faded.

Again, Paul emphasizes the surpassing glory of the new covenant over the old. The old covenant had a glorious past, but the new covenant has an even more glorious present and future because of Christ's work.

Verse 11: "For if what was being brought to an end came with glory, much more will what is permanent have glory."

Here, Paul emphasizes the permanency of the new covenant. The old covenant was temporary, but the new covenant, through the Spirit, is permanent and brings infinite glory.

Verse 12: "Since we have such a hope, we are very bold,"

In light of the surpassing glory and permanency of the new covenant, Paul encourages the believers to be bold in their faith and proclaim the gospel without fear. The hope we have in Christ gives us confidence to boldly share the good news with the world.

Verse 13: "not like Moses, who would put a veil over his face so that the Israelites might not gaze at the outcome of what was being brought to an end." The age of Moses has ended!

Paul uses the example of Moses and the veil over his face to illustrate the temporary nature of the old covenant. The veil was meant to hide the fading glory and also symbolizes the spiritual blindness of the Israelites to the true purpose of the law.

Verse 14: "But their minds were hardened. For to this day, when they read the old covenant, that same veil remains unlifted, because only through Christ is the veil taken away."

The spiritual blindness of the Israelites is not completely lifted until they turn to Christ. Only through Christ can the veil be taken away, and the true understanding of the law be revealed.

Verse 15: "Yes, to this day whenever Moses is read a veil lies over their hearts."

Paul emphasizes the importance of understanding the true purpose of the law, and how only through Christ can the veil be lifted. Without a proper understanding of the law, one cannot fully understand the surpassing glory of the new covenant.

Verse 16: "But when one turns to the Lord, the veil is removed." Oh that there would be more turning in our daily lives, we would be full of light and understanding receiving revelation on a daily basis just by turning our hearts to Him. Like an old hymn we used to sing in the 70's, "Calling His name O Lord Jesus, saying Amen when He speaks, filling my spirit with His love, filling my whole with His life". Turning our hearts is just saying His name, calling Him, and this is how we are changed.

Verse 17: "Now the Lord is the Spirit, and where the Spirit of the Lord is, there is freedom."

Why is the Lord NOW the Spirit? It is because the Lord Jesus has become the life-giving Spirit. 1 Cor. 15:45

In this verse, Paul equates the Lord with the Spirit. They are one and the same, and where the Spirit resides, there is freedom. This freedom is found in the new covenant in Christ, where we are no longer bound by the law but instead we are guided by the Holy Spirit.

Verse 18: "And we all, with unveiled face, beholding the glory of the Lord, are being transformed into the same image from one degree of glory to another. For this comes from the Lord who is the Spirit."

Through Christ, the veil has been removed, and we can now behold the glory of the Lord. As we continue to behold His glory, through the work of the Holy Spirit, we are transformed into His image and reflect His glory more and more each day.

Applications:

1. Boldness in sharing the gospel: Paul encourages us to be bold in sharing the gospel, knowing that our hope in Christ gives us confidence and courage to proclaim the good news to others.
2. Spiritual understanding: Just as the Israelites had a veil over their hearts, we too can have a spiritual veil over our minds until we turn to Christ. Only through Him can we fully understand the true purpose of the law and the glory of the new covenant.

In this passage, we see the surpassing glory and permanency of the new covenant in Christ. Through faith in Him, we are set free from the bondage of the law and are transformed into His image through the work of the Holy Spirit. Let us be bold in sharing the good news of this new covenant, and continue to behold the glory of the Lord, reflecting it in our lives.

Chapter 4 – The God of this Age blinded the minds

It is hard for us to understand that the God of this age, in Paul's day was the old covenant age, and it was Yahweh instead of the devil. I am not saying that the devil does not blind people through deception, but this verse in 2 Cor. is not speaking of the devil. The unbelieving Jews of that day were experiencing Isaiah's prophecy and what Jesus and Paul applied to their day.

Powerful prophecies and warnings from Yahweh to His people, specifically the nation of Israel. In Isaiah chapter six of this book, we see a powerful vision that Isaiah receives from God, in which Yahweh commissions him to be a messenger to the people of Israel. Within this vision, there is a specific passage that speaks to Yahweh's blinding of Israel.

And he said, Go and tell this people: Keep on hearing, but do not understand; keep on seeing, but do not perceive. Make the heart of this people dull, and their ears heavy, and blind their eyes; lest they see with their eyes, and hear with their ears, and understand with their hearts, and return and be healed. (Isaiah 6:9-10) Isaiah 6:9-10 is quoted once each by the four gospel writers—Matt. 13:14-15; Mark 4:11- 12; Luke 8:10; John 12:40—and by Paul in Acts 28:26-27. And Paul uses another reference in Romans from Isaiah 29. 7 What then? What Israel is seeking, it has not obtained, but those who were chosen obtained it, and the rest were hardened; 8 just as it is written, "God gave them a spirit of stupor, Eyes to see not and ears to hear not, Down to this very day."[36]

Contextually, this passage is set during a time when the nation of Israel had turned away from Yahweh and turned to idolatry and wickedness. In the previous chapters, Isaiah delivers warnings and judgments from God to the people, calling them to repent and turn back to Him. However, the people refuse to listen and continue in their rebellion. In this passage, Yahweh declares that He will continue to blind the people, and they will not see or understand the truth of His words.

Historically, this prophecy was fulfilled during the reign of King Nebuchadnezzar when he conquered Judah and took the people into captivity in Babylon. The eyes of the people were blinded as they were forced to leave their homeland and live in a foreign land. However, this was also a spiritual blindness as they were unable to see the truth and understand the consequences of their actions.

---

[36] *New American Standard Bible, 1995 Edition: Paragraph Version* (Ro 11:7–8). (1995). The Lockman Foundation.

In terms of exegesis, it is essential to note the use of parallelism in this passage. The repetition of keep on hearing and keep on seeing emphasizes the stubbornness and unwillingness of the people to listen to God's message. The use of heart, ears, and eyes also suggests a holistic blindness – both physical and spiritual. This is why when Christ showed up many in Israel were physically blind. Matt. 9:27; 12:22; 20:30; John 5:3[37] As one blind man said, 32" Nobody has ever heard of anyone opening the eyes of a person born blind. 33If this man had not come from God; he could do nothing."[38]

From a theological standpoint, this passage reveals the sovereignty of Yahweh. He is not only the one who gives sight and understanding but also the one who withholds it. This reminds us that our understanding and knowledge of God's truth are ultimately in His hands and not in our own.

In terms of application, this passage speaks to us today, as much as it did to the people of Israel in the past. It serves as a warning against spiritual blindness and the consequences of turning away from God. When we reject Gods message and continue in our own ways, we too can become blinded to the truth and unable to see Gods hand at work in our lives. Therefore, we are called to continually seek Gods wisdom and truth, humbling ourselves before Him and allowing Him to guide us.

Furthermore, this passage is a call to action for us as Christians to be messengers of Gods truth. As Yahweh commissioned Isaiah to be a messenger to the people of Israel, we too are called to share the Gospel and bring light to those who are spiritually blind. This passage also reminds us of the power of prayer – that we can intercede on behalf of those who are blinded by sin and ask God to open their eyes and hearts to His truth. The passage in Isaiah 6 serves as a powerful reminder of Yahweh's sovereignty and the consequences of ignoring His message. This passage speaks to us about both physical and spiritual blindness and the importance of seeking God's truth and sharing it with others. Let us be reminded to continually seek God's guidance and to be messengers of His truth in a world that is blinded in sin. The concept of God blinding Israel can be found in several passages in the New Testament, including Romans 11:7-10, 2 Corinthians 3:14, and John 12:40. In these passages, we can see a pattern of God blinding the eyes and hardening the hearts of the people of Israel. This concept can be difficult to understand and may raise questions about God's character and actions. However, upon deeper examination and exegesis, we can see the purpose and message behind God's decision to blind Israel.

---

[37] Easton, M. G. (1893). In *Illustrated Bible Dictionary and Treasury of Biblical History, Biography, Geography, Doctrine, and Literature* (p. 102). Harper & Brothers.
[38] *New International Reader's Version* (1st ed., Jn 9:32–33). (1998). Zondervan.

Context:

In Romans 11, the apostle Paul is writing to the church in Rome, a predominantly Gentile church. He is addressing the tension and division that exists between Jewish and Gentile believers. Paul explains that God has not rejected His chosen people, the Jews, but has instead opened the door for Gentiles to be grafted into the family of God through faith in Jesus Christ. Paul goes on to quote from Isaiah 29:10 and Deuteronomy 29:4, showing that God had always foretold of a time when Israel's hearts would be hardened and their eyes blinded.

Historicity:

Historically, we can see the fulfillment of God's actions in the life of Israel. Throughout the Old Testament, we see a pattern of Israel's disobedience and rejection of God, despite His faithfulness and provision. This continued until eventually, they rejected and crucified their own promised Messiah, Jesus Christ. As a result, their eyes were blinded, and their hearts were hardened, causing them to reject the Gospel message.

Exegesis:

In 2 Corinthians 3:14, Paul compares the veil over the hearts of the Jews to the veil that covered Moses' face in the Old Testament. Just as Moses' face was veiled to prevent the Israelites from seeing the fading glory, the Jews' hearts were veiled, preventing them from seeing the true glory of God in Jesus Christ. This blindness and hardening of hearts was a judgment from God, as He allowed them to continue in their rejection of Him.

In John 12:40, John quotes from Isaiah 6:10, where God commissions Isaiah to speak to the people of Israel, knowing that they will not listen or understand. This is a poignant reminder of Israel's stubbornness and hardness of heart, despite God reaching out to them repeatedly through His prophets.

1. Understanding God's sovereignty: God's decision to blind the eyes and harden the hearts of Israel may seem harsh and unfair. However, we must remember that God is sovereign and has the right to do as He pleases. He had warned Israel repeatedly of the consequences of disobedience, and their actions were a fulfillment of that warning.

2. God's mercy and grace towards Gentiles: In blinding Israel, God opened the door for Gentiles to be grafted into His family through faith in Jesus. This is a reminder of God's mercy and grace towards us, as we were once strangers and aliens but have now been included in God's kingdom and the commonwealth of Israel of those that received their Messiah.

3. Humility and gratitude: As Gentile believers, we must approach God with humility and gratitude, knowing that we have been grafted into the family of God through no merit of our own.

4. A warning against unbelief: The concept of Israel's blindness serves as a warning for us to not harden our hearts against God and His word. We must constantly examine our hearts and guard against the dangers of unbelief and disobedience.

The concept of God blinding Israel may seem puzzling, but upon closer examination, we can see the purpose and message behind His actions. It serves as a reminder of God's sovereignty, mercy, and grace towards us as Gentile believers and a warning against unbelief. In light of this, may we approach God with humility, gratitude, and a desire for His will to be done in and through our lives.

Chapter 4:6 God who said, "Let light shine out of darkness has shone into our hearts". In 2 Corinthians 4:6, Paul emphasizes the power of the gospel of God and how creative speech is in bringing light into the darkness. By quoting Genesis 1:3 ("Let light shine out of darkness"), Paul is drawing a parallel between the act of creation in the old creation realm and the new spiritual realm. The gospel creates a new dimension within us, and Paul is enlightening the Corinthians' eyes to see this kingdom dimension within them.

Paul goes on to explain that just as God created light to shine out of darkness at the beginning, He has also shone His light in the hearts of believers to give them the knowledge of the glory of God in the face of Jesus Christ. This spiritual transformation is a new creation that takes place within the hearts of believers, illuminating their understanding and revealing the truth of God's glory. We will see later that if the new creation is a people, perhaps we must reconsider the idea of an old creation being a people also.

By quoting Genesis 1:3 and relating it to the creation in our hearts, Paul is emphasizing the transformative power of God's light, the gospel of glory, and the ongoing work of creation that He is doing in the lives of believers. It serves as a reminder of the continual renewal and transformation that comes from having a relationship with God.

2 Cor. 4:7-14 - These verses highlight the paradoxical nature of the Christian life, where believers are described as "earthen vessels" containing the treasure of God's power, the gospel. The weakness and fragility of human beings are contrasted with the surpassing greatness of God's power, which works through believers despite their limitations. The imagery of being afflicted but not crushed, perplexed but not despairing, persecuted but not forsaken, and struck down but not destroyed emphasizes the resilience of believers in the face of challenges and hardships. It speaks to the reality that Christians may face trials and tribulations, but through their faith in God, they are able to endure and overcome.

The concept of carrying about in the body the dying of Jesus so that the life of Jesus may be manifested in our bodies points to the idea of dying to self and living for Christ. As believers undergo suffering and persecution for the sake of Jesus, it is ultimately a means for the life of Jesus to be made evident in them and through them.

The verse concludes with the assurance that believers have the spirit of faith and the hope of resurrection, knowing that just as God raised Jesus from the dead, He will also raise them and present them with Jesus. This provides comfort and encouragement to believers facing trials and suffering, reminding them of the ultimate victory and redemption that awaits them in Christ. Though their body may perish because of the murderous persecutors in their day, their faith in Christ guarantees that they will never die.

An Analysis of the External and Internal Man as in 2 Corinthians 4:10–17

In 2 Corinthians 4:10–17, Paul employs the symbolism of the External and Internal Man to illustrate the paradoxical essence of the Christian existence. The External Man signifies the earthly body of Christ, susceptible to decay and able to be physically destroyed. Conversely, the Inner Man symbolizes the glorification process that is happening in every believer of the faithful, undergoing daily renewal. Paul understood that even as Christ suffered in His physical body and then sacrificed Himself, so also the church joined to the Lord in her earthly state will experience a momentary light affliction is not worthy to be compared to the glory that awaited them. Paul was defining the transition they were experiencing of the suffering servant. Not the individual human body, but the corporate body of Christ in its mortality and encouraging them that the body of Christ will be honored in resurrection and glory. Paul uses the plural "our" and the singular "outer man". Even though many look at this verse on an individual level, Paul is drawing from the motif from the songs of the Servant in Isaiah.

2 Cor. 4:16-18 - In these passages, the Apostle Paul is encouraging believers to not lose heart in the face of suffering and trials because our outer body may be experiencing decay and affliction, but our inner man is being renewed and transformed day by day. This transformation leads to an infinite weight of glory that far surpasses any temporal suffering we may endure. Paul reminds us to fix our eyes not on the temporary things of this world, but on the unseen infinite realities of God's kingdom. This perspective helps us endure and persevere through difficulties, knowing that they are producing a greater and infinite glory in us. The outer man may refer to the corporate, suffering, servant body of Christ and as the church moves towards the new covenant age it will come into the reigning body of Christ and experience some fashion of glory. Those that pass before A.D. 70 that are martyred will enter an infinite glory and be rewarded for their faithfulness. Normally, these verses are applied to the individual, but a careful analysis begs me to understand that the word for renewed is a verb in the present passive voice where the action is coming on the recipient. The renewal is happening to the inner man. The inner man isn't making it happen, it is happening sovereignly. Some that are more skilled in the Greek language should take this up and expand upon it.

Chapter 5

1 For we know that if our earthly house of this tabernacle were dissolved, we have a building of God, a house not made with hands, infinite in the heavens. 2 For in this we are groaning, earnestly desiring to put on our house which is out of heaven: 3 If indeed, being clothed we will not be found naked. 4 For we that are in the tabernacle do groan, being burdened: not that we want to be stripped, but to put on in order that the mortality may be consumed by life. 5 Now He that has prepared us for the very same thing is God, who also has given to us the guarantee of the Spirit. 6 Therefore being courageous always, seeing that, while we are among our own people in the body, earthly house, we are away from the new covenant people of the Lord: 7 For we walk by faith, not by sight: 8 We are confident, I say, and wanting more to be away from my own people among the body, earthly house, and to be among the people of the Lord. 9 Therefore we are ambitious, that, whether being among my own people or away, may we be well-pleasing to Him. 2 Cor. 5:1-9 TKB Translation – Terry Kashian.

This is how I translated this portion of scripture with the intention of capturing the spirit of Paul as he contrasted the old covenant and new covenant and the old covenant ministry with the new covenant ministry. Following his train of thought we must see that the earthly house is the old covenant people of God, and the building not made with hands is the new creation, the new covenant people of God. Paul is contrasting the nature of the two houses. This is his method throughout the New Testament. Two covenants, two mountains, two Jerusalem's, two sons, two priesthoods, two laws, two temples and two lands. One is earthly and one is heavenly. One is temporal and one is perpetual. Over and over throughout the New Testament he contrasts the old with the new. What earthly house was going to be dissolved? The Greek word is kataluo and some have translated it destroyed, demolished and it is ok to do that they are synonyms of the word dissolved. The latter part of the word kataluo is in 2 Peter 3:10,11,12 and those three times the luo is used, but in the ESV it is translated dissolve. Kata means down and luo means loosed, or destroyed, and dissolve. So kataluo could means destroyed down to nothing.

Or the word picture of something dissolving and being visible and then vanishing. The problem with the ESV in 2 Peter 3 is the ignorance of what the heavens and earth were. Not physical but the symbol of the old covenant house and people of God. The building of God that is coming down out of heaven is the consummation of the tabernacle of God among men, the bride, the wife of the Lamb, the city of God, the New Jerusalem. Paul was saying that as long as we identify with old covenant Israel and that house, we are away from the new covenant people of the Lord. This was the transition of moving away from the law, the old covenant system and those that were clinging to the old. The last sign miracle in the Gospel of John was raising Lazarus from the dead and this is the picture of old covenant Israel being dead and Christ calling him forth from the tomb. Lazarus was alive but he was still bound by grave clothes. Jesus said to His disciples, "loose him" When he had said these things, he cried out with a loud voice, "Lazarus, come out." The man who had died came out, his hands and feet bound with linen strips, and his face wrapped with a cloth. Jesus said to them, "Unbind him, and let him go."[39] The word unbind or loose in the KJV is luo.

In the beginning of the church at Pentecost the church was alive but still had the grave clothes of Judaism on. They were still wearing the old covenant clothes and still bound up. Slowly the Lord started taking off the grave clothes of them and they were becoming freer as time went on and false teachers were still trying to get the saints to wear those old grave clothes. These were the garments of death and condemnation. Paul says we are groaning, sound familiar, this is the creation groaning that was subject to futility not of its own will, but in hope that what was mortal would be consumed by life. This idea of not wanting to be naked and unclothed is possibly the idea of a lawbreaker i.e. Adam in the garden as a lawbreaker was found by God naked and ashamed. The burden of the law has always been the undoing of God's people because of the flesh. Paul is saying we are putting on this new garment so death will be swallowed up by life. The mixing of metaphors is common with Paul, but this concept is all over the New Testament. Put on the new man, put on the armor of light, put on the Lord Jesus Christ. The baptism of the Holy Spirit was being clothed with power.

The New Covenant clothing was available to the believers to put on so that the ministry of death would be swallowed and consumed by the New. Putting on Christ means abiding in Jesus and living to please Him. John Wesley described it as "a strong and beautiful expression for the most intimate union with Him and being clothed with all the graces which were in Him" (quoted by L. Morris in The Epistle to the Romans, Inter-Varsity Press, 1988, p. 473). We are clothed in Christ when we become so closely united with Jesus that others see Him and not us. Just as when we wear clothes and people say, "what are you wearing", "cool shirt", we are clothed with spiritual realities that are invisible until we put them on and animate those realities.

The building of God, house of God, the clothing is spiritual and invisible and as believers we make them visible when we put them on. There are two words in the Greek I want to focus on which are ekdemeo and endemeo. 2 Cor. 5:6 is where these two words are first commonly translated and very different than how I translated this verse. For example: So, we are always confident, knowing that while we are at home in the body we are absent from the Lord.[40] The phrase "while we are at home in the body we are absent from the Lord" …. Consider this phrase and check it out to see if that is true. When you are in your physical body, you are absent from the Lord? Is this true? Or is He always with you and in you? I am proposing that perhaps this is not speaking about our physical body. The word at home is the Greek word endemeo, from a compound of <G1722> (en) and <G1218> (demos);

---

[39] The Holy Bible: English Standard Version (Jn 11:43–44). (2016). Crossway Bibles.
[40] *The New King James Version* (2 Co 5:6). (1982). Thomas Nelson.

to be in one's own country, i.e. home (figurative): - be at home (present).⁴¹ The two words that make up this Greek word is en= in, among, at. The word demos are people, endemos is defined as (1736)), lit., to be among one's people (en, in, dēmos, people; endēmos, one who is in his own place or land), is used metaphorically of the life on earth of believers,⁴² This definition is by two of the top scholars in Greek, W.E. Vines and F.F. Bruce. I am persuaded that the phrase "at home in the body" should be understood as being among the Old Covenant people we are absent or away from the people of the Lord. The word absent is ekdemeo in Greek. from a compound of <G1537> (ek) and <G1218> (demos); to emigrate, i.e. (figurative) vacate or quit: - be absent.⁴³ We are confident, yes, well pleased preferring to be absent from the body (old covenant people) and to be among the people of the Lord. 2 Cor. 5:8

What Paul is explaining is that if the true believers leave or emigrate to the old covenant realm and Judaizers they will be away from the true people of the Lord. Only those who accepted Christ as their Messiah were the true children of God. Paul says in Romans that it is not the children of the flesh who are the children of God, but those born of the promise (Spirit). This is why Paul said we walk by faith and not by sight because the real spiritual items in the Christian life were invisible compared to the accouterments of the Jewish religion. We have never seen the blood of Jesus and yet it washed all our sins away. Not having seen Him we still love Him. We have touched the spiritual realities of the New Covenant. We are a spiritual house made of living stones, we are the body of Christ, not metaphorically, but actually. There is more, but I think you get what I mean. We walk by faith, not blind faith, but divinely enlightened faith.

For the love of Christ controls us, because we have concluded this: that one has died for all, therefore all have died; and he died for all, that those who live might no longer live for themselves but for him who for their sake died and was raised.⁴⁴

In essence, the resonance of 2 Corinthians 5:14-15 within contemporary theology is undeniable. These verses challenge the Church to embody a countercultural standard of sacrificial love, to champion restorative justice and conciliation, and to reimagine its practices in alignment with the transformative power of the gospel. By embracing these profound truths, believers are equipped to navigate the complexities of the modern world, bearing witness to the enduring relevance of Paul's teachings and the timeless message of Christ's redemptive love.

At the heart of these teachings lies the concept of divine love, a sacrificial and all-encompassing force that compels believers to embrace a radically different way of living. Paul's depiction of this love as a constraining power that governs the motivations and

---

⁴¹ Strong, J. (2020). ἐνδημέω. In *Strong's Talking Greek and Hebrew Dictionary*. WORDsearch.
⁴² Vine, W. E., & Bruce, F. F. (1981). In *Vine's Expository dictionary of Old and New Testament words* (Vol. 2, p. 228). Revell.
⁴³ Strong, J. (2020). ἐκδημέω. In *Strong's Talking Greek and Hebrew Dictionary*. WORDsearch.
⁴⁴ *The Holy Bible: English Standard Version* (2 Co 5:14–15). (2016). Crossway Bibles.

actions of the redeemed resonates profoundly, challenging the self-centered tendencies of the human condition and inviting a Christ-centered existence marked by selflessness and service.

Therefore, from now on we recognize no one according to the flesh; even though we have known Christ according to the flesh, yet now we know Him in this way no longer.[45]

One that envisions Christ not merely as a historical figure but as the embodiment of the divine life or God's very being. This viewpoint has had far-reaching ethical implications for believers, redefining moral and ethical conduct as an outflow of the indwelling Spirit rather than adherence to external codes. How this understanding has reshaped personal spiritual growth, communal ethics, and interpersonal dynamics within the church.

Moreover, this research analyzes the transformative impact of this theological lens on contemporary church teachings and rituals. It explores how the recognition of Christ as the Life-giving Spirit has reshaped worship practices, church leadership and governance models, and the understanding and observance of rituals and sacraments. Exploring the evolution of educational programs, theological training, catechism, and member integration processes, all of which have been influenced by this profound Christological perspective.

Drawing from a diverse array of sources, including scholarly works, theological treatises, and brother Lee's extensive writings, my aim is to provide a comprehensive understanding of how the concept of Christ as the Life-giving Spirit has transformed the landscape of Christian thought and practice. By synthesizing insights from New Testament exegesis, philosophical traditions, and contemporary ecclesiastical developments, the paper offers a holistic exploration of this transformative theological concept and its far-reaching implications for the life and witness of the church. We cannot remain with the understanding that Jesus is a 5-foot something Jewish man sitting on a chair in heaven. We must see Him as He is and how the perfect humanity of Christ has been added to the Godhead and this additive of perfect humanity is blended into the new spirit that has been given to us who believe. The concept of the Life-giving Spirit originates from the theological teachings of the New Testament, specifically from the writings of the apostle Paul. In one of his letters, 1 Corinthians 15:45, Paul draws a comparison between the first Man, Adam, who was given life as a living soul, and Christ, referred to as the last Adam, who embodies the essence of God and became the life-giving Spirit. On the cross, Christ was the last Adam and in resurrection He became the life-giving Spirit so He could fill all things. Eph. 3:10. Understanding the nature of Christ today is imperative, otherwise we will have a carnal or fleshly understanding of who He is today. Christ is omnipresent and the next verses are even more profound because Paul is now going to reveal the new creation in Christ. If Jesus is a 5-foot something Jewish man in resurrection and ascension, how can anyone be in Him? My point is as the life-giving Spirit, He is in us, and we are in Him. We are mingled with

---

[45] *New American Standard Bible: 1995 update* (2 Co 5:16). (1995). The Lockman Foundation.

God and God is mingled with us infused with a perfect humanity. Our perception of one another and Christ should be "there is a new creation", Hallelujah! Anyone in Christ is a new creation.

2 Corinthians 5:17-21 is part of a letter written by Paul, the apostle, to the church in Corinth. In this passage, Paul is addressing the believers and reminding them of their new identity in Christ. He emphasizes the fact that anyone who is in Christ is a new creation, and the old has passed away. He also discusses the role of believers as ambassadors of Christ, tasked with the ministry of conciliation.

Verse 17: Therefore, if anyone is in Christ, the new creation has come: The old has gone, the new is here! The word old is an interesting word and interpreters mostly apply this to our old life. But is that true, when we first get saved, are the old things passed away. It takes time to be transformed and if we are honest, even after we are saved there are still some old things hanging around. I want to comfort you with an explanation of this verse, "old things have passed away, behold the new has come". Paul just said when He died, we all died. This is an explanation of 1 Cor. 15:45, stating that Jesus is the last Adam. Jesus is not the second Adam, He is the second man, a new species of humanity. A God-Man starting a new people, a new race, a new humanity. The old that has passed away is the Old Man, Adam. There is a termination in the death of Christ and a germination in the resurrection. The word for old things is Archaios in the Greek and used in the NAS - 11 times - that has been from the beginning, original, primal, old ancient of men, things, times, conditions. Paul was contrasting the old and new in the covenants, ministries, the glory, the houses and concludes his train of thought, he says the old passed away. The ancient, the original, the former and long standing things of the old creation have passed away. Behold new things have come. The new creation was present within the old creation and the new was emerging and the old was already dead.

This verse highlights the drastic transformation that takes place when someone becomes a follower of Christ. The phrase in Christ refers to being one with Him through faith. This oneness brings about a new creation, not just a reformation of the old. The old that Paul is referring to is not subjective but related to the context of the last few chapters. The old covenant and all its components. The new covenant was being established in the midst of the old covenant age. Paul says this is from God.

Verse 18: All this is from God, who conciliated us to Himself through Christ and gave us the ministry of conciliation.

Here, Paul emphasizes that this transformation is not a result of our own efforts, but it is from God. Paul is saying that God is the source It is through the sacrifice of Christ that we are conciliated to God and brought into a relationship with Him. This conciliation also gives believers the responsibility of sharing this message of conciliation with others, resulting in a genuine and internal communion with God. Faith connects us to Him and faith keeps us in fellowship.

Verse 19: That God was conciliating the world to Himself in Christ, not counting peoples sins against them. And he has committed to us the message of conciliation.

This verse further highlights the heart of God for all people to be conciliated, made one with Him through Christ. It also emphasizes that through Christ, our sins are not counted against us. As ambassadors of Christ, we are entrusted with the message of conciliation to share with the world.

Verse 20: We are therefore Christ's ambassadors, as though God were making His appeal through us. We implore you on Christ's behalf: Be conciliated to God.

Paul uses the imagery of ambassadors to illustrate the role of believers in representing Christ to the world. As ambassadors, we carry the authority and message of Christ, and our actions and words are expressing and representing Him. We are also urged to implore others to be conciliated to God, demonstrating the urgency and importance of this ministry.

Verse 21: God made Him who had no sin to be sin for us so that in Him we might become the righteousness of God.

This powerful verse highlights the ultimate sacrifice of Jesus, who took on our sins and became sin for us in order for us to be made right with God. Our righteousness is not earned, but it is gifted to us through Christ. This reminds us of the overwhelming love and grace of God towards us.

Applications:

1. Recognize your new identity in Christ: As believers, we are no longer bound by our past sins and failures. We have a new identity in Christ, and we should live in accordance with it. We are the righteousness of God! In Him.

2. Be conciliated and share the message of conciliation: We have been conciliated to God through Christ, and it is our responsibility to share this message with others. We should persevere to live as ambassadors of Christ, representing Him well and inviting others to be conciliated to God.

3. We are called to a ministry of conciliation: This passage highlights the importance of the ministry of conciliation and reminds us that it is not just the role of church leaders, but of every believer. We should actively seek opportunities to share the message of God's love and conciliation with those around us.

4. Remember the sacrifice of Christ: The final verse of this passage reminds us of the ultimate sacrifice Jesus made for us. We should never take for granted the forgiveness and righteousness we have received through Him and always live in gratefulness and awe of His love for us.

2 Corinthians 5:17-21 highlights the transformative power of Christ and our role as ambassadors of conciliation. I use the word conciliation instead of reconciliated which to some it may be a hair splitter, but with precise and accurate understanding that reconciliation is being brought back into a relationship that we once had. I have never had a relationship with God before I got saved. So, I use the word conciliate which means to be made one with. We are now one with God through Christ. He that is joined to the Lord is one spirit. It is not that I was one with God in my past and I had to get in good standing with God, no I fell short of the glory of God and while I was helpless in sin, God conciliated me and saved me through Christ. We have been conciliated to God and that is our message to the world, Christ made it possible to be one with God.

Chapter 6

Paul is calling the church to work together with the Lord, cooperate and not receive the grace of God in vain. Cooperation with the Lord is the way to maintain a grace filled life.

2 Cor. 6:3-12 These verses are urging believers to live in a way that does not cause offense to others in order to uphold the credibility of their ministry. They are encouraged to display qualities such as endurance, patience, kindness, and genuine love in the face of afflictions, hardships, and distress. The verses also emphasize the importance of relying on the power of God and using the weapons of righteousness to navigate through challenges. Ultimately, believers are called to serve as representatives of God, demonstrating his truth and love in all they do.

The "weapons of righteousness for the right hand and the left" mentioned in these verses likely refer to spiritual weapons or tools that believers can use to uphold righteousness and defend against spiritual attacks or challenges. This imagery evokes the idea of being fully equipped and prepared to stand firm in the face of adversity. Perhaps the righteous weapons for the right and left hand may depict the sword of the Spirit, which Spirit is the word of God in the right hand and the shield of faith in the left hand. Our warfare is offensive and defensive. The word and faith are our weapons.

Paul now is going back to the original thought in chapter 5, 8we have courage, and are well pleased rather to be away from the home of the body, and to be at home with the Lord. 9Wherefore also we are ambitious, whether at home or away from home, to be well pleasing to him,[46] Remember the words endemeo (with the people) and ekdemeo (away from the people) translated by Young as "at home" and "away from home". Two houses, two peoples, two covenants. Paul was dealing with the Corinthian Jews about their compromise. This is why Paul mentioned that the Judgment seat of Christ will determine their compromise and how it will affect them. In chapter 6, 14 Do not be bound together with unbelievers; for what partnership have righteousness and lawlessness, or what fellowship has light with darkness?

---

[46] Young, R. (1997). *Young's Literal Translation* (2 Co 5:7–10). Logos Bible Software.

15 Or what harmony has Christ with Belial, or what has a believer in common with an unbeliever? 16 Or what agreement has the temple of God with idols? For we are the temple of the living God; just as God said, "I will dwell in them and walk among them; And I will be their God, and they shall be My people.17 "Therefore, come out from their midst and be separate," says the Lord. "And do not touch what is unclean; And I will welcome you. 18 "And I will be a father to you, And you shall be sons and daughters to Me," Says the Lord Almighty.[47] Paul is admonishing the Jewish Christians to break ties with the old covenant people.

The six contrasts Paul defines are remarkable because these are practical comparisons of what we need to have to make boundaries in our walk with the Lord. The physical temple in Jerusalem had become an idol, place of darkness, a den of thieves. It was a dead body and those that touched it became unclean. Paul is quoting the Old Testament verses from Exodus, Ezekiel and specifically Isaiah 52:11, Depart, depart, go out from there! Touch no unclean thing; go out from the midst of her, purify yourselves, you who carry the vessels of the LORD. Paul knew that to remain with the old covenant people that he would touch the dead carcass of Judaism and would be unclean. A reference to the book of Revelation, John in Rev. 18:4, says, "Come out of her My people". And he cried out with a mighty voice, saying, "Fallen, fallen is Babylon the great! She has become a dwelling place of demons and a prison of every unclean spirit, and a prison of every unclean and hateful bird.[48] God would receive them if they separated from old covenant Israel who rejected their Messiah. They would be His sons and daughters. There is so much more to share in this epistle and because of space I will prepare something for the future with a preterist and practical view of this epistle. Thank you!

Terry Kashian

---

[47] *New American Standard Bible, 1995 Edition: Paragraph Version* (2 Co 6:14–18). (1995). The Lockman Foundation.
[48] *New American Standard Bible: 1995 update* (Re 18:2). (1995). The Lockman Foundation.

2 Corinthians

Chapter 1

1. Paul, an apostle of Jesus Christ by the will of God, and Timothy our brother, to the Assembly of God which is at Corinth, with all the saints who are in all Achaia:
2. Grace be to you and peace from God our Father, and from the Lord Jesus Christ.
3. Blessed be God, even the Father of our Lord Jesus Christ, the Father of mercies, and the God of all comfort;
4. Who comforts us in all our tribulation, that we may be able to comfort those who are in any trouble, by the comfort with which we ourselves are comforted of God.
5. For as the sufferings of Christ abound in us, so our consolation also abounds by Christ.
6. Whether we are afflicted, it is for your consolation and salvation, which is effective in the enduring of the same sufferings which we also suffer: or whether we are comforted, it is for your consolation and salvation.
7. So, our hope of you is steadfast, knowing, that as you are partakers of the sufferings, so will you be also of the consolation.
8. For we would not, brothers, have you ignorant of our trouble which came to us in Asia, that we were burdened beyond measure, above strength, so that we despaired even of life:
9. But we had the sentence of death in ourselves, that we should not trust in ourselves, but in God which raises the dead:
10. Who delivered us from so great a death, and does deliver: in whom we trust that He will yet deliver us;
11. You also helping together by prayer for us, that for the gift granted to us by the means of many persons, thanks may be given by many on our behalf.
12. For our rejoicing is this, the testimony of our conscience, that in simplicity and godly sincerity, not with fleshly wisdom, but by the grace of God, we have had our conduct in the world, and more abundantly toward you.
13. For we write none other things to you, than what you read or acknowledge; and I trust you will acknowledge even to the end;
14. As also you have acknowledged us in part, that we are your rejoicing, even as you also are ours in the day of the Lord Jesus.
15. And in this confidence, I was minded to come to you before, that you might have a second benefit;
16. And to pass by you into Macedonia, and to come again out of Macedonia to you, and of you to be brought on my way toward Judea.
17. Therefore, when I was planning this, did I do it lightly? Or the things that I plan, do I plan according to the flesh, that with me there should be yes yes, and no no?
18. But as God is reliable, our word to you was not yes and no.
19. For the Son of God, Jesus Christ, who was preached among you by us, even by me and Silvanus and Timotheus, was not yes and no, but in Him was yes.

20. For all the promises of God in Him are yes, and because of Him Amen, to the glory of God through us.
21. Now He which establishes us with you in Christ, and has anointed us, is God;
22. Who has also sealed us, and given the guarantee of the Spirit in our hearts.
23. Moreover, I call God for a witness on my soul, that to spare you I came not as yet to Corinth.
24. Not for that we have dominion over your faith, but are helpers of your joy: for by faith you stand.

Chapter 2

1. But I determined this myself that I would not come to you again in sorrow.
2. For if I make you sad, who is he then that makes me glad, but the same which is made sad by me?
3. And I wrote this same to you, unless, when I came, I should have sadness from them of whom I should rejoice; having confidence in you all, that my joy is of you all.
4. For out of much affliction and anguish of heart I wrote to you with many tears; not that you should be sad, but that you might know the love which I have more abundantly to you.
5. But if any have caused sadness, he has not saddened me, but all of you to some extent: that I may not be too harsh.
6. Sufficient to such a man is this punishment, which was inflicted by the majority.
7. So that on the contrary you should rather forgive him, and comfort him, unless perhaps such a one should be swallowed up with too much sadness.
8. Therefore, I implore you that you would confirm your love toward him.
9. For to this end also I did write, that I might know the proof of you, whether you be obedient in all things.
10. To whom you forgive anything, I forgive also: for if I forgave anything, to whom I forgave it, for your sakes I forgave it in the person of Christ;
11. Unless Satan should get an advantage over us: for we are not ignorant of his devices.
12. Furthermore, when I came to Troas to preach Christ's gospel, and a door was opened to me of the Lord,
13. I had no rest in my spirit, because I did not find Titus my brother: but taking my leave of them, I went from there into Macedonia.
14. Now thanks be to God, which always causes us to triumph in Christ, and makes manifest the fragrance of His knowledge in us in every place.
15. For we are to God a sweet fragrance of Christ, in them that are saved, and in them that perish:
16. To the one we are the aroma of death to death; and to the other the aroma of life to life. And who is sufficient for these things?
17. For we are not as many, which corrupt the word of God: but as of sincerity, but as of God, in the sight of God we speak in Christ.

Chapter 3

1. Do we begin again to commend ourselves? Or need we, as some others, letters of commendation to you, or letters of commendation from you?
2. You are our letter written in our hearts, known and read of all men:
3. Since as you are manifestly declared to be the letter of Christ ministered by us, written not with ink, but with the Spirit of the living God; not in tables of stone, but in fleshy tables of the heart.
4. And such trust have we through Christ toward God:
5. Not that we are sufficient of ourselves to think anything as of ourselves; but our sufficiency is of God;
6. Who also has made us capable ministers of the New Covenant; not of the letter, but of the Spirit: for the letter kills, but the Spirit gives life.
7. But if the ministry of death, written and engraved on stones, was glorious, so that the children of Israel could not steadfastly behold the face of Moses for the glory of his countenance; which glory is passing away:
8. How the ministry of the Spirit will be in glory?
9. For if the ministry of condemnation had glory, how much more does the ministry of righteousness exceed in glory?
10. For even that which was made glorious had no glory in this respect, because of the glory that surpasses.
11. For if what is being done away was with glory, then what remains is in glory.
12. Seeing then that we have such hope, we use great boldness of speech:
13. And not as Moses, who put a veil over his face, so that the children of Israel could not look steadily at the end of what is being done away:
14. But their minds were blinded: for until this day remains the same veil unlifted in the reading of the Old Testament; which veil is done away in Christ.
15. But even to this day, when Moses is read, the veil is on their heart.
16. Nevertheless, when one turns to the Lord, the veil is taken away.
17. Moreover, the Lord is the Spirit: and where the Spirit of the Lord is, there is freedom.
18. But we all, with open face beholding as in a glass the glory of the Lord, are changed into the same image from glory to glory, just as from the Lord Spirit.

Chapter 4

1. Therefore, seeing we have this ministry, as we have received mercy, we do not lose heart;
2. But have renounced the hidden things of dishonesty, not walking in craftiness, nor handling the word of God deceitfully; but by manifestation of the truth commending ourselves to every man's conscience in the sight of God.
3. But if our gospel be veiled, it is veiled to them that are lost:

2 Corinthians 4:4

4. In whom the God of this age has blinded the minds of those who believe not, unless the light of the glorious gospel of Christ, who is the image of God, should make them see clearly.

5. For we preach not ourselves, but Christ Jesus the Lord; and ourselves your servants for Jesus' sake.

6. For God, who commanded the light to shine out of darkness, has shined in our hearts, to give the light of the knowledge of the glory of God in the face of Jesus Christ.

7. But we have this treasure in earthen vessels, that the excellency of the power may be of God, and not of us.

8. We are troubled on every side, yet not distressed; we are perplexed, but not in despair;

9. Persecuted, but not forsaken; cast down, but not destroyed;

10. Always bearing about in the body the dying of the Lord Jesus, that the life also of Jesus might be made manifest in our body.

11. For we which live are always delivered to death for Jesus' sake, that the life also of Jesus might be made manifest in our mortal flesh.

12. So, then death works in us, but life in you.

13. Now we having the same spirit of faith, according as it is writen, I believed, and therefore have I spoken; we also believe, and therefore speak;

14. Knowing that He which raised up the Lord Jesus will raise up us also by Jesus, and will present us with you.

15. For all things are for your sakes that the abundant grace might through the thanksgiving of many abound to the glory of God.

16. For which reason we do not lose heart; but though our outward man perish, yet the inward man is renewed daily.

17. For our light affliction, which is but for a moment, works for us a far more exceedingly and eternal weight of glory;

18. While we look not at the things which are seen, but at the things which are not seen: for the things which are seen are temporary; but the things which are not seen are perpetual.

Chapter 5

1. For we know that if our earthly house of this tabernacle be dissolved, we have a building of God, a house not made with hands, perpetual in the heavens.

2. For in this we are groaning, desiring to put on our dwelling place which is out of the heavens:

3. Whether in fact after we have put it on we will not be found naked.

4. For we that are in this tabernacle do groan, being burdened: not that we want to be unclothed, but to put on so that the mortality may be consumed by life.

5. Now He that has prepared us for the very same thing is God, who also has given to us the guarantee of the Spirit.

6. Therefore, being courageous always, seeing that, while we are among our own people in the body, earthly house, we are away from the New Covenant people of the Lord:

2 Corinthians 5:7

7. For we walk by faith, not by sight:
8. We are confident, I say, and wanting more to be away from my own people among the body, earthly house, and to be among the people of the Lord.
9. Therefore, we are ambitious, that, whether being among my own people or away, we may be well-pleasing to Him.
10. For we must all appear before the judgment seat of Christ; that everyone may receive the things done in the body, according to what he has done, whether it be good or evil.
11. Knowing therefore the fear of the Lord, we persuade men; but we are made manifest to God; and I trust also are made manifest in your consciences.
12. For we commend not ourselves again to you, but give you occasion to glory on our behalf, that you may have something to answer those who glory in appearance, and not in heart.
13. For whether we are beside ourselves, it is to God: or whether we are alert, it is for your cause.
14. For the love of Christ constrains us; because we thus judge, that if one died for all, then we are all dead:
15. And that He died for all, that they which live should not after this live to themselves, but to Him which died for them, and rose again.
16. Therefore, from now on, we regard no man according to the flesh: yes, even though we have known Christ after the flesh, yet now we know Him thus no more.
17. Therefore, if anyone is in Christ, there is a new creation: the old has come to an end; behold, all things are new.

18. And all is out from God, who has conciliated us to Himself by Jesus Christ, and has given to us the ministry of conciliation;
19. That is, that God was in Christ, conciliating the world to Himself, not counting their trespasses to them; and has placed in us the Word of conciliation.
20. Now then we are ambassadors for Christ, as though God did implore you through us: we plead with you in Christ's place, be conciliated to God!
21. For He has made Him to be sin for us, who knew no sin; that we might be made the righteousness of God in Him.

Chapter 6

1. We then, as workers together with Him, implore you also that you receive not the grace of God in vain.
2. For He says, I have heard you in an acceptable time, and in the day of salvation have I heard you: behold, now is the acceptable time; behold, now is the day of salvation.
3. Giving no offense in anything, that the ministry be not blamed:
4. But in all things approving ourselves as the ministers of God, in much patience, in afflictions, in necessities, in distresses,
5. In stripes, in imprisonments, in tumults, in labors, in watching's, in fasts;
6. By pureness, by knowledge, by longsuffering, by kindness, by the Holy Spirit, by love unfeigned,
7. By the word of truth, by the power of God, by the armor of righteousness on the right hand and on the left,

8. By honor and dishonor, by evil report and good report: as deceivers, and yet true;
9. As unknown, and yet well known; as dying, and, behold, we live; as disciplined, and not put to death;
10. As sorrowful, yet always rejoicing; as poor, yet making many rich; as having nothing, and yet possessing all things.
11. O you Corinthians, our mouth is open to you, our heart is enlarged.
12. You are not restricted in us, but you are restricted in your own affections.
13. Now for the same reward, (I speak as to my children), you be open too.
14. Be not unequally yoked together with unbelievers: for what fellowship has righteousness with unrighteousness? And what communion has light with darkness?
15. And what fellowship has Christ with Belial? Or what part has he that believes with an unbeliever?
16. And what agreement has the temple of God with idols? For you are the temple of the living God; as God has said, I will dwell in them, and walk in them; and I will be their God, and they will be My people.
17. Therefore, come out from among them, and be separate, says the Lord, and touch not the unclean thing; and I will receive you.
18. And will be a Father to you, and you will be My sons and daughters, says the Lord Almighty.

Chapter 7

1. Having therefore these promises, dearly beloved, let us cleanse ourselves from all filthiness of the flesh and spirit, maturing holiness in the fear of God.
2. Receive us; we have wronged no man, we have corrupted no man, we have defrauded no man.
3. I speak not this to condemn you: for I have said before, that you are in our hearts to die and live with you.
4. Great is my boldness of speech toward you, great is my glorying of you: I am filled with comfort, I am exceedingly joyful in all our tribulation.
5. For, when we had come into Macedonia, our flesh had no rest, but we were troubled on every side; outside were conflicts, within were fears.
6. Nevertheless God, that comforts those that are cast down, comforted us in the presence of Titus;
7. And not by his presence only, but by the consolation with which he was comforted in you, when he told us your sincere desire, your mourning, your zeal toward me; so that I rejoiced the more.
8. For though I made you sorry with a letter, I do not repent, though I did repent: for I perceive that the same letter has made you sorry, though it were but for a season.
9. Now I rejoice, not that you were made sorry, but that you sorrowed to repentance: for you were made sorry after a godly manner, that you might receive damage by us in nothing.
10. For godly sorrow works repentance to salvation not to be repented of: but the sorrow of the world works death.

11. For behold this very same thing, that you sorrowed after a godly sort, what diligence it brought in you, yes, what introspection, yes, what indignation, yes, what fear, yes, what vehement desire, yes, what zeal, yes, what vindication! In all things you have approved yourselves to be clear in this matter.
12. Therefore, though I wrote to you, I did it not for his reason that had done the wrong, nor for his reason that suffered wrong, but that our care for you in the sight of God might appear to you.
13. Therefore, we were comforted in your comfort: yes, and exceedingly the more we rejoiced for the joy of Titus, because his spirit was refreshed by you all.
14. For if I have boasted anything to him of you, I am not ashamed; but as we spoke all things to you in truth, even so our boasting, which I made before Titus, is found a truth.
15. And his inward affection is more abundant toward you, while he remembers the obedience of you all, how with fear and trembling you received him.
16. I rejoice therefore that I have confidence in you in all things.

Chapter 8

1. Moreover, brothers, we do you to know of the grace of God bestowed on the Assemblies of Macedonia;
2. That in a great trial of affliction the abundance of their joy and their deep poverty abounded to the riches of their generosity.
3. For to their ability, I bear record, yes, and beyond their ability they were willing of themselves;
4. Praying us with much entreaty that we would receive the gift, and take on us the fellowship of the ministering to the saints.
5. And this they did, not as we hoped, but first gave their own selves to the Lord, and to us by the will of God.
6. So that we desired Titus, that as he had begun, so he would also finish in you the same grace also.
7. Therefore, as you abound in everything, in faith, and speech, and knowledge, and in all diligence, and in your love to us, see that you abound in this grace also.
8. I speak not by commandment, but by occasion of the forwardness of others, and to prove the sincerity of your love.
9. For you know the grace of our Lord Jesus Christ, that, though He was rich, yet for your sakes He became poor, that you through His poverty might be rich.
10. And in this I give my advice: for this is expedient for you, who have begun before, not only to do, but also to be forward a year ago.
11. Now therefore perform the doing of it; that as there was a readiness to will, so there may be a performance also out of that which you have.
12. For if there be first a willing mind, it is accepted according to that a man has, and not according to that he has not.
13. For I mean not that other men be eased, and you burdened:

14. But by an equality, that now at this time your abundance may be a supply for their want, that their abundance also may be a supply for your want: that there may be equality:
15. As it is written, he that had gathered much had nothing over; and he that had gathered little had no lack.
16. But thanks be to God, which put the same sincere care into the heart of Titus for you.
17. For indeed he accepted the exhortation; but being more forward, of his own accord he went to you.
18. And we have sent with him the brother, whose praise is in the gospel throughout all the Assemblies;
19. And not that only, but who was also chosen of the Assemblies to travel with us with this grace, which is administered by us to the glory of the same Lord, and declaration of your alacrity:
20. Avoiding this, that no man should blame us in this abundance which is administered by us:
21. Providing for honest things, not only in the sight of the Lord, but also in the sight of men.
22. And we have sent with them our brother, who we have often times proved diligent in many things, but now much more diligent, on the great confidence which I have in you.
23. Whether any do inquire of Titus, he is my partner and fellow helper concerning you: or our brothers be inquired of, they are the apostles of the Assemblies, and the glory of Christ.
24. Therefore, show to them, and to the Assemblies, the proof of your love, and of our boasting on your behalf.

Chapter 9

1. For as concerning the ministering to the saints, it is superfluous for me to write to you:
2. For I know your willingness, for which I boast of you to them of Macedonia, that Achaia was ready a year ago; and your zeal has provoked very many.
3. Yet have I sent the brothers, unless our boasting of you should be in vain in this behalf; that, as I said, you may be ready:
4. Unless if they of Macedonia come with me, and find you unprepared, we (not to mention you) should be ashamed in this same confident boasting.
5. Therefore, I thought it necessary to exhort the brothers that they would go before to you, and prepare your generous gift, of which you had prior notice, that the same might be ready, as a matter of generosity, and not as a grudging obligation.
6. But this I say, he which sows sparingly will reap also sparingly; and he which sows bountifully will reap also bountifully.
7. Every man according as he purposes in his heart, so let him give; not as a grudging obligation: for God loves a cheerful giver.
8. And God is able to make all grace abound toward you; that you, always having all sufficiency in all things, may abound to every good work:

9. As it is written, he has dispersed abroad; he has given to the poor: his righteousness remains forever.
10. Now he that ministers seed to the sower both minister bread for your food, and multiply your seed sown, and increase the fruits of your righteousness;
11. Being enriched in everything to all bountifulness, which causes through us thanksgiving to God.
12. For the administration of this service not only supplies the need of the saints, but is abundant also by many thanksgivings to God;
13. While by the experiment of this ministry they glorify God for your professed obedience to the gospel of Christ, and for your free distribution to them, and to all men;
14. And by their prayer for you, which long after you for the exceedingly grace of God in you.
15. Thanks be to God for His unspeakable gift.

Chapter 10

1. Now I Paul myself implore you by the meekness and gentleness of Christ, who in presence am humble among you, but being absent am bold toward you:
2. But I implore you, that I may not be bold when I am present with that confidence, with which I think to be bold against some, which think of us as if we walked according to the flesh.
3. For though we walk in the flesh, we do not war after the flesh:
4. For the weapons of our warfare are not fleshly, but mighty through God to the pulling down of strong holds;
5. Casting down arguments, and every high thing that exalts itself against the knowledge of God, and bringing into captivity every thought to the obedience of Christ;
6. And being ready to punish all disobedience, when your obedience is fulfilled.
7. Do you look on things after the outward appearance? If any man is persuaded himself that he is Christ's, let him be reminded of this again, that, as he is Christ's, even so are we Christ's.
8. For though I should boast somewhat more of our authority, which the Lord has given us for building up, and not for demolition, I will not be ashamed:
9. That I may not seem like I would terrify you by my letters.
10. For his letters, they say, are severe and strong; but his bodily presence is weak, and his speech despicable.
11. Let such a one think this that, such as we are in word by letters when we are absent, likewise we will also be in deed when we are present.
12. For we dare not classify ourselves, or compare ourselves with some that approve themselves: but they measure themselves between themselves, and comparing themselves among themselves, are not understanding.
13. But we will not take pride in things immeasurable, but according to the measure of the standard which God has assigned to us, a standard to reach even to you.

14. For we did not over extend ourselves beyond our measure, as though we did not reach you: for we have come as far as you, also in preaching the gospel of Christ:

15. Not taking pride in things beyond measure, that is, of other men's labors; but having hope, when your faith is increasing abundantly, then we will be enlarged in you according to our assignment,

16. To preach the gospel in the regions beyond you, and not to take pride in another man's assignment.

17. But he that takes pride, let him take pride in the Lord.

18. For not he that approves himself is approved, but who the Lord approves.

Chapter 11

1. Would to God you could put up with me a little folly: and indeed, put up with me.

2. For I am jealous over you with godly jealousy: for I have betrothed you to one husband that I may present you as a pure virgin to Christ.

3. But I fear, unless by any means, as the serpent beguiled Eve through his trickery, so your minds should be corrupted from the simplicity that is in Christ.

4. For if he that comes preaches another Jesus, whom we have not preached, or if you receive another spirit, which you have not received, or another gospel, which you have not accepted, you might well put up with him.

5. For I suppose I was not inferior to the very chief apostles.

6. But though I am unskilled in speech, yet not in knowledge; but we have been thoroughly made manifest among you in all things.

7. Have I committed an offense in humbling myself that you might be exalted, because I have preached to you the gospel of God freely?

8. I robbed other Assemblies, taking wages of them, to serve you.

9. And when I was present with you, and lacked, I was not burdensome to anyone: for that which I was lacking the brothers which came from Macedonia. Supplied: and in all things I have kept myself from being a burden to you, and so I will be vigilant with myself.

10. As the reality of Christ is in me, no one will stop me from boasting in the regions of Achaia.

11. Why? Because I do not love you? God knows.

12. But what I do, that I will do, that I may cut off an opportunity from those who desire an opportunity; that in which they take pride in, they may be found just as we.

13. For such are false apostles, deceitful workers, masquerading themselves into the apostles of Christ.

14. And no marvel; for Satan himself is masquerading into an angel of light.

15. Therefore, it is no great thing if his ministers also are masquerading as the ministers of righteousness; whose end will be according to their works.

16. I say again, let no one think that I a fool; if otherwise, yet as a fool receive me that I may brag myself a little.

17. That which I speak, I speak it not after the Lord, but as it were foolishly, in this confidence of bragging.
18. Seeing that many take pride according to the flesh, I will brag also.
19. For you tolerate fools gladly, seeing you yourselves are wise.
20. For you tolerate, if someone brings you into bondage, if someone devours you, if someone takes from you, if someone exalts himself, if someone strikes you on the face.
21. To our shame I say that we were too weak for that. But in whatever anyone is bold, I speak foolishly, I am bold also.
22. Are they Hebrews? So am I. Are they Israelites? So am I. Are they the seed of Abraham? So am I.
23. Are they ministers of Christ? I speak as a fool - I am more; in labors more abundant, in stripes above measure, in prisons more frequent, in deaths often.
24. Of the Jews five times I received I forty lashes less one.
25. Three times was I beaten with rods, once was I stoned, three times I suffered shipwreck, a night and a day I have been in the deep sea;
26. In journeying often, in perils of waters, in perils of robbers, in perils by my own countrymen, in perils by the nations, in perils in the city, in perils in the wilderness, in perils in the sea, in perils among false brothers;
27. In weariness and painfulness, in sleeplessness often, in hunger and thirst, in fasting often, in cold and nakedness.
28. Beside those things that are external, that daily pressure, the anxiety for all the Assemblies.
29. Who is weak, and I am not weak? Who is stumbled, and I not burn with distress?
30. If I have a need to brag, I will brag concerning my weaknesses.
31. The God and Father of our Lord Jesus Christ, who is blessed into the New Covenant Age, knows that I lie not.
32. In Damascus the governor under Aretas the king kept the city of the Damascenes with a garrison, desirous to apprehend me:
33. And through a window in a basket was I let down by the wall, and escaped his hands.

Chapter 12

1. It is not expedient for me doubtless to glory. I will come to visions and revelations of the Lord.
2. I know such a man in Christ above fourteen years ago, (whether in the body, I cannot tell; or whether out of the body, I cannot tell; God knows) such a one was seized to the third heaven.
3. And I know such a man (whether in the body, or out of the body, I cannot tell; God knows)
4. That he was seized into paradise, and heard unspeakable words, which it is not allowed for anyone to speak.
5. Of such a one will I boast: yet of myself I will not brag, but in my weaknesses.
6. For though I would desire to boast, I will not be a fool; for I will say the truth: but now I hold back, unless anyone should think of me above that which he sees me to be, or that he hears of me.

2 Corinthians 12:7

7. And unless I should be exalted above measure through the abundance of the revelations, there was given to me a thorn in the flesh, the messenger of Satan to abuse me, unless I should be exalted above measure.
8. For this thing I asked the Lord three times, that it might depart from me.
9. Yet He said to me, My grace is adequate for you: for My strength is made complete in weakness. Most gladly therefore will I rather brag of my weaknesses, that the power of Christ may tabernacle over me.
10. Therefore, I take pleasure in weaknesses, in reproaches, in necessities, in persecutions, in distresses for Christ's sake: for when I am weak, then am I am powerful.
11. I have become a fool in bragging; you forced me: for I should have been approved by you: because in nothing am I inferior to the preeminent apostles, though I am nobody.
12. Truly the signs of an apostle were performed thoroughly in you in all patience, in signs, and wonders, and miracles.
13. For what is it in which you were inferior to other Assemblies, except it be that I myself was not burdensome to you? Forgive me this wrong.
14. Behold, the third time I am ready to come to you; and I will not be burdensome to you: for I am not seeking from you, but you yourselves; for the children should not lay up for the parents, but the parents for the children.
15. And I will very gladly spend and be entirely spent for you; even though the more abundantly I love you, the less I am loved.
16. On the other hand, let it be so, I did not burden you: nevertheless, being cunning, I caught you with deceit.
17. Did I covet from you by any of them whom I sent to you?
18. I desired Titus, and with him I sent a brother. Did Titus covet from you? Did we not walk in the same spirit? Did we not walk in the same steps?
19. Again, do you think that we are defending ourselves to you? We speak before God in Christ: but we do all things, dearly beloved, for your building up.
20. For I fear, unless, when I come, I will not find you such as I desire, and that I will be found to you such as you not desire: unless there be strife, envying, outbursts of anger, cliques, slanderers, gossipers, puffed up with pride, anarchy:
21. And unless, when I come again, my God will humble me among you, and that I will mourn for many who have sinned already, and have not repented of the uncleanness and sexual immorality and lasciviousness which they have committed.

Chapter 13

1. This is the third time I am coming to you. In the mouth of two or three witnesses every word will be confirmed.
2. I told you before, and foretell you, as if I were present, the second time; and being absent now I write to those who have sinned before, and to all others, that, if I come again, I will not spare:

3. Since you seek a proof of Christ speaking in me, which toward you is not weak, but is powerful in you.

4. For though He was crucified through weakness, yet He lives by the power of God. For we also are weak in Him, but we will live with Him by the power of God toward you.

5. Investigate yourselves, whether you are in the faith; test yourselves. Do you not fully know yourselves that Jesus Christ is in you, unless you are unapproved?

6. But I trust that you will know that we are not unapproved.

7. Now I pray to God that you do no evil; not that we should shine as sterling, but that you should do that which is honest, though we may seem unapproved.

8. For we have no power against the reality, but for the reality.

9. For we are glad, when we are weak, and you are powerful: and this also we pray, even your completion.

10. Therefore, I write these things being absent, unless being present I should act with harshness, according to the power which the Lord has given me for building up, and not to demolition.

11. Finally, brothers, farewell. Be restored, be of good comfort, think the same thing, live in peace; and the God of love and peace will be with you.

12. Greet one another with a holy kiss.

13. All the saints greet you.

14. The grace of the Lord Jesus Christ, and the love of God, and the imparting participation of the Holy Spirit, be in the midst of you all. Amen.

Galatians Commentary

The epistle to the Galatians is a letter written by Paul, an apostle by Jesus Christ (Galatians 1:1), to the churches in the region of Galatia. There were four city churches in this region, Lystra, Derbe, Iconium, and Antioch Pisidia (Acts 14:6-8,21), which Paul had ministered to during his missionary journey. Paul's sole concern for the Galatian churches was in regard to the influence of the Old Covenant Law being taught (Galatians 1:6-9) to them as something to live under, rather than living under the grace of God, through the rule of the Spirit of God. They are corrected strongly by Paul, "This is the only thing I want to find out from you: did you receive the Spirit by the works of the Law, or by hearing with faith? Are you so foolish? Having begun by the Spirit, are you now being perfected by the flesh? Did you suffer so many things in vain — if indeed it was in vain (Galatians 3:2-4)?"

We must understand that the façade of the flesh was coming to the Galatians in the form of "religious flesh", the Judaizers. Paul's solution to their error was simply for them to walk according to the Spirit as Paul states, "But I say, walk in the Spirit, and you will not carry out the desires of the flesh (Galatians 5:16-17)."

In Acts 14:8-10, where we read, "and there sat a certain man at Lystra, impotent in his feet, being a cripple from his mother's womb, who never had walked: the same heard Paul speak: who steadfastly beholding him, perceiving that he had faith to be healed, said with a loud voice stand upright on thy feet. And he leaped and walked." In Galatia here, Paul said with a loud voice, (The hearing of faith), "stand upright on thy feet. And he leaped and walked (working miracles among the Galatians, and empowering one of them to walk, one who never had walked)." This first miracle in Lystra was a picture of the true condition of man in Lystra and universally. This was the problem with the Law; it didn't empower one to walk with God. It is only by the hearing of faith, not by the works of the Law (Galatians 3:5), which enables one to do so. No one is ever empowered to walk with God, except through a miracle of God!

We see this same theme in the phrase, "from his mother's womb" here in Acts 14:8. It is also in Galatians 1:16 when Paul says, "but when it pleased God, who separated me from my mother's womb, and called me by His grace, to reveal His Son in me, that I might preach Him among the heathen; immediately I conferred not with flesh and blood." It was an act of the grace of God, planned from his mother's womb, which intervened to cause both Paul and the crippled man in Galatia to walk by the grace and power of God. The picture becomes clear in this portion of scripture that one's natural birth could never allow one to walk with God. The natural birth produces one who is spiritually crippled. Only after an encounter with the grace and power of God, could one ever walk with God.

The natural birth is not enough, one has to be born again (John 3:3), from the mother of us all (Galatians 4:26), the Lamb's wife (Revelation 21:9), the church. Yes the church produces children, which are born from above (John 3:3), not by entering a second time into his mother's womb (John 3:4), but by being born of the Spirit (John 3:6, 8). The church proclaims the word of God, verbally, or in written form (John 17:20), and she gives birth. Being born again, not of corruptible seed (natural birth), but of incorruptible, by the word of God, which lives and abides forever (1 Peter 1:23). Psalm 87 communicates this clearly, "Zion … O city of God" (Psalm 87:2-3, Hebrews 12:22, Galatians 4:26), "and of Zion it will be said, "This one and that one were born in her; and the Most High Himself shall establish her." The Lord will record, when He registers the peoples: "this one was born there (Psalm 87:5-6)."

It truly takes an act of God in order for one to rise from their crippled state and walk with God. We see this with the man who was crippled for 38 years, where he was not able to lift himself up, and only Jesus was willing and able to do so for him (John 5:1-9). This was the problem with the Law. One could not walk with God, in the promises of God. Even Moses, the representative of the Law, could not even walk into the Promised Land, but was of that generation that had to die off (the first generation of the Law, with no faith), and be replaced with a new generation (the second generation and faith) with Joshua (Yeshua). It is not a coincidence that it took 38 years (Deuteronomy 2:14) in the wilderness of not walking with God until a new generation in Israel rose up in faith and entered into the promises of God. Only a remnant endured through faith, Joshua and Caleb. It is the same in the transition period, approximately 40 years (the crucifixion until AD 70), one generation's faith was tested (Matthew 24:9,13,21; Acts 14:22; Hebrews 3:19-4:11;12:25-26), and only a scarce number would endure and persevere (Matthew 10:22,34) through faith, "… when the Son of man cometh, shall he find the faith on the land (Luke 18:1- 8)"? There was a great falling away in that generation, led by the Jewish zealots (2 Thessalonians 2:3,4; Hebrews 6:6), which involved a deception of confessing Christians turning from the faith in order to go back to the Old Covenant, and even back to its practice of animal sacrifices in the temple. The Galatian churches had been bewitched, (Galatians 3:1), with this same influence as they were returning to the Old Covenant practices (Galatians 1:6; 2:4, 18, 21; 4:9-11; 5:1).

There was such peer pressure in Galatia that even Peter and Barnabas had to be corrected from its influence (Galatians 2:11-16). Peter, "… withdrew and separated himself, insomuch that Barnabas also was carried away (think of being carried away into Babylonian bondage, Babylon, that great city, Jerusalem, Revelation 11:8; 14:8; Galatians 4:25) with their dissimulation". The word withdrew (Greek, hupostello: to withdraw, shrink from declaring, with "stello" (Strongs, 4724) meaning to haul down, lower, referring to a sail, to contract, thus not able to be moved by the wind of the Spirit, John 3:8) is very fitting here. Here is another resource for this Greek word, (Strongs,5288) hupostello, "to draw back, withdraw," perhaps a metaphor from lowering a sail and so slackening the course, and hence of being remiss in holding the reality; in the active voice, rendered "drew back" in Galatians 2:12 (from Vine's Expository Dictionary of Biblical Words, it is the same word used in Hebrews where the exhortation was toward faith in the unseen, and away from the visible things of the Old Covenant. Now the just shall live by faith: but if any man draw back (hupostello), My soul shall have no pleasure in him. But we are not of them who draw back unto perdition, but of them that believe to the saving of the soul. Now faith is the substance of things hoped for, the evidence of things not seen (Hebrews 10:38-11:1).

The challenge was to not withdraw and shrink back into the shadows of the Law. It took revelation and the faith of God to declare those shadows as fulfilled in Christ. The Hebrew Christians were to, "hold fast the profession of our faith without wavering; (for He is faithful that promised) … as ye see that day approaching (Hebrews 10:23-25)." Faith was what was required (Luke 18:8) to prevent shrinking back and declaring Jesus' name and words. The Lord says, "whosoever therefore shall be ashamed of Me and of My words in this adulteress and sinful generation; of him also shall the Son of man be ashamed, when He cometh in the glory of His Father with the holy angels (Mark 8:38). The very next verse tells us that this coming with the glory of His Father and the angels would occur in the lifetime of these first century disciples, "and He said unto them, Verily I say unto you, … there are some that stand here, which shall not taste of death, till they have seen the kingdom of God come with power (Mark 9:1; Matthew 16:27-28)." This was not fulfilled in the following verse through the transfiguration, which was only six days later. In that amount of time not one of the twelve disciples had died, and Christ did not reward every man according to their works on the mount of transfiguration (Matthew 16:27)! This same evil influence may have even affected Paul, where we read in Acts 16:1-3, "Then he came to Derbe and Lystra. And behold, a certain disciple was there, named Timothy, the son of a certain Jewish woman who believed, but his father was Greek.

He was well-spoken of by the brothers who were at Lystra and Iconium. Paul wanted to have him go on with him. And he took him and circumcised him because of the Jews who were in that region, for they all knew that his father was Greek." This action by Paul in his early ministry was corrected by the Lord Jesus when he says, "for in Christ Jesus neither circumcision nor uncircumcision avails anything, but faith working through love (Galatians 5:6). He states it again in Galatians 6:15, "For in Christ Jesus neither circumcision nor uncircumcision avails anything, but a new creation." Perhaps Paul was attempting to simply become as a Jew that he might gain the Jews; to them that are under the Law that he might gain them that are under the Law (1 Corinthians 9:20). When Paul circumcised Timothy, this created a problem down the road for him. When he emphasized something other than

Christ in order to have a normal Christian life. Paul's revelation was developing, and he was understanding better that it is "faith in the working of Christ in order to have a normal Christian life. Paul s revelation that it is faith working through love" in a "new creation" that is the reality. He then considers circumcision to be as nothing and only the new creation in the New Covenant nation as something (Galatians 2:3, 4:24- 26, 6:15- 16). Nevertheless, the pressure was overwhelming to conform to the age, the Old Covenant age. An age which Galatians 1:4 refers to as an "evil age", "… that He might deliver us from this present evil age". It was an evil and adulterous generation, which was to be condemned shortly for its lack of faith and disobedience. (Matthew 3:7-10; 12:39- 42; 23:36; 24:34, Luke 18:8). Destruction (desolation) was about to be poured out upon that age which had chosen the broad way (Matthew 7:13-14), as opposed to the narrow way, a persecuted way, which leads to life. Relatively speaking, few were choosing the latter.

This was the struggle the Galatian churches were facing. So quickly had they gone back, fallen from grace (Galatians 5:4, same idea as fallen away, 2 Thessalonians 2:3, Hebrews 6:6, 10:38), and were, "…so soon removed from Him that called you into the grace of Christ unto another gospel (Galatians 1:6)." The Greek word for removed here is, metatithemi, which means to transfer, to change one's place, one thing that is put in the place of another, to fall away to desert from one person or thing to another. In Galatians 1:6, "I marvel that ye are … removing," RV (not as KJV, "removed"); the present tense suggests that the abandonment of the Galatian believers from the reality was not yet complete, but they were gradually being infected with a crippling disease unless they returned to the faith alone and the Spirit. The middle voice specifies that the believers themselves were liable for their deterioration, rather than the Judaizers who had influenced them. We can see how a believer can be healed and set free and then fall back into bad and unhealthy habits of dieting on the Law and regulations. Their self-righteousness or condemnation affects their lives, and they contract a disease spiritually, a crippling disease that prevents them from being able to walk. The corrupting influence of the leaven of legalism cannot empower one to walk with God. (Galatians 5:9). Herein lies the problem, the Old Covenant Law. The Law only revealed emphatically that one cannot walk with God because men are sinners, "wherefore the Law was our school master to bring us to Christ, that we might be justified by faith (Galatians 3:24)."

Adam being under the law, one law, "… thou shalt not eat from the tree of the knowledge of good and evil" (Genesis 2:17, Hosea 6:7), is never portrayed as walking with God. In fact, only God did the walking in that day and Adam hid from God and then blamed everyone else, including God, for his shortcomings. Adam was a spiritual cripple and could not walk with God because he was the natural man. But the natural (soulish) man received not the things of the Spirit of God: for they are foolishness unto him: neither can he know them, because they are spiritually discerned. (1 Corinthians 2:14). It wasn't until men began to call upon the name of the Lord in faith (Genesis 4:26), that we read of Enoch walking with

God (Genesis 5:24)! Noah walked with God (Genesis. 6:9). And he blessed Joseph, and said: "God, before whom my fathers, Abraham and Isaac walked (Genesis. 48:15)."

The Galatians were coming under the influence of the present evil age, which was connected to the Law, and none would be justified by the works of the Law, but by the faith of Jesus Christ, even we have believed in Jesus Christ, that we might be justified by the faith of Christ, and not by the works of the Law: for by the works of the Law shall no flesh be justified (Galatians 2:16). Christ is become of no effect unto you, whosoever of you are justified by the Law; you are fallen from grace (Galatians 5:4). The word fallen here is also used in Mark 13:25 of stars falling from the heavens. As a believer is saved and justified by faith they are like stars set in the firmament (Daniel 12:3; Matthew 5:14; 13:43, Philippians 2:15) to testify of God's grace to this dark world by holding forth the word of life. Paul says in Philippians, "that you may become blameless and harmless, children of God without fault in the midst of a crooked and perverse generation, among whom you shine as lights (a luminary, a star) in the world, holding forth the word of life, so that I may rejoice in the day of Christ that I have not run in vain or labored in vain … (Philippians 2:15-16)." Even Peter, and those with him, had come under the influence, the leaven of that evil age (Old Covenant Age) as they, "walked not uprightly according to the reality of the gospel (Galatians 2:14)." Paul had the serum to vaccinate Peter and those who were being infected, and he rebuked Peter to his face and was, in effect, saying to him, "take your medicine and don't allow what you have to spread to the others." Paul was not going to stand by and let Peter, or anyone, build a wall of partition between the Jews and the Gentiles. The Law builds that wall, while the gospel tears it down and makes us one (Ephesians 2:12-14). Death is separation and division, while life is found in union and oneness.

Those who live according to that evil age (Galatians 1:4) were seeking to build again matters of the Old Covenant age in the hearts and minds of Christians. Paul said, "For if I build again the things which I destroyed, I make myself a transgressor (Galatians 2:18)." The Law puts us to death as it is the ministry of death, it receives its ransom through Jesus' death, and we in turn partake of Jesus' death (2 Corinthians 3:7). For as many as are of the works of the Law are under the curse: for it is written, cursed is everyone that continues not in all things which are written in the book of the Law to do them (Galatians 3:10). The criterion for being under the Law is to do all of the Law, not just some of it. No one can do all the Law; therefore, all fall short of the glory of God and are lawbreakers (Romans 3:23). Christ has redeemed us from the curse of the Law, having become a curse for us (for it is written, "cursed is everyone who hangs on a tree … (Galatians 3:13)." We are faced with true opposites and the battle in the Christian life is between the Law and the gospel. Then we have the works of the Law versus grace and faith. Paul is saying to choose the blessing over the curse, "… that the blessing of Abraham might come upon the Gentiles in Christ Jesus, that we might receive the promise of the Spirit through faith (Galatians 3:14). Ultimately, we have the choice to walk according to the flesh or according to the Spirit. But when the fullness of the time had come, God sent forth His Son, born of a woman, born under the Law, to redeem those who were under the Law, that we might receive the adoption as sons. (Galatians 4:4). Christ fulfilled the Law (Matthew 5:17-18), and now dwells in us (Galatians 4:19), that the righteousness of the Law might be fulfilled IN US (not by us), who walk not after the flesh, but after the Spirit (Romans 8:4). We who come short of the glory of God (Romans 3:23), now have Christ in us, the hope of glory (Colossians 1:27)! Therefore, "For through the Law I died to the Law, that I might live to God. I have been crucified with Christ; it is no longer I who live; but Christ lives in me: and the life which I now live in the flesh I live by the faith of the Son of God, who loved me and gave Himself up for me (Galatians 2:19-20)."

"What purpose then does the Law serve? It was added because of transgressions, till the seed should come to whom the promise was made ... (Galatians 3:19)." Once the seed comes then the need for the Law is obsolete. We have a predicament in the world today. Jews claim to be the promised seed for all the promises of God. While Muslims claim the rights to all the promises of God. This is due to the fact that they both claim to be descendants of Abraham. Paul clarifies who this seed is, yet it is so overlooked and rejected in our day. Paul states emphatically, "Now to Abraham and his Seed were the promises made. He does not say, "and to seeds," as of many, but as of one, "and to your Seed," who is Christ (Galatians 3:16)." Paul surely identifies the rightful heir of the promises, plural, as Christ Jesus our Lord. It is not the Jews or the Muslims that have a right to the promises of God which He spoke to Abraham and to his SEED. Only Christ has a right and the claim. Paul adds to this with such accuracy, it's amazing! "For you are all sons of God through faith in Christ Jesus. For as many of you as were baptized into Christ have put on Christ. There is neither Jew nor Greek, there is neither slave nor free, there is neither male nor female; for you are all one in Christ Jesus. And if you are Christ's, then you are Abraham's seed, and heirs according to the promise (Galatians 3:26-29)." This is so wonderful! How it would solve so many problems today in our world if this revelation was promoted with love and faith. Christ is the promised SEED and those who belong to Christ are the true seed of Abraham, and we are called to inherit all things.

The inheritance was based on covenant, and the Old Covenant had its inheritance which was fulfilled in the earthly realm. The Old Covenant inheritance was a type and shadow of the heavenly promises which are not temporal, but perpetual, spiritual, invisible and superior. Paul uses the Law as an allegory and lays out the scenario where Abraham had two sons (Galatians 4:22-31). The two sons each had a different mother. He says the two women are two covenants. He names one woman as Hagar. Paul says this Hagar is Mount Sinai bearing children of bondage. The question to ask at this point is what covenant came from Mount Sinai? The Law of Moses and it gives birth to children of bondage. Now pay close attention at this point of Paul's allegory. Now this Hagar is Mount Sinai in Arabia and corresponds to the present Jerusalem, (first century Jerusalem) for she is in slavery with her children (Galatians 4:25). Paul is allegorizing his present situation with Judaism and the current Jerusalem as a house of bondage. He reveals that those under the Law in first century Judaism are in bondage. Then Paul mentions the Jerusalem above which is free, and she is our mother (Galatians 4:26). Paul is very specific here to contrast those bound under the Law, with those of the Jerusalem, which is above and free, which is the mother of us all. What covenant is the woman not mentioned by name? She is Sarah and corresponds to the New Covenant and her children, which are free.

Hagar's son is Ishmael and Sarah's son is Isaac. Where many go astray here is when they don't understand the allegory which Paul is stressing. The son of Hagar to the first century are the Jews under the Law of Moses in the Old Covenant. Paul is using this literal story as an allegory to paint a picture for the Galatian believers. The sons of Hagar are the Jews under the Law. The sons of Sarah are they that are under the New Covenant who have come to Mount Zion and the heavenly Jerusalem which is above. (Hebrews 12:22). Now Paul's defines these two sons, "… and you brothers, like Isaac, are children of promise. But as at that time (back in Genesis), he who was born according to the flesh persecuted him who was born according to the Spirit, so it is now (first century) also (Galatians 4:28- 30)." This is also an ongoing experience of the believers with the religious and irreligious. What is Paul's instruction concerning Hagar and her son? But what does the Scripture say? "CAST OUT THE BONDWOMAN AND HER SON, FOR THE SON OF THE BONDWOMAN SHALL NOT BE AN HEIR WITH THE SON OF THE FREE WOMAN.

So then, brothers, we are not children of a bondwoman, but of the free woman (Galatians 4:30- 31)." Paul says to cast out the Old Covenant as a guide for our lives, because he wants us to be free. If we live under the Law with its influence, we will fight against God's glorious purpose and reject God's ways and persecute those who are according to the Spirit.

The most devastating of all is that it will keep us immature and dwarfed in our spiritual growth, we will not be able to live in the Spirit so as to inherit the kingdom of God. "But if you are led by the Spirit, you are not under the Law. Now the deeds of the flesh are these… (Galatians 5:18-19), just as I have forewarned you, that those who practice such things will not inherit the kingdom of God (Galatians 5:21-22)." The deeds of the flesh will keep us stunted and we will not be able to grow to maturity. Look closely at this verse where Paul is explaining the difference between an heir as a child and an heir who inherits. "Now I say, as long as the heir is a child, he does not differ at all from a slave although he is owner of everything, but he is under guardians and managers until the date set by the father (Galatians 4:1-2)." An immature believer does not discontinue being a child of the father, but as an heir he must grow to maturity in order to inherit. It is crucial, and one must be motivated to live according to the Spirit and not according to the flesh or the Law. Our conflict is between our own flesh and the flesh of others and the enemy to keep us in our flesh and fulfill its desires, which keeps us in shackles. Our victory is to live in the Spirit and walk according to the Spirit and we will know the true meaning of being a free person.

This is why our freedom is in the cross of Christ. He set us free to be yoked to Him alone and not to a list of regulations. He wants to regulate in our lives so we can through love serve one another. Set free to serve in the capacity of restoring and mending the lives that God has put in our lives. We serve in the Spirit sacrificially by taking the cross which is the Spirit and with His empowering we are responsible to bear our own burden, which our Lord says is light and our yoke with Him is easy. The more mature we are the more we will be able to help others and bear their overwhelming loads and burdens so as to be a blessing to them. The Law free believer will sow to the Spirit and from the Spirit will he, or she, reap infinite life (Galatians 6:7- 8). Those who are under Law will sow to the flesh and from the flesh reap corruption. The Judaizers were sowing to the flesh, and they could only expect corruption, (destruction, ruin, waste). Those who are not weary in well doing will be rewarded in God's proper time (Galatians 6:9). So, we glory in the Cross of Christ! "But God forbid that I should glory, save in the cross of our Lord Jesus Christ, by whom the world (Greek: Kosmos, the arrangement, constitution, order and government, in this case that of the Old Covenant world) is crucified unto me, and I unto the world (Galatians 6:15)." This Old Covenant world is (was passing and did pass away) passing away along with its desires, but whoever does the will of God abides forever. Children it is the last hour, and as you have heard that antichrists (against Christ) are coming, so now many antichrists have come, therefore we know that it is the last hour (1 John 2:17-18)." TKB The last days of the Old Covenant system countdown had begun, from the last days to the last day, to the last hour, relatively speaking, nothing to do with twenty-four hours or sixty minutes! It was that Old Covenant system that was "ready to pass away (Hebrews 8:13)." It would be left desolate (Matthew 23:38; 24:15), not one stone would be left upon another (Matthew 24:2), it would all be thrown down (Mark 13:2; Luke 21:6) and destroyed (Acts 6:14)! All of the works under the Law would burn up (2 Peter 3:10).

The elements, Greek: Stoicheion: rudiments, principles, elements (think of the elementary school master) would all be burned up (2 Peter 3:10). The heavens shall pass away (Old Covenant heavens and earth replaced with a New Covenant heavens and earth (Matthew 5:17-18; 2 Peter 3:13, Deuteronomy 31:2, Isaiah 1:2; 51:16, Hebrews 12:25-28) with a great noise, and the elements (Stoicheion, Galatians 4:3,9; Heb. 5:12; Colossians 2:8,20) shall melt with fervent heat, the earth also and the works that are therein shall be burned up (2 Peter 3:10). The old creation passed and the new creation was emerging. The children of the wicked one, the tares, were to be burned up at the end of the age, the Old Covenant age (Matthew 13:38-40). John the Baptist warns of the wrath to come upon these trees, that they will be cut down and cast into the fire (Matthew 3:7-10). This same chaff would God burn up with unquenchable fire (Matthew 3:12). Baptized in fire! After they seized His (King

Jesus') servants, treated them shamefully, and killed them. The King (Jesus) was angry and sent His troops, and destroyed those murderers and burned their city (Matthew 22:6-7)!"

So, the contrasts are so clear in Galatians. Those who were removing themselves from Him (Galatians 1:6), rather than God Revealing His Son in me that I might preach Him… (Galatians 1:16). The only tool for change and dominion is the gospel, the cross, which is grace as opposed to works under the Law. We can be afraid, as Peter was subjected to fear, or faith to influence our actions (Galatians 2:12). We can be cursed in our works under the Law (Galatians 3:10) or blessed in the blessings of Abraham by faith (Galatians 3:14). We can be a slave, or a son (Galatians 4:7), present our works, or receive His grace (Galatians 2:21; 3:2-5), be in bondage, or in freedom (Galatians 5:1), in the flesh, or in the Spirit (Galatians 5:16-25), in the Old Covenant, or the New Covenant (Galatians 4:24- 26), in the Old Israel, or the New Israel (Galatians 4:24-26; 6:16; Matthew 2:15; Ephesians 2:12-14), in the Old Creation, or in the New Creation (Galatians 6:15), in the Old Jerusalem (how many dispensationalists dwell here in our day), or in the New Jerusalem (Galatians 4:25-26; Hebrews 12:22- 23), children of the harlot, or of the mother that is free and above (Galatians 4:25,-26; Revelation 11:8, Babylon THE GREAT Harlot, Jerusalem,1 Peter 5:13), living for selfish ambitions, or for the cross and resurrection life in the new creation (Galatians 2:18-20).

-Garrett Paul Parrish & Terry Kashian

Galatians

Chapter 1

1. Paul, an apostle, (not of men, neither by man, but by Jesus Christ, and God the Father, who raised Him out from the dead)
2. And all the brothers which are with me, to the Assemblies of Galatia:
3. Grace be to you and peace from God the Father, and from our Lord Jesus Christ,
4. Who gave Himself for our sins, that He might deliver us from this present evil age, according to the will of God and our Father:
5. To whom be glory forever and ever. Amen.
6. I marvel that you are so soon turning away from Him that called you into the grace of Christ to another gospel:
7. Which is not another; but there be some that trouble you and would pervert the gospel of Christ.
8. But though we, or an angel from heaven, preach any other gospel to you than that which we have preached to you, let him be accursed.
9. As we said before, so I say now again, if any man preach any other gospel to you than that you have received, let him be accursed.
10. For do I now persuade men, or God? Or do I seek to please men? For if I yet pleased men, I should not be the slave of Christ.
11. But I certify brothers, that the gospel which was preached of me is not after man.
12. For I neither received it of man, neither was I taught it, but by the revelation of Jesus Christ.
13. For you have heard of my manner of life in time past in the Judaism, that beyond measure I persecuted the Assembly of God, and wasted it:
14. And profited in the Judaism above many my equals in my own nation, being more exceedingly zealous of the traditions of my fathers.
15. But when it pleased God, who separated me from my mother's womb, and called me by His grace,
16. To reveal his Son in me, that I might preach and returned to Damascus. Him among the nations; immediately I conferred not with flesh and blood:
17. Neither went I up to Jerusalem to those who were apostles before me; but I went into Arabia.
18. Then after three years I went up to Jerusalem to see Peter and stayed with him fifteen days.
19. I saw none of the other apostles, except James the Lord's brother.
20. Now the things which I write to you, behold, before God, I am not lying.
21. Afterwards I came into the regions of Syria and Cilicia;
22. And was unknown by face to the Assemblies of Judea who were in Christ:
23. But they had heard only, that he which persecuted us in times past now preaches the faith which once he destroyed.
24. And they glorified God in me.

Chapter 2

1. Then fourteen years after I went up again to Jerusalem with Barnabas, and took Titus with me also.
2. And I went up by revelation, and communicated to them that gospel which I preach among the nations, but privately to those who were of reputation, unless by any means I should run, or had run, in vain.
3. But not even Titus, who was with me, being a Greek, was compelled to be circumcised:
4. And because of false brothers brought in secretly, who came in to spy out our freedom which we have in Christ Jesus, that they might reduce us to slaves:
5. To them we gave no place for subjection, no, not for an hour; that the reality of the gospel might remain permanent with you.
6. But those who seemed to be something, whatever they were, it makes no matter to me: God shows no man personal favoritism: for they who seemed to be something added nothing to me:
7. On the contrary, when they saw that the gospel of the uncircumcision was committed to me, as the gospel of the circumcision was to Peter;
8. (For He that worked effectively in Peter into the apostleship of the circumcision, the same was operating in me toward the nations)
9. So, when James, Cephas, and John, who seemed to be pillars, perceived the grace that was given to me, they gave to me and Barnabas the right hands of fellowship; that we should go to the nations, and they to the circumcision.
10. Only they desired that we should remember the poor; the same which I also was eager to do.
11. But when Peter had come to Antioch, I stood against him to his face, because he was reprehensible.
12. For prior to the coming of certain ones from James, he did eat with the nations: but when they had come, he withdrew and separated himself, fearing those who were of the circumcision.
13. Then the other Jews played the hypocrite with him; that even Barnabas was also lead away together with their hypocrisy.
14. But when I saw that they walked not uprightly according to the reality of the gospel, I said to Peter before them all, If you, being a Jew, live after the manner of nations, and not as do the Jews, why do you compel the nations to live as do the Jews?
15. We who are Jews by nature, and not sinners from among the nations,
16. Knowing that a man is not justified by the works of the Law, but by the faith of Jesus Christ, even we have believed in Jesus Christ, that we might be justified by the faith of Christ, and not by the works of the Law: for by the works of the Law will no flesh be justified.
17. But if, while we seek to be justified by Christ, we ourselves also are found sinners, is therefore Christ the minister of sin? God forbid.
18. For if I build again the things which I threw down, I make myself a transgressor.

19. For I through the Law am dead to the Law, that I might live to God.
20. I am crucified with Christ: nevertheless, I live; yet not I, but Christ lives in me: and the life which I now live in the flesh I live by the faith of the Son of God, who loved me, and gave Himself for me.
21. I do not frustrate the grace of God: for if righteousness came by the Law, then Christ died in vain.

Chapter 3

1. Foolish Galatians, who has bewitched you, that you should not obey the reality, before whose eyes Jesus Christ has been evidently set forth, crucified among you?
2. This only would I learn from you, did you receive the Spirit by the works of the Law, or by the hearing of faith?
3. Are you so foolish? Having begun in the Spirit, are you now made mature by the flesh?
4. Have you suffered so many things in vain? If it be yet in vain.
5. He therefore that ministers to you the Spirit, and works miracles among you, does he do it by the works of the Law, or by the hearing of faith?
6. Just as Abraham believed God, and it was accounted to him for righteousness.
7. Know you therefore that they which are of faith, the same are the children of Abraham.
8. For the Scripture, foreseeing that God would justify the nations through faith, preached before the gospel to Abraham, saying, in you all nations will be blessed.
9. So, then they which are of the faith are blessed with faithful Abraham.
10. For as many as are of the works of the Law are under the curse: for it is written, cursed is everyone that continues not in all things which are written in the book of the Law to do them.
11. But that no man is justified by the Law in the sight of God, it is evident: for, the just will live by faith.
12. Yet the Law is not of faith: but, the man that does them will live in them.
13. Christ has redeemed us from the curse of the Law, being made a curse for us: for it is written, cursed is every one that hangs on a tree:
14. That the blessing of Abraham might come on the nations through Jesus Christ; that we might receive the promise of the Spirit through faith.
15. Brothers, I speak after the manner of men; though it be but a man's covenant, yet if it be confirmed, no man cancels, or adds to it.
16. Now to Abraham and his seed were the promises made. He says not, and to seeds, as of many; but as of one, and to your seed, which is Christ.
17. This I say, that the covenant, that was confirmed before by God in Christ, the Law, which was four hundred and thirty years after, cannot cancel, that it should make the promise void.
18. For if the inheritance be of the Law, it is no more of promise: but God gave it to Abraham by promise.

19. Why then serves the Law? It was added because of transgressions, until the seed should come to whom the promise was made; and it was ordained by angels in the hand of a mediator.
20. Now a mediator is not a mediator of one, but God is one.
21. Is the Law then against the promises of God? God forbid: for if there had been a Law given which could have given life, truthfully righteousness should have been by the Law.
22. But the Scripture has concluded all under sin that the promise by faith of Jesus Christ might be given to them that believe.
23. But before faith came, we were kept under the Law, shut up to the faith which should afterwards be revealed.
24. Therefore, the Law was our schoolmaster to bring us to Christ, that we might be justified by faith.
25. But after faith is come, we are no longer under a schoolmaster.
26. For you are all the children of God by faith in Christ Jesus.
27. For as many of you as have been immersed into Christ have put on Christ.
28. There is neither Jew nor Greek, there is neither slave nor free, there is neither male nor female: for you are all one in Christ Jesus.
29. And if you are Christ's, then you are Abraham's seed, and heirs according to the promise.

Chapter 4

1. Now I say, that the heir, as long as he is a babe, differs nothing from a slave, though he be master of all;
2. But is under tutors and guardians until the time appointed by the father.
3. Even so we, when we were babes, were in bondage under the elements of the world:
4. But when the fullness of the time had come, God sent forth his Son, come of a woman, come under the Law,
5. To redeem them that were under the Law, that we might receive being placed as sons.
6. And because you are sons, God has sent out
7. the Spirit of His Son into your hearts, crying, Abba, Father.
8. Therefore, you are no more a slave, but a son; and if a son, then an heir of God through Christ. 8.But then, when you did not know God, you did service to those who by nature are not gods.
9. But now, after you have known God, or rather are known of God, how do you turn again to the weak and beggarly elements, where you desire again to be in bondage?
10. You observe days, and months, and times, and years.
11. I am afraid for you, perhaps I have bestowed on you my labor in vain.
12. Brothers, I urge you, be as I am; for I am as you are: you have not injured me at all.
13. You know how through infirmity of the flesh I preached the gospel to you at the first.

14. And my temptation which was in my flesh you looked down on not, nor rejected; but received me as an angel of God, just as Christ Jesus.

15. Where is then the blessedness you spoke of? For I bear you record, that, if it had been possible, you would have plucked out your own eyes, and have given them to me.

16. Am I therefore become your enemy, because I am being faithful to you?

17. They zealously affect you, but not well; yes, they would exclude you, that you might affect them.

18. But it is good to be zealously affected always in a good thing, and not only when I am present with you.

19. My little children, of whom I labor in birth again until Christ is formed in you,

20. I desire to be present with you now, and to change my voice; for I stand in doubt of you.

21. Tell me, you that desire to be under the Law, do you not hear the Law?

22. For it is written, that Abraham had two sons, the one by a bond woman, the other by a free woman.

23. But he who was of the bond woman was born after the flesh; but he of the free woman was by promise.

24. Which things are symbolic: for these are the two covenants; the one from the Mount Sinai, which gives birth to bondage, which is Hagar.

25. For this Hagar is Mount Sinai in Arabia, and is analogous of Jerusalem who at this moment is in bondage with her children.

26. But Jerusalem that which is above is free, which is the mother of us all.

27. For it is written, rejoice, you barren that bear not; break out and cry, you that labor not: for the desolate has many more children than she which has a husband.

28. Now we, brothers, as Isaac was, are the children of promise.

29. But as then he that was born after the flesh persecuted him that was born after the Spirit, even so it is now.

30. Nevertheless, what does the Scripture say? Cast out the bond woman and her son: for the son of the bond woman will not be heir with the son of the free woman.

31. So then, brothers, we are not children of the bond woman, but of the free.

Chapter 5

1. Stand fast therefore in the freedom with which Christ has made us free, and be not entangled again with the yoke of bondage.

2. Behold, I Paul say to you, that if you be circumcised, Christ will profit you nothing.

3. For I testify again to every man that is circumcised, that he is a debtor to do the whole Law.

4. Christ is become of no effect to you, whoever of you are justified by the Law; you are fallen from grace.

5. For we through the Spirit expect the hope of righteousness out of faith.

6. For in Jesus Christ neither circumcision adds anything, nor uncircumcision; but faith which works through love.

7. You were running properly; who obstructed you that you should not be persuaded by the reality?

8. This persuasion does not come from Him who calls you.
9. A little leaven is leavening the whole lump.
10. I have confidence in you through the Lord, that you will not have any other mindset: but he that troubles you will receive his judgment, whoever he is.
11. And I, brothers, if I yet preach circumcision, why do I still suffer persecution? Then the scandal of the cross would cease.
12. I wish they would mutilate themselves who disturb you.
13. For, brothers, you have been called over to freedom; only use not your freedom for an occasion to the flesh, but through love serve one another.
14. For all the Law is fulfilled in one word, even in this; you will love your neighbor as yourself.
15. But if you bite and devour one another, take heed that you be not consumed one of another.
16. This I say then, walk in the Spirit, and you will not fulfill the desire of the flesh.
17. For the flesh sets it desire against the Spirit, and the Spirit against the flesh: and these are contrary to one another: so that you cannot do the things that you intend.
18. But if you be led of the Spirit, you are not under the Law.
19. Now the works of the flesh are manifest, which are these; adultery, fornication, uncleanness, lasciviousness,
20. Idolatry, witchcraft, enmities, contention, jealousy, outbursts of anger, factions, cliques, heresies, Envying, drunkenness, murders,
21. drinking parties, and similar things: of which I told you before, as I have also told you in time past, that they which practice such things will not inherit the kingdom of God.
22. But the fruit of the Spirit is love; joy, peace, patience, gentleness, goodness, faithfulness,
23. Gentleness, self-control: against such there is no Law.
24. For they that are Christ's have crucified the flesh with the affections and lusts.
25. If we live in the Spirit, let us also walk in the Spirit.
26. Let us not become egotistical, provoking one another, envying one another.

Chapter 6

1. Brothers, if a man be overtaken in a false step, you who are spiritual, restore such a one in the spirit of gentleness; checking yourself, lest you also be tempted.
2. Carry one another's burdens, and so fulfill the Law of Christ.
3. For if a man think himself to be something, when he is nothing, he deceives himself.
4. But let every man prove his own work, and then he will have rejoicing in himself alone, and not in another.
5. For everyone will carry his own burden.
6. Let him that is taught in the word contribute to him that teaches in all good things.

7. Be not deceived; God is not mocked: for whatever a man sows that will he also reap.
8. For he that sows into his flesh will out of the flesh reap corruption; but he that sows into the Spirit will out of the Spirit reap infinite life.
9. So, let us not be weary in well doing: for in due season we will reap, if we do not quit.
10. As we have therefore opportunity, let us do good to all men, especially to them who are of the household of the faith.
11. You see how large a letter I have written to you with my own hand.
12. As many as desire to make a good showing in the flesh, they constrain you to be circumcised; only so they should not suffer persecution for the cross of Christ.
13. For neither they themselves who are circumcised keep the Law; but desire to have you circumcised, that they may glory in your flesh.
14. But God forbid that I should glory, save in the cross of our Lord Jesus Christ, by who the world is crucified to me, and I to the world.
15. For in Christ Jesus neither circumcision adds anything, nor uncircumcision, but a new creation.
16. And as many as march in rank according to this rule, peace be on them, and mercy, and on the Israel of God.
17. From now on let no man trouble me: for I carry in my body the scars of the Lord Jesus.
18. Brothers, the grace of our Lord Jesus Christ be with your spirit. Amen.

Corporate Identity in Ephesians

I. Introduction
   A. Background information on the letter of Ephesians
   B. Purpose and significance of the paper
   C. Research objectives and questions
   D. Methodology and sources employed
II. Corporate Identity in Ephesians: A Thematic Overview
   A. Definition and understanding of corporate identity
   B. Examination of the theme of corporate identity in Ephesians
      1. Chapter 1: The identity of believers in Christ
      2. Chapter 2: The unity and conciliation of Jew and Gentile
      3. Chapter 3: The mystery of Christ and the participation of all believers
      4. Chapter 4: The diversity and unity of ascension gifts within the body of Christ
      5. Chapter 5: The instructions for righteous living in the community
      6. Chapter 6: The armor of God for spiritual warfare
   C. Analysis of the significance of corporate identity in understanding God's perpetual purpose
      1. The communal nature of God's work in salvation history
      2. The fulfillment and embodiment of God's redemptive plan in the corporate identity of believers
III. Analysis of Corporate Identity in Ephesians
   A. Chapter 1: The identity of believers in Christ
      1. The predestination and sonship of believers
      2. The sealing and guarantee of the Holy Spirit
   B. Chapter 2: The unity and conciliation of Jew and Gentile
      1. The dividing wall of hostility broken down in Christ
      2. The creation of one new man through the cross

- C. Chapter 3: The mystery of Christ and the participation of all believers
    1. The revelation of the mystery to Paul
    2. The inclusion of all believers in Christ's inheritance
- D. Chapter 4: The diversity and unity of ascension gifts within the body of Christ
    1. The diversity of ascension gifts given by Christ to equip and build up the body
    2. The call to unity and maturity in the body
- E. Chapter 5: The instructions for righteous living in the community
    1. The call to imitate God and walk in love
    2. The contrast between light and darkness in the Christian community
- F. Chapter 6: The armor of God for spiritual warfare
    1. The spiritual battle against evil forces
    2. The importance of prayer and perseverance in the corporate identity of believers

In the realm of corporate identity, one text that holds significant value is the letter of Ephesians. Situated among the Pauline epistles in the New Testament of the Bible, this letter, attributed to the Apostle Paul, was composed during his time of imprisonment in Rome between 60-62 AD. The recipients of this correspondence were the believers residing in Ephesus, a prominent city known for trade and religious practices dating back to the first century. The primary intent of this epistle was to uplift and instruct these Ephesian believers, providing them with both theological and practical teachings. The purpose of this study is to delve into the theme of corporate identity as conveyed in the letter of Ephesians and explore its theological significance. By undertaking a comprehensive examination of the various chapters, we shall gain insight into Paul's portrayal and understanding of corporate identity within the Christian community. Moreover, we will scrutinize how this theme intertwines with God's perpetual purpose and the communal nature of His redemptive plan. To achieve this objective, this treatise posits several crucial questions. First and foremost, it aims to define and apprehend the concept of corporate identity within the context of Ephesians. Second, it seeks to analyze the significance of corporate identity as it manifests in each chapter of this epistle. Lastly, it endeavors to examine the relationship between corporate identity and the comprehension of God's perpetual purpose. To conduct this research, a textual analysis approach will be employed. This methodology emphasizes thorough exegesis and interpretation of the letter of Ephesians. The primary sources utilized for this analysis will encompass the original Greek text, various English translations, as well as reputable commentaries by biblical scholars. Additionally, secondary sources, such as scholarly articles and books, which provide insights and theological perspectives on the theme of corporate identity, will also be incorporated. Through this comprehensive exploration of the biblical text and the integration of pertinent scholarly perspectives, a deeper understanding of corporate identity within this epistle can be attained.

I. Corporate Identity in Ephesians: A Thematic Overview

A. Definition and Understanding of Corporate Identity

Within the context of the book of Ephesians, the concept of corporate identity refers to the collective identity and unity of believers in Christ as a cohesive body. This encompasses various facets, such as their shared identity as family, sons of God, the conciliation between Jews and Gentiles, the involvement of all believers in the mystery of Christ's work, the diversity and unity of ascension gifts within the body of Christ, and the guidelines for righteous living within the community. Each chapter in the book contributes to the development and comprehension of corporate identity, accentuating the interconnected nature of the believers' identity and their essential unity in Christ.

B. Examination of the Theme of Corporate Identity in Ephesians 1

Chapter 1: The Identity of Believers in Christ

In the first chapter, the apostle Paul places emphasis on the predestination and sonship of believers as sons and daughters of God, perpetually sealed and assured by the Holy Spirit (Ephesians 1:3-14). This highlights the collective dimension of their identity, as they are united as a chosen and redeemed community in Christ. Our corporate identity is we are family, brothers and sisters. Genuinely! Our human family is a shadow of what we are in the Spirit. We are also the body of Christ, the fullness of Him who fills all in all. We are not a metaphor, but the authentic body of Jesus! This is Paul's unique revelation which he received on the road to Damascus. Who are You, Lord? The Lord responded, "I am Jesus whom you are persecuting". We touch a believer, we touch Jesus. Whatever I do to you, I do to Jesus. Not metaphorically but actually.

Chapter 2: The Unity and conciliation of Jew and Gentile

In the second chapter, Paul addresses the conciliation and unity between Jews and Gentiles through the redemptive work of Christ, dismantling the walls of hostility and establishing a new man (Ephesians 2:11-22). This emphasizes the corporate identity of believers, united as one body in Christ, irrespective of cultural or ethnic differences. We are a New Man not a new self and we are called to put on the New Man. The practical way to experience this is to engage in daily fellowship with devoted believers, sharing your life and love with them. This new man expresses the heavenly culture that needs to be exhibited in this world. When we practice putting on the new man, we experience the heavenly life, a heavenly humanity showing a practical example of His kingdom and will on earth as it is in Heaven.[49]

---

[49] John Nelson Darby. Synopsis of the Books of the Bible: Ephesians.

Chapter 4 Practical Expression of the New Man

Our calling to walk worthy is humility, gently considering one another with longsuffering and being diligent to maintain the unity of the Spirit. Jesus' prayer was answered concerning the oneness we have in Christ. We are one and our calling is to be diligent to maintain it. Then we have the 7 cardinal principals of our oneness. One body, One Spirit, One hope of our calling, One faith, One baptism, One God and Father. These 7 are challenging. One Body that's who we are. This is rich if we can accept it. One body is denominational, and it is not a body of believers it is the body of Christ, the one new man. You get my point concerning these. One God and Father who is above all and through you all, and in you all. Do you believe that the Father is in you because you are a believer. The denomination is ONE BODY, not you name it. Once we get this it's game over for all opposers!

But to each one of us grace was given according to the measure of Christ's gift. Therefore He says: "When He ascended on high, He led captivity captive And gave gifts to men."

(Now this, "He ascended"—what does it mean but that He also first descended into the lower parts of the earth? He who descended is also the One who ascended far above all the heavens, that He might fill all things.)

The gifts He gave are ministry ascension gifts to equip the saints to do the work of the ministry, the ministry of building up the body of Christ. The fivefold ascension gifts are equippers, not directly doing all the work and the assembly is not a spectator. The whole assembly are builders, and the goal is the unity of the faith (the heavenly culture), the full knowledge of the Son of God, unto a mature man, (a mature new man), unto the measure of the stature of the fullness of Christ. See how important this revelation of our corporate identity is? The experience of our corporate identity is the only way to come into full sonship, full maturity. Where every joint supplies because we are joined and knit together with Him.

Chapter 5: The Instructions for Righteous Living in the Community

In the fifth chapter, Paul imparts instructions for righteous living within the community, emphasizing the call to represent and express God, to demonstrate love in action, and to live in stark contrast to darkness (Ephesians 5:1-21). This underscores the communal nature of believers' identity, urging them to lead lives that reflect their collective identity and bear witness to the world.[50]

Chapter 6: The Armor of God for Spiritual Warfare

In the sixth and final chapter, Paul addresses the spiritual warfare faced by believers, highlighting the importance of putting on the armor of God and emphasizing the necessity of prayer and perseverance in the corporate identity of believers (Ephesians 6:10-20). This

---

[50] .K. Beale. The Book of Ephesians: New International Commentary on the New Testament (Eerdmans, 2008).

underscores the collective responsibility of believers to engage in spiritual battle together, united in their corporate identity and reliance on God's strength.[51]

Analysis of the Significance of Corporate Identity in Understanding God's Perpetual Purpose

The Cooperative Nature of God's Work in Salvation History

The concept of corporate identity in Ephesians highlights the cooperative nature of God's work in the resolution of salvation history. It illustrates that God's redemptive plan extends beyond individual salvation to encompass the formation and unity of a corporate body of Christ. The identity of each believer in Christ is intricately interwoven with the identity of the entire body, forging a unified people of God who are collectively being built into a dwelling place for God (Ephesians 2:19-22).

The Fulfillment and Embodiment of God's Redemptive Plan in the Corporate Identity of Believers

The theme of corporate identity in Ephesians reveals the fulfillment and embodiment of God's redemptive plan within the collective identity of believers. Through the conciliation and unity of diverse groups, the participation of all believers in Christ's work, and the diversity and unity of spiritual gifts, the corporate body of Christ incarnates God's purpose of creating a diverse and unified community that manifests His righteousness and love and life.[52] Corporate identity serves as a visible witness to God's perpetual purpose in bringing forth His kingdom through His people.

In this descriptive essay, we will delve into an analysis of the corporate identity in the book of Ephesians. The complexity of this topic is explored through various themes and concepts.

Chapter 1 focuses on the identity of believers in Christ. The author highlights two key concepts: predestination and adoption (literally "placed as sons). These concepts play a crucial role in establishing the identity of believers. According to the apostle Paul, believers were predestined by God for sonship even before the downfall of the world. This divine predestination emphasizes God's sovereign plan and His initiative in salvation. Additionally, believers are placed as sons and daughters of God through Christ, signifying a deep relational aspect of intimacy and belonging within the family of God. Furthermore, the first chapter of Ephesians emphasizes the sealing and guarantee of the Holy Spirit as another foundational aspect of believers' identity. [53]We are describing believers as being sealed with the Holy Spirit after hearing the word of truth, the gospel of their salvation. This sealing serves as a mark of authenticity and ownership by God, protecting believers

---

[51] Witness Lee. Life-study of Ephesians (Living Stream Ministry, 1986).

[52] F.F. Bruce. The Epistle to the Ephesians: A Verse-by-Verse Exposition (Eerdmans, 1984).

[53] Lee, W. (2017). Life-study of Ephesians. Living Stream Ministry.

from spiritual harm. [54] Moreover, it serves as a guarantee of believers' future inheritance, providing assurance of their perpetual security in Christ. Moving on to Chapter 2, the theme shifts to the unity and conciliation between Jews and Gentiles. The author explores the transformation of their relationship through the work of Christ. Paul highlights the historical division and enmity between these two groups, symbolized by the "dividing wall of hostility."[55] However, through Christ, this barrier has been dismantled, leading to a new relationship between Jews and Gentiles. The sacrificial death of Jesus not only conciliates individuals to God but also brings diverse groups together, eliminating the barriers that once kept them apart. Additionally, the work of Christ creates a new humanity and species on the earth. Through the cross, God conciliates both Jews and Gentiles in Himself, forming them into one new man. This new humanity introduces a new culture made up of beliefs, values, ideas and norms of the kingdom as spiritual laws, creating a new corporate identity in Christ. This cooperative enterprise reflects God's redemptive purpose and plan, highlighting the inclusive nature of His salvation and the peaceful power of Christ's cross.[56] In conclusion, the book of Ephesians delves into the complexity of corporate identity. Through themes such as predestination, adoption, the sealing of the Holy Spirit, unity, and conciliation, this text offers profound insights into the believers' identity in Christ. It emphasizes God's sovereign plan and His redemptive work, showcasing the profound and transformative nature of corporate identity in the context of faith.

IV. Theological and Scholarly Perspectives on Corporate Identity in Ephesians

A. Interpretations and insights from theological scholars

Significant attention has been given by theological scholars to the theme of corporate identity in the letter of Ephesians, and they have offered valuable interpretations and insights. One theologian known for distinct views on biblical interpretation, Witness Lee, believes that corporate identity is fundamental to God's redemptive plan. According to Lee, the identity of believers in Christ is not just an individualistic concept, but a corporate reality where believers are united in Christ as one body.[57] Another influential figure in theology, John Nelson Darby, a prominent 19th-century theologian and involved in the Brethren movement, stressed the centrality of corporate identity in the unity and fellowship of the body of Christ. [58] Darby argued that the collective nature of the church is vital for expressing the fullness of Christ and manifesting God's perpetual purpose.

---

[54] Darby, J. N. (2019). Synopsis of the Books of the Bible: The Book of Ephesians. Irving Bible-Publishing.

[55] Bruce, F. F. (1990). The Epistles to the Colossians, to Philemon, and to the Ephesians. Wm. B. Eerdmans Publishing.

[56] Beale, G. K. (2014). Ephesians. Baker Academic.

[57] Witness Lee, The Mystery of Christ and His Church: Life-Study of Ephesians (Living Stream Ministry, 1990).

[58] John Nelson Darby, Synopsis of the Books of the Bible: Ephesians (Bible Truth Publishers, 1996).

In addition, F.F. Bruce, a renowned biblical scholar, has explored the theme of corporate identity in Ephesians, highlighting the communal aspects of believers' participation in Christ. Bruce asserts that individual experiences of salvation are inseparable from the collective identity of the body of Christ.

G.K. Beale, another influential scholar, has examined the theme of corporate identity in relation to the cosmic dimensions of God's redemptive plan. Beale has suggested that the corporate identity of the church reflects and fulfills God's perpetual purpose, which encompasses the redemption and restoration of all things in Christ.

B. Comparative analysis of different exegetical approaches to corporate identity in Ephesians

To comprehensively understand corporate identity in Ephesians, various exegetical approaches, including socio-historical and theological perspectives, need to be taken into consideration. The socio-historical context of Ephesus significantly influences the comprehension of corporate identity in the letter. Ephesus was a diverse city with unique cultural, religious, and social dynamics.

This context shaped the understanding of corporate identity, particularly in relation to the unity and conciliation of Jews and Gentiles within the church. By considering the historical background of the intended audience, scholars can interpret the portrayal of corporate identity in a nuanced manner that reflects the challenges and dynamics of the Ephesian community. In addition, the relevance of other biblical texts and themes contributes to the interpretation of corporate identity in Ephesians. The concept of the body of Christ, for instance, is explored in other writings by Paul, such as 1 Corinthians, and provides a framework for understanding the diversity and unity of ascension gifts and spiritual gifts, manifestation and motivational within the body (Ephesians 4:11-13; 1 Cor. 12; Rom. 12). The theme of redemption and inheritance, pervasive throughout the Old Testament and the New Testament, sheds light on the mystery of Christ and the participation of all believers in His redemptive work (Ephesians 3:6).

V. Conclusion

Summary of key findings and insights from the analysis

Throughout this work, we have delved into the intricate concept of corporate identity in the letter of Ephesians as presented by the Apostle Paul within the Christian community. Each chapter of Ephesians has been thoroughly examined, allowing us to uncover significant insights and findings:

In Chapter 1, we discovered that the identity of believers in Christ is firmly established through predestination, sonship, sealing, and the guarantee of the Holy Spirit.

Chapter 2 emphasizes the unity and conciliation of both Jew and Gentile, highlighting the breaking down of the dividing wall of hostility and the creation of one new man in Christ.

In Chapter 3, we explore the revelation of the mystery of Christ and the participation of all believers, showcasing the inclusion of all believers in Christ's inheritance.

Chapter 4 emphasizes the importance of understanding the diversity and unity of all spiritual gifts within the body of Christ, calling for unity and maturity in the body.

In Chapter 5, we uncover instructions for righteous living within the community, emphasizing the call to model God, walk in love, and live in light.

Chapter 6 presents the necessity of the armor of God for spiritual warfare, stressing the significance of prayer and perseverance in the corporate identity of believers.

Reiteration of the significance of corporate identity in Ephesians

By conducting this analysis, we have gained a profound understanding of the role played by corporate identity in the letter of Ephesians. It is now evident that the identity of believers in Christ, the unity and reconciliation of diverse groups, the revelation of the mystery of Christ's work, the diversity and unity of spiritual gifts, the instructions for righteous living, and the call to spiritual warfare all contribute to a deeper understanding of this concept. We must acknowledge that corporate identity in Ephesians extends beyond a mere social or cultural construct within the Christian community: it reflects God's redemptive plan and His perpetual purpose.

Implications for the understanding of God's perpetual purpose

The exploration of corporate identity in Ephesians has profound implications for our comprehension of God's perpetual purpose. The communal nature of God's work throughout salvation history becomes clear through the emphasis on unity, conciliation, and the participation of all believers. The corporate identity of believers embodies and fulfills God's redemptive plan, effectively reflecting His desire for a unified and diverse community that upholds righteousness, demonstrates love, and engages in spiritual warfare. Through our enhanced understanding of corporate identity in Ephesians, we are now able to appreciate the vast breadth and profound depth of God's perpetual purpose as He establishes His kingdom through His people.

Suggestions for further research and study on corporate identity in biblical literature

While this study provides a panoramic examination of corporate identity in the letter of Ephesians, there remains ample opportunity for further research and study in this area. Future scholarship can expand on this concept by exploring corporate identity in other biblical texts and evaluating its implications for contemporary local churches and the Christian community. Additionally, comparative analyses across different epistles or within the broader biblical literature can shed further light on the development and significance of corporate identity as a recurring theme. Continued research in these domains will greatly contribute to the advancement of our understanding of corporate identity and its theological implications within biblical literature.

Another aspect that I did not develop in Ephesians is the corporate identity of the church being the bride of Christ. Let me give some overview of this glorious figure in God's word.

Introduction

Background information on the concept of the church as the bride of Christ

The concept of the church as the bride of Christ is of utmost significance and carries immense symbolism within the realm of Christian theology. It draws upon biblical imagery and various theological perspectives in order to explore the profound and intimate relationship between Christ and His faithful followers, as well as the collective identity of the church as a community of devoted believers.

Significance of delving into the corporate identity of the church

Gaining a comprehensive understanding of the corporate identity of the church as the bride of Christ is indispensable in grasping the profound implications it holds for both individual believers and the broader community of the faithful. Through the exploration of this concept, we are able to delve deep into the realms of Christian spirituality and critically analyze the diverse theological viewpoints and symbolic interpretations associated with the bride of Christ.

Biblical Perspectives on the Bride of Christ

Examination of relevant biblical passages that portray the church as the bride of Christ

The church is vividly portrayed as the bride of Christ in relevant biblical passages. These passages offer insights into the intimate relationship between Christ and believers, shedding light on the corporate identity of the church as a community of faithful followers. One such passage, Ephesians 5:25-27, draws a comparison between Christ and the church to that of a husband and wife. In this analogy, the apostle Paul highlights the sacrificial nature of Christ's love for the church, using the imagery of a bridegroom who selflessly gives Himself up for the sake of His bride. This imagery serves to emphasize the depth of Christ's love and His willingness to lay down His life for His beloved church. The book of Revelation also presents rich imagery of the bride of Christ. Revelation 19:7-8 depicts the church as the bride adorned in fine linen, symbolizing the righteousness's of the saints.

This imagery accentuates the purity and holiness of the church as she prepares for the perpetual union with Christ, the consummation. It must be understood that as Paul tells the Corinthians that he betrothed them to Christ as a pure virgin. For I feel a divine jealousy for you, since I betrothed you to one husband, to present you as a pure virgin to Christ. 2

Cor. 12:2. This betrothal was inaugurated and would be consummated at the end of the Old Covenant age in A.D. 70. Today we are not waiting to be married and attend a marriage supper of the Lamb. We generations later enter this divine union when we get saved. Today we that are His are enjoying the intimacy of this perpetual union that consummated 2000 years ago. Additionally, Revelation 21:2 describes the new Jerusalem as a bride beautifully dressed for her husband, signifying the ultimate union between Christ and His redeemed community. Furthermore, another passage such as Matthew 25:1-13 also portray the church as the bride of Christ. This parable is a past event.

Profoundly grasping the concept of corporate identity in Ephesians invites us into a deeper appreciation for the unparalleled breadth, height, and astounding depth of God's perpetual purpose in bringing forth His glorious kingdom in and through His cherished people.[59]

Analysis of the intimate relationship between Christ and believers depicted in these passages

An examination of the biblical passages that depict the church as the bride of Christ reveals a profound intimacy and love between Christ and believers. The imagery of the bride and bridegroom symbolizes the union of two hearts, the devotion of Christ to His church, and the unconditional love He has for His bride. These passages prominently showcase Christ's sacrificial love, as evident in Ephesians 5:25-27. Christ's selfless act of surrendering Himself for the church exemplifies His deep affection and desire for the well-being and sanctification of His beloved bride. This intimate fellowship is characterized by love, sacrificial commitment, and a longing for the spiritual growth and flourishing of the church.[60] The wedding imagery found in Revelation emphasizes the joyful anticipation and union between Christ and the church in the 1st Century. The fine linen worn by the bride in Revelation 19:7-8 symbolizes the righteousness of the saints, underscoring the purity and holiness of the bride that originates from Christ's redemptive work. This imagery reinforces the notion that the intimate relationship between Christ and the church is rooted in His grace and the transformative power of His love. Ultimately, the biblical passages that depict the church as the bride of Christ portray a deep and intimate relationship characterized by sacrificial love, devotion, and the eager anticipation of a perpetual union. These passages lay a biblical foundation for comprehending the corporate identity of the church as the bride of Christ, serving as a reminder of the profound extent of Christ's love and His longing for an intimate communion with His followers.[61]

---

[59] Sparks, T. Austin. Our Heavenly Calling: An Exposition of the Epistle to the Hebrews. Christian Publications, 1992, p. 41.

[60] Schmidt, Dottie. "The Bride of Christ: A Symbol of the Church."

[61] In The Role of Women in the Church: Biblical Principles and Contemporary Insights, edited by Witness Lee, pp. 82-95. Living Stream Ministry, 1990.

Theological Perspectives on the Bride of Christ

Exploration of different theological viewpoints on the corporate identity of the church as the bride or wife of Christ When examining the concept of the church as the bride of Christ from a theological perspective, several viewpoints emerge. T. Austin Sparks emphasizes the intimate relationship between Christ and believers.

He describes the corporate identity of the church as the "correspondence of His own divine union with His Bride, being the product and expression of His own relationship."[62]

On the other hand, Witness Lee highlights the corporate aspect of the church as the bride. He emphasizes that "the bride must be a corporate entity, not just individual believers."[63]

Overview of theological interpretations and symbolism associated with the bride of Christ

Various theologians have delved into the symbolic interpretations associated with the bride of Christ. Dottie Schmidt asserts that the bride of Christ symbolizes the perpetual and inseparable union between Christ and the church, evoking imagery of a sacred marriage bond.[64] Watchman Nee expands on this symbolic representation, suggesting that the church as the bride signifies the perfect oneness and harmonious relationship between Christ and believers.[65] These interpretations emphasize the deep spiritual meaning embedded in the symbolism of the bride of Christ. They draw attention to the transformative power of this motif within Christian theology.

In the next section, we will explore the symbolic representation of the bride of Christ in Christian spirituality. Furthermore, we will discuss the implications of this symbolism for individual believers as well as the community of believers.

Symbolic Representation of the Bride of Christ

Examining the Symbolic Representation of the Bride of Christ in Christian Spirituality

The symbolic representation of the bride of Christ in Christian spirituality is multifaceted and draws upon various sources and interpretations. It takes inspiration from biblical imagery found in the Old and New Testaments. The apostle Paul, in his letter to the Ephesians, compares the relationship between Christ and the church to a marital bond, highlighting the depth of intimacy and love that exists between them (Ephesians 5:22-33). This imagery conveys the profound connection between Christ and believers. Another significant source of symbolism lies in visual representations found in Christian art and iconography. Artists throughout history have depicted the bride of Christ in diverse forms, such as a radiant bride adorned in white garments or as a collective body of believers united in worship. These

---

[62] T. Austin Sparks, "The Church as the Vehicle of the Corporate Christ" (1946), p. 33.

[63] Witness Lee, "The Glorious Church" (2011), p. 55.

[64] Dottie Schmidt, "The Symbolism of the Bride of Christ", Theological Journal, 70(2), 2018, p. 124.

[65] Watchman Nee, "The Normal Christian Church Life" (1948), p. 92

visual representations evoke a sense of awe, reverence, and devotion among believers, reminding them of their identity as the bride of Christ and their calling to pursue a deep and intimate communion with Him.[66]

Exploring the Implications of this Symbolism for Individual Believers and the Community

The symbolism associated with the bride of Christ holds profound implications for both individual believers and the community as a whole. For individual believers, the symbolism serves as a constant reminder of their unique and cherished relationship with Christ. Just as a bride trustingly loves and submits to her husband, believers are called to trust, love, and submit to Christ as their spiritual husband. This symbolism emphasizes the need for personal devotion, surrender, and an ongoing pursuit of intimacy with Christ in every aspect of life. It encourages believers to deepen their understanding of Christ's love and to respond with wholehearted commitment and obedience. For the community of believers, the symbolism of the bride of Christ promotes unity, love, and fellowship.[67]

As individual believers come together to practice the corporate body of Christ, they become a diverse yet unified bride. This symbolism underscores the importance of embracing diversity within the church and working together towards a common purpose. It reminds believers of their shared identity and mission as the bride of Christ, fostering mutual support, accountability, and sacrificial love.[68]

Section V: Intimacy between Christ and Believers

One of the most profound aspects of the Christian faith lies in the intimate relationship between Christ and individual believers. This section delves into the depth and complexity of this connection by exploring the concept of the bride of Christ and its impact on our understanding of this divine union. The concept of the bride of Christ enhances the understanding of the intimate relationship between Christ and individual **believers**. The concept of the bride of Christ serves as a powerful lens through which we can grasp the extraordinary love and commitment that Christ has for each follower.[69] When we contemplate the church as the bride, we inevitably plunge into the depths of this intimate relationship characterized by adoration and devotion. It mirrors the profound affection a husband has for his wife, with Christ wholeheartedly loving and cherishing every single believer. Biblical passages such as Ephesians 5:25, where Christ's selfless sacrifice for the church is

---

[66] T. Austin Sparks, The Bride, the Lamb's Wife, and Her Pleasure

[67] Watchman Nee, The Normal Christian Church Life

[68] Lee, W. (1995). The Bride of Christ: The Transformation of the Believers For the New Jerusalem (3rd ed.). Living Stream Ministry.

[69] Nee, W. (1973). The Song of Songs. Christian Fellowship Publishers.

highlighted, and Revelation 19:7-8, depicting the sacred union of Christ and His bride at the marriage supper of the Lamb, beautifully illustrates this sacrificial love and profound intimacy. This understanding of the bride of Christ serves to deepen our appreciation of the boundless love that Christ has for each individual believer. It serves as a powerful reminder that we are not mere followers or servants, but precious members of His beloved bride, united with Him through a covenant of unwavering love and perpetual commitment.

Ephesians 5:25 The apostle Paul eloquently captures the essence of Christ's love for the church in Ephesians 5:25: "Husbands, love your wives, just as Christ loved the church and gave Himself up for her" (Sparks, 1970, p. 25).[70]

Revelation 19:7-8 Revelation 19:7-8 provides a vivid depiction of the profound and intimate union between Christ and his bride, the church, symbolized by the marriage supper of the Lamb (Schmidt, 2021, p. 37). Look at the parable of the King who planned a wedding for His son. Matt. 22:1-14. Especially in verse seven, you find the timing of the wedding. Discussion of how this intimacy impacts the spiritual journey and growth of believers. The profound intimacy found within the concept of the bride of Christ permeates every aspect of believers' spiritual journey and growth. Understanding the depth of Christ's love and unwavering commitment to His bride empowers believers to place their trust in His faithfulness, fostering a desire for deeper intimacy with him. This profoundly intimate relationship brings a sense of security, knowing that we are enveloped in the boundless love of our Bridegroom[71]. Moreover, this deep sense of intimacy with Christ serves as a catalyst for believers to cultivate a rich and vibrant spiritual life through prayer, worship, and the study of God's Word. Embracing our identity as the bride of Christ compels us to draw nearer to him, yearning to know Him more intimately and obediently aligning our lives with His teachings. This extraordinary intimacy also profoundly impacts the growth and transformation of believers. As we embrace our identity as the bride of Christ, we are called to exemplify the qualities of a loving and faithful spouse, including selflessness, forgiveness, and unwavering commitment.

This transformative journey of becoming more Christlike strengthens our faith, deepens our relationship with Christ, and propels us toward spiritual maturity.

Intimacy among Believers

One of the intriguing aspects of exploring intimacy among believers is the recognition of the corporate identity of the church as the bride of Christ. This concept serves as a powerful motif that not only promotes intimacy, but also fosters a sense of mutual love, support, and belonging among believers within the body of Christ. It is fascinating to observe that this intimacy not only stems from each individual's personal relationship with Christ, but

---

[70] Sparks, T. A. (1970). The Church as the Body of Christ (Excerpts) (2nd ed.). Ministry Books.
[71] Schmidt, D. The Bride of Christ: Unveiling the Beauty of the Church. Authors Press, 2020.

also from the divine connection that exists among believers within the church.[72] Just like a bride and groom are intimately joined together in holy matrimony, believers too are united through their shared identity as the bride of Christ. This shared identity creates a profound bond of unity and intimacy where believers can find solace, encouragement, and a sense of community. It cultivates an environment where believers can grow in their faith, come together to share in each other's joys and sorrows, and embark on their spiritual journey as a unified body.[73]

B. Analysis of the implications of this intimacy for Christian community and fellowship

Delving into the implications of the intimacy fostered by the corporate identity of the church as the bride of Christ reveals profound effects on Christian community and fellowship. This unique sense of intimacy cultivates an environment where genuine relationships flourish, enabling individuals to authentically share their lives, struggles, and joys with one another. Within this context, the church becomes a supportive and nurturing space where believers can seek and provide encouragement, guidance, and comfort. Furthermore, this depth of intimacy fosters a deep sense of unity and acceptance within the Christian community. [74]Believers are encouraged to wholeheartedly embrace one another as valuable members of the same body, recognizing and appreciating their individual gifts and contributions that ultimately enrich and edify the entire church.

Implications for Christian Spirituality and Community

An Exploration into the Influence of the Concept of the Bride of Christ on Christian Spirituality
The idea of the church being referred to as the bride of Christ holds deep significance for Christian spirituality. It functions as a potent symbol of the intimate bond between Christ and believers, serving as a constant reminder of the immense love and sacrifice that Christ has bestowed upon them. This symbolic representation invites and encourages believers to forge a deeper, more personal connection with Christ, as they strive to comprehend and embrace their identity as part of the bride of Christ.

As believers deeply contemplate this concept, they are prompted to reflect upon the profound nature of Christ's love, which is akin to the love shared between a husband and wife. This deeper reflection opens up new pathways for spiritual growth and transformation, as individuals endeavor to emulate the selfless love and unwavering commitment that Christ exemplified during his earthly ministry and ultimately on the cross.

---

[72] Lee, W. (1995). The Bride of Christ: The Transformation of the Believers For the New Jerusalem (3rd ed.). Living Stream Ministry.

[73] Schmidt, D. (2021). The Bride, The Groom with a Flaming Pen, and the Friends of the Bride in Songs of Songs: A Diachronic Analysis. 'Parângâl' - Journal of Protestant Theology, 38(1), 37-54.

[74] Lee, W. The Believer's Intimate Relationship with Christ. Living Stream Ministry, 1983.

Conclusion

In wrapping up this insightful presentation, we have embarked on an exploration of the captivating concept of the church as the bride of Christ through lenses of both biblical and theological perspectives. Additionally, we have delved into its symbolic representation within the realm of Christian spirituality. By closely examining pertinent biblical passages and intricately analyzing the profound connection between Christ and believers, we have gained a profound and comprehensive understanding of the immense significance that this concept holds. As we dug into diverse theological viewpoints and interpretations, we were presented with a kaleidoscope of symbolism tied to the bride of Christ, enlightening us to the plethora of ways in which this concept has been embraced and understood within the realms of Christian theology and tradition. Moreover, we have embarked on an exploration of how the symbolic representation of the bride of Christ within the realm of Christian spirituality has far-reaching implications, not just for individuals but also for the entire community of faithful followers. This symbolism serves as an ever-present reminder of the profound connection between Christ and believers, greatly impacting their spiritual journey and fostering personal growth. Furthermore, the corporate identity of the church, defined as the bride of Christ, lays a foundation for intimacy among believers, giving rise to a sense of unity, love, and fellowship within the Christian assembly. Through this deep sense of connection, believers are inspired to cultivate spiritual closeness with one another and with Christ, thus strengthening the bonds that foster mutual support within the body of Christ. In conclusion, exploring the corporate identity of the church as the bride of Christ engenders profound implications for Christian spirituality and the body at large. It pushes believers to embrace the notion of an intimate relationship with Christ, thereby acknowledging the depths of His love and the sacrifices He made for them. Additionally, it urges believers to highly value their fellow brothers and sisters in Christ, recognizing them as integral members of the same body, thereby promoting a sense of community and purposeful unity. Ultimately, this work not only encapsulates key findings and invaluable insights but also accentuates the magnitude of exploring the corporate identity of the church as the bride of Christ. Through such exploration, our understanding of spirituality deepens, while the bonds within the community of believers strengthen, facilitating growth and laying the groundwork for an environment where the transformative power of Christ's love and Spirit can fervently flourish.

Terry Kashian

Ephesians

Chapter 1

1. Paul, an apostle of Jesus Christ by the will of God, to the saints who are at Ephesus, and to the faithful in Christ Jesus:
2. Grace be to you, and peace, from God our Father, and the Lord Jesus Christ.
3. Blessed be the God and Father of our Lord Jesus Christ, who has blessed us with all spiritual blessings in the heavenlies in Christ:
4. According as He has chosen us in Him before the downfall of the world, that we should be holy and without blame before Him in love:
5. Having determined us in advance to sonship through Jesus Christ to Himself, according to the good pleasure of His will,
6. To the praise of the glory of His grace, in which He has made and graced us in the beloved.
7. In Whom we have redemption through His blood, the forgiveness of sins, according to the riches of His grace;
8. He has abounded toward us in all wisdom and prudence;
9. Having made known to us the mystery of His will, according to His good pleasure that He has brought forth in Himself:
10. Into the administration of the completion of the proper time that He might gather together in one all in Christ, both which are in heaven, and which are on earth; even in Him:
11. In Whom also we have obtained an inheritance, being predestinated according to the purpose of Him who works all things after the counsel of His own will:
12. That we should be to the praise of His glory, who first hoped in Christ.
13. In Whom also you believed after you heard the word of reality, the gospel of your salvation: in Whom also after you believed, you were sealed with that Holy Spirit of promise,
14. Which is the guarantee of our inheritance until the redemption of the purchased possession, to the praise of His glory.
15. Therefore, I also, after I heard of your faith in the Lord Jesus, and love for all the saints,
16. Do not stop giving thanks for you, making mention of you in my prayers;
17. That the God of our Lord Jesus Christ, the Father of glory, may give to you the spirit of wisdom and revelation in the full knowledge of Him:
18. The eyes of your understanding being enlightened; that you may know what is the hope of His calling, and what the riches of the glory of His inheritance in the saints,
19. And what is the exceeding greatness of His power toward us who believe, according to the working of His mighty power,
20. Which He worked in Christ when He raised Him from the dead and set Him at His own right hand in the heavenlies,
21. Far above all government, and authority, and power, and dominion, and every name that is named, not only in this Old Covenant Age but also in that New Covenant Age which is about to come:

22. And has put all things under His feet, and gave Him to be the head over all things to the Assembly,
23. Which is His body, the fullness of Him that fills all in all.

Chapter 2

1. He has made you alive, who were dead in trespasses and sins;
2. Which in time past you walked according to the age of this world, according to the prince of the power of the air, the spirit that now works in the sons of stubbornness:
3. Among whom also we all had our conduct in times past in the lusts of our flesh, fulfilling the desires of the flesh and of the mind; and were by nature the children of wrath, just as others.
4. But God, who is rich in mercy, for His great love with which He loved us,
5. Even when we were dead in sins, has given life to us together with Christ, (by grace you are saved;)
6. And has raised us up together, and made us sit together in the heavenlies in Christ Jesus:
7. That in the coming age, He might show the exceeding riches of His grace in His kindness toward us through Christ Jesus.
8. For by grace are you saved through faith; and that not of yourselves: it is the gift of God:
9. Not of works, so that no one can boast.
10. For we are His workmanship, created in Christ Jesus for good works, which God has prepared beforehand that we should walk in them.
11. Therefore, remember, that you being in time past nations in the flesh, who are called uncircumcision by that which is called the circumcision in the flesh made by hands;
12. That at that time you were without Christ, being aliens from the commonwealth of Israel, and strangers from the covenants of promise, having no hope, and without God in the world:
13. But now in Christ Jesus you who sometimes were far off are made close by the blood of Christ.
14. For He is our peace, who has made both one, and has broken down the middle wall of separation between us;
15. Having abolished in His flesh the enmity, even the Law of commandments contained in ordinances; to create in Himself of the two, one new man, so making peace;
16. So that He might conciliate both to God in one body by the cross, having slain the enmity in Himself:
17. And came and preached peace to you who were afar off, and to them that were close.
18. For through Him we both have access by one Spirit to the Father.
19. Now therefore you are no more strangers and foreigners, but fellow citizens with the saints, and of the household of God;
20. And are built on the foundation of the apostles and prophets, Jesus Christ Himself being the chief cornerstone;
21. In whom all the building fitly framed together is growing into a holy temple in the Lord:

22. In whom you also are built together into a dwelling place of God in the Spirit.

Chapter 3

1. For this reason, I Paul, the prisoner of Jesus Christ for you nations,
2. If you have heard of the stewardship of the grace of God which is given me toward you:
3. That by revelation He made known to me the mystery; (as I wrote before in few words,
4. Whereby, when you read, you may understand my knowledge into the mystery of Christ)
5. Which in other generations was not made known to the sons of men, as it is now revealed to His holy apostles and prophets in the Spirit;
6. That the nations should be fellow heirs, and of the same body, and partakers of His promise in Christ by the gospel:
7. Which I was made a minister, according to the gift of the grace of God given to me by the effective working of His power.
8. To me, who is inferior to all the saints, is this grace given, that I should preach among the nations the untraceable riches of Christ;
9. Then to make all men see what is the stewardship of the mystery, which from the beginning of the age has been hidden in God, who created all things by Jesus Christ:
10. To the intent that now to the rulers and authorities in the heavenlies might be made known through the Assembly, the multifarious wisdom of God,
11. According to the purpose of the New Covenant age which He brought about in Christ Jesus our Lord:
12. In whom we have boldness and access with confidence through faith in Him.
13. Therefore, I ask that you do not lose heart at my tribulations for you, which is your glory.
14. For this reason I bow my knees to the Father of our Lord Jesus Christ,
15. Of whom the whole family in heaven and earth is named
16. That He would grant you, according to the riches of His glory, to be strengthened with power through His Spirit into the inner man,
17. That Christ may make His home in your hearts through faith, that you, being rooted and grounded in love,
18. May be powerful to apprehend with all the saints what the breadth and length and height and depth are and
19. To know the knowledge-surpassing love of Christ, that you may be complete into all the fullness of God.
20. Now, to Him that is able to do exceedingly abundantly above all that we ask or think, according to the power that works in us,
21. To Him be the glory in the Assembly in Christ Jesus throughout all generations, in this age, and into the New Covenant age. Amen.

Chapter 4

1. I, therefore, the prisoner of the Lord, beg you that you walk worthy of the calling with which you are called,
2. With all lowliness and meekness, with longsuffering restraint with one another in love;
3. being diligent to guard the unity of the Spirit in the bond of peace.
4. There is one body and one Spirit, just as you are called in one hope of your calling:
5. One Lord, one faith, one baptism,
6. One God and Father of all, who is above all, and through all, and in you all.
7. But to every one of us is given grace according to the measure of the gift of Christ.
8. Therefore, he says, when He ascended up on high, He led captivity captive and gave gifts to men.
9. 9.(Now that He ascended, what is it but that He also descended first into the lower parts of the earth?
10. He that descended is the same also that ascended up far above all the heavens, that He might fill all things),
11. For He gave some, apostles; and some, prophets; and some, evangelists; and some, shepherds and teachers;
12. For the maturing of the saints, for the work of the ministry, for the building of the body of Christ:
13. Until we all come in the unity of the faith, and of the full knowledge of the Son of God, to a mature man, to the measure of the stature of the fullness of Christ:
14. That after this we are babes no more, tossed back and forth, and carried about by waves and every wind of doctrine, by the chicanery of men, by a clever method of leading astray;
15. But speaking the reality in love, may grow up into Him in all things, which is the head, even Christ:
16. From whom the whole body, joined and held together by every joint with which it is equipped when each part is working properly, makes the body grow so that it builds itself up in love.
17. This I say, therefore, and testify in the Lord, that you do not walk any longer like the nations walk, in the futility of their mind,
18. Having their understanding darkened, being alienated from the life of God through the ignorance that is in them, because of the callousness of their heart:
19. Who being past feeling have given themselves over to unbridled desires, to work all uncleanness with greediness.
20. But you have not so learned Christ;
21. If so be that you have heard Him, and have been taught in Him, as the reality is in Jesus:
22. That you put off concerning the former conduct of the old man, which is corrupt according to the deceitful lusts;
23. But be renewed in the spirit of your mind;
24. So that you put on the new man, which after God is created in righteousness and true holiness.
25. Therefore, putting away lying, speak every man truthfully with his neighbor: for we are members one of another.

26. Be angry, and do not sin: let not the sun go down on your anger:
27. Neither give the devil a foothold.
28. Let him that stole steal no more: but rather let him labor, working with his hands in that which is good, that he may be able to give to him that is in need.
29. Let no putrid words proceed out of your mouth, but that which is good to the use of building up, that it may be giving grace to the hearers.
30. And do not grieve the Holy Spirit of God, by whom you were sealed into the day of redemption.
31. Let all bitterness, and wrath, and anger, and clamor, and evil speaking, be put away from you, with all malice:
32. Then be kind to one another, tenderhearted, forgiving one another, just as God for Christ's sake has forgiven you.

Chapter 5

1. Be you therefore models of God, as dear children;
2. And walk in love, as Christ also has loved us, and has given Himself for us an offering and a sacrifice to God for a sweet-smelling aroma.
3. But fornication, and all uncleanness, or covetousness, let it not even be mentioned among you, as is proper for saints;
4. Neither filthiness, nor foolish talking, nor jesting, which are improper, but rather giving of thanks.
5. For this you know that no fornicator, nor unclean person, nor covetous man, who is an any inheritance in the kingdom of Christ and of God.
6. Let no man deceive you with empty words: for because of these things comes the wrath of God on the sons of stubbornness.
7. Be not therefore partakers with them.
8. For you were sometimes darkness, but now you are light in the Lord: walk as children of light:
9. 9.(For the fruit of the Spirit is in all goodness and righteousness and reality)
10. Proving what is acceptable to the Lord.
11. And do not participate with the unfruitful works of darkness, but rather reprove them.
12. For it is a shame even to speak of those things which are done of them in secret.
13. But all are being convicted and are made manifest by the light: for the light exposes all.
14. Therefore, He says, awake you that sleep, and arise from the dead, and Christ will give you light.
15. See then that you walk accurately, not as fools, but as wise,
16. Buying up the opportunities, because the days are evil.
17. Therefore, do not be unwise but understand what the will of the Lord is.
18. And do not be drunk with wine, in which is dissolution; but be continually filled full in spirit;
19. Speaking to yourselves in psalms and hymns and spiritual songs, singing and making melody in your heart to the Lord;

20. Giving thanks always for all things to God and the Father in the name of our Lord Jesus Christ;
21. Place yourselves under one another in the fear of God.
22. Wives, place yourselves under your own husbands, as to the Lord.
23. For the husband is the head of the wife, just as Christ is the head of the Assembly: and He is the Savior of the body.
24. Therefore, as the Assembly is subject to Christ, so let the wives be to their own husbands in everything. idolater, has Husbands love your wives, just as Christ also loved the Assembly, and gave Himself for her;
25. That He might sanctify and cleanse her with the washing of water by the word,
26. That He might present her to Himself a glorious Assembly, not having spot, or wrinkle, or any such thing; but that she should be holy and without blemish.
27. So, ought men to love their wives as their own bodies. He who loves his wife loves himself.
28. For no man ever yet hated his own flesh; but
29. Nourishes and cherishes it, just as the Lord the Assembly:
30. For we are members of His body, of His flesh, and of His bones.
31. For this reason, a man will leave his father and mother and will be joined to his wife, and they two will be one flesh.
32. This mystery is great: but I speak concerning Christ and the Assembly.
33. Nevertheless, let every one of you in the same way so love his wife just as himself; and the wife see that she respect her husband.

Chapter 6

1. Children, obey your parents in the Lord: for this is right.
2. Honor your father and mother; which is the first commandment with promise;
3. That it may be well with you, and you may live long on the land.
4. And, you fathers, provoke not your children to anger: but bring them up in the training and admonition of the Lord.
5. Servants, be obedient to them that are your masters according to the flesh, with fear and trembling, in singleness of your heart, as to Christ;
6. Not with eye service, as man-pleasers; but as the servants of Christ, doing the will of God out from the soul;
7. With goodwill doing service, as to the Lord, and not to men:
8. Knowing that whatever good thing any man does, the same he will receive of the Lord, whether he be slave or free.
9. And, you masters do the same things to them, giving up threatening: knowing that your own Master also is in heaven; neither is there respect of persons with Him.
10. For the rest, my brothers, be strong in the Lord, and in the power of His might.
11. Put on the whole armor of God that you may be able to stand against the schemes of the devil.

12. For we wrestle not against flesh and blood, but against governments, against authorities, against the world rulers of this Old Covenant Age, against spiritual wickedness in the heavenlies.

13. Therefore, you take up the whole armor of God that you may be able to withstand in the evil day, and having done all, to stand.

14. Stand, therefore, having your waist wrapped about with reality, and putting on the breastplate of righteousness;

15. And your feet shod with the firm footing of the gospel of peace;

16. Above all, taking up the shield of faith, with which you can quench all the fiery arrows of the wicked.

17. And receive the helmet of salvation, and the sword of the Spirit, which is the declaration of God:

18. Through prayer and supplication with all praying in spirit at every appointed time, and staying vigilant in all perseverance and supplication for all the saints;

19. And for me, that the word may be given to me, that I may open my mouth boldly, to make known the mystery of the gospel,

20. For which I am an ambassador in a shackle: I may speak boldly in it as I ought to speak.

21. But that you also may know my affairs, and how I am doing, Tychicus, a beloved brother, and faithful minister in the Lord, will make known to you all things:

22. Who I have sent to you for the same purpose, that you might know our affairs, and that he might comfort your hearts.

23. Peace be to the brothers, and love with faith, from God the Father and the Lord Jesus Christ.

24. Grace be with all them that are loving our Lord Jesus Christ with integrity. Amen.

Philippians Synopsis

Introduction

The Apostle Paul's epistle, the book of Philippians, stands as a profound testament to the transformative power of Christ and the unifying force among believers.

Penned during the trying times of Paul's incarceration, the book of Philippians offers a unique window into the early Christian community, their trials, and their unwavering faith. It is a treasure trove of theological revelations, traversing themes such as the encounter with Christ, the fellowship of believers, divine righteousness, spiritual maturation, transformation, unity under Christ, mutual care, and the secret to contentment.

This essay intends to delve into these intricate themes and concepts, illuminating their significance within the book's context and their pertinence to the modern Christian life. The encounter with Christ and the fellowship of believers will be scrutinized, as they lay the foundation for the teachings in Philippians.

The exploration of these themes will not only enrich our understanding of the book of Philippians but also offer invaluable insights into the core of Christian faith and practice. Despite the passage of centuries, the teachings from the Philippians continue to reverberate with believers today, underscoring their timeless relevance and applicability.

II. The Experience of Christ and Communion of Believers

I. The Crucial Role of Fellowship and Engagement in the Gospel

The Epistle to the Philippians underscores the profound importance of fellowship and active engagement in the gospel. In his heartfelt letter to the Philippians, the Apostle Paul sheds light on the transformative potential of collective worship and a shared mission. This fellowship, a binding force among believers, fosters a unified devotion to Christ and a shared commitment to propagate the message of salvation. This unity not only fortifies the ties within the Christian community but also acts as a beacon of hope and support during challenging times.

II. Existence in Christ and the Profound Significance of Enduring Suffering for His Cause

The concept of existence in Christ is a recurring theme in the book of Philippians. Paul inspires believers to accept suffering as a means to glorify Christ and further His divine kingdom. The life of Christ Himself, marked by voluntary suffering and ultimate sacrifice on the cross, serves as a guiding light for believers. By partaking in Christ's sufferings, believers not only deepen their bond with Him but also contribute to His redemptive mission. Enduring suffering for the cause of Christ is perceived as a journey towards spiritual growth and maturity, refining and fortifying the believer's faith (Smith, Year).

III. The Attitude of Humility and Selflessness as Embodied by Jesus

The book of Philippians persistently accentuates the attitude of humility and selflessness, as embodied by Jesus. Paul implores believers to emulate the mindset of Christ, who epitomized humility and placed the needs of others before His own. This attitude of humility and selflessness cultivates unity among believers and solidifies the ties within the Christian community. It challenges believers to relinquish selfish desires and arrogance, and instead, to regard others as more significant than themselves. By mirroring Christ's humility, believers reflect His character and manifest His love to the world.

III. Righteousness from God and Spiritual Growth

I. Understanding Divine Righteousness

The philosophical exploration of divine righteousness is a central theme in the book of Philippians. It underscores the transformative power of God's grace and the continual journey of spiritual evolution. In Philippians 3:9, Apostle Paul articulates his aspiration to be found in Christ, without his own righteousness, but possessing the righteousness that comes from God by faith in Christ. This notion underscores that righteousness is not a product of human endeavor or compliance to the law, but rather a result of faith in Christ and the gift of His righteousness to the faithful. It is a gift! Can't emphasize that enough.

II. The Journey of Spiritual Development and Maturity

Philippians further delineate the journey of spiritual development and maturity that the faithful are encouraged to undertake. In Philippians 1:6, Paul expresses his conviction that God, who initiated a noble work in the faithful, will persist in it until its culmination at the advent of Christ Jesus at the end of the Old Covenant age. This implies that spiritual advancement is a lifelong journey, encompassing continuous metamorphosis and maturation in Christ. The journey of spiritual transformation comprises:

- The initial encounter with Christ
- A deepening bond and an expanding comprehension of His truth and ways

- Producing fruit (win souls), cultivating a Christ-like character, and participating in the mission of God's kingdom

As the faithful mature spiritually, they are encouraged to produce fruit (win souls), cultivate a Christ-like character, and participate in the mission of God's kingdom.

III. The Divine Calling in Christ Jesus and the Opposition from the Cross's Adversaries

Philippians underscores the divine calling in Christ Jesus and the opposition encountered from the cross's adversaries. In Philippians 3:14, Paul talks about his relentless pursuit of the goal to secure the reward for which God has summoned him heavenward in Christ Jesus. This divine calling necessitates a life of commitment, endurance, and the pursuit of Christ-likeness. However, the faithful also confront resistance from those who are preoccupied with worldly matters and oppose the cross's message. These adversaries of the cross may attempt to destabilize the faith of the faithful and obstruct their spiritual transformation. Consequently, the faithful are encouraged to:

- Remain steadfast in their faith.
- Resist worldly influences.
- Stay focused on the divine calling in Christ Jesus

IV. Transformation and Unity in Christ

I. The Significance of Solidarity Among the Faithful

The theme of unity among believers is a recurring motif in the book of Philippians. Apostle Paul underscores the significance of harmony within the Christian community, urging the faithful to share a common mindset and love for each other. He passionately declares, "Complete my joy by thinking alike, sharing the same love, and being united in spirit and purpose" (Philippians 2:2, Holy Bible: New International Version, 2011). The unity among believers is not only a mirror reflecting the unity of the Holy Trinity but also a compelling testament to the world of the transformative power of the gospel.

II. The Influence of Prayer in Cultivating Unity and Spiritual Maturation

Prayer holds a pivotal role in cultivating unity and fostering spiritual maturation among the faithful. Apostle Paul inspires the Philippians to intercede for each other and to express their desires to God with a heart full of gratitude. He advises, "Do not be burdened by any worry, but in every circumstance, through prayer and supplication, with a heart of gratitude, present your desires to God" (Philippians 4:6, Holy Bible: New International Version, 2011). Prayer not only fortifies the bond of unity among believers but also deepens their connection with God, aligning their hearts with His divine will.

V. Caring for One Another and the Secret of Contentment

I. Emulating Mutual Care in the Christian Fellowship: An Exemplary Model

The book of Philippians places a significant emphasis on the virtue of mutual care within the Christian fellowship. The apostle Paul, through his actions and teachings, provides a compelling illustration of this principle.

1. Paul, in Philippians 2:4, encourages believers to not merely focus on their own needs but to also consider the needs of others. This appeal to selflessness and empathy for others is further accentuated in Philippians 2:3, where Paul advises believers to act not out of self-interest or empty pride, but to humbly regard others as superior to themselves.

Paul's commitment to caring for others is also manifested in his relationship with the Philippian church. Throughout the letter, Paul conveys his profound affection and gratitude for the Philippians, affectionately referring to them as his "joy and crown" (Philippians 4:1). He applauds them for their generosity and support, acknowledging that they have been his partners in spreading the gospel from the outset (Philippians 1:5).

This model of mutual care serves as a blueprint for believers in the present day. It underscores the significance of nurturing a community characterized by love, support, and encouragement within the body of Christ. By emulating Paul's example and prioritizing the needs of others, we can foster an environment where individuals feel cherished, cared for, and supported in their spiritual journey.

II. Unveiling the Secret to Contentment as Articulated by the Apostle Paul

Another prominent theme in the book of Philippians is the secret to contentment, as articulated by the apostle Paul.

1. In Philippians 4:11-13, Paul states, "I have learned to be content in any situation. I understand what it means to be in need, and I know what it means to have abundance. I have discovered the secret to being content in every circumstance, whether well-nourished or hungry, whether living in abundance or in scarcity. I can endure all things through him who strengthens me."

Paul's contentment is anchored in his unwavering faith in Christ and his trust in God's provision. Despite enduring various trials and tribulations, including imprisonment, Paul finds tranquility and satisfaction in his relationship with Christ. He understands that true contentment is not derived from external circumstances or material possessions but from a profound and enduring faith in God.

This secret to contentment has profound implications for believers in the present day. It prompts us to reassess our priorities and seek fulfillment in our relationship with Christ rather than in worldly pursuits. It reminds us that true contentment is not found in the accumulation of wealth or possessions, but in the assurance that we are loved and cared for by a faithful God.

I. Revisiting the Central Themes and Concepts Explored in the Discourse

This discourse has been a journey through the profound themes and theological concepts embedded in the book of Philippians. We have navigated the depths of Christ's experience and the communion of believers, underscoring the significance of fellowship and active participation in the gospel. The discourse has illuminated the path of living in Christ and embracing suffering for His glory as avenues toward spiritual evolution and maturity. The ethos of humility and selflessness, as embodied by Jesus, has been underscored as a cardinal virtue for believers to internalize. We have scrutinized the concept of divine righteousness and the phases of spiritual evolution and maturity. The lofty calling of God in Christ Jesus and the trials posed by adversaries of the cross have been investigated. The metamorphosis from the body of humiliation to the body of glory has been portrayed as a beacon of hope for believers, while the unity among believers and the role of prayer in nurturing unity and spiritual growth have been deliberated. Finally, we have reflected on the paradigm of mutual care within the Christian community and the secret of contentment as articulated by the apostle Paul.

II. Reemphasizing the Significance of Christ's Experience and the Communion of Believers

The doctrines in Philippians persistently underscore the transformative potency of encountering Christ and the importance of the communion of believers. The experience of Christ and the fellowship of believers form the bedrock of the Christian faith, endowing believers with a sense of purpose, belonging, and spiritual evolution. As believers engage in fellowship and partake in the gospel, they are metamorphosed by the power of Christ's love and grace, and they are galvanized to live their faith in a manner that glorifies God and enriches others.

III. Concluding Reflections on the Pertinence and Application of the Teachings from Philippians

The teachings from the Philippians continue to reverberate with believers today, offering direction and inspiration in steering through the complexities of the contemporary world. The encounter with Christ and the communion of believers remains the cornerstone of the Christian faith, reminding us of the transformative power of encountering Christ and the importance of nurturing unity and care within the Christian community. The concepts dissected in Philippians, such as humility, selflessness, righteousness, spiritual growth, and unity, are not merely theoretical constructs but practical principles that can be integrated into our daily lives. By embracing these teachings and striving to live them out, believers can experience a more profound relationship with Christ, find fulfillment in their faith, and make a positive imprint on the world around them.

I. The Suffering Servant Pattern in Philippians

The cornerstone of biblical literature, the book of Isaiah, presents a profound and captivating concept that has intrigued theologians for centuries - the suffering servant and the reigning Messiah. Paul sources his epistle to the Philippians from these four servant songs in Isaiah.

This emblematic figure, vividly portrayed in Isaiah's prophetic verses, serves as a potent symbol of sacrifice and redemption. It weaves a compelling narrative of humiliation and exaltation. The journey of the suffering servant is not merely a central theme in Isaiah. Still, it also echoes profoundly within the Christian tradition, especially in the interpretation of Christ's role and the church's mission.

The objective of this paper is to delve deeply into the depiction of the suffering servant in Isaiah and its profound implications for the church. It aims to unravel the complex interconnections between the narrative of the suffering servant and the church's journey, particularly viewed through the prism of kenosis, or self-emptying. Moreover, it will scrutinize the ramifications of this theme for the believers, who are the body of Christ, and their role in the realization of their salvation with purpose.

II. The Suffering Servant in Isaiah

I. An Exploration of Isaiah 42:1–4 and its Illustration of the Suffering Servant

Isaiah's book offers a striking depiction of the suffering servant in verses 42:1–4. The servant, chosen and blessed with God's Spirit, is painted with strokes of gentleness, humility, and justice. The servant's mission, to set in place justice in the nations, is not achieved through brute force or violence, but through a compassionate and gentle approach. This portrayal of the suffering servant lays the foundation for comprehending the sacrificial essence of Christ's mission and the church's mandate to mirror this servant-like demeanor in its global mission. Matthew in his gospel shows clearly that Jesus is the real Israel and the real SON that Yahweh calls out of Egypt. Matt. 2:14 When he arose, he took the young Child and His mother by night and departed for Egypt, and was there until the death of Herod, **that it might be fulfilled** which was spoken by the Lord through the prophet, saying, *"Out of Egypt I called My Son."*[75] Matthew quotes Hosea 11:1. This is the beginning of the suffering servant coming on the scene. Later Matthew in chapter 12:12-21 quotes the song in Isa. 42. And great multitudes followed Him, and He healed them all. Yet He warned them not to make Him known, **that it might be fulfilled** which was spoken by Isaiah the prophet,

---

[75] *The New King James Version* (Mt 2:14–15). (1982). Thomas Nelson

saying: ***"Behold! My Servant*** *whom I have chosen, My Beloved in whom My soul is well pleased! I will put My Spirit upon Him, And He will declare justice to the Gentiles. He will not quarrel nor cry out, Nor will anyone hear His voice in the streets. A bruised reed He will not break, And smoking flax He will not quench, Till He sends forth justice to victory; And in His name, Gentiles will trust."*[76]

I will keep You and give You as a covenant to the people, As a light to the Gentiles, To open blind eyes,[77] … This quote from Isaiah is echoed in Matthew 12 as Jesus is fulfilling this prophetic song. ²²Then **a demon-possessed man *who* was blind and mute was brought to Jesus, and He healed him** so that the mute man spoke and saw. ²³All the crowds were amazed and were saying, "This man cannot be the Son of David, can he?" [78]Jesus was kept by the Father and presented as a Covenant to His people Israel, and a light to the nations. The Lord symbolically opened the eyes of the blind, he literally healed the blind man and was demonstrating it as a symbol of the condition of Israel. They were blind and had nothing to say. No good news!

32 Since this Old Covenant Age began, it has not been heard that anyone opened the eyes of one who was born blind. 33 If this man were not of God, He could do nothing. John 9:32-33 TKB – Translation – Terry Kashian. No one before Christ had opened the eyes of the blind, this was a new thing, and it was sprouting in the land of Israel. Jesus was proclaiming that Israel was blind and He was the cure for their blindness. Isaiah 42:16 predicted that Jesus would lead the blind in a way they do not know. But Old Covenant Israel was blind and deaf and unless they came to their only savior and God, they would remain blind and deaf and have nothing to say to the world. Isaiah states that Israel as Yahweh's servant is in a deplorable condition.¹⁹ **Who is blind but my servant,** or **deaf as my messenger whom I send?** Who is blind as my dedicated one, or blind as the servant of the LORD? ²⁰ He **sees many things but does not observe them; his ears are open, but he does not hear.**[79]

The prophets like Isaiah, and Ezekiel proclaimed Israel's condition over and over. When you get to the New Testament Jesus says in Matthew. 14 With them indeed is fulfilled the prophecy of Isaiah which says: 'You **shall indeed hear but never understand,** and you **shall indeed see but never perceive.** 15 For this people's heart has grown dull, and **their ears are heavy of hearing, and their eyes they have closed,** lest they should perceive with their eyes, and hear with their ears, and understand with their heart, and turn to Me to heal them.'[80] **WHILE SEEING, THEY MAY SEE AND NOT PERCEIVE, AND WHILE HEARING, THEY MAY HEAR AND NOT UNDERSTAND,** OTHERWISE, THEY

---

[76] *The New King James Version* (Mt 12:15–21). (1982). Thomas Nelson.

[77] *The New King James Version* (Is 42:6–7). (1982). Thomas Nelson.

[78] *New American Standard Bible,* 1995 Edition: Paragraph Version (Mt 12:22–23). (1995). The Lockman Foundation.

[79] *The Revised Standard Version* (Is 42:19–20). (1971). Logos Research Systems, Inc.

[80] *The Revised Standard Version* (Mt 13:13–15). (1971). Logos Research Systems, Inc.

MIGHT RETURN AND BE FORGIVEN."⁸¹ ³⁸*This was* to fulfill the word of Isaiah the prophet which he spoke:⁸² ³⁹For this reason they could not believe, for Isaiah said again, ⁴⁰**"HE HAS BLINDED THEIR EYES** AND HE HARDENED THEIR HEART SO THAT THEY WOULD **NOT SEE WITH THEIR EYES AND PERCEIVE WITH THEIR HEART,** AND BE CONVERTED AND I HEAL THEM."⁸³

    Old Covenant Israel can only be healed if they forsook their idolatry and believed in the Lord Jesus. These verses were applied by the apostle Paul when dealing with Old Covenant Israel. The ministry of Christ is continued in His body. This is the pattern in the New Testament. Christ the head ministers to the nation of Israel and the Body of Christ ministers to the nations. This is the one new man, Christ the head, and the church as the body. Just as the Lord Jesus is the suffering servant in Isaiah 42, the body takes on the same role. This is the light to the nations to bring revelation of God's perpetual purpose to them. The hope of glory which is the Messiah in them! We can see the application of Isaiah 42:6. Luke applies this in Acts 13 where he says, 46 And Paul and Barnabas spoke out boldly, saying, "It was **necessary that the word of God should be spoken first to you.** Since you thrust it from you, and judge yourselves unworthy of eternal life, behold, we turn to the Gentiles. 47 For so **the Lord has commanded us**, saying, '**I have set you to be a light for the Gentiles**, that you may be salvation to the uttermost parts of the earth. Now the suffering servant is an US instead of just Him. Paul embodies the concept of the suffering servant. Paul explicitly is the model and pattern the church will go through. The Lord told Ananias about Paul, ¹⁵ But the Lord said to him, "Go, for he is a chosen instrument of mine to carry my name before the Gentiles and kings and the sons of Israel; ¹⁶for **I will show him how much he must suffer for the sake of my name**⁸⁴

    As a light to the Gentiles, To open blind eyes, To bring out prisoners from the prison, Those who sit in darkness from the prison house.⁸⁵ Compare this verse to Acts 26, ¹⁶ But rise and stand upon your feet; for I have appeared to you for this purpose, **to appoint you to serve** and bear witness to the things in which you have seen in Me and to those in which I will appear to you, 17 delivering you from the people and from the Gentiles— **to whom I send you 18 to open their eyes, that they may turn from darkness to light and from the power of Satan to God**, that they may receive forgiveness of sins and a place among those who are sanctified by faith in me.'⁸⁶ The suffering servant in Isaiah 42 is Jesus and the blind servant is Old Covenant Israel. Jesus is replacing the blind servant and as Head and body, the corporate Christ is fulfilling this prophecy. 1 Cor. 12:12. Many members, one body, so

---

⁸¹ *New American Standard Bible, 1995 Edition: Paragraph Version* (Mk 4:12). (1995). The Lockman Foundation.

⁸² *New American Standard Bible, 1995 Edition: Paragraph Version* (Jn 12:38). (1995). The Lockman Foundation.

⁸³ *New American Standard Bible, 1995 Edition: Paragraph Version* (Jn 12:39–40). (1995). The Lockman Foundation.
⁸⁴ *The Revised Standard Version* (Ac 9:15–16). (1971). Logos Research Systems, Inc.
⁸⁵ *The New King James Version* (Is 42:6–7). (1982). Thomas Nelson.
⁸⁶ *The Revised Standard Version* (Ac 26:15–18). (1971). Logos Research Systems, Inc.

also is the Messiah or the Christ! Paul's message to the Philippians is directly tied to these prophecies in Isaiah.

II. Delving into Isaiah 49:1–6 and its Link to Christ as the Church's Head

Isaiah 49:1–6 identifies the suffering servant as Israel, yet the passage also alludes to a broader fulfillment in Christ as the church's leader. The servant, called from birth to be a beacon to the nations, brings salvation to the world's farthest corners. This passage underscores the global reach of the suffering servant's mission and its tie to the church's mandate to spread the gospel universally. Christ, as the ultimate embodiment of the suffering servant, realizes this mission through his sacrificial demise and resurrection, and the church, as Christ's body, is tasked with perpetuating this mission in the world. Even Paul related his calling to this song in Isaiah in the letter to the Galatians. [15] But when God, who had **set me apart *even* from my mother's womb** and called me through His grace, was pleased [16] to reveal His Son in me so that I might preach Him among the Gentiles,[87] I will say again Paul's life echoes the life of Christ as the suffering servant and is the pattern that he called the church to emulate. What has puzzled scholars throughout the generations when attempting to interpret this song, Isaiah goes from the individual servant to the corporate servant. Unless we understand that Jesus becomes the new Israel, the reality, and embodiment of all that Yahweh desired of Israel, and that this Israel is Jesus as the head and his church as His body. Paul said it clearly in Philippians, "For me to live is Christ". Paul saw his life as an expression of the life of the Messiah. The early church apostles saw Christ as the true Israel, and the Old Covenant Israel as a shadow of reality. Paul's expectation for the church was for them to see as he shared in Colossians, "Christ is our life". This is the mystery and wisdom of God. He installed the Messiah inside of a people that received Him to be His body. This is not metaphorical! We are the body of Christ. Yahweh was glorified in Jesus as the head and He was glorified in His body, the corporate Messiah. So, in verse 3, of Isaiah 49, Yahweh says you are My servant in whom I will be glorified.

Another application of this chapter in Isaiah by Paul and John. 8 Thus says Yahweh, "in an acceptable time have I answered you, and in a day of salvation I have helped you; and I will preserve You, and give You for a covenant of the people, to establish the land, to make them take possession of the destroyed inheritances: 9 saying to those who are bound, 'come out!'; to those who are in darkness, 'show yourselves!' "They will feed in the ways, and on all bare heights will be their pasture. 10 They will not hunger nor thirst; neither will the heat nor sun strike them: for He who has mercy on them will lead them, even by springs of water He will guide them. Isaiah 49:8-10. TKB – Translation – Terry Kashian. In 2 Cor. 6:2, Paul quotes this passage in verse 8. For He says: *"In an acceptable time I have heard you, And in the day of salvation I have helped you."* **Behold, now** *is* the accepted time; behold,

---
[87] *New American Standard Bible, 1995 Edition: Paragraph Version* (Ga 1:15–16). (1995). The Lockman Foundation.

now *is* the day of salvation[88] The acceptable time is the appointed time of fulfillment. Paul says it is NOW in his day. Paul admonishes the Corinthians not to receive the grace of God in vain, but to work together with Him. This is the head and body cooperating in the **NOW** of the day of salvation. This application of the suffering body of the Servant is profound. He assures the Corinthian believers that they have not caused an occasion of stumbling to them as he relates their experiences of suffering. In the middle of chapter 6 Paul makes a statement," ... **as dying**, and **behold we live**[89]".

Even as Christ went through the dying stage into resurrection and the suffering stage into exaltation. Paul had this in mind when he applied Isaiah 49 to their experiences. The Ministry of Conciliation was given to the church for the whole world. The head died for the sins of the world and the church with her head was made a covenant to all nations to set creation free and bring them out into His marvelous light. John quotes verse 10 in his Revelation 7:14-17. So he said to me, "**These are the ones** who **come out of the great tribulation** and **washed their robes** and **made them white** in **the blood of the Lamb**. Therefore, they are before the throne of God and serve Him day and night in His temple. And He who sits on the throne will dwell among them. **They shall neither hunger anymore nor thirst anymore; the sun shall not strike them, nor any heat**; for **the Lamb** who is in the midst of the throne **will shepherd them** and **lead them to living fountains of waters. And God will wipe away every tear from their eyes**[90] **God promises to wipe their tears away because they were martyred for the faith.** These are the many of the body of the suffering Servant that Isaiah predicted that Yahweh had compassion on. The stages that Paul wrote to the Philippians of knowing Him, the power of His resurrection, **the fellowship of His sufferings**, and **being made conformable to His death** is exactly what the first-century saints went through to the goal of ultimate exaltation.

III. Inspecting Isaiah 50:4–11 and its Depiction of the Suffering Servant's Path from Humiliation to Glory

Isaiah 50:4–11 offers a window into the suffering servant's path from humiliation to glory. The servant is depicted as one who remains obedient to God's call, even when faced with opposition and suffering. The servant's dedication to God's mission is steadfast, and despite the trials faced, the servant places unwavering trust in God's faithfulness. This passage anticipates Christ's own path of suffering and glory, as he willingly submits to the Father's will, even to the point of death on the cross. The church, in turn, is called to adopt the path of self-sacrifice and trust in God's faithfulness, confident that glory and vindication will arrive in due course.

---

[88] *The New King James Version* (2 Co 6:1–2). (1982). Thomas Nelson.

[89] *The New King James Version* (2 Co 6:9). (1982). Thomas Nelson.

[90] *The New King James Version* (Re 7:14–17). (1982). Thomas Nelson.

IV. Probing Isaiah 52:13–53:12 and its Realization in Christ and the Church

Isaiah 52:13–53:12 is arguably the most renowned passage illustrating the suffering servant in Isaiah. This passage vividly portrays the suffering servant's sacrificial death and the redemptive significance of his suffering. The suffering servant is depicted as one who is scorned, shunned, and afflicted, carrying the weight of humanity's sins. Through his suffering, the servant paves the way for salvation and healing. This passage finds its ultimate realization in Christ's crucifixion and resurrection, as he becomes the propitiation for the world's sins. The church, as Christ's body, partakes in this redemptive work by spreading the message of salvation and embodying the sacrificial love of the suffering servant.

III. The Process of Kenosis and Its Reflection in the Church

I. Explaining Kenosis: A Journey of Self-Emptying

Kenosis, a term rooted in the Greek language, translates to "to empty." It is a theological concept that encapsulates the self-emptying of Christ during His incarnation and earthly ministry. This term paints a vivid picture of the Son of God voluntarily surrendering His divine attributes and privileges, taking on a human form to execute God's redemptive plan. The humility, obedience, and self-sacrifice exhibited by Christ, who willingly relinquished His divine glory and power to identify with humanity and offer salvation, are the core elements of Kenosis. Kenosis is a profound theological concept that underscores the selflessness and love of God, as manifested in Christ's life and ministry. It serves as a beacon for believers, urging them to mirror Christ's humility and self-emptying in their own lives.

II. Tracing Parallels: Isaiah's Suffering Servant and the Church's Journey

The journey of the church finds a parallel in Isaiah's portrayal of the suffering servant. The suffering servant's narrative of humiliation and exaltation echoes in the church's journey of self-emptying and transformation. The servant's role as a sacrificial figure, bearing the sins of others and facilitating redemption, aligns with the church's mission to proclaim the gospel and bring salvation to the world.

Isaiah's depiction of the suffering servant serves as a prophetic precursor to Christ's redemptive work and the subsequent mission of the church. The servant's journey of self-emptying and ultimate exaltation mirrors the transformative process that believers undergo as they heed the call to deny themselves, take up their cross, and follow Christ.

III. Unpacking the Significance: The 40 years from AD 30 to AD 70 in the Role of the Suffering Servant

The 40-year span from AD 30 to AD 70 carries immense significance in fulfilling the role of the suffering servant. This period encapsulates the life, death, and resurrection of Christ, as well as the establishment and growth of the early Christian church. It marks the generation tasked with fulfilling the prophecies of the suffering servant, bringing the light of God's Kingdom to the Gentiles. I call this the generational model for every generation that follows.

During this period, the transformative power of the cross is evident in the lives of believers. The apostle Paul, as an example, experienced a personal transformation through his encounter with Christ on the road to Damascus. His journey of suffering and exaltation, marked by persecution and the proclamation of the gospel, exemplifies the pattern of the suffering servant portrayed in Isaiah.

IV. Spotlight on Transformation: The Power of the Cross in Believers' Lives through the Lens of the Apostle Paul

The life of the apostle Paul serves as a compelling testament to the transformative power of the cross in the lives of believers. Through his encounter with Christ and subsequent conversion, Paul underwent a radical transformation from a persecutor of the church to a devoted follower of Christ. His journey of suffering and exaltation, marked by trials, hardships, and the proclamation of the gospel, mirrors the pattern of the suffering servant portrayed in Isaiah.

Paul's example underscores the transformative impact of the cross on believers, as they are called to die to self, crucify their old nature, the flesh, and live in the power of Christ's resurrection. The cross becomes the central symbol of their faith, representing both the suffering and the victory of Christ, and serving as a catalyst for personal and communal transformation.

IV. The Church as the Body of Christ

A. Prologue to the notion of the faithful as the Body of Christ

The notion of the faithful as the body of Christ is a pivotal theme in the New Testament, predominantly in the epistles of the apostle Paul. This metaphorical expression underscores the unity and interdependence of the faithful in their bond with Christ. Analogous to the physical body, composed of diverse parts functioning in harmony, the body of Christ is an assembly of diverse individuals, unified in their faith and objective.

B. Dissection of the External and Internal Man as depicted in 2 Corinthians 4:10–17

In 2 Corinthians 4:10–17, Paul employs the symbolism of the External and Internal Man to illustrate the paradoxical essence of the Christian existence. The External Man signifies the earthly body of Christ, susceptible to decay and able to be physically destroyed. Conversely, the Inner Man symbolizes the glorification process that is happening in every believer of the faithful, undergoing daily renewal. Paul understood that even as Christ suffered in His physical body and then sacrificed Himself, so also the church joined to the Lord in her earthly state will experience a momentary light affliction is not worthy to be compared to the glory that awaited them. Paul was defining the transition they were experiencing of the suffering servant. Not the individual human body, but the corporate body of Christ in its mortality and encouraging them that the body of Christ will be honored in resurrection and glory. Paul uses the plural "our" and the singular "outer man". Even though many look at this verse on an individual level, Paul is drawing from the motif from the songs of the Servant in Isaiah.

C. Scrutiny of the model of suffering and glorification exemplified by Christ in Philippians 2:5-11

In Philippians 2:5-9b, Paul introduces the model of suffering and glorification exemplified by Christ as the ultimate paradigm for the faithful. 5 Let this mindset be in us, the one in Christ Jesus: 6 Who, being in essence God, not leading the way to seize to be equal with God: 7 but He emptied Himself, and accepting the essence of a slave, and came in the resemblance of men: 8 and being found in the external appearance as a man, He humbled Himself and became obedient even to death, even the death of the cross. 9 Therefore God also has highly exalted Him and given Him a name which is above every name: TKB Translation Terry Kashian. However, due to His obedience and self-abnegation, God exalted Him supremely and conferred upon Him the name surpassing all names. This model of suffering and glorification serves as a blueprint for the faithful to experience in their personal lives.

D. Implementation of this model to the Body of Christ and its repercussions for the faithful

The model of suffering and glorification exemplified by Christ bears significant repercussions for the Body of Christ, the church, and its individual members. Just as Christ suffered and was glorified, so too are the faithful summoned to adopt the path of denying the Self and sacrificial love. This entails the willingness to withstand hardships and persecution for the gospel's sake, and confident that God will ultimately glorify and reward those who follow Him faithfully. The implementation of this model to the body of Christ cultivates unity, humility, and a collective sense of purpose among the faithful as they endeavor to accomplish their mission in the world.

V. Working out Salvation in Fear and Trembling
I. Delving into the Practical Consequences of the Journey of Salvation

The journey of salvation, a pivotal theme in Christianity, is not a singular event but a continuous process that demands active engagement and effort from the faithful. The journey of salvation entails:

- Nurturing an intimate bond with the Divine
- Seeking His divine counsel
- Endeavoring to lead a life that is in harmony with His wishes.
- Consistently submitting to the will of God
- Aligning one's thoughts, words, and deeds with His teachings.
- Constantly evolving in faith and obedience

The journey of salvation also necessitates the cultivation of spiritual disciplines such as:

- Prayer
- Studying the Bible
- Worship
- Communion and fellowship daily with fellow believers
- Practicing daily sharing your faith with unbelievers to win them to Christ.

These practices aid believers in deepening their comprehension of God's Word, fortifying their bond with Him, and maturing spiritually. They provide a structure for believers to engage in reflection, repentance, and transformation, enabling them to embody Christ-like character and behavior.

II. Highlighting God's Role in Inspiring and Enabling His Good Pleasure within Believers

While the journey of salvation demands personal dedication and commitment, it is crucial to acknowledge that it is ultimately God who equips and empowers believers to do so. Philippians 2:13 proclaims, "For it is God who works in you both to will and to do for His good pleasure" (NKJV). This verse underscores the divine collaboration between God and believers in the process of salvation.

God's role in the journey of salvation is multifaceted. He:

- Commences the work of salvation by drawing individuals towards Himself.
- Convicts them of their sins.
- Bestows upon them the gift of salvation through faith in Jesus Christ
- Continues to work in their lives, transforming their hearts and renewing their minds.
- Empowers them to live by His purpose.

God's work in believers permeates every facet of their lives. He:
- Supplies the necessary grace, wisdom, and strength to surmount challenges.
- Guides believers through His Holy Spirit, illuminating His Word
- Equips believers with spiritual gifts to serve others and contribute to the building up of His body in the kingdom.

VI. Endearing Relationships Within the Body of Christ

I. An Overview of the Deeply Rooted Relationships of Paul with Timothy and Epaphroditus

Within the Christian community, the Apostle Paul's profound connections with Timothy and Epaphroditus stand as compelling illustrations of deep-seated relationships, marked by selfless love and unwavering commitment. The depth of Paul's relationship with Timothy is palpable in his epistles, where he affectionately refers to Timothy as his "cherished and loyal child in the Lord" (1 Corinthians 4:17) and articulates his intention to dispatch Timothy to the Philippians, asserting, "I have no one like him, who will genuinely care for your well-being" (Philippians 2:20). In a similar vein, Paul's bond with Epaphroditus is characterized by mutual respect and self-sacrifice, as Epaphroditus risked his own life in service to Paul and the church, even to the point of near death (Philippians 2:27).

II. Dissecting the Selfless Nature of Paul's Life Dedicated to God and the Church

Paul's life is a testament to selfless love and unwavering dedication to God and the church. In his epistle to the Philippians, Paul pens, "Even if I am to be poured out as a libation upon the sacrificial offering of your faith, I am glad and rejoice with you all" (Philippians 2:17). This metaphor of being poured out as a libation underscores Paul's readiness to sacrifice his life for the propagation of the gospel and the advancement of the church. Paul's selfless nature is further accentuated in his letter to the Corinthians, where he outlines the trials he faced for Christ, stating, "We are afflicted in every way, but not crushed; perplexed, but not driven to despair; persecuted, but not forsaken; struck down, but not destroyed" (2 Corinthians 4:8-9).

III. Underlining the Importance of These Relationships as the Standard Within the Christian Community

The bonds between Paul, Timothy, and Epaphroditus serve as significant exemplars within the Christian community, underscoring the importance of unity, selfless love, and self-sacrifice. These relationships exemplify the power of genuine empathy and concern for others, as well as the readiness to sacrifice one's life for the benefit of others. They inspire believers to nurture similar bonds within the church, fostering an atmosphere of love, support, and mutual edification. By emulating the example set by Paul, Timothy, and Epaphroditus, the Christian community can embody the selfless love and enduring relationships that echo the essence of the suffering servant motif in Isaiah and fulfill its mission in the world.

VII. Conclusion

A. Revisiting the primary arguments presented in the discourse.

This discourse has embarked on a journey through the depiction of the suffering servant in the book of Isaiah, shedding light on its profound implications for the church's identity and mission. The suffering servant, as portrayed in Isaiah's prophetic verses, stands as a potent symbol of sacrifice, redemption, and transformation.

By delving into pivotal passages such as Isaiah 42:1–4, 49:1–6, 50:4–11, and 52:13–53:12, we have observed the realization of these prophecies in the figure of Christ and the ensuing influence on the church. The suffering servant's path from humiliation to exaltation reflects the transformative process of kenosis, or self-emptying, which is mirrored in the church's own journey.

In addition, we have debated the importance of the 40 years from AD 30 to AD 70 in fulfilling the role of the suffering servant, underscoring the transformative power of the cross in the lives of believers. The apostle Paul's life serves as a testament to the pattern of suffering and exaltation, accentuating the necessity of pursuing one's salvation with reverence and awe.

Furthermore, we have navigated the notion of believers as the body of Christ, scrutinizing passages such as 2 Corinthians 4:10–17 and Philippians 2:5-11. These passages unveil the external and internal man, the pattern of suffering and exaltation, and the implications for the body of Christ and its individual constituents.

Finally, we have probed the affectionate relationships within the body of Christ, drawing inspiration from Paul's relationships with Timothy and Epaphroditus. These relationships exemplify sacrificial love and commitment, emphasizing the importance of unity and selflessness within the church.

B. Reemphasizing the importance of the suffering servant motif in Isaiah for the church's identity and mission.

To conclude, the suffering servant motif in Isaiah carries immense importance for the church's identity and mission. It acts as a potent reminder of Christ's sacrifice and redemption, and a call to believers to undertake the transformative journey of self-emptying and to live out their salvation with reverence and awe. The body of Christ is urged to embody sacrificial love and enduring relationships, expressing the example set by the suffering servant and fulfilling its mission in the world.

Examination

The Apostle Paul's Epistle to the Philippians stands as a beacon of spiritual enlightenment and theological wisdom, having influenced countless generations over the centuries. This essay ventures into the profound essence of Paul's teachings, with a particular emphasis on the verses Philippians 3:20-21.

These verses, embedded in the core of the epistle, portray a captivating depiction of Christ's bond with the church and the transformative odyssey of its followers. The essay endeavors to illuminate the historical and cultural backdrop of these verses, their immediate context within the epistle, and the pivotal terms and concepts they encapsulate.

The objective of this essay is to delve into the metaphor of Christ as the head of the body, the church, scrutinize the relationship between Christ and the collective body of believers, and probe into the implications of Christ's leadership for the church. Moreover, it aspires to comprehend the church's experience of suffering in the context of Christ's redemptive actions and its eventual glorification.

The essay is partitioned into five primary sections: a contextual analysis of Philippians 3:20-21, an investigation of Christ as the head of the body, a study of the church's experience of suffering, an examination of the church's ultimate glorification, and a conclusion encapsulating the primary discoveries and arguments. Each section is designed to enhance our comprehension of Paul's teachings and their pertinence for modern readers. By scrutinizing these verses within their historical and cultural milieu, and by dissecting the metaphor of Christ as the head of the body, this essay aims to enrich the ongoing academic discourse surrounding the Epistle to the Philippians and its timeless relevance.

II. Contextual Analysis of Philippians 3:20-21

    I. <u>Unraveling the Historical and Cultural Tapestry of Paul's Epistle</u>

To fully appreciate the profound implications of Philippians 3:20-21, one must delve into the historical and cultural context that shaped the Apostle Paul's writings. Penned during his confinement, likely in Rome around 60-62 AD, the Epistle to the Philippians is a testament to the circumstances that molded Paul's teachings, and the hurdles encountered by the blossoming Christian community in Philippi.

The Roman Empire, during this epoch, wielded considerable sway over the region, with Philippi being a Roman colony. This status conferred certain privileges and rights upon the Philippians as Roman citizens. However, it also subjected them to Roman laws and traditions, often at odds with Christian teachings.

Moreover, Philippi was a melting pot of diverse cultures, housing both Jews and Gentiles. This diversity undoubtedly added to the unique challenges faced by the Philippian church, as they strived to reconcile the differences between various cultural and religious backgrounds.

II. A Synopsis of the Verses Preceding Philippians 3:20-21

Before dissecting the nuances of Philippians 3:20-21, it is crucial to sketch an outline of the preceding verses. In Philippians 3:17-19, Paul cautions the Philippians against false teachers who foster a self-absorbed and worldly perspective. These individuals place their own desires and earthly accomplishments above the perpetual hope offered by Christ.

This is not a metamorphosis of individual bodies but the corporate body of Christ fulfilling the suffering servant in Isaiah 42:1–4; Isaiah 49:1–6; Isaiah 50:4–11; and Isaiah 52:13–53:12. The church does not fulfill the redemptive work of the Cross, only Christ as the head fulfills this part. But the church continues the ministry of conciliation to the Gentiles.

The concept of the corporate body of Christ refers to the collective body of believers who make up the Church. In this understanding, each believer is considered a member of this body and contributes to its overall functioning. The suffering servant passages in the book of Isaiah (Isaiah 42:1–4; Isaiah 49:1–6; Isaiah 50:4–11; and Isaiah 52:13–53:12) are often seen as foreshadowing the role of Christ as the ultimate suffering servant who brings redemption to humanity. While it is true that the Church, as the corporate body of Christ, participates in the ministry of conciliation to the Gentiles, it is important to note that only Christ as the head of the Church fulfills the redemptive work of the Cross. The sacrifice of Christ on the Cross is considered unique and sufficient for the salvation of humanity. The Church, as the body of Christ, carries out the mission of spreading the message of salvation and conciliation to all people. This mission involves proclaiming the good news of Christ's sacrifice and offering an invitation to all people to enter into a relationship with God through faith in Christ. However, it is essential to understand that the Church does not take on the role of personally redeeming individuals; it is Christ alone who accomplishes that through His sacrifice on the Cross. In summary, the corporate body of Christ, which is the Church, continues the ministry of conciliation to the Gentiles, spreading the message of salvation and reconciliation. However, it is Christ as the head of the Church who fulfills the redemptive work of the Cross, and it is through faith in Him that individuals are personally redeemed.

III. Probing the Immediate Context of the Verses

To truly comprehend the essence of Philippians 3:20-21, one must scrutinize the immediate context of these verses within the epistle. In the preceding verses, Paul underscores the importance of emulating Christ and adhering to his example of selflessness and humility.

Paul then segues into the theme of heavenly citizenship, accentuating the stark contrast between the Philippians' terrestrial citizenship as Romans and their ultimate citizenship in the celestial kingdom.[91] This notion of heavenly citizenship lays the groundwork for the exploration of the church's ultimate glorification in Philippians 3:20- 21.

IV. Deciphering Key Terms and Concepts in the Passage

Philippians 3:20-21 is replete with key terms and concepts that necessitate identification and elucidation for a comprehensive understanding of their significance. The term "citizenship" (politeuma) alludes to the rights and privileges associated with being a citizen of a specific city or state. In this context, Paul employs the term to underscore the heavenly citizenship of believers, which transcends any terrestrial citizenship. The concept of the "body" (soma) is also pivotal in interpreting these verses. Paul frequently uses the metaphor of the body to depict the collective body of believers, underscoring their unity and interconnectedness.[92] In Philippians 3:21, Paul specifically alludes to the transformation of the believers' bodies to mirror the glorious body of Christ.

III. Christ as the Head of the Body

I. Delving into the reality of Christ as the pinnacle of the church (the body)

Within the verses of Philippians 3:20-21, the Apostle Paul utilizes the metaphor of Christ as the pinnacle of the body, a metaphor that paints a vivid picture of the profound relationship between Christ and the church. This example is rooted in the imagery of the human body, where the head acts as the central command, orchestrating and synchronizing the various components of the body. In a similar vein, Christ is portrayed as the ultimate authority and the compass for the church. This metaphor underscores the unity and interdependence of believers, spotlighting their reliance on Christ for direction and purpose.

II. Dissecting the relationship between Christ and the collective body of believers

By casting Christ as the pinnacle of the body, Paul accentuates the organic unity between Christ and the congregation of believers. The church is not simply an assembly of individuals, but a harmonious entity with Christ at its helm. This relationship suggests a profound intimacy and reciprocal dependence between Christ and the church. Just as the head breathes life and sustenance into the body, Christ bestows spiritual life and nourishment upon the church. The church, reciprocally, draws its identity and purpose from its bond with Christ, serving as the tangible embodiment of Christ's presence in the world.

---

[91] Carson, D. A. The Epistle to the Philippians. Eerdmans, 2000.

[92] Wuest, Kenneth S. Wuest's Word Studies from the Greek New Testament: For the English Reader. Eerdmans, 1997.

III. Probing the implications of Christ's leadership for the church

The metaphor of Christ as the pinnacle of the body bears significant implications for the church. Primarily, it underlines the necessity of submission and obedience to Christ's authority. Just as the body heeds the direction of the head, believers are urged to submit to Christ's sovereignty and adhere to His teachings. Secondly, it underscores the need for unity and collaboration among believers. Just as the diverse parts of the body operate in harmony, the church is urged to function as a unified entity, with each member contributing their unique abilities and talents for the upliftment of the whole.[93] Lastly, it emphasizes the church's mission to mirror Christ to the world. As the visible manifestation of Christ's presence, the church is tasked with reflecting His character and broadcasting His message of redemption and reconciliation.

IV. Debating the church's role in mirroring Christ to the world

As the embodiment of Christ, the church plays a pivotal role in mirroring Christ to the world. Just as the head steers and governs the body, Christ empowers and equips the church to accomplish its mission. The church is tasked with personifying the love, grace, and truth of Christ, acting as His emissaries in a fractured and suffering world. Through acts of compassion, justice, and proclamation of the Gospel, the church showcases the transformative power of Christ's redemptive work. By faithfully executing its calling, the church becomes a tangible expression of Christ's presence and a beacon of hope for those in need.[94]

IV. The Church's Experience of Suffering

I. Parallels between the Church's Suffering and the Suffering Servant in Isaiah 42:1-4

Grasping the church's encounter with suffering necessitates an exploration of the parallels with the Suffering Servant delineated in Isaiah 42:1-4. This particular excerpt from Isaiah paints a vivid picture of a servant who endures suffering for the sake of others, thereby facilitating redemption and restoration. In a similar vein, the church undergoes suffering in its quest to propagate the gospel and embody the teachings of Christ.

II. The Church's Suffering: A Link to Christ's Redemptive Endeavor

The suffering experienced by the church is intrinsically linked to Christ's redemptive endeavor. Mirroring Christ's suffering on the cross to effectuate salvation, the church partakes in this redemptive process through its own trials and tribulations. The Apostle Paul, in Philippians 3:10, articulates, "that I may know Him and the power of His resurrection, and the fellowship of His sufferings, being conformed to His death" (NASB). Thus, the

---

[93] Carson, D. A. The Epistle to the Philippians. Eerdmans, 2000.
[94] Wuest, Kenneth S. Wuest's Word Studies from the Greek New Testament: For the English Reader. Eerdmans, 1997.

church's suffering is not a futile endeavor, but rather, it serves a grander purpose in God's divine plan.[95]

III. Understanding the Church's Suffering in the Context of Christ's Leadership

Christ's leadership over the church does not shield it from suffering. Instead, it offers a framework for comprehending the reasons behind its trials. One such reason is the resistance it encounters from the world. Jesus Himself cautioned His disciples about the impending persecution for their faith (John 15:18-21). Moreover, the church's suffering can be perceived as a tool for refining and purifying believers, molding them into the likeness of Christ (Romans 8:17; 1 Peter 4:12-13).

IV. The Importance of the Church's Perseverance amidst Suffering

The church's perseverance in the face of suffering carries immense significance. It bears witness to the faithfulness and might of God, as believers maintain their allegiance to Christ despite the hurdles they encounter. The Apostle Peter emboldens believers, stating, "But even if you should suffer for righteousness' sake, you are blessed. And do not be afraid of their threats, nor be troubled" (1 Peter 3:14, NASB). The church's perseverance amidst suffering serves as a potent testament to the world, showcasing the transformative power of Christ's redemptive endeavor.[96]

V. The Church's Ultimate Glorification

I. A Scrutiny of the Church's Ultimate Exaltation in the Context of Christ

Paul, in Philippians 3:20-21, introduces the notion of the church's ultimate exaltation in the context of Christ. The term "exaltation" signifies the transformation and elevation of believers, both individually and as a collective, into a state of shepherding and reigning with Christ. This metamorphosis is intrinsically linked to the transition of the suffering servant body of Christ to the reigning body of Christ in the New Covenant age after AD 70, as Paul asserts that Christ will change our body of humiliation, that it may be like His body of glory, according to the energy where He can even place the whole under Himself. (Philippians 3:21, TKB).

II. Dissection of the Parallel References to the Suffering Servant in Isaiah

To comprehend the significance of the church's ultimate exaltation, it is crucial to dissect the parallel references to the Suffering Servant in Isaiah. These references, located in Isaiah 42:1-4, 49:1-6, 50:4-9, and 52:13-53:12, offer a blueprint for understanding the transformative journey from suffering to exaltation. The Suffering Servant in Isaiah is

---

[95] Carson, D. A. Exegesis on the New Testament's Utilization of the Old Testament. Baker Academic, 2007.

[96] Wuest, Kenneth S. Wuest's Word Studies from the Greek New Testament: For the English Reader. Eerdmans, 1997.

depicted as one who bears suffering and humiliation for the benefit of others, culminating in exaltation and triumph. This parallel underscores the redemptive quality of the church's suffering and its ultimate exaltation in Christ.

III. Investigation of the Progression from Suffering to Exaltation in the Church

The transition from suffering to exaltation in the church is a pivotal theme in Philippians 3:20-21. Paul underscores that the church's current experience of suffering is not futile, but rather a necessary stage in the transformative journey towards exaltation. The church's suffering is deeply connected to Christ's redemptive work, as believers are summoned to partake in His sufferings and engage in His victory over sin and death. Through this engagement, the church is being molded into the likeness of Christ and readied for its ultimate exaltation.

IV. Deliberation on the Implications of the Church's Exaltation for its Mission

The church's exaltation carries substantial implications for its mission in the world. As the body of Christ, the church is tasked to represent Him and His kingdom on earth. The church's exaltation serves as a potent testament to the transformative power of the gospel and the hope that believers harbor in Christ. It is a reminder that the present sufferings of the church are transient and will be eclipsed by the eternal glory that lies ahead. This knowledge emboldens believers to persist in their mission, aware that their efforts are not futile and that their ultimate exaltation is guaranteed.

VI. Conclusion

A. Recapitulation of the Central Discoveries and Arguments

This discourse has embarked on an in-depth journey into the profound wisdom of Apostle Paul, as encapsulated in his Epistle to the Philippians, with a special emphasis on Philippians 3:20-21. A contextual dissection of these verses has allowed us to delve into their historical and cultural relevance, as well as their immediate context within the epistle.

We have meticulously dissected the meaning of Christ as the head of the body, the church, unveiling the intimate bond between Christ and the collective body of believers. This exploration has illuminated the implications of Christ's leadership and headship for the church, accentuating its role in embodying Christ to the world.

Moreover, we have probed into the church's experience of suffering, drawing parallels with the Suffering Servant in Isaiah 42:1-4 and underscoring the connection between the church's suffering and Christ's redemptive work. We have scrutinized the reasons behind the church's suffering in the light of Christ's headship and acknowledged the significance of the church's perseverance through suffering.

The ultimate glorification of the church has also been analyzed, considering its relationship with Christ and the parallel references to the Suffering Servant in Isaiah. This exploration has unveiled a progression from suffering to glorification in the church, highlighting the transformative journey that believers undertake.

B. Reflection on the Study's Significance in Understanding the Letter to the Philippians

Reflecting on the central discoveries and arguments presented in this discourse, it is clear that Paul's letter to the Philippians holds immense significance for understanding the essence of the church and how she is related to Christ. By studying these teachings, we gain insight into the timeless message of Paul and its relevance for contemporary readers. The relevance of Paul's message transcends the boundaries of the ancient world, as it addresses the challenges and aspirations of believers today. Christ as the head of the body underscores the importance of unity and the church's mission to embody Christ in the world. The church's experience of suffering serves as a reminder of the redemptive power of Christ's sacrifice and the endurance required of believers. Lastly, the church's ultimate glorification provides hope and encouragement amidst trials and tribulations.

C. Concluding Remarks on the Relevance of Paul's Message for Contemporary Readers

As we conclude this discourse, it is crucial to acknowledge that there is still a vast expanse to explore and research regarding Christ's headship and the church's suffering. Further investigation into these topics will undoubtedly enrich the ongoing academic discourse surrounding the Epistle to the Philippians and its timeless relevance. The teachings of Paul in his letter to the Philippians continue to resonate with contemporary readers, offering guidance and inspiration in navigating the complexities of faith and the challenges of the world. By engaging with these teachings, we can deepen our understanding of the church's role in embodying Christ, the redemptive power of suffering, and the hope of ultimate glorification.

D. Proposals for Further Research and Exploration on Christ's Headship and the Church's Suffering

As we draw this discourse to a close, it is crucial to recognize that there is still a vast landscape to be explored and understood regarding Christ's headship and the church's experience of suffering. Further research and exploration in these areas can contribute to a deeper understanding of the Epistle to the Philippians and its implications for contemporary theology and practice. Specifically, future research could probe into the theological implications of Christ's headship for the church's mission and identity. Additionally, further exploration of the reasons for the church's suffering in light of Christ's redemptive work can illuminate the transformative power of suffering in the life of believers. These avenues of research hold the potential to enrich our understanding of the Epistle to the Philippians and its relevance for contemporary readers.

1. Carson, D. A. (1994). Commentary on the Epistle to the Philippians. Eerdmans.
2. Wuest, K. S. (1997). Wuest's Word Studies from the Greek New Testament: For the English Reader. Eerdmans.

Terry Kashian

Philippians

Chapter 1

1. Paul and Timothy, the servants of Jesus Christ, to all the saints in Christ Jesus which are at Philippi, with the elders and deacons:
2. Grace be to you, and peace, from God our Father, and the Lord Jesus Christ.
3. I thank my God on every remembrance of you,
4. Always in every prayer of mine for you, making all requests with joy,
5. For your participation in the gospel from the first day until now;
6. Being confident of this very thing, that He which has begun a good work in you will complete it until the day of Jesus Christ:
7. Just as it is right for me to have this mindset of you all because I have you in my heart; in as much as both in my chains and in the defense and confirmation of the gospel, you all are joint participants with me of grace.
8. For God is my witness, how greatly I long for you all in the affections of Jesus Christ.
9. So, this I pray, that your love may abound yet more and more in full knowledge and in all discernment;
10. That you may distinguish between the things that differ; that you may be sincere and without offense until the day of Christ.
11. Being filled with the fruits of righteousness, which are through Jesus Christ, to the glory and praise of God.
12. But I would have you understand, brothers, that the things which happened to me have turned out for the advancement of the gospel;
13. So that my chains are manifest in Christ in all the Praetorium, and in all other places;
14. For many of the brothers in the Lord, growing confident because of my chains, are much bolder to speak the word without fear.
15. Some indeed preach Christ even of envy and strife, and some also of good will:
16. The one indeed preaches Christ for contention, not sincerely, supposing to add affliction to my chains:
17. But the other out of love, knowing that I am appointed for the defense of the gospel.
18. What then? Only that, in every way, whether in pretense, or in reality, Christ is preached; and I in this I rejoice, yes, and will rejoice.
19. For I know that this will turn to my deliverance through your prayer and the supply of the Spirit of Jesus Christ,
20. According to my earnest expectation and my hope, that in nothing will I be ashamed, but that with all boldness, as always, so now also Christ will be magnified in my body, whether it be by life, or by death.
21. For to me to live is Christ, and to die is gain.
22. But if I live on in the flesh, this is the fruit of my labor: yet what I will choose I do not know.
23. For I am hard-pressed between the two, having a desire to depart, and to be with Christ; which is far better:
24. Nevertheless, to stay on in the flesh is more needed by you.

Philippians 1:25

25. So, having this confidence, I know that I will stay and continue with you all for your progress and joy of faith;
26. That your boasting may be more abundant in Jesus Christ in me through my presence with you again.
27. Only be a citizen worthy of the gospel of Christ: that whether I come and see you, or else be absent, I may hear of your affairs, that you stand fast in one spirit, with one soul striving together for the faith of the gospel;
28. In nothing terrified by your adversaries: which is to them an obvious proof of destruction, but to you your salvation, and that from God.
29. For to you it is given in behalf of Christ, not only to believe in Him, but also to suffer for His sake;
30. Having the same conflict which you saw in me, and now hear is in me.

Chapter 2

1. If there be therefore any consolation in Christ, if any comfort of love, if any participation in the Spirit if any affection and mercies,
2. You make my joy complete, by being mutually minded, having reciprocal love, being joined in soul and the one intention.
3. Let nothing be done through selfish ambition or conceit, but in lowliness of mind let each esteem others surpassing ourselves.
4. Not considering the self, but even on another.
5. Let this mindset be in us, the one in Christ Jesus:
6. Who, being in essence God, not leading the way to seize to be equal with God:
7. But He emptied Himself, and accepting the essence of a slave, and came in the resemblance of men:
8. And being found in the external appearance as a man, He humbled Himself and became obedient even to death, even the death of the cross.
9. Therefore, God also has highly exalted Him and given Him a name which is above every name:
10. That at the name of Jesus every knee should bow, of things in heaven, and things in earth, and things under the earth;
11. And that every tongue should confess that Jesus Christ is Lord, to the glory of God the Father.
12. Therefore, my beloved, as you have always obeyed, not as in my presence only, but now much more in my absence, work out your own salvation with fear and trembling.
13. For it is God which energizes in you both the willing and the doing of His good pleasure.
14. Do all things without complaining and arguing:
15. That you may be blameless and pure, the children of God, without reproach, in the midst of a crooked and perverse generation, among whom you give light as stars in the world;
16. Holding forth the word of life; that I may rejoice in the day of Christ, that I have not run in vain, either labored in vain.

17. Yes, and if I am poured out upon the sacrifice and service of your faith, I joy and rejoice with you all.

18. For the same reason also do you joy and rejoice with me.

19. But I trust in the Lord Jesus to send Timothy to you shortly, that I also may be of good comfort when I know your state.

20. For I have no man equal in soul, who will naturally care for your state.

21. Or all seek their own, not the things which are Jesus Christ's.

22. But you know his proven character, that, as a son with the father, he has served with me in the gospel.

23. Therefore, I hope to send him at once as soon as I see how it will go with me.

24. But I trust in the Lord that I also myself will come shortly.

25. Yet I supposed it necessary to send to you Epaphroditus, my brother, and companion in labor, and fellow soldier, but your apostle, and he ministered to my need.

26. For he longed after you all and was full of heaviness because you had heard that he had been sick.

27. For indeed he was sick close to death: but God had mercy on him; and not on him only, but also on me, unless I should have sorrow upon sorrow.

28. I sent him therefore the more carefully, that, when you see him again, you may rejoice, and that I may be the less sorrowful.

29. Receive him therefore in the Lord with all gladness, and hold such in esteem:

30. Because for the work of Christ, he was close to death, not regarding his soul, to supply your lack of service toward me.

Chapter 3

1. Finally, my brothers, rejoice in the Lord. To write the same things to you, to me indeed is not grievous, but it is for your safety.

2. Beware of dogs, beware of evil workers, beware of the mutilators.

3. For we are the circumcision, which worship God in spirit, and glory in Christ Jesus, and put no confidence in the flesh.

4. Even though I have confidence in the flesh. If any other man thinks that he has confidence and might trust in the flesh, I more:

5. Circumcised the eighth day, out of the stock of Israel, the tribe of Benjamin, a Hebrew of the Hebrews; as concerning the Law, a Pharisee;

6. Concerning zeal, persecuting the Assembly; concerning the righteousness which is in the Law, blameless.

7. But what things were gain to me, those I count as loss for Christ.

8. Yes doubtless, and I count all things but loss for the excellency of the knowledge of Christ Jesus my Lord: for who I have suffered the loss of all things, and do count them but dung, that I may win Christ,

9. And be found in Him, not having my own righteousness, which is from the Law, but that which is through the faith of Christ, the righteousness which comes from God by faith:

10. That I may know Him, and the power of His resurrection, and the fellowship of His sufferings, being conformed to His death;
11. If by any means I might attain to the out-resurrection, out from the dead.
12. Not as though I had already attained, either were already complete: but I ensue after, moreover, that I also may lay hold of that for which Christ Jesus has also laid hold of me.
13. Brethren, I do not count myself to have apprehended: but this one thing I do, forgetting those things which are behind, and reaching forward to those things which are before,
14. I press toward the goal for the prize of the on- high calling of God in Christ Jesus.
15. Let us therefore, as many as are mature, have this mindset: and if in anything you are otherwise minded, God will reveal that also to you.
16. However, into that which we have already attained, let us walk by the same standard, let us have the same mindset.
17. Brothers, be joint imitators of me and pay attention to those who walk about, you have a pattern in us.
18. For many walk, of whom I have told you often, and now tell you even weeping, that they are the enemies of the cross of Christ:
19. Whose end is destruction, whose god is their appetites, and whose glory is in their shame, having an earthly mindset.
20. For our citizenship we have is in the heavens; from where also we eagerly expect the Savior, the Lord Jesus Christ:
21. Who will change together our body of humiliation, that it becomes conformed with His body of glory, according to the energy of His power to even place the whole under Himself.

Chapter 4

1. Therefore, my brothers dearly beloved and longed for, my joy and crown, so stand fast in the Lord, my dearly beloved.
2. I implore Euodias, and implore Syntyche, that they are of the same mindset in the Lord.
3. And I entreat you also, true companion, help those women who labored with me in the gospel, with Clement also, and with my other fellow laborers, whose names are in the Book of Life.
4. Rejoice in the Lord always: and again, I say, rejoice.
5. Let your gentleness be known to all men. The Lord is near.
6. Don't be anxious about anything, but in everything by prayer and supplication with thanksgiving let your requests be made known to God.
7. And the peace of God, which is superior to all mental processes, will keep your hearts and minds through Christ Jesus.
8. Finally, brothers, whatsoever things are real, whatever things are honorable, whatsoever things are right, whatsoever things are unmixed, whatsoever things are agreeable, whatsoever things are well spoken of; if there be any moral excellencies, and if there be any applause, calculate the value of these things.

9. Those things, which you have both learned, and received, and heard, and seen in me, practice: and the God of peace will be with you.

10. Moreover, I rejoiced in the Lord greatly, that now at last, your thoughtfulness over me has revived; in which you were also before, but you lacked opportunity.

11. Not that I speak in respect of need: for I have learned, in whatever state I am, there to be content.

12. I know both how to be without, and I know how to abound: everywhere and in all things I am instructed both to be full and to be hungry, both to abound and to suffer need.

13. I can do all things through Christ who strengthens me.

14. Nonetheless you have done well, that you did have a joint- participation in my tribulations.

15. Now you Philippians know also, that in the beginning of the gospel, when I departed from Macedonia, no Assembly had participated with me in the matter of giving and receiving, but only you.

16. For even in Thessalonica, you sent once and again for my necessities.

17. Not because I desire a gift: but I desire fruit that may increase to your account.

18. But I have all and abound: I am full, having received of Epaphroditus the things which were sent from you, an aroma of a sweet smell, an acceptable sacrifice, well pleasing to God.

19. But my God will fulfill all you need according to His riches in glory in Christ Jesus.

20. Now to God and our Father be glory into the New Covenant Age from the Old Covenant Age. Amen.

21. Embrace every saint in Christ Jesus. The brothers who are with me embrace you.

22. All the saints embrace you, especially they that are of Nero Caesar's household.

23. The grace of our Lord Jesus Christ be in the midst of you all. Amen.

Colossians Synopsis

Paul wrote this epistle in AD 63, prior to all, you know what, was going to take place with Nero and his insanity. He starts this epistle with a different twist than many of his letters. He greets the saints in Colossae instead of the church in that city, and tacks on the faithful. Paul looked at these saints and addresses the faithful in a special way. This impresses me greatly as I see that there is in the church those we would call faithful. There is a great need to have reliable brothers and sisters in the church. Those that we can trust are precious to us. It reminds me of the proverb, Many a man proclaims his own steadfast love, **but a faithful man who can find**?[97] Faithfulness is the very nature and character of God. In Psalm 136 it is used 26 times and normally translated Mercy, Hesed in Hebrew. It is covenant love or steadfast love. It is constant and not fickle. The best definition I found in regard to man being faithful is, the kind of man who displays an overall consistency between his words and his actions, between what he professes to believe and how he carries himself, between what he promises and what he performs. May the Lord help us be faithful to the end of our lives!

Paul's letter to the Colossians is a significant piece of biblical literature that holds immense importance in the understanding of Christian theology. One of the unique aspects of this letter is Paul's sourcing from Old Testament passages, particularly in relation to Israel's feast days and the concept of Christ being our life. Through a thorough analysis of this letter, one can see how Paul draws connections between the Old Testament and the reality of Christ, highlighting the fulfillment of prophecy and the divine plan of redemption with a view to God's building.

The first place I want to focus on is Col. 1:3-6. 3 We give thanks to God and the Father of our Lord Jesus Christ, praying at all times for you, 4 **since we heard of your faith in Christ Jesus**, and of **the love which you have for all the saints**, 5 for the hope which is laid up for you in the heavens, of which you heard before in **the word of the reality of the gospel;** 6 **that is coming into you, as it is in all the world**; and **is being fruitful** and **multiplying**, as it does also in you, since the day you heard of it, and **knew the grace of God in reality:** …TKB

I have highlighted parts of these verses to show the reference in Gen. 1:26-28 specifically, And **God blessed them.** And **God said to them,** "**Be fruitful and multiply and fill the**

---

[97] _The Holy Bible: English Standard Version_ (Pr 20:6). (2016). Crossway Bibles.

earth and subdue it[98],…. The gospel in Colossae was producing children of God and being fruitful and multiplying as it was in all the world. The prophecy of the Man in God's image and the Female in God's image is Christ and the church. Their union is producing children of God, the fruit of heaven. God blessed them and spoke to them, be fruitful and multiply. O how wonderful this is, and I can hardly sit still! These Colossian saints were on fire and full of faith and they had the goods, the love for all the saints. The gospel is the reality of the grace of God to conquer the world. We conquer with the gospel of grace; the Kingdom of God is the reign of God in LIFE and GRACE. The tool of dominion is the reality of the gospel.

In this portion of Colossians, a few Old Testament references that help get Paul's intentions and theological points. One of the key references is in Colossians 1:15-20, where the author describes Jesus Christ as the image of the invisible God, the firstborn over all creation, and the one in whom all things hold together. Beale traces this language back to Genesis 1, where God creates man in His image and pronounces them "very good. Christ is the image of God, Adam was made in the image, very much like a glove is made in the image of a hand. When you look inside the glove it is empty, it is missing the hand. Adam was missing the hand and that is why he failed. The hand is Christ and in reality, God was in Christ conciliating the world to Himself. This is why in the Lord's great plan He had a secret to put the hand in us, the hope of Glory. What a God we have! Adam failed for lack of a hand, but we now have the hand, and we can only succeed and glorify the Lord. The firstborn of all creation is not the old creation, but the brand-new creation that has been created in Christ. He is the new creation, and we are in Him as the new creation.

Focusing on the references in Colossians 1:25-27, where the apostle Paul declares that he became a minister to complete the word of God, which was hidden from the old covenant age but has now been revealed to the saints. Let's look into the Old Testament background of this passage, particularly focusing on the theme of mystery and revelation found in the Hebrew Scriptures. Paul is bold in saying that he is completing the word of God. The Lord used Paul for this very purpose and handed him a stewardship to unveil the long-hidden mystery of the Messiah. He revealed to Paul that the Messiah was going to be installed inwardly, in the deepest part of the believers' being. This is something that the prophets and especially the Jewish people of Jesus' day could not fathom. The Messiah came to be our indwelling Savior, God, Life. This was fantastic and incredible for the Jewish mind.

This idea of mystery in the Old Testament is not merely something unknown, but rather something hidden by God until the appointed time for its unveiling. He highlights that the revelation of this mystery among the nations, namely the indwelling of Christ in believers as the hope of glory, is the secret that was hidden from the Jewish nation and the world. The Messiah in you the hope of glory.

---

[98] *The Holy Bible: English Standard Version* (Ge 1:28). (2016). Crossway Bibles.

The connections between Colossians 1:25-27 and various Old Testament passages such as Isaiah 45:15, Daniel 2:22, and Daniel 2:47, which speak of God's wisdom and knowledge being beyond human comprehension. By incorporating these references, there is this continuity of God's redemptive plan from the Old Testament to the New Testament, showcasing how Christ fulfills the promises and prophecies of the Old Testament.

Moreover, exploring Old Testament references in Colossians serves to underscore the universal scope of God's plan of salvation with a view to the building of His temple and city. By revealing the mystery of Christ dwelling in all believers, where is Christ? In the church at Colossae! In them! The Messiah in them the hope of glory! Paul affirms that salvation is not limited to the Jewish people but extends to all who put their faith in Christ. This universal message of redemption is deeply planted in the Old Testament promises of God's covenant love for all nations.

One key Old Testament references in Colossians identified is the use of Isaiah 45:23 in Colossians 2:10, where Paul quotes, "Every knee will bow to me, and every tongue will confess allegiance to God." This reference emphasizes the universal lordship of Christ. He is preeminent in all things. The context of Isaiah 45 is profound. And there is no other God besides Me, A just God and a Savior; There is none besides Me. "Look to Me, and be saved, all you ends of the earth! For I am God, and there is no other. I have sworn by Myself; The word has gone out of My mouth in righteousness, and shall not return, That to Me every knee shall bow, every tongue shall take an oath. He shall say, 'Surely **in the Lord** I have righteousness and strength. To Him men shall come, and all shall be ashamed Who are incensed against Him. **In the Lord** all the descendants of Israel Shall be justified and shall glory.'". The word for Lord is Yahweh and Paul is connecting the dots to say Jesus is Yahweh and every knee will bow.

In Colossians 2:6-8, Paul exhorts the believers in Colossae to be rooted and built up in Christ, being established in their faith and not being beguiled and taken captive by empty philosophy and deceitful human tradition. This admonition draws upon key Old Testament references pointing to the spiritual realities of the believers' union with Christ and the dangers of straying from the truth. Not only straying, being taken captive. The deception that the Old Testament false prophets spoke caused the Israelites **to be taken captive to Babylon.** Jeremiah 14:13-16 is about the false prophets giving Israel a false hope and that no judgment would come because of their idolatry and wickedness. The Jews of Paul's day were the same as the false prophets, they were babbling on about a false hope. Their hope was in Moses and the temple and sacrificial system. Their hope was in a Messiah that would come and conquer Rome. And the Lord said to me: **"The prophets are prophesying lies in my name.** I did not send them, nor did I command them or speak to them. **They are prophesying to you a lying vision**, worthless divination, and **the deceit of their own minds.** Therefore, thus says the Lord concerning **the prophets who prophesy** in my name although **I did not send them**, and **who say, 'Sword and famine shall not come upon this land': By sword and famine those prophets shall be consumed**. And the people to whom they prophesy shall be cast out in the streets of Jerusalem, victims of famine and sword, with none to bury them—them, their wives, their sons, and their daughters. **For I will pour out their evil upon them.**[99]

One of the references Beale highlights is the imagery of being rooted in the promised land, which has its origins in the Old Testament book of Deuteronomy. In Deuteronomy 11:10-12, the land flowing with milk and honey is described as a place where the Israelites are to be planted and flourish, under the covenant blessings of God. This imagery is echoed in Colossians 2:6-8, where believers are encouraged to be firmly rooted in Christ, who is the true fulfillment of the promised land. Christ is our land and in Him is the spiritual realm. This is Paul's view, and we are called to abide in Him, rooted so we can be built up in Him. What is being built, a spiritual house made of living stones. We are these stones, and we need to stay put and not be destroyed so there is no temple. A corporate dwelling place.

Another Old Testament reference to point out is the warning against being captivated by empty philosophy and human tradition, which mirrors the prophetic warnings of Isaiah and Jeremiah. In Isaiah 29:13, the prophet rebukes the people of Israel for honoring God with their lips while their hearts are far from Him, being led astray by human precepts. Similarly, Jeremiah 4:22 warns against the folly of relying on human wisdom and neglecting the true wisdom that comes from God. These Old Testament warnings serve as a backdrop for Paul's caution in Colossians 2:6-8 against being deluded by deceptive philosophies and the Jewish elements of the law that can lead to spiritual captivity and bondage.

The historical context of Colossians provides further insight into the significance in the letter. The church in Colossae was facing threats from false teachers who were promoting a mix of Jewish legalism and Greek philosophies, undermining the believers' firm foundation in Christ. By referencing Old Testament passages that speak to the dangers of straying from God's truth and the blessings of being rooted in Him, Paul reinforces the importance of remaining steadfast in the faith and not being swayed by deceptive teachings.

A crucial Old Testament reference in Colossians is in Colossians 2:11-14, where Paul writes about the spiritual circumcision that takes place in Christ. Paul draws on the Old Testament imagery of circumcision as a sign of belonging to God's covenant people (Genesis 17:9-14) and applies it to the believers' union with Christ. Beale unpacks this passage by highlighting the symbolic significance of circumcision as a removal of the flesh, signifying a new creation in Christ. This removal of the flesh is the removing of all that is related to the flesh, the Law of Moses, the ethical philosophies of the Greeks, everything that is natural and part of the fallen humanity. Whether it is religious or sophisticated flesh, this circumcision eradicates all but Christ and the new creation.

---

[99] *The Holy Bible: English Standard Version* (Je 14:13–16). (2016). Crossway Bibles.

In Colossians, Paul references Israel's last three feast days as a shadow of the good things **about to come**, with Christ being the ultimate reality. He demonstrates how these feasts were a foreshadowing of the coming Messiah and how Christ fulfills the specifics of these celebrations. What needs to be understood here is that Paul is saying that the last three feasts hadn't yet been fulfilled. He said they were about to be fulfilled. We are not waiting for Rosh Hashanah Trumpets, the Day of Atonement, or the Feast of Tabernacles. There is much to say about these celebrations and Paul is saying don't get tangled up in these because they are about to be fulfilled in Christ. The new moons is where the Old MOON fades out and the trumpets blow when the New MOON appears. The old is passing and the new is coming. It is a picture of the old being judged and the announcement that the new has come. The Day of Atonement has a positive and negative connotation in it. Judgment and rejection and acceptance and forgiveness. The feast of tabernacles, ingathering, harvest is resurrection and the manifestation of God's glory. His abiding presence with us. Emmanuel! The letter to the Colossians, written by the apostle Paul, is a rich text that emphasizes the Old Testament usage to convey the message of the supremacy of Christ. Paul draws on the Old Testament scriptures to highlight how Christ fulfills and surpasses the shadow of the good things that were about to come. In the Old Testament, Israel's last three feast days - Feast of Trumpets, Day of Atonement, and Feast of Tabernacles - were shadows of the reality that is in Christ. These feasts pointed to the coming of Christ as the ultimate sacrifice, the atonement for sins in judgment and salvation, and the dwelling of God with His people. His Parousia is His presence in fulness!

By pointing to these Old Testament practices, Paul shows the continuity between the Old and New Testaments, emphasizing the overarching narrative of God's plan for salvation and the building up of His people into His dwelling place. Not just redemption, that is half the story. We need the full picture of God's perpetual purpose. He saves us for His building. Just like He saved Israel from Egypt and brought them into the promised land and out of the land emerged a temple, a glorious dwelling place. The son of David, Solomon was the apex of God's purpose in saving Israel and that picture foreshadows what God was doing in the first century. Our SON of DAVID enthroned and all His enemies under His feet.

Furthermore, Paul highlights the idea that Christ is our life, a shared life with a corporate expression. He explains that when Christ is manifest in us, His presence is also manifest in others, creating a beautiful corporate body, His body that radiates with the living presence of Christ. This concept of the shared life and corporate expression points to the interconnectedness of believers and emphasizes the unity that is found in Christ. In verses 3-4, Paul uses the expression *"phaneroō"* translated as appeared or manifest to signify that all believers are to be expressions of Christ. When Christ who is OUR LIFE is manifested in us, His presence is not only seen in us but in others as well. This shared life with Christ transforms the corporate body of believers into a living expression of Christ's life. In verse 5, Paul highlights the contrast between who we are outwardly and the true life that is hidden within God. This mysterious life in Christ is a testament to the profound reality of our **fusion** with Him. In Christ there is a new ethnicity, in the New Creation there **CANNOT BE** ... where there is neither Greek nor Jew, circumcised nor uncircumcised, barbarian, Scythian, slave *nor* free, but Christ *is* all and in all.[100]

In verses 3-4 of Colossians of chapter 3, Paul emphasizes the importance of expressing Christ in all aspects of life, so that believers may be manifestations of Him. This idea reinforces the notion that Christ's presence should be evident not only in individual believers but in the living body of Christ as well. Through this shared life and expression of Christ, the true beauty of the corporate body is revealed, with individuality not highlighted, but not lost to the unity found in Christ.

Additionally, Paul delves into the mystery of the Christian life, highlighting how believers have obtained Christ through His death and resurrection. He asserts that believers have died with Christ and have been raised with Him, symbolizing a new life in Christ and a transformation of the self. This concept of dying with Christ and being raised with Him speaks to the life-changing power of the gospel and the radical transformation that occurs when one enters into a relationship with Christ.

"Another important reference is in Colossians 2:16-17, where the author warns against being judged by human rules and regulations regarding food, drink, or religious festivals. This is an explanation of the Old Testament laws and customs that the Colossians were being influenced by, pointing to passages like Leviticus 23 and Deuteronomy 16 that outline the Jewish feasts and sacrifices.

In Colossians 3:9-10, the author urges believers to put off the old man and put on the new man, which is being renewed in knowledge after the image of its Creator. Some translations of the bible translate old man and new man as old self and new self. The word for self in the Greek is autos and the word for man in this case is anthropos. It is not the old self, but the old man. It is not the new self, but the new man we are to put on. What is the New Man? In Ephesians we have a definition of the New Man. Eph. 2:14 For He is our peace, **who has made both one**, and has **broken down the middle wall of separation between us**; 15 having abolished in His flesh the enmity, even the Law of commandments contained in ordinances; to **create in Himself of the two, one new man**, so making peace; 16 **so that He might conciliate both to God in one body by the cross**, having slain the enmity in Himself: ... TKB. Christ created in Himself from the two, Jews and Gentiles, one new man. The new man is not an individual, but a corporate man. How do we put on the new man if it is not individual? Paul understood the need for Christians to have a corporate life and this revelation was unique to Paul, since his visitation on the road to Damascus. Paul fell to the ground in the presence of the Great Light, and he said, who are you Lord? And the Lord said, I am Jesus whom you are persecuting. This was the seed that the Lord planted in Paul

---

[100] The New King James Version (Col 3:11). (1982). Thomas Nelson.

that would grow into the revelation of each believer being Jesus, His body. Putting on the new man is being covered and surrounded like a garment with other believers.

This is how we as followers of Christ become the testimony of the risen Christ and express His shared life and live connected and accountable. Someone once said to me that he didn't need anyone but Jesus in his life and I'm accountable to God. I explained to him that accountability is not having a policeman in your life, it's having an experience with Christ that is higher than our individual experience. Every joint supplies and that means a joint is when two members come together, and our joining creates a supply that we would miss from being individualistic. I am not the whole, just a part of the body of Christ. Paul says, "one member is not the body", so putting on the New Man is experiencing the corporate life of Christ. The corporate life is hidden in the Old Testament, but it is there, and I am not just talking about community or social gatherings. For example, So he said to Him, "O my Lord, **how can I save Israel**? Indeed my clan *is* the weakest in Manasseh, and I *am* the least in my father's house." And the Lord said to him, "Surely I will be with you, and **you shall defeat the Midianites as one man."**[101] Gideon's 300 men were as ONE MAN. Again, Now **all the people gathered together as one man** in the open square that *was* in front of the Water Gate;[102] Judges 20:8, So **all the people arose as one man,** saying, **"None of us will go to his tent, nor will any turn back to his house;** …,. This is how evil was overcome in the day of the Judges. We can see that victory comes when we practice being one instead of going to our own tent or turning back to our own house. This is marvelous to see!

We are learning to connect this language to passages in the prophets like Isaiah 65 and Ezekiel 36, where God promises to give His people a new heart and a new spirit, leading to a renewed relationship with Him. One thing that irks me is the many modern translations translate the word in Greek "Anthropos" as self, when the Greek word for self is "autos". We do not put on the new self, but the New Man. This is a corporate man, we put on togetherness that is made of a divine humanity. Our corporate experience is something we take in a personal way, not in a private way. This is difficult for most people to understand because we are very independent and terribly individualistic. The Christian life is a life surrounded by Christian people where we encourage one another daily in the faith. This is putting on the New Man.

Furthermore, Colossians 3:16-17 instructs believers to let the word of Christ dwell in them richly, teaching and admonishing one another with psalms, hymns, and spiritual songs. Beale sees this as a call to worship and fellowship rooted in the Old Testament's rich tradition of music and praise, exemplified in books like Psalms and Isaiah. This is the earmark of a spiritual people.

---

[101] *The New King James Version* (Jdgs. 6:15–16). (1982). Thomas Nelson.

[102] *The New King James Version* (Ne 8:1). (1982). Thomas Nelson.

In Colossians 4:6, the author urges believers to let their speech always be gracious, seasoned with salt, so that they may know how to answer each person. Beale sees this as a reflection of the wisdom literature in the Old Testament, particularly Proverbs, which emphasizes the importance of wise and gracious speech. In the Lord's little parable that we are the salt of the earth we can confirm Beale's connection to the wisdom literature. Jesus said if the salt 'loses it flavor' it is good for nothing, and men trample it under their feet. The phrase 'lose its flavor' is one Greek word, Greek Word: μωραίνω Transliteration: mōrainō.[103] Vine's defines this word as foolish. This is the opposite of wisdom. When God's people become silly, foolish, stupid they lose their flavor, saltiness. Even the root word for this Greek word is 'moros', where we get the English word 'moron'. So as our brother James says, keep asking for wisdom from God who is generous. Help us Lord!

Finally, in Colossians 4:18, the author sends greetings from Paul, who writes in his own hand. Beale notes that Paul's practice of signing his letters in this way was consistent with the cultural norms of his time and can be seen in other ancient documents.

G.K. Beale's references in the letter of Colossians from the Old Testament provide valuable insights into the author's theological perspectives and arguments. By tracing these references back to their Old Testament roots, Beale helps readers better understand the rich tapestry of biblical thought that are foundational in the New Testament writings. As scholars continue to explore the connections between the Old and New Testaments, Beale's work stands as a significant contribution to the field of biblical studies.

In conclusion, Paul's letter to the Colossians provides valuable insights into the relationship between the Old Testament and the reality of Christ, as well as the significance of Christ being our life. Through his commentary on Israel's feast days and the shared life of believers, Paul offers a profound perspective on the transformative nature of the Christian faith and the oneness that is found in Christ. By drawing connections between the Old Testament and the New Testament, Paul underscores the cohesive narrative of God's redemptive plan and His building and most of all the centrality of Christ in the life of believers. Overall, Colossians serves as a rich source of theological insight and spiritual nourishment for all who seek to deepen their understanding of the Christian faith. Through the lens of Old Testament imagery and prophecy, Paul reveals that Christ is the fulfillment of all that was foreshadowed in the law and the prophets. The sacrificial system, the priesthood, and the temple all find their ultimate fulfillment in the person of Jesus Christ. Christ is the true Passover lamb whose blood redeems us from sin, the high priest who intercedes on our behalf, and the temple in whom the fullness of God dwells, the Father's house where we have a place perpetually.

Overall, Paul's commentary on the Old Testament usage in his letter to the Colossians underscores the central theme of Christ's preeminence and the shared life that believers

---

Strong, J. (2020). μωραίνω. In Strong's Talking Greek and Hebrew Dictionary. WORDsearch.

have in Him. The Old Testament foreshadowed the coming of Christ, and Paul reveals how Christ fulfills and surpasses all that was prophesied. Through a deep dive into Old Testament imagery and prophecy, Paul conveys the profound truth that everything in the Old Testament points to Christ as the reality behind the shadows of the Old Testament.

References:1. Beale, G.K. The Use of the Old Testament in the New Testament. Grand Rapids: Baker Academic, 2008.

Terry Kashian

Colossians

Chapter 1

1. Paul, an apostle of Jesus Christ by the will of God, and Timothy our brother,
2. To the saints and faithful brothers in Christ who are at Colosse: grace be to you, and peace, from God our Father and the Lord Jesus Christ.
3. We give thanks to God and the Father of our Lord Jesus Christ, praying at all times for you,
4. Since we heard of your faith in Christ Jesus, and of the love which you have for all the saints,
5. For the hope which is laid up for you in the heavens, of which you heard before in the word of the reality of the gospel;
6. That is coming into you, as it is in all the world; and is being fruitful and multiplying, as it does also in you, since the day you heard of it, and knew the grace of God in reality:
7. As you also learned from Epaphras our dear fellow slave, who is for you a faithful servant of Christ;
8. Who also affirmed to us your love in the Spirit.
9. For this reason we also, since the day we heard it, do not pause praying for you, and desire that you might be filled with the full knowledge of His will in all wisdom and spiritual understanding;
10. That you might walk worthy of the Lord fully pleasing Him, being fruitful in every good work, and growing by the experiential knowledge of God;
11. Strengthened with all power, according to the force of His glory, into all patience and a long fuse, with joyfulness;
12. Giving thanks to the Father, who has made us adequate to be participants in the inheritance of the saints in light:
13. Who has rescued us from the power of darkness, and has transferred us into the kingdom of the Son of His love:
14. In Whom we have redemption through His blood, even the forgiveness of sins:
15. Who is the image of the invisible God, the firstborn of all creation:
16. For in Him were all things created, that are in the heavens, and that are in earth, visible and invisible, whether they be thrones, or dominions, or rulers, or powers: all things were created through Him, and unto Himself:
17. And He is before all things, and in Him all things inhere.
18. He is the head of the body, the Assembly: Who is the beginning, the firstborn out from the dead; that in all things He might have the preeminence.
19. For in Him was pleased all the fullness to dwell;
20. And having made peace through the blood of His cross, through Him to conciliate all things to Himself; through Him, I say, whether they be things on earth or things in the heavens.
21. And you, that were at one time alienated and hostile with your thinking in evil works, and now He has conciliated
22. In the body of His flesh through death, to present you holy and without blemish and impeccable in His sight:

23. If you continue in the faith grounded and settled, and not moved away from the hope of the gospel, which you have heard, and which was preached to all creation which is under the heavens; of which I Paul became a servant;
24. I am now rejoicing in my sufferings for you, and filling up that which is deficient of the sufferings of Christ in my flesh for His body's sake, which is the Assembly:
25. Of which I became a servant according to God's stewardship bestowed upon me and placed into you, to complete the written word of God,
26. The mystery which has been concealed from this Old Covenant Age and this generation, but now is made evident to His saints:
27. To whom God would make known what is the riches of the glory of this mystery in the nations; which is Christ in you, the hope of glory:
28. Whom we preach, warning every man, and teaching every man in all wisdom; that we may present every man fully mature in Christ Jesus:
29. Into which I also strenuously toil, contending according to His working, energizing me in power.

Chapter 2

1. For I would that you knew what great struggle I have for you, and for them at Laodicea, and for as many as have not seen my face;
2. That their hearts might be comforted, being knit together in love, and into all the riches of the full certainty of understanding and into the full knowledge of the mystery of God, Christ;
3. In Whom are concealed all the treasures of wisdom and knowledge.
4. And this I say, so that no one should mislead you by false reasoning and persuasive speech.
5. For though I am absent in the flesh, yet I am with you in spirit; joyfully witnessing your good order, and the steadfastness of your faith in Christ.
6. As you have therefore received Christ Jesus the Lord, in Him walk:
7. Take root and build further in Him, and be established in the faith, according as you have been instructed, overflowing in thanksgiving.
8. Beware unless anyone manipulates and fleeces you through philosophy and empty deceit, after the traditions of men, after the Jewish elements of the Old Covenant order, and not according to Christ.
9. For in Him dwells all the fullness of the Godhead bodily.
10. And you are complete in Him, who is the head of all rulers and authorities:
11. In Whom also you are circumcised with the circumcision made without hands, in the stripping off the body of the flesh by the circumcision of Christ:
12. Buried with Him in immersion, in which also you have risen with Him out of the faith of the operation of God, who has raised Him from the dead.
13. And you, being dead in your sins and the uncircumcision of your flesh, He has made us alive together, joined to Him, having forgiven us all our trespasses;

14. Having wiped out the handwriting of debts that were against us, which were antagonistic to us, and took it out of the way, nailing it to His cross;
15. And completely stripped rulers and authorities, He made a show of them openly, triumphing over them in Himself.
16. Let no one therefore judge you in food, or drink, or a component of the festival, or a new moon, or the Sabbaths:
17. That are a shadow of things about to come; but the reality is the Christ.
18. Let no one judge against you by depriving you of your prize in taking pleasure in esteeming ourselves small and the worshiping of the angels, stepping into that which he has not seen, inflated with pride by his fleshly mind,
19. And not taking hold of the Head, out from whom all the body is nourished and knit together by joints and ligaments, is growing with the increase of God.
20. Therefore, if you are dead with Christ from the Jewish elements of the Old Covenant order, why, as though living in the Old Covenant order, are you subject to regulations,
21. Touch not; taste not; handle not;
22. Which will all be destroyed with the using; after the commandments and teachings of men?
23. Which things have indeed an appearance of wisdom in self-imposed religion, false humility, and neglect of the body: but are of no value against the indulgence of the flesh.

Chapter 3

1. If you then be risen with Christ, seek those things which are above, where Christ is sitting in the right hand of God.
2. Set your heart on things above, not on things on the land.
3. For you died, and your life is hidden with Christ in God.
4. When Christ, who is our life, is revealed, then you also will be revealed together with Him in glory.
5. Therefore, put to death your members which are on the earth; fornication, uncleanness, inordinate affection, evil sexual desire, and covetousness, which is idolatry:
6. For this reason, the wrath of God is coming on the sons of stubbornness:
7. In which yourselves also walked some time, when you lived in them.
8. But now you also put off all these, anger, wrath, malice, blasphemy, foul abusive language out of your mouth.
9. Do not lie to one another, seeing that you have put off the old man with his deeds;
10. But have put on the new man, which is renewed in full knowledge after the image of Him that created Him:
11. Where Greek nor Jew have no place, circumcision nor uncircumcision, Barbarian, Scythian, slave nor free: but Christ is all, and in all.
12. Put on, therefore, as the elect of God, holy and beloved, deep inner mercies, kindness, humbleness of mind, meekness, long fuse;

13. Forbearing one another, and forgiving one another, if any man has a quarrel against anyone: just as Christ forgave you, so also do you.

14. And above all these things put on love, which is the uniting bond of maturity.

15. So, let the peace of God rule in your hearts, to the which also you are called in one body: and be you thankful.

16. Let the word of Christ dwell in you richly in all wisdom, teaching and admonishing one another in psalms and hymns and spiritual songs, singing with grace in your passion to the Lord.

17. For whatever you do in word or deed, do all in the name of the Lord Jesus, giving thanks to God and the Father through Him.

18. Wives, submit yourselves to your own husbands, as it is proper in the Lord.

19. Husbands, love your wives and be not bitter against them.

20. Children obey your parents in all things: for this is well pleasing to the Lord.

21. Fathers do not irritate your children unless they become dispirited.

22. Slaves, obey in all things your masters according to the flesh; not with eye service, as man pleasers; but in singleness of heart, fearing God;

23. Whatever you do, labor out from your soul, as to the Lord, and not to men;

24. Knowing that of the Lord you will receive the reward of the inheritance: for you serve the Lord Christ.

25. But he that does wrong will receive for the wrong which he has done: and there is no favoritism.

Chapter 4

1. Masters, give to your slaves that which is just and equal; knowing that you also have a Master in heaven.

2. Continue in prayer, being diligent in it with thanks giving;

3. Meanwhile praying also for us, that God would open to us a door for the word, to speak the mystery of Christ, for which I am also in chains:

4. That I may make it manifest, as I ought to speak.

5. Walk in wisdom toward those who are without, buying up the opportunity.

6. Let your speech always be with grace, seasoned with salt, that you may know how you ought to answer every man.

7. All my undertakings Tychicus will make known to you, who is a beloved brother, and a faithful minister and fellow servant in the Lord:

8. Who I have sent to you for the same purpose, that he might know your concerns, and comfort your hearts;

9. With Onesimus, a faithful and beloved brother, who is one of you. They will make known to you all things which are done here.

10. Aristarchus my fellow prisoner greets you, and Marcus, Barnabas' cousin, concerning whom you received instructions: if he come to you, receive him.

11. And Jesus, which is called Justus, who are of the circumcision. These only are my co-workers within the kingdom of God, who have been a soothing balm to me.

12. Epaphras, who is one of you, a slave of Christ, greets you, always laboring fervently for you in prayers, that you may stand mature and complete in all the will of God.

13. For I testify of him, that he has a great zeal for you, and them that are in Laodicea, and them in Hierapolis.

14. Luke, the beloved physician, and Demas greet you.

15. Greet the brothers who are in Laodicea, and Nymphas, and the Assembly in his house.

16. When this letter is read among you, cause that it be read also in the Assembly of the Laodiceans; and that you likewise read the letter from Laodicea.

17. And say to Archippus, pay attention to the ministry which you have received in the Lord, that you may be completing it.

18. This salutation is by my hand, Paul. Remember my chains. Grace be with you. Amen.

1st Thessalonians Synopsis

The letter that Paul was writing was the freshest work of inspiration in the first century. Scholars worth their salt say that Paul wrote this letter around (AD 52) and the persecution of Rome hadn't fully emerged in the empire. He is writing to a church that has made a great sacrifice and in faith and they are suffering and being persecuted. Most likely they are being persecuted by the local Judaizers who are instigating all kinds of lies about the Thessalonians. Some have been killed and the pressure the saints experienced was to test their faith.

However, "since the Jews were continually making disturbances at the instigations of Chrestus, he [Claudius] expelled them from Rome " So writes the Roman historian Suetonius about events in Rome around 52. "Chrestus" may have been a thorn in the side of Roman politicos anxious to be rid of him and his cohorts. Or "Chrestus" may be the way uninformed bureaucrats pronounced the name about which Jews argued: Christus. Such arguments between Jews and Christians were not unknown (e.g., in Ephesus; Acts 19). Claudius likely and inadvertently was the first emperor, then, to persecute Christians (who were perceived as a Jewish sect)—for, it seems, disturbing the peace. The fact that the term "Christians" (Christianoi) was most plausibly coined by Latin speakers suggests that the followers of Jesus had come to the attention of city magistrates in Antioch, as had happened in Jerusalem in the past and would happen in other cities in the future. While the exact circumstances are unknown, it is plausible to assume that the encounter which required labelling the new Jewish movement and which involved the Roman magistrates was a hostile event.

Either Jewish citizens of Antioch brought legal charges before the magistrates of the city (as happened in Thessalonica; cf. Acts 17:5–9) or before the Roman governor of the province (as happened in Corinth; cf. Acts 18:12–14). Or Syrian citizens of Antioch who felt threatened by the missionary work of the Christians brought legal charges before the magistrates of the city (as happened in Philippi; cf. Acts 16:19–39). These events could have taken place in AD 37/38 or, if Paul was active in Antioch at the time, in AD 39/40. Some of the Jews in Thessalonica responded to Paul's preaching by recruiting "bad characters" (NIV), organizing a crowd who started a riot, probably a reference to an unofficial demonstration that got out of hand; they looked for Paul and Silas with the intention to drag them before the assembly of the city, evidently hoping that the citizens would indict and sanction the visiting teachers (Acts 17:5). After they failed to locate Paul and Silas, they took Jason, presumably Paul's host, before the politarchs, the senior magistrates of the city who were responsible for convening the assembly of the people (ekklēsia) as well as the city council (boulē) and who had judicial authority. The citizens whom the Jewish agitators had managed to organize accuse Paul and Silas of two offenses: first, they are people who upset the stability in other regions of the empire and who have now come to Thessalonica where they are also upsetting the stability of peace and order; second, they violate the decrees of the emperor by advocating loyalty to a certain Jesus rather than to the emperor in Rome (Acts 17:6–7). Reference: THE PERSECUTION OF CHRISTIANS IN THE FIRST CENTURY ECKHARD J. SCHNABEL. This is a great work on the history of the persecution in the first century in chronological order.

… we sent Timothy, our brother and co-worker for God in proclaiming the gospel of Christ, to strengthen and encourage you for the sake of your faith, 3 so that no one would be shaken by these persecutions[104] For this reason, brothers and sisters, during all our distress and persecution we have been encouraged about you through your faith.[105]

14 For you, brothers and sisters, became imitators of the churches of God in Christ Jesus that are in Judea, for you suffered the same things from your own compatriots as they did from the Jews, 15 who killed both the Lord Jesus and the prophets, and drove us out; they displease God and oppose everyone 16 by hindering us from speaking to the Gentiles so that they may be saved. Thus they have constantly been filling up the measure of their sins; but God's wrath has overtaken them at last.[106]

The Thessalonians were being persecuted just as the saints in Judea and Paul is saying that, they displease God, that is Old Covenant Israel, and they are opposers to everyone and dogging the steps of those who are preaching the kingdom of God. This phrase filling up the measure of their sins is similar to the words of our Lord in Matt. 23:31-33, 31So that you testify to yourselves, that you are sons of them who did murder the prophets; 32and you—you fill up the measure of your fathers.33 'Serpents! brood of vipers! How may you escape from the judgment of the Gehenna?[107] 35that on you may come all the righteous blood being poured out on the earth from the blood of Abel the righteous, unto the blood of Zacharias son of Barachias, whom you slew between the sanctuary and the altar: 36verily I say to you, all these things shall come upon this generation. [108]Just like Paul was saying to the Thessalonians that wrath has come upon them to the uttermost, Jesus predicted that the generation that He warned would experience the wrath of God. This was imminent and with certainty as the Lord goes on to cry out O Jerusalem, Jerusalem who kills the prophets!

---

[104] *The Holy Bible: New Revised Standard Version* (1 Th 3:2–3). (1989). Thomas Nelson Publishers.

[105] *The Holy Bible: New Revised Standard Version* (1 Th 3:7). (1989). Thomas Nelson Publishers.

[106] *The Holy Bible: New Revised Standard Version* (1 Th 2:14–16). (1989). Thomas Nelson Publishers.

[107] Young, R. (1997). *Young's Literal Translation* (Mt 23:31–33). Logos Bible Software.

[108] Young, R. (1997). *Young's Literal Translation* (Mt 23:35–36). Logos Bible Software.

Paul is so impressed with the steadfastness of these Thessalonian believers that he is praising them, and he knew they needed these words of affirmation.

The threefold expressions of the Thessalonians character, - the work of faith, labor of love, and endurance of hope - hold significant importance. These expressions, as outlined in 1 Thessalonians 1:3, serve as foundational principles for the Christian walk.

The work of faith emphasizes the active demonstration of one's faith through practical obedience and righteous living. It involves not only professing faith but also living it out in a way that glorifies God and aligns with His Word. True faith manifests itself in works, as James 2:26 teaches, and drives believers to follow God's voice with diligence and sincerity.

The labor of love is the central aspect and heart of Christian living, characterized by selfless service and sacrificial care for others. This love goes beyond mere sentiments or emotions, prompting believers to act in kindness and compassion towards those in need. Just as Christ selflessly gave Himself for us, believers are called to sacrificially love and serve others, reflecting the love of Christ in their interactions and deeds.

The endurance of hope is a steadfast perseverance in the face of trials and difficulties, rooted in the secure hope we have in Christ. This hope is not fleeting or uncertain but is anchored in the promises of God and the assurance of His faithfulness. By remaining steadfast in hope, believers can withstand hardships and challenges, trusting in God's sovereign control and His ultimate plan for their lives.

In summary, the threefold expressions of the Thessalonians - work of faith, labor of love, and endurance of hope - are foundational principles in the Christian walk. By embodying these attributes, believers can demonstrate a vibrant and consistent faith, selfless love for others, and unwavering hope in God's promises, bearing witness to the transforming power of the gospel in their lives.

4 For we know, brothers and sister's beloved by God, that he has chosen you, 5 because our message of the gospel came to you not in word only, but also in power and in the Holy Spirit and with full conviction; just as you know what kind of persons we proved to be among you for your sake. 6 And you became imitators of us and of the Lord, for in spite of persecution you received the word with joy inspired by the Holy Spirit[109]

This phrase 'not in word only' is quite telling. Our message needs to be in power and in the Holy Spirit. Just like then, we need today an anointed word with power.

I want to bring something to your attention concerning the level of maturity of these young saints in Thessalonica. The phrase 'became imitators of us and of the Lord', is really profound. In spiritual growth there are three stages whereby we are developing. As it is in our physical life. Childhood, Adolescence, and Adulthood. Using this word imitate we can see something of these stages in the letters of Paul. In 1 Cor. 11:1, Paul is addressing

---

[109] *The Holy Bible: New Revised Standard Version* (1 Th 1:3–6). (1989). Thomas Nelson Publishers.

an assembly of believers in the childhood stage of the Christian life. This self-centered, self-seeking church was childish and immature. So Paul writes, "Imitate me, just as I also imitate Christ".[110] As those who minister to immature believers we need to understand the capacity of new or immature believers. They need a human model to follow. Their spiritual eyes are not yet focused. Naturally a child's eyesight does not fully develop until 8 yrs. old. They can see but not fully. Isn't this true in our spiritual life. This is why when you were in 1st grade the letters A, B, C's were giant because educators know that straining the eyes in our formative years will cause us to damage our eyes and we will need glasses at a very young age. The Corinthians were children, and their spiritual eyesight was not fully developed so they needed a human example of someone that is following Christ. Paul says imitate me as I Christ.

When you come to the Thessalonians we see an advancement and Paul says, 'imitate us and the Lord'. This is the adolescent stage of growth where we see those that are excellent examples of following Christ, and not just one person, it is now us with the added spiritual discernment of and the Lord.

The adulthood stage is really wonderful as Paul addresses the Ephesian church. Therefore, be imitators of God as dear children. And walk in love, as Christ also has loved us and given Himself for us, an offering and a sacrifice to God for a sweet-smelling aroma.[111] Here he is addressing these saints as mature believers. Their eyes are open as he prayed that the eyes of their heart would be opened to the full knowledge of Him. Paul is saying to imitate God in the matters of forgiveness, proper speaking, kindness in the way God was in Christ. Paul's exhortation is to increase and abound in love for one another.

10 You are witnesses, and God also, how pure, upright, and blameless our conduct was toward you believers. 11 As you know, we dealt with each one of you like a father with his children, 12 urging and encouraging you and pleading that you lead a life worthy of God, who calls you into his own kingdom and glory.[112]

But we were gentle among you, like a nursing mother taking care of her own children.

1 Thessalonians 2:7 ESV

These two verses describe for us and nature of true ministry. There is a fathering side of ministry and a mothering side. Each side is imperative for effective ministry in the lives of the saints. In these verses, the apostle Paul reveals to us the tender heart of a true shepherd. Just as a father lovingly guides and instructs his children, so too did Paul and his fellow workers minister to the Thessalonian believers. They urged, encouraged, and pleaded with

---

[110] *The New King James Version* (1 Co 11:1). (1982). Thomas Nelson.

[111] *The New King James Version* (Eph 5:1–2). (1982). Thomas Nelson.

[112] *The Holy Bible: New Revised Standard Version* (1 Th 2:9–12). (1989). Thomas Nelson Publishers.

them to walk in a manner worthy of the God who had called them into His kingdom and glory.

But it is not with harshness or severity that they exhorted them, but with gentleness and compassion, like a nursing mother caring for her own children. Just as a mother tenderly nurtures and protects her little ones, so did Paul and his companions care for the spiritual well-being of the Thessalonian believers.

May we too, dear ones, learn from this example of genuine ministry. Let us not lord it over one another, but instead let us humbly and lovingly serve and encourage one another in the ways of the Lord. And may we always remember that it is God who calls us into His kingdom and glory, and it is He who will empower us to live lives worthy of that high calling.

17 But we, brothers, being separated and deprived of you for a short season in person, not in heart, endeavored the more abundantly to see your face with great desire. 18 Therefore we would have come to you, even I Paul, once and again; yet Satan impeded us. 19 For what is our hope, our joy, or crown we are proud of? Surely it is you before our Lord Jesus Christ in His Presence? 20 For you are our glory and joy. TKB Translation

Paul longing for the saints is very touching and he mentions that he was impeded by Satan from coming to them, but he has them in his heart. He with spectacular words says that they were his hope, and joy, even crown. Their faithfulness was an extension of the kingdom's presence, and he didn't want that to disappear and vanish. The testimony of their standing was evidence of God advancing. When we stand for the Lord in our city, we become the evidence of God's kingdom. Let's stand together to claim what is the Lord's. The earth and the world and all it contains is His and that makes it ours.

Chapter three is Paul sending Timothy to establish the testimony and encourage them and reminding them that afflictions were going to come. That was their destiny, and it was inevitable. In verse 8, which is an amazing verse. 8 for now we live if you are standing in the Lord. TKB Translation. Paul is saying we live if you are standing in the Lord. Many don't see the vital connection in the body of Christ, that our standing, our steadfastness, our faithfulness impacts the vitality of our brothers and sisters in Christ. When one member suffers we all suffer and when one member is glorified we rejoice with that member. We are integrally connected organically.

The chapter we are going to look at now is one of the most popular portions of scripture in our current time which is 1 Thess. Chapter 4. It is also the most misused portion of scripture with no rhyme or reason. I first of all want to thank Don K Preston for his diligence in tying the Olivet Discourse Matthew 23-25 and the Thessalonian letters together, it is such a masterpiece. Personally I don't think I would have connected the dots so neatly without his help. I thank God for him and for all the writings he has been blessed to produce.

His book "We Shall Meet Him in the Air: The Wedding of the King of Kings" is by far the most convincing book I have ever read on the quote "rapture doctrine". It is thorough and compelling in so many ways. I say in agreement with the Lord, "Give honor where honor is due". Thank you Don!

Since the Olivet Discourse is the source of Paul's 1st Thessalonians' chapter 4, let's start with it. The Olivet discourse is primarily dealing with old covenant Israel's history of sin and defiance of God and His will. The Lord Jesus says that He is going to destroy the city and the sanctuary. This was fulfilled in AD 70 and Jerusalem was leveled. No longer a temple, priesthood, holy city, or holy land. God was doing a new thing predicted by Isaiah in Isaiah 43. Paul uses a phrase in 1 Thess. 4:15.

For this we say to you by the word of the Lord, that we who are alive and are surviving into the Presence of the Lord did not at all come beforehand of them that have fallen asleep. This is not some rhema word from the Lord but a reference to a portion of the sermon on the Mount of Olives in Matthew 24. In this short synopsis I will not expound on the discourse only highlight the section that Paul is using as a source.

29 'Immediately after the tribulation of those days will the sun be darkened, and the moon shall not reflect her light, and the stars will fall from the heavens, and the powers of the heavens will be shaken; 30 and then will appear the sign of the Son of Man in the heaven; and then will all the tribes of the land mourn, and they will see the Son of Man coming in the cloud of the heavens, with power and great glory; 31 and He will send His messengers with a great sound of a trumpet, and they will gather together His elect from the four winds, from one extreme of heaven to the other extremity. TKB Translation.

Now let's compare 1st Thessalonians 4 with this. 16 For the Lord Himself will descend from heaven with a shout, with the voice of the chief messenger, and with the trumpet of God: and the dead in Christ will rise first: 17 after that, we the living and surviving, will be caught up together with Him in the cloud, to meet the Lord in the air, so we will at all times be with the Lord. 18 Therefore comfort one another with these words. We can see that the cloud, trumpet, and gathering the dead from the ends of the heavens and unto the ends thereof. I want to establish the timing of this event. The context of Matthew is the destruction of Jerusalem and the temple.

The Lord said that His generation would not pass until all these things come to pass or are fulfilled. The event of the Son of Man coming on the clouds and the sound of the trumpet and gathering the dead from the heavens would happen before that generation passed. Truly, I say to you, this generation will not pass away until all these things take place.[113] One of the things is His coming in the cloud and the sound of the trumpet and

---

[113] *The Holy Bible: English Standard Version* (Mt 24:34). (2016). Crossway Bibles.

gathering of the dead from the heavens. So, we see that the timing of this event is within the generation that Christ said would not pass away.

Paul uses the same language when he says, 'we who are alive and remain will be caught up together with Him in the cloud. Jesus' timing is in the first century and Paul is in full alignment with Christ's word in the discourse. Refer to Don's book WE SHALL MEET HIM IN THE AIR for more details. Excerpts from the book We Shall Meet Him in the Air, The Wedding of the King of Kings Don K Preston 2009 (Used with permission)

Temple Sermon and Olivet Discourse	1st & 2nd Thessalonians
1. Matt. 23:29f – Jews had slain the prophets	1 Thess. 2:15 – Jews had slain the prophets
2. 23:34 – Would kill Jesus' "prophets"	1:2:15 – Had killed Jesus' prophets
3. 23:32 – Would fill up the measure of their sin by persecuting.	1:2:15-16 – Were filling up the measure of their sin by persecuting.
4. 23:36 – Judgment would come in that generation. (cf. Luke 21:23)	1:2:16 – Wrath has come on them to the uttermost.
5. 24:9 – Shall deliver you to be afflicted – (thlipsis) (first section)	Received the word in much affliction (thlipsis, cf. 2:1:5-7)
6. 24:10-12 – Apostasy (v. 12) love of most people will grow cold, (NASB) (First section)	2 Thess. 2:3 – Paul had told them of this when he was with them (v.5). Paul is basing his prediction on the Olivet Discourse.
7. Lawlessness (anomia) will abound (24:12)	Spirit of lawlessness (anomia) is already at work (2 Thess.2:5)
8. 24:14 – Gospel Mission	1 Thessalonians 1:8 – Gospel mission being fulfilled.
9. Mark 13:11 – Miraculous presence of the Spirit	1 Thess. 1:5; 5:19 Miraculous presence of the Spirit

Matthew 24 comparing 1st Thessalonians 4:13-18

Matthew 24:29-31	1st Thessalonians 4:13-18
Coming on the Son of Man	Coming on the Son of Man
With the angels v. 30-31	With the angels v. 16
With the trumpet v. 31	With the trumpet v. 16
Coming on the cloud v. 30	Descending from heaven in the air v. 16-17
Gathering of the redeemed v. 31	Gathering of the redeemed v. 17
This generation shall not pass until all these things are fulfilled v. 34	"We who are alive and remain until the coming of the Lord v. 15,17

This event that is coined the rapture is a threefold event that cannot be separated. The rapture, the return, and the resurrection. All three of these components of the Parousia are invisible to the natural eye. The Parousia is invisible because this is the consummation of the manifestation of the kingdom of God. Here is a question that the Pharisees asked: Now when He was asked by the Pharisees when the kingdom of God would come[114] … He answered them and said, "The kingdom of God does not come with observation; nor will they say, 'See here!' or 'See there!' For indeed, the kingdom of God is inside you." You must be born again to see the kingdom of God. If the kingdom of God was obvious to all then why would Jesus say, 'you must be born again to see'? It is because it is invisible. The kingdom coming and Christ coming are synonymous and when the church gets this it will be a bondage breaker into looking at the kingdom in a fleshly way. We will see Jesus in a different way too. 22 And He said to the disciples, the days will come when you will want to see one of the days of the Son of man, and you will not see it. 23 And they will say to you, see here; or see there: go not after them, nor follow them. 24 For as the lightning, that lightens out of the one part under the heavens, shines to the other part under the heavens; so also will the Son of man be in His day. 25 But first He must suffer many things and be rejected by this generation. Lk. 17:22-25 TKB. 16 Therefore, from now on, we regard no man according to the flesh: yes, even though we have known Christ after the flesh, yet now we know Him thus no more. 2 Cor. 5:16 TKB. This is a gamechanger when we view Christ, the last Adam became the life-giving Spirit. 1 Cor. 15:45b.

---

114 *The New King James Version* (Lk 17:20). (1982). Thomas Nelson.

1 Thess. 4:17; Revelation 9:2; Revelation 16:17; ὁ ἄρχων τῆς ἐξουσίας τοῦ ἀέρος in Ephesians 2:2 signifies 'the ruler of the powers (spirits, see ἐξουσία 4 c. ββ.) in the air,' i. e. the devil, the prince of the demons that according to Jewish opinion fill the realm of air … Strong's G109. When reading the context of Ephesians chapter two the aer is described in two ways. On the positive side it is called the heavenlies where those who were dead in sins were made alive and raised and made to sit in the heavenlies. Those who walk according to the course of the age of this world are under the influence of the ruler who has the authority of the air. The word aer is translated air. Paul shows the clash between those two rulers in chapter six of Ephesians. In Thessalonians those of the dead and those who were alive were caught up into that realm where those wicked forces in the air were conquered. This what Paul noted earlier in Ephesians regarding God's perpetual purpose: 8 He has abounded toward us in all wisdom and prudence; 9 having made known to us the mystery of His will, according to His good pleasure that He has brought forth in Himself: 10 into the administration of the completion of the proper time that He might gather together in one all in Christ, both which are in heaven, and which are on earth; even in Him: 11 in Whom also we have obtained an inheritance, being predestinated according to the purpose of Him who works all things after the counsel of His own will: 12 that we should be to the praise of His glory, who first hoped in Christ. Eph. 1:8-12 TKB. The gathering and being caught up both the dead and those who are alive when He came were victorious in the manifestation of His Kingdom. This was all fulfilled at the end of the first generation and completed in AD 70. The sons of disobedience were destroyed and this ruler, prince was defeated completely.

The two spheres in Ephesians chapter 1 is a prediction of the perpetual purpose of God and the goal that He was working towards. The first sphere is gathering all things in Christ both in heaven and on earth. The second sphere is the conquered sphere. 20 which He worked in Christ when He raised Him from the dead and set Him at His own right hand in the heavenlies, 21 far above all government, and authority, and power, and dominion, and every name that is named, not only in this Old Covenant Age but also in that New Covenant Age which is about to come: 22 and has put all things under His feet, and gave Him to be the head over all things to the Assembly, 23 which is His body, the fullness of Him that fills all in all. Here we see the unique description of the assembly as the body of Christ, the fullness of HIM and this full-grown man that God is working all things after the counsel of His will is the goal of every generation. If every generation is cooperative and compliant to God's will forces of darkness are subdued, but if the church remains immature and weak by disobedience and walking according to flesh those forces of darkness are not subdued. If we don't see the first century as a generational model for to understand God's purpose for each generation we will fail in our journey and destiny with God. God did not just do something so wonderful in the first century and then, now that it's fulfilled, we just invent church and our own purpose. We must be those that turn the world upside down but are we willing to pay the price for that to be realized.

The New Testament is a progressive unfolding of transitioning from the old to the new, from the flesh to the Spirit, from the physical to the perpetual, from the visible to the invisible, from the temporary to the infinite. The rapture, return, and resurrection was the capstone and climax of God's purpose. I will never be able to look at the New Testament any other way than this. It was not written to us; it was written for us.

In chapter 5 which is a continuation of Paul's thought. He is telling the Thessalonians that the day of the Lord will not be a surprise to you, but to those in darkness it will be like a thief in the night, and they won't get out of that situation.

1 But of the times and the appointed times, brothers, you have no need that I write to you. 2 For yourselves know fully that the day of the Lord so comes as a thief in the night. 3 For when they will say, Peace and safety; then sudden destruction stands on them, as pains on a woman with child; and they will not get out. 1st Thess. 5:1-3. I translate the word about sudden destruction as standing on them. They are defeated and conquered. Paul assures the saints that they will not be surprised because they are not in the dark. 4 But you, brothers, are not in darkness, so that day will not be seizing you as a thief. 5 You are all the children of light, and the children of the day: we are not of the night, nor darkness. 1st Thess. 5:4-5 TKB. The general understanding of the saints in Thessalonica were not ignorant of the times. They were like the sons of Issachar who understood the times and knew what Israel ought to do. It amazes me when those that teach the bible say the first century saints and servants of God didn't know what time it was. That they were mixed up. There are too many verses that say the opposite. In the beginning, they were not clear as time went on after 20 – 30 years the New Testament was written is became glaringly clear to the saints, especially to the apostles. John says in 1 John 2:18, Little children it is the last hour. He knew what time it was. I ask you, what last hour was John talking about? The last hour of what? We need to understand these things, the last days of what. The last hour and last days of the completion of God's perpetual purpose. There is so much to say about the night and the day. The old covenant age was a place of shadows and types and considered as the night and Jesus as the morning star was rising in the hearts of those first century saints, the new day was approaching, the new covenant age. In the new Jerusalem there is no night there. No old covenant, no wrinkles from old age, no spots which are false teachers. No blemishes nothing that is a defect of the image of God. Now the new Jerusalem is not a place but a people. The wife of the Lamb!

9 For God has not appointed us to wrath, but to obtain salvation by our Lord Jesus Christ, 10 who died for us, that, whether we are awake or asleep, we should live together with Him. 11 Therefore comfort yourselves together, and build up one another, just as also you do. 1st Thess. 5:9-11. 1st Thess. 5:9-11 TKB.

The wrath of God was coming in their lifetime and Paul is encouraging them that they were not appointed to wrath but to obtain salvation. It did not matter whether they were alive or dead they would not miss this event.

12 For we urge you, brothers, to know those who labor among you, and are standing before you in the Lord, and admonish you; 13 and to esteem them very highly in love for their work's sake. And be at peace among yourselves. 1st Thess. 5:12-13 TKB. Know those who labor among you. Now this is a word. Those who minister the word and stand before us need to be transparent before us so we can know them. I asked a brother not too long ago, who attends a rather large congregation of believers. Do you know your pastor? He said not really. I asked him if he had ever been to his home? He laughed at me and said, 'that would never happen'. It should happen. We need to know those who labor among us. Not to judge them, but to build a relationship with those who serve us. This is the problem with a CEO type of church. This only works in a business not in an organic testimony of Jesus!

Brothers and sisters in Christ, let us meditate on the words of the Apostle Paul in 1 Thessalonians 5:23. May we remember that our God is the God of peace, and He desires to sanctify us completely. It is His will that every part of our being—spirit, soul, and body—be kept blameless and faultless before our Lord Jesus Christ. Let us pursue holiness and purity in all areas of our lives, seeking to be set apart for God's purpose. This verse has relevance to the saints then living. This is a prayer of Paul for God to preserve these saints from being killed during the persecution and that their spirit, soul, and body be preserved at the coming of the Lord. Paul wanted them to live into the New Covenant age to carry on the work of the kingdom. He who calls you is faithful and He will do it. 25 Brethren, pray for us. 26 Greet all the brothers with a holy kiss as a token of friendship. 27 I adjure you by the Lord that this letter be read to all the holy brothers. 28 The grace of our Lord Jesus Christ be with you. Amen

Paul asks the saints for prayer and closes with an affectionate goodbye saying greet the brothers with a holy kiss as a token of friendship. Commanding them to have this letter read to all the holy brothers and closing in his usual fashion, "the grace of our Lord Jesus Christ be with you".

Terry Kashian

1 Thessalonians

Chapter 1

1. Paul, and Silvanus, and Timothy, to the Assembly of the Thessalonians whom is in God the Father and in the Lord Jesus Christ: grace be to you, and peace, from God our Father, and the Lord Jesus Christ.
2. We give thanks to God always for you all, making mention of you in our prayers;
3. Remembering without stopping your work of faith, and labor of love, and patience of hope in our Lord Jesus Christ, in the sight of God and our Father;
4. Knowing, brothers beloved, your election of God.
5. For our gospel came not to you in word only, but also in power, and in the Holy Spirit, and in much assurance; as you know what manner of men we were among you for your sake.
6. So, you became followers of us, and of the Lord, having received the word in much affliction, with the joy of the Holy Spirit.
7. So that you were a model to all that believe in Macedonia and Achaia.
8. For from you sounded out the word of the Lord not only in Macedonia and Achaia, but also in every place your faith toward God is spread abroad; so that we need not to speak anything.
9. For they themselves show of us what manner of entry we had toward you, and how you turned to God from idols to serve the living and true God;
10. And to wait for His Son from heaven, who He raised out from the dead, who is Jesus, who delivers us out of the coming wrath.

Chapter 2

1. For yourselves, brothers, know our coming to you, that it was not for nothing:
2. But even after we had suffered before, and were outrageously treated, as you know, at Philippi, we were bold in our God to speak to you the gospel of God with great opposition.
3. 3. For our exhortation was not out of deceit, nor of uncleanness, nor in error.
4. But as we were allowed of God to be put in trust with the gospel, even so, we speak; not as pleasing men, but God, who is testing our hearts.
5. For neither at any time did we use flattering words, as you know, nor a cloak of covetousness; God is witness:
6. Nor of men did we seek glory, neither of you nor yet of others when we might have been burdensome, as the apostles of Christ.
7. But we were gentle in your midst, just as a nursing mother nourishes her children:
8. So being affectionately passionate for you, we were gratified to impart to you, not the gospel of God only, but also our own souls, because you became dear to us.
9. For you remember, brothers, our labor and toil: for laboring night and day, because we would not overload any of you, we preached to you the gospel of God.

10. You are witnesses, and God also, how in a sacred manner and justly and blamelessly we behaved ourselves among you that believe:

11. As you know how we advised and comforted and urged every one of you, as a father does his children,

12. That you are to be walking worthy of the God, who has called you into His kingdom and glory.

13. For this reason also we thank God continually, because, when you received the word of God which you heard from us, you received it not as the word of men, but as it is in reality, the word of God, which is actively working also in you who are believing.

14. For you, brothers, became followers of the Assemblies of God which in Judea are in Christ Jesus: for you also have suffered like things of your own countrymen, just as they have of the Jews:

15. Who both killed the Lord Jesus, and their own prophets, and have expelled us; and they are not pleasing God, and are contrary to all men:

16. Forbidding us to speak to the nations that they might be saved, filling up the measure of sins all this time: for the wrath has come suddenly on them into the consummation.

17. But we, brothers, being separated and deprived of you for a short season in person, not in heart, endeavored the more abundantly to see your face with great desire.

18. Therefore we would have come to you, even I Paul, once and again; yet Satan impeded us.

19. For what is our hope, our joy, or crown we are proud of? Surely it is you before our Lord Jesus Christ in His Presence?

20. For you are our glory and joy.

Chapter 3

1. Therefore, when we could no longer hold back, we thought it good to be left at Athens alone;

2. So, sent Timothy, our brother, and minister of God, and our fellow laborer in the gospel of Christ, to establish you, and to comfort you concerning your faith:

3. That no man should be shaken by these afflictions: for yourselves know that we are appointed for this.

4. For truthfully, when we were with you, we told you before that we are about to suffer tribulation; just as it came to pass, and you know.

5. For this reason, when I could no longer hold back, I sent to know your faith, unless by some means the tempter had tempted you, and our labor had been for nothing.

6. But now when Timothy came from you to us, and brought us good tidings of your faith and love, and that you have good remembrance of us always, desiring greatly to see us, as we also to see you:

7. Therefore, brothers, we were comforted concerning you in all our affliction and distress by your faith:

8. For now, we live, if you are standing in the Lord.

9. For what thanks can we render to God again for you, for all the joy with which we rejoice for your sakes before our God;

10. Night and day praying exceedingly that we might see your face, and complete the mending of that which is lacking in your faith?

11. Now, God Himself and our Father, and our Lord Jesus Christ, direct our way to you.

12. And the Lord make you to increase and abound in love one toward another, and toward all men, just as we do toward you:

13. To the end He may establish your hearts blamelessly in holiness before God, even our Father, in the Presence of our Lord Jesus Christ with all His saints.

Chapter 4

1. Furthermore, then we implore you, brothers, and exhort you by the Lord Jesus, that as you have received of us how you ought to walk and to please God, so you would abound more and more.

2. For you know what commandments we gave you by the Lord Jesus.

3. For this is the will of God, even your sanctification, that you should abstain from fornication:

4. That each one of you should know how to possess his vessel in sanctification and honor;

5. Not in the lust of sexual desire, just as the nations whom know not God:

6. That no man go beyond and defraud his brother in any matter: because that the Lord is the avenger of all such, as we also have forewarned you and testified.

7. For God has not called us to uncleanness, but to holiness.

8. He therefore that despises, despises not man, but God, who has also given to us His Holy Spirit.

9. But as concerning brotherly love you need not that I write to you: for you yourselves are taught by God to love one another.

10. And indeed, you do it toward all the brothers whom are in all Macedonia: but we urge you, brothers, that you increase more and more;

11. That you aspire to be quiet, and to do your own business, and to work with your own hands, as we commanded you;

12. That you may walk honestly toward them that are outside, and that you may have lack of nothing.

13. But I would not have you to be ignorant, brothers, concerning them which slept, that you sorrow not, just as others which have no hope.

14. For if we believe that Jesus died and rose again, even so them which slept in Jesus, God brought with Him.

15. For this we say to you by the word of the Lord, that we who are alive and are surviving unto the Presence of the Lord did not at all prevent them that slept.

16. For the Lord Himself will descend from heaven with a shout, with the voice of the archangel, and with a trump of God: and the dead in Christ will rise first:

17. After that, we the living and surviving, will be caught up together with Him in the cloud, to meet the Lord in the air, so we will be perpetually with the Lord.

18. Therefore, comfort one another with these words.

Chapter 5

1. But of the times and the seasons, brothers, you have no need that I write to you.
2. For yourselves know fully that the day of the Lord so comes as a thief in the night.
3. For when they will say, Peace and safety; then sudden destruction comes on them, as pains on a woman with child; and they will not escape.
4. But you, brothers, are not in darkness, so that day should be overtaking you as a thief.
5. You are all the children of light, and the children of the day: we are not of the night, nor of darkness.
6. Therefore, let us not sleep, as do others; but let us watch and be sober.
7. For they that sleep, are sleeping in the night; and they that be drunken are drunken in the night.
8. But let us, who are of the day, be sober, putting on the breastplate of faith and love, and for a helmet, the hope of salvation.
9. For God has not appointed us to wrath, but to obtain salvation by our Lord Jesus Christ,
10. Who died for us, that, whether we wake or sleep, we should live together with Him.
11. Therefore, comfort yourselves together, and build up one another, just as also you do.
12. For we urge you, brothers, to know those who labor among you, and are over you in the Lord, and admonish you;
13. And to esteem them very highly in love for their work's sake. And be at peace among yourselves.
14. Now we exhort you, brothers, warn them that are unruly, comfort the fainthearted, support the weak and be patient toward all men.
15. See that no one gives back evil for evil to anyone; but pursue that which is good, both among yourselves, and to all men.
16. Rejoice at all times.
17. Pray without intermission.
18. In everything give thanks: for this is the will of God in Christ Jesus concerning you.
19. Quench not the Spirit.
20. Despise not prophesying.
21. Test all things; hold fast that which is good.
22. Abstain from all appearance of evil.
23. And the very God of peace sanctify you completely; and may all your parts, spirit and soul and body be kept faultless in the presence of our Lord Jesus Christ.
24. Faithful is He that is calling you, who also will be doing it.
25. Brethren, pray for us.
26. Greet all the brothers with a holy kiss as a token of friendship.
27. I charge you by the Lord that this letter be read to all the holy brothers.
28. The grace of our Lord Jesus Christ be with you. Amen.

2nd Thessalonians Synopsis

Introduction (1:1-2)

I. Paul introduces himself as the writer of the letter shortly after 1 Thessalonians around 54 AD

   1. Mentions Silvanus and Timothy his coworkers

   2. offers a greeting to the recipients in Thessalonica

II. Thanksgiving for the Thessalonians' Faith and Perseverance (1:3-4)

   1. Paul expresses gratitude for the Thessalonians' strong faith and perseverance in the face of persecution

   2. Commends them for their love for one another

III. Assurance of God's Righteous Judgment (1:5-10)

   1. Paul reassures the Thessalonians that God will bring justice to those who are persecuting them

   2. Describes the future judgment of the wicked and the reward of the righteous

IV. Prayers for the Thessalonians (1:11-12)

   1. Paul prays for God to fulfill the Thessalonians' desire to do good and to strengthen their faith

   2. Expresses his desire for them to be worthy of God's calling

V. The Day of the Lord (2:1-12)

   1. Paul addresses concerns about the coming of the day of the Lord

   2. Describes the events that will precede the day of the Lord, including the rise of the men of lawlessness, the sons of perdition

   3. Urges the Thessalonians to stand firm in their faith and not be deceived by false teachings

VI. Stand Firm in Your Faith (2:13-3:5)

   1. Paul reminds the Thessalonians of their calling as God's chosen people

   2. Encourages them to hold fast to the traditions they were taught

   3. Urges them to be diligent in their work and to avoid idleness

VII. Dealing with Unruly Believers (3:6-15)

1. Paul instructs the Thessalonians on how to deal with believers who are living in disobedience

2. Encourages them to maintain discipline and not grow weary in doing good

3. Emphasizes the importance of living in obedience and working diligently VIII.

VIII. Final Greetings and Benediction (3:16-18)

1. Paul closes the letter with final greetings and a blessing for the Thessalonians

2. Urges them to have peace and to remain faithful to the Lord

This outline provides a structured overview of the key themes and teachings found in the letter of 2 Thessalonians.

This letter, penned by the apostle Paul, was likely written shortly after the first epistle to the Thessalonians. Scholars suggest that 2 Thessalonians was written around the mid-50s AD, during Paul's missionary journeys as he spread the gospel throughout various regions.

As we delve into the historical context of this epistle, we find that Paul's purpose in writing to the Thessalonian believers was to address some misunderstandings that had arisen concerning the return of Christ. In 1 Thessalonians, Paul had spoken about the second coming of Christ, and some within the church had become confused about the timing and nature of this event.

Therefore, in 2 Thessalonians, Paul seeks to clarify and reassure the Thessalonians regarding the return of Christ, emphasizing the need for steadfastness and faithfulness in the face of persecution and trials. The themes of eschatology and endurance permeate this epistle, with Paul's words serving as a source of comfort and encouragement to the early Christian community. Let us journey back to the first decades of the Christian church, as we explore the hope and perseverance contained within the pages of 2nd Thessalonians.

The Epistles of First and Second Thessalonians have often been seen as evidence supporting a future, world-ending return of Christ. These two letters extensively address the Parousia, with nearly every chapter containing a reference to this event. However, challenging this traditional view, we will examine whether Thessalonians truly points to a future return of Christ. Specifically, in this analysis, we will argue that the subject matter of II Thessalonians aligns with that of Matthew 24, particularly the 'first section' (verses 4-35), acknowledged by many Amillennialists as focusing exclusively on Christ's coming in the destruction of Jerusalem.

Our disagreement is that if Matthew 24:4-35 exclusively relates to the coming of Christ in Jerusalem's destruction and if Paul drew from this passage in II Thessalonians 2, then the subject matter of II Thessalonians 2 also pertains to Christ's coming in the context of Jerusalem's destruction. Not only do we seek to establish a thematic link between the two passages, but we also aim to explore their chronological framework. Scholars have noted striking similarities between Paul's discussion of Christ's coming and Jesus' Olivet discourse. While some parallels are more apparent in the original language, there are clear similarities between Matthew 24 and Thessalonians, detailed in Don K Preston's book 'II Peter 3: The Late Great Kingdom.'

In Matthew 24:29-31; Mark 13:26, Jesus prophesies his return in judgment at the end of the old covenant age, emphasizing the gathering of the saints from all corners of the earth and from the ends of heaven. Paul's concept of the saints' gathering at Christ's coming likely drew from this passage. The persecution and anticipated vindication described in Matthew and Thessalonians reveal a significant correspondence. Paul addressed the Thessalonians' persecution instigated by the Jews, promising their vindication at the Lord's coming in fire and vengeance, matching the judgment foreseen by Jesus. Therefore, the vindication of the Thessalonians aligns with the judgment in Matthew 24:29-31 and Mark 13:26.

An important point of comparison between Matthew 24:31 and II Thessalonians 2:1ff lies in the word 'gathering.' The distinctive term 'episunago' used by Jesus in Matthew 24 is crucial in emphasizing the eschatological gathering at Christ's coming in Jerusalem's judgment. This same term is employed by Paul in II Thessalonians, suggesting a parallel in the gathering of the saints for judgment. Since Jesus primarily utilized 'episunago' in reference to his coming in judgment over Jerusalem, the application of this term in II Thessalonians necessitates a similar interpretation. The consistent usage of this term across these passages mandates careful consideration of their shared eschatological significance.

Ultimately, the unity in language and thematic content between Matthew and Thessalonians underscores a coherent narrative surrounding Christ's coming and the gathering of the saints. The question remains: How many comings of the Lord, with his angels, in power and glory, to gather the saints, are depicted in the New Testament?

In his book "We Shall Meet Him in the Air: The Wedding of the King of Kings," Don K. Preston brings a unique perspective to eschatological passages such as 2 Thessalonians. In interpreting these verses, he may focus on the imminent nature of the judgment described by the Apostle Paul and its relevance to the first-century audience.

Paul's words to the Thessalonian believers regarding their patience and faith in the face of persecution and tribulation are seen as evidence of the righteous judgment of God. Preston does emphasize the idea that the suffering endured by the Thessalonian church was not only a sign of their faithfulness but also a precursor to the impending judgment that would vindicate them as faithful followers of Christ.

The mention of God repaying those who trouble the believers with tribulation is understood in the context of the imminent judgment that was to come upon those who rejected the gospel message. Preston interprets the language of the Lord Jesus being revealed from heaven with His mighty angels in flaming fire as symbolic of the impending judgment upon Jerusalem in AD 70, a key event in his eschatological framework known as "Covenant Eschatology."

The emphasis on vengeance upon those who do not know God or obey the gospel of Jesus Christ is seen by Preston as a reference to the judgment that befell unbelieving Jerusalem and the Jewish authorities who rejected Jesus as the Messiah. The promise of rest for the troubled believers when the Lord Jesus is revealed could be understood in light of the relief and vindication that would come with the destruction of Jerusalem and the establishment of the new covenant age.

In summary, Don K. Preston's interpretation of 2 Thessalonians 1:4-8 from the perspective of his eschatological framework focuses on the imminent judgment upon Jerusalem in AD 70 and its significance for the early Christian community as evidence of God's righteous judgment and vindication of the faithful believers and martyrs.

Chapter 2

The concept of 'the day of the Lord' is a pivotal aspect of biblical prophecy, particularly in the Old Testament. It is a day of divine judgment and reckoning, where God's justice and righteousness are fully revealed. In the prophetic scriptures, 'the day of the Lord' is described as a day of darkness, destruction, and ultimately, salvation.

However, in my study of eschatology, particularly through the lens of covenant eschatology, I have come to understand 'the day of the Lord' in a different light. I believe that 'the day of the Lord' is not just a singular event in the future, but rather a pattern of judgment and deliverance throughout history. As the Lord's people are obedient and taking the ground we will see prosperity righteousness, joy and peace flourish, but on the other hand if the Lord's people compromise and become apathetic darkness will creep in and as His church we will lose ground calling for the discipline of the church and judgment on the ungodly.

I make the claim that the day of the Lord was fulfilled in the destruction of Jerusalem in AD 70, when God poured out his judgment on the unbelieving Jews and established the new covenant kingdom. This event marked the end of the old covenant age, the last days of old covenant Israel and the beginning of the new covenant age, where Christ reigns as King.

Therefore, I believe that we are currently living in 'the new covenant age,' where God's kingdom is advancing, and His justice is being fulfilled. We do not need to anxiously await a future day of judgment, but rather live in the reality that Christ has already won the victory and established his perpetual kingdom.

In conclusion, the concept of 'the day of the Lord' is a powerful reminder of God's sovereignty and justice. Through my study of covenant eschatology, I have come to see 'the day of the Lord' as a present reality, where God's kingdom is gaining ground, and His justice is being fulfilled. Let us embrace this truth and live as citizens of God's perpetual kingdom, knowing that Christ has already conquered sin and death.

In 2 Thessalonians 2:1-2, the Apostle Paul addresses concerns among the Thessalonian Christians about the coming of the Lord Jesus Christ and their gathering together with Him. Paul is cautioning them not to be quickly shaken or troubled by false teachings or messages claiming that the day of Christ has already arrived.

It is clear from Paul's exhortation that some in the early church believed that the day of Christ had already come. This belief likely stemmed from a misunderstanding or misinterpreting prophetic teachings about the end times.

Paul's reminder to the Thessalonians serves as a corrective to this erroneous belief. He goes on to explain in the following verses that certain events, such as the 'men of sin' being revealed, must take place and the great falling away from the faith before the coming of the Lord Jesus Christ and their gathering together to Him.

Therefore, the Thessalonians' mistaken belief that the day of Christ had already arrived highlights the importance of proper understanding and interpretation of biblical prophecy. It also underscores the need for vigilance against false teachings and the importance of holding fast to the true teachings of the apostles.

Overall, Paul's words to the Thessalonians serve as a reminder for us today to be discerning in our understanding of prophecy and to remain steadfast in our faith, knowing that the day of the Lord came at the appointed time according to God's sovereign plan.

Now we urge you, brothers, on behalf of the Presence of our Lord Jesus Christ, and by our gathering together to Him, 2 that you be not soon shaken in mind, or be troubled, neither by spirit, nor by word, nor by letter as if from us, that the day of the Lord is present. 3 Let no one deceive you by any means: for that day will not come, unless there come the apostasy first, and the men of sin unveiled, the sons of perdition; 4 opposing and exalting themselves above all that is called God, or that is worshiped; so that they like God, take their seat in the temple of God, exhibiting themselves that they are God. 2nd Thessalonians -TKB Translation

Paul is urging the brothers to not be disturbed by a spirit or letter that supposedly came from them that the day of the Lord had arrived or was present. The day of the Lord was a day of judgment on the wicked and a deliverance of the righteous believers. As brother Don puts it, it was not a time-ending, earth burning event where people were coming out of their graves. If this was what the Thessalonians were taught they would never have been deceived or fooled by such a letter. The nature of the day of the Lord was not what we are taught today in the majority of churches. Paul says that day will not happen until there is a great falling away from the faith. Men's hearts will grow cold and the agape love of many will freeze up. The amount of deception that existed in the first century was overwhelming and our Lord said that even the elect would be deceived. "Then if anyone says to you, 'Look, here is the Christ!' or 'There!' do not believe it. For false Christs and false prophets will rise and show great signs and wonders to deceive, if possible, even the elect. See, I have told you beforehand.[115] The term apostasy is derived from Ancient Greek: ἀποστάτης, meaning "rebellious", and it reminds me of the verses in Daniel regarding the 70 weeks. Daniel 9:24 Seventy sevens mark the end concerning your people and concerning your holy city, **to put an end to the rebellion**, and to **make an end of sin-offerings,** and to **make conciliation for iniquity,** and to **bring in perpetual righteousness,** and to **finalize the visions and the prophets,** and to **anoint the Holy of Holies.** 25 Know therefore and understand, that from the going forth of the commandment to return and to rebuild Jerusalem to the Messiah the Prince will be **seven sevens, and sixty-two sevens:** it will be built again, the public square and waterways, even in times of distress. 26 **After the sixty-two sevens the Messiah will be cut off** and have nothing: and the **people of the Prince that will come will destroy the city and the sanctuary; and its end will be with a flood,** and even up to the end of the war, desolations are decided. 27 He will reinforce the covenant with the many, one seven, **and in the middle of the seven,** He will **cause the sacrifice and the grain offering to discontinue;** and because of the extreme abominations He will make it desolate; even until the complete desolation, and that order will be poured out on the desolate. TKB Translation.

The starting point of this glorious prophecy is the rebuilding of the city of Jerusalem and the end is the destruction of the temple and the city. These two points entail the entire purpose of bringing in the Messiah and the New Covenant. Many scholars do not add up the weeks properly about when the Messiah is crucified. There are seven weeks or sevens and then there are sixty-two sevens which add up to sixty-nine sevens. Daniel was told after the sixty-two sevens Messiah is cut off. That is seven sevens plus sixty-two sevens adding up to sixty-nine sevens. So after the sixty-nine sevens Messiah is crucified and we are left with one seven left. All scholars agree that each of the sevens are years. The last seven years is regarding the war of the Jews with Rome. The war lasted seven years from AD 66 to AD 73. In the middle of the seven the sanctuary was destroyed and God put an end to sin-offerings for good. The insurgents who remained held out for many months. Herod's Palace was laid to siege and finally destroyed, and by the next summer, even as Titus and Vespasian were celebrating a triumph in Rome, their forces were still clearing Judea of fighters. Captured Jewish men were sent to either live out their lives in forced labor in Egypt or to be torn apart by animals in gladiatorial games, while their women and children were dispersed and sold as slaves. The whims of the new regime also meant that the rebel leaders met with different fates. John was sentenced to life imprisonment, while Simon was systematically tortured and scourged before being strangled. In Judea in AD 73 and 74, the Romans conquered the

---

[115] The New King James Version (Mt 24:23–25). (1982).

hilltop fortress of Masada, bringing the First Jewish War to a bloody conclusion.[116] 2 The Old Covenant was fulfilled, and all the promises and prophecies were completed at the destruction of Jerusalem in AD 70 and all that was written. All the types and shadows came to an end. In AD 70, the rebellion, the sacrificial system and all that it entailed was removed for the better covenant. All the six items in Daniel's prophetic word found their fulfillment at the consummation of AD 70. Paul is summing up what will happen to the Old Covenant Israel in her final days and what will transpire when the city is taken over by the criminals.

During the first century, the Jewish historian Josephus recorded several instances of false prophets and false messiahs who arose in Judea and ultimately led to the conquest of Jerusalem in 70 AD. Some of the names associated with false signs and wonders during this period include:

1. Simon bar Giora - A prominent leader of the Zealot movement who declared himself the messiah and led the rebellion against the Romans in Jerusalem in the 60s AD. He was known for his ruthless tactics and fierce resistance against the Roman forces.

2. John of Gischala - Another Zealot leader who vied for control of Jerusalem during the siege. He engaged in power struggles with Simon bar Giora and contributed to the internal conflict within the city.

3. Menahem ben Judah - A false messiah who initially led a rebellion against the Romans in 66 AD and later returned to Jerusalem during the siege. He was eventually captured and killed by the Roman forces. These men, along with other false prophets and leaders, played significant roles in the events leading up to the fall of Jerusalem in 70 AD. He was reported to have performed acts that were believed to be signs of his divine favor. Their actions and conflicts with each other further contributed to the chaos and devastation that ultimately befell the city and its inhabitants.

4. Eleazar ben Simon - A leader of the Sicarii faction, Eleazar ben Simon also played a role in the events of the siege. He and his followers were known for their extremist tactics, including acts of violence and terrorism against both the Romans and their fellow Jews.

Other unnamed individuals - Josephus records several instances of false prophets and magicians who emerged during the siege of Jerusalem, claiming to possess supernatural powers or the ability to perform miracles. These individuals, whether through deception or genuine belief in their own abilities, played significant roles in the unfolding events of the siege and contributed to the religious and political turmoil. These false prophets and messianic figures played significant roles in the escalating tensions between the Jews and the Roman authorities, ultimately leading to the destruction of Jerusalem and the Second

---

[116] Thomas Nelson. https://warfarehistorynetwork.com/article/the-fall-of-jerusalem-in-70-ce-a-story-of-roman-revenge/

Temple in 70 AD. During the siege of Jerusalem in 70 AD. Some of the key figures during this time included: These leaders, among others, set themselves up in the Temple and exercised significant influence over the population during the siege of Jerusalem, contributing to the chaos and destruction that ultimately led to the fall of the city.

The modern-day concept of a quote "man of sin" is so far-fetched and the church since the reformation has always looked for a man, whether it was the pope or any public ruler in their generation. This is a Hollywood version of what happened in the siege of Jerusalem. Men took over the temple as Josephus records his eyewitness report. These leaders, not leader, set themselves up in the Temple and exercised significant influence over the people. This is what Paul was predicting in 2nd Thess. 2 - the men of sin unveiled, the sons of perdition; 4 opposing and exalting themselves above all that is called God, or that is worshiped; so that they like God, take their seat in the temple of God … TKB Translation.

Strong's # 444 thrown out and trampled underfoot by men. Mt 5:13 444 "Let your light shine before men in Mt 5:16 444 before men to be noticed by them; Mt 6:1 444 that they may be honored by men. Mt 6:2 444… New American Standard Exhaustive Update Edition Concordance of the Bible (78 times)

There are many times where this Greek word for man is translated men. I am under the persuasion that this is not an individual, but an organized group of criminals who ruthlessly took over the temple and deceived the people. Even the word that is translated lawlessness can refer to an individual or a group. We might that say, "he is lawless, or the lawless will be exposed. I added ones to emphasize the collective as of those who were being lawless. One person did not take over the temple. Even leaders have dogs. I read Animal Farm! Out of the 382 times the Greek word huios is used, 85 of those times it is plural. So I am saying there is a possibility that it is this organized group of criminals versus one man. In most translations of verse 4 where is says, "who opposes and exalts". The word that is translated "who" is the definite article and thousands of times translated 'the'.

7. For the mystery of lawlessness does already work: only he who presently restrains will do so until they emerge out of the midst.

8. Then will the lawless ones be exposed, whom the Lord will consume with the spirit of His mouth and will render useless with the full manifestation of His Presence. 9 Whose coming is according to the activity of Satan with all power and signs and pseudo wonders, 10 and with all deceivableness of unrighteousness in those that perish; because they were not receiving the love of the reality, that they might be being saved. 11 For this reason God will send them an effectual wandering, that they should believe the lie: 12 that they all may be judicially condemned who believed not the reality but had pleasure in unrighteousness. 2nd Thess. 2:8-12 TKB Translation.

During the siege of Jerusalem it became the dwelling place of every unclean spirit every deceitful spirit, and hateful bird. And he cried out with a mighty voice, saying, "Fallen, fallen is Babylon the great! She has become a dwelling place of demons and a prison of every unclean spirit, and a prison of every unclean and hateful bird. Rev. 18:2 NASB. Jerusalem the great city where our Lord was crucified, Babylon the great.

Paul closes this chapter with it is a great privilege to give thanks to God for each of you who have been chosen by Him for salvation and sanctification. Through the gospel, you have been called to share in the glory of our Lord Jesus Christ. I urge you to stand firm in the truth you have been taught, whether through spoken word or letter. Our Lord Jesus Christ and our Father, who loves us deeply, provide us with comfort, hope, and grace. Let their words strengthen you and guide you in every good work. Keep the faith, my dear friends, and may the Lord be glorified in all you do.

Chapter 3

Verse 1:

"Brothers, I beseech you to fervently pray for us without ceasing. Our desire is for the word of the Lord to spread quickly and be magnified, just as it was manifested among you. We long for the glorious advancement of God's word in every corner of the earth, and your prayers play a vital role in accomplishing this divine purpose."

Verse 2:

"It is crucial that we are shielded from the devious schemes and wicked intentions of those who oppose the truth. Not all individuals possess a steadfast faith, or even faith itself. It is imperative that we are delivered from the influences of those who seek to hinder the work of the Lord in our lives and in our churches. Let us unite in prayer, seeking God's protection and deliverance from all evil forces."

Verse 3:

"Even in the midst of trials and tribulations, we can trust in the unchanging faithfulness of our Lord. He is the steadfast foundation upon which we stand, offering us strength and security in the face of adversity. Rest assured, dear brethren, that God is faithful to establish and safeguard us from all forms of wickedness and wrongdoing."

Verse 4:

"Having witnessed your unwavering commitment to following the Lord's commands, we are filled with confidence and assurance in your faithfulness. Your obedience and dedication to the work of the Lord inspire us, and we are convinced that you will continue to walk in His ways. May the Lord bless and empower you to persevere in faith and obedience." Paul was amazed and so encouraged by who the Thessalonians had become.

Verse 5:

"May the love of God envelop your hearts and lead you into a deeper relationship with Him. As you walk in His love, may you also embrace the steadfast endurance and perseverance displayed by our Lord Jesus Christ. Let His example be your guiding light, empowering you to remain steadfast in faith and unwavering in your commitment to Him."

Verse 6:

"Now, in the authority of our Lord Jesus Christ, we issue this command to you, my brothers: separate yourselves from any fellow believer who lives in disobedience and does not follow the teachings we imparted to you. Stand firm in the faith and do not tolerate unrighteous behavior among your brethren."

Verse 7:

"You have witnessed firsthand the example we set for you. We did not live in disobedience but led lives of sincerity and integrity. We did not rely on others for support but labored diligently day and night to provide for ourselves. Follow our lead and strive to emulate our commitment to hard work and self-sufficiency."

Verse 8:

"We did not seek handouts or burden anyone with our needs, even though we were entitled to support. Our aim was to set a positive example for you to follow, showing that self-sufficiency and hard work are commendable virtues worthy of emulation."

Verse 9:

"Our actions were not driven by a lack of entitlement, but rather by a desire to set a precedent for you to imitate. Let our lives serve as a model for you to emulate, demonstrating the importance of diligence, self-reliance, and integrity in all your endeavors."

Verse 10:

"During our time with you, we emphasized the importance of diligence and hard work. We made it clear that those who refuse to work should not expect to reap the benefits of their community's labor. Work diligently and contribute positively to society."

Verse 11:

"Unfortunately, we have heard reports of some among you who are living in idleness and causing strife within the community. These individuals are not pulling their weight and are instead meddling in the affairs of others. Such behavior is unacceptable and must be addressed."

Verse 12:

"Therefore, we command and exhort those who refuse to work to change their ways and to earn their own sustenance. Work diligently and conduct yourselves in a peaceful manner, providing for your own needs and refraining from causing discord within the community."

Verse 13:

"My brothers, do not grow weary or disheartened in doing good. Stay steadfast in your commitment to righteousness, even in the face of adversity and disobedience among your peers. Persevere in your efforts to live honorably and ethically."

Verse 14:

"If anyone disregards our instructions communicated in this letter, take note of that person and do not associate with them. It is important to hold one another accountable and to address wrongdoing within the community. Treat them not as enemies but as brothers in need of correction and guidance."

Verse 15:

"Despite their disobedience, do not view them as adversaries but rather as fellow believers in need of correction and restoration. Lovingly rebuke and admonish them, with the goal of leading them back to the right path and fostering reconciliation within the community." Deal with them redemptively and not punitively, this will resound in the hearts of those who need adjustment.

Verse 16:

"May the Lord of peace Himself grant you peace always and in every way. May His presence be with you at all times, comforting and upholding you in the midst of trials and tribulations. Rest in the peace that surpasses all understanding, knowing that the Lord is with you."

Verse 17:

"I, Paul, write this greeting with my own hand, underscoring its importance and authenticity. This signature is a hallmark of genuineness in all my letters, serving as a reminder of my personal investment in your spiritual growth and well-being."

Verse 18:

"May the grace of our Lord Jesus Christ be with you all, sustaining and strengthening you in your faith journey. Embrace His unmerited favor and divine influence and let Him guide you in all aspects of your life. Amen."

Terry Kashian

2nd Thessalonians

Chapter 1

1. Paul, and Silvanus, and Timothy, to the Assembly of the Thessalonians in God our Father and the Lord Jesus Christ:
2. Grace to you, and peace, from God our Father and the Lord Jesus Christ.
3. We are constrained to be thanking God at all times for you, brothers, as it is proper, because your faith is flourishing abundantly, and the love of each one of you all toward one another is increasing;
4. So that we ourselves glory in you in the Assemblies of God for your perseverance and faith in all your persecutions and the tribulation that you endure:
5. Which is a manifest evidence of the righteous judgment of God, that you may be counted worthy of the kingdom of God, for which you also suffer:
6. Seeing it is a righteous thing for God to pay with tribulation them that afflict you;
7. And to you who are afflicted rest with us, in the unveiling of the Lord Jesus from heaven with His mighty angels,
8. In flaming fire taking vengeance on them that do not know God, and that obey not the gospel of our Lord Jesus Christ:
9. Who will pay the punishment of perpetual ruin away from the Presence of the Lord, and from the glory of His power;
10. When He comes to be glorified in His saints, and to be a wonder in all them that believe because our testimony among you was believed in that day.
11. Therefore, also we pray at all times for you, that our God would count you worthy of this calling, and fulfill all the good pleasure of His goodness, and the work of faith in power:
12. That the name of our Lord Jesus Christ may be glorified in you, and you in Him, according to the grace of our God and the Lord Jesus Christ.

Chapter 2

1. Now we urge you, brothers, regarding the Presence of our Lord Jesus Christ, and by our gathering together unto Him,
2. That you be not soon shaken in mind, or be troubled, neither by spirit, nor by word, nor by letter as if from us, that the day of the Lord is present.
3. Let no one deceive you by any means: for that day will not come, unless there come the apostasy first, and the men of sin unveiled, the sons of perdition;
4. Opposing and exalting themselves above all that is called God, or that is worshiped; so that they like God, take their seat in the temple of God, exhibiting themselves that they are God.
5. Do you not remember, that, when I was yet with you, I told you these things?
6. And now you know what restrains that they might be unveiled in their season.
7. For the mystery of lawlessness does already work: only he who presently restrains will do so, until they begin to come out of the midst.

8. Then will the lawless ones be exposed, whom the Lord will consume with the spirit of His mouth and will render useless with the full manifestation of His Presence.
9. Whose coming is according to the activity of Satan with all power and signs and pseudo wonders,
10. And with all deceivableness of unrighteousness in those that perish; because they were not receiving the love of the reality, that they might be being saved.
11. For this reason, God will send them an effectual wandering, that they should believe the lie:
12. That they all may be judicially condemned who believed not the reality but had pleasure in unrighteousness.
13. But we are bound to give thanks always to God for you, brothers beloved of the Lord, into salvation in sanctification of spirit and faith in the reality:
14. To which He called you through our gospel, to the acquiring of the glory of our Lord Jesus Christ.
15. Therefore, brothers, stand fast, and hold to the things which were handed down to you and which you have been taught, whether by word, or our letter.
16. Now our Lord Jesus Christ Himself, and God, even our Father, who has loved us, and has given us perpetual comfort and good hope through grace,
17. Comfort your hearts, and establish you in every good word and work.

Chapter 3

1. Finally, brothers, pray continually for us, that the word of the Lord may run swiftly and be glorified, just as it is among you:
2. That we may be delivered from abnormal and evil men: for all men do not have faith.
3. But the Lord is faithful, who is establishing you, and holding you close, away from evil.
4. And we are convinced in the Lord regarding you, the things which we command, you are doing and will do.
5. And the Lord direct your hearts into the love of God, and into the persevering for Christ.
6. Now we command you, brothers, in the name of our Lord Jesus Christ, that you withdraw yourselves from every brother that walks disorderly, and not after the things which were given, which you received from us.
7. For yourselves know how you ought to imitate us: for we did not behave ourselves disorderly among you;
8. Neither did we eat any man's bread for nothing; but labored in toil and hard labor night and day, that we might not be a burden to any of you:
9. Not because we have no right, but to make ourselves an example for you to imitate us.
10. For even when we were with you, we commanded this to you, that if any will not work, neither should he eat.
11. For we hear that there are some which walk among you disorderly, not working at all, but are meddlers.

12. Now we order them that are so and urge by our Lord Jesus Christ, that having tranquility, they labor for their own bread and eat.

13. But you, brothers, do not be discouraged in doing good.

14. And if anyone does not obey our word by this letter, mark this one, and do not mingle with him, that he may be ashamed.

15. Yet count them not as an enemy, but reprimand as a brother.

16. Now the Lord of peace Himself give you peace at all times in all ways. The Lord be with you all.

17. The greeting of Paul with my own hand, which is the sign in every letter: so I write.

18. The grace of our Lord Jesus Christ be with you all. Amen.

1st Timothy Commentary

1 Timothy 1:1-14 - TKB Translation

The 1st Letter of Paul to Timothy – Written from Macedonia in about AD 64 just after Paul was released from a two-year house arrest.

Chapter 1

1 Paul, an apostle of Jesus Christ by the mandate of God our Savior, and Lord Jesus Christ, who is our hope; 2 to Timothy, my authentic son in faith: grace, mercy, and peace, from God our Father and Jesus Christ our Lord. 3 As I called upon you to remain at Ephesus, when I went into Macedonia that you might charge some that they do not teach different teachings, 4 neither give heed to myths and incomplete genealogies, which present arguments, rather than God's building which is in faith: so, do. 5 Now the goal of the mandate is love out of a pure heart, a good conscience, and authentic faith: 6 from which some having missed the goal; having turned aside to meaningless speaking; 7 desiring to be teachers of the Law; comprehending neither what they say, nor concerning what they positively assert. 8 But we know that the Law is good if a man uses it lawfully; 9 knowing this, that the Law is not made for a righteous man, but for the lawless and disobedient, for the ungodly and sinners, for unholy and profane, for murderers of fathers and murderers of mothers, for manslayers, 10 for fornicators, for homosexuals, for kidnappers, for liars, for perjured persons, and if there be any other thing that is set against healthy teaching; 11 according to the glorious gospel of the blessed God, which was entrusted to me. 12 And I thank Christ Jesus our Lord, who empowers me, for He counted me faithful, placing me into service; 13 who was before a blasphemer, and a persecutor, and injurious: but I obtained mercy because I did it ignorantly in unbelief. 14 And the grace of our Lord was exceedingly abundant with faith and love which is in Christ Jesus.

In this portion of Scripture, the apostle Paul begins his first letter to Timothy by identifying himself as an apostle of Christ Jesus according to the command of God our Savior. He greets Timothy as his true son in the faith, emphasizing the importance of healthy doctrine and teaching in the church.

4 neither give heed to myths and incomplete genealogies, which present arguments, rather than God's building which is in faith: so do. 5 Now the goal of the mandate is love out of a pure heart, a good conscience, and authentic faith: 6 from which some having missed

the goal; having turned aside to meaningless speaking; 7 desiring to be teachers of the Law; comprehending neither what they say, nor concerning what they positively assert. TKB

The rampant fables and myths that infiltrated the church was like a virus and because the saints in those days did not have a written bible, they were dependent on the teachers to get the truth. And many in that day were illiterate so the disadvantage was monumental. Paul is instructing Timothy to avoid these myths and genealogies and focus on God's building. As Paul wrote about this to the Corinthians being the building of God in 1 Cor. 3:9, he is steering Timothy to center on the main thing. God's building is the vision for the church then and now. Only a healthy church can be immune to the spiritual disease of false and unhealthy teaching. Paul is directing Timothy to teach, healthy teaching that will immunize the saints from this disease that makes the church sick and weak and ultimately kill it. The Law is called by Paul the ministry of death and condemnation. We must be clear regarding this matter. God's building can only be built by Christ's life, the Spirit, and His word of grace, not legalism and fables.: "And now I commend you to God and to the word of His grace, which is able to build you up and to give you the inheritance among all those who are sanctified." The apostle mentions some have missed the goal to nonsensical teaching and not even understanding what they are talking about even though they speak with great confidence. The truth immunizes us as it did in that day. On the other hand Paul says, "the Law is good if one uses it lawfully". A phrase that needs to be digested in our lives is, "the Law was not made for the righteous, but the lawless". The righteous requirement of the Law is fulfilled in us, not by us if we walk according to the Spirit. Our need is to live by the right source, the Spirit not the Law. Paul says a few verses before that in Romans 8, "what the Law could not do, God did" …. Amen! Do we see the tense of that, God did, not He is going to do. Paul then goes on to warn against false teachers who promote speculations and vain discussions that cause divisions within the body of Christ. He emphasizes the need for love that comes from a pure heart, a good conscience, and a sincere faith. The teaching that immunizes the church is a pure heart which means an undivided heart, singleness, and a guarded heart which out of it flows the issues of life. The preaching of the Law affects our conscience, and the rules show our shortcomings and the vaccine for the spiritual disease of death and condemnation is Christ is our righteousness, we have received the gift of righteousness. We have infinite life! Not one day we will get it. He who has the son has the LIFE! That is healthy teaching. Authentic faith is the life source of our walk with God, and it needs to be authentic and genuine without hypocrisy. Real faith transforms us in every part of our being. We must not pretend to trust God and if we have doubts, believe God enough to tell Him and ask Him to help our unbelief and we will be surprised how He responds to an honest heart to dispel our doubts.

Paul shares his testimony of how he was once a blasphemer, persecutor, and insolent opponent of the faith, but by the grace of our Lord Jesus Christ, he was shown mercy and appointed as a minister of the gospel. He highlights the incredible patience and mercy of

God towards sinners, demonstrating his desire for all people to come to repentance and faith in Christ.

15. This is a faithful saying, and worthy of all acceptance, that Christ Jesus came into the world to save sinners; of who I am chief.

16. However for this reason I obtained mercy, that in me first, Jesus Christ might show forth all longsuffering, for a pattern to those who are about to be believing on Him to life infinite. 17 Now to the King infinite, immortal, invisible, the only wise God, be honor and glory in this age and into the New Covenant Age. Amen. 18 This mandate I set before you, child Timothy, according to the prophecies which went before on you, that in them you might be fighting a good warfare; 19 possessing faith, and a good conscience; which some having pushed away concerning the faith have shipwrecked: 20 of whom is Hymenaeus and Alexander; whom I have given over to Satan, that they may learn not to blaspheme. These verses highlight the central message of Christianity - that Jesus came into the world to save sinners.

The Apostle Paul recognizes himself as the chief of sinners, but he received mercy from Jesus Christ to serve as an example of God's longsuffering and grace. The verses also emphasize the importance of faith and a good conscience in maintaining a strong spiritual life. Paul warns against pushing away these qualities, as seen in the cases of Hymenaeus and Alexander who have shipwrecked their faith by blaspheming. The winds of teaching and waves blow us off course and hinder us from growing to spiritual maturity. The example of the apostle Paul is quite unique and an exercise of Kingdom authority to deliver these two men to Satan for discipline to teach them not to speak against the ministry or Christ and His grace. He writes this to Timothy for instruction on what to do with certain opposers in the church. This is Kingdom authority, and it must be practiced carefully and discerningly.

17. Now to the King of the ages, immortal, invisible, the only wise God, be honor and glory in this age and into the New Covenant Age. Amen. 1 Tim. 1;17 TKB

The verses conclude with a declaration of honor and glory to God, who is the King of the ages, immortal, invisible, and the only wise King. The King of two ages, the Old Covenant age and the New Covenant age. The Old covenant age was temporary, and the New Covenant age is endless, perpetual. He is the King of two ages and Paul is declaring honor and glory to Him.

1 Tim. 1:18 – Fight the Good Fight

Just as Paul exhorted Timothy to fight the good fight of faith, I also encourage you to stand firm in the face of opposition and spiritual warfare. The prophecies spoken over you are a reminder of the promises and blessings that God has in store for you as you walk in obedience and faith. It is sad when some in the body say there is no prophecies on a personal level any longer. We need to be built up, stirred up, and cheered up in our Christian life.

When someone prophetic comes into your life to confirm what God is speaking to you, cause you to focus clearly on a direction that is essential in your life, or to comfort and console you when you are having a hard time. This has happened to me so many times during my 50 years of walking with God. Jesus is the same yesterday, today, and forever! Just for FYI. We don't necessarily need someone to say, "Thus says the Lord", or order to get a prophetic word. It can happen while fellowshipping and casual conversation when the Spirit is accenting something to us, and we sense that the Lord is speaking to us. Some do prophesy without even knowing it and they are comforting and consoling someone in the body. We can't limit the way God wants to speak through us or to us. But we must believe He is still speaking to be built up, stirred up, and cheered up.

Do not be discouraged by the challenges that may come your way, for the prophecies serve as a source of strength and courage in difficult times. Trust in the Lord's guidance and leading as you navigate through the spiritual battles ahead. Hold fast to your faith and maintain a good conscience, for these are key weapons in the warfare you are called to fight.

May the prophecies that went before you serve as a beacon of light, guiding you in the path that God has prepared for you. Embrace your calling with boldness and perseverance, knowing that God's grace and power are with you as you engage in the good warfare set before you.

As witnesses and disciples of Christ, we must strive to hold fast to the healthy teaching of the gospel, reject false teachings, and live out our faith with love and sincerity. We must remember the grace and mercy that has been shown to us and extend that same grace and mercy to others as we proclaim the good news of salvation through Jesus Christ. May we be faithful stewards of the gospel, sharing it boldly and living it out daily in our lives.

Instruction about approaching God - 1 Tim. 2:1-7

Prayer is defined as a heartfelt communication with God, conveying our deepest desires, needs, and praises. Scripture teaches us that prayer is a vital part of our relationship with God and that it has the power to bring about miraculous results. In this passage, Paul is writing to Timothy, encouraging him to lead the church in Ephesus to prioritize prayer in their gatherings. As we dive deeper into this passage, we will explore the different types of prayer mentioned, namely: petitions, intercession, and thanksgiving.

Petitions refer to specific requests made to God, often regarding our own needs and desires. In prayer, we can come to God boldly, laying out our needs and desires before Him. Jesus Himself instructs us to come to God with our requests, saying in Matthew 7:7, Ask, and it will be given to you; seek, and you will find; knock, and it will be opened to you. We see in Scripture how God lovingly responds to His children's petitions, as we read in Luke 11:13, If you then, who are evil, know how to give good gifts to your children, how much more will the heavenly Father give the Holy Spirit to those who ask him! As we engage in the practice of prayer, we must remember that God is our loving Father, and He desires to care for us and provide for our needs.

Intercession is seen as a more selfless form of prayer. It involves praying on behalf of others, standing in the gap for them and their needs. In verse 1, Paul urges that supplications, prayers, intercessions, and thanksgivings be made for all people. This reminds us that prayer is not just about our own needs, but it is also about lifting others before the throne of God. In intercession, we can pray for our family, friends, leaders, and even our enemies. We see this beautiful example in the life of Jesus, who interceded for His disciples and all believers in John 17:9, I am praying for them. I am not praying for the world but for those whom you have given me, for they are yours.

Thanksgiving is an essential aspect of prayer as it acknowledges and expresses gratitude for what God has done for us. Throughout the Bible, we are commanded to give thanks to God, for He is good, and His steadfast love endures forever (Psalm 118:1). In verse 2, Paul urges that thanksgivings be made for all people. This may seem challenging, especially when we encounter difficult people or situations. But, as we cultivate a grateful heart through prayer, we can see how God is working in and through those situations and people to bring about His purpose. Thanksgiving in prayer also keeps us humble, recognizing that all good things come from God, not from our own doing.

In looking at the historical context of this passage, the church in Ephesus was facing persecution, and many false teachers had infiltrated the church, causing division and confusion. In this letter, Paul reminds Timothy of the importance of prayer, especially in such challenging times. He urges Timothy to lead the church in prayer, both individually and corporately, to remain strong in their faith and witness for Christ.

In terms of exegesis, we see that Paul emphasizes the universality of prayer by using the words all people repeatedly. He emphasizes that prayer is not limited to specific individuals or situations but should encompass every aspect of our lives. Paul also highlights the different types of prayer, encouraging believers to approach God with a variety of requests, not just their own personal needs.

As we consider the applications of this passage, we can see how vital prayer is in our personal lives and in the life of the church. Prayer positions us to hear from God, receive His guidance, and see His will fulfilled. It also reminds us of our dependence on God and builds our faith as we see His faithfulness in answering our prayers. In our individual prayer lives, we should make time to bring our petitions, intercede for others, and offer thanksgiving. In our corporate prayer, we should come together as the body, interceding for our communities, nations, and the world. We must also guard against false teaching and division, continually lifting our leaders and fellow believers in prayer.

In conclusion, this passage serves as a reminder of the power of prayer and its various forms. As we engage in petition, intercession, and thanksgiving, we can see God move in miraculous ways in our lives and in the world around us. Let us heed Paul's exhortation and make prayer a vital part of our Christian walk, trusting in God's love and faithfulness to hear and answer our prayers.

In this passage, Paul specifically addresses the issue of prayer and the role of leaders in the church. In verse 8, Paul moves on to address the issue of prayer, specifically in the context of public worship. In the first century, most public prayers were led by men, and Paul gives instructions to Timothy on how men and women should conduct themselves during prayer.

Verse 1 - Paul begins by exhorting Timothy to pray for all people, without exception. The Greek word used for all in this verse is pas, which not only means all in a general sense, but also emphasizes that no one should be excluded from the prayers. This includes believers and non-believers, gentiles and Jews, slave and free. Paul's instruction to pray for all people reflects the heart of God, who desires for everyone to be saved (2 Peter 3:9).

Verse 2 - Paul specifies that prayers should be made for kings and all those in authority. During this time, Christians were facing persecution from the Roman government, and Paul reminds them to pray for their leaders, even if they are hostile towards the church. This aligns with Jesus command to pray for our enemies (Matthew 5:44). Paul also gives the reason for praying for leaders, which is to lead a peaceful and quiet life, free from persecution. This is not only beneficial for believers but also for the spread of the gospel.

Verse 3 - Paul explains that praying for all people and specifically for those in authority is pleasing to God our Savior. This shows that prayer is not just a duty, but it is a way to please and honor God. It also highlights the importance of intercession for others, as it is a crucial part of the Christians life and expresses the character of Jesus, who intercedes for us (Romans 8:34).

Verse 4 - In this verse, Paul gives another reason for praying for all people, which is that it is Gods desire for all to be saved and come to the knowledge of the truth. This aligns with 2 Peter 3:9, which states that God is patient, not wanting anyone to perish but for all to come to repentance. Through prayer, we align ourselves with Gods desire and join Him in the work of salvation.

Verse 5 - Paul reminds the readers of the one mediator between God and men, the MAN Jesus Christ. This verse affirms that there is no other way to the Father except through Jesus. It also contradicts the false teaching that was spreading in Ephesus, which claimed that there were multiple mediators between God and men. This verse also highlights the importance of our faith in Jesus Christ as the only way to salvation.

Verse 6 - Paul continues to emphasize the uniqueness of Jesus as the mediator by stating that he gave himself as a ransom for all people. This is a reminder of the ultimate sacrifice that Jesus made on the cross to redeem us from our sins. It also shows that salvation is available to all, regardless of their social status or background.

Verse 7 - Paul ends this section by reminding Timothy that he was appointed as a preacher and apostle, and teacher to proclaim the truth to the Gentiles. This is a cluster gifting that we need to understand. Paul's gift to preach as an exhorter is more prophetic, and his calling as an apostle is foundational for church planting and establishing God's people. The teacher in him was to clarify and give instruction to the Gentiles on how to live the Christian life. This verse reinforces Paul's authority to give instructions and also reminds us that the gospel is for all people, Jew or Gentile.

Roles of Husbands and Wives 1 Tim. 2:8-

Paul addresses the wives after he instructs the husbands to be men of prayer with self-control. He then instructs wives to be modest and discreet. Our culture today has lost this wisdom of being modest and discreet. These are lost treasures of virtue that women need to find in order to express the heavenly culture. These are Kingdom virtues that godly wives exhibit, and they are aware of not giving signals to men for attention. Many women have shunned modesty and discreet apparel and become temptress' for weak and fleshly men. Even the matter of costly or expensive clothing can be a form of haughtiness and can produce envy in others. I am not saying that we cannot wear jewelry or designer clothes, but to use wisdom in our appearance. I fellowshipped with an apostolic denomination where the women could not wear jewelry or pants, or make-up and I always felt sorry for those in that bondage. But as a godly people we must find the perfect balance. This is where we need to follow the registrations of the Lord in us. Asking Him, what do you think Lord. Some may mock me in this regard, but I believe it will deepen our intimacy with the Lord. Paul closes these thoughts with "this is right for wives professing godliness with good works". Please understand I am not saying that our wives need to wear a burlap sack and look like they were baptized in lemon juice.[117]

hēsuchia (ἡσυχία, (2271)), akin to A, No. 2, and B. No. 1, denotes quietness, 2 Thess. 3:12; it is so translated in the R.V. of 1Tim. 2:11, 12 (A.V., "silence"); in Acts 22:2, R.V., "(they, were the more) quiet," A.V., "(they kept the more) silence," lit., 'they kept quietness the more. 68 hēsuchios (ἡσύχιος, (2272)) has much the same meaning as No. 1, but indicates tranquility arising from within, causing no disturbance to others. It is translated "quiet" in 1 Tim. 2:2,[118]

---

[117] Vine, W. E., & Bruce, F. F. (1981). In Vine's Expository dictionary of Old and New Testament words (Vol. 2, p. 242). Revell.

[118] Vine, W. E., & Bruce, F. F. (1981). In Vine's Expository dictionary of Old and New Testament words (Vol. 2, p. 242). Revell.

This is a difficult portion of scripture to translate, and I pray for God's wisdom in conveying the spirit of the apostle Paul in this regard. Paul gets a bad rap about women. In verse 11, I sense that Paul is instructing wives to learn about this matter of modesty and discretion from their husbands with a receptive, teachable, spirit. The silence that Paul is exhorting is the way a wife should receive this instruction from her husband. He would give understanding to his wife regarding not giving signals to other men and to be wise with her appearance. This is where the wife needs to come under her husband for protection and peace. The next verse says that a wife is not permitted to teach or domineer over her husband. Look at the context of what Paul is instructing. The word "But" begins a transition not a new subject with Paul. δές: a marker of contrast—'but, on the other hand.'[119] A wife is not permitted to teach or domineer over her husband, but to be submissive and tranquil about this matter of modesty and soberness. Paul mentions Adam and Eve. They are not just man and woman, but they are husband and wife.

Therefore, in the context Paul is not saying that a woman is not permitted to teach in a general sense, but in relationship and specifically about the matter of virtuous conduct and attitude in her appearance. Paul says that Adam was not deceived. 13 For it was Adam who was first created, and then Eve. 14 And it was not Adam who was deceived, but the woman being deceived, fell into transgression. 15 But will be preserved through the bearing of children if they continue in faith and love and sanctity with discretion. I hope you are seeing the context down to the last word. Discretion. Adam's fault in this matter was not protecting his wife from being approached by someone else to tempt her. His abdication of his role allowed his wife to be deceived and disobey the Lord. So many of the Lord's servants have been hindered by this portion of scripture regarding women teaching and yet many churches today have women teaching Sunday school. Those who are misinformed have used these scriptures to hamstring women from being a part of the ministry. Watchmen Nee tells the story of a woman that became so influential in his life that it left an indelible mark on his life and ministry, and not only that, but he became a Christian under the ministry of a woman evangelist. We need to set the women free in our midst to exercise their gifts and callings so we can benefit from the whole body of Christ.

Aspiring to Oversee the Lord's People – 1 Tim. 3:1-16

In 1 Timothy 3, the concept of a bishop is discussed in terms of the qualifications necessary for someone to fulfill this role. It is important to note that a bishop is not an official office, but rather a function of overseeing and leading within the church community.

---

[119] Louw, J. P., & Nida, E. A. (1996). In Greek-English lexicon of the New Testament: based on semantic domains (electronic ed. of the 2nd edition., Vol. 1, p. 793). United Bible Societies.

The passage outlines the qualities that a bishop or overseer should possess, including being above reproach, married with one wife, temperate, self-controlled, respectable, hospitable, able to teach, not given to drunkenness or violence, and not a lover of money. These characteristics emphasize the importance of an overseer being a moral and ethical leader within the church, setting a positive example for others to follow.

Furthermore, the chapter breaks down the roles and responsibilities of deacons within the church, outlining similar qualifications for those who serve in this capacity. Deacons are called to be dignified, sincere, not indulging in excessive wine or pursuing dishonest gain, holding to the mystery of the faith with a clear conscience.

Overall, 1 Timothy 3 underscores the importance of selecting qualified and righteous individuals to serve in leadership within the church. By upholding high standards and moral integrity, these leaders can effectively guide and nurture the local assembly, promoting growth and spiritual development among its members.

Seeing the church as the house of God being the pillar and base of the truth holds significant spiritual depth. The church, as the dwelling place of God's presence, is called to be a living testimony to the marvelous truths of God's Word.

The church, when functioning according to God's design, stands as a pillar, supporting and upholding the truth of God's revelation in Christ. It is in the context of the church that the reality of the gospel is embodied and proclaimed to a world in desperate need of hope and redemption. The truth of God's Word is the solid foundation upon which the church is built, providing stability and direction in a world of shifting ideologies and philosophies.

As the pillar and base of the truth, the church serves as a beacon of light, overcoming the darkness and pointing others to the reality of God's grace and love. It is within the community of believers, gathered together as the house of God, that the transformative power of the gospel is displayed and experienced. The church is called to be a witness to the reality of Christ, both in word and deed, reflecting His character and nature to a watching world.

In essence, the church's identity as the pillar and base of the truth is a sacred trust and responsibility. As believers, we are called to steward and uphold the truths of God's Word with humility, grace, and integrity. By faithfully embodying the truth in our lives and relationships, we fulfill the purpose of the church to glorify God and make known His redemptive plan to all creation. Let us, therefore, strive to walk in the light of His truth, expressing His glory in the world around us.

In the Final Appointed Times 1 Tim. 4:1-16

The first verse really needs to be understood in the light of the first century and not our time or future. Most translations are bias and miss this important prophetic word. The phrase "later times", first we will look at the word later, but not later, we will look at it now.

Sorry! This word is husteros (ὕστερος, (5306)) denotes later or latter and is used in 1 Tim. 4:1.

1. Sometimes this word is translated "last of all". I want to be clear in this explanation. It is the last part of the appointed times that Paul is speaking to Timothy. Something that was quite near to the time Paul was writing. In fact all the apostles' in their writings speak of the appointed time. This was the time of fulfillment of all that was written. Paul is speaking about the apostasy that was coming. John wrote of the last hour in 1 John 2:18, Peter spoke of the end of all things is at hand in 1 Pet. 4:7.

2. Peter uses "kairos" in 1 Peter 1:5 - "who by God's power are being guarded through faith for a salvation ready to be revealed in the last time (kairo)." Here, Peter uses "kairo" derived from "kairos" to refer to the appointed time or season determined by God for the revelation of salvation.

3. John uses "kairos" in his writing in Revelation 1:3 - "Blessed is the one who reads aloud the words of this prophecy, and blessed are those who hear it and take to heart what is written in it, because the time (kairos) is near." In this verse, John uses "kairos" to indicate that the prophetic events described in Revelation are approaching or at hand.

Perhaps Peter's understanding of the last time is related to the times, time, and a half a time. It's an interesting connection to consider! The phrase "a time, times, and half a time" is commonly associated with end times prophecy in the Bible, particularly in the book of Daniel and also mentioned in the book of Revelation. This phrase is understood to symbolize a period of persecution or tribulation lasting for a specified time before the end of all things. Peter was in tune with the time. He could be considered those of the sons of Issachar who understood the times and knew what Israel ought to do. The apostles understood their times and unfortunately many in the ministry are not clear regarding the times we are living in. If only we would look at the first century generation and see the generational model.

These passages here in 1 Timothy is a powerful reminder of the importance of staying true to the faith and not falling away. The Spirit warns us that there will be those who will be led astray by deceitful spirits and false teachings. These false teachers will be hypocrites, claiming to have a deep knowledge of the truth but in reality, they are only leading people away from God.

One of the key things these false teachers will do is advocate for things like forbidding marriage and abstaining from certain foods that God has created for us to enjoy. Now, we have to understand that everything created by God is good and meant to be received with gratitude. We are to sanctify these things through prayer and the word of God, not to reject them as the false teachers would have us do.

So, let us be vigilant and discerning, not being swayed by false teachings but holding fast to the truth of God's word. Remember, everything God has created is good, and we should gratefully receive it as such. Stay strong in your faith and do not let anyone lead you astray.

Dear saints, in these verses from 1 Timothy, the apostle Paul is exhorting us to remain faithful to healthy teaching and to avoid being entangled in worldly teachings and myths. As servants of Christ Jesus, we are to be constantly nourished by the words of faith and healthy teaching that we have been following.

Paul instructs us to discipline ourselves for the purpose of godliness, emphasizing that while bodily discipline may have some benefit, godliness is profitable for both this life and the life to come. We must not get caught up in trivial matters or distractions, but rather focus on cultivating a heart of godliness that is pleasing to the Lord.

It is crucial for us to fix our hope on the living God, who is the Savior of all, especially of those who believe. Our labor and striving in the faith are directed towards this ultimate goal of glorifying God and experiencing the promises of eternal life.

In these verses, the apostle Paul is exhorting Timothy to be diligent in his service to the Lord and to the believers. He instructs Timothy to prescribe and teach the truths of the faith and to not let anyone look down on his youthfulness. Instead, Timothy is called to be an example to all believers in his speech, conduct, love, faith, and purity.

Furthermore, Paul encourages Timothy to give attention to the public reading of Scripture, exhortation, and teaching. He emphasizes the importance of not neglecting the spiritual gift within him, which was bestowed upon him through prophetic utterance and the laying on of hands.

Timothy is urged to take pains with these things, to be fully absorbed in them, so that his progress in the faith will be evident to all. He is to pay close attention to himself and to his teaching, persevering in these things, knowing that by doing so he will ensure salvation both for himself and for those who hear him.

Let us also take these exhortations to heart and strive to be examples of believers in all areas of our lives. May we immerse ourselves in the Word of God, exhortation, and teaching, never neglecting the spiritual gifts that the Lord has bestowed upon us. Yes He has, and I encourage you to find those in your life. May our progress in the faith be evident to all, as we pay close attention to ourselves and persevere in our service to the Lord.

May the Lord grant us grace and strength to walk in obedience and faithfulness, so that we may bring glory to His name and lead others to salvation. Amen.

Let us, therefore, heed these words of wisdom from Paul and dedicate ourselves to pursuing godliness and holiness in all aspects of our lives. Through disciplined living and unwavering faith in the living God, we can be assured of His salvation and blessings both now and in the future.

1 Tim 5:1-25

In these verses, Paul gives us instructions on how to treat different categories of people within the church. He emphasizes the importance of showing respect and honor to older men, treating them as fathers, and younger men as brothers, older women as mothers, and younger women as sisters, in all purity.

Paul also highlights the responsibility of the church to care for widows who are truly in need, especially those who have no children or family to support them. He stresses the importance of family members taking care of their own, especially parents, as a way of showing godly piety and honoring God.

Paul points out the distinction between widows who are truly dependent and those who are younger and should remarry and care for their families instead of burdening the church. He warns against idleness and gossip among younger widows and urges them to fulfill their God-given roles as wives and mothers.

Overall, Paul's instructions remind us of the importance of showing respect, honor, and care to different members of the church, and of the church's responsibility to care for those in need while maintaining order and godly conduct within the body of believers.

In these verses, we are reminded of the importance of honoring and respecting the elders within the church who rule well, especially those who diligently labor in preaching and teaching. The scripture emphasizes the principle of not withholding support from those who work hard, drawing an analogy from the commandment not to muzzle the ox while it is threshing. This teaches us that those who labor in teaching and preaching the Word of God are deserving of support and honor for their work.

Paul's instructions regarding accusations against elders underscore the need for evidence and proper procedure in dealing with such matters, in order to preserve the integrity and unity of the church. Furthermore, addressing sin openly and holding believers accountable serves to promote a culture of holiness and reverence within the community.

Paul's charge to maintain these principles without bias or partiality reflects the importance of upholding justice and righteousness in the church. The warning against hasty appointments to leadership roles reminds us to exercise discernment and diligence in selecting qualified individuals to serve in responsibility, ensuring the purity and effectiveness of the church's ministry.

In these verses, Paul highlights the reality that the sins of some individuals are evident and known even before they face judgment, while for others, their sins become evident only later on. This emphasizes the principle that one's character and actions will ultimately come to light and have consequences.

Similarly, Paul points out that good deeds are also unmistakably evident, and those who engage in righteous behavior cannot hide their virtuous actions. This underscores the importance of living a life of integrity and good works, as they will be visible for all to see and will ultimately be rewarded.

Ultimately, Paul's words serve as a reminder that one's true character and actions will be revealed whether they are good or bad. It is important for believers to live in a manner that reflects the values of the Kingdom of God and to practice righteousness and holiness in all aspects of their lives.

In these verses, Paul provides practical instruction for slaves and masters within the church community. He emphasizes the importance of slaves regarding their masters as worthy of honor, regardless of their circumstances, so that the name of Christ and the Christian teaching are not blasphemed. He also reminds those who have Christian masters to serve them with even greater respect and diligence, recognizing the shared bond of faith and love.

Furthermore, Paul warns against those who promote false teachings that deviate from the healthy words of Jesus Christ and the teaching of godliness. Those who focus on controversial debates and worldly gain rather than the truth of the gospel reveal their lack of understanding and spiritual immaturity. Paul highlights the dangers of pursuing wealth and material gain, as it often leads to temptation, snare, and ruin. The love of money is identified as a root cause of various evils, causing some to stray from the faith and experience unnecessary suffering.

Paul ultimately encourages believers to pursue godliness accompanied by contentment, recognizing that true gain comes from a heart that is satisfied with basic necessities. Contentment, rather than the pursuit of wealth, leads to a life characterized by peace and fulfillment, without the snares that come with the love of money.

1 Tim. 6:1-21

In these verses, Paul encourages Timothy, a man of God, to turn away from the distractions and deceptions of the world and to actively pursue righteousness, godliness, faith, love, endurance, and meekness. He urges Timothy to engage in the good fight of faith, seizing hold of the eternal life to which he has been called and holding fast to his confession of faith in the presence of many witnesses.

Paul solemnly charges Timothy before God, the source of all life, and Christ Jesus, who faithfully testified before Pontius Pilate. He exhorts Timothy to keep the commandment blameless and pure, looking forward to the appearing of our Lord Jesus Christ at the appointed time. Paul paints a vivid picture of the glorious and majestic nature of God, describing Him as the blessed and unparalleled Sovereign. In my translation of King of kings and Lord of lords, I found a different rendering that I thought was unique. 15 which in His own proper time He will exhibit, the blessed and only Sovereign, the King of the ones reigning, and Lord of the ones exercising lordship; Since the word kings and lords are verbs instead of nouns I translated as a verb. King of kings is literally "king of those who are ruling," since kings translates a present participle of the verb "to rule." The title appears first in the Old Testament as a title used for Babylonian and Persian emperors (see, for example, Ezek. 26.7; Dan. 2.37; Ezra 7.12); its first application to God appears in one of the writings in the period before New Testament times, namely the second book of Maccabees (see 2 Maccabees 13.4).

This usage is found here and in other parts of the New Testament. Rev. 17:14; 19:16. This is why the translators translated it as a noun instead of a verb. In Revelation 17 and 19 they are nouns.

Timothy is reminded to honor and give glory to God, acknowledging His perpetual dominion and supreme authority. Through these exhortations, Paul encourages Timothy to remain steadfast in his faith, to zealously pursue godliness, and to await with anticipation the glorious Parousia of the Lord Jesus Christ. In these verses, the Apostle Paul instructs Timothy concerning the proper attitude towards those who are wealthy in this present age. Paul urges Timothy to not allow the rich to become arrogant or to put their trust in uncertain riches, but rather to place their confidence in the living God who abundantly provides all things for our enjoyment.

Paul exhorts the wealthy to be active in doing good, to be rich in good works, ready to share with others, and willing to be generous. By living in this way, they are storing up for themselves a sure foundation for the future, laying hold of the life that is truly life.

Timothy is charged with safeguarding the trust that has been placed in him, steering clear of meaningless and empty talk, as well as the opposing ideas of false knowledge that leads astray from the genuine faith. Some have missed the mark from the truth, but Paul encourages Timothy by reminding him that grace is with him to keep him from swerving and missing the mark.

In summary, Paul emphasizes the importance of handling wealth and knowledge in alignment with God's principles. He urges Timothy to stand firm in guarding the truth, rejecting empty distractions and false teachings, and remaining steadfast in the grace that is found in Christ.

Terry Kashian

1 Timothy

Chapter 1

1. Paul, an apostle of Jesus Christ by the mandate of God our Savior, and Lord Jesus Christ, who is our hope;
2. To Timothy, my authentic son in faith: grace, mercy, and peace, from God our Father and Jesus Christ our Lord.
3. As I called upon you to remain at Ephesus, when I went into Macedonia that you might charge some that they do not teach different teachings,
4. Neither give heed to myths and incomplete genealogies, which present arguments, rather than God's building which is in faith: so do.
5. Now the goal of the mandate is love out of a pure heart, a good conscience, and authentic faith:
6. From which some having missed the goal; having turned aside to meaningless speaking;
7. Desiring to be teachers of the Law; comprehending neither what they say, nor concerning what they positively assert.
8. But we know that the Law is good if a man uses it lawfully;
9. Knowing this, that the Law is not made for a righteous man, but for the lawless and disobedient, for the ungodly and sinners, for unholy and profane, for murderers of fathers and murderers of mothers, for manslayers,
10. For fornicators, for homosexuals, for kidnappers, for liars, for perjured persons, and if there be any other thing that is set against healthy teaching;
11. According to the glorious gospel of the blessed God, which was entrusted to me.
12. And I thank Christ Jesus our Lord, who empowers me, for He counted me faithful, placing me into service;
13. Who was before a blasphemer, and a persecutor, and injurious: but I obtained mercy because I did it ignorantly in unbelief.
14. And the grace of our Lord was exceedingly abundant with faith and love which is in Christ Jesus.
15. This is a faithful saying, and worthy of all acceptance, that Christ Jesus came into the world to save sinners; of who I am chief.
16. However, for this reason I obtained mercy, that in me first, Jesus Christ might show forth all longsuffering, for a pattern to those who are about to be believing on Him to life infinite.
17. Now to the King of the ages, immortal, invisible, the only wise God, be honor and glory in this age and into the New Covenant Age. Amen.
18. This mandate I set before you, child Timothy, according to the prophecies which went before on you, that in them you might be fighting a good warfare;
19. Possessing faith, and a good conscience; which some having pushed away concerning the faith have shipwrecked:
20. Of whom is Hymenaeus and Alexander; whom I have given over to Satan, that they may learn not to blaspheme.

Chapter 2

1. I want, therefore, that, first of all, supplications, prayers, intercessions, and giving of thanks, be made for all men;
2. For kings, and for all that are in authority; that we may lead a quiet and peaceable life in all godliness and honesty.
3. For this is good and acceptable in the sight of God our Savior;
4. Who will have all men to be saved, and to come to the full knowledge of the reality.
5. For there is one God, and one mediator between God and men, the Man Christ Jesus;
6. Who gave Himself a ransom for all, to be a testimony in His own time.
7. Into which I have been placed a herald and an apostle, I speak the reality in Christ and do not lie, a teacher of the nations in faith and reality.
8. Therefore, I want husbands to pray everywhere, lifting holy hands, apart from rage and discord.
9. In like manner also, that wives adorn themselves in appropriate clothing, with modesty and sober-mindedness; not with braided hair, or gold, or pearls, or costly clothing;
10. But that which is proper for wives promising godly respect with good works.
11. Let the wives learn in tranquility with all submission.
12. But I do not turn over to a wife the matter of teaching, nor to domineer her husband, but to be tranquil.
13. For Adam was first formed, then Eve
14. And Adam was not deceived, but the wife being thoroughly deceived was in violation.
15. Nonetheless, they will be saved in childbearing if they abide in faith and love and sanctification with a sound mind.

Chapter 3

1. This is a worthy saying, if anyone yearns to oversee, he has set his passion upon a noble work.
2. An overseer then must be blameless, the husband of one wife, vigilant, self-controlled, of good behavior, given to hospitality, able to teach;
3. Not given to wine, no striker, not greedy of money; but patient, not a brawler, not covetous;
4. One that leads with care well before his own house, having his children in subjection with all reverence;
5. 5.(For if a man does not know how to lead with care his own house, how will he take care of the Assembly of God?)
6. Not a new believer, unless being lifted up with pride he falls into the condemnation by the Devil.
7. Moreover, he must have a good reputation with those who are outside, lest he fall into reproach and the snare of the Devil.
8. Likewise, the deacons must be reverent, not double-tongued, not obsessed with much wine, and not greedy for money;
9. Holding the mystery of the faith in a pure conscience.

10. And let these also first be tested; then let them serve, being found blameless.
11. Even so must their wives be respectable, not slanderers, sober, faithful in all things.
12. Let the deacons be the husbands of one wife, lead with care for their children and their own houses well.
13. For they that have served well gain for themselves a good status, and great boldness in the faith which is in Christ Jesus.
14. These things I write to you, hoping to come to you shortly:
15. But if postponed, that you may know how you ought to behave yourself in the house of God, which is the Assembly of the living God, the pillar and base of the reality.
16. And without controversy great is the mystery of godliness: God was manifest in the flesh, justified in the Spirit, seen of angels, preached to the nations, believed on in the world, received up into glory.

Chapter 4

1. Now the Spirit speaks expressly, that in the latter times some will depart from the faith, giving heed to seducing spirits, and teachings of demons;
2. Speaking lies in hypocrisy; having their conscience seared with a hot iron;
3. Forbidding to marry, and commanding to abstain from foods, which God has created to be received with thanksgiving by those who believe and fully know the reality.
4. For every creature of God is good, and nothing to be rejected, if it be received with thanksgiving:
5. For it is made clean by the word of God and intercession.
6. Layout to the brothers these things, you will be a good minister of Jesus Christ, nourished up in the words of faith and healthy teaching, which you have followed closely.
7. But refuse profane and old wives' tales and exercise yourself toward godliness.
8. For bodily exercise profits a little: but godliness is profitable for all things, having promise of the life that now is, and of that which is about to be.
9. This is a faithful saying and worthy of all acceptance.
10. Therefore, we both labor and suffer reproach, because we trust in the living God, who is the Savior of all men, especially of those who believe.
11. These things command and teach.
12. Let no man despise your youth; but be a pattern to the believers, in word, in conduct, in love, in spirit, in faith, in purity.
13. Until I come, give attention to reading, to exhortation, to teaching.
14. Neglect, not the gift that is in you, which was given to you by prophecy, with the laying on of the hands by the eldership.
15. Meditate on these things; give yourself wholly to them; that your progress may appear to all.
16. Take heed to yourself, and the teaching; continue in them: for in doing this you will both save yourself and them that hear you.

Chapter 5

1. Rebuke not an elder but entreat him as a father, and the younger men as brothers;
2. The elder women as mothers; the younger as sisters, with all purity.
3. Honor widows that are widows indeed.
4. But if any widow has children or nephews, let them learn first to show respect at home, and to repay their parents: for that is good and acceptable before God.
5. Now she that is a widow indeed, and desolate, trusts in God, and continues in supplications and prayers night and day.
6. But she that lives in pleasure is dead while she lives.
7. And these things charge, that they may be blameless.
8. But if anyone does not provide for his own and especially for those of his own house, he has denied the faith and is worse than an unbeliever.
9. Let a widow not be taken into the number under sixty years old, having been the wife of one man.
10. Well known for good works; if she has raised children if she has lodged strangers, if she has washed the saints' feet, if she has relieved the afflicted, if she has diligently followed every good work.
11. But the younger widow's refuse: for when they have begun to grow wanton against Christ, they will marry;
12. Having damnation, because they have cast off their first faith.
13. And beside this they learn to be idle, wandering about from house to house; and not only idle, but gossips also and busybodies, speaking things which they ought not.
14. Therefore, I desire that the younger women marry, bear children, manage the house, and give no occasion to the adversary to speak reproachfully.
15. For some are already turned aside after Satan.
16. If any man or woman that believes has widows, let them help them, and let not the Assembly be charged; that it may help them that are widows indeed.
17. Let the elders that rule well be counted worthy of double honor, especially they who labor in the word and teaching.
18. For the scripture says, you will not muzzle the ox that treads out the corn. And the laborer is worthy of his reward.
19. Do not receive an accusation against an elder, unless before two or three witnesses.
20. Them that sin rebuke before all, that others also may fear.
21. I charge you before God, and the Lord Jesus Christ, and the elect angels, that you observe these things without prejudice, doing nothing by partiality.
22. On no man lay hands hastily, neither be a partner of other men's sins: guard your innocence.
23. Drink no longer only water but use a little wine for your stomach's sake and your often infirmities.
24. Some men's sins are open beforehand, going before judgment; and some follow after.

25. Likewise, also the good works of some are manifest beforehand, and they that are otherwise cannot be hidden.

Chapter 6

1. Let all that are slaves under the yoke, esteem their own masters worthy of all honor, that the name of God and His teaching is not blasphemed.
2. And they that have believing masters, let them not despise them because they are brothers; but rather do them service, because they are faithful and beloved, partakers of the benefit. These things teach and exhort.
3. If any man teach otherwise, and consent not to wholesome words, even the words of our Lord Jesus Christ, and to the teaching which is according to godliness;
4. He is proud, knowing nothing, but obsessed about disputes and strife of words, of which comes envy, slanders, strife, evil suspicions,
5. Useless arguments of men with corrupt minds, and destitute of the reality, supposing that godliness is a means of gain: from such remove yourselves.
6. But godliness with contentment is great gain.
7. For we brought nothing into this world, and it is certain we can carry nothing out.
8. And having food and clothing let us be therefore content.
9. But they that will be rich fall into temptation and a snare, and into many foolish and hurtful lusts, which drown men in destruction and perdition.
10. For the love of money is the root of all kinds of evil: which while some coveted after, they have erred from the faith, and pierced themselves through with many sorrows.
11. But you, O man of God, flee these things; and follow after righteousness, godliness, faith, love, patience, meekness.
12. Fight the good fight of faith, lay hold on infinite life, to which you are also called, and have professed a good profession before many witnesses.
13. I give you charge in the sight of God, who gives life to all things, and before Christ Jesus, who before Pontius Pilate witnessed a good confession;
14. That you keep this command unblemished and irreprehensible, until the appearing of our Lord Jesus Christ:
15. Which in His own proper time He will exhibit, the blessed and only Sovereign, the King of the ones reigning, and Lord of the ones exercising lordship;
16. Who alone possesses immortality, dwelling in light inaccessible; whom no man perceived, nor are even able to be perceiving: to who be honor and power infinitely! Amen!
17. Charge them that are rich in this present age, that they are not conceited, nor trust in uncertain wealth, but in the living God, who gives us richly all things to enjoy;
18. That they do good, that they are rich in good works, ready to distribute, willing to share;
19. Laying up in store for themselves a good foundation against the time about to come, that they may lay hold of infinite life.

20. O Timothy, guard the entrusted deposit, turn away from profane and empty speaking, and contrary positions of pseudo knowledge. 21. Which some publicly declare have missed the goal regarding the faith. Grace be with you. Amen.

2nd Timothy Commentary

Paul had previously written to Timothy, emphasizing that the local church serves as a foundation and pillar for God's truth (1 Tim. 3:15). He had explained that the purpose of the church is to proclaim God's truth to the world and for church leaders to explain God's truth to the congregation. As the conditions in the New Testament churches worsened, with signs of the last days becoming more apparent (2 Tim. 3:1-7), Paul was concerned that godlessness and worldliness were infiltrating the church through false teaching and heresy. He knew that if the church failed to fulfill its purpose, the truth of God would not be shared with the world. Therefore, he wrote a letter to Timothy to encourage him to fulfill his responsibilities as a church leader and create a heavenly culture in the city of Ephesus. The church does not adapt to the cultures or subcultures of the cities they are planted in. They are mandated with the purpose of establishing a heavenly culture wherever they are planted. Leaders must have a heavenly vision and Paul's burden was to instill in Timothy this vision.

This letter is specifically for church leaders, addressing their duties and responsibilities. It highlights the essential resources of a Christian leader, which are God's gifts and grace. Paul emphasized that one can only become a servant of God's truth when Jesus Christ bestows a gift through the Holy Spirit. Grace, which refers to all of God's provisions through Christ, is also essential for ministry. It is through these gifts and grace that ministers are able to carry out their work effectively. As Peter states, In 1 Peter 4:10, it says, "**As each one** has received a gift, minister it to one another, **as good stewards** of the manifold grace of God." This verse emphasizes the importance of using the gifts and abilities that God has given us to serve others in the body of Christ. The heavenly culture is a selfless culture being exemplified by our own Savior when He said I came not to be served but to serve and give my life as a ransom for others.

Being a good steward of the multifarious grace of God means recognizing that everything we have, including our gifts and talents, comes from the direct influence of God. It also means understanding that these gifts are not meant for our own selfish gain, but for the benefit of others and ultimately for the glory of God.

As believers, we are called to use our gifts to minister to one another in the body of Christ. This includes using our words to encourage, uplift, and edify those around us. There are no giftless believers, each one of us has been graced with a measure of Christ.

By being good stewards of the grace of God in both our words and in our serving, we can contribute to the growth and unity of the body of Christ. We have a responsibility to use our gifts wisely and diligently, always keeping in mind that they are ultimately a manifestation and evidence of God's grace and love towards us.

In view of the quality of Timothy's faith, Paul urged his son in the ministry not to neglect, but instead "fan the flame" the use of his God-given gifts for the service of Christ. Any person can become less effective in the exercise of his gifts if he or she does not use them regularly. This was Paul's concern. He wanted Timothy to keep active. He was not implying that Timothy's gift had left him. Paul reminded him of the time he laid hands on him and through the laying on hands Paul discerned Timothy's gifting and activated it. Paul encourages Timothy saying he had not received a spirit of fear or cowardice, but of love, power, and a healthy mind. He then goes on to say do not be ashamed of me or of the gospel according to the power of God. Paul is appealing to him to suffer with him The miraculous working of the gospel is what changed Paul and all those who received the gospel. Called with a holy calling before the ages of time. The gospel was God's way, which Paul in another place called it the foolishness of God which is wiser than men. Preaching the cross is foolishness to the world, but unto us who are being saved it is the power of God.

The methods of a Christian minister, as outlined in 2 Timothy, involve construction and demonstration. Ministers are responsible for developing holy character and conduct in those under their care, as well as providing a good example of godliness in their own lives. The most important work of a minister is to know and proclaim the Scriptures. Knowledge of the Word of God is crucial in building up believers and transforming lives.

In order to fulfill their ministry effectively, ministers must continuously stir up their gifts and draw strength from God's grace. They must be diligent in their work, using their resources wisely, and constantly seeking to advance in love and faith. Ministers must also be ready at all times to proclaim the Scriptures and provide help to those in need. Paul's letter to Timothy serves as a guide for church leaders on how to succeed in ministry and remain steadfast in their faith.

Overall, the message of the epistle applies not only to church leaders but to all believers. It emphasizes the importance of proclaiming God's truth, both within the church and to the world, by maintaining the heavenly culture in strength and beauty that the house of God may be a real testimony of Christ. By remaining faithful to their calling and using their gifts effectively, believers can fulfill their ministry and bring glory to God.

I emphasize the heavenly culture that needs to be established. Sociologically, the definition of a culture has four components. This is a simplified version for the sake of space. The first component is belief with the idea of a conviction of what is real. The second is values with the understanding of what is important and worthy. The third component is ideas and in the Christian culture this is revelation whereby God infuses creativity, and lastly number four is norms which is the standard of behavior expected or the pattern or model. These four components make up every culture and subculture in the world. The world has its culture and subcultures, and the church has its culture. The nature of the church's culture is heavenly, and the nature of the world's cultures is earthly. Paul's letter to Timothy is woven with heavenly culture definitions.

1. The importance of staying strong in the faith and enduring hardship as a good soldier of Christ.
2. The need to faithfully preach the gospel and to always be prepared to do so, even in the face of opposition.
3. The importance of studying and correctly interpreting scripture in order to avoid false teachings.
4. The need to live a godly life and to strive for righteousness, resisting the temptations of the world.
5. The promise of eternal life for those who remain faithful to Christ and endure until the end.
6. The importance of teaching and training others in the faith, passing on the teachings of Christ to future generations.
7. The reality of persecution for those who follow Christ, and the assurance that God will deliver and protect his faithful followers.
1. The cultural context of the Roman Empire at the time of 2nd Timothy would have influenced the way in which Paul and Timothy understood and communicated about their beliefs. The Roman Empire was often hostile to Christianity, and followers of Christ faced persecution and opposition from the Judaizers and the Roman government and society at large.
2. In the 1st century Greco-Roman world, there were various philosophical and religious beliefs that influenced people's understanding of the world and their place in it. Paul's teachings in 2nd Timothy would have been in contrast to these competing beliefs, emphasizing the uniqueness of Christ and the need for salvation through faith in Him.
3. The cultural expectations of masculinity and honor in the ancient world would have informed Paul's language about Timothy being a good soldier, a hard-working farmer, and an athlete striving for victory. These metaphors would have resonated with Timothy and the broader audience, drawing on familiar images of strength, endurance, and disciplined training.
4. The cultural practices of teaching and mentorship in the ancient world would have also influenced Paul's instructions to Timothy to pass on the teachings he had

received to others who could carry on the faith. The idea of training and equipping others in the faith would have been a common practice in Greco-Roman society, and Paul used this cultural norm to emphasize the importance of passing on the gospel message to future generations.

Several key values of the heavenly culture to Timothy in his epistles, particularly in 2 Timothy. These values include:

1. Endurance and perseverance in the face of persecution and hardships: Paul emphasizes the importance of enduring suffering for the sake of the gospel and remaining steadfast in faith even in difficult circumstances.

2. Healthy teaching: Paul instructs Timothy to hold fast to the teachings he has received and to accurately handle the word of truth. This emphasizes the importance of staying true to the gospel message and avoiding false teachings.

3. Moral integrity and godly living: Paul encourages Timothy to live a godly life, free from sin and devoted to righteousness. This includes avoiding the temptations of the world and striving to live in a way that is pleasing to God.

4. Faithfulness in ministry: Paul urges Timothy to fulfill his ministry and to continue preaching the gospel and proclaiming the message of Christ, even in the face of opposition and persecution.

In defining the testimony of Christ in Ephesus, Paul would have emphasized the centrality of Jesus Christ as the Savior and Lord. He would have likely highlighted the importance of faith in Christ for salvation, the need for repentance and forgiveness of sins, and the transformative power of the gospel in the lives of believers. Paul may have also emphasized the unity of believers in Christ, regardless of their cultural or social backgrounds, and the importance of loving one another as Christ loved the church. The testimony of Christ in Ephesus would have been a powerful witness to the grace and truth of Jesus Christ, transforming lives and communities in accordance with the values of the heavenly kingdom.

In 2nd Timothy, Paul conveys several specific revelations to Timothy that are meant to encourage, instruct, and exhort him in his ministry. Some of these revelations include:

1. The revelation of the power of God: Paul reminds Timothy of the power of God that has saved and called believers to a holy calling, not because of their works but because of God's own purpose and grace (2 Timothy 1:9).

2. The revelation of God's faithfulness: Paul encourages Timothy to remember the genuine faith that is in him, which first dwelt in his grandmother Lois and his mother Eunice, and to continue in what he has learned and firmly believed, knowing from whom he learned it (2 Timothy 1:5).

3. The revelation of God's Word: Paul instructs Timothy to rightly handle the word of truth, avoiding irreverent babble and contradictions of what is falsely called "knowledge," and to continue in the sacred writings, which are able to make him wise for salvation through faith in Christ Jesus (2 Timothy 2:15, 3:15).

4. The revelation of suffering for the gospel: Paul reminds Timothy that all who desire to live a godly life in Christ Jesus will be persecuted and that he must endure suffering as a good soldier of Christ, realizing that the gospel is worth any hardship or sacrifice (2 Timothy 3:12, 2:3).

5. The revelation of the coming judgment: Paul warns Timothy that there will be a time when people will not endure sound teaching but will turn away from the truth, and that the Lord will judge the living and the dead when he appears (2 Timothy 4:3-4, 1:12).

These specific revelations in 2nd Timothy serve to strengthen Timothy's faith, remind him of the truths of the gospel, and equip him for the challenges and responsibilities of his ministry. They also emphasize the importance of staying true to the teachings of the faith, enduring in the face of opposition, and remaining steadfast in the grace and power of God.

In 2nd Timothy, the apostle Paul unpacked several spiritual norms and principles for Timothy to follow in his ministry and personal life. Some of these spiritual norms include:

1. Faithfulness: Paul emphasizes the importance of remaining faithful to the teachings of the gospel and to the calling that Timothy has received. He encourages Timothy to guard the deposit of faith that has been entrusted to him and to follow the example of Paul in enduring suffering for the sake of Christ (2 Timothy 1:13-14).

2. Endurance: Paul instructs Timothy to endure suffering as a good soldier of Christ and to not be ashamed of the gospel, even in the face of opposition and persecution. He reminds Timothy that God has not given us a spirit of fear but of power, love, and self-discipline (2 Timothy 1:7).

3. Healthy Teaching: Paul emphasizes the importance of teaching and upholding healthy doctrine, avoiding irreverent babble and empty chatter that leads to ungodliness. He instructs Timothy to rightly handle the word of truth and to preach the word in season and out of season (2 Timothy 2:16, 4:2).

4. Flee from sin: Paul warns Timothy to avoid youthful passions and to pursue righteousness, faith, love, and peace, along with those who call on the Lord from a pure heart. He urges Timothy to flee from the love of money and the desires of the flesh, and to pursue a godly life (2 Timothy 2:22, 3:4).

5. Training and Equipping: Paul encourages Timothy to continue in the things he has learned and to entrust them to faithful men who will be able to teach others also. He

emphasizes the importance of training and equipping others in the faith, passing on the teachings of Christ to future generations (2 Timothy 2:2).

By unpacking these spiritual norms for Timothy, Paul provides practical guidance and encouragement for Timothy's ministry and personal walk with the Lord. These principles continue to serve as a source of inspiration and instruction for believers today, reminding us of the importance of faithfulness, endurance, sound doctrine, righteousness, and equipping others in the faith.

In the preterist interpretation of 2 Timothy 3, the focus is often on understanding the passage within the context of the first century rather than as a prediction of events in the distant future. Preterists typically view the references to "the last days" in this passage as referring to the period leading up to the destruction of Jerusalem in 70 AD, rather than to a far-off end times scenario.

In 2 Timothy 3:1-9, the apostle Paul warns Timothy about the difficult times that will come, characterized by people who are lovers of self, lovers of money, abusive, disobedient to their parents, and so on. Preterists may see these descriptions as reflective of the moral and spiritual decay present in the society of the first century, particularly in the lead-up to the destruction of Jerusalem.

As for the reference to Jannes and Jambres in 2 Timothy 3:8, preterists may interpret this as a symbolic or allegorical reference rather than as a literal recounting of historical figures. Jannes and Jambres are not mentioned by name in the Old Testament, but they are traditionally associated with the magicians or sorcerers who opposed Moses in the court of Pharaoh (Exodus 7-8). Preterists may see the mention of these names as symbolic of the opposition faced by the early Christian church, perhaps in the form of false teachers or opponents of the gospel message.

In relation to the idea of Egypt being a type of Jerusalem, as it says in Rev. 11:8 that the city where our Lord was crucified is spiritually called Sodom and Egypt. Preterists may draw parallels between the historical events of the Old Testament (such as the Israelites' exodus from Egypt) and the events of the first century, particularly the fall of Jerusalem in 70 AD. Like Paul did in 1 Cor. 10:11 saying that the children of Israel in the wilderness was a type of us. Not a type of 21st century people but a type of 1st Century saints going through the wilderness of the 40 years from the cross to the destruction of Jerusalem. We see Jerusalem as symbolically representing the old order of Judaism, which was being judged and replaced by the new covenant community of believers in Christ. This interpretation would emphasize the typological significance of Jerusalem and its destruction as a fulfillment of prophetic patterns established in the Old Testament. Origen says that there was an apocryphal book called The Book of Jannes and Jambres, containing details of their exploits, and that Paul the Apostle was quoting from it. In the story of Exodus, Aaron through down his rod and it turned into a serpent and the soothsayer priests, which Origen says was Jannes and Jambres through down their rods and they became serpents. Aaron's rod as a serpent swallowed up those two serpents that were an imitation of truth. Paul is relating this story to Timothy indicating the real gospel will overcome the lies and falsehood. Christ is our serpent on the pole that was lifted up and He has swallowed up death forever and triumphed. Nothing can stand before our Christ, embrace the Christ on the cross and realize in resurrection the serpent has been defeated and death has been conquered and now He holds the keys of death and of Hades.

The Greek word "mellō" in 2 Timothy 4:1 is a significant term that can indicate imminence or the idea of something about to happen. The translation of this word can impact the interpretation of the verse, particularly in relation to the timing of the judgment mentioned by Paul.

While some translations may choose to render "mellō" as "about to," "on the point of," or with similar immediacy, others may choose to translate it in a more general sense to convey the overall meaning without specifically highlighting the concept of imminence. Translation decisions are often based on a variety of factors, including the overall understanding of the passage, the context of the surrounding verses, and the theological perspective of the translators.

The omission of the word "mellō" in certain translations does not necessarily negate the concept of imminence in the passage. The broader context of Paul's exhortation to Timothy to preach the word and be ready for the judgment still conveys a sense of urgency and readiness for the events that are to come.

(mello) (through the idea of *expectation*); to *intend*, i.e. *be about* to be, do, or suffer something (of persons or things, especially events; in the sense of *purpose, duty, necessity, probability, possibility*, or *hesitation*)[120]

In Acts 28:3-6, Paul and the ship he was on was stranded on an Island and as he was getting firewood to warm up, a poisonous snake bit him on the hand and he instantly shook it off into the fire. Those that were present watched with expectation that he would swell up and die. But they were expecting that he was **about to** swell up or suddenly fall down dead.[121] The phrase about to in this verse is mello. See how this word is used here, something was about to happen. When Paul was imprisoned and was called upon by Felix and he spoke to Felix regarding the gospel. But some days later Felix arrived with Drusilla, his wife who was a Jewess, and sent for Paul and heard him *speak* about faith in Christ Jesus. But as he was discussing righteousness, self-control and **the judgment to come**, Felix became frightened and said, "Go away for the present, and when I find time I will summon you."[122] This version omits the translation of mello when it should have been translated,

---

[120] Strong, J. (2020). μέλλω. In *Strong's Talking Greek and Hebrew Dictionary*. WORDsearch.

[121] *New American Standard Bible: 1995 update* (Ac 28:6). (1995). The Lockman Foundation.

[122] *New American Standard Bible: 1995 update* (Ac 24:24–25). (1995). The Lockman Foundation.

"the judgment **about to come**". Why was Felix frightened? If Paul was vague about the judgment as in "someday", but not in your lifetime Felix, he wouldn't have gotten shaken up. Felix was frightened because Paul used the word "mello" and Paul was saying to Felix, the judgment is about to happen. Likewise, in 2 Tim. 4:1, the resurrection and judgment was about to happen. There is so much more to address in this letter but for the sake of space I will endeavor to build on this in the future.

Terry Kashian

2nd Timothy

Chapter 1

1. Paul, an apostle of Jesus Christ by the will of God, according to the promise of life which is in Christ Jesus,
2. To Timothy, my dearly beloved son: grace, mercy, and peace, from God the Father and Christ Jesus our Lord.
3. I thank God, who I serve from my forefathers with pure conscience, that without stopping I have remembrance of you in my prayers night and day;
4. Greatly desiring to see you, being mindful of your tears, that I may be filled with joy;
5. When I call to remembrance the genuine faith that is in you, which made its home first in your grandmother Lois, and your mother Eunice; and I am convinced that in you also.
6. Therefore, I put you in remembrance that you stir up the gift of God, which is in you by the laying on of my hands.
7. For God has not given us the spirit of fear; but of power, and love, and a sound mind.
8. Therefore, be not ashamed of the testimony of our Lord, nor of me his prisoner: but be you, partakers of the afflictions of the gospel, according to the power of God;
9. Who has saved us, and called us with a holy calling, not according to our works, but according to His own purpose and grace, which was given to us in Christ Jesus before measured time began,
10. But is now made apparent through the manifestation of our Savior Jesus Christ, who has abolished the death, and has brought the life and immortality to light through the gospel:
11. To which I am appointed a preacher, and an apostle, and a teacher of the nations.
12. For which reason I also suffer these things: nevertheless, I am not ashamed: for I know in whom I have believed, and am convinced that He can safeguard that which I have committed to Him until that day.
13. Hold fast the pattern of healthy words, which you have heard by me, in faith and love which is in Christ Jesus.
14. That good deposit entrusted to you, safeguard through the Holy Spirit who is at home in us.
15. This you know that all they which are in Asia turned away from me; of whom are Phygellus and Hermogenes.
16. The Lord give mercy to the house of Onesiphorus; for he often refreshed me, and was not ashamed of my shackle:
17. But, when he was in Rome, he sought me out very diligently and found me.
18. The Lord grant to him that he may find mercy of the Lord in that day: and in how extensive he served in Ephesus, you know very well.

Chapter 2

1. Therefore, my son, be vitalized in the grace that is in Christ Jesus.
2. The things that you have heard from me among many witnesses, these entrust to faithful men, who will be adequate to teach others also.

3. You now then suffer evil as a good soldier of Jesus Christ.
4. No man that wars entangles himself with the business of his livelihood; that he may please him who has enlisted him.
5. And if anyone contends as an athlete, yet he is not crowned unless he contends lawfully.
6. The laboring farmer must be first to partake of the fruits.
7. Consider what I say, and the Lord will give you understanding in all these things.
8. Remember that Jesus Christ out of the seed of David was raised out from the dead according to my gospel:
9. For which I suffer evil, even to bonds as a criminal; but the word of God is not being bound.
10. Therefore, I am enduring all things for the elect's sakes that they may also obtain the salvation which is in Christ Jesus with infinite glory.
11. It is a faithful saying: For if we died together, we will also live together:
12. If we are persevering, we will be reigning also: if we are denying, He will also be denying us:
13. If we are disbelieving, that One is remaining faithful: He cannot be rejecting Himself.
14. Of these things remind them, charging them before the Lord that they contend not about words to no profit, but to the ruin of the hearers.
15. Be diligent to show yourself certified by God, a workman who does not need to be disgraced, cutting straight the word of reality.
16. But shun profane and idle babblings: for they will increase to more ungodliness.
17. And their word will take hold and spread like an infection: of whom are Hymenaeus and Philetus;
18. Who concerning the reality have missed the goal, saying that the resurrection already happened; and undermining the faith of some.
19. Nevertheless, the foundation of God stands firm, having this seal, the Lord knew them that are His. And let everyone that names the name of Christ stand apart from unrighteousness.
20. But in a great house there are not only vessels of gold and silver, but also of wood and earthen; and some into honor, and some into disgrace.
21. Therefore, if anyone rid themselves of these, they will be vessels for honor, consecrated, and profitable for the master's use, and prepared for every good work.
22. Flee also youthful lusts: now follow righteousness, faith, love, peace, with those calling upon the Lord out of a pure heart.
23. But foolish and ignorant questions disallow, knowing that they create battles.
24. And the slave of the Lord must not be combatant; but be gentle to all men, able to teach, patient,
25. In meekness instructing those that opposing; if God will perhaps give them repentance into the full knowledge of the reality;
26. And that they may return to sober-mindedness out of the snare of the Devil, who is entrapped by him into his will.

Chapter 3

1. This know also, that in the last days terrifying times will come.
2. For men will be self-lovers, money-lovers, boasters, proud, blasphemers, disobedient to parents, unthankful, unholy,
3. Without natural affection, trucebreakers, false accusers, without self-control, untamed, despisers of those that are good,
4. Traitors, reckless, blinded with pride, pleasure-lovers more than God-lovers;
5. Holding an external godliness, but denying His power: turn away from these.
6. For these are they which sneak into homes, and dominate little housewives overwhelmed with sins, led along with manifold sexual desires,
7. Always learning, and not even able to come to the full knowledge of the reality.
8. Now, as Jannes and Jambres withstood Moses, so do these also resist the reality: men of depraved minds, unapproved concerning the faith.
9. But they will advance no further: for their folly will be manifest to all men, as theirs also was.
10. But you have fully known my teaching, manner of life, purpose, faith, longsuffering, love, patience,
11. Persecutions, afflictions, which came to me at Antioch, at Iconium, at Lystra; what persecutions I endured: but out of them all the Lord delivered me.
12. Yes, and all that will live godly in Christ Jesus will be persecuted.
13. But evil men and charlatans will grow worse and worse, deceiving, and being deceived.
14. But you continue in the things which you have learned and have been assured of, knowing of whom you have learned them;
15. And that from a newborn you have known the Holy Scriptures, which can make you wise into salvation through faith which is in Christ Jesus.
16. All Scripture is God breathing, and is profitable for teaching, for reproof, for correction, for instruction in righteousness:
17. That the man of God may be complete, equipped fully for every good work.

Chapter 4

1. I charge you therefore before God, and the Lord Jesus Christ, who is about to be judging the living and the dead at His full manifestation and His kingdom;
2. Preach the word; be instant in season, out of season; reprove, rebuke, exhort with all longsuffering and teaching.
3. For the time will come when they will not endure sound teaching; but after their own lusts will they heap to themselves teachers, having itching ears;
4. And they will turn away their ears from the reality and will be put out of joint to fiction.
5. Be lucid in everything, endure evil, commit to the work of an evangelist, and fully accomplish your ministry.
6. For I am now ready to be offered, and the time of my departure is at hand.

7. I have fought the good fight, I have finished my race, I have kept the faith:
8. After this there is laid up for me a crown of righteousness, who the Lord, the righteous judge, will give me at that day: and not to me only, to all them also having loved His appearing.
9. Be diligent to come to me soon:
10. For Demas has deserted me, having loved this present age, and set sail to Thessalonica; Crescens to Galatia, Titus to Dalmatia.
11. Only Luke is with me. Take Mark and bring him with you: for he is profitable to me for the ministry.
12. And Tychicus have I sent to Ephesus.
13. The cloak that I left at Troas with Carpus, when you come, bring it with you, and the books, but especially the parchments.
14. Alexander the coppersmith did me much evil: The Lord will repay him according to his works:
15. Of whom be on guard also; for he has greatly resisted our words.
16. At my first defense no man stood together with me, but all men forsook me: I pray God that it may not be counted against them.
17. Nonetheless, the Lord stood with me, and inwardly strengthened me; that through me the preaching might be thoroughly fulfilled, and that all the nations might hear: and I was rescued out of the lion's mouth.
18. For the Lord will deliver me from every evil work and will preserve me to His heavenly kingdom: to Whom be the glory for this age and the New Covenant Age. Amen!
19. Greet Prisca and Aquila, and the household of Onesiphorus.
20. Erastus stayed at Corinth: but Trophimus I left at Miletus sick.
21. Do your best to come before winter. Eubulus greets you, and Pudens, and Linus, and Claudia, and all the brothers.
22. The Lord Jesus Christ be with your spirit. Grace be with you. Amen!

Titus Synopsis

This personal letter from the Apostle Paul to Titus was most likely written at or around 63 AD. These were the latter days of the life of the Apostle and a very pertinent time in a world that had no absolutes, in a world lost and void of moral standards. This was the condition of those days with the heavy weight of Roman rule and the burden of Jewish religious authority.

Titus 1:5 For this reason I left you in Crete, that you should set in order the things that are deficient, and constitute elders in every city, as I had directed you:

Paul leaves Titus in Crete which was an island in the Mediterranean. An early Christian community was established at Gortyn c. 60 A.D. whose apostle was Titus, trained by the apostle Paul. Gortyn thrived with a population reaching 300,000. There was about 15 cites in Crete that were thriving in the first century. There was a great need to establish authentic spiritual authority in Crete.

Titus is called a genuine child not a natural born child, but a child in the ministry. In Corinthians Paul speaks about not many fathers and he says that the Corinthians were fathered by him. For I became your father in Christ Jesus through the gospel. I urge you, then, be imitators of me. Literally, xerox me inside you. That is why I sent you Timothy, my beloved and faithful child in the Lord, to remind you of my ways in Christ, as I teach them everywhere in every church[123]. In this verse we see two aspects of fathering. One is related to being offspring of the gospel. Those we lead to Christ become our children. The other aspect of fathering is bringing up a person in the ministry. Paul raised up Timothy in his gifting and nurtured him and trained him. Titus was exactly the same as Timothy to Paul and he raised him up in the ministry and he fathered him. This verse in 1 Corinthians reveals fathering in the gospel and fathering in the ministry. Paul left Titus in Crete to continue in the ministry to constitute elders in every city.

The church had an understanding that there can only be one administration in each city. This is why Paul did not say constitute elders in every church. Paul's vision of the church was one church, one city with one administration. This is kingdom thinking and I don't believe that God wanted little kingdoms of men thinking it's their flock or church. This was a glorious task given to Titus by Paul. If we practice this model think of the work, we would accomplish and the power of such unity. I know the question, "who going to be in

---

[123] *The Holy Bible: English Standard Version* (1 Co 4:15–17). (2016). Crossway Bibles.

charge"? This is where leadership needs to understand the Kingship and Headship of Christ. Humble men need to lead the church and those who have a revelation of His headship and the one body of Christ. WE do not need to meet under one roof, but we need to meet in His name knowing that He rules in the midst of us. When leaders are networking in each city with the desire to find the Lord's mind and heart they will make an impact on their cities while submitting to the headship of Christ and establishing a single administration in each of those cities. This is what will turn the world upside down!

Bondservants are to be submissive to their own masters in everything; they are to be well-pleasing, not argumentative, not pilfering, but showing all good faith, so that in everything they may adorn the doctrine of God our Savior.[124]

The institution of slavery in the first century of the Roman Empire was a pervasive and multifaceted system that permeated nearly every aspect of society. This research delves into the intricate tapestry of historical context, social conditions, and personal experiences that shaped the realities of slavery during this pivotal time. Drawing upon a comprehensive analysis of scholarly works and primary sources, including the seminal studies of Brent Shaw, Judith Evans Grubbs, C.A. Yeo, M.I. Finley, and Jane Webster, among others, this exploration illuminates the origins, legal frameworks, and economic underpinnings of Roman slavery, as well as the profound impact it had on families, communities, and the psyche of the enslaved.

At the heart of this inquiry lie the fundamental questions that have long challenged our understanding of this dark chapter in human history: What were the driving forces behind the rise and perpetuation of slavery in the first century? How did the institution both uphold and disrupt the hierarchical structures of Roman society? What were the daily lived experiences of those condemned to servitude, and how did they navigate the oppressive realities of their existence? Through a meticulous examination of these inquiries, this research seeks to shed light on the intricate dynamics of power, resistance, and survival that defined the lives of slaves and their masters alike.

The findings presented herein are the product of a comprehensive analysis of a diverse array of sources, including historical texts, legal documents, philosophical treatises, archaeological evidence, and literary works. By synthesizing these varied perspectives, a nuanced and multidimensional portrait emerges, one that captures the complexities of a society deeply entrenched in the practice of human bondage, yet rife with contradictions, subversions, and glimmers of human agency amidst the oppressive confines of servitude.

Through this exploration, we bear witness to the resilience of the human spirit, the enduring quest for dignity and freedom, and the profound impact that institutions of oppression can have on the very fabric of a civilization. It is a tale that resonates across

---

[124] *The Holy Bible: English Standard Version* (Tt 2:9–10). (2016). Crossway Bibles.

time, serving as a disturbing reminder of the consequences of dehumanization and the vital importance of upholding the fundamental rights and liberties of all individuals, regardless of their circumstances or societal standing.

The origins of slavery in the Roman Empire can be traced back to the Republic, where the practice was deeply entrenched and accepted as a fundamental component of society. As Rome's military campaigns expanded its territories, the influx of captives from conquered lands fueled the growth of the slave population (A Study of Roman Society and Its Dependence on Slaves). The insatiable demand for labor on vast agricultural estates and within the burgeoning urban centers of the empire ensured a steady stream of human property, effectively normalizing the commodification of human beings.

The legal framework governing slavery in the first century was intricate and multifaceted. Roman law granted slaves a peculiar status, acknowledging their humanity while simultaneously denying them personhood. Slaves were considered property, subject to the authority and whims of their masters, yet they possessed limited rights and could accumulate peculium, a form of personal property (A Study of Roman Society and Its Dependence on Slaves). The Theodosian Code, a comprehensive legal compendium, grappled with the complexities of slave status, addressing issues such as the wrongful enslavement of freeborn individuals and the precarious position of freedmen, who remained tethered to their former masters.

Slavery's economic impact was profound, intertwining with the intricate web of trade routes that spanned the Mediterranean and beyond. The thriving slave markets facilitated the exchange of human commodities, sustaining the demand for labor across the empire (A Study of Roman Society and Its Dependence on Slaves). Slaves were not merely passive recipients of this trade but actively participated as producers, merchants, and facilitators of commerce, reflecting the complex dynamics of their roles within Roman society. The imbalance between imports and exports further fueled the reliance on slave labor, solidifying their pivotal position within the economic foundations of the empire.

Political influences and power structures were inextricably linked to the institution of slavery. The elite strata of Roman society, comprising influential citizens and political leaders, relied on the exploitation of slaves to consolidate their wealth and status (A Study of Roman Society and Its Dependence on Slaves). Public slaves, employed in various governmental roles, exemplified the state's dependency on this subjugated workforce. Simultaneously, the specter of slave revolts, such as the uprising led by Spartacus, instilled fear within the ruling class, prompting the development of oppressive legal frameworks and harsh punitive measures to maintain control over the enslaved populace.

Despite the pervasive acceptance of slavery, philosophical and religious movements offered alternative perspectives, though their impact on the institution's decline remains a subject of scholarly debate. Stoic thinkers promoted a notion of virtue transcending physical circumstances, while early Christian leaders like Paul advocated for a more benevolent treatment of slaves within the emerging Christian community, albeit without directly challenging the institution itself.

The daily existence of slaves in the first century was a relentless cycle of hardship and oppression. From the rise of the sun until its setting, their lives were defined by unwavering submission to the whims of their masters. Slaves were tasked with a myriad of labors, ranging from domestic chores to intellectual pursuits, their roles spanning every facet of Roman society (A Study of Roman Society and Its Dependence on Slaves). In households, they attended to the most intimate needs of their owners, from bathing and grooming to taking dictation, while on plantations, they toiled in the fields and oversaw the management of supplies.

Discipline and punishment were ever-present specters, looming over the lives of the enslaved. Roman law permitted the harsh treatment of slaves, sanctioning brutal practices such as whipping, physical abuse, and deprivation of food. The consequences for failure or disobedience were severe, with accounts detailing punishments as extreme as having tongues cut out or being thrown to lampreys, eel like creatures with sucking mouths and sharp tiny teeth. It would be compared being thrown to a school of piranhas. This systemic terror served to maintain order and ensure compliance, reinforcing the subhuman status afforded to slaves within Roman society.

The institution of slavery did not merely impact individuals but fractured the very fabric of family and community life. Families were torn asunder as slave owners exercised their authority to sell or reallocate slaves at whim, cleaving apart bonds of family and marriages, inflicting profound psychological and emotional distress). As slavery proliferated, the lines between free and enslaved individuals blurred, fostering a pervasive sense of status confusion that permeated all strata of society.

Yet, amidst the oppression, pockets of resistance and rebellion emerged. The uprising led by Spartacus stands as an iconic testament to the unyielding desire for freedom that burned within the hearts of the enslaved. On an individual level, acts of defiance manifested in the form of runaways, with slaves risking brutal punishments, including torture, to escape the shackles of bondage. The apostle Paul, in his epistles, grappled with the complex dynamics of the master-slave relationship, advocating for a more benevolent treatment of slaves within the Christian community, though stopping short of explicitly condemning the institution itself.

The psychological toll exacted by slavery was profound and enduring. Slaves developed coping mechanisms to survive the dehumanizing realities of their existence, often retreating into a state of mute obedience and docility to shield themselves from further abuse (A Study of Roman Society and Its Dependence on Slaves). Yet, even as they adapted to their circumstances, the trauma of their lived experiences left indelible marks on their psyches, echoing through the generations that followed.

The institution of slavery in the first century of the Roman Empire was a pervasive and deeply entrenched phenomenon that left an indelible mark on the fabric of ancient society. From its origins in the incessant military campaigns of the Republic to its perpetuation through economic necessity and cultural norms, slavery became an integral thread woven into the tapestry of Roman life, shaping the dynamics of power, labor, and social hierarchies.

As this research has illuminated, the factors that contributed to the rise and continuation of slavery during this period were multifaceted and interconnected. Warfare and territorial expansion fueled the influx of captives, while the insatiable demand for labor on agricultural estates and urban centers created an ever-growing market for human commodities. The legal framework, though acknowledging the humanity of slaves to a limited extent, ultimately reinforced their status as property, subject to the whims and cruelties of their masters.

The economic impact of slavery was profound, intertwining with the intricate web of trade routes that spanned the Mediterranean world and beyond. Slaves were not merely passive recipients of this trade but active participants, their labor driving the production and exchange of goods that sustained the Roman economy. This interdependence between slavery and commerce further entrenched the institution, rendering its abolition a perceived threat to the very foundations of the Empire's prosperity.

Yet, the harsh realities of slavery extended far beyond mere economic considerations. The daily lives of the enslaved were marked by unrelenting hardship, brutality, and the constant specter of punishment. Families were torn asunder, communities fractured, and the lines between free and enslaved individuals became increasingly blurred, fostering a pervasive sense of status confusion that permeated all strata of Roman society.

Amidst this oppression, however, the indomitable human spirit found ways to resist and rebel. From the iconic uprising led by Spartacus to the subtle acts of defiance woven into daily existence, the enslaved refused to surrender their quest for freedom and dignity. Philosophical and religious movements, though rarely challenging the institution outright, offered alternative perspectives on the treatment of slaves and the nature of true liberty.

As we reflect on this dark chapter in human history, we are reminded of the resilience of the human spirit and the enduring struggle for justice and equality. The echoes of the past reverberate through the ages, reminding us of the profound consequences of dehumanization and the vital importance of upholding the fundamental rights and liberties of all individuals, regardless of their circumstances or societal standing. Paul's exhortation for divine infused character and action is Paul calling those in servitude to exemplify this kind of Christian life which was above all expectations. This way was what Jesus meant when he said if someone asks you to carry their load for a mile, which was Roman law to any Jew, He said, "go an extra mile". The slave had the opportunity to be a testimony of having Christ in their life. The lessons gleaned from this exploration of slavery in the first century of the Roman Empire serve as a poignant reminder of the enduring need to confront oppression, challenge injustice, and strive for a world where the inherent dignity of every human being is recognized and celebrated. It is a call to action, a clarion call to honor the sacrifices and struggles of those who came before us and to build a more just, equitable, and compassionate society for generations to come.

Being Trained By the Grace of God

For the grace of God has appeared, bringing salvation for all people, training us to renounce ungodliness and worldly passions, and to live self-controlled, upright, and godly lives in the present age, waiting for our blessed hope, the appearing of the glory of our great God and Savior Jesus Christ, who gave himself for us to redeem us from all lawlessness and to purify for Himself a people for His own possession who are zealous for good works.[125]

The grace of God is not just unmerited favor but as James Strong puts it, "the divine influence of God upon the heart to reflect the glory of God". Grace has a training aspect that is virtually ignored by those that are propagating the grace message. I will give you a picture of what I think grace truly is. In the book of Revelation, John saw a Lamb on the throne. This symbol is marvelous! The Lamb is Christ full of grace and reality, the throne is a symbol of government, the kingdom. Grace without the throne is incomplete and the throne without grace is pure legalism. The combination is the true balance, grace and government is how grace trains us to renounce ungodliness and worldly passions and live a proper upright and godly life. When Paul uses the phrase "present age". The Lord Jesus spoke about the present age and the age to come.

Salvation by the costly grace of God was beckoning the 1st century church to change lifestyles, mindsets and motives in response to God's grace. Anyone who receives grace and refuses to pursue righteousness demonstrates either his / her ignorance or their hardness of heart. The same is true in our day, in our time, to be saved means to pursue righteousness -- not so that we may earn our salvation, but so that God's saving grace will not be fruitless in us.

After Paul was released from prison in Rome (see Acts 28:30), he continued his ministry work. Companions and fellow servants in his mission work included Timothy and Titus. Paul left Titus to oversee the administration of churches in Crete (Titus 1:5). Similar to the other ministry letters (1 and 2 Timothy), this one to Titus contains practical advice meant for Titus but well applied to the contemporary Christian as well.

---

[125] *The Holy Bible: English Standard Version* (Tt 2:11–14). (2016). Crossway Bibles.

Leadership with a Golden Character

A notable aspect of the epistle is its focused discussion on the qualifications and responsibilities of church leaders. If Titus is to ordain elders in every city, he must have a standard to point them out in the midst of the assemblies. The apostle Paul outlines specific requirements for the selection of elders, emphasizing the significance of integrity, godly conduct, and the ability to teach healthy teachings. This emphasis on leadership reflects the early church's necessity for strong and trustworthy individuals to guide its development. Additionally, the letter skillfully explores the correlation between faith and actions in a believer's life. Paul emphasizes the power of divine grace and salvation, promoting a lifestyle characterized by good works and adherence to God's commands. This practical demonstration of faith is crucial, underscoring the importance of living out one's faith in daily practice.

(1). God wants and equips people of high spiritual character to serve as leaders and teachers among the saints.

(2). Leaders in the church should serve as examples for others, not lording over the fellow believer but in one mind striving together to achieve abiding love.

(3). Every Christian should be self-controlled, eager to oppose sin and to do that which is pleasing to the Lord.

Consequently, Paul conceived of his calling not simply as sowing seeds of faith, but also as cultivating a soon to be harvest of strong, mature and fruitful believers. Paul accomplished the purpose of his calling and paved the way for leaders and fellow laborers, as was Titus, presenting life in Christ to the known world in which the result was increasing in maturity.

Allyn Morton & Terry Kashian

Titus

Chapter 1

1. Paul, a slave of God, and an apostle of Jesus Christ, according to the faith of the chosen by God and the full knowledge of the reality, which is according to godliness;
2. In expectation of infinite life, which God, who cannot lie, promised before the times of the ages;
3. But has in these appointed times manifested His word through preaching, which was committed to me according to the command of God our Savior;
4. To Titus, my genuine child, according to a shared faith: grace, mercy, and peace, from God the Father and the Lord Jesus Christ our Savior.
5. For this reason, I left you in Crete, that you should set in order the things that are deficient and constitute elders in every city, as I had directed you:
6. If any be blameless, the husband of one wife, having believing children not accused of being incorrigible or defiant.
7. For an overseer must be impeccable, as the steward of God; not self-willed, not quick-tempered, not given to wine, not violent, not greedy for dishonest gain;
8. But a lover of hospitality, a lover of good, sober, just, holy, temperate;
9. Cleaving to the faithful word according to the teaching, that he may be able by healthy teaching both advising and convicting the opponents.
10. For there are many unable to sit and be governed and empty prattlers and con artists, especially those out from the circumcision:
11. Whose mouths must be stopped, who overturn whole houses, teaching things which they ought not, in favor of dishonorable gain.
12. One of themselves, even a prophet of their own, said, the Cretans are continually lying, evil wild beasts, and lazy gluttons.
13. This witness is true. Therefore, rebuke them sharply, that they may be healthy in the faith;
14. Not giving heed to Jewish fables, and commandments of men, who are perverting the reality.
15. To the clean all things are clean: but to them that have been stained and are unfaithful, nothing is clean; both their minds and consciences are stained.
16. They confess that they see God; but in works they are denying Him, being disgusting, and unwilling to be persuaded, unsanctioned for all good works.

Chapter 2

1. But you speak the things which are proper for healthy teaching:
2. That the senior men be sober, reverent, temperate, and healthy in faith, love, and patience.
3. The senior women likewise, that they have sacred behavior as to their demeanor, not devilish, not addicted to much wine, teachers of what is good;
4. That they may train the new wives to be sensible, to be affectionate to their husbands, to be loving their children,

5. To be healthy-minded, chaste, homemakers, good, submissive to their own husbands, that the word of God is not spoken against.

6. Young men likewise exhort to be sensible.

7. In all things showing yourself a pattern of good works: in teaching with no alloy, venerable, incorruptible,

8. Healthy speaking, that cannot be condemned; that the opponent may be ashamed, having no evil thing to say of us.

9. Exhort slaves to be submissive to their own masters, and to please them well in all things; not talking back;

10. Not stealing but showing all good faith; that they may adorn the teaching that is of God our Savior in all things.

11. Because the grace of God's salvation has shined upon all men,

12. Training us to refuse all godless and worldly desires, living judiciously, righteously, and godly in this present age;

13. Receiving the blessed hope, and the full manifest glory of our great God and Savior, Christ Jesus;

14. Who gave Himself for us, that He might ransom us from all lawlessness, and purify for Himself a treasured people, zealous for good works.

15. These things speak and exhort, and reprove with all injunctions. Let no one be guessing about you.

Chapter 3

1. Remind them to be in submission to rulers and authorities, to be obedient, to be ready for all good works,

2. To speak against no one, to not be belligerent, but gentle, showing all clemency to all men.

3. For we also were sometimes foolish, disobedient, deceived, in bondage to numerous lusts and pleasures, passing through life in evil and envy, despicable, and hating one another.

4. But when the kindness and friendship of God our Savior for men illuminated us,

5. Not by works of righteousness which we have done, but according to His mercy He saved us, by the washing of regeneration, and renewing of the Holy Spirit;

6. Which He pours out on us lavishly through Jesus Christ our Savior;

7. That being justified by His grace, we begin to become inheritors according to the expectation of infinite life.

8. This is a faithful saying and these things I want you to affirm constantly, that they who have believed God consider practicing good works. These things are good and profitable for men.

9. But avoid foolish questions, and genealogies, and contentions, and strivings about the law; for they are unprofitable and useless.

10. A man that is causing formal divisions by opinion, after the first and second warning, reject;

11. Knowing that he that is such has turned out of the way and continually sins, being self-condemned.

12. When I send Artemas to you, or Tychicus, be diligent to come to me at Nicopolis: for I decided to stay there for the winter.

13. Bring Zenas the lawyer and Apollos on their journey with speed, that they may be lacking in nothing.

14. Let our own also learn to preside in honorable occupations for the essential needs, that they are not unprofitable.

15. All that are with me greet you. Greet them that are fond of us in the faith. Grace be with you all. Amen.

Philemon Commentary

The letter of Paul to Philemon is a poignant and powerful piece of scripture that provides insight into relationships, forgiveness, and the value of personal responsibility. The epistle is a unique testament to the character of the apostle Paul, who intercedes on behalf of a runaway slave named Onesimus, appealing to Philemon, a wealthy Christian in Colossae, to welcome Onesimus back as a brother in Christ.

To Philemon our beloved *friend* and fellow laborer, to the beloved Apphia, Archippus our fellow soldier, and to the church in your house:[126] A phrase in this letter that stands out in the beginning is "to the church in your house". Philemon had the gathering of the saints in his home. It was not until the late 3rd century that the church shifted from being the people of God to a physical building and since hospitality has been on the degrading scale. This shift has confused many throughout the centuries and the children of God have lost their corporate identity. The church is an organic, living group of regenerated human beings that are called into fellowship with His son to express Christ to the world, to their neighborhood. The church has had her identity stolen and replaced with a physical building when she is the building of God. 1 Cor. 3:9, For we are God's fellow workers; you are God's field, *you are* **God's building**.[127] Paul was a master builder, and his goal was to build with gold, silver, and precious stones. In the case of Philemon Paul is going to build with silver. Silver is for redemption. It was used in redeeming and had a precious value to purchase. Num. 3:46-51. The word translated as money is the Hebrew word for silver. Paul was building in Philemon as Paul's tongue was the ready writer building something redemptive in Philemon. *The tongue of the righteous is choice* **silver***, but the heart of the wicked is of little value." – Proverbs 10:20.* Silver holds a rich symbolic significance in the Bible, representing purity, redemption, value, wisdom, and knowledge. As believers, we are called to reflect the qualities of silver in our lives – to be refined, valuable, and filled with the wisdom and knowledge that comes from God. Forgiveness and acceptance is edifying to those who need to be conciliated with God and reconciled to others.

This is Paul's burden for Onesimus and his relationship to Philemon. Paul always prayed for Philemon and Philemon's testimony was he loved all the saints. His virtuous character encouraged Paul to honor Philemon because of his love and faith toward the church.

---

[126] *The New King James Version* (Phm 1–2). (1982). Thomas Nelson.
[127] *The New King James Version* (1 Co 3:9). (1982). Thomas Nelson.

Philemon refreshed the church by giving them a safe place to meet and find encouragement amid the turmoil in the Roman Empire.

The historical context of the letter is crucial in understanding its significance. During the first century A.D., slavery was a common practice in the Roman Empire, and it was not uncommon for slaves to seek liberation through running away. In this context, Paul's letter to Philemon takes on added weight, as it challenges social norms and calls for a radical reevaluation of the relationship between master and slave.

Key figures in the letter include Paul, Philemon, and Onesimus. Paul, as the author, demonstrates his compassion and empathy for Onesimus by advocating on his behalf. Philemon, as the recipient of the letter, is urged to act with grace and forgiveness towards his runaway slave. Onesimus, the subject of the letter, is ultimately the catalyst for reconciliation between the two men.

Chuck Swindoll, a renowned pastor, author, and radio preacher, has provided valuable insight into the letter of Paul to Philemon. In his commentary on the book of Philemon, Swindoll emphasizes the themes of forgiveness, reconciliation, and redemption. He highlights the transformative power of grace and the importance of extending mercy to others, even when it is difficult. Swindoll's perspective on the letter of Paul to Philemon underscores the timeless relevance of its message. In a world plagued by division and conflict, the call for grace and forgiveness remains as urgent as ever. Swindoll's commentary serves as a reminder of the radical love of Christ, which transcends societal barriers and calls for unity among believers.

Influential individuals who have contributed to the field of commentary on the letter of Paul to Philemon include theologians, scholars, and pastors. William Barclay, a Scottish author and theologian, offered a scholarly analysis of the letter in his book "The Letters to the Galatians and Philemon." Barclay's commentary delves into the historical context of the letter and provides valuable insights into its meaning and significance.

Another influential figure in the field of commentary on Philemon is N.T. Wright, a prominent New Testament scholar and Anglican bishop. Wright's work on the letter of Paul to Philemon offers a fresh perspective on the themes of reconciliation and justice. By examining the social dynamics of the first-century Roman Empire, Wright sheds light on the complexities of the master-slave relationship and the implications of Paul's message for contemporary readers.

Overall, the letter of Paul to Philemon is a profound testament to the power of forgiveness and reconciliation. Through the lens of Chuck Swindoll's commentary, we gain a deeper understanding of the transformative impact of grace and the enduring relevance of Paul's message. As we consider the various perspectives and analyses of influential individuals in the field, we are reminded of the universal call to love our neighbors as ourselves and extend forgiveness to those who have wronged us. The letter of Paul to Philemon serves as a timeless reminder of the redemptive power of Christ's love and the imperative to extend that love to others.

Terry Kashian

Philemon

Chapter 1

1. Paul, a prisoner of Jesus Christ, and Timothy our brother, to Philemon our dearly beloved, and coworker,
2. And to our beloved Apphia, and Archippus our fellow soldier, and the Assembly at your home:
3. Grace to you, and peace, from God our Father and the Lord Jesus Christ.
4. I thank my God, making mention of you always in my prayers,
5. It is being reported about your love and faith, which you have toward the Lord Jesus, and for all the saints;
6. That the fellowship of your faith may become effective in the full knowledge of every good thing which is in you in Christ Jesus.
7. For we have great joy and comfort in your love because the inner parts of the saints are revitalized by you, brother.
8. Therefore, though I might be very bold in Christ to command you to do what is proper,
9. Yet through love I would rather entreat you, being such a one as Paul, an old man, and now also a prisoner of Jesus Christ.
10. I beg you for my child Onesimus, who I have begotten in my shackles:
11. Which in time past was to you useless, but now useful to you and me:
12. Who I have sent back to you, therefore receive him, that is, as my very own inner parts:
13. Who I would have kept with me, that in your place he might have ministered to me as I am shackled for the gospel:
14. But without your consent, I would do nothing; that your kindness might not be done out of compulsion, but willingly.
15. For perhaps he therefore was separated for a period, that you should receive him perpetually;
16. Not now as a slave, but above a slave, a beloved brother, especially to me, but how much more to you, both in flesh and in the Lord?
17. If you count me therefore as a companion, receive him as myself.
18. If he has wronged you, or owes you anything, put that on my account;
19. I Paul have written it with my own hand, I will repay it: yet I do not say to you how you owe me even your own self besides.
20. Yes, brother, let me profit from you in the Lord: revitalize my inner parts in the Lord.
21. Having confidence in your obedience, I wrote to you, knowing that you will also do more than I say.
22. Also prepare hospitality for me: for I trust that through your prayers I will be given to you.
23. Greetings to you from Epaphras, my fellow prisoner in Christ Jesus;
24. And Marcus, Aristarchus, Demas, Lucas, my coworkers.
25. The grace of our Lord Jesus Christ be with your spirit. Amen.

The Truth of Two Ages

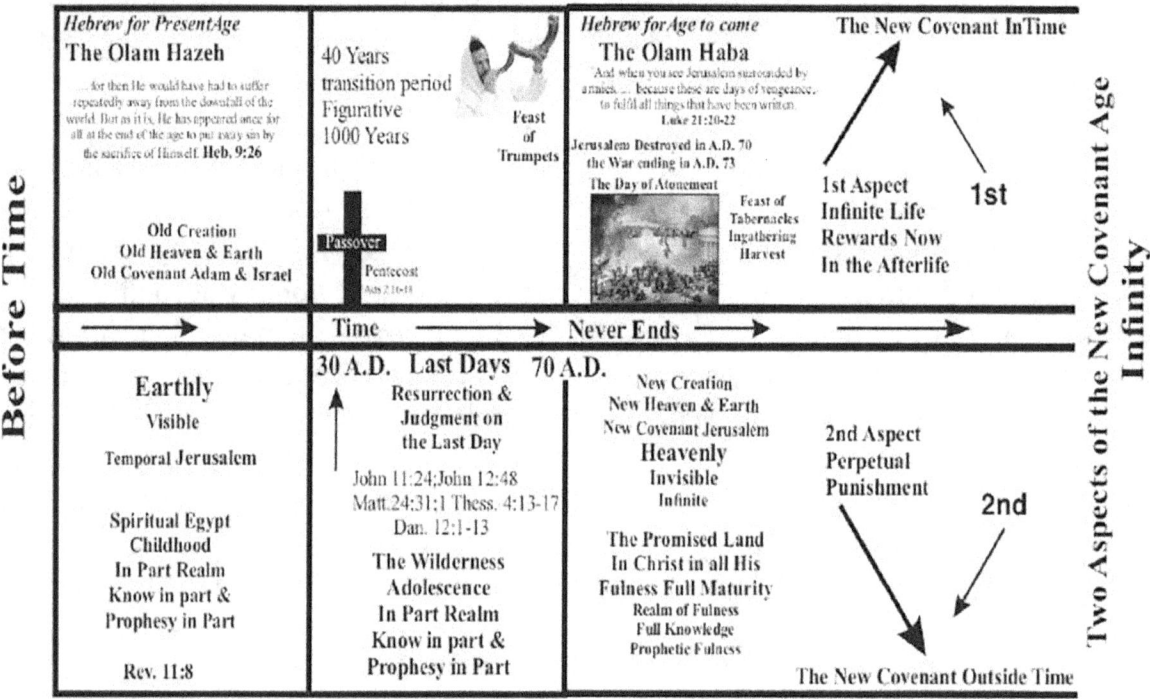

Hebrews Synopsis

Overview:

Hebrews is an epistle that holds significant implications when viewed through a preterist lens. This interpretation asserts that all of the prophecies and events described in the New Testament, including those in Hebrews, were fulfilled in the first century, particularly around the destruction of the Jewish Temple in AD 70 and the decentralization of the true worship of our Lord. In spirit and reality for all time.

Hebrews emphasizes the superiority of Christ and the New Covenant over the Old Covenant and the Mosaic Law. From a fulfilled perspective, this superiority was demonstrated through the events of the first century, especially the destruction of the Temple in Jerusalem by the Romans. This event signaled the end of the Old Covenant system of worship, as the Temple was central and the very heart to Jewish religious practices. The modern version of Judaism is an artificial religion because of what is missing to practice true Judaism has been destroyed. No temple, no priesthood, no sacrifice to take away their sins according to the Law of Moses. This is what the writer of Hebrews highlights in this letter. The more perfect temple or tabernacle not made with hands, the Melchizedek priesthood in Christ, and the perfect sacrifice, the Lamb of God, our Lord Jesus, to take away, not just cover our sins, but to fully cleanse us of all our sins and make us righteous in the eyes of God.

Key verses in Hebrews that align with a fulfilled interpretation include:

Hebrews 1:1 – "Long ago, at many times and in many ways, God spoke to our fathers by the prophets, **but in these last days** He has spoken to us in His Son, whom He appointed the heir of all things, through whom also He created the world." These last days indicates that they were in the last days of the old covenant age which was about to end. All the speaking of God is embodied in its fullness in Jesus.

Hebrews 8:13 - "In speaking of a new covenant, he makes the first one obsolete. And what is becoming obsolete and growing old is ready to vanish away." This verse suggests that the Old Covenant was coming to an end, which could be seen as fulfilled in the destruction of the Temple.

Luke 21:20-22, **"… because these are the days of vengeance that all things that are written will be fulfilled"**.

2. Hebrews 9:26 - "But as it is, He has appeared once for all at the goal of the ages to put away sin by the sacrifice of Himself." The mention of "the goal of the ages" can be interpreted as referring to the end of the Jewish age, culminating in the destruction of the city and the sanctuary. And the **people of the prince who is to come shall destroy the city and the sanctuary.** Its end shall come with a flood, and **to the end there shall be war. Desolations are decreed**[128]

3. Hebrews 10:37 - "For, 'Yet a little while, and the coming one will come and will not delay.'" This verse is seen as a reference to the imminent judgment and coming of Christ in the first century, which included the destruction of Jerusalem. The phrase "For yet in a very little while, He who is coming will come, and will not delay" in Hebrews 10:37 is a quotation from the Old Testament book of Habakkuk. Habakkuk 2:3 (NASB) reads: "For the vision is yet for the appointed time; **It hastens toward the goal**, and **it will not fail**. Though it tarries, wait for it; For it will certainly come, it will not delay." The author of Hebrews references this verse from Habakkuk to convey the idea of an at hand, close, near, fulfillment of God's promises, emphasizing that the coming of the Lord would not be delayed and urging believers to patiently wait for it. The phrase "But my righteous one shall live by faith" in Hebrews 10:38 is a quotation from the Old Testament. Also in Habakkuk 2:4 (NASB) reads: "Behold, as for the proud one, His soul is not right within him; But **the righteous will live by His faith**." The author of Hebrews quotes this verse from Habakkuk to emphasize the importance of faith and righteousness in the lives of believers, highlighting the contrast between those who live by faith and those who do not. In Hebrews 10:39, the author expresses confidence that the audience to whom he is writing is not among those who "shrink back to destruction."

This statement can be understood in the context of the historical situation facing Jewish Christians at that time. The Jewish Christians to whom the letter of Hebrews was addressed were facing significant challenges and pressure to return to Judaism, particularly as the destruction of Jerusalem and the Temple by the Romans was imminent. Some believers may have been tempted to abandon their faith in Christ and revert to the practices of the Old Covenant in order to escape persecution or align themselves with the prevailing religious authorities. By stating that **"we are not of those who shrink back to destruction,"** the author is affirming the steadfastness and faithfulness of the recipients of the letter. He is reassuring them that they are not turning away from their faith in Christ and risking total destruction by returning to the Old Covenant practices that were about to be destroyed along with those who rejected Jesus their Messiah.

Instead, the author highlights that the audience possesses faith that leads to the preservation and salvation of the soul. They are encouraged to remain firm in their commitment to Christ, trusting in the saving power of God by faith, even in the face of external pressures and

---

[128] *The Holy Bible: English Standard Version* (Da 9:26). (2016). Crossway Bibles.

persecution. This statement serves as a reminder to the Jewish Christians that their ultimate security and preservation lie in their faith in Christ, rather than in the fading practices and rituals of the Old Covenant that were about to be brought to an end.

4. Hebrews 12:26-27 – "At that time his voice shook the earth, but now he has promised, 'Yet once more I will shake not only the earth but also the heavens.' This phrase, 'Yet once more,' indicates the removal of things that are shaken—that is, things that have been made—in order that the things that cannot be shaken may remain." These verses are to be interpreted as describing the shaking and removal of the old Jewish system, including the Temple, to make way for the enduring Kingdom of God. Hebrews 12:26 quotes from the Old Testament verse found in Haggai 2:6, which reads: "For thus says the Lord of hosts, 'Once more in a little while, I am going to shake the heavens and the earth, the sea also and the dry land.'" When Hebrews 12:26 states, "Yet once more I will shake not only the earth but also the heaven," it is referring to a divine shaking or upheaval that signifies a significant change in the order and structure of things. In the context of Hebrews, this shaking is related to the removal of the sacrificial system of Judaism and the establishment of the New Covenant through Christ. The **writer of Hebrews uses this imagery of shaking the heavens and the earth to convey the idea of a cosmic event that will bring about a fundamental shift in the religious and spiritual landscape.** This is what Peter was referring to in 2 Peter 3:7,10, - **the present heavens and earth** are being reserved for fire, **kept for the day of judgment and destruction of ungodly men**[129] **10** But **the day of the Lord will come** like a thief, **in which the heavens will pass away** with a roar and the elements will be destroyed with intense heat, and **the earth and its works will be burned up**[130] This shaking symbolizes the end of the old order of things, including the sacrificial system of Judaism, and the inauguration of a new age through the redemptive work of Christ. A new age with a new heavens and earth where in righteousness dwells.

By quoting from Haggai and applying it to the situation of the Hebrew Christians, the author of Hebrews emphasizes **the imminent and transformative nature of the changes occurring in their religious practices.** The shaking of the heavens and the earth signifies the upheaval and displacement of the old religious structures, paving the way for the establishment of the New Covenant in Christ.

I. Introduction

The Epistle to the Hebrews emerges as a profound exploration of early Christian theological thought, intricately blending notions of faith, endurance, and Christ's unrivaled supremacy.

Distinct in both its narrative style and theological depth, the text engages a community ensnared by critical theological dilemmas within their unique socio-historical milieu.

---

[129] *New American Standard Bible, 1995 Edition: Paragraph Version* (2 Pe 3:7). (1995). The Lockman Foundation.

[130] *New American Standard Bible, 1995 Edition: Paragraph Version* (2 Pe 3:10). (1995). The Lockman Foundation.

Hebrews delivers a nuanced portrayal of Jesus as the quintessential high priest and the consummation of Old Testament prophecies, heralding a new covenant that eclipses the former in both splendor and commitment.

This paper intends to delve into the predominant themes and theological insights offered in the Book of Hebrews, scrutinize its historical backdrop, and evaluate its lasting influence on Christian ideology and teachings. By examining these components, the research endeavors to furnish a detailed comprehension of Hebrews' theological importance and its instrumental role in molding Christian identity and convictions.

II. Key Themes in the Book of Hebrews

A. Faith and Perseverance

In the Book of Hebrews, the resounding call to faith and perseverance surfaces as a cornerstone theme, urging believers to cling tightly to their faith amidst adversities. The narrative vividly recounts the steadfastness of Old Testament icons like Abraham, Moses, and Rahab, who, despite facing daunting uncertainties, never wavered in their trust in God.

B. Superiority of Christ

Portraying Jesus as the consummate manifestation of God's glory and the prophesied Messiah, the author of Hebrews establishes His supremacy over angels, notable prophets, and the Levitical priesthood. Christ's role as the ultimate sacrifice for sins and as the mediator of a superior, new covenant is intricately detailed, underscoring His unparalleled authority and uniqueness within the Christian doctrine.

C. Covenant Theology

The discourse on covenant theology within Hebrews provides a profound examination of the transition from the old covenant, rooted in Mosaic Law, to the revolutionary new covenant brought forth in Christ. Employing rich symbolism from the Old Testament, particularly the sacrificial system and the Day of Atonement, the text elucidates the transformative implications of Christ's death and resurrection, celebrating the enduring superiority of the new covenant.

D. High Priesthood of Jesus

Central to the theological narrative of Hebrews is the high priesthood of Jesus, positioned as the ultimate mediator who offers an unblemished sacrifice for humanity's sins and intercedes for believers. By drawing parallels with the Levitical priesthood, the text highlights the efficacy and superiority of Christ's priestly office, emphasizing the profound access it grants believers to God and magnifying the significance of His sacrificial work on the cross.

E. Warnings Against Apostasy

Interspersed with stern warnings against apostasy, Hebrews calls upon its readers to maintain a vigorous and unwavering faith, alerting them to the perils of deviating from the truth. These admonitions underscore the severe repercussions of renouncing Christ and serve as a poignant reminder of the essentiality of perseverance and adherence to Jesus' teachings.

F. Rest for God's People

The recurring motif of rest, promised by God to the Israelites in the Promised Land, is re-envisioned in Hebrews as a prelude to the ultimate rest believers will find in Christ. This theme invites the faithful to embrace the spiritual repose offered by Jesus, who alleviates the burdens of striving and secures a tranquil and everlasting future for His followers. This rest is related to the resurrection and because of space I will have to address this in another article. The rest has two aspects on in time and one outside of time. The picture is clear in the Exodus from Egypt to the Promised land. At the end of the 40 years all Israel was at the banks of the Jordan river. Jordan means descent and as Israel descended onto the dry ground of Jordan and rose up into the promised land, it was a picture of death, burial, and resurrection. The resurrected state is in time and experienced to take possession of their inheritance. There is also an experience of rest when we physically die, and it is a fulness of resurrection outside of time and it never ends. Life and rest is our outside of time experience. In time rest and resurrection our experience is to take possession and fight the giants and "ites" of the spiritual realm where our inheritance is with the saints in light. Just a little to consider and develop it more. The promised land is not heaven, otherwise the picture would indicate that we have some giants to fight to enter the promised land. Not going to happen when we physically die. The fight is over!

III. Theological Perspectives in Hebrews

Within the rich tapestry of Christian theology, the Book of Hebrews stands out for its depth and doctrinal sophistication. It explores a spectrum of theological dimensions, including Christology, soteriology, eschatology, pneumatology, and their intersections with the Pauline epistles, weaving a complex narrative that enriches our understanding of Christian thought.

A. Christology

At the heart of Hebrews lies Christology, which scrutinizes the nature and deeds of Jesus Christ. Portrayed as the supreme high priest, Jesus transcends the traditional Levitical priesthood by offering a once-and-for-all sacrifice for sin. And His priesthood is of the order of Melchizedek, and it is an endless priesthood with an indestructible, incorruptible life. This portrayal not only affirms His divinity but also underscores His pivotal role as the mediator between God and man, a cornerstone of redemption.

B. Soteriology

Soteriology in Hebrews delves into the mechanics of salvation through Christ's sacrifice, which is portrayed as both effective and sufficient for humanity's redemption. The storyline stresses the importance of faith in Jesus as the pathway to salvation and cautions against the perils of apostasy or falling back, painting a vivid picture of salvation's transformative potential.

C. Eschatology

Hebrews also addresses eschatology, presenting Jesus as the fulfillment of prophetic visions and the precursor to a new covenant. This theological angle not only reinforces those believers' hope but also instills a sense of urgency, encouraging steadfastness in faith amidst the anticipation of God's ultimate dominion and the final judgment which was imminent in the 1st Century.

D. Pneumatology

Though less explicitly tackled, pneumatology is nonetheless a significant thread within Hebrews. It subtly permeates the text through exhortations that hint at the Holy Spirit's role in empowering and sustaining believers, facilitating their spiritual growth and resilience.

E. Comparative Analysis with Pauline Epistles

The theological narratives of Hebrews invite comparisons with the Pauline epistles, particularly in their common themes of faith and salvation. However, Hebrews distinguishes itself through its rhetorical flourish and its adept use of Old Testament imagery to articulate profound theological truths, offering a unique lens through which to view the early Christian theological landscape.

The exploration of these theological perspectives in the Book of Hebrews offers a comprehensive and nuanced understanding of its enduring significance in Christian doctrine. From the deep dives into Christology and soteriology to the broader implications of eschatology and pneumatology, each aspect enriches our comprehension of early Christian thought. The comparative analysis with the Pauline epistles further illuminates the diverse theological contours of early Christianity.

The forthcoming section will explore the historical context of Hebrews, shedding light on aspects such as authorship, dating, audience, purpose, socio-political background, and its intricate relationship with Judaism. This historical examination promises to deepen our grasp of the theological insights and intentions behind the text.

IV. Historical Context of Hebrews

A. Authorship and Dating

The origins of the Book of Hebrews, enveloped in mystery, have long sparked vigorous debates among scholars. Lacking a clear attribution within its texts, the authorship remains speculative, with early church traditions pointing towards Paul, though figures like Apollos or Barnabas have also been considered. In contemporary scholarship, the notion of an anonymous author, possibly compiling teachings from various sources, gains the most traction.

I lean towards an early date and many notable scholars do also lean towards the early 60s AD, predating the destruction of the Jerusalem Temple in 70 AD.

B. Audience and Purpose

The intended recipients of Hebrews, though not explicitly named, are generally believed to be Jewish Christians grappling with persecution and wavering faith. The author's profound grasp of Jewish customs and the emphasized preeminence of Christ over all the Old Testament's players and components give us the clue they are predominantly a Jewish audience.

Hebrews serves multiple purposes: it is a source of solace and encouragement for believers to hold steadfast against persecution; it articulates the supremacy of Christ and the new covenant, contrasting with the Old Testament's limitations; and it warns against apostasy while offering theological insights into the early Jewish Christian community's struggles.

C. Socio-Political Background

Understanding the socio-political landscape during which Hebrews was written is crucial. Likely penned under Roman dominion, which was marked by growing animosity towards Christians, the text reflects the pressures Jewish believers faced, including persecution for their non-conformity to the culture of the Jews but also the Roman religious norms. Jews that converted and believed Jesus was the Messiah lost everything, family, property, status, and all the advantages in their former life.

This age also saw complex interactions within the Jewish community concerning Jesus's identity and role, debates that Hebrews addresses by advocating for the supremacy of Christ and the new covenant, aiming to define the Jewish Christians' place within the larger Jewish tradition.

D. Relationship to Judaism

Hebrews navigates a nuanced relationship with Judaism. While deeply rooted in Jewish scriptures and traditions, it rejects the Old Testament sacrificial system and positions Jesus as the ultimate high priest of a new covenant. This assessment is a replacement of Judaism in the light of Christ's life and mission, asserting Jesus as the fulfillment of the Law of Moses and the prophets and the zenith of God's salvation plan.

E. Historical Impact on Early Christianity

The Book of Hebrews profoundly influenced early Christian thought, enriching theological discourse with its unique interpretations of Jesus's life and work. It bolstered the community's faith, urging resilience amidst persecution and significantly shaped the perception of Christ as the ultimate mediator and high priest. Christ became the all in all, and the Judaizers hated what they were seeing.

Moreover, Hebrews contributed to the evolving discourse on Christianity's separation from Judaism, challenging established Jewish doctrines and practices, thereby setting the stage for a distinct Christian identity. The historical context of the Book of Hebrews is essential for understanding Christianity. The audience of Hebrews consisted of Jewish Christians facing persecution and struggling with their faith. The book's socio-political background reflects the challenges faced by Jewish believers under Roman rule and their relationship with the broader Jewish community. Regarding its relationship to Judaism, Hebrews presents a revelation of key Jewish elements in light of Jesus Christ. The book argues for the superiority of Christ and the new covenant He established, while also affirming the continuity between the Old Testament and the new covenant. Finally, the Book of Hebrews had a lasting impact on early Christianity, shaping Christian theology, providing inspiration for believers. Just as there were five warnings in this letter to not go back to Judaism, we see that many factions sprung up over the centuries that combine Judaism and Christianity, trying to blend them together creating a mixture that will never produce a full expression of the glorious and holy Son of God.

V. Conclusion

The Book of Hebrews weaves a complex and intricate theological fabric that resonates deeply within the sphere of Christian thought and practice. Through meticulous examination of its central themes, this paper unveils the pivotal roles of faith and perseverance, the unparalleled supremacy of Christ, and the nuanced theories of covenant theology. It also delves into the high priesthood of Jesus, the stern warnings against apostasy, and the comforting promise of eternal rest promised to the followers of God, all of which anchor this profound epistle.

Further enriching this exploration, the theological dimensions of Christology, soteriology, eschatology, and pneumatology are dissected alongside a comparative study with Pauline epistles. These examinations shed light on the deep theological insights the text harbors, enhancing our understanding and underscoring its significance amid the broader expanse of early Christian doctrine. The profound theological depth and the sweeping exploration of Jesus Christ's person and works have indelibly shaped the Christian identity and ethos across time. By portraying Jesus as the magnificent high priest in the order of Melchizedek and the fulfillment of ancient prophecies, the book of Hebrews lays a robust foundation for believers' faith, offering them a persuasive cause to persist amid adversities.

Ultimately, the Book of Hebrews stands as a formidable testament to the power and pertinence of biblical theology. Its discourse on faith, Christ's supremacy, covenant theology, the high priesthood of Jesus, warnings against apostasy, and the assured rest for God's adherents continues to inspire and provoke thought among believers. Engaging with its theological perspectives and historical contexts allows scholars and devout readers alike to unearth its profound insights and appreciate its enduring legacy within the Christian faith.

Terry Kashian

Hebrews

Chapter 1

1. God, who at various times and in different ways spoke of old to the fathers in the prophets,
2. Has at these last days spoken to us in the Son, Whom He has placed as the legal owner of all things, through Whom also He made the Old Covenant Age;
3. Who being the brilliance of His glory, and the exact duplicate of His essence, and carrying upon Himself everyone, by the power of His speaking, making a cleansing of our sins by Himself, and sat in the right hand of the Majesty in the highest:
4. Becoming so much better than the angels, as He has received as an inheritance, a superior name than they.
5. For to which of the angels did He ever say, You are My Son, today I have begotten You? And again, I will be a Father to Him, and He will be a Son to Me?
6. And again, when He brings the firstborn into the Roman world, He is saying, and let all the angels of God worship Him.
7. But of the angels He is saying, who is making His angels spirits and His ministers a flame of fire.
8. But to the Son He is saying, Your throne, O God, into the New Covenant Age from the Old Covenant Age: a scepter of righteousness is the scepter of Your kingdom.
9. You have loved righteousness, and hated lawlessness; therefore God, even Your God, has anointed You with the oil of gladness above your companions.
10. So, You, Lord, in the beginning, have founded the earth; and the heavens are the works of your hands:
11. They will be destroyed, but You remain, and they all will be made old like a garment;
12. And as a cloak You fold them up, and they will be changed: but You are the same, and Your years will not cease.
13. Which of the angels did He ever say, sit at My right hand, until I make Your enemies Your footstool?
14. Are they not all ministering spirits, sent out to minister to them who are about to be heirs of salvation?

Chapter 2

1. Therefore, we ought to give abundant attentiveness to the things which we have heard, unless perhaps we could be wandering away.
2. For if the word spoken by angels was steadfast, and every violation and refusing to hear received a fair compensation;
3. Then how will we escape, if we neglect so great a salvation; which at first began to be spoken by the Lord, and was confirmed to us by them that heard Him;
4. God also giving them witness, both with signs and wonders, and with various miracles, and allocations of the Holy Spirit, according to His own will?
5. For to the angels He has not put in subjection the inhabited earth about to come, of which we speak.

6. But one in a certain place testified, saying, what is Man, that You are conscious of Him? Or the Son of Man that You watch over Him?
7. You made Him a little lower than the angels; You crowned Him with glory and honor, and installed Him over the works of Your hands:
8. You have put all things in subjection under His feet. For in that He put all in subjection under Him, He left nothing that is not put under Him. But now we do not yet see all things put under Him.
9. But we see Jesus, who was made a little lower than the angels by the suffering of death, crowned with glory and honor; so that He by the grace of God experienced death in the place of all.
10. For it was appropriate for Him, for whom are all things, and by whom are all things, in leading many sons into glory, to make the Captain of their salvation complete through sufferings.
11. For both He that sanctifies and they who are sanctified are all out of One: for which reason He is not ashamed to call them brothers,
12. Saying I will proclaim Your name to My brothers, within the Assembly, I will be singing hymns to You.
13. And again, I will have My confidence in Him. And again, behold I and the children who God has given Me.
14. Since the little children are partakers of blood and flesh, He also Himself nearly pertaining to them; that through death, He might make inactive him that had the power of death, that is the devil;
15. And deliver them who through fear of death all their lives were subject to bondage.
16. For certain He did not take possession of angels, but He did take possession of the offspring of Abraham.
17. Therefore, He was obligated in all things to be prepared externally like the brothers, that He might be a merciful and faithful high priest in things pertaining to God, to make a complete appeasement for the sins of the people.
18. For in that He Himself has suffered being tempted, He has the ability to help those who are being tempted.

Chapter 3

1. Therefore, holy brothers, companions of the heavenly calling, consider the Apostle and High Priest of our confession, Jesus;
2. Who was faithful to Him who makes Him, as also Moses was faithful in all his house.
3. For He has been counted worthy of more recognition than Moses, inasmuch, as He who has built the house has more value than the house.
4. For every house is fully prepared by someone, but He that fully prepared all things is God.
5. And Moses truly was faithful in all His house, as a serving companion, for a testimony of those things which were to be spoken in the future;
6. But Christ as a Son over His own house; whose house we are if we hold fast the confidence and the rejoicing of the hope firm until the end.

7. Therefore, as the Holy Spirit says, today if you will hear His voice,
8. Do not harden your hearts, as in the day of testing in the wilderness:
9. When your fathers tried Me and tested Me and saw My works for forty years.
10. Therefore, I was nauseous with that generation, and said, they continually wander in their hearts; and they have not known My ways.
11. So, I swore in My wrath, they will not enter into My rest.
12. See the warning, brothers, unless there be in any of you an evil heart of unbelief, in withdrawing from the living God.
13. But exhort one another daily, while it is called today; unless any of you be hardened through the deceitfulness of sin.
14. For we have become companions of Christ if we hold the beginning of our assurance steadfast to the end;
15. While it is said, today if you will hear His voice, harden not your hearts, as in the bitter exasperation.
16. For some, when they had heard, did exasperate: however, not all that came out of Egypt by Moses.
17. But with whom was He nauseous for forty years? Was it not with those who kept sinning, whose corpses fell in the wilderness?
18. And to whom did He swear that they should not enter into His rest, but to those that did not believe?
19. So, we see that they could not enter in because of unbelief.

Chapter 4

1. Let us fear for sure, unless at any time, the promise being forsaken of entering into His rest, anyone should seem to come short of it.
2. For to us was the good news announced, as well as to them: but the word heard did not profit them, not being mixed with faith in them that heard it.
3. For we who have believed are coming into rest, as He said, as I have sworn in My wrath, they will not enter into My rest: although the works apart from the downfall of the world were occurring.
4. For He spoke in a certain way concerning the seventh day, and God did rest the seventh day from all His works.
5. And in this place again, they will not enter into My rest.
6. Therefore, seeing it remains that some must enter in it, and they to whom it was first evangelized, entered not in because of disobedience:
7. Again, He defined a certain day, saying in David, today, after so long a time; as it is said, today if you will hear His voice, do not harden your hearts.
8. For if Joshua had given them rest, then He would not afterward have spoken of another day?
9. Therefore, there remains a rest for the people of God.
10. For he that is entering into His rest, he also has ceased from his own works, as God did from His.

11. Therefore, let us be diligent to enter into that rest, unless anyone falls after the same pattern of stubbornness.
12. For the Word of God is living, and energetic, and sharper than any two-edged sword, penetrating even to the dividing apart of soul and spirit, and of the joints and marrow, and is a discerner of the thoughts and intentions of the heart.
13. There is nothing in creation that is unseen by Him: but all things are naked and exposed to the eyes of Him before whom we are accountable.
14. Seeing then that we have a great high priest, that is passed into the heavens, Jesus the Son of God, let us hold fast our confession.
15. For we do not have a high priest who cannot be compassionate of our weaknesses; but was in all aspects tempted just as we are, yet without sin.
16. Therefore, let us advance boldly to the throne of grace, that we may obtain mercy, and find grace to help in a needy time.

Chapter 5

1. For every high priest chosen from among men is inaugurated for men in the things of God, that he may offer both gifts and sacrifices for sins:
2. Who can be moderate on the ignorant, and on them that are wandering; for he also is encompassed with weaknesses.
3. And for this reason, he is obligated, concerning the people, so also for himself, to offer for sins.
4. And no man chooses this honor for himself, but he that is called of God, as was Aaron.
5. So, also Christ glorified not Himself to be made a high priest; but He that said to Him, You are My Son, today have I begotten You.
6. As He says also in another place, You are a priest into the New Covenant Age after the order of Melchizedek.
7. This One in the days of His flesh, when He had offered up prayers and supplications with strong crying and tears unto Him that was able to save Him out of death and was heard in that He was devoted;
8. Though He was a Son, yet He learned obedience by the things which He suffered;
9. And being made complete, He became the source of perpetual salvation to all them that are obeying Him;
10. Called of God a high priest after the order of Melchizedek.
11. Concerning whom we have many things to say, and difficult to interpret, seeing you are obtuse in hearing.
12. For by this time you ought to be teachers, you have need that one teach you again the basic parts of the beginning of the oracles of God; and have become such that need milk, and not of solid food.
13. For every one that uses milk is inexperienced in the word of righteousness: for he is a babe that cannot speak.
14. But solid food belongs to those that are fully grown, even those who through experience have their intuitive powers trained to discern both good and evil.

Chapter 6

1. For this reason, break away from the beginning word of the Christ, let us be brought forth to completion; not laying down again the foundation of repentance from dead works, and of faith toward God,
2. Of the teaching of washings, and of laying on of hands, and of the resurrection of the dead, and perpetual judgment.
3. And this we will be doing if God is allowing.
4. For it is impossible for those who were once enlightened, and have tasted of the heavenly gift, and were made partakers of the Holy Spirit,
5. And have tasted the good word of God, and the powers of the New Covenant Age about to be coming,
6. If they fall aside, to renew them again into repentance; seeing they crucify to themselves the Son of God again and are exposed to an open shame.
7. For the ground which drinks in the rain that often comes on it, brings forth vegetation suitable for them by whom it is cultivated, receives a blessing from God:
8. But that which bears thorns and thistles is rejected, and is near cursing; whose end is to be a place of burning.
9. But, beloved, we are persuaded better things of you, and things that accompany salvation, though we are speaking this.
10. For God is not unrighteous to forget your work and labor of love, which you have shown toward His name, in that you have served the saints, and are serving still.
11. And we want everyone to show the same diligence to the full assurance of hope to the end:
12. That you be not obtuse, but followers of those who through faith and patience inherit the promises.
13. For when God made a promise to Abraham because He could swear by no one greater, He swore by Himself,
14. Saying, surely blessing I will bless you, and multiplying I will multiply you.
15. And so, after he had patiently endured, he obtained the promise.
16. For men swear by the greater: and an oath for confirmation is to them an end of all contradictions.
17. Therefore God, willing more abundantly to show to the heirs of promise the unchangeableness of His counsel, confirmed it by an oath:
18. That by two unchangeable things, in which God can not lie, we might have a strong consolation, who are fleeing for refuge to take hold of the hope set before us:
19. Which hope we have as an anchor of the soul, both immovable and fixed, and which enters into within the veil;
20. Where the forerunner has for us entered, Jesus, beginning to be the high priest into the New Covenant Age after the order of Melchizedek.

Chapter 7

1. For this Melchizedek, king of Salem, priest of the Most High God, who met Abraham returning from the slaughter of the kings, and blessed him;

2. To who also Abraham gave a tenth part of all; first being by interpretation King of righteousness, and after that also King of Salem, which is, King of peace;
3. Without father, without mother, without descent, having neither beginning of days, nor end of life, but made like to the Son of God; remains a priest perpetually.
4. Now consider how great this one was, to whom even the patriarch Abraham gave a tenth of the choice goods.
5. And indeed those of the sons of Levi, who receive the priesthood, have a command to receive a tenth from the people according to the Law, that is, of their brothers, though they come out of the reproductive system of Abraham.
6. However, he whose genealogy is not counted from them, received a tenth from Abraham, and he blessed him that had the promises.
7. And without any dispute the lesser is blessed by the greater.
8. And here men that die receive tenths; but there he receives them, of whom it is witnessed that he lives.
9. And as I may say so, Levi also, who receives tenths, paid a tenth in Abraham.
10. For he was yet in the reproductive system of his father when Melchizedek met him.
11. Therefore, if completion was by the Levitical priesthood, (for under it the people received the Law) what further need was there that another priest should arise after the order of Melchizedek, and not be called after the order of Aaron?
12. For the priesthood being removed, there is beginning to be by necessity a removing also of the Law.
13. For he of whom these things are spoken pertains to another tribe, of which no man served at the altar.
14. For it is evident that our Lord sprang out of Judah; of which tribe Moses spoke nothing concerning priesthood.
15. And it is yet far more evident: for that after the likeness of Melchizedek there arises another priest,
16. Who is made, not after the Law of a fleshly commandment, but according to the power of an invincible life.
17. For it is testified, You are a priest going into the New Covenant Age after the order of Melchizedek.
18. On one hand there is a cancellation of the commandment before us because of the weakness and fruitlessness of it.
19. For the Law made nothing complete, but the bringing in of a better hope did; through which we are drawing near to God.
20. And in as much as not separate from an oath,
21. (for those became priests without an oath; but this with an oath by Him that said to Him, the Lord swore and will not be regretting, You are a priest going into the New Covenant Age after the order of Melchizedek:)
22. By so much was Jesus made a guarantee of a better covenant.
23. And there were indeed many priests because they were not permitted to continue because of death:

24. But this One, because He continues into the New Covenant Age, has an inviolable priesthood.
25. Therefore, He is able also to save them completely that are advancing to God through Him, seeing He is always living to make intercession for them.
26. For such a high priest stands out to us, who is holy, harmless, undefiled, separate from sinners, and made higher than the heavens;
27. Who does not need daily, as those high priests, to offer up sacrifice, first for their own sins, and then for the peoples: for He did this once when He offered up Himself.
28. For the Law makes men high priests who have feebleness; but the word of the promise, which is in the Law, makes the Son into the New Covenant Age complete.

Chapter 8

1. Now of the things which we have spoken the epitome is this: we have such a high priest, who sat in the right hand of the throne of the Majesty in the heavens;
2. A minister of the sanctuary, and of the true tabernacle, which the Lord pitched, and not man.
3. For every high priest is ordained to offer gifts and sacrifices: therefore, it is of necessity that this Man have somewhat also to offer.
4. For if He remained upon the land, He would not be a priest, some offer gifts according to the Law:
5. Who serve as a pattern and shadow of the heavenly, as Moses was advised when he was about to complete the tabernacle: then, see to it, He says, that you make all things according to the pattern presented to you on the mountain.
6. But now He has achieved a more excellent ministry, so much greater is He also, the Mediator of a superior covenant, which was established on superior promises.
7. For if that first covenant had been blameless, then no place would have been sought for the second.
8. Then blaming them, He says, behold, the days are coming, says the Lord, when I will make a New Covenant with the house of Israel and with the house of Judah:
9. Not according to the covenant which I made with their fathers in the day when I took them by the hand to lead them out of the land of Egypt; because they continued not in My covenant, and I showed no care for them, says the Lord.
10. For this is the covenant that I will arrange with the house of Israel after those days, says the Lord; I will supply My Laws into their mind, and write them upon their hearts: and I will be to them God, and they will be to Me a people:
11. And they will not teach everyone his neighbor, and everyone his brother, saying, know the Lord: for all will know Me, from the least to the greatest.
12. For I will be merciful to their unrighteousness, and their sins and their lawlessness's will I remember no more.

Hebrews 8:13

13. In that He says, a new covenant, He has rendered the first obsolete. Now that which decays and is growing old is near vanishing away.

Chapter 9

1. Therefore indeed, the first even had ordinances of divine service and a worldly sanctuary.
2. For there was a tabernacle built; the first, in which was the candlestick, and the table, and the setting forth of the bread; which is called holy place.
3. And after the second veil, the tabernacle which is called the Holiest of Holies;
4. Which had the golden censer, and the Ark of the Covenant covered around every place with gold, in which was the golden container that had manna, and Aaron's rod that blossomed, and the tablets of the covenant;
5. And over it the cherubim of glory shadowing the mercy seat; of which we cannot now speak in detail.
6. Now, when these were built in this way, the priests always went into the first Tabernacle, accomplishing the service of God.
7. But into the second went the high priest alone once every year, not without blood, which he offered for himself, and the ignorance's of the people:
8. The Holy Spirit is signifying this, that the way into the Holiest of all was not yet made manifest, while the first tabernacle has its existence:

9. Which is a parable for the present time, according to which both gifts and sacrifices are being offered and are not able to complete in respect to the conscience of the one serving;
10. Consisting only of foods and drinks, and different washings, and fleshly ordinances, imposed on them until the time of the amendment.
11. But Christ having come a high priest of good things about to come, by a greater and more complete tabernacle, not made with hands, that is not of this creation;
12. Neither by the blood of goats and calves, but by His own blood, He entered in once for all into the Holy of Holies, having obtained perpetual redemption for us!
13. For if the blood of bulls and goats, and the ashes of a heifer sprinkling the unclean, sanctifies to the purifying of the flesh:
14. How much more will the blood of Christ, who through the Infinite Spirit offered Himself unblemished to God, purge your conscience from dead works to serve the living God?
15. So, for this reason He is the Mediator of the New Covenant that through death, for the redemption of the transgressions that were under the first covenant, those who are called might take the promise of a perpetual inheritance.
16. For where a testament is, there must also of necessity be the death of the will-maker.
17. For a testament is of force after men are dead: otherwise, it is of no value at all while the will-maker lives.

18. Where neither the first covenant was dedicated without blood.

19. For when Moses had spoken every precept to all the people according to the Law, he took the blood of calves and goats, with water, and scarlet wool, and hyssop, and sprinkled both the book and all the people,

20. Saying, this is the blood of the covenant which God has commanded to you.

21. Moreover, he sprinkled with blood both the tabernacle and all the vessels of the ministry.

22. And almost all things by the Law are being cleansed with blood, and without the shedding of blood, there is no forgiveness.

23. Therefore, it was necessary that the copies of the things in the heavens should be purified with these; but the heavenly things themselves with better sacrifices than these.

24. For Christ has not entered into the holy of holies made with hands, which are copies of the real; but into heaven itself, now to appear in the presence of God for us:

25. Nor yet that He should offer Himself frequently, as the high priest enters into the holy of holies every year with the blood of others;

26. For then He certainly would be suffering frequently from the downfall of the world: but now once at the completion of the Old Covenant Age He has appeared to put away sin by the sacrifice of Himself.

27. And as it is reserved for men to die once, but after this judgment:

28. So, Christ also, being offered once to bear the sins of many; and to those who are looking for Him, He will be seen out from the second time, apart from sin for deliverance.

Chapter 10

1. For the Law having a shadow of good things about to come, and not the very image of the things, can never with those sacrifices which they offered year by year continually make the comers complete.

2. For then they would not have ceased to be offered? They would no longer have sins on their conscience.

3. But in those sacrifices, there is a remembrance of sins every year.

4. For it is impossible that the blood of bulls and goats should remove sins.

5. Therefore, when He came into the world, He said, sacrifice and offering You do not desire, but a body You have prepared for Me:

6. In wholly burned offerings and sacrifices for sin You are not well pleased.

7. Then I said, behold, I come (in the volume of the book it is written of Me) to do Your will, O God.

8. Above when He said, sacrifice and offering and wholly burned offerings and offering for sin You do not desire, neither are well pleased; by what is offered by the Law;

9. Then I said, behold, I come to do Your will, O God. He is removing the first, so that He may establish the second.

10. By this one will we are sanctified through the offering of the body of Jesus Christ once and for all.

11. For every priest stands daily ministering and offering oftentimes the same sacrifices, which can never take away sins:
12. But this One, after He had offered one sacrifice for sins for perpetuity, sat down in the right hand of God;
13. From now on expecting until His enemies are put as a footstool under His feet.
14. For by one offering He has completed into perpetuity those that are sanctified.
15. Of whom the Holy Spirit also is a witness to us: for after that He had said before,
16. This is the covenant that I will make with them after those days, says the Lord, I will put My Laws into their hearts, and in their minds will I write them;
17. And their sins and lawlessness's I will remember no more.
18. Now, where forgiveness of these is, there is no longer an offering for sin.
19. Therefore brothers, having boldness to enter into the Holy of Holies by the blood of Jesus,
20. By a freshly slain and living way, which He has consecrated for us, through the veil, that is to say, His flesh;
21. And having a great priest over the house of God;
22. Let us advance with a true heart in full assurance of faith, having our hearts sprinkled from an evil conscience, and our bodies washed with pure water.
23. Let us hold fast the confession of our faith without wavering; for He is faithful that promised.
24. And let us perceive one another clearly to stimulate love and good works:
25. Not forsaking the assembling of ourselves together, as the usual practice of some; but exhorting one another: and so much the more, as you see that Day coming near.
26. For if we sin willfully after we have received the knowledge of the reality, there are no longer sacrifices for sins left,
27. But a certain terrible expectation of judgment and fiery indignation, which is about to devour the adversaries.
28. He that rejected Moses' Law died without mercy under two or three witnesses:
29. Of how much worse vengeance, do you think, will he be counted deserving, who has trampled underfoot the Son of God, and has counted the blood of the covenant, with which he was sanctified, an unholy thing, and has insulted the Spirit of grace?
30. For we know Him who has said, vengeance belongs to Me, I will pay back, says the Lord. And again, the Lord will judge His people.
31. It is a fearful thing to fall into the hands of the living God!
32. But remember the former days in which, after you were elucidated, you endured a great conflict of sufferings;
33. Partly while you were made a spectacle both by insults and afflictions; and partly, while you became companions of them that were so treated.

34. For you had compassion for me in my chains, and accepted joyfully the plundering of your possessions, knowing in yourselves that you have a better possession and one that is abiding.
35. Therefore, do not lose your courage, which has a huge reward.
36. For you need endurance, that, after you have done the will of God, you acquire the promise.
37. For yet a little while, and He that will come will come, and He will not delay.
38. Now, the just will live by faith: but if anyone withdraws, My soul will not be well pleasing in him.
39. But we are not of those who are shrinking back into perdition; but of those who are believing into taking possession of the soul.

Chapter 11

1. Now, faith is the authentication of things expected, the convincing of things being done that are not seen.
2. For by it the elders obtained a good testimony.
3. Through faith we understand that the Old Covenant Age was furnished completely by the speaking of God regarding the things which are visible and it does not have its origin out of that which is appearing.
4. By faith Abel offered to God a more excellent sacrifice than Cain, by which he obtained the testimony that he was righteous, God testifying of his gifts: and by it, he being dead yet speaks.
5. By faith Enoch was removed that he should not know death; and was not found, because God had translated him: for before his removal he had this testimony, that he pleased God.
6. But without faith it is impossible to please Him: for he that advances to God must believe that He is, and that He is rewarding them that diligently seek Him out.
7. By faith Noah, being warned by God of things not yet seen, moved with fear, built an ark for the salvation of his house; by which he condemned the world, and became heir of the righteousness which is by faith.
8. By faith Abraham, when he was called to go out into a place which he was about to receive for an inheritance, obeyed; and he went out, not knowing to where he was going.
9. By faith he dwelt as a foreigner in the land of promise, as in a strange country, dwelling in tabernacles with Isaac and Jacob, the heirs with him of the same promise:
10. For he looked for a city which has foundations, whose Designer and Builder is God.
11. Through faith also Sarah herself received the power to conceive an offspring and was delivered of a child when she was past age because she judged Him faithful who had promised.
12. Therefore, sprang there even one, and him as good as dead, so many as the stars of the heavens in multitude, and as the sand which is by the seashore innumerable.

Hebrews 11:13

13. These all died in faith, not having received the promises, but having seen them far off, and were persuaded by them, and embraced them, and confessed that they were strangers and pilgrims on the land.
14. For they that say such things declare plainly that they seek a fatherland.
15. And truly, if they had been mindful of from where they came out, they might have had an opportunity to have returned.
16. But now they desire a better, that is, a heavenly: therefore, God is not ashamed to be called their God: for He made ready for them a city.
17. By faith Abraham, when he was tested, offered up Isaac: and he that had received the promises offered up his only begotten son,
18. Of whom it was said, that in Isaac will your offspring be called:
19. Counting that God was able to raise him up, even from the dead; from where also he received him back as a parable.
20. By faith Isaac blessed Jacob and Esau about things that are about to come.
21. By faith Jacob, when he was dying, blessed both the sons of Joseph; and worshipped, leaning on the top of his staff.
22. By faith Joseph, when he died, made mention of the exodus of the children of Israel; and gave a command concerning his bones.
23. By faith Moses, when he was born, was hidden for three months by his parents, because they saw he was a handsome child; and they were not afraid of the king's decree.
24. By faith Moses, when he had become great, disowned Pharaoh's daughter and to be called her son,
25. Choosing rather to be treated with adversity with the people of God than to have the enjoyment of sin for a season;
26. Counting the revilement of Christ greater wealth than the treasures in Egypt: for he fixed his eyes earnestly on the reward.
27. By faith he left Egypt, not fearing the wrath of Pharaoh: for he endured, as seeing Him who is invisible.
28. Through faith he kept the Passover, and the sprinkling of blood, so that the destroying one should not touch the firstborns.
29. By faith they passed through the Red Sea as on dry land: when the Egyptians attempted were drowned.
30. By faith the walls of Jericho collapsed after they encircled them seven days.
31. By faith the prostitute Rahab did not perish with them that believed not, having received the spies with peace.
32. And what more will I say? For the time would fail me to tell of Gideon, and of Barak, and Samson, and Jephthah; of David also, and Samuel, and of the prophets:
33. Who through faith subdued kingdoms, worked righteousness, obtained promises, and stopped the mouths of lions.
34. Quenched the violence of fire, escaped the edge of the sword, out of weakness were made strong, grown valiant in war, the armies of the foreigners were caused to back down.
35. Women received their dead raised to life again: and others were tortured, not accepting deliverance; that they might obtain a better resurrection:

Hebrews 11:36

36. And others had trials of cruel mocking and scourging, yes, moreover of chains and prison:
37. They were stoned, they were sawn in pieces, were tempted, and were slain with the sword: they wandered about in sheepskins and goatskins; being homeless, afflicted, tormented;
38. (Of whom the world was not worthy:) they wandered in deserted places, and mountains, and in dens and caves of the land.
39. So, these all, having obtained a good testimony through faith, received not the promise:
40. God having provided some better thing for us, that they without us should not be made complete.

Chapter 12

1. Therefore, seeing we also are surrounded by so great a cloud of witnesses, let us lay aside every weight, and the sin which does so easily entangle us, and let us run with endurance the race that is set before us,
2. Looking away into Jesus the chief leader and consummator of faith; who for the joy that was set before Him suffered the cross, despising the shame, and has sat down at the right hand of the throne of God.
3. Examine Him that suffered such a contradiction of sinners against Himself, that you do not faint in your souls and let go.
4. You have not yet laid down your life, contending against sin.
5. And you have forgotten the exhortation which speaks to you as sons, My son, despise not the child training of the Lord, nor lose heart when you are rebuked by Him:
6. For whom the Lord loves He corrects, and punishes every son whom He embraces.
7. If you endure child training, God deals with you as with sons; for what son is he who the father corrects not?
8. But if you be without child training, of which all are partakers, then you are illegitimate, and not sons.
9. Furthermore, we have had fathers in our flesh who corrected us, and we gave them respect: should we not be even more willing to be subject to the Father of spirits and live?
10. For they truthfully for a few days were child training us as it seemed good to them; but He for our development, that participating into His holiness.
11. Now, no child training for the present seems to be joyous, but sorrowful: nevertheless, afterward, it yields the peaceable fruit of righteousness to those who have been trained through it.
12. Therefore, the hands which hang down, and the paralyzed knees make upright;
13. And make upright paths for your feet, so that which is lame be not put out of joint; but let it rather be made whole.
14. Go after peace with all men, and holiness, without it no one will be seeing the Lord:
15. Overseeing that no one comes too late for the grace of God, nor any root of bitterness springing up agitating, and through this, many are contaminated;

16. Nor any fornicator, or godless person, as Esau, who for one meal sold his birthright.

17. For you know that afterward when he desired to inherit the blessing, he was rejected: for he found no place of repentance, though he sought it earnestly with tears.

18. For you have not advanced to the mountain that may be touched, and that burned with fire, nor to blackness, and darkness, and whirlwind,

19. And the sound of a trumpet, and the voice of words; which voice they who heard begged that no further word should be added to them:

20. For they could not hold up under what was commanded, and if so, much as a beast touched the mountain, it would be stoned, or shot with an arrow:

21. And so terrible was the sight, that Moses said, I exceedingly fear and tremble:

22. But you have advanced to Mount Zion, and the city of the living God, the heavenly Jerusalem, and to an innumerable company of angels,

23. To the Assembly of the firstborn ones, having been written in the heavens, and to God the Judge of all, and the spirits of the just made complete,

24. And to Jesus the Mediator of the new covenant, and to the blood of sprinkling, that speaks better things than that of Abel.

25. See that you are not refusing Him that is speaking. For if they escaped not who refused Him who warned them on the earth, much more we will not escape, if we turn away from Him in the heavens:

26. Whose voice then shook the earth: but now He has promised, saying, yet once more I shake not the earth only, but also the heavens.

27. And this word, yet once more, signifies the removing of those things which are being shaken, as of things that are made, that those things which are not being shaken may remain.

28. Therefore, we are taking the unmovable kingdom, let us possess grace, through which we may serve God well pleasingly with respect and godly fear:

29. For our God is a consuming fire!

Chapter 13

1. Let brotherly love continue.

2. Do not be forgetful to show hospitality to strangers: for through this some have lodged messengers not knowing it.

3. Remember them that are in chains, as chained with them; and those who are tortured, as being also in the body yourselves.

4. Marriage is to be held precious in all, and the bed undefiled: but fornicators and adulterers God will judge.

5. Let your conduct be without covetousness, and be content with such things as you have: for He has said, I will never leave you, nor forsake you.

6. So that we may boldly say, the Lord is my helper, and I will not fear what man will do to me.

7. Remember those who have taken the lead among you, who have spoken to you the word of God: follow their faith, contemplating the outcome of their demeanor.

8. Jesus Christ the same yesterday, and today, and into the New Covenant Age.

9. Be not carried about with various strange teachings. It is good that the heart be established by grace; not with food, which is not profitable to those who have walked that way.

10. We have an altar, where they have no right to eat who serve the tabernacle.

11. For the bodies of those animals, whose blood is brought into the Holy of Holies by the high priest for sin, are burned outside the camp.

12. Therefore, Jesus also, that He might sanctify the people with His own blood, suffered outside the gate.

13. Therefore, let us go out to Him outside the camp, bearing His reproach.

14. For here have we no continuing city, but we seek one about to come.

15. Therefore, through Him let us offer the sacrifice of praise to God continually, that is, the fruit of our lips that confess His name.

16. Now, well-doing and contributing do not forget: for with such sacrifices God is well pleased.

17. Be persuaded by them that have taken the lead among you and yield yourselves: for they are watchful over your souls, as they that must give a report, that they may do it with joy, and not with groaning: for that is fruitless for you.

18. Pray for us: for we are persuaded we have a good conscience in all things willing to live honorably.

19. But I urge you to rather do this, that I may be restored to you more swiftly.

20. Now, the God of peace, who brought out from among the dead our Lord Jesus, the great Shepherd of the sheep, through the blood of the perpetual covenant,

21. Furnish you completely in every good work to do His will, working in you that which is well pleasing in His sight, through Jesus Christ; to whom be glory into the New Covenant Age from the Old Covenant Age. Amen.

22. And I urge you, brothers, receive the word of exhortation: for I have written a letter to you in few words.

23. Know that our brother Timothy is now released; with whom if I come promptly, I will be seeing you.

24. Greet all those that are leading you, and all the saints. They of Italy greet you.

25. Grace be with you all. Amen.

James Commentary

I. Introduction (James 1:1)

   A. Greeting to the twelve tribes
   B. Authorship attributed to James, the Lord's brother and written in AD 62

II. Trials and Maturity (James 1:2-18)

   A. Joy in trials, producing steadfastness
   B. Wisdom and faith in times of testing
   C. True religion is caring for the vulnerable

III. Hearing and Doing (James 1:19-27)

   A. Be quick to listen, slow to speak, and slow to anger
   B. Doers of the word, not just hearers

IV. Showing No Partiality (James 2:1-13)

   A. Do not show favoritism
   B. Mercy triumphs over judgment

V. Faith and Works (James 2:14-26)

   A. Faith without works is dead
   B. Abraham and Rahab as examples of faith and works

VI. Taming the Tongue (James 3:1-12)

   A. Warning against the power of the tongue
   B. The need for self-control and purity in speech

VII. Wisdom from Above (James 3:13-18)

   A. True wisdom from God is pure, peaceable, and gentle
   B. The fruit of righteousness is sown in peace by those who make peace

VIII. Friendship with the World (James 4:1-10)

    A. Warning against worldly desires and pleasures

    B. Drawing near to God and resisting the devil

IX. The Uncertainty of Life (James 4:13-17)

    A. Boasting about the future is foolish

    B. The need for humility and dependence on God

X. Rich Oppressors Condemned (James 5:1-6)

    A. Warnings to the wealthy oppressors

    B. The cries of the oppressed heard by the Lord

XI. Patience in Suffering (James 5:7-12)

    A. Exhortation to be patient in suffering

    B. Let your yes be yes and your no be no

XII. Prayer and Mutual Confession (James 5:13-20)

    A. Call to prayer in all circumstances

    B. The power of prayer and confession for healing and restoration

Overall Theme: Endurance in the face of trials, the importance of faith accompanied by works, and the call to maturity in Christ.

Martin Luther's most popular statements about the Epistle of James, "I will not have it in my Bible" and "[James] mangles the Scriptures and thus contradicts Paul and all of Scripture" or "St. James' epistle is a real epistle of straw [...] for it has no evangelical way about it," suggest that the message of James was inconsistent with the Reformer's theology. These are some quotes from Martin Luther who was considered a giant in the faith. It is important for us to realize that when God uses anyone in a large or small way, they can have opinions that are not of God. In this case Luther, he was dead wrong. Anyone with a little spiritual acumen would recognize that the epistle of James was right out of the sermon on the mount. I counted at least 26 times James alludes to the sermon on the mount. There are 108 verses in the letter of James and 26 references to Jesus. Twenty-five percent of the letter of James is Jesus' direct teaching. The is just the sermon on the mount unpacked and some of the other references are also from the teachings of Jesus. I don't have room to list them, but the diligent student will find this quite interesting and profitable. Many bible teachers have given James a bad rap, mainly because of his, 'faith and works' idea in his letter.

Remember audience relevance is key to looking at this letter. The twelve tribes scattered throughout the Roman Empire. Jewish minded people, and this letter is written to saved and unsaved Jews. He covers both in this epistle. I will identify his applications. James has a burden for all of Old Covenant Israel.

James 1:2 My brothers, consider it all joy when you fall into various trials; 3 knowing that the testing of your faith develops persistence. 4 But let persistence have her complete work, that you may be complete and whole, lacking nothing. Matthew 5:12, Matt. 5:48 is James referencing Jesus. Being perfect is being complete, mature, and perfect.

My understanding of this letter is that James is explaining how the Lord is maturing and perfecting His church, and He will get a ripe harvest in the end. In this passage from James, the author is emphasizing the idea that trials and difficulties are opportunities for growth and maturity in our lives. He states that we should "consider it pure joy" when we face trials because they have the potential to produce persistent endurance and develop our character and bring us to full maturity.

James is encouraging his readers to view struggles as a refining process that ultimately leads to a deeper level of spiritual maturity. Just as the process of refining gold requires just as intense heat and pressure purify by removing impurities, our trials and challenges refine and strengthen us.

By persevering through trials and relying on God for strength and wisdom, we can cultivate a sense of perseverance and steadfastness in our faith. This process of growth and maturation leads us to become more complete and whole individuals, able to handle adversity with grace and resilience.

Ultimately, James is reminding us that trials are not to be feared or avoided, but rather embraced as opportunities for growth. Through facing and overcoming challenges, we can develop a deeper faith and a more mature character, ultimately becoming more like Christ in the process. These trials provide opportunities for the saints to lack nothing, they are perfected by them.

1:5 If any of you are lacking wisdom, let him be asking of God, who is giving to all generously, without finding fault; and it will be given to him. Matt. 7:7 'Ask, and it shall be given to you; seek, and you shall find; knock, and it shall be opened to you; 8 for everyone who is asking does receive, and he who is seeking does find, and to him who is knocking it shall be opened.[131]

James now says if you are lacking, ask continually to God to supply wisdom. Wisdom is the ability to use your experience and knowledge in order to make sensible decisions or judgments. Keep asking continually God to supply the ability to make sensible decisions and good judgments. James emphasizes the generosity of God in this matter. This is God's

---

[131] Young, R. (1997). *Young's Literal Translation* (Mt 7:7–8). Logos Bible Software.

open hand, and He will not find any fault in you asking. A humble person asks for help. When we ask God for wisdom we are expressing true humility in His presence.

1:6 But let him be asking in faith, without doubting. For he that is doubting is like a wave of the sea driven with the wind and tossed. 7 Do not let that man think that he will be receiving anything from the Lord. 8 A two-souled man is fickle in all his ways.

In Matthew 7:8, it is said that everyone who asks, receives. James warns that doubt can divide our soul, comprising our mind, emotions, and will. Doubt can lead to a fractured experience, with conflicting thoughts, desires, and feelings. A person in doubt is not whole, and when doubt or unbelief creeps in, they become incomplete. Like the man in the gospel who asked for help with his unbelief, we must seek to overcome doubt. Doubt arises when we struggle to accept God's ways in our lives, leading to inner conflict. By surrendering to Him and trusting in His ways, we can experience a glorious outcome. Doubt can pull us away from faith, causing us to lose focus on God. We must be like the man in the gospel that said to the Lord, "help my unbelief" so we can be whole. Doubting happens in our life when we have a disagreement with God. If we yield in our circumstances and trust we will gain wisdom of His ways. Doubt pulls us in all directions, and we lose sight of Him who is the author of faith. James is pointing these saints to pray and trust in these precarious circumstances and to be persistent in trusting Him all the way to the end. Matt. 6:13 is in James mind. "Do not lead us into temptation but deliver us from evil".

1:9 Let the brother of lowly status rejoice in that he is exalted: 10 and the rich, in that he is humbled: because as the flower of the grass, he will pass away. 11 For the sun is as soon as it rises with a burning heat and withers the grass, and the flower of it falls, and the gracefulness of the appearance of it perishes: so also will the rich man wither away in his journey. Matt. 6:19-21, 19 'Treasure not up to yourselves treasures on the earth, where moth and rust disfigure, and where thieves break through and steal, 20but treasure up to yourselves treasures in heaven, where neither moth nor rust doth disfigure, and where thieves do not break through nor steal, 21for where your treasure is, there will be also your heart[132]

James is instructing believers to find their true source of glory and exaltation in their spiritual riches, not in worldly wealth or status. The lowly brother is encouraged to boast in the fact that he has been exalted by God through his position in Christ. Pointing the believers to their identity in Christ. Conversely, the rich are to take pride in their lowly state, recognizing the temporal nature of their material possessions. He knew that the possessions that the rich had acquired were going to be destroyed in the near future in the destruction of the cities of Israel and the confiscation of their property by the Roman authorities. James uses the analogy of a wilting flower in the field, which quickly fades and loses its beauty when exposed to the scorching heat of the sun. The scorching heat was the persecution that was coming and in many cases had already happened. For you had compassion on those in

---

[132] Young, R. (1997). *Young's Literal Translation* (Mt 6:19–21). Logos Bible Software.

prison, and you joyfully accepted the plundering of your property, since you knew that you yourselves had a better possession and an abiding one. Heb. 10:34. Just as the flower fades away, so too will the rich man's pursuit of wealth come to nothing in the current situation. The message is clear: true glory and exaltation come from a humble reliance on Christ, not from the temporary riches of this world.

1: 12 Blessed is the man that endures temptation: for when he has been approved, he will receive the crown of life, which the Lord has promised to those who are loving Him. 13 Let no man say when he is being tempted, I am being tempted by God: for God is not tempted with wrongdoings, neither does He tempt anyone: 14 but everyone is tempted, when he is taken away by his own unrestrained desires and enticed. 15 Then, when unrestrained desires have conceived, it gives birth to sin: and sin, when it is fully grown, gives birth to death. 16 Do not be deceived, my beloved brothers. TKB.

We find James exalting the individual who perseveres through trials and temptations, illustrating the idea of receiving a crown of divine life as a symbol of authority in our Christian walk. Those who endure and overcome temptation are considered blessed, for they have demonstrated faithfulness and trust in the Lord. Through the process of being tested and approved, believers can receive the promised reward of the crown of life, signifying their dedication and love for God. This crown of life serves as a symbol of victory and authority in the Christian life, showcasing the believer's commitment to following Christ and overcoming the challenges that come their way. Ultimately, James encourages us to remain steadfast in our faith, for in doing so, we are granted the privilege of receiving the crown of life promised by the Lord to those who love Him.

James delivers a crucial message regarding the nature of temptation and sin. He addresses the misconception that temptation originates from God, emphasizing that God is not tempted by evil and does not tempt anyone to sin. Instead, James explains that temptation arises when individuals are lured and enticed by their own unchecked desires and passions. This internal struggle leads to the conception of sin, and when sin is fully cultivated, it results in spiritual death.

James sternly warns his beloved brothers not to be misled or deceived by the allure of temptation and the false narrative that blames God for human transgressions. Instead, he urges believers to recognize the source of temptation within themselves and to exercise self-control and spiritual discernment to resist sin. By acknowledging the dangers of unrestrained desires and the destructive paths of sin. Imagine a seed planted in the fertile soil of a garden. This seed represents desire - a longing or craving within us. As this seed is nurtured and watered, it begins to grow and take root in our hearts and minds, much like how desires can consume our thoughts and drive our actions.

As time passes, the seed grows into a small sapling, representing the temptation that arises from our desires. Just as the sapling begins to branch out and spread its leaves, temptation starts to entice and lure us away from what we know to be right and good. It beckons us with promises of fulfillment and satisfaction, leading us down a path that may ultimately lead to sin.

If we allow the sapling of temptation to continue to grow unchecked, it eventually matures into a towering tree of sin. This tree casts a shadow over our spiritual life, blocking out the light of God's truth and love. Like a tree that bears poisonous fruit, sin brings forth death - not just physical death, but a spiritual distance from God and the abundant life He offers.

Just as a gardener must uproot a poisonous tree to protect the rest of the garden, we must uproot and deal with these sinful desires in our lives before it chokes out the fruit of righteousness and life. By recognizing the progression from desire to temptation to sin and to death, we can be vigilant in guarding our hearts and minds against the destructive nature of temptation. When we pass the test of temptations we experience God's authority in our walk with Him.

1:17 Every good and complete gift is from above, and coming down from the Father of lights, with whom is no change or shadow thrown off by circular motion. Matt. 5:22 is the reference. 18 By His own will He birthed us out by the word of reality, that we should be the first fruits of a certain species, His own created ones.

These verses from the book of James illuminate the divine nature of God and His gifts bestowed upon His children. James declares that all good and perfect gifts originate from above, emanating from the Father of lights, who remains constant and unchanging in His character and essence. Unlike shifting shadows that change with the movement of the sun, God's gifts are steadfast and unwavering, a reflection of His infinite and immutable nature.

Further delving into the theological depth of these verses, James emphasizes the spiritual rebirth and new creation that believers experience through God's will and the transformative power of His Word. By His own volition and purpose, God brings forth a new existence in His children, birthing them through the living and powerful Word of truth. This divine birth marks believers as the first fruits of a unique and special kind, a chosen people set apart by God as His own created beings, His new creation, a new species.

James highlights God's role as the ultimate source of goodness and perfection, showcasing His unchanging character and infinite nature. He underscores the transformative power of God's Word in birthing believers into a new spiritual reality, enabling them to fulfill their purpose as God's chosen ones and bear witness as the first fruits of a distinct and sacred creation by the Father of lights.

James offers practical wisdom on communication and behavior in these verses. He begins by addressing his beloved brothers, urging them to prioritize listening over speaking and to exercise patience and self-control in times of anger. James emphasizes that quickness to listen, accompanied by restraint in speech and emotion, is essential for fostering understanding and fostering harmonious relationships. This advice is rooted in the understanding that human anger typically does not align with the righteous standards of God, often leading to harmful outcomes. The source of James thoughts here in Matt. 5:22.

Building upon this foundation, James encourages believers to rid themselves of moral impurities and the abundance of ill will, that can hinder spiritual growth. Instead, he advocates for a posture of humility and openness to receive the transformative power of God's Word. By cultivating a spirit of meekness and receptivity, individuals can internalize and integrate the Word of God, which has the capacity to bring about salvation and renewal to their souls. James is focusing on the latter stages of spiritual growth using the analogy the implanted word which is able to save the soul. As I previously mentioned in the two-souled experience of the doubter, receiving the word saves our mind, emotions, and will. When we first experience regeneration our spirit is saved, then God works to renew our minds, stabilize our emotions, and fortify our will to align with His will. This is the process of conforming us to the image of His son.

Through these verses, James underscores the importance of active listening, restraint in communication, and emotional composure in interpersonal interactions. He emphasizes the necessity of purifying oneself from negative influences and embracing the transformative message of God's Word with humility and openness. By following this guidance, individuals can cultivate a spirit of harmony, righteousness, and spiritual growth in their lives.

1: 22 But be doers of the word, and not hearers only, deluding yourselves. 23 For if any be a hearer of the word and not a doer, he resembles a man observing his natural face in a mirror: 24 For he sees himself, and goes his way, and immediately forgets what manner of man he was. 25 But whoever looks into the complete law, the law of freedom, and continues in it, he being not a forgetful hearer, but a doer of the work, this man will be blessed in his creativity. 26 If anyone among you seems to be religious and bridles not his tongue, but is deluding his own heart, this one's religion is fruitless. 27 Pure and undefiled religion before God and the Father is this, to visit the fatherless and widows in their affliction, and to keep oneself unstained from the world.

This where Jesus tells the parable of the man who builds his house on the rock or the sand. "Therefore, whoever hears these sayings of Mine, and does them, I will liken him to a wise man who built his house on the rock: and the rain descended, the floods came, and the winds blew and beat on that house; and it did not fall, for it was founded on the rock. "But everyone who hears these sayings of Mine, and does not do them, will be like a foolish man who built his house on the sand: and the rain descended, the floods came, and the winds blew and beat on that house; and it fell. And great was its fall." Matt. 7:24-28.

In this parable we have two men, both are hearers, but only one is a doer. The rock is not Jesus in this parable, but obedience. The sand is indifference and disobedience. The rain, the floods and the winds come on both houses. Jesus is saying that the storm will come. The two houses represent the New Covenant House of Israel, and the other house is the Old Covenant House of Israel. Old Covenant Israel did not heed the words of their Messiah; therefore, their house would fall and great would be that fall. James is brilliant in bringing up this reference of being a doer and encouraging them to obey the words of Christ and they will endure the storm that is coming, the tribulation that is coming and their house will stand. James uses the phrase "the law of freedom or liberty". Paul said where the Spirit of the Lord is there is liberty, freedom. James is not telling the twelves tribes to keep the Law of Moses, there is no freedom in the law of Moses, it was a law that kept them in bondage. James is referring to the Law of the Spirit of life in Christ Jesus that has set us free from the law of sin and of death.

In these verses, James presents a vivid contrast between empty religious practices and true, authentic devotion to God. He cautions against a mere appearance of religious piety if it is not matched by control over one's speech. James highlights the significance of controlling the tongue as a litmus test for the sincerity of one's faith. Those who fail to bridle their speech, despite outward displays of religiosity, are ultimately deceiving themselves, revealing the emptiness of their faith.

James then proceeds to define genuine, unadulterated religion as expressed in acts of compassion and morality. He asserts that true religion is not confined to ritualistic observances but is demonstrated through practical acts of kindness and service. Specifically, James identifies caring for the most vulnerable members of society – the fatherless and widows in their distress – as a hallmark of authentic faith. Furthermore, remaining unpolluted by the corrupt influences of the world is emphasized as an essential aspect of pure religion.

By reaching out to those in need and maintaining a moral purity that sets believers apart from the world's corrupting influences, individuals can exemplify the true essence of faith that pleases God. James's words challenge believers to go beyond superficial appearances and engage in practical expressions of love, mercy, and righteousness as evidence to their authentic devotion to God. He also mentions to be unstained by the world. This word unstained truly means unspotted, without spots. In my synopsis of Jude I mention the spots being false, apostate law teachers but there is another aspect of spots and that is world's contaminations. Their ideologies, philosophies, and standards when accepted we become stained. Paul talks about a bride without spot or blemish. We see James is ministering to the house of Israel to be like the wise virgins and not the foolish ones. Matt. 25.

Chapter 2

James begins by cautioning his audience against showing partiality or favoritism within their faith community. He emphasizes that holding the faith of our Lord Jesus Christ, the Lord of glory, should be done without bias or discrimination. James then presents a vivid scenario where a man richly dressed receives preferential treatment over a poor man dressed in shabby clothing. By showing favoritism towards the wealthy individual and treating the poor man with disrespect, the community members reveal a deep-seated prejudice and a lack of genuine love for their neighbors.

The writer goes on to highlight the paradoxical nature of their actions, noting that while God has chosen the poor to be rich in faith and heirs of His kingdom, the community members have mistreated and dishonored the poor among them. James challenges his audience to reconsider their behavior, pointing out that the very individuals they exalt – the rich who may oppress and mistreat them – are the ones who blaspheme the worthy name of Christ that they bear. By failing to show love and compassion to their neighbor, regardless of social status, they are in violation of the royal law to love one's neighbor as oneself. Matt. 5:3.

Through these verses, James's impassioned plea for impartiality, compassion, and adherence to the royal law of love. He urges believers to examine their attitudes and behaviors, cautioning against the sin of favoritism and discrimination within the community of faith. The interconnectedness of faith and works, emphasizing that true faith is evidenced by deeds of love and impartiality towards others. James's message serves as a timeless reminder of the importance of living out one's faith through genuine love and equality, reflecting the teachings and example of Christ.

2:10 For whoever will keep the whole law, and yet stumbles once, is guilty of all. 11 For He that said, do not commit adultery, also said, do not murder. Now if you are not committing adultery, yet if you are murdering, you have become a transgressor of the law. 12 In this way be speaking, and be doing, as they that are about to be judged by the law of freedom. 13 For judgment is without mercy, to the one that has shown no mercy, and mercy gloats against judgment! James is dealing with the Jewish mindset with what they were familiar with regarding religion. The Jewish paradigm was in order to be religious you needed to keep the Law of Moses. James is writing to them that if they want to keep the whole law and stumble once, they are guilty of the whole law. The Jews were famous for keeping the parts of the law that was convenient for them. Jesus said, Woe to you scribes and Pharisees, hypocrites; because you tithe mint, and anise, and cummin, and have left the weightier things of the law; judgment, and mercy, and faith. These things you ought to have done, and not to leave those undone. Matt. 23:23. James is now going to expound on the weightier aspects of the law and show them that judgment, mercy, and faith were the most important aspects of the law which they had neglected. James is not saying you need to keep the whole law as means of salvation. He is saying that if you want to live that way, do it all. I believe he is speaking to those who were still under the influence of Judaism, and some may not have come to true faith in the Messiah. You are about to be judged. Judgment was coming he says, and judgment will be without mercy to those who have rejected the Messiah. How will they be judged? By the Law of Freedom, the Law of the Spirit. Judgment without mercy is to those who have shown no mercy. James is admonishing them to be a merciful people, and he is referencing the teachings of Jesus in the sermon on the mount. Matt. 5:7. In the phrase "mercy gloats against judgment," there is a powerful and profound message conveyed. The concept of mercy triumphing over judgment is a central theme in Christian theology and morality.

To "gloat" means to take great pleasure or satisfaction in one's own success or superiority. In this context, the idea is that mercy, in its essence and practice, stands in triumph over judgment. This means that when mercy is extended, it goes beyond mere justice or retribution. It triumphs over condemnation and punishment, offering empathy, compassion, and grace instead.

In Christian teaching, God's mercy is often portrayed as being greater than His judgment. While God upholds justice and righteousness, His mercy and forgiveness are extended to those who seek it. This idea is encapsulated in the belief that through Christ's sacrifice, humanity can receive redemption and salvation, not through judgment, but through mercy.

Therefore, the phrase "mercy gloats against judgment" can be understood as a celebration of the triumph of compassion and forgiveness over condemnation and harshness. It reflects the grace and love that are at the heart of the Christian message, emphasizing the transformative and redemptive power of mercy in the face of judgment.

2:15 If a brother or sister is without clothing, and lacks daily food, 16 and one of you say to them, depart in peace, be warmed and filled; nonetheless, you do not give them those things which are necessary for the body; what does it profit? 17 Even so faith, if it has no works, it is dead, by itself. 18 Yes, someone may say, you have faith, and I have works: show me your faith without your works, and I will show you my faith out of the works.

In this passage from James 2:14-26, the author presents a comparison between the initial stage of justification exemplified by Abraham and the mature stage of justification that manifests through works in the life of Abraham and Rahab. The key message conveyed is the critical relationship between faith and works in the life of a believer, emphasizing that true faith is evidenced by actions and deeds. Matt. 6:1-3; 7:21-23.

James begins by questioning the value of a professed faith that lacks corresponding works, highlighting the inadequacy of a faith that does not produce tangible expressions of love and compassion towards others. He illustrates this point with the example of someone claiming to have faith but failing to meet the practical needs of a brother or sister in need. James argues that genuine faith is living and active, reflected in deeds of kindness and service towards others.

Drawing upon the example of Abraham, James illustrates a transformative journey from initial faith-based justification to a mature stage where faith is demonstrated through actions. He references Abraham's obedience in offering Isaac on the altar as evidence of his faith being "made complete" or perfected or mature through works. This example shows that true faith is not merely a cognitive belief but a dynamic force that produces tangible results in obedience and selfless acts of righteousness.

James further asserts that faith without works is dead, emphasizing the inseparable connection between faith and deeds in the life of a believer. By referencing Rahab's justification through her actions of sheltering the spies, James underscores that genuine faith is always accompanied by corresponding deeds that reflect a transformed heart and a living relationship with God.

In summary, James's teaching harmoniously combines the concepts of initial justification by faith demonstrated through belief in God (as seen in Abraham's case) and the mature stage of justification where faith is evidenced through practical works and deeds. This holistic view emphasizes the life-changing power of real faith that leads to a life marked by love, compassion, and obedience. Through this perspective, James presents a coherent and complementary understanding of faith and works in the Christian life, highlighting the necessity of both for a vibrant and authentic relationship with God. I hope we can see that Paul and James are not in conflict. Abraham in the beginning received a living faith that was deposited as the seed of faith for justification and as that seed germinated and grew, his faith bore the fruit of works.

This is the final stage of justification; it is mature faith in action and his works were the evidence of his faith and he was justified by those works. The first stage was believing for the impossible, count the stars, that's how many children you are going to have, and Abraham believed God. Then he offered his son to God who contained all the promises of God. The time between Abraham having no children and the time Isaac grew is an example of how our faith matures and how justification comes in stages. Instead, Abraham accepted the substitute of the ram caught in the thornbush for Isaac and was justified. Rahab hid the spies by faith and therefore was justified, this was the initial aspect of justification, this is her confession, "And as soon as we heard it, our hearts melted, and there was no spirit left in any man because of you, for the Lord your God, he is God in the heavens above and on the earth beneath.[133] This was her faith speaking and it was initial justification. Her works were: Behold, when we come into the land, you shall tie this scarlet cord in the window through which you let us down, and you shall gather into your house your father and mother, your brothers, and all your father's household.[134] But to the two men who had spied out the land, Joshua said, "Go into the prostitute's house and bring out from there the woman and all who belong to her, as you swore to her." So the young men who had been spies went in and brought out Rahab and her father and mother and brothers and all who belonged to her.

---

[133] *The Holy Bible: English Standard Version* (Jos 2:11). (2016). Crossway Bibles.
[134] *The Holy Bible: English Standard Version* (Jos 2:18). (2016). Crossway Bibles.

And they brought all her relatives and put them outside the camp of Israel. And they burned the city with fire, and everything in it. Only the silver and gold, and the vessels of bronze and of iron, they put into the treasury of the house of the Lord. But Rahab the prostitute and her father's household and all who belonged to her, Joshua saved alive. And she has lived in Israel to this day, because she hid the messengers whom Joshua sent to spy out Jericho.[135] In both cases with Abraham and Rahab we see faith working with their works for justification. This was the obedience of faith which resulted in the final stage of justification. The overall picture of the story of Rahab is quite profound, since the city that destroyed was a type of Jerusalem and the prostitute that had faith was saved with all those that believed and belonged to her. It is a true picture of Old Covenant Israel depicted as the city of Jericho and the prostitute that was in her (Jericho) was saved because of faith initially and mature faith finally.

Chapter 3

In James 3:1-2, the author is issuing a solemn warning regarding the role of teaching within the Christian community. The emphasis is placed on the weighty responsibility that comes with being a teacher, as they will be held to a higher standard and face a stricter judgment due to their influential position. This highlights the importance of humility, diligence, and accountability in the teaching ministry.

The passage continues by acknowledging the universal human experience of stumbling and making mistakes, underscoring the inherent imperfection of humanity. This serves as a reminder of our constant need for God's grace and forgiveness, despite our best efforts. The ability to control one's speech is portrayed as a sign of maturity and wisdom, indicating that one who can govern their words demonstrates a higher level of spiritual growth and discipline.

They mark the importance of humility, self-awareness, and spiritual maturity in all areas of ministry and personal conduct. Darby's interpretation would likely highlight the need for believers to approach teaching and communication with reverence, integrity, and a deep sense of reliance on God's wisdom and guidance.

In explaining the concept that one who does not stumble in their words is a mature individual capable of controlling their entire being, The power and significance of the tongue. James highlights the challenge and significance of maintaining control over one's speech, as it often reflects the inner state of the heart. I can't stress enough the maturity that comes with mastering one's words and the impact it can have on one's overall character and behavior.

---

[135] *The Holy Bible: English Standard Version* (Jos 6:22–25). (2016). Crossway Bibles.

This is our shared struggle with sin and imperfection, and the importance of controlling one's verbal communication as an earmark of maturity and self-discipline in the Christian walk.

In this passage from James 3:3-12, the author uses powerful analogies to illustrate the immense impact of the tongue and the importance of guarding one's speech. Let's explore the analogies used by James and provide an illustration for each:

1. Bits in Horses' Mouths: James compares the tongue to the bit used in a horse's mouth to control and direct the animal. Just as a small bit can influence the movement and behavior of a large horse, the tongue, though a small part of the body, can guide and shape one's actions and interactions.

Illustration: Imagine a skilled equestrian riding a powerful horse. By using the bit in the horse's mouth, the rider can effectively communicate commands to guide the horse's movements. Similarly, when we exercise control over our words and language, we can steer our actions and influence our relationships in a positive direction.

2. Ships and Rudders: James draws a parallel between the tongue and the rudder of a ship. Despite the massive size of a ship, it is the small rudder that determines its course. Likewise, the tongue, though a small part of the body, can have a significant impact on the direction and outcome of our words and interactions.

Illustration: Picture a vast ocean with a large ship navigating through turbulent waters. The experienced steersman uses the rudder to maneuver the ship through challenging conditions and guide it to its desired destination. Just as the rudder directs the course of the ship, our words and communication can shape the trajectory of our relationships and impact those around us.

Through these powerful analogies, James emphasizes the importance of exercising restraint and wisdom in the use of our words. Just as a bit controls a horse's movements and a rudder steers a ship, our tongue has the power to influence our actions, relationships, and the atmosphere around us. By recognizing the magnitude of the impact of our words and striving for consistency in our speech, we can cultivate a spirit of kindness, respect, and positivity in our interactions with others.

Let us not be deceived by the wisdom of this world, for it leads to envy and strife, which only bring about confusion and evil deeds. True wisdom comes from above, it is pure, peaceable, and full of mercy and good fruits. The natural man operates with the wisdom from below and the spiritual man operates from the wisdom from above. Even Jesus told the leaders of Israel, 'you are from below and I am from above', He said to them, "You are from below; I am from above. You are of this world; I am not of this world. I told you that you would die in your sins, for unless you believe that I am He you will die in your sins."[136]

---

[136] *The Holy Bible: English Standard Version* (Jn 8:23–24). (2016). Crossway Bibles.

The leaders of Israel operated in the wisdom below and they didn't know that the Wisdom of God was standing right there in their midst. 1 Cor. 1:30.

If you find bitterness and selfish ambition in your hearts, do not boast in it, for such wisdom is not from God. Instead, humble yourselves and seek the wisdom that comes from the Lord, for it brings forth righteousness and peace.

Let God produce in us a spirit of humility and meekness, displaying wisdom through our actions and always seeking to make peace with others. May our lives be a reflection of the wisdom that comes from above, shining brightly in a dark and tumultuous world.

James describes the 7 attributes of the wisdom from above and I was reminded of the proverbs.

In Proverbs 9:1, King Solomon speaks of wisdom as having built her house, setting up seven pillars. These seven pillars represent essential characteristics of divine wisdom that come from above:

1. Fear of the Lord: The foundation of wisdom is the fear of the Lord, recognizing His sovereignty, holiness, and authority in our lives. A fountain of life able to keep us from the snares of death.
2. Knowledge: True wisdom is grounded in knowledge, understanding, and discernment, allowing us to make wise decisions and choices.
3. Understanding: Wisdom goes beyond mere knowledge to a deep understanding of God's ways, His purpose, and His will for our lives.
4. Discernment: Wisdom enables us to discern between right and wrong, good and evil, truth and falsehood, guiding us in making righteous decisions.
5. Prudence: Wisdom is marked by prudence, foresight, and sound judgment, leading us to act with caution and wisdom in all circumstances.
6. Strength: True wisdom gives us strength and courage to withstand trials, challenges, and temptations, empowering us to live according to God's divine life.
7. Honor: The final pillar of wisdom is honor, which expresses a life of integrity, humility, and reverence for God, leading to a life that glorifies Him.

James says that the wisdom from above is first: first pure, then peaceable, gentle, not biased, full of mercy and good fruits, and authentic.

As we seek for God to build these seven pillars of wisdom into our being, we align ourselves with the divine wisdom that comes from above, guiding us in righteousness, peace, and the fulfillment of God's purpose for us with stability and steadfastness.

Chapter 4

Let us consider the profound truth conveyed in this passage from James that addresses the root cause of conflicts and wars among believers. James draws our attention to the internal struggle within the heart, where our own selfish desires and cravings lead us into sin and discord. It is this inner turmoil, driven by pleasure-seeking and covetousness, that manifests itself outwardly in quarrels, battles, and strife.

Furthermore, James admonishes us for our misplaced priorities and improper motives in our prayers. When we seek God's blessings primarily for the fulfillment of our own gratifications rather than aligning with His will, we hinder the reception of His blessings. Our friendship with the world, characterized by worldly pursuits and values, stands in direct opposition to our relationship with God, leading to enmity and conflict.

In light of these insights, let us reflect on our own hearts and actions, recognizing the need to submit our desires and ambitions to God's will. May we strive to seek after the things of the Kingdom above all else, forsaking the fleeting pleasures of this world and embracing a life of obedience and surrender to our Creator. Jesus told the story of the parable of the Sower and said some soil (hearts), 7 Other seed fell among thorns, which grew up with it and choked the plants. Jesus explains the parable:

11 "This is the meaning of the parable: The seed is the word of God. 14 The seed that fell among thorns stands for those who hear, but as they go on their way they are choke by life's worries, riches and pleasures, and they do not mature. Haven't we been studying the letter to James and do we see this pattern outlined in this epistle of these three things. The believers that James is writing to need to weed out the anxieties, desire for riches and now deal with the weed out these passions and pleasures that choke out the seed of the kingdom and the things of the kingdom that are growing and not fully mature. So they can be perfected and become mature.

The scripture in James 4:5 poses a thought-provoking question: "Do you think that the Scripture speaks to no purpose? He jealously desires the spirit which He has made to dwell in us." This verse points to the profound truth that God, in His infinite love and jealousy for His people, longs for the human spirit that He has placed within us, which bears His likeness.

The human spirit, created in the likeness of God, is a precious gift from the Almighty, reflecting His nature and character in each and every one of us. It is this spirit that enables us to connect with God on a deeper level, to worship Him in spirit and truth, and to experience His presence and guidance in our lives.

God's jealousy for the spirit within us stems from His desire for a close and intimate relationship with His beloved children. Just as a loving parent longs for the well-being and flourishing of their offspring, so too does God yearn for us to walk in harmony with His Spirit, to reflect His glory and grace in all that we do.

We might think that jealousy is a negative thing, but God has perfect jealousy for the human spirit in man. The human spirit is connected to worship, and this has been God's heart's desire from the beginning. One thing that is incredible is that Adam is never seen worshiping or praying to God. Psalm 150:6 ESV Let everything that has breath praise the Lord! Praise the Lord!

As we contemplate the depth of God's jealousy and longing for the spirit within us, may we respond with humility, gratitude, and a renewed commitment to honor and glorify Him in every aspect of our lives. Let us cherish the spiritual imprint within us and seek to cultivate a spirit of reverence, obedience, and love towards our Father, who jealously desires the fullness of our hearts and spirits for His perpetual purpose.

In these verses as translated by Kenneth S. Wuest, the depth of God's grace and the call to humble submission are beautifully expounded:

"But He gives the ultimate grace! Therefore He says, God is opposed to the arrogant but gives grace to the humble. Therefore submit yourselves to God. Take a stand against the Devil, and he will flee from you. Be drawing near to God, and He will be drawing near to you. Cleanse your hands, you sinners; and purify your hearts, you two-souled ones. Be miserable, and mourn, and wail: let your laughter be changed into mourning, and your joy to depression. Be humiliated in the sight of the Lord, and He will be lifting you up." James 4:6-17.

In these powerful words, we are reminded of God's abundant grace that He extends to the humble of heart. The call to submit ourselves to God, to resist the enemy, and to draw near to Him with clean hands and pure hearts, reveals the radical change of His work of transformation that God desires to do within us. This is the pattern for victory. We cannot resist the Devil if we are prideful, we must submit ourselves to God and then we are empowered to resist the devil resulting in our experience of a breakthrough to Him with clean hands and pure heart.

Wuest's translation brings out the urgency and sincerity in the exhortation to humble ourselves before the Lord, to mourn over our sins, and to allow God to lift us up in His grace. The reminder of the fleeting nature of life and the necessity of aligning our will with God's will marks the importance of acknowledging our utter dependence on Him and submitting our plans and desires to His sovereign will.

Let us heed the call to humility, submission, and obedience to the law of the Spirit of life in Christ Jesus, recognizing His authority and sovereignty over our lives. May we embrace His grace with grateful hearts, seeking His will above our own.

In this verse, James is highlighting the responsibility that comes with knowledge and understanding of what is good and right according to God's standards. The concept expressed here is that if one knows what is right and good but fails to act on it or neglects to do what is within their power to bring about that good, it is considered sin.

This verse emphasizes the importance of not only knowing what is good, but actively pursuing it and putting it into practice. It speaks to the idea that passivity or inaction in the face of knowing what is right can be just as sinful as actively doing what is wrong.

James is calling believers to a higher standard of accountability and action. It challenges us to be intentional in seeking and promoting good, righteousness, and justice in the world around us. It reminds us that knowledge without corresponding action is incomplete and falls short of God's glory.

The twelve tribes were given much, and Jesus said this about the faithful and wise steward … Everyone to whom much was given, of him much will be required, and from him to whom they entrusted much, they will demand the more.[137] It serves as a reminder that to whom much is given, much is required, and that a failure to act on what we know to be good, and right is considered sin in the sight of God. This was a stern warning to the twelve tribes. They are Israelites, and to them belong the adoption, the glory, the covenants, the giving of the law, the worship, and the promises. To them belong the patriarchs, and from their race, according to the flesh, is the Christ, who is God over all, blessed forever. Amen.[138] The twelve tribes were given much, and much was required, and this is why out of over a 100 verses, James is commanding these twelve tribes to do what is right on almost 50 of those verses it is in the imperative mood. They know right from wrong!

Chapter 5

1 Come now, oh rich, weep and be shrieking over your miseries which are coming upon you. 2 Your riches have rotted away, and your garments are moth-eaten. 3 Your gold and silver have corroded from disuse, and the corrosion of them will be a witness against you and will eat your flesh as it were fire. You have accumulated treasure in the last days. 4 Behold, the wages of the workers who have reaped your lands, which you are depriving, cries out: and the cries of those who have reaped have entered into the ears of the Lord of armies. 5 You have lived in luxury on the land, and been unrestrained; you have nourished your hearts, as in a day of slaughter. 6 You have condemned and murdered the righteous, and he does not resist you.

Indeed, the warning given by James in these verses can be seen as a prophetic message concerning the impending judgment and destruction that befell Jerusalem and the land of Israel in AD 70. The denunciation of the wealthy oppressors, the call to repentance, and

---

[137] *The Holy Bible: English Standard Version* (Lk 12:48). (2016). Crossway Bibles.
[138] *The Holy Bible: English Standard Version* (Ro 9:4–5). (2016). Crossway Bibles.

the emphasis on imminent miseries align with the historical events surrounding the fall of Jerusalem to the Romans.

During the last days of the Old Covenant, leading up to the destruction of Jerusalem in AD 70, the city faced internal strife, corruption, and political unrest. The rich and powerful exploited the poor, disregarded justice, and lived in luxury while neglecting the needs of the marginalized and oppressed. James said they accumulated treasure in the LAST DAYS. They were in the last days. We are not in the last days today. This societal decadence and moral decay set the stage for the catastrophic judgment that would come upon Jerusalem in Israel's latter days according to the song of Moses. Deut. 32.29 If they were wise, they would understand this; they would discern their latter end!

The imagery of decaying riches, moth-eaten garments, and corroded gold and silver symbolizes the transience and emptiness of material wealth that would offer no protection against the impending devastation. The cries of the oppressed workers and the condemnation of the righteous reflect the social injustices and moral corruption prevalent in Jerusalem at that time.

The call to repentance and mourning for the miseries to come echo the urgent need for the people to turn back to God, seek His forgiveness, and change their ways before it was too late. The impending destruction of Jerusalem and the desolation that followed served as a sobering reminder of the consequences of disobedience, unrighteousness, and rejection of God's ways.

In light of the historical context and the events that unfolded in AD 70, the warning given by James in these verses carries a distressing call of repentance, judgment, and the importance of aligning with God's will to avoid the impending miseries that awaited Jerusalem and the people of Israel.

5:7 Therefore be long-suffering, brothers, until the presence of the Lord. Behold, the farmer waits for the precious fruit of the land, and perseveres for it, until he receives the early and latter rain. 8 Be long-suffering also and stabilize your hearts: for the presence of the Lord is approaching.[139] Grumble not against one another, brothers, unless you be condemned: behold, the Judge stands before the door! 10 My brothers, copy the prophets, who have spoken in the name of the Lord, for an example of suffering and of patience. 11 Behold, we count them blessed who endure. You have heard of the patience of Job and have seen the goal intended by the Lord; that the Lord is very compassionate and rich in mercy. The Parousia is in view in James mind and the end of the Old Covenant age. He was expecting the Lord to come and judge and separate the wheat from the tares.

In the context of the parable of the wheat and tares and the impending destruction of Jerusalem, James' exhortation for long-suffering, patience, and endurance takes on

---

[139] *The New King James Version* (Mt 7:24–28). (1982). Thomas Nelson.

added significance. The parable of the wheat and tares, where the wheat (representing the righteous) is gathered into the barn (symbolizing being gathered in Christ) and the tares (representing the unrighteous Old Covenant people) are thrown into the fire (symbolizing judgment and destruction on Jerusalem), can be seen as the events leading up to the end of the Old Covenant age in AD 70.

James urges believers to be patient and steadfast in their faith, like the farmer who patiently waits for the precious fruit of the land, enduring through the early and latter rains until the harvest. This echoes the need for the those righteous to persevere and endure through difficult times, remaining faithful and trusting in the Lord's timing and provision.

The reference to not grumbling against one another ties in with the idea of separating the wheat from the tares, avoiding divisions and conflicts within the community of believers. The Judge, symbolic of Christ's imminent presence and judgment, stands before the door, underscoring the urgency of leading lives of righteousness, unity, and love before His Parousia, coming, presence.

James encourages believers to follow the example of the prophets who endured suffering and remained patient while faithfully proclaiming the word of the Lord. The patience of Job is highlighted as a model of enduring faithfulness, with the outcome demonstrating the Lord's compassion and mercy towards those who persevere.

As the Old Covenant age draws to a close, with the impending destruction of Jerusalem and the fulfillment of prophecies, James' message serves as a reminder for those believers to remain steadfast in their faith, patient in times of trial, and focused on living lives that honor God.

In these words of James, we are reminded by the Holy Spirit of the importance of integrity and truthfulness in our words and actions. As believers, we are called to a higher standard of honesty and reliability, reflecting the character of our Lord and Savior, Jesus Christ. We approach this passage with a focus on the foundational principles of integrity and righteousness found in Scripture.

James is basically saying let our yes be yes and our no be no, highlighting the necessity of speaking truthfully and keeping our word. By upholding this principle, we demonstrate our faithfulness, reliability, and commitment to honesty in all areas of our lives.

James is cautioning against the dangers of making frivolous oaths or vows, pointing out that such actions can lead to a lack of credibility and a diminishing of trustworthiness. By emphasizing the need for straightforward and sincere communication. James' exhortation is a call to the twelve tribes to live in a way marked by authenticity, truthfulness, and unwavering honesty.

In this letter he gives instruction on the power of prayer, both in times of affliction and in times of joy. As we face trials and tribulations, we are called to turn to God in prayer, seeking His comfort, guidance, and healing. On the other hand, in moments of happiness and celebration, we are encouraged to express our thankfulness to the Lord through singing praises and songs of worship.

My strong emphasis on faith and the supernatural power of God through prayer, I am sharing the importance of approaching God in faith and with unwavering belief in His ability to heal and restore. The significance of the elders of a local gathering of God's people coming together to pray over the sick, anointing them with oil in the name of the Lord, and expressing confidence in the Lord's ability to bring about healing and forgiveness. We need elders who believe this and practice it, exercising spiritual authority as a kingdom people.

James also exhorts the believers to confess their faults to one another, emphasizing the power of transparency, accountability, and intercessory prayer in the process of healing and restoration. By praying for one another with fervency and righteousness, believers can tap into the healing power of God and the effective nature of prayer, drawing inspiration from the example of Elijah, a man of faith who fervently prayed for miraculous interventions from God.

Through these words I would command the vital role of prayer in the life of a believer, showcasing its ability to bring about healing, forgiveness, restoration, and deliverance. By turning to prayer in times of need and in times of joy, we demonstrate our trust in God's sovereignty, faithfulness, and unwavering love towards His children.

Terry Kashian

James

Chapter 1

1. James, a slave of God and of the Lord Jesus Christ, to the twelve tribes which are in the Dispersion, greeting.
2. My brothers, consider it all joy when you fall into various trials;
3. Knowing that the testing of your faith develops persistence.
4. But let persistence have her complete work, that you may be complete and whole, lacking nothing.
5. If any of you are lacking wisdom, let him ask of God, who is giving to all freely, without finding fault; and it will be given to him.
6. But let him ask in faith, without doubting. For he that is doubting is like a wave of the sea driven with the wind and tossed.
7. Do not let that man think that he will receive anything from the Lord.
8. 8.A double minded man is unstable in all his ways.
9. Let the brother of lowly status rejoice in that he is exalted:
10. But the rich, in that he is humbled: because as the flower of the grass, he will pass away.
11. For the sun is no sooner risen with a burning heat, but it withers the grass, and the flower of it falls, and the gracefulness of the appearance of it perishes: so also will the rich man wither away in his journey.
12. Blessed is the man that endures temptation: for when he has been approved, he will receive the crown of life, which the Lord has promised to those who are loving Him.
13. Let no man say when he is tempted, I am tempted by God: for God is not tempted with evil, neither does He tempt anyone:
14. But everyone is tempted, when he is taken away by his own unrestrained desires, and enticed.
15. Then, when unrestrained desires have conceived, it gives birth to sin: and sin, when it is fully grown, gives birth to death.
16. Do not be deceived, my beloved brothers.
17. Every good and complete gift is from above, and coming down from the Father of lights, with whom is no change or shadow thrown off by circular motion.
18. By His own will He produced us out by the word of reality, that we should be a kind of first-fruits of His own creation.
19. Therefore, my beloved brothers, let everyone be swift to hear, slow to speak, slow to anger:
20. For the anger of man does not work the righteousness of God.
21. Therefore, put aside all filthiness and abundance of malice, and receive with meekness the implanted word, which is able to save your souls.
22. But be doers of the word, and not hearers only, deceiving yourselves.
23. For if any be a hearer of the word, and not a doer, he is like a man observing his natural face in a mirror:
24. For he sees himself, and goes his way, and immediately forgets what manner of man he was.

25. But whoever looks into the complete law of freedom, and continues in it, he being not a forgetful hearer, but a doer of the work, this man will be blessed in his doing.

26. If anyone among you seems to be religious and bridles not his tongue, but deceives his own heart, this one's religion is fruitless.

27. Pure and undefiled religion before God and the Father is this, to visit the fatherless and widows in their affliction, and to keep oneself unspotted from the world.

Chapter 2

1. My brothers, do not hold the faith of our Lord Jesus Christ, the Lord of glory, with favoritism.

2. For if there come to your gathering a man with a gold ring, in fine apparel, and there come in also a poor man in dirty clothing;

3. Then you have respect for him that wears the rich clothing, and say to him, sit here in a good place; but say to the poor, Stand you there, or sit here under my footstool:

4. Are you not showing discrimination among yourselves, and have become judges with evil reasonings?

5. Listen, my beloved brothers, has not God chosen the poor of this world to be rich in faith, and heirs of the kingdom which He has promised to them that are loving Him?

6. But you have looked down on the poor. Do not rich men oppress you, and drag you before the courts?

7. Do they not blaspheme that worthy name by which you are called?

8. If you fulfill the royal law according to the Scripture, you will love your neighbor as yourself, you do well:

9. But if you show favoritism, you commit sin, and are convicted by the law as transgressors.

10. For whoever will keep the whole law, and yet stumble in one thing, he is guilty of all.

11. For He that said, do not commit adultery, also said, do not murder. Now if you do not commit adultery, yet if you murder, you have become a transgressor of the law.

12. In this way be speaking, and be doing, as they that are about to be judged by the law of freedom.

13. For judgment is without mercy, to the one that has shown no mercy; and mercy boasts against judgment!

14. What does it profit, my brothers, though a man say he has faith, and have not works? Can such faith save him?

15. If a brother or sister is without clothing, and lacks daily food,

16. And one of you say to them, depart in peace, be warmed and filled; nonetheless you give them not those things which are necessary to the body; what does it profit?

17. Even so faith, if it has no works, it is dead, by itself.

18. Yes, someone may say, you have faith, and I have works: show me your faith without your works, and I will show you my faith out of the works.

19. You believe that there is one God; you do well: the demons also believe, and tremble!

James 2:20

20. But do you want to know, oh foolish man, that faith without works is dead?
21. Was not Abraham our father justified by works, when he had offered Isaac his son upon the altar?
22. See how faith worked with his works, and out of the works, faith was made complete?
23. So, the Scripture was fulfilled which said, Abraham believed God, and it was accounted to him for righteousness: and he was called the friend of God.
24. You see then that out of the works a man is justified, and not out of faith only.
25. Likewise, and was not Rahab the harlot justified out of the works, when she had received the messengers, and had sent them out another way?
26. For as the body without the spirit is dead, so faith without works is also dead.

Chapter 3

1. My brothers, let not many become teachers, knowing that we will receive a greater judgment.
2. For we all stumble in many things. If any man stumble not in word, the same is a mature man, and able also to bridle the whole body.
3. Behold, we put bits in horses' mouths that they may obey us; and we turn around their whole body.
4. Behold also the ships, which though they be so great, and are driven of fierce winds, yet are they turned around with a very small rudder, wherever the pilot wants.
5. Even so the tongue is a little member, yet boasts great things. Behold how great a matter a little fire kindles.
6. For the tongue is a fire, a world of iniquity: so is the tongue among our members, that it defiles the whole body, and sets on fire the course of nature; and it is set on fire by Gehenna.
7. For every kind of beast, and bird, and serpent, and things in the sea, is subdued, and has been subdued by human nature:
8. But the tongue no man can subdue; it is an unruly evil, full of deadly poison.
9. With it we bless God, even the Father; and with it we curse men, who are made according to the likeness of God.
10. Out of the same mouth proceeds blessing and cursing. My brothers, these things should not be.
11. Does a fountain send out at the same place sweet water and bitter?
12. Can the fig tree, my brothers, bear olive berries? Either a vine, figs? Thus no fountain can provide both sweet and bitter.
13. Who is the wise man and understanding among you? Let him display by good conduct that his works are done in the meekness of wisdom.
14. But if you have bitter envying and strife in your hearts, glory not, and lie not against the reality.
15. This wisdom descends not from above, but is earthly, sensual, and demonic.
16. Therefore, where envying and strife exist, there is confusion and every evil work.
17. But the wisdom that is from above is first pure, then peaceable, gentle, without favoritism, full of mercy and good fruits, and without hypocrisy.

18. And the fruit of righteousness is sown in peace by them that make peace.

Chapter 4

1. From what source are wars and battles among you? Are they not from this, even your own gratifications that wage war in your members?
2. You are coveting, and do not have: you are murdering, and zealous, and cannot acquire: you are battling and contending, but not possessing, because you are not asking.
3. You are asking, and not receiving, because you are asking improperly that you may squander it on your gratifications.
4. You adulteresses, are you not clear that friendship with the world is antagonism with God? Therefore, whoever purposes to be a friend of the world is constituted the enemy of God.
5. Do you think that the Scripture says with no cause? He jealously longs for the spirit that resides in us.
6. But He gives the ultimate grace! Therefore He says, God resists the proud, but gives grace to the humble.
7. Therefore, submit yourselves to God. Resist the Devil, and he will flee from you.
8. Be drawing near to God, and He will be drawing near to you. Cleanse your hands, you sinners; and purify your hearts, you double-minded.
9. Be miserable, and mourn, and wail: let your laughter be changed into mourning, and your joy to depression.
10. Be humiliated in the sight of the Lord, and He will be lifting you up.
11. Do not be speaking against one another, brothers. He that is speaking against his brother, and is judging his brother, speaks against the law, and is judging the law: but if you are judging the law, you are not a doer of the law, but a judge.
12. There is one lawgiver, who is able to save and to destroy: who are you that judges others?
13. Come now, you who say, today or tomorrow we will go into such a city, and continue there a year, and buy and sell, and make a profit:
14. But you do not know what will be on the next day. For what is your life? You are even a vapor that appears for a little time, and then vanishes away.
15. For you ought to say, if the Lord wills, we will live, and do this, or that.
16. But now you boast in your pretensions: all such boasting is evil.
17. Therefore, to him that is clear to bring about good, and does not bring it about, to him it is sin.

Chapter 5

1. Come now, oh rich, weep and be shrieking over your miseries that are coming upon you.
2. Your riches have rotted away, and your garments are moth eaten.
3. Your gold and silver has corroded from disuse; and the corrosion of them will be a witness against you, and will eat your flesh as it were fire. You have accumulated treasure in the last days.

4. Behold, the wages of the workers who having reaped your lands, which you are depriving, cries out: and the cries of those who have reaped have entered into the ears of the Lord of armies.

5. You have lived in luxury on the land, and been unrestrained; you have nourished your hearts, as in a day of slaughter.

6. You have condemned and murdered the righteous; and he does not resist you.

7. Therefore, be long-suffering, brothers, until the presence of the Lord. Behold, the farmer waits for the precious fruit of the land, and has long-suffering for it, until he receive the early and latter rain.

8. Be long-suffering also and establish your hearts: for the presence of the Lord is drawing near.

9. Grumble not against one another, brothers, unless you be condemned: behold, the Judge stands before the door!

10. My brothers, examine the prophets, who have spoken in the name of the Lord, for an example of suffering and of patience.

11. Behold, we count them blessed who endure. You have heard of the patience of Job, and have seen the goal intended by the Lord; that the Lord is very compassionate and rich in mercy.

12. But above all things, my brothers, swear not, neither by heaven, neither by the earth, neither by any other oath: but let your yes be yes; and your no, no; unless you fall into condemnation.

13. Are any among you afflicted? Let him pray. Are any happy? Let him sing psalms.

14. Are any sick among you? Let him call for the elders of the Assembly; and let them pray over him, anointing him with oil in the name of the Lord:

15. For the prayer of faith will save the sick, and the Lord will raise him up; and if he has committed sins, they will be forgiven.

16. Confess your faults to one another, and pray for one another, that you may be healed. The fervent prayer of a righteous man is powerful and effective.

17. Elijah was a man with a nature like ours, and he prayed earnestly that it might not rain: and it rained not on the land for three and a half years.

18. Then he prayed again, and the heavens gave rain, and the land brought forth her fruit.

19. Brethren, if any of you wanders from the reality, and one turns him back;

20. Let him know, that he who returns a sinner from wandering out of the right way will be delivering his soul from death, and will cover over a great many sins.

1st Peter Commentary

As we contemplate the insights of Peter's first epistle, we are transported back to a time when the apostle's character was being refined and honed by the sovereign hand of God. We are granted a glimpse into the challenges and obstacles that Peter faced - the impurities in the clay that required breaking, adjusting, and aligning with the divine will. This was a transformative process, a journey of sanctification and maturation. We are reading a man that has come into a full knowledge of the Son of God, who has spiritually grown a beard in his walk and understanding of God's perpetual purpose. He knows he is at the consummation of this purpose.

In examining Peter's epistles, we discern a radical shift that has transpired within him. He has adopted a new mindset, a fresh perspective, perceiving the Kingdom through a lens that is vastly different from his previous worldly and natural viewpoint. Where once his desires were fixed on temporal power and recognition, Peter now understands that the Kingdom entails suffering in his present age, coupled with the promise of future glories.

Peter's letters delve into weighty theological concepts such as election, redemption, priesthood, and the nature of the house of God. Yet, these truths are no longer viewed through the narrow prism of earthly things. They belong to a transcendent sphere, a spiritual realm that Peter now inhabits and walks in. He was called a stone, then he became a living stone, and the finished work he is a precious stone. Our calling too!

The transformation in Peter's worldview came at a cost - a dismantling of his former expectations of an earthly king and fleshly aspirations at the foot of the cross of Christ. It was a wrenching process, but one that ultimately yielded immeasurable spiritual gain. As he addresses the scattered sojourners, Peter reminds them of their heavenly inheritance, their living hope anchored in the resurrection power of Jesus Christ.

Let us, like Peter, embrace this transformative journey, recognizing that the trials we encounter are the means through which the Lord refines us and leads us into the newness of life. May we rejoice in the living hope we possess.

In the early days of Christianity, Peter played a significant role and frequently incorporated elements from the Old Testament in his writings. This practice served to connect the teachings of Christ with the established Jewish religious customs, resulting in rich spiritual revelations. However, Peter's utilization of the Old Testament went beyond mere references; he employed artistic expression and storytelling techniques to convey his message. In this essay, we will thoroughly analyze how Peter applies the Old Testament in his first letter. Our goal is to shed light on how Peter uses allusions to the Old Testament to reinforce divine acts, establish moral principles, and present familiar quotations as accepted truths. Through our exploration, we will delve into Peter's incorporation of prophetic texts, examine the scriptures he references, and interpret his nuanced implications. Ultimately, our objective is to make sense of Peter's unique interpretive methods and understand their contribution to the overall message and impact of his epistle.

Three things are bundled together in verse two:

The foreknowledge of God, the Father – This is quite impressive from a Jewish perspective. Peter is expounding on God's foreknowing that He would sprinkle with the blood of the Messiah, not only Israel but the nations. And sandwiched between these two thoughts is being sanctified by the Spirit into obedience. Isa. 52 appears to be in the mind of Peter. The Hebrew writer quotes Leviticus: For when every commandment of the law had been declared by Moses to all the people, he **took the blood** of calves and goats, with water and scarlet wool and hyssop, **and sprinkled** both the book itself and **all the people**, … Hebrews 9:19; let us draw near with a true heart in full assurance of faith, **having our hearts sprinkled** from an evil conscience and our bodies washed with pure water. Hebrews 10:22. Isa. 52-15, So shall He startle *and* **sprinkle many nations**, and kings shall shut their mouths because of Him; for that which has not been told them shall they see, and that which they have not heard shall they consider *and* understand. Paul quotes the latter part of Isa. 52:15b in Rom. 15:21.

The next three items that Peter bundles are:

1. Living hope – The realization that this life is a shadow and not even compared to the next.
2. Incorruptible Inheritance – The inheritance is not geography that can be taken by anyone, and it is guarded by Him who can never die.
3. A deliverance as the last time – I understand that sometimes when we see the word salvation, we have a religious concept, but in this case Peter is saying there is a deliverance coming at the last time. This will be the sign of the Son of Man sitting and coming with the glory of the Father. The revealing of the Son of Man!

6 In this **you greatly rejoice**, even though now for a little while, if necessary, you have been distressed by various trials, **7** so that the proof of your faith, *being* more precious than gold which is perishable, even though tested by fire, **may be found to result in praise and glory and honor at the revelation of Jesus Christ**; **8** and **though you have not seen Him**, **you love Him**, and though you do not see Him now, but believe in Him, you greatly rejoice with joy inexpressible and full of glory, **9 obtaining as the outcome of your faith the salvation of your souls**[140]

[10] As to this salvation, the prophets who prophesied of the grace that *would come* to you made careful searches and inquiries, [11] seeking to know what person or time **the Spirit of Christ within them** was indicating as He **predicted the sufferings of Christ and the glories to follow.** [12] **It was revealed to them that they were not serving themselves, but you**[141] This salvation was predicted by the prophets, and they had the Spirit of Christ within them, not upon them, and they realized that they were not serving themselves, but the 1st Century generation. Peter said the same thing in Acts 3:24, [24] And likewise, **all the prophets who have spoken**, from Samuel and *his* successors onward, also **announced these days.**[142]

[44] For I am the Lord your God. **Consecrate yourselves** therefore, and **be holy, for I am holy**. And you shall not make yourselves unclean with any of the swarming things that swarm on the earth. [45] For I am the Lord who brought you up from the land of Egypt to be your God; thus **you shall be holy, for I am holy.**' "[143] Peter quotes the verse 'be holy for I am holy, instruction on consecrating themselves. The phrase gird up the loins of your mind is used in the Gospel of Luke 12:35-40. The context is "Therefore you also be ready, for the Son of Man is coming at an hour you do not expect."[144] Peter was expecting the Lord to wrap things up very soon. He is instructing the saints to not be pushed back in the mold of their lusts. Be sober, vigilant, and be holy separated unto the Lord. He advises his readers to "abstain from the passions of the flesh" (1 Peter 2:11), echoing the call for holiness and self-discipline prevalent in the Old Testament.

By stressing the importance of self-control, Peter aims to arm his readers with the tools necessary to fend off temptation and live in alignment with God's will. Additionally, Peter advocates for his readers to "honor everyone" (1 Peter 2:17), mirroring the commandment to love one's neighbor as oneself found in Leviticus. This counsel underscores the importance of treating everyone with respect and dignity, irrespective of their societal standing or background. When we read the Old Testament or even the New Testament writings and we see exemplary qualities and virtues. We must recognize that this is Christ in them, even the Spirit of Christ in them. Our prayer should be since we have the Spirit of Christ in us, Lord manifest these qualities and virtues in and through me. He is greater that is in you than he that is in the world. Be specific what you want the Lord to manifest in you. There was a time when I experienced the friendship of the Lord, and I began to pray for that friendship to manifest in my life. I was amazed that shortly after this I had met some brothers and

---

[140] *New American Standard Bible, 1995 Edition: Paragraph Version* (1 Pe 1:5–9). (1995). The Lockman Foundation.

[141] *New American Standard Bible, 1995 Edition: Paragraph Version* (1 Pe 1:10–12). (1995). The Lockman Foundation.

[142] *New American Standard Bible, 1995 Edition: Paragraph Version* (Ac 3:23–24). (1995). The Lockman Foundation.

[143] *New American Standard Bible, 1995 Edition: Paragraph Version* (Le 11:44–45). (1995). The Lockman Foundation.

[144] *The New King James Version* (Lk 12:40). (1982). Thomas Nelson.

after almost 40 years we are still friends and talk and fellowship and eat meals together. He manifested His friendship in me.

The inspired words of the apostle Peter in verses 22-23. We have not been born again of corruptible seed, but of incorruptible seed - the living and enduring word of God. This seed is incorruptible and infinite, bringing forth life and transformation within us. As believers, we must realize the power and significance of the living word of God in our lives. It is through this word that we have been regenerated and made new creations in Christ. The word of God is not merely a collection of letters and stories, but a living and active force that works within us to bring about spiritual growth and maturity. Let us therefore immerse ourselves in the word of God, allowing it to penetrate deep into our hearts and minds. By abiding in the word and allowing it to dwell richly in us, we will continue to experience the ongoing work of transformation and renewal by the Spirit of God. May the indestructible seed of the living word bring forth abundant fruit in our lives, to the glory of God.

In 1 Peter 1:24-25, Peter provides an example of his utilization of Old Testament quotations by referring to Isaiah 40:6-8. He cites the passage, stating, "All flesh is like grass, and all its glory like the flower of grass. The grass withers, and the flower falls, but the word of the Lord remains forever." By incorporating this renowned quote from Isaiah, Peter emphasizes the temporary nature of human existence and the enduring nature of God's word. This inclusion in his epistle enables Peter to effectively convey the timeless truth of God's word and its profound significance in the lives of believers. Peter is building confidence in what God has spoken and reminding the saints of the transient nature of their human lives.

In Chapter two he continues with the exhortation for newborn babes. To put all aside five destructive attitudes and actions. Malice, deceit, hypocrisy, envy, evil speaking like slander. Put these asides is casting off these ways. We pick up and long for the pure milk of the word. Since Peter is talking to newborn babes, we must understand that a newborn cannot feed itself. When we see newborns, we must embrace them and bring them close to the breast of faith and love so they will be nourished and grow. The word in the Greek language for the word as in milk of the word is "logikos" and we get our English word 'logical'. The newborn must drink in God's logic instead of the world's logic. The life of faith is sometimes illogical, but as new believers we must trust and learn God's ways. The components of God's logic is knowledge, wisdom, faith, love, and power.

These five components of God's logic combat the five negative degraded attitudes and actions. The little parable of the saints being the salt of the earth may help us understand God's ways. Salt is commonly taught as a preservative or taste enhancer which is true. Jesus connects His disciples to salt. In Matthew 5:13 He tells them explicitly, "You are the salt of the earth; but if the salt loses its flavor, how shall it be seasoned? It is then good for nothing but to be thrown out and trampled underfoot by men." What is profound about this little parable is the phrase "if salt loses it flavor". W.E. Vines dictionary defines this phrase as: 1. mōrainō (μωραίνω, (3471)) is used (*a*) in the causal sense, to make foolish, 1 Cor. 1:20; (*b*) in the passive sense, to become foolish, Rom. 1:22; in Matt. 5:13 and Luke 14:34 it is said of salt that has lost its flavor, becoming tasteless.[145] If salt losing its flavor means becoming a moron or foolish, then being salty would indicate wisdom, knowledge, faith, love, and power. These attributes are the contents of grace and peace.

New believers must desire the pure milk of God's logic and used believers need to maintain their saltiness. Not maintaining this saltiness makes God's people good for nothing and they become defeated saints under the foot of their enemies. Our prayer should be, Lord, continue to make us salty! We have tasted that the Lord is good. As we taste Him we see! Tasting is all about our mouth and we need to open it. Even the word for worship is pictured as a dog licking. In 60 of the 91 occurrences of "worship" in the NT, it is the Greek word proskuneo. It means **"to kiss, like a dog licking his master's hand."** Literally & figuratively, to proskuneo is to *fawn over, crouch to, & fall down to kiss the ground before.* Nobody is as salty as the Lord and as we worship and praise the Lord we are licking the divine salt block, and we are continually thirsty for more of Him.

These next verses open up to us the revelation of Jesus Christ and His people. This understanding came to Peter when he received the revelation of Christ from the Father. Flesh and blood did not reveal this to you, Simon Barjonah, … you will be called Peter, "a stone". This was the first time Peter had received the revelation of who Christ was, but it also is the first revelation of Peter's spiritual identity. He was building material for God's house. Here Peter says, coming to Him as a living stone, you also are living stones built into a spiritual house. Peter's revelation of his identity enlarged to the corporate identity of God's people. This was a radical revelation as Peter had transitioned from an earthly house, temple to a spiritual house made up of people who belonged and were coming to Christ. 4 **Coming towards Him, as to a living stone**, being rejected indeed by men, but chosen of God and precious, 5 **you also, as living stones**, are being built up as **a spiritual house, a holy priesthood,** to **offer up spiritual sacrifices**, acceptable to God through Jesus Christ. 6 Therefore also it is contained in the Scripture, behold, I lay in Zion a chief cornerstone, chosen and precious: and he that is believing on Him will in no way be disgraced. 1 Pet. 2:4-6 TKB. The new paradigm Peter has is the people of God are the temple and they are the priests, and they offer spiritual sacrifices.

My understanding of this nugget of scripture is the means whereby we grow corporately. A pile of stones is not a building, it is only material. Our commitment to one another and our giftedness is essential to the ability to be built up. We are not automatically built as a spiritual house. This is an allegiance with a revelation of who we are and the need to function in our

---

[145] Vine, W. E., & Bruce, F. F. (1981). In *Vine's Expository dictionary of Old and New Testament words* (Vol. 2, p. 114). Revell.

giftedness to build one another in relationship to Christ and each other. Out of our being built up the priesthood emerges, not a couple of priests, but a body of priests functioning in the anointing and calling in their lives. The unveiling of our corporate identity expands from being a temple to a priesthood. You are priests but that reality will not fully manifest if we are not built together. This understanding changed my entire Christian life. I am not a Rambo Christian or a rogue believer, I was called to have sacred relationships in His body. What are spiritual sacrifices? Peter has made the full transition from the Old Covenant to the New. The sacrificial system is no longer a physical thing, but a spiritual reality. Each locality is challenged to be built together and emerge as a spiritual priesthood to minister to the Lord and to each other, and to those who are unsaved of their locality. The priestly order today is the order of Melchizedek, king priests. A royal priesthood. A kingdom of priests who offer spiritual sacrifices. There are at least five spiritual sacrifices that I am aware of in the scriptures.

1. We offer **our bodies as a living sacrifice**. God is so wise, and He knows if He gets our bodies, He gets everything that is inside us. Rom. 12:1

2. The sacrifice of praise. 15 Therefore through Him let us offer the sacrifice of praise to God continually, that is, the fruit of our lips **that confess His name.** Heb. 13:15 TKB. Our sacrifice of praise is our **upreach**, but there is also the sacrifice of the fruit of our lips. Our confession of His name is our in reach to those we meet with on a regular basis, and outreach to those who don't know His name.

3. Righteous works - 16 Now **well-doing and contributing** do not forget: for with **such sacrifices God is well pleased.** Heb. 13:16 TKB. The writer of Hebrews calls Spirit motivated works and giving sacrifices that are pleasing to God.

4. Winning Souls - 16 that I should be the servant of Jesus Christ to the nations, **ministering as a priest the gospel of God**, **that the offering up of the nations** might be acceptable, being sanctified by the Holy Spirit. Rom. 15:16 TKB. When the house is built, and the altar is established we bring people to the altar, the (cross) and they discover their salvation. They are a sacrifice to God to begin their journey of being built into the house of God to emerge as a priest to offer up spiritual sacrifices that are pleasing to God.

5. A priest is engaged in loving people especially the household of faith

Be you therefore **followers of God**, as dear children; 2 and **walk in love**, as Christ **also has loved us**, and **has given Himself for us an offering and a sacrifice to God for a sweet-smelling aroma**. Paul is highlighting the life of Christ as an example for to walk in. When we are loving we are a sweet-smelling aroma to God. Love builds up! You and I are building in the lives of those we are loving.

The Chief Cornerstone: This is one of the most significant descriptions of the Lord Jesus and it quoted multiple times in the New Testament. First of all, the concept of a cornerstone is amazing. This is the first stone that is laid in a new building connecting two walls of the building. This picture is marvelous, since one wall is pictured by the Jewish believers and the other wall is pictured by the Gentile believers. There is no longer a dividing wall between Jews and Gentile believers. They have been connected to the Messiah as the chief cornerstone in the New Building, the New Covenant Temple. In Psalm 118:22 is the first mention of the chief cornerstone. **²²The stone which the builders rejected** Has become the chief cornerstone. ²³This is the Lord's doing; It is marvelous in our eyes. ²⁴This is the day which the Lord has made; Let us rejoice and be glad in it.[146] The Lord Jesus quoted this verse to the scribes and Pharisees after telling the parable of the renters and the vineyard in Matt. 21. He exposed the murderous hearts of the scribes and Pharisees. They were the builders that wanted to continue to build the Old Covenant system when God was doing a new thing that they wanted to have no part in what God was doing. Therefore, later in the chapter 21, Jesus said the kingdom of God will be taken away from you and given to a nation that will produce the fruits thereof. The scribes and Pharisees knew He was talking about them. In the New Testament it is quoted: Matt 21:42; Mark 12:10, 11; Luke 20:17; Acts 4:11; Eph 2:20; 1 Pet 2:7.[147] It will bless you to look up these verses and notice the context. Isa 28:16 and its context is also a great resource to the way the apostles thought about the cornerstone. Peter's use of these verses solidify the idea that Christ was rejected and despised, but precious in the sight of God. The saints that were scattered throughout the Roman Empire might find solace in the fact that they will be or are treated the same way.

6 Therefore also it is contained in the Scripture, behold, **I lay in Zion a chief cornerstone**, chosen and precious: and he that is believing on Him will in no way be disgraced. 1 Pet. 2:6.

Zion is the spiritual Zion as the writer of the Hebrews states saying "**we have come to Mount Zion, the city of the living God**, the **heavenly Jerusalem**. Heb. 12:22. This is a heavenly place, and the Christ was placed in the realm of the Spirit in resurrection and ascension, not the earthly Jerusalem or Judaism. This Zion is not a geographic place but has a universal and cosmic delineation.

⁹But you are a chosen race, a royal priesthood, a holy nation, a people for *God's* own possession, so that you may proclaim the excellencies of Him who has called you out of darkness into His marvelous light; ¹⁰for you once were not a people, but now you are the people of God; you had not received mercy, but now you have received mercy[148].

In these verses from 1 Peter, the apostle Peter is quoting from the prophet Hosea to emphasize the profound shift in identity and status that has occurred for believers in Christ.

---

[146] *New American Standard Bible, 1995 Edition: Paragraph Version* (Ps 118:22–24). (1995). The Lockman Foundation.

[147] *New American Standard Bible, 1995 Edition: Paragraph Version*. (1995). The Lockman Foundation.

[148] *New American Standard Bible, 1995 Edition: Paragraph Version* (1 Pe 2:9–10). (1995). The Lockman Foundation.

The original context of the quote in Hosea refers to the restoration of Israel after they had been judged and rejected by God. Despite their disobedience and unfaithfulness, God shows mercy and restores them as His people.

Likewise, Peter is applying this message to the Christian community, highlighting the transformative power of God's mercy in their lives. Previously, they were not recipients of God's mercy, living in rebellion and sin. But now, through their faith in Jesus Christ, they have been brought into a new covenant relationship with God and are recognized as His chosen people.

This shift from being outside of God's mercy to receiving His abundant grace signifies a radical change in status and identity for believers. It demonstrates the undeserved favor and love that God has shown towards His people, inviting them into a new way of life marked by forgiveness, redemption, and restoration.

Peter goes on to exhort the scattered saints to keep away from fleshly lusts and where the battleground is against our souls. Be an example in godly behavior among the nations so they will be ashamed of their prejudice and bias and when they see your good works, they will glorify God in the day of visitation.

Ultimately, these verses serve as a reminder of the transformative power of God's mercy and the incredible privilege of being called the people of God. It is a call to live in gratitude and obedience, recognizing the depth of God's love and the significance of our new identity in Christ.

In these verses from 1 Peter chapter 2, we are reminded of the importance of honoring authority and submitting to human institutions for the Lord's sake. The apostle Peter instructs believers to respect and obey the governing authorities, whether it be a king, or governors appointed by him. This submission is not based on the character or actions of the rulers, but on our reverence for God and our desire to do what is right in His eyes.

It is God's will that we conduct ourselves in a manner that is honorable and upstanding, walking in His righteousness and silencing the criticisms of those who do not understand the ways of God. As followers of Christ, we are called to act as free men and women, not using our freedom as a license or cloak for sinful behavior, but instead as slaves of God, dedicated to His will and purpose.

Furthermore, Peter emphasizes the importance of honoring all people, showing love to fellow believers, maintaining a healthy fear of God, and honoring the authority of the king. This comprehensive approach to relationships and societal structures reflects a commitment to living in harmony and obedience within the framework of God's ordained order. In essence, these verses remind us of the need to respect and obey authority, not out of fear or obligation, but out of a desire to honor God and express His character in our lives. By following these instructions, we demonstrate our faithfulness to God and contribute to the advancement of His kingdom here on earth.

The historical context in which Peter was writing, with Emperor Nero reigning alongside other corrupt governors and authorities, adds an extra layer of significance to his instructions regarding honoring authority. Nero was known for his extravagance, cruelty, and persecution of Christians, making him one of the most infamous rulers in Roman history.

Despite the difficult and oppressive environment in which believers found themselves under Nero's rule, Peter's exhortation to submit to governing authorities and honor the king takes on even greater meaning. It demonstrates the timeless and transcendent nature of biblical principles, emphasizing the importance of obedience and respect for authority regardless of the ruler's character or conduct. It must be understood that difference between submission and obedience. Shadrach, Meshach, and Abednego were submissive to Nebuchadnezzar, but they did not obey him. When any authority demands you disobey God, you must submit which is an attitude, but you should not obey, which is an action. We can be submissive and not obey. In our submission we must accept the consequences of not obeying. This is the proper Christian conduct in relation to authority.

In light of Nero's wickedness and the presence of other corrupt governors, Peter's words carry a weight of conviction and courage for believers to stand firm in their faith, trusting in God's sovereignty and justice even in the midst of persecution and injustice. It serves as a reminder that our ultimate hope and security lie in God's perpetual kingdom, where true righteousness and justice does reign supreme.

In these verses from 1 Peter 2:18-25, we are exhorted to demonstrate a spirit of submission and honor not only to those in authority but also to our masters and employers, even if they are unreasonable.

The text reminds us that when we endure suffering unjustly and bear the sorrows of mistreatment with patience for the sake of our conscience towards God, we find favor in His sight. It is easy to respond with patience when we are mistreated for our own wrongdoings, but it is a higher calling to endure suffering when we do what is right, following the example of Christ.

Christ is held up as the ultimate example of suffering unjustly and responding in grace and humility. He committed no sin, spoke no deceit, and did not retaliate when reviled or threatened. Instead, He entrusted Himself to God, bearing the weight of being treated unjustly. Through Christ's sacrificial death and resurrection, we are healed and restored, like lost sheep returning to the care of our Shepherd. Peter uses the example of Christ's in our lives, urging believers to follow His footsteps in enduring suffering with grace and trust in God's righteous judgment.

In conclusion, Peter's words, encourage us to imitate Christ's humility, patience, and trust in times of suffering, honoring God through our obedience and endurance. Through Christ's redemptive work, we are called back to the Shepherd and Guardian of our souls, finding healing and restoration in His loving care.

In these verses from 1 Peter, it is important to understand the unique dynamics of marriage and the significance of a wife's role in cultivating a healthy relationship with her husband. Peter instructs wives to be submissive to their husbands, even if they are unbelievers or disobedient to the word. I would encourage wives to look for opportunities to influence their husbands through their behavior and attitudes, demonstrating respect and honor in a way that speaks louder than words. The focus on inner beauty and character, rather than external appearances, would resonate on the importance of emotional and spiritual connections in marriage. He would likely encourage wives to cultivate a gentle and quiet spirit, reflecting the heart of God and creating a peaceful and loving atmosphere in the home.

By drawing parallels to the example of Sarah and other holy women of old, Peter underscores the timeless principles of faith and trust in God that are essential for a harmonious marriage. He might encourage wives to seek God's guidance in honoring and respecting their husbands, even when faced with challenges or disagreements. I would likely highlight the divine influence of a wife's respectful and submissive behavior in creating a strong foundation for a healthy and loving relationship. By following the biblical principles outlined by Peter, wives have the opportunity to nurture a strong and enduring marriage that reflects God's design for the union between a man and his wife.

In these verses from 1 Peter 3:8-12, we see principles that apply not only to marriage but to all relationships, emphasizing the importance of harmony, kindness, humility, and forgiveness in our interactions with others. Peter exhorts believers to be harmonious, sympathetic, brotherly, kindhearted, and humble in spirit towards one another. These qualities are foundational for fostering healthy and strong relationships, whether in marriage, friendships, or within the larger community. By embodying these virtues, we create an atmosphere of love, understanding, and mutual respect.

The instruction to not repay evil with evil or insult with insult, but instead to offer a blessing, speaks to the transformative power of forgiveness and grace in relationships. When we choose to respond with kindness and blessing, we break the cycle of negativity and pave the way for reconciliation and healing. In Psalm 34:12-16, the psalmist exhorts his audience to listen and learn the fear of the Lord, to keep their tongues from evil and deceit, to turn away from evil and do good, to seek peace and pursue it, for the eyes of the Lord are on the righteous and His ears attentive to their cry, but the face of the Lord is against those who do evil. Peter draws from this psalm in his first epistle to emphasize the importance of righteous living and moral conduct in the lives of believers. He highlights the need for believers to align themselves with God's standards of righteousness and holiness, to refrain from deceitful speech, to actively pursue peace, and to turn away from evil.

Peter reminds his audience that God's favor is upon those who adhere to His ways and seek righteousness, while His judgment is against those who choose to do evil and engage in deceitful behavior. By referencing the words of the psalmist, Peter underscores the enduring relevance of these principles in the lives of believers, encouraging them to live in a manner that reflects the fear and reverence of the Lord.

In essence, Peter's use of Psalm 34 serves as a reminder to his audience and to all believers of the timeless importance of walking in righteousness, speaking truth, pursuing peace, and turning away from evil. It is a call to live lives that honor God, knowing that His eyes are upon the righteous and His ears attentive to their cries for help and guidance. Through obedience to God's commands and a commitment to righteous living, believers can experience the blessings of God's favor and the assurance of His presence in their lives.

In these verses from 1 Peter, focuses on the theme of suffering for the sake of righteousness and the importance of maintaining a strong faith and witness in the face of opposition.

Peter begins by questioning who could harm those who are zealous for what is good, implying that God's protection is upon those who walk in righteousness. Peter emphasizes the promise of blessings for those who endure sufferings for the sake of righteousness, reminding believers to not fear intimidation or trouble, but to trust in God's sovereign protection.

The apostle instructs believers to sanctify Christ as Lord in their hearts, always being prepared to give a defense for their faith with gentleness and respect. highlight the call for believers to be ready to share their hope in Christ, even in the midst of opposition, maintaining a posture of humility and grace in their interactions.

Peter urges believers to keep a good conscience, so that even in the face of slander or reviling, their good behavior in Christ will silence their accusers. Peter underscores the importance of living a life of integrity and righteousness, knowing that suffering for doing what is right is preferable in God's eyes than suffering for wrongdoing.

The passage also references Christ's sacrificial death and resurrection, His proclamation to the spirits in prison, and the symbolism of baptism as an appeal to God for a good conscience through the resurrection of Jesus Christ. The theological significance of these references, highlighting Christ's victory over sin and death and the believer's identification with Him through baptism. This for sure is not referring to water baptism, but a baptism of fire. A baptism of judgment. Those who were saved were baptized with the Holy Spirit and those who rejected the gospel and what God was doing in their generation experienced being baptized in fire. The fiery trial that the saints were going through was not going to burn them or destroy them. He will baptize you with the Holy Spirit and fire. His winnowing fork is in his hand, and he will clear his threshing floor and gather his wheat into the barn, but the chaff he will burn with unquenchable fire."[149]

Overall, I would stress the importance of standing firm in faith, being prepared to defend one's hope in Christ, and maintaining a good conscience and a life of righteousness, even in the face of persecution and suffering. He would encourage believers to trust in God's sovereignty, cling to the hope of Christ's resurrection, and live out their faith with boldness and humility in a world that may oppose them.

It is an intriguing perspective to view the disobedient sons of God in the time of Noah as a type of Old Covenant Israel. Just as the sons of God rebelled against God's commands and were judged in the flood, Old Covenant Israel also rebelled against God and faced judgment in AD 70 when Jerusalem was destroyed by the Roman army.

The parallel between the judgment of the sons of God in the flood and the judgment of Old Covenant Israel in AD 70 can be seen as a warning of the consequences of disobedience and rebellion against God. Just as the flood was a cataclysmic event that wiped out the sinful generation in Noah's time, the destruction of Jerusalem in AD 70 was a devastating consequence of Israel's rejection of Christ and refusal to repent.

In referencing the days of Noah, Christ was alluding to the similarities between the moral decay and judgment of that time and the impending judgment that Old Covenant Israel would face. The destruction of Jerusalem in AD 70 served as a sobering reminder of the consequences of rejecting God and failing to uphold the covenant.

Ultimately, the parallels between the disobedience of the sons of God in the time of Noah and the judgment of Old Covenant Israel in AD 70 is a wonderful picture of what God was going to bring about on the Jews that held on to the old system and old world of Judaism.

I am of the persuasion that those that rose with Christ and appeared to many in Jerusalem testified of the impending judgment that was coming as a warning from their own experience of not joining with Noah and his family before the flood. The tombs were also opened. And many bodies of the saints who had fallen asleep were raised, and coming out of the tombs after His resurrection they went into the holy city and appeared to many[150] Some believe that these sons of God were fallen angels based on the book of Enoch, but I am of this persuasion. Peter uses the ark of Noah as going through the judgment as the waters of the flood caused the ark to be submerged in the flood, Peter uses this picture as a baptism, death, burial, and resurrection into the new creation. This baptism of fire of God's judgment did not affect the 1st Century saints because they were in Christ and were safe as Peter points through water is through the judgment.

---

[149] *The Holy Bible: English Standard Version* (Mt 3:11–12). (2016). Crossway Bibles.
[150] *The Holy Bible: English Standard Version* (Mt 27:51–53). (2016). Crossway Bibles.

This is not being saved as in salvation and being born again, but saved from the wrath of God which the believers were not destined for. 1 Thessalonians 5:9-11 English Standard Version 2016 (ESV) **For God has not destined us for wrath**, but to obtain salvation through our Lord Jesus Christ, who died for us so that whether we are awake or asleep we might live with him. Therefore encourage one another and build one another up, just as you are doing. Christ during His descension into the lower parts of the earth preached to the spirits in prison. In the original language the word "now" is not in there, "he made a proclamation to the spirits in prison". When Peter wrote this the antediluvian sons of God were not in their graves. They ascended when Christ ascended in the cloud awaiting the time of the end. His ascension Peter writes has caused angels, all authorities and powers who were now subject to Him. Today He is still on the throne, and no one is going to kick Him off of it. His kingdom knows no end.

In these verses from 1 Peter 4:4-7, the apostle Peter talks about the reaction of unbelievers towards Christians who do not participate in their sinful behaviors and excesses of dissipation. He emphasizes that these unbelievers will be held accountable by God, who is ready to judge both the living and the dead. Peter then goes on to explain that the gospel has been preached even to those who have died, so that even though they were judged in the flesh as men, they may live in the spirit according to the will of God. Peter is highlighting the importance of living a life that is distinct from the world, even when faced with persecution and ridicule from unbelievers. He emphasizes the imminent judgment that all will face, whether they are living or dead.

Peter focuses on the nearness of the time of the end, as Peter mentions that "the end of all things is near." This sense of urgency underscores that those believers were to remain faithful to God, to preach the gospel to those who have not heard it, and to live according to the will of God despite the opposition they may face from the world.

He is stressing the importance of remaining steadfast in the face of persecution, proclaiming the gospel to all, and living in anticipation of the imminent return of Christ and the final judgment.

Since the end was near and the Lord Jesus predicted that the agape love of many would grow cold, Peter writes; be of sound judgment and sober *spirit* for the purpose of prayer. **8** Above all, **keep fervent in your love for one another,** because love covers a multitude of sins. **9 Be hospitable** to one another **without complaint.**[151] In the midst of persecution where many were losing their homes and livelihood, Peter urges believers to practice hospitality towards one another without grumbling or complaint. This directive emphasizes the importance of extending kindness and generosity to those in need, even in the face of personal loss and hardship. By showing hospitality with a willing and cheerful spirit,

---

[151] <u>New American Standard Bible, 1995 Edition: Paragraph Version</u> (1 Pe 4:7–10). (1995). The Lockman Foundation.

believers demonstrate their genuine care and compassion for one another, reflecting the love and selflessness exemplified by Christ.

10 As each one has received the gift of grace, even so serving this to one another, as good stewards of the multifarious grace of God. 11 If any man speaks let him speak as the oracles of God; if any man serves, let him do as out of the ability which God supplies: that God in all things may be glorified through Jesus Christ, to Whom be praise and dominion into the New Covenant age from the Old Covenant age. Amen. 1 Pet. 4:10-11 TKB. In these verses from 1 Peter 4:10-11, the apostle Peter highlights the importance of using the charisma gifts of grace that each believer has received to serve one another and glorify God. Peter is giving the saints a sense of stewardship and responsibility that comes with receiving God's grace.

The idea that each believer is entrusted with a unique gift of grace, which should be used to benefit and support others in the body of Christ. This stewardship requires faithful and diligent service, as well as using the gifts in a manner that aligns with the will of God.

Furthermore, Peter's exhortation for believers to speak as the oracles of God and to serve with the ability that God provides underscores the importance of relying on God's strength and guidance in all aspects of ministry. The need for all believers to speak and serve in alignment with God's truth and to depend on His empowerment to carry out their service effectively. The priesthood didn't stop at AD 70, we still need to build one another up in Christ. There still needs to be a spiritual house in every generation, in every city, town, and hamlet shining with the testimony of Christ as light, life, and love.

Ultimately, Peter is encouraging believers to discover and utilize the charisma gifts of grace that God has bestowed upon them, to serve one another faithfully, and to bring glory to God through their words and works. By acknowledging God's provision and seeking to glorify Him in all things, believers can fulfill their role as stewards of the multifarious grace of God and supply for the advancement of His kingdom.

In these verses from 1 Peter 4:12-18, the apostle Peter addresses the challenges and trials that believers may face as they live out their faith in a world that is often hostile to the message of Christ. Once we understand the historical and cultural context of the Scriptures, we can expound on these verses by delving into the significance of persecution and suffering in the early Christian community. Peter was reassuring the believers not to be surprised by the fiery ordeal or the trials that they are facing, as it is a common experience for those who follow Christ. The early Christians were facing intense persecution and opposition from the Roman authorities and society at large, Nero was on the rampage, and Peter's words were meant to encourage them to stand firm in their faith amidst adversity. Furthermore, Peter is exhorting them to rejoice in the midst of suffering, as it is an opportunity to share in the sufferings of Christ and to participate in His redemptive work in the world. By enduring persecution with joy and steadfastness, believers demonstrate their allegiance to Christ and their trust in His ultimate victory and His sovereignty.

In 1 Peter 4:13, the mention of "the revelation of His glory" can also be understood in the context of the events surrounding AD 70, particularly the destruction of Jerusalem and the temple. In this interpretation, the fulfillment of the revelation of His glory can be seen as pointing to the judgment and vindication that occurred during this significant historical event.

When we draw from the understanding of AD 70 as a key moment in biblical prophecy, we may expound on this verse by connecting the revelation of His glory to the events of the destruction of Jerusalem. In this view, the dramatic and catastrophic events of AD 70 served as a manifestation of God's judgment and sovereignty, revealing His glory and vindicating the early Christians who had faced persecution and martyrdom.

The fall of Jerusalem and the temple marked a significant turning point in the history of God's people, demonstrating His justice and faithfulness in fulfilling His promises. The events of AD 70, with the devastation brought upon the city and the end of the Jewish sacrificial system, can be seen as a revelation of God's glory in His righteous judgment and establishment of the new covenant.

We need to see how the events of AD 70 underscored the importance of endurance, faithfulness, and perseverance in the face of trials and tribulations. Believers who had remained steadfast in their faith despite persecution would have seen the fulfillment of God's purpose and the revelation of His glory through the events of that time.

Additionally, Peter also cautions against suffering as a result of wrongdoing or sinful behavior, emphasizing the importance of living a life that is honorable and in accordance with the teachings of Christ. Believers are encouraged to glorify God even in the midst of suffering, knowing that their faithfulness will bear witness to the life changing power of the gospel.

In these verses from 1 Peter 4:16-19, the apostle Peter alludes to the impending judgment that was to come upon the house of God. Peter's understanding of AD 70, which culminated in the destruction of Jerusalem and the temple, can provide a lens through which to interpret these verses.

Peter warns that judgment will begin with the household of God, indicating that the Jewish community, particularly those who rejected Jesus as the Messiah, would face severe consequences for their disobedience and unbelief. The events of AD 70, which saw the destruction of the temple and the dispersion of the Jewish people, served as a fulfillment of this prophetic warning. Additionally, Peter's contemplation of the difficulties faced by the righteous in being saved can be understood in light of the turmoil and persecution that Christians faced leading up to and during the events of AD 70. The apostle's words may reflect the challenges and hardships that believers encountered as they remained faithful to their beliefs amidst societal unrest and upheaval.

Furthermore, Peter's encouragement for those who suffer according to the will of God to entrust their souls to a faithful Creator takes on added significance in the context of the judgment of AD 70. Believers who endured persecution and hardship during this tumultuous period were called to maintain their trust in God's providence and sovereignty, even in the face of adversity.

Overall, Peter's belief that AD 70 signified judgment on the house of God influences his encouragement for believers to stay faithful, endure in righteousness, and rely on God's faithfulness amidst tribulation.

Chapter 5

In these verses from 1 Peter 5:1-5, the apostle Peter provides guidance to the elders and younger members of the early Christian community. The focus is on the importance of leadership, humility, and mutual respect within the church. It is quite a revelation when you understand that to be an elder in the church, you must be the husband of one wife. Paul was never addressed as an elder. This means that when Peter said as a fellow-elder, he must have been married. We know that Peter's mother-in-law was sick with a fever Jesus healed her. There is a portion of scripture I would like to address regarding elders, bishops, pastors. It wasn't until the 3rd Century that these roles were separated, but in the 1st Century these were a description of three in one. For instance, Acts 20, [17]From Miletus **he sent to Ephesus and called to him the elders of the church**. [18]And when they had come to him, he said to them[152]... [28]Be on guard for yourselves and for all the flock, among which **the Holy Spirit has made you overseers**, **to shepherd the church** of God which He purchased with His own blood. [29]I know that after my departure savage wolves will come in among you, not sparing the flock; [30]and from among your own selves men will arise, speaking perverse things, to draw away the disciples after them.[153] In this portion of scripture we see Elders from the church in Ephesus.

Paul says to the elders, the holy spirit has made you Overseers (bishops), to shepherd the church. The word shepherd is pastor. These men were elders, bishops, pastors. Three in one I call it. The elder is a mature saint, so the quality of these elders was there maturity. Their function was to oversee, 'episkope', epi over, skope, see. This was the elders function. Their gift was a pastor. We see these men collegiately were taking care of the church with their maturity, functioning, with their gifting. Towards the middle of the 3rd century, pastors and bishops became two different offices, and the hierarchy began until a pastor and priest were locally over the elders, and it was no longer three in one but now three separate offices. Then the bishops were over the pastors and priests. What a mess!

---

[152] *New American Standard Bible, 1995 Edition: Paragraph Version* (Ac 20:17–18). (1995). The Lockman Foundation.

[153] *New American Standard Bible, 1995 Edition: Paragraph Version* (Ac 20:28–30). (1995). The Lockman Foundation.

Peter's exhortation to the elders to shepherd the flock of God among them with diligence and care, modeling their leadership after Jesus Christ, the Chief Pastor. By exercising oversight willingly and eagerly, and by setting an example of humility and service, the elders can effectively guide and nurture the spiritual growth of the community. Peter's emphasis on the importance of humility in relationships within the church. Younger members are encouraged to respect and submit to their elders, while all members are called to clothe themselves with humility toward one another. This attitude of humility reflects a posture of dependence on God's grace and a willingness to serve one another in love. Additionally, Peter's warning against pride, noting that God opposes the proud but gives grace to the humble. This reminder reinforces the call to humility and mutual submission within the community, as well as the recognition of God's sovereignty and favor upon those who walk in humility and obedience.

In 1 Peter chapter 5 the church is addressed in terms of the role and responsibility of the elders or overseers within the community. The use of the Greek word "kleros" in this passage, translated as "clergy" in English, has its origins in the concept of the portion or inheritance assigned to the church. The church is God's inheritance. And as we take pleasure in God, we become integrated with God, and He as our inheritance becomes one; the result is that we are God's people, that is, we are God's inheritance and God's portion. His inheritance is in the saints, not just the leaders of the church. The church is a special people as God's allotment. The Roman church and many non-Roman churches have muddied the waters in making a special priesthood the clergy, this is wrong, and we need to see the church as the clergy. These verses reveal that truth. (Eph. 1:18). having the **eyes of your hearts enlightened, that you may know** what is the hope to which he has called you, **what are the riches** of **His glorious inheritance in the saints.** His inheritance is in the saints. His legal clergy "kleronomia", His special class of people. Kleronomia comes from two Greek words. Kleros and nomos. We know what 'kleros' means and 'nomos' is law. The legal heirship, legal clergy. Just like in the Old Covenant there was a special class of priests called Levites, many of the churches today have adopted this model to our shame. Originally Yahweh desired a kingdom of priests, a royal priesthood and now He has it in the New Covenant. Let's strip ourselves of the old model and start practicing the New Covenant model. For us to be God's people means that we're His inheritance; we not only inherit God as our inheritance for our pleasure, but we also become God's inheritance for His pleasure. There is a mutual enjoyment of each other. The term "kleros" carries the connotation of being a portion, lot, or inheritance, and it was used in the New Testament to refer to the church who were chosen or appointed for a specific task or role within the community of unbelievers. The leaders were to shepherd the church and oversee her well-being.

W.E. Vine, a renowned biblical scholar and lexicographer, likely emphasizes the connection between the Greek word "kleros" and the English word "clergy" to underscore the idea that those appointed to leadership roles within the church are seen as having a specific portion or allotment of responsibility in caring for the spiritual well-being of the community. The concept of clergy, derived from "kleros," carries with it the idea of those who are set apart for a particular ministry or service within the church. Peter calls the church the clergy. ³nor yet as lording it over those **allotted to your charge**,[154] … In this verse the words allotted to your charge is one Greek word, "kleros". This is the traditional concept of 1 Peter 5:3, the use of the term "kleros" to describe the elders or overseers within the church is a grave mistake. God has appointed shepherds and overseers to the flock of God. The leaders can't be the clergy since they are being admonished to not lord over the clergy. Vine's connection to the English word "clergy" serves to emphasize the idea of those who have been set apart for a specific ministry within the community, not of believers but of unbelievers. Look at the Greek text and you tell me if we have fallen for tradition or not.

³μηδ	ως	κατακυριευοντες	των	κληρων	αλλα	γινομενοι	του	ποιμνιου	τυποι
not	as	lording over	the	clergy	but	being	of the	flock.	patterns
μηδέ	ὡς	κατακυριεύω	ὁ	κλῆρος	ἀλλά	γίνομαι	ὁ	ποίμνιον	τύπος
3366	5613	2634	3588	2819	235	1096	3588	4168	5179

You will see that there is a lot of creativity in translating this verse to give the impression that the clergy is something different than the church. Listen I believe in leadership, and I believe in spiritual authority. I believe in the fivefold ascension gifts that the bible says, "He gave some to be". I am not throwing the baby out with the bathwater. We must be clear that all God's people are the treasured possession, God's inheritance and they are priests of God. There are gifted men and women in the body and yes, I said women. These gifted people have a responsibility for the people of God, but they are not the clergy, they are part of the clergy.

As Peter closes this letter, let us consider these words of wisdom from the apostle Peter through the lens of the first century Church. In the early days of Christianity, believers faced intense persecution and hardship for their allegiance to Christ.

As they humbled themselves under the mighty hand of God, they were often at odds with the powerful forces of the Roman Empire and the religious authorities of the day. They were marginalized, oppressed, and even killed for their faith. Yet, they took solace in the promise that God would exalt them at the proper time, even if it meant enduring suffering in this present life.

---

[154] *New American Standard Bible, 1995 Edition: Paragraph Version* (1 Pe 5:3). (1995). The Lockman Foundation.

In the face of anxiety and fear, these early Christians cast all their cares upon the Lord, finding comfort in the knowledge that He cared for them deeply. They leaned on their faith in the midst of trials, knowing that God was faithful and would never abandon them, even in the face of persecution from their adversaries.

The first century Church understood all too well the reality of spiritual warfare. They were alert and vigilant against the schemes of the devil, who sought to devour them and lead them away from the truth of the Gospel. They stood firm in their faith, drawing strength from the knowledge that they were not alone in their struggles.

Despite the suffering and trials, they faced, these early Christians found hope in the promise of God's grace. They knew that after enduring a little while, the God of all grace would perfect, confirm, strengthen, and establish them in their faith, leading them to perpetual glory in Christ.

Let us look to the example of our first-century brothers and sisters in the faith, who endured great hardships and persecution with steadfastness and courage. May we draw strength from their example as we face our own struggles and trials in the world today. And let us give honor and praise to the God who sustains us, to whom belongs dominion forever and ever. Amen.

Beloved brethren, let us consider the closing words of the apostle Peter as he shares his final exhortations and greetings with the early Christian community. Through the faithful messenger Silvanus, Peter has penned this brief letter to encourage and testify to the true grace of God that sustains and empowers us in our journey of faith. He urges us to stand firm in this grace, knowing that it is the very foundation of our salvation and the source of our strength.

Peter sends greetings from "She who is in Babylon," a symbolic name that John was given by the Lord as the great city, where our Lord was crucified. The church in Jerusalem was she who was in Babylon. Babylon was the embodiment of Old Covenant Israel who murdered the prophets in the Old Testament and continued her bloodlust into the New Testament period to destroy the apostles and saints. Old Jerusalem is the mother of harlots. That means she has daughters who imitate and practice the same spirit of hatred and murder towards what is of God.

This is a reminder that we, as believers, are chosen and set apart by God, called to live boldly and faithfully in the face of opposition and hardship. Let us take heart in the solidarity of our fellow brothers and sisters in Christ, knowing that we are united in our shared experiences of suffering and triumph.

The apostle also remembers to convey the greetings of his son in the faith, Mark, a fellow laborer in the Gospel ministry. It is a reminder that we are not alone in our journey but are surrounded by a community of believers who offer support, encouragement, and love along the way. Let us greet one another with a kiss of love, demonstrating the unity and affection that binds us together as members of the body of Christ.

In conclusion, Peter offers a blessing of peace to all who are in Christ. May this peace, which surpasses all understanding, guard our hearts and minds as we navigate the trials and tribulations of this world. Let us hold fast to the true grace of God, stand firm in our faith, and continue to love and support one another in the name of Christ. Peace be with you all, dear brothers and sisters in the faith. Amen.

By alluding to past events and prophecies, Peter underscores the unbroken continuity and realization of God's grand design across the generations. These allusions not only fortify the theological foundation of his message, but they also bolster the authenticity and pertinence of his teachings to his contemporary audience.

Terry Kashian

1 Peter

Chapter 1

1. Peter, an apostle of Jesus Christ, to those outsiders residing alongside the people, as scattered seed in Pontus, Galatia, Cappadocia, Asia, and Bithynia,
2. Chosen according to the foreknowledge of God the Father, in sanctification of the Spirit, into obedience of Jesus Christ and the sprinkling blood: grace to you, and peace be multiplied.
3. Blessed is the God and Father of our Lord Jesus Christ, who according to His overflowing mercy has regenerated us into a lively anticipation through the resurrection of Jesus Christ out from the dead,
4. To an inheritance incorruptible, flawless, unable to fade, guarded in the heavens for you,
5. Those protected in the power of God through faith into salvation ready to be revealed in the final appointed time.
6. In which you greatly rejoice, though now for a little while, if need be, you have grievances in numerous trials:
7. That the proving of your faith, being much more precious than of gold that perishes, though it is tested with fire, may be found for acclamation and honor and glory at the revelation of Jesus Christ:
8. Whom having not seen, you are loving; in Whom, though now you do not see Him, yet believing, you rejoice with joy unspeakable and being glorified:
9. Receiving the goal of your faith, even the salvation of your souls.
10. Of which salvation the prophets have inquired and searched diligently, who prophesied of the grace that should come into you:
11. Searching what, or what manner of time the Spirit of Christ which was in them did make known when they predicted the sufferings of Christ and the glories that would come after.
12. To whom it was revealed, that it was not for themselves, but they were serving us these things, who are now declaring to you by them that have preached the gospel to you in the Holy Spirit sent down from heaven; into which angels desire to look.
13. Therefore, having prepared your minds thoroughly, being sober, and expecting the completion of the grace that is to be brought to you at the revelation of Jesus Christ;
14. As obedient children, not conforming yourselves to the patterns according to your previous desires in ignorance:
15. But as He which has called you is holy, so be holy in all behavior;
16. Because it is written, you be holy; for I am holy.
17. And if you are calling to the Father, who judges fairly according to each one's work, act properly throughout the time of your journey in fear:
18. Since as you know that you were not redeemed with corruptible things, as silver and gold, from your aimless manner of life handed down from your fathers;
19. But with the precious blood of Christ, as of a lamb flawless and spotless:

20. Who indeed was foreknown before the downfall of the world, but was made clear in the time of the end for you,

21. Who through Him are believing into God, that raised Him out from the dead, and gave Him glory; that your faith and expectation be in God.

22. Having consecrated your souls in obeying the reality through the Spirit into authentic love for the brothers, love one another intensely with a pure heart:

23. Having been regenerated, not of corruptible seed, but of incorruptible, by the word of God, which lives and continues into the New Covenant age.

24. For all flesh is as grass and all the glory of man as the flower of the fields. The grass withers and the flower fades away,

25. But the word of the Lord continues into the new covenant age. And this present word is the gospel to you.

Chapter 2

1. Therefore, laying aside all malice, and all guile, and hypocrisies, and envies, all slandering,

2. As newborn babes, yearn for the unadulterated milk of the word that you may grow into salvation:

3. If so you have tasted that the Lord is gracious.

4. Coming towards Him, as to a living stone, being rejected indeed by men, but chosen of God and precious,

5. You also, as living stones, are being built up as a spiritual house, a holy priesthood, to offer up spiritual sacrifices, acceptable to God through Jesus Christ.

6. Therefore, also it is contained in the Scripture, behold, I lay in Zion a chief cornerstone, chosen and precious: and he that is believing on Him will in no way be disgraced.

7. To you believing then, He is priceless: but the unbelieving, the stone which the builders rejected, the same is made the chief cornerstone,

8. And a stone of stumbling, and a rock causing scandal, even to those who get tripped up against the word, refusing to believe into which also they were appointed.

9. But you are a chosen species, a regal priesthood, a holy nation, a purchased people; that you should declare far and wide the moral excellencies of Him who has called you out of darkness into His marvelous light;

10. Which at one time were not a people, but are now the people of God: which had not obtained mercy, but now have obtained mercy.

11. Dearly beloved, I implore you as strangers and outsiders residing alongside the people, to abstain from fleshly cravings, which war against the soul;

12. Having your conduct exemplary among the nations: that, when they speak against you as evildoers, they may by your good works, which they will behold, glorify God in the day of visitation.

13. Submit yourselves to every constitution of man for the Lord's sake: whether it be to the king, as supreme;

14. Or to governors, as to them that are sent by him for the punishment of evildoers, and for the praise of them that do well.
15. For so is the will of God, that with well doing you may put to silence the ignorance of foolish men:
16. As free, and not using your freedom even as a covering for wickedness, but as the servants of God.
17. Honor all men. Love the brotherhood. Fear God. Honor the King.
18. Servants, be subject to your masters with all respect; not only to the good and gentle but also to the perverse.
19. Indeed, this is grace, if a man endures grievances, suffering unjustly because of conscience towards God.
20. For what credit is it, if, when you are mistreated for sinning, you endure it? But if, when you do well, and suffer for it, you endure it, this is acceptable with God.
21. For even to this you were called: because Christ also suffered for us, leaving us an example, that you should follow in His footprints:
22. Who did not sin, neither was guile found in his mouth:
23. Who, when He was reviled, did not revile back; when He suffered, He threatened not; but committed Himself to Him that judge righteously:
24. Who Himself bore our sins in His own body on the tree, that we, being separated from sins, are to be living to righteousness: by His wounds, you were healed.
25. For you were as sheep going astray; but now turned toward the Shepherd and Overseer of your souls.

Chapter 3

1. In the same way, you wives, being in subjection to your own husbands; that, if any are obstinate to the word, they also may without a word, be gained by the conduct of the wives;
2. While they behold your pure and respectful conduct.
3. Whose beauty should not come from merely outward adorning of braiding the hair, and of wearing of gold, or of putting on of fine apparel;
4. But let it be the hidden man of the heart, in that incorruptible part, even the ornament of a gentle and tranquil spirit, which is surpassing value in the presence of God.
5. For in this manner formerly the holy women also, who trusted in God, adorned themselves, being in subjection to their own husbands:
6. Just as Sarah obeyed Abraham, calling him lord: whose children you have become, showing yourself beneficent, and not frightened away by any fear.
7. Likewise, you husbands, make a home together according to knowledge, giving honor to the wife, as to the weaker vessel, and as being co-heirs of the grace of life; that your prayer life is not impeded.
8. Finally, all of you be of one mind, sympathetic, with brotherly love, be tender-hearted, be friendly:
9. Not returning evil for evil, or insult for insult: but with continual blessing; knowing that you are called, that you should inherit a blessing.

10. For he that will love life, and see good days, let him refrain his tongue from evil, and his lips that they speak no deceit:

11. Let him turn away from evil, and do good; let him seek peace, and pursue it.

12. For the eyes of the Lord are upon the righteous, and His ears are open to their prayers: but the face of the Lord is against them that do evil.

13. And who is he that will harm you, if you be followers of that which is good?

14. But even if you suffer for righteousness sake, blessed are you: and do not be frightened away of their terror, neither be agitated;

15. But sanctify the Lord God in your hearts: and be always prepared to give a defense to everyone that asks you for the word concerning the hope that is in you with gentleness and respect:

16. Having a good conscience; that, though they speak evil of you, as of evildoers, they may be ashamed that falsely accuse your good conduct in Christ.

17. For it is better, if the will of God be so, that you suffer for well doing, than for evil doing.

18. For Christ also has once suffered for sins, the just for the unjust, that he might bring us to God, being put to death in the flesh, but made alive in Spirit:

19. By which also he went and preached to the spirits in prison;

20. Which at one time were disobedient, when the long-suffering of God once waited in the days of Noah, while the ark was being prepared, in which a few, that is, eight souls were saved by water.

21. The symbol to which even baptism also now is saving us (not the putting away of the filth of the flesh, but the appeal of a good conscience toward God) by the resurrection of Jesus Christ:

22. Who is gone into heaven, and is at the right hand of God; angels and authorities and powers being made subject to Him.

Chapter 4

1. Since Christ has suffered for us in the flesh, arm yourselves fully likewise with the same mind: for he that has suffered in the flesh has ceased from sin;

2. To no longer spend the remaining time in the flesh to the lusts of men but to the will of God.

3. For sufficient for us was the passing of the time of our life to work out the purpose of the nations, when we walked in debauchery, lusts, drunkenness, orgies, carousing, and abominable idolatries:

4. While they are stunned that you do not run around with them to the same extreme, being out of control and blaspheming.

5. They will give an account to Him that is ready to judge the living and the dead.

6. For this purpose was the gospel also preached to them that are dead, that they might be judged according to men in the flesh and be living according to God in the Spirit.

7. Now of all things the end is approaching: therefore, now be sober-minded and watchful into prayer.

8. And before all things have intense love inside yourselves: for love will cover the multitude of sins.
9. Offer hospitality to one another without complaining.
10 As each one has received the gift of grace, even so serving this to one another, as good stewards of the multifarious grace of God.
11 If any man speaks let him speak as the oracles of God; if any man serves, let him do as out of the ability which God supplies: that God in all things may be glorified through Jesus Christ, to Whom be praise and dominion into the New Covenant age from the Old Covenant age. Amen.
12. Though some strange thing happened to you:
13. But rejoice, so much as you are in the fellowship of Christ's sufferings; continue rejoicing that at the revealing of His glory, you may be elated and leap for joy.
14. If you are being verbally abused in the name of Christ, you are blessed; for the spirit of glory and of God rests upon you: on their part, He is blasphemed, but on your part, He is glorified.
15. But let none of you suffer as a murderer, or as a thief, or as an evildoer, or as a busybody in other men's matters.
16. Yet if any man suffers as a Christian, let him not be ashamed; but let him glorify God on this behalf.
17. For the time has come that the judgment must begin at the house of God: and if it first begins with us, what will the end be of them that disobey the gospel of God?
18. And if the righteous is being saved with difficulty, in what place will the ungodly and the sinner appear?
19. Therefore, let them that suffer according to the will of God commit the keeping of their souls to Him in well doing, as to a faithful Creator.

Chapter 5

1. The elders which are among you I exhort, who am also an elder, and a witness of the sufferings of Christ, and also a companion of the glory that is about to be revealed:
2. Shepherd the flock of God which is in your midst, taking the oversight of it, not by obligation, but willingly; not for avaricious gain, but enthusiastically;
3. Neither as being lords over God's clergy, but being patterns to the flock.
4. And when the Chief Pastor is manifested, you will receive a crown of glory that will not fade away.
5. Likewise, you younger, submit yourselves to the older. Yes, all of you be subject one to another, and be clothed with humility: for God resists the proud and gives grace to the humble.
6. Therefore, humble yourselves under the mighty hand of God, that He may exalt you in the appointed time:
7. Casting all your cares upon Him; for He cares for you.
8. Be sober-minded, be watchful; because your adversary the Devil, as a roaring lion, walks about, seeking who he may devour:
9. Who resist steadfast in the faith, knowing that the same afflictions are accomplished in your brothers that are in the world.

10. But the God of all grace, who has called us into His infinite glory in Christ Jesus, after you have suffered a little, make you entirely complete, resolute, strengthened, and stable.
11. His is the dominion and the glory into the New Covenant Age from the Old Covenant Age. Amen.
12. Through Silvanus, a faithful brother to you, as I maintain, I have written few things, exhorting, and testifying that this is the true grace of God in which you are standing.
13. The Assembly that is in Babylon, chosen together with you, greets you; and so does Mark, my son.
14. Greet one another with a kiss of love. Peace be with you all that are in Christ Jesus. Amen.

2nd Peter Synopsis

2 Pet. 1:1-2

Beloved readers, let us meditate on the words of the apostle Peter as he addresses those who have received the precious gift of faith through the righteousness of our God and Savior Jesus Christ. Peter, a humble slave and apostle of Jesus Christ, extends his greetings and blessings to all who have embraced this life changing faith.

He speaks of the abundance of grace and peace that is available to us through the full knowledge of God and our Lord Jesus Christ. This knowledge is not merely intellectual, but experiential and intimate, leading us into deeper communion with our Creator and Savior. In this full knowledge, we find the fountainhead of grace that sustains us in times of trial and the peace that transcends all understanding.

As recipients of this precious faith, let us treasure it as a priceless gift, recognizing the righteousness of our God and Savior Jesus Christ that has brought us into relationship with Him. May we continually seek to grow in the full knowledge of God and Jesus our Lord, allowing His grace and peace to flow abundantly in our lives and manifest through our actions and attitudes.

May we be encouraged and strengthened by the words of Peter, remembering the richness of our faith and the immeasurable blessings that come from walking in relationship with our God and Savior. Let us strive to deepen our knowledge of Him, so that His grace and peace may overflow in our hearts and spill over into the lives of those around us. May grace and peace be yours in abundance, dear brothers and sisters, as you walk in the full knowledge of God and Jesus our Lord.

2 Pet. 1:3-4

Precious saints, let us consider the profound truth revealed to us by the apostle Peter. He reveals to us the magnificent reality that by His divine power and He declares that through the divine power of God, we have been granted all things necessary for life and godliness. This provision is not based on our own efforts or abilities but is a gracious gift from our heavenly Father.

It is through our full knowledge of Him, the One who has called us to share in His glory and moral excellence, that we are able to partake of this abundance. As we grow in our understanding of God and His ways, we are equipped to live a life that is pleasing to Him and shine forth His character.

The promises of God are described as peerless and precious, offering us the opportunity to become companions of the divine nature. Through these promises, we are able to escape the corruption that is inherent in the world's desires and live lives that are pleasing to God. Let us then treasure these promises and allow them to shape and transform us into vessels of honor that display the beauty and character of our Lord. By walking in obedience and holiness, we can express the divine nature to a world that is in desperate need of light and truth. May we hold fast to these promises, allowing them to guide us in our journey of faith and draw us closer to the heart of our Father.

2 Pet. 1:5-8

Beloved brothers and sisters, let us dive into the rich imagery of choreography as we explore the concept of divine provision and the orchestration of our spiritual walk. The Greek word for "supply" carries the nuance of furnishing upon, giving generously, and providing beyond measure. Just as a choreographer meticulously plans the sequence of steps and movements in a dance production, God lavishly supplies us with everything we need for life and godliness.

Imagine your spiritual journey as a grand, divinely choreographed dance, where God is the Master Choreographer who has intricately designed every movement and step of our lives even before the downfall of the world. As followers of Christ, we are called to diligently seek to fulfill the unique parts He has prepared for us in this grand production of the Christian life. Our ultimate goal is to bring honor and glory to the Author of faith, who has scripted the music, the words, and the movements of our lives. Eph. 2:10.

In 2 Peter 1:5-8, we are presented with a beautiful progression of virtues that form the choreography of our spiritual growth. From faith to moral excellence, from knowledge to self-control, from perseverance to dedication, and from brotherly love to divine love. These virtues are the intricate steps that shape our Christian walk and lead us closer to the full knowledge of our Lord Jesus Christ.

Let us, then, diligently pursue these virtues, allowing them to intensify and grow within us, so that we may not be inactive or unfruitful in the full knowledge of Christ. Just as a well-executed dance captures the attention and admiration of its audience, may our lives radiate with the beauty and harmony of God's divine choreography, drawing others to the glory of our Lord Jesus Christ.

Kenneth S. Wuest adds that epichoregeo was... derived from chorus, a chorus, such as was employed in the representation of Greek tragic dramas. The verb originally meant 'to bear the expense of a chorus,' which was done by a person selected by the state, who was obliged to defray all the expense of training and maintenance." Strachan adds, "It was a duty that prompted to lavishness in execution. Hence choregeo came to mean 'supplying costs for any purpose,' a public duty or religious service, with a tending, as here, towards the meaning, 'providing more than is barely demanded.'" Thus, the word means "to supply in copious measure, to provide beyond the need, to supply more than generously.""(Wuest, K. S. Wuest's Word Studies from the Greek New Testament: Logos). What a beautiful picture Peter is painting about someone else supplying what we need to become godly and virtuous. Supply is in the aorist imperative word and it is a peremptory command to carry out this "abundant furnishing" with a sense of urgency. Do this now and do not delay! What Peter is commanding by using the aorist imperative is that spiritual growth demands that we make a choice, and that such growth will not come automatically or inevitably. We are to receive the fully supply all that is needed to make the "production" (the virtues in 2 Pe 1:5-7) a "success" so to speak. And what God requires of us, God's grace provides for us (copiously, abundantly, amazingly). In other words every divine commandment is based on divine enablement (the indwelling Holy Spirit's empowerment). If we look at the word choreography - The root verb choregeo gives us our English word choreography which is defined as the **sequence of steps and movements in dance, the arrangement of movements that the audience sees on the stage.** We are God's masterpiece better than any of the plays of the Greeks or Romans. Think of a dance. Someone leads and the other follows. The GUIDANCE is an interesting word. Peter is guiding the saints to the source in the beginning of this epistle, and he wants the saints to follow his lead. This is guidance at its apex! We may not know this dance therefore God has supplied richly someone to lead us in the steps. The letters of guidance start with G, so the G is preeminent. This is God and then the second letter is U and that's where you come in, and the third is I, and that's where I come in. After those three letters you have the word DANCE. Guidance is following the Lord together as we learn the steps and we are supplied to exhibit on the stage of life so those in the world who are looking on can be blessed with a glorious performance of the divine nature being expressed. We need to trust our benefactor, the Lord Jesus to supply and lead us in every step.

2 Pet. 1:9-11

These verses remind us of the importance of growing in faith and embodying the qualities of a faithful follower of Christ, especially leading up to the fulfillment of the prophesied events in AD 70. It is crucial to actively pursue virtue, knowledge, self-control, endurance, godliness, mutual affection, and love in order to maintain spiritual clarity and avoid nearsightedness and spiritual blindness during this significant time.

As believers, they were called to confirm their call and election and to ensure they were walking in alignment with God's will as they approached the events of AD 70. By doing so, they would be assured that they would stand firm and not stumble during the challenging times that they were in and what was coming. Their entrance into the perpetual kingdom of our Lord and Savior Jesus Christ will be abundantly supplied for them. The word 'epichoregeo' is the word supplied. A totally financed entrance into the kingdom is promised in the face of these impending events. We need to see the that these saints were in the midst of the Neronic rage and insanity that was rampant in the Roman Empire. Peter is on fire and has such an encouraging word for them. Let us eagerly cultivate these qualities in our lives and deepen our relationship with Christ.

2 Pet. 1:12-15

From a preterist viewpoint, the verses 12-15 in 2 Peter 1 convey a sense of urgency and impending fulfillment of prophetic events. The apostle Peter, writing to the early Christian community, emphasizes the importance of being reminded of the teachings and truths of the faith, even though they may already be established in them.

Peter likens his physical body to a tent, symbolizing its temporary and transient nature. This imagery suggests that Peter is aware of his impending death and departure from this world. In verse 14, Peter mentions that he must shortly "put away" his tent, indicating his awareness of his imminent martyrdom or death. This echoes Jesus' prediction in John 21:18-19 regarding Peter's death. The apostle expresses his intention to continue reminding and waking up the believers through his teachings and exhortations. By highlighting the brevity of his own life and the certainty of his departure, Peter underscores the urgent need for the believers to internalize and pass on the teachings he has imparted to them.

Furthermore, in verse 15, Peter expresses his desire that the believers will have a lasting memory of his teachings even after his decease. This reflects Peter's commitment to ensuring the preservation and transmission of the gospel message and the truths of the faith to future generations.

Overall, from a preterist perspective, these verses in 2 Peter 1 serve as a poignant reminder of the imminent fulfillment of prophetic events, the urgency of the apostolic message, and the need for believers to remain steadfast in their faith even in the face of impending trials and persecutions. Peter's words convey a sense of urgency and purpose in preparing the early Christian community for the challenges that lie ahead.

2 Pet. 1:16-21

Let's unpack these powerful verses in 2 Peter 1 from a preterist perspective, tying them back to the Mount Transfiguration experience where Peter, James, and John were given a glimpse of the end of the Old Covenant age and the preeminence of Christ in the new covenant age.

Peter starts by emphasizing that the teachings he and the apostles shared about the power and presence of Jesus Christ were not made up myths but were based on their own firsthand experiences. These experiences included witnessing the majesty of Christ in the Transfiguration event where Jesus was revealed in His glory and received honor and glory from God the Father. The voice from heaven confirmed Jesus as the beloved Son of God, who was to be the central figure in the transition from the Old Covenant to the New Covenant age. Remember the story as these men saw Moses and Elijah which represent the Law and the Prophets. Peter was so excited that he told the Lord it was good that he was there. He wanted to build a tabernacle for Moses, Elijah, and Jesus. Suddenly the Majestic Voice thundered out of the cloud and Moses and Elijah disappeared and ONLY Jesus was in view. God was revealing that Jesus was the focus and the fading glory of the Old Covenant represented in Moses and Elijah is fading away.

The Transfiguration served as a powerful confirmation of the authority and divine nature of Jesus, foreshadowing His role as the preeminent figure in the new covenant age. Peter, in referencing this event, highlights the importance of paying attention to the word of prophecy as a guiding light in a dark world. Just as the Transfiguration revealed the glory of Christ, so too does the prophetic word shine as a beacon of hope and guidance until the full realization of the new covenant age. Peter uses the Morning Star rising in our hearts as picture. The morning star is the first light to appear before the new day. Peter was saying … where **you do well to pay attention**, as **to a lamp** that **shines in a dismal place, until the day dawn** and **the morning star rises in your hearts**:. On the canvas of Peter's thoughts here the church is the lamp which contains the sure word of prophecy, but it is shining in a dismal place. In the night, which is still the Old Covenant age, but their expectation is the day dawning. The New Covenant Age! The day is the New Covenant age which in the present time of Peter's writing, the **day was dawning**, the day was breaking through and the morning star was rising in their hearts. The morning star is Christ within them. Rev. 22:16 reveals Christ as the bright and morning star. In Rev. 2:28, those who overcome are promised the morning star which may be that they were going to enter the New Covenant age to reign in the spiritual authority over the nations. Some have suggested that the day dawning refers to the resurrection, which in my understanding, the Parousia, resurrection, and the coming of the new covenant age are all simultaneous. Resurrection is a rising and, in the morning, just like our Lord rose in the morning. I will need to study more on this to unpack it properly.

Moreover, Peter emphasizes the reliability and authenticity of the prophetic word, asserting that it does not come from human invention but is inspired by God through the Holy Spirit. This underscores the divine authority behind the prophecies that foretold the transition from the Old Covenant to the New Covenant, with Christ at the center of God's redemptive plan.

In conclusion, Peter's words serve as a powerful reminder of the transformative and authoritative nature of Christ, as revealed in the Transfiguration event and confirmed by the prophetic word. The Mount Transfiguration experience foreshadowed the coming of the new covenant age, where Christ would reign supreme, fulfilling the promises of old and ushering in a new beginning of redemption and glory.

2 Pet. 2:1-3

These verses from 2 Peter chapter 2 vividly warn against the rise of false teachers and prophets within the church, whose deceitful and destructive teachings threaten to lead believers astray. Just as there were false prophets among the people in the past, Peter cautions that false teachers will inevitably infiltrate the church, spreading dangerous and disruptive doctrines.

These false teachers, Peter explains, will stealthily introduce destructive heresies, subtly distorting and denying the sovereign authority of the Master, Jesus Christ, who purchased them with His own blood. By rejecting Christ and His teachings, these deceitful individuals bring swift destruction upon themselves, as they are held accountable for leading others astray and perverting the truth.

Furthermore, Peter warns that many will follow after these false teachers, succumbing to their deceptive words and ultimately facing their own spiritual destruction. The credibility and integrity of the true way of salvation, the gospel of Christ, will be maligned and spoken against by the influence of these deceitful individuals within the church.

The motivation behind the actions of these false teachers is revealed to be rooted in covetousness, as they exploit and manipulate believers for their own gain. With flattering and superficial words, they seek to take advantage of unsuspecting followers, turning the gospel into a means of profit and personal enrichment.

Peter concludes by emphasizing that the judgment and destruction awaiting these false teachers is imminent and inevitable. Their deception and exploitation will not go unpunished, as the day of reckoning was swiftly approaching. The apostle's sobering warning serves as a stern reminder to remain vigilant and discerning against the dangers posed by false teachers, safeguarding the truth of the gospel and protecting the flock from spiritual harm.

2 Pet. 2:4-10

In these verses, Peter is warning the church about the consequences of following false prophets and teachers, drawing parallels to historical events in the Old Testament. By interpreting the "messengers that sinned" as referring to the spies sent by Moses into the promised land, Peter is emphasizing the importance of faithfulness and obedience to God. In this context we should look at Peter's point in mentioning the quote "angels that sinned".

At first glance, we usually have the myth that some good angels rebelled against God. Something like they ganged up with each other thinking they could sneak up on God and take His throne. Ludicrous! The New Testament uses the Greek word aggelos for angel several times referring to human messengers. For example, James Likewise, was not Rahab the harlot also justified by works when she received the **messengers** and sent *them* out another way? [155] This is the word aggelos. The 12 spies were angels sent by Moses. Ten of them were sinful with their evil report of unbelief. Here are some references of human angels. Mt 11:10, Mk 1:2, Lk 7:24, Lk 9:52,

Just as God did not spare the spies who brought back an evil report and led the Israelites astray, He will also judge and punish false teachers and prophets in the church. Peter further illustrates this point by referencing the examples of Noah, who preached righteousness in the midst of a wicked world, and Lot, who was righteous but tormented by the sinful actions of those around him.

Ultimately, Peter assures the believers that God knows how to deliver the godly out of trials and will judge and punish the unrighteous. Peter is taking the past ways of God and making them relevant to those who were discouraged and wanting justice in their day. He specifically highlights those who walk after the flesh and hold contempt for authority, describing them as presumptuous, self-willed, and blasphemous. By drawing these parallels and examples, Peter is urging the church to remain faithful, resist false teachings, and trust in God's judgment and deliverance that was imminent.

2 Peter 2:11-19

In these verses from 2 Peter 2:11-19, the focus shifts to false teachers within the church who are characterized by their perverse and corrupt behavior. Peter contrasts these false teachers with even heavenly angels, emphasizing that angels, who are greater in power and might, do not bring a blaspheming judgment upon them before the Lord. Peter is using the angels as an example of giving the final say to God and not taking it into their own hands even though they are mightier than these false teachers. Instruction to those who want to judge these false teachers. This comparison serves to highlight the extreme nature of the false teachers' actions and the severity of their sins.

The false teachers are described as behaving like physically unreasonable animals, speaking evil of things they do not understand, and being ultimately corrupted by their own actions. They are portrayed as indulging in self-indulgence, luxury, and sinful behavior, leading others astray with their deceitful ways. They are likened to spots and blemishes, fully possessed with eyes of an adulteress, constantly seeking after their own desires and pleasures. These have the harlot spirit.

---

[155] *The New King James Version* (Jas 2:25). (1982). Thomas Nelson.

Peter further condemns these false teachers for forsaking the straight path of righteousness and following in the footsteps of Balaam, who was motivated by greed and the love of unrighteousness. He highlights how even Balaam, who was rebuked for his wickedness, was restrained by a dumb donkey speaking with a man's voice, emphasizing the absurdity of the false teachers' actions.

The false teachers are likened to waterless wells and clouds driven by the wind, empty and lacking substance. Peter's reference to waterless wells and clouds reminds me of the Proverb. He who boasts of his gift falsely is like a cloud without water. In the Hebrew language, the **word** for leader or prince is pictured as a mist that rises above the people and forms a cloud. These false teachers were those that exalted themselves and appear to people as leaders. Just like God comes in the cloud to speak to the children of Israel because He was in the cloud, these men are clouds without God in them. They are wells without God as the living water in them. They are just smooth talkers. Jude refers to these same types of people. They are condemned to darkness and are described as slaves of corruption, promising freedom but leading others into bondage and slavery to sin. Peter warns the believers to be wary of these deceptive teachers who speak great words of emptiness and allure through the lusts of the flesh, urging them to stay true to the genuine teachings of the faith and to resist the temptations of those who seek to lead them astray.

2 Pet. 2:19-22

Peter is painting a picture of a person who, after having received the holy commandment and tasted the righteousness of God, chooses to disregard it and return to their former ways. He uses the example of a dog that, after vomiting, goes back to eat it again, or a pig that has been washed clean only to return to wallowing in the mud. A reference to a proverb: Proverbs 26:11 American Standard Version (ASV) As a dog that returneth to his vomit, So is a fool that repeats his folly. These illustrations serve to highlight the folly and destructiveness of turning away from the truth and returning to a life of sin and corruption.

Peter is urging believers to remain steadfast in their faith, continue to follow the Lord, and avoid the pitfalls of false teachings and deceptive practices that can lead them astray. He emphasizes the need for consistent growth, maturity, and perseverance in the Christian walk to avoid the tragic outcome that awaits those who turn away from the truth they once knew.

2 Pet. 3:1-4

From a preterist perspective, 2 Peter 3 is addressing the doubts and skepticism of the recipients concerning the imminent return of Christ and the fulfillment of His promised presence. Peter is reminding the believers to remember the teachings of the prophets and apostles, pointing to the signs and events that were unfolding in their time as evidence of the coming eschatological fulfillment.

Peter is explaining that the mockers mentioned were individuals who were dismissing the idea of a future return of Christ, questioning the delay and wondering where the promised presence of the Lord was. We must understand the context of the first-century audience and the challenges they faced in maintaining their faith in the face of persecution and doubt.

Using this knowledge of historical context and the fulfillment of prophecies in the events leading up to and following the destruction of Jerusalem in 70 AD, the mockers' claims were refuted by the unfolding of history. The destruction of the temple and the city of Jerusalem was a significant sign of the end times, demonstrating the validity of the prophetic warnings given by Jesus and the apostles.

Peter is encouraging the believers to hold fast to their faith, remain steadfast in their understanding of the prophetic timeline, and trust in the fulfillment of God's promises despite the challenges and doubts they may face. He was emphasizing the importance of remaining attentive to the signs of the times and being prepared for the coming of the Lord, recognizing that the final days were indeed unfolding in their midst.

2 Pet. 3:5

What were the mockers ignoring? Peter says, 5 For this they willingly ignore, that by the word of God, the heavens were of old, and the earth standing out of the water and in the water: 6 in which **that world then was, being flooded with water, was destroyed**:. They are ignoring the fact that God saw the world and its evil and flooded it and destroyed it. The word destroyed is an interesting word that necessitates we look at it. It is the word apollumi in Greek.

1. apollumi (ἀπόλλυμι , (622)), a strengthened form of *ollumi,* signifies to destroy utterly; in Middle Voice, to perish. The idea is not extinction but ruin, loss, not of being, but of well–being[156] The world of Noah's time was destroyed, and he came into a new world. It was the living things that were destroyed, the wicked, but the planet was not destroyed.

7 but the heavens and the earth, which are now, by the same word are kept in store, reserved for fire into the day of judgment and destruction of godless men.

The word for destruction in this verse is the Greek Word: ἀπώλεια Transliteration: apōleia.[157] destruction (act) — the termination of something by causing so much damage to it that it cannot be repaired or no longer exists.

---

[156] Vine, W. E., & Bruce, F. F. (1981). In Vine's Expository dictionary of Old and New Testament words (Vol. 2, p. 302). Revell.
[157] Strong, J. (2020). ἀπώλεια. In Strong's Talking Greek and Hebrew Dictionary. WORDsearch.

8 But, beloved, do not ignore this one thing, that one day with the Lord is as a thousand years, and a thousand years is as one day. 9 Concerning His promise, the Lord is not postponing, as some men regard postponement; but is forbearing toward us, not desiring that any would be destroyed, but that all would come to repentance.

Most scholars agree that the thousand years as one day is taken from: **Psalm 90:1- 17** ESV. A Prayer of Moses, the man of God. Lord, you have been our dwelling place in all generations. Before the mountains were brought forth, or ever you had formed the earth and the world, from everlasting to everlasting you are God. You return man to dust and say, "Return, O children of man!" **For a thousand years in your sight are but as yesterday** when it is past, or as a watch in the night. **You sweep them away as with a flood**; they are like a dream, like grass that is renewed in the morning In the Psalm the thousand years and the word flood are in the same context and because Peter just wrote about Noah's flood. Noah's flood was a judgment. Peter mentions the thousand years and says there is a judgment, the day of the Lord. Peter is comparing the world of Noah with the destruction of Jerusalem. Daniel also uses this imagery. And the people of the prince who is to come shall destroy the city and the sanctuary. **The end of it *shall be* with a flood**, And till the end of the war desolations are determined.[158] Daniel predicted the destruction of the temple and city of Jerusalem with the imagery of a flood. We know it was not a literal deluge of water, but an army that flooded the cities of Israel in the mid-sixties AD. Because of space I will not go into too much detail, but Peter is connecting the thousand years as one day with the destruction of Jerusalem. The Jewish believers would connect these dots and understand his reference.

The preterist view of these passages interprets them as referring to the destruction of Jerusalem in AD 70. According to this view, the "day of the Lord" coming as a thief in the night symbolizes the unexpected and swift destruction of Jerusalem by the Roman armies. The heavens passing away with roaring thunder and the elements being released with fervent heat are seen as symbolic language for the destruction of the Jewish temple and the city of Jerusalem. The burning of the earth and the works in it represents the devastation and destruction caused by the Roman siege and destruction of Jerusalem and the cities of Israel.

The call for believers to be consecrated in conduct and devotion is seen as a reminder to live holy and faithful lives in anticipation of the impending judgment upon Jerusalem. The expectation and speeding up of the day of God's presence is understood as a call for believers to actively participate in spreading the gospel and bringing about the fulfillment of God's purposes.

Looking at these verses and understanding they are referring to the destruction of the Temple in Jerusalem in 70 AD. This event marked the end of the Old Covenant age and the beginning of the New Covenant age. The language of the heavens being dissolved and the

---

[158] The New King James Version (Da 9:26). (1982). Thomas Nelson.

elements melting with fervent heat is symbolic of the profound change and transformation that took place at this time. Specifically, when it comes to 2 Peter 3:11- 13, these verses are referring to the coming of the day of the Lord in judgment upon Jerusalem and the Old Covenant system, rather than a literal end of the world scenario.

In light of this understanding, the exhortation to live lives of holy conduct and godliness takes on added significance. Those 1st Century saints were called to live in such a way that reflects the new reality brought about by the destruction of the Temple and the establishment of the New Covenant. This includes eagerly anticipating and actively working towards the enjoyment of God's promises, such as living in the new creation of the new heavens and new earth in which righteousness dwells.

Stressing the importance of understanding the time frame and audience relevance of biblical passages in order to properly grasp their meaning. Overall, his view of 2 Peter 3:11-13 definitely aligns with this broader theological framework of full preterism and the belief that all biblical prophecies were fulfilled in the first century.

In these verses from 2 Peter 3:14-18, the author addresses the audience as "beloved" and emphasizes the importance of being found by Christ in peace, without spot, and blameless. Peter's perspective of this is seen as a call to maintain faithfulness and live in accordance with the teachings of Jesus and the apostles in light of the impending judgment upon Jerusalem and the end of the Old Covenant age.

The reference to "the Lord's patience" and the salvation brought by Him may be interpreted as referring to the delay in the coming judgment, giving people time to repent and turn to Christ before the destruction of the Temple in 70 AD. The mention of Paul and his writings being difficult to understand and subject to distortion by the unlearned and unstable could be seen as a warning against false teachings and the need for careful interpretation of Scripture in the face of impending events. Peter's reference to Paul's writings makes the claim that they are scripture.

The exhortation to "grow in grace and the knowledge of our Lord and Savior Jesus Christ" can be understood as a call to spiritual maturity and deepening understanding of the New Covenant teachings as the transition from the Old Covenant age to the New Covenant age takes place. The doxology at the end, giving glory to Jesus both now and into the New Covenant Age, reinforces the idea of the ongoing relevance and impact of Christ's redemptive work throughout history, including the fulfillment of Old Covenant prophecies in the events of 70 AD.

Terry Kashian

2 Peter

Chapter 1

1. Simon Peter, a slave and an apostle of Jesus Christ, to them that have obtained an equally priceless faith with us through the righteousness of God and our Savior Jesus Christ:
2. Grace and peace be multiplied to you through the full knowledge of God, and of Jesus our Lord,
3. Therefore, His divine power has given to us all things that pertain to life and godliness, through the knowledge of Him that has called us to glory and moral excellence:
4. Through which are given to us peerless and precious promises: that through these you might become companions of the divine nature, escaping from the corruption that is in the world's cravings.
5. Now these things also, bringing in all diligence, supply in your faith moral excellence; and to moral excellence knowledge;
6. And to knowledge self-control; and to self-control perseverance; and to perseverance dedication;
7. And to dedication brotherly love; and brotherly love divine love.
8. For these things being present in you, and intensifying, they constitute you not inactive nor unfruitful in the full knowledge of our Lord Jesus Christ.
9. But he that these things are not present is blind, and is nearsighted, and being forgetful that he was cleansed from his past sins.
10. Therefore instead, brothers, be diligent to make your calling and choice certain: for if you practice these things, you will not ever stumble:
11. Therefore, in this manner the way in will be supplied to you richly into the perpetual kingdom of our Lord and Savior Jesus Christ.
12. Therefore, I will always be reminding you of these things, though you know them, and having been established in the present reality.
13. Yes, I regard it right, as long as I am in this tent, to wake you up by putting you in remembrance;
14. 14. Knowing that I must shortly put away my tent, just as our Lord Jesus Christ has revealed to me.
15. Moreover, I will endeavor that you may be able after my exodus to make a memory of these things always.
16. For we have not carried out expertly concocted myths when we made known to you the power and presence of our Lord Jesus Christ, but were eyewitnesses of His Majesty.
17. For He received from God the Father honor and glory, when there came such a voice to Him from the Excellent Glory, this is My beloved Son, in whom I am well pleased.
18. And this voice which came from heaven we heard when we were with Him on the holy mountain.
19. We have also a more sure word of prophecy; where you do well to pay attention, as to a lamp that shines in a dismal place, until the day dawn and the morning star rises in your hearts:

20. Knowing this first, that not ever is the prophecy of the Scripture brought forth from a private source.

21. For no prophecy was ever produced any time by the will of man: but men spoke from God as they were moved along by the Holy Spirit.

Chapter 2

1. But there were false prophets also among the people, just as there will be false teachers among you, who covertly will bring in alongside fatal opinions, even rejecting the Master that bought them and bring upon themselves swift destruction.

2. And many will carry out their destruction; because of whom the way of reality will be spoken against.

3. And through covetousness they will with superficial words make merchandise of you: whose judgment now of a long time will not delay, and their destruction is not dozing off.

4. For if God spared not the messengers that sinned, but hurled them down to Tartarus, and delivered them into depths of gloom, to be guarded for judgment;

5. And spared not the ancient world, but saved Noah the eighth person, a preacher of righteousness, bringing in the flood upon the world of the ungodly;

6. And turning the cities of Sodom and Gomorrah into ashes condemned them with a catastrophe, making them an example to those that live ungodly, the things about to be;

7. And delivered righteous Lot, worn down with the filthy conduct of the wicked:

8. 8.(For that righteous man dwelling among them, in seeing and hearing, tormented his righteous soul daily with their lawless deeds).

9. The Lord knows how to deliver the godly out of trial, and to reserve the unrighteous for judgment day to be punished:

10. But especially them that walk after the flesh in polluted desires, and hold in contempt lordship. These are presumptuous, self-willed, they are not afraid to be blaspheming honored ones.

11. Even angels, which are greater in power and might, bring not a blaspheming judgment down upon them before the Lord.

12. But these, as physically unreasonable animals, born to be captured and slaughtered, speak evil of the things that they understand not; and will utterly be corrupted in their own corruption;

13. And will receive the wages of unrighteousness, as they lead the way in the daytime in self-indulgence. They are spots and blemishes, indulging themselves in luxury with their own delusion while they feast with you;

14. Fully possessed with eyes of an adulteress, and unable to stop from sin; baiting unstable souls: a heart that has been trained in covetousness; cursed children:

15. Which have forsaken the straight way, and have wandered away, following the way of Balaam, the son of Beor, who loved the wages of unrighteousness.

16. On the other hand, he was rebuked for his unrighteousness: the dumb donkey speaking with a man's voice restrained the madness of the prophet.

17. These are waterless wells, clouds that are driven by the strong winds; for whom the murkiness of darkness has been reserved into the new covenant age.

18. For when they speak great swelling words of emptiness, they allure through the lusts of the flesh, through much sexual lawlessness, but those that were genuine escaped from those behaving in delusion.

19. While they promise them freedom, they are the slaves of corruption: for by whom a man is overcome, by the same is he brought into slavery.

20. For if after they have escaped the pollutions of the world through the knowledge of the Lord and Savior Jesus Christ, they are entangled again in it, and overcome, the latter end is worse with them than the beginning.

21. For it would have been better for them not to have known the way of righteousness, than, after they have known it, to turn from the holy commandment delivered to them.

22. But it has happened to them according to the true proverb, the dog returns to his own vomit, and the pig that was washed goes back to her wallowing in the mud.

Chapter 3

1. I now write to you, beloved, this second letter; in which I stir up your pure minds by way of remembrance:

2. That you may be mindful of the words which were spoken before by the holy prophets, and of our command as the apostles of the Lord and Savior:

3. Knowing this first, that there will be coming at the final days, mockers will come mocking, walking after their own lusts,

4. And saying, where is the promise of His Presence? For since the fathers fell asleep, all things are ongoing as they were from the beginning of the creation.

5. For this they willingly ignore, that by the word of God, the heavens were of old, and the earth standing out of the water and in the water:

6. In which that world then was, being flooded with water, was destroyed:

7. But the heavens and the earth, which are now, by the same word are kept in store, reserved for fire into the day of judgment and destruction of godless men.

8. But, beloved, do not ignore this one thing, that one day with the Lord is as a thousand years, and a thousand years is as one day.

9. Concerning His promise, the Lord is not postponing, as some men regard postponement; but is forbearing toward us, not desiring that any would be destroyed, but that all would come to repentance.

10. But the day of the Lord will come as a thief in the night; in which the heavens will pass away with roaring thunder, and the (Jewish) elements will be released with fervent heat, the land also and the works that are in it will be burned utterly.

2 Peter 3:11

11. Now then that all these things will be dissolved, what manner of persons ought you to be in consecrated conduct and devotion,
12. Expecting and speeding up the Presence of the day of God, in which the heavens being set on fire will be dissolved, and the (Jewish) elements will disintegrate by melting?
13. Nevertheless we, according to His promise, look for new heavens and a new earth, in which dwells righteousness.
14. Therefore, beloved, since you are expecting this, be diligent that you may be found by Him in peace, without spot, and blameless.
15. And regard the self-restraint of our Lord salvation; even as our beloved brother Paul also according to the wisdom given to him has written to you;
16. As also in all his letters, speaking in them of these things; in which some things are hard to understand, which they that are unlearned and unstable distort, as they do also the rest of the Scriptures, to their own destruction.
17. You, therefore, beloved, seeing you knew these things previously, be on guard unless you also, being led away by the wandering of the degenerates, fall from your own stability.
18. But grow in grace and the knowledge of our Lord and Savior Jesus Christ. To Him be glory both now and into the New Covenant Age from the Old Covenant Age, Amen.

1st Letter of John Commentary

There is much debate on the dating of this letter and traditionally men have dated this letter way to far outside of the inspiration of the other writings of the New Testament. We know that the Lord Jesus said in Luke 21:20-22, when you see Jerusalem surrounded by armies know that her desolation is at hand … because these are the days of vengeance that **all things that are written** will be fulfilled. John states in his letter in 1 John 2:17, For **the world order is disappearing**, and the lust of it: but he that does the will of God abides into the New Covenant Age. TKB. This verse is in the present tense, and it is not our world, it was the world that John new, the Jewish world and arrangement. The desire for that world was passing away. Therefore, it is my conviction from this verse that it had to be written before the Jewish world passed away and disappeared. So many common taters, have neglected the framework of the forty-year period or the generation of Jesus' day to fit the inspired records in their proper place. Before we get into this study, John is writing in a style full of conviction and absolutes with no mixture. This kind of message infuses and inspires confidence. John is really authoritative in this letter. I was dumbfounded when I was doing a word study and discovered that out of the 105 verses in this letter, the word KNOW, Greek - ginosko is in this letter 38 times. That's 36% of the Letter. Those of you that are real miners in the word will love this study.

That which was from the beginning, which **we have heard**, which **we have seen with our eyes**, **which we have looked upon**, and **our hands have handled**, concerning the Word of life—the life was manifested, and **we have seen**, and **bear witness**, and declare to you that eternal life which was with the Father and **was manifested to us**—that **which we have seen and heard** we declare to you, **that you also may have fellowship with us**; and truly **our fellowship *is* with the Father and with His Son Jesus Christ.**[159]

These verses speak of the personal experience and intimate relationship that the author and others were having with Jesus Christ. They emphasize the tangible nature of their experience - they heard, saw, looked upon, and even handled Jesus, the Word of life. This was not just some distant, abstract concept for them, but a real, lived experience. And even in their present state they didn't have some remote Jesus. He said, He would never leave them or forsake them. The last Adam became the life-giving Spirit.1 Cor. 15:45. Paul says,

---

[159] *The New King James Version* (1 Jn 1:1–3). (1982). Thomas Nelson.

NOW the Lord is the Spirit and where the Spirit of the Lord is there is freedom. 2 Cor. 3:17. We have the present Jesus and can experience Him daily!

John starts this epistle declaring that this life, which was manifested in Jesus Christ, was with the Father and has now been revealed to them. They bear witness to this life and proclaim it to others so that they too may have fellowship with them and with God. He emphasizes the importance of sharing their experience and knowledge of Jesus Christ so that others may come into relationship with Him.

This passage reminds us that our faith is not just a set of beliefs or doctrines, and it is not private but personal and our faith is to be shared. It is a lived experience of intimacy with God. It invites us to reflect on our own relationship with Jesus Christ and to seek to deepen our fellowship with Him and with others who share in this experience. Ultimately, it challenges us to live out our faith in a way that bears witness to the reality of Jesus Christ and His profound life-changing power in our lives. This is the real meaning of knowing, ginosko. In 1 John 1:4, the apostle John is expressing his purpose for writing this letter to his audience. He wants to bring them joy, not just any kind of joy, but an abundance of joy. John understands the struggles and challenges that his readers may be facing, whether it be persecution, doubts, temptations, or spiritual warfare. And so, he wants to encourage them and uplift their spirits by sharing with them the truth of God's love, grace, and salvation.

In 1 John 1:5, the Apostle John declares that God is light and in Him there is no darkness at all. This powerful statement is not only a characteristic of God's nature, but it also serves as a metaphor for truth, goodness, purity, and righteousness.

Throughout the Bible, light is often used to represent God's presence, truth, and holiness. In the book of Psalms, we read, "The Lord is my light and my salvation" (Psalm 27:1), highlighting God's guidance and protection in our lives. In the New Testament, Jesus refers to Himself as the "light of the world" (John 8:12), indicating His role as the source of spiritual illumination and salvation.

On the other hand, darkness symbolizes sin, ignorance, evil, and separation from God. In Ephesians 5:11, Paul exhorts believers to "have no fellowship with the unfruitful works of darkness, but rather expose them." He even goes deeper and saying that we were once darkness, but now we are light in the Lord. Prior to that verse …for at **one time you were darkness, but now you are light in the Lord.** Walk as children of light (for the fruit of light is in all goodness and righteousness and reality) discerning what is pleasing to the Lord. Eph. 5:8 TKB. This verse underscores the importance of walking in the light of God's reality and rejecting the ways of darkness.

Ultimately, the contrast between light and darkness serves as a spiritual and a moral imagery in the Bible. As believers, we are called to walk in the light of God's presence, allowing reality and righteousness to guide our thoughts, words, and actions. In doing so, we express the character of God, who is the ultimate source of light and goodness.

In 1 John 1:5-7, the Apostle John emphasizes the crucial connection between walking in the light, fellowship with God and other believers, and the cleansing power of Jesus Christ's blood. These three items are the practical characteristics of the heavenly culture that God wants to establish in the lives of the saints. The verses begin by stating that if we claim to have fellowship with God but continue to walk in darkness (sin, ignorance, evil), we are essentially lying and not practicing the reality. This highlights the inconsistency between claiming to be in relationship with God while living in a manner that is contrary to His character and will.

On the other hand, if we walk in the light as God is in the light, we experience true fellowship with God and with other believers. Walking in the light signifies living in alignment with God's actual reality, righteousness, and holiness. This leads to a deep sense of communion and unity with God and fellow believers, as we share the same beliefs, values, and purpose, the heavenly culture emerges in our communities and all the facets of our daily life are affected.

Furthermore, the passage emphasizes the cleansing power of Jesus Christ's blood. When we walk in the light and have fellowship with God, His Son's blood continually cleanses us from all sin. This cleansing is not a one-time event but an ongoing process in the life of a believer. The blood of Jesus purifies us from our sins, maintains our relationship with God, and empowers us to live victoriously in this world.

In conclusion, 1 John 1:5-7 underscores the importance of walking in the light of God's truth, experiencing fellowship with Him and other believers, and being continually cleansed by the redemptive power of Jesus Christ's blood. As we are diligent to walk in the light, we grow in intimacy with God, build community with other believers, and experience the genuine life-changing power of Christ's sacrifice in our lives.

In 1 John 1:8-10, the Apostle John addresses the importance of acknowledging our sinfulness, the necessity of confession for maintaining a healthy relationship with God, and the truthfulness of God's Word in contrast to human deception. Firstly, John warns against the deception of denying our own sinfulness. He states that if we claim to be without sin, we are deceiving ourselves, and the reality is not in us. This highlights the danger of living in a state of denial or self-delusion regarding our need for forgiveness and redemption. Recognizing and admitting our sinfulness is the first step towards receiving God's grace and mercy.

It is also a continual practice of confessing our faults to God to receive on going mercy and forgiveness. God sprinkles our conscience during confession, and this helps our spirit remain clear so our intuition can function, and our creativity can flow, and our communion deepens. Many believers today do not know how to live up to date in their relationship with the Lord. Confession keeps us up to date. This is also true in our human relationships. When we sin, and we do sometimes unknowingly, this brings static and interference in our being. It affects all areas of relationship. Confession clears the air and the slate, to start fresh in our relationships with the Lord and other people in our lives. John emphasizes the importance of confessing our sins to God. He reassures believers that if we confess our sins, God is faithful and just to forgive us and cleanse us from all unrighteousness. It involves acknowledging our wrongdoings, seeking forgiveness, and turning away from sin. Through confession, we open the door for God's forgiveness, restoration, and ongoing transformation in our lives.

Secondly, John warns against the grave error of claiming to be without sin. He asserts that if we deny or ignore our sinfulness, we are essentially accusing God of falsehood, as His Word clearly highlights the reality of human sinfulness and the need for redemption through Christ. Making God out to be a liar not only distorts the reality but also hinders our ability to receive the grace and mercy He offers to all of us.

Lastly, 1 John 1:8-10. By humbly admitting our need for forgiveness, seeking God's mercy through confession, and aligning ourselves with the reality, we can experience the fullness of His grace, restoration, and transformative power in our lives.

In 1 John 2:1-2, the apostle John addresses believers as "my little children" and explains that he is writing to them so that they may not sin. He encourages them that if anyone does sin, they have an Advocate with the Father, Jesus Christ the righteous. This passage makes the point of Jesus as our Advocate and the atonement for our sins.

The term "Advocate" used by John carries a strong Jewish flavor. In Jewish culture, an advocate was someone who stood beside an accused person, defending them and representing their interests. In John's context, Jesus is our Advocate before the Father, interceding on our behalf and pleading our case. He is righteous and blameless, ensuring that our sins are forgiven and pardoned.

Furthermore, John introduces the concept of atonement by stating that Jesus is the atonement for our sins. The Greek word used for atonement in this passage is ἱλασμός (hilasmos), which carries a deep significance rooted in Jewish sacrificial practices. The word ἱλασμός is translated in the Septuagint (the Greek translation of the Hebrew Scriptures) as atonement. It is also associated with the Day of Atonement, the most significant day in the Jewish religious calendar for the atoning of sins.

By using the term ἱλασμός, John brings to mind the concept of sacrificial atonement found in the Old Testament, where animals were offered as sacrifices to atone for sin. However, Jesus, as the perfect and ultimate sacrifice, fulfills and surpasses the need for all other sacrifices. He atones not only for the sins of believers but also for the sins of the entire world, highlighting the all-encompassing nature of His atoning work. Seeing John use this language in his writing gives us a clue who his audience is and as the Old Covenant age is coming to a close, and Jerusalem being the target of God's wrath which took place during the last three feasts of Israel. The atonement would strike a hopeful cord in the Jewish mind if they understood that Jesus was there atonement and that the need for the temple and sacrifices under the Law would be unnecessary to bring them into God's good graces.

In conclusion, 1 John 2:1-2 portrays Jesus as our righteous Advocate before the Father and the atonement for our sins. By understanding the Jewish undertones of the terms "Advocate" and "atonement" in this passage, believers can appreciate the depth of Jesus' role in interceding for and conciliating humanity to God through His sacrificial atonement.

In 1 John 2:3-8, the apostle John emphasizes the importance of obedience to God's commands as a sign of knowing and walking in relationship with Him. He contrasts darkness with light, representing the Old Covenant age and the presence of Christ in believers, respectively.

John begins by stating that our knowledge of God is validated by our obedience to His commands. This obedience is a demonstration of our love for God and our desire to walk in His ways. Those who claim to know God but do not obey His commands are considered liars, as their actions do not align with their profession of faith.

John further explains that keeping God's word and obeying His commands is a manifestation of the love of God being completed in us. This love is not just a feeling but a practical demonstration of our relationship with God. By obeying His commands, we show that we are truly in Him and connected to His love.

The apostle then introduces the concept of an old commandment and a new commandment. The old commandment refers to the word that the believers had heard from the beginning, which the teachings of Moses and the moral law given by God in the Old Testament.

However, John now presents a new commandment that is real in Christ and in believers. This new commandment is characterized by the disappearance of darkness and the shining of the true light, which represents the transformative power of Christ in believers' lives. As Christ's light shines in and through believers, they are empowered to walk in righteousness and love as He did.

In conclusion, 1 John 2:3-8 highlights the significance of obedience to God's commands as evidence of knowing and abiding in Him. The contrast between darkness and light symbolizes the shift from the Old Covenant age to the reality of Christ's presence in the New Covenant age in believers. By walking in obedience and allowing Christ's light to shine through us, we demonstrate our love for God and our unity with Him and each other in this world.

In 1 John 2:9-11, the Apostle John addresses the connection between walking in the light of God and demonstrating love towards others, specifically fellow believers. These verses highlight the essential nature of love in the Christian life and the stark contrast between love and hatred in relation to spiritual light and darkness.

Firstly, John states that anyone who claims to be in the light of God but harbors hatred towards their brother or sister is actually still walking in darkness. Hatred is antithetical to the nature of God, who is love (1 John 4:8), and as such, it indicates a lack of true fellowship with God. This individual remains in a state of spiritual blindness, unable to see the way ahead.

Conversely, John explains that one who loves their brother remains in the light. By demonstrating love towards others, especially fellow believers, they are embodying the character of God and walking in alignment with His truth and righteousness. Love is a powerful expression of walking in the light, as it reflects the selfless and sacrificial nature of Christ's love towards humanity.

Moreover, John emphasizes that those who walk in hatred towards their brother are not only in darkness but are also walking in the darkness, further illustrating their state of spiritual blindness and confusion. Hatred not only separates individuals from God but also distorts their perception of reality and hinders their ability to discern God's will and direction for their lives.

The correlation between walking in the light and demonstrating love towards others is foundational in the Christian faith. As believers align themselves with the light of God's truth, grace, and love, they are transformed to become vessels of that love in the world. Walking in the light cultivates a heart of compassion, forgiveness, and empathy towards others, enabling love to flow naturally and abundantly from their lives.

1 John 2:9-11 he underscores the inseparable connection between walking in the light of God and manifesting love towards others. As believers abide in God's light, His love permeates their hearts and spills over into their relationships, demonstrating the transformative power of God's love in action.

In 1 John 2:12-14, the Apostle John addresses different stages of spiritual growth within the Christian community, using the terms children, young men, and fathers. These stages signify varying levels of maturity, experience, and depth in one's relationship with God.

1. Children:

John addresses the "children" first, highlighting their position as newcomers or beginners in the faith. These individuals are characterized by their need for foundational knowledge, protection, and guidance. They are still learning the basics of the Christian faith, such as understanding their need for salvation, the foundational doctrines of Christianity, and the importance of obedience to God's commands. Children in the faith require nurturing, instruction, and care from more mature believers to help them grow and develop in their walk with God.

2. Young Men:

The term "young men" signifies a stage of growth beyond childhood, where believers have moved past basic knowledge and are now actively engaging in spiritual battle and service. Young men are characterized by their strength, vitality, and courage in the face of spiritual challenges. They are involved in active ministry, serving others, and contending against spiritual opposition. Young men have a fervent passion for living out their faith and making a difference in the world. They are developing spiritual maturity and resilience, growing in their understanding of spiritual warfare and the deeper truths of the faith.

3. Fathers:

The term "fathers" represents a stage of spiritual maturity and depth in one's relationship with God. Fathers are characterized by their wisdom, experience, and deep intimacy with the Lord. They have weathered many spiritual storms, overcome numerous challenges, and have a profound understanding of God's ways and purposes. Fathers in the faith serve as mentors, guides, and examples to younger believers, offering wisdom, counsel, and spiritual insight gleaned from their years of walking with God. They display a mature faith marked by humility, love, and a deep abiding trust in the Lord. We may consider Paul's statement with regard to the idea of fathers, "not many fathers, but ten thousand teachers". 1 Cor. 4:15.

1 John 2:12-14 outlines the different stages of spiritual growth within the Christian community, ranging from children who are new to the faith, young men actively engaging in spiritual battle, to fathers who exhibit maturity and depth in their relationship with God. Each stage represents a progression in one's spiritual journey, with the goal of growing in intimacy with God, developing spiritual maturity, and becoming effective witnesses for Christ in the world.

1 John 2:15-17 In these verses, John warns against loving the world order of his day, which was characterized by the physical and temporal elements of Judaism. The Old Covenant world, with its rituals, traditions, and physical manifestations, was passing away as God was ushering in a new world order under the New Covenant age.

John's admonition to not love the world order is a call to prioritize spiritual values and heavenly reality over material possessions and earthly desires. He emphasizes that if one's love is focused on the things of this world, particularly the religious practices and external trappings of the Old Covenant, then the love of the Father is not in that person.

From a preterist perspective, which views the prophecies in the Bible as already fulfilled in the past, the passage in 1 John 2:15-17 can be interpreted in the context of the Old Covenant world of John's day. In this view, John is addressing the attachment of some Jewish believers to the physical and visible elements of the Old Covenant system, which was coming to an end with the destruction of the Temple in AD 70.

The desire of the flesh, desire of the eyes, and boastful pride of life can be understood as the inclination of some Jewish Christians to hold on to the external rituals, ceremonies, and practices of Judaism. This attachment to the outward forms of religion, including the pride in their Jewish heritage and the belief that they were chosen and superior to others, was not in line with the teachings of the New Covenant brought by Jesus. All humanity was leveled at the foot of the cross.

As the Old Covenant world was passing away with the destruction of the Temple in AD 70, John was reminding the believers to focus on the spiritual truths and never-ending realities of the New Covenant age.

John's message in these verses serves as a call to believers to let go of their attachment to the physical and outward aspects of religion and to embrace the spiritual and invisible kingdom of God. By recognizing that the Old Covenant world was fading away and embracing the new realities of the New Covenant age, believers could find true fulfillment and purpose in the genuine realities of God's kingdom

John clarifies that these worldly desires are not of the Father but are part of the passing world order. As the physical elements of Judaism were fading away, God was calling His people to align themselves with His will and the spiritual realities of the New Covenant age. Those who do the will of God, who focus on the invisible, spiritual, and heavenly kingdom, will abide in the enduring reality of the New Covenant age.

Overall, John's message serves as a reminder to believers to detach themselves from the temporal and physical aspects of the old-world order and to embrace the spiritual and perpetual realities of God's kingdom. By rejecting worldly desires and aligning with God's will, believers can find true fulfillment and lasting significance in the New Covenant age. There is also an application of the desires of the flesh, and desires of the eyes, and the boastful pride of life from a Gentile perspective and is valid in dealing with the heart. Paul defines the works of the flesh in Gal.5, and we can see that when we live according to the world, we live according to the flesh. The mind set on the flesh is death. The mind set on the spirit is life and peace. The desire of the eyes is related to covetousness and envy and greed. The lust of the eyes creates this experience in our lives, and if we walk in the Spirit, not by sight but by faith we will learn the secret of being content and satisfied. The boastful pride of life is in the list of what the Lord says issues out of the heart of man. Pride contaminates our being, pride … "[23]all these evils do come forth from within, and they defile the man."[160] This stain affects every part of us and as we humble ourselves and confess our pride we experience the stain remover in the blood of Jesus. So, this is the other viewpoint of these three items that are of the world from a non-Jewish point of view.

---

[160] Young, R. (1997). *Young's Literal Translation* (Mk 7:22–23). Logos Bible Software.

1 John 2:18-19 In these verses, John is warning the believers about the presence of many antichrists in the world. By using the plural form of the word "antichrists," John is emphasizing the widespread and varied nature of these false teachers who are opposed to Christ and seek to deceive believers. Jesus himself warned about false Christs and false prophets in the plural in Matthew 24:11, indicating that there would be many deceivers in the last days.

John's emphasis on the last hour signifies that he believed he was living in the final days before the culmination of God's redemptive plan. He saw the presence of these antichrists as a clear sign that the end times were near.

The statement "They went out from us, but they were not of us" highlights the fact that these false teachers had once been within the Christian community but had departed from the faith and revealed their true nature. If they had truly been part of the genuine followers of Christ, they would have remained in fellowship with other believers. However, their departure exposed their falsehood and showed that they were never truly aligned with the true people of God.

Overall, John's warning serves as a reminder to believers to be vigilant and discerning in recognizing and rejecting false teachings and false prophets. By remaining steadfast in the truth of the Gospel and in fellowship with other believers, they can guard against deception and remain faithful to Christ in the midst of the challenges of the many voices in our day.

2:20 But you have an anointing from the Holy One, and you perceive all things. 21 I have not written to you because you do not understand the reality, but because you know it, and that no lie is out of the reality. 22 Who is a liar but the one that denies that Jesus is the Christ? This one is an antichrist that denies the Father and the Son. 23 All who reject the Son, the same has not the Father: he that confesses the Son has the Father also. 24 Therefore let that continue in you, which you have heard from the beginning. If that which you have heard from the beginning will continue in you, you also will continue in the Son, and in the Father. TKB

In 1 John 2:20-24, John is addressing the believers and reminding them of the anointing they have received from the Holy One, which enables them to have spiritual discernment and understanding of the truth. The term "anointing" here comes from the Greek word "chrisma," which is related to the person of Christ. This anointing signifies that believers have been chosen and set apart by God for His purpose, and it empowers them to perceive spiritual realities and discern between what is real and the imagination and falsehood. All believers have an anointing, not just special people in the body of Christ. What John is saying here is the anointing sends registrations in our spirit that help us determine what is true and what is not. As we grow in our experience with the Lord those registrations become clearer and clearer. The immature are dull and somewhat numb to these spiritual senses. Many saints live in the outer part of their being, mind, emotions and will, their soul, and are soulish believers, instead of in their spirit where the anointing abides. Rom. 1:9. Paul says in MY spirit!

John reassures the believers that he did not write to them because they lacked understanding, but rather to affirm their knowledge and to guard them against deception. He emphasizes that those who deny Jesus as the Christ are liars and antichrists because they reject both the Father and the Son. This underscores the inseparable connection between Jesus and the Father in the Christian faith. Furthermore, John highlights the importance of confessing and acknowledging Jesus as the Son of God. Those who reject the Son also do not have the Father, but those who confess the Son have the Father as well. This establishes the central role of Jesus mediating between humanity and God and the essential nature of faith in Him for salvation.

In verse 24, John encourages the believers to remain steadfast in the teachings they have received from the beginning. By continuing in the reality of the Gospel message and holding fast to their faith in Christ, they will remain in a close relationship with the Son and the Father.

Overall, John's message in these verses highlights the foundational importance of recognizing and confessing Jesus as the Son of God. Through the anointing we maintain our faith in the face of deception and opposition. By abiding in the reality and our confession of Jesus as the Christ, believers can and experience the fullness of His presence and grace.

The teaching of the anointing in this passage refers to the Holy Spirit, who is often symbolically represented as anointing oil in the Bible. The anointing refers to the empowering and guiding presence of the Holy Spirit in the lives of believers. Through the Holy Spirit, believers receive wisdom, understanding, and discernment to navigate through life and discern reality from non-reality and deception.

The passage emphasizes that believers do not need external teachers to guide them because they have the Holy Spirit dwelling within them. The Holy Spirit teaches believers all things and guides them into the reality. The anointing is described as real and not a lie, ensuring that the guidance provided by the Holy Spirit is reliable and trustworthy. This can be a dangerous verse for those that may be a little rebellious or unteachable. They may say that "I don't need teachers in my life, I have the anointing". Teachers in the bible train the minds of believers to understand God's logic and pertinent doctrines of the bible. They were given for equipping the saints for the work of ministry. Their gift will help you be able to teach the scriptures to others. When John says we don't need anyone to teach us, he is referring to practical guidance in life. If the Lord wanted you to go to the Circle K because there was a person in need. You wouldn't find that direction in the bible. You would find that in your spirit as the Lord was registering and revealing His direction for you. The anointing has a practical value to teach us what to do and where to go and warn us if something is wrong. We don't have a relationship with the bible only, but we have a living Christ in our spirit to bear witness of the truth. For example, imagine you are driving through a dense fog on a winding road. The visibility is extremely poor, and you can hardly see what lies ahead. Suddenly, a small voice inside your heart whispers, "Slow down, there's danger ahead." You listen to the voice and slow down, avoiding a potential accident. In this illustration, you represent the believer, the fog symbolizes the confusion and deceptions in the world, and the small voice represents the anointing of the Holy Spirit within you. The Holy Spirit guides and directs you, providing insights and warnings to help you navigate through life's challenges and avoid pitfalls. Just as the small voice inside guided you to safety in the fog, the Holy Spirit's anointing teaches and empowers believers to discern truth and abide in God's truth.

1 John 2:28-29 From a fulfilled view of these verses they can be interpreted as exhorting believers to remain faithful to Christ until his second coming, which did happen in the first century, typically in A.D. 70 with the destruction of the Jerusalem temple.

Verse 28 encourages believers to abide in Christ so that when he appears (in his judgment on Jerusalem or in a spiritual sense), they can speak boldly and confidently before him without shame. This refers to the idea that those who remained faithful to Christ during the tumultuous events leading up to the destruction of Jerusalem would be vindicated and rewarded for their righteousness. Abiding in Christ would enable them to be bold and speak freely and as they abided, they would not shrink back in shame or be embarrassed in His presence for not trusting His prediction.

Verse 29 emphasizes the importance of recognizing and practicing righteousness as a sign of being born of God. In the fulfilled view, this means that those who lived righteous lives in accordance with the teachings of Christ were demonstrating their true spiritual lineage and connection to God. Ultimately, the message is about remaining steadfast in faith and practicing righteousness in anticipation of His Parousia.

1 John 3:1-2 is such a delightful section of scripture. I have written many times in my commentaries about the word, 'behold' in the bible. This word is what I call a window word. It's a window that allows us see into the spiritual realm. Here John is saying, "Behold what manner of love". What sort of love is this? This is the Father's love; it is so deep that even the Lord Jesus said in His high priestly prayer in John 17 ... and **loved them** even as **You loved me.** [161]Have you ever considered that as the Father loved Jesus, He loves you the same. We are looking through this glorious window and are seeing how deep the Father loves us. This is marvelous! And through this window we see another aspect of our identity. Called to be children of God. You are God's child, you're His! Now through this window we not see a wonderful aspect of our identity, but a vision of what we will become. We are not clear now what we will be like, but when He appears we will be the same as Him

---

[161] *The Holy Bible: English Standard Version* (Jn 17:23). (2016). Crossway Bibles.

for we will see Him as He is. Prior to this verse there is a phrase, "if you know that He is righteous."

And He said to him, arise, go your way: your faith has made you whole. 20 When the **Pharisees demanded of Him saying, when will the kingdom of God come?** He answered them and said, **the kingdom of God does not come with observation:** 21 neither will they say, look here! Or look there! **For, behold, the kingdom of God is inside you.** 22 And He said to the disciples, **the days will come when you will want to see one of the days of the Son of man, and you will not see it.** 23 And **they will say to you, see here; or see there: go not after them, nor follow them.** 24 For as the lightning, that lightens out of the one part under the heavens, shines to the other part under the heavens; **so also will the Son of man be in His day.** 25 But first **He must suffer many things and be rejected by this generation.** 26 As it was in the days of Noah, so will it also be in the days of the Son of man. 27 They did eat, they drank, they married wives, they were given in marriage, **until the day that Noah entered into the ark, and the flood came, and destroyed them all.** 28 In the same way as it was in the days of Lot; they did eat, they drank, they bought, they sold, they planted, they built; 29 **but the same day that Lot went out of Sodom it rained fire and brimstone from the heavens and destroyed them all.** 30 **Even so will it be in the day when the Son of man is revealed.**

Even though I am applying this verse in a devotional sense, actually this verse is interpreted in Luke 17: 19. In 1 John 3:2, **but we know that, when He will appear ...,** what is this appearing, it is the day the Son of man is revealed. Remember my analogy of the window. It is behold and one of things we behold is when He appears. This is not a physical seeing. It is something that is unveiled in the Spirit. Luke 17 makes perfectly clear; the kingdom does not come with observation. The deceivers will say 'see here' and 'see there', **go not after them, nor follow them.** Jesus is saying in My day I will be the cosmic Christ, like the lightning from one end of heaven to the other. The Lord said that they would long to see one of the days of the SON of MAN and **they will not see it.** Ask yourself this question. Why? Because Jesus is not a finite confined human being. We know Him thus no longer. He is the life-giving Spirit. This is why in Ephesians Paul says (Now this, "He ascended"—**what does it mean** but that He also first descended into the lower parts of the earth? He who descended is also the One who ascended far above all the heavens, **that He might fill all things.**)[162] What is Christ filling all things with? He is filling all things with Himself. **That Christ may be all in all.** We will be like Him. His righteous, He is pure, His is love, He is light. John is saying this hope is purifying us. This indicates that we are in a process that is unimaginable. The context of Luke 17 is quite revealing. The Son of Man is revealed in the context of judgment and deliverance. Luke uses the analogy of the days of Noah and God judged the wicked and delivered Noah and his family. The son of man is revealed like in

---

[162] *The New King James Version* (Eph 4:9–10). (1982). Thomas Nelson.

the days of Lot. God judged Sodom and Gomorrah and delivered Lot. So the appearing and revealing of the Son of Man is both positive and negative and John's audience is encouraged to keep this hope and practice righteousness, and the result will be, we will be like Him.

1 John 3:4-10 In these verses, John is emphasizing the importance of our will in choosing to abide in God and live righteously. He explains that sin is essentially lawlessness, going against God's commands and principles. Those who habitually sin are considered lawless because they continuously go against God's will.

On the other hand, those who remain in God, who strive to do righteousness and love their brothers, are considered children of God. This is a matter of choice and will - we have the ability to choose to abide in Him and follow His ways.

John also highlights the work of Jesus in taking away our sins and undoing the works of the Devil. Through Jesus, we are able to overcome sin and live a righteous life. Those who are born of God, who have accepted Jesus as their Savior, are able to overcome sin and live a life pleasing to God because the seed of God remains in them.

Ultimately, John is drawing a clear distinction between the children of God and the children of the Devil based on their actions and choices. The children of God are those who choose to abide in Him, do righteousness, and love others, while the children of the Devil are those who continue to sin and go against God's will. Our will plays a crucial role in determining which category we fall into, and it is through our choices and actions that we demonstrate our true identity as children of God. Now I am not talking about will power but using our will to tap into the divine life to be empowered to live according to God's will. If I could live the Christian life without God then I wouldn't need God. He has chosen this way for us to connect to the source of all this is good, righteous, and holy. We use our will to tap into the proper source and then we have success in our spiritual life.

1 John 3:11-16 In these verses, John uses the example of Cain and Abel to illustrate the destructive consequences of jealousy and unrighteousness. Cain, representing Old Covenant Israel, tried to earn God's favor through his works, but his jealousy of his brother Abel led him to commit a heinous act of murder. This serves as a stark reminder of how Old Covenant Israel rejected the sacrifice of Jesus, the Lamb of God, and ultimately played a role in His crucifixion.

John's message is a caution to his Jewish audience, warning them not to follow the path of Cain by trusting in their own works and rejecting the sacrifice of Jesus. This rejection of Jesus and persecution of His followers throughout the Roman Empire is akin to the murder of Abel, demonstrating the destructive nature of sin and unbelief.

By emphasizing the parallel between Cain's actions and the rejection of Jesus by Old Covenant Israel, John urges his audience to embrace the sacrificial love of God exemplified by Jesus' death on the cross. Just as Jesus laid down His life for us, we are called to love one another sacrificially and to stand firm in our faith, even in the face of persecution and opposition.

Through this message, John highlights the importance of choosing love, righteousness, and faith in Jesus, rather than following the path of Cain and rejecting the ultimate sacrifice that Jesus made for our salvation. It serves as a powerful reminder of the consequences of unbelief and the imperative of embracing the love and grace of God through Jesus Christ.

These verses in 1 John 3:17-24 focus on the importance of genuine love and the practical demonstration of that love through action. John begins by highlighting the contradiction of someone who has material wealth and resources but closes their heart to the needs of their brother or sister in Christ. This lack of compassion and generosity raises the question of whether the love of God truly dwells in that person. John emphasizes that love should not be merely expressed through words or empty speech but should be demonstrated through tangible actions and deeds. True love requires a genuine concern for others' well-being and a willingness to help when there is a need.

The apostle goes on to discuss the assurance that comes from living a life of love and obedience to God. When our actions align with God's commands and we strive to please Him, we can have confidence in approaching God and presenting our requests to Him. John emphasizes that one of God's primary commands is to believe in Jesus Christ and to love one another, just as Jesus has commanded us. By keeping God's commands and walking in love, we experience a deep fellowship with Him. This fellowship is marked by the indwelling of the Holy Spirit, who enables us to love sacrificially and to live in alignment with God's will. The presence of the Spirit in our lives is a confirmation that God is indeed dwelling within us.

In summary, these verses teach us that true love is not merely a concept or sentiment but is demonstrated through our actions and interactions with others. By living a life of love and obedience, we experience a close relationship with God and receive the assurance that He is with us, guiding us through His Spirit. By believing in Jesus and loving one another, we fulfill God's commands and experience the transformative power of His love in our lives.

In these verses from 1 John 4:1-6, the apostle John warns believers to be discerning and test the spirits to determine whether they are from God or not. He highlights the presence of false prophets who have emerged in the world, spreading deceit and leading people astray. John instructs his audience to pay attention to the confession of Jesus Christ in the flesh as a key indicator of the Spirit of God. Those who deny the incarnation of Jesus are identified as antichrists and are not aligned with God. John is the only one that uses this term antichrist, and you would think according to modern day prophecy teachers that the word antichrist is all over the New Testament. Technically this word should be translated in the plural which in these verses it is. Jesus called the antichrists, false Christs. We need to drop the Hollywood version of the antichrist and see that the world were not considered the antichrists. It was

Old Covenant Israel that propped up their own version of saving the world and it was without the nations. Their prejudice, exclusion, and separateness was contrary to all the prophets since they were supposed to be a light to the nations. The antichrist in the New Testament is not one man, it is a collective of those who oppose God and try to take from God what is His. Now I understand that certain people in the world have an antichrist spirt. I am interpreting in the context of the first generation where many antichrists were rampant in the land of Israel. There is no record of a Messiah in Rome or other parts of the world. Their polytheistic culture was not even looking for a Messiah, they had their Emperors who claim to be sons of God and divine. This was a phenomenon only in Israel because Israel was expecting a Messiah. These were the antichrists were already in the world. This world was the world of the Jews that was passing away.

John reassures his readers that they belong to God and have the strength to overcome these false prophets and antichrists, as the presence of God within them is greater than the forces of the world that oppose them. He distinguishes between those who are of the world and therefore speak in accordance with worldly values, and those who are of God and listen to the teachings of the apostles.

In the context of Old Covenant Israel, this passage can be seen as a reflection of their rejection of the message of the gospel and their resistance to the Holy Spirit. This is exemplified by Stephen's words in Acts 7, where he confronts the Jewish leaders for their stubbornness and refusal to accept the prophets who foretold the coming of Jesus. Despite being entrusted with the Law and the prophecies, they ultimately betrayed and killed the Just One, Jesus Christ. The parallel drawn between the rejection of Jesus by Old Covenant Israel and the warning against false prophets and antichrists in John's letter underscores the importance of discernment and faithfulness to the truth of the gospel. Just as the early believers had to navigate the presence of deceptive teachings and false spirits, Christians today are called to stay grounded in the truth of Christ's incarnation and resist the influences of the world and its false ideologies. Through discernment and reliance on the Spirit of God, believers can recognize and reject deceitful spirits and remain steadfast in their faith.

1 John 4:7-19 - The profound truth that love emanates from God Himself. Those who possess love are born of God, intimately acquainted with His very essence. Conversely, those who do not demonstrate love lack a true understanding of God, for God is love personified. The ultimate demonstration of God's love for us was manifest in the sending of His Son, His very heart poured out for us so that we may experience abundant life through Him. This love is not based on our futile attempts to love God, but arises from the unconditional, sacrificial love that God lavishly bestows upon us through His Son, making conciliation for our sins.

In response to God's boundless love for us, we are called to extend that same love to one another. No one has visually encountered God, yet when we love one another, we bear witness to God's tangible presence dwelling with us. This mutual love among believers gives evidence that we are abiding in God and that His love is reaching its full expression in us, a testimony to His abiding Spirit.

The Father's act of sending His Son as the Savior of the world attests to the profound nature of His love for all humanity. When we openly confess Jesus as the Son of God, we enter into a reciprocal and intimate relationship with God, a mutual indwelling where His love flows unreservedly in and out of us. We dwell in Him and He dwells in us. As we immerse ourselves in the love of God and walk in love towards others, we find ourselves firmly enveloped in God's presence. In this divine exchange of love, fear dissipates, for perfect love banishes all fear and anxiety. When we abide in this complete love, we are empowered to stand boldly and without reservations in the Day of Judgment, for we radiate with God's love in the world and mirror His love in our dealings with others. Our love for one another stems from the initial outpouring of God's love towards us. It is this foundational love that propels us to love others, to love unconditionally and unreservedly, following the example set forth by our loving Father.

Let's imagine two villagers, Tony and Rick, living in a small community in ancient times. Both Tony and Rick are known for their devotion to God, whom they worship daily at the village meeting. Tony is a well-respected member of the community, always ready to help his neighbors with their farming tasks, share his harvest during hard times, and offer a listening ear to those in need. His love for the Lord is evident in his selfless actions towards others, including his close friend Rick.

On the other hand, Rick, while also professing his love and devotion to the Lord, often shows disdain towards Tony. He refuses to work alongside Tony in the fields, speaks ill of him behind his back, and shows no concern for Tony's well-being. Despite his outward displays of religious fervor, Rick's treatment of Tony reveals a lack of genuine love and compassion. In this ancient village setting, the contrasting behaviors of Tony and Rick serve as a clear illustration of the message in 1 John 4:20-21. Tony's love for the Lord is exemplified through his actions towards his neighbor, Tony, demonstrating that true devotion to the Lord includes demonstrating love and care for others in the community. His practical acts of kindness and generosity reflect his genuine love for Christ.

In contrast, Rick's failure to show love and kindness towards Tony exposes the hollowness of his professed devotion to Christ. His hypocritical behavior highlights the disconnect between his words of love for the Lord and his actions towards his neighbor. Through the story of Tony and Rick, we see the timeless truth that true love for God must be lived out in our influence with others. Just as Tony's love for the village god is intertwined with his love for his neighbor, our love for God is evidenced by how we treat those around us. The command to love God and love others goes hand in hand, revealing the inseparable connection between our vertical relationship with God and our horizontal relationships with our fellow neighbors in our community.

In these verses from 1 John 5:1-5, the concept of conquering the world and the role of faith in achieving victory in our lives are emphasized. John begins by highlighting the connection between believing that Jesus is the Christ and being born of God. Faith in Jesus as the Messiah is the starting point of our spiritual journey and marks our rebirth as children of God. This belief is not merely intellectual but touches the depths of our hearts and souls, transforming our relationship with the Father and leading us to love Him with all our being. John goes on to explain that our love for God and obedience to His commands are evidence of our love for the children of God. By keeping God's commands, which are not burdensome but lead to life and freedom, we demonstrate our love for Him and for His people. This obedience flows from a heart filled with love for God and a desire to walk in His ways. The apostle then introduces the idea that those born of God are able to subdue the world order. This conquest over the world, its values, and its temptations is described as our triumph, and the key to this victory is our faith. Faith acts as the driving force that empowers us to overcome the challenges and struggles of the world, enabling us to walk in victory as children of God. The ultimate conqueror of the world, as John declares, is the one who believes that Jesus is the Son of God. This foundational belief in Jesus as the Son of God is the cornerstone of our faith and the key to our victory over the world. It is through this faith in Jesus, our Savior and Lord, that we are empowered to subdue the world order and walk in triumph as conquerors.

In conclusion, these verses underscore the essential role of faith in our journey as conquerors over the world. Through genuine faith in Jesus as the Christ, love for God, obedience to His commands, and faith in His Son, we find the strength and victory to overcome the challenges of the world and experience the triumph that comes from being born of God. A strong and unwavering faith in Jesus enables us to conquer the world and live victorious lives as children of God.

During Jesus' time, the Jewish people had longstanding hopes and expectations regarding the Messiah. They believed that the Messiah would be a powerful political leader who would deliver them from Roman oppression, restore their national sovereignty, and establish a kingdom that would reign over the nations of the world. The Jews of that time longed for conquest and dominance, envisioning a time when they would be elevated to a position of power and influence over other nations. However, their understanding of how this conquest would take place and the nature of their superiority was misaligned with God's intentions. The Jewish people focused on earthly power, military might, and political dominance as the means to achieve their desired status in the world. They viewed the Messiah as a conquering hero who would lead them in military victory over their enemies and establish a kingdom characterized by earthly glory and wealth. Contrary to their expectations, Jesus came as a humble and servant-hearted Messiah, whose kingdom was not of this world.

He challenged the conventional understanding of power and authority, teaching that true greatness comes through humility, service, and sacrificial love. Jesus emphasized that His kingdom was spiritual in nature, based on principles of love, mercy, and righteousness rather than military conquest and earthly dominance. Through His teachings and actions, Jesus revealed that God's kingdom operates on different principles than those of the world. The path to true greatness and victory in God's kingdom involves surrendering worldly ambitions and embracing a mindset of humility, service, and love. Rather than seeking to conquer the world through military might and political power, Jesus showed that true conquest comes through spiritual transformation, love for God and others, and obedience to His commands. The Jews of Jesus' day, with their focus on earthly conquest and political power, missed the profound truth that God's kingdom operates on spiritual laws and principles that transcend human understanding. The way in which God would make them "the head and not the tail" was through humility, faith, and obedience to His ways, rather than through worldly conquest and domination. Jesus came to establish a kingdom of hearts, where God reigns supreme, and His people are elevated through spiritual transformation and a deep relationship with Him.

1 John 5: 6-10. These verses speak about the testimony of God concerning His Son, Jesus Christ, and the confirmation of this testimony through various witnesses. The passage emphasizes the reliability and authority of God's testimony and the importance of believing in Jesus as the Son of God. Verse 6 highlights Jesus' identity as the One who came through water and blood. I believe this verse is the clearest verse regarding the virgin birth of Christ. Jesus' response emphasizes the necessity of being born twice to enter the kingdom of God. The fact that unborn babies reside in a sack of amniotic fluid. We even use the expression "her water broke" when it's time for birth. There is much controversy over this verse in John 3. Looking at John's gospel, he repeatedly contrasts the things that are physical to the reality of the things of the Spirit. Why wouldn't we think of the two births in this light. And why did Nicodemus say, "do I need to go back into my mother's womb and be born?" So I am suggesting that born of water is childbirth but there is no ancient record of this being an idiom of ancient culture. The fascinating thing about 1 John is the trio of Spirt, water, and blood. John says they bear witness on earth. I want you to ponder on this matter for a moment regarding the virgin birth. Jesus' birth was like no other and never will be. The Holy Spirit came upon Mary, and she conceived, and Jesus was growing in her. She was a virgin and when she gave birth her water broke, but also the hymen when Christ came out of her. Jesus was born of water and blood. I could be way off on this, but I feel persuaded that if the hymen didn't break from natural causes, then the birth of Christ was very unique in this way. The trio of the Spirit first, then the water, and then the blood seem to coincide with the

process of a unique birth from a virgin. He is the son of God, and the Spirit bears witness to the truth of Jesus' identity and mission, confirming His divine nature and role as the Savior.

In verses 7-8, the concept of three witnesses is presented, both in heaven and on earth. In heaven, the Father, the Word, and the Holy Spirit bear witness to the truth of Jesus' identity and mission. On earth, the Spirit, the water, and the blood provide additional testimony that attests to the truth of Jesus as the Son of God and the Savior of the world. Verse 9 emphasizes the superiority of God's testimony over that of men and marks the significance of believing in the testimony that God has given concerning His Son. Those who believe in Jesus as the Son of God carry this testimony within themselves and affirm the truth of God's word. On the other hand, those who reject this testimony make God out to be a liar, denying the truth of His testimony concerning Jesus.

In summary, these verses stress the importance of believing in Jesus as the Son of God and the Savior of the world. The testimony of God, confirmed by a multitude of witnesses, attests to the truth of Jesus' identity and mission, and those who believe in Him align themselves with God's testimony, while those who reject Him stand in opposition to God's truth. John is warning his audience to believe or there will be consequences.

In these verses from 1 John 5:10-15, the apostle emphasizes the foundational importance of believing in Jesus as the Son of God and the source of infinite life. This text marks the critical choice between believing, which results in possessing abundant life in Christ, and unbelief, which rejects God's testimony and His gift of infinite life. The believer in the Son of God carries the testimony of God within themselves, a witness to the reality of Jesus as the Messiah and Savior. By contrast, those who do not believe in God's testimony regarding His Son are essentially calling Him a liar, denying the truth of His revelation. The essence of God's testimony to humanity is centered on the gift of infinite life, a life that is found in His Son, Jesus Christ. Those who have received the Son have also received this infinite life, while those who reject Him miss out on this life-giving relationship with God.

John writes to reassure those who believe in the Son of God, affirming that they indeed possess infinite life through their faith in Jesus. This assurance is grounded in the confidence that believers have in God, knowing that He hears their prayers and responds according to His will. This confidence and trust in God's faithfulness enable believers to approach Him with boldness and expectancy, knowing that He grants the desires of their hearts that align with His purpose.

These verses speak to the transformative power of faith in Jesus as the Son of God, leading to the possession of eternal life and the assurance of answered prayers when aligned with God's will. The core message is one of confidence in God's faithfulness, the inheritance of infinite life through Christ, and the ongoing communion with God through prayer and reliance on His promises.

A Jew in the 1st century would likely approach these verses from a different perspective compared to a Christian believer. The Jewish people of that time had a different understanding of faith, infinite life, and the nature of God's testimony. For a Jew in the 1st century, the concept of faith in a divine Son of God would have been challenging, as traditional Jewish monotheism emphasized the oneness of God without a divine Son figure. The idea of Jesus as the Son of God and the source of infinite life would have been viewed as incompatible from their established beliefs and teachings. Additionally, Jewish understanding of infinite life often centered around concepts of future resurrection and eschatological hope rather than a present reality experienced through faith in Jesus as the Son of God. Since the Jewish teachers were divided into two main factions, the Pharisees and Sadducees. The Pharisees believed in a resurrection, but their belief as a national resurrection and the Sadducees did not believe the soul went on after the body died. The concept of time was succinct involving two ages.

The Old Covenant age and the age of the Messiah. Their view was that the Messiah would come, and the resurrection would take place and there would be no pain, no tears, no suffering, but a paradise would be created by the Messiah. The Jewish people anticipated a Messiah who would bring about political liberation and establish a kingdom on earth, rather than emphasizing a personal relationship with God and the gift of infinite life through faith in Jesus. Furthermore, the notion of God's testimony being revealed through Jesus as the Son of God would have been seen as a departure from the traditional understanding of God's revelation through the Law and the Prophets. Jewish theology emphasized adherence to the Torah and the teachings of the prophetic tradition as a means of remaining in covenant relationship with God, rather than placing faith in a specific individual as the Son of God.

Overall, a Jew in the 1st century would likely approach these verses with a different theological framework and perspective than a Christian believer, highlighting the theological and interpretative differences between Jewish and Christian understandings of faith, infinite life, and God's testimony.

1 John 5:16-17 - The mention of a sin toward death underscores the seriousness and gravity of certain sins that can have perpetual consequences. The author advises against questioning or praying for those engaged in such sinful behavior. This firm stance suggests a tone of caution and discernment in dealing with sins that could potentially lead to death. The passage also reiterates the belief that all unrighteousness is sin but distinguishes between sins that lead to death and those that do not. By acknowledging the presence of sin in various forms, the author emphasizes the need for believers to both support and hold each other accountable within the Christian community. The overall message of these verses underscores the importance of prayer, discernment, and understanding the gravity of certain sins in the context of Christian fellowship.

The situation with Saul in the Old Testament can be seen as a parallel to the concept of sin unto death and sin not unto death discussed in the verses from 1 John. In the case of Saul, he was the first king of Israel chosen by God but eventually fell out of favor due to his disobedience and sinful actions. Throughout Saul's reign, he made several poor choices, including disobeying God's commands and seeking guidance from mediums. Despite warnings and opportunities for repentance, Saul persisted in his sinful behavior, ultimately leading to God's decision to reject him as king. In 1 Samuel 15:28, after Saul's continued disobedience, Samuel receives a message from God saying, "I regret that I have made Saul king, for he has turned back from following me and has not performed my commandments." This indicates that Saul's actions had crossed a threshold where his sins had led to a point of no return, ultimately leading to his downfall. In a similar way, the concept of sin unto death in the New Testament warns of sins that can have severe spiritual consequences, potentially leading to separation from God. Just as Samuel was instructed to stop praying for Saul in his situation, believers may be guided to exercise discernment and refrain from praying for individuals who persist in unrepentant, destructive behavior that leads to spiritual death. The story of Saul serves as a cautionary anecdote about the consequences of persistent sin and disobedience. It highlights the importance of recognizing when prayers for certain individuals may not align with God's will, requiring believers to exercise discernment and wisdom in their intercession.

1 John 5:20-21 - In the closing of his letter, John reinforces the idea of the believer's identity and relationship with God. He emphasizes that those who are born of God do not continually practice sin, indicating a transformed nature and a commitment to righteousness. This transformation is attributed to the protective presence of God within believers, guarding them against the influence and manipulation of the wicked one. John contrasts the nature of those born of God with the corrupt state of the world, highlighting the pervasive hold of wickedness in society. Despite this, believers are reassured of their connection to God through His Son, Jesus Christ. Through Christ, believers have been granted understanding and knowledge of the true God, establishing a relationship with Him and experiencing infinite uncreated life. The passage concludes with a warning to beware of idols, reminding believers to guard against anything that may take the place of God in their lives. By acknowledging the real God and His Son, Jesus Christ, believers are encouraged to remain steadfast in their faith and resist the temptations of false gods and distractions. Wrapping up these verses, John's writing serves as a reminder of the believer's secure position in God, the transformative power of Christ, and the need for spiritual vigilance in a world filled with deception and idolatry. The exhortation to stay focused on the real God and to avoid distractions targets the importance of maintaining a strong, authentic relationship with God through His Son, Jesus Christ.

Terry Kashian

1 John

Chapter 1

1. That which was from the beginning, which we have heard, which we have seen with our eyes, which we have looked upon, and our hands have handled, concerning the Word of life;
2. For the life was made visible, and we have seen it, and bear witness, and make known to you this infinite life, who was with the Father, and was made visible to us;
3. What we have seen and heard we make known to you, that you also may have fellowship with us: and truly our fellowship is with the Father, and with His Son Jesus Christ.
4. We write these things to you, how your joy may be abundantly supplied.
5. This is the message which we have heard from Him, and disclose to you, that God is light, and in Him is no darkness at all.
6. If we say that we have fellowship with Him, and walk in darkness, we are false, and do not practice the reality:
7. But if we walk in the light, as He is in the light, we have fellowship with one another, and the blood of Jesus Christ His Son is cleansing us from all sin.
8. If we say that we have no sin, we deceive ourselves, and the reality is not in us.
9. If we confess our sins, He is faithful and just to forgive us our sins, and to cleanse us from all unrighteousness.
10. If we say we have not sinned, we make Him a liar, and His word is not in us.

Chapter 2

1. My little children, these things I write to you, that you may not be sinning. And if any man is sinning, we have an Advocate with the Father, Jesus Christ the righteous:
2. For He is the conciliation for our sins: and not for ours only, but also for all the world.
3. Now by this we know that we know Him if we obey His commands.
4. He that says, I know Him, and does not obey His commands, is a liar, and the reality is not in him.
5. But whoever keeps His word, in this one, in reality, is the love of God completed: by this we know that we are in Him.
6. He who says he remains in Him ought himself also to walk, just as He walked.
7. Brothers, I write no new command to you, but an old command which you had from the beginning. The old command is the word that you have heard from the beginning.
8. Again, a new command I write to you, which is real in Him and in you: because the darkness is disappearing, and the real light already shines.
9. He that says he is in the light and is hating his brother, is in darkness even until now.
10. He that is loving his brother remains in the light, and there is no entrapment in him.
11. But he that hating his brother is in darkness and is walking in darkness, and does not know where he is going, because the darkness has blinded his eyes.

12. I write to you, little children because your sins are forgiven for His name's sake.
13. I write to you, fathers because you have known Him who is from the beginning. I write to you, young men because you have overcome the wicked one. I write to you, little children because you have known the Father.
14. I have written to you, fathers, because you have known Him who is from the beginning. I have written to you, young men, because you are powerful, and the word of God dwells in you, and you have overcome the wicked one.
15. Do not love the world order, nor the accouterments that are in the world order. If any man is loving the world, the love of the Father is not in him.
16. For all that is in the world, the lust of the flesh, and the lust of the eyes, and the pride of life, is not of the Father but is of the world order.
17. For the world order is disappearing, and the lust of it: but he that does the will of God abides into the New Covenant Age.
18. Little children, it is the last hour: and as you have heard that antichrists are coming, even now there are many antichrists; by this, we know that it is the last hour.
19. They went out from us, but they were not of us; for if they had been of us, they would have continued with us: but they went out, that they may be exposed that they all were not of us.
20. But you have an anointing from the Holy One, and you perceive all things.
21. I have not written to you because you do not understand the reality, but because you know it, and that no lie is out of the reality.
22. Who is a liar but the one that denies that Jesus is the Christ? This one is an antichrist that denies the Father and the Son.
23. All who reject the Son, the same has not the Father: he that confesses the Son has the Father also.
24. Therefore, let that continue in you, which you have heard from the beginning. If that which you have heard from the beginning will continue in you, you also will continue in the Son, and in the Father.
25. For this is the promise that He has promised us, even infinite life.
26. These things have I written to you concerning them that try to deceive you.
27. But the anointing which you have received from Him is remaining in you, and you do not need anyone to teach you: but as the same anointing is teaching you about all things, and is real, and is not false, and just as you have been taught, remain in Him.
28. So now, little children, remain in Him; that when He will appear, we may speak freely, and not shrink away in shame in His Presence.
29. If you know that He is righteous, you know that everyone that is practicing righteousness is born of Him.

Chapter 3

1. Behold, what manner of love the Father has given unto us, to be called the children of God: therefore the world does not know us, because it did not know Him.

2. Beloved, now are we the children of God, and has not made known yet what we will be: but we know that, when He will appear, we will be the same as Him; for we will see Him as He is.

3. And everyone that has this expectation in Him purifies himself, even as He is pure.

4. Whoever habitually sins is habitually lawless: for sin is lawlessness.

5. For you know that He was made known to take away our sins; and in Him is no sin.

6. Whoever remains in Him is not sinning: whoever is sinning has not seen Him, neither knows Him.

7. Little children, let no man deceive you: he that is doing righteousness is righteous, just as He is righteous.

8. He that habitually sins is of the Devil; for the Devil sins from his origin. For this purpose, the Son of God was made known, that He might undo the works of the Devil.

9. Whoever is born of God does not habitually sin; for His seed is remaining in him: and he is not able to be sinning, because he is born of God.

10. In this the children of God are evident, and the children of the Devil: whoever is not doing righteousness is not of God, neither he that is not loving his brother.

11. For this is the message that you heard from the beginning, that we should be loving one another.

12. Not as Cain, who was of that wicked one, and slew his brother. And why did he slay him? Because his own works were evil, and his brothers righteous.

13. Do not be astonished, my brothers, if the world is hating you.

14. We know that we have walked out of death into life because we are loving the brothers. He that is not loving his brother stays in death.

15. Everyone who hates his brother is a murderer: and you know that no murderer has infinite life dwelling in him.

16. By this we know the love of God because He laid down His life for us: and we ought to lay down our lives for the brothers.

17. But whoever has this world's subsistence, and sees his brother has needs, and closes up his inner parts away from him, how is the love of God dwelling in him?

18. My little children, let us not love in word, neither in speech, but in action and reality.

19. Therefore, in this we know that we are out from the reality and will persuade our hearts before His face.

20. For if our heart condemns us, God is greater than our heart and knows all things.

21. Beloved, if our heart does not condemn us, then we can speak freely in the presence of God.

22. And whatever we ask, we receive from Him, because we keep His commands, and do those things that are pleasing in His sight.

23. Then this is His command that we should believe in the name of His Son Jesus Christ, and love one another, as He gave us this command.

24. And he that is keeping His commands is dwelling in Him, and He in him. Therefore, in this, we know that He is dwelling in us, out from the Spirit Whom He is giving us.

Chapter 4

1. Beloved do not believe every spirit but be testing the spirits whether they are of God: because many false prophets have come out into the world.
2. By this you will know the Spirit of God: every spirit that confesses that Jesus Christ is come in the flesh is of God:
3. Therefore, every spirit that does not confess this Jesus is not of God: and these are antichrists, which you have heard they are coming; and are now already in the world.
4. You are of God, little children, and have conquered them: because greater is He that is in us, than the ones that are in the world order.
5. They are of the world order: therefore, they speak of the world order, and the world listens to them.
6. We are of God: he that is knowing God is hearing us; he that is not of God is not hearing us. In this, we know the spirit of reality and the spirit of the delusion.
7. Beloved, let us be loving one another: for love is of God, and everyone that is loving is born of God and knows God.
8. He who is not loving does not know God; for God is love.
9. In this is the love of God is made apparent in us, because God sent His only begotten Son into the world, that we might be living through Him.
10. This is love, not that we loved God, but that He loved us, and sent his Son to be the conciliation for our sins.
11. Beloved, if God so loves us, we ought also to be loving one another.
12. No man has beheld God at any time. If we are loving one another, God dwells in us, and His love has been completed in us.
13. In this we know that we are dwelling in Him and He in us because He has given us out of the same Spirit.
14. For we have seen and do testify that the Father sent the Son to be the Savior of the world.
15. Whoever will confess that Jesus is the Son of God, God is dwelling in him, and he in God.
16. And we have known and believed the love that God has in us. God is love, and he that is dwelling in love is dwelling in God, and God in him.
17. In this, love has been made complete with us, that we may speak freely in the Day of Judgment: because as He is, so are we in this world.
18. There is no fear in love, but complete love casts out fear: because fear has punishment. He who is fearful is not made complete in love.
19. We are loving, because He first loved us.
20. If a man says, I am loving God, and hating his brother, he is a liar: For he that is not loving his brother whom he has seen, how can he have the power to be loving God whom he has not seen?
21. And this is the command we have from Him, that he who is loving God is also loving his brother.

Chapter 5

1. Everyone believing that Jesus is the Christ is born of God: and everyone that is loving the Father is loving Him also, that is born of Him.
2. In this we know that we are loving the children of God when we love God and obey His commands.
3. Since this is the love of God we are keeping His commands: and His commands are not oppressive.
4. Because all that are born of God are subduing the world order: and this is the triumph that is subduing the world order, our faith!
5. Who is he that is subduing the world, but he that is believing that Jesus is the Son of God?
6. This is the One that came through water and blood, Jesus Christ, not in water only, but in water and in blood. And it is the Spirit that is bearing witness because the Spirit is the reality.
7. For there are three that are bearing witness in the heavens, the Father, the Word, and the Holy Spirit: and these three are one.
8. And there are three that are bearing witness in earth, the Spirit, and the water, and the blood: and these three agree in one.
9. If we receive the testimony of men, the testimony of God is greater: for this is the testimony of God which He has testified of His Son.
10. He that believes in the Son of God has the testimony in himself: he that believes not God has made Him a liar; because he believes not the testimony that God gave of His Son.
11. Then this is the testimony that God has given us infinite life, and this life is in His Son!
12. He that has the Son has the life, and he that does not have the Son of God does not have the life.
13. I have written these things to you that believe in the name of the Son of God; that you may know you have infinite life, and that you may believe in the name of the Son of God.
14. For this is the confidence that we have in Him, that, if we ask anything according to His will, He hears us:
15. And if we know that He hears us, whatever we ask, we know that we have the requests that we desire of Him.
16. If anyone notices his brother sinning a sin toward death, he should be pleading, and He will be giving him life that is not sinning toward death. There is a sin toward death: I do not say that he should question this.
17. All unrighteousness is sin: and there is a sin not toward death.
18. We know all who are born out from God are not sinning, but He that is born out of God guards them, and that wicked one is not manipulating them.
19. For we know that we are out from God, and the whole world order is prostrate in wickedness.
20. And we know that the Son of God is present, and has given us an understanding, that we may know Him that is real, and we are in Him who is real, even in His Son Jesus Christ. This is the real God and life infinite.
21. Little children, look out for yourselves from idols. Amen.

2nd Letter of John Synopsis

In these verses from the second epistle of John, the writer identifies himself as "the elder" and addresses his letter to "the chosen noble lady and her children." While the identities of the recipients are not explicitly mentioned, some scholars interpret the "chosen noble lady" as a metaphorical reference to a specific church or group of believers, with her "children" in the community. The writer expresses his deep love for the saints in reality, emphasizing the genuine affection and care he has for them. This love is not limited to himself but is shared by all who have experienced and understood the reality of the gospel. The letter speaks of the presence of truth, referred to as "reality," that dwells in the writer and the recipients, guiding them into the New Covenant Age. This truth is not merely a concept but a living reality that shapes their beliefs, actions, and relationships. The truth shapes our culture and the purer the truth a heavenly culture emerges. John continues the passage with a prayer for grace, mercy, and peace from God the Father and the Lord Jesus Christ. This blessing is wished upon the readers in reality and love, underscoring the greatness of experiencing and embodying these attributes in their lives. Grace represents God's divine influence and empowerment, mercy signifies His compassion and forgiveness, and peace signifies the harmony and wholeness found in the bond with Him.

Overall, these verses convey a message of love, truth, and blessing bestowed upon the recipients by the writer, rooted in the reality of their shared faith in Jesus Christ. The emphasis on the life-changing power of truth and the importance of grace, mercy, and peace highlights the foundational principles of the Christian faith and the relational aspect of believers' connection with God and one another.

These verses from the second epistle of John can be understood in the context of the early Christian community and the challenges they faced during that time. In verses 5 and 6, the writer emphasizes the priority of continuing to love one another and walking in obedience to God's commands. This viewpoint can be seen as a reflection of the practical instructions given to the early Christian believers to maintain unity, love, and adherence to the teachings of Jesus. The call to love one another and walk in obedience is viewed as the core values of the faith that were essential for the unity and strength of the early church.

Verse 7, which warns about the presence of deceivers who deny the incarnation of Jesus Christ, can be understood as a reference to specific challenges or heresies that arose within the early Christian community. In a preterist interpretation, this may be seen as a warning against false teachings and ideologies that undermined the belief in the humanity and divinity of Jesus Christ. These false teachings were present during the time of the apostles and posed a threat to the foundational tenets of the Christian faith. I truly believe we as 21st century believers need to understand that the Roman world was not infested with false prophets and antichrists. It was the land of Israel. This was an epidemic to Judaism. The Roman world were polytheistic and full of wicked deities and most of the emperors declared themselves as gods and as sons of God. They were considered pagans and Gentiles to the Jewish world. John is writing to Jewish believers warning them of the deceivers and antichrists.

These are Jesus' warnings who warned of false prophets and false christ's who would try to deceive before that generation passed away. And Jesus answered them, "See that no one leads you astray. For many will come in my name, saying, **'I am the Christ,'** and **they will lead many astray.**[163] And **many false prophets** will arise and **lead many astray.**[164] John is just echoing Jesus' teaching. Overall, these verses can be viewed as practical instructions and warnings specifically relevant to the early Jewish Christian community, addressing the need for love, unity, obedience, and vigilance against false teachings. We must focus on the historical context of the early church and the challenges they faced rather than viewing these verses as exclusively speaking to future events for our time or prophetic fulfillments that are yet to be. Remember **the scriptures were not written to us, they were written for us** and as we **learn the principles, we can apply them**. I do know there is a timeless application for our day, because after the first generation of believers, false teaching didn't stop, but we need to see the relevance and urgency that John was referring to.

Let's consider a practical illustration to break down these verses from the second epistle of John 8-11, particularly focusing on the warnings against false teaching and the importance of remaining steadfast in the true teachings of Christ. Imagine a close-knit Christian community that has been thriving and growing in their faith together. The members of this community have worked hard to build relationships, support one another, and diligently study and experience the teachings of Jesus Christ. One day, an influential person who has great speaking ability arrives in the community, claiming to be a teacher of spiritual truths. However, upon closer examination of his teachings, it becomes apparent that his message deviates from the core tenets of the faith. He denies the divinity of Jesus Christ and distorts essential biblical teachings. The leaders of the community, aware of the warnings in John's letter, recognize the danger of allowing this false teacher to influence their community. They remember the instruction to be vigilant and to guard against false teachings that could lead members astray. They understand the importance of preserving the purity of the gospel message that they have labored to uphold. In adherence to the guidance provided in these verses, the community leaders take a firm stance. They do not welcome the false teacher into their gatherings or homes, refusing to endorse or support his teachings.

[163] _The Holy Bible: English Standard Version_ (Mt 24:3–5). (2016). Crossway Bibles.
[164] _The Holy Bible: English Standard Version_ (Mt 24:11). (2016). Crossway Bibles.

They prioritize the spiritual well-being of the members and protect them from the influence of deceptive teachings. By remaining steadfast in the true teachings of Christ and rejecting false ones, the saints safeguards the integrity of the faith and ensures that they continue to walk in the light of God's truth. They understand that to compromise on core beliefs and values and embrace falsehood would not only jeopardize their own spiritual growth but also risk leading others astray. Through this practical illustration, we can see the importance of discernment, vigilance, and adherence to sound biblical teaching in maintaining the unity and spiritual health of the gathering of the saints. In these closing verses of 2 John 12-13, John expresses his desire to have more to communicate with the saints but prefers to do so in person rather than through writing. This personal touch demonstrates the importance of face-to-face interaction and the value of direct communication in fostering relationships and deepening understanding. His intention to visit in person reflects a desire for genuine connection and mutual joy with the saints. By speaking to them directly, he hopes to enhance their relationship and share in the fullness of joy that comes from fellowship and shared faith.

The mention of the children of the chosen sister extending greetings serves as a warm and personal conclusion to the letter. In touching this section, we can see that the decision to forego further written communication in favor of a personal visit prioritizes the importance of building and maintaining authentic relationships within the Christian community. The reference to the children of the chosen sister conveys a sense of family affection and unity among believers, highlighting the interconnectedness and mutual support found in the body of Christ. Overall, these closing verses of 2 John emphasize the significance of personal connection, joy in fellowship, and the shared bond of faith that unites believers. John's desire and determination to visit in person and the warm greetings exchanged serve as a reminder of the importance of relationship-building and community within the context of the early Christian church.

Terry Kashian

2 John

Chapter 1

1. The elder, to the chosen noble lady and her children, whom I love in reality; and not only I but also all they that have known the reality;
2. Through the reality dwelling in us, and into the New Covenant Age.
3. Grace be with you, mercy, and peace, from God the Father, and the Lord Jesus Christ, the Son of the Father, in reality and love.
4. I rejoiced greatly to find your children walking in reality, as we received the command from the Father.
5. And now I am asking you, noble lady, not as though I wrote a new command to you, but that which we had from the beginning, that we continue loving one another.
6. And this is love that we walk according to His commands. This is the command, that, as you have heard from the beginning, you should walk in it.
7. For many deceivers have entered into the world order who confess that Jesus Christ has not come in the flesh. These are deceivers and antichrists.
8. Lookout for yourselves that you do not destroy those things with which you have labored, but that you receive a full reward.
9. Whoever falls away, and is not continuing in the teaching of Christ, does not have God. He that continues in the teaching of Christ, he has also the Father and the Son.
10. If anyone comes to you, and does not bring this teaching, do not take him into your home and do not rejoice with him:
11. For he that rejoices with him participates in his wicked works.
12. Having many things to write to you, I will not with pen and paper: but I trust to be brought to you, and speak to you personally, that our joy may be full.
13. The children of your chosen sister are greeting you. Amen.

3rd Letter of John Synopsis

In these verses from the third epistle of John, John, who identifies himself as the aged one, addresses Gaius, whom he refers to as beloved and whom he loves genuinely. He expresses his desire for Gaius's well-being and success, both physically and spiritually. He wishes for Gaius to prosper in his journey and health, paralleling this with the prosperity of his soul.

John rejoices greatly upon hearing positive reports about Gaius from fellow believers who have borne witness to the authenticity of his faith and his commitment to walking in the reality of the gospel. This affirmation brings John immense joy, as he feels a deep connection to Gaius and takes pride in witnessing his spiritual growth and dedication to living out the reality. The author commends Gaius f4or his faithful service to the brothers and newcomers in the Church. Gaius's loving and generous actions towards these individuals, as witnessed by others in the church, are seen as exemplary and praiseworthy. John shouts out encouragement to Gaius to continue this admirable behavior and to support these messengers whom Gaius has sent out in a manner worthy of God. The messengers mentioned in the passage are commended for their selfless dedication to the work of the gospel, as they have gone out for the sake of Christ's name, relying on the support and hospitality of fellow believers. John put point on this emphasis and the importance of supporting such workers in their mission, as it enables them to continue their work effectively and be fellow workers in spreading the reality of the gospel. Overall, these verses highlight themes of love, faithfulness, hospitality, and support within the church. John's interactions with Gaius and the messengers demonstrate the importance of genuine relationships with other men of God, mutual encouragement, and collaborative efforts in furthering the mission of sharing the reality of the gospel. The passage encourages believers to continue walking in the reality, supporting one another in love, and actively participating in the work of God in spreading the reality of the faith.

In the passage from the third epistle of John, the writer addresses the issue of Diotrephes, a prominent individual in the church community who seeks to assert his authority and position of prominence above others. This behavior is in direct conflict with the teachings of Christ, which emphasize humility, servanthood, and prioritizing the needs of others over self-interest. Diotrephes, on the other hand, loves himself more than anything else, so that the Apostle John describes him as a "lover of putting himself first" (3 John 1:9) John highlights the actions of Diotrephes, who not only refuses to welcome him and his companions but also goes as far as spreading malicious words against them. Additionally,

Diotrephes hinders and expels fellow believers who desire to be part of the community, displaying a lack of hospitality, love, and acceptance towards others.

The behavior of Diotrephes stands in stark contrast to the teachings of Jesus Christ, who exemplified humility and servanthood throughout His ministry. Jesus taught His disciples to serve one another, to humble themselves, and to prioritize love and unity within the fellowship of believers. The desire to be first, to seek personal recognition or power within the church, is condemned in the teachings of Christ. Jesus preached about the importance of humility, sacrificial love, and selflessness, instructing His followers to prioritize the needs of others and to serve with a heart of humility and compassion. The importance of receiving and welcoming fellow believers aligns with the teachings of Jesus, who emphasized the significance of hospitality, kindness, and acceptance towards others. In Matthew 10:40, Jesus said, "Whoever receives you receives Me," highlighting the interconnectedness and unity within the body of Christ. Jesus said if you want to be first you must be the slave of all. Matt.20:26

The shamefulness of wanting to be first, as demonstrated by Diotrephes, lies in the violation of core Christian values of humility, love, and unity. Seeking personal glory and power at the expense of others goes against the spirit of Christ's teachings and undermines the essence of the faith, which is centered on selfless love, mutual respect, and unity in Christ. John continues to address the issue of Diotrephes, who displays pride, arrogance, and a lack of hospitality towards fellow believers. The apostle expresses his intention to address Diotrephes' harmful actions directly when he visits, as Diotrephes has been spreading malicious words and refusing to receive or support other believers within the fellowship. The writer contrasts the behavior of Diotrephes with the admonition to not imitate evil but instead to follow what is good.

Those who do good are described as being aligned with God, while those who do evil are depicted as not having truly seen or experienced God's presence in their lives. John then singles out Demetrius as an example of someone who is well-regarded by others, being testified to by everyone and proven to be devoted to the reality. The commendation of Demetrius serves as a contrast to the negative actions of Diotrephes, highlighting the importance of living out one's faith with integrity and authenticity. He then expresses his desire to communicate further with the saints but indicates that he prefers a personal visit over written communication. This personal touch underscores the value of face-to-face interaction and direct communication in addressing issues and fostering strong relationships within the fellowship of believers.

In conclusion, the passage emphasizes the importance of discerning between good and evil behavior, following the path of righteousness, and upholding the reality in one's actions. The contrast between Diotrephes' negative behavior and Demetrius' positive example serves as a lesson in integrity, authenticity, and the importance of walking in the reality of the gospel. The writer's intention to address the situation personally underscores the significance of directly confronting issues within the church and working to maintain unity, peace, and genuine fellowship among believers.

Terry Kashian

3 John

Chapter 1

1. The aged one to Gaius the beloved, whom I am loving in reality.
2. Beloved, I want in all things that you may have a prosperous journey along the way and be in good health, just as your soul prospers.
3. Therefore, I rejoiced exceedingly in the brothers coming and having bore witness of the reality that is in you, just as you are walking in the reality.
4. I have no greater joy than to hear that my children are walking in the reality.
5. Beloved, you are doing faithfully in which you are laboring into the brothers and newcomers;
6. Who have given witness of your love before the Assembly: whom if you send them forward in a worthy manner of God, you will do well:
7. Because that for His name they went out, taking nothing from the nations.
8. Therefore, such men ought to receive from us, that we might be fellow workers in the reality.
9. I wrote to the Assembly: but Diotrephes, who strives to be first among them, does not receive us.
10. Therefore, if I come, I will bring his actions to his attention, talking nonsense against us with malicious words: and not satisfied over these, neither does he receive the brothers and impedes them who desire to, and expels them out of the Assembly.
11. Beloved, do not copy that which is evil, but that which is good. He that is doing good is out from God: but he that is doing evil has not beheld God.
12. To Demetrius it's been witnessed by everyone, and with the reality itself: yes, and we also bear witness, and you know that our testimony is real.
13. I had many things to write, but I will not with pen and paper write to you:
14. But I am hoping to see you without delay, and we will be talking personally. Peace to you. Our dear ones are greeting you. Greet the friends by name.

Synopsis of Jude

This epistle is quite remarkable for a little postcard as some preachers would call it. This letter is a call to arms for the faithful in order to battle the false teachers, Judaizers, and false prophets. This was the battle in the wilderness with those within who were departing from the faith and perverting the faith. In order to maintain victory these first century saints needed mercy to avoid being deceived and lead astray. They needed peace in order to not be frightened so their hearts could be guarded. And without a doubt they needed agape love in order to overcome the rebellion in which many hearts would grow cold during this time. Jude wrote, may the mercy, peace and love be multiplied to you. These three attributes of God must increase and abound in us to be overcomers. Jude is calling an army to rise up to secure the faith, the heavenly culture, and battle to defeat all enemies against it.

    The apostle Paul warned the elders of the Ephesian church in Miletus of enemies from within saying, "For I know this that after my departure savage wolves will come in among you, not sparing the flock. Also, from among yourselves men will rise up, speaking perverse things, to draw away the disciples after themselves. Acts 20:29-31.

    The Apostle points out that not only from the outside will enemies come in, but from their very own. Who were the very own in the audience of Jude? This is the same audience the Lord Jesus addressed when he said, "I know that you are Abraham's seed, but you seek to kill Me because My word has no place in you. I speak what I have seen with My Father, and you do what you have seen with your father." John 8:37-38. The key to maintaining the heavenly culture and being free in Christ is continuing in His word so we can know the reality and the reality will set us free. Deceivers and those who are false deviate from the word of God and it has no place in them. They do the deeds of their father. Jesus said, "you are of your father the devil, and the desires of your father you want to do. He was a murderer from his origin, and does not stand in the reality, because there is no reality in him.

    When he speaks a lie, he speaks out of himself, for he is a liar and the father of it." John 8:44. Jesus is talking about the sons of serpents as John the Baptist did when he said, 'who warned you to flee from the wrath to come you brood of vipers and sons of snakes. The leaders in Israel were deceivers and they spoke lies with their mixture of the traditions of men invalidating the word of God. Not pure lies, but just enough mixture to cancel out the effectiveness of the word of God. These were the sons of the evil one, the tares, the goats, and the citizens that hated the King's son and did not want this man to reign over them.

Jude is dealing with the enemy and his strategy to corrupt the heavenly culture, the faith, with lies, perversion, and religion. These were the tactics in the wilderness in the days of Moses. Jude is passionate about getting this message out to his companions. You can sense his urgency to reveal what the Lord is saying to him. He writes in verse four, "for certain men have crept in unnoticed". This is literally, "some men have slithered in stealthily". When I saw this, I at once thought of a snake slipping in unawares to cause a fatality.

This was predicted by the prophets, by our Lord Jesus, and by Paul and Peter. Some came in to make a mockery of the grace of God and change it into a license for sexual perversion. These that came in were even rejecting Christ as the Lord and Owner of their bodies. Lawlessness and no boundaries were the enticing message that called for soldiers of the cross to pull out their sword of the Spirit and cut in pieces those irreverent messages that would produce fatalities among the saints. The enemy knows that sexual immorality of any kind will contaminate and weaken the testimony of Jesus on this earth. It is the negative leaven that leavens the whole lump and changes a loving community of believers into a selfish, self-seeking group with little expression and experience of Christ. Jude, prompted by the Holy Spirit reminds them of the days of Moses.

The days of Moses are crucial to our understanding of what the first century saints went through in their journey during the time of the cross to the destruction of the city of Jerusalem and the sanctuary. The Apostle Paul states in 1 Cor. 10:11, now all these things happened to them as examples, (types of us), and they were written for our admonition, upon whom the goal of the ages has come. The time of Moses was a type of the first century church. The first century church was the chosen generation which I gather is the generational model for us to learn the ways of God. From the cross in 30 A.D. to the destruction of the city of Jerusalem and the sanctuary in 70 A.D., forty years in the wilderness.

Jude was writing right at the end of the forty-year period with only a little time left before the end of all things were to happen. The old world of the Mosaic Covenant was about to end, and the new world of New Covenant and Kingdom was about to appear. So, Jude writes to these precious Jews who had put their faith in Jesus the Messiah. You are all aware that one time the Lord saved a people out of the land of Egypt, then secondly, destroyed those who did not continue to believe. There truly was a mixed multitude and though they were saved out of the land of Egypt they never came into their inheritance.

"How long shall I bear with this evil congregation who are grumbling against Me? I have heard the complaints of the sons of Israel, which they are making against Me. "Say to them, 'as I live,' says the Lord, 'just as you have spoken in My hearing, so I will surely do to you; your corpses will fall in this wilderness, even all your numbered men, according to your complete number from twenty years old and upward, who have grumbled against Me. 'Surely you shall not come into the land in which I swore to settle you, except Caleb the son of Jephunneh and Joshua the son of Nun. 'Your children, however, whom you said would become a prey — I will bring them in, and they will know the land which you have rejected. 'But as for you, your corpses will fall in this wilderness. 'Your sons shall be shepherds for forty years in the wilderness, and they will suffer for your unfaithfulness, until your corpses lie in the wilderness. 'According to the number of days which you spied out the land, forty days, for every day you shall bear your guilt a year, even forty years, and you will know My opposition. 'I, the Lord, have spoken, surely this I will do to all this evil congregation who are gathered together against Me. In this wilderness they shall be destroyed, and there they will die. 'Num. 14:27-35

You can see from these verses in Numbers that the relevance of the forty years in the wilderness is so related to the transition period between the cross and destruction of Jerusalem. What is quite amazing about Jude is that most of this epistle is drawn from chapters 13 and 14 of Numbers as we will see going further into this letter.

Now here is where things get a little thorny because I will be dealing with some deep ingrained tradition, and I ask for your patience as you consider this part of the summary of Jude. We are going to look at verse 6 and we must consider the train of thought that Jude is conveying. He is talking about Israel and their deliverance and their destruction. The question I have is, is he talking about angels or messengers? I propose this question because he may have been talking about some messengers and not necessarily heavenly angels. The Greek word for angel is aggelos ("a messenger"). In the bible there are earthly and heavenly messengers. I will be honest with you in this section. I could be wrong, but I have a gut feeling about this and I have not ever felt right about angels from heaven going bad.

In my experience that seems more like the Hollywood version of angels than the Bible version. I will now attempt to persuade you regarding these angels which did not keep their first estate and left their habitation. First of all, let's keep in mind the context of Jude's train of thought. Those that were destroyed in the wilderness were influenced by ten angels. Let me illustrate my point. In Joshua, Moses had sent out 12 spies to bring a report back to the people of Israel. These 12 men are called angels in Joshua two times. Now the city shall be doomed by the Lord to destruction, it and all who are in it. Only Rahab the harlot shall live, she and all who are with her in the house, because she hid the messengers (angels: malak in Hebrew) that we sent. Josh. 6:17. And Joshua spared Rahab the harlot, her father's household, and all that she had. So, she dwells in Israel to this day, because she hid the messengers whom Joshua sent to spy out Jericho.

Josh. 6:25. This is quoted by James in his letter to the twelve tribes in Chapter 2. Likewise, was Rahab the harlot not also justified by works, when she had received the messengers (aggelos: messenger), and had sent them out another way? James 2:25.

In the New Testament this word for angel is used about 175 times. It is more commonly used for heavenly angels than earthly ones. It takes some discernment to rightly divide the word here. John the Baptist is called the angel from Malachi 3:1 in Matthew, Mark, and

Luke. Also, in Luke 7:24 John's disciples are called angels when asking the Lord Jesus if He was the One or should they look for another. They went back to John in prison and delivered the message. In Luke 9:52 the Lord sent angels to the Samaritans to see if they would receive Him and they would not. These angels were His disciples. The angels of the seven churches are leaders of the assemblies in those cities. Now from this we should be able to see that there are distinctions between heavenly and earthly angels. It is not one-sided. Therefore, we must examine these verses a little more carefully to get Jude's point. I mentioned above that ten angels caused the death of an entire generation except for two men and their families of that generation.

This is quite shocking!

Here are some verses to explain the nature of the messengers. 'Let us send men before us, that they may explore the land for us and bring us word again of the way by which we must go up and the cities into which we shall come.' The thing seemed good to me, and I took twelve men from you, one man from each tribe. Deut. 1:22-23.

Then the Lord spoke to Moses saying, "send out for yourself men so that they may spy out the land of Canaan, which I am going to give to the sons of Israel; you shall send a man from each of their fathers' tribes, everyone a leader among them." So, Moses sent them from the wilderness of Paran at the command of the Lord, all of them men who were heads of the sons of Israel. Num. 13:1-3.

Thus, they told him, and said, "we went into the land where you sent us; and it certainly does flow with milk and honey, and this is its fruit. "Nevertheless, the people who live in the land are strong, and the cities are fortified and very large; and moreover, we saw the descendants of Anak there. "Amalek is living in the land of the Negev and the Hittites and the Jebusites and the Amorites are living in the hill country, and the Canaanites are living by the sea and by the side of the Jordan." Num. 13:27-29.

Then Caleb quieted the people before Moses and said, "we should by all means go up and take possession of it, for we will surely overcome it." Num. 13:30-31.

But the men who had gone up with him said, "we are not able to come against the people, for they are too strong for us." So they gave out to the sons of Israel an evil report of the land which they had spied out, saying, "the land through which we have gone, in spying it out, is a land that devours its inhabitants; and all the people whom we saw in it are men of great size. "There also we saw the Nephilim (the sons of Anak are part of the Nephilim); and we became like grasshoppers in our own sight, and so we were in their sight." Num. 13:31-33. ... and you complained in your tents, and said, 'because the Lord hates us, He has brought us out of the land of Egypt to deliver us into the hand of the Amorites, to destroy us. 28 Where can we go up? Our brothers have discouraged our hearts, saying, "the people are greater and taller than we; the cities are great and fortified up to heaven; moreover, we have seen the sons of the Anakim there." Deut. 1:27-28.

It is important that the messengers with the evil report caused the hearts of the people to melt and lose courage. Here we see two distinct messages being delivered to the people in the wilderness. One message is giving faith and courage, and the other is a slanderous lie that defames God and imparts unbelief and discouragement to the people of God. This is what Jude was dealing with in his day. This is why he is encouraging them to fight for the faith once delivered to the saints.

The angels that did not keep their first estate. Let us go back to Jude 6 and identify what is the first estate. I hope by now you can see the possibility that these angels are the spies that were sent to the Promised Land. The phrase in Jude 6 "did not keep their first estate" is very significant as we look at the word first. This word in Greek is 'arche', which is translated beginning, head, ruler, first, principalities, and prince. The idea is a leader or prince or position of authority. Other translations or versions translate this word for first estate as 'domain, position of authority, principality, original position, etc. We can draw from these admirable attempts to find the most fitting word to help us understand this word better.

In Numbers 13:2 when the leaders were picked to spy out the land. Moses said everyone must be a leader. The word leader in Hebrew is 'nasi' and it means prince, something that is lifted up, a mist like a cloud rising up to proclaim that rain is coming. The King James translates this as ruler and Young as prince. Now going into verse 3 of Numbers we find the phrase, "all those men were heads of the children of Israel." The Hebrew word for heads is 'rosh' which means head, beginning, chief, leader, the place at the head, principal. The result of my findings was that the angels did not keep their position of authority or princely position. They lost it because God destroyed them for slandering Him and causing the people to doubt the ability of God to give them the victory. Their evil report caused them to lose their position of authority.

As for the men whom Moses sent to spy out the land and who returned and made all the congregation grumble against him by bringing out an evil report concerning the land, even those men who brought out the very evil report of the land died by a plague before the Lord. But Joshua the son of Nun and Caleb the son of Jephunneh remained alive out of those men who went to spy out the land. Num. 14:36-38.

Ten angels died by a plague for giving an evil report, a contradicting message to the people of God. These ten angels had families and they left behind their families and lost their position of authority. The word for habitation in Jude 6 is quite interesting. It is the word: 'oiketerion' and it means habitation, dwelling, residence, home and abode. This word is made up of two Greek parts. The first is 'oiketer' meaning an inhabitant or resident. The 'ion' makes this word change from resident to residence. When a person dies, they leave behind their family, residence, etc. and in this case the ten angels were judged for their wickedness, lost their authority, and left their family and residence behind. This is my presentation on the angels that did not keep their first estate and left behind their homes. I hope this is a little more practical than the Jewish fables we are fed by Christendom and the speculators of fallen angels.

Next, we have Sodom and Gomorrah as an illustration of God's judgment on those that are great sinners against Him and against His righteous ones. As we follow the train of thought that Jude has, we can see that Egypt and Sodom are specific examples to the Jews. The apostle John in his book of the Revelation in Rev 11:8; … and their dead bodies will lie in the street of the great city which spiritually is called Sodom and Egypt, where also their Lord was crucified. We can see very clearly that Jerusalem, 'where our Lord was crucified', is spiritually called Egypt and Sodom. I am not stretching this. This is what John says and Jude is on the same page. Egypt is the place of bondage, terrorizing the people of God. Sodom means in Hebrew according to J.B. Jackson's Dictionary of Scripture Proper Names, fettered and Gomorrah means bondage. The righteous soul of Lot was vexed and oppressed by the perversion of Sodom and Lot was so bound that it took two angels to drag him out of the city and blinded those that would not repent of their great wickedness against the Lord and was later destroyed.

The development of the doctrine of archangels has its basis in the tendency to give prominence to certain leading and individualized angels. It is worth noting, however, that there is virtually no interest in this aspect in the NT. The paucity of occurrences is striking.

1.Above is a quote concerning archangels and it is important to note that this term is used only one time in reference to Michael in the New Testament. The other time it is used is in 1 Thess. 4:17, the theoretical rapture verse. The Lord descends with the voice of the archangel. Could it be that the Lord Jesus is given the symbolic name of Michael, 'One who is like God'? I am not saying that the Lord Jesus is an angel in the sense of a created being separate from God, Jude is using symbolic language and drawing from the types in the Old Testament to make a point.

Michael the Archangel, Archangel is two Greek words, archon = chief, prince and aggelos – angel. So, this Michael is the chief or prince of the angels. Jesus would be the prince or chief of the messengers. In Thessalonians, He descends with the voice of the Archangel. Connect the dots where Jesus is shouting with the voice of the Archangel. The dead in Christ shall rise first. In John 5:25, 28. The dead hear the voice of the Son of God and come to life. In Jude it says, Michael contending with Satan concerning the body of Moses. Again, we must realize that Jude is using many symbols in this little postcard, so let's continue to understand the symbolism of Moses' body. When I was a young believer, I assumed this was speaking about the physical body of Moses, which is normal when we in the beginning do not see the corporate aspect of God's people. Paul uses this same symbolism in 1 Cor. 10.

He says to the Corinthians, "I don't want you to be ignorant that all our fathers were under the cloud and passed through the sea and were baptized or immersed into Moses. Israel became the body of Moses, just like the church is the body of Christ. Satan was wanting to possess the body of Moses, just like he was trying to fill the body of Christ with his demons and demonic teachings. Someone might say, how can Satan fill the believers? Remember the story of Ananias and his wife, Acts5:3, but Peter said, "Ananias, why has Satan filled your heart to lie to the Holy Spirit NASU. Satan is always fighting to get into the church. This is the motivation of Jude's letter. My conclusion to this is that, in type Jude is using the picture of the children of wilderness as an example of what the early believers were going through.

Tying back the original idea that Jesus is Michael, one might say, why did Jesus say the Lord rebuke you? If Michael was the Lord, why didn't He just say, "I rebuke you"! In Zech. 3:2 The Lord said to Satan, "The Lord rebuke you, Satan! NASU. There are other verses that would further prove this topic, but my main thought is the message of Jude. As I pointed out above, Jude is conveying that what happened in the Old Testament is a picture of what was going on in his day.

Jude says, these speak evil of the things they do not understand. The phrase speak evil is the Greek word, 'blasphemeo'. This is a common phrase that is used throughout the New Testament. One such verse as an example is, but when they resisted and blasphemed, he shook out his garments and said to them, "Your blood be on your own heads! I am clean. From now on I will go to the Gentiles." 2 Paul says that 'they' were the unbelieving Jews and now he was going to the nations. Jude says in verse 11, Woe to them! For they have gone the way of Cain, and for pay they have rushed headlong into the error of Balaam and perished in the rebellion of Korah.3

This is the threefold process of apostasy. The first is the way of Cain. Cain did not love his brother. This is how it starts. He was jealous of his brother.

4 By faith Abel offered to God a more excellent sacrifice than Cain, through which he obtained witness that he was righteous, God testifying of his gifts; and through it he being dead still speaks.4

11 For this is the message that you heard from the beginning, that we should love one another, 12 not as Cain who was of the wicked one and murdered his brother. And why did he murder him? Because his works were evil and his brother's righteous.5

Abel was offering to God by faith in the blood of the lamb and Cain was offering to God by the works of his hands. The principle of Law is trusting in your Law works to be accepted by God, which can only produce self-righteousness and pride or if you have an honest heart condemnation and defeat. Cain through his jealousy and envy and hatred killed his brother. The Jews of the 1st century had a choice to practice the way of Cain or the example of Abel. They could be free by trusting in the blood of the Lamb or the works of the Law.

Acts 17:5-8, But the Jews, becoming jealous and taking along some wicked men from the marketplace, formed a mob and set the city in an uproar; and attacking the house of Jason, they were seeking to bring them out to the people. 6 When they did not find them, they began dragging Jason and some brothers before the city authorities, shouting, "These men who have caused the Roman world to rise up, have come here also; 7 and Jason has accepted them, and they all are opposed to the set of the beliefs of Caesar, saying that there is another king, Jesus." These unbelieving Jews were taking the way of Cain and many of the believers when rebellion abounded the agape love was growing cold and there were many that betrayed their own brothers and sisters and family members.

Secondly, the error of Balaam. Balaam's name in the Dictionary of Scripture Proper Names by J.B. Jackson says that his name means, 'swallower of the people; confounding the people'. Charles Spurgeon writes on the matter in the book called 'Well Intentioned Dragons' by Marshall Shelley. In Chapter 7, Spurgeon says, in 'When the Dragon May Be Right'. The first test is to see if the dragon is right, consider the source. What is motivating this person? Is this person a person of integrity? Is this person for the people or is he hungry to swallow and feed on the people for himself? This is a paraphrase of his comments. Balaam was tempted to follow his own will instead of God's will. The self-willed starts out not loving his brother and loving himself above all others. Then he will be tempted to be self-willed, seeking a reward for himself. This is child gone wrong.

The error of Balaam is the adolescence of spiritual life. This kind of person will truly turn out to be a dragon. We are supposed to love people and use things. This is the opposite of the person that is growing improperly in a spiritual way. We are not to use people and love things. Peter says that 2 Peter 2:15-16 … the way of Balaam, the son of Beor, who loved the wages of unrighteousness; 16 but he received a rebuke for his own transgression, for a mute donkey, speaking with a voice of a man, restrained the madness of the prophet. NASU. Here Peter says that he was a prophet. The prophet Balaam and this is the key, Peter did not say false prophet Balaam and it is documented where God spoke through him and spoke to him. But eventually in Joshua 13:22, he is called Balaam the soothsayer or diviner. Joshua pierces him with the sword. Only the sword can put an end to the error of Balaam. Remember the symbolism! The sword of the Spirit, which Spirit is the Word of God.

Lastly, this is the adult apostate, the rebellion or contradiction of Korah. This is when a person has decided not to submit to authority that God has appointed. Many times, these are self-appointed men or women instead of God anointed. It is also important to understand this point because Korah accused Moses of lifting himself up over the congregation. Korah was a Levite and part of the holy priesthood. And 250 men were standing with Korah and

Moses said because they were opposing Moses that they were against the Lord. The proof of a real and genuine leader is the matter of resurrection life. Does the leader have life in his ministry? It is not an official position, otherwise Korah would have already had that. He was a leader. Also, with him 250 men stood against the Lord. Moses said let's see who God chooses to come near to Him and who belongs to Him. So, Moses had them take their sensors and fill them with incense and there were 250 of them in all before the Lord. He also said to Korah, you and Aaron take your censors too and place them before the Lord. They put fire in all of them, can you imagine the smoke from 252 censors burning incense, what a cloud of smoke! Then it says the glory of the Lord appeared at the doorway of the tent of meeting.

The Lord said to Moses, you and Aaron separate yourselves from this gathering that I may consume this whole congregation. Moses and Aaron fell on their faces and pleaded with the Lord not to destroy the whole congregation. The Lord then told Moses and Aaron to tell everyone to get away from Korah and his company. So, Moses said this is the test if the Lord sent me to do all these things, if they die a normal death, like old age the Lord has not sent me. But if they die by the earth opening and swallowing them then you will know by this new thing that the Lord has sent me. So, all the people left where these rebels were dwelling. Then suddenly the earth opened its mouth and swallowed Korah and his company because they despised the Lord.

Korah and other leaders despised the Lord and the true land that flows with milk and honey. They wanted people to go back to slavery. "Is it not enough that you have brought us up out of a land flowing with milk and honey to have us die in the wilderness, but you would also lord it over us?6 These accusations are serious! This is the contradiction of Korah and his followers. These leaders were saying that Egypt is the land flowing with milk and honey. This is the contradiction! Since Egypt is a type of Jerusalem, (Rev.11:8), it represents Judaism and the temple worship. Applying this to the 1st century there were teachers and false prophets saying that Judaism is the land flowing with milk and honey. Even today we have these same things where people are saying the Israel in the Mideast is the holy land. When in fact, the holy land is in Christ and is Christ. We are in Him therefore we are in the holy land enjoying this land. Milk is for babes in Christ and honey is called meat for those who are growing and mature. Korah's men were leaders, but their leadership was to lead them backwards instead of onward with God's purpose. Don't be fooled by those today that want you to go back to the types and shadows claiming that these are the real things.

There are two types of leaders in this little epistle. Those like Jude and those like Korah! Those like Jude are going to lead you into the real Promised Land and those like Korah are going to lead you back into bondage. Jude says, 12 These are hidden rocky reefs in your love-feasts, when they feast together with you, shepherding themselves fearlessly; they are clouds without water, carried around by winds; trees who are rotting, fruitless, twice dying, rooted out; 13 wild waves of the sea, foaming out their own shame; wandering stars, for whom is reserved the blackness of darkness into the New Covenant Age. TKB. People like this cause many to be shipwrecked because they are self-willed, shepherding themselves. Jude uses the phrase, 'clouds without water'.

The word leader in Hebrew is a beautiful picture of how one becomes a leader in a sovereign way. OT: 5387 - Some scholars have proposed that the term refers to elected officials, contending that these were common people who were elevated or lifted up. They often buttress their argument with Num. 1:16, which talks of these leaders as the ones called, chosen, or appointed from the congregation. In a few instances, this word also indicates a mist or vapors that rise from the earth to form clouds and herald the coming of rain (from The Complete Word Study Dictionary: Old Testament Copyright ©2003 by AMG Publishers. All rights reserved.) In this word picture we can see that when God wants real leaders he will begin to shine upon their lives, and they become like vapor and they rise to form a cloud. Sometimes in Scripture teaching is like rain from a cloud. Deut. 32:2. Sow with a view to righteousness, reap in accordance with kindness; break up your fallow ground, for it is time to seek the Lord until He comes to rain righteousness on you.7 False leaders are like the verse in Proverbs 25:14, like clouds and wind without rain is a man who boasts of his gifts falsely.8 Jude says of these false teachers that they are like clouds without water carried about by winds (false teaching). Eph.4:14. These are people that Jude says are twice dead.

Jude condemns those who are spiritually dead, referring to them as "twice dead." This concept is derived from the teachings of Christ, who emphasized the importance of spiritual life and the consequences of spiritual death. In the Bible, being "dead in sins and trespasses" is a state of separation from God, as mentioned in Ephesians 2:1. The idea of experiencing the second death, as mentioned by Jude, aligns with the teachings of Christ on the reality of perpetual punishment for those who reject Him. In the New Testament, Jesus warns about the consequences of not accepting Him as the Messiah, which includes facing the second death (Revelation 21:8). Jude highlights the danger faced by the Judaizers who rejected their Messiah. By rejecting Christ, they wandered in the spiritual wilderness, akin to the Israelites wandering for forty years. This spiritual wanderlust, according to Jude, leads to being uprooted and facing the second death. The mention of "wandering stars" in Jude's writing alludes to the promise God made to Abraham, Isaac, and Jacob regarding their descendants being as numerous as stars. However, those who stray from the path of righteousness and reject the Messiah become like wandering stars, lost in darkness and confusion, and propagate that confusion to the body of Christ. Overall, Jude's message warns against the consequences of rejecting Christ and emphasizes the need for a new covenant life with God, rather than the old covenant. This aligns with the teachings of Christ on the importance of faith, repentance, and following Him to avoid spiritual death and perpetual separation from God.

This should put the fear of God in us as leaders! My God will cast them away because they have not listened to Him; and they will be wanderers among the nations.9 It is quite interesting that when Cain murdered his brother, he was sent out from the presence of the Lord to a place called Nod. Nod in Hebrew means wandering. The dictionary defines 'wandering', like this; moving from place to place without a fixed plan; roaming; rambling. These false teachers have no roots, and they are fruitless, rotting trees, like wild waves casting up their shame like foam. Perpetual darkness is their lot. Thank God He knows those who are His. This foundation stands sure!

We have next a quote from the pseudo book of Enoch. It is not proven that this book is genuinely the Book of Enoch the seventh from Adam. It is littered with false concepts of creation and redemption and angels, and you name it. It mentions hell in this book which is not an Old Testament term and not really a New Testament term either. The word in our English translations is the Greek word, 'Gehenna'. There are just too many erroneous things in this Enoch I that was discovered in 1956 among the other Dead Sea Scrolls. Even as Paul quoted: Acts 17:28 … for in Him we live, move, and exist, as even some of your own poets have said, 'For we also are His children.' NASU. Although we are creations of God as His, we are only real children of God in the sense of being born again. Adam was the first earthly son of God. Therefore, all humans as follows would be considered earthly children of God. To enter the kingdom of God we must be born from above, again, of His Spirit. In a generic sense we are God's children, but only in the sense of creation. This does not prove that everything the Greek poet, Epimenides wrote was inspired by God. So, I would dismiss the book of Enoch as the Old Covenant leaders rejected it and as the church fathers excluded it. I have read it many times and find some truths in it, but as a consistent record of inspired thoughts, I would have to pass on some of those ideas.

The pertinence of Jude quoting this prophecy of Enoch was in my understanding, to encourage the saints then in his day that God was about to judge the ungodly and to endure the hostility to the end. Just like God judged Sodom and Gomorrah and Egypt, He was ready to judge the opponents quickly. Jude: 17 But, beloved, remember the words which were spoken before by the apostles of our Lord Jesus Christ; 18 that they told you there would be mockers in the time of the end, who should walk after their own godless lusts. 19 These are they who isolate themselves, soulish, not possessing the Spirit. TKB. This is the same time that Daniel spoke of, "the time of the end". Dan 8:17; … "Son of man, understand that the vision pertains to the time of the end." NASU. Dan 8:16a, 18- 19; I heard a human voice calling from the middle of the Ulai: "Gabriel, explain the vision to this man." … and said, "I am here to tell you what will happen at the conclusion of the time of wrath, because it refers to the appointed time of the end. (From Holman Christian Standard Bible® Copyright © 1999, 2000,2002, 2003, 2005 by Holman Bible Publishers.) The end of the age was upon them and the natural man, soulish man was trying to take over and lead the church back into bondage and misery.

The true leader instructs the saints in a way to inoculate them against this religious disease of Law-works and superstition and countless other strange teachings which the apostles warned them about. Jude's direction was simple, keep building up yourselves upon your holy faith. This concentration of building one another up is the key to being under the controlling vision. Where there is no vision, revelation, the people run wild, cast-off restraint, and go to pieces. We need to see how important the early church needed this vision of corporate life to survive the ongoing rejection, persecution, and physical destruction. The word for 'your' is plural. It is not just my holy faith, but the corporate faith, the heavenly culture that needs further building up. A continuous extension of the faith in every place.

The next component of being preserved from the false teachers and prophets was praying in the Holy Spirit. Keep praying in the Holy Spirit. Stay connected to the Spirit. Apart from the Spirit we have no power or ability to overcome. Praying and accountability, i.e. being subject one to another is the way to be continuously filled in spirit. Thirdly, keep yourselves in the love of God. This implies watching, guarding your heart that it is not hardened for out of it spring forth the issues of life. Guard our hearts from resentment, unforgiveness, bitterness, and retaliation. This is what Jude's audience was to do by expecting and anticipating the mercy of the Lord Jesus Christ into infinite life. This wasn't all up to them, but Jude says, NOW is the possibility of Him to guard you, protect you from stumbling and present you flawless before His glory and cause you to stand in His presence now and into all the New Covenant Age.

Terry Kashian

Jude

Chapter 1

1. Jude, the slave of Jesus Christ, and brother of James, to those who are the called, beloved in Father God, and guarded by Jesus Christ;
2. Mercy to you, and peace, and love, be multiplied.
3. Beloved, when I was making every urgency to write to you concerning our collective deliverance, it was necessary for me to write to you, and entreat you that you compete over the prize for the faith that was once handed over to the saints.
4. For there are certain men who slithered in stealthily, who were written about previously long ago for this condemnation, godless men, changing the grace of our God into unrestrained sexual lust, and rejecting our only Master and Lord Jesus Christ.
5. Therefore, I desire to remind you, though you know all this, one time the Lord saved the people out of the land of Egypt, then secondly destroyed those who did not believe.
6. Even the messengers who did not keep their princely position, but left behind their own homes, He has guarded in perpetual bonds under darkness for the great Day of Judgment.
7. Just as Sodom and Gomorrah, and the cities around them in like manner, gave themselves over to excessive fornication and going after other flesh, are set before us as an illustration, undergoing the punishment of perpetual fire.
8. Likewise, also these dreamers are polluting the body, rejecting authority, and blaspheming the glory.
9. Yet Michael, the chief of the messengers, when contending with the Devil, he disputed regarding the body of Moses and did not challenge to bring a blasphemous judgment against him, but said, may the Lord rebuke you!
10. But these blaspheme the things which they do not understand; but what these understand instinctively, as illogical animals, in these things they corrupt themselves.
11. Woe to them! For they have gone in the way of Cain, and moved toward the deception of Balaam poured out for compensation, and were utterly destroyed in Korah's contradiction.
12. These are spots in your love feasts, when they feast together with you, shepherding themselves fearlessly; they are clouds without water, carried around by winds; trees who are rotting, fruitless, twice dead, rooted out;
13. Wild waves of the sea, foaming out their own shame; wandering stars, for whom is reserved the blackness of darkness into the New Covenant Age.
14. And Enoch also, the seventh from Adam, prophesied and also to these, saying, behold, the Lord comes with countless of His saints,
15. To execute judgment against all, and to prove guilty all that are godless among them of all their godless deeds which they have committed in a godless way; and of all their cruel words which ungodly sinners have spoken against Him.

Jude 1:16

16. These are grumblers, complainers, walking after their own lusts; and their mouth speaks great swelling words, complimenting faces with flattery for their own profit.
17. But, beloved, remember the words which were spoken before by the apostles of our Lord Jesus Christ;
18. That they told you there would be mockers in the final time, who would walk after their own godless lusts.
19. These are they who isolate themselves, soulish, not possessing the Spirit.
20. But you, beloved, building up yourselves upon your holy faith, praying in the Holy Spirit,
21. Keep yourselves in the love of God, anticipating the mercy of our Lord Jesus Christ into infinite life.
22. And on some having compassion, examining carefully;
23. And others saving with fear, seizing them out of the fire; hating even the garment spotted by the flesh.
24. Now is the possibility of Him guarding you against stumbling, and presenting you flawless in the very presence of His glory with exuberant joy,
25. To the only wise God our Savior, be glory and majesty, dominion and power, both now and into all the New Covenant Age. Amen.

Revelation Commentary

Revelation Commentary

The book of Revelation is the revealing of Jesus Christ. First century Christians are encouraged in it, as they see Jesus Christ on the throne ruling the nations (1:5), which was difficult to see in the midst of a horrific persecution, which to the natural eye, appeared not to be the case. All that was seen in the natural was this persecution being carried out by a beast on the throne. The Apostle John sees what's really going on, as he is in this persecution, the tribulation (1:9), and is given heaven's perspective. John is encouraged as he sees judgment and vindication (Luke 21:22), which is soon to be poured out upon the persecutors. The book of Revelation is a vision being recorded by John, "what thou sees, write in a book… (Revelation 1:11)". Visions often contain much symbolism. Therefore, symbolism, and what R.C. Sproul refers to as "Apocalyptic Language" (Read, The Last Days According to Jesus), must be highly considered when interpreting the book. The book brings us into a world of green horses ("Chloros", 6:8), red dragons (12:2), an eagle (4:7), a woman standing on the moon without astronaut attire (12:1), hippy locusts shaped like horses (Revelation 9:7, See 1 Chronicles 12:8 and Joel 1:6 for the meaning here), dogs (22:15), a harlot (17:1), a lion (5:5), a lamb (5:6, 14:1), a leopard, a bear (13:2) and a seven-headed beast with ten horns (13:1), oh my! So, when we see, for instance, a sea beast arises from the sea (13:1), we must not entertain our Sci-Fi fancies in beholding Godzilla's ascension. The sea itself, must be understood metaphorically as the place of the Gentiles, or the barrier dividing them from the Promised Land people, (Revelation 8:8; 13:1; 16:3; 21:1; Ephesians 2:12, 14; Genesis 10:5; Psalm 72:10; Isaiah 11:10; 11; 24:14-16; 60:5).

Charles Spurgeon comments on "The Sea" in Revelation 21:1, "Is not the text to be read as a metaphor? … There must be a spiritual meaning here… The sea separates nations and sunders peoples from each other". So, to avoid the David Koresh or any other cult leader commentary on Revelation, we must understand that there are many more such metaphors to be considered. For example, let's consider the imagery conveyed when mountains are used in the vision (1:11). We see them in Revelation 8:8 and 16:20. One "mountain" is cast into the sea in the former, and one is not found in the latter. Because Revelation's contents are primarily taken from the Old Testament, 278 out of its 404 verses are Old Testament references or inferences, we must follow the interpretive method of, "Let Scripture interpret Scripture", and not like that of modern interpreters, which is, "Let newspaper headlines interpret Scripture". So, for instance, how does the rest of the Bible communicate the word "mountains" in prophecy? Did John the Baptist interpret the prophecy from Isaiah 40:3,4, which he was fulfilling, as an excavation project in Israel, where "Every valley shall be filled, and every mountain and hill shall be brought low…" (Luke 3:4,5)? How does the rest of the Bible use "mountain" in prophecy, in a figurative sense?

Daniel 2, a chief passage in Bible prophecy, communicates a mountain, as a kingdom, which fills the whole earth (Daniel 2:35). Psalm 46:2-6 communicates mountains synonymously with kingdoms as well, as does Hebrews 12:22, 27-28. Galatians 4:24-26 communicates the two covenant kingdoms as mountains. While both Isaiah 41:15-16, and Daniel 2:35, speak of mountains /kingdoms being carried away by the wind. Isaiah 64:1-3 reveals "the mountains" as synonymous with "the nations". Isaiah 51:24-25 refers to the kingdom of Babylon as the "destroying mountain". Jesus communicates this same figurative mountain in Matthew 21:21/Revelation 8:8, where he speaks of a mountain being removed (Hebrews 12:27) and cast into the sea.

APOCALYPTIC LANGUAGE is throughout Revelation, with much of it borrowed from the Old Testament. Consider sayings, such as coming in the cloud, and the sun, moon, and stars being darkened. Let's examine the latter in Isaiah 13:10, quoted by Jesus in Matthew 24:29. Remember, that the Olivet Discourse (Matthew 24, Mark 13, and Luke 21) is a highlighted version of the book of Revelation. Isaiah describes the Lord coming (13:9) in judgment upon Babylon (13:1) by using these same words, "For the stars of heaven and the constellations thereof shall not give their light: the sun shall be darkened in his going forth, and the moon shall not cause her light to shine (Isaiah 13:10)." Any sound scholar understands this judgment to be fulfilled by the Medes (13:17), bringing Babylon down (Daniel 2:39). All should understand, therefore, that nothing transpired in Babylon regarding the physical heavens. The physical sun, moon, and stars remained unchanged. Therefore, when Jesus quotes this same passage (Matthew 24:29), why do we then think that He is describing physical and astronomical occurrences? Yet, it was a judgment that was "astronomical". We even describe large scale events in our day with such metaphorical words.

To a Jew in the first century, "The sun, moon, and stars" communicated astronomical events. In our day, we still use the sun, moon, and stars, in a figurative and symbolic sense. National flags commonly use the sun, moon, and stars, to signify ruling authority (Genesis 1:16-18). The sun rules the day, while the moon and stars rule the night. Joseph's dream communicated this figurative understanding of the sun, moon, and stars (Genesis 37:9, 10). Consider the same metaphorical understanding when a judgment against Egypt (Ezek. 32:2) uses this same imagery, "And when I shall put thee out, I will cover the heaven, and make the stars thereof dark; I will cover the sun with the cloud and the moon shall not give her light (Ezekiel 32:7)."

It was lights out for Egypt (vs 8)! Nothing to do with the firmament! So, when Revelation 6:9-10 speaks of, "the sun becoming black, the moon as blood, and the stars of heaven falling to the earth", we must see how the rest of the Bible interprets these things, including Matthew 24:29 and considering Isaiah 13:9-10. Physical stars, by the way, cannot plummet into the earth. It would take only one literal star to incinerate the physical earth, which would transpire well before it ever fell down and touched ground.

We must avoid stubbornness and pharisaical attitudes when interpreting the scriptures. Refusing to consider alternative interpretations and rigidly insisting on a "literal" understanding of the Bible is a trap we must avoid. We must examine how the scriptures use various terms and phrases to communicate their message effectively. So, when Revelation 8:12 states that a third part of the sun was darkened, this cannot be communicating a scientific event. If 1/3 of the sun did not shine, the planet would become a giant ice ball! In fact, Revelation 16:8, says that the sun scorched men with fire. These two extremes cannot both occur in a scientific sense. The wooden literalist cannot have it both ways!" So, when Revelation 6:9, 10, and Acts 2:16-21, mention the sun, moon, and stars being darkened, astronomy is not the subject. In fact, Acts 2:16-21 tells us that this passage, quoted from Joel 2:28-32, is fulfilled at that time in the first century! "But this is that (This event is that passage's fulfillment) which was spoken by the prophet Joel; and it shall come to pass (be fulfilled) in the last days (The last days of the old covenant) …The sun shall be turned to darkness, and the moon into blood…" Now as for Revelation 6:9-10, "the sun became black…the moon became as blood, and the stars of heaven fell…" what's astounding here is that verses 15 and 16 give us the clearest of timelines for this event! In Revelation 6:15, they go into the caves of the earth/land to hide, which is a quote from Isaiah 2:19.

Josephus literally hid in one of these caves. In the next verse (Revelation 6:16), they call for the mountains to fall upon themselves, to be put out of their misery. This is a quote from Hosea 10:8 and is also quoted in Luke 23:30. Let's let Scripture interpret Scripture. Luke 23:28-30 states, "… daughters of JERUSALEM, weep not for me, but weep for yourselves, and for your children. For behold the days (Matthew 24:19, Luke 21:22-same days) are coming in the which they shall say, Blessed are the barren, and the wombs that never bare, and the breasts which never gave suck (same nursing going on as in Matthew 24:19). Then shall they (the first century citizens of Jerusalem) say to the mountains, fall on us; and the hills, cover us." These are the same citizens of Jerusalem, the same nursing mothers, calling for the same mountains to fall on them, in the same days! Those days were the days of the great tribulation period. John tells us this when he says that he is, "in the tribulation", in the first century (Revelation 1:9)! Paul says the same in 1 Corinthians 7:29-31 because of "the present distress" (A.D. 57), Christians shouldn't even be considering marriage! ^{29}But this I say, brethren, THE TIME IS SHORT, so that from now on even those who have wives should be as though they had none, ^{30}those who weep as though they did not weep, those who rejoice as though they did not rejoice, those who buy as though they did not possess,

³¹and those who use this world as not misusing it. FOR THE FORM OF THIS WORLD **IS** PASSING AWAY.[165]

HOW does the rest of the Bible interpret the Lord (Jesus) coming in the cloud in Revelation 1:7 and Matthew 24:30? To start with, Revelation 1:7 says, "Behold, he comes with the cloud; and every eye shall "see" (Greek, Optanomai, word origin, Horao: To discern, perceive, experience, and understand something) Him, and they also who pierced Him (they're not around today); and all the tribes (The 12 tribes are no longer in account) of the land (not the globe) shall wail because of Him." See, ironically, Darby's Translation, The Complete Jewish Bible, and Young's Literal Translation for this exact wording regarding the tribes and the land. Throughout the Bible the Lord comes in the cloud (Isaiah 19:1), or it is a cloudy day (Ezekiel 30:3) for this, or that, nation, and it has nothing to do with a weather report.

It is a time of judgment for that land, or even for an individual (Ecclesiastes 12:2). Jesus uses this same language concerning His coming judgment (Matthew 22:7) upon Jerusalem. In fact, the Greek word for Jesus' coming (Matthew 24:3) is Parousia, which literally means, coming presence. It literally (for the literalist) does not mean to come bodily, physically, or visibly. Addressing Caiaphas, Jesus says, "Hereafter shall you (a first century individual) see (Optanomai / Horao-discern) the Son of man sitting on the right hand of power and coming in the cloud of heaven" (Matthew 26:64). Caiaphas was enraged (vs.65) because he understood that it was only "The Lord" who would come in the cloud of judgment throughout the O.T., and that Jesus, therefore, was saying that He was that Lord who would be judging Caiaphas and the nation, rather than the current dynamics of Caiaphas judging Jesus!

WHEN would this coming (Revelation 1:7, Matthew 24:3) of Jesus occur? Revelation chapter one gives us the clearest of timelines (1:1, 3; 22:10), as does Matthew 24:34. The very first verse of the book tells us, "to show unto His servant's things which must shortly come to pass (1:1)." Shortly (Greek, Tachos) is defined as, Quickness, speed. That's it, no wiggle room to try to make this word mean something more than this. Tachos and its variations, Tachu, Tachista, Tachion, Tachinos, Tachoes, NEVER once suggests the idea that the subject being discussed is something that will happen a millennium or two later. The first and last chapter of Revelation has such clear time indicators. In 1:3, and 22:10, we see the word at hand (Eggus) used, "for the time is at hand".

This word is defined as, near, imminent, soon to come to pass". Now, for "the teaching of imminence", did this word (Eggus) mean the same thing in the first century as it does in the twenty first century? Was it imminent for them, or for us? Dispensationalists, against all logic and reasoning capacities, contend that it means imminent for both! Their own reasoning implodes upon itself, in that they claim that there are 7 ages, within a so called

---

[165] *The New King James Version* (1 Co 7:29–31). (1982). Thomas Nelson.

"Church Age", and that we are now living in the final, seventh, era of "the church age". Therefore, first century disciples could not have lived in a time to expect an imminent coming of Jesus, because they were in the first era of the seven stages of "the church age". Once more, dispensationalists claim that Israel becoming a nation in 1948 had to occur, before the imminent rapture of the church, therefore, imminence could only be applied since 1948, and not for the previous centuries, including the first century, when John used the word "at hand/near" (Eggus)! These two words, tachos (quickness, speed) and eggus (near, imminent, soon to come to pass), are consistently used in the N.T. to mean what they say and say what they mean. They NEVER communicate the idea of something that will take place some 2000 years from the time they were penned. These words, their definitions and N.T. usages, exclude the possibility of "A THOUSAND YEAR", mathematically speaking, reign!

A THOUSAND mathematical years are not permitted within the definitions and usages of shortly (tachos) and at /near/soon (eggus). To allow Scripture to interpret Scripture, we can understand that "A THOUSAND" year reign is only used in Revelation Chapter 20. It is used nowhere else in Revelation, nowhere in the epistles, gospels, prophets, psalms, or in the law!!! The rest of Scripture does tell us how "A THOUSAND" is used repeatedly. It is used figuratively, to communicate completeness or totality of something. Consider the following passages, Deuteronomy 7:9," …God, who keeps covenant and mercy with them that love Him and keep His commandments to "A THOUSAND" generations." Mathematics here gives us 36,000 years till any last day's concepts. 1 Chronicles 16:15, "the word which He commanded to "A THOUSAND" generations". Job 9:3, "If someone wanted to take God to court, would it be possible to answer Him once in "A THOUSAND" times?" So, mathematically speaking, after A THOUSAND times, one could answer God in Court and prove Him wrong? Psalm 50:10, "For every beast of the forest is mine, and the cattle upon "A THOUSAND" hills".

The thousand and first mathematic hill is His as well. This verse has nothing to do with cattle, "A THOUSAND", or hills. It has everything to do with God's total ownership of everything. Psalm 84:10, "Better is one day in Your courts, than "A THOUSAND" elsewhere…" After a thousand mathematical days, would a day in His courts still be better? No, a day there is completely better than anywhere else! Mathematics is not involved with this expression! Psalm 105:8, "the word which He commanded to "A THOUSAND" generations." I can give "A THOUSAND" examples of mathematics being excluded from the usage of this expression, this phrase. For example, "I've told you "A THOUSAND" times, that this thing weighs a ton." I may have mentioned it a few times, and the thing weighs 40 pounds, not 2000 lbs.! So, in the book of Revelation, either shortly (tachos) and at hand/near (eggus) must be taken figuratively, or "A THOUSAND" years must be taken figuratively! Both cannot!

Therefore, when we consider the Bible's usages of tachos and eggus, and its usages of "A THOUSAND", we must conclude that tachos and eggus are NEVER used figuratively throughout the Scriptures, and that "A THOUSAND" is virtually ALWAYS used figuratively! So, when was this non-mathematical reign of Christ? When might the kingdom, in which He reigns, hit the earth, that is, the stone cut out without hands, which becomes a mountain and fills the earth (Daniel 2:35)? And, where does Revelation 20 say that Jesus is reigning bodily, physically, and visibly? Did His kingdom not hit at the time of the Roman Empire, according to Daniel 2:34? Is it not a kingdom that comes without observation (Luke 17:20-21)? Was not Paul, the Colossians, and John, in it (Romans 14:17, Colossians 1:13, Revelation 1:9)? Was there ever a promised earthly utopia to be involved with it, according to Luke 17:20-21, and Revelation 21:1/ Isaiah 65:17-20, the latter involving people physically dying under the new heavens and new earth, as dogs and murderers prowl outside the new covenant city (Revelation 22:15; Hebrews 12:22; Galatians 4:26; Matthew 5:14), as nations are still in need of healing (22:2), and while evangelism is still going on (22:17, Daniel 12:2-3)? How is this describing a physical utopia? Did not this kingdom spread like leaven (Matthew 13:33)? Was it not preached to every creature under heaven, fulfilling Matthew 24:14 (Colossians 1:5, 6, 23; Acts 28:31; Romans 1:8; 10:18; 16:25-26)? Did not the stone/ the rock/the word of God smite the Roman Empire, turn it upside down (Acts 17:6), and crush Satan under the church's feet in the first century (Romans 16:20)? Was not Satan bound through the free speech given by Claudius Caesar (Religio Licita), resulting in the gospel conquering an empire (Revelation 6:2;19:11-16; Romans 8:37), even though he was loosed out of his prison for a short time thereafter (Revelation 20:7), when Nero changed that law (Daniel 7:25)? Is not the gospel the power of God (Romans 1:16)? Is not the power of God in the church greater than that of Satan's (Luke 11:18, 19, Matthew 16:18-19; 28:18-20; Ephesians 3:10, James 4:7; Romans 16:20; Revelation 2:26-27, fulfilling Psalm 2)? Does not the kingdom of God bind the strong man (Matthew 12:29; Revelation 20:2)? Should not "THE THOUSAND "year reign be interpreted figuratively, just like the key, the chain, and the serpent, in the very same passage (Revelation 20:2-3)?

Revelation cannot be speaking of a steel key and chain, binding a slithering reptile! Neither can it be speaking of a mathematical "THOUSAND YEAR" reign! This reign is spoken of by the Apostle Paul, as he quotes Isaiah 11:10 in Romans 15:12, "there shall be a root of Jesse, and He that shall rise TO REIGN over the Gentiles, in Him shall the Gentiles trust"! Note also, that Isaiah states in the word before this, "AND IN THAT DAY, there shall be a root of Jesse..." What day? Paul's day, the same day when the wolf, lamb, leopard, kid, calf, lion, fatling, a little child, a cow, and a bear, are all getting along just fine. The Gentile nations would miraculously be living together, along with the true Jews of Israel (Ephesians 2:12-14), as the Prince of Peace breaks down every barrier between them! This is also how Peter understood the various beasts, that they were communicating about the Gentiles in Acts 10 in Peter's vision! Noah's ark is another example of a dwelling place of refuge, where miraculous peace existed between those who would otherwise be at one another's throats! The clean and unclean animals in Noah's ark, two by two unclean and the clean by sevens. The Jews are the clean animals and the Gentile Nations are the unclean and they become one in one **vessel** being brought in by Noah into the new creation.

TIMING is everything and the timing of the described events within the book of Revelation is never so clear as it is in the last chapter, 22:10, where John clearly instructs his first century readers to, "SEAL NOT THE sayings of the prophecy of this BOOK: for the time is at hand (Eggus)." Again, "A THOUSAND" mathematical years away contradicts at hand (Eggus). This verse creates a real problem for futurists as well as for Partial Preterists. With futurists, it's evident with the New Testament usages of Eggus. For Partial Preterists, now they face the same problem, as well as the problem of thousands of years (Post Millennialism) stretching out the word "at hand" (Eggus)! Does this verse instruct us to, "seal not some of the sayings of this book, or most of the sayings of this book?" Or, does it clearly say, and mean, "THE sayings" of the prophecy of this book?" Contrast this verse, with Daniel 12:4,9, where Daniel is instructed, with his vision/ book, to do the opposite of John, and, "SEAL THE BOOK", because its fulfillment would not be in Daniel's own day (12:13), but at the time of the end (Note, that it doesn't say, "the end of time"), that, "it refers to many days in the future", (NIV), "the distant future" (Daniel 8:26). So, Daniel's contents were hundreds of years away, the five kingdoms, the fifth being the kingdom of God in Chapter 2. The Messiah being cut off in Chapter 9, and the temple being left desolate, all prophecies that were in the distant future, not in Daniel's day, his prophecy was SEALED! These prophecies would all be fulfilled in less than six hundred years, and they are labeled SEALED in Daniel's day. However, John is told the opposite, "SEAL NOT the book, the time is AT HAND", in John's Day (22:10)! Therefore, the prophecy of John's book is much less than hundreds of years into the future, never mind A THOUSAND or two years into the future, it is in his day (John 21:23).

Consider the contrast in another prophecy found in Ezekiel 12. Israel is corrected to realize that the pronounced judgment upon them was to occur "in your days" (vs.25), it was "AT HAND" (vs.23), it was not "far off" (vs.27), or "prolonged" (vs.22, 25, 28). Can "AT HAND" mean thousands of years away? Can "prolonged" and "far off" mean tomorrow? These words must mean something in Bible Prophecy! Matthew 24 also gives us the clearest of timelines for the same events as Revelation. It states, "Verily I say unto you (You, meaning first century disciples, vs 3), THIS GENERATION shall not pass, till all these things be fulfilled." Here are two words used together, "THIS GENERATION", about a dozen and a half **times** in the New Testament. Each time they're used together, futurist teachers admit that they are communicating a first century generation of people. Every time, except for the time they're used in the Olivet Discourse (Matthew 24:34; Mark 13:30; Luke 21:32).

There, they claim that it means something entirely different. Some futurist teachers change the words, and they redefine the context. They will say, "The (changed word from this) generation that sees (that sees are added words) these things (changed sentence structure), shall not pass away till all these things be fulfilled." Other futurist teachers claim that the Greek word for generation, Genea, can mean race, as in, "This Race shall not pass away, till all these things be fulfilled." This doesn't make any logical since, so this race will pass away once these things are fulfilled, is that true? Once more, they have yet to come up with a single verse (there are none) where Genea is communicating race in the N.T.! The only N.T. Greek word that could communicate race is Genos. This Watch Tower like denial will even go so far as to say that Genea, used nearly 40 times in the New Testament, is always referring to those living in that first-century generation, that it's not a race or distant generation, except for the one time it's used in the Olivet Discourse! Consider the following verses using "THIS GENERATION."

Matthew 11:16, "But whereunto shall I liken THIS GENERATION", Matthew 12:41, Nineveh shall rise in judgment with THIS GENERATION", Matthew 12:42, "The queen of the south shall rise in judgment with THIS GENERATION", Matthew 12:45, "THIS wicked GENERATION", Matthew 23:36, "All these things shall come upon THIS GENERATION", Matthew 24:34, "THIS GENERATION shall not pass, till all these things be fulfilled", Mark 8:12, "..no sign be given to THIS GENERATION", Mark 8:38, "THIS adulterous, and sinful GENERATION", Luke 11:50, "blood of all the prophets, which was shed from the foundation of the world, may be required of THIS GENERATION.", Mark 11:51, "blood of Abel unto Zacharias …shall be required of THIS GENERATION." Mark 17:25, "be rejected of THIS GENERATION, Acts 2:40, "THIS perverse GENERATION." See also, Matthew 3:7, 16:4, 23:33, Mark 9:19; Luke 7:31; 9:41; 11:30-32. "THIS GENERATION" lines up perfectly with John's "AT HAND" (Eggus), "SHORTLY", "QUICKLY" (Tachos), and "SEAL NOT", all time indicators. It lines up perfectly with, … **when they persecute you in one town, flee to the next**, for truly, I say to you, **you will not have gone through all the towns of Israel before the Son of Man comes.**[166] (Matthew 10:22-23)." And with, "There be some standing here, which shall not taste of death till they see the Son of man coming in His kingdom (Matthew 16:28)." By the way, this is not referring to The Transfiguration in the next chapter, because that took place only six days later, and NONE of the disciples had died, but most had died by A.D. 66-70. Also, rewards weren't handed out at The Transfiguration (16:27). These time indicators are consistent with nothing but a first century fulfillment!

WHO are the players in the book of Revelation? First off, who was the book written to? First century Christians, many of whom were Jewish, therefore, Audience Relevance must be understood. Who was the beast, whose number was six hundred and sixty-six (13:18)?

---

[166] *The Holy Bible: English Standard Version* (Mt 10:23). (2016). Crossway Bibles.

Again, first century Christians were commanded to apply wisdom and understanding and to count the number of his name. The Hebrews used letters of the alphabet for their numbering system. The name Caesar Nero equates exactly to six hundred and sixty-six, using the Hebrew letter number calculation. His name can be spelled, in the Hebrew, Neron Kaiser NRWN QWR (N=50, R=200 W=6 N=50 Q=100 S=60 R=200), which equates to six hundred and sixty-six, this is the exact way in which Jastow's Lexicon of the Talmud spells it. Or it can be spelled Nero Kaiser NRW QSR (- 50 without the extra N), equaling six hundred and sixteen.

Many manuscripts use this number, rather than six hundred and sixty-six, proving that there is no doubt as to whom the numbers were identifying! Nero was the sixth Caesar (17:10), six, signifying man who was created the sixth day (Genesis 1:31). He had his palace interior walls painted, which can be seen to this day, with hundreds of images of a half-man half-beast creature! He would cloth himself with animal skins and act out the role of an animal by doing unspeakable perversions and mutilations against political opponents, including Christians. Nero was often referred to by his political contemporaries as "THE BEAST"! God was not asking first century disciples to spend their precious time under persecution, being fed to lions, figuring out who a 21st century beast was! That would be the cruelest of hoaxes! For more on the significance of the number of six, consider that man was created on the sixth day (Genesis 1:31). Consider that the beast Goliath's height was six cubits and a span, six and grasping for more, who's spear weighed six hundred shekels (1 Samuel 17:4, 7). He also had six fingers. Also remember Nebuchadnezzar, another beast (Daniel 4:16), who demanded the worship of an image of himself, which was sixty cubits high and six cubits wide.

WHAT was the mark of this same beast (13:16-17), which these first century disciples were warned to not take nor be deceived by (19:20)? Interpreting Scripture with Scripture, we understand that the rest of the Bible consistently speaks of a mark of ownership, separating those on the Lord's side, and His ways, from those opposing Him. This mark on the forehead begins with Adam and the fall, whose forehead had turned away from the Lord's blessing and would be cursed, covered with sweat (Genesis 3:19). Cain would become a marked man, a mark declaring the mercy of the Lord upon him (Genesis 4:15). Exodus 28:36- 38 shows progression toward the restoration from the curse, where we see the MITRE of gold placed on the Priest's forehead, restoring from the glory that had been lost, "HOLINESS TO THE LORD." The process continues in Numbers 6:25-26 when the priesthood is blessed by God with The Lord making His face (His image, contrasting Adams, mans, and the beasts in Revelation 13:14-15) to shine upon them, resulting in a change in their countenance, in their forehead. In Deuteronomy 6:8, marking the Lord's ownership of Israel and covenant with them, they are instructed to bind His words upon their hand, and upon their foreheads, between their eyes as frontlets (Hebrew: Towphaphah, meaning Phylacteries, marks).

This same thing was said, concerning their hand and forehead, and frontlets, in Exodus 13:9, 16. In Ezekiel's day, those who were repentant in Israel were given a mark of ownership upon their foreheads, signifying that they were on the Lord's side. Those without this mark were to be slain (Ezekiel 9:4-6). In Revelation 14:1, this same mark is written upon the foreheads of those belonging to, and were on the side of the Lamb, as opposed to those belonging to, and on the side of, the beast with his mark (13:16). Note, that there are no tattoos or computer chips involved in the writing upon the foreheads in Revelation 14:1. Why then is such nonsense insisted upon, by today's Sci-Fi prophets, just two verses prior to this in Revelation 13:17? By the way, the mark is "upon" (Greek: Epi) not "in", such as a computer chip under the skin. We even say in our day, "He's a marked man", for this or that purpose. The mark of ownership, loyalty, and worship of the beast is clearly seen in the emperor and state worship dynamics of the first century. Individuals were given a choice, "is Caesar Lord, or is Jesus Lord?" This ultimatum could result in death if one chose allegiance to Jesus over Caesar! The very minimum result would be the ostracizing of one from market activity. If one did not declare allegiance to Caesar by stating "Hail Caesar" (a statement of worship) with each transaction, one could not participate in the marketplace buying or selling (13:17)!

The majority in Israel chose Caesar over Jesus, "we have no king but Caesar" (John 19:15). The persecution seen throughout the New Testament Scriptures reveal Jewish authorities working with the Roman government. The harlot, Israel (Isaiah 1:21) rode the beast that was Rome (17:3, 7), manipulating the persecution, until the beast turns on her (in mid A.D. 66), makes her desolate (Matthew 23:38; 24:15; Luke 21:20), eats her flesh, and burns her with fire (Revelation 17:16, Leviticus 21:9). In fact, Herod who massacred the male children under 2 in Bethlehem, and murdered John the Baptist and James, were circumcised Jews! One cannot be more in bed (fornication-17:4; 18:3) with Rome than they! Israel chose the king of Rome over the king of Israel (John 19:15), the King of Kings (Revelation 17:14; 1 Timothy 6:15)! They rejected the name above names (Philippians 2:9) and received the one who came in his own name (John 5:43), whose name amounts to six hundred and sixty-six! They chose to be marked for the service of the beast with their hand (signifying service), and the worship from their heart, soul, mind (forehead) and strength. Complete allegiance was given to emperor and state worship! Those choosing to serve and worship the Lamb were marked with His seal in their foreheads (Revelation 7:2, 3; 3:12; 9:4; 14:1; 22:4; 2 Corinthians 1:22)!

WHO IS BABYLON, THE GREAT CITY? Revelation 11:8 identifies "THIS GREAT CITY", "...THE GREAT CITY, which spiritually is called Sodom (Isaiah 1:10) and Egypt, WHERE ALSO OUR LORD WAS CRUCIFIED." Jesus was crucified in JERUSALEM (Luke 13:33, Matthew 16:21)! THE/THAT/THIS GREAT CITY IS MENTIONED ABOUT A DOZEN TIMES IN REVELATION AND IS IDENTIFIED AS BABYLON. THEREFORE, BABYLON, THE GREAT CITY, IS JERUSALEM! Peter identifies it as well, writing from

Jerusalem (Acts 15:2, 7; Galatians 2:8; 1 Peter 1:1), he states, "The church that is at BABYLON ... salutes you (1 Peter 5:13). The following is a complete list of references, with overwhelming proofs, which declares that THE GREAT CITY, BABYLON is unquestionably JERUSALEM! "THE GREAT CITY...WHERE ALSO OUR LORD WAS CRUCIFIED (Revelation 11:8)", "BABYLON...THAT GREAT CITY (Revelation 14:8)", "THE GREAT CITY...GREAT BABYLON (Revelation 16:19)", "THE GREAT PROSTITUTE (Revelation 17:1), "And upon her FOREHEAD...BABYLON THE GREAT..., the mother of HARLOTS (Revelation 17:5)", "THE WOMEN you saw IS THAT GREAT CITY (Revelation 17:18)", "BABYLON THE GREAT... (Revelation 18:2)", "THAT GREAT CITY BABYLON (Revelation 18:10)", "THIS GREAT CITY (Revelation 18:18)", "THAT GREAT CITY (Revelation 18:19), "THAT GREAT CITY BABYLON (Revelation 18:21)", "THE GREAT PROSTITUTE (Revelation 19:2)", "The church that is AT BABYLON... salutes you (1 Peter 5:13), How is THE FAITHFUL CITY (Jerusalem) become an HARLOT (Isaiah 1:21)", "JERUSALEM...PLAYING THE HARLOT (Jeremiah 2:2,20), "But you (Jerusalem) have PLAYED THE HARLOT (Jeremiah 3:1)", "You (Jerusalem) have A PROSTITUTE'S FOREHEAD (Jeremiah 3:3, same FOREHEAD as Revelation 17:5), "... have played THE HARLOT (Jeremiah 3:6)", "played THE HARLOT (Jeremiah 3:8)", "Wherefore hath the Lord done thus unto THIS GREAT CITY (Jeremiah 22:8)."

Here are some more positive I.D.'s, pointing the finger at Jerusalem. "how has the FAITHFUL CITY become a HARLOT. It was full of judgment; righteousness lodged in it, but now MURDERERS (Isaiah 1:21)", connect this with, "scribes and Pharisees…you build the TOMBS of the prophets, and garnish the SEPULCHERS of the righteous … BLOOD of the prophets, KILLED the prophets…you shall KILL and CRUCIFY … that upon you may come ALL THE RIGHTEOUS BLOOD SHED UPON THE EARTH … O JERUSALEM, JERUSALEM, you that KILL the prophets, and STONE them which are sent to you …" (Matthew 23:29-37 it was blood for blood with Jerusalem - Genesis 9:6), "And in her was found THE BLOOD of prophets, and of saints, and of ALL THAT WERE SLAIN UPON THE EARTH (Revelation 18:24)!"

Jerusalem had become, "the HABITATION OF DEVILS…of every HATEFUL BIRD (Revelation 18:2; 1 John 3:15), "THE UNCLEAN SPIRIT…SEVEN OTHER SPIRITS… EVEN SO SHALL IT BE ALSO UNTO THIS WICKED GENERATION (Matthew 12:43-45)!" THE GREAT CITY'S TEMPLE is clearly identified in Chapter 18:11- 24, where the "MERCHANTS" of the land, and their MERCHANDISE, are revealed (18:11-15). These are the same temple MERCHANTS that we read of in John 2:16, "…make not My Father's house a house of MERCHANDISE!" "THE MERCHANDISE of gold, and silver, and precious stones, and of pearls, and fine linen, and purple, and silk, and scarlet, and all your wood, and all manner of vessels of ivory, and all manner of most precious wood, and of brass, and iron, and marble, and cinnamon, and odors, and ointments, and frankincense, and wine, and oil and fine flour, and wheat, and BEASTS, and SHEEP (the sacrificial system), and horses, and chariots (used for transporting the sacrifices), and slaves (They built and maintained the temple at the command of Herod), and souls of men (Revelation 18:11-13)."

These are all things that were contained within the temple!

WHO is the Sea Beast of Revelation 13:1? Remember that the place of the Gentiles is "The Sea" (Genesis 10:5; Psalm 72:10; Isaiah 11:10; 24:14-16; 60:5), and that the Gentile rule at the time of Revelation's penning was that of the Roman Empire (Daniel 2:40- 45), it had complete (seven heads), and total (10 horns, 10 provinces with the Roman Empire) authority. Rome is identified as the city of seven hills, upon which the harlot sits (Revelation 17:9). The harlot (Israel) works in unison with Rome, the beast (John 19:15), she rides the beast (Revelation 17:3), manipulating the beast's actions, until the beast turns on the harlot (Revelation 17:16) in mid A.D. 66, when Roman Armies invade Jerusalem. Rome had opposed Christianity, because of its proclamation of another king of kings and another Son of God, titles which Nero claimed for himself. In A.D. 64, Nero went completely mad in opposing Christians, and used the Coliseum fire as a political opportunity to turn the empire completely against them. By A.D. 66, Titus states, "The Temple is distinguished above all human achievements, its destruction will take care of the root (Judaism), and the offshoot (Christianity)". Because Christianity's temple existed in the Spirit (Ephesians 2:21-22; John 4:21-22), he could not destroy the true Jews (Romans 2:28-29, Revelation 2:9; 3:9) and their temple (Hebrews 9:8).

WHO is the Land Beast of Revelation 13:11? The people of the land are the people of the Promised Land. Again, they are in cahoots with Rome, the Sea Beast.

WHO is the false prophet of Revelation 16:13; 19:20; 20:10? Josephus speaks of many false prophets in Israel promising deliverance over the Romans. Those prophets were opposing the prophet of prophets, and were, of course, false prophets. Corporately, Old Covenant Israel was THE false prophet.

WHO are the two witnesses of Revelation 11? Both could very well have been raised physically and ascended from Jerusalem, without any recorded history of the event. There would have been no surviving witness who came out of Jerusalem. They would have been killed by either the Romans, or by the Jewish Zealots, who slaughtered fellow Jews by the thousands. They are witnesses who would appear "shortly," "quickly", and "soon" (Revelation 1:1, 3; 22:10), within the generation of the Apostles (Matthew 24:34)! Revelation 11:9 states that, "The people, and kindreds, and tongues, and nations shall see their dead bodies…", that is, those dwelling in Jerusalem would see their dead bodies, as identified in the previous verse (11:8). Jerusalem was an international city (Acts 2:5). Note, that the text says nothing about every nation on the planet seeing them through modern technologies as modern-day Sci-Fi prophets proclaim. It simply, and literally, says that "THEY OF (KJV)", or "THOSE FROM (NASB)", various peoples, kindreds, tongues, and nations, shall see them, and does not say that every nation on the planet would see them! Who then are these two witnesses?

We know that fire proceeds from their mouths (11:5), and that those proclaiming the word of the Lord are described exactly in this way (Jeremiah 5:14), therefore, it is not the depiction of a circus act! The word they were preaching was THE LAW AND THE PROPHETS (ELIJAH AND MOSES' ministries -11:6), which are two witnesses. It was the APOSTLES AND PROPHETS (Revelation 18:20), two witnesses, preaching that word, as well as THE SAINTS AND PROPHETS, two witnesses (Revelation 18:24). All of whom were thought to be completely stamped out through the intense persecution, yet all were resurrected after it had looked like complete defeat! They did not reach complete, seven days, defeat/death! That seven was broken, three and a half days (11:9), by the continued work of the Spirit through the next wave of enduring and persevering saints! Take your pick; there were two witnesses at that time, including, some would contend, PETER AND JAMES, living in Jerusalem. This would categorize Peter's alleged crucifixion in Rome as "Catholic Fiction".

If this be the case, Peter surely fits the Prophet mold (Elijah), and James the law (Moses). Both could very well have been raised and physically ascended out of Jerusalem, since there would have been no witnesses to record such an event, being that they would all most likely have been slaughtered by the Romans, or by the mad Jewish Zealots, who slaughtered fellow Jews by the thousands? WHERE (location, location, location) are the judgments in Revelation to occur? Again, it's a judgment upon the land (1:7), not the globe! The Greek word "Kosmos", which can mean the entire earth, is never once used in describing the judgments in Revelation. The "earth" is always equated to the "land". Young's Literal Translation often gets this right in Revelation by using the "land", rather than the "earth". The "globe" wasn't clearly established as a concept until Kepler in the 17th century. In fact, the book of Revelation even pinpoints the "land" which it is referring to. Three times, we see the word for "world", which in the Greek is, "Oikoumene", and defined as, "The inhabited Roman world". This same word is used in Luke 2:1, where a census went throughout the "world". The census went only throughout the Roman world. Therefore, "world" (Oikoumene), also used in Acts 17:5 where they turned the "world" upside down, is not used to describe the globe, or even nations outside the Roman Empire! We see the "Oikoumene" world used in Revelation 3:10, "the hour of trial, which shall come upon all the world (Oikoumene)". Here we clearly understand that Revelation is not describing a global tribulation! Matthew 24:16 clarifies this, when believers in Judea are instructed to flee from there to the mountains for refuge. What good would fleeing from Judea to the mountains do in a global war, in an era of F-16's and Hydrogen bombs? The "Oikoumene" world is also mentioned in Revelation 12:9, and 16:14. The latter, is where the whole "world" (Oikoumene) is gathered in a place called Armageddon (16:14, 16). Therefore, Armageddon is not worldwide!

In Revelation, A CITY, THE GREAT CITY (Revelation 17&18; 16:19; 11:8,13) is identified as the recipient of judgment, not the planet! The city is surrounded (Luke 21:20-21), and the inhabitants of it are warned to flee from it to the mountains. WHERE then is Armageddon and what is this name communicating in Revelation 16:16? The name

Armageddon comes from two Hebrew words, "Har", meaning a mountain, a mount, a mountainous range, sometimes used figuratively, says Strongs. The other Hebrew word is "Megiddon" or "Megiddo", a plain in Israel, also referred to as "The valley of Jehoshaphat". Strong's first describes "Har-Meggidon" as, "A SYMBOIC NAME"! The very meaning of the name makes this evident, "a mountain, plain". Megiddo was the location of multiple judgments carried out by the Lord against Israel's enemies, and upon Israel herself. Debra's victory, Barak's, and Gideon's are just a few. Saul, Josiah, and Jehoshaphat himself, were all judged there. To the Jewish mind, the name Armageddon would sir up these memories, as would Waterloo for the French, or Pearl Harbor, Omaha Beach, and Valley Forge, would for Americans. The closest mountain to this plain is Mount Carmel, where Elijah was used to carry out the Lord's judgment on, that unfaithful women, Jezebel's (Revelation 3:20-22) false prophets. The dynamics of that event fit those of the first century dynamics like a glove! This unfaithful woman was thrown down and consumed by the dogs (Gentiles)! The judgment carried out at the battle of Armageddon was upon a city, "THE GREAT CITY", Jerusalem, as we read forward three verses (16:19). "Armageddon's" only usage in the Bible is in Revelation 16:16. And it is "the whole WORLD (Oikoumene) to gather" (Revelation 16:14) for this battle, THE WHOLE "OIKOUMENE" WORLD, THE ROMAN WORLD!

WHAT do the NEW HEAVENS AND NEW EARTH communicate in Revelation 21:1? Let us allow Scripture to interpret Scripture here and consider a common understanding associated with the HEAVENS and the EARTH throughout the Bible. Consider the following passages. Deuteronomy 32:1, "Give ear O ye HEAVENS, and I will speak; and hear O EARTH, the words of my mouth." Moses is addressing the covenant people, the congregation, in the verse prior (31:30). Isaiah 1:2, "Hear, O HEAVENS, and give earth, O EARTH, for the Lord has spoken…" Jerusalem, the covenant people are being addressed (1:1). Isaiah 49:13, "Sing, O HEAVENS; and be joyful, O EARTH; and break forth into singing O MOUNTAINS (of ISRAEL): for the Lord has comforted HIS PEOPLE…" The HEAVENS AND EARTH singing is ISRAEL, HIS PEOPLE! Isaiah 51:16, "…that I may plant THE HEAVENS, and lay the foundation of THE EARTH, and say unto ZION, THOU ART MY PEOPLE." THE HEAVENS and THE EARTH are clearly ZION, his covenant PEOPLE." The puritan theologian John Owen uses this verse to explain 2 Peter 3's NEW HEAVEN and NEW EARTH. Hosea 2:18-21, "And in that day will I make A COVENANT for them…And I will BETROTH thee unto me in faithfulness: and thou shalt know the Lord. And it shall come to pass in that day, I will hear, saith the Lord, I will hear THE HEAVENS, and they shall hear THE EARTH." Covenant is very clear here.

Joel 2:30, "And I will show wonders in THE HEAVENS and in THE EARTH, blood, and fire, and pillars of smoke." Peter quotes this passage in Acts 2:16-21 and begins by saying, "This is that which was spoken by the prophet Joel, and it shall come to pass in the last days …". This Scripture in Joel is fulfilled here and now in "the last days", the last days of the Old Covenant, and the first days of the New Covenant. In fact, the words "blood" and "fire" and "smoke" are the exact words used by Josephus to describe the events of A.D.66-A.D.70! Joel 3:16, "the Lord shall roar out of ZION, and utter His voice from JERUSALEM; and THE HEAVENS and THE EARTH shall shake (Hebrews 12:26), but the Lord will be the hope of HIS PEOPLE, and the strength of THE CHILDREN OF ISRAEL." The passage clearly speaks for itself. Zechariah 12:1, "The burden of the word of the Lord for ISRAEL, saith the Lord, who stretches forth THE HEAVENS and lays the foundations of THE EARTH …"

Matthew 5:17-18, "Do not think that I have come to abolish the Law or the Prophets; I have not come to abolish them but to fulfill them. For truly, I say to you, until heaven and earth pass away, not an iota, not a dot, will pass from the Law until all is accomplished.[167] Did Jesus fulfill the law and the prophets? If He did, HEAVEN and EARTH have then passed! That is, the Old Covenant law and the prophets have passed away, the OLD passes away, and all things become NEW in Christ, whose contractual words of the new covenant will never become dormant and pass away (2 Corinthians 5:17; Revelation 21:5; Matthew 24:35)!

2 Peter 3:10, "… THE HEAVENS shall pass away with a great noise, and the ELEMENTS shall melt with fervent heat, THE EARTH also and the works that are therein shall be burned up." The key here is in the Greek word for "elements", which is "Stoicheon", defined as rudiments, principles, and philosophies (Jewish Components of Judaism). Used only seven times in the New Testament, twice here in 2 Peter 3, twice in Galatians, "were in bondage under the elements of the age (Galatians 4:3)", "the weak and beggarly elements (Galatians 4:9)", twice in Colossians, "after the rudiments of the age (Colossians 2:8)", "from the rudiments of the age (Colossians 2:20)", and once in Hebrews, "the first principles of the oracles of God…(Hebrews 5:12)". So, there was to be a forsaking of the "elements", the principles, philosophies, and rudiments of the Old Covenant AGE, because they were all about to go up in flames (Matthew 22:7)! Revelation 21:1,5, "And I saw a NEW HEAVEN and NEW EARTH, for THE FIRST HEAVEN and the FIRST EARTH were PASSED AWAY…" Did not the Old Covenant pass away entirely in A.D. 70, an event which first century Christians were longing for, "A New Covenant, He has made THE FIRST OLD. Now that which decaying and waxes OLD is ready (Greek Eggus, Revelation 1:3) to VANISH/PASS AWAY (Hebrews 8:13)"!

WHEN was the book of Revelation written? It was written before A.D. 70. We know this, because Nero Caesar is identified as the sixth (sixth, how fitting) king (Emperor) in Chapter 17:10. The book was written before the destruction of the temple, as the temple is discussed in detail by John in Chapter 11. We know that the Apostles teaching always expounds on any prophecy which is fulfilled. John would never address the temple in Jerusalem without mentioning the fulfillment of Jesus' prophecy concerning it. Given the

---

[167] *The Holy Bible: English Standard Version* (Mt 5:17–18). (2016). Crossway Bibles.

imminency of the foretold events of Revelation, what occurred shortly, quickly, and was near, at hand (1:1, 3; 22:10), from the time Revelation was written? Nothing occurred in the late 90's to fit the descriptions in the book, yet from mid A.D. 66 to A.D. 70 (3 1/2 years), the tribulation (1:9) can be seen clearly. Also, the 90's goes beyond the biblical definition of a generation (40 years), "this generation" in Matthew 24:34, which chapter describes the same events as those of Revelation. The Murdock Syriac Version of Revelation makes this clear, "The Revelation, which was made by God to John the Evangelist, in the Island of Patmos, to which he was banished by Nero the Emperor". Nero committed suicide in A.D. 68 (he stabbed himself with a knife to prove he was God on earth in human form), therefore Revelation was written prior to this. Also, John would have many more nations to bring the word of the Lord to (10:11), which would be impossible for a man to reach on horseback since that man was so advanced in age, that is, if Revelation were written in A.D. 96. John did not write Revelation, or his gospel (John 5:2), after A.D. 70, because all Scripture would be fulfilled by this time (Luke 21:22). "Prophet and vision" are "sealed", or fulfilled, at the point and time of the temples' destruction (Daniel 9:24-27).

Hundreds of Scholars have understood the early date of Revelation, contrary to the popular opinions of our day. Here is a brief list of early date scholars.

Robert Young (Young's Literal Translation),

Sir Isaac Newton,

Adam Clark,

FW Farrar,

FF Bruce,

James Stuart Russell,

Philip Schaff,

R.C. Sproul,

Hank Hanegraaff,

David Chilton,

Gary Demar,

Steve Gregg,

and Kenneth Gentry.

Gentry examines the internal and external evidence for the date and puts the matter to rest in his book, Before Jerusalem Fell. Gary Demar adds historical evidence with his book The Early Church and The End of the World. Babylon is identified clearly as Jerusalem (See above), and 1st-century Christians were exhorted to apply wisdom and decipher the number of the beast (13:18), not 21st-century Christians! They which pierced Him, and the tribes of the land (1:7), are no longer with us today but were about to see and experience the events described in the book in their day. Sir Isaac Newton makes the point concerning the book's appeal and reach toward the Jewish nation, for example, the interchanging of Greek and Hebrew words, and the fact that three-fourths of its contents are quotes and references from the Old Testament, as proof positive that the book was written before Israel's destruction in A.D. 70!

The book of Revelation does NOT contain a seven-year tribulation period. Nor does it use the word "Antichrist". Jesus is never revealed as reigning physically on the earth in Chapter 20. A "church age" with seven eras, represented by the seven churches, is an entire fabrication forced into the text! A rapture is nowhere to be found in 4:1, John alone is told in the vision, to come up here, no one else is with him! There is no 200-million-man army in 9:16, a Greek interlinear reveals the Greek words, "duos murias murias", meaning two myriad of myriads, where murias is defined as an innumerable multitude, excluding any specific number. We see a similar description of an army, whose number was as the sand of the sea (20:8). It does not describe an army of quadrillions. There is not a Magog invasion before the thousand-year reign but after it (20:7-8). There are no satellites, tectonic plates, cobra helicopters, flame throwers, ICBMs, or computer chips. These have all been ADDED TO THE "DO NOT ADD LIST (22:18)"! The book may best be described as the story of two women, the harlot, and the bride, or of two cities, the Old Jerusalem and the New Jerusalem.

Chapters 21 and 22

New Heaven and New Earth = New Creation - New Israel - spiritual creation

Old Heaven and Old Earth = Old Creation - Old Covenant Israel - natural creation

A New Creation without a sea means that Gentiles and Jews are no longer separated.

New Jerusalem = bride made ready and decked out for her husband, the wife of the Lamb

New Jerusalem = a city depicted as the Kingdom of God and God's administration

The Tabernacle of God among men = God's dwelling place - Lev 26:11; Ezek. 37:27; 48:35; Rev. 7:15

Comfort the Martyrs

Wipe away every tear - Isa. 25:8; Rev. 7:17

No longer death - Isa. 25:8; 1 Cor. 15:26; Hosea 13:14

No more mourning - Is 35:10; 51:11; 65:19

The ransomed, redeemed come to Zion, the New Jerusalem no more crying or pain. The meaning of this crying and pain is the relief from the persecution and final rest that awaited the martyrs. God will relieve the suffering of those who are persecuted. All sadness, injustice and lies will be gone forever for those saints who experienced the trial of persecution and saw their loved ones murdered. Rev 21:4.

As in 2nd Thess. ... for which you also suffer; since it is a righteous thing with God to repay with tribulation those who trouble you, and to give you who are troubled rest with us when the Lord Jesus is revealed from heaven with His mighty angels, in flaming fire taking vengeance on those who do not know God, and on those who do not obey the gospel of our Lord Jesus Christ.

These shall be punished with everlasting destruction from the presence of the Lord and from the glory of His power, when He comes, in that Day, to be glorified in His saints and to be admired among all those who believe, because our testimony among you was believed. The New King James Version (2 Th 1:5–10). (1982). Thomas Nelson.

And I have put My words in your mouth; I have covered you with the shadow of My hand, That I may plant the heavens, Lay the earth's foundations, and say to Zion, 'You are My people.'" The New King James Version (Is 51:16). (1982). Thomas Nelson. First things pass away - Old Covenant, Old Sacrificial system, Old Priesthood, Old Temple, Old Jerusalem.

And He who sits on the throne said, "Behold, I am making all things new." New American Standard Bible, 1995 Edition: Paragraph Version (Re 21:5). (1995). The Lockman Foundation.

The Contrast

He who overcomes - the conqueror, the one who subdues - inherits all things – He comes into Sonship. The Second Death - 8 But for the cowardly and unbelieving and abominable and murderers and immoral persons and sorcerers and idolaters and all liars, their part will be in the lake that burns with fire and brimstone, which is the second death." New American Standard Bible, 1995 Edition: Paragraph Version (Re 21:8). (1995). The Lockman

Foundation. 1 Cor 6:9; Gal 5:19–21; Rev 9:21; 21:27; 22:15

Description of the New Jerusalem, the bride, wife of the Lamb, tabernacle of God 10 And he carried me away in spirit to a great and high mountain, and showed me the holy city, Jerusalem, coming down out of heaven from God, 11 having the glory of God. Her brilliance was like a very costly stone, as a stone of crystal-clear jasper. 12 It had a great and high wall, with twelve gates, and at the gates twelve angels; and names were written on them, which are the names of the twelve tribes of the sons of Israel. 13 There were three gates on the east and three gates on the north and three gates on the south and three gates on the west. 14 And the wall of the city had twelve foundation stones, and on them were the twelve names of the twelve apostles of the Lamb. New American Standard Bible, 1995 Edition: Paragraph Version (Re 21:10–14). (1995). The Lockman Foundation.

Something holy is coming down, descending from Heaven. This is coming from the invisible to the visible. This is His kingdom coming to earth and His will being done on earth as it is in Heaven. Not an outer holiness imposed by religious rules, but an intrinsic holiness that expresses God's uniqueness, His separateness, and otherworldliness. We're not just going to the New Jerusalem; we're becoming the New Jerusalem. Being in the New Jerusalem is not a location change. It is an "intrinsic" or "essential" matter—a change of our essence or constitution to that of Christ. As we are in the New Jerusalem (the kingdom), we become the New Jerusalem. In our commitment to corporate life, we are transformed. This does not happen if we are individualistic! Hermits are never transformed, they rot! The New Jerusalem is the ruling class, the kings, and priests after the order of Melchizedek and judges unto God: those who have followed the Lamb wherever He goes and have attained to the highest position of honor and might and true greatness in the Spirit. It comprises those who have attained experientially the reign with Christ upon His throne and those who will enlighten, nurture, feed, and bless all the nations with the life of Christ. God's called and chosen elect, therefore, whether bride or sons, who supremely love Christ, who are submitted completely and only to His Lordship, who are accounted worthy to suffer with Christ and through our trials, testing, grow up into Him in all things, is the New Jerusalem which shall rule over God's infinite realm into the New Covenant AGE, and all nations and peoples shall walk in the light of this city and shall enter through its gates to partake of the living water and the tree of Life! We become citizens of the New Jerusalem by being born of the Spirit and then brought into a responsible place in the family of God, by the workings of His Spirit within us.

The spiritual New Jerusalem is a glorious realm in the Divine, far more glorious and spectacular than anything earthly of Jerusalem has ever been! It is the free city, free from the old Mosaic law, free from the old Aaronic priesthood, free from the old fleshly Davidic kingship, and free from all the religious traditions, regulations, creeds, liturgies, methods, systems, and bondages of men. And when the New Jerusalem realm has come from God out of heaven to be manifested in all its fullness here in the earthly realm, with all her glorious kingdom components fully established and spiritually realized, she shall indeed be, and certainly be, "the joy of the whole earth." Beautiful in elevation, the joy of the whole earth, is Mount Zion on the sides of the north, the city of the great King. As the entire city symbolizes the perfected bride of Christ, the glorified sons of God, and the fully established kingdom of God—invested, manifested, and operating in and through them—so the various parts of the city described signify special attributes, characteristics, and conditions that will exist in the divine kingdom in its consummation at the completion of the Old Covenant age. And yet, it will continue to manifest as His people apprehend the revelation and vision of their corporate identity into the ongoing generations. **John was in spirit** - this is the unique part of our being where we see the things of God on the great and high mountain - John was brought to Mt. Zion as in Heb 12:22.

Her Appearance is like Jasper - the same appearance of Him who sat on the throne - Rev 4:3; 21:18, 19 - the image of His son - the city has the same appearance as Christ. Immediately I was in spirit; and behold, a throne set in heaven, and One sat on the throne. **2 The New King James Version (Ps 48:2). (1982). Thomas Nelson. sat on the throne.** And He who sat there was like a jasper and a sardius stone in appearance, and there was a rainbow around the throne, in appearance like an emerald. The city has reached God's goal to conform her to the image of His SON! A Great and High Wall - But understood spiritually, the wall has a deep meaning and wonderful significance. The walls of this city are SALVATION. "In that day shall this song be sung in the land of Judah: We have a strong city; salvation will God appoint for walls and bulwarks" (Isa. 26:1). "Violence shall no more be heard in your land, wasting nor destruction within your borders; but You will call Your walls Salvation, and Your gates Praise" (Isa. 60:18). "For I, says the Lord, will be unto her a wall of fire round about, and will be the glory in the midst of her" (Zech. 2:5). "The name of the Lord is a strong tower (a place within walls, a safe place)" (Prov. 18:10). The walls are for protection and boundaries. Twelve Gates – Eze. 48:31-34 Ezekiel's vision of the temple city is the same as John's vision. Also, she had a great and high wall with twelve gates, and twelve messengers at the gates, and names written on them, which are the names of the twelve tribes of the children of Israel: three gates on the east, three gates on the north, three gates on the south, and three gates on the west. The twelve gates were twelve pearls: each individual gate was made of one pearl. Its gates shall not be shut at all by day (there shall be no night there). And they shall bring glory and the honor of the nations into it. Rev. 21:12-13, 21, 25-26

The Gates - the Place of Government - The gates were seats of authority (Ruth 4:11). At the gates wisdom was uttered (Proverbs 1:21). Judges and officers served at the gates administering justice (Deuteronomy 16:18) and the councils of state were held at the gates (2 Chronicles 18:9 12 gates – signify a governmental number for Kingdom entrance for wisdom, counsel, authority, guidance, and judgment. 12 angels – Governing what comes in, inspection. They are the porters who guard the gates. 12 tribes of Israel – Old covenant believers, remnant being complete with the N.T. saints. … 40 God having provided some better thing for us, that they without us should not be made complete. Heb. 11:40 TKB – Translation – Terry Kashian 3 gates on each side of the compass – Never shut and all-inclusive in every direction welcoming all into the kingdom. Christ is always ready to receive all who come to him; and the gate of mercy is always open, night and day. These are the gates of Mercy and Grace! Perhaps the three on each side can be related to 2 Cor. 11:14 … The grace of the Lord Jesus Christ, and the love of God, and the fellowship of the Holy Spirit, be with you all.

Gate of one pearl – Each gate is one pearl – the pearl is made by a single foreign object that gets inside an oyster or mollusk like a grain of sand with eight cutting sides and begins to cut the creature and the creature secretes fluid from within itself and it coats the grain of sand and wraps itself around that grain until it is smooth and shiny and there it is, a pearl is secured within the creature. It is faith and love that produces the secretion to endure the suffering. According to the Encyclopedia Britannica, only 2 out of 20 of these creatures produce a pearl. The creature dies and produces this pearl. The creature is transformed into something precious and is symbolically recreated in the pearl. Perhaps we can see the suffering, death, and resurrection of Christ in this process. We can also see the believers' experience of entering the fellowship of His sufferings. And when they had preached the gospel to that city and made many disciples, they returned to Lystra, Iconium, and Antioch, strengthening the souls of the disciples, exhorting them to continue in the faith, and saying, "We must through many tribulations enter the kingdom of God. Acts 14:21-22.

In the city, each gate is a pearl and symbolizes our entrance and what we become. If we suffer with Him we will also reign with Him. 2 Timothy 2:12. Now the wall of the city had twelve foundations, and on them were the names of the twelve apostles of the Lamb.[168] 12 foundations are the apostles of the Lamb. (Eph. 2:20). So, we see that the apostles and prophets are the foundation and that we are to build upon this foundation. The very truth I am presenting to you today is rooted in the word and ministry of those early apostles! The very work that God is doing in you today to bring you to the measure of the stature of the fullness of Christ is rooted in that foundation laid down by the apostles both that day and in this day! And we, the body of Christ, are God's building, God's house, God's temple, and we are the Holy City that He is building in the spiritual realm of His Spirit! The early church devoted themselves continually to the apostles' teaching. They were being established on a good foundation.

I mentioned that jasper was the expression of the city, and that Christ in Rev.4 has the appearance of jasper. Out of the twelve foundations, the first is the jasper stone of the twelve apostles of the Lamb. The first foundation stone may have been Peter. In the beginning, he was called a "stone". Then later in his ministry, he wrote about living stones. We can see a transformation in the lives of the apostles by this progression. A stone, to a living stone, and ultimately to a precious stone. This is my thought only that Peter was so transformed that in the end, he looked just like Christ. For what it's worth. Precious stones are not something on the surface, not superficial. If you only look for what is on the surface, you will only find dirt. Wood, hay, and stubble. But the deeper you go the more valuable items you will find. The gold, and the jewels, are all from the land. The pearls are from the sea. A lot could be said about this but allow the Lord to inspire you as you contemplate these two environments.

---

[168] New American Standard Bible, 1995 Edition: Paragraph Version (Eze 47:9). (1995). The Lockman Foundation.

Measuring The City

The city is four square ... the length, and the breadth, and the height, of it are equal.[169] This is a picture of perfection, and the corporate life of the church is how we are perfected. WE cannot attain this separately and independently from a committed life together in Christ. The outcome is evenness on every side and every angle. Harmony, agreement, symmetry. A glorious church! That He would grant you, according to the riches of His glory, to be strengthened with power through His Spirit into the inner man, that Christ may make His home in your hearts through faith, that you, being rooted and grounded in love, may be full of strength to apprehend with all the saints what the breadth and length and height and depth are and to know the knowledge-surpassing love of Christ, that you may be filled unto all the fullness of God. Eph. 3:16-19. Being foursquare has dimensions that convey evenness on all sides and that's how the Holy of Holies was built. If you notice that the book of Revelation starts with the imagery in the holy place. The seven lampstands and the stars. As we move towards the end of the book of Revelation, we see the vision climax at the most holy place, the holy of holies. In the city, John saw no temple in it.[170]

For the Lord God Almighty and the Lamb are its temple. Our worship is not in a place but in the mingled Godhead of the Father and the Son. We are in Him, and our worship is not in old Jerusalem or some mountain, but in spirit and reality. This is what Jesus was referring to when He told the Samaritan woman. John says, But I saw no temple in it, for the Lord God Almighty and the Lamb are its temple. The city had no need for the sun or of the moon to shine in it, for the glory of God illuminated it. The Lamb is its light.[171] There shall be no night there: They need no lamp nor the light of the sun, for the Lord God gives them light. And they shall reign forever.[172] This is the holy of holies and no outer court no holy place. In the city, there is no night. The Old Covenant age symbolized the time of night and when the day is approaching, it is dawning into the New Covenant age. The New Covenant Age is the day and in the New Jerusalem, the first-century saints with the faithful of the Old Covenant saints entered the day.

They were joined and compacted together into the finished product of history. The generation of the early church is the generational model starting at the cross (altar) to the foundation (Christ and the apostles of the Lamb) to the holy Temple in the Lord (Church), to the City of God, the New Jerusalem (Kingdom, Bride, Tabernacle of God, Sons of God). I will circle back to the generational model because we must see God's pattern and the work of His Spirit in every generation following. God has a beginning, a planting, and a harvest in every generation. God's goal is fullness, full maturity, something that matches Him in every

---

[169] Young, R. (1997). Young's Literal Translation (Re 21:16). Logos Bible Software.
[170] The New King James Version (Rev 21:22–23). (1982). Thomas Nelson.
[171] New American Standard Bible, 1995 Edition: Paragraph Version (Eze 47:12). (1995). The Lockman Foundation.
[172] The New King James Version (Re 22:5). (1982). Thomas Nelson.

generation in every city in the world and He desires to bring the city out of the invisible to the visible. 24 And the nations will walk by its light, and the kings of the earth will bring their glory into it.[173]

The nations will walk by the city's light – wisdom, insight, vision, prudence, justice. 9 then to make all men see what is the stewardship of the mystery, which from the beginning of the age has been hidden in God, who created all things by Jesus Christ: 10 to the intent that now to the rulers and authorities in the heavenlies might be made known through the Assembly, the multifarious wisdom of God, 11 according to the purpose of the New Covenant age which He brought about in Christ Jesus our Lord: Eph. 3:9-11 TKB Translation. The city (church) is to display the multifarious wisdom of God to those in authority, those that rule our cities, states, countries. We are to show God's ways, kingdom ways to bring order and prosperity into societies and communities in these areas of family, faith, education, media, entertainment, business, and government. When God's people are loving each other and God, this will cause this city of God to appear and manifest within the cities of the world. A spiritual city within a natural city influencing it to surrender to the King of Kings.

The Walls The purpose of the wall and the watchman at the gates is to guard it: 27 And every unclean thing and the one who practices detestable things and falsehood will never enter into it [1]. Never enter means those who practice such things can never experience this reality. Many who are living hidden lives cannot experience corporate life because it is a life exposed by the Spirit and the body of Christ. The Proverb says, "He that separates himself seeks his own desire and quarrels against all sound wisdom. The independent and rebellious argue with corporate life, they reject it. The spiritual realm must stay clean and pure. The words that describe this city, are pure gold, transparent like glass, glory, honor, wealth, precious, bright, and clear as crystal. These attributes are divine attributes that are worked into the lives of God's people as they are submitted to the work of the Holy Spirit. These attributes are expressed in relationships in the body of Christ with each other who are overcoming in their daily life. Those who are overcoming are being supplied by the Spirit of Jesus Christ and infused with His life and attributes. Overcomers are not improving themselves or adjusting their behavior, they are being transformed by the power of God and wisdom of God. Later in this paper I will discuss how to stay clean.

THE BOOK OF THE LIFE OF THE LAMB is the autobiography of God's Lamb, the account of who He is, what He is like, and what He does. Everything you always wanted to know about the Son of God is contained in this wonderful Book of the Life of the Lamb! It is not a literal book, of course, for the sons and daughters of the MOST HIGH are the LIVING PUBLICATIONS AND REVELATIONS of the life of the indwelling Lamb of God. It was to the apostle Paul that the revelation was given that the Book of Life, the Book

---
[173] Harris, W. H., III, Ritzema, E., Brannan, R., Mangum, D., Dunham, J., Reimer, J. A., & Wierenga, M., eds. (2012). The Lexham English Bible (Rev 21:24). Lexham Press.

of the Life of the Lamb, the Book of the Son of God is a people in Christ. 2 You are our letter written in our hearts, known and read of all men: 3 since as you are manifestly declared to be the letter of Christ ministered by us, written not with ink, but with the Spirit of the living God; not in tables of stone, but in fleshy tables of the heart. 4 And such trust have we through Christ toward God: 5 Not that we are sufficient of ourselves to think anything as of ourselves; but our sufficiency is of God; 2 Cor. 3:2-5 TKB – Translation - Terry Kashian Figuratively when the Lord opens the book of life or the Lamb's book of life. He is looking for us and our identities in Christ. As we are inscribed by the Spirit, and He writes the life of the Lamb into our lives, we become the city, the bride, the Tabernacle, the Temple, the sons of God, the kingdom expressed and made visible in the spiritual realm. But all things become visible when they are exposed by the light, for everything that becomes visible is light. Eph. 5:13. We were once darkness but now we are light in the Lord. Eph.5:8.

The River of the Water of Life

And he showed me a river of water of life, bright as crystal, proceeding out of the throne of God and of the Lamb in the middle of its street. Rev. 22:1. One thought about the street of gold. You can't walk on it because the river flows down the middle of it. It represents one way, one walk, in a transparent way. Since there is a river flowing on the street of the one way, it is to walk in the Spirit and not in the flesh. Jesus stood and cried, saying, if any man thirst, let him come unto me, and drink. He that believeth on me, as the scripture hath said, out of his innermost being shall flow rivers of living water" But this He spoke of the Spirit, whom those who believed in Him were to receive; for the Spirit was not yet, because Jesus was not yet glorified. (John 7:37-39). John was seeing this river of life as the Spirit flowing out from the throne of God and of the Lamb. The city is the people of God and within the city in the innermost parts of the city is the throne, just like within us the center of our being is the kingdom, the throne and they have come to make their abode in us, the Father, Son, and Spirit and the Spirit flows out of those who are full of faith and are governed by Him.

From John's gospel do we see the location of the rivers of living water? It is within us who believe! Marvelous isn't it? At this point Ezekiel comes wonderfully to our rescue, as we attempt to picture what is here. You remember how the river came out from beneath the threshold of the house, flowing by way of the altar, out through the whole sacred area, and down through the land, gaining in breadth and gaining in depth. 1 Then he brought me back to the door of the house; and behold, water was flowing from under the threshold of the house toward the east, for the house faced east. And the water was flowing down from under, from the right side of the house, from south of the altar.2 He brought me out by way of the north gate and led me around on the outside to the outer gate by way of the gate that faces east. And behold, water was trickling from the south side.3 When the man went out toward the east with a line in his hand, he measured a thousand cubits, and he led me through the water, water reaching the ankles.4 Again he measured a thousand and led me through the water, water reaching the knees.

Again, he measured a thousand and led me through the water, water reaching the loins. 5 Again he measured a thousand; and it was a river that I could not ford, for the water had risen, enough water to swim in, a river that could not be forded.[2] (Ezek. 47:1-5). This vision of Ezekiel is very similar to John's vision of the New Jerusalem. Ezekiel's vision starts with the temple and then the temple city. and the name of the city from that day shall be: THE LORD IS THERE.3 Yahweh Shammah! The New Testament starts with the Temple, the Spiritual House, on Pentecost, and then the city. Ezekiel then goes on to describe the trees on either side of the river. In John's vision it is the tree of life on this side and that side. The symbolism in Ezekiel is that the trees are plural on each side of the river. In Revelation, the trees become one tree on this side and that side. Many of us know the Tree of Life is God in Christ as infinite life to man.

The trees in Ezekiel are two groups of people and in Revelation, they become one as the Corporate Christ, one new man. To understand the tree of life in Revelation we need to see the corporate Christ as the soulwinners in Proverbs. "The fruit of the righteous is a tree of life, and he that wins souls is wise." Proverbs 11:30. This verse reminds me of John 15 where Christ says, He is the vine, and we are the branches. We are the vine tree of life that grows on either side of the river. It is the Tree of Life that bears fruit. The Tree of Life lives from the river, and we live by the Spirit and as we are abiding in the vine and river, we bear fruit. Wherever the river goes there is life in Ezekiel. "So, everything will live where the river goes."[174] 12 By the river on its bank, on one side and on the other, will grow all kinds of trees for food. Their leaves will not wither, and their fruit will not fail. They will bear every month because their water flows from the sanctuary, and their fruit will be for food and their leaves for healing." [2] In Revelation, "on either side of the river was the tree of life, bearing twelve kinds of fruit, yielding its fruit every month; and the leaves of the tree were for the healing of the nations."[175] [3] We know that this is not a natural tree since no tree bears a different fruit every month. I propose that the fruit the Tree of Life bears is souls that are made disciples. The great commission in Matthew, Mark, and Luke is Go and preach, make disciples, but in John 15:16 it is Go and bear fruit.[176]

"You have not chosen Me, but I have chosen you and I have appointed and placed and purposefully planted you, so that you would go and bear fruit and keep on bearing, and that your fruit will remain and be lasting, so that whatever you ask of the Father in My name [as My representative] He may give to you. John 15:16 AMP. This fruit is the souls of men, as

---

[174] Harris, W. H., III, Ritzema, E., Brannan, R., Mangum, D., Dunham, J., Reimer, J. A., & Wierenga, M., eds. (2012). The Lexham English Bible (Rev 21:27). Lexham Press. [2] New American Standard Bible, 1995 Edition: Paragraph Version (Eze 47:1–5). (1995). The Lockman Foundation.

[175] New American Standard Bible, 1995 Edition: Paragraph Version (Re 22:2). (1995). The Lockman Foundation.

[176] The New King James Version (Eze 48:35). (1982). Thomas Nelson.

the righteous we become the Tree of Life, and our fruit are the souls of those we have won to Him. 3 We give thanks to God and the Father of our Lord Jesus Christ, praying always for you, 4 since we heard of your faith in Christ Jesus, and of the love which you have for all the saints, 5 for the hope which is laid up for you in heaven, of which you heard before in the word of the reality of the gospel; 6 that has come to you, as it is in all the known world; and is being fruitful and multiplying, as it does also in you, since the day you heard of it, and knew the grace of God in reality: 7 as you also learned of Epaphras our dear fellow servant, who is for you a faithful minister of Christ; 8 who also declared to us your love in the Spirit. TKB – Col. 1:3-8 – Translation – Terry Kashian. This was the experience of the Tree of Life being fruitful and multiplying. This is very similar to Gen. - Then God blessed them, and God said to them, "Be fruitful and multiply; fill the earth and subdue it; have dominion [4] This prophecy in Genesis is the man corporately as the tree of life being fruitful and multiplying, the one new man producing children as fruit. Rom. 7 - … that you may be married to another—to Him who was raised from the dead, that we should bear fruit to God.[5] This is marvelous when we understand the symbolism.

The leaves are for the healing of the nations.

Let's recognize that this experience is in the New Heavens and New Earth. This is not heaven and if it was, why would we need to heal the nations in heaven? As the corporate Christ, the tree of life, our leaves are for healing. In Judaism, leaves are a metaphor for people. While leaves have their unique character, not sameness and distinct significance, they're inextricably linked to a larger community – coexisting with others to create beauty in togetherness. Leaves mean many things in different cultures, but the most common symbolism they are used for is related to fertility, hope, abundance, growth, peace, victory, and rebirth. Leaves are the hands on the branches and as we reach out and touch the nations, we bring all these things to them through the laying on of hands and giving what is of God to them.

No longer any curse

Jerusalem shall be raised up and inhabited in her place from Benjamin's Gate to the place of the First Gate and the Corner Gate, and from the Tower of Hananel to the king's winepresses. The people shall dwell in it; And no longer shall there be utter destruction, But Jerusalem shall be safely inhabited.[6] This verse from Zechariah is referring to the New Jerusalem. The encouragement is this Jerusalem will never be utterly destroyed. The word, "destroyed" here in Zechariah in Hebrew is ḥērem: A masculine noun meaning devoted things, devoted to destruction, devotion, things under ban, cursed [7] This curse in Rev.22:3 is no longer any curse. This Jerusalem will dwell securely from generation to generation where time never ends. 52 because it is for you that paradise is opened, the tree of life is planted, the age to come is prepared, plenty is provided, a city is built, rest is appointed, goodness is established, and wisdom perfected beforehand. 53 The root of evil is sealed up from you, illness is banished from you, and death is hidden; Hades has fled, and corruption has been forgotten; 54 sorrows have passed away, and in the end, the treasure of immortality is made manifest.[177] [8] So, there will be no curse any longer, but the throne of God and of the Lamb will be in her, and His slaves will serve Him; TKB – Translation – Terry Kashian

The curse that Adam brought to humanity could also be looked at through the redemption in Christ becoming a curse for us as He fulfilled "cursed is the man who hangs on a tree". On the cross, He became a curse for us so we would become blessed. Hallelujah! The mingled God-Man Jesus is on the throne in her. This is the location of Christ today. He is not some remote Christ or an objective God in the universe, but a personal, touchable God that governs us from within. We must recognize these registrations of Him who dwells in our midst. This is how we will know experientially His authority and we will reign with Him. His slaves will serve Him. But Jesus called them to Himself and said, "You know that the rulers of the Gentiles lord it over them, and their great men exercise authority over them. "It is not this way among you, but whoever wishes to become great among you shall be your servant, and whoever wishes to be first among you shall be your slave; just as the Son of Man did not come to be served, but to serve, and to give His life a ransom for many."[178] We must understand that being a slave has modern negative connotations and it was a low-class status in the ancient world. Only in the Kingdom of God, it is an honor to be a servant and it is the highest status to be a slave in the kingdom. We need to have a renewed mind because this is what it means to be like Christ.

They will see His face

Nothing blocking our view when it comes to our relationship. Seeing God face to face is the most intimate fellowship we can have with the Lord. No veil, living in the Shekinah glory with Him. This Hebraic idiom is quite amazing since the priests serving in the Tabernacle and Temple under the Old Covenant were not allowed to go into the Holy of Holies only the High Priest could enter once a year. The veil was the barrier and set the distance under the Old Covenant. Inside the Temple in the Holy of Holies everything was painted with pure gold. So Solomon overlaid the inside of the temple with pure gold. He stretched gold chains across the front of the inner sanctuary and overlaid it with gold. The whole temple he overlaid with gold until he had finished all the temple; also he overlaid with gold the entire altar that was by the inner sanctuary.[179]

When the High priest would enter the Holy of Holies he would see his reflection in the gold. He would see himself as the image of God in the gold. In this place He would see the

---

[177] The Holy Bible: New Revised Standard Version (2 Esd. 8:52–54). (1989). Thomas Nelson Publishers.
[178] New American Standard Bible: 1995 update (Mt 20:25–28). (1995). The Lockman Foundation.
[179] The New King James Version (1 Ki 6:21–22). (1982). Thomas Nelson.

Shekinah glory and meet with God face to face. This is the meaning of seeing God face to face. Even when he would approach the mercy seat and apply the blood, he would see himself in the golden cherubim overshadowing the mercy seat. For now, we see in a mirror, dimly, but then face to face. Now I know in part, but then I shall know just as I also am known.6 In the first century, the saints were growing to maturity and as they matured, they would ultimately come to the place of seeing God face to face. Knowing in part was the beginning of God's goal and He progressively unveils to us who He is and what He is doing until that goal is reached.

In the vision of the New Jerusalem, these ones had fully matured and were seeing God's face. When that which is perfect is come in 1 Cor. 13 I believe it is related to the consummation of God's goal and the New Jerusalem in that generation as God's goal to have a glorious church - His wife, a perfect city-kingdom, a magnificent dwelling place with His people. His name in their foreheads There is a contrast here between the bride and the harlot. The harlot is full of blasphemous names and on her forehead is the name, a mystery, Babylon the Great, the mother of harlots. The great city is where our Lord was crucified. Rev. 11:8. We conclude that this Mystery, Babylon is Old Covenant Jerusalem. She is stamped with this name, Mother of Harlots. Her character is treacherous and unfaithful. She is drunk with the blood of the saints and martyrs of Jesus. She has slain the Old Testament prophets. 24 And in her was found the blood of prophets and of saints and of all who have been slain on the land." TKB – Translation – Terry Kashian The name on the foreheads is the sealing and character of those where the name is stamped. The name of the Lord on the foreheads of the slaves who serve and minister to Him who sits on the throne is the Lord's character worked into those lives who are overcomers. 3 saying, hurt not the land, neither the sea, nor the trees, until we have sealed the slaves of our God on their foreheads. Rev. 7:3 TKB - Translation – Terry Kashian 12 He that is overcoming I will make a pillar in the temple of My God, and he will go no more out; and I will write on him the name of My God, and the name of the city of My God, which is New Jerusalem, which continually comes down out of the heavens from My God; and I will write on him My new name. Rev. 3:12 TKB – Translation – Terry Kashian.

The sons also of them that afflicted thee shall come bending unto thee; and all they that despised thee shall bow themselves down at the soles of thy feet; and they will call you, the city of the LORD, the Zion of the Holy One of Israel. Isaiah 60:14. This contrast between the harlot and the bride is alarming since Old Covenant Jerusalem is called the mother of harlots. She gives birth to daughters and those daughters carry the same blasphemous names in her and are marked with the stigma of unfaithfulness and hatred of all that is holy and spiritual. On the other hand, the bride is beautiful, holy, pure, clean, and blessed. The harlot is full of spots, wrinkles, and blemishes. Paul's vision of Christ and the Church portrays the Lord presenting to Himself a glorious church without spots, wrinkles, or blemishes. Spots in the scriptures are described as false teachers. Like clouds and wind without rain is a man who boasts of his gifts falsely. Prov. 25:14. These are self-appointed teachers and no anointing to teach and build up the people of God. They build with wood, hay, and straw, not with gold, silver, or precious stones. But there were also false prophets among the people, even as there will be false teachers among you [180] ... They are spots and blemishes, carousing in their own deceptions while they feast with you, having eyes full of adultery and that cannot cease from sin, enticing unstable souls. They have a heart trained in covetous practices and are accursed children.[181] They have forsaken the right way and gone astray, following the way of Balaam the son of Beor, who loved the wages of unrighteousness; but he was rebuked for his iniquity: a dumb donkey speaking with a man's voice restrained the madness of the prophet.[182] 8 Likewise also these dreamers are polluting the body, rejecting authority, and speaking evil of glorious ones … 12 These are spots in your love-feasts, when they feast together with you, shepherding themselves fearlessly; they are clouds without water, carried around by winds; trees who are rotting, fruitless, twice dying, rooted out; 13 wild waves of the sea, foaming out their own shame; wandering stars, for whom is reserved the blackness of darkness into the New Covenant Age. Jude 8,12-13 TKB – Translation – Terry Kashian

These spots and blemishes are false teachers who teach legalism or license (grace without boundaries). These false teachers cause the church to have wrinkles. Wrinkles are the signs of old age. The Church is a new creation, no wrinkles and these teachers who teach the church to go back to the old, Eden, natural Israel, traditions of men, and philosophies of the world create wrinkles. Also, those teachers who teach worldliness and license create wrinkles from the Old Man and flesh. The New Jerusalem has no spots, no wrinkles, and no blemishes. She is ready for her bridegroom. This is what we are in the Spirit, and it becomes visible in our maturity corporately. The New Jerusalem is the universal church in her perfected form, her mature state. It took one generation to bring this beautiful woman to maturity. This is our generational model. Every generation has this goal to reach full maturity in Christ and the leadership has a responsibility to get rid of the spots and blemishes in order that her maturity is not stunted. The universal church is expressed in local city churches.

Each city church can express the spiritual realities of the universal church. When this happens the city of God emerges within any specific city of the world as light and healing, salt and food, and the multifarious wisdom of God is transmitted to that community. The key to manifesting the New Jerusalem. is one administration in every city. Paul sent Titus to Crete to ordain elders in every city. Some things to know about Crete, it was an Island in the Mediterranean Sea. Crete became known to ancient writers as the 'Island with a hundred cities' (ekatompolis). And truly, it had perhaps even more than one hundred. It is believed that there were more than 300,000 people on the island serving all of these cities and there

---

[180] The New King James Version (2 Pe 2:1). (1982). Thomas Nelson.

[181] The New King James Version (2 Pe 2:13–14). (1982). Thomas Nelson.

[182] The New King James Version (2 Pe 2:15–16). (1982). Thomas Nelson.

was very little land that was not tilled to grow food. Back then Crete also had huge, forested areas right up to the mountain's tree line, and there was much fruit gathered from these forests. There was also plenty of wild game, and there were many hunters. In Acts …
And there were dwelling in Jerusalem Jews, devout men, from every nation under heaven. Acts 2:5. Cretans and Arabs were among those who witnessed the outpouring of the Spirit. Acts 2:11. My point is that Paul instructed Titus to ordain elders in every city not in every church, the boundary of the church is the city, and it should only have one administration in every city. This is kingdom thinking and it takes a mature leadership to understand this and to learn accountability and submission to one another. For this reason, I left you in Crete, that you would set in order what remains and appoint elders in every city as I directed you, 10 After Paul was shipwrecked, he instructed Titus to take care of the saints in the cities of Crete by putting things in order. This is how the New Jerusalem comes down and is made visible! New American Standard Bible: 1995 update (Tit. 1:5). (1995). The Lockman Foundation, New American Standard Bible, 1995 Edition: Paragraph Version (Re 22:5). (1995). The Lockman Foundation.

This reality is in the Spirit. Again, No Longer will there be any night 5 And there will no longer be any night; and they will not have need of the light of a lamp nor the light of the sun, because the Lord God will illumine them, and they will reign forever and ever.11 This is the second time it is mentioned, no night. My thought on this is because there is no need of a lamp nor light of the sun it creates in my mind the reality of the Holy of Holies. The Shekinah glory of God gives light and illuminates them. The city is the Holy of Holies, no veil. No outer court so no need of the sun. No holy place so no need of the lamp. God Himself is their light and He gives that light to them for a purpose. That light is to rule. As God gives us light, we will have insight, revelation, guidance, wisdom, and know-how into the assignments where He wants us to rule with Him.

This reigning is exercising kingdom authority on earth in our sphere of influence to make an impact in the lives of people. This was the original prophecy in 26 God said, "let us make man in our image, after our likeness: and let them have dominion over the fish of the sea, and over the birds of the heavens, and over the beasts, and over all the earth, and over every creeping thing that creeps on the earth." Gen.1:26 TKB – Translation – Terry Kashian There are four realms where dominion is exercised. The fish are souls that need to be caught for the kingdom. Jesus makes us fishers of men! Birds of the air is the spiritual realm where spirit activity moves. Jesus' parable of the Sower, "he sowed, some seed fell by the wayside, and the birds came and devoured them."[183] Kingdom authority is taking dominion over the birds of the air, these wicked spirits that are antagonistic to His word. Over the beasts which are wild kingdoms in the world, the nations that need to be subdued in subjection to King Jesus bowing their knees to the Lord of lords. Then lastly, to

---

[183] The New King James Version (Mt 13:4–5). (1982). Thomas Nelson.

take dominion over every creeping thing that creeps upon the earth. These are the sneaky things in life, slithering, clinging to us to supplant and harm us. The Lord has given us all authority over serpents and scorpions and over all the power of the enemy. These four realms need to be conquered and can only be conquered by the corporate Christ.[184] But God, who is rich in mercy, for His great love with which He loved us,[185] even when we were dead in sins, has given life to us together with Christ, (by grace you are saved;)[186] and has raised us up together, and made us sit together in the heavenlies in Christ Jesus:[187] that in the coming age He might show the exceeding riches of His grace in His kindness toward us through Christ Jesus. TKB - Translation – Terry Kashian. … much more those who receive abundance of grace and of the gift of righteousness will reign in life through the One, Jesus Christ.)[188]

Things which must shortly take place.

Then he said to me, "These words are faithful and true." And the Lord God of the holy prophets sent His angel to show His servants the things which must shortly take place.[189] If these words are faithful and true, why do so many teachers and preachers doubt the nearness of fulfillment of the following words? This is exactly how the beginning of the prophecy is in chapter one. These are faithful words and true words! Many Bible teachers that I have been exposed to say the first three chapters are to the seven churches, but the fourth chapter is about our future. This is nonsense because the entire book of Revelation is a prophecy that was about to happen. "And behold, I am coming soon. Blessed is the one who keeps the words of the prophecy of this book."[190] Here is a tidbit, whenever you see the word "behold" in the bible think of it as a window into the spiritual realm. This word wants you to look closely through the window of the following words. In this case, it is, "I am coming soon". The word soon here is an adjective in Greek Usage 1. Ταχύς - tachys prompt — performed with little or no delay. This is critical and it does go against our grain, if we have a preconceived idea of the coming of Christ. John was told this would be prompt, not 2000-plus years later. The book of Revelation uses the word taxos (Rev. 1:1; 22:6) and taxhys (2:5, 16; 3:11; 11:14; 22:7, 12, 20) a total of nine times. We find in Revelation 11:14 that the "third woe is coming quickly." Futurists like Rhodes believe Revelation 11 describes events of the last days during a concentrated period of seven years. If "quickly" and "soon" can

---

[184] The New King James Version (Ge 1:28). (1982). Thomas Nelson.
[185] The New King James Version (Ro 7:4). (1982). Thomas Nelson.
[186] The New King James Version (Zec 14:10–11). (1982). Thomas Nelson.
[187] Baker, W., & Carpenter, E. E. (2003). In The complete word study dictionary: Old Testament (p. 380). AMG Publishers.
[188] The New King James Version (Ro 5:17). (1982). Thomas Nelson.
[189] The New King James Version (Re 22:6). (1982). Thomas Nelson.
[190] The Holy Bible: English Standard Version (Re 22:7). (2016). Crossway Bibles.

mean an extended period of nearly 2000 years (so far), then how should the use of "quickly" be interpreted in Revelation 11:14? If "quickly" can mean nearly 2000 years in Revelation 1:1, then it should mean the same thing in 11:14, and yet, what's being described in 11:14 happens in a short period of time. Given Rhodes' definition of "quickly," the time between the past two woes (9:12) and the woe to come could be thousands of years, and yet the time span of Revelation 4-19 is only seven years. Gary Demar 8 So I John saw these things and heard them. And when I had heard and seen, I fell down to worship before the feet of the messenger who showed me these things.[191] 9 Then he said to me, behold do not do that; for I am your fellow slave, and of your brothers' the prophets and of those who keep the sayings of this book, worship God!

Rev. 22:8-9 – TKB – Translation – Terry Kashian

I have a few things to say about this regarding honoring and adoring those who bring revelation and insight into the things of God in our lives. As leaders we must have the same attitude as this messenger, pointing people to God and not ourselves. Paul says we preach Christ and not ourselves. For we preach not ourselves, but Christ Jesus as Lord, and ourselves as your slaves for Jesus' sake. 2 Cor. 4:5. This is the proper disposition for those in leadership. Also as followers of Christ, it is important not to idolize those who are gifted and not to exalt them too highly to their demise. The exhortation is 'worship God'.

Do Not Seal The Prophecy Of This Book

10 Then he said to me, seal not the sayings of the prophecy of this book, for the time is near! TKB – Translation – Terry Kashian

The relevance of the prophecy in this book is of the utmost importance to understand it. The audience needed this message, and it was written to them not to us, but for us. Most readers of the bible recognize the distinction from Daniel to seal up the prophecy that he received because the time was not yet. It was for the time of the end. We might ask what end is the Lord revealing to Daniel? The end was the end of Old Covenant Israel and the sacrificial system and all that entailed. The fulfillment of the Mosaic Law. So, Daniel sealed it up. Now the Lord is revealing to John to not seal up the sayings of this prophecy. Notice it is not prophecies, but singular prophecy. The whole book is a prophecy of the time of the end, the removing of the old and bringing in of the new. We could say this is a good reference to the dating of this prophecy. The sacrificial system was still up and operating and if it wasn't the theme of removing the old and bringing in the new would be senseless. Also, the reference in the first chapter states the time is near. Blessed is the one who reads and those who hear the words of this prophecy, and who keep what is written in it, for the time is near. The word translated as 'near' is Strong's 1451 – ἐγγύς (eggus), indicating something close at hand, imminent, and not distant. In the early Christian understanding,

---

[191] New American Standard Bible, 1995 Edition: Paragraph Version (Re 22:3). (1995). The Lockman Foundation.

there was a strong anticipation of the telos – the final goal or fulfillment. These words reflect the sacred hope in the immediate coming of God's promised future. The term is used with sanctity in connection to the great hope of consummation. Whenever ἐγγύς appears in the New Testament – it occurs thirty times – it refers to something close in time or space. It never suggests a long delay. Specifically, when used in regard to time, it implies immediacy and readiness. The Greek language distinguishes between two types of time: chronos and kairos. Chronos is sequential, measurable time – seconds, minutes, hours, and years. Kairos, on the other hand, is qualitative. It speaks of the right or opportune moment, a significant or appointed season. In Revelation 22:10, the word used is kairos, not chronos. Understanding this distinction is crucial. Kairos signifies a divine moment, the critical or opportune time when something must occur. Paul emphasizes this when he wrote to the Romans, saying: 'so that, knowing the time (kairos), that now it is the hour to wake from sleep, for now our deliverance is nearer than when we first believed' (Romans 13:11, TKB translation). Paul recognized the kairos – the sacred moment. John also identified the urgency of the moment: 'Little children, it is the last hour; and as you have heard, the Antichrists are coming, even now many Antichrists have come, by which we know it is the last hour' (1 John 2:18, TKB translation). Similarly, Peter understood the time, writing: 'But the end of all things is at hand; therefore be serious and watchful in your prayers' (1 Peter 4:7, TKB translation). In Christian thought, the terms ἐγγύς and ἐγγίζειν carry a sense of sacred urgency and reverent expectation – they are used when the fulness of the divine plan is about to unfold.

The Warning

11 He that is being harmful, let him be harmful still; and he who is being filthy, let him be filthy still; and he that is righteous, let him be affirmed righteous still, and he that is holy, let him be holy still. 12 And, Behold I am coming quickly, and My wages are with Me to repay each one according to their works. TKB – Translation – Terry Kashian This is an unusual verse, and many have ignored it in commentaries or skimmed over it. It is a warning that the judgment is pending, near and the Lord is coming to repay those according to their works. We can learn something valuable from the wording, "according to their works". This is an Old Covenant context being judged according to our works. The Old Covenant is all about works and it is a meritorious system that depends on our behavior. 2 For if Abraham was justified by works, he has something to boast about, but not before God. 3 For what does the Scripture say? "ABRAHAM BELIEVED GOD, AND IT WAS CREDITED TO HIM AS RIGHTEOUSNESS." 4 Now to the one who works, his wage is not credited as a favor, but as what is due. 5 But to the one who does not work, but believes in Him who justifies the ungodly, his faith is credited as righteousness, 6 just as David also speaks of the blessing on the man to whom God credits righteousness apart from works: 7 "BLESSED ARE THOSE WHOSE LAWLESS DEEDS HAVE BEEN FORGIVEN, AND WHOSE SINS HAVE BEEN COVERED. 8 "BLESSED IS THE MAN WHOSE SIN THE LORD WILL NOT TAKE INTO ACCOUNT."

In the New Covenant Age, the judgment will be based on rewards, not punishments. Believing that we will be punished or rewarded based on works is a mixture of Old Covenant and New Covenant concepts. The entire Old Covenant was based on works of the Law. The intrinsic difference under the Old Covenant which is connected to the flesh was the demands that were put on the flesh and finding man faulty and unable to carry out His commands was a dismal failure. Under the New Covenant righteousness is a gift, justification is free and in the process of believing God, He empowers us to obey Him and supplies us with all that we need to please Him which is the life of Christ within us. Eternal or Infinite life is a gift to those who receive the gift of grace. In understanding this idea of judging according to works we must understand that it is a judgment within the Old Covenant Age that ended in AD 70. The gospel of the kingdom is embodied in two events that are a generational model. The first event is the cross – death, burial, resurrection, and ascension. The second event is the destruction of Jerusalem and the removal of the Old Covenant elements that condemned and held Israel in bondage. Those who accepted the first event experienced salvation, deliverance, and inheritance with the saints in light, the kingdom. Those who reject the first event experience the second event. Jesus predicted in Matthew, 27 For the Son of Man is going to come in the glory of His Father with His angels and WILL THEN REPAY EVERY MAN ACCORDING TO HIS DEEDS. 28 "Truly I say to you, there are some of those who are standing here who will not taste death until they see the Son of Man coming in His kingdom."[192] Preisker, H. (1964–). ἐγγύς, ἐγγίζω, προσεγγίζω. In G. Kittel, G. W. Bromiley, & G. Friedrich (Eds.), Theological dictionary of the New Testament (electronic ed., Vol. 2, p. 332). Eerdmans.

This verse in Rev. 22:12 echoes Jesus' words in Matthew. The generation then living would see His coming and the judgment according to works. Only in the Old Covenant age is there a judgment based on works. In the New Covenant age, the judgment is based on whether someone has faith in Christ and is born again. If not, then their future is sealed to experience the perpetual judgment of God for rejecting the only payment for their sins which is the glorious Lamb of God. If God says that His forgiveness for sins is final and that He remembers our sins no more. What is He going to bring up when we are judged if He threw our sins in the sea of forgetfulness. He will judge us in the matter of rewards done in His body. This is critical to our understanding of judgment. The person not born again has not had his sins washed away; therefore, his sin will condemn him. We on the other hand have the righteousness of Christ and are the righteousness of God in Him. It is a gift! We receive it by faith in Christ. At the coming of Christ, He is judging according to the Old Covenant standard because it is still the Old Covenant age. If those in the Old Covenant age received Christ for their payment for sins they will be ok.

---

[192] New American Standard Bible, 1995 Edition: Paragraph Version (Mt 16:27–28). (1995). The Lockman Foundation.

In Psa. 62:12, while David is waiting for God's salvation and declaring that He only is his rock, he states that God will, "Also to You, O Lord, belongs mercy; For You render to each one according to his work." [193] And will He not render to each man according to his deeds?[194] The context of Romans chapter 1 & 2 is intense in the context of God's righteous judgment. But we know that the judgment of God is according to truth against those who practice such things. And do you think this, O man, you who judge those practicing such things, and doing the same, that you will escape the judgment of God? Or do you despise the riches of His goodness, forbearance, and longsuffering, not knowing that the goodness of God leads you to repentance? (Only Israel would be familiar with this about God TK) But in accordance with your hardness and your impenitent heart you are treasuring up for yourself wrath in the day of wrath and revelation of the righteous judgment of God, who "will render to each one according to his deeds": eternal life to those who by patient continuance in doing good seek for glory, honor, and immortality; but to those who are self-seeking and do not obey the truth, but obey unrighteousness—indignation and wrath, tribulation and anguish, on every soul of man who does evil, of the Jew first and also of the Greek; but glory, honor, and peace to everyone who works what is good, to the Jew first and also to the Greek. For there is no partiality with God.[195] Mat. 25:46; Ro. 2:6–9; 1 Th. 1:7– 10; Da. 12:2. The sword is dividing here between the wicked and the righteous. There is an unmovable and fixed condition contrasted in these verses and the revelation of who God is should cause repentance, but in those who do harm and are morally filthy, there is no change of mind or heart. For there is no partiality with God.22 Mat. 25:46; Ro. 2:6–9; 1 Th. 1:7– 10; Da. 12:2. The sword is dividing here between the wicked and the righteous. There is an unmovable and fixed condition contrasted in these verses and the revelation of who God is should cause repentance, but in those who do harm and are morally filthy, there is no change of mind or heart.

13 I am the Alpha and the Omega, the first and the last, the beginning and the end."[196] "I am the Alpha and the Omega, saith the Lord God, which is and which was and which is to come, the Almighty" (Rev. 1:8). "And He said unto me... I am the Alpha and the Omega, the Beginning and the End" (Rev. 21:6). "I am the Alpha and the Omega, the First and the Last, the Beginning and the End" (Rev. 22:13).

"I am the Alpha and the Omega, the First and the Last, the Beginning and the End" (Rev. 22:13). The book of Revelation is called the Revelation of Jesus Christ. This is the revelation of Jesus Christ in all His aspects and relation to the players and people and

---

[193] The New King James Version (Ps 62:12). (1982). Thomas Nelson.
[194] The New King James Version (Pr 24:12). (1982). Thomas Nelson.
[195] The New King James Version (Ro 2:1–11). (1982). Thomas Nelson.
[196] New American Standard Bible, 1995 Edition: Paragraph Version (Re 22:13). (1995). The Lockman Foundation.

entities in this book. All of these things will take place quickly with the first generation revealing who He is.

One of the titles which the Lord takes to Himself in His glorified state is: "the Alpha and the Omega". The Lord Jesus here presents Himself as "the Living One", Who was dead, and is alive again - alive for evermore (Rev. 1:18). Those two letters, Alpha and Omega, are, as we know, the first and the last letters of the Greek alphabet. The one is the same in form as the first letter in our own alphabet; the other is unlike any of our letters. Alpha and Omega - First and Last. In every alphabet there is something which corresponds to an 'A' and a 'Z', an Alpha and an Omega, a beginning and an end. It does not matter how complicated the alphabet may be, or if it only contains a poor twenty-six letters as in English: everything is bounded by the 'A' and the 'Z', the Alpha and the Omega. You cannot get anything outside of that; all is within that. The Alpha and the Omega incorporate all speaking and writing; there is no communication possible in any language outside of what comes between those two letters. All that can be said has to come between these parameters; outside of this range, nothing can be said. Nothing outside of Christ's communication has worth and meaning with infinite value.

Who is saying He is the first and the last? Yahweh, the God of Israel is I, Jesus who has sent my angel and said He was coming? Jesus is revealed as Yahweh! Isa. 44:6; 48:12.

The Last Beatitude in the Bible

Blessed are they who are washing their robes, so that they may have the authority to the Tree of Life and may enter in through the gates into the city. TKB – Translation – Terry Kashian Rev. 22:14, 14 So I said to him, sir, you know. And he said to me, these are they who are coming out of the great tribulation and have washed their robes and made them white in the blood of the Lamb. TKB – Translation – Terry Kashian Rev. 7:14 These are those who have made their robes white in the blood of Jesus. This is the only way for anyone to become clean and righteous. David Aune in the Word Biblical Commentary says this... In the phrase οἱ ἐρχόμενοι ἐκ τῆς θλίψεως τῆς μεγάλης, "those who have emerged from the great tribulation," οἱ ἐρχόμενοι is translated in a past tense because it represents action simultaneous with the two main verbs ἔπλυναν, "washed," and ἐλεύκαναν, "made white," both of which are aorists (see Note 7:14. d-d.; Beckwith, 545). It is therefore grammatically improbable to translate the present substantival participle οἱ ἐρχόμενοι as "those who are coming," as if the scene in 7:9–17 was occurring precisely when it was narrated by the author .... Rev. 7 is written in a past tense and Rev. 22 is in the present. Having this in mind we need to realize that those martyrs were killed, and they had been washed in the blood of the Lamb. In Rev. 22 John is indicating that those who were washing their robes were in the present being saved by the light of the city and being washed to have authority to eat from the Tree of Life and coming into the city of God to be a part of the Lamb's wife. This is not a scene of eternity or outside of time. This is the purpose of God in its practical means of being the kingdom of God in the first century. This is why outside the city are those who are not saved. Remember this is the New Heavens and Earth motif, not a literal new planet, but imagery of the function of the New Creation and its components. The city is the Lord's testimony in the New Creation calling the lost to come which we will see later.

Outside the City

15 For outside are the dogs, and sorcerers, and the sexually immoral, and murderers, and idolaters, and whoever loves even to fabricate falsehood. TKB – Translation – Terry Kashian Rev. 22:15

What and who are these degenerate people outside the city? First let's look at the dogs and let scripture interpret scripture. I was surprised when I saw the description of the first type of person and the usage of dogs. 2 Beware of the dogs, beware of the evil workers, beware of the false circumcision; 3 for we are the true circumcision, who worship in the Spirit of God and glory in Christ Jesus and put no confidence in the flesh 24. Paul's usage of dogs exposes the Judaizers and calls them evil workers and false circumcision. These dogs are false teachers teaching contrary to the message of grace and righteousness apart from the Law of Moses. These dogs were also those who perverted Paul's emphasis on grace to the point of license. This is what Galatians is all about. The balance of grace is walking in the Spirit. These dogs were sorcerers and immoral and even murderers because they idolized themselves and fabricated every falsehood. After Nineveh had repented and come into covenant with God, she played the harlot. A type of Old Covenant Israel which God was trying to show to Jonah. Nahum defines this sorcery about Nineveh which is exactly what Israel did in the first century to incur God's final stroke of wrath on Jerusalem the perfect example of harlotry. All because of the many acts of prostitution of [Nineveh], the prostitute, the charming and well-favored one, the mistress of sorceries, Who betrays nations by her acts of prostitution (idolatry) And families by her sorceries. Nahum 3:4 Amplified Bible. Israel became the same in the generation of Christ.24 (Php. 3:2–3). So will Babylon, the great city, be thrown down with violence, and will not be found any longer. 22 And the sound of harpists and musicians and flute players and trumpeters will not be heard in you any longer, and no craftsman of any craft will be found in you any longer, and the sound of a mill will not be heard in you any longer; 23 and the light of a lamp will not shine in you any longer; and the voice of the bridegroom and bride will not be heard in you any longer; for your merchants were the great men of the earth, because all the nations were deceived by your sorcery. 24 And in her was found the blood of prophets and of saints and of all who have been slain on the land."25 Rev. 18:21-25. This great city was the sorceress and those in her were masters at sorcery and this great city is where our Lord was crucified. Rev. 11:8. Those who were connected to her were also immoral and murderers and propagators of all that was false. They were outside the city-kingdom.

The Root and Offspring of David

16 I Jesus have sent My messenger to testify to you these things in the Assemblies. I am the Root and the Offspring of David, and the bright Morning Star. TKB – Translation – Terry Kashian Rev. 22:15 He is the I am in His divinity, the root of David. Before time, before anything, He is. Then stealthily He slips into humanity and becomes the offspring of David. What a God we have! We see the process that God put Himself through. Divine always, incarnation Man, death, resurrection, and becoming the Life-giving Spirit. Imparting Himself into us as our all in all, our supply, our fortification, our life. This message is to the seven churches or assemblies. This is not some addendum to a future generation. Even though the word of God has a timeless application it is specific to the generation it was sent to. Understanding this will help us see the generational model of the first century.

Christ reveals who He is as the root of David. 10 Then in that day the nations will resort to the root of Jesse, who will stand as a standard for the peoples; And His resting place will be glorious.26 This is the glorious church in Eph. 5 where Christ presents to Himself a glorious church without spot or wrinkle. Jews and Gentiles resorting to the root of Jesse. The root is before the person or plant. It is the source. Jesus is revealing that He is the source of David, even the source of David's father. He is also the offspring of David. As the source He is Yahweh and as the offspring, He is the Son of God. Jesus is the magnificent God-Man! It is spectacular that He is the Morning Star. The Morning Star's appearance has fascinated cultures for centuries, symbolizing hope and new beginnings. It is often one of the brightest objects in the night sky which is why it is often called the bright morning star.

The morning star is known to be a sign of hope, that the darkness will soon give way to the light. The apostle Paul writes in Romans 13. "12 The night is almost gone, and the day is near. [197] 19 So we have the prophetic word made more sure, to which you do well to pay attention as to a lamp shining in a dark place, until the day dawns and the morning star arises in your hearts.[198] 28 We can see from these two verses that Paul and Peter were on the same page about the day coming. It was a new day; it was the New Covenant age breaking forth from the darkness and night of the Old Covenant. Peter's reference to the morning star is unique because he says, "until the day and morning star arises in your hearts". The Lord Jesus says He is bright morning star, and I am amazed where He is arising from. He is within us wanting to be glorified in His saints.

The context of Peter's word is he is reminding the saints of the time he was on the holy mountain, and he had the vision of Moses, Elijah, Jesus in Matt. 17. This was an unforgettable moment for Peter. He writes … "we made known to you the power and coming of our Lord Jesus Christ",.[199] He said to Jesus, let's make three tabernacles "one for You, and

---

[197] New American Standard Bible, 1995 Edition: Paragraph Version (Ro 13:12). (1995). The Lockman Foundation.

[198] New American Standard Bible, 1995 Edition: Paragraph Version (2 Pe 1:19). (1995). The Lockman Foundation.

[199] New American Standard Bible, 1995 Edition: Paragraph Version (2 Pe 1:16). (1995). The Lockman Foundation.

one for Moses, and one for Elijah.[200] This is when he heard the majestic voice. Hear Him! 8 And lifting up their eyes, they saw no one except Jesus Himself alone.[201] Moses and Elijah had faded, just like the Old Covenant Law and Prophets were going to vanish away at the coming of the Lord. The bright and Morning Star was coming in the glory of the New Day. John saw that day!

The Spirit and Bride say Come

As the consummation of God's judgment and the manifestation of His kingdom in glory climaxed John reverts back to the purpose of the church. We have seen the city and who they are and the components that make up the mature church, the effective church at the end of the first generation and how this will become the model for generations to come. The bride and Spirit are one. This oneness is so marvelous, and they are saying the same thing. The bride has the mind of the Spirit. She is speaking only what the Spirit is saying and that word is 'come'.

17 And the Spirit and the bride say, "come." And let the one who hears say, "come."

And let the one who is thirsty come; let the one who desires, receive the water of life as a gift. The word 'come' is found three times in this verse. This verse covers three matters: the response of the Spirit and the Bride; the word of the one who hears the announcement and invitation of the Spirit and the Bride; and the desire of the sinner, the unsaved one, to come and receive the water of life. The first matter is the most important. As the church we need to learn how to cooperate with the Spirit, he that is joined to the Lord is one spirit. This is a fact, 1 Cor. 6:17.

The more we believe this verse the more we experience the reality of it. I declare I am one with you Lord, I am one with you! This is a fact! Our oneness with the Lord should flow out of us with the same speaking and same thoughts. The church is calling out to all in all directions, east, west, north, and south to COME. This is the corporate purpose of the church, then there is the individual who hears what the Spirit and bride say and that individual cries out, COME. And as the world gets thirsty, they will come and the one who desires will receive the water of life as a gift. God's purpose is to give us life as a gift. His purpose is the give us righteousness as a gift, and Christ is that gift. The bride is our corporate identity and is present in time to cooperate with the Spirit calling out to bring all who are thirsty into His kingdom.

John's Witness and the Stern Warning

18 For I witness together with everyone that is hearing the words of the prophecy of this book, if anyone adds to these things, God will add to him the calamities that are written in

---

[200] New American Standard Bible, 1995 Edition: Paragraph Version (Mt 17:4). (1995). The Lockman Foundation
[201] New American Standard Bible, 1995 Edition: Paragraph Version (Mt 17:8). (1995). The Lockman Foundation.

this book; 19 And if anyone takes away from the words of the book of this prophecy, God will take away his part away from the Tree of Life, and out of the holy city, and from the things which are written in this book. John is closing the revelation given to him with a stern warning not to add or take away from the book of this prophecy. Firstly, not to add which means to put something more into the message.

The one who adds will have God put the plagues and calamities of this prophecy on their lives. Secondly, the one who takes away or cuts something out or cuts off some of the message will be cut off from the Tree of Life and out of the city of God. Many try to say that this applies to the whole bible, and we can understand their concerns not to corrupt the word of God, but this specifically addresses the book of Revelation. It is wise not to handle God's word with prejudice or creativity. Doing so would prove we are false witnesses.

Surely, I am Coming Soon

20 He who bears witness to these things says, yes, I am coming quickly. Amen. Yes, come, Lord Jesus. 21 The grace of our Lord Jesus Christ be with you all! Amen. Rev.22:20 TKB -Translation – Terry Kashian The Lord's promise of coming quickly is reiterated as He promised at the beginning of the prophecy of this book. "…to show to His bondservants, the things which must shortly take place." Rev. 1:1 "The time is near." Rev. 1:3 "Nevertheless, what you have, hold fast until I come." Rev. 2:25 "…to show to His bondservants the things which must shortly take place." Rev. 22:6 The emphasis in the last chapter the word quickly is mentioned three times. Rev. 22:7, Rev. 22:12. Vines Dictionary: TACHUS (ταχύς, (5036) It means speedily, without delay, a short and measurable period. It is a specific time statement. … for yet in a very little while, He who is coming will come, and will not delay. Hebrews 10:27 Other verses that show the world and times were about to change. "The darkness is passing away, and the true light is already shining." I Jn. 2:8 "The world is passing away, and its desires." I Jn. 2:17 "It is the last hour." I Jn. 2:18

All these verses show that Jesus was about to come and that what is revealed in this book is the Lord carrying out His perpetual purpose and He is showing the consummation of His purpose. It is not about heaven, but the heavenly realities that are possible when He gets a people that cooperate with Him to develop into mature believers. The mature stage of God's purpose manifests His kingdom in every generation. This is the generational model and when we understand this paradigm, we will see the need to coordinate with God's people and with the Lord of Glory. This is how we become light and salt to the nations. This is how the city-kingdom, tabernacle, and bride, move from the invisible to visible realm. This is His kingdom and His will coming on earth as it is in Heaven. This is what happened in the first century. The church transformed the culture of the Roman Empire, and we can transform the culture of our world. Grace to All!

The grace of our Lord Jesus Christ be with you all. Amen.[202]

John closes the book with the "grace" that is needed to make all this happen. Grace is not some objective things, not like the Sunday school definition. Unmerited favor only! Grace is the divine influence of God upon the heart of man to reflect the glory of God. For us to become the city in reality, it will take the divine influence of God upon us. The city coming down out of heaven, "having the glory of God". That's the result of grace! Hallelujah!

Garrett Paul Parrish 2016 - 12/22/2023 Terry Kashian

---

[202] *The New King James Version (Re 22:21). (1982). Thomas Nelson.*

Revelation

Chapter 1

1. The Revelation of Jesus Christ, which God gave to him, to show to His slaves things which must shortly take place; and He made it known through signs, sending it by His angel to His slave John;
2. Who bore witness to the Word of God, and to the testimony of Jesus Christ, and to all things that he saw.
3. Blessed is he that reads, and they that hear the words of this prophecy, and keep those things which are written in it; for the appointed time is at near.
4. John to the seven Assemblies who are in Asia; grace to you, and peace, from Him who is, and who was, and who is to come; and from the seven Spirits who are before His throne;
5. And from Jesus Christ, who is the Faithful Witness, the Firstborn of the dead, and the Ruler of the kings of the earth. To Him that is loving us and having eradicated our sins in His own blood,
6. And made us kings and priests to God and His Father; to Him be glory and dominion into the New Covenant age from the Old Covenant age. Amen.
7. Behold, He comes with the cloud; and every eye will see Him, and also they who pierced Him, and all the tribes of the land will grieve because of Him. Even so, Amen.
8. I am Alpha and Omega, the Beginning and the Ending, says the Lord, Who is, and Who was, and Who is coming, the Almighty.
9. I John, who also am your brother, and companion in the tribulation, and in the kingdom and endurance of Jesus Christ, was on the isle that is called Patmos, for the Word of God, and for the testimony of Jesus Christ.
10. I was in spirit on the Day of the Lord, and heard behind me a great voice, as of a trumpet,
11. Saying I am Alpha and Omega, the First and the Last; and, what you see, write in a book, and send it to the seven Assemblies in Asia; to Ephesus, and Smyrna, and Pergamum, and Thyatira, and Sardis, and Philadelphia, and Laodicea.
12. So, I turned to see the voice that spoke with me. And turning around, I saw seven golden lampstands;
13. In the midst of the seven lampstands one like the Son of man, clothed with a robe down to the foot and wrapped about the chest with a golden sash.
14. His head and His hair are white like wool, as white as snow; and His eyes as a flame of fire;
15. And His feet like polished bronze, as if they burned in a furnace; and His voice as the sound of many waters.
16. And He had in His right hand seven stars; and out of His mouth went a sharp two-edged sword; and His countenance was as the sun shining in its strength.
17. When I saw Him, I fell at His feet as dead. But He laid His right hand on me, saying to me, fear not; I am the first and the last;
18. I am He that lives, and was dead; and, behold, I am alive into the New Covenant Age from the Old Covenant Age, Amen; and have the keys of Hades and Death.

19. Write the things which you have seen, and the things which are, and the things which are about to be in the midst of these things;
20. The mystery of the seven stars which you saw in My right hand, and the seven golden lampstands. The seven stars are the messengers of the seven Assemblies, and the seven lampstands which you saw are the seven Assemblies.

Chapter 2

1. To the messenger of the Assembly of Ephesus write; these things says He that holds the seven stars in His right hand, who walks in the midst of the seven golden lampstands;
2. I know your works, and your labor, and your patience, and how you cannot bear those who are evil; and you have tried those who say they are apostles and are not, and have found them, liars;
3. And have endured, and have patience, and for My name's sake have labored, and have not fainted.
4. Nevertheless, I have something against you because you have forsaken your first love.
5. Therefore, remember from where you have fallen, and repent, and do the first works, or else I will come to you quickly, and will remove your lampstand out of its place unless you repent.
6. But you have this that you hate the deeds of the Laity-Conquerors, which I also hate.
7. He that has an ear, let him hear what the Spirit says to the Assemblies; to him, that is overcoming will I give to eat of the Tree of Life, which is in the midst of the Paradise of God.
8. To the messenger of the Assembly in Smyrna write; these things says the First and the Last, who was dead, and is alive;
9. I know your works, and tribulation, and poverty, (but you are rich) and I know the blasphemy of those who say they are Jews, and are not, but are the synagogue of Satan.
10. Fear none of those things which you are about to suffer; behold, the Devil is about to cast some of you into prison, that you may be tried; and you will have tribulation ten days; be faithful to death, and I will give you a crown of life.
11. He that has an ear, let him hear what the Spirit says to the Assemblies; he who is overcoming will not be hurt by the second death.
12. And to the messenger of the Assembly in Pergamum write; these things says He who has the sharp two-edged sword;
13. I know your works, and where you dwell, even where Satan's throne is; and you clinging to My name, and have not denied My faith, even in those days in which Antipas was My faithful martyr, who was slain among you, where Satan dwells.
14. But I have a few things against you because you have them there that prevailed by the teaching of Balaam, who taught Balak to cast a stumbling block before the children of Israel, to eat things sacrificed to idols, and to commit sexual immorality.

15. So, in like manner you also have those who prevail by the teaching of the Laity-Conquerors, which is what I hate.
16. Repent, or else I will come to you quickly, and will fight against them with the sword of My mouth.
17. He that has an ear, let him hear what the Spirit says to the Assemblies; to him who is overcoming will I give to eat of the hidden manna, and will give him a white stone, and in the stone, a new name is written, which no one knows except he that receives it.
18. And to the messenger of the Assembly in Thyatira write; these things says the Son of God, who has His eyes like a flame of fire, and His feet are like burnished bronze;
19. I know your works, and love, and service, and faith, and your patience, and your works; and the last to be more than the first.
20. Nonetheless, I have a few things against you, because you permitted that woman Jezebel, who calls herself a prophetess, to teach and to seduce My slaves to commit sexual immorality and to eat things sacrificed to idols.
21. I gave her time to repent of her sexual immorality, and she repented not.
22. Behold, I will cast her into a bed of anguish, and them that commit adultery with her into great tribulation, unless they repent of their deeds.
23. And I will strike her children with death, and all the Assemblies will know that I am He who searches minds and hearts, and I will give to everyone according to your deeds.
24. But to you I say, and to the rest in Thyatira, as many as have not this teaching, and who have not known the depths of Satan, as they are saying; I will place on you no other burden.
25. But that which you already have prevailed until I come.
26. And he that is overcoming and keeping My works to the end, to him, I will give authority over the nations;
27. And he will shepherd them with a staff of iron; as the vessels of a potter will they be broken to pieces; just as I received authority from My Father.
28. And I will give him the Morning Star.
29. He that has an ear, let him hear what the Spirit says to the Assemblies.

Chapter 3

1. And to the messenger of the Assembly in Sardis write; these things says He that has the seven Spirits of God, and the seven stars; I know your works, that you have a name that you live, but are dead.
2. Be watchful, and strengthen the things which remain, that are about to die; for I have not found your works complete before God.
3. Therefore, remember how you have received and heard, and keep watch, and repent. Therefore, if you will not watch, I will come on you as a thief, and you will not know what hour I will come on you.
4. You have a few names in Sardis who have not stained their garments, and they will walk with Me in white; for they are worthy.

5. He that is overcoming, the same will be clothed in white clothing, and I will not erase his name out of the Book of Life, but I will confess his name before My Father, and before His angels.

6. He that has an ear, let him hear what the Spirit says to the Assemblies.

7. And to the messenger of the Assembly in Philadelphia write; these things say He that is Holy, He that is true, He that has the key of David, He that opens, and no one shuts; and shuts, and no one opens;

8. I know your works; behold, I have set before you an open door, and no man can shut it; for you have a little power, and have kept My word, and have not denied My name.

9. Behold, I will make them of the synagogue of Satan, who say they are Jews and are not, but do lie; behold, I will make them come and prostrate before your feet, and they will know that I love you.

10. Because you have kept the word of My endurance, I also will keep you from the hour of trial, which is about to come on the entire Roman world, to test them that dwell upon the land.

11. Behold, I come quickly; take possession of that which you have, that no one may take your crown.

12. He that is overcoming I will make a pillar in the temple of My God, and he will go no more out; and I will write on him the name of My God, and the name of the city of My God, which is New Jerusalem, which continually comes down out of the heavens from My God; and I will write on him My new name.

13. He that has an ear, let him hear what the Spirit says to the Assemblies.

14. And to the messenger of the Assembly of the Laodiceans write; these things says the Amen, the faithful and true Witness, the beginning of the creation of God;

15. I know your works, that you are neither cold nor hot; I would rather you were either cold or hot.

16. So then because you are lukewarm, and neither cold nor hot, I am about to spit you out of My mouth.

17. Because you say, I am rich, and increased with possessions, and need nothing; and do not know that you are wretched and miserable, and poor, and blind, and naked;

18. I advise you to buy from Me gold tried in the fire, that you may be rich; and white clothing, that you may be clothed, and that the shame of your nakedness does not appear; and anoint your eyes with eye salve, that you may see.

19. As many as I love, I rebuke and discipline; therefore, be zealous and repent.

20. Behold, I stand at the door, and knock; if anyone hears My voice, and opens the door, I will come into him, and will eat with him, and he with Me.

21. To him that is overcoming will I grant to sit with Me on My throne, just as I also overcame, and have sat down with My Father on His throne.

22. He that has an ear, let him hear what the Spirit says to the Assemblies.

Chapter 4

1. After this I looked, and, behold, a door was opened in the heavens; and the first voice which I heard was as it were of a trumpet talking with me; which said, come up here, and I will show you things which must be afterward.
2. Immediately I was in spirit; and, behold, a throne was set in heaven, and One sat on the throne.
3. He that sat was to look upon like a jasper and a carnelian stone; and there was a rainbow around the throne, in appearance like an emerald.
4. Around the throne were twenty-four thrones; and on the thrones, I saw twenty-four elders sitting, clothed in white garments; and they had on their heads crowns of gold.
5. And out of the throne proceeded bolts of lightning and the noise of thunders; and there were seven lamps of fire burning before the throne, which are the seven Spirits of God.
6. Before the throne there was a sea of glass like crystal; and in the midst of the throne, and around the throne, were four living creatures full of eyes before and behind.
7. The first creature was like a lion, the second creature like a bull, the third creature had a face like a man, and the fourth creature was like a flying eagle.
8. And the four living creatures each had six wings about him; and they were full of eyes around and within; and they do not rest day and night, saying, holy, holy, holy Lord God Almighty, who was, and is, and is to come.
9. And when those living creatures give glory and honor and thanks to Him who sits on the throne, who is living into the New Covenant Age from the Old Covenant Age.
10. The twenty-four elders fall down before Him who sits on the throne, and worship Him who is living into the New Covenant Age from the Old Covenant Age, and cast their crowns before the throne, saying,
11. You are worthy, O Lord, to receive glory and honor and power; for You have created all things and for Your will they exist and were created.

Chapter 5

1. So, I saw in the right hand of Him that sat on the throne a book written inside and on the backside, sealed with seven seals.
2. Then I saw a strong angel proclaiming with a loud voice, who is worthy to open the book, and to loosen the seals?
3. And no one in the heavens, nor the earth, neither under the earth, was able to open the book, neither to behold it.
4. So, I wept much because no one was found worthy to open and to read the book, neither to behold it.
5. Then one of the elders says to me, cease weeping; behold, the Lion of the tribe of Judah, the Root of David, has overcome to open the book, and to loosen the seven seals.

Revelation 5:6

6. And I perceived, and, behold, in the midst of the throne and of the four living creatures, and in the midst of the elders, a Lamb standing as having been slain, having seven horns and seven eyes which are the seven Spirits of God sent out into all the land.
7. Then He came and took the book out of the right hand of Him that sat upon the throne.
8. And when He had taken the book, the four living creatures and twenty-four elders fell down before the Lamb, having every one of them harps, and golden bowls full of incense, which are the prayers of saints.
9. So, they sang a new song, saying, You are worthy to take the book and to open the seals; for You were slain, and have redeemed us to God by Your blood out of every tribe, and tongue, and people, and nation;
10. And have made us to our God, a kingdom and priests; and we will be reigning over the earth.
11. So, I beheld, and I heard the voice of many angels around the throne and the living creatures and the elders, and the number of them was countless upon countless, and thousands upon thousands;
12. Saying with a loud voice, worthy is the Lamb who was slain to receive power, and riches, and wisdom, and strength, and honor, and glory, and blessing.
13. Then all creation which is in the heavens, and over the earth, and subduing the earth, and such as are in the sea, and all that are in them, I heard saying, blessing, and honor, and glory, and power, be to Him that is sitting upon the throne, and to the Lamb into the New Covenant Age from the Old Covenant Age.
14. The four living creatures said, Amen. And the elders fell down and worshipped.

Chapter 6

1. Then I saw when the Lamb opened one of the seals, and I heard, as it were the voice of thunder, one of the four living creatures saying, come and see!
2. And I saw, and behold a white horse, and he that sat on him had a bow; and a crown was given to him, and he went out conquering, and that he would be conquering.
3. And when He had opened the second seal, I heard the second living creature say, come and see!
4. And there went out another red horse, and power was given to him that sat on it to take peace from the land and that they should kill one another, and there was given to him a mammoth sword.
5. And when He had opened the third seal, I heard the third living creature say, come and see! And I beheld, and look a black horse, and he that sat on him had a pair of balances in his hand.
6. Then I heard a voice in the midst of the four living creatures say, a measure of wheat for a denarius, and three measures of barley for a denarius; and see you hurt not the oil and the wine.

7. And when He had opened the fourth seal, I heard the voice of the fourth living creature say, come and see!
8. And I looked, and behold a pale green horse, and his name that sat on him was Death, and Hades followed with him. And authority was given to them over a fourth of the land, to kill in sword, and in famine, and in death, and through the wild beasts of the land.
9. When He had opened the fifth seal, I saw underneath the altar the souls of them that were slaughtered for the Word of God, and for the testimony which they held;
10. so, they cried with a loud voice, saying, how long, O Lord, holy and true, are you not judging and avenging our blood on them that dwell on the land?
11. Then white robes were given to all of them; and it was said to them, that they should rest yet for a little time, until their fellow slaves also and their brothers, who were about to be killed as they were, should be completed.
12. And I beheld when He had opened the sixth seal, and, behold, there was a great earthquake, and the sun became black as sackcloth of hair, and the whole moon became as blood;
13. And the stars of the heavens fell into the land, just as a fig tree casts her untimely figs when she is shaken by a mighty wind.
14. And the heavens depart apart as a scroll when it is rolled up, and every mountain and island were moved out of their places.
15. Then the kings of the land, and the great men, and the rich men, and the chief captains, and the mighty men, and every slave, and every free man, hid themselves in the caves and the rocks of the mountains;
16. And said to the mountains and rocks, fall on us, and hide us from the face of Him that sits on the throne, and from the wrath of the Lamb;
17. For the great day of His wrath has come; and who will be able to stand?

Chapter 7

1. After these things I saw four angels standing on the four corners of the land, holding the four winds of the land, that the wind should not blow on the land, nor the sea, nor any tree.
2. And I saw another angel ascending from the east, having the seal of the living God; and he cried with a loud voice to the four angels, to whom it was given to hurt the land and the sea,
3. Saying, hurt not the land, neither the sea nor the trees until we have sealed the slaves of our God on their foreheads.
4. For I heard the number of those who were sealed; and there were sealed one hundred and forty-four thousand of all the tribes of the children of Israel.
5. Of the tribe of Judah were sealed twelve thousand. Of the tribe of Reuben were sealed twelve thousand. Of the tribe of Gad were sealed twelve thousand.
6. Of the tribe of Asher were sealed twelve thousand. Of the tribe of Naphtali were sealed twelve thousand. Of the tribe of Manasseh were sealed twelve thousand.

7. Of the tribe of Simeon were sealed twelve thousand. Of the tribe of Levi were sealed twelve thousand. Of the tribe of Issachar were sealed twelve thousand.
8. Of the tribe of Zebulon were sealed twelve thousand. Of the tribe of Joseph were sealed twelve thousand. Of the tribe of Benjamin were sealed twelve thousand.
9. After this I saw, and, behold, a great multitude, who no man could number, of all nations, and tribes, and people, and tongues, stood before the throne, and before the Lamb, clothed with white robes, and palms in their hands;
10. And cried with a loud voice, saying, salvation to our God who is sitting on the throne, and to the Lamb.
11. And all the angels stood around the throne, and about the elders and the four living creatures, and fell before the throne on their faces, and worshiped God,
12. Saying, Amen; blessing, and glory, and wisdom, and thanksgiving, and honor, and power, and might, be to our God into the New Covenant Age from the Old Covenant Age. Amen.
13. And one of the elders answered, saying to me, who are these who are arrayed in white robes? From where do they come?
14. So, I said to him, sir, you know. And he said to me, these are they who are coming out of the great tribulation and have washed their robes, and made them white in the blood of the Lamb.
15. Therefore, they are before the throne of God, and serving Him day and night in His temple, and He that is sitting on the throne will stretch His tabernacle over them.
16. They will hunger no more, neither thirst any longer; neither will the sun beat downward on them, nor any heat.
17. For the Lamb who is in the midst of the throne will be shepherding them, and leading them over to the fountains of living waters, and God will be wiping away every tear from their eyes.

Chapter 8

1. When He had opened the seventh seal, there was silence in the heavens for about a half hour.
2. And I saw the seven angels who stood before God, and to them were given seven trumpets.
3. Another angel came and stood at the altar, having a golden censer; and there was given to him much incense, that he should offer it with the prayers of all saints on the golden altar which was before the throne.
4. For the smoke of the incense, which came with the prayers of the saints, ascended up before God out of the hand of the angel.
5. And the angel took the censer, and loaded it with fire from the altar, and hurled it into the land, and there were voices, and thundering, and lightning, and an earthquake.
6. Then the seven angels who had the seven trumpets prepared themselves for trumpeting.

7. The first angel trumpeted, and there came hail and fire mingled with blood, and they were hurled on the land; and the third part of the land was burnt up, a third of the trees was burnt up, and all green grass was burnt up.
8. And the second angel trumpeted, and something like a great mountain burning with fire was hurled into the sea, and the third part of the sea became blood;
9. And the third part of the creatures which were in the sea, and had life, died; and the third part of the ships were destroyed.
10. Then the third angel trumpeted, and there fell a great star from the heavens, burning as it were a torch, and it fell on the third part of the rivers, and the fountains of waters;
11. The name of the star is called Wormwood, and the third part of the waters became Wormwood, and many men died of the waters because they were made bitter.
12. And the fourth angel trumpeted, and the third part of the sun was smitten, and the third part of the moon, and the third part of the stars; so as the third part of them was darkened, and the day shone not for a third part of it, and the night likewise.
13. So, I beheld, and heard an eagle flying through the mid-heavens, saying with a loud voice, woe, woe, woe, to those that dwell upon the land because of the remaining blasts of the trumpet of the other three angels, which are about to be trumpeting!

Chapter 9

1. And the fifth angel trumpeted, and I saw a star fall from the heavens to the earth, and to him was given the key of the bottomless pit.
2. So, he opened the Abyss; and there arose a smoke out of the well, as the smoke of a burning furnace; and the sun and the air were darkened because of the smoke of the well.
3. Then there came out of the smoke locusts on the land; and to them was given authority, as the scorpions of the land have authority.
4. For it was commanded them that they should not hurt the grass of the land, neither any green thing, neither any tree; but only those men which have not the seal of God on their foreheads.
5. And to them it was given that they should not kill them, but that they should be tormented five months, and their torment was as the torment of a scorpion when he strikes a man.
6. And in those days will men seek death, and will not find it; and will desire to die, and death will flee from them.
7. The shapes of the locusts were like horses prepared for battle, and on their heads were crowns like gold, and their faces were like the faces of men.
8. They had hair as the hair of women, and their teeth were like the teeth of lions.
9. They had breastplates, as it were breastplates of iron; and the sound of their wings was as the sound of chariots, of many horses running to battle.

10. They had tails like scorpions, and there were stings in their tails, and they were authorized to hurt men for five months.

11. They had a king over them, which is the angel of the Abyss, whose name in the Hebrew tongue is Abaddon, but in the Greek tongue has his name Apollyon.

12. One woe is past; and, behold, there come two woes more after that.

13. Then the sixth angel sounded, and I heard a voice from the four horns of the golden altar which is before God,

14. Saying to the sixth angel who had the trumpet, loosen the four angels who are bound in the great river Euphrates.

15. So, the four angels were released, who were prepared for an hour, and a day, and a month, and a year, to slay the third of men.

16. And the number of the army of the horsemen were myriads upon myriads, and I heard the number of them.

17. Thus, I saw the horses in the vision, and them that sat on them, having breastplates of fire, and of hyacinth, and sulfur; and the heads of the horses were as the heads of lions; and out of their mouths issued fire and smoke and brimstone.

18. By these three the third of men were killed, out of the fire, and out of the smoke, and out of the brimstone, which issued out of their mouths.

19. Because their authority is in their mouths, and their tails; for their tails were like serpents and had heads, and in them they do damage.

20. And the rest of the men which were not put to death in these calamities did not repent of the works of their hands, that they should not worship demons, and idols of gold, and silver, and brass, and stone, and of wood; which neither can see, nor hear, nor walk;

21. Neither did they repent of their murders, nor from their sorceries, nor their sexual immoralities, nor their thefts.

Chapter 10

1. Then I saw another powerful angel come down from the heavens, clothed with the cloud; and a rainbow was on His head, and His face was as the sun, and His legs as pillars of fire;

2. He had in His hand a little open book, and He put His right foot on the sea, and His left foot on the land,

3. And cried with a loud voice, as when a lion roars; and when He had cried, seven thunders uttered their voices.

4. And when the seven thunders had uttered their voices, I was about to write; and I heard a voice from the heavens saying to me, seal up those things which the seven thunders uttered, and do not write them.

5. And the angel whom I saw stand on the sea and the land lifts up His right hand to the heavens,

6. And swore in Him that is living into the New Covenant Age from the Old Covenant Age, who created the heavens, and the things that are in it, and the earth, and the things that are in it, and the sea, and the things which are in it, that time will not be delayed any longer;

7. But in the days of the seventh angel's voice, when he is about to trumpet, the mystery of God is fulfilled, as He has declared to His slaves the prophets.
8. Then the voice which I heard from the heavens spoke to me again, and said, go and take the little book which is open in the hand of the angel who stands on the sea and upon the land.
9. So, I went to the angel, and said to him, give me the little book. And he said to me, take it, and eat it up; and it will make your stomach bitter, but it will be in your mouth sweet as honey.
10. So, I took the little book out of the hand of the angel, and ate it up, and it was in my mouth sweet as honey; and as soon as I had eaten it, my stomach was made bitter.
11. Then he said to me, you must prophesy again before many peoples, and nations, and tongues, and kings.

Chapter 11

1. Then there was given me a measuring rod like unto a pole; and the angel stood, saying, rise, and measure the temple of God, and the altar, and them that worship in it.
2. But the court which is outside the temple leave out, and do not measure it; for it is given to the nations; and the holy city they will be treading it under foot for forty-two months.
3. And I will give to My two witnesses, and they will prophesy a thousand two hundred and sixty days, clothed in sackcloth.
4. These are the two olive trees, and the two lampstands standing before the God of the land.
5. And if anyone will injure them, fire proceeds out of their mouth, and devours their enemies; and if anyone will injure them, he must in this manner be put to death.
6. These have authority to shut the heavens that no rain falls in the days of their prophesying; and have authority over waters to change them into blood, and to smite the land with all calamities, as often as they will.
7. When they have finished their testimony, the wild beast that ascends out of the Abyss will make war against them, and will overcome them, and put them to death.
8. And their dead bodies will lie in the street of the great city, which spiritually is called Sodom and Egypt, where also our Lord was crucified.
9. And out of the people and tribes and tongues and nations will behold their dead bodies three and a half days, and will not permit their dead bodies to be put into tombs.
10. So, they that dwell on the land will rejoice over them, and make merry, and will send gifts one to another; because these two prophets tormented them that reside upon the land.
11. But after three and a half days the Spirit of life out of God entered in them, and they stood on their feet; and great fear fell upon those who beheld them.
12. And they heard a great voice from the heavens saying to them, come up here. And they ascended up to the heavens in the cloud; and their enemies beheld them.

Revelation 11:13

13. The same hour there was a great earthquake, and the tenth part of the city fell, and in the earthquake were seven thousand men slain; and those remaining were terrified, and gave glory to the God of the heavens.
14. The second woe is past; and, behold, the third woe comes rapidly.
15. And the seventh angel trumpeted; and there were great voices in the heavens, saying, the kingdom of this world have become to be of our Lord and of His Christ; and He will reign into the New Covenant Age
16. from the Old Covenant Age.
17. So, the twenty-four elders, who sat before God on their thrones, fell on their faces, and worshiped God,
18. Saying, we are thanking You, O Lord God Almighty, who is, and was, and is to come; because You have taken Your great power, and have begun to reign.
19. The people were furious; therefore Your wrath has come, and the time of the dead that they should be judged, and that You should give rewards to Your slaves the prophets, and to the saints, and them that fear Your name, small and great; and should destroy those who corrupt the land.
20. And the temple of God was opened in the heavens, and there was seen in His temple, the Ark of the Covenant; and there were lightnings, and voices, and thunders, and an earthquake, and a great hail.

Revelation 12:9

Chapter 12

1. And there appeared a great sign in the heavens; a woman clothed with the sun, and the moon under her feet, and on her head a crown of twelve stars;
2. So, she had in her womb crying out, travailing in labor, and being distressed to bring forth.
3. Then there appeared another sign in the heavens; and behold a great fiery red dragon, having seven heads and ten horns, and seven crowns on his heads.
4. And his tail dragging the third of the stars of the heavens, and did hurl them into the land; and the dragon stood before the woman who was about to give birth, to devour her son as soon as it was born.
5. For she brought out a male son, who was about to shepherd all the nations with a staff of iron; and her son was caught up to God, and to His throne.
6. Then the woman escaped into the wilderness, where she had a place prepared by God that they should nurture her there a thousand two hundred and sixty days.
7. So, there was war in the heavens; Michael and His messengers fought against the dragon; and the dragon fought and his messengers,
8. And prevailed not; neither was their place found anymore in the heavens.
9. For the great dragon was cast out, that old serpent, called the devil, and Satan, who is deceiving the Roman world; he was cast out into the land, and his messengers were cast out with him.

10. Then I heard a loud voice saying in the heavens, now has come salvation, and power, and the kingdom of our God, and the authority of His Christ; for the accuser of our brothers was hurled down, who accused them before our God Day and night.

11. So, they overcame him by the blood of the Lamb, and by the word of their testimony, and they loved not their soul lives even to death.

12. Therefore, rejoice, you heavens, and you that dwell in them. Woe to the inhabitants of the land and of the sea! For the devil has come down to you, having great wrath, because he knows that he has but a little time appointed.

13. When the dragon saw that he was cast to the land, he persecuted the woman who brought forth the man child.

14. And the woman was given two wings of a great eagle that she might fly into the wilderness, into her place, where she is nurtured for a time, and times, and half a time, from the presence of the serpent.

15. And the serpent cast out of his mouth water as a flood after the woman that he might cause her to be carried away by the flood.

16. But the land opened her mouth, which helped the woman, and swallowed up the flood which the dragon cast out of his mouth.

17. And the dragon was very angry with the woman and went to make war with those remaining of her offspring, who keep the commandments of God, and have the testimony of Jesus Christ.

Chapter 13

1. So, I stood on the sand of the sea and saw a wild beast rise up out of the sea, having seven heads and ten horns, and on his horns ten crowns, and on his heads the name of blasphemy.

2. For the wild beast which I saw was like a leopard, and his feet were as the feet of a bear, and his mouth as the mouth of a lion, and the dragon gave him his power, and his throne, and great authority.

3. Then I saw one of his heads that it had been slaughtered to death, and his death blow was healed, and the whole land wondered after the wild beast.

4. So, they worshiped the dragon which gave authority to the wild beast; and they worshiped the wild beast, saying, who is like the wild beast? Who can make war with him?

5. For there was given to him a mouth speaking great things and blasphemies; and authority was given to him to continue forty-two months.

6. Then he opened his mouth in blasphemy against God, to blaspheme His name and His tabernacle, those that tabernacle in the heavens.

7. And it was granted to him to make war with the saints, and to overcome them, and authority was given to him over all tribes, and tongues, and nations.

8. So, all that dwell on the land will worship him, whose names are not written in the book of the life of the Lamb slain from the downfall of the world.

9. If anyone has an ear, let him hear.
10. He that leads into captivity will go into captivity; he that kills with the sword must be killed with the sword. Here is the perseverance and the faith of the saints.
11. And I beheld another beast coming up out of the land, and he had two horns like a lamb, and he spoke as a dragon.
12. And he exercises all the authority of the first wild beast before him and causes those who dwell in the land to worship the first wild beast, whose death blow was healed.
13. And he does great wonders so that he makes fire come down from the heavens on the land in the sight of men,
14. But deceives them that dwell on the land through those signs which he had been given to do in front of the wild beast; saying to them that dwell on the land, that they should make an image to the wild beast, who was struck by the sword, and is alive.
15. For he had been granted to give breath to the image of the wild beast, that the image of the wild beast would both speak and cause as many as would not worship the image of the wild beast would be killed.
16. So, he causes all, both small and great, rich and poor, free and slave, to receive a mark on their right hand, or on their foreheads;
17. So that no man might buy or sell, except he that had the mark, or the name of the wild beast, or the number of his name.
18. Here is wisdom. Let him that has understanding calculate the number of the wild beast; for it is the number of a man, and his number is six hundred sixty-six.

Chapter 14

1. Then I looked, and behold, a Lamb stood on the mount Zion, and with Him a hundred and forty-four thousand, having His Father's name written on their foreheads.
2. And I heard a voice out of the heavens, as the voice of many waters, and as the voice of a great thunder; and I heard the voice of harp singers playing upon their harps;
3. And they were singing a new song before the throne, and before the four living creatures, and the elders; and no one could learn that song but the hundred and forty-four thousand, who were redeemed from the land.
4. These are they who were not defiled with women; for they are the virgins. These are they which follow the Lamb wherever He is going. These were redeemed from among men, the first fruits of God, and to the Lamb.
5. And in their mouth was found no falsehood; for they are flawless before the throne of God.
6. Then I saw another messenger fly in the midst of the heavens, having the perpetual gospel to preach to them that dwell on the land, and even the whole nation, and kindred, and tongue, and people.
7. Saying with a loud voice, be terrified of God, and give glory to Him; for the hour of His judgment has come; and worship Him that made the heavens, and the earth, and the sea, and the fountains of waters!
8. Then there followed another angel, saying, Babylon is fallen, is fallen, that great city, because she made all nations drink of the wine of the passion of her fornication.

9. And the third angel followed them, saying with a loud voice, if any man worships the wild beast and his image, and receive his mark on his forehead, or on his hand,
10. The same will drink of the wine of the wrath of God, which is poured out unmixed into the cup of His indignation; and he will be tormented with fire and brimstone in the presence of the holy angels, and in the presence of the Lamb;
11. For the smoke of their torment is ascending up into the New Covenant Age from the Old Covenant Age; and they have no rest either day or night, who worship the wild beast and his image, and whoever receives the mark of his name.
12. Here is the perseverance of the saints; here are they that obey the commandments of God, and the faith of Jesus.
13. Then I heard a voice out of the heavens saying to me, write, blessed are the dead which are dying in the Lord from now on; yes, says the Spirit that they may rest from their labors, and their works do follow them.
14. So, I looked, and behold a white cloud, and on the cloud, one sat like the Son of man, having on His head a golden crown, and in His hand a sharp sickle.
15. Yet another angel came out of the temple, crying with a loud voice to Him that sat on the cloud, thrust in your sickle, and reap; for the time has come for you to reap; for the harvest of the land is withering away.
16. So, He that sat on the cloud thrust in His sickle on the land; and the land was reaped.
17. Then another angel came out of the temple which is in the heavens, he also had a sharp sickle.
18. Yet another angel came out from the altar, who had authority over fire; and cried with a loud cry to him that had the sharp sickle, saying, thrust in your sharp sickle, and gather the clusters of the vine of the land; for her grape clusters have come to maturity.
19. So, the angel thrust in his sickle into the land, and gathered the vine of the land, and cast it into the great winepress of the wrath of God.
20. For the winepress was trodden outside the city, and blood came out of the winepress, even to the horse bridles, by the space of a thousand six hundred stadia.

Chapter 15

1. Then I saw another sign in the heavens, great and marvelous, seven angels having the seven last calamities; for in them is completed the wrath of God.
2. For I saw as it were a sea of glass mingled with fire; and those that had gained the victory over the wild beast, and over his image, and over his mark, and over the number of his name, standing on the sea of glass, having the harps of God.
3. So, they sing the song of Moses the servant of God, and the song of the Lamb, saying, great and marvelous are Your works, Lord God Almighty; just and true are Your ways, You King of the nations.
4. Who will not fear you, O Lord, and glorify Your name? For You only are holy; for all nations will come and worship before You; for Your judgments are made manifest.

5. And after that I looked, and, behold, the temple of the tabernacle of the testimony in the heavens was opened;
6. Then the seven angels came out of the temple, having the seven calamities, clothed in pure and white linen, and having their chests wrapped with golden sashes.
7. So, one of the four living creatures gave to the seven angels seven golden bowls full of the wrath of God, who is living into the New Covenant Age from the Old Covenant Age.
8. For the temple was filled with smoke from the glory of God, and from His power, and no one was able to enter into the temple until the seven calamities of the seven angels were completed.

Chapter 16

1. I heard a great voice out of the temple saying to the seven angels, go and pour out the seven bowls of the wrath of God into the land.
2. So, the first went, and poured out his bowl into the land, and there fell loathsome and malignant sores on the men who had the mark of the wild beast, and on those who worshiped his image.
3. Then the second poured out his bowl into the sea, and it became as the blood of a dead man, and every living soul died in the sea.
4. And the third poured out his bowl into the rivers and fountains of waters, and they became blood.
5. Then I heard the angel of the waters say, You are righteous, O Lord who is and was because You have so judged these.
6. For they have shed the blood of saints and prophets, and You have given them blood to drink; for they deserve it!
7. And I heard another out of the altar say, even so, Lord God Almighty, true and righteous are Your judgments.
8. So, the fourth poured out his bowl upon the sun, and it was given to scorch men with fire.
9. And men were scorched with great heat, and blasphemed the name of God, Who holds the authority over these calamities; yet they did not repent to give Him glory.
10. Then the fifth poured out his bowl upon the throne of the wild beast, and his dominion was full of darkness, and they gnawed their tongues for pain,
11. And blasphemed the God of the heavens because of their pains and their sores, and did not repent of their deeds.
12. So, the sixth poured out his bowl upon the great river Euphrates; and the waters themselves dried up, that the way of the kings of the rising of the sun might be prepared.
13. For I saw three unclean spirits like frogs come out of the mouth of the dragon, and out of the mouth of the beast, and out of the mouth of the false prophet.
14. For they are the spirits of demons, doing signs, who go out to the rulers of the land and the Roman world, to gather them to the battle of that great day of God Almighty.

15. Behold, I am coming as a thief. Blessed is he that is watching, and keeping his garments, unless he is walking naked, and they are seeing his indecency.
16. So, he gathered them together into a place called in Hebrew, Armageddon.
17. And the seventh poured out his bowl into the air; and there came a great voice out of the temple from the throne, saying, it is done!
18. So there were voices, and thunders, and bolts of lightning; and there was a great earthquake, such as was not since men were upon the land, so mighty an earthquake, and so great.
19. Then the great city was divided into three parts, and the city of the people fell; and great Babylon was remembered before God, to give to her the cup of the wine of the fierceness of His wrath.
20. For every island fled away, and the mountains were not found.
21. And there fell on men a great hail out of the heavens, every stone about the weight of a talent; and men blasphemed God because of the calamity of the hail; for the calamity of it was intensely significant.

Chapter 17

1. Then there came one of the seven angels who had the seven bowls, and spoke with me, saying to me, here; I will show to you the judgment of the great prostitute that is sitting on many waters;
2. With whom the kings of the land have practiced prostitution and the inhabitants of the land have been made drunk with the wine of her fornication.
3. Then he transported me in spirit into the wilderness; and I saw a woman sitting on a scarlet wild beast, full of names of blasphemy, having seven heads and ten horns.
4. For the woman was arrayed in purple and scarlet, and decked with gold and precious stones and pearls, having a golden cup in her hand full of abominations and the uncleanness of her fornications;
5. And on her forehead was a name written, MYSTERY, BABYLON THE GREAT, THE MOTHER OF PROSTITUTES AND ABOMINATIONS OF THE LAND.
6. So, I saw the woman drunk with the blood of the saints, and with the blood of the witnesses of Jesus; and when I saw her, I wondered greatly.
7. For the angel said to me, why did you wonder? I will tell you the mystery of the woman, and of the wild beast that carries her, which has the seven heads and ten horns.
8. The wild beast that you saw was, and is not; and is about to be ascending out of the Abyss, and going away into destruction; and they that are dwelling upon the land will marvel, whose names were not written in the Book of Life from the downfall of the world, when they behold the wild beast that was and is not, and although is.
9. And here is the mind which has wisdom. The seven heads are seven mountains, which the woman is sitting upon.

10. And there are seven kings; five are fallen, and one is, and the other is not yet come; and when he comes, he must continue briefly.
11. For the wild beast that was, and is not, even he is the eighth and is of the seven, and going into destruction.
12. And the ten horns which you saw are ten kings, who have received no kingdom as yet; but receive authority as kings for one season with the wild beast.
13. These have one purpose and will give their power and authority to the wild beast.
14. These will make war with the Lamb, and the Lamb will overcome them; for He is Lord of lords, and King of kings, and they that are with Him are called, and chosen, and faithful.
15. And he said to me, the waters which you saw, where the prostitute is sitting, are people, and multitudes, and nations, and tongues.
16. For the ten horns which you saw upon the beast, these will hate the prostitute, and will make her desolate and naked, and will eat her flesh, and burn her with fire.
17. For God has put in their hearts to perform His will, and to agree, and give their kingdom to the wild beast, until the words of God will be completed.
18. And the woman which you saw is that great city, which reigns over the kings of the land.

Chapter 18

1. After these things I saw another angel come down from the heavens, having great authority; and the land was irradiated with his glory.
2. And he cried mightily with a strong voice, saying, "fallen, fallen is Babylon the great", and has become the dwelling of demons, and the prison of every foul spirit, and a prison of every unclean and hateful bird.
3. For all the nations have drunk of the wine of the passion of her fornication, and the kings of the region have practiced prostitution with her, and the merchants of the region have grown rich through the influence of her luxuries.
4. Then I heard another voice from the heavens, saying, come out of her My people, so that you will not be an accomplice of her sins, and not receive of her calamities.
5. For her sins have accumulated as far as the heavens, and God has remembered her crimes.
6. Give to her just as she was given to you, and pay her double according to her works; in the cup which she has mixed, pour out to her twice as much.
7. As much as she has glorified herself, and lived luxuriously, so give her much torment and sorrow; for she says in her heart, I sit as a queen, and am no widow, and will see no sorrow.
8. Therefore, her calamities will come in one day, pestilence, and mourning, and famine; and she will be utterly burned with fire; for strong is the Lord God who judges her.
9. For the kings of the region, who have practiced prostitution and lived luxuriously with her, will weep for her, and wail for her, when they see the smoke of her burning,

10. Standing afar off because of the terror of her torment, saying, alas, alas that great city Babylon, that mighty city! For in one hour your judgment has come.

11. So, the merchants of the region will weep and mourn over her; for no one buys their merchandise anymore;

12. The merchandise of gold, and silver, precious stones, pearls, fine linen, and purple, and silk, and scarlet, and all citron wood, and all vessels of ivory, and all vessels of costly wood, and of bronze, and iron, and marble,

13. And cinnamon, and incense, and myrrh, and frankincense, and wine, and olive oil, and fine flour, and wheat, and cattle, and sheep, and horses, and chariots, and bodies and souls of men.

14. For the juicy fruits that your soul desired greatly have departed from you, and all things which were expensive and resplendent have departed from you, and you will not find them anymore.

15. The merchants of these things, who were made rich by her, will stand afar off for the fear of her torment, weeping and wailing,

16. And saying, alas, alas that great city, that was clothed in fine linen, and purple, and scarlet, and decked with gold, and precious stones, and pearls!

17. For in one hour so many riches have been made desolate. And every shipmaster, and all the voyagers in ships, and sailors, and as many as trade by sea, stood far off,

18. And cried when they saw the smoke of her burning, saying, what city is like this great city?

19. So, they threw dust on their heads, and cried, weeping and wailing, saying, alas, alas that great city, in which were made rich all that had ships in the sea because of her wealth! For in one hour, she was made desolate.

20. Rejoice over her, you heavens, and you saints and apostles and prophets; for God has condemned and passed judgment on her.

21. A mighty angel took up a stone like a great millstone, and threw it into the sea, saying, in this way with sudden violence that great city Babylon will be thrown down, and will no longer be found.

22. So, the voice of harpers and musicians, and flute players, and trumpeters, will be heard no longer in you; and no craftsman, of whatever trade he is, will be found any longer in you and the sound of a millstone will be heard no longer in you;

23. Then the light of a lamp will shine no longer in you, and the voice of the bridegroom and the bride will be heard no longer in you; for your merchants were the great men of the land; for by your sorceries were all nations deceived.

24. For in her was found the blood of prophets, and of saints, and of all that were slain upon the land.

Chapter 19

1. And after these things I heard a great voice of many people in the heavens, saying, Alleluia; salvation, and glory, and honor, and power, to the Lord our God;

2. Because real and righteous are His decisions; because He has judged the great prostitute, who did corrupt the land with her fornication, and has avenged the blood of His slaves.
3. Yet again they said, Alleluia and her smoke is ascending into the New Covenant Age from the Old Covenant Age.
4. Then the twenty-four elders and the four living creatures fell down and worshiped God who sat on the throne, saying, Amen; Alleluia.
5. And a voice came out of the throne, saying, praise our God, all you His slaves, and you that fear Him, both small and great.
6. And I heard as it were the voice of a great multitude, and as the voice of many waters, and as the voice of mighty thundering, saying, Alleluia; for the Lord God Almighty reigns.
7. Let us be glad and rejoice, and give honor to Him; for the marriage of the Lamb has come, His wife has prepared herself.
8. So, to her was granted that she should be arrayed in fine linen, clean and white; for the fine linen is the righteousness's of the saints.
9. Then he said to me, write, blessed are they which are called to the marriage supper of the Lamb. So, he said to me, these are the real sayings of God.
10. So, I fell at his feet to worship him. Then he said to me, look, no, I am your fellow servant, and of your brothers that have the testimony of Jesus; worship God; for the testimony of Jesus is the spirit of prophecy.

11. And I saw the heavens opened, and behold a white horse, and He that sat on him was called Faithful and Genuine, and in righteousness, He is judging and making war.
12. His eyes were as a flame of fire, and on His head were many crowns, and He had a name written, that no one knew, but He Himself.
13. For He was clothed with a robe dipped in blood, and His name is called The Word of God.
14. Then the armies who were in the heavens followed Him on white horses, clothed in fine linen, white and clean.
15. And out of His mouth goes a sharp sword, that with it He may smite the people; and He will shepherd them with a staff of iron, and He treads the winepress of the fierceness and wrath of Almighty God.
16. And He has a name written on His garment and His thigh, KING OF KINGS, AND LORD OF LORDS.
17. Then I saw an angel standing in the sun; and he cried with a loud voice, saying to all the birds that fly in the midst of the heavens, come and gather yourselves together to the supper of the great God;
18. That you may eat the flesh of kings, and the flesh of captains, and the flesh of mighty men, and the flesh of horses, and of those that sit on them, and the flesh of all men, both free and slave, both small and great.
19. So, I saw the wild beast, and the kings of the land, and their armies, gathered together to make war against Him who sat on the horse, and against His army.

20. For the wild beast was taken and with him the false prophet that worked miracles before him, with which he deceived those who had received the mark of the wild beast and those who worshiped his image. These both were cast alive into the lake of fire burning with brimstone.

21. And those remaining were put to death with the sword of Him that sat on the horse, which proceeded out of His mouth; and all the birds were satisfied with their flesh.

Chapter 20

1. Then I saw an angel come down from the heavens, having the key of the Abyss and an enormous chain in his hand.

2. So, he overpowered the dragon, that old serpent, who is the Devil, and Satan, and bound him a thousand years,

3. And threw him into the Abyss, and shut him up, and set a seal on him, that he should deceive the people no further until the thousand years should be fulfilled; and after that, he must be unleashed a short time.

4. So, I saw thrones, and they sat on them, and judgment was given to them, and I saw the souls of them that were decapitated for the witness of Jesus, and for the Word of God, and who had not worshiped the wild beast, neither his image, neither had received his mark upon their forehead and their hand; and they lived and reigned with Christ a thousand years.

5. But the remainder of the dead did not live again until the thousand years were completed. This is the first resurrection.

6. Blessed and holy is he that has a part in the first resurrection; on such the second death has no authority, but they will be priests of God and Christ and will reign with Him for a thousand years.

7. When the thousand years have been completed, Satan will be freed from his prison,

8. And will come out to deceive the people which are in the four corners of the land, Gog, and Magog, to gather them together to battle; the number of whom is as the sand of the sea.

9. For they went up on the breadth of the land, and encircled the stronghold of the saints, and the beloved city; and fire came down from God out of the heavens and devoured them.

10. Then the Devil that deceived them was thrown into the lake of fire and brimstone, where the wild beast and the false prophet are, and will be tormented day and night into the New Covenant Age from the Old Covenant Age.

11. So, I saw a great white throne, and Him that sat on it, from whose face the earth and the heavens fled away; and there was no place found for them.

12. And I saw the dead, small and great, stand before God; and the books were opened; and another book was opened, Who is the Life; and the dead were judged out of those things which were written in the books, according to their works.

13. For the sea gave up the dead which was in it, and Death and Hades delivered up the dead who were in them, and they were judged each one according to his works.

14. Then Death and Hades were cast into the lake of fire. This is the second death.
15. And anyone not found written in the Book of Life was thrown into the lake of fire.

Chapter 21

1. And I saw a new heavens and a new earth; for the first heavens and the first earth had passed away; and there was no sea anymore.
2. Then I John saw the holy city, New Jerusalem, descending from God out of the heavens, prepared as a bride adorned for her husband.
3. Then I heard a great voice out of the heavens saying, Behold, the tabernacle of God is with men, and He will dwell with them, and they will be His people, and God Himself will be with them, and be their God.
4. So, God will wipe away all tears from their eyes; and there will be no more death, neither sorrow, nor crying, neither will there be pain anymore; for the former things have passed away.
5. He that sat on the throne said, behold, I am making all things new! He said to me, write; for these words are faithful and true.
6. And He said to me, it is done! I have become the Alpha and Omega, the Beginning and the End. I will give to him who thirsts out of the fountain of the water of life freely.
7. He that is overcoming will inherit all things, and I will be His God, and he will be My son.
8. But the fearful, and unbelieving, and the abominable, and murderers, and sexually immoral, and sorcerers, and idolaters, and all liars, will have their part in the lake which burns with fire and brimstone; which is the second death.
9. So, there came to me one of the seven angels who had the seven bowls full of the seven last calamities, and spoke with me, saying, here! I will show you the bride, the Lamb's wife.
10. And he transported me in spirit to a massive and high mountain, and showed me the holy city, Jerusalem, descending from God, out of the heavens,
11. Having the glory of God; and her radiance is like a stone most precious, even like a jasper stone, clear as crystal;
12. And had a wall massive and high, and had twelve gates, and at the gates twelve angels, and names inscribed, which are the names of the twelve tribes of the sons of Israel;
13. On the east three gates; on the north three gates; on the south three gates; and the west three gates.
14. For the walls of the city had twelve foundations and in them the names of the twelve apostles of the Lamb.
15. And he that spoke with me had a golden reed to measure the city, and her gates, and her walls.
16. The city lies four corners, and the length is as huge as the width; and he measured the city with the reed, twelve thousand stadia. The length, width, and height of her are equal.
17. Then he measured the walls of her, a hundred and forty-four cubits, a man's measure who is the messenger.

18. So, the building of her walls was of jasper; and the city was pure gold, like clear glass.
19. And the foundations of the walls of the city were garnished with all manner of precious stones. The first foundation was jasper; the second, sapphire; the third, a chalcedony; the fourth, an emerald;
20. The fifth, sardonyx; the sixth, sardius; the seventh, chrysolite; the eighth, beryl; the ninth, a topaz; the tenth, a chrysoprasus; the eleventh, a jacinth; the twelfth, an amethyst.
21. And the twelve gates were twelve pearls; each of the gates was of one pearl; and the street of the city was pure gold, like transparent glass.
22. But I saw no temple in her; for the Lord God Almighty and the Lamb is the temple of her.
23. For the city did not need the sun, neither the moon, to shine in it; for the glory of God did lighten it, and the Lamb is the light of it.
24. And the nations will walk in the light of her, and the kings of the earth will bring their glory and honor into her.
25. And the gates of it will not be shut at all by day; for there will be no night there.
26. For they will bring the glory and honor of the nations into her.
27. And any that are unclean will not ever enter into it, neither whoever practices an abomination, nor fabricating falsehood; but they who are written in the Lamb's Book of Life.

Chapter 22

1. Then he pointed out to me a river of the water of life, shining like crystal, bursting out of the throne of God and of the Lamb.
2. In the midst of her, and on each side of the river, there was the Tree of Life, which bore twelve fruits, and yielded her fruit every month; and the leaves of the tree were for the healing of the nations.
3. So, there will be no curse any longer, but the throne of God and the Lamb will be in her, and His slaves will serve Him;
4. For they will see His face; and His name will be upon their foreheads.
5. And there will be no night there, and they need no lamp, neither light of the sun; for the Lord God gives them light; and they will reign into the New Covenant Age from the Old Covenant Age.
6. Then he said to me, these sayings are faithful and true, and the Lord God of the holy prophets sent His angel to show to His slaves the things which must shortly take place.
7. Behold, I come quickly; blessed is he that keeps the sayings of the prophecy of this book.
8. So, I John saw these things and heard them. And when I had heard and seen, I fell down to worship before the feet of the messenger who showed me these things.
9. Then he said to me, behold do not do that; for I am your fellow slave, and of your brothers the prophets and of those who keep the sayings of this book; worship God!

10. Then he said to me, seal not the sayings of the prophecy of this book; for the time is near!

11. He that is being harmful, let him be harmful still; and he who is being filthy, let him be filthy still; and he that is righteous, let him be affirmed righteous still, and he that is holy, let him be holy still.

12. And, Behold I am coming quickly and my wages are with Me to repay each one according to their works.

13. I am Alpha and Omega, the Beginning and the End, the First and the Last.

14. Blessed are they who are washing their robes, so that they may have the authority to the Tree of Life, and may enter in through the gates into the city.

15. For outside are the dogs, and sorcerers, and the sexually immoral, and murderers, and idolaters, and whoever loves even to fabricate falsehood.

16. I Jesus have sent My messenger to testify to you these things in the Assemblies. I am the Root and the Offspring of David, and the bright Morning Star.

17. And the Spirit and the bride say, "come." And let the one who hears say, "come." And let the thirsty one come; let the one who desires, receive the water of life as a gift.

18. For I witness together with everyone that is hearing the words of the prophecy of this book, if anyone will add to these things, God will add to him the calamities that are written in this book;

19. And if anyone will take away from the words of the book of this prophecy, God will take away his part away from the Tree of Life, and out of the holy city, and from the things which are written in this book.

20. He who bears witness to these things says, yes, I am coming quickly. Amen. Yes, come, Lord Jesus.

21. The grace of our Lord Jesus Christ be with you all! Amen.

Olivet Discourse Charts - Riley Powell

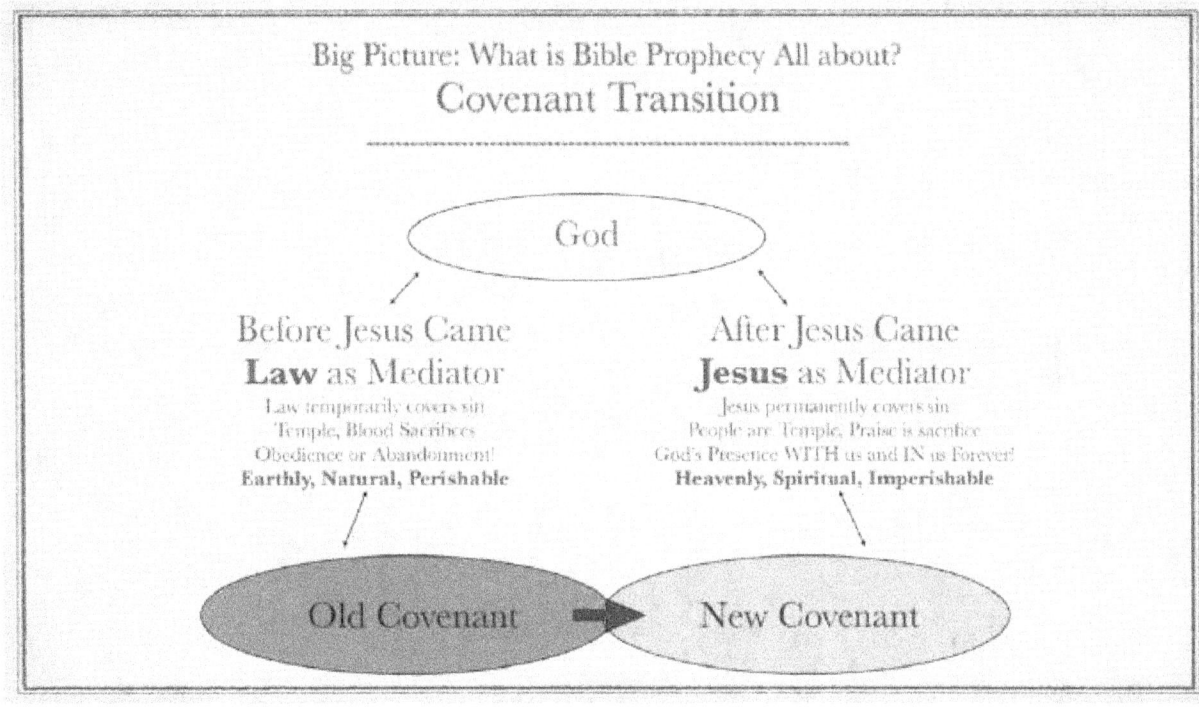

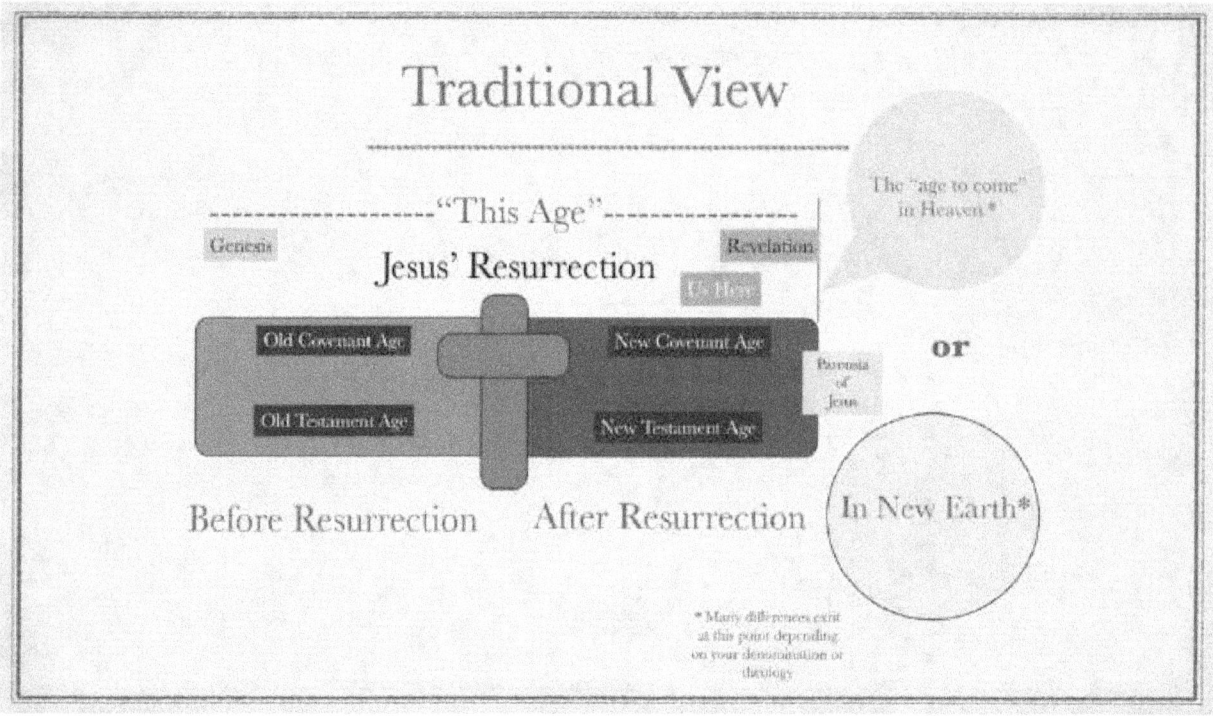

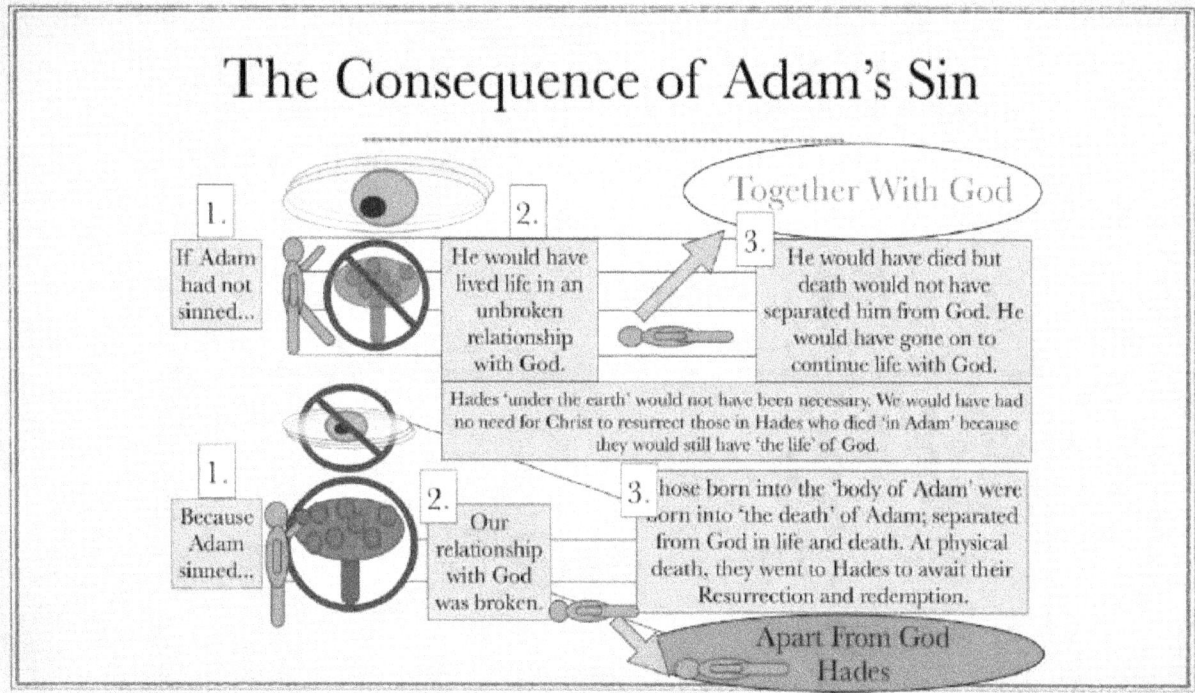

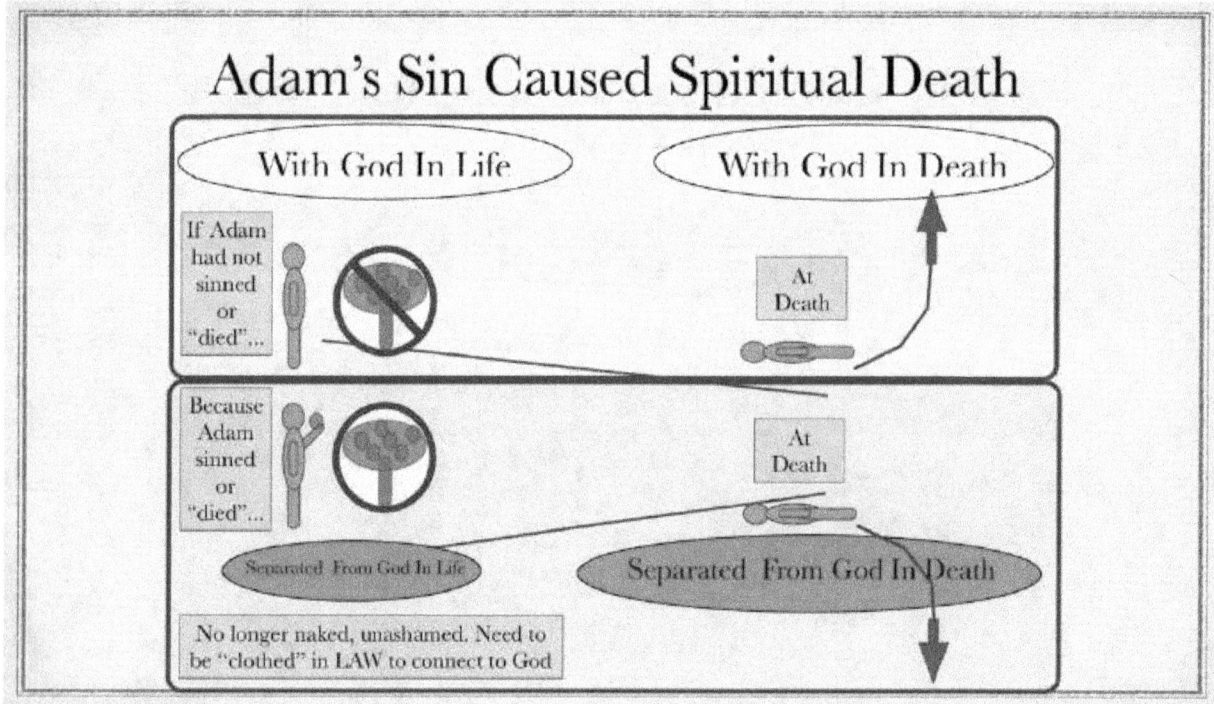

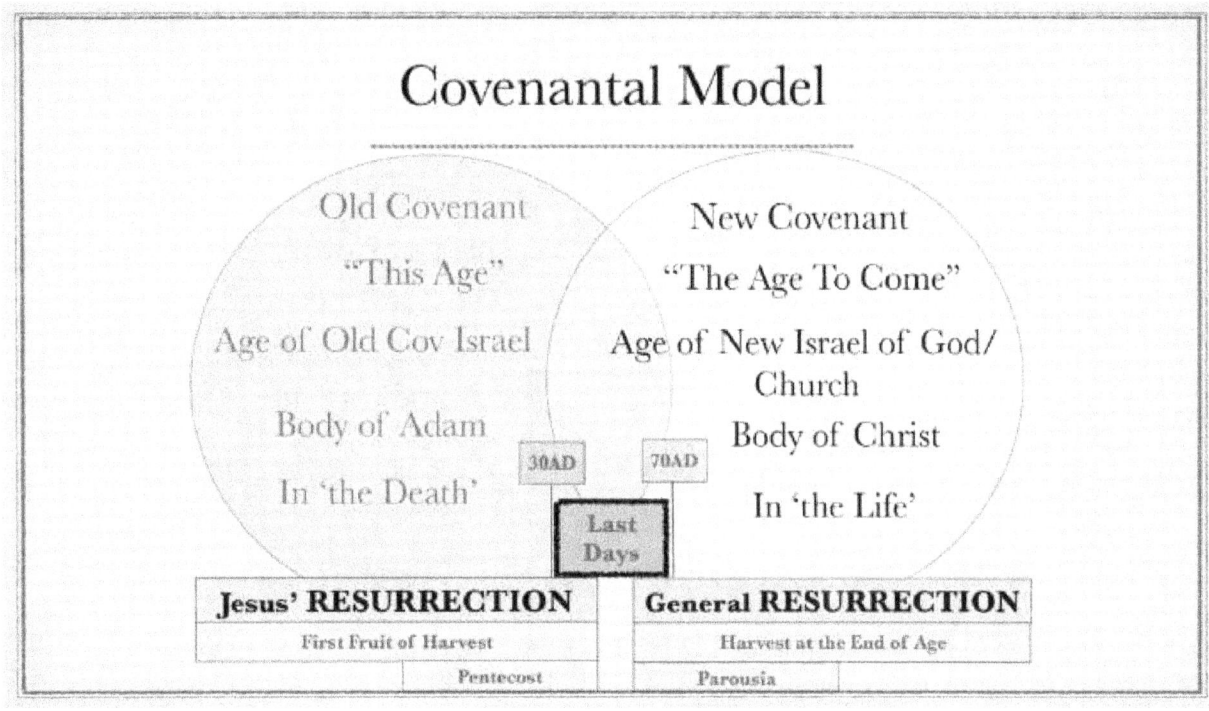

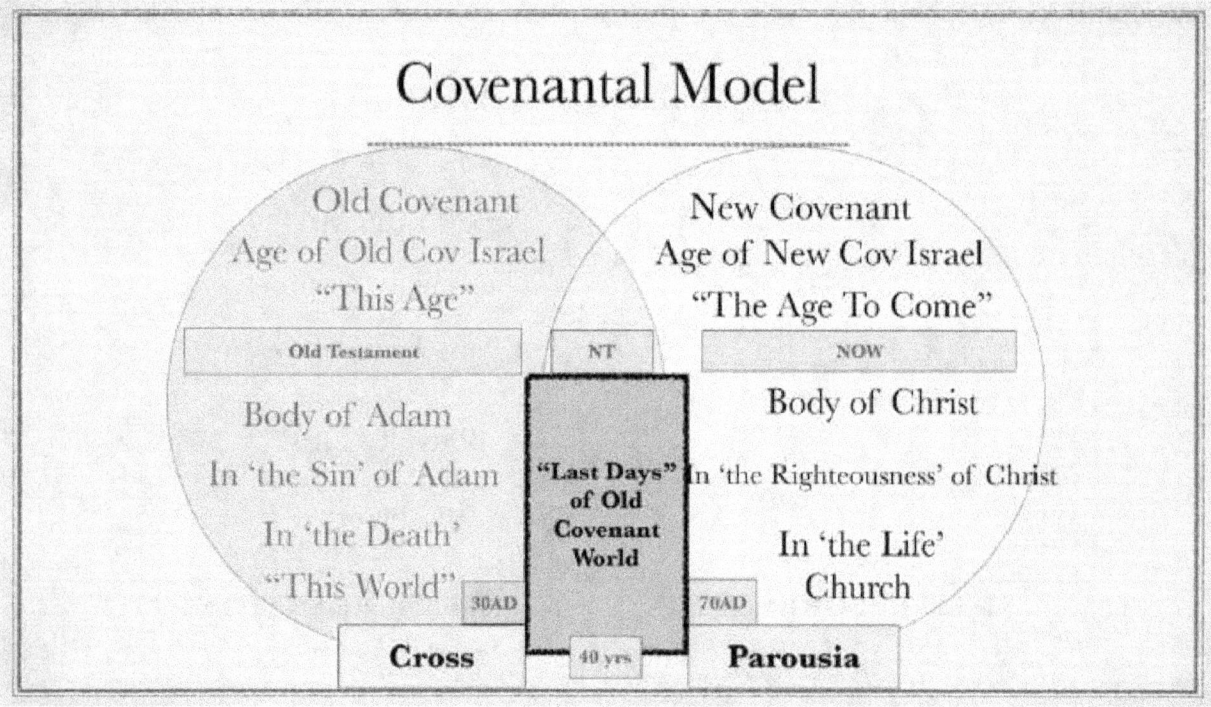

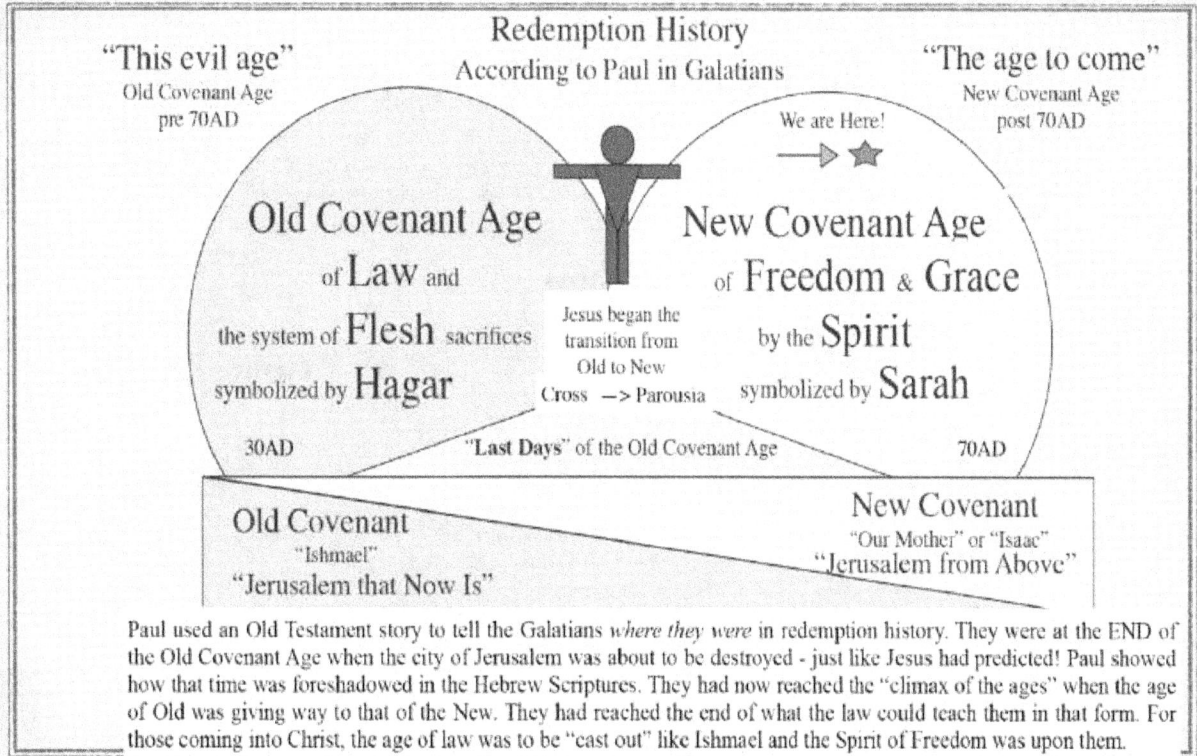

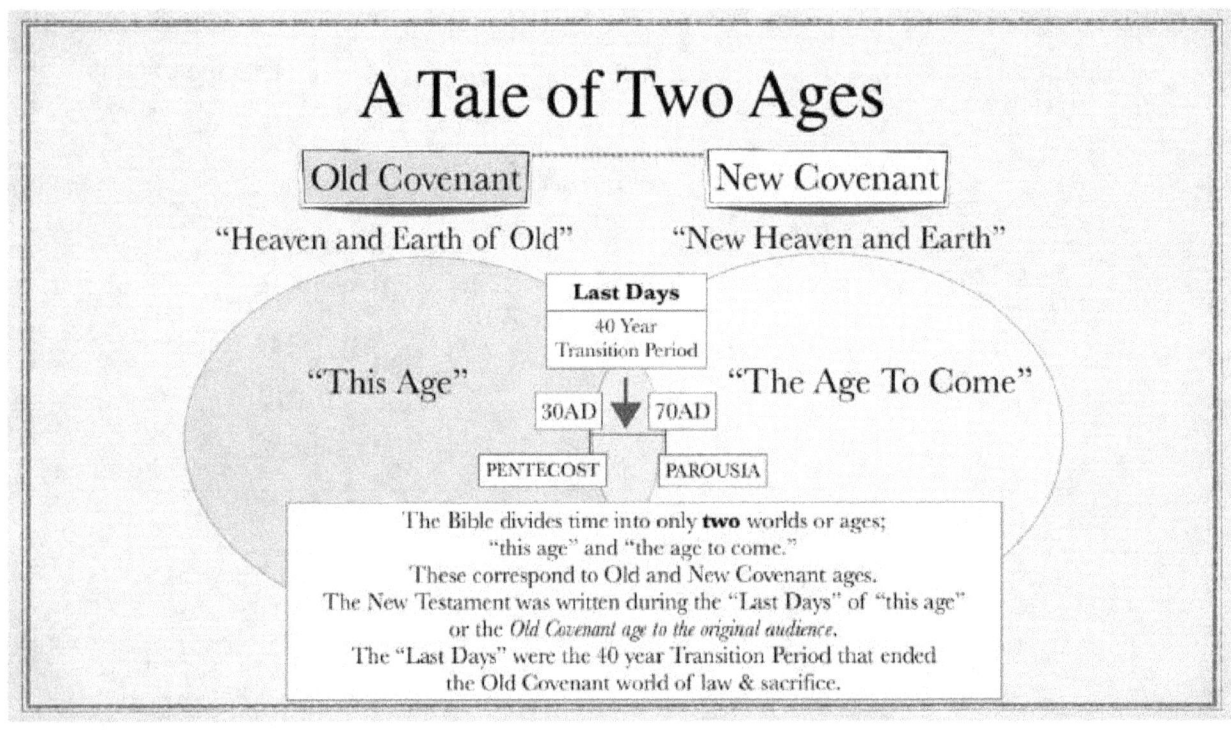

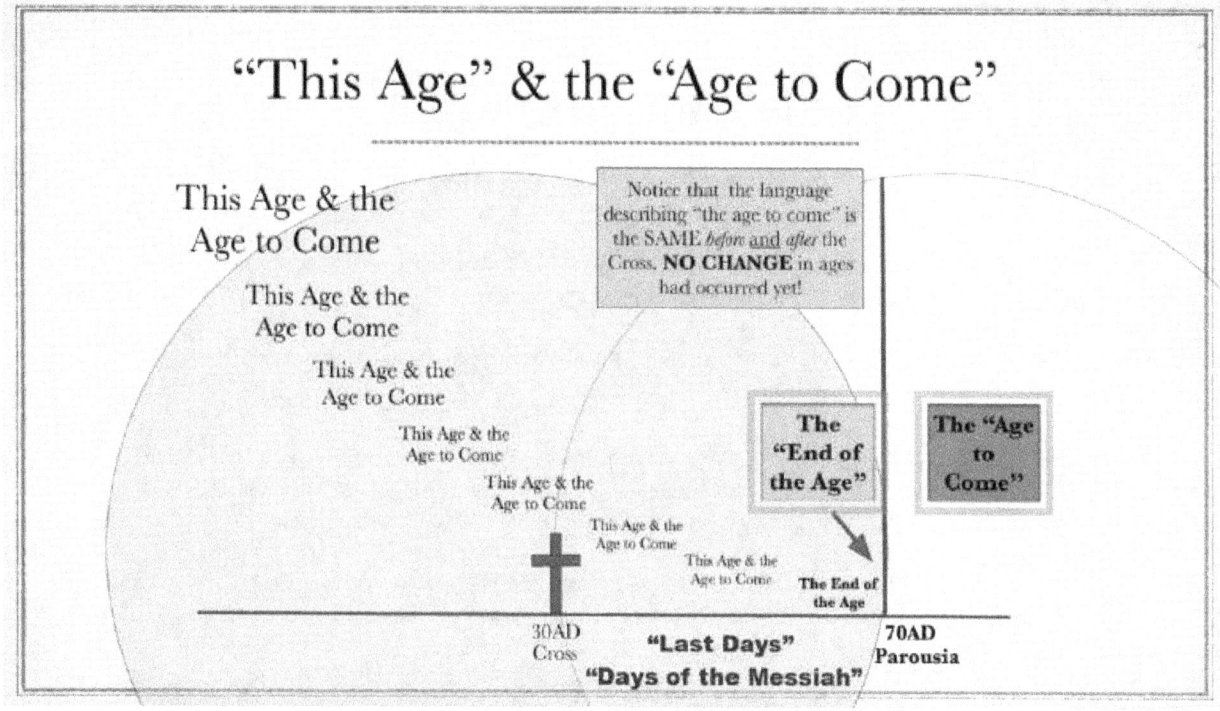

What Age Are We In?

- Matthew 12:32 And whoever speaks a word against the Son of Man will be forgiven, but whoever speaks against the Holy Spirit will not be forgiven, either in **this age** or in **the age to come**.

- Matthew 13:39 ....and the enemy who sowed them is the devil. The **harvest** is the **end of the age**, and the reapers are angels.

- Matthew 24:3 As he sat on the Mount of Olives, the disciples came to him privately, saying, "Tell us, **when** will these things be, and **what** will be the sign of your Coming [*parousia*] and of the end of the age?" [the destruction of the Temple and Jerusalem would be the sign of Jesus' coming and the end of the Old Covenant age].

- Matthew 28:20...teaching them to observe all that I have commanded **YOU**. And behold, I am with you always, to the **end of the age**." [how could Jesus be with them if the End of the Age was something in the far distant future? He taught that the end of the age was coming upon *them*]

What Age Are We In?

- Mark 10:30 ...who will not receive a hundredfold now in **this time**, houses and brothers and sisters and mothers and children and lands, with persecutions, and in the **age to come**, age-life [or the resurrection life of the age to come].

- Luke 20:35-36 ...or neither are they able to die [the death of Adam] any more -- for they are **like messengers** -- and they are sons of God, being **sons of the rising again [us in Christ]**. But those accounted worthy to obtain **that age**, and the **rising again that is out of the dead**, neither marry, nor are they given in marriage [meaning the Levirite marriage, or having to keep the law] (YLT)

- 1 Corinthians 2:6-7 ...And wisdom we speak among the perfect, and wisdom not of **this age**, nor of the rulers of **this age** -- of *those becoming useless [think: "obsolete" like the Old Covenant from the letter to the Hebrews]*, but we speak the hidden wisdom of God in a secret, that God foreordained **before the ages** to our glory...

- 1 Corinthians 10:11 These things happened *to them* as examples and were written down as warnings *for us* <u>**ON WHOM**</u> the **final end of the ages** *HAS COME*.

THE BIG PICTURE
Of Covenant Transition

BIG PICTURE

Luke 21:22, "For **THESE** are the days of vengeance, that ALL THINGS WHICH ARE WRITTEN MAY BE **FULFILLED**."

Parable of the Vineyard
Matthew 21

- The "Kingdom" is transferring...and Resurrecting anew!

Kingdom of God with OC Nation Israel → **Is Transferring** → **Kingdom of God with NC "Nation" of Jesus Followers**

- Mt 21:42-43 "The **Kingdom** will be <u>taken</u> from **you** and given to a **people** producing its fruits."

- **Taken** = Gk: *AIRO* = "<u>1. to raise up from the ground,</u>"

- **"You"** = Old Covenant Israel,

- **"People"** = New Covenant Israel of God, the Kingdom, the body of Christ

- Meaning: The people of God will be <u>raised up</u> from the "land" and will <u>inherit 'the life'</u> and will <u>bear the fruit</u> of God in this new restored Garden, land, Kingdom, etc.

cf: 1 Pet 2:9 "...you are a chosen race (genos), a holy **nation** (ethnos)", Isaiah 65:15 "...God shall slay ... and call his servants by another name.", Mt 11:29 "Take (airo/resurrect) my yoke upon you, and learn from me, for I am gentle and lowly in heart, and you will find rest for your souls.

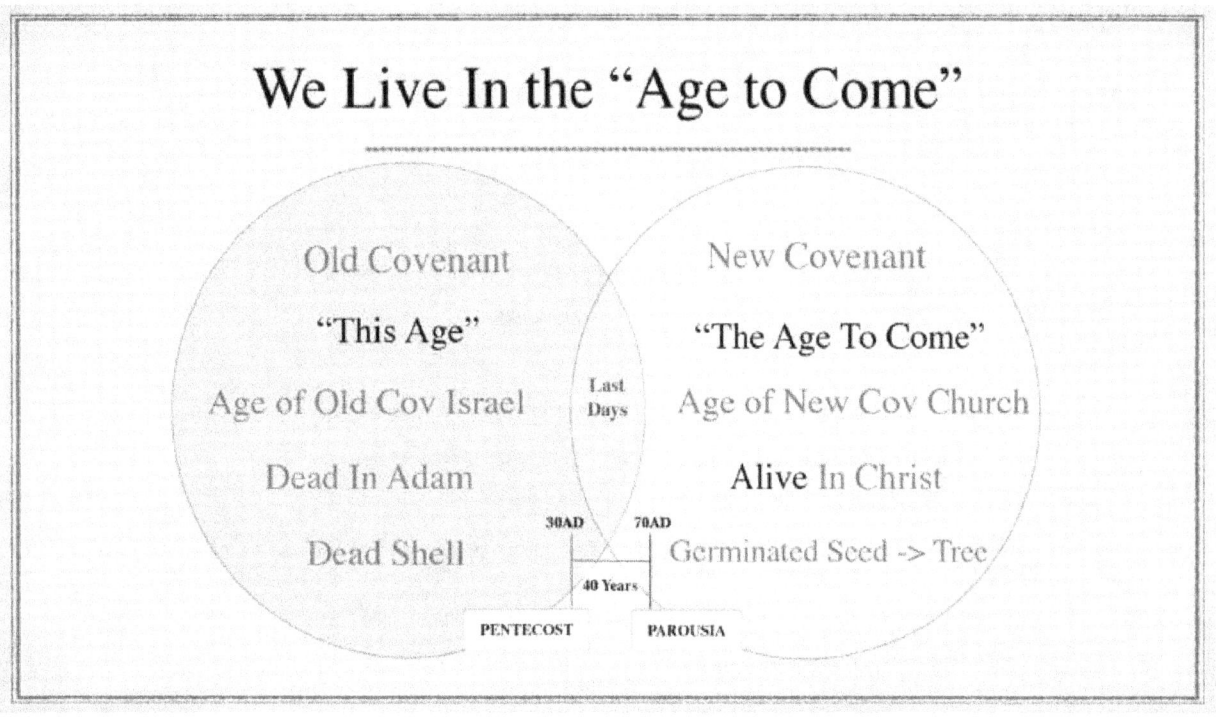

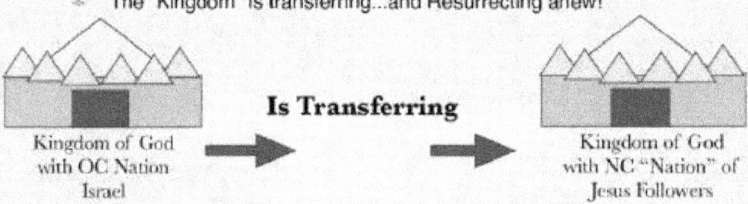

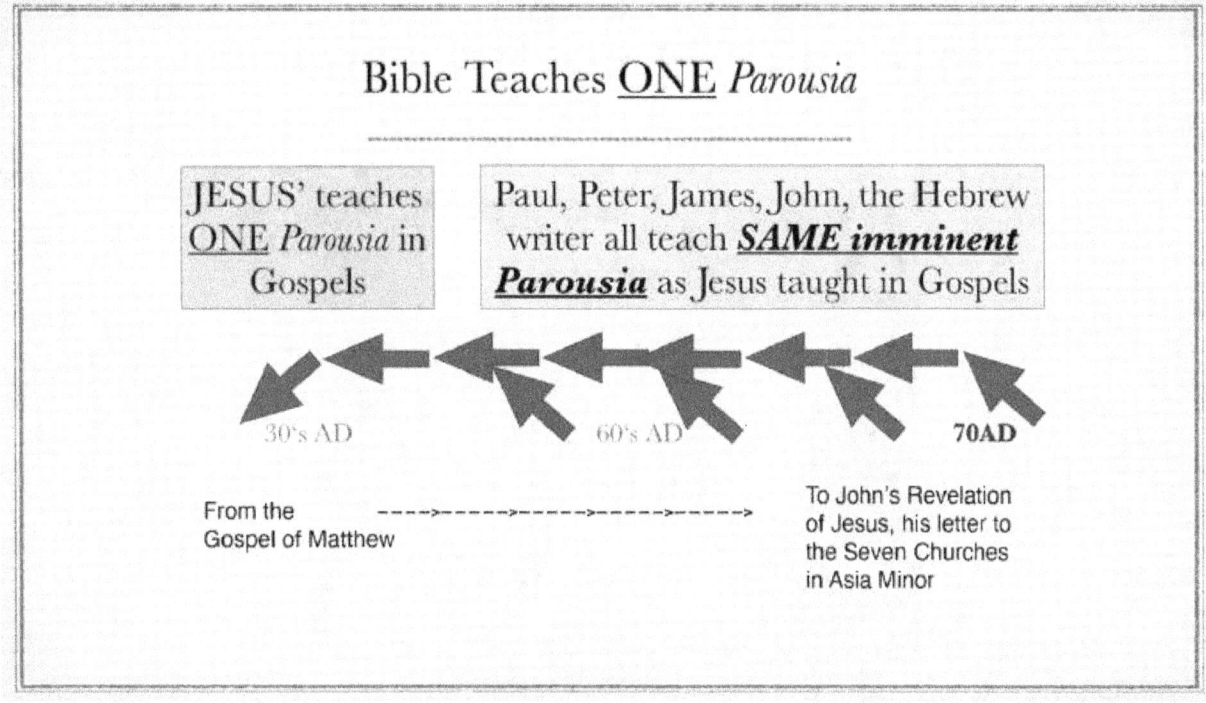

THE DISCIPLES QUESTIONS

Matthew 24:1-3 "Their Question"

- Jesus left the **Temple** and was walking away when his disciples came up to him to call his attention to its **buildings**. And Jesus said unto them, "Do **YOU see** all these things?" he asked. "I tell you the truth, not one stone here will be left on another; <u>every one will be thrown down."</u>

- As Jesus was sitting on the Mount of Olives, the disciples came to him privately. "Tell us," they said, <u>"**When** will this happen, and **what** will be the sign of **your COMING** and of the **end of the AGE**?"</u>

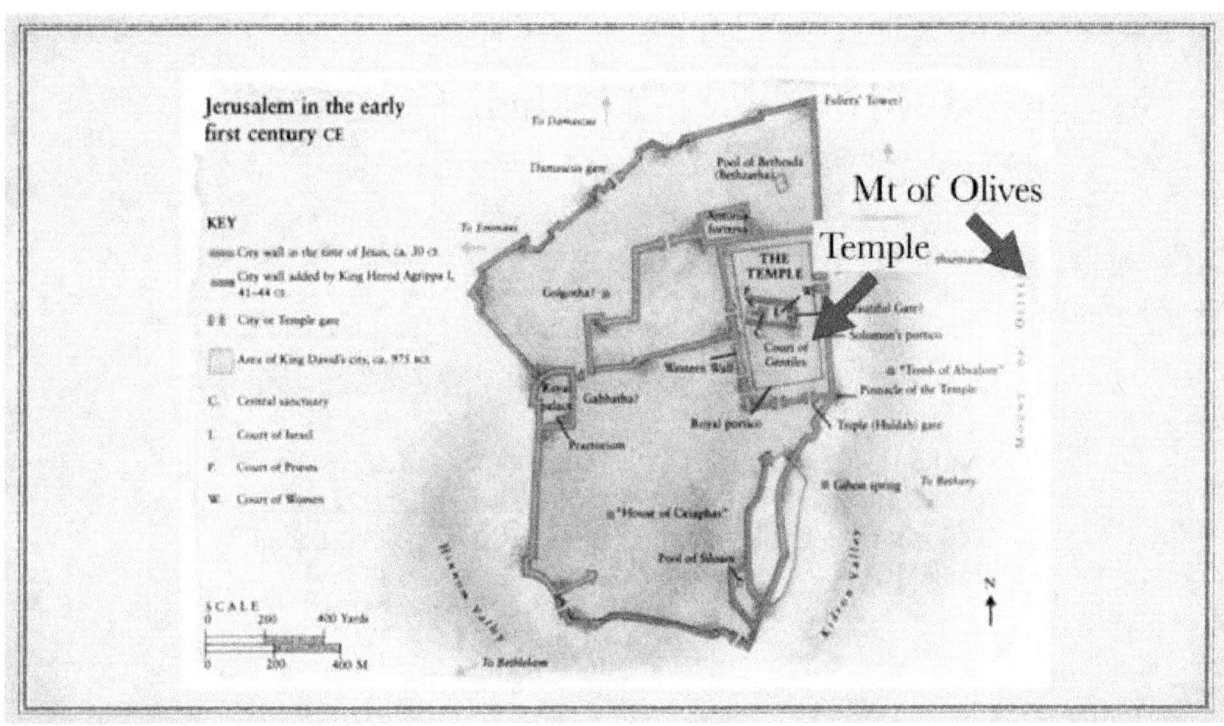

shocked and confused

Parallel Passage:

Luke 21:7

And they asked him, "Teacher, **when** will these things be, and **what** will be the sign when

these things are

about to take place?"

Olivet Discourse: "Jesus' Answer"

- Mt 24:4-6 Jesus answered: "Watch out that no one deceives **YOU**. For many will come in my name, claiming, 'I am the Christ,' and will deceive many.

- **YOU** will hear of <u>**wars and rumors of wars,**</u> but see to it that **you** are not alarmed. Such things must happen, but <u>**THE END**</u> is still to come.

    - Question: 'The **END**' of what? **What** is the nature of this 'end'? **Who** does Jesus say would experience it?

    - It must be the end of something associated with the Temple. Notice that the end of time, the world, or history have never been mentioned.

The Birth Pains

There are six parts to Jesus' reply. Collectively they are known as "the beginning of birth pains." And what was being birthed? The church and God's Kingdom in the "age to come". Notice the reference to the "end of the age." If one age ends another must begin.

The Birth Pains included:

1. false Christs
2. wars and rumors of wars (also "tribe against tribe")
3. famines
4. earthquakes
5. pestilences
6. signs from heaven

Note that every event above is a "sign" answer, but each is a negative sign – they showed "the end" was "not yet". In other words, He had not yet specifically answered their question. Notice also that the Olivet Discourse if addressed to the disciples who were the ones that would see and hear these things. That they did see these things is a matter of historical record. So why do people continue today to look for their "fulfillment" almost 2,000 years later? Too many people have not been made aware of when and how Jesus' predictions, including His coming and the 'end of the age', all came to pass *in that generation* to whom Jesus spoke.

The End of What?

- To what do these terms refer?
- Last Days
- Last Day
- Time of the End

The END of What?

Heb 1:1, 8:13 "In **these Last Days** He has spoken through His Son...In saying a New Covenant He has made the Old obsolete. But whatever is becoming obsolete and growing old is **ready to disappear**"

Heb 9:26 "But **NOW** once at the **CONSUMMATION (or final END) of the AGES** He has been manifested to put away sin..."

Heb 10:25, 37 "As **YOU** see **the Day drawing near**... For yet in a **VERY LITTLE WHILE** He who is **coming will come** and **will NOT DELAY**." (quoting Habbakuk)

Rom 13:12 "the night is almost gone, the **Day is at hand**")

1 Peter 4:7 "The **END** of ALL THINGS is **at hand**"

1 Cor 7:31 "the form of this world/age **IS PASSING AWAY**"

1 Cor 10:10 "...these things were written for OUR instruction, upon whom the **ENDS of the AGES have come**."

James 5:8 "Be patient, brothers, for the **coming of the Lord is AT HAND**"

O. T. Comings of God

- **What were they?**
  - Judgment of a people and city via an enemy army
- **What did they look like?**
  - War, clouds, fire, death ...judgment
- **How did people know God's presence? What did they see?**
  - Clouds, storms, fire, soldiers fighting
- **How were they described?**
  - The same way Jesus describes the destruction of the Temple. World-ending, earth-burning utter destruction of the planet and people.

Parousia

- ***Parousia*** is a Greek word meaning "presence". Their question was, literally, "What will be the **sign** of **_your presence_** and the **end** of the [Jewish] **age**?"

- Q: Why did Jesus' coming presence need a sign?

  - What does this need for a sign **say** about the **nature** of the **presence** and the way they heard Jesus say he was 'coming'? What kind of coming did they expect?

  - A: Look to the Old Testament 'comings of God' to see what was already in the disciples' minds when they asked this of Jesus.

What had Jesus already said about His *Parousia*?

- Matt 10:22-23, "And YOU will be hated by all on account of my name, but the one who endures to **the END** will be saved. But whenever they persecute you in one city, flee to the next; for truly I say to **YOU, YOU** <u>will not finish going through the cities of Israel until the</u> **Son of Man comes**."

- Mt 16:27-28, "For the Son of Man is going to come in the glory of his Father with his angels; and will then recompense every man according to his deeds. Truly I say to you, there are <u>some of</u> **YOU standing HERE who shall NOT TASTE DEATH until YOU see the Son of Man coming** <u>in his Kingdom</u>."

- Jesus told Peter and John that **John would remain alive** until his coming. John was the ONLY Apostle to live past 70 AD!

- Jesus told the --leaders-- that they would not see him again until **they saw** him coming on the clouds of heaven (at which they tore their robes, understanding Jesus to be aligning Himself with God, who 'came on clouds' in the Old Testament).

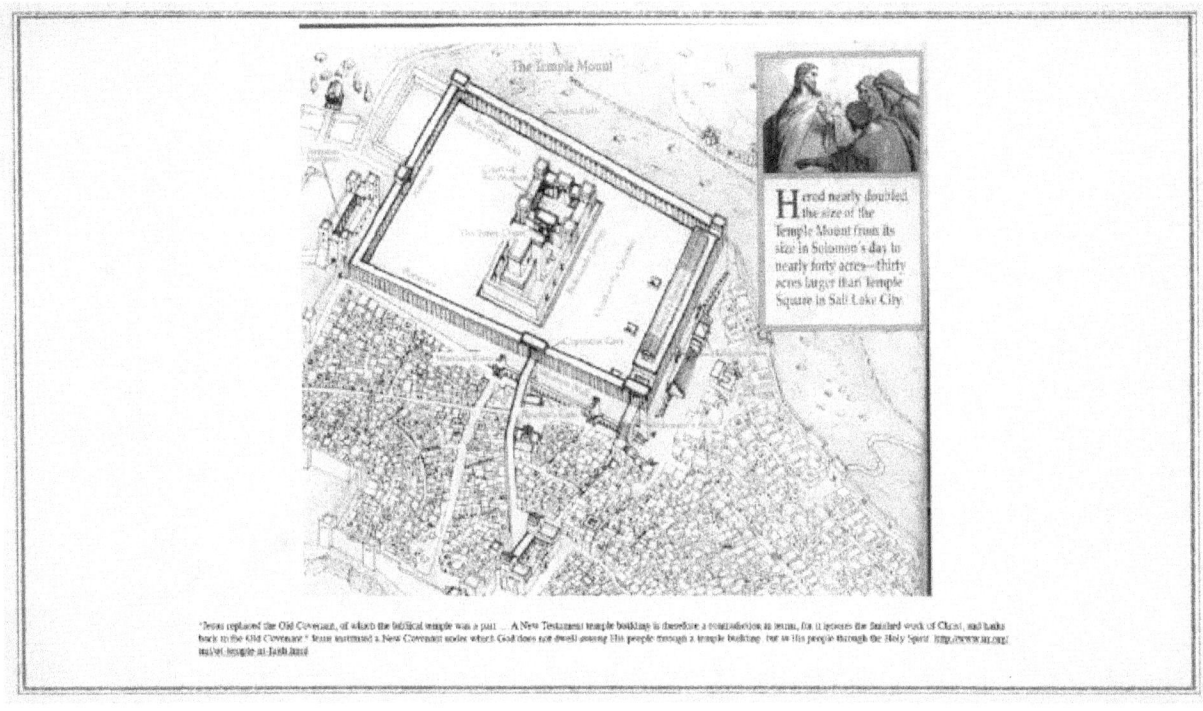

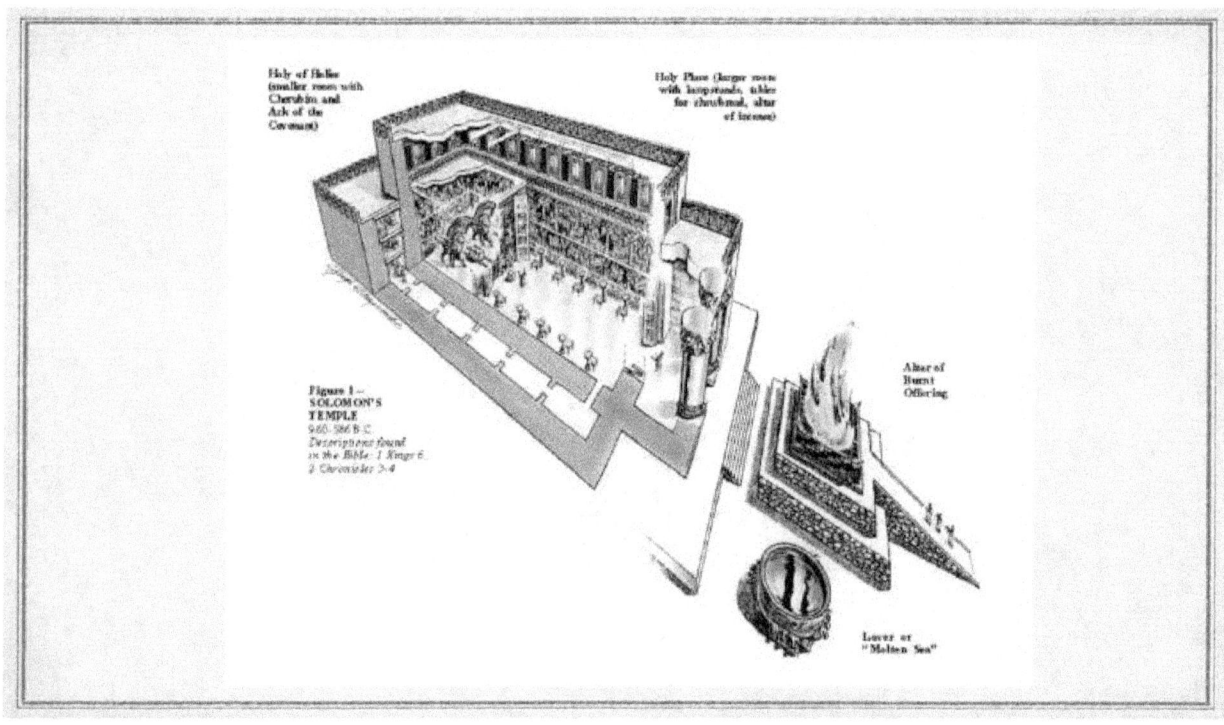

Herod's Temple

The "Birth Pains"

There are six parts to Jesus' reply. Collectively they are known as "the beginning of birth pains." And what was being birthed? The church and God's Kingdom in the "age to come." Notice the reference to the "end of the age." If one age ends another must begin.

The Birth Pains included:

1. false Christs
2. wars and rumors of wars (also "tribe against tribe")
3. famines
4. earthquakes
5. pestilences.
6. signs from heaven

Note that every event above is a "sign," but each is also a negative sign – they showed that "the end" was "not yet". In other words, Jesus had not yet specifically answered their question. Notice also that the Olivet Discourse is addressed to the disciples who He said were the ones that would see and hear these things. And they *did* see these things.

So why do people continue today to look for their "fulfillment" almost 2,000 years later? Too many people have not been made aware of when and how Jesus' predictions, including His coming and the 'end of the age', all came to pass *in that generation* to whom Jesus spoke.

Wars and Rumors of War

- **Tacitus**, the 1st c Roman historian, wrote his annals covering the period from 14AD-68AD when Nero died. He said there were:

- "**disturbances** in Germany," "**commotions** in Africa," "**commotions** in Thrace," "**insurrections** in Gaul," "**intrigues** among the Parthians," "the **WAR** in Britain," "the **WAR** in Armenia" and that the period following Nero's death was "rich in **disaster**, terrible with **battle**, torn by **civil struggles**, horrible..." *(Annals of Tacitus (Rome's greatest historian), 17-68AD, LDM 78-79).*

Wars and Rumors of War

- "At Caesarea, the Jews and Syrians **contended for the mastery** of the city. 20,000 Jews were put to death, and the rest were expelled. Every city in Samaria was then divided into two armies, and *multitudes were slaughtered*.

- Alexandria and Damascus presented a similar **scene of bloodshed**. About 50,000 of the Jews fell in the former, and 10,000 in the latter. The Jewish **nation rebelled** against the Romans; Italy **convulsed with contentions** for the empire; and, as a proof of the troublous and **warlike character of the period**, within the brief space of two years, **four emperors**, Nero, Galba, Otho and Vitellius, suffered **death**." Alexander Keith, *The Evidence of the Truth of the Christian Religion Derived from the Literal Fulfillment of Prophecy Particularly as Illustrated by the History of the Jews, Philadelphia, PA: Presbyterian Board of Publication, 1826,* 59-60.

Wars and Rumors of War

- Josephus writes that **civil wars were so common** in the empire that there was no need to write about them in any great detail: "I have omitted to give an exact account of them, because they are **well known by all**, and they are described by a great number of Greek and Roman authors; yet for the sake of the connection of matters, and that my history may not be incoherent, I have just touched upon everything briefly." (Flavius Josephus, The Wars of the Jews, trans. by William Whiston (Peabody, MA: Hendrickson Publishers, 1987), 4:9:2, 688.

- "...**every city was divided into two armies** encamped against one another, and the preservation of the one party was in the destruction of the other; so that the **day-time was spent in the shedding of blood, and the night in fear.** It was then common to see *cities filled with dead bodies,* still lying unburied, and those of old men, mixed with infants, **all dead**, scattered about together; women also lay amongst them, without any covering for their nakedness..." (Wars, 2:18:2)

Chart of Wars

DATE	LOCATION	DETAILS
AD 40	Mesopotamia	50,000 killed (Josephus)
AD 49	Jerusalem	20,000 killed at Passover
Unknown (30's-70's)	Caesarea	40,000 Jewish killed
Unknown (30's-70's)	Alexandria	50,000 killed
Unknown (30's-70's)	Scythopolis	13,000 Jewish killed
Unknown (30's-70's)	Damascus	10,000 killed in 1 hour
AD 67	Gadara	60,000 Vespasian "slew all the youth" - Josephus
AD 67	Jotapata	15,000 killed, 2130 made slaves
AD 67	Mt Gerizzim	11,600 killed

Chart of Wars

DATE	LOCATION	DETAILS
AD 67	Taricheae	6500 killed
AD 67	Gamala	4000 killed, 5000 mass suicide
AD 67	Gischala	6000 women&children
AD 67	Jerusalem	Idumeans sieged J, killed 12000, including high priest Ananus

"...enemies are destroying each other with their own hands...vast numbers of dead bodies lay in heaps" and Zealots would not allow them to be buried - Josephus (*Wars*, p.320. (Bray))

Vespasian and Titus took other cities, and there were "disorders and civil **wars** in **every city**" Josephus (*Wars*, p.291. (Bray))

"I shall not mistake if I said that the death of Ananus was the beginning of the destruction of the city, and that from this very day may be dated the overthrow of her walls, and the ruin of her affairs" - Josephus (*Wars*, p.314 (Bray)

Earthquakes Mt 24:7

Where	When
Crete	46 AD
Rome	51 AD
Phrygia	53 AD
Laodiciea	60 AD
Campania	62 AD
Pompeii	63 AD
Tacitus, *Annals*, XV, xxii Tacitus, *Histories*, II, lxii	Josephus, *Antiquities*, XX, vii2

Signs From Heaven

- The third paragraph of the fifth chapter of Book 6 of the War contains a fascinating series of **omens** that **foretold the fall of the Temple well in advance** of the beginning of the revolt. God gave people plenty of warning. Josephus stresses the theme that the destruction was predestined to happen. Notice the similarity between some of the signs of Jesus' first coming, his birth, and his second coming, in 70AD.

Star shaped like a sword hovered over Jerusalem a year
Hailey's Comet around Jerusalem for a year
Light around the Altar lit up the Temple 1/2 an hour like day at night
Cow gave birth to lamb
The Temple's eastern gate opened on its own
Flaming CHARIOTS whirling and SOLDIERS fighting in the air
Outline of a man's face, most beautiful, above the Holiest of Holies
Sound of a Great Multitude or God Departing the Temple
Jesus son of Ananias: A Voice from the East

False Prophets Mt 24:11

1	2 Pet 2:1	But **false prophets** also arose among the people, just as there will also be false teachers among you, who will secretly introduce destructive heresies, even denying the Master who bought them, bringing swift destruction upon themselves
2	2 Cor 11:13	For such men are **false apostles**, deceitful workers, disguising themselves as apostles of Christ
3	Acts 13:6	When they had gone through the whole island as far as Paphos, they found a magician, a Jewish **false prophet** whose name was Bar-Jesus...

Gospel Preached Mt 24:14

PROPHECY	FULFILLMENT
MT 24:14 "And this gospel of the kingdom will be proclaimed throughout the **whole WORLD** (*oikoumene*) as a testimony to all nations, and then the end will come."	Romans 10:18 "But I ask, have they not heard? Indeed they *HAVE*, for "Their voice *HAS* gone out to *ALL* the earth, and their words to the *ends of the WORLD* (*oikoumene*)."
MARK 13:10 "And the gospel must first be proclaimed to **ALL NATIONS** (*ethnos*)."	Romans 16:26 "...the mystery that was kept secret for long ages but has now been disclosed... *HAS BEEN* made known to **ALL NATIONS** (*ethnos*) according to the command of the eternal God..."
MARK 16:15 "And he said to them, "Go into **ALL THE WORLD** (*kosmos*) and proclaim the gospel to the whole creation."	Colossians 1:6 "...the gospel, which *HAS COME* to you, as indeed in **ALL THE WORLD** (*kosmos*) it *IS* bearing fruit and growing--as it also *DOES* among you..."

Gospel Preached Mt 24:14

PROPHECY	FULFILLMENT
MARK 16:15 "And he said to them, "Go into all the world and proclaim the gospel to **ALL CREATION** (*ktisis*)."	Colossians 1:23 "...if indeed you continue in the faith, stable and steadfast, not shifting from the hope of the gospel that you heard, which *HAS BEEN PROCLAIMED* in **ALL CREATION** (*ktisis*) under heaven
ACTS 1:8 "But you will receive power when the Holy Spirit has come upon you, and you will be my witnesses in Jerusalem and in all Judea and Samaria, and to the **end of THE EARTH** (*ge/land*)."	Romans 10:18 "But I ask, have they not heard? Indeed they *HAVE* for "Their voice *HAS GONE* out to all **THE EARTH** (*ge/land*), and their words to the ends of the world."
	Romans 1:8 "First, I thank my God through Jesus Christ for all of you, because your faith *IS* being reported *all over the WORLD*."
	2 Timothy 4:17, "...But the Lord stood by me, and strengthened me; that *through me* the message might be *FULLY proclaimed*, and that *ALL the Gentiles* might hear."

Compare Moses' 40 year "Generation"

❖ Hebrews 3:5-19

❖ "Now Moses was faithful in all God's house as a servant, to testify to the things that were to be spoken later, but Christ is faithful over God's house as a son. And we are his house if indeed we hold fast our confidence and our boasting in our hope. Therefore, as the Holy Spirit says, "Today, if you hear his voice, *do not harden your hearts as in* **the rebellion**, *on the day of testing* **in the wilderness**, *where your fathers put me to the test and saw my works* **for forty years**. Therefore I was provoked with **that generation**, and said, 'They always go astray in their heart; they have not known my ways.' As I swore in my wrath, 'They shall not enter my rest.'"

Compare Moses' 40 year "Generation"

- Hebrews 3:5-19 continued,

- "...Take care, brothers, lest there be in any of you an evil, unbelieving heart, leading you to fall away from the living God. But exhort one another every day, as long as it is called "today," that none of you may be hardened by the deceitfulness of sin. For we have come to share in Christ, if indeed we hold our original confidence firm to the end.

- As it is said, "Today, if you hear his voice, do not harden your hearts **as in the rebellion**." *For who were those who heard and yet **rebelled**? Was it not all those who left Egypt **led by Moses**? And with whom was he provoked **for forty years**?* Was it not with those who sinned, whose bodies fell in the wilderness? And to whom did he swear that they would not enter his rest, but to those who were disobedient? So we see that they were unable to enter because of unbelief."

In the Old Covenant, Moses set the pattern that foreshadowed the **sequence** and **timing** of Jesus' work in establishing the New Covenant

MOSES	JESUS
Moses freed people from bondage to Pharoah	Jesus freed people from bondage to sin
Delivered people through the Red Sea	Delivered people through His red blood
After 50 days then -> Law Given at Sinai	After 50 days then -> Spirit Given at Pentecost
3000 people Died at Sinai because of idolatry	3000 received life at Pentecost because of repentance
Then God's people wandered 40 years before entering the material Promised Land	Then God's people evangelized 40 years before entering the *true* **spiritual Promised Land in 70AD!**
Established a temporary Covenant of law	Established a permanent Covenant of love, grace and life

Old ← 40 Year Transition Period → New

Temple = Heaven, Earth, Sea

* The Jews of Jesus' time considered their **Temple to be a model of their universe, representing their 'heaven and earth and sea'**. They called the holiest place 'heaven,' where God met man, and where heaven and earth met. The inner court where Jews worshiped was 'earth' and the outer bath where Gentiles could go was called "the sea".

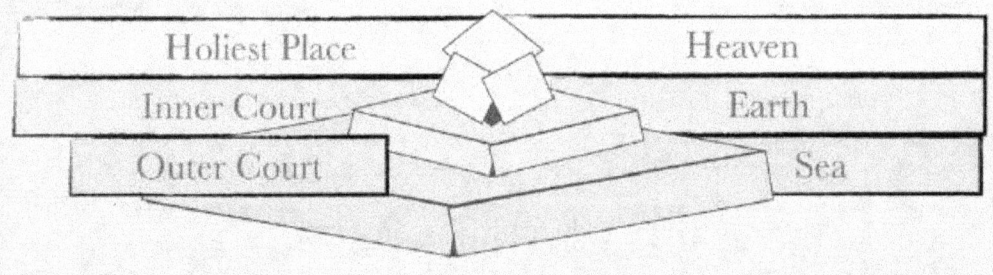

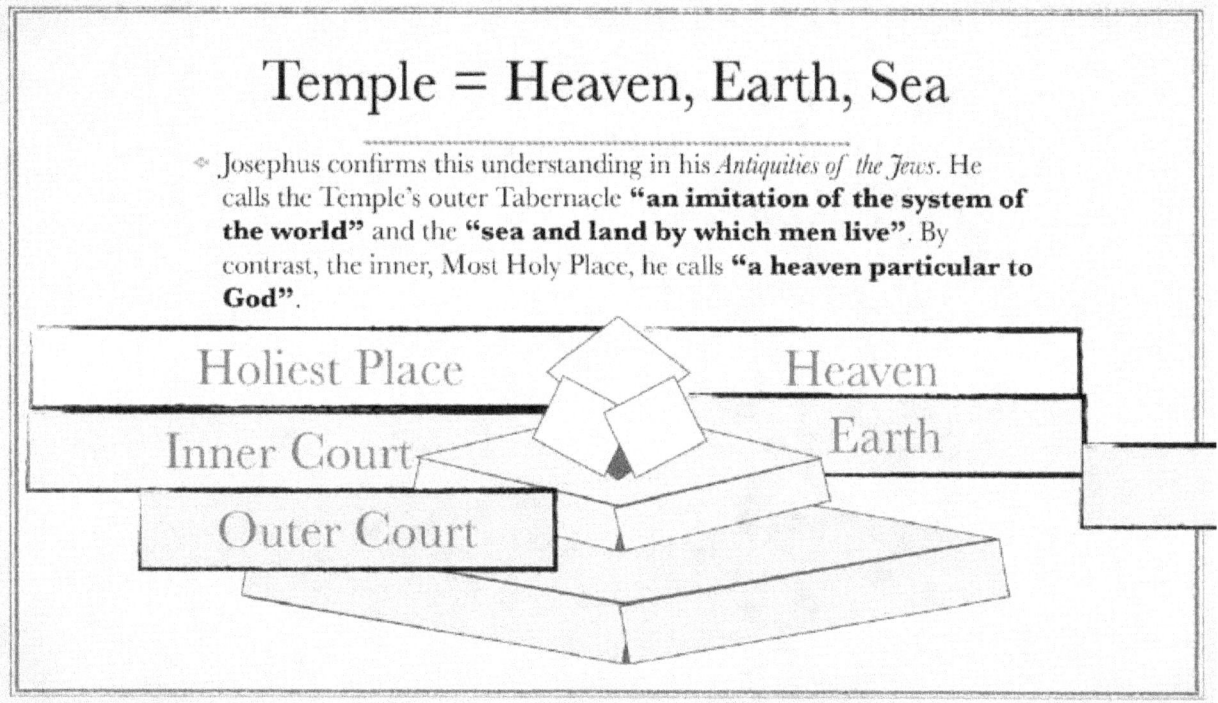

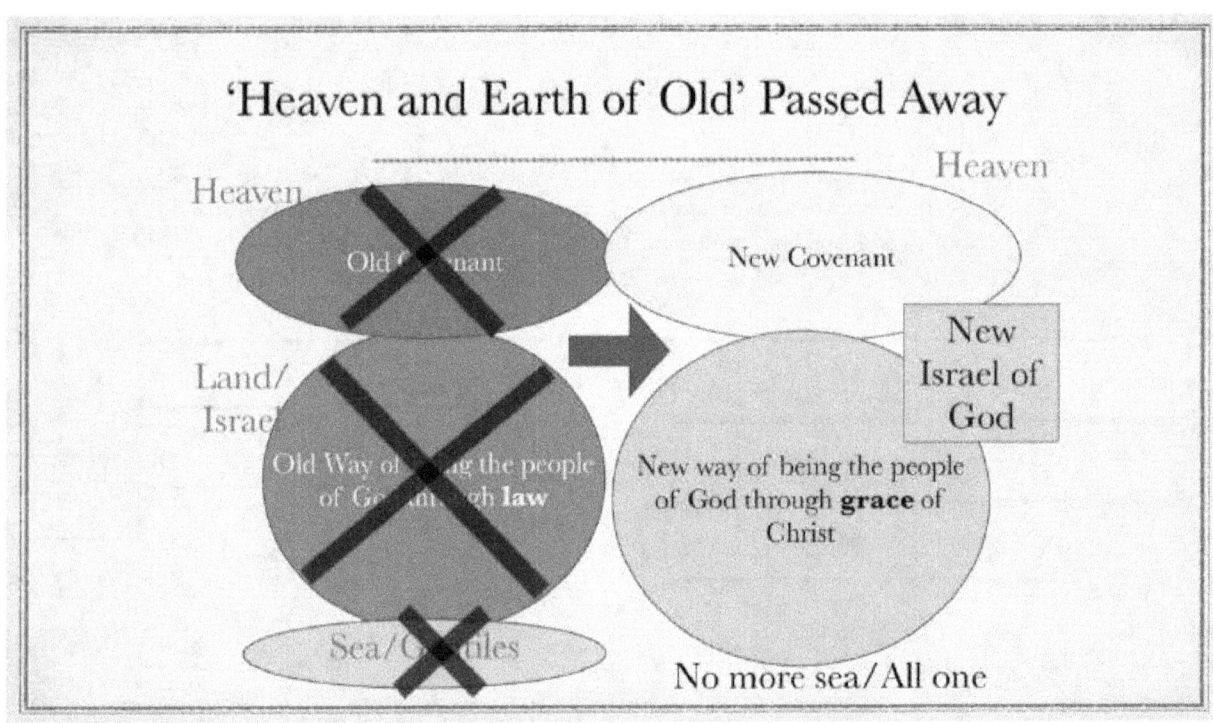

Covenant Map Analogy

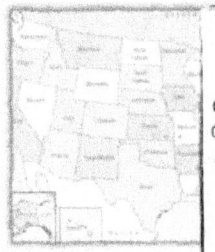

What kind of a map is this? A true map? Yes. Is it a *literal* map of *physical* land? No. What is it trying to tell us? It is a map expressing **legal** and **covenantal** *realities* in the world. But it is NOT a map that describes the physical land. This is a **map of covenants** between entities like states, countries, **people and laws**. This is a map of the American world. *Just like the Bible is a map of Israel's covenant world*. Similarly, the United States had a beginning in 1776. Then a Transition Period of transitional government; and in 1789 it became **a new country** with the ratification or "consummation" of the Constitution. It will someday have an 'end' too.

But for a physical description of the land or geology you need a different kind of map! If you tried to take it literally, you might ask, "Is Minnesota green? Can you see the lines between the states?" No, you cannot. Why? Because this is a *covenant map*. It is not trying to teach a physical picture. It is representing the *"legal and covenantal world"* of America. The physical land of North America existed long before the idea of America. So, too, the physical world existed long before the Old Covenant world of Israel.

First presented by Tim Martin, co-author of *Beyond Creation Science*, at the 2010 Covenant Creation Conference

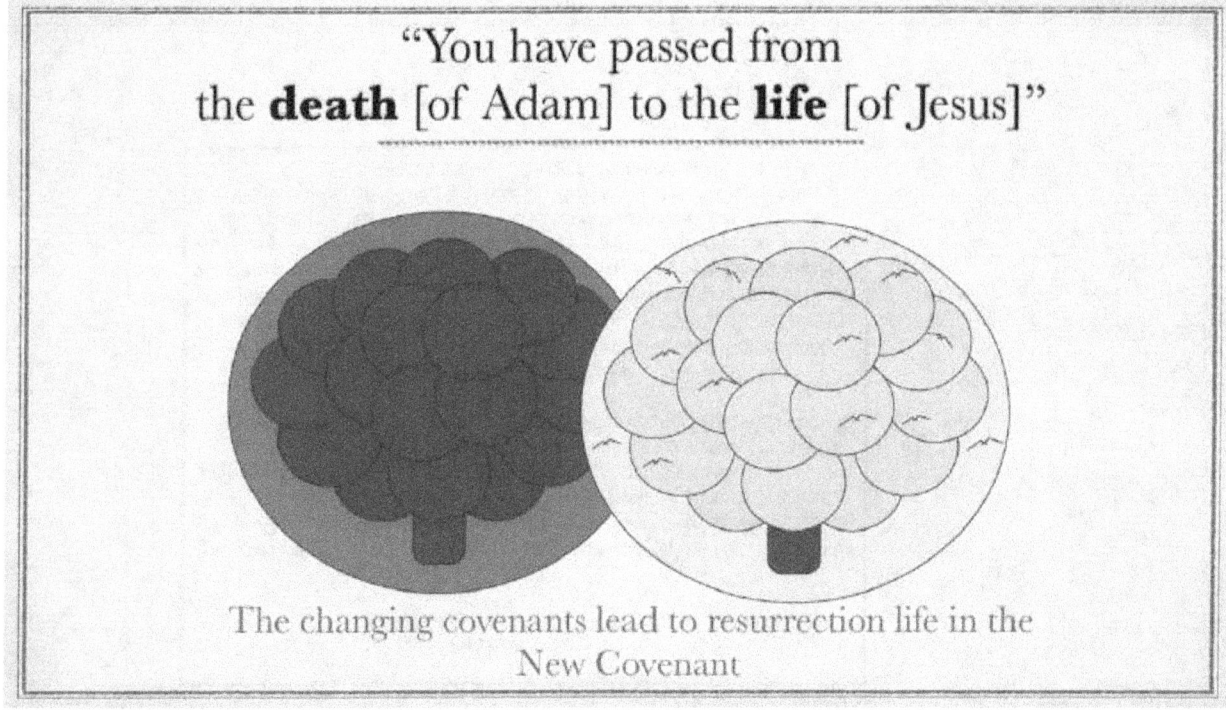

Hebrews: Change Your Clothes!

- Change your clothes! Clothe yourself in righteousness. Wash your "robe" in the blood of the Lamb (Rev) in order to enter the New Jerusalem, in the New Heavens and Earth. *Put on* the "new man" - Christ. Don't be found without the right 'wedding clothes'.

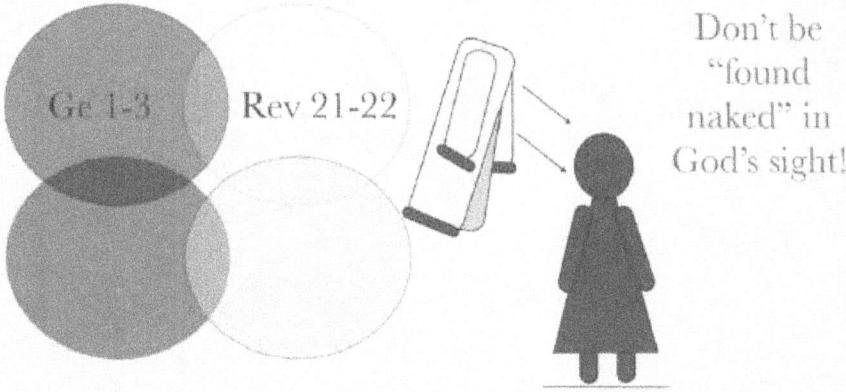

Don't be "found naked" in God's sight!

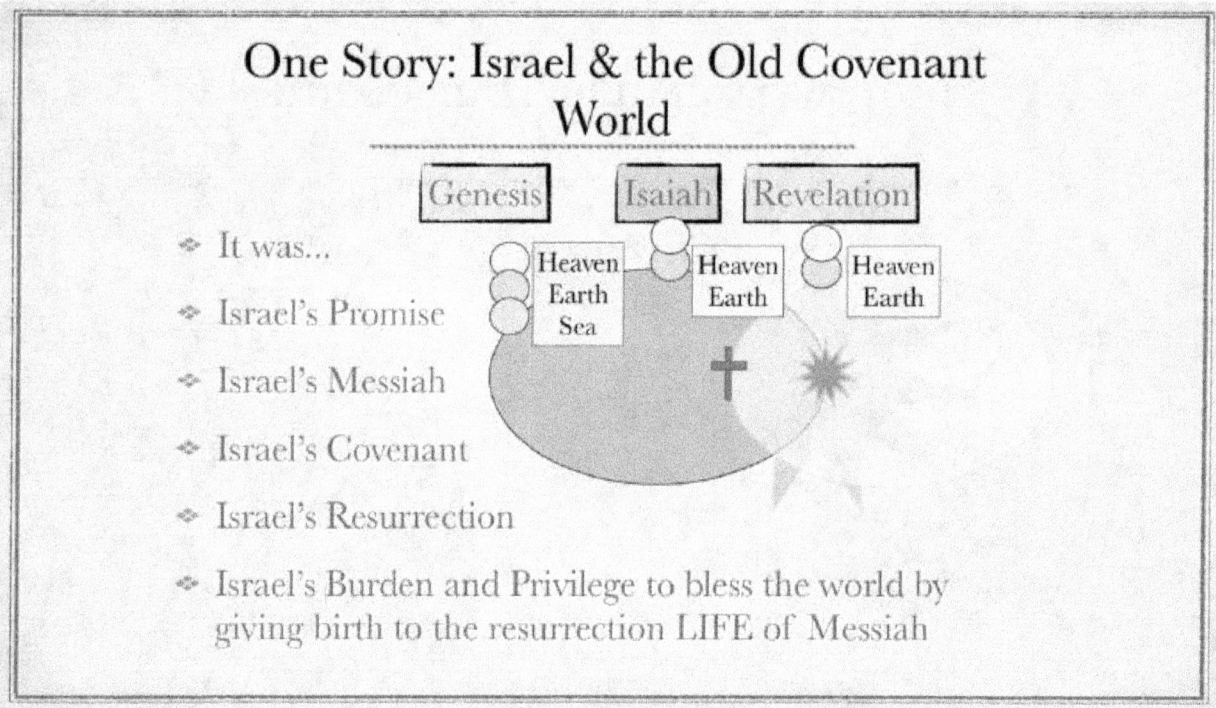

Elements - Stoicheia

<u>Gal 4:3</u> Even so we, when we were children, were in <u>bondage under the **elements** of the world</u>...

<u>Gal 4:9</u> But now, after that ye have known God, or rather are known of God, how turn ye again to the <u>weak and beggarly</u> **elements**, whereunto ye desire again to be <u>in bondage</u>?

<u>Col 2:8</u> Beware lest any man spoil you through philosophy and vain deceit, after the tradition of men, after the **principles** <u>of the world</u>, and not after Christ.

<u>Col 2:20</u> Wherefore if ye be dead with Christ from the **principles** <u>of the world</u>, why, as though living in the world, are ye subject to ordinances?

Elements - Stoicheia

Hbr 5:12 For though by this time you ought to be teachers, you need someone to teach you again the basic **principles** of the oracles of God; you need milk, not meat...

2Pe 3:10 But the day of the Lord will come as a thief in the night; in the which the heavens shall pass away with a great noise, and the **elements** shall melt with fervent heat, the earth also and the **works** that are therein shall be burned up.

2Pe 3:12 Looking for and hasting unto the coming of the day of God, wherein the heavens being on fire shall be dissolved, and the elements shall melt with fervent heat?

Thousand Years Simile

<u>2 Peter 3:8</u> But do not let this one thing escape your notice, beloved, that with the Lord one day is like a thousand years, and a thousand years like one day.

Peter is referencing Ps 90:4 "A thousand years *in your sight* are like a day that has just gone by, or like a watch in the night."

> People often quote this verse in order to avoid taking the time statements in Scripture at face value. You will hear people say "God's time is different than ours" to dismiss over a hundred imminent time statements in Scripture which point to a first century fulfillment of eschatological events. While it may be true that God is outside of time, this single quote of a poetic Psalm should not be used to dismiss Jesus' repeated "Generation Promise" - the Promise of Jesus' Coming to judge *his generation*.

Thousand Years = 30-70AD?

	Revelation	Peter
1	Rev 1:4 church in Asia	1 Peter 1:1 church in Asia
2	Rev 1:6, Rev 20:6 kingdom of priests	1 Peter 2:9 made a priesthood
3	Rev 11, and 20 soon to judge the living and the dead	1 Peter 4:5 ready to judge living and the dead
4	Rev 13:8 foundation of the world	1 Peter 1:20 foundation of the world
5	Rev 4 warnings about judging churches	1 Peter 4:17 judging family of God (church)
6	Rev 14, 16, 17, and 18 Babylon	1 Peter 5:13 Babylon
7	Rev 20:3 Satan released for a short time	1 Peter 5:8-10 resist the Devil, suffer a short time
8	Rev 20:1-3 chains	2 Peter 2:4 angels, chains
9	Rev 20:11, 21 new heaven and new earth	2 Peter 3:13 new heaven and new earth
10	**Rev 20:2. a thousand years**	**2 Peter 3:8 a day a thousand years**
11	Rev 3:3, 16:15 coming like a thief	2 Peter 3:10 coming like a thief

Are 1st Peter and John in Revelation talking about the same event? Was the timeframe John wrote about in Revelation the same time frame that Peter wrote about when he said "a day is as a thousand years and a thousand years is as a day"? It seems they may both be describing what the readers could expect to happen during the upcoming transition period to Christ's reign.

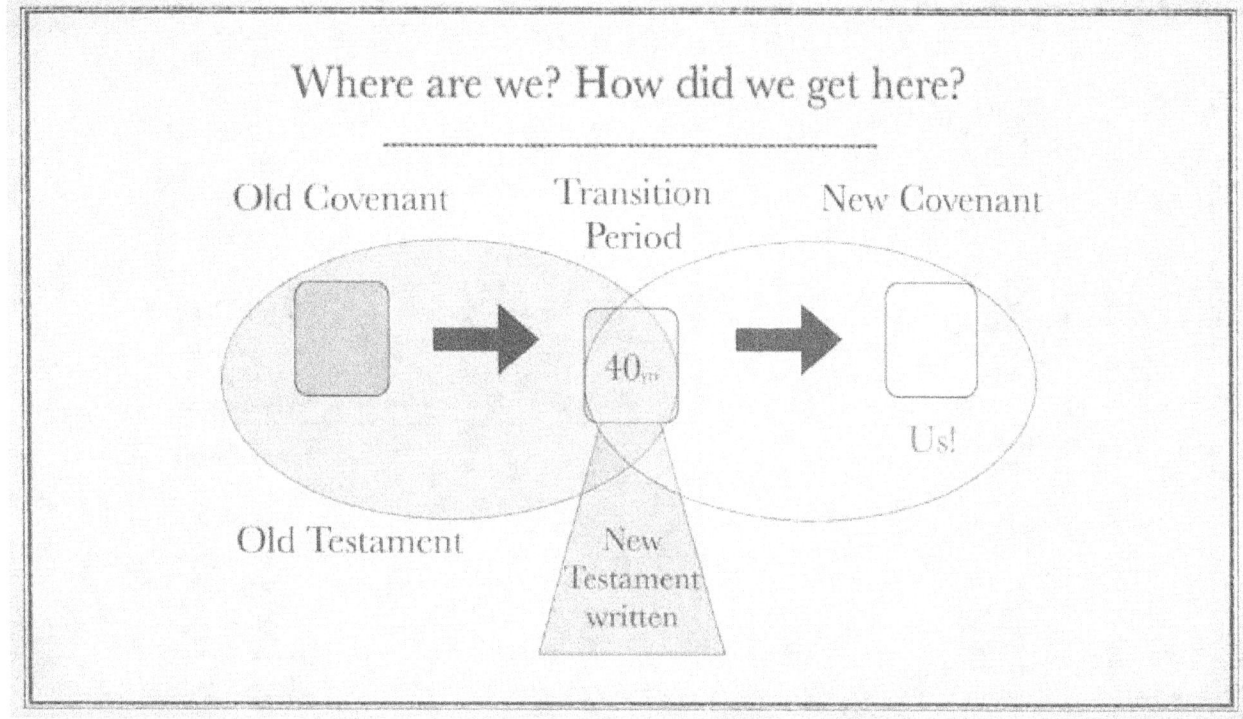

Transformation in Christ

		Cross		Parousia
Our Exodus	In Bondage to Sin	Passover	Seeking Promise Land, Kingdom of God	**Our Arrival**
Our Stature	Old, Die with Christ	Born Again	"Growing in **Christ's righteousness**" Going from milk to meat Putting off childish things	**Fully Grown**
Our Clothing	"Wholly Old, Filthy Rags"	Resurrection Life	Put off Old Man, put on New Man One New Man "What kind of body? A *Spiritual Body*"	**Wholly New**
His Building	Earthly Temple	Jesus Chief Cornerstone	"Living Stones, being built up as a Spiritual House"	**Living in Mansion**
Tree of Life	Inert Seed	Seed Germinated	"First the grain, then the head, then the blade"	**Harvested**
Chronology	Year ~ "0"	Year ~"30"	"…as *you* see the Day approaching" "The end of all things is at hand!"	Year 70
Identity/ Body	In Adam	Cross	Believe, shed circumcision into Adam, be baptized into Jesus	In Christ
"This Age" Old Covenant Age	Old Covenant	Transformaiton	Transition Period Already/Not Yet (*to them*)	"Age to Come" New Cov Age

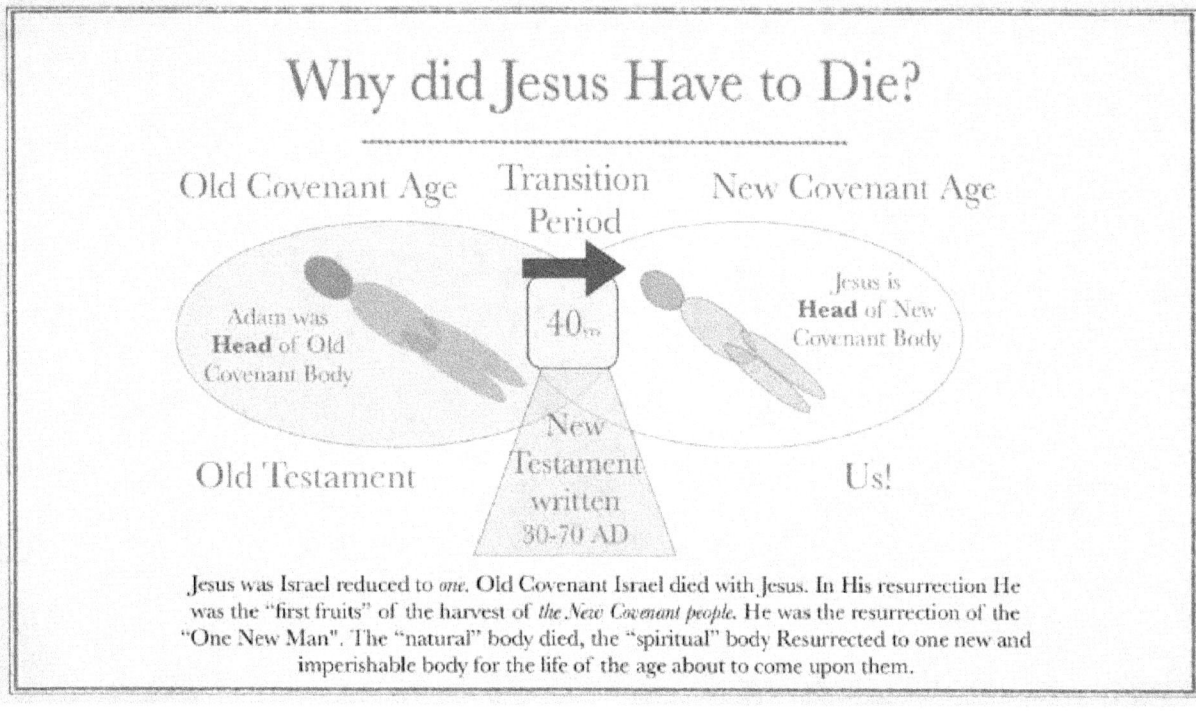

MILLENNIUM

Eusebius on Millennium Madness

- 325AD Eusebius Pamphilius, Ecclesiastical History: (On the 'Millennial Reign' of Christ) "This same historian (Papias) also gives other accounts, which he says he adds as received by him from **unwritten tradition**, likewise certain **strange parables** of our Lord, and of His doctrine and some other matters rather too fabulous. In these he says there would be a certain **millennium after the resurrection**, and that there would be a corporeal **reign of Christ on this very earth**; which things he appears to have **IMAGINED**, as if they were authorized by the apostolic narrations, **NOT UNDERSTANDING CORRECTLY** those matters which they propounded **MYSTICALLY** in their representations. For he was very **LIMITED IN HIS COMPREHENSION**, as is evident from his discourses; yet he was the **cause why MOST** of the ecclesiastical writers, urging the antiquity of man, **were carried away by a SIMILAR OPINION**; as, for instance, **Irenaeus**, or any other that **adopted such sentiments**. (Book III, Ch. 39)

- Notice that Eusebius, the "Father of Church History" acknowledges that many theologians think like Papias - and yet he believes that they are WRONG. He sees them as taking too literal and not "mystical" enough of a view on Jesus' teachings.

"1000 Years"

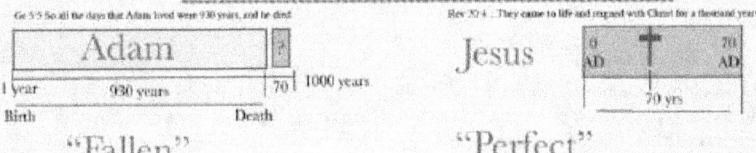

"Fallen"   "Perfect"

- 1000s years = Number of Perfection, considered to represent a perfect reign of perfect king in ancient thought and literature

- "First Adam" reigned only 930 years, which is almost 1000. But he fell short of the perfect reign, demonstrating his sin.

- "Second Adam" and those "in Him" "came to life and reigned with Christ 1000s years" demonstrating their restored righteousness in contrast with Adam's fallenness.

1000's of Years

- I've also heard from linguists that the 1000 years in Revelation transcripts is plural. So it is actually the 1000s of years.

- This gives weight to the idea that it is a symbolic tool used to describe the **quality** of a reign rather than the **quantity** of years or duration of a reign.

Millennium

Peter and John are talking about the same imminent first-century eschatological events.

PETER	REVELATION
1 Peter 1:1 church in asia	Rev 1:4 church in asia
1 Peter 2:9 made a priesthood	Rev 1:6, Rev 20:6 kingdom of priests
1 Peter 4:5 *ready* to judge living and the dead	Rev 11, and 20 *soon* judge the living and the dead
1 Peter 1:20 foundation of the world	Rev 13:8 foundation of the world
1 Peter 4:17 judging the family of God (churches)	Rev 4 warnings about judging churches
1 Peter 5:13 Babylon	Rev 14, 16, 17, 18 Babylon
1 Peter 5:8-10 resist Devil, suffer a little while	Rev 20:3 Devil released for a little while
2 Peter 2:4 angels, chains, tartarus/ "hell", judgment	Rev 20:1-3 angel, chains, bottomless pit, judgment
2 Peter 3:12 Old Heaven & Earth destroyed	Rev 20:11 Old Heaven & Earth flee
2 Peter 3:13 New Heaven and Earth	**Rev 21 New Heaven and Earth**
2 Peter 3:8 one day a 1000 years, 1000 years a day	**Rev 20:2 a 1000 years**
2 Peter 3:10 the Day will come like a thief in night	Rev 3:3, 16:15 Jesus will come like a thief in night

John and Peter wrote to their audiences in apocalyptic language about eschatological events that would happen soon - to *THEM*. The close of the age-changing eschaton was upon them! The Day, the Coming of Jesus, the Judgment and the New World were on the brink of arrival. With reference to the "1000 years" mentioned by Peter and John, both use the term figuratively and **qualitatively**, *not literally and not quantitatively*, to describe the Transition Period through which they were living, when the Old Covenant world was giving way to the New Covenant world of life and righteousness in Christ.

Millennium

Revelation 20

vs. 1 - An angel descends from heaven with a key and a chain.

vs. 2 - He binds Satan for 1000 years.

vs. 3 - During the 1000 years Satan cannot deceive the nations any more [so the Gospel can spread].

vs. 4 - **Martyrs are resurrected to reign with Jesus Christ for 1000 years.**

vs. 5a - **The rest of the dead raised at the end of the 1000 years.**

vs. 6 - **Those in the first resurrection reign with Jesus for 1000 years.**

vs. 7 - Satan loosed at the end of the 1000 years.

vs. 8 - After the rest of the dead are raised, Satan deceives them again. They are great in number - like the sand of the sea. Satan gathers them for a final battle, Gog and Magog.

vs. 9 - Satan and this host surround God's City. Fire comes down and devours them.

vs. 10 - Satan, the Beast, and the False Prophet end up in this lake of fire.

vs. 11 - Before this fire falls, a great judgment occurs.

vs. 12 - All the resurrected lost are judged.

vs. 13 - Another description of the resurrected lost being judged.

vs. 14 - Death and Hell [Hades-Grave] are cast into the lake of fire, which is the second death.

vs. 15 - All the resurrected lost are cast into the lake of fire.

After the first and second Resurrections and the Judgment, then the old earth passes, and the new earth comes (Revelation 21:1). This old earth is the Old Covenant passing away and the new earth coming is the New Covenant being fully established or consummated. Just like the consummation of a marriage covenant signifies the change from the engagement to the establishment of the marriage relationship, so too, this New Covenant consummation fully established God's marriage to His bride, the Church universal. This Millennium period was like the engagement period between God and God's people, before the great wedding feast of the Lamb.

Two more significant points should be noted:

1. *Revelation 20 doesn't say there will be peace on earth during the 1000 years.* For it is not speaking of the state of the material world, but rather the realities in the New Covenant world for those "in Christ". Jesus is our peace and our righteousness. In this sense there is peace and righteousness in the New Covenant world for all those who are in Christ.

2. *Revelation 20 doesn't say Jesus Christ will rule during the 1000 years from the present city of Jerusalem.* Rather, Jesus rules the hearts of the people of the New Covenant, the church, who *is* New Jerusalem.

The saints and priests reigning with Christ during the Millennium are the believers who were in Christ during the 40 year Transition Period between 30AD-70AD.

1000 Years in Contemporary Thought

- Greeks and Romans believed that after people died, they lived in Hades 1000 years and then were resurrected to earthly life

- Virgil (19BC), in his poem *The Aeneid*, portrays the lead character, Aeneas, founder of Rome, descending to Hades, or the underworld, where the soul wanders for 1000 years. Aeneas' father describes it like this:

  - "...not even when the last flicker of life has left us does evil...relinquish our souls...Therefore the dead are disciplined in purgatory, and **pay the penalty of old evil**...in the next world...a few of us are later released to wander at will...until, in the **fulness of time**, the ages have **purged that ingrown stain**, and nothing is left but pure ethereal sentience and the spirit's essential flame. All these souls, when they have finished their **THOUSAND YEAR CYCLE**, *God sends for, and they come in crowds to* the river Lethe, so, you see, with **memory washed out**, they may revisit the earth above and begin to wish to be **born again**." (1)

Greco-Roman 1000 Years

- Voltaire, the famous French historian and writer, notes the connection between John's imagery in Revelation and Greco-Roman beliefs about Hades and 1000 years.

- "The belief in this reign of a thousand years was long prevalent among the Christians. This period was also in great credit among the Gentiles. The souls of the Egyptians also returned to their bodies at the end of a thousand years; and, according to Virgil, the souls in purgatory were exorcised for the same space of time - a thousand years." - Voltaire quoting "The Epistle of Dioysius of Alexandria"

- Revelation was written to groups of Greek and Latin speaking people in Asia minor who would surely have been familiar with literary notions of 1000 years and associated John's millenium period with their beliefs about Hades and beliefs of a 1000 year reign of people after they died.

"1000 Years" in ANE Thought

- Egyptians also believed that they returned to their bodies after 1000 years.

- ANE documents like records of the reigns of kings use the term "1000 years" to describe the reign of a "perfect" king. Saying X king "reigned 1000" or more years is synonymous with saying that he was a perfect king. The records were not trying to say that the king literally lived 1000 years. People writing and reading these records at the time understood this. This use of "1000" was used in a similar location and time as the Old Testament was assembled. John quotes from the Old Testament more than any other NT writer. He borrows symbolism from the OT throughout his letter. Chances are that John was aware of this symbolic use of the term 1000 and applied it to *Jesus' perfect reign in contrast to Adam's imperfect reign of 930 years*.

- We see many symbolic uses of the term 1000 throughout the OT.
  - God owns the sheep on 1000 hills. God is faithful to 1000 generations...etc

God Speaking in Context

- What do you think about Scripture quoting, alluding to and borrowing from other famous and contemporary works?

- Does it add to or take away from the *specialness* of Scripture for you?

- What if God wanted you to share His story with a group of rappers. Might he inspire you to look at their lyrics and poetry and draw from it in order to make your points and be relevant, contextual and speak their language?

Eusebius on Millennium Madness

- 325AD Eusebius Pamphilius, in his *Ecclesiastical History*, has this to say about the 'Millennial Reign' of Christ. "This same historian [Papias] also gives other accounts, which he says he adds as received by him from unwritten tradition, likewise certain strange parables of our Lord, and of His doctrine and some other matters rather too fabulous. In these *he says there would be a certain millennium after the resurrection*, and that there would be *a corporeal reign of Christ on this very earth*; which things he appears to have imagined, as if they were authorized by the apostolic narrations, *not understanding correctly those matters which they propounded mystically in their representations*. For he was very *limited in his comprehension*, as is evident from his discourses; *yet he was the cause why most of the ecclesiastical writers…were carried away by a similar opinion*; as, for instance, Irenaeus, or any other that adopted such sentiments." Book III, Ch. 39

- Notice that Eusebius, the "Father of Church History," says that Papias is the reason that many theologians believed in a literal "millennium reign." And yet *he asserts that they are WRONG*. He says they mistakenly interpret the millennium idea as too literal and not "mystical" enough.

| Ge 5:5 "So all the days that Adam lived were 930 years, and he died" | "1000 Years" | Rev 20:4 "...They **came to life** and reigned with Christ for a thousand[s] years" |

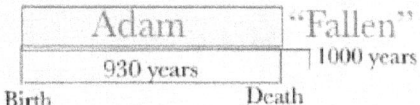 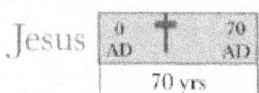 "Perfect"

Adam | "Fallen" | Jesus
930 years / 1000 years / 70 yrs
Birth — Death

- 1000s years = A number of perfection, is considered to represent "a perfect reign" of a king in ancient thought and literature. Describing Christ's reign as 1000 is another way of saying it is the reign of a perfect king. Seen this way, it is more of a qualitative statement about the perfect quality of Christ's reign and may not be intended as a quantitative statement about the numbers of years of his reign.

- The "First Adam" reigned only 930 years, which is almost 1000. But he "fell short" of achieving the perfect reign, demonstrating his imperfection.

- The "Second Adam" and those "in Him" "came to life and reigned with Christ 1000s years," demonstrating their restored perfection in righteousness and spiritual life in contrast with Adam's imperfection and spiritual death. It is interesting that the number of Adam's 930 years of life and the approximately 30 years of Jesus' earthly life and the 40 years of Transition Period add up to an actual 1000 years.

Does the Thousand Years = 30-70AD?

	Revelation	Peter
1	Rev 1:4 church in Asia	1 Peter 1:1 church in Asia
2	Rev 1:6, Rev 20:6 kingdom of priests	1 Peter 2:9 made a priesthood
3	Rev 11, and 20 soon to judge the living and the dead	1 Peter 4:5 ready to judge living and the dead
4	Rev 13:8 foundation of the world	1 Peter 1:20 foundation of the world
5	Rev 4 warnings about judging churches	1 Peter 4:17 judging family of God (church)
6	Rev 14, 16, 17, and 18 Babylon	1 Peter 5:13 Babylon
7	Rev 20:3 Satan released for a short time	1 Peter 5:8-10 resist the Devil, suffer a short time
8	Rev 20:1-3 chains	2 Peter 2:4 angels, chains
9	Rev 20:11, 21 new heaven and new earth	2 Peter 3:13 new heaven and new earth
10	**Rev 20:2. a thousand years**	**2 Peter 3:8 a day a thousand years**
11	Rev 3:3, 16:15 coming like a thief	2 Peter 3:10 coming like a thief

John and Peter wrote to their audiences in apocalyptic language about eschatological events that would happen soon to *THEM*. With reference to the "1000 years" mentioned by Peter and John, both use the term **qualitatively**, *not literally and **not quantitatively***, to describe the Transition Period through which they were living, when the Old Covenant world was giving way to the New Covenant world of life and righteousness in Christ.

Millennium Insight

Revelation Chapter 20

vs. 1 - An angel descends from heaven with a key and a chain.
vs. 2 - He binds Satan for 1000 years.
vs. 3 - During the 1000 years Satan cannot deceive the nations any more [so the Gospel can spread].
vs. 4 - **Martyrs are resurrected to reign with Jesus Christ for 1000 years.**
vs. 5a - **The rest of the dead raised at the end of the 1000 years.**
vs. 6 - **Those in the first resurrection reign with Jesus for 1000 years.**

Two more significant points should be noted:

1. *Revelation 20 doesn't say there will be peace on earth during the 1000 years.* For it is not speaking of the state of the material world, but rather the realities in the New Covenant world for those "in Christ". Jesus is our peace and our righteousness. In this sense there is peace and righteousness in the New Covenant world for all those who are in Christ.
2. *Revelation 20 doesn't say Jesus Christ will rule during the 1000 years from the present city of Jerusalem.* Rather, Jesus rules the hearts of the people of the New Covenant, the church, who *is* New Jerusalem.

The saints and priests reigning with Christ during the Millennium seem to be the believers who were in Christ during the 40 year Transition Period between 30AD-70AD.

1000 Years in Contemporary Thought

- Greeks and Romans believed that after people died, they lived in Hades 1000 years and then were resurrected to earthly life

- Virgil (19BC), in his poem *The Aeneid*, portrays the lead character, Aeneas, founder of Rome, descending to Hades, or the underworld, where the soul wanders for 1000 years. Aeneas' father describes it like this:

    - "...not even when the last flicker of life has left us does evil...relinquish our souls...Therefore the dead are disciplined in purgatory, and **pay the penalty of old evil**...in the next world...a few of us are later released to wander at will...until, in the **fulness of time**, the ages have **purged that ingrown stain**, and nothing is left but pure ethereal sentience and the spirit's essential flame. All these souls, when they have finished their **THOUSAND YEAR CYCLE**, *God sends for, and they come in crowds to* the river Lethe, so, you see, with **memory washed out**, they may revisit the earth above and begin to wish to be **born again**." (1)

Greco-Roman 1000 Years

- Voltaire, the famous French historian and writer, notes the connection between John's imagery in Revelation and Greco-Roman beliefs about Hades and 1000 years.

- "The belief in this reign of a thousand years was long prevalent among the Christians. This period was also in great credit among the Gentiles. The souls of the Egyptians also returned to their bodies at the end of a thousand years; and, according to Virgil, the souls in purgatory were exorcised for the same space of time - a thousand years." - Voltaire quoting "The Epistle of Dioysius of Alexandria"

- Revelation was written to groups of Greek and Latin speaking people in Asia minor who would surely have been familiar with literary notions of 1000 years and associated John's millenium period with their beliefs about Hades and beliefs of a 1000 year reign of people after they died.

"1000 Years" in ANE Thought

- Egyptians also believed that they returned to their bodies after 1000 years.

- ANE documents like records of the reigns of kings use the term "1000 years" to describe the reign of a "perfect" king. Saying X king "reigned 1000" or more years is synonymous with saying that he was a perfect king. The records were not trying to say that the king literally lived 1000 years. People writing and reading these records at the time understood this. This use of "1000" was used in a similar location and time as the Old Testament was assembled. John quotes from the Old Testament more than any other NT writer. He borrows symbolism from the OT throughout his letter. Chances are that John was aware of this symbolic use of the term 1000 and applied it to *Jesus' perfect reign in contrast to Adam's imperfect reign of 930 years*.

- We see many symbolic uses of the term 1000 throughout the OT.
  - God owns the sheep on 1000 hills. God is faithful to 1000 generations...etc

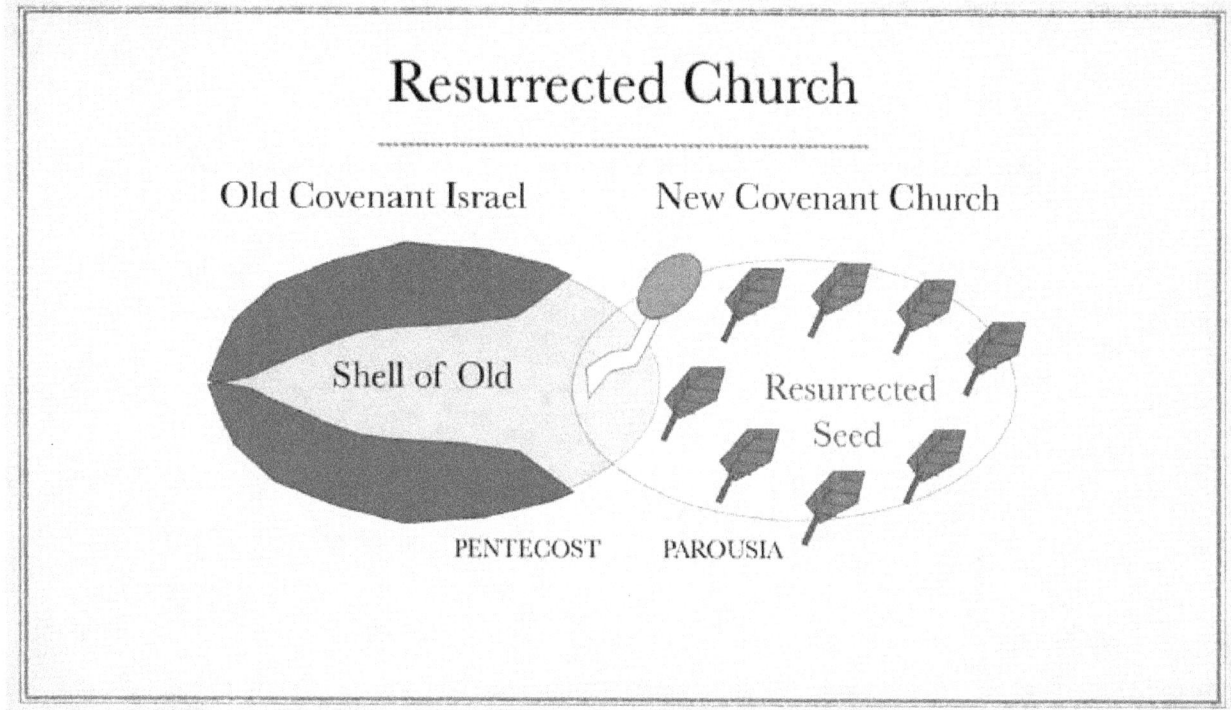

Early Daters

Ancient Scholars	Modern Scholars	At Living the Question
Moses Stuart	A.A. Bell	62 SCHOLARS FOR THE EARLY DATE OF REVELATION
Frederick Deusterdig	F.F. Bruce	20TH-21ST CENTURIES
Westcott	Rudolph Bultmann	
Horjt	C.C. Torrey	122 SCHOLARS FOR THE EARLY DATE OF REVELATION
Lightfoot	John A.T. Robinson	PRIOR TO THE 20TH CENTURY
F.W. Farrar	J.A. Fitzmeier	
Ederscheim	J.M. Ford	
Phillip Schaff	C.F.D. Moule	EARLY CHURCH ADVOCATES FOR THE EARLY DATE OF REVELATION
Milton Terry	Cornelius VanderWaal	
Augustus Strong	Max King	

The Same Resurrection Events:
Matthew 24, 1 Thessalonians 4 & 1 Corinthians 15

	Event	Matthew 24	1 Thess 4	1 Corinthians 15
1	**Christ Comes - Parousia**	Matt. 24:30	I Thess. 4:16	1 Corinthians 15:23
2	**From Heaven**	Matt. 24:30	I Thess. 4:16	1 Corinthians 15:23
3	**With a Shout / Power**	Matt. 24:30	I Thess. 4:16	1 Corinthians 15:52
4	**With Angels**	Matt. 24:31	I Thess. 4:16	
5	**With Trumpet of God**	Matt. 24:31	I Thess. 4:16	1 Corinthians 15:52
6	**Believers Gathered with Christ**	Matt. 24:31	I Thess. 4:17	1 Corinthians 15:51
7	**In Clouds**	Matt. 24:30, 25:6	I Thess. 4:17	
8	**Time Unknown**	Matt. 24:36	I Thess. 5:1-2	1 Corinthians 15:51
9	**Christ Comes as a Thief**	Matt. 24:43	I Thess. 5:2, 4	
10	**Believers Unaware of Impending Judgment**	Matt. 24:37-39	I Thess. 5:3	
11	**Judgment Comes Like Birth Pains**	Matt. 24:8	I Thess. 5:3	
12	**Believers to Watch**	Matt. 24:42	I Thess. 5:4, 6	1 Corinthians 15:58
13	**Warning Against Drunkenness**	Matt. 24:49	I Thess. 5:7	
14	**The Day**			

Timing of Resurrection from the Dead

- 1 Cor 15:20-24 "But now is Christ risen from the dead, and become the firstfruits of them that slept. For since by man came 'the death,' by man came also 'the resurrection of the dead'. For as **in Adam** all die [the death], even so **in Christ** shall all be made alive [resurrected in 'the life']. But everyman in his own order: Christ the firstfruits; afterward they that are Christ's **AT HIS COMING [PAROUSIA]**. Then comes **THE END [of the Old Covenant age]**, when he shall have delivered up the kingdom to God, even the Father; when he shall have put down all rule [law] and all authority and power [priesthood]...the last enemy 'the death'..." (author's emphasis)

Question	Answers	Cross Reference
Q: **When** does Paul say the Resurrection will be?	A: At the *Parousia*, or when Jesus' *Presence* is manifested at the **END of the AGE**	Disciples' *question*: "What will be the sign of your **Presence/*Parousia*** and the **END of the AGE**?" Mt 24
Q: **When** does Jesus say the *Parousia/Presence* and the **END** will be?	A: At the time of the Destruction of the Temple and Jerusalem, in **70AD**	Mt 24, Mk 13, Lk 21

What kind of "death"?

- How many times have you heard that a central part of the Gospel message is: "Because Adam sinned -> death entered the world -> therefore all people die now. This is not God's plan that we should die, so God will someday resurrect all dead bodies and make us alive forever when he defeats physical death". This is what many churches teach today. But is it what the Bible *actually says*?

- 1 Cor 15:55-56 "O death, where is thy sting? O **Hades** where is thy victory? The sting of 'the **death**' is 'the **sin**'; and the strength of 'the **sin**' is the **law**."

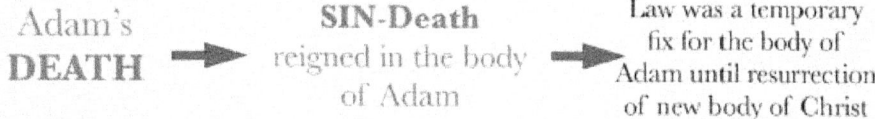

Adam's **DEATH** → **SIN-Death** reigned in the body of Adam → Law was a temporary fix for the body of Adam until resurrection of new body of Christ

Because Adam died 'in the day' he ate the fruit, he lost connection to the presence of God. Essentially, being the head of the body of Israel, *he cut off the life or "oxygen" to the body*. The law was like being hooked up to oxygen...propping it up until Jesus restored the BREATH

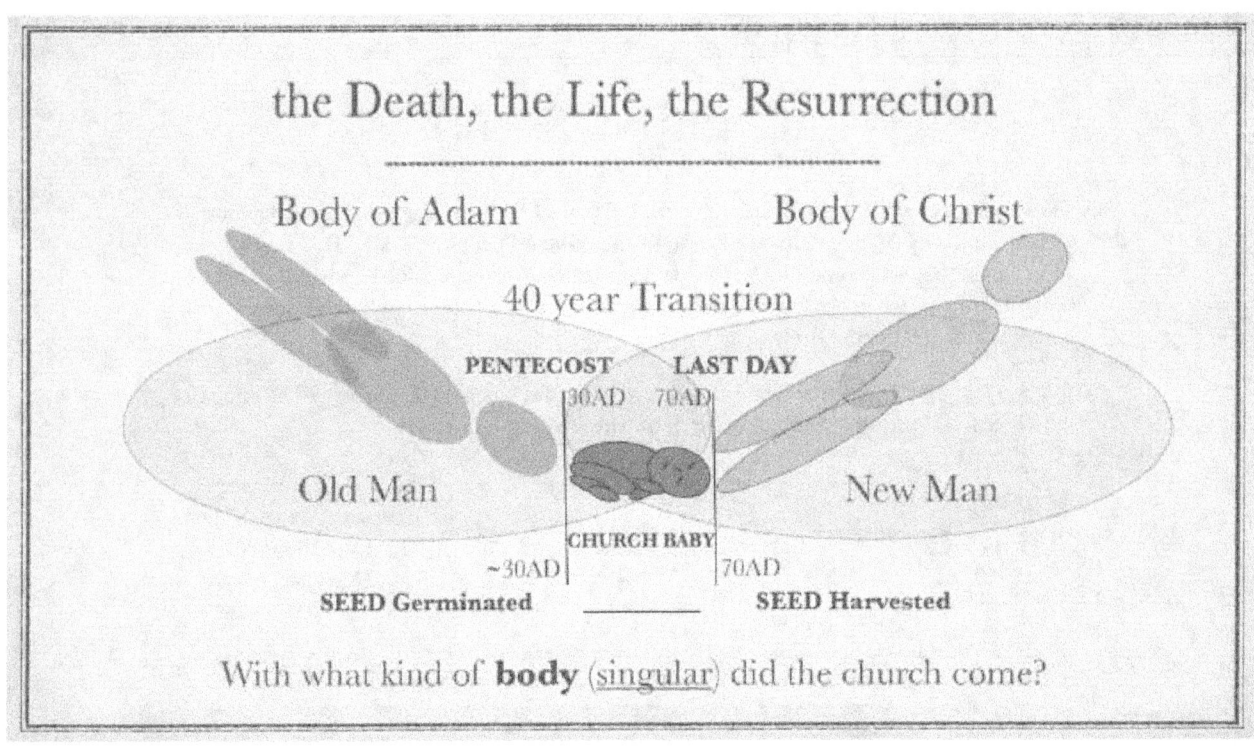

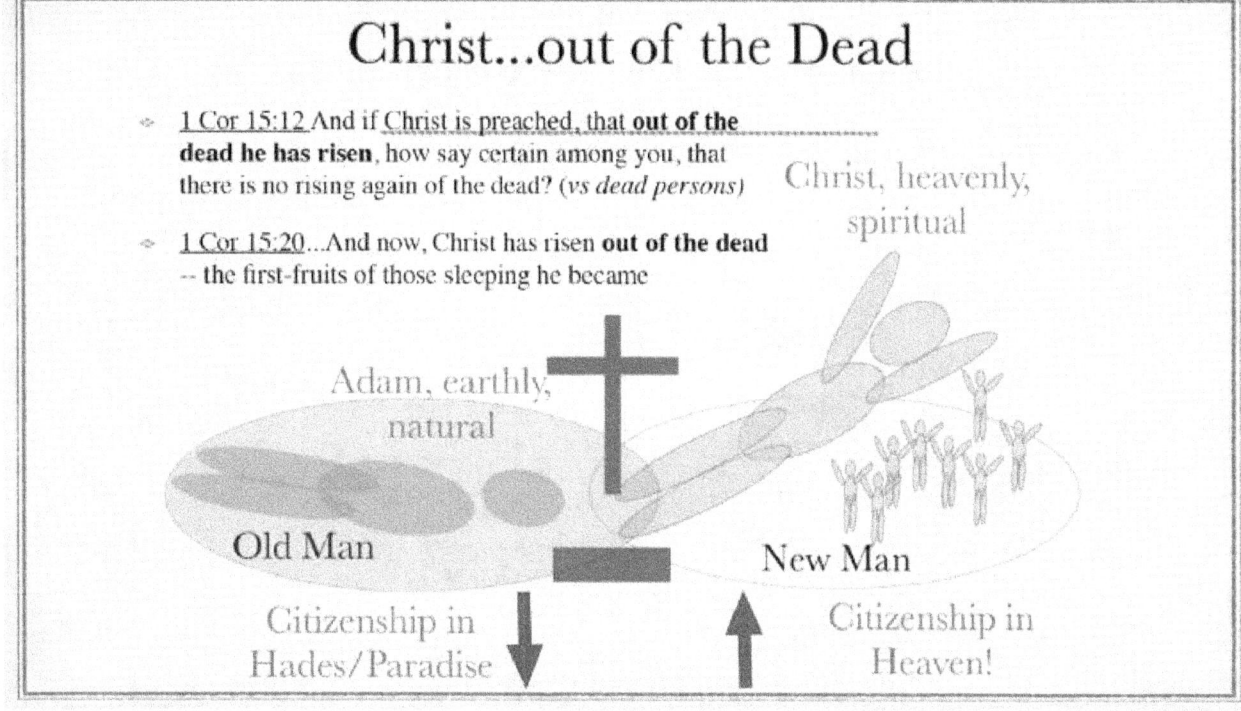

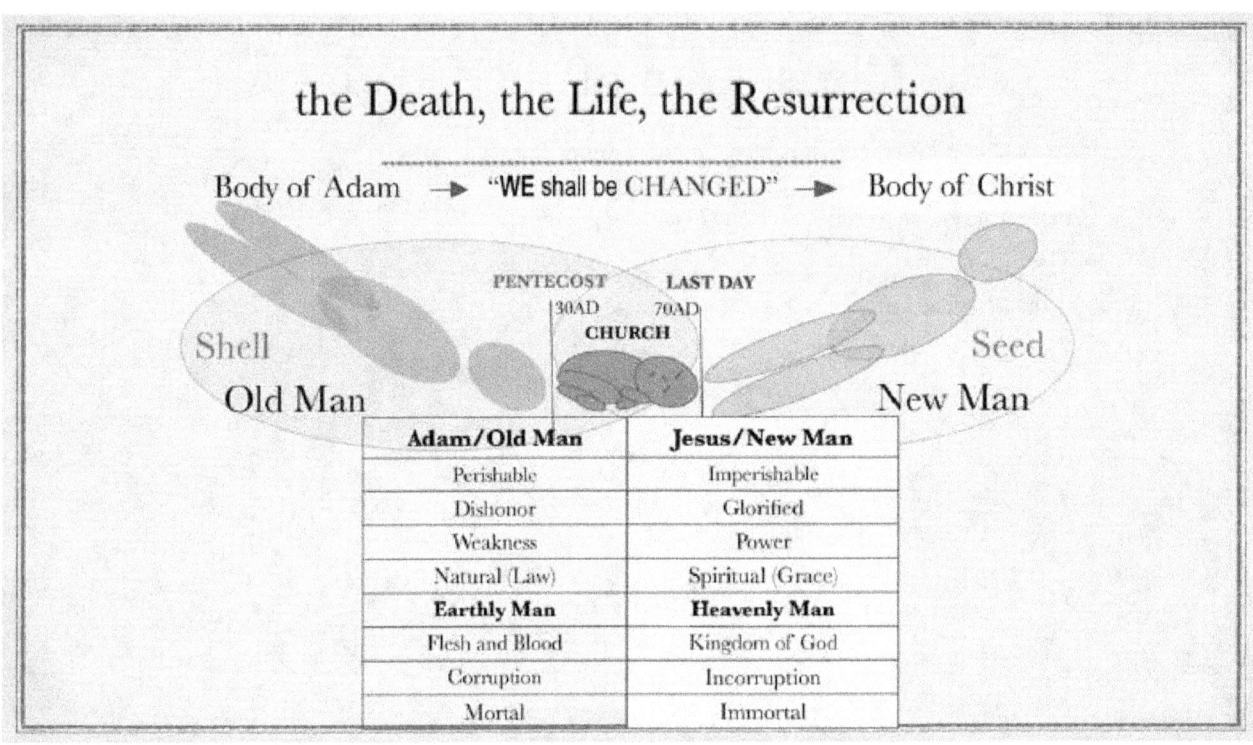

These Seed References Refer to People in Adam and Christ

1 Cor 15:38	...and God gives to it a body according to His will, and to **each of the seeds** its proper body.
Rom 1:3	Concerning his Son Jesus Christ our Lord, which was made of the **seed** of David according to the **flesh**...
Rom 4:13	For the **promise**, that he should be the heir of the world, was not to Abraham, or to his seed, through the **law**, but through the **righteousness of faith**.
Rom 9:8	that is, the children of the flesh -- these [are] not children of God; but the **children of the promise** are reckoned for **SEED**;
Gal 3:16	...and to Abraham were the promises spoken, and to his seed; He does NOT say, `And to seeds,' as of many, but **as of ONE**, `And to thy **seed**,' which **is Christ**;
Gal 3:19	Why, then, the **law**? On account of the **transgressions it was added, till the seed** might come to which the **promise** hath been made, having been set in order through messengers in the hand of a mediator...

Cross References About 'the Dead' and Resurrection Life

- **Question: What are you hearing in these verses?**

- Mt 8:22 But Jesus said unto him, Follow me; and let 'the dead' bury their dead [think: those who are 'in Adam']

- Mt 22:32 I am the God of Abraham, and the God of Isaac, and the God of Jacob? God is not the God of 'the dead, but of the living.

- Mk 9:10 And they kept that saying with themselves, **questioning one with another** what the rising from 'the dead' should mean.

- Mk 12:25 For when they shall rise from 'the dead', they neither marry, nor are given in marriage *[they are speaking of keeping the law of Levirite marriage, in the resurrected church, they do not have to keep that law]*; but are as the angels which are in heaven. [*Angels are FREE from the law because they are In Christ*]

- 1 Jn 3:14 ...we have known that **we have passed out of 'the death'** into '**the life'** because we love one another; he who is not loving his brother remains in '**the death'**.

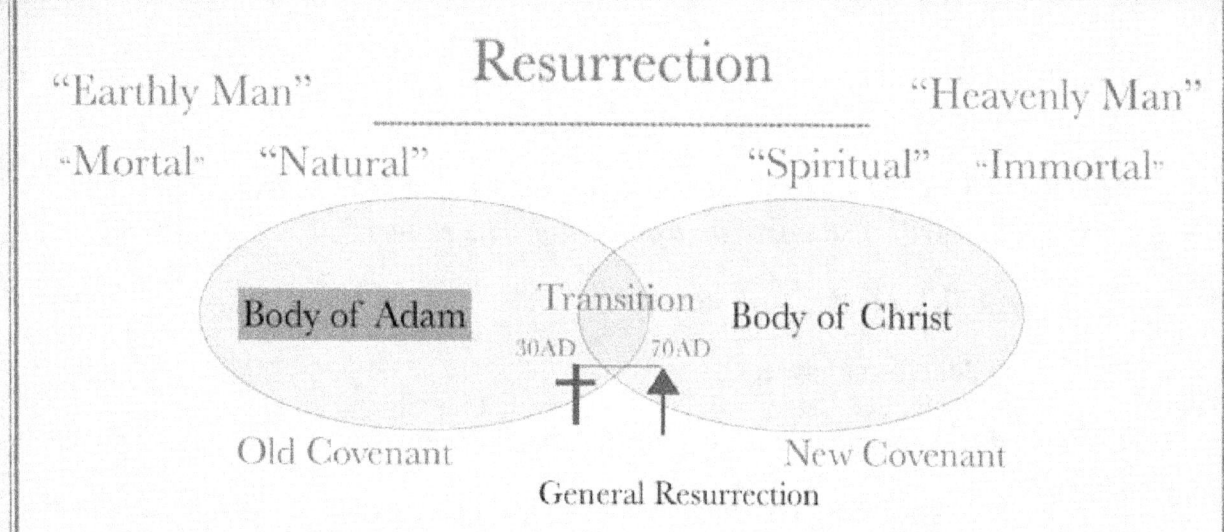

1 Corinthians 6:14

- **1 Cor 6:14** *"Now God has not only raised the Lord, but will also **raise us up** through His power."*

- Q: Who is the "us" here?

  - Possible answers:

  - 1. Each physical body individually someday

  - 2. The 'new Israel of God' or 'the body of Christ,' at Christ's coming in 70ad, an event in which the Corinthians participated, just as they had been told

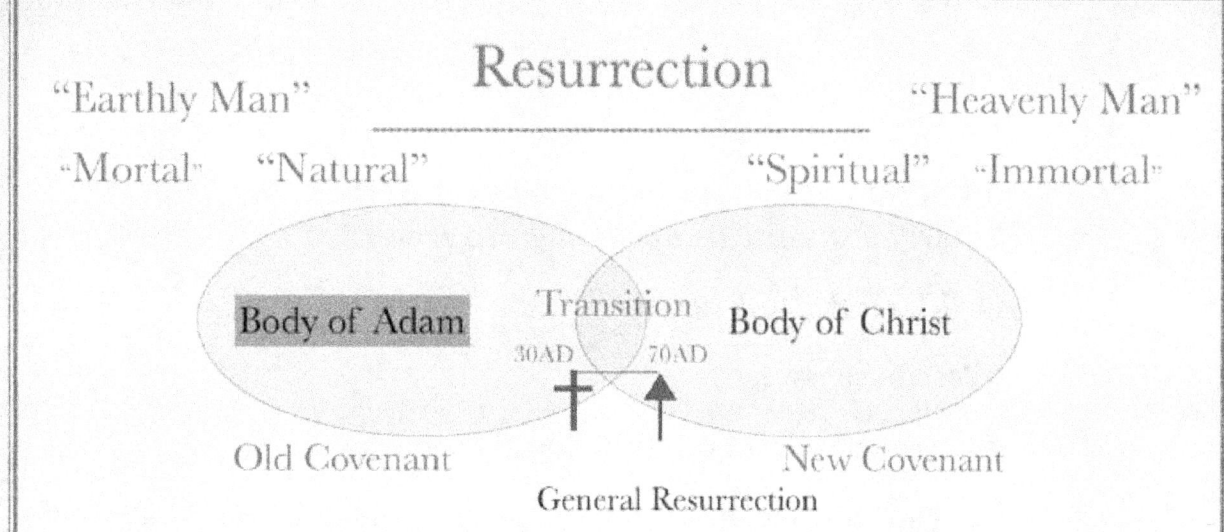

1 Corinthians 6:14

- **1 Cor 6:14** *"Now God has not only raised the Lord, but will also **raise us up** through His power."*

- Q: Who is the "us" here?

  - Possible answers:

  - 1. Each physical body individually someday

  - 2. The 'new Israel of God' or 'the body of Christ,' at Christ's coming in 70ad, an event in which the Corinthians participated, just as they had been told

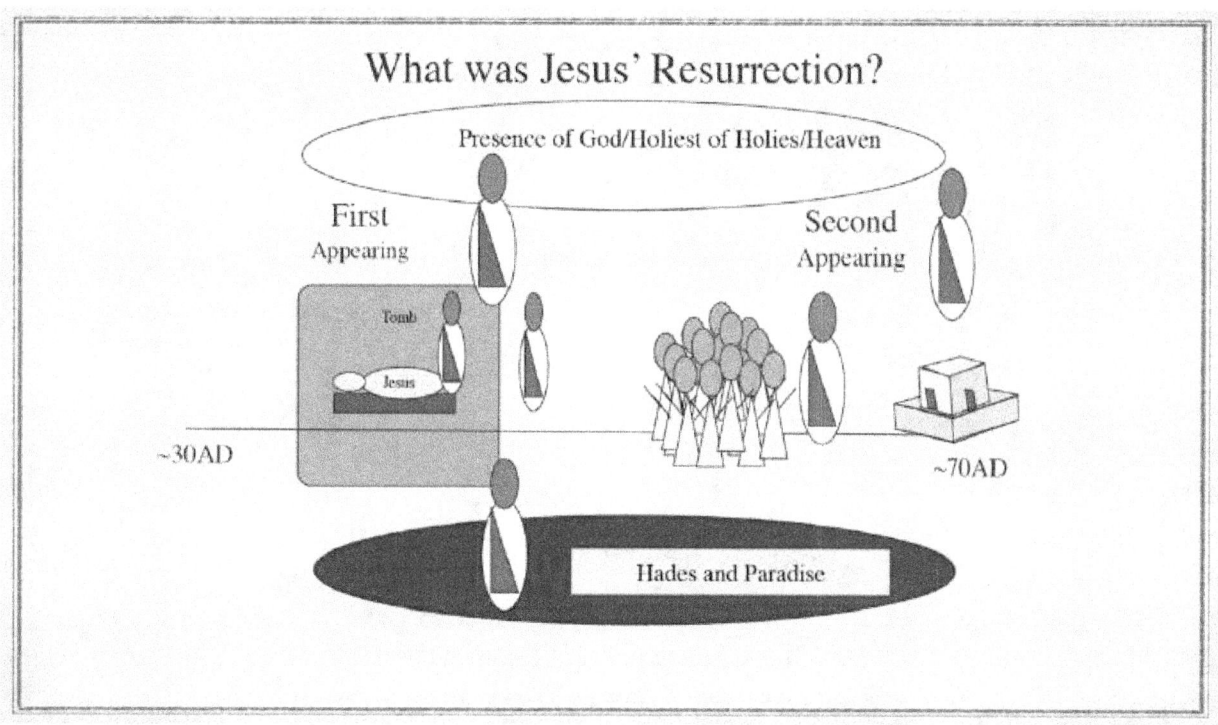

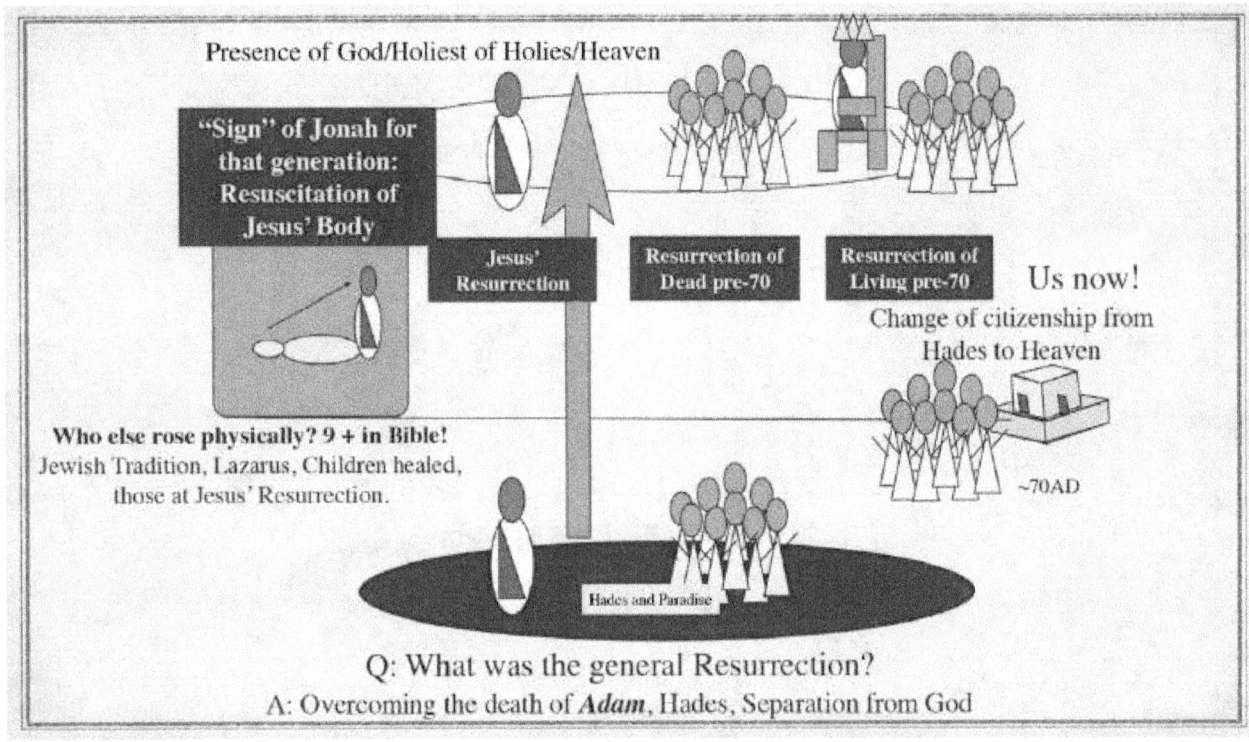

7 Kings/Caesars of Rome

	7 Caesars	
1	Julius Caesar (49 BC)	"five fallen"
2	Augustus	
3	Tiberius	
4	Caius	
5	Claudius	
6	**Nero**	**"the one who is"**
7	Vespasian (68 AD)	"one not yet come...little while"
		He reigned 7 months, shortest Roman reign

The "five fallen" are the Caesars who died prior to the Roman-Jewish war of 67-70AD. This includes the first five emperors, making Nero the one who "is" and Vespasian the one "not yet come." (for more info Suetonius, Lives of the Twelve Emperors")

666 or 616?

Revelation 13:15–18

- Most manuscripts of the New Testament and in English translations of the Bible, the number of the Beast is 666. In critical editions of the **Greek text**, such as the Novum Testamentum Graece, it is noted that **616 is a variant**.

- Although Irenaeus (2nd century AD) affirmed the number to be 666 and reported several scribal errors of the number, there is still doubt by theologians about the original reading because of the figure 616 being given in Codex Ephraemi Rescriptus, one of the four great uncial codices, as well as by the **Latin version of Tyconius** and by an **ancient Armenian version**.

- "The number 666 has been substituted for 616 either by analogy with 888, the [Greek] number of Jesus or because it is a triangular number, the sum of the first 36 numbers (1+2+3+4+5+6...+36 = 666)" The NRSV translation for Rev 13:18 includes this translation note: "Other ancient authorities read six hundred and sixteen".

- Around 2005, a fragment from **Papyrus 115,** taken from the Oxyrhynchus site, was discovered at the Oxford University's Ashmolean Museum. It **gave the beast's number as 616. This fragment happens to be the oldest manuscript (about 1,700 years old) of Revelation 13 to date.**

- **Codex** Ephraemi Rescriptus, known before the P115 finding but dating to after it, **has 616 written in full**: ἑξακόσιοι δέκα ἕξ, *hexakosioi deka hex* (lit. "six hundred and sixteen").

- *Papyrus 115* **and** *Ephraemi Rescriptus* **has led some scholars to conclude that 616 is the original number of the beast. If this variant is the original number of the Beast, it would be catastrophic to existing dispensational literature.** *Wikipedia*

Calculating 666 = Nero

- In Greek isopsephy and Hebrew gematria, every letter has a corresponding number. Summing these numbers gives a numeric value to a word or name. The use of isopsephy to calculate "the number of the beast" is used in many of the below interpretations.

- An Aramaic scroll from Murabba'at, dated to "the second year of Emperor Nero", refers to him by his name and title. In Hebrew it is *Nron Qsr* (Pronounced "Nerōn Kaisar"). In Latin it is *Nro Qsr* (Pronounced "Nerō Kaisar").

- **Nron Qsr** The **Greek** version of the name and title transliterates into Hebrew as נרון קסר, and yields a numerical value of **666**, as shown:

Resh (ר)	*Samekh* (ס)	*Qoph* (ק)	*Nun* (נ)	*Vav* (ו)	*Resh* (ר)	*Nun* (נ)	Sum
200	60	100	50	6	200	50	**666**

Nro Qsr: The Latin version of the name appears as *Nro* and transliterates into Hebrew as נרו קסר, yielding **616**

Resh (ר)	*Samekh* (ס)	*Qoph* (ק)	*Vav* (ו)	*Resh* (ר)	*Nun* (נ)	Sum
200	60	100	6	200	50	**616**

Eleven Imminent Time references in Revelation

"quickly, all at once, without delay."	"at hand, near"	"about to, on the verge of"
tachos & en tachei	εγγυς, engus	μελλει, mello, mellei
Revelation 1:1 – "...things which MUST shortly take place"	Revelation 1:3 – "The time is near."	Revelation 1:19 – "Write ... the things that are about to take place."
Revelation 2:16 – "Repent, or else I will come to you quickly"	Revelation 22:10 – "The time is at hand."	Revelation 3:10 – "the hour of trial...is about to come upon the whole world."
Revelation 3:11 – "Behold, I come quickly!"		
Revelation 22:6 – "...things which MUST shortly take place."		
Revelation 22:7 – "Behold, I am coming quickly!"		
Revelation 22:12 – "Behold, I am coming quickly."		**Time statements like book ends**
Revelation 22:20 – "Surely I am coming quickly."